SHOW TUNES

SHOW TUNES

THE SONGS, SHOWS, AND CAREERS
OF BROADWAY'S MAJOR COMPOSERS

Revised and Expanded Third Edition

With a Foreword by Michael Feinstein

STEVEN SUSKIN

New York • Oxford

Oxford University Press

2000

Oxford University Press

Oxford   New York

Athens   Auckland   Bangkok   Bogotá   Buenos Aires   Calcutta
Cape Town   Chennai   Dar es Salaam   Delhi   Florence   Hong Kong   Istanbul
Karachi   Kuala Lumpur   Madrid   Melbourne   Mexico City   Mumbai
Nairobi   Paris   São Paulo   Singapore   Taipei   Tokyo   Toronto   Warsaw

and associated companies in
Berlin   Ibadan

Published by Oxford University Press, Inc.
198 Madison Avenue, New York, New York 10016

Oxford is a registered trademark of Oxford University Press.

Library of Congress Cataloging-in-Publication Data
Suskin, Steven.
Show tunes : the songs, shows, and careers of Broadway's
major composers / Steven Suskin. —Rev. and expanded 3rd ed.
p.   cm.
Rev. ed. of: Show tunes, 1905–1991. 1st Limelight ed. 1992.
Includes bibliographical references and indexes.
ISBN 978-0-19-512599-3

1. Musicals—United States—Bibliography.   2. Popular music—
United States—Bibliography.   I. Suskin, Steven. Show tunes,
1905–1991.   II. Title.
ML 128.M78586   1999
782.1'4'0973—dc21   98-34048

7 9 8

Printed in the United States of America
on acid-free paper

For
Helen, Johanna, and Charlie

CONTENTS

Foreword by Michael Feinstein   ix

Preface to the Third Edition   xi

Prefaces to the Earlier Editions   xiii

Acknowledgments   xv

How to Use This Book   xvii

PART I
COMPOSERS OF THE EARLY YEARS

Introduction   1

Jerome Kern   3

Irving Berlin   37

George Gershwin   57

Vincent Youmans   77

Richard Rodgers   85

Cole Porter   117

Arthur Schwartz   135

Harold Arlen   149

Vernon Duke   159

Burton Lane   169

Kurt Weill   173

Marc Blitzstein   185

Harold Rome   193

PART II
NEW COMPOSERS OF THE 1940S AND 1950S

Introduction   203

Hugh Martin   205

Leonard Bernstein   211

Frederick Loewe   221

Jule Styne   227

Frank Loesser   243

Richard Adler   251

Jerry Bock   255

Bob Merrill   263

Meredith Willson   269

Stephen Sondheim   273

PART III
NEW COMPOSERS OF THE 1960S AND BEYOND

Introduction   291

Charles Strouse   293

Harvey Schmidt   305

Cy Coleman   313

Jerry Herman   323

John Kander   331

Mitch Leigh   343

Larry Grossman   349

Stephen Schwartz   355

Marvin Hamlisch   359

Alan Menken   363

William Finn   369

Maury Yeston   375

Stephen Flaherty   381

PART IV
NOTABLE SCORES BY OTHER COMPOSERS

Introduction   385

IRENE   387

SHUFFLE ALONG   387

GEORGE WHITE'S SCANDALS
OF 1926   388

CONTENTS

GOOD NEWS!   388

BLACKBIRDS OF 1928   389

WHOOPEE   389

FINE AND DANDY   390

WALK WITH MUSIC   390

EARLY TO BED   391

BEGGAR'S HOLIDAY   391

FLAHOOLEY   392

TOP BANANA   392

KISMET   393

THE GOLDEN APPLE   394

PLAIN AND FANCY   394

LI'L ABNER   395

GOLDILOCKS   396

REDHEAD   396

ONCE UPON A MATTRESS   397

YOU'RE A GOOD MAN, CHARLIE
   BROWN   397

JACQUES BREL IS ALIVE AND WELL
   AND LIVING IN PARIS   398

HAIR   399

PROMISES, PROMISES   400

1776   400

PROMENADE   401

PURLIE   402

GREASE   402

THE WIZ   403

SHENANDOAH   403

THE ROBBER BRIDEGROOM   404

THE BEST LITTLE WHOREHOUSE
   IN TEXAS   404

DREAMGIRLS   405

BABY   405

BIG RIVER   406

THE SECRET GARDEN   406

JELLY'S LAST JAM   407

VICTOR/VICTORIA   408

FLOYD COLLINS   408

BRING IN 'DA NOISE, BRING IN
   'DA FUNK   409

BIG   409

RENT   410

JEKYLL & HYDE   411

SIDE SHOW   412

THE LION KING   413

SATURN RETURNS: A CONCERT   413

PARADE   414

APPENDICES

Appendix 1 • Chronological Listing of
   Productions   417

Appendix 2 • Collaborator Reference
   Listing   441

Appendix 3 • Bibliography and a Word
   about Finding Music   463

Song Title Index   467

Show Index   543

People Index   557

FOREWORD

One of the happiest memories of my second Broadway engagement (in October of 1988) was the gift of a book from the property master of the Booth Theatre, the late Leo Herbert. Leo (a descendant of Victor Herbert) had been around the theater scene for a long time and described himself as "an old guy who usually smiles and pisses ice water." But he was moved enough by my performance of well-known and lesser-known Broadway and Hollywood songs to give me a copy of Steven Suskin's book *Show Tunes*. It was a perfect gift. The book had a very personal effect on me. Let me explain why.

I have spent most of my life not as a performer but as an archivist . . . someone who spends hours on end burrowing through stacks of musty papers and manuscripts in libraries and private collections (and sometimes other locales too exotic to mention). One's hope, of course, is to expand the general knowledge of the golden age of popular music and also to find some unknown treasure adding to the somewhat limited storehouse of knowledge about show music. We do know a lot, but there is also a lot that we don't know. Many songs are lost forever because of carelessness or simply lack of foresight.

During my six-year stint as assistant to Ira Gershwin, I gained a better perspective on why many songs created only a few decades ago no longer survive. Ira explained that theatre songs enjoyed a limited shelf life. They were written for a show that, if it was lucky, might run for a couple hundred performances—and that was the end of it. Nobody thought about preserving the music and no one was particularly concerned about what happened to original orchestrations after a show died. The orchestral parts were useless—dead weight that took up space. Ira told

me that if a show failed, after the last performance, all the musicians in the pit would gleefully tear up the music. Good riddance! Sometimes a successful show would go on tour, but when the tour was over, the music would again fall into oblivion.

Authors of songs don't always have copies of their own work, either. When I first went to work for Ira Gershwin, I was amazed at what he had in his private archive, but also at what he didn't have. On the plus side, there were lyric sheets for most of his works, including extra words for some of the famous ones. He also had a cache of manuscripts of some unpublished songs in his brother George's own hand. There were, however, many holes in Ira's collection. Where were the original first edition copies of some of these songs? What happened to all the music written for several hundred of those lyric sheets? What happened to the lyrics not penciled in on some of the copies of George's manuscripts? Where were the copies of Ira's earliest songs written with Gus Edwards and Al Sherman?

Sometimes I would find a lyric sheet and a separate copy of the music for a particular song and "marry" the two, as I did with the song *Gather Ye Rosebuds*. One time I found the music for an earlier version of the title song *Strike Up the Band*, but I never found the lyrics. Ditto with a song called *Leave It to Love*, cut from LADY, BE GOOD! Ira would ask me once every couple of months if I had located the lyrics for that one—he couldn't believe that he didn't have the text for one of his favorite songs—but it never turned up.

Of course, sometimes treasures do turn up, as they did in 1982 at the Warner Brothers Music warehouse in Secaucus, New Jersey. Boxes and boxes of "lost" songs and orchestrations by the Broadway greats and not-so-greats turned up—over eighty boxes, as I recall. Ira sent me to see what material written by the brothers Gershwin might have surfaced, not thinking that anything of consequence would be there. When I called to tell him that, for starters, I had counted thirty-seven manuscripts in George's hand, he truly did not believe it, and it took a couple of months for the discovery to really sink in.

But the Lord giveth and the Lord taketh away. Shortly after the discovery in Secaucus, I learned that many boxes of unique and irreplaceable musical theatre scores housed in an old theatre basement in London had been destroyed. The theatre had been taken over by Andrew Lloyd Webber, and somebody had cleaned out the "useless" stuff taking up so much space in the basement. They saved the scores of all the old warhorses like ANNIE GET YOUR GUN (those might be of use, they thought) but destroyed the obscure material—including several complete Gershwin scores and orchestrations!

So in view of the above, if you want to find out what is available in the way of songs from a particular Broadway show, where do you look? Most Broadway songs live on in two primary forms, as sheet music or on record. Before the publication of *Show Tunes*, it was very hard to determine exactly what material exists in either of these formats. Thanks to Steven's meticulous research, we now have a complete chronicle of what is out there, combined with much pertinent information about the shows and their creators. His book was the first of its kind and is obviously a labor of love. It has only become more valuable through the years, as more of our Broadway heritage has disappeared. Many of the songs listed in *Show Tunes* are so obscure that many of their publishers do not even possess a copy of them. (EMI Music Publishers, for example, can only supply you with a blurry microfilm copy of many of their old songs. They didn't bother to save any of the originals.)

Steven's magnum opus gives me a burst of adrenaline every time I open it. It is clearly and thoughtfully organized, and is a pleasure to read. I also get a burst of adrenaline when I read some of his comments about various songwriters. I certainly don't agree with all of his opinions. But I do respect his commentary.

I'm sure you will enjoy this revised edition of *Show Tunes*.

Michael Feinstein

PREFACE TO THE THIRD EDITION

As I write this preface to the Third Edition of *Show Tunes*, some girl is on my mind. Not a certain girl; rather, *Some Girl Is on Your Mind* is on my mind. That being the title of a song by Jerome Kern and Oscar Hammerstein from the 1929 musical SWEET ADELINE.

When shows of that era opened, the publishers automatically published any songs from the show which they thought would sell any copies whatsoever. Especially when the composer himself was his own publisher. Kern and his partners at T. B. Harms published eight songs from SWEET ADELINE, including two interpolations by Lulu Franklin, the featured comedienne. They didn't bother with *Some Girl Is on Your Mind*, though, except to include it in what they used to call the piano selection, a medley of (mostly) song refrains printed without lyrics.

In compiling the first edition of *Show Tunes*, I found and fell in love with the piano selection excerpt of *Some Girl*. Several years later I thought to call Tams-Witmark, which had controlled the stock & amateur rights back when people still did stock & amateur productions of SWEET ADELINE. They went through their materials, coming back to report that they could find no such song. After a bit of creative jockeying, we found something entitled "Hoffman House"; the song was sung in a scene set at the famous turn-of-the-century watering hole. There it was, as exquisite a song as you'd want to find. We almost got the long-forgotten *Some Girl* a hearing in 1990, when I put together a demo at RCA of a dozen similarly forgotten "trunk songs." Nothing happened with the project, though, and *Some Girl* went back into hibernation. Two years later John McGlinn included it on one of his Broadway omnibus albums: finally, in all its

glory and the original arrangements, the exquisite *Some Girl Is on Your Mind*. Unfortunately, that album is already out of print. Move forward to the spring of 1997: The City Center Encores series mounted a concert version of SWEET ADELINE. Critics and audiences alike stopped in amazement, stunned by that stunning song—which to this day, after seventy years, is still unpublished. (And is likely to remain so; unlike the catalogues of Berlin, Gershwin, Rodgers, Porter, etc., Kern's publication rights are owned by an international conglomerate with little interest in issuing 1920s Broadway sheet music.)

The point of all this: There are dozens of similarly forgotten, similarly wonderful songs. "A song is no song till you sing it," as *Some Girl*'s lyricist once said; and how old is a seventy-year-old song on the day when you first hear it? All of us who work with show tunes—writing about them, performing them, recording them—have but one goal: to find small treasures as we sift through stacks and storehouses, simply so that we can bring them to your attention. (I have reformatted *Show Tunes* in this new edition to specifically point out wonderful songs, although many of them are already deservedly known.)

Happily, more and more long-forgotten songs are being rediscovered and performed. When first updating *Show Tunes*, I found that I was not only adding song listings of the new shows; I was also going back and revising song listings of old shows. In the years since I finished the First Edition in 1985, in fact, some two hundred never-before-published show tunes have received their initial recording. More than fifty by Gershwin alone, thanks to the recording series implemented by Leonore (Mrs. Ira) Gershwin; and dozens by other composers, from Berlin to Rodgers to Sondheim to Strouse to Schmidt. And as the market in song folios has expanded, publishers have started digging through their archives. What better way to get people to buy yet another Frank Loesser song book than by adding unknown treasures like the fascinatingly jaunty *Travelin' Light*, a song cut from GUYS AND DOLLS and long forgotten?

The First Edition of *Show Tunes* discussed the careers of thirty important Broadway composers, the criteria for inclusion including quality, quantity, or in some cases the luck of writing one phenomenal hit. The number of new composers added for the Second Edition in 1991? None—which is to say that things were pretty dire along Broadway. (The street was dominated by British musicals, so a section of "Notable Imported Shows"—half of them by Lloyd Webber—was added, albeit with misgivings, as the focus of this book is properly on Broadway show tunes. All of the British imports since the Second Edition have failed; thus, I have seen fit to excise the import section and concentrate on matters of more interest.) I am pleased to report that I have been able to justify the addition of six more composers to this new edition, four of whom were previously represented in brief in the "Notable Scores by Other Composers" section and two of whom are altogether new to these pages. As we move warily ahead into the twenty-first century, it seems that the health of the Broadway musical is not quite so dire as previously supposed.

New York   Steven Suskin
June 1999

First Edition

It is probably true that a few people are not interested in show tunes. This book isn't for them.

A veritable mountain of material has been written about Broadway musicals. Some volumes focus on individual creators or performers; others discuss shows in general or certain selected shows. Distinct musical theatre forms have been examined, as has the total work of an era. There are biographies—some excellent, some not—of specific composers, or groups of composers, or composers and their lyricists. All concentrate on the hit shows, with summaries of plots, excerpts from reviews, etc.

But the Broadway musical is built on Show Tunes.

Song soothes the soul. Personal favorites express our feelings better than we can in our own words. Truths captured in music and lyric by the Messrs. Rodgers and Hart, or Gershwin and Gershwin, or Arlen (and on) remain constant. Their songs are on our lips, or in our ears, or at the touch of our fingers whenever we want them, whenever we need them. *Dancing in the Dark* at twilight, *Time on My Hands* at dawn. The plaintive *Someone to Watch Over Me*, the importunate *I Can't Get Started*. *All the Things You Are* in times rhapsodic, *Spring Is Here* in times unrequited, and *I've Got the World on a String* any old time at all.

This book grew from the assumption that for every well-known Kern or Duke or Youmans treasure, there were two or three unknown gems hidden from view. (An assumption that proved, for the most part, to be correct!) It was quickly discovered that there was no accurate list of what to look for. The works of Gershwin and Porter have been fairly well catalogued; information on other composers is inconsistent, haphazard, or simply nonexistent. Shows which closed out of town and "plays with music," particularly, have heretofore been ignored.

The search grew into a quest. Pursuit of accuracy eventually led to a piece-by-piece search through the copyright deposits at the Library of Congress. The Library's vast collection of uncatalogued material inconveniently mixes together all theatre, vaudeville, and motion picture music from America, England, France, Austria, Germany, Italy, Mexico, etc., registered since the turn of the century. In the interests of providing a fairly complete guide to important musical theatre, the number of examined composers trebled.

A list of song titles, though, is ultimately of limited interest, no matter how extensive. Personal involvement in and enthusiasm for the musical theatre led to an investigation of why these composers wrote what they did. How did they come to work with their various collaborators? Did the songs work in the theatre? What were the effects of success and failure on future work (and the work of others)? The Broadway musical has been examined from the perspective of scholars and musicologists, but rarely from a theatrical viewpoint; this book does so.

Show Tunes is my personal paean to (and investigation of) the music that makes me, figuratively, dance on the ceiling. I was born in a trunk full of original cast albums, and I have spent many a night and day—vocationally and avocationally—in the Broadway theatre. I have examined many thousands of songs for this book, listening with a highly analytical musical ear. Shows by the hundreds were researched in my guise as musical-comedy detective, discovering coincidences, contradictions, surprises and curiosities. Finally, I liberally laced my accounts of songs, shows, and careers with random observations accumulated during my long years as a Broadway production manager. (Editor's note: The author appears to have been born sometime between WISH YOU WERE HERE and WONDERFUL TOWN).

The reader will find favorite and (nonfavorite) composers within, and perhaps even a few unknowns. For one discriminating individual to enjoy all their songs is virtually impossible. Tastes, even among drama critics, vary. Whether you agree with my comments or not, I trust you will find them provocative and informative.

My reward has been the discovery of hundreds of good songs. The reader's rewards will be a better acquaintance with the show tunes he or she already enjoys, and a guide to new favorites.

New York
June 1985

Second Edition

I'm somewhat surprised to find how much new material has crept into this "updated and expanded" edition. There has been a surprising increase in musical theatre activity over the last few years. Sixteen of the thirty composers discussed in this book are still around, although five are no longer active. New musicals by all of the others (except, oddly enough, Jerry Herman) have been produced since 1985! Only two of the shows had any success, alas. Several obscure, early productions by these composers have also come to my attention.

The section of "Notable Scores by Other Composers"—which was added to the First Edition as an afterthought—received so much favorable comment that it has been expanded; some worthy shows which were omitted from the First Edition due to space constraints are now deservedly recognized.

Finally—and importantly—it will be seen that quite a few never-before-available songs have recently been published or recorded. Let us hope this practice continues, as there are still many long-lost treasures waiting to be "discovered."

New York
July 1991

ACKNOWLEDGMENTS

There are many existing sources for statistics, facts, and the like. Songs, though, could not be examined until they were found. The following people were of help in locating materials and clarifying information.

The late Jule Styne, the late Harold Rome, Hugh Martin, the late Bob Merrill, Billy Finn, Jerry Herman, Charles Strouse, and Larry Grossman were all generous with their time and helpful. Stephen Sondheim graciously went to the trouble of fact-checking and correcting his chapter for this Third Edition. Early encouragement came from Theodore S. Chapin of the Rodgers and Hammerstein Organization and the late Ceciley Youmans Collins. The late Stanley Green and the late Alfred Simon were generous with their time and knowledge, while Edward Jablonski was—and remains—a gracious source of knowledge and a gentleman. Michael Feinstein answered pages-full of Gershwin questions back when I was first writing this book. (He also confided that he hoped to break into the performing world as a cabaret singer. Lots of luck, said I.) He was kind enough to provide an enthusiastic foreword to the Second Edition, which he has updated for the Third. Also providing information and insight were Robert Kimball, Frank Military, the late John Fearnley, Jack Gottlieb, Michael Kerker of ASCAP, Dr. Leonard Lehrman, Paul McKibbins, Lys Simonette and David Farneth of the Kurt Weill Foundation, and Joseph Weiss.

A number of advanced music collectors have shared their knowledge of the field and helped track down obscure material: Bill Simon, the late Lawrence Jay Taylor, the late Bill Tynes, Joe Friedman, Vi Foerster, Stan White, and the late Irv Gerst. James J. Fuld provided helpful suggestions and was responsible for the unexpected discovery of certain important items. Special thanks go to Donald J. Stubblebine, who continually offered access to his extensive collections. Don's 1996 book *Broadway Sheet Music* is a fine supplemental guide to published sheet music.

Much of the initial research for this book was done at the following institutions: the Billy Rose Theatre Collection and the Music Division of The Performing Arts Research Center at Lincoln Center; the Music Reference Collection of The New York Public Library at Lincoln Center; the Music Division of the Library of Congress in Washington, D.C.; the now-defunct Songwriters Hall of Fame Museum (where Frankie MacCormack was of great help); and other private collections that wish to remain private.

Quite a few readers of the first two editions took the time to send in suggestions, comments, and corrections which have resulted in changes, additions, and clarifications. I thank all of them for their efforts and kind words. If *Show Tunes* has provided critical song information unavailable elsewhere, I can only say that that's precisely why I went to the trouble of writing it in the first place!

Much credit for the existence of this book goes to the enthusiasm and care of Jerry Gross of the now-departed Dodd, Mead & Company. (In business since 1839, publishers of G. B. Shaw, A. Christie, and S. Sondheim, they published my first book and disappeared in a sea of red ink. My *second* book was published by a fellow who jumped off his yacht and disappeared in a sea, too; but I digress.) Jerry Gross's ideas and suggestions helped make this book as comprehensive and usable as it is; he also encouraged me to "personalize" it into something more interesting and entertaining (hopefully) than a mere book of lists. Mel Zerman of the invaluable Limelight Editions published and edited the Second Edition, and I am grateful to him for the care and dedication he lavished on the project.

For all sorts of assistance, support, and encouragement, the following are gratefully acknowledged: Mitchell Erickson, Kate Glasner, the late Arlene Grayson, Janice Herbert, the late Leo Herbert, Carol Patella, Amy Pell, Skipp Porteous, Stephanie Ross, William Rosenfield, Kim Sellon, Mark Sendroff, Dr. Barbara Ann Simon, Mary Jo Slater, Marion Finkler Taylor, and Max Woodward. William W. Appleton has been an enthusiastic part of this project since its inception. A discerning theatregoer since 1925—how many people do you know who can describe his favorite numbers from THE GARRICK GAITIES?—he has graciously spent many hours double-checking song listings and consulting on commentary. His efforts and interest are deeply appreciated.

Finally, I couldn't have written this book without the assistance of my wife Helen and daughter Johanna. I could have, actually, but I doubt that I would have. Johanna had the patience to delay her première until after the 1997 Tony Award–voting deadline, so that we didn't have to miss any shows. She's a very discriminating child, actually; her first words were "Please, don't make me see *Cats*."

S. S.

HOW TO USE THIS BOOK

Thirty-six major composers have been selected for discussion, six of whom have been newly added to this Third Edition of *Show Tunes*. They are divided into three generational groups—Composers of the Early Years, New Composers of the 1940s and 1950s, and New Composers of the 1960s and Beyond—with each career discussed separately.

This study of the musical theatre starts at the very beginning, with Jerome Kern. Kern entered a theatre dominated by operetta and slowly incorporated radical changes. Other successful early American composers chose to continue working in an earlier tradition: Victor Herbert, Rudolf Friml, and Sigmund Romberg all retain a (tiny) measure of popularity today. But they wrote operetta and light opera, with few show tunes, and therefore are not included. The one early composer who did try to create a primitive American musical comedy was George M. Cohan; but his work was, well, primitive.

Hundreds of American composers have been represented on Broadway since Kern began interpolating songs in 1904. Selecting thirty-six out of the pack for discussion has not been all that difficult, though; most of the choices are obvious. (Also-rans whom I have been unable to muster the enthusiasm to include include Louis Hirsch, Sammy Fain, and Albert Hague.) The major criteria are importance of work, in terms of quality or popular success, and a sustained concentration on the musical stage. The lack of a theatre career does not signify the inability to write important musical theatre work, of course. Such composers are included in a separate section of "Notable Scores by Other Composers."

For purposes of chronology, composers are arranged (roughly) by date of their first impor-

tant work. Not year of birth, or first produced musical, but what one might consider their date of "arrival." George Gershwin, Vincent Youmans, and Richard Rodgers were all firmly established with multiple hit musicals before Cole Porter finally achieved recognition in 1928 and are therefore discussed prior to Porter; this despite the fact that Cole Porter was considerably older than the others—eleven years older than Rodgers—and had his initial Broadway hearing back in 1915. Porter's eventual acceptance was prepared, in some ways, by the mid-1920s success of Lorenz Hart and Ira Gershwin. For these reasons, he is introduced into our chronicle after the younger Gershwin, Youmans, and Rodgers.

The individual work of each composer is examined show by show, from the earliest interpolation by Kern in January 1904 up through January 1, 1999. Each production is discussed in three parts: show data, song information, and (usually) commentary.

Show Data

The Shows

All stage productions from which songs were published or recorded are listed. These include shows that closed during pre-Broadway tryouts, others written specifically for London, and others that weren't intended for Broadway presentation. The majority are musicals and revues, but any organized stage production for which the composer wrote specific material is included. These include Off Broadway shows, nightclub shows, World's Fair shows, Armed Forces shows, vaudeville acts, arena shows, and even a few ice shows. In addition, many productions for which no songs were published are included. Movie and television work are discussed in passing; subsequent stage versions of movie or television musicals are listed in cases where the composer wrote new material for the adaptation or previously unheard songs were used. Thus, the 1973 Broadway version of GIGI (for which Loewe and Lerner wrote additional songs) and the 1996 version of STATE FAIR (which included previously unused Rodgers and Hammerstein material) are included; British productions of Porter's TV musical "Aladdin" or Loesser's film *Hans Christian Andersen*—filled out with interpolations by other composers—are not.

Revivals are separately discussed only when the show included new material by the composer or was significantly rewritten, as in the case of the 1974 CANDIDE and the 1954 Off Broadway version of THE THREEPENNY OPERA. Otherwise, Broadway and Off Broadway revivals are mentioned after the credits of the original production, as are some "concert versions" and other revivals relevant to the discussion. (Opera and light opera company revivals are generally not included.) Credits of the key people involved in the revival are given, with the major cast members followed by the names of the actors who originated the role. We thus see at a glance—rather than having to look it up elsewhere—that the role written-to-order for Nancy Walker in ON THE TOWN [Bernstein: December 28, 1944] was recreated by Pat Carroll (1959), Bernadette Peters (1971), and Lea DeLaria (1998).

Amateur shows, unproduced musicals, unfinished musicals, and workshops are given separate listings when songs were published (or recorded); much of the stronger material, of course, was reused in other productions and published at that time. With respect to unfinished or unproduced shows, the credit section lists not only the authors but others who were involved with the project. These people have been placed in brackets; you could not say that Jerome Robbins directed and Zero Mostel starred in A PRAY BY BLECHT [Bernstein: circa February 16, 1969], as the piece was ultimately never mounted. Robbins and Mostel were key elements in the development of the piece, though, and are there-

fore credited. The date given is that of the announced (but canceled) Broadway opening. Most of the dates of these unproduced shows are less exact, as few went so far as to book a theatre.

The subtitles or colorfully descriptive slogans which appear beneath some of the titles (e.g., "A Bubbling Satirical Musical Revue of Plays, Problems and Persons") are taken from original advertising materials.

Date

The date of the official Broadway (or London) opening is used. For shows which closed during tryout or were not intended to play Broadway or London, date of the out-of-town opening or first public performance is given. Where exact date is unknown, approximate year and month are given.

Theatre and Number of Performances

The theatre where the show officially opened is listed, followed by the "official" number of performances. Published figures are, unfortunately, often contradictory. The most accurate-seeming number has been listed, usually from the earliest reliable reference source. All shows were produced in New York City unless otherwise indicated. Complete information is sometimes unknown, particularly for shows that did not play Broadway. This applies to credits, number of performances, and other data as well. In such cases, the listings herein are necessarily incomplete.

Credits

Composers The composer under discussion wrote all music unless specifically noted. In the Gershwin chapter, for example, "Music also by Sigmund Romberg" (ROSALIE) means that Gershwin and Romberg each wrote substantial parts of the score. "Music mostly by Sigmund Romberg" (THE DANCING GIRL) means that Gershwin supplied an interpolated song (or songs) to a Romberg score. "Music mostly by Gershwin" (LADY, BE GOOD!) means that other composers provided interpolations. "Music by

Gershwin and Herbert Stothart" (SONG OF THE FLAME) indicates that the pair collaborated on the score, with songs written by Gershwin alone so labeled. "Music by others (see Arlen: February 11, 1930)" (NINE-FIFTEEN REVUE) indicates that the score had no principal composer, although additional information on the same show can be found in the Arlen chapter.

Lyricists   The overall lyricist for the production is named in the credit section; exceptions for specific songs are noted following the song title. In cases of partial scores, the principal composer and lyricist are named; only songs written by the composer under discussion are listed. Some of the composers wrote their own lyrics; this is mentioned at the beginning of their chapters, with specific exceptions noted. Songs for which the composer wrote lyrics but not music are included, except that collaborations with other composers in this book are discussed under the career of the composer (but cross-referenced). Thus, Stephen Sondheim's collaborations with composer Mary Rodgers are discussed in the Sondheim chapter; his work with Leonard Bernstein, Jule Styne, and Richard Rodgers are discussed in the composers' chapters. The most important lyricists are featured—along with key directors, choreographers, and producers—in appendix 2, "Collaborator Reference Listing," which gives a chronological overview of their careers.

Others   Librettists, directors, and producers are listed where information is available. Choreographers are listed for many (but not all) of the shows. Certain cast members are listed: stars, supporting performers, and others of interest. Future stars in the chorus are specifically not included. Standardized terms are used: "directed" rather than "staged," "choreographed" rather than "dances by," "with" rather than "starring."

Alternate Show Titles

When a show underwent a name change during tryouts, songs were sometimes issued using both the original and the final show title. In dealing with such shows, the alternate show title is noted. Songs cut from these shows might, in fact, have been issued using the earlier show title only.

Song Listings

Song listings for each production include all material that was published or recorded. Information is given on lyricists, other uses of the same material, and related details. The purpose of the section is to provide a complete guide to all songs that exist and that, theoretically, can be found. (Not all are found easily, sad to say; if only someone would gather all this rare material in one accessible place!)

Some other reference books list titles of published and unpublished songs, usually without any differentiation. Unfortunately, few unpublished manuscripts are viewable by the general public, and in many cases they have long since disappeared. These "unpublished" titles are sometimes songs that actually were published—with a different lyric, or merely a different title. Theatre programs can provide unreliable information, as shows-in-crisis make changes faster than a good press agent can keep track of (or wants to). Sometimes proposed titles for never-written songs find their way onto these lists. Accurate information and authorship of unpublished material, therefore, is simply not verifiable. I have chosen to concentrate only on what is verifiably real. Unpublished songs and manuscripts I've come across in the course of research have been examined and mentioned where relevant.

Almost all the composers wrote songs for purposes other than stage shows. A few wrote as carefully for these assignments as they did for the theatre. Due to space restrictions, it is impossible to include non-show songs. Those that are especially notable have been noted, however.

Within the listings of each production, only songs written by the composer under discussion are included (although contributions by other composers with their own chapters in the book are cross-referenced). Thus, songs written by Chick Endor for the Gershwins' LADY, BE GOOD! is not listed; a song written by Vincent Youmans for the Gershwins' SHOW GIRL is cross-referenced to the Youmans chapter.

Non-song material is listed where it is a separate composition: *Overture to Candide* as opposed to song-medley overtures, *Slaughter on Tenth Avenue* as opposed to dance music arrangements. Certain songs were published with subtitles: *The Impossible Dream (The Quest)*. In other cases, logical subtitles follow the official title for purposes of identification; thus, Sondheim's *Any Moment* from INTO THE WOODS is also labeled and indexed as *Anything Can Happen in the Woods*. Someone looking for CAROUSEL's *My Boy Bill* or *My Little Girl* will thus be able to find it, although they were published under the title *Soliloquy*. (As it happens, they were originally registered for copyright separately.) Vocal scores sometimes neglected to print song titles in favor of *Opening Act Two*, *Scene and Song*, or *Entrance of Cowgirls*. Where necessary, a suitable title or subtitle has been taken from the lyric. Where a composer wrote completely different songs with the same title— Porter's *Just One of Those Things* or Rodgers' *Spring Is Here*, for example, or Coleman's three title songs for SWEET CHARITY—I have numbered the songs as [1st] and [2nd] (and [3rd]); this does not apply to identically titled songs by different composers, like the four *Maria*s. (How many can you name?)

The majority of the songs in this book have been published individually as sheet music. Other songs have appeared in other guises, though. These have been listed accordingly, the major formats being:

Published Songs

Sheet music of individual songs, for sale in stores and theatre lobbies.

Songs Published in Vocal Selection(s)

Collections of selected songs, sometimes including titles not published individually. American and British vocal selections for the same show sometimes have different contents; revised editions of long out-of-print vocal selections in some cases add previously unpublished songs. The use of the plural, "selections," in the heading indicates that different editions have slightly different contents.

Songs Published in Vocal Score(s)

Collections of all musical material needed for performance: songs, dances, underscoring, and so on. These frequently include more complete versions of the songs than the individual sheet or vocal selection, with additional lyrics. Again, the use of the plural, "scores," indicates different contents in different editions.

Songs Published in Non-show Folio

Otherwise unpublished material contained in songbooks, collections, scripts, or other publications. A few show tunes have appeared only in so-called fakebooks; they are so noted.

Songs Published (No Lyric) in Piano Selection

Medleys of songs issued without lyrics, sometimes piano reductions of the overtures. Dozens of believed-to-be-vanished songs by Gershwin, Rodgers, Kern, and others were published in this manner (and are here catalogued for the first time). In some cases American and British editions of the piano selection have different contents.

Songs Recorded

Otherwise unpublished songs that have been recorded (and are thus, technically, published on the recording). In olden days, the publisher usually issued the "best" (i.e., most likely to sell) songs even before the tryout began. More titles were added as demand was shown—if the show ran long enough. Leftover songs appeared only in the vocal score, if any; otherwise they were forgotten or eventually reused in another show. Since the advent of the original cast album, many otherwise unpublished songs have been salvaged on disc.

While this book concentrates on printed music, songs preserved only on recordings are certainly to the point. Therefore, unpublished-but-recorded songs that appear on original (or studio) cast albums, "songwriter anthologies," pirated albums, and other special collections, are listed at the end of the song listings. Live tapes and noncommercial demonstration records are sometimes obtainable: imaginative readers interested in this material can easily track down sources. Due to space limitations and the desire to concentrate on more important matters, I do not supply label and number information on unpublished-but-recorded songs; most can be found on original cast or studio cast albums.

Classification of Publications

Many songs were printed in more than one format: an individually published song was almost always also included in the vocal selection (if any), in the vocal score (if any), cast recording (if any), and in other formats. These listings are cumulative, the key word being "additional." Thus, you can expect the vocal score to include most of the songs published individually or in the vocal selection; this doesn't hold for cut songs, though, which were usually withdrawn after the initial printing.

Song Explanations

While most of the songs were simply written to order, performed as planned, and published forthwith, others followed a not-so-straightforward path:

Cut Songs

Cut material includes songs dropped during previews, during rehearsals, and sometimes even before rehearsals began. As these cases were not accurately chronicled in programs or anywhere else, such listings cannot be complete.

Reused Songs

Songs were occasionally used in more than one show, especially those that were cut from (or unused in) the show for which they were initially intended. In some cases a song was reused with the same lyric but a different title, such as *Dancing on the Ceiling*, which was originally published as *He Dances on My Ceiling*.

New (or Revised) Lyrics

These are cases where a new (or revised) lyric was set to music from an earlier song. Often

there are minor changes in the music of the refrain, and sometimes a whole new verse; but the refrain is for the most part identical.

Revised Music

At the least, these songs have basically similar music that appears to have been consciously reworked: the same song in a different tempo with a new bridge, for example. At the most, these songs have virtually new music which is nevertheless clearly derived from the earlier song. (And why not? A good musical idea is well worth rescuing from ignominious obscurity.)

Advertised but Not Published

A fair number of songs were advertised by the publishers but not actually printed and distributed. They were clearly intended to be issued, and in some cases final "printers' proofs" have been found; before the songs went to press they were cut from the show, perhaps, or the show might have closed altogether. It is impossible to prove nonexistence, of course, but the songs thus listed seem definitely not to exist. Other mysterious titles have indeed been found—and discovered to be interpolations by other composers.

Issued as Professional Copy (Only)

Prior to actual publication, many songs were distributed to singers and recording companies in hopes of arranging performances outside the theatre. For any number of reasons—(premature closing of the show, song cut on the road, etc.)—some songs were never ultimately issued for sale and can be found only as "professional copies," usually printed without covers, often on poor-quality paper.

Initial Publication

Certain songs were not published until long after the production closed, usually in connection with a successful movie version or revival. These are listed as such. Because the individually published sheet is our primary source, "initial individual publication" supersedes an earlier printing in a vocal score or selection. It is regretted that current availability is impossible to indicate; happily, numerous long-out-of-print individual sheets are now reappearing in selections and folios.

Additional Songs

Songs by the composer in question not originally written for the show in question are sometimes interpolated into revivals or movie versions. These are listed when it marked the initial use, publication, or recording of previously unpublished material.

Commentary

Pertinent—and sometimes impertinent—comments are given on the shows, songs, and careers. Other publications can be consulted for plot summaries and the like; my concern is with the composers: What they wrote and with whom they wrote; why and how they came to be involved with their chosen projects. All were influenced and/or affected by their counterparts and competitors. They shared the same collaborators and producers, wrote for the same performers. And, the shows were performed in the same theatres for the same audiences (and the same reviewers).

Critical comments on contemporary shows come from actual viewing. Opinions on older productions have been derived from analysis of existing material, reviews, and first-hand reports. Certain critics, one finds, can be relied upon for generally insightful comments. Statements of commercial success or failure are derived from financial records.

Show Tunes is not meant to be a total history of the American musical theatre. Rather, it is a look at the more important composers and their work, with incidental miscellania of curiosity and interest included.

Cross-Referencing

Reference to any of the productions discussed in this book is printed with the show title in capital letters, followed by composer and date:

SHOW BOAT [Kern: December 27, 1927]

The date refers to the chapter on Kern, where the listing can be found chronologically. When ref-

erence is to a show written by the composer under discussion, his name is not repeated. For example, in the chapter on Jerome Kern:

SHOW BOAT [December 27, 1927]

When more than one composer wrote for the same production, contributions are discussed in their respective chapters. This is indicated by naming the other composer; show title and date are not repeated.

It will not always be necessary to check the reference, of course; often the date alone is the relevant factor. Finding the location of the most-referred-to chapters might take some getting used to. Specific page numbers for cross-referenced productions can be found in the "Chronological Listing of Productions" (appendix 1).

A number of musicals mentioned in passing were not written by the composers under discussion or included in the "Notable Scores" section, and thus do not have listings in this book. They are listed in capital letters—indicating that they are musicals—followed by a dagger. This also applies to imported musicals written by non-Americans. Thus:

ROSE-MARIE†
THE MERRY WIDOW†
LES MISÉRABLES†

Sources and Contradictions

Standard reference sources—often compiled from earlier standard sources—can contain contradictory information. Titles and names with different spelling or punctuation; different dates, varying "official" numbers of performances; different facts, different facts about the same facts; and more.

Wherever possible, information has been taken directly from published music, theatre programs, reviews, and advertising material. Even primary source materials are often in disagreement. A piece of music can have different titles (or authors) listed on the cover and the first page.

Obvious misspellings and errors have been corrected; alternate spellings have been standardized. In dealing with contradictions, the most likely information—usually from the earliest source—has been used. It will be noted that certain "experts" in the field are consistently reliable, while others are just as consistently not.

To verify song existence and to provide correct authorship and as-complete-as-practical reuse information, I have personally examined the great majority of individual sheets, scores, selections, and other sources. Copyright records and registration deposit copies have been checked to ensure the greatest possible accuracy. Even so, I am fairly certain that this volume will contain an error or two.

Exact titles and composer/lyricist information are taken from the published songs, as given at the top of the page with the copyright notice. Where reason exists to doubt authorship as credited, copyright and performing-rights organization records have been consulted. Such discrepancies have been included in the interests of completeness and accuracy.

About Those Asterisks (*)

Readers of past editions of *Show Tunes* will notice a new feature: the song listings are now littered with asterisks*. Let us say that you, the reader, have just discovered Rodgers & Hart or Arthur Schwartz, Vincent Youmans, or Vernon Duke. Amazed, you start out to find other songs (most of which are long out-of-print and difficult to find) by the above-mentioned gentlemen. Assuming that you have some constraints on your time and patience, it will not be possible or practical to go after all 220 published Schwartz songs, or the 190 by Duke. Thus, the *s. Songs so marked are recommended to you, dear reader, as being worthy of note. Wonderful songs in themselves; wonderful songs in context, which handily accomplish what they set out to do; or merely songs which remain ever delightful no matter how many times I hear them. A limited number of songs—mostly older songs—are marked with double asterisks (**). These, obviously, are songs which I find extra special.

Now I can already hear some readers criticize this system: it is unfair, they'll say, being based solely on my personal opinions. Well, *of course* it's based on my personal opinions. How could it be otherwise? But I have nevertheless decided to institute this system; it gives the reader and song-searcher a starting point, at least. I would guess that two-thirds of the songs—especially in the ** category—are obvious choices, anyway. For the rest, readers should take my commentary as their guide. If they do not like Harold Arlen or Stephen Sondheim as much as I seem to, they might wish to discount my many *s in those sections; they can also write in their own *s for the likes of Charles Strouse and Jerry Herman, if they see fit. In pencil.

PART I

Composers of the Early Years

The twentieth century began with American musical theatre dominated by European operettas—English, German, and Austrian. This held firm until 1914, when the Great War quickly ended popularity of things foreign. Jerome Kern, a practiced hand at "Americanizing" imports, finally had a chance to explore his own style; the result was the "modern musical comedy" form (actually, the first of many "modern musical comedy" forms). Irving Berlin, already known along Broadway for pop song hits, tried his hand at complete scores; he was less adventurous than Kern, but highly successful. The postwar years brought three young Kern protégés: George Gershwin, Vincent Youmans, and Richard Rodgers. They surpassed the master with a newer "modern musical comedy" built on dance rhythms; Kern, meanwhile, began development of "musical drama." Cole Porter, of the Kern/Berlin generation, was next to make his mark on Broadway after a long, unapplied apprenticeship. Then came Arthur Schwartz, establishing himself in the months just before the stock market crash. The year 1930 saw the entrance of three talented Gershwin protégés: Harold Arlen, Vernon Duke, and Burton Lane. But the worsening depression brought Broadway musical opportunity to a near halt. Broadway's top composers spent most of the bleak depression in Hollywood. The only important new voices of the 1930s were introduced, fittingly, in politically slanted propaganda musicals. The already renowned Kurt Weill arrived on Broadway in 1936, exiled from Germany (where his work had been radical both musically and politically). Marc Blitzstein was even more outspoken, arriving on Broadway amidst a swirl of controversy. Harold Rome, on the other hand, used comedy and charm to make similar points for the proletariat; not surprisingly, he met with greater popular success than Weill or Blitzstein.

Jerome Kern   3

Irving Berlin   37

George Gershwin   57

Vincent Youmans   77

Richard Rodgers   85

Cole Porter   117

Arthur Schwartz   135

Harold Arlen   149

Vernon Duke   159

Burton Lane   169

Kurt Weill   173

Marc Blitzstein   185

Harold Rome   193

JEROME KERN

Born: January 27, 1885, New York, New York
Died: November 11, 1945, New York, New York

JEROME KERN was raised in Newark, New Jersey, where his father was a merchant. In 1902, Kern left high school to become a song plugger for Edward B. Marks's Lyceum Publishing Company. Kern was already writing songs for amateur groups, and Lyceum shortly issued his first published piece, the 1902 piano solo *At the Casino.* Already determined to write for Broadway, Kern went looking for a theatre music publisher and in 1903 signed on with (and soon bought an interest in) a small house named T. B. Harms. T. B. Harms was owned by the remarkable Max Dreyfus, whose future imprints included Harms, Inc., and Chappell. When Kern's Broadway success began attracting novice composers, Dreyfus selected the most promising of them and convinced producers to hire newcomers like Gershwin, Youmans, Porter, Rodgers, and Schwartz. Back in 1903 Dreyfus published American editions of many of the European operettas prevalent at the time. Interpolations were often needed to "Americanize" the material, so Dreyfus went about getting some assignments for Kern.

AN ENGLISH DAISY
January 18, 1904
Casino Theatre • 41 performances
Music mostly by A. M. Norden; Lyrics to Kern songs by Edgar Smith; Book by Seymour Hicks and Walter Slaughter; Directed by Ben Teal; Produced by (Joe) Weber and (Lew) Fields.

Published Songs
The Downcast Eye—added to post-Broadway tour
Wine, Wine! (Champagne Song)

MR. WIX OF WICKHAM
September 19, 1904
Bijou Theatre • 41 performances
Music mostly by Herbert Darnley and George Everard; Lyrics mostly by John H. Wagner; Book by Herbert Darnley and John H. Wagner; Directed and Produced by Edward E. Rice; With Julian Eltinge.

Published Songs
Angling by the Babbling Brook [lyric by Kern]
From Saturday to Monday
Susan [lyric by Kern]
Waiting for You

THE SILVER SLIPPER
[circa April 1905]
Post-Broadway tour
Music mostly by Leslie Stuart; Lyrics by W. H. Risqué; Book by Clay M. Greene (based on the British book by Owen Hall); Directed by Cyril Scott; Produced by John C. Fisher; With Samuel Collins, Ben Lodge, and George Tennery.

Published Song
My Celia (by John Golden and Kern)—added during tour

THE CATCH OF THE SEASON
August 28, 1905
Daly's Theatre • 104 performances
Music mostly by W. T. Francis and others; Book by Seymour Hicks and Cosmo Hamilton; Directed by Ben Teal; Produced by Charles Frohman; With Edna May.

Published Songs
Frolic of a Breeze [lyric by Clifford Harris]—see
   THE BEAUTY OF BATH [March 19, 1906]

Molly O'Hallerhan (*"Edna May's Irish Song"*)
[lyric by Kern]
Oh, Mr. Chamberlain [lyric by Charles H.
Taylor]—see THE BEAUTY OF BATH
Raining [lyric by Harris]
Take Me on the Merry-Go-Round [lyric by
Kern]
Tulips (*Two Lips*) [lyric by Kern]
Won't You Kiss Me Once before I Go? [lyric by
Fred W. Leigh]

Charles Frohman revolutionized the haphazard
American theatre business with innovations still
in effect today. By 1900 he was equally active
in London, mounting and remounting his hits on
both sides of the Atlantic. Specializing in British plays and operettas, he regularly refused
Kern's offered interpolations until he met the
composer in England and assumed he was British. Kern was soon Frohman's favorite interpo-
lator and good friend—but he never gave Kern
a chance at a complete score.

THE BABES AND THE BARON
October 14, 1905
{London}
Music mostly by H. E. Haines; Lyrics mostly
by Charles H. Taylor; Book by A. M. Thompson
and Robert Courtneidge. Post-Broadway title:
BABES IN THE WOOD.

Published Song
Farewell, Dear Toys (March) [instrumental
with partial lyric by Kern]

THE EARL AND THE GIRL
November 4, 1905
Casino Theatre • 148 performances
Music mostly by Ivan Caryll; Lyrics mostly by
Percy Greenbank; Book by Seymour Hicks;
Directed by R. H. Burnside; Produced by Sam
S. and Lee Shubert, Inc.; With Eddie Foy.

Published Songs
How'd You Like to Spoon with Me? [lyric by
Edward Laska]—also used in THE RICH
MR. HOGGENHEIMER [October 22, 1906]
My Southern Belle [music by Max Eugene (Max
Dreyfus), lyric by Kern]

How'd You Like to Spoon with Me? quickly became Kern's first hit song. ("I'd like to," the boy
sings back.) The Shubert Brothers (Lee, Sam S.,
and J. J.) arrived on Broadway in 1901 and built
an empire which has lasted a century. Sam, the
"good" brother, died May 12, 1905, in a train
crash en route from THE EARL AND THE GIRL
tryout in Cincinnati. Lee opted to keep Sam
billed for the next few years as coproducer rather
than credit J. J. This greatly annoyed little brother
Jake, which was Lee's intention.

THE BEAUTY OF BATH
March 19, 1906
Aldwych Theatre {London} •
287 performances
Music mostly by H. E. Haines; Book by
Seymour Hicks and Cosmo Hamilton;
Choreographed by Edward Royce; Produced
by Charles Frohman; With Seymour Hicks
and Ellaline Terriss (Hicks).

Published Song
Mr. Chamberlain [lyric by P. G. Wodehouse
and Kern]—revised lyric for *Oh, Mr.
Chamberlain* from CATCH OF THE
SEASON [August 28, 1905]

Additional Song Published in Vocal Score
The Frolic of a Breeze [lyric by Wodehouse and
Charles H. Taylor]—revised lyric for song
from CATCH OF THE SEASON

Astute British showman Seymour Hicks brought
Kern and Pelham Grenville Wodehouse together
for these interpolations. The young humorist was
working as a newspaper columnist; his contributions here indicated lyrical skill, but it wasn't
till after the beginning of World War I that the
two resumed collaboration—with revolutionary
(for musical comedy) results.

THE SPRING CHICKEN
[circa March 1906]
Gaiety Theatre {London} • 401 performances
Music mostly by Ivan Caryll and Lionel
Monckton; Lyrics mostly by Adrian Ross and
Percy Greenbank; Book by George Grossmith
(based on *Coquin de Printemps* [play] by Jaimé
and Duval); With Richard Carle.

Published Song
Rosalie [lyric by Grossmith]—added after
London opening; see THE LAUGHING
HUSBAND [February 2, 1914]

Although THE SPRING CHICKEN opened May
30, 1905, Kern's contribution wasn't written
until the following year. For purposes of chronology, the show listing uses the date *Rosalie*
was interpolated.

THE LITTLE CHERUB
August 6, 1906
Criterion Theatre • 155 performances
Music mostly by Ivan Caryll; Lyrics mostly by
Adrian Ross; Book by Owen Hall; Directed by
Ben Teal; Produced by Charles Frohman; With
Hattie Williams.

Published Songs
Meet Me at Twilight [lyric by F. Clifford
Harris]
A Plain Rustic Ride ('Neath the Silv'ry Moon)
[music by Jackson Gouraud and Kern, lyric
by Kern]
Under the Linden Tree [lyric by M. E. Rourke]

Michael Elder Rourke, an Irishman (born in
England), began his Broadway career as a press
agent before moving on to songwriting. Rourke
—who changed his name in 1913 to Herbert
Reynolds—was Kern's major collaborator until
he rejoined with P. G. Wodehouse in 1916.

MY LADY'S MAID
September 20, 1906
Casino Theatre • 44 performances
Music mostly by Paul Rubens; Lyrics by Paul
Rubens and Percy Greenbank; Book by
Edward Paulton and R. H. Burnside (based on
the British musical by Paul Rubens and N.
Newnham Davis); Directed by R. H. Burnside;
Produced by Sam S. and Lee Shubert; With
Madge Crichton.

Published Song
All I Want Is You [lyric by Paul West]

THE RICH MR. HOGGENHEIMER
October 22, 1906
Wallack's Theatre • 187 performances
Music mostly by Ludwig Englander; Book and
Lyrics mostly by Harry B. Smith (based on a
character from *The Girl from Kay's* [musical] by
Owen Hall); Directed by Ben Teal; Produced by
Charles Frohman; With Sam Bernard.

Published Songs
Bagpipe Serenade [lyric by Kern]
Blue, Blue [lyric by Paul West]
Don't You Want a Paper Dearie? [lyric by
West]
How'd You Like to Spoon with Me? [lyric by
Edward Laska]—originally used in THE
EARL AND THE GIRL [November 4, 1905]
I've a Little Favor [lyric by M. E. Rourke]
My Hungarian Irish Girl [lyric by West]
Poker Love (Card Duet) [lyric by West and
Kern]
A Recipe [lyric by Kern and West]—added
after opening, also used in THE ORCHID
[April 8, 1907]

THE WHITE CHRYSANTHEMUM
March 25, 1907
Garrick Theatre {Philadephia} •
Closed during tryout
Music mostly by Howard Talbot; Lyrics mostly
by Arthur Anderson; Book by Leedham
Hantock and Arthur Anderson; With Edna
Wallace Hopper and Lawrence Grossmith.

Published Songs
Bill's a Liar [lyric by M. E. Rourke]
I Just Couldn't Do without You [lyric by Paul
West]

THE ORCHID
April 8, 1907
Herald Square Theatre • 178 performances
Music mostly by Ivan Caryll and Lionel
Monckton; Lyrics mostly by Adrian Ross and
Percy Greenbank; Book by James T. Tanner
and Joseph W. Herbert; Directed by Frank
Smithson; Produced by Sam S. and Lee
Shubert, Inc.; With Eddie Foy.

Published Songs

Come Around on Our Veranda [lyric by Paul West and Kern]

I'm Well Known [lyric by Kern]

A Recipe [lyric by Kern and West]—originally used in THE RICH MR. HOGGENHEIMER [October 22, 1906]

FASCINATING FLORA

May 20, 1907
Casino Theatre • 113 performances
Music mostly by Gustave Kerker; Book by R. H. Burnside and Joseph W. Herbert; Staged by R. H. Burnside; Produced by R. H. Burnside and F. Ray Comstock.

Published Songs

Ballooning [lyric by Paul West]

Katy Was a Business Girl [lyric by West]

The Little Church around the Corner [lyric by M. E. Rourke]

Right Now [music by Fred Fisher, lyric by Kern]

The Subway Express [lyric by James O'Dea]

Producer F. Ray Comstock, an early Kern fan, ultimately devised the Princess Theatre series—and gave Kern the assignment that established him as Broadway's leading composer (see NOBODY HOME [April 20, 1915]). But not until Kern had slogged his way through eight more years of interpolations.

THE DAIRYMAIDS

August 26, 1907
Criterion Theatre • 86 performances
Music mostly by Paul A. Rubens and Frank A. Tours; Lyrics to Kern songs by M. E. Rourke; Book by A. M. Thompson and Robert Courtneidge; Directed by A. E. Dodson; Produced by Charles Frohman; With Julia Sanderson.

Published Songs

Cheer Up Girls
The Hay Ride
I'd Like to Meet Your Father
I've a Million Reasons Why I Love You
Little Eva
Mary McGee
Never Marry a Girl with Cold Feet

THE GAY WHITE WAY

October 7, 1907
Casino Theatre • 105 performances
Music mostly by Ludwig Englander; Book by Sydney Rosenfeld and J. Clarence Harvey; Directed by R. H. Burnside; Produced by Sam S. and Lee Shubert, Inc.; With Melville Ellis.

Published Song

Without the Girl—Inside! [lyric by M. E. Rourke and Kern]

THE MORALS OF MARCUS

November 18, 1907
Criterion Theatre • 44 performances
Play by William J. Locke; Produced by Charles Frohman; With Marie Doro.

Published Song

Eastern Moon [lyric by M. E. Rourke]

PETER PAN, OR THE BOY WHO WOULDN'T GROW UP [1907]

[circa December 1907]
Post-Broadway tour
Play by J. M. Barrie; Produced by Charles Frohman; With Maude Adams and Ernest Lawford.

Published Song

Won't You Have a Little Feather? [lyric by Paul West]—added during tour

Producer Charles Frohman, actress Maude Adams, and playwright J. M. Barrie formed an unlikely but enduring friendship. Written specifically for the great American star Adams, PETER PAN cast something of a spell over each of their lives (see ROSY RAPTURE [March 22, 1915]). Adams's debut in the role had been November 6, 1905; she toured in the play for years. Kern also provided a song for Broadway's first non-Adams production of the play, Marilyn Miller's unsuccessful attempt [November 6, 1924].

A WALTZ DREAM

January 27, 1908
Broadway Theatre • 111 performances
Music mostly by Oscar Straus; Lyrics mostly by Joseph W. Herbert; Book by Felix

Doermann and Leopold Jacobson (based on the Austrian musical by Hans Müeller); Directed by Herbert Gresham; Produced by The Inter-State Amusement Co., Inc.

Published Songs
The Gay Lothario [lyric by C. H. Bovill]
I'd Much Rather Stay at Home [lyric by Bovill]
Vienna [lyric by Adrian Ross]

The musical theatre world changed abruptly with the success of Franz Lehar's Viennese operetta *Die Lustige Witwe* [December 30, 1905]. (Tenor Edmund Loewe starred in the Berlin première; his nineteen-month-old son wrote MY FAIR LADY [Loewe: March 15, 1956], though not until fifty years later.) THE MERRY WIDOW† waltzed into London [June 8, 1907], then on to New York [October 21, 1907]. Kern's "American" interpolations into British imports had given him a name, of sorts, and he was ready for his big break; but now audiences only wanted Viennese operetta. So Kern began a new round of interpolations.

THE GIRLS OF GOTTENBERG
September 2, 1908
Knickerbocker Theatre • 103 performances
Music mostly by Ivan Caryll and Lionel Monckton; Lyrics mostly by C. H. Bovill; Book by George Grossmith and L. E. Berman; Directed by J. A. E. Malone; Produced by Charles Frohman; With Gertie Millar.

Published Songs
Freida [lyric by M. E. Rourke]
I Can't Say You're the Only One
Nothing at All [lyric by Rourke]

FLUFFY RUFFLES
September 7, 1908
Criterion Theatre • 48 performances
Music mostly by W. T. Francis; Lyrics mostly by Wallace Irwin; Lyrics to Kern songs mostly by C. H. Bovill; Book by John J. McNally; Directed by Ben Teal; Produced by Charles Frohman; With Hattie Williams.

Published Songs
Aida McCluskie
Dining Out [lyric by George Grossmith]

Meet Her with a Taximeter
Mrs. Cockatoo
Sweetest Girl, Silly Boy, I Love You [lyric by Irwin]
Take Care
There's Something Rather Odd about Augustus
Won't You Let Me Carry Your Parcel?

KITTIE GREY
January 25, 1909
New Amsterdam Theatre • 48 performances
Music mostly by Augustus Barratt, Howard Talbot, and Lionel Monckton; Lyrics to Kern songs by M. E. Rourke; Book by J. Smyth Pigott (based on *Les Fêtards* [play] by Antony Mars and Maurice Hennequin); Directed by Austin Hurgon; Produced by Charles Frohman; With Julia Sanderson and G. P. Huntley.

Published Songs
Eulalie
If the Girl Wants You (Never Mind the Color of Her Eyes)
Just Good Friends

THE GAY HUSSARS
July 29, 1909
Knickerbocker Theatre • 44 performances
Music by Emmerich Kalman; English lyrics by Grant Stewart; Book by Maurice Browne Kirby (based on the Austrian musical by Karl Von Bakonyi and Robert Bodansky); Directed by George Marion; Produced by Henry W. Savage.

Published Song
Shine Out All You Little Stars [lyric by M. E. Rourke]

THE DOLLAR PRINCESS
September 6, 1909
Knickerbocker Theatre • 288 performances
Music mostly by Leo Fall; Book by George Grossmith (based on the Austrian musical by A. M. Willner and Fritz Grunbaum); Directed by J. A. E. Malone; Produced by Charles Frohman; With Donald Brian and Valli Valli.

Published Songs
A Boat Sails on Wednesday [quartet] [lyric by Adrian Ross and Grossmith]—written for London production [September 25, 1909]

Not Here! Not Here! [lyric by M. E. Rourke]—see THE GIRL FROM UTAH [August 24, 1914]

Red, White, and Blue [lyric by Ross]—written for London production

THE GIRL AND THE WIZARD
September 27, 1909
Casino Theatre • 96 performances
Music mostly by Julian Edwards [see Berlin: September 27, 1909]; Lyrics mostly by Robert B. Smith and Edward Madden; Lyrics to Kern songs by Percival Knight; Book by J. Hartley Manners; Directed by Ned Wayburn; Produced by the Messrs. Shubert; With Sam Bernard.

Published Songs
By the Blue Lagoon
Frantzi
Suzette and Her Pet

THE GOLDEN WIDOW
October 26, 1909
Belasco Theatre {Washington, D.C.} • Closed during tryout
Music mostly by Melville Gideon and Louis Hirsch; Lyrics mostly by Edward Madden; Book by Joseph Herbert; Produced by Sam S. and Lee Shubert; With Louise Dresser.

Published Song
Howdy! How D'You Do? [lyric by M. E. Rourke]

KING OF CADONIA
January 10, 1910
Daly's Theatre • 16 performances
Music also by Sidney Jones; Lyrics to Kern songs by M. E. Rourke; Book by Frederick Lonsdale; Directed by Joseph Herbert; Produced by the Messrs. Shubert; With Marguerite Clark.

Published Songs
The Blue Bulgarian Band
Catamarang [lyric by Percival Knight]—see SALLY [December 21, 1920]
Come Along, Pretty Girl—also used in THE GIRL AND THE DRUMMER [circa August 1910]

Coo-coo Coo-coo (Marie) [lyric by Maurice Stonehill]
Every Girl I Meet [lyric by Percival Knight]
Hippopotamus
Lena, Lena
Mother and Father

THE ECHO
August 17, 1910
Globe Theatre • 53 performances
Music mostly by Deems Taylor; Book by William Le Baron; Directed by Fred G. Latham; Produced by Charles B. Dillingham; With John E. Hazzard, Bessie McCoy, and George White.

Published Song
Whistle When You're Lonely [lyric by M. E. Rourke]

Charles Dillingham, former aide to Charles Frohman, began his producing career in 1903 with a series of Victor Herbert musicals (including THE RED MILL† [September 24, 1906]). He remained the most respected producer of American musicals until the stock market crash, often in competition with sometime partner (and co-manager of the New Amsterdam Theatre) Florenz Ziegfeld, Jr.

OUR MISS GIBBS
August 29, 1910
Knickerbocker Theatre • 64 performances
Music mostly by Ivan Caryll and Lionel Monckton; Book by James T. Tanner; Directed by Thomas Reynolds; Produced by Charles Frohman; With Pauline Chase.

Published Songs
Come Tiny Goldfish to Me [music by Harry Marlow, lyric by Kern]
Eight Little Girls [lyric by M. E. Rourke]
I Don't Want You to Be a Sister to Me [lyric by Frederick Day]

THE GIRL AND THE DRUMMER
[circa August 1910]
Closed during tryout
Music mostly by Augustus Barratt (see Berlin: circa August 1910); Book and Lyrics mostly by

George Broadhurst (based on *What Happened to Jones* [play] by George Broadhurst); Produced by Wm. A. Brady, Ltd.; With Herbert Corthell and Belle Gold.

Published Song

Come Along, Pretty Girl [lyric by M. E. Rourke]—originally used in KING OF CADONIA [January 10, 1910]

THE HENPECKS

February 4, 1911
Broadway Theatre • 137 performances
"Notes" mostly by A. Baldwin Sloane; "Rhymes" mostly by E. Ray Goetz; "Words" by Glen MacDonough; Directed by Ned Wayburn; Produced by Lew Fields; With Mr. and Mrs. Sam Watson and Gertrude Quinlan.

Published Song

The Manicure Girl [lyric by Frederick Day]

LA BELLE PAREE

March 20, 1911
Winter Garden Theatre • 104 performances
"A Jumble of Jollity." Music also by Frank Tours; Lyrics by Edward Madden; Book by Edgar Smith; Produced by the Messrs. Shubert; With Stella Mayhew, Kitty Gordon, Al Jolson, and Mitzi Hajos.

Published Songs

De Goblin's Glide [lyric by Frederick Day]
The Edinboro Wriggle [lyric by M. E. Rourke]
   —originally printed in a newspaper supplement as *The Edinboro Jig*
I'm the Human Brush (*That Paints the Crimson on Paree*)
Look Me Over Dearie—added after opening
Paris Is a Paradise for Coons
Sing Trovatore
That s All Right for McGilligan [lyric by Rourke]—added after opening

The Shuberts opened their lavish new musical showplace—formerly a stable—with a vaudeville show featuring the two-act revue LA BELLE PAREE. The hit of the evening was Shubert discovery Al Jolson (singing, needless to say, *Paris Is a Paradise for Coons*). He became a Winter Garden fixture and was quickly elevated to stardom.

LITTLE MISS FIX-IT

April 3, 1911
Globe Theatre • 56 performances
Music and Lyrics mostly by Jack Norworth; Book by William J. Hurlbut and Harry B. Smith; Directed by Gustav von Seyfferitz; Produced by Louis F. Werba and Mark A. Luescher; With Nora Bayes and Jack Norworth.

Published Songs

There Is a Happy Land (*Tale of Woe*) [lyric by Norworth]
Turkey Trot [instrumental] [music by Kern and Dave Stamper]

ZIEGFELD FOLLIES OF 1911

June 26, 1911
Jardin de Paris • 80 performances
Music mostly by Maurice Levi and Raymond Hubbell (see Berlin: June 26, 1911); Book and Lyrics mostly by George V. Hobart; Staged by Julian Mitchell; Produced by Florenz Ziegfeld, Jr.; With Bessie McCoy.

Published Song

I'm a Crazy Daffydil [lyric by Bessie McCoy]

This fifth edition of the series marked Kern's first association with Ziegfeld. Despite the producer's indifferent musical ear, he was later responsible for mounting two of Kern's biggest hits.

THE SIREN

August 28, 1911
Knickerbocker Theatre • 136 performances
Music mostly by Leo Fall; Book and Lyrics mostly by Harry B. Smith (based on the Austrian musical by Leo Stein and A. M. Willner); Produced by Charles Frohman; With Donald Brian and Julia Sanderson.

Published Songs

Follow Me Round [music by Fall, lyric by Adrian Ross and Kern]
In the Valley of Montbijou [lyric by M. E. Rourke]
I Want to Sing in Opera [music and lyric by Morton David, George Arthurs, and Kern]
My Heart I Cannot Give to You [lyric by Matthew Woodward]

Donald Brian—star of the Broadway MERRY WIDOW† [October 21, 1907]—and Julia Sanderson played together in several Kern shows, including the composer's breakthrough hit THE GIRL FROM UTAH [August 24, 1914].

THE KISS WALTZ
September 18, 1911
Casino Theatre • 88 performances
Music mostly by C. M. Ziehrer; Lyrics by Matthew Woodward; Book by Edgar Smith; Directed by J. C. Huffman; Produced by the Messrs. Shubert; With Adele Rowland.

Published Songs
Fan Me with a Movement Slow
Love Is Like a Rubber Band (*Hoop Song*)
Love's Charming Art
Ta-Ta, Little Girl
There's a Resting Place for Every Girl (*Sun Chair Song*)

THE OPERA BALL
February 12, 1912
Liberty Theatre • 32 performances
Music mostly by Richard Heuberger; Book by Sydney Rosenfeld (based on the Austrian musical by Victor Leon and H. von Waldbaum); With Marie Cahill.

Songs Published (No Lyrics) in Piano Selection
Marie-Louise
Nurses Are We—advertised but not published separately
Sergeant Philip of the Dancers—advertised but not published separately

A WINSOME WIDOW
April 11, 1912
Moulin Rouge Theatre • 172 performances
Music mostly by Raymond Hubbell; Lyrics mostly by Harry B. and Robert B. Smith (based on *A Trip to Chinatown* [musical] by Charles Hoyt); Directed by Julian Mitchell; Produced by Florenz Ziegfeld, Jr.

Published Song
Call Me Flo [words and music by John Golden and Kern]

THE GIRL FROM MONTMARTRE
August 5, 1912
Criterion Theatre • 64 performances
Music mostly by Henry Bereny and Kern; Book and Lyrics mostly by Harry B. and Robert B. Smith (based on the French musical by Henry Bereny and Rodolph Schanzer, from *La Dame de Chez Maxim* [farce] by Georges Feydeau); Directed by Tom Reynolds; Produced by Charles Frohman; With Hattie Williams and Richard Carle.

Published Songs
Bohemia [lyric by Robert B. Smith]
Don't Turn My Picture to the Wall [lyric by Smith]
Hoop-La-La, Papa! [lyric by M. E. Rourke]
I'll Be Waiting 'neath Your Window ["written and composed" by James Duffy and Kern]
I've Taken Such a Fancy to You [lyric by Clifford Harris]
Ooo, Ooo, Lena! ["written and composed" by John Golden and Kern]

A POLISH WEDDING
August 31, 1912
Empire Theatre {Syracuse, N.Y.} • Closed during tryout
"A Fascinating Farce with Dainty Music."
Music mostly by Jean Gilbert; Book and Lyrics mostly by George V. Hobart (based on *Die Polnische Wirtschaft* [musical] by Kraatz and Okonkowski); Produced by George M. Cohan and Sam H. Harris; With Valli Valli, Ann Pennington, and Genevieve Tobin.

Published Songs
Bygone Days [lyric by Kern]
He Must Be Nice to Mother
Let Us Build a Little Nest [lyric by Kern and Hobart]—see HEAD OVER HEELS [August 29, 1918]
You're the Only Girl He Loves—see OH LADY! LADY!! [February 1, 1918]

THE "MIND-THE-PAINT" GIRL
September 9, 1912
Lyceum Theatre • 136 performances
Play by Sir Arthur Wing Pinero; Directed by

Dion G. Boucicault; Produced by Charles Frohman; With Billie Burke.

Published Songs
If You Would Only Love Me [words and music by John Crook and Kern]
Mind the Paint [lyric by Pinero]

Billie Burke was one of Charles Frohman's major stars. The producer demanded his leading ladies live chaste, scandal-free lives. He banished Burke when she clandestinely married Flo Ziegfeld in 1914.

THE WOMAN HATERS
October 7, 1912
Astor Theatre • 32 performances
Music mostly by Edmund Eysler; Book and Lyrics by George V. Hobart (based on *Die Frauenfresser* [musical] by Leo Stein and Karl Lindau); Directed by George Marion; Produced by A. H. Woods; With Dolly Castles.

Published Song
Come on Over Here [music by Walter Kollo, lyric by Kern and Hobart]—also used in THE DOLL GIRL [August 25, 1913]

THE RED PETTICOAT
November 13, 1912
Daly's Theatre • 61 performances
Lyrics by Paul West; Book by Rida Johnson Young (based on *Next* [play] by Rida Johnson Young); Directed by Joseph W. Herbert; Produced by Sam S. and Lee Shubert, Inc.; With Helen Lowell. Pre-Broadway title: LOOK WHO'S HERE.

Published Songs
I Wonder
Little Golden Maid
My Peaches and Cream
Oh, You Beautiful Spring [lyric by M. E. Rourke]
The Ragtime Restaurant
Since the Days of Grandmama

After eight years on Broadway, Kern was given a chance by Lee Shubert to write a complete, original score. Not successfully, though. Kern had heretofore cloaked his individual style with English and Viennese overtones. Now, as the developing political situation ended the popularity of things Continental and English imports gradually halted, Kern's originality launched him into Broadway prominence.

THE SUNSHINE GIRL
February 3, 1913
Knickerbocker Theatre • 160 performances
Music mostly by Paul A. Rubens; Lyrics mostly by Arthur Wimperis and Paul A. Rubens; Book by Paul A. Rubens and Cecil Raleigh; Directed by J. A. E. Malone; Produced by Charles Frohman; With Julia Sanderson and Joseph Cawthorn.

Published Song
Honeymoon Lane [lyric by M. E. Rourke]

THE AMAZONS
April 28, 1913
Empire Theatre • 48 performances
Play by Sir Arthur Wing Pinero; Directed by William Seymour; Produced by Charles Frohman; With Billie Burke.

Published Song
My Otaheitee Lady [lyric by Charles Taylor]

THE DOLL GIRL
August 25, 1913
Globe Theatre • 88 performances
Music mostly by Leo Fall; Book and Lyrics mostly by Harry B. Smith (based on the Austrian musical by Leo Stein and A. M. Willner, from *Riquette et sa Mère* [play] by Caillavet and de Flers); Produced by Charles Frohman; With Hattie Williams and Richard Carle.

Published Songs
Come on Over Here [music by Walter Kollo, lyric by Smith and Kern]—revised lyric for song of same title from THE WOMAN HATERS [October 7, 1912]
If We Were on Our Honeymoon (Railway Duet)
A Little Thing Like a Kiss—see OH LADY! LADY!! [February 1, 1918]

When Three Is Company (Cupid Song) [lyric by
M. E. Rourke]—see ZIEGFELD FOLLIES
OF 1917 [April 13, 1917]
Will It All End in Smoke?

Additional Songs Published (No Lyrics) in
Piano Selection
I'm Going Away
Opening Act Two (Russian Dance)

Harry Bache Smith was the most prolific writer
in American musical theatre history, with lyrics
and librettos for over three hundred (pretty much
forgotten) shows. His early collaboration with
Reginald DeKoven (THE BEGUM [November 21,
1887]) is considered by many the first "American"
comic operetta. In the course of his long career
he also did notable work with Victor Herbert.
Smith's close friendship with Kern included a
shared passion for collecting antique books. Kern
auctioned off most of his collection in January
1929 for an unprecedented $1.7 million. Kern
knew enough not to invest in show business, so
he took the money and put it in the stock market.

LIEBER AUGUSTIN
September 3, 1913
Casino Theatre • 37 performances
Music mostly by Leo Fall; Book by Edgar
Smith (based on the Austrian musical by Ernst
Welisch and Rudolf Bernauer); Directed by Al
Holbrook and Julian Alfred; Produced by Sam
S. and Lee Shubert, Inc.; With DeWolf Hopper
and George MacFarlane. Post-opening title:
MISS CAPRICE.

Published Song
Look in Her Eyes [lyric by Herbert Reynolds
(M. E. Rourke)]—also used (as *Look in His
Eyes*) in HAVE A HEART [January 11,
1917]

The Shuberts anglicized LIEBER AUGUSTIN's
name after the opening, this being a bad time for
things German, but to no avail.

THE MARRIAGE MARKET
September 22, 1913
Knickerbocker Theatre • 80 performances
Music mostly by Victor Jacobi; Lyrics to Kern
songs by M. E. Rourke; Book by Gladys Unger

(based on the Austrian musical by M. Brody
and F. Martos); Directed by Edward Royce;
Produced by Charles Frohman; With Donald
Brian.

Published Songs
By the Country Stile [lyric by Kern]
I'm Looking for an Irish Husband—cut after
opening
I've Got Money in the Bank
A Little Bit of Silk—cut after opening
You're Here and I'm Here [lyric by Harry B.
Smith]—added to post-Broadway tour;
originally used in THE LAUGHING
HUSBAND [February 2, 1914]

DIE BALLKÖNIGIN
[circa September 1913]
{Vienna, Austria}
Music mostly by H. E. Haines and Evelyn
Baker; Book and Lyrics by Fritz Luner and
Karl Tuschl (based on a libretto by Seymour
Hicks and Cosmo Hamilton).

Published Song
Die Süsse Pariserin (Fraulein de Loraine) [lyric
by Luner]—see THE STEPPING STONES
[November 6, 1923] and LADY MARY
[February 23, 1928]

Die Süsse Pariserin (the sweet Parisian) seems to
be one of Kern's early British interpolations; it's
highly unlikely that he wrote it specifically for
this Viennese operetta. DIE BALLKÖNIGIN (The
King's Ball) could well have been an adaptation
of THE BEAUTY OF BATH [March 19, 1906].
However, *Die Süsse Pariserin* is not related to the
published Kern songs from that show.

OH, I SAY!
October 30, 1913
Casino Theatre • 68 performances
"*A Riotous Musical Comedy.*" Music mostly by
Kern; Lyrics mostly by Harry B. Smith; Book
by Sydney Blowe and Douglas Hoare (based on
a play by Keroul and Barré); Directed by J. C.
Huffman; Produced by the Messrs. Shubert;
With Joseph W. Herbert and Cecil Cunningham.
Post-Broadway title: THE WEDDING NIGHT.

Published Songs

Alone at Last [1st]—different than song with
    same title from VERY GOOD EDDIE [1915]
    [December 23, 1915]; also see BLUE EYES
    [April 27, 1928]
Each Pearl a Thought
I Can't Forget Your Eyes—see SUNNY [Septem-
    ber 22, 1925] and CRISS-CROSS [October
    12, 1926]
I Know and She Knows
Katy-did
A Wifie of Your Own

Kern's second complete score—again for the
Shuberts—was more successful than THE RED
PETTICOAT [November 13, 1912], if not particu-
larly distinguished.

THE LAUGHING HUSBAND
February 2, 1914
Knickerbocker Theatre • 48 performances
Music mostly by Edmund Eysler; Lyrics to
Kern songs by Harry B. Smith; Book by Arthur
Wimperis (based on the Austrian musical by
Julius Brammer and Alfred Grunwald); Directed
by Edward Royce; Produced by Charles
Frohman; With Courtice Pounds.

Published Songs

Bought and Paid For—see SUNNY [September
    22, 1925] and CRISS-CROSS [October 12,
    1926]
Love Is Like a Violin
Take a Step with Me—new lyric for *Rosalie*
    from THE SPRING CHICKEN [circa
    March 1906]
*You're Here and I'm Here—also used in THE
    MARRIAGE MARKET [September 22, 1913]

You're Here and I'm Here was another American-
flavored Kern song hit. THE LAUGHING HUS-
BAND had a brief life, so the song was inserted
into the successfully touring MARRIAGE MAR-
KET to help sell tickets (and music sheets).

WHEN CLAUDIA SMILES
February 2, 1914
39th Street Theatre • 56 performances
Play by Anne Caldwell (based on a play by Leo
Ditrichstein); Produced by Frederic McKay;
With Blanche Ring and Charles Winninger.

Published Song
Ssh . . . You'll Waken Mister Doyle [music by
    John L. Golden; lyric by E. W. Rogers,
    Golden, and Kern]

THE GIRL FROM UTAH
August 24, 1914
Knickerbocker Theatre • 120 performances
"The Acme of Musical Comedy." Music mostly
by Paul Rubens and Sydney Jones; Lyrics to
Kern songs by Harry B. Smith; Book by James
T. Tanner; Directed by J. A. E. Malone;
Produced by Charles Frohman; With Donald
Brian, Julia Sanderson, and Joseph Cawthorn.

Published Songs
Alice in Wonderland
The Land of "Let's Pretend"—revised version
    of *Not Here! Not Here!* from THE DOLLAR
    PRINCESS [September 6, 1909]
The Same Sort of Girl—see ROSY RAPTURE
    [March 22, 1915]
*They Didn't Believe Me [lyric by Herbert
    Reynolds]—also used in TONIGHT'S THE
    NIGHT! [April 28, 1915]
We'll Take Care of You All—cut; also used in
    FADS AND FANCIES [March 8, 1915]
Why Don't They Dance the Polka Anymore?
You Never Can Tell—cut

Although Kern merely interpolated songs to
THE GIRL FROM UTAH, the show's popularity rested on one of his songs. *They Didn't Believe Me* was unlike anything that preceded it,
featuring a couple of unusual but catchy musical devices (like the delicious chromatics in the
B section). Already well known to theatre audiences, within the year Kern was established as
Broadway's leading "modern" composer, in a
pack with the likes of Victor Herbert, Rudolf
Friml, and George M. Cohan.

NINETY IN THE SHADE
January 25, 1915
Knickerbocker Theatre • 40 performances
Music and Lyrics also by Clare Kummer;
Lyrics to Kern songs by Harry B. Smith; Book
by Guy Bolton; Directed by Robert Milton;
Produced by Daniel V. Arthur; With Marie
Cahill and Richard Carle.

Published Songs

Can't You See I Mean You? [lyric by Herbert Reynolds]—see VERY GOOD EDDIE [1915] [December 23, 1915] and THEODORE AND CO. [September 19, 1916]

It Isn't Your Fault [lyric by Reynolds]—initial publication upon reuse in LOVE O' MIKE [January 15, 1917]

Love Blossoms—advertised but not published

A Package of Seeds—initial publication upon reuse in OH, BOY! [February 20, 1917]

The Triangle [musical scene] [lyric by Bolton]—initial publication upon reuse in VERY GOOD EDDIE [1915]

Where's the Girl for Me?—advertised but not published; initial publication upon reuse in THE LADY IN RED [May 12, 1919]

Whistling Dan—advertised but not published; see LEAVE IT TO JANE [August 28, 1917]

The thirty-year-old Kern entered the second phase of his career, divorcing himself from all operetta influences (except Arthur Sullivan). At the same time, his collaborators—led by librettist Guy Bolton—began using more realistic situations and contemporary American locales and characters. Bolton, born in England of American parents, followed his father into architecture before entering the theatre in 1912. NINETY IN THE SHADE was a failure, but Kern and Bolton were already at work on the first show of the Princess Theatre series.

A GIRL OF TODAY

February 8, 1915
{Washington, D.C.} • Closed during tryout
Play by Porter Emerson Browne; Produced by Charles Frohman; With Ann Murdock.

Published Song

You Know and I Know [lyric by Schuyler Greene]—see NOBODY HOME [April 20, 1915]

FADS AND FANCIES

March 8, 1915
Knickerbocker Theatre • 48 performances
Music mostly by Raymond Hubbell; Book and Lyrics mostly by Glen MacDonough; Directed

by Herbert Gresham; Produced by Klaw and Erlanger; With Frank Moulan.

Published Song

We'll Take Care of You All (*Refugee Song*) [lyric by Harry B. Smith]—originally used (cut) in THE GIRL FROM UTAH [August 24, 1914]

ROSY RAPTURE, THE PRIDE OF THE BEAUTY CHORUS

March 22, 1915
Duke of York's Theatre {London}
Burlesque by J. M. Barrie; Produced by Charles Frohman; With Gaby Deslys and Jack Norworth.

Published Song

Best Sort of Mother, Best Sort of Child [lyric by F. W. Mark]—new lyric for *The Same Sort of Girl* from THE GIRL FROM UTAH [August 24, 1914]

A legendary (but unconfirmable) story says that Frohman and Kern booked passage to sail together to England. Kern overslept and missed the departure. On May 7, 1915, the Lusitania was sunk by a German torpedo; the gentle Frohman paraphrased his friend Barrie's PETER PAN [circa December 1907]—"Why fear Death? It is the most beautiful adventure of Life"—as the ship went down.

NOBODY HOME

April 20, 1915
Princess Theatre • 135 performances
Lyrics mostly by Schuyler Greene; Book by Guy Bolton (based on *Mr. Popple (of Ippleton)* [musical] by Paul A. Rubens); Directed by J. H. Benrimo; Produced by F. Ray Comstock; With Adele Rowland.

Published Songs

Another Little Girl [lyric by Herbert Reynolds]

Any Old Night (*Is a Wonderful Night*) [music by Otto Motzan and Kern, lyric by Greene and Harry B. Smith]—also used in TONIGHT'S THE NIGHT! [April 28, 1915]

At That San Francisco Fair [music by Ford Dabney, James Reese Europe, and Kern]

The Chaplin Walk [music by Motzan and Kern]

In Arcady [lyric by Reynolds]

The Magic Melody

That Peculiar Tune [music by Kern and Motzan, lyric by Greene and Reynolds]—cut; initial publication as 1916 non-show song

Wedding Bells Are Calling Me [lyric by Smith]—added after opening; also used in VERY GOOD EDDIE [1915] [December 23, 1915]

You Know and I Know—originally used in A GIRL OF TODAY [February 8, 1915]

F. Ray Comstock managed the 299-seat Princess for the Shuberts. Having been unable to find suitable attractions for the two-year-old jewel-box theatre, Comstock and play agent Elisabeth Marbury (see SEE AMERICA FIRST [Porter: March 28, 1916]) decided to try a small scale, contemporary musical comedy. NOBODY HOME, adapted from a 1905 British musical, was not successful; but the Princess Theatre series concept took off with its second offering, the very good VERY GOOD EDDIE [1915].

TONIGHT'S THE NIGHT!

April 28, 1915

Gaiety Theatre {London} • 460 performances

Music mostly by Paul A. Rubens; Lyrics mostly by Paul A. Rubens and Percy Greenbank; Book by Fred Thompson (based on *The Pink Dominos* [play] by James Albery); Produced by George Grossmith and Edward Laurillard; With George Grossmith and Madge Saunders.

Published Songs

Any Old Night (*Is a Wonderful Night*) [music by Otto Motzan and Kern, lyric by Schuyler Greene and Harry B. Smith]—originally used in NOBODY HOME [April 20, 1915]

They Didn't Believe Me [lyric by Herbert Reynolds]—originally used in THE GIRL FROM UTAH [August 24, 1914]

A MODERN EVE

May 3, 1915

Casino Theatre • 56 performances

Music mostly by Jean Gilbert and Victor Hollaender; Lyrics to Kern songs by Harry B. Smith; Book by Will M. Hough and Benjamin

Hapgood Burt (based on the German musical by Georg Okonkowski and Alfred Schönfeld); Directed by Frank Smithson; Produced by Mort H. Singer.

Published Songs

I'd Love to Dance through Life with You

I've Just Been Waiting for You

COUSIN LUCY

August 27, 1915

George M. Cohan Theatre • 43 performances

Play by Charles Klein; Lyrics by Schuyler Greene; Directed by Robert Milton; Produced by A. H. Woods; With Julian Eltinge.

Published Songs

Society

Those "Come Hither" Eyes—see THEODORE AND CO. [September 19, 1916]

Two Heads Are Better Than One [lyric by Kern and Greene]—see ROCK-A-BYE BABY [May 22, 1918]

Julian Eltinge was Broadway's finest female impersonator and immensely popular with the family trade. In 1912 he became only the second performer to have a Broadway theatre built in his honor; Maxine Elliott, a Lee Shubert mistress, was the first. The charming Eltinge—which for many years was called the Empire—survived more than eighty years of 42nd Street abuse. In 1998 it was lifted, moved 130 feet westward, and transformed into the entrance lobby for a new multiplex.

MISS INFORMATION

October 5, 1915

George M. Cohan Theatre • 47 performances

"A Little Comedy with Music." Play by Paul Dickey and Charles W. Goddard; Music mostly by Kern [see Porter: October 5, 1915]; Lyrics mostly by Elsie Janis; Book by Paul Dickey and Charles W. Goddard; Directed by Robert Milton; Produced by Charles B. Dillingham; With Elsie Janis and Irene Bordoni.

Published Songs

A Little Love (*But Not for Me*)—also used in VERY GOOD EDDIE [1915] [December 23, 1915]

On the Sands of Wa-Ki-Ki [music by Henry Kailimai and Kern]—also used in VERY GOOD EDDIE [1915]

Some Sort of Somebody—also used in VERY GOOD EDDIE [1915]

Cole Porter—the first of the Gershwin/Youmans/Rodgers group to reach Broadway—had his second interpolation in this little comedy, with little success. Eldest member of the oncoming new generation, Porter was the only one not particularly influenced by Kern.

VERY GOOD EDDIE [1915]

December 23, 1915

Princess Theatre • 341 performances

Lyrics mostly by Schuyler Greene and Herbert Reynolds [M. E. Rourke] (also see Porter: May 18, 1918); Book by Philip Bartholomae and Guy Bolton (based on *Over Night* [play] by Philip Bartholomae); Directed by Frank McCormick; Produced by the Marbury-Comstock Co.; With Ernest Truex, Alice Dovey, and John E. Hazzard

Revival

December 21, 1975

Booth Theatre • 288 performances

Directed by Bill Gile; Choreographed by Dan Siretta; Produced by David Merrick, Max Brown, and Byron Goldman; Transferred from the Goodspeed Opera House; With Charles Repole [Truex], Virginia Seidel [Dovey], and James Harder [Hazzard].

Published Songs

*Babes in the Wood [lyric by Kern and Greene]

Babes in the Wood (*"Fox-Trot"*)—non-show dance version

I'd Like to Have a Million in the Bank [lyric by Reynolds]

If I Find the Girl [lyric by John E. Hazzard and Reynolds]

Isn't It Great to Be Married? [lyric by Greene]—new lyric for *Can't You See I Mean You?* from NINETY IN THE SHADE [January 25, 1915]; also see THEODORE AND CO. [September 19, 1916]

I've Got to Dance [lyric by Greene]—cut

Nodding Roses [lyric by Greene and Reynolds]

Old Bill Baker (the Undertaker) [lyric by Ring Lardner]—added after opening

Old Boy Neutral [lyric by Greene]—music revised from *A Little Love* from MISS INFORMATION [October 5, 1915]

On the Shore at Le Lei Wi [music by Henry Kailimai and Kern, lyric by Reynolds]—new lyric for *On the Sands of Wa-Ki-Ki* from MISS INFORMATION

Some Sort of Somebody (*All of the Time*) [lyric by Elsie Janis]—originally used in MISS INFORMATION

Thirteen Collar [lyric by Greene]

Wedding Bells Are Calling Me [lyric by Harry B. Smith]—originally used in NOBODY HOME [April 20, 1915]

Additional Songs Published in Vocal Score

Alone at Last [2nd] [lyric by Reynolds]—different than song with same title from OH, I SAY! [October 30, 1913]

Buffo Dance [instrumental]

Dance Trio [instrumental]

The Triangle [musical scene] [lyric by Bolton]—originally used (unpublished) in NINETY IN THE SHADE

We're on Our Way [lyric by Greene]

The first Princess Theatre show had been an Americanized import. Beginning with VERY GOOD EDDIE, Kern and Bolton—soon joined by Wodehouse—concentrated on making comedy and song spring directly from situation and character (as opposed to finding a loose framework and inserting whatever jokes and songs turned up). The difference was immediately noted, and Kern and company went on to a creative showmaking spree. *Babes in the Wood*, a "modern" lullaby, joined *They Didn't Believe Me* as Kern's second major song hit in his newly developing style. Ring Lardner's *Old Bill Baker*—about a popular undertaker in Rye, New York (which rhymes with die)—quickly disappeared, but it's sure amusing.

ZIEGFELD FOLLIES OF 1916

June 12, 1916

New Amsterdam Theatre • 112 performances

Music mostly by Louis Hirsch and Dave Stamper [see Berlin: June 12, 1916; Book and

Lyrics mostly by George V. Hobart and Gene Buck; Lyrics to Kern songs by Gene Buck; Directed by Ned Wayburn; Produced by Florenz Ziegfeld, Jr.

Published Songs

Ain't It Funny What a Difference Just a Few Drinks Make?
Have a Heart [1st]—different than song from HAVE A HEART [January 11, 1917]
My Lady of the Nile
When the Lights Are Low

THEODORE AND CO.

September 19, 1916
Gaiety Theatre {London} • 503 performances
Music mostly by Ivor Novello; Lyrics by Clifford Grey; Book by H. M. Harwood and George Grossmith; Produced by George Grossmith and Edward Laurillard.

Published Song

Isn't There a Crowd Everywhere? [music by Kern and Novello, lyric by Grey and Adrian Ross]

Additional Songs Published in Vocal Score

All That I Want Is Somebody to Love Me—new lyric for *Can't You See I Mean You?* from NINETY IN THE SHADE [January 25, 1915] and *Isn't It Great to Be Married?* from VERY GOOD EDDIE [1915] [December 23, 1915]
The Casino Music Hall
That "Come Hither" Look—new lyric for *Those "Come Hither" Eyes* from COUSIN LUCY [August 27, 1915]
365 Days

MISS SPRINGTIME

September 25, 1916
New Amsterdam Theatre • 224 performances
Music mostly by Emmerich Kalman; Lyrics by P. G. Wodehouse; Book by Guy Bolton; Directed by Herbert Gresham; Produced by Klaw and Erlanger. Pre-Broadway title: LITTLE MISS SPRINGTIME.

Published Songs

All Full of Talk
My Castle in the Air
Saturday Night
Some One [lyric by Herbert Reynolds]

At the opening night party for NOBODY HOME [April 20, 1915], Kern ran into P. G. Wodehouse (from THE BEAUTY OF BATH [March 19, 1906]) and introduced him to Guy Bolton, who was adapting this Viennese Kalman operetta. Wodehouse got the lyric assignment, and Kern, suddenly very popular, helped out with a few songs, including *My Castle in the Air*.

GO TO IT

October 24, 1916
Princess Theatre • 23 performances
Music, Lyrics, and Book mostly by John L. Golden, John E. Hazzard, and Anne Caldwell (based on *A Milk White Flag* [play] by Charles Hoyt); Directed by William H. Post; Produced by the Comstock-Elliott Co.

Published Song

When You're in Love You'll Know [music by Golden and Kern, lyric by Golden]

Kern and Bolton disliked the source material for this third Princess Theatre show and turned down the assignment; the song contributed was presumably adapted from a prior song written with John Golden. GO TO IT was a quick flop. Kern, Bolton, and Wodehouse—already working together on a full-scale musical—agreed to also devise a fourth Princess show.

HAVE A HEART

January 11, 1917
Liberty Theatre • 76 performances
"The Up-to-the-Minute Musical Comedy."
Lyrics by P. G. Wodehouse; Book by Guy Bolton and P. G. Wodehouse; Directed by Edward Royce; Produced by Henry W. Savage; With Louise Dresser.

Published Songs

*And I Am All Alone [lyric by Kern and Wodehouse]

Daisy
Have a Heart [2nd]—different than song from
    ZIEGFELD FOLLIES OF 1916 [June 12,
    1916]
Honeymoon Inn
I'm So Busy [lyric by Schuyler Greene and
    Wodehouse]
Look in His Eyes [lyric by Herbert Reynolds]—
    same song as *Look in Her Eyes* from
    LIEBER AUGUSTIN [September 3, 1913]
Napoleon
Polly Believed in Preparedness—cut
The Road That Lies Before
They All Look Alike
You Said Something [lyric by Kern and
    Wodehouse]

Additional Songs Published in Vocal Score

Bright Lights
Finale Act One
I'm Here, Little Girls, I'm Here
It's a Sure Sign [by R. P. Weston and Kern]
The Nightingale (*Turk's Song*)
Opening Act Two
Reminiscences [instrumental]
Shop

The Kern/Wodehouse collaboration burst on the scene with their first complete score. The lyricist's humor and crisp language perfectly matched the composer's sprightliness, a modern-day equivalent to Gilbert and Sullivan. The run of HAVE A HEART was disappointingly short, but other projects were underway.

LOVE O' MIKE

January 15, 1917
Shubert Theatre • 192 performances
Lyrics by Harry B. Smith; Book by Thomas
Sydney; Directed by J. H. Benrimo; Produced
by Elisabeth Marbury and Lee Shubert; With
Peggy Wood, Luella Gear, and Clifton Webb.
Pre-Broadway titles: FOR LOVE OF MIKE and
GIRLS WILL BE GIRLS.

Published Songs

The Baby Vampire
Don't Tempt Me
Drift with Me

I Wonder Why
It Can't Be Done—cut
It Wasn't My Fault [lyric by Herbert
    Reynolds]—same song as *It Isn't Your
    Fault* (unpublished) from NINETY IN THE
    SHADE [January 25, 1915]
Simple Little Tune
We'll See
Who Cares?—cut

Additional Songs Published (No Lyrics) in Piano Selection

Life's a Dance
Look in the Book

While the Princess formula called for intimacy, LOVE O' MIKE was a full-scale piece which had to play large houses (1,500 seats instead of 300). The show was not particularly memorable, but it managed a decent run.

OH, BOY!

February 20, 1917
Princess Theatre • 463 performances
Lyrics by P. G. Wodehouse; Book by Guy
Bolton and P. G. Wodehouse; Directed by
Edward Royce and Robert Milton; Produced
by Comstock and Elliott Co.; With Anna
Wheaton, Edna May Oliver, and Dorothy
Dickson.

Published Songs

Ain't It a Grand and Glorious Feeling?—cut
Be a Little Sunbeam
The First Day of May—written for British
    version, retitled OH, JOY! [† January 27,
    1919]
Nesting Time in Flatbush [1st]
Nesting Time in Flatbush [2nd] [lyric by
    Wodehouse and Kern]—version with
    extended lyric
An Old Fashioned Wife
A Package of Seeds [lyric by Herbert
    Reynolds and Wodehouse]—revised lyric
    for song with same title (unpublished)
    from NINETY IN THE SHADE [January
    25, 1915]
A Pal Like You—originally issued as *We're
    Going to Be Pals*
Rolled into One

Till the Clouds Roll By [lyric by Kern and
  Wodehouse]
Words Are Not Needed—originally issued as
  Every Day
You Never Knew about Me

Additional Songs Published (No Lyrics) in Piano Selection

Flubby Dub
Opening Act One

The most successful of the Princess Theatre shows.
OH, BOY! set the standard for early musical comedy, with the songs reasonably interpolated into
entertainingly humorous (though often slight)
stories. *Till the Clouds Roll By*—a ballad with a
markedly pure melody—joined *They Didn't Believe Me* and *Babes in the Wood* as Kern's three
biggest pre-1920s hits.

ZIEGFELD FOLLIES OF 1917

June 12, 1917
New Amsterdam Theatre • 111 performances
Music mostly by Raymond Hubbell and Dave
Stamper; Lyrics mostly by Gene Buck; Book
by Gene Buck and George V. Hobart; Directed
by Ned Wayburn; Produced by Florenz
Ziegfeld, Jr.

Published Song

Just Because You're You—new lyric for *When
  Three Is Company* from THE DOLL GIRL
  [August 25, 1913]

LEAVE IT TO JANE

August 28, 1917
Longacre Theatre • 167 performances
Lyrics by P. G. Wodehouse; Book by Guy
Bolton and P. G. Wodehouse (based on *The
College Widow* [play] by George Ade); Directed
by Edward Royce; Produced by William
Elliott, F. Ray Comstock, and Morris Gest;
With Edith Hallor and Oscar Shaw.

Revival
May 25, 1959
Sheridan Square Theatre {Off Broadway} •
  928 performances
Directed by Lawrence Carra; With Kathleen
Murray [Hallor] and Dorothy Greener
[O'Ramey].

Published Songs

*Cleopatterer
The Crickets Are Calling
I'm Going to Find a Girl*—song version of
  Little Billie [instrumental], a silent picture
  accompaniment theme for the 1916 Billie
  Burke film *Gloria's Romance*
*It's a Great Big Land
Just You Watch My Step
Leave It to Jane*—revised version of *Whistling
  Dan* (unpublished) from NINETY IN THE
  SHADE [January 25, 1915]
*A Peach of a Wife
Poor Prune*—cut
**Sir Galahad
*The Siren's Song
The Sun Shines Brighter
There It Is Again (When Your Favorite Girl's
  Not There)
What I'm Longing to Say
Why?*—cut

Additional Song Published in Vocal Selection

Wait till Tomorrow—initial publication upon
  reuse in revival

Additional Songs Recorded

*Football Song (Opening Act Two)
Good Old Atwater*

With the tremendously successful OH, BOY! [Feb-
ruary 20, 1917] still going strong, this next Princess
Theatre show was booked instead into a standard-
sized, 1,000-seat theatre (which accounts for the
considerably shorter run). The score is filled with
bright tunes and pert lyrics, including *The Siren's
Song, Cleopatterer,* and the delectable *Sir Galahad.*
JANE served as model for the college-football
musicals of the future—specifically GOOD NEWS!
[Notables: September 6, 1927], TOO MANY GIRLS
[Rodgers: October 18, 1939], and BEST FOOT FOR-
WARD [Martin: October 1, 1941]. In 1959 the
forty-one-year-old JANE came back for an impressively successful Off Broadway revival.

THE RIVIERA GIRL

September 24, 1917
New Amsterdam Theatre • 78 performances
Music mostly by Emmerich Kalman; Lyrics
by P. G. Wodehouse; Book by Guy Bolton and

P. G. Wodehouse; Produced by Klaw and Erlanger.

Published Song
*Bungalow in Quogue

MISS 1917
November 5, 1917
Century Theatre • 48 performances
Music also by Victor Herbert; Lyrics by P. G. Wodehouse; Book by Guy Bolton and P. G. Wodehouse; Directed by Ned Wayburn; Produced by Charles B. Dillingham and Florenz Ziegfeld, Jr.; With Lew Fields, Vivienne Segal, Bessie McCoy Davis, and Irene Castle.

Published Songs
Go Little Boat—cut; also used in OH, MY DEAR! [November 27, 1918]
I'm the Old Man in the Moon
The Land Where the Good Songs Go
Peaches
The Picture I Want to See—also used in OH LADY! LADY!! [February 1, 1918]
Tell Me All Your Troubles, Cutie
We're Crooks

Dillingham and Ziegfeld had successfully taken over the Century Theatre with THE CENTURY GIRL [Berlin: November 6, 1916]. For their second presentation they kept co-composer Victor Herbert on and substituted Kern for Irving Berlin. Kern and Herbert did not mix well, though, and THE CENTURY GIRL gave up after six weeks. Rehearsal pianist was nineteen-year-old George Gershwin. Harry Askins, the company manager, was impressed and sent him over to Max Dreyfus.

OH LADY! LADY!!
February 1, 1918
Princess Theatre • 219 performances
Lyrics by P. G. Wodehouse; Book by Guy Bolton and P. G. Wodehouse; Directed by Robert Milton and Edward Royce; Produced by F. Ray Comstock and William Elliott; With Vivienne Segal and Carl Randall.

Published Songs
Before I Met You
Bill [1st]—cut; see ZIP, GOES A MILLION [December 8, 1919] and SHOW BOAT [December 27, 1927]

Dear Old Prison Days
Greenwich Village—revised version of A Little Thing Like a Kiss from THE DOLL GIRL [August 25, 1913]
It's a Hard Hard World
Moon Song
Not Yet—revised version of You're the Only Girl He Loves from A POLISH WEDDING [August 31, 1912]
Oh Lady! Lady!!
Our Little Nest
The Picture I Want to See—originally used in MISS 1917 [November 5, 1917]
The Sun Starts to Shine Again
Waiting around the Corner—initially issued as Some Little Girl
Wheatless Day
When the Ships Come Home
You Found Me and I Found You

Additional Songs Published in Vocal Score
Do It Now
Do Look at Him
Finale Act One
Opening Chorus Act One (Wedding Day)

Despite their enormous success, major disagreements—centering on money and billing—developed between Kern and Wodehouse, and the precedent-setting partnership suddenly ceased. Both men continued to work individually with Bolton and were to reunite briefly. The Kern, Bolton, and Wodehouse collaboration made its contributions to the musical theatre in a period of just sixteen months. As influential as their work was, I find that Kern's music often seems melodically restrained, as though he were standing aside to make room for Wodehouse's verbal acrobatics.

TOOT-TOOT!
March 11, 1918
George M. Cohan Theatre • 40 performances
"A Train of Mirth and Melody." Lyrics by Berton Braley; Book by Edgar Allan Woolf (based on Excuse Me [play] by Rupert Hughes); Directed by Edgar Allan Woolf and Edward Rose; Produced by Henry W. Savage; With Louise Groody and William Kent.

Published Songs
Every Girl in All America
Girlie
Honeymoon Land—cut; see THE NIGHT BOAT
  [February 2, 1920]
I Will Knit a Suit o' Dreams—cut; originally
  issued as *Teepee*
If (There's Anything You Want)—cut
If You Only Care Enough—revised lyric for *If*
  (There's Anything You Want)
Let's Go
When You Wake Up Dancing

Additional Songs Published (No Lyrics) in Piano Selection
It's Greek to Me
Yankee Doodle on the Line

ROCK-A-BYE BABY
May 22, 1918
Astor Theatre • 85 performances
Lyrics by Herbert Reynolds; Book by Edgar
Allan Woolf and Margaret Mayo (based on
Baby Mine [play] by Margaret Mayo); Directed
by Edward Royce; Produced by Selwyn and
Co.; With Louise Dresser, Frank Morgan, and
Dorothy Dickson.

Published Songs
The Big Spring Drive
I Believed All They Said
I Never Thought
The Kettle Song
Little Tune, Go Away
Lullaby
My Boy
Not You—cut
Nursery Fanfare
One, Two, Three
There's No Better Use for Time Than Kissing—
  revised version of *Two Heads Are Better Than
  One* from COUSIN LUCY [August 27, 1915]

The success of the Princess shows put Kern in
great demand. After ten frustrating years of interpolation chores, he composed an unprecedented seven-and-a-half full scores for shows
opening within eighteen months. Some of his
best early work was done in this period; a considerable portion was rather weak, though, filled
with songs of little enduring interest.

HEAD OVER HEELS
August 29, 1918
George M. Cohan Theatre • 100 performances
Book and Lyrics by Edgar Allan Woolf (based
on *Shadows* [play] by Lee Arthur and [story]
by Nalbro Bartley); Directed by George
Marion; Produced by Henry W. Savage; With
Mitzi [Hajos], "The Little Human Dynamo."

Published Songs
All the World Is Swaying
The Big Show
Funny Little Something
Head over Heels
Head over Heels ("Fox Trot")—non-show
  dance version
I Was Lonely
Let's Build a Little Nest [lyric by Kern and
  Woolf]—cut; revised lyric for song from A
  POLISH WEDDING [August 31, 1912]
Mitzi's Lullaby
Moments of the Dance

Additional Song Published (No Lyric) in Piano Selection
Spring

THE CANARY
November 4, 1918
Globe Theatre • 152 performances
Music mostly by Ivan Caryll (see Berlin:
November 4, 1918); Book and Lyrics mostly by
Harry B. Smith (based on a play by Georges
Barr and Louis Vermeuil); Directed by Fred C.
Latham and Edward Royce; Produced by
Charles B. Dillingham; With Julia Sanderson
and Joseph Cawthorn.

Published Songs
Oh Promise Me You'll Write to Him Today
  [lyric by Harry Clarke]—cut; see SHE'S A
  GOOD FELLOW [May 5, 1919]
Take a Chance (Little Girl and Learn to Dance)

OH, MY DEAR!
November 27, 1918
Princess Theatre • 189 performances
Music mostly by Louis Hirsch; Lyrics by P. G.
Wodehouse; Book by Guy Bolton and P. G.
Wodehouse; Directed by Robert Milton and

Edward Royce; Produced by F. Ray Comstock and William Elliott; With Joseph Santley and Ivy Sawyer (Santley).

Published Song

Go Little Boat—originally used (cut) in MISS 1917 [November 5, 1917]
A non-Kern Princess show, interpolating a previously used Kern/Wodehouse song.

SHE'S A GOOD FELLOW

May 5, 1919
Globe Theatre • 120 performances
Book and Lyrics by Anne Caldwell; Directed by Fred G. Latham and Edward Royce; Produced by Charles B. Dillingham; With Joseph Santley and Ivy Sawyer (Santley). Pre-Broadway title: A NEW GIRL.

Published Songs

*The Bull Frog Patrol
First Rose of Summer—see THE CABARET GIRL [September 19, 1921]
Ginger Town—cut
A Happy Wedding Day
Home Sweet Home
I Want My Little Gob
I've Been Waiting for You All the Time—new lyric for *Oh Promise Me You'll Write to Him Today* from THE CANARY [November 4, 1918]
Jubilo—refrain from *Kingdom Comin'* by Henry Clay Work
Just a Little Line
Letter Song—cut
Oh! You Beautiful Person
Some Party
Teacher, Teacher

Kern began a series of more-lavish-than-the-Princess shows for producer Charles Dillingham: six of eight were commercial hits, albeit with undistinguished scores. Kern's new lyricist/librettist was Anne Caldwell, the first and (frighteningly, to this day) most successful woman writer in Broadway musical history with over twenty first-class (but forgotten) shows to her credit. The score contained one fine song, *The Bull Frog Patrol*, an exceedingly delightful counterpoint duet with a splash of rag.

THE LADY IN RED

May 12, 1919
Lyric Theatre • 48 performances
Music mostly by Robert Winterberg (see Gershwin: May 12, 1919); Book and Lyrics mostly by Anne Caldwell; Directed by Frank Smithson; Produced by John P. Slocum.

Published Song

Where's the Girl for Me? [lyric by Harry B. Smith]—originally used (unpublished) in NINETY IN THE SHADE [January 25, 1915]

ZIP, GOES A MILLION

December 8, 1919
Worcester Theatre {Worcester, Mass.} • Closed during tryout
Lyrics by Bud (B. G.) DeSylva; Book by Guy Bolton (based on *Brewster's Millions* [play] by Winchell Smith and Byron Ongley, from the novel by George Barr McCutcheon); Directed by Oscar Eagle; Produced by F. Ray Comstock and Morris Gest; With Harry Fox.

Published Songs

Bill [2nd]—unpublished but recorded; new lyric for song originally used (cut) in OH LADY! LADY!! [February 1, 1918]; also see SHOW BOAT [December 27, 1927]
A Business of Our Own
Forget Me Not
Give a Little Thought to Me
The Language of Love
The Little Back-Yard Band
**Look for the Silver Lining*—initial publication upon reuse in SALLY [December 21, 1920]
A Man around the House
Telephone Girls
***Whip-Poor-Will*—cut; also used in SALLY
You Tell 'Em

The final Princess Theatre show closed before reaching the Princess. The series had included eight shows (counting LEAVE IT TO JANE [August 28, 1917] and ZIP, GOES A MILLION, neither of which actually played the Princess) in only four years. But the innovative work accomplished—introducing contemporary sounds and themes into the heretofore make-believe terrain of musical comedy—had immediate and far-reaching effects. The oncoming younger generation (composers George Gershwin, Vincent Youmans, and Richard Rodgers along with lyricists Ira Gershwin and Lorenz Hart—were all great fans, and their early work was to show an admitted indebtedness to Kern, Bolton, and Wodehouse. ZIP, GOES A MILLION was soon forgotten, but the score included two of Kern's best songs yet: the anthem-like *Look for the Silver Lining*, and the misterioso *Whip-Poor-Will*—one of my favorite Kern songs—which were soon rescued and properly launched in SALLY.

THE NIGHT BOAT
February 2, 1920
Liberty Theatre • 313 performances
Book and Lyrics by Anne Caldwell; Directed by Fred G. Latham; Produced by Charles B. Dillingham; With Louise Groody and John E. Hazzard.

Published Songs
Bob White—cut
Chick! Chick! Chick!—cut; also used in
    HITCHY-KOO 1920 [4th] [October 19, 1920]
Don't You Want to Take Me?
Good-Night Boat [lyric by Caldwell and Frank Craven]
A Heart for Sale
I'd Like a Lighthouse—new lyric for *Honeymoon Land* (cut) from TOOT-TOOT! [March 11, 1918]
I Love the Lassies (*I Love 'Em All*)
Left All Alone Again Blues
The Lorelei—cut; initial publication upon reuse in SALLY [December 21, 1920]
Rip Van Winkle and His Little Men—cut
Whose Baby Are You?

Additional Song Published (No Lyric) in Piano Selection
Some Fine Day

Additional Song Recorded
Girls Are Like a Rainbow—see THE CABARET GIRL [September 19, 1921]

Another hit show, another score of little interest except for the playful *Whose Baby Are You?* and the rapid fire *Left All Alone Again Blues*.

THE CHARM SCHOOL
August 2, 1920
Bijou Theatre • 87 performances
Play by Alice Duer Miller and Robert Milton;
"With a Wee Bit of Music by Jerome Kern";
Produced and Directed by Robert Milton;
With Sam Hardy and James Gleason.

Published Song
When I Discover My Man [lyric by Miller]

HITCHY-KOO 1920 ✦ Fourth Edition
October 19, 1920
New Amsterdam Theatre • 71 performances
Lyrics by Anne Caldwell; Book by Glen MacDonough; Directed by Ned Wayburn; Produced by Raymond Hitchcock; With Raymond Hitchcock and Julia Sanderson.

Published Songs
Bring 'Em Back—see SHOW BOAT [December 27, 1927]
Buggy Riding
Chick! Chick! Chick!—cut; originally used in THE NIGHT BOAT [February 2, 1920]
Cupid, the Winner
Ding Dong, It's Kissing Time
Girls in the Sea
Moon of Love
The Old Town
The Star of Hitchy-Koo
Sweetie

Kern contributed one of his blandest scores to this edition of comedian Raymond Hitchcock's occasional revue series.

SALLY
December 21, 1920
New Amsterdam Theatre • 570 performances
Lyrics mostly by Clifford Grey; Book by Guy Bolton; Directed by Edward Royce; Produced by Florenz Ziegfeld, Jr.; With Marilyn(n) Miller, Leon Errol, and Walter Catlett.

Revival
May 6, 1948
Martin Beck Theatre • 36 performances
Directed by Billy Gilbert; With Willie Howard [Errol], Bambi Linn [Miller], and Robert Shackleton [Catlett].

Published Songs

The Church 'round the Corner [lyric by P. G. Wodehouse and Grey]

*Look for the Silver Lining [lyric by B. G. DeSylva]—originally used (cut/unpublished) in ZIP, GOES A MILLION [December 8, 1919]

The Lorelei [lyric by Anne Caldwell]—originally used (cut/unpublished) in THE NIGHT BOAT [February 2, 1920]

On with the Dance

Sally—revised version of *Catamarang* from KING OF CADONIA [January 10, 1910]

The Schnitza Komisski

**Whip-Poor-Will [lyric by B. G. DeSylva]—originally used (cut) in ZIP, GOES A MILLION

Wild Rose

You Can't Keep a Good Girl Down (*Joan of Arc*) [lyric by Wodehouse and Grey]

Additional Songs Published in British Vocal Score

The Night Time

Opening Act Two (*In Society*)

Ziegfeld, king of the revue, wanted to attain a similar position in the world of musical comedy. He determined to produce the most lavish, successful musical comedy to date. Taking advantage of his FOLLIES performers, facilities, and money, he did just that with SALLY. He also established his favorite mistress as Broadway's favorite musical comedy star. Marilynn Miller (originally Mary Ellen; soon to be further contracted to Marilyn, originating the now popular name) had been discovered in a Winter Garden Revue by none other than Mrs. Billie Burke Ziegfeld. Flo stole her from the Shuberts and placed her in the FOLLIES OF 1918 [Berlin: June 18, 1918]. Miller turned on Ziegfeld by marrying costar Frank Carter; Ziegfeld retaliated by sending husband Carter on the road. When Carter was killed in a car crash on May 9, 1920, Ziegfeld made up with Miller and built SALLY around her. For Kern the success of SALLY was deceptive: the better parts of the score were leftovers from earlier shows (notably *Look for the Silver Lining* and *Whip-Poor-Will*).

ZIEGFELD FOLLIES OF 1921

June 21, 1921

Globe Theatre • 119 performances

Music mostly by Victor Herbert, Rudolf Friml, and Dave Stamper; Lyrics mostly by Gene Buck; Directed by Edward Royce; Produced by Florenz Ziegfeld, Jr.

Published Song

You Must Come Over [lyric by B. G. DeSylva]

THE CABARET GIRL

September 19, 1921

Winter Garden Theatre {London} • 361 performances

Lyrics mostly by P. G. Wodehouse; Book by George Grossmith and P. G. Wodehouse; Directed by George Grossmith; Produced by George Grossmith and J. A. E. Malone; With Dorothy Dickson, George Grossmith, and Heather Thatcher.

Published Songs

Dancing Time [lyric by Grossmith]

First Rose of Summer [lyric by Wodehouse and Anne Caldwell]—new lyric for song of same title from SHE'S A GOOD FELLOW [May 5, 1919]

Journey's End—also used in THE CITY CHAP [October 26, 1925]

Ka-Lu-A [lyric by Anne Caldwell]—added after opening; originally used in GOOD MORNING DEARIE [November 1, 1921]

Looking All Over for You

Oriental Dreams [lyric by Grossmith]

Shimmy with Me

Additional Songs Published in Vocal Score

At the Ball [lyric by Grossmith]—alternate lyric for *Dancing Time*

Chopin Ad Lib (*Opening Chorus*)

Finaletto Act One

Finale Act Two (*Vicar Song*)

London, Dear Old London—new lyric for *Girls Are Like a Rainbow* (unpublished) from THE NIGHT BOAT [February 2, 1920]

Mr. Gravvins—Mr. Gripps

Nerves

The Pergola Patrol—(see SITTING PRETTY
    [April 8, 1924]
Those Days Are Gone Forever
Whoop-De-Oodle-Do!
You Want the Best Seats, We Have 'Em

The producers decided to follow the 387-performance run of their London production [September 10, 1921] of SALLY [December 21, 1920] with an original Kern musical. Wodehouse proved amenable, so THE CABARET GIRL was written for the local SALLY stars—American Dorothy Dickson, who had been featured in Broadway's OH, BOY! [February 20, 1917] and ROCK-A-BYE BABY [May 22, 1918], and producer/director/librettist/lyricist George Grossmith. The success of the venture paved the way for future London musicals by Kern, Gershwin, Rodgers, and Schwartz. The score, nevertheless, was exceedingly commonplace.

GOOD MORNING DEARIE
November 1, 1921
Globe Theatre • 347 performances
Book and Lyrics by Anne Caldwell; Directed by Edward Royce; Produced by Charles B. Dillingham; With Louise Groody and Oscar Shaw.

Published Songs
Blue Danube Blues
Didn't You Believe?
Easy Pickin's
Good Morning Dearie
Ka-Lu-A—also used in THE CABARET GIRL
    [September 19, 1921]
My Lady's Dress—cut
Niagara Falls
Rose Marie
Sing-Song Girl
Toddle
Way down Town

Another Kern/Caldwell hit for Dillingham. Though Kern's shows in this period were successful, the music was generally stale and uninteresting. At the same time, younger Harms composers George Gershwin and Vincent Youmans were attracting notice with their first Broadway hits. Kern didn't recover from his fallow period until SHOW BOAT

[December 27, 1927]—when he once again led the pack onto new musical theatre ground. *Ka-Lu-A*—Kern's most popular song between *Look for the Silver Lining* (ZIP, GOES A MILLION [December 8, 1919]) and *Who?* (SUNNY [September 22, 1925])—caused the composer to be sued for plagiarism. Songwriter and one-time Kern collaborator Fred Fisher claimed infringement on his 1919 hit *Dardanella*. The songs were determined similar enough for Kern to be ruled technically (though unintentionally) guilty; he was fined a token $250 rather than the million sought by Fisher.

THE BUNCH AND JUDY
November 28, 1922
Globe Theatre • 65 performances
Book and Lyrics by Anne Caldwell; Directed by Fred G. Latham and Edward Royce; Produced by Charles B. Dillingham; With Fred and Adele Astaire.

Published Songs
Every Day in Every Way
"Have You Forgotten Me?" Blues
Hot Dog!—cut
How Do You Do, Katinka?
Morning Glory
The Pale Venetian Moon
Peach Girl

Producer Charles Dillingham found brother Fred and sister Adele Astaire in vaudeville and nurtured them toward stardom, hoping to create a successor to his team of David Montgomery and Fred Stone. But THE BUNCH AND JUDY didn't work, and the aging Dillingham let the Astaires get away—to immediate success with George Gershwin and producer Alex Aarons (see FOR GOODNESS SAKE [Gershwin: February 20, 1922]).

ROSE BRIAR
December 25, 1922
Empire Theatre • 89 performances
Play by Booth Tarkington; Produced by Florenz Ziegfeld, Jr.; With Billie Burke (Ziegfeld).

Published Song
Love and the Moon [lyric by Tarkington]

THE BEAUTY PRIZE

September 5, 1923
Winter Garden Theatre {London} •
    213 performances
Book and Lyrics by George Grossmith and P. G.
Wodehouse; Directed by George Grossmith;
Produced by George Grossmith and J. A. E.
Malone; With Dorothy Dickson, Leslie
Henson, and George Grossmith.

Published Songs
Honeymoon Isle
I'm a Prize
It's a Long, Long Day
Meet Me Down on Main Street
Moon Love
Non-Stop Dancing [lyric by Wodehouse]
When You Take the Road with Me [lyric by
    Wodehouse]
You Can't Make Love by Wireless—see BLUE
    EYES [April 27, 1928] [lyric by Wodehouse]

Additional Songs Published in Vocal Score
A Cottage in Kent
For the Man I Love
Joy Bells [lyric by Wodehouse]
We Will Take the Road Together (*Finale*)
You'll Find Me Playing Mah-Jongg [lyric by
    Wodehouse]

Another London success for the CABARET GIRL
[September 19, 1922] group. Grossmith, as can
be seen above, was a versatile man of the theatre. He had been associated with Kern on numerous London shows since 1906.

THE STEPPING STONES

November 6, 1923
Globe Theatre • 241 performances
Lyrics by Anne Caldwell; Book by Anne
Caldwell and R. H. Burnside; Directed by R. H.
Burnside; Produced by Charles B. Dillingham;
With Fred Stone, Aileen Crater (Stone), and
(introducing) Dorothy Stone.

Published Songs
Everybody Calls Me Little Red Riding Hood
I Saw the Roses and Remembered You [lyric by
    Herbert Reynolds]
*In Love with Love—revised version of *Die
    Süsse Pariserin* from DIE BALLKÖNIGIN

[circa September 1913]; also see LADY
    MARY [February 23, 1928]
Once in a Blue Moon
Our Lovely Rose
Pie
*Raggedy Ann
Stepping Stones
Wonderful Dad

Additional Songs Published in Vocal Score
Babbling Babette
Because You Love the Singer
Cane Dance [instrumental]
Dear Little Peter Pan
Little Angel Cake
Nursery Clock
Palace Dance [instrumental]
Prelude

The title was a pun, as the show was built around
the talents of eccentric dancing star Fred Stone,
with wife Aileen Crater and eighteen-year-old
daughter Dorothy. Stone and his partner Dave
Montgomery (who died in 1917) had been major
family-trade stars for producer Dillingham since
Victor Herbert's THE RED MILL[†] [September 24,
1906]. Ivan Caryll was Anne Caldwell's collaborator on the later Stone shows; when he died in
1921, Dillingham and Caldwell turned to Kern.
STEPPING STONES contained an especially infectious rag, *Raggedy Ann*.

SITTING PRETTY

April 8, 1924
Fulton Theatre • 95 performances
Lyrics by P. G. Wodehouse; Book by Guy
Bolton and P. G. Wodehouse; Directed by Fred
G. Latham and Julian Alfred; Produced by F.
Ray Comstock and Morris Gest; With Queenie
Smith and Gertrude Bryan.

Published Songs
All You Need Is a Girl
*Bongo on the Congo
*The Enchanted Train
Mr. and Mrs. Rorer
On a Desert Island with You
Shadow of the Moon
Shufflin' Sam
Sitting Pretty [lyric by Kern and Wodehouse]
*Tulip Time in Sing-Sing

Worries
A Year from Today

Additional Songs Recorded
All the World Is Dancing Mad—cut; music
    recorded only
Days Gone By
I'm Wise—cut; music recorded only
Is This Not a Lovely Spot?—new lyric for *The
    Pergola Patrol* from THE CABARET GIRL
    [September 19, 1921]
Just Wait—cut
Opening Act One (Coaching)—cut; music
    recorded with partial lyric
Opening Act Two (Ancient Tunes)
There Isn't One Girl
You Alone Would Do (I'd Want Only You)

What was to have been a happy return of the
Princess Theatre triumvirate fell short of expec-
tations. This reunion of Kern, Wodehouse, and
Bolton (with producer Comstock) was poorly received, despite a clever and amusing (if mild)
score. The highly polished set of lyrics was
Wodehouse's final work with Kern; he soon
ceased songwriting altogether.

DEAR SIR
September 23, 1924
Times Square Theatre • 15 performances
Lyrics by Howard Dietz; Book by Edgar
Selwyn; Directed by David Burton; Produced
by Philip Goodman; With Genevieve Tobin,
Walter Catlett, and Oscar Shaw.

Published Songs
All Lanes Must Reach a Turning—see BLUE
    EYES [April 27, 1928]
Gypsy Caravan
If You Think It's Love You're Right
I Want to Be There
Weeping Willow Tree—see BLUE EYES

Additional Song Recorded
Wishing Well Scene (including reprises)

Kern seems to have sensed the need to work with
younger collaborators; Wodehouse, Rourke,
Smith, and Caldwell were his seniors, by as many
as twenty-five years. Max Dreyfus paired him
with beginner Bud DeSylva on the ill-fated ZIP,
GOES A MILLION [December 8, 1919]. Next came

young Noël Coward, who wrote a few songs with
Kern, including *If You Will Be My Morganatic
Wife* (rewritten by Dietz for DEAR SIR as *If We
Could Lead a Merry Mormon Life*; both unpub-
lished) and an early version of the song we know
as *Where's the Mate for Me?* from SHOW BOAT
[December 27, 1927]. Howard Dietz, a movie pub-
licist who displayed a knack for wordplay, pro-
vided a more than respectable set of lyrics for
DEAR SIR, but the poorly produced show was a
quick fiasco. Dietz faced several bleak years until
THE LITTLE SHOW [Schwartz: April 30, 1929].

PETER PAN [1924]
November 6, 1924
Knickerbocker Theatre • 120 performances
Revival of play by J. M. Barrie; Directed
by Basil Dean; Produced by Charles B.
Dillingham; With Marilyn Miller.

Published Song
The Sweetest Thing in Life [lyric by B. G.
    DeSylva]—new lyric for *When Three Is
    Company* from THE DOLL GIRL [August
    25, 1913] and *Just Because You're You* from
    ZIEGFELD FOLLIES OF 1917 [June 12,
    1917]

Marilyn Miller temporarily deserted Ziegfeld—
star and producer were spatting—and signed
with competitor Dillingham. While they worked
to devise another SALLY [December 21, 1920],
Dillingham placed his new star in this revival.
Marilyn Miller was somewhat out of place in
Maude Adams's role of the boy who wouldn't
grow up, but the musical in preparation made
up for that.

SUNNY
September 22, 1925
New Amsterdam Theatre • 517 performances
Music mostly by Kern; Book and Lyrics
mostly by Otto Harbach and Oscar Hammerstein
2nd; Directed by Hassard Short; Produced by
Charles B. Dillingham; With Marilyn Miller
and Jack Donahue.

Published Songs
D'ye Love Me?
Dream a Dream—cut

I Might Grow Fond of You [lyric by Desmond
Carter]—written for London production
[October 7, 1926]

I Was Alone—written for 1930 movie version

I've Looked for Trouble [lyric by Carter]—
written for London production; revised
version of *Bought and Paid For* from THE
LAUGHING HUSBAND [February 2, 1914];
also see CRISS-CROSS [October 12, 1926]

Let's Say Good-Night—initial publication upon
use in London production

Sunny

Sunshine—revised version of *I Can't Forget
Your Eyes* from OH, I SAY! [October 30,
1913]; also see CRISS-CROSS

Two Little Bluebirds

When We Get Our Divorce—initial publication
upon use in London production

*Who?

Additional Songs Published in British Vocal Score

The Chase

The Fox Has Left His Lair—written for
London production

Here We Are Together Again (*Opening Act One*)

The Hunt Ball [instrumental]

It Won't Mean a Thing

So's Your Old Man

We're Gymnastic

Wedding Knell

Wedding Scene (*Finale Act One*)

Dillingham succeeded in out-Ziegfelding Ziegfeld
with this extravaganza. Hiring the Harbach and
Hammerstein team on the heels of two long-running hits—WILDFLOWER [Youmans: February
7, 1923] and the Friml/Stothart ROSE-MARIE†
[September 2, 1924]—Dillingham joined Kern
with his two most important future collaborators. Everything about SUNNY was spectacular,
in fact, except the score: nothing worth noting
other than the breezy and immensely popular
Who?

THE CITY CHAP
October 26, 1925
Liberty Theatre • 72 performances
Music mostly by Kern; Lyrics mostly by Anne
Caldwell; Book by James Montgomery (based

on *The Fortune Hunter* [play] by Winchell
Smith); Directed by R. H. Burnside; Produced
by Charles B. Dillingham; With Richard "Skeet"
Gallagher, Irene Dunne, and George Raft.

Published Songs
He Is the Type

Journey's End [lyric by P. G. Wodehouse]—
originally used in THE CABARET GIRL
[September 19, 1922]

No One Knows (*How Much I'm in Love*)

Sympathetic Someone

Walking Home with Josie

When I Fell in Love with You—cut after
opening

CRISS-CROSS
October 12, 1926
Globe Theatre • 206 performances
Book and Lyrics by Otto Harbach and Anne
Caldwell; Directed by R. H. Burnside; Pro-
duced by Charles B. Dillingham; With Fred
and Dorothy Stone.

Published Songs
Bread and Butter—cut

Cinderella Girl

In Araby with You—new lyric for *Sunshine*
from SUNNY [September 22, 1925], a
revised version of *I Can't Forget Your Eyes*
from OH, I SAY! [October 30, 1913]

Kiss a Four Leaf Clover—cut

Susie (*Camel Song*) [lyric by Caldwell]

That Little Something [lyric by Bert Kalmar and
Harry Ruby]—added to post-Broadway
tour; originally used in LUCKY [March 22,
1927]

You Will—Won't You?—new lyric for *I've
Looked for Trouble* from London production of SUNNY, a revised version of *Bought
and Paid For* from THE LAUGHING
HUSBAND [February 2, 1914]

LUCKY
March 22, 1927
New Amsterdam Theatre • 71 performances
Music mostly by Bert Kalmar and Harry Ruby;
Lyrics by Bert Kalmar and Harry Ruby; Book
by Otto Harbach, Bert Kalmar, and Harry

Ruby; Directed by Hassard Short; Produced
by Charles B. Dillingham; With Mary Eaton,
Walter Catlett, Ruby Keeler, and Paul Whiteman.

Published Songs
That Little Something—see CRISS-CROSS
[October 12, 1926]
When the Bo-Tree Blossoms Again

Additional Song Published (No Lyric) in Piano Selection
Ballet (Pearl of Ceylon) (probably by Kern)

SHOW BOAT
December 27, 1927
Ziegfeld Theatre • 575 performances
Music mostly by Kern; Book and Lyrics
(mostly) by Oscar Hammerstein 2nd (based on
the novel by Edna Ferber); Directed by Zeke
Colvan; Produced by Florenz Ziegfeld, Jr.;
With Charles Winninger, Helen Morgan,
Norma Terris, Howard Marsh, Edna May
Oliver, and Jules Bledsoe.

Revivals
May 19, 1932
Casino Theatre • 180 performances
With Charles Winninger, Helen Morgan,
Norma Terris, Dennis King [Marsh], Edna
May Oliver, and Paul Robeson [Bledsoe].

January 5, 1946
Ziegfeld Theatre • 417 performances
Book directed by Oscar Hammerstein
2nd; Staged by Hassard Short; Choreo-
graphed by Helen Tamiris; Produced
by Kern (posthumously) and Oscar
Hammerstein 2nd; With Jan Clayton
[Terris], Ralph Dumke [Winninger], Carol
Bruce [Morgan], and Charles Fredericks
[Marsh].

July 19, 1966
New York State Theater • 64 performances
Directed by Lawrence Kasha; Choreo-
graphed by Ronald Field; Produced by
Music Theater of Lincoln Center (Richard
Rodgers); With Barbara Cook [Terris],
Constance Towers [Morgan], Stephen
Douglass [Marsh], David Wayne
[Winninger], Margaret Hamilton [Oliver],
and William Warfield [Bledsoe].

April 24, 1983
Uris Theatre • 73 performances
Directed by Michael Kahn; Choreographed
by Dorothy Danner; With Donald O'Connor
[Winninger], Sheryl Woods [Terris], Lonette
McKee [Morgan], and Ron Raines [Marsh].

October 2, 1994
Gershwin Theatre • 949 performances
Directed by Harold Prince; Choreographed
by Susan Stroman; Produced by Livent
(U.S.); With John McMartin [Winninger],
Elaine Stritch [Oliver], Rebecca Luker
[Terris], Lonette McKee [Morgan], and
Mark Jacoby [Marsh].

Published Songs
Bill [3rd] [lyric by P. G. Wodehouse and
Hammerstein]—revised version of [1st] cut
from OH LADY! LADY!! [February 1,
1918] [lyric by Wodehouse]; also used in
[2nd] version (unpublished but recorded)
in ZIP, GOES A MILLION [December 8,
1919] [lyric by B. G. DeSylva]
**Can't Help Lovin' Dat Man*
Dance Away the Night—written for London
production [May 3, 1928]
I Have the Room Above—written for 1936
movie version
I Might Fall Back on You—initial individual
publication upon use in 1936 movie
version
I Still Suits Me—written for 1936 movie
version
Life upon the Wicked Stage—initial individual
publication upon use in 1936 movie
version
Make Believe
Nobody Else but Me—written for revival
[January 5, 1946]; revised version of
Dream of a Ladies Cloak Room Attendant
[instrumental] (unpublished) from
unproduced 1935 movie *The Flame Within*
***Ol' Man River*
Why Do I Love You?—see THE CAT AND THE
FIDDLE [October 15, 1931]
You Are Love

Additional Songs Published in Vocal Scores (Several Different Editions)
Captain Andy's Entrance and Ballyhoo
Cotton Blossom

Dahomey—revised version of *Bring 'Em Back* from HITCHY-KOO 1920 [4th] [October 19, 1920]

Dandies on Parade (*The Sports of Gay Chicago*)

Finale Act I (*Wedding*)

Hey, Fellah!

**Mis'ry's Comin' Aroun'* (*Act I, Scene IV*)

Queenie's Ballyhoo (*C'mon Folks, We'se Rarin' to Go*)

'Til Good Luck Comes My Way

Villain Dance [instrumental]

When We Tell Them about It All (*Opening Act II*)

Where's the Mate for Me?

Additional Songs Recorded

The Creole Love Song—cut

Gallivantin' Aroun'—written for 1936 movie version

It's Getting Hotter in the North—cut

I Would Like to Play a Lover's Part—cut

Out There in an Orchard [possibly by Kern and Hammerstein]—cut

A Pack of Cards [possibly by Kern and Hammerstein]—cut

Pantry Scene—cut

Trocadero Opening Chorus (*New Year Song*)—cut

Yes, Ma'am! (*You're from the Show Boat*)—cut

Kern and Hammerstein knew they were onto something monumental with SHOW BOAT. In the musical theatre of the day, other hands—or Kern and Hammerstein two years earlier—might have woven Ferber's setting and romances into a moldy operetta, excising the miscegenation, prejudice, unhappy marriages, and so on. (As it was, the authors opted for a weak, happy ending.) But Kern and Hammerstein otherwise stayed close to the novel, creating a new musicodramatic form. In a period when shows were quickly written and put together, Kern dedicated a full year to SHOW BOAT. Hammerstein also lavished an uncommon amount of care on the project, displaying unique theatrical talents for the first time in his heretofore successful (but hacklike) career. The score was incredibly rich, with Kern developing his highly melodic operetta style in *Make Believe* and *You Are Love. Can't Help Lovin' Dat Man* and *Life upon the Wicked Stage* were perfect in their genre, while *Bill* finally found a home (on his third try).

With *Ol' Man River,* Hammerstein wasn't trying to make a far-reaching social statement: his primary concern was to bring the action downstage while the massive cotton-blossom set was being struck. (Kern wasn't interested in the spot at all. He suggested merely taking the already-written *Cotton Blossom* theme and inverting it—which is what they did.) Ziegfeld's lavishness was evident in the physical production, but Hammerstein—who more or less served as director—kept the showboat from overwhelming the powerful material.

LADY MARY

February 23, 1928

Daly's Theatre {London} • 181 performances

Music mostly by Albert Sirmay and Philip Charig; Lyrics by Harry Graham; Book by Frederick Lonsdale and John Hastings Turner.

Published Song

If You're a Friend of Mine—new lyric for *In Love with Love* from THE STEPPING STONES [November 6, 1923], revised from *Die Süsse Pariserin* (*Fraulein de Loraine*) from DIE BALLKÖNIGIN [circa September 1913]

Composer Albert Sirmay apparently remembered *Die Süsse Pariserin* and had it interpolated here in revised form. As Albert Szirmai, he had also been a contributor to the score of DIE BALLKÖNIGIN. After emigrating to America, he became an important editor for Max Dreyfus's publishing house, working with Gershwin, Rodgers, Porter, and others.

BLUE EYES

April 27, 1928

Piccadilly Theatre {London} •
276 performances

Lyrics by Graham John; Book by Guy Bolton and Graham John; Directed by John Harwood; Produced by Lee Ephraim; With Evelyn Laye.

Published Songs

Back to the Heather

Blue Eyes—revised version of *All Lanes Must Reach a Turning* from DEAR SIR [September 23, 1924]

Bow Belles—revised version of *You Can't Make Love by Wireless* from THE BEAUTY PRIZE [September 5, 1923]

Do I Do Wrong—see ROBERTA [November 18, 1933]

Henry

In Love—revised version of *Alone at Last* from OH, I SAY! [October 30, 1913]

No One Else but You

Additional Songs Published in Vocal Score

Charlie (Opening Act One)

The Curtsey—revised version of *Weeping Willow Tree* from DEAR SIR

A Fair Lady (Opening Act Two)

Finale Act One

His Majesty's Dragoons

Long Live Nancy

Praise the Day

Romeo and Juliet

Someone

Trouble about the Drama

A British historical romance, moderately successful but nonexportable. As with so many of Kern's pre–SHOW BOAT musicals, the score is full of uninteresting songs.

SWEET ADELINE

September 3, 1929

Hammerstein's Theatre • 234 performances

"Musical Romance of the Gay Nineties." Music mostly by Kern; Book and Lyrics (mostly) by Oscar Hammerstein 2nd; Directed by Reginald Hammerstein; Produced by Arthur Hammerstein; With Helen Morgan, Lulu Ward, Robert Chisholm, and Charles Butterworth

Concert Version

February 13, 1997

City Center • 5 performances

Directed by Eric D. Schaeffer; Produced by City Center Encores; With Patti Cohenour [Morgan], Dorothy Loudon [Ward], Stephen Bogardus [Chisholm], and Tony Randall [Butterworth].

Published Songs

*Don't Ever Leave Me

*Here Am I

Lonely Feet—added to 1935 movie version; originally used in THREE SISTERS [April 19, 1934]

Out of the Blue

The Sun about to Rise

'Twas Not So Long Ago

We Were So Young—written for movie version

**Why Was I Born?

Additional Songs Recorded

**Some Girl Is on Your Mind*—also published (no lyric) in piano selection

Kern and Hammerstein followed their precedent-breaking SHOW BOAT [December 27, 1927] with this nostalgic look at the gay '90s. (The 1890s, that is.) Written for torch-singing Helen Morgan (of SHOW BOAT), the lovely score is particularly plaintive. There are no fewer than *five* absolutely stunning songs: *Why Was I Born?*, *Here Am I*, *Don't Ever Leave Me*, *Lonely Feet* (added to the film version), and *Some Girl Is on Your Mind*. Unforunately, the favorably received SWEET ADELINE ran headlong into the stock market crash and could not recoup its costs. Producer Arthur Hammerstein, responsible for some of Broadway's most successful operettas (see WILDFLOWER [Youmans: February 7, 1923]), was bankrupt within a year. The family theatre on Broadway at 53rd Street was lost; it's now named for Ed Sullivan. More importantly, the lucrative rights to the Hammerstein operettas—including NAUGHTY MARIETTA† [November 7, 1910], THE FIREFLY† [December 2, 1912], and ROSE-MARIE† [September 2, 1924] —were auctioned off. The sole bidder at the auction, which nobody else seems to have known about, was a fellow named Shubert—who got the lot for $684.

RIPPLES

February 11, 1930

New Amsterdam Theatre • 55 performances

"The New Musical Extravaganza." Music mostly by Oscar Levant and Albert Sirmay; Lyrics by Irving Caesar and Graham John; Book and Direction by William Anthony McGuire; Produced by Charles B. Dillingham; With Fred Stone, Dorothy Stone, and (introducing) Paula Stone.

Published Song
Anything May Happen Any Day [lyric by John]

A circus acrobat in his youth, Fred Stone's shows always featured daredevil stunts—like his entrance in THE RED MILL[†] [September 24, 1906], where he fell backwards down an eighteen-foot ladder. In his mid-fifties, Stone and neighbor/friend Will ("Let's go flying") Rogers took up the daredevil hobby of flying. A crash landing crushed Stone's legs, forcing him to miss the next scheduled show, the Raymond Hubbell/Roy Henderson THREE CHEERS[†] [October 15, 1928]. Daughter Dorothy proved star material on her own, and Rogers—who was to be killed in a 1935 plane crash—stepped into Fred's role. Stone returned to the stage with RIPPLES, bringing along Dorothy and his other dancing daughter, Paula. But the accident had aged the ageless Stone, and the times had made the innocent Stone shows obsolete. There was to be one last unsuccessful attempt, Harry Revel and Mack Gordon's SMILING FACES[†] [August 30, 1932].

Kern joined Otto Harbach for this successful integrated-score experiment, with song arising naturally from the action. (The leading characters, conveniently, were composers, singers, and street musicians.) The songs are somewhat disappointing, though, filled with lovely melodic phrases which are unresolved. Only *Try to Forget* stands out, with its strong, Kern-like melody. Kern turned to a new producer: Max Gordon, who had cheered the depressed Broadway scene with THREE'S A CROWD [Schwartz: October 15, 1930] and THE BAND WAGON [Schwartz: June 3, 1931]. An unhappy footnote: the financially bereft Charles Dillingham, crushed by the Depression, retained only his beloved (and mortgaged) Globe Theatre. In May 1932 he unaccountably absconded with the box office receipts and fled; his well-deserved reputation was such that Broadway pitied rather than censured him. He existed on charity from still-solvent former associates (including Kern) until his death on August 30, 1934.

THE CAT AND THE FIDDLE
October 15, 1931
Globe Theatre • 395 performances
"A Musical Love Story." Book and Lyrics by Otto Harbach; Directed by José Ruben; Produced by Max Gordon; With Bettina Hall, Georges Metaxa, and José Ruben.

Published Songs
Don't Ask Me Not to Sing—cut; also used in
    ROBERTA [November 18, 1933]
I Watch the Love Parade
Misunderstood—advertised but not published
    (apparently a misprint)
A New Love Is Old
The Night Was Made for Love
One Moment Alone
Poor Pierrot
She Didn't Say "Yes"
Try to Forget

Additional Songs Published in Vocal Score
The Breeze Kissed Your Hair
Hh! Cha Cha!—countermelody for *Why Do I Love You?* from SHOW BOAT [December 27, 1927]
Opening Act One (Street Vendors)

MUSIC IN THE AIR
November 8, 1932
Alvin Theatre • 342 performances
Book and Lyrics by Oscar Hammerstein 2nd;
Directed by Kern and Hammerstein; Produced by Peggy Fears; With Natalie Hall, Tullio Carminati, Walter Slezak, Katherine Carrington, and Al Shean.

Revival
October 8, 1951
Ziegfeld Theatre • 56 performances
Directed by Oscar Hammerstein 2nd;
Produced by Reginald Hammerstein (for Billy Rose); With Dennis King [Carminati], Jane Pickens [Hall], and Charles Winninger [Shean].

Published Songs
*And Love Was Born
I Am So Eager
I'm Alone
In Egern on the Tegern Sea
*I've Told Ev'ry Little Star
One More Dance
**The Song Is You*
There's a Hill beyond a Hill

We Belong Together
When the Spring Is in the Air

Additional Songs Published in Vocal Score

At Stony Brook
Hold Your Head Up High [hymn]
Melodies of May [music by Beethoven, arranged by Kern]
Prayer

Working again with Hammerstein, Kern turned out one of his richest scores for this charming Bavarian tale. As in CAT AND THE FIDDLE [October 15 1931], the European setting and musical subject matter again enabled close integration of score and book. There are three especially lovely songs: *I've Told Ev'ry Little Star* (Kern claimed he borrowed the melody of the title phrase from a Nantucket sparrow); *And Love Was Born*; and *The Song Is You*, one of Kern's finest, most rapturous ballads. The authors felt they needed Ziegfeld for the show, but he was in hopeless financial/physical shape and died July 22, 1932. Dillingham and Arthur Hammerstein were bankrupt; even the Shuberts were bankrupt; and Kern had fought with Max Gordon on CAT AND THE FIDDLE. Along came former Follies girl Peggy Fears with rich husband A. C. Blumenthal who had kept Ziegfeld afloat during his final production (the May 19, 1932, revival of SHOW BOAT [December 27, 1927]). Fears—with Blumenthal's money—presented MUSIC IN THE AIR, with Hammerstein and Kern doing the actual producing. Hammerstein followed this hit with a ten-year string of flops, until Dick Rodgers called looking to replace Larry Hart for the project that became OKLAHOMA! [Rodgers: March 31, 1943].

ROBERTA
November 18, 1933
New Amsterdam Theatre • 295 performances
Book and Lyrics by Otto Harbach (based on *Gowns by Roberta* [novel] by Alice Duer Miller); Produced by Max Gordon; With Lyda Roberti, Fay Templeton, Tamara, Sydney Greenstreet, and Bob Hope. Pre-Broadway title: GOWNS BY ROBERTA.

Published Songs

Armful of Trouble—cut
I Won't Dance [lyric by Oscar Hammerstein 2nd, Harbach, Dorothy Fields, and Jimmy McHugh]—added to 1935 movie version; new lyric for song from THREE SISTERS [April 19, 1934]
I'll Be Hard to Handle [lyric by Bernard Dougall]
Let's Begin
Lovely to Look At [lyric by Fields and McHugh]—written for 1935 movie version
Smoke Gets in Your Eyes
Something Had to Happen
The Touch of Your Hand
Yesterdays
You're Devastating—new lyric for *Do I Do Wrong* from BLUE EYES [April 27, 1927]

Additional Songs Published in Vocal Score

Don't Ask Me Not to Sing—originally used (cut) in THE CAT AND THE FIDDLE [October 15, 1931]
Hot Spot
Madrigal

A dreary fashion show/musical comedy with many problems and few positive attributes. Gordon temporarily patched his shaky relationship with Kern by allowing the composer to direct the show; then he fired Kern out of town and brought in Hassard Short. (No one ultimately received director billing.) ROBERTA managed a fair run, with minimal competition, drastically cut-rate tickets, and the song hit *Smoke Gets in Your Eyes*. Another fine song, *Lovely to Look At*, was written for the film version. The lyrics were by Dorothy Fields, although her writing partner Jimmy McHugh was contractually entitled to coauthor billing.

THREE SISTERS
April 19, 1934
Theatre Royal, Drury Lane {London} • 72 performances
Book and Lyrics by Oscar Hammerstein 2nd; Directed and Produced by Kern and Hammerstein; With Charlotte Greenwood, Adele Dixon, and Stanley Holloway.

Published Songs

Funny Old House—initial publication as 1945 non-show song in the United States

*Hand in Hand

I Won't Dance—see ROBERTA [November 18, 1933]

Keep Smiling

*Lonely Feet—also used in 1935 motion picture version of SWEET ADELINE [September 3, 1929]

Roll On, Rolling Road

What Good Are Words?

You Are Doing Very Well

Additional Songs Published (No Lyrics) in Piano Selection

Circus Queen

Here It Comes

Now That I Have Springtime

Somebody Wants to Go to Sleep

THREE SISTERS—not related to the Chekhov play—was an original musical written for the Drury Lane, London home of Hammerstein's hit 1920s operettas. The score contained some particularly lovely work, including the plaintive *Lonely Feet* and the hymn-like *Hand in Hand;* but the disappointing failure of THREE SISTERS sent Kern to Hollywood for (almost) the rest of his life. His score for the film *Swing Time* [1936, lyrics by Dorothy Fields] is especially sterling, with **A Fine Romance, **Pick Yourself Up, *Never Gonna Dance*, and another brilliant ballad, the Oscar-winning ***The Way You Look Tonight*.

GENTLEMEN UNAFRAID

June 3, 1938

Municipal Opera {St. Louis, Mo.} •
6 performances • Summer stock tryout
Book and Lyrics by Oscar Hammerstein 2nd and Otto Harbach (based on a story by Edward Boykin); Directed by Zeke Colvan; Produced by St. Louis Municipal Opera; With Ronald Graham, Vicki Cummings, Hope Manning, Avon Long, and Richard (Red) Skelton. Title of 1942 stock & amateur release: HAYFOOT, STRAWFOOT.

Published Songs

Abe Lincoln Had Just One Country—added to stock and amateur version; original

publication as 1941 non-show song for War Bond drive

Cantabile (Song without Words)—cut; for initial publication see VERY WARM FOR MAY [May 17, 1939]

When a New Star [lyric by Harbach]—initial publication upon release of HAYFOOT, STRAWFOOT

Your Dream (Is the Same As My Dream)—only publication upon reuse in 1940 movie *One Night in the Tropics*

This Civil War operetta never got further than its one-week tryout, with no one even bothering to attempt a Broadway transfer. GENTLEMEN UNAFRAID was yet another theatrical disappointment for Kern. HAYFOOT, STRAWFOOT, a revised 1942 version released for stock & amateur groups, didn't create much more interest either. (The score, let it be added, is surprisingly bland.)

MAMBA'S DAUGHTERS

January 3, 1939

Empire Theatre • 162 performances
Play by Dorothy and DuBose Heyward (based on the novel by DuBose Heyward); Produced and Directed by Guthrie McClintic; With Ethel Waters.

Published Songs

*Lonesome Walls [lyric by DuBose Heyward]

Kern and Hammerstein had once expressed interest in musicalizing Heyward's earlier novel *Porgy* (as an Al Jolson vehicle). By the time MAMBA'S DAUGHTERS was produced, Gershwin was no longer alive. Kern was asked to write the one original song used in the play and came up with the highly effective *Lonesome Walls,* a worthy companion to Ethel Waters's *Supper Time* from AS THOUSANDS CHEER [Berlin: September 30, 1933].

VERY WARM FOR MAY

May 17, 1939

Alvin Theatre • 59 performances
Book and Lyrics by Oscar Hammerstein 2nd; Production staged by Vincente Minnelli; Book

staged by Oscar Hammerstein 2nd; Produced by Max Gordon; With Grace McDonald, Jack Whiting, Eve Arden, Hiram Sherman, Avon Long, and Donald Brian.

Published Songs

All in Fun
***All the Things You Are*—full version; revised from *Cantabile* (*Song without Words*) (cut/ unpublished) from GENTLEMEN UNAFRAID [June 3, 1938]
All the Things You Are—abridged version (without extended verse)
**Heaven in My Arms* (*Music in My Heart*)
In Other Words, Seventeen
**In the Heart of the Dark*
That Lucky Fellow

Additional Songs Recorded

Harlem Boogie-Woogie [instrumental]—non-song version of *High Up in Harlem* (cut, unpublished)
L'Histoire de Madame de la Tour [instrumental]

Without a Broadway appearance since ROBERTA [November 18, 1933], Kern was in no position to hold out when Max Gordon called again. Things went even worse than on the previous show. Gordon was in Hollywood during the production period; he arrived at the tryout and panicked, demanding radical changes and once again calling Hassard Short for help. VERY WARM FOR MAY arrived on Broadway in dismal shape and quickly closed. Kern's final theatre score contained some lovely work, although only *All the Things You Are*—one of the very best show tunes ever—managed to escape the wreckage. (*In the Heart of the Dark* and *Heaven in My Arms* are also stunning.) Kern returned to Hollywood for the rest of his life, where his work included another two brilliant ballads, **I'm Old Fashioned* [1942, lyric by Johnny Mercer] and

**Long Ago (*And Far Away*) [1944, lyric by Ira Gershwin]. He also picked up a second Oscar, with Hammerstein, for **The Last Time I Saw Paris* [1941]. In 1945 Hammerstein and Richard Rodgers—who had established themselves as Broadway producers—commissioned Kern and Dorothy Fields to write an Annie Oakley bio-musical for Ethel Merman (see ANNIE GET YOUR GUN [Berlin: May 16, 1946]).

Simultaneously, Kern and Hammerstein planned to revive SHOW BOAT [December 27, 1927], writing a new song (*Nobody Else but Me*) for the final scene. Returning to New York for SHOW BOAT auditions, Kern suffered a cerebral hemorrhage on November 5, 1945, and collapsed in the street. (Unrecognized and without proper identification, he was taken to the derelict ward on Welfare Island.) Jerome Kern died six days later, on November 11, 1945.

Kern entered a musical theatre dominated by British and Continental operettas. During his thirty-five-year career, the American musical theatre first established its own identity during World War I, with the Kern, Bolton, and Wodehouse Princess Theatre shows. The early twenties saw the arrival of the more sophisticated, jazz-influenced Gershwin and Youmans, with Kern (momentarily) passed by. But in 1927 Kern (with Hammerstein) discovered the dramatic potential of musical theatre, with SHOW BOAT [December 27, 1927] and succeeding scores. If much of Kern's earlier work—with a very few exceptions—is hopelessly dated, it is a case of the developmental and experimental being outmoded by the perfected finished product. Moving into the twenty-first century, Kern's best songs retain their place among the very finest songs of the American musical theatre.

IRVING BERLIN

Born: May 11, 1888, Mohilev, Russia
Died: September 22, 1989, New York, New York

I RVING BERLIN's family fled from religious persecution and came to America, when Berlin was
a mere lad of five. The son of a part-time cantor,
Izzy Baline took to the streets as a singing pan-
handler and went on to become a singing waiter
at a Chinatown saloon. It was here, at "Nigger
Mike's," that he wrote his first published song:
Marie from Sunny Italy [1907, music by Nick
Nicholson and lyrics by "I. Berlin"]. In 1908
came his first composer/lyricist effort, *Best of
Friends Must Part*. Berlin went to work as a staff
lyricist (and occasional composer) for publisher/
songwriter Ted Snyder, soon becoming a partner in Waterson, Berlin & Snyder Co. As it was
then common practice to interpolate Tin Pan
Alley songs in Broadway shows, Berlin found a
natural showcase for a portion of his increasingly
enormous output.

*All Music and Lyrics by Irving Berlin unless other-
wise indicated.*

THE BOYS AND BETTY
November 2, 1908
Wallack's Theatre • 112 performances
Music mostly by Silvio Hein; Book and Lyrics
mostly by George V. Hobart; Directed by
George Marion; Produced by Daniel V.
Arthur; With Marie Cahill.

Published Song
She Was a Dear Little Girl [music by Ted
Snyder, lyric by Berlin]

THE GIRL AND THE WIZARD
September 27, 1909
Casino Theatre • 96 performances
Music mostly by Julian Edwards (see Kern:
September 27, 1909); Lyrics mostly by Robert B.

Smith and Edward Madden; Book by J. Hartley
Manners; Directed by Ned Wayburn; Produced
by the Messrs. Shubert; With Sam Bernard.

Published Song
Oh, How That German Could Love [music by
Ted Snyder, lyric by Berlin]

THE JOLLY BACHELORS
January 6, 1910
Broadway Theatre • 84 performances
Music mostly by Raymond Hubbell; Music
to Berlin lyrics by Ted Snyder; Book and Lyrics
mostly by Glen MacDonough; Directed by Ned
Wayburn; Produced by Lew Fields; With Stella
Mayhew, Nora Bayes (Norworth), Jack
Norworth, and Emma Carus.

Published Berlin/Snyder Songs
*If the Managers Only Thought the Same As
Mother*
Oh, That Beautiful Rag—also used in UP AND
DOWN BROADWAY [July 19, 1910]
Stop That Rag (Keep on Playing, Honey)
*Sweet Marie, Make-a Rag-a-Time Dance
wid Me*

ARE YOU A MASON?
[circa April 1910]
Closed during tryout
Play by Leo Ditrichstein; Produced by Charles
Rich and Sam H. Harris; With Leo Ditrichstein
and Beth Tate.

Published Song
I'm Going on a Long Vacation [music by Ted
Snyder]

ZIEGFELD FOLLIES OF 1910
June 20, 1910
Jardin de Paris Theatre • 88 performances
Music mostly by others; Book and Lyrics
mostly by Harry B. Smith and Gus Edwards;
Directed by Julian Mitchell; Produced by
Florenz Ziegfeld, Jr.; With Bert Williams,
Lillian Lorraine, and Fanny Brice.

Published Songs
The Dance of the Grizzly Bear [music by George
    Botsford]
Good-Bye Becky Cohen—advertised but not
    published (not by Berlin)

Florenz Ziegfeld, Jr., began his Broadway career
in 1896 by importing and featuring (and marrying) Parisian star Anna Held in a series of musicals. He came up with his successful revue format with FOLLIES OF 1907 [July 8, 1907]. The
scores were generally contributed by a throng
of songwriters, the only exception being Berlin's
ZIEGFELD FOLLIES OF 1927 [August 16, 1927].

UP AND DOWN BROADWAY
July 18, 1910
Casino Theatre • 72 performances
Music mostly by Jean Schwartz; Lyrics mostly
by William Jerome; Music to Berlin lyrics by
Ted Snyder; Book by Edgar Smith; Directed
by William J. Wilson; Produced by the
Messrs. Shubert; With Eddie Foy, Ted Snyder,
and Irving Berlin.

Published Berlin/Snyder Songs
Sweet Italian Love
Oh, That Beautiful Rag—originally used in THE
    JOLLY BACHELORS [January 6, 1910]

The popularity of the early Berlin and Snyder
"rags" was such that the writers were hired to
perform some of their work in this Shubert revue.

THE GIRL AND THE DRUMMER
[circa August 1910]
Closed during tryout
Music mostly by Augustus Barrett (see Kern:
circa August 1910); Music to Berlin lyrics by
Ted Snyder; Book and Lyrics mostly by George
Broadhurst (based on his play *What Happened to

Jones); Produced by William A. Brady, Ltd.;
With Herbert Corthell and Belle Gold.

Published Berlin/Snyder Songs
Herman, Let's Dance That Beautiful Waltz—
    also used in TWO MEN AND A GIRL [circa
    December 1910]
Wishing

HE CAME FROM MILWAUKEE
September 21, 1910
Casino Theatre • 117 performances
Music mostly by Ben M. Jerome and Louis A.
Hirsch; Lyrics mostly by Edward Madden;
Book by Mark Swan; Directed by Sidney
Ellison; Produced by the Messrs. Shubert;
With Sam Bernard.

Published Song
Bring Back My Lena to Me [music and lyric by
    Berlin and Ted Snyder]

GETTING A POLISH
November 7, 1910
Wallack's Theatre • 48 performances
Play by Booth Tarkington and Harry Leon
Wilson; Music by Ted Snyder; Lyrics by
Berlin; Directed by Hugh Ford; Produced by
Liebler and Company; With May Irwin. Pre-
Broadway title: MRS. JIM.

Published Berlin/Snyder Songs
He Sympathized with Me
My Wife Bridget [music and lyric by Berlin]
That Opera Rag

TWO MEN AND A GIRL
[circa December 1910]
Closed during tryout
Music mostly by Julian Edwards; Book and
Lyrics mostly by Charles Campbell and Ralph
Skinner; With Fred Bailey, Ralph Austin, and
Belle Gold.

Published Song
Herman, Let's Dance That Beautiful Waltz
    [music by Ted Snyder, lyric by Berlin]—
    originally used in THE GIRL AND THE
    DRUMMER [circa August 1910]

JUMPING JUPITER
March 6, 1911
New York Theatre • 24 performances
Music mostly by Karl Hoschna; Lyrics mostly
by Richard Carle; Music to Berlin lyrics by Ted
Snyder; Book by Richard Carle and Sydney
Rosenfeld; Directed by Richard Carle; Produced
by H. H. Frazee and George W. Lederer; With
Richard Carle and Edna Wallace Hopper.

Published Berlin/Snyder Songs
Angelo
It Can't Be Did
"Thank You Kind Sir!" Said She

GABY ✦ Part of FOLIES BERGÈRE REVUE
April 27, 1911
Folies Bergère Theatre • 92 performances
Music and Lyrics by Vincent Bryan, Berlin,
Ted Snyder, and others; Book by Harry B. and
Robert B. Smith; Directed by George Marion;
Produced by Henry B. Harris and Jesse L.
Lasky; With Ethel Levey and Otis Harlan.

Published Berlin/Bryan/Snyder Songs
Answer Me—advertised but not published
Down to the Folies Bergère
I Beg Your Pardon, Dear Old Broadway [music
   and lyric by Berlin]
Keep a Taxi Waiting Dear
Spanish Love

The Folies Bergère on West 46th Street opened
as a dinner theatre featuring a three-part vaudeville show, including Berlin's GABY. Within five
months the house was transformed into a legitimate theatre, the Fulton. It was renamed in honor
of Helen Hayes in 1955 and demolished in 1981.

FRIARS' FROLIC OF 1911
May 28, 1911
New Amsterdam Theatre • 1 performance
Music and Lyrics mostly by others; Directed
by George M. Cohan; Produced by A. L.
Erlanger; With George M. Cohan, Berlin,
Julian Eltinge, and William Collier.

Published Song
Alexander's Ragtime Band—published as
   1911 non-show song; see HOKEY-POKEY
   [February 8, 1912]

Berlin himself sang his one-month-old syncopated song hit at this benefit for the Friars' Club.
Alexander's Ragtime Band ushered a new sound
into popular music; not ragtime, though, as it's
not a rag. Throughout his career, Berlin had the
uncanny ability to express in song what the public
was about to feel—just ahead of the competition.

ZIEGFELD FOLLIES OF 1911
June 26, 1911
Jardin de Paris Theatre • 80 performances
Music mostly by Maurice Levi and Raymond
Hubbell (see Kern: June 26, 1911); Book and
Lyrics mostly by George V. Hobart; Directed
by Julian Mitchell; Produced by Florenz
Ziegfeld, Jr.; With Bessie McCoy, Bert Wil-
liams, and Fanny Brice.

Published Songs
Dog Gone That Chilly Man
Ephraham Played upon the Piano [by Berlin
   and Vincent Bryan]
Woodman, Woodman, Spare That Tree! [by
   Berlin and Bryan]
You've Built a Fire Down in My Heart—also
   used in THE FASCINATING WIDOW [Sep-
   tember 11, 1911]

THE FASCINATING WIDOW
September 11, 1911
Liberty Theatre • 56 performances
Music mostly by others; Book and Lyrics
mostly by Otto Hauerbach (Harbach); Directed
by George Marion; Produced by A. H. Woods;
With Julian Eltinge.

Published Songs
Don't Take Your Beau to the Seashore [by E.
   Ray Goetz and Berlin]
You've Built a Fire Down in My Heart—
   originally used in ZIEGFELD FOLLIES OF
   1911 [June 26, 1911]

Songwriter/producer E. Ray Goetz was an early
collaborator with Berlin, Gershwin, and Porter.
Goetz's sister Dorothy became Berlin's bride in
1912. She contracted typhoid fever on their
honeymoon, though, and died—an event memo-
rialized in the top-selling tear-jerker *When I Lost*

You. (An ad features the smiling, tuxedoed tune-smith pointing to a copy, with the caption "Irving Berlin, song genius of the world, says this is the best song I ever wrote.")

THE LITTLE MILLIONAIRE
September 25, 1911
George M. Cohan Theatre • 102 performances
Book, Music, and Lyrics mostly by George M. Cohan; Directed by George M. Cohan; Produced by George M. Cohan and Sam H. Harris; With George M. Cohan, Jerry Cohan, and Donald Crisp.

Published Song
Down in My Heart—different song than *You've Built a Fire Down in My Heart* from ZIEGFELD FOLLIES OF 1911 [June 26, 1911]

Cohan, recognizing Berlin as his natural successor in the popular music field, befriended and encouraged him. Producer Sam H. Harris joined Cohan for the hit LITTLE JOHNNY JONES [November 7, 1904]. They became a major producing firm, presenting not only Cohan's plays and musicals but the work of others as well. (They built two 42nd Street theatres just before World War I, the George M. Cohan and the Cohan & Harris.) After he broke up with Cohan in 1919, Harris formed similar partnerships with Berlin and, later, George S. Kaufman.

THE NEVER HOMES
October 5, 1911
Broadway Theatre • 92 performances
Music mostly by A. Baldwin Sloane; "Rhymes" mostly by E. Ray Goetz; "Words" by Glen MacDonough; Directed by Ned Wayburn; Produced by Lew Fields.

Published Song
There's a Girl in Havana [by Goetz, Berlin, and Ted Snyder]

A REAL GIRL
[circa October 1911]
Closed during tryout
Music and Lyrics also by others; Produced by Bonita Amusement Co.; With Bonita and Lew Hearn.

Published Songs
Cuddle Up
One o'Clock in the Morning
That Mysterious Rag [by Berlin and Ted Snyder]
When You're in Town

WINTER GARDEN VAUDEVILLE
[circa November 1911]
Winter Garden Theatre
Music and Lyrics mostly by others; Produced by the Messrs. Shubert; With Dolly Jardon.

Published Song
Sombrero Land [by E. Ray Goetz, Berlin, and Ted Snyder]

SHE KNOWS BETTER NOW
January 15, 1912
Plymouth Theatre {Chicago} •
    Closed during tryout
Play by Agnes L. Crimmins; Songs also by others; Directed by William Collier; Produced by Eisfeldt and Anhalt; With May Irwin and Arthur Byron.

Published Songs
I'm Going Back to Dixie [music and lyrics by Berlin and Ted Snyder]
The Ragtime Mocking Bird

HOKEY-POKEY AND BUNTY, BULLS, AND STRINGS
February 8, 1912
Broadway Theatre • 108 performances
"*A Potpourri in Two Acts.*" Music mostly by John Stromberg and A. Baldwin Sloane; Lyrics mostly by E. Ray Goetz; Sketches by Edgar Smith; Directed by Gus Sohlke; Produced by Weber and Fields; With Joe Weber, Lew Fields, William Collier, Lillian Russell, and Fay Templeton.

Published Song
Alexander's Bag-Pipe Band [by Goetz, Berlin, and Sloane]—revised version (take-off) of *Alexander's Ragtime Band* from FRIARS' FROLIC [May 28, 1911]

The famous acting/producing team of Weber and Fields broke up in 1904, after twenty-four years of partnership. Both continued successfully on their own and with HOKEY-POKEY began occasional "all-star" reunions of their famous music-hall company. Fields remained a major musical theatre force into the twenties, when he discovered and nurtured his librettist-son Herbert and his collaborators Richard Rodgers and Lorenz Hart (see A LONELY ROMEO [Rodgers: June 10, 1919]).

THE WHIRL OF SOCIETY
March 5, 1912
Winter Garden Theatre • 136 performances
Music mostly by Louis A. Hirsch; Lyrics mostly by Harold Atteridge; Book by Harrison Rhodes; Directed by J. C. Huffman; Produced by Winter Garden Co. (the Messrs. Shubert); With Stella Mayhew and Al Jolson.

Published Songs
I Want to Be in Dixie [by Berlin and Ted Snyder]—also used in HULLO, RAGTIME [December 23, 1912]
Opera Burlesque (*On the Sextette from Lucia de Lammermoor*)—initial publication upon reuse in HANKY PANKY [August 5, 1912]
That Society Bear

COHAN AND HARRIS MINSTRELS
[circa April 1912]
Post-Broadway tour
Music and Lyrics mostly by others; Produced by George M. Cohan and Sam H. Harris; With "Happy" Lambert.

Published Song
Lead Me to That Beautiful Band [lyric by E. Ray Goetz]

THE PASSING SHOW OF 1912
July 22, 1912
Winter Garden Theatre • 136 performances
Produced by the Messrs. Shubert; With Eugene and Willie Howard, Charlotte Greenwood, and Trixie Fraganza.

Published Song
The Ragtime Jockey Man

HANKY PANKY
August 5, 1912
Broadway Theatre • 104 performances
"A Jumble of Jollification." Music mostly by A. Baldwin Sloane; Lyrics mostly by E. Ray Goetz; Book by Edgar Smith; Directed by Gus Sohlke; Produced by Lew Fields; With Carter De Haven, Myrtle Gilbert, and Bobby North.

Published Songs
The Million Dollar Ball [by Goetz and Berlin]
Opera Burlesque (*On the Sextette from Lucia de Lammermoor*)—originally used (unpublished) in THE WHIRL OF SOCIETY [March 8, 1912]

MY BEST GIRL
September 12, 1912
Park Theatre • 68 performances
Music mostly by Clifton Crawford and Augustus Barratt; Book and Lyrics mostly by Channing Pollock and Rennold Wolf; Directed by Sidney Ellison; Produced by Henry B. Harris; With Clifton Crawford.

Published Song
Follow Me Around

ZIEGFELD FOLLIES OF 1912
October 21, 1912
Moulin Rouge Theatre • 88 performances
Music mostly by Raymond Hubbell; Lyrics mostly by Harry B. Smith; Directed by Julian Mitchell; Produced by Florenz Ziegfeld, Jr.

Published Song
A Little Bit of Everything

THE SUN DODGERS
November 30, 1912
Broadway Theatre • 29 performances
"Fanfare of Frivolity." Music mostly by A. Baldwin Sloane; Lyrics mostly by E. Ray Goetz; Book by Edgar Smith and Mark Swan; Directed by Ned Wayburn; Produced by Lew Fields; With Eva Tanguay and George Monroe.

Published Songs
At the Picture Show [by Goetz and Berlin; issued as by Goetz and Sloane]

Hiram's Band [music by Goetz and Sloane, lyric
by Berlin; issued as by Goetz and Sloane]

Exact authorship of a number of early Berlin
songs is uncertain, as Berlin did not take public
credit. Copyright records show that he wrote
these two with Ray Goetz. Baldwin Sloane, the
main composer of the show, allowed them to be
interpolated but insisted on taking sole credit for
all the music in the score.

HULLO, RAGTIME!
December 23, 1912
Hippodrome {London} • 451 performances
Music mostly by Louis Hirsch; Sketches by
Max Pemberton and Albert P. De Courville;
Directed by Austen Hurgon; Produced by
Albert P. De Courville; With Ethel Levey,
Bonita, and Lew Hearn.

Published Songs
I Want to Be in Dixie [by Berlin and Ted
Snyder]—originally used in THE WHIRL
OF SOCIETY [March 5, 1912]
The Ragtime Soldier Man—initial publication
as 1912 non-show song

ALL ABOARD!
June 5, 1913
44th Street Roof Garden Theatre •
108 performances
Music mostly by E. Ray Goetz and Malvin
Franklin; Lyrics mostly by E. Ray Goetz; Book
by Mark Swan; Directed by Wm. J. Wilson and
W. H. Post; Produced by Lew Fields; With
Fields, Carter De Haven, and Claire Rochester.

Published Songs
The Monkey Doodle Doo [1st]—different than song
from THE COCOANUTS [December 8, 1925]
Somebody's Coming to My House
Take Me Back

THE TRAINED NURSES
[circa September 1913]
Vaudeville act
"Jesse L. Lasky's Most Pretentious Production."
Produced by Jesse L. Lasky; With Gladys
Clark and Henry Bergman.

Published Song
*If You Don't Want Me (Why Do You Hang
Around)*

THE QUEEN OF THE MOVIES
January 12, 1914
Globe Theatre • 104 performances
Music mostly by Jean Gilbert; Book and
Lyrics mostly by Glen MacDonough (based on
the German musical by Freund and
Okonkowski); Directed by Herbert Gresham;
Produced by Thomas W. Ryley.

Published Song
Follow the Crowd

ALONG CAME RUTH
February 23, 1914
Gaiety Theatre • 56 performances
Play by Holman Day (based on the French
play by Fonson and Wicheler); Directed by
George Marion; Produced by Henry W.
Savage; With Irene Fenwick.

Published Song
Along Came Ruth

THE SOCIETY BUDS
[circa October 1914]
Vaudeville act
Produced by Jesse L. Lasky; With Gladys
Clark and Henry Bergman.

Published Songs
Furnishing a House for Two
That's My Idea of Paradise

WATCH YOUR STEP
December 8, 1914
Globe Theatre • 175 performances
Book by Harry B. Smith; Directed by R. H.
Burnside; Produced by Charles B. Dillingham;
With Irene and Vernon Castle, and Frank
Tinney.

Published Songs
Come to the Land of the Argentine
Homeward Bound

I Hate You

I Love to Have the Boys around Me

I'm a Dancing Teacher Now—advertised but not published

I've Got A Go Back to Texas

Lead Me to Love [music by Ted Snyder]

Let's Go 'round the Town

Lock Me in Your Harem and Throw Away the Key

The Minstrel Parade

Move Over

Ragtime Opera Medley—published in separate edition

Settle Down in a One-Horse Town

Show Us How to Do the Fox Trot

*Simple Melody

The Syncopated Walk

They Always Follow Me Around

Watch Your Step—published in separate edition

What Is Love?

When I Discovered You [music and lyrics by Berlin and E. Ray Goetz]

When It's Night Time in Dixie Land

Additional Songs Published in Vocal Score

Metropolitan Nights

Opening Chorus (Office Hours)

Polka (Mr. and Mrs. Castle's Specialty) [instrumental]

Berlin wrote his first full score for this "syncopated musical," which brought the new pop rhythms to the dignified stage and made Broadway stars of society dancers Vernon and Irene Castle. Producer Charles Dillingham began his career a decade earlier with hit Victor Herbert operettas and was to remain Broadway's most respected producer until the stock market crash. Berlin, who had been providing all the profits for publishers Waterson, Berlin & Snyder Co., broke with his partners and started Irving Berlin, Inc.

WINTER GARDEN VAUDEVILLE ✦
DID YOU EVER?
[circa April 1915]
Winter Garden Theatre
Music and Lyrics mostly by others; Produced by the Messrs. Shubert; With Blossom Seeley.

Published Song
Bird of Paradise (My Honolulu Girl)

STOP! LOOK! LISTEN!
December 25, 1915
Globe Theatre • 105 performances
Book by Harry B. Smith; Directed by R. H. Burnside; Produced by Charles B. Dillingham; With Gaby Deslys, Harry Fox, and Justine Johnstone.

Published Songs
And Father Wanted Me to Learn a Trade

Blow Your Horn

England Every Time for Me—written for London version, FOLLOW THE CROWD [February 19, 1916]

Everything in America Is Ragtime

The Girl on the Magazine

*I Love a Piano

I Love to Dance—advertised but not published

The Law Must Be Obeyed

A Pair of Ordinary Coons—published in separate edition

Sailor Song

Skating Song—advertised but not published

Stop! Look! Listen!

Take Off a Little Bit

Teach Me How to Love

That Hula Hula

Until I Fell in Love with You

When I Get Back to the U.S.A.

When I'm Out with You

Why Don't They Give Us a Chance?—advertised but not published

Additional Song Published (No Lyric) in Piano Selection
I Love to Dance—initial publication in FOLLOW THE CROW selection

A follow-up to WATCH YOUR STEP [December 8, 1914], not quite as successful but with a more satisfying score—including Berlin's jaunty *I Love a Piano.*

FRIARS' FROLIC OF 1916
May 28, 1916
New Amsterdam Theatre • 1 performance
Music and Lyrics mostly by others; Directed by George M. Cohan; Produced by Sam H.

Harris and A. L. Erlanger; With George M. Cohan, Berlin, William Collier, and Frank Tinney.

Published Song
Friars' Parade

STEP THIS WAY
May 29, 1916
Shubert Theatre • 88 performances
Music mostly by E. Ray Goetz and Bert Grant; Lyrics mostly by E. Ray Goetz; Book by Edgar Smith (based on *The Girl behind the Counter* [musical] by Edgar Smith); Directed by Frank McCormack; Produced by Lew Fields; With Lew Fields, Gladys Clark, and Henry Bergman.

Published Songs
I've Got a Sweet Tooth Bothering Me
In Florida among the Palms—also used in
    ZIEGFELD FOLLIES OF 1916 [June 12, 1916]
Step This Way [not by Berlin]

ZIEGFELD FOLLIES OF 1916
June 12, 1916
New Amsterdam Theatre • 112 performances
Music mostly by Louis Hirsch and Dave Stamper (see Kern: June 12, 1916); Book and Lyrics mostly by George V. Hobart and Gene Buck; Directed by Ned Wayburn; Produced by Florenz Ziegfeld, Jr.

Published Song
In Florida among the Palms—originally used in
    STEP THIS WAY [May 29, 1916]

THE CENTURY GIRL
November 6, 1916
Century Theatre • 200 performances
Music also by Victor Herbert; Lyrics also by Henry Blossom; Produced by Charles B. Dillingham and Florenz Ziegfeld, Jr.; With Elsie Janis, Hazel Dawn, Frank Tinney, and Sam Bernard.

Published Songs
Alice in Wonderland [1st]—different than song
    from MUSIC BOX REVUE [4th] [December 1, 1924]

The Chicken Walk
It Takes an Irishman to Make Love [lyric by Elsie Janis and Berlin]

Dillingham and Ziegfeld took the lease on the failed New Theatre, a white elephant of a theatre built to house the short-lived dramatic equivalent to the Metropolitan Opera. Renamed the Century, it opened with this successful wartime extravaganza. But with the failure of MISS 1917 [Kern: November 5, 1917], Dillingham and Ziegfeld gave up on the theatre. The Shuberts eventually bought and demolished it, replacing it with their Century Apartments (at 25 Central Park West). During the depression, Shubert employees were "encouraged" to lease apartments.

DANCE AND GROW THIN
[circa April 1917]
Cocoanut Grove (Atop the Century Theatre) • Nightclub show
Music and Lyrics mostly by others; Directed by Ned Wayburn; Produced by Charles B. Dillingham and Florenz Ziegfeld, Jr.

Published Songs
Dance and Grow Thin [music by George W. Meyer]
There's Something Nice about the South

RAMBLER ROSE
September 10, 1917
Empire Theatre • 72 performances
Music mostly by Victor Jacobi; Book and Lyrics mostly by Harry B. Smith; Produced by Charles Frohman, Inc.; With Julia Sanderson and Joseph Cawthorn.

Published Song
Poor Little Rich Girl's Dog

JACK O'LANTERN
October 16, 1917
Globe Theatre • 265 performances
Music mostly by Ivan Caryll; Lyrics mostly by Anne Caldwell; Book by Anne Caldwell and R. H. Burnside; Directed by R. H. Burnside; Produced by Charles B. Dillingham; With Fred Stone.

Published Song
I'll Take You Back to Italy

GOING UP
December 25, 1917
Liberty Theatre • 351 performances
Music mostly by Louis A. Hirsch; Book and
Lyrics mostly by Otto Harbach (based on *The
Aviator* [play] by James Montgomery);
Directed by Edward Royce and James Mont-
gomery; Produced by George M. Cohan and
Sam H. Harris; With Frank Craven and Edith
Day.

Published Songs
Come along to Toy Town—also used in EVERY-
    THING [August 22, 1918]
When the Curtain Falls

THE COHAN REVUE OF 1918
December 31, 1917
New Amsterdam Theatre • 96 performances
*"A Hit and Run Play Batted out by George M.
Cohan."* "Some of the Songs by Irving Berlin,
Others by George M. Cohan"; Directed by
George M. Cohan; Produced by George M.
Cohan and Sam H. Harris; With Nora Bayes
and Charles Winninger.

Published Songs
Down Where the Jack O'Lanterns Grow
The Eyes of Youth See the Truth [music by
    Cohan and Berlin, lyric by Cohan; issued as
    by Cohan]
Polly Pretty Polly (*Polly with a Past*) [lyric by
    Cohan]
Spanish [music by Cohan and Berlin, lyric by
    Cohan; issued as by Cohan]
Wedding of Words and Music—advertised but
    not published

ZIEGFELD FOLLIES OF 1918
June 18, 1918
New Amsterdam Theatre • 151 performances
Music mostly by Louis A. Hirsch; "Lines and
Lyrics" mostly by Rennold Wolf and Gene
Buck; Directed by Ned Wayburn; Produced
by Florenz Ziegfeld, Jr.; With Eddie Cantor,
Frank Carter, Marilyn(n) Miller, and W. C.
Fields.

Published Songs
The Blue Devils of France [by "Private Irving
    Berlin"]
I'm Gonna Pin a Medal on the Girl I Left Behind
Oh, How I Hate to Get up in the Morning—
    added three months after opening;
    originally used in YIP-YIP-YAPHANK
    [August 19, 1918]

YIP-YIP-YAPHANK
August 19, 1918
Century Theatre • 32 performances
*"A Military Musical 'Mess' Cooked up by the
Boys of Camp Upton."* Words and Music by
Sergeant Irving Berlin; Directed by Private
William Smith; Produced by Uncle Sam; With
Danny Healy, Sammy Lee, and Berlin.

Published Songs
Bevo—also used in ZIEGFELD FOLLIES OF
    1919 [June 23, 1919]
Ding Dong—also used in THE CANARY
    [November 4, 1918]
Dream On Little Soldier Boy [lyric by Jean
    Havez]
Ever Since I Put on a Uniform—advertised but
    not published
*I Can Always Find a Little Sunshine in the
    Y.M.C.A.*
Kitchen Police (*Poor Little Me*)
*Mandy—also used in ZIEGFELD FOLLIES OF
    1919; originally issued as *Sterling Silver
    Moon*
Oh, How I Hate to Get Up in the Morning—
    also used in ZIEGFELD FOLLIES OF 1918
    [June 18, 1918] and THIS IS THE ARMY
    [July 4, 1942]
Ragtime Razor Brigade
Send a Lot of Jazz Bands over There
We're on Our Way to France

Additional Song Published in THIS IS
    THE ARMY [Special Edition] Vocal
    Selection
Ladies of the Chorus

Berlin's contribution to the war effort was this
successful service show. Berlin appeared, intro-

ducing *Oh, How I Hate to Get Up in the Morning*—
which he was to revive for the next war in THIS
IS THE ARMY.

EVERYTHING
August 22, 1918
Hippodrome Theatre • 461 performances
Music mostly by John Philip Sousa and
others; Lyrics mostly by John Golden and
others; Book and Direction by R. H. Burnside;
Produced by Charles B. Dillingham; With De
Wolf Hopper.

Published Songs
The Circus Is Coming to Town
Come along to Toy Town—originally used in
  GOING UP [December 25, 1917]

THE CANARY
November 4, 1918
Globe Theatre • 152 performances
Music mostly by Ivan Caryll (see Kern:
November 4, 1918); Book and Lyrics mostly by
Harry B. Smith (based on the French play by
George Barr and Louis Vermeuil); Directed by
Fred C. Latham and Edward Royce; Produced
by Charles B. Dillingham; With Julia
Sanderson and Joseph Cawthorn.

Published Songs
Ding Dong—cut; originally used in YIP-YIP-
  YAPHANK [August 19, 1918]
I Have Just One Heart for Just One Boy
It's the Little Bit of Irish—cut
*I Wouldn't Give That for the Man Who
  Couldn't Dance*
You're So Beautiful

THE ROYAL VAGABOND
February 17, 1919
Cohan and Harris Theatre • 208 performances
"*Opéra Comique*." Music mostly by Anselm
Goetzl and George M. Cohan; Lyrics mostly by
William Cary Duncan and George M. Cohan;
Book by Stephen Ivor Szinnyey and William
Cary Duncan; Directed by George M. Cohan;
Produced by George M. Cohan and Sam H.
Harris.

Published Song
That Revolutionary Rag

Berlin's musical secretary for a very brief time
was George Gershwin, who wrote the arrangement for *That Revolutionary Rag*. Berlin suggested Gershwin might be better off composing
on his own (but did not offer to publish him).

ZIEGFELD FOLLIES OF 1919
June 23, 1919
New Amsterdam Theatre • 171 performances
Music and Lyrics also by others; Sketches by
Rennold Wolf, Gene Buck, and others;
Directed by Ned Wayburn; Produced by
Florenz Ziegfeld, Jr.; With Bert Williams,
Eddie Cantor, Marilyn(n) Miller, and Eddie
Dowling.

Published Songs
Bevo—originally used in YIP-YIP-YAPHANK
  [August 19, 1918]
Harem Life (*Outside of That Every Little
  Thing's All Right*)
I'd Rather See a Minstrel Show
I'm the Guy That Guards the Harem (*And My
  Heart's in My Work*)
Look Out for the Bolsheviki Man—published in
  separate edition
*Mandy—originally used in YIP-YIP-YAPHANK
My Tambourine Girl
A Pretty Girl Is Like a Melody
A Syncopated Cocktail
You Cannot Make Your Shimmy Shake on Tea
  [lyric by Rennold Wolf and Berlin]
You'd Be Surprised—added after opening;
  published in separate edition

Considered the best edition of the FOLLIES, Berlin contributed a significant amount of the score
—including the series' most famous song, *A
Pretty Girl Is Like a Melody*.

ZIEGFELD MIDNIGHT FROLIC
October 2, 1919
New Amsterdam Roof • 171 performances
Music mostly by Dave Stamper; Book and
Lyrics mostly by Gene Buck; Directed by Ned
Wayburn; Produced by Florenz Ziegfeld, Jr.;
With Fanny Brice, Ted Lewis, and W. C. Fields.

Published Song
I'll See You in C-U-B-A

THE PASSION FLOWER
January 13, 1920
Greenwich Village Theatre
{Off Broadway} • 144 performances
Play by Jacinto Benavente, as translated by
John Garrett Underhill; With Nance O'Neil.

Published Song
The Passion Flower

ZIEGFELD GIRLS OF 1920
March 8, 1920
New Amsterdam Roof • 78 performances
"A 9 O'Clock Revue." Music mostly by Dave
Stamper; Book and Lyrics mostly by Gene
Buck; Directed by Ned Wayburn; Produced
by Florenz Ziegfeld, Jr.; With Fanny Brice,
Lillian Lorraine, and W. C. Fields.

Published Song
Metropolitan Ladies—advertised but not
   published

ZIEGFELD FOLLIES OF 1920
June 22, 1920
New Amsterdam Theatre • 123 performances
Music and Lyrics also by others; Sketches by
George V. Hobart, James Montgomery, and
W. C. Fields; Directed by Edward Royce;
Produced by Florenz Ziegfeld, Jr.; With Fanny
Brice, W. C. Fields, Mary Eaton, and Charles
Winninger.

Published Songs
Bells
Chinese Firecrackers
Come Along Sextette
The Girls of My Dreams
The Leg of Nations
The Syncopated Vamp
Tell Me Little Gypsy

BROADWAY BREVITIES OF 1920
September 29, 1920
Winter Garden Theatre • 105 performances
Music mostly by Archie Gottler (see Gershwin:
September 29, 1920); Lyrics mostly by Blair

Treynor; Book by George LeMaire; Produced
by Rufus LeMaire; With George LeMaire,
Eddie Cantor, Edith Hallor, and Bert Williams.

Published Song
Beautiful Faces

MUSIC BOX REVUE ✦ First Edition
September 22, 1921
Music Box Theatre • 440 performances
Sketches by William Collier, George V.
Hobart, and others; Directed by Hassard
Short; Produced by Sam H. Harris (and Berlin);
With William Collier, Sam Bernard, and Berlin.

Published Songs
At the Court around the Corner
Behind the Fan
Everybody Step
I'm a Dumb-Bell—advertised but not
   published
In a Cozy Kitchenette Apartment
Legend of the Pearls
My Little Book of Poetry
*Say It with Music
The Schoolhouse Blues
Tell Me with a Melody—written for London
   version [May 15, 1923]
They Call It Dancing

Sam Harris (see THE LITTLE MILLIONAIRE [September 25, 1911]) and Berlin began their partnership by building the intimate Music Box Theatre to house their own revue series. The MUSIC BOX REVUES headed away from the overblown, lavish productions of Ziegfeld, White, and Carroll, opting for style and sophistication. Guiding the MUSIC BOX REVUES was innovative director/designer Hassard Short, whose taste and talent were first demonstrated here.

MUSIC BOX REVUE ✦ Second Edition
October 23, 1922
Music Box Theatre • 330 performances
Sketches by George V. Hobart, Walter Catlett,
and others; Directed by Hassard Short;
Produced by Sam H. Harris (and Berlin); With
William Gaxton, Charlotte Greenwood, and
Bobby Clark & Paul McCullough.

Published Songs

Bring on the Pepper
Crinoline Days
Dancing Honeymoon
Diamond Horseshoe
I'm Looking for a Daddy Long Legs
Lady of the Evening
The Little Red Lacquer Cage
Mont Martre
Pack Up Your Sins and Go to the Devil
Porcelain Maid
Take a Little Wife
Three Cheers for the Red, White, and Blue—
    advertised but not published
Will She Come from the East? (East-North-
    West or South)

This edition featured vaudevillians William Gaxton and Bobby Clark, both of whom were to become major musical comedy stars by the end of the decade.

MUSIC BOX REVUE ✦ Third Edition

September 22, 1923
Music Box Theatre • 273 performances
Sketches by George S. Kaufman, Robert Benchley, and others; Directed by Hassard Short; Produced by Sam H. Harris (and Berlin); With Frank Tinney, Grace Moore, and Robert Benchley.

Published Songs

Climbing up the Scale
Learn to Do the Strut
Little Butterfly
Maid of Mesh
One Girl
An Orange Grove in California
Tell Me a Bedtime Story
Too Many Sweethearts—cut; for initial
    publication see THE COCOANUTS
    [December 8, 1925]
The Waltz of Long Ago
What'll I Do?—added after opening; initial
    publication as 1924 non-show song

As the series continued, a marked improvement was noticeable in the quality of the sketches. George S. Kaufman had already collaborated with Marc Connelly on two successful comedies; his first musical, with Connelly, Kalmar,

and Ruby, had been the unsuccessful HELEN OF TROY, N.Y.† [June 19, 1923]. His contributions to this MUSIC BOX REVUE included the near-legendary sketch "If Men Played Cards As Women Do." Soprano Grace Moore went on to stardom, but popular Irish song-and-dance man Frank Tinney went on to obscurity. His career was destroyed in Broadway's equivalent to the Fatty Arbuckle sex scandal. The faded, forgotten Tinney served as inspiration for Charles Chaplin's 1952 film *Limelight*.

THE PUNCH BOWL

May 21, 1924
Duke of York's Theatre {London} •
    565 performances
Music and Lyrics mostly by others; Produced by Archibald De Bears; With Norah Blaney.

Published Songs

All Alone—added after opening; initial
    publication as 1924 non-show song; also
    added to MUSIC BOX REVUE [4th]
    [December 1, 1924]
What'll I Do?—1924 non-show song; also
    added after opening to MUSIC BOX
    REVUE [3rd] [September 22, 1923]

The romance of immigrant Berlin and socialite heiress Ellin Mackay created international headlines until their elopement in 1926. *Always*, *What'll I Do*, and *All Alone* served as courtship songs and immensely popular hits. Berlin interpolated the last two in his then-running revues.

MUSIC BOX REVUE ✦ Fourth Edition

December 1, 1924
Music Box Theatre • 184 performances
Sketches by Bert Kalmar, Harry Ruby, and others; Directed by John Murray Anderson; Produced by Sam H. Harris (and Berlin); With Fanny Brice, Bobby Clark and Paul McCullough, Grace Moore, and Oscar Shaw.

Published Songs

Alice in Wonderland [2nd]—different than
    song from THE CENTURY GIRL [November
    6, 1916]
All Alone—see THE PUNCH BOWL [May 21,
    1924]

The Call of the South
*Don't Send Me Back (To Petrograd)
Don't Wait Too Long
In the Shade of a Sheltering Tree
I Want to Be a Ballet Dancer—advertised but
    not published
Listening
Rockabye Baby
Tell Her in the Springtime
Tokio Blues
Unlucky in Love
Where Is My Little Old New York?
Who

The MUSIC BOX REVUES had been expensively and tastefully produced; but with the costs increasing and the runs decreasing, Harris and Berlin decided to end the series. Berlin retained control of the Music Box for the rest of his life, in partnership with the Shuberts (who bought the Harris share from his estate).

THE COCOANUTS
December 8, 1925
Lyric Theatre • 377 performances
Book by George S. Kaufman; Directed by Oscar Eagle; Produced by Sam H. Harris; With The Marx Brothers and Margaret Dumont.

Published Songs
Can't You Tell?—advertised but not published
Everyone in the World Is Doing the Charles-
    ton—added to "New Summer Edition"
    [1926]; issued as professional copy only
Five o'Clock Tea
Florida by the Sea
Gentlemen Prefer Blondes—added to "New
    Summer Edition"; issued as professional
    copy only
A Hit with the Ladies—advertised but not
    published
A Little Bungalow
Lucky Boy
Minstrel Days—advertised but not published
*The Monkey Doodle-Doo [2nd]—different than
    song from ALL ABOARD [June 5, 1913]
Take 'Im Away (He's Breakin' My Heart)—
    advertised but not published
Tango Melody
Ting-a-Ling, the Bells'll Ring—added to "New
    Summer Edition"

Too Many Sweethearts—originally used
    (unpublished) in MUSIC BOX REVUE [3rd]
    [September 22, 1923]
We Should Care (Let the Lazy Sun Refuse to
    Care) [1st]—cut
We Should Care (Let the Sky Start to Cry) [2nd]
What's There about Me?—advertised but not
    published
When My Dreams Come True—written for
    1929 movie version
When We're Running a Little Hotel of Our
    Own—advertised but not published
Why Do You Want to Know Why?—added to
    "New Summer Edition"
With a Family Reputation

Berlin, George Kaufman, Alex Woolcott, and other members of the 1920s intelligentsia were captivated by the zany lunacy of the Marx Brothers, resulting in THE COCOANUTS. The comedy was superb but the score uninspired, except for the raggy Monkey Doodle-Doo.

BETSY
December 28, 1926
New Amsterdam Theatre • 39 performances
Music mostly by Richard Rodgers (see Rodgers: December 28, 1926); Lyrics mostly by Lorenz Hart; Book by Irving Caesar and David Freedman; Directed by Wm. Anthony McGuire; Produced by Florenz Ziegfeld, Jr.; With Belle Baker and Al Shean.

Published Song
**Blue Skies

Belter Belle Baker, about to open in the mediocre BETSY, called Berlin for help. He pulled Blue Skies out of the trunk, fixed it up, and Baker interpolated it on opening night (much to Richard Rodgers's displeasure). The show flopped —but the song sure didn't!

ZIEGFELD FOLLIES OF 1927
August 16, 1927
New Amsterdam Theatre • 167 performances
Sketches by Harold Atteridge and Eddie Cantor; Directed by Zeke Colvan; Produced by Florenz Ziegfeld, Jr.; With Eddie Cantor, Ruth Etting, and Dan Healy.

Published Songs
It—advertised but not published (probably a misprint)
It All Belongs to Me
It's up to the Band
Jimmy
Jungle Jingle—advertised but not published
Learn to Sing a Love Song
My New York
Ooh, Maybe It's You
Rainbow of Girls
Ribbons and Bows—advertised but not published
Shaking the Blues Away
What Makes Me Love You?—advertised but not published

Additional Song Recorded
Tickling the Ivories

Berlin wrote most of the songs for this edition of the FOLLIES, all mediocre. Eddie Cantor was featured as the sole star, also a departure from FOLLIES tradition. The show was very lavish and far from the best of the series; Ziegfeld was only able to mount one more edition [July 1, 1931] before his death. Berlin, meanwhile, was in a creative drought which was only exacerbated by the depression. He spent time the next years mostly in Hollywood, with little to show for them other than two exceptional songs for otherwise forgotten films: ***Puttin' on the Ritz** (1929) and *Let Me Sing and I'm Happy* (1930).

SHOOT THE WORKS
July 21, 1931
George M. Cohan Theatre • 87 performances
Music and Lyrics mostly by others (see Duke: July 21, 1931); Sketches by Nunnally Johnson, Heywood Broun, and others; Directed by Ted Hammerstein; Produced by Heywood Broun, with Milton Raison; With Heywood Broun, George Murphy, and Imogene Coca.

Published Song
Begging for Love—published in separate edition

FACE THE MUSIC
February 17, 1932
New Amsterdam Theatre • 165 performances
Book by Moss Hart; Book directed by George S. Kaufman; Production staged by Hassard Short; Produced by Sam H. Harris; With Mary Boland, J. Harold Murray, and Katherine Carrington.

Published Songs
I Say It's Spinach
*Let's Have Another Cup of Coffee
Manhattan Madness
My Rhinestone Girl—advertised but not published
On a Roof in Manhattan
Soft Lights and Sweet Music

Additional Song Published in Non-show Folio
I Don't Wanna Be Married, I Just Wanna Be Friends

Additional Song Recorded
Two Cheers instead of Three

Berlin's career picked up with this mildly satirical success, produced concurrently with director Kaufman and producer Harris's highly satirical smash OF THEE I SING [Gershwin: December 26, 1931]. Moss Hart, collaborator with Kaufman on the 1930 comedy *Once in a Lifetime*, provided the book; like Kaufman, he went on to become an important musical theatre librettist/director. Berlin once again exhibited his ability to sense the public's mood with *Let's Have Another Cup of Coffee*.

AS THOUSANDS CHEER
September 30, 1933
Music Box Theatre • 400 performances
Sketches by Moss Hart; Directed by Hassard Short; Choreographed by Charles Weidman; Produced by Sam H. Harris; With Marilyn Miller, Clifton Webb, Helen Broderick, and Ethel Waters.

Revival
June 14, 1998
Greenwich House Theatre {Off Off Broadway}
Directed by Christopher Ashley; Choreo-

graphed by Kathleen Marshall; Produced by the Drama Dept. (Ira Weitzman); With Kevin Chamberlin, Judy Kuhn, Howard McGillin, Paula Newsome, Mary Beth Peil, and B. D. Wong.

Published Songs

*Easter Parade—revised version of 1917 non-show song *Smile and Show Your Dimple*
The Funnies
Harlem on My Mind
*Heat Wave
How's Chances
Lonely Heart
Not for All the Rice in China
**Supper Time

Additional Song Published (No Lyric) in Piano Selection

Revolt in Cuba [instrumental]—initial publication upon reuse in the London revue STOP PRESS† (February 21, 1935)

Additional Songs Recorded

Debts
Man Bites Dog
Metropolitan Opening
Our Wedding Day
Through a Keyhole

Berlin and Moss Hart used the concept of newspaper—with news headlines, weather reports, and even the funnies page—for their topical revue AS THOUSANDS CHEER. With a stylish production and an especially stellar cast, the show was Berlin's only Broadway hit of the 1930s. The score included the staggeringly powerful *Supper Time*, a tragic lament about a lynching. This is a great song and a highly dramatic one, totally unlike anything else Berlin ever wrote. (He had *Stormy Weather* to model it upon; Berlin saw Ethel Waters in the COTTON CLUB PARADE [22nd] [Arlen: April 6, 1933] and brought her to Broadway, making her the first black to star in a "white" show.) He also provided Waters with the sizzling tropical *Heat Wave*. The song hit of the show, though, was for the rotogravure section of the paper: a fashionable glimpse at the Fifth Avenue swells strolling in their finery at the *Easter Parade*. STOP PRESS† was a Moss Hart/Hassard Short British revue which used the CHEER format and

several of the songs. MORE CHEERS†, a Broadway sequel to AS THOUSANDS CHEER, was announced for early 1935 but never produced; Berlin published a professional copy of one song, *Moon over Napoli*. For Marilyn Miller, Broadway's favorite (and highest paid) star of the 1920s, CHEER was to be the end of the road. She died of a mysterious medical malady on April 7, 1936, at the age of thirty-seven. Berlin spent the rest of the thirties writing for the movies, his output including some great songs like **Cheek to Cheek, **Top Hat, White Tie and Tails, **Let's Face the Music and Dance, and *Now It Can Be Told.

LOUISIANA PURCHASE

May 28, 1940
Imperial Theatre • 444 performances
Book by Morrie Ryskind (based on a story by B. G. DeSylva); Directed by Edgar MacGregor; Choreographed by George Balanchine and Carl Randall; Produced by B. G. DeSylva; With William Gaxton, Victor Moore, Vera Zorina, Irene Bordoni, and Carol Bruce.

Concert Version
June 19, 1996
Weill Recital Hall, Carnegie Hall • 4 performances
Produced by Carnegie Hall; With Michael McGrath [Gaxton], Judy Blazer [Zorina], George S. Irving [Moore], Taina Elg [Bordoni], and Debbie (Shapiro) Gravitte [Bruce].

Published Songs

Dance with Me (Tonight at the Mardi Gras)— originally issued as *Tonight at the Mardi Gras*
Fools Fall in Love
I'd Love to Be Shot out of a Cannon with You— cut; issued as professional copy, also published in 1996 vocal selection
It'll Come to You
It's a Lovely Day Tomorrow
Latins Know How
The Lord Done Fixed Up My Soul
*Louisiana Purchase
Outside of That I Love You
Sex Marches On—issued as professional copy
What Chance Have I with Love?

Wild about You
You Can't Brush Me Off
You're Lonely and I'm Lonely

Additional Songs Published in "Special Edition" Vocal Selection

Opening Chorus
Opening Letter

An entertaining musical comedy, loosely satirizing Louisiana governor Huey Long. The team of William Gaxton and Victor Moore appeared in their final hit, ably supported by choreographer George Balanchine's wife, Vera Zorina, and Irene Bordoni (of PARIS [Porter: October 8, 1928], Berlin's former brother-in-law's former wife). The songs are pretty much all pleasant, fun, and highly tuneful—like *Fools Fall in Love* and the infectious title song—though not especially memorable. Berlin then went back to Hollywood for the 1942 film *Holiday Inn*, including the imperishable *White Christmas.

THIS IS THE ARMY

July 4, 1942
Broadway Theatre • 113 performances
Directed by Ezra Stone; Produced by Uncle Sam; With Ezra Stone, Julie Oshins, Anthony Ross, and Berlin.

Published Songs

American Eagles
The Army's Made a Man out of Me
How about a Cheer for the Navy
I Left My Heart at the Stage Door Canteen
I'm Getting Tired So I Can Sleep
Jap-German Sextet—issued as professional copy
My Sergeant and I Are Buddies
Oh, How I Hate to Get Up in the Morning—originally used in YIP-YIP-YAPHANK [August 19, 1918]
That Russian Winter
That's What the Well-Dressed Man in Harlem Will Wear
This Is the Army, Mr. Jones
What Does He Look Like—written for 1943 movie version
With My Head in the Clouds

Additional Songs Published in "Special Edition" Vocal Selection

Closing
Ladies of the Chorus—initial publication of song from YIP-YIP-YAPHANK
Opening (The Army and the Shuberts Depend on You)
Opening Chorus (Some Dough for the Army Relief)
Opening of Second Act (Jane Cowl Number)
Yip-Yip-Yaphanker's Introduction

Additional Published Songs Added to Overseas Touring Productions

The Fifth Army's Where My Heart Is [1944]—issued as professional copy only
I Get Along with the Aussies [1945]—issued as professional copy only
The Kick in the Pants [1943]—issued as professional copy only
My British Buddy [1943]
There Are No Wings on a Foxhole [1944]
This Time—initial publication as 1942 non-show song
Ve Don't Like It [1943]—issued as professional copy only
What Are We Going to Do with All the Jeeps? [1944]

Additional Song Published in Non-show Folio

Take Me with You, Soldier Boy—cut; written for 1943 movie version

Another war, another service show—this time the ultimate wartime service show, which earned millions of dollars for the Army Emergency Relief Fund. YIP-YIP-YAPHANK [August 19, 1918] had run merely a month, opening just before the end of World War I. THIS IS THE ARMY, however, toured Army bases around the world until the fall of 1945—usually with the composer in attendance. Berlin kept things topical, adding special material along the way. The score is generally rambunctious, with a few pleasant ballads (*I Left My Heart at the Stage Door Canteen* and *I'm Getting Tired So I Can Sleep*) and quite a bit of good comedy material (*That Russian Winter*, *That's What the Well-Dressed Man in Harlem Will Wear*, *The Kick in the Pants*, and *Ve Don't Like It*).

ANNIE GET YOUR GUN
May 16, 1946
Imperial Theatre • 1,147 performances
Book by Herbert and Dorothy Fields;
Directed by Joshua Logan; Choreographed
by Helen Tamiris; Produced by Rodgers and
Hammerstein; With Ethel Merman and Ray
Middleton.

Revivals
September 21, 1966
Broadway Theatre • 77 performances
Directed by Jack Sydow; Choreographed
by Danny Daniels; Produced by Music
Theater of Lincoln Center (Richard
Rodgers); With Ethel Merman, Bruce
Yarnell [Middleton], Jerry Orbach, and
Benay Venuta.

March 4, 1999
Marquis Theatre • Still playing
    April 1, 1999
Additional book material by Peter Stone;
Directed by Graciela Daniele; Choreographed
by Graciela Daniele and Jeff Calhoun; With
Bernadette Peters (Merman), Tom Wopat
(Middleton), Ron Holgate, and Valerie
Wright.

Published Songs
*Anything You Can Do
Colonel Buffalo Bill
*Doin' What Comes Natur'lly
The Girl That I Marry
I Got Lost in His Arms
*I Got the Sun in the Morning
I'll Share It All with You
I'm a Bad, Bad Man
I'm an Indian Too
Let's Go West Again—written for 1950 movie
    version (cut); issued as professional copy
    and in orchestral arrangement only
*Moonshine Lullaby
My Defenses Are Down
An Old Fashioned Wedding—written for
    revival
*There's No Business Like Show Business
They Say It's Wonderful
Who Do You Love, I Hope
*You Can't Get a Man with a Gun

Additional Songs Recorded
Take It in Your Stride—cut; advertised but not
    published
With Music—cut

Berlin wrote his best score (by far) for this enter-
taining, highly professional musical bull's-eye.
Rodgers and Hammerstein had begun their pro-
ducing career in 1944 (see HAPPY BIRTHDAY
[Rodgers: October 31, 1946]). Dorothy Fields came
to them with a surefire idea: Ethel Merman as
Annie Oakley. They concurred, enlisting Jerome
Kern to write the music (see VERY WARM FOR
MAY [Kern: November 17, 1939]). Following
Kern's death, Berlin agreed to take on the score
(with Fields relinquishing her lyric assignment).
Rodgers brought along Joshua Logan, his fre-
quent director since I MARRIED AN ANGEL
[Rodgers: May 11, 1938]. The combination of tal-
ents promised a rip-roarin' success, and they
turned up a first-rate crowd-pleaser (though not
a well-made, well-constructed musical like CAR-
OUSEL [Rodgers: April 19, 1945] or BRIGADOON
[Loewe: March 13, 1947]). Still, with *Anything
You Can Do, Doin' What Comes Natur'lly, I
Got the Sun in the Morning, Moonshine Lullaby,
There's No Business Like Show Business*, and *You
Can't Get a Man with a Gun*, there were few
complaints.

STARS ON MY SHOULDERS
[circa 1948]
Unfinished musical. Book by Norman
    Krasna.

Published Songs
It Gets Lonely in the White House—initial
    publication upon use in MR. PRESIDENT
    [October 20, 1962]
What Can You Do with a General?—initial
    publication upon use in 1954 movie *White
    Christmas*

Additional Songs Published in Non-show
    Folio
*A Beautiful Day in Brooklyn
It's a Lovely Day for a Walk*—initially
    intended for the 1946 movie *Blue Skies*
Nothing More to Say

STARS ON MY SHOULDERS dealt with a retired general—not unlike Eisenhower—adjusting to postwar peace and retirement. Vestiges of the main character found their way into the film *White Christmas* and the musical MR. PRESIDENT.

MISS LIBERTY

July 15, 1949
Imperial Theatre • 308 performances
Book by Robert E. Sherwood; Directed by Moss Hart; Choreographed by Jerome Robbins; Produced by Berlin, Robert E. Sherwood, and Moss Hart; With Allyn McLerie, Eddie Albert, and Mary McCarty.

Published Songs

Business for a Good Girl Is Bad—cut; issued as professional copy only
Extra! Extra!
Falling out of Love Can Be Fun
Give Me Your Tired, Your Poor (poem by Emma Lazarus)
Homework
The Hon'rable Profession of the Fourth Estate—cut
I'd Like My Picture Took
Just One Way to Say I Love You
*Let's Take an Old-Fashioned Walk—revised version of 1945 non-show song *The Race Horse and the Flea*
Little Fish in a Big Pond
Me an' My Bundle
Miss Liberty
*Mr. Monotony—cut, initially issued as *Mrs. Monotony*; written for 1948 movie *Easter Parade* (also cut), initial use in JEROME ROBBINS' BROADWAY [February 26, 1989]
The Most Expensive Statue in the World
Only for Americans
Paris Wakes Up and Smiles
The Policeman's Ball
The Pulitzer Prize—cut; advertised but not published
What Do I Have to Do to Get My Picture in the Paper?—cut
You Can Have Him

A patriotic flag-waver about the Statue of Liberty from Berlin, Hart, and Pulitzer Prize–win-

ner/Roosevelt speechwriter Robert E. Sherwood. The combination of talents promised another rip-roarin' success, so much so that the boys went and produced it by themselves. So much for promises. There is one pretty pop ballad, *Let's Take an Old-Fashioned Walk*, and two likeable up-tunes (*Falling out of Love Can Be Fun* and *Homework*); but MISS LIBERTY was a distinct disappointment.

CALL ME MADAM

October 12, 1950
Imperial Theatre • 644 performances
Book by Howard Lindsay and Russel Crouse; Directed by George Abbott; Choreographed by Jerome Robbins; Produced by Leland Hayward; With Ethel Merman, Paul Lukas, Russell Nype, and Galina Talva.

Concert Version
February 16, 1995
City Center • 4 performances
Directed by Charles Repole; Choreographed by Kathleen Marshall; Produced by City Center Encores; With Tyne Daly [Merman], Walter Charles [Lukas], Lewis Cleale [Nype], and Melissa Errico [Talva].

Published Songs

Anthem for Presentation—cut; advertised but not published
The Best Thing for You
Can You Use Any Money Today?—initial individual publication upon use in 1953 movie version
For the Very First Time—cut; initially published in 1952 in non-show edition
Free—cut; revised for 1954 movie *White Christmas* with new lyric, as *Snow*
The Hostess with the Mostes' on the Ball
It's a Lovely Day Today
Lichtenburg—advertised but not published (except in vocal score)
Marrying for Love
Mrs. Sally Adams—advertised but not published (except in vocal score)
(Dance to the Music Of) The Ocarina
Once upon a Time Today
Our Day of Independence—cut; advertised but not published

Something to Dance About
They Like Ike
Washington Square Dance
*You're Just in Love (I Wonder Why?)

This slick entertainment was Berlin's final Broadway hit, carried by Ethel Merman's performance, some pleasant tunes, and the knockout eleven-o'clock duet *You're Just in Love*. After some final motion picture work, Berlin went into virtual retirement—which for him meant writing outdated, unpublishable pop songs and continuing his publishing activities. He wrote some additional MADAM songs—*You've Got to Be Way Out to Be Way In, We Still Like Ike*, and a title number—for a proposed 1967 television version but was unable to get it produced.

THE MIZNER STORY
[circa December 1956]
Unfinished musical. Book by S. N. Behrman and George S. Kaufman (based on *The Legendary Mizners* [biography] by Alva Johnston); [Produced by Max Gordon; With José Ferrer]. Alternate titles: SENTIMENTAL GUY and WISE GUY.

Song Published in Non-show Folio
Love Leads to Marriage
You're a Sentimental Guy
You're a Sucker for a Dame

This musical biography of a pair of real-life con men was abandoned when the authors couldn't figure out just what to do with the material. Forty years later, Stephen Sondheim and librettist John Weidman undertook their own version of the same material (currently entitled WISE GUYS, scheduled for the 1999–2000 season).

MR. PRESIDENT
October 20, 1962
St. James Theatre • 265 performances
Book by Howard Lindsay and Russel Crouse; Directed by Joshua Logan; Choreographed by Peter Gennaro; Produced by Leland Hayward; With Robert Ryan, Nanette Fabray, and Anita Gillette.

Published Songs
Don't Be Afraid of Romance
Empty Pockets Filled with Love
The First Lady
Glad to Be Home
I'm Gonna Get Him
In Our Hide-Away
Is He the Only Man in the World?—revised version of *Where Is the Song of Songs for Me?* from 1929 movie *Lady of the Pavements*; lyric revised from the 1954 non-show song *Is She the Only Girl in the World?*
It Gets Lonely in the White House—initial publication of song written for STARS ON MY SHOULDERS [circa 1948]
I've Got to Be Around
Laugh It Up
Let's Go Back to the Waltz
Meat and Potatoes
Once Every Four Years—cut
Opening of "Mr. President"—issued as professional copy only
Pigtails and Freckles
Poor Joe—cut
The Secret Service
Song for Belly Dancer (The Only Dance I Know)
They Love Me
This Is a Great Country
The Washington Twist

Additional Song Published in Non-show Folio
*If You Haven't Got an Ear for Music—cut

Additional Song Recorded
You Need a Hobby

After a twelve-year hiatus, the seventy-four year old Berlin returned to Broadway with what was supposed to be a topical, satirical, political musical. But Berlin and his collaborators were old and tired. MR. PRESIDENT and Mr. Berlin both received a severe critical drubbing, with the supersensitive songsmith going into virtual seclusion for the next quarter century, though he resurfaced in 1966 with a final contrapuntal duet, *An Old-Fashioned Wedding*, for Ethel Merman's revival of ANNIE GET YOUR GUN [May 16, 1946]. Irving Berlin died on September 22, 1989, at the age of 101.

Irving Berlin remains America's most popular composer, with handfuls of all-time hits to his credit (including a number of very fine songs). His contributions to Broadway were often entertaining and usually successful—not a bad combination. But Berlin rarely attempted well-rounded musical theatre scores; he always seemed more interested in parades of song hits, which kept his publisher (i.e., himself) happy.

An exception was ANNIE GET YOUR GUN, where he was motivated, intimidated, and prodded by the presence of producers Rodgers and Hammerstein. In 1914–15, Jerome Kern and Irving Berlin led musical theatre into a new era. While Kern made musico-dramatic innovation his lifelong quest, Berlin seemed content just writing song hit after song hit (after song hit).

GEORGE GERSHWIN

Born: September 26, 1898, Brooklyn, New York
Died: July 11, 1937, Beverly Hills, California

GEORGE GERSHWIN grew up in Manhattan, where his Russian immigrant father attempted a succession of unsuccessful businesses. Gershwin displayed a sudden musical aptitude at the age of eleven, quitting school at fifteen to work as a song plugger for Tin Pan Alley publisher Jerome H. Remick. A highly distinctive pianist, Gershwin began supplementing his income by making player-piano rolls. He also began writing music of his own, the first published song being the 1916 *When You Want 'Em, You Can't Get 'Em* (*When You've Got 'Em, You Don't Want 'Em*) [lyric by Murray Roth]. Gershwin was ready for Broadway, making his debut at the age of seventeen.

PASSING SHOW OF 1916

June 22, 1916
Winter Garden Theatre • 140 performances
"The Annual Summer Review." Music mostly by Sigmund Romberg and Otto Motzan; Book and Lyrics mostly by Harold Atteridge; Directed by J. C. Huffman; Produced by The Winter Garden Company (the Messrs. Shubert).

Published Song
The Making of a Girl [music by Romberg and Gershwin]

Shubert staff composer Sigmund Romberg listened to some of Gershwin's material and liked one tune enough to use it, taking co-composer credit for himself. Leaving song plugging, Gershwin was hired as rehearsal pianist for the Ziegfeld/Dillingham extravaganza MISS 1917 [Kern: November 5, 1917]. Gershwin was a fan of Kern's Princess Theatre shows, while Kern was impressed with the young Gershwin.

Kern's publishing partner Max Dreyfus signed up Gershwin and began placing his work.

HITCHY-KOO OF 1918 ✦ Second Edition

June 6, 1918
Globe Theatre • 68 performances
Music mostly by Raymond Hubbell; Book and Lyrics mostly by Glen MacDonough; Directed by Leon Errol; Produced by Raymond Hitchcock; With Raymond Hitchcock, Leon Errol, and Irene Bordoni.

Published Song
You-oo Just You [lyric by Irving Caesar]— initially published as 1918 non-show song

Gershwin served as concert accompanist for Vivienne Segal (star of MISS 1917 [Kern: November 5, 1917]). He prevailed upon her to introduce *You-oo Just You,* and the song soon found its way into HITCHY-KOO OF 1918. Gershwin and childhood friend Irving Caesar collaborated on several early songs, including the breakthrough hit *Swanee* (CAPITOL REVUE [October 24, 1919]).

LADIES FIRST

October 24, 1918
Broadhurst Theatre • 164 performances
Music mostly by A. Baldwin Sloane; Book and Lyrics mostly by Harry B. Smith (based on *A Contented Woman* [play] by Charles Hoyt); Directed by Frank Smithson; Produced by H. H. Frazee; With Nora Bayes. Pre-Broadway title: LOOK WHO'S HERE.

Published Songs

The Real American Folk Song (*Is a Rag*) [lyric
by Arthur Francis (Ira Gershwin)]—initial
publication in 1958 as non-show song
Some Wonderful Sort of Someone [lyric by
Schuyler Greene]—see THE LADY IN RED
[May 12, 1919]

Early in his career Gershwin wrote with many
different lyricists, including his older brother
Ira. (Wishing to avoid the appearance of a sibling team, Ira chose to combine the names of his
younger siblings into the pseudonym Arthur
Francis.) After dropping out of college, Ira
drifted through a series of odd jobs in the same
unsuccessful manner as his father had until his
first success (see TWO LITTLE GIRLS IN BLUE
[Youmans: May 3, 1921]. *Some Wonderful Sort of
Someone* is the first interesting Gershwin song,
a fairly pretty ballad with an arresting, slightly
melancholy strain.

HALF PAST EIGHT
December 9, 1918
Empire Theatre {Syracuse, N.Y.} •
    Closed during tryout
Music mostly by Gershwin; Lyrics by Fred
Caryll [Edward B. Perkins]; Produced by
Edward B. Perkins; With Joe Cook, Sybil
Vane, and the Famous Original Clef Club Band.

Published Songs
None

Gershwin wrote his first full score for this ill-
assembled revue. Things went so badly that at one
of the six performances Gershwin himself was sent
on stage to play a medley of his "hits." Producer
Perkins borrowed the title from a Paul Rubens
revue [August 19, 1916], claiming his show was
direct from a nine-month London run; he even
billed the lyricist—himself—as "Fred Caryll."
(Brother of popular British composer Ivan Caryll,
perhaps?) Some of the music resurfaced, with new
lyrics, in LA, LA LUCILLE [May 26, 1919].

GOOD MORNING JUDGE
February 6, 1919
Shubert Theatre • 140 performances
Music mostly by Lionel Monckton and
Howard Talbot; Book by Fred Thompson

(based on *The Magistrate* [play] by Sir Arthur
Wing Pinero); Directed by Wybert Stamford;
Produced by the Messrs. Shubert; With Mollie
King and Charles King.

Published Songs
I Was So Young (*You Were So Beautiful*) [lyric
by Irving Caesar and Alfred Bryan]
There's More to the Kiss Than the X-X-X [lyric
by Caesar]—see LA, LA LUCILLE [May 26,
1919]

THE LADY IN RED
May 12, 1919
Lyric Theatre • 48 performances
Music mostly by Robert Winterberg (see Kern:
May 12, 1919); Book and Lyrics mostly by
Anne Caldwell; Directed by Frank Smithson;
Produced by John P. Slocum; With Adele
Rowland.

Published Songs
Something about Love [lyric by Lou Paley]—also
used in London production [April 14, 1926]
of LADY, BE GOOD! [December 1, 1924]
Some Wonderful Sort of Someone [lyric by
Schuyler Greene]—revised version of song
from LADIES FIRST [October 24, 1918]

LA, LA LUCILLE
May 26, 1919
Henry Miller's Theatre • 104 performances
"*A New, Up-to-the-Minute Musical Comedy of
Class and Distinction.*" Lyrics by Arthur J.
Jackson and B. G. DeSylva; Book by Fred
Jackson; Directed by Herbert Gresham and
Julian Alfred; Produced by Alfred E. Aarons;
With Janet Velie and John E. Hazzard.

Published Songs
The Best of Everything—see FOR GOODNESS
SAKE [February 20, 1922]
From Now On
The Love of a Wife—cut
Nobody but You—added after opening
Somehow It Seldom Comes True
Tee-Oodle-Um-Bum-Bo
There's More to the Kiss Than the Sound [lyric
by Irving Caesar]—issued in separate

edition; revised lyric for *There's More to the Kiss Than the X-X-X* from GOOD MORNING JUDGE [February 6, 1919]

Gershwin wrote his first complete Broadway score for this moderately successful intimate musical. Best of the songs: *Nobody but You*, an early attempt at the type of up-tempo ballad which would become a Gershwin specialty (i.e., *Do-Do-Do*). Twenty-four-year-old B. G. DeSylva had already written several Al Jolson song hits; he became Gershwin's primary lyricist for five years. The up-and-coming Gershwin was chosen for the assignment (over the over-the-hill Victor Herbert) by Alex Aarons, son of producer Alfred E. Aarons. Alex produced the post-Broadway tour of LA, LA LUCILLE and joined with Vinton Freedley in 1924 to produce a successful string of hit Gershwin musicals.

DEMI TASSE ✦ Part of CAPITOL REVUE
October 24, 1919
Capitol Theatre • Vaudeville revue
Directed and Produced by Ned Wayburn;
With Paul Frawley and Muriel DeForrest.

Published Songs
Come to the Moon [lyric by Ned Wayburn and Lou Paley]—see THE RAINBOW [April 3, 1923]
*Swanee [lyric by Irving Caesar]—also used in SINBAD [circa December 1919]

The opening bill for this movie palace included a quickly forgotten stage show. *Swanee*—sung by a stageful of girls with electric lights on their toes—made little impression, but Al Jolson heard the song and decided to record it. The driving, up-tempo tune became a spectacular success, and Gershwin had his first hit. (Had Jolson actually introduced *Swanee*, he no doubt would have demanded—and received—authorship credit and a chunk of the royalties.)

MORRIS GEST'S MIDNIGHT WHIRL
December 27, 1919
Century Grove Theatre • 110 performances
Book and Lyrics by Bud (B. G.) DeSylva and John Henry Mears; Directed by Julian

Mitchell and Dave Bennett; Produced by Morris Gest; With Bessie McCoy Davis and Bernard Granville.

Published Songs
Limehouse Nights
Poppyland

SINBAD
[circa December 1919]
Post-Broadway tour
"The Winter Garden's Latest Extravaganza."
Music mostly by Sigmund Romberg; Book and Lyrics mostly by Harold Atteridge; Directed by J. C. Huffman; Produced by the Messrs. Shubert; With Al Jolson.

Published Songs
*Swanee [lyric by Irving Caesar]—originally used in DEMI TASSE [October 24, 1919]
Swanee Rose [lyric by Caesar and B. G. DeSylva]—published in non-show edition; originally issued as *Dixie Rose*

With his recording of *Swanee* an immense hit, Jolson interpolated it into his current show (the better to sell records).

DERE MABLE
February 2, 1920
Academy of Music {Baltimore, Md.} •
    Closed during tryout
Music mostly by Rosamond Hodges; Lyrics mostly by John Hodges; Book by Edward Streeter and John Hodges (based on the books by Edward Streeter); Directed by George Marion; Produced by Marc Klaw; With Louis Bennison.

Published Song
We're Pals [lyric by Irving Caesar]

Gershwin also contributed a second song, *Back Home* [lyric by Arthur Francis (Ira Gershwin)], which was unpublished.

THE ED WYNN CARNIVAL
April 5, 1920
New Amsterdam Theatre • 150 performances
Book and Songs mostly by Ed Wynn; Directed by Ned Wayburn; Produced by B. C. Whitney; With Ed Wynn.

Published Song
Oo, How I Love to Be Loved by You [lyric by
    Lou Paley]

GEORGE WHITE'S SCANDALS ✦
Second Annual Event
June 7, 1920
Globe Theatre • 134 performances
Music mostly by Gershwin; Lyrics by Arthur
Jackson; Book by Andy Rice and George
White; Directed by George White and Willie
Collier; Produced by George White; With Ann
Pennington, Lou Holtz, and George White.

Published Songs
Idle Dreams
My Lady
My Old Love Is My New Love—advertised but
    not published
On My Mind the Whole Night Long
Queen Isabella—advertised but not published
Scandal Walk
The Songs of Long Ago
Tum On and Tiss Me

ZIEGFELD FOLLIES song-and-dance man George
White decided to go into competition with his
former boss, stealing FOLLIES star Ann Pennington for the first GEORGE WHITE'S SCAN-
DALS[†] [June 2, 1919], [with songs by Richard
Whiting and Arthur Jackson]. The SCANDALS
ran neck and neck (and leg) with the FOLLIES
until the depression effectively ended both
series. Ziegfeld's shows were typically lavish,
star-laden, and indistinguishable. White could
be counted on for better music and exciting
dancing (see GEORGE WHITE'S SCANDALS OF
1926 [8th] [Notables: June 14, 1926]).

THE SWEETHEART SHOP
August 31, 1920
Knickerbocker Theatre • 55 performances
"The Fascinating Musical Play." Music mostly
by Hugo Felix; Book and Lyrics mostly by
Anne Caldwell; Directed by Herbert Gresham;
Produced by Edgar J. MacGregor and William
Moore Patch; With Helen Ford.

Published Song
Waiting for the Sun to Come Out [lyric by
    Arthur Francis (Ira Gershwin)]

This moderately successful interpolation was Ira
Gershwin's first published song.

PICCADILLY TO BROADWAY
September 27, 1920
Globe Theatre {Atlantic City, N.J.} •
    Closed during tryout
"All Anglo-American Musical Review." Music
also by William Daly, Vincent Youmans (see
Youmans: September 27, 1920), and others;
Sketches and Lyrics mostly by Glen Mac-
Donough and E. Ray Goetz; Directed by
George Marion and Julian Alfred; Produced
by E. Ray Goetz; With Johnny Dooley, Anna
Wheaton, Clifton Webb, and Helen Broderick.

Published Songs
None

Gershwin collaborated with Ray Goetz on two
songs: *On the Brim of Her Old-Fashioned Bonnet*
and *Baby Blues* (both unpublished, also used in
SNAPSHOTS OF 1921 [June 2, 1921]). Among
the other songwriters represented were William
Daly—an important future Gershwin musical
associate—and the budding new team of Vincent
Youmans and Arthur Francis (Ira Gershwin).

BROADWAY BREVITIES OF 1920
September 29, 1920
Winter Garden Theatre • 105 performances
Music mostly by Archie Gottler (see Berlin:
September 29, 1920); Lyrics mostly by Blair
Treynor; Book by George LeMaire; Produced
by Rufus LeMaire; With George LeMaire,
Eddie Cantor, Edith Hallor, and Bert Williams.

Published Songs
Lu Lu [lyric by Arthur Jackson]
Snow Flakes [lyric by Jackson]
Spanish Love [lyric by Irving Caesar]

A DANGEROUS MAID
March 21, 1921
Nixon's Apollo Theatre {Atlantic City, N.J.} •
    Closed during tryout
"A New TNT Laugh Fest." Lyrics by Arthur
Francis [Ira Gershwin]; Book by Charles W.
Bell (based on his play *A Dislocated Honey-*

moon); Produced by Edgar MacGregor; With Vivienne Segal, Amelia Bingham, and Vinton Freedley.

Published Songs
*Boy Wanted—see PRIMROSE [September 11, 1924]
Dancing Shoes
Just to Know You Are Mine
The Simple Life
The Sirens—for initial publication see PRIMROSE
Some Rain Must Fall

Additional Song Recorded
Anything for You

The first complete score written by the brothers Gershwin was for this quick failure. *Boy Wanted*, though, is a fine, wistful ballad. Ira, meanwhile, wrote his first hit show, TWO LITTLE GIRLS IN BLUE [1921] [Youmans: May 3, 1921].

SNAPSHOTS OF 1921
June 2, 1921
Selwyn Theatre • 44 performances
Music mostly by others; Gershwin lyrics by E. Ray Goetz; Directed by Leon Errol; Produced by the Selwyns and Lew Fields; With Nora Bayes, Lew Fields, and DeWolf Hopper.

Published Songs
None

The two Gershwin/Goetz songs from PICCADILLY TO BROADWAY [September 27, 1920] were interpolated into this revue. For the post-Broadway tour, Lew Fields assigned the conducting job to his nineteen-year-old discovery Richard Rodgers.

GEORGE WHITE'S SCANDALS ✦
Third Annual Production
July 11, 1921
Liberty Theatre • 97 performances
Music mostly by Gershwin; Lyrics by Arthur Jackson; Book by Arthur "Bugs" Baer and George White; Directed by George White and John Meehan; Produced by George White; With Ann Pennington, Lester Allen, and George White.

Published Songs
Drifting along with the Tide
I Love You
She's Just a Baby
South Sea Isles
Where East Meets West

Additional Song Published (No Lyric) in Piano Selection
Russian Dance [instrumental]

THE PERFECT FOOL
November 7, 1921
George M. Cohan Theatre • 256 performances
Book, Music, and Lyrics mostly by Ed Wynn; Directed by Julian Alfred; Produced by B. C. Whitney; Presented by A. L. Erlanger; With Ed Wynn and Janet Velie.

Published Songs
My Log-Cabin Home [lyric by Irving Caesar and B. G. DeSylva]
No One Else but That Girl of Mine [lyric by Caesar]—see THE DANCING GIRL [January 24, 1923]

FOR GOODNESS SAKE
February 20, 1922
Lyric Theatre • 103 performances
Music mostly by William Daly and Paul Lannin; Lyrics mostly by Arthur Jackson; Lyrics to Gershwin songs by Arthur Francis [Ira Gershwin]; Book by Fred Jackson; Directed by Priestly Morrison; Produced by Alex A. Aarons; With Adele & Fred Astaire, Helen Ford, and Vinton Freedley. London title: STOP FLIRTING!

Published Songs
The Best of Everything [lyric by Arthur J. Jackson and B. G. DeSylva]—added to London production; revised lyric for song originally used in LA, LA LUCILLE [May 26, 1919]
*I'll Build a Stairway to Paradise [lyric by DeSylva and Arthur Francis (Ira Gershwin)]—added to London production; originally used in GEORGE WHITE'S SCANDALS [4th] [August 28, 1922]

Someone
Tra-La-La

Additional Songs Published (No Lyrics) in Piano Selection

All by Myself—written for London production
Opening Chorus Act One—written for London production

Alex Aarons's second musical featured the sibling act of Adele and Fred Astaire. Though unsuccessful on Broadway, the show—supplemented with additional Gershwin tunes—was a major London hit. Retitled STOP FLIRTING!, it opened on May 30, 1923, for an impressive 418 performances. The Nebraska-born sister-and-brother act suddenly found themselves major transatlantic stage stars. Aarons set the Gershwins to work on a vehicle to bring the Astaires back to Broadway.

THE FRENCH DOLL

February 20, 1922
Lyceum Theatre • 120 performances
Play by A. E. Thomas (based on a play by Paul Armont and Marcel Gerbidon); Produced by E. Ray Goetz; With Irene Bordoni (Goetz).

Published Song

Do It Again [lyric by B. G. DeSylva]

SPICE OF 1922

July 6, 1922
Winter Garden Theatre • 73 performances
"Lyrics and Music by Everybody"; Book by Jack Lait; Directed by Allan K. Foster; Produced by Arman Kaliz; With Georgie Price.

Published Song

The Yankee Doodle Blues [lyric by Irving Caesar and B. G. DeSylva]

GEORGE WHITE'S SCANDALS ✦
Fourth Annual Production

August 28, 1922
Globe Theatre • 88 performances
Music mostly by Gershwin; Lyrics by B. G. DeSylva and E. Ray Goetz; Book by Andy Rice and George White; Directed and Produced by George White; With W. C. Fields, Jack MacGowan, George White, and Paul Whiteman and His Orchestra.

Published Songs

Across the Sea
Argentina [lyric by DeSylva]
Cinderelatives [lyric by DeSylva]
I Found a Four Leaf Clover [lyric by DeSylva]
*I'll Build a Stairway to Paradise [lyric by DeSylva and Arthur Francis (Ira Gershwin)]—see FOR GOODNESS SAKE [February 20, 1922]
She Hangs Out in Our Alley—initially published as *Oh, What She Hangs Out*
Where Is the Man of My Dreams?

Additional Songs Published in 1993 in Vocal Score of *Blue Monday*

*Blue Monday Blues
Has One of You Seen Joe?—revised version of 1919 string quartet *Lullaby* (published 1968)
I'm Goin' to See My Mother

The strongly driving *I'll Build a Stairway to Paradise* became Gershwin's second major hit song, and it's a good one. This SCANDALS included the one-act opera *Blue Monday*, which was withdrawn after the opening night performance. A primitive forerunner of PORGY AND BESS [October 10, 1935], the work marked Gershwin's first attempt at the extended musical form (and included one of Gershwin's finest early songs, the lazy *Blue Monday Blues*).

OUR NELL

December 4, 1922
Nora Bayes Theatre • 40 performances
"A Musical Mellow Drayma." Music also by William Daly; Lyrics by Brian Hooker; Book by A. E. Thomas and Brian Hooker; Directed by W. H. Gilmore; Produced by Hayseed Productions (Ed Davidow and Rufus LeMaire). Pre-Broadway title: HAYSEED.

Published Songs

By and By
Innocent Ingenue Baby [music by Gershwin and William Daly]—see THE RAINBOW [April 3, 1923]
Walking Home with Angeline

Bill Daly, principal composer of FOR GOODNESS SAKE [February 20, 1922], became Gershwin's close friend and musical colleague. He was to conduct many of Gershwin's future shows. For OUR NELL they collaborated on the playfully chromatic *Innocent Ingenue Baby*.

THE DANCING GIRL
January 24, 1923
Winter Garden Theatre • 126 performances
Music mostly by Sigmund Romberg and Alfred Goodman; Book and Lyrics mostly by Harold Atteridge; Directed by J. C. Huffman; Produced by the Messrs. Shubert; With Trini, Marie Dressler, and Jack Pearl.

Published Songs
That American Boy of Mine [lyric by Irving Caesar]—revised lyric for *No One Else but That Girl of Mine* from THE PERFECT FOOL [November 7, 1921]

THE RAINBOW
April 3, 1923
Empire Theatre {London} • 113 performances
Lyrics mostly by Clifford Grey; Book by Albert De Courville, Edgar Wallace, and Noel Scott; Produced by Albert De Courville; With Grace Hayes.

Published Songs
All over Town [lyric by Lou Paley and Grey]— cut; new lyric for *Come to the Moon* from DEMI TASSE [October 24, 1919]
Any Little Tune—advertised but not published
Beneath the Eastern Moon
Give Me My Mammy—advertised but not published
Good-Night, My Dear
In the Rain
Innocent Lonesome Blue Baby [music by Gershwin and William Daly, lyric by Brian Hooker and Grey]—revised lyric for *Innocent Ingenue Baby* from OUR NELL [December 4, 1922]
Moonlight in Versailles
Oh! Nina
Strut Lady with Me

Sunday in London Town—cut
Sweetheart, I'm So Glad That I Met You—see TELL ME MORE! [April 13, 1925]

Gershwin wrote one of his blandest scores for this uninspired, unsuccessful British musical.

GEORGE WHITE'S SCANDALS ✦
Fifth Annual Production
June 18, 1923
Globe Theatre • 168 performances
Music mostly by Gershwin; Lyrics mostly by B. G. DeSylva; Book by George White and William K. Wells; Directed and Produced by George White; With Winnie Lightner and Lester Allen.

Published Songs
Let's Be Lonesome Together [lyric by DeSylva and E. Ray Goetz]
The Life of a Rose
Lo-La-Lo
(On the Beach At) How've You Been
There Is Nothing Too Good for You [lyric by DeSylva and Goetz]
Throw 'Er in High! [lyric by DeSylva and Goetz]
Where Is She?
You and I (In Old Versailles) [music by Gershwin and Jack Green]

Jack Green, brother of symphonic composer Louis Gruenberg, was the SCANDALS' rehearsal pianist; he presumably contributed a musical idea which Gershwin fashioned into *You and I*, meriting shared credit. The following winter he worked as a music copyist on the rushed preparation of **Rhapsody in Blue—afterwards suing Gershwin for coauthorship, unsuccessfully.

LITTLE MISS BLUEBEARD
August 28, 1923
Lyceum Theatre • 175 performances
Play by Avery Hopwood; Produced by Charles Frohman [Inc.] in association with E. Ray Goetz; With Irene Bordoni (Goetz).

Published Song
I Won't Say I Will (But I Won't Say I Won't) [lyric by B. G. DeSylva and Arthur Francis (Ira Gershwin)]

NIFTIES OF 1923
September 25, 1923
Fulton Theatre • 47 performances
Music mostly by others; Produced by Charles
B. Dillingham; With Sam Bernard and William
Collier.

Published Songs
At Half Past Seven [lyric by B. G. DeSylva]—
    see PRIMROSE [September 11, 1924]
Nashville Nightingale [lyric by Irving Caesar]

SWEET LITTLE DEVIL
January 21, 1924
Astor Theatre • 120 performances
"The Gayest of Musical Comedies." Lyrics by
B. G. DeSylva; Book by Frank Mandel and
Laurence Schwab; Directed by Edgar
MacGregor; Produced by Laurence Schwab;
With Constance Binney. Pre-Broadway title:
A PERFECT LADY.

Published Songs
Hey! Hey! Let 'Er Go!
The Jijibo
Mah-Jongg—cut; also used in GEORGE
    WHITE'S SCANDALS [6th] [June 30, 1924]
Pepita—cut; new lyric and verse for 1921
    non-show song *Tomale* [lyric by DeSylva]
Someone Believes in You
Under a One-Man Top
Virginia (Don't Go Too Far)

Gershwin had heretofore only hinted at the
modern rhythms and colorings which soon distinguished him from his contemporaries. Then
came **Rhapsody in Blue*, which was first performed on February 12, 1924. This "assault by
jazz on the concert hall" brought Gershwin sudden fame—and soon eased him away from
accepting hackwork (like the SCANDALS).

GEORGE WHITE'S SCANDALS ✦
    Sixth Annual Production
June 30, 1924
Apollo Theatre • 192 performances
Music mostly by Gershwin; Lyrics mostly by
B. G. DeSylva; Book by George White and
William K. Wells; Directed and Produced by

George White; With Winnie Lightner and
Lester Allen.

Published Songs
I Need a Garden
Kongo Kate
Mah-Jongg—originally used (cut) in SWEET
    LITTLE DEVIL [January 21, 1924]
Night Time in Araby
Rose of Madrid
***Somebody Loves Me* [lyric by DeSylva and
    Ballard MacDonald]
Tune In to Station J. O. Y.
Year after Year

With the success of the *Rhapsody*, Gershwin
made this his final SCANDALS. His work for the
series had never been more than adequate, with
Somebody Loves Me (joining *I'll Build a Stairway to Paradise*) as only his second SCANDALS
song hit in five scores. It's a warmly emotional
ballad, perhaps the best Gershwin song up until
that time. Gershwin turned his attention to contemporary musical comedy—with immediately
gratifying results.

PRIMROSE
September 11, 1924
Winter Garden Theatre {London} •
    225 performances
Lyrics mostly by Desmond Carter; Book by
George Grossmith and Guy Bolton; Directed
by Charles A. Maynard; Produced by George
Grossmith and J. A. E. Malone; With Heather
Thatcher and Leslie Henson.

Published Songs
**Boy Wanted* [lyric by Ira Gershwin and
    Carter]—revised lyric for the song from
    A DANGEROUS MAID [March 21, 1921]
Isn't It Wonderful [lyric by Ira Gershwin and
    Carter]
Naughty Baby [lyric by Ira Gershwin and
    Carter]
Some Far-Away Someone [lyric by Ira
    Gershwin and B. G. DeSylva]—new
    Gershwin lyric for *At Half Past Seven* from
    NIFTIES OF 1923 [September 25, 1923]
That New-Fangled Mother of Mine
This Is the Life for a Man (The Country Side)

Wait a Bit, Susie [lyric by Ira Gershwin and Carter]—see ROSALIE [January 10, 1928]

Additional Songs Published in Vocal Score
Beau Brummel
Berkeley Square and Kew
Can We Do Anything? [lyric by Ira Gershwin and Carter]
Four Little Sirens [lyric by Ira Gershwin]— initial publication of *The Sirens* from A DANGEROUS MAID
I Make Hay When the Moon Shines
It Is the Fourteenth of July
Leaving Town While We May
The Mophams
Roses of France
Till I Meet Someone Like You
When Toby Is out of Town

Additional Song Recorded
Isn't It Terrible What They Did to Mary Queen of Scots?

STOP FLIRTING!, the highly successful 1923 British version of FOR GOODNESS SAKE [February 20, 1922], made Gershwin extremely popular in England; thus, a West End original, PRIMROSE. Ira, meanwhile, dropped his pseudonym and began to write under his own name.

LADY, BE GOOD!
December 1, 1924
Liberty Theatre • 330 performances
Music mostly by Gershwin; Lyrics mostly by Ira Gershwin; Book by Guy Bolton and Fred Thompson; Directed by Felix Edwardes; Produced by Alex A. Aarons and Vinton Freedley; With Fred and Adele Astaire, Walter Catlett, and Cliff Edwards.

Published Songs
**Fascinating Rhythm*
The "Half of It, Dearie" Blues
Hang On to Me
I'd Rather Charleston [lyric by Desmond Carter]—written for London production [April 14, 1926; 326 performances]
Little Jazz Bird
***The Man I Love*—cut; also cut from STRIKE UP THE BAND [1927] [August 29, 1927] and ROSALIE [January 10, 1928]

Oh, Lady Be Good
So Am I
Something about Love [lyric by Lou Paley]— added to London production; originally used in THE LADY IN RED [May 12, 1919]
Swiss Miss (The Cab-Horse Trot) [lyric by Ira Gershwin and Arthur Jackson]—piano solo version (no lyric) published upon use in London production.

Additional Song Published (No Lyric) in Piano Selection
Evening Star—cut; for initial publication see TELL ME MORE! [April 13, 1925]

Additional Songs Recorded
Carnival Time [instrumental]
End of a String
Juanita
Linger in the Lobby
Swiss Miss (The Cab-Horse Trot) [lyric by Ira Gershwin and Arthur Jackson]
We're Here Because
Will You Remember Me?—cut

Alex Aarons and his new partner Vinton Freedley —who had danced in A DANGEROUS MAID [March 21, 1921] and FOR GOODNESS SAKE [February 20, 1922]—commissioned this musical for the Astaires, who were returning as stars from the London production of the latter show. LADY, BE GOOD! was Gershwin's first major Broadway success, his score filled with fascinating rhythms, jazzy harmonies, and lively melodies (with a touch of humor). *Fascinating Rhythm* is as good a rhythm number as you're likely to find; the little-known *Little Jazz Bird* is jauntily playful; and *Oh, Lady Be Good* was highly successful (though rather tame). And then there's the stunning *The Man I Love*, which was cut from this and other shows but managed to work its way into a deserved classic.

TELL ME MORE!
April 13, 1925
Gaiety Theatre • 100 performances
Lyrics by B. G. DeSylva and Ira Gershwin; Book by Fred Thompson and William K. Wells; Directed by John Harwood; Produced by Alfred E. Aarons; With Phyllis Cleveland,

Alexander Gray, and Lou Holtz. Pre-Broadway title: MY FAIR LADY.

Published Songs

Baby! [1st]—new lyric for *Sweetheart, I'm So Glad That I Met You* from THE RAINBOW [April 3, 1923]

Baby! [2nd]—written for London production [May 6, 1925]; revised music for lyric of *Baby!* [1st]

Kickin' the Clouds Away

Murderous Monty (*And Light-Fingered Jane*) [lyric by Desmond Carter]—written for London production

My Fair Lady

Tell Me More

Three Times a Day

Why Do I Love You?

Additional Songs Published (No Lyrics) in Piano Selections

Love I Never Knew [lyric by Carter]—London lyric for *Evening Star* (cut) from LADY, BE GOOD! [December 1, 1924]

Opening Chorus Act One

Where the Delicatessen Flows (*In Sardinia*)

Additional Song Recorded

Love Is in the Air

TELL ME MORE's original title was changed during the pre-Broadway tryout—not because they felt MY FAIR LADY wouldn't sell but because audiences were cold to the anticipated hit title song. (Musicals are occasionally renamed for songs that work well during tryouts, OKLA-HOMA! [Rodgers: March 31, 1943] being a famous example.) The best song of the show, though, was the rhythmic dance tune *Kickin' the Clouds Away*. Alex Aarons's father Alfred produced this modest musical, which couldn't compete with the snazzy LADY, BE GOOD! [December 1, 1924]; it's hard to believe that this drab score is by the post-*Rhapsody* Gershwin. The composer's British popularity made the London production of TELL ME MORE! a 261-performance hit, though, as LADY was delayed until the Astaires could make the trip. There has been confusion as to the proper credits of father and son Aarons, not helped by some pro-grams reading "Al Aarons presents." For the record, Alfred was responsible—under Alex's prodding—for giving Gershwin, Ira, and You-mans their first Broadway opportunities with LA, LA LUCILLE [May 26, 1919] and TWO LITTLE GIRLS IN BLUE [1921] [Youmans: May 3, 1921]. Alex produced the road tour of LUCILLE as well as FOR GOODNESS SAKE [February 20, 1922]. Then he joined Vinton Freedley to produce five George and Ira hits, beginning with LADY, BE GOOD!

TIP-TOES

December 28, 1925
Liberty Theatre • 194 performances
Lyrics by Ira Gershwin; Book by Guy Bolton and Fred Thompson; Directed by John Harwood; Produced by Alex A. Aarons and Vinton Freedley; With Queenie Smith and Allen Kearns.

Published Songs

It's a Great Little World—cut

Harlem River Chanty—initial publication in 1968 non-show choral arrangement

Looking for a Boy

Nice Baby

Nightie-Night

Sweet and Low-Down

That Certain Feeling

These Charming People

When Do We Dance?

Additional Song Published (No Lyric) in Piano Selection

Opening Act One

Another hit for the Gershwins, Aarons, and Freedley. Like LADY, BE GOOD! [December 1, 1924] and the upcoming OH, KAY! [November 8, 1926], TIP-TOES had a mindless but fast-paced book coauthored by Guy Bolton (Kern's Princess Theatre librettist). The score was Gersh-win's best yet, with the plaintive *Looking for a Boy*, the charming *That Certain Feeling*, and the sweet and low-down *Sweet and Low-Down*. During the TIP-TOES tryout, Gershwin introduced his **Concerto in F* at Carnegie Hall on December 3, 1925.

SONG OF THE FLAME
December 30, 1925
44th Street Theatre • 219 performances
Music by Gershwin and Herbert Stothart;
Book and Lyrics by Otto Harbach and Oscar
Hammerstein 2nd; Directed by Frank Reicher;
Produced by Arthur Hammerstein; With Tessa
Kosta and Guy Robertson.

Published Songs
Cossack Love Song
Midnight Bells [music by Gershwin only]
The Signal [music by Gershwin only]
Song of the Flame
Vodka
You Are You—cut

Additional Song Published (No Lyric) in Piano Selection
Tartar

Producer Arthur Hammerstein had great success
teaming "star" composers with his house staff of
Herbert Stothart, Otto Harbach, and nephew
Oscar Hammerstein for modern-ish operettas (including WILDFLOWER [Youmans: February 7,
1923] and Rudolf Friml's ROSE-MARIE† [Sep-
tember 2, 1924]). Gershwin was chosen for this
Russian opus, which opened just two days after
TIP-TOES [December 28, 1925]. The result was
successful but pedestrian.

AMERICANA ✦ First Edition
July 26, 1926
Belmont Theatre • 224 performances
Music mostly by Con Conrad and Henry
Souvaine; Book by J. P. McEvoy; Directed by
Allan Dinehart; Produced by Richard
Herndon; With Lew Brice and Roy Atwell.

Published Song
That Lost Barber Shop Chord [lyric by Ira
Gershwin]

OH, KAY!
November 8, 1926
Imperial Theatre • 256 performances
Lyrics mostly by Ira Gershwin; Book by
Guy Bolton and P. G. Wodehouse;

Directed by John Harwood; Produced by Alex
A. Aarons and Vinton Freedley; With
Gertrude Lawrence, Oscar Shaw, and Victor
Moore.

Revivals
April 16, 1960
East 74th Street Theatre {Off Broadway} •
    89 performances
Directed by Bertram Yarborough;
Choreographed by Dania Krupska;
With Marti Stevens [Lawrence],
David Daniels [Shaw], and Bernie West
[Moore].

July 20, 1978
Royal Alexandra Theatre {Toronto} •
    Closed during tryout
[New] Book by Thomas Meehan; Directed and
Choreographed by Donald Saddler; Produced
by Cyma Rubin; With Jack Weston [Moore],
Jane Summerhays [Lawrence], and David-
James Carroll [Shaw].

November 1, 1990
Richard Rodgers Theatre •
    77 performances
Adaptation by James Racheff; Directed,
Choreographed, and Conceived by Dan
Siretta; Produced by David Merrick; Trans-
ferred from Goodspeed Opera House; With
Angela Teek [Lawrence] and Brian (Stokes)
Mitchell [Shaw].

Published Songs
Ask Me Again—initial publication of non-
    show song (written circa 1929) upon use in
    1990 revival
Clap Yo' Hands
Dear Little Girl—initial publication upon
    reuse in 1968 movie *Star*
Do-Do-Do
Fidgety Feet
Heaven on Earth [lyric by Ira Gershwin and
    Howard Dietz]—see ROSALIE [January 10,
    1928]
Maybe
Oh, Kay [lyric by Ira Gershwin and Dietz]
Show Me the Town—cut; also used in
    ROSALIE
**Someone to Watch over Me*

Additional Songs Published in 1984 Vocal
Selection
Bride and Groom
Don't Ask
A Woman's Touch

Additional Songs Recorded
Ain't It Romantic?
When Our Ship Comes Sailing In [lyric by Ira
Gershwin and Dietz]

Gertrude Lawrence conquered New York with
Beatrice Lillie and Jack Buchanan in CHARLOT'S
REVUE [January 9, 1924]. With OH, KAY! she
became a major star on her own. So did bumbling
character comedian Victor Moore, whose last important Broadway role had been in George M.
Cohan's THE TALK OF NEW YORK [December
3, 1907]. The Gershwins provided another popular score, with the young Howard Dietz stepping
in when Ira underwent an appendectomy. Hit
songs included *Do-Do-Do*, *Maybe*, and the exquisite *Someone to Watch over Me*.

STRIKE UP THE BAND [1927]
August 29, 1927
Broadway Theatre {Long Branch, N.J.} •
Closed during tryout
*"The Gershwin-Kaufman Musical Play." Also
see January 14, 1930.* Lyrics by Ira Gershwin;
Book by George S. Kaufman; Directed by R. H.
Burnside; Produced by Edgar Selwyn; With
Jimmy Savo and Edna May Oliver.

Concert Version
February 12, 1998
City Center • 5 performances
Adaptation by David Ives; Directed by John
Rando; Choreographed by Jeff Calhoun;
Produced by City Center Encores; With Lynn
Redgrave, Philip Bosco, Judy Kuhn, David
Schramm, Jason Danieley, and David Garrison.

Published Songs
**The Man I Love*—also cut from LADY, BE
GOOD! [December 1, 1924] and ROSALIE
[January 10, 1928]
Military Dancing Drill—also used in STRIKE
UP THE BAND [1930]
Seventeen and Twenty-One

Strike Up the Band—also used in STRIKE UP
THE BAND [1930]
Yankee Doodle Rhythm—also used in ROSALIE

Additional Songs Published in 1999 Vocal
Score
Come-Look-at-the-War Choral Society
Fletcher's American Cheese Choral Society
Homeward Bound
Hoping That Someday You'd Care
How about a Man
Meadow Serenade—cut; lost music for the
refrain reconstructed by Kay Swift, new
music for the verse composed by Burton
Lane in 1990
Oh, This Is Such a Lovely War
Patriotic Rally
A Typical Self-Made American
The Unofficial Spokesman
The War That Ended War

This bitter satire—about war with Switzerland
over Grade B cheese—met a stony reception
and was quickly withdrawn for repairs. *The Man
I Love* never made it back to Broadway, although
Marilyn Miller briefly gave it a try in ROSALIE
[January 10, 1928]. Fortunately, it found a well-
deserved life of its own outside the theatre.

FUNNY FACE
November 22, 1927
Alvin Theatre • 244 performances
Lyrics by Ira Gershwin; Book by Fred Thomp-
son and Paul Gerard Smith; Directed by Edgar
MacGregor; Produced by Alex A. Aarons and
Vinton Freedley; With Fred and Adele Astaire,
William Kent, Victor Moore, and Allen Kearns.
Pre-Broadway title: SMARTY.

Revival
As MY ONE AND ONLY: May 1, 1983
St. James Theatre • 762 performances
[New] Book by Peter Stone and Timothy S.
Mayer; Directed and Choreographed by
Thommie Walsh and Tommy Tune; With
Tommy Tune, Twiggy, Charles "Honi" Coles,
and Denny Dillon.

Published Songs
The Babbitt and the Bromide
Dance Alone with You—cut; see ROSALIE
[January 10, 1928]

Funny Face
He Loves and She Loves
High Hat
**How Long Has This Been Going On?*—cut; also
    used in ROSALIE
Let's Kiss and Make Up
*My One and Only—originally published as
    What Am I Gonna Do?
*'S Wonderful
Tell the Doc—issued in vocal arrangement; initial
    publication upon use in London production
    [November 8, 1928; 263 performances]
The World Is Mine—cut; see NINE-FIFTEEN
    REVUE [February 11, 1930]

Additional Song Published in Vocal Selection

In the Swim—initial publication upon reuse in
    MY ONE AND ONLY

With profits from their three Gershwin musicals, "Al" Aarons and "Vin" Freedley built the Alvin Theatre and determined to open with another Gershwin/Astaire hit. But SMARTY—like STRIKE UP THE BAND [1927] [August 29, 1927]—faced grave tryout troubles. Drastic measures were taken: half the score was discarded, colibrettist Robert Benchley was replaced, and Victor Moore (from the cast of OH, KAY! [November 8, 1926]) was rushed in for support. The miracle was achieved, and FUNNY FACE came in for a long run, followed by an even longer run in London. The brothers came up with another strong score, highlighted by the charming *'S Wonderful*, the rhythmic *My One and Only*, and the poignant *How Long Has This Been Going On?* (which was lost on the road). Fifty-five years later, the troubled-but-salvaged FUNNY FACE was more or less recycled into another troubled-but-salvaged entertainment, MY ONE AND ONLY.

ROSALIE
January 10, 1928
New Amsterdam Theatre • 335 performances
Music also by Sigmund Romberg; Lyrics by
P. G. Wodehouse and Ira Gershwin; Lyrics to
Gershwin songs by Ira Gershwin; Book by
Wm. Anthony McGuire and Guy Bolton;
Directed by Wm. Anthony McGuire; Produced by Florenz Ziegfeld, Jr.; With Marilyn Miller, Jack Donahue, and Frank Morgan.

Published Songs
Beautiful Gypsy—cut; new lyric for *Wait a Bit,*
    Susie from PRIMROSE [September 11, 1924]
Ev'rybody Knows I Love Somebody—added after
    opening; new lyric for *Dance Alone with You*
    from FUNNY FACE [November 22, 1927]
**How Long Has This Been Going On?*—
    originally used (cut) in FUNNY FACE
The Man I Love—cut; published only as from
    LADY, BE GOOD! [December 1, 1924] and
    STRIKE UP THE BAND [1927] [August 29,
    1927]
Oh Gee! Oh Joy! [lyric by Ira and Wodehouse]
Rosalie—cut
Say So! [lyric by Ira and Wodehouse]
Setting Up Exercises [instrumental]—initial
    publication in 1967 as non-show piano solo
    Merry Andrew
Show Me the Town—originally used in (cut)
    and only published as from OH, KAY!
    [November 8, 1926]
Yankee Doodle Rhythm—cut; originally used in
    STRIKE UP THE BAND [1927]

Additional Song Published (No Lyric) in Piano Selection

Follow the Drum—added after opening;
    revised version of *Heaven on Earth* from
    OH, KAY!

After three years under contract to Charles Dillingham (see PETER PAN [1924] [Kern: November 6, 1924]), Marilyn Miller returned to Flo Ziegfeld. The great glorifier, flush with the success of SHOW BOAT [Kern: December 27, 1927], combined Sigmund Romberg (who had three other shows that fall) and Gershwin (with two) for this modern-day fairy-tale romance. The results were altogether bland with a throw-away score, though Miller's popularity allowed a successful run.

TREASURE GIRL
November 8, 1928
Alvin Theatre • 68 performances
Lyrics by Ira Gershwin; Book by Fred Thompson and Vincent Lawrence; Directed by
Bertram Harrison; Produced by Alex A.
Aarons and Vinton Freedley; With Gertrude
Lawrence, Paul Frawley, and Walter Catlett.

Published Songs
Feeling I'm Falling
Got a Rainbow
*I Don't Think I'll Fall in Love Today
*I've Got a Crush on You—initial publication
    upon reuse in STRIKE UP THE BAND
    [1930] [January 14, 1930]
K-ra-zy for You
Oh, So Nice
What Are We Here For?
*Where's the Boy? Here's the Girl

Additional Song Published in Vocal Selection
What Causes That?—initial publication upon
    reuse in CRAZY FOR YOU [February 19, 1992]

Closely copying the OH, KAY! [November 8, 1926] formula, this "sure thing" was a resounding failure. There are three rather nice songs, though: the breezy *I've Got a Crush on You* —which was rescued from oblivion to become a standard—and the now forgotten *I Don't Think I'll Fall in Love Today* and *Where's the Boy? Here's the Girl*. Gershwin's third and final major symphonic work, the tone poem **An American in Paris*, premiered on December 13, 1928.

EAST IS WEST
[circa January 1929]
Unfinished musical. Lyrics by Ira Gershwin; Book by Wm. Anthony McGuire (based on the play by Samuel Shipman and John B. Hymer); [Produced by Florenz Ziegfeld]. Alternate title: MING TOY.

Published Song
In the Mandarin's Orchid Garden—publication
    as a non-show "art" song in 1930

SHOW GIRL
July 2, 1929
Ziegfeld Theatre • 111 performances
Music mostly by Gershwin (see Youmans: July 2, 1929); Lyrics mostly by Gus Kahn and Ira Gershwin; Book and Direction by Wm. Anthony McGuire (based on the novel by J. P. McEvoy); Produced by Florenz Ziegfeld, Jr.; With Ruby Keeler Jolson and

"(Lew) Clayton, (Eddie) Jackson & (Jimmy) Durante."

Published Songs
Do What You Do!
Feeling Sentimental—cut
Harlem Serenade
I Must Be Home by Twelve o'Clock
*Liza (All the Clouds'll Roll Away)
*So Are You! (The Rose Is Red—Violets Are
    Blue)*

Additional Song Published in Vocal Selection
Tonight's the Night—cut; initial publication
    upon reuse in CRAZY FOR YOU [February
    19, 1992]

Additional Songs Recorded
Home Blues—lyric for *Blues Theme* from *An
    American in Paris*
Somebody Stole My Heart Away

Virtually all the great stage performers of the twenties—Miller, Cantor, Williams, Fields, Rogers, Brice—starred for Ziegfeld. The sole exception was Al Jolson, who had been discovered by the Shuberts and stayed with them (as long as they paid him regally). So Ziegfeld decided to make a star out of Jolson's new wife, nineteen-year-old tap dancer Ruby Keeler. He didn't succeed; SHOW GIRL was poor, and the "Ziegfeld touch" was by now lost. But he did manage to finally get hold of Jolson, who often dropped by (gratis) to serenade his bride as she descended the full-stage staircase to Gershwin's *Liza*. She was, it seems, afraid of heights.

STRIKE UP THE BAND [1930]
January 14, 1930
Times Square Theatre • 191 performances
Also see August 29, 1927. Lyrics by Ira Gershwin; Book by Morrie Ryskind (based on a libretto by George S. Kaufman); Directed by Alexander Leftwich; Produced by Edgar Selwyn; With Bobby Clark & Paul McCullough.

Published Songs
Hangin' Around with You
I Mean to Say

I've Got a Crush on You—originally used (unpublished) in TREASURE GIRL [November 8, 1928]
I Want to Be a War Bride
Mademoiselle in New Rochelle
*Soon
Strike up the Band—originally used in STRIKE UP THE BAND [1927]

Additional Songs Published in Vocal Score
Ding Dong
Fletcher's American Chocolate Choral Society (Opening Act One)
He Knows Milk
How about a Boy Like Me?—also published in piano selection (no lyric) as *How about a Man*
If I Became the President
In the Rattle of the Battle
A Man of High Degree
Military Dancing Drill (Opening Act Two)—originally used (with different verse) in STRIKE UP THE BAND [1927]
Official Resume (First There Was Fletcher)
Soldiers' March
This Could Go on for Years
Three Cheers for the Union!
A Typical Self-Made American
The Unofficial Spokesman

Hoping to salvage STRIKE UP THE BAND despite its quick failure in 1927, producer Edgar Selwyn asked the authors for a friendlier, less-bitter rewrite. Kaufman, who was strongly anti-war, couldn't in good conscience tone down the satire. He withdrew from active involvement, authorizing Morrie Ryskind—his collaborator on the Marx Brothers' Broadway hit ANIMAL CRACKERS† [October 23, 1928]—to write a new book. Ryskind and the Gershwins came up with a significantly sweeter show, changing the source of the plot's international dispute from bad cheese to bad chocolate. Besides, the public mood had changed with the stock market crash. With a heavily revised score and star comedians, the new STRIKE UP THE BAND was a hit. More importantly, it prodded the Gershwins, Kaufman, and Ryskind to move on to a new form of Broadway musical satire.

NINE-FIFTEEN REVUE
February 11, 1930
George M. Cohan Theatre • 7 performances
Music mostly by others (see Arlen: February 11, 1930); Lyric to Gershwin song by Ira Gershwin; Directed by Alexander Leftwich; Produced by Ruth Selwyn; With Ruth Etting.

Published Song
Toddlin' Along—new title for *The World Is Mine*, published only as from FUNNY FACE [November 22, 1927]

GIRL CRAZY
October 14, 1930
Alvin Theatre • 272 performances
Lyrics by Ira Gershwin; Book by Guy Bolton and John McGowan; Directed by Alexander Leftwich; Produced by Alex A. Aarons and Vinton Freedley; With Ginger Rogers, Allen Kearns, Willie Howard, Ethel Merman, and William Kent.

Revival
As CRAZY FOR YOU: February 19, 1992
Shubert Theatre • 1,622 performances
[New] Book by Ken Ludwig; Conception by Ken Ludwig and Mike Ockrent; Directed by Mike Ockrent; Choreographed by Susan Stroman; With Harry Groener [Kearns], Jodi Benson [Rogers], and Bruce Adler.

Published Songs
Bidin' My Time
Boy! What Love Has Done to Me!
But Not for Me!
Could You Use Me?
Embraceable You
**I Got Rhythm*
Sam and Delilah
Treat Me Rough!—initial publication upon reuse in 1943 movie version
You've Got What Gets Me—written for 1932 movie version

Additional Songs Published in Vocal Score
Barbary Coast
Broncho Busters
Goldfarb, That's I'm
Land of the Gay Caballero

The Lonesome Cowboy
When It's Cactus Time in Arizona

The last of the great Gershwin/Aarons and Freedley hits, enhanced by the strong score and stronger singing voice of Ethel Merman (on *I Got Rhythm, Boy! What Love Has Done to Me!*, and *Sam and Delilah*). Ginger Rogers, in her second and final Broadway musical, introduced *But Not for Me, Could You Use Me?*, and *Embraceable You*. (When help was needed to stage the dance for the latter song, Gershwin/Aarons and Freedley alumnus Fred Astaire stopped by to show Ginger what to do.) CRAZY FOR YOU [February 19, 1992], a revised, stripped, and rewritten version of GIRL CRAZY, proved a major 1,622-performance hit, although in places it violated the artistic integrity of both music and lyrics.

OF THEE I SING
December 26, 1931
Music Box Theatre • 441 performances
Lyrics by Ira Gershwin; Book by George S. Kaufman and Morrie Ryskind; Directed by George S. Kaufman; Produced by Sam H. Harris; With William Gaxton, Lois Moran, and Victor Moore.

Revivals
May 5, 1952
Ziegfeld Theatre • 72 performances
Directed by George S. Kaufman; Choreographed by Jack Donohue; With Jack Carson [Gaxton], Paul Hartman [Moore], and Betty Oakes [Moran].

March 7, 1969
New Anderson Theatre {Off Broadway} •
  21 performances
Directed by Michael Gordon; With Hal Holden [Gaxton], Lloyd Hubbard [Moore], and Joy Franz [Moran].

Concert Version
March 18, 1987
Brooklyn Academy of Music
Produced by the Brooklyn Academy of Music;
With Maureen McGovern [Moran],
Larry Kert [Gaxton], and Jack Gilford [Moore].

Published Songs
Because, Because
The Illegitimate Daughter

*Love Is Sweeping the Country
*Of Thee I Sing
*Who Cares?
*Wintergreen for President—initial individual
  publication upon 1952 revival

Additional Songs Published in Vocal Score
The Dimple on My Knee
Garçon, S'il Vous Plaît
*Hello, Good Morning
I Was the Most Beautiful Blossom
Jilted, Jilted!
*A Kiss for Cinderella
Never Was There a Girl So Fair
On That Matter No One Budges
Prosperity Is Just around the Corner
The Senatorial Roll Call
Some Girls Can Bake a Pie (Corn Muffins)
Trumpeter, Blow Your Golden Horn!
Who Is the Lucky Girl to Be?

Having forged new ground in musical satire with STRIKE UP THE BAND [1930] [January 14, 1930], Kaufman and Ryskind rejoined the Gershwins on this epochal piece of musical theatre. As the nation headed into the first presidential election of the Depression, the choice target for satire was politics. The score was remarkably cohesive, as the brothers forged—with a bow to Gilbert and Sullivan—a form of extended musical scenes (as opposed to typical Broadway show tunes). There was a handful of hit tunes, actually—*Love Is Sweeping the Country, Who Cares?*, and *Of Thee I Sing*—but most of the score was intrinsically linked to the plot, including such delights as *Some Girls Can Bake a Pie, The Illegitimate Daughter, A Kiss for Cinderella*, and *Hello, Good Morning*. Ira turned in especially strong work. All elements combined to make OF THEE I SING the most important musical of its time, and the first to win the Pulitzer Prize—which went to the librettists and Ira, but not George.

PARDON MY ENGLISH
January 20, 1933
Majestic Theatre • 46 performances
Lyrics by Ira Gershwin; Book by Herbert Fields; Directed by Vinton Freedley; Produced by Alex A. Aarons and Vinton Freedley; With Jack Pearl, Lyda Roberti, and George Givot.

Published Songs
**Isn't It a Pity?*
I've Got to Be There
The Lorelei
The Luckiest Man in the World
My Cousin in Milwaukee
So What?
Tonight—initial publication as 1971 non-show
   instrumental, retitled *Two Waltzes in C*
Where You Go, I Go

Additional Songs Published in 1999 Vocal Score
Dancing in the Streets
Dresden Northwest Mounted
Fatherland, Mother of the Band
Freud, Jung and Adler
Hail the Happy Couple
He's Not Himself
He's Oversexed
In Three-Quarter Time
No Tickee, No Washee (*Opening Act Two*)
Together at Last
Tonight [song version]
Watch Your Head—see LET 'EM EAT CAKE
   [October 21, 1933]
What Sort of Wedding Is This?

PARDON MY ENGLISH was one of those hopeless musicals which, in retrospect, should never have been mounted. But producers Aarons and Freedley —who had already lost their Alvin Theatre--were desperate for a hit to stave off bankruptcy, and the Gershwins felt a loyalty to them. The show underwent a troubled tryout, saw the departure of star Jack Buchanan and librettist Morrie Ryskind, and stumbled through a painful six-week Broadway run. Buried in the wreckage, though, was a fine, slyly playful score. Two songs stand on their own, *Isn't It a Pity*—one of the boys' great ballads—and the hot and squawky *My Cousin in Milwaukee*. The rest were perhaps too closely integrated into the mixed-up plot for popularity, but the pleasures abound. As for the producers, Aarons never recovered from bankruptcy. Freedley, on the other hand, rebounded with some of the biggest hits of the 1930s starting with ANYTHING GOES [Porter: November 21, 1934].

LET 'EM EAT CAKE
October 21, 1933
Imperial Theatre • 90 performances

Lyrics by Ira Gershwin; Book by George S. Kaufman and Morrie Ryskind (based on characters from OF THEE I SING [December 26, 1931]); Directed by George S. Kaufman; Produced by Sam H. Harris; With William Gaxton, Lois Moran, and Victor Moore.

Concert Version
March 18, 1987
Brooklyn Academy of Music
Produced by the Brooklyn Academy of Music; With Maureen McGovern [Moran], Larry Kert [Gaxton], and Jack Gilford [Moore].

Published Songs
**Blue, Blue, Blue*
Let 'Em Eat Cake
**Mine*
On and On and On
Union Square

Additional Songs Recorded
Climb up the Social Ladder
**Comes the Revolution*—new lyric for *Watch Your Head* from PARDON MY ENGLISH
   [January 20, 1933]
First Lady and First Gent—lost music reconstructed by Kay Swift
The General's Gone to a Party
Hanging Throttlebottom in the Morning
I Know a Foul Ball
Introduction to Finale Act One (*Dignitary's Song*)
It Isn't What You Did (*It's What You Didn't Do*)
I've Brushed My Teeth
The League of Nations
Mothers of the Nation
No Comprenez, No Capish, No Versteh!
Shirts by the Millions
That's What He Did
Throttle Throttlebottom
Tweedledee for President—countermelody to *Wintergreen for President* from OF THEE I SING
The Union League
Up and At 'Em
When Nations Get Together
Who's the Greatest?
Why Speak of Money?

This eagerly awaited sequel to OF THEE I SING proved a total bust, as eagerly awaited sequels tend to do. More bitter than comic, the satire was forced. By the time the authors realized the fundamental creative problems, though, it was too late to cancel the production. Ironically, the LET 'EM EAT CAKE score contains some of the best and most intricate work by the Gershwins, including the stunningly chromatic *Blue, Blue, Blue* and *Comes the Revolution*. The score is highly integrated, though, and aside from the counterpoint ballad *Mine* pretty much non-extractable. LET 'EM EAT CAKE—like PARDON MY ENGLISH—was pretty much lost for more than fifty years, until a 1987 concert version (in tandem with OF THEE I SING) led to a full recording of the score.

PORGY AND BESS

October 10, 1935
Alvin Theatre • 124 performances
Lyrics by DuBose Heyward and Ira Gershwin; Libretto by DuBose Heyward (based on *Porgy* [novel] by DuBose Heyward and [play] by DuBose and Dorothy Heyward); Directed by Rouben Mamoulian; Produced by The Theatre Guild; With Todd Duncan, Anne Brown, John W. Bubbles, and Warren Coleman.

Revivals
January 22, 1942
Majestic Theatre • 286 performances
Directed by Robert Ross; Produced by Cheryl Crawford in association with John Wildberg; With Todd Duncan, Anne Brown, Avon Long [Bubbles], and Warren Coleman.

March 10, 1953
Ziegfeld Theatre • 312 performances
Directed by Robert Breen; With Leslie Scott [Duncan], Leontyne Price [Brown], and Cab Calloway [Bubbles].

September 25, 1976
Uris Theatre • 122 performances
Directed by Jack O'Brien; With Donnie Ray Albert [Duncan], Clemma Dale [Brown], and Larry Marshall [Bubbles].

Note: All lyrics by DuBose Heyward unless otherwise noted.

Published Songs

**Bess, You Is My Woman* [lyric by Ira Gershwin and Heyward]
I Got Plenty o' Nuttin' [lyric by Ira Gershwin and Heyward]
***I Loves You Porgy* [lyric by Ira Gershwin and Heyward]—initial individual publication upon use in 1959 movie version
***It Ain't Necessarily So* [lyric by Ira Gershwin]
***My Man's Gone Now*
Oh Bess, Oh Where's My Bess? [lyric by Ira Gershwin]
***Summertime*
There's a Boat Dat's Leavin' Soon for New York [lyric by Ira Gershwin]
A Woman Is a Sometime Thing

Additional Songs Published in Vocal Score

Buzzard Song—cut
Clara, Clara
Crap Game
Gone, Gone, Gone
I Ain't Got No Shame
It Takes a Long Pull to Get There
Lawyer Frazier Scene
Leavin' fo' de Promise' Lan'
Oh de Lawd Shake de Heavens
Oh, Doctor Jesus
Oh, I Can't Sit Down [lyric by Ira Gershwin]
Oh Lawd, I'm on My Way
Overflow
A Red Headed Woman [lyric by Ira Gershwin]
Storm Prayers
Street Cries
They Pass by Singin'
What You Want wid Bess?

Additional Song Recorded

Lonely Boy—cut

Gershwin was intrigued by the musical possibilities of the novel *Porgy* when it was first published in 1926, but the Theatre Guild already had the stage rights. The one-time song plugger had been training, experimenting, and stretching himself since his early days on Tin Pan Alley, reaching important plateaus with *Blue Monday* (1922), *Rhapsody in Blue* (1924), *Concerto in F* (1925), *An American in Paris* (1928), STRIKE UP THE BAND

[1930] and OF THEE I SING [December 26, 1931]. In 1935 he finally began work on the piece, collaborating with novelist DuBose Heyward. (Ira ultimately stepped in to handle the more sophisticated lyric needs, notably the Sportin' Life material.) Gershwin immersed himself in the world of Catfish Row, writing an unparalleled score which is unlike anything he—or, I think it safe to say, anyone else—ever wrote. I needn't point out high spots of the score as it speaks for itself, although I can't resist citing the tumultuous *My Man's Gone Now* as a personal favorite. Rouben Mamoulian, director of the play version, made a remarkable Broadway musical debut. Demanding an exacting control over all production elements, his strong theatricality and sense of movement took Broadway in new directions (as did his next musical, OKLAHOMA! [Rodgers: March 31, 1943]). The initial commercial failure of PORGY AND BESS can be ascribed to several reasons, including subject matter, economic conditions, and the overuse of operatic conventions. The piece has been continually successful since producer Cheryl Crawford's 1942 revival, which cut the recitatives and presented it as more of a book musical. Broadway has enjoyed subsequent PORGY visits by two highly successful touring companies: the 1953 Robert Breen/Blevins Davis production, with a cast including Leontyne Price and Cab Calloway (playing Sportin' Life—not Porgy!), and a 1976 mounting by the Houston Grand Opera. Gershwin finally made it to the Met—in 1985, when PORGY AND BESS entered the repertory. The Met imprimatur doesn't matter to some of us, perhaps, but it would surely have mattered to Gershwin. At the time of the composer's death, incidentally, the residuary value of PORGY AND BESS was appraised at $250.

THE SHOW IS ON
December 25, 1936
Winter Garden Theatre • 237 performances
Music mostly by Vernon Duke (see Duke: December 25, 1936; also Arlen, Rodgers, and Schwartz); Lyric to Gershwin song by Ira Gershwin; Sketches mostly by David Freedman and Moss Hart; Directed by Vincente Minnelli; Produced by Lee Shubert; With Beatrice Lillie and Bert Lahr.

Published Song
By Strauss

Gershwin contributed his final theatre song to this revue devised by his friend and protégé Vernon Duke. Following PORGY AND BESS [October 10, 1935], Gershwin made his first—and only—foray to Hollywood, where he wrote three film scores. *Shall We Dance* (1937) reunited the brothers with Fred Astaire (as well as Ginger Rogers of GIRL CRAZY [October 14, 1930]). The score included some of three of their best songs: **Let's Call the Whole Thing Off*, **They All Laughed*, and **They Can't Take That Away from Me*. The film *A Damsel in Distress* (1937), also with Astaire, contained two more: *A Foggy Day (in London Town)* and *Nice Work If You Can Get It*. Gershwin's final completed song, for the posthumously produced film *Goldwyn Follies* (1938), was *Love Is Here to Stay*. At the age of thirty-eight, Gershwin developed a brain tumor and died on July 11, 1937, in Beverly Hills.

LET ME HEAR THE MELODY
March 9, 1951
Playhouse Theatre {Wilmington, Del.} •
    Closed during tryout
Play by S. N. Behrman; Incidental music by George Gershwin; Lyric by Ira Gershwin; Directed by Burgess Meredith; Produced by Harold Clurman and Walter Fried; With Melvyn Douglas, Anthony Quinn, Mike Kellin, and Morris Carnovsky.

Published Song
Hi-Ho!—initial publication as 1967 non-show
    song

LET ME HEAR THE MELODY, about a songwriter in Hollywood, made use of a considerable amount of Gershwin material. The jaunty *Hi-Ho* was the only never-before-heard song, and it's a fine one. It had been written for (but unused in) the 1937 Fred Astaire movie *Shall We Dance*.

The Gershwin section in the first edition of *Show Tunes* ended with the statement: "With familiarity and increased exposure to Arlen, Youmans Duke, and Weill, Gershwin love diminishes to

Gershwin respect. But Gershwin respect never diminishes"—for which I seem to have been drummed out of the Gershwin lovers society. I repeat here that Gershwin respect never diminishes. (I'll also add that I grow more and more impressed with Ira's later work, much of which is unpublished; had he not withdrawn after LADY IN THE DARK [Weill: January 23, 1941] and THE FIREBRAND OF FLORENCE [Weill: March 22, 1945], he might have done for the comedy musical what Oscar Hammerstein did for the serious musical.) George brought new rhythms and colors into the musical theatre, a significant and far-reaching contribution without which we might never have been able to appreciate the work of his followers. Gershwin's distinctive trademarks were jazz-influenced syncopation and "blue-note" chromaticism, marvelous devices developed during his apprentice years (1919–23) and showcased to the musical world's astonishment in *Rhapsody in Blue* (1924). As wonderful as Gershwin's early great songs are, though, I'm constantly reminded that the devices are conscious—the delicious parts are caused by an unexpected blue note here or a fascinating rhythmic figure

there. Out-of-key notes in musical terminology are called accidentals. To Gershwin, they always were accidental—deliberately used to jar our ear and create the desired effect. To Arlen and Weill, these seemed not to be attention-getting accidentals but a natural part of the musical fabric. (This can be explained to some extent by the fact that both men were sons of cantors, the improvisatory melodists of the Jewish faith.) My favorite Gershwin songs simply don't enthrall me the way the best of Arlen, Kern, or Rodgers does. *Fascinating Rhythm*, *Someone to Watch over Me*, and *Isn't It a Pity?* are among my favorites by Gershwin or anyone; but when did he ever write a song like *Stormy Weather*, *Spring Is Here*, or *All the Things You Are?* Where did Gershwin ever display such a pure stream of melodic freeness? (In the stunning *Summertime*, that's where, but nowhere else; and it is my theory that he was consciously emulating the style of his young friend Arlen.) It is pointless to ponder what might have happened had Gershwin continued working past PORGY AND BESS [October 10, 1935]. As it is, he left us with dozens of *'s wonderful* songs to be forever cherished.

VINCENT YOUMANS

Born: September 27, 1898 New York, New York
Died: April 5, 1946 Denver, Colorado

VINCENT YOUMANS was born the day after George Gershwin. Both played an important part in developing the new musical comedy of the 1920s; both tried to move into more serious theatre work; and both were cut short by illness in their mid-thirties. Unlike Gershwin, Youmans was born on the right side of the New York City tracks (on the Central Park West site of what is now the Mayflower Hotel). His father, a prosperous hat manufacturer, moved the family to upper-class Larchmont, New York. After wartime service in the Navy, Youmans became a song plugger at Remick's—where civilian Gershwin had started three years earlier—and wrote his first published song in 1920, *Country Cousin* [lyric by Alfred Bryan]. Youmans moved on to play rehearsal piano for Victor Herbert's 1920 OUI MADAME[†], produced by Alfred E. Aarons. Aarons had intended to hire operetta-great Herbert for his previous musical, but his son-and-associate Alex convinced him to gamble on novice Gershwin (see LA, LA LUCILLE [Gershwin: May 26, 1919]). After the Herbert musical closed during its tryout, Aarons gave Youmans the composing chore on his next musical. Meanwhile, the ever-alert-for-talent music publisher Max Dreyfus of Harms signed up Youmans (at just about the same time he told Richard Rodgers to "come back in a few years"). Unlike Gershwin, Rodgers, Porter, and Kern, Youmans established himself with a hit Broadway musical within the year.

PICCADILLY TO BROADWAY
September 27, 1920
Globe Theatre {Atlantic City, N.J.} •
    Closed during tryout
"All Anglo-American Musical Review." Music also by William Daly, George Gershwin (see Gershwin: September 27, 1920), and others; Sketches and Lyrics mostly by Glen MacDonough and E. Ray Goetz; Lyrics to Youmans songs by Arthur Francis [Ira Gershwin]; Directed by George Marion and Julian Alfred; Produced by E. Ray Goetz; With Johnny Dooley, Anna Wheaton, Clifton Webb, and Helen Broderick.

Published Song
Who's Who with You?—initial publication upon reuse in TWO LITTLE GIRLS IN BLUE [1921] [May 3, 1921]

Max Dreyfus placed interpolations by his two up-and-coming composers into this thrown-together revue. George collaborated with established producer/lyricist Ray Goetz, while Youmans was paired with Gershwin's lyric-writing older brother Ira (using the pseudonym Arthur Francis). After the PICCADILLY TO BROADWAY failure, Dreyfus held the playfully catchy *Who's Who with You?* as bait while scouting another opportunity. The other Youmans/Francis offering, for the record, was *Now That We're Mr. and Mrs* (unpublished).

TWO LITTLE GIRLS IN BLUE [1921]
May 3, 1921
George M. Cohan Theatre • 135 performances
Music also by Paul Lannin; Lyrics mostly by Arthur Francis [Ira Gershwin]; Book by Fred Jackson; Directed by Ned Wayburn; Produced by A. L. Erlanger [replacing Alfred E. Aarons]; With The Fairbanks Twins (Madeline and Marion) and Oscar Shaw.

Published Songs
Dolly [lyric by Arthur Francis and Schuyler Greene]
Oh Me! Oh My!

Orienta [lyric by Irving Caesar and Greene]
Rice and Shoes [lyric by Francis and Greene]
Who's Who with You?—originally used
    (unpublished) in PICCADILLY TO BROAD-
    WAY [September 27, 1920]
You Started Something—see NO, NO,
    NANETTE [September 16, 1925]

Having done fairly well with LA, LA LUCILLE
[Gershwin: May 26, 1919], producer Alfred
Aarons offered Gershwin his next contemporary
musical. The composer was already contracted
for two simultaneous shows, so he and Max
Dreyfus and Alex Aarons steered the job to Ira
and Youmans. Prior to the tryout, the elder
Aarons's producing credit was taken over by
tyrannical theatre-czar A. L. Erlanger; Aarons
was Erlanger's general manager, and it appears
that his productions were owned in fact by A. L.
(for Abraham Lincoln, no less). TWO LITTLE
GIRLS was a moderate hit—more popular than
George's "sophisticated" LUCILLE—with two of
the Youmans/Francis songs proving fairly popular (if unexceptional), *Oh Me! Oh My!* and *Dolly*.

WILDFLOWER
February 7, 1923
Casino Theatre • 477 performances
Music also by Herbert Stothart; Book and
Lyrics by Otto Harbach and Oscar
Hammerstein 2nd; Directed by Oscar Eagle;
Produced by Arthur Hammerstein; With Edith
Day and Guy Robertson. Pre-Broadway title:
THE WILDFLOWER.

Published Songs
*Bambalina
I Can Always Find Another Partner
If I Told You—cut; see RAINBOW [November
    21, 1928]
I Love You I Love You I Love You
Wildflower
You Never Can Blame a Girl for Dreaming—
    added after opening

Additional Songs Published in Vocal Score
The Chase (*Opening Act II*) [probably by
    Youmans]
Come Let's Dance through the Night [probably
    by Stothart]
'Course I Will [probably by Youmans]

Note: All songs issued as by Youmans and
Stothart, although written separately. Those
listed were Youmans's actual contributions.

The competent but unremarkable composer/
arranger Herbert Stothart had collaborated
with Otto Harbach, Oscar Hammerstein, and
producer Arthur Hammerstein on four competent but unremarkable musicals since 1920.
Arthur decided to add a more inventive co-
composer into the mix, resulting in the first of
several immensely successful operettas. Otto
Harbach had collaborated with Rudolf Friml on
several smash hits, including Arthur Hammerstein's first production THE FIREFLY† [De-
cember 2, 1912]. Oscar Greeley Clendenning
Hammerstein 2nd—for that was his name—
went to work for his uncle as a stage manager
in 1917. Arthur produced Oscar's first play, *The
Light*, in 1919 (it closed in New Haven), after
which he teamed his novice nephew with the
veteran Harbach; the new team would make
invaluable contributions to the musical theatre.
With the immense success of WILDFLOWER,
Broadway and Tin Pan Alley embraced Youmans. His unconventional rhythmic style made
Bambalina, a top song hit of the 1920s, as was
the somewhat Kernish title tune. A third song,
If I Told You, was cut but is worth noting for
its strong, chromatic melody. George Gershwin
had been intriguing Broadway audiences for
several years with his contributions to second-
rank revues, but WILDFLOWER established
Youmans as the leader of the new breed of
composers.

HAMMERSTEIN'S NINE O'CLOCK REVUE
October 4, 1923
Century Roof Theatre • 12 performances
Music and Lyrics mostly by Harold Simpson
and Morris Harvey; Produced by Arthur
Hammerstein.

Published Song
Flannel Petticoat Girl [lyric by Oscar
    Hammerstein 2nd and Wm. Cary
    Duncan]—initial publication upon reuse in
    MARY JANE McKANE [December 25,
    1923]

MARY JANE MCKANE
December 25, 1923
Imperial Theatre • 151 performances
Music also by Herbert Stothart; Book and
Lyrics by Oscar Hammerstein 2nd and Wm.
Cary Duncan; Directed by Alonzo Price;
Produced by Arthur Hammerstein; With Mary
Hay and Hal Skelly.

Published Songs
Come On and Pet Me—see A NIGHT OUT
    [September 7, 1925]
Flannel Petticoat Girl—originally used
    (unpublished) in HAMMERSTEIN'S NINE
    O'CLOCK REVUE [October 4, 1923]
My Boy and I—see NO, NO, NANETTE
    [September 16, 1925]
Toodle-Oo

This moderate success opened the Shubert's
new Imperial Theatre. Youmans began to constantly revise songs and reuse them in future
shows. While a standard practice of the day,
Youmans came up with several major songs in
this manner.

LOLLIPOP
January 21, 1924
Knickerbocker Theatre • 152 performances
Book and Lyrics by Zelda Sears; Directed by
Ira Hards; Produced by Henry W. Savage;
With Ada May (Weeks), Harry Puck, and
Zelda Sears. Pre-Broadway title: THE LEFT
OVER.

Published Songs
Deep in My Heart
Going Rowing
Honey-Bun
It Must Be Love—cut; see A NIGHT OUT
    [September 7, 1925]
Take a Little One-Step
Tie a String around Your Finger

Additional Songs Published (No Lyric) in
    Piano Selection
Orphan Girl
Spanish [instrumental]

A non-adventurous effort aimed at the family
trade, LOLLIPOP enjoyed a moderate success.

CHARLOT'S REVUE
September 23, 1924
Prince of Wales' Theatre {London} •
    518 performances
Music mostly by others; Book by Ronald
Jeans; Produced by André Charlot.

Published Song
That Forgotten Melody [lyric by Douglas
    Furber]

A NIGHT OUT [1925]
September 7, 1925
Garrick Theatre {Philadelphia} •
    Closed during tryout
Lyrics mostly by Clifford Grey and Irving
Caesar; Book by George Grossmith and Arthur
Miller (based on the British musical by Willie
Redstone, George Grossmith, and Arthur
Miller [see Porter: September 18, 1920]);
Directed by Thomas Reynolds; Produced by
Alfred E. Aarons in association with Edward
Laurillard.

Published Songs
I Want a Yes Man [lyric by Grey, Caesar, and
    Ira Gershwin]
Kissing—revised version of *It Must Be Love*
    from LOLLIPOP [January 21, 1924]
Like a Bird on the Wing
*Sometimes I'm Happy [lyric by Caesar]—
    revised version of *Come On and Pet Me*
    from MARY JANE McKANE [December
    25, 1923]; also used in HIT THE DECK
    [April 25, 1927]

Youmans wrote his greatest success in 1924, featuring two of Broadway's all-time song hits; but
a prolonged and highly popular tryout kept NO,
NO, NANETTE [September 16, 1925] out of New
York for the better part of a year. In the mean-
while Alfred Aarons enlisted Youmans to Ameri-
canize A NIGHT OUT, with negligible results.
(Son Alex Aarons had hit the jackpot with
George & Ira and Fred & Adele and LADY, BE
GOOD! [Gershwin: December 1, 1924]; Papa
Alfred produced 1925 flops by both Gershwin
and Youmans.) Ira, now working full-time with
brother George, received co-lyricist credit for *I
Want a Yes Man*. This was reworked from the

Youmans/Arthur Francis *Robbing Your Father*, a cut from TWO LITTLE GIRLS IN BLUE [1921] [May 3, 1921]; Ira wasn't even aware of the new use until after A NIGHT OUT closed. The genial Ira Gershwin was a hard man to alienate, but Youmans managed to do it. Another rewritten tune fared much better, the perky and altogether excellent *Sometimes I'm Happy*.

NO, NO, NANETTE
September 16, 1925
Globe Theatre • 321 performances
Lyrics mostly by Irving Caesar; Book by Otto Harbach and Frank Mandel (based on *My Lady Friends* [play] by Emil Nyitray and Frank Mandel); Produced and Directed by H. H. Frazee; With Louise Groody, Charles Winninger, and Georgia O'Ramey.

Revival
January 19, 1971
46th Street Theatre • 861 performances
Directed and Book Adapted by Burt Shevelove; Choreographed by Donald Saddler; Produced by Cyma Rubin; With Ruby Keeler, Jack Gilford [Winninger], Bobby Van, Helen Gallagher, Susan Watson [Groody], and Patsy Kelly [O'Ramey].

Published Songs
The Boy Next Door [lyric by Schuyler Greene and Harbach]—cut
I Don't Want a Girlie [lyric by B. G. DeSylva]—cut
*I Want to Be Happy
I've Confessed to the Breeze [lyric by Harbach]—cut
No, No, Nanette! [lyric by Harbach]—revised version of *My Boy and I* from MARY JANE McKANE [December 25, 1923]
Santa Claus [lyric by Harbach]—cut
*Tea for Two
*Too Many Rings around Rosie
*"Where Has My Hubby Gone?" Blues
You Can Dance with Any Girl at All

Additional Songs Published in Vocal Selection of Revival
Call of the Sea
Peach on the Beach [lyric by Harbach]
Telephone Girlie [lyric by Harbach]

Waiting for You—new lyric for *You Started Something* from TWO LITTLE GIRLS IN BLUE [1921] [May 3, 1921]

Additional Songs Published in British Vocal Score
Fight over Me
Flappers Are We (*Opening Act I*)
We're All of Us Excited (*Finale Act II*)
When You're Sad

Additional Song Recorded
Only a Moment Ago [lyric by Burt Shevelove] —new lyric for unpublished song; cut

NO, NO, NANETTE played a short tryout in Detroit [beginning April 23, 1924] before moving on to phenomenal success in Chicago. The show nevertheless underwent major changes: Irving Caesar was brought in to replace half of Harbach's lyrics, and producer Harry Frazee—best known as the man who sold Babe Ruth (he owned the Boston Red Sox)—fired director Edward Royce after all the work was done and took credit himself. By the time NANETTE reached Broadway, there were two road companies as well as a London production [March 11, 1925], which enjoyed an unprecedented 665-performance run. As with WILDFLOWER [February 7, 1923], the show was driven by two smash song hits, *Tea for Two* and *I Want to Be Happy*. Unlike in the earlier musicals, though, the hits were supplemented by a fine assortment of interesting numbers like the dance-happy *Too Many Rings around Rosie* and *You Can Dance with Any Girl at All* and the delicious mock-torch song *"Where Has My Hubby Gone?" Blues*. A stylish Broadway revival of NANETTE launched a nostalgia craze (and a string of not-so-successful revivals of rewritten old musicals with old-time stars).

OH, PLEASE!
December 17, 1926
Fulton Theatre • 75 performances
Lyrics by Anne Caldwell; Book by Otto Harbach and Anne Caldwell (based on a play by Maurice Hennequin and Pierre Veber); Directed by Hassard Short; Produced by Charles B. Dillingham; With Beatrice Lillie, Charles Winninger, and Charles Purcell.

Published Songs
I Know That You Know
I'm Waiting for a Wonderful Girl
Like He Loves Me
Nicodemus

Having taken New York by storm in an imported edition of CHARLOT'S REVUE [January 29, 1924], Beatrice Lillie and Gertrude Lawrence signed with New York producers Charles Dillingham (on one hand) and Aarons & Freedley (on the other). Lawrence met immediate success (see OH, KAY! [Gershwin: November 8, 1926]); the Canadian-born Lillie suffered inappropriate vehicles until the 1930s revue provided a more suitable format for her considerable talents. Youmans had a difficult time writing for and dealing with Lillie, as did Rodgers and Hart on SHE'S MY BABY [Rodgers: January 3, 1928]. Youmans, incidentally, married two girls from the OH, PLEASE! chorus (not at the same time).

HIT THE DECK
April 25, 1927
Belasco Theatre • 352 performances
"A Nautical Musical Comedy." Lyrics by Leo Robin and Clifford Grey; Book by Herbert Fields (based on *Shore Leave* [play] by Hubert Osborne); Directed by Alexander Leftwich; Produced by Youmans (with Lew Fields); With Louise Groody, Charles King, and Stella Mayhew.

Published Songs
Armful of You—cut
Hallelujah!—revised version of a 1918 march (unpublished) written for John Philip Sousa's U.S. Navy Band
Harbor of My Heart
Join the Navy!
*Keepin' Myself for You [lyric by Sidney Clare]—written for 1929 movie version
Loo-Loo
Lucky Bird
Nothing Could Be Sweeter—cut; see *Why, Oh Why?*
*Sometimes I'm Happy [lyric by Irving Caesar]—see A NIGHT OUT [1925] [September 7, 1925]
*Why, Oh Why?—new lyric for *Nothing Could Be Sweeter*

Having suffered from several indifferently mounted productions—and having seen the financial returns generated by his mother's substantial investment in NO, NO, NANETTE [September 16, 1925]—Youmans resolved to henceforth present his own shows. For experienced advice, librettist Herb Fields's father Lew was invited to coproduce HIT THE DECK; Youmans bought him out immediately after the opening. Youman's successful producing debut proved to be the disastrous turning point in his career: with his best music yet to come, HIT THE DECK was to be his last successful show. Youmans was still in the lead among Broadway's "new" composers, with HIT THE DECK providing yet another two tuneful standards (the ingratiating *Sometimes I'm Happy* and the revivalist *Hallelujah!*). But George Gershwin had startled the musical world in 1924 with *Rhapsody in Blue*, followed up by his own string of song hits; the young Richard Rodgers burst upon *Manhattan* in 1925; and Kern and Berlin were still very much in evidence. Youmans felt self-conscious as the only "real" American among this highly talented group of Jewish immigrants and sons of immigrants. Competition prodded him to move away from his reliance on catchy, rhythmic phrases and develop a new style of soaring melodies and complexly colored harmonies, as in *Why, Oh Why?* and (for HIT THE DECK's movie version) *Keepin' Myself for You*.

RAINBOW
November 21, 1928
Gallo Theatre • 29 performances
Lyrics by Oscar Hammerstein 2nd; Book by Laurence Stallings and Oscar Hammerstein 2nd; Directed by Oscar Hammerstein 2nd; Produced by Philip Goodman; With Libby Holman, Brian Donlevy, and Charles Ruggles.

Published Songs
The Bride Was Dressed in White—initial publication upon use in 1929 movie version (retitled *Song of the West*)
Faded Rose—advertised but not published
Hay, Straw
I Like You As You Are
I Look for Love—advertised but not published
I Want a Man
Let Me Give All My Love to Thee—initial publication upon use in movie version

My Mother Told Me Not to Trust a Soldier—
initial publication upon use in movie
version
The One Girl
Virginia—unpublished; new lyric for *If I Told
You* (cut) from WILDFLOWER [February 7,
1923]
West Wind [lyric by J. Russel Robinson]—
written for movie version
Who Am I? (That You Should Care for Me)
[lyric by Gus Kahn]—cut

Following his groundbreaking work on SHOW
BOAT [Kern: February 27, 1927], Oscar Hammerstein rejoined with Youmans for the ambitious RAINBOW. Disastrously under-rehearsed,
the opening night was a shambles (highlighted
by the onstage contribution of Fanny the don-
key!). Surprisingly patient critics saw the piece
as a successor to SHOW BOAT and hoped RAIN-
BOW could run long enough to be put into
shape. It didn't, it wasn't. The score seems somewhat pedestrian for Youmans; only two songs are
notable, the torchy *I Want a Man* and especially
the cut *Who Am I? (That You Should Care for Me)*.
The failure of RAINBOW sent Hammerstein—an
ideal collaborator for perfectionist Youmans—
back to other composers and fifteen years of flops
(relieved only by MUSIC IN THE AIR [Kern:
November 8, 1932]). This was a crucial loss for
Youmans. Unable to sustain relationships with
Ira Gershwin, Hammerstein, or Harbach, the rest
of his career was spent working with uninspired
and uninspiring pop-song lyricists. Jealous and
insecure with publisher Max Dreyfus—whom he
felt favored Kern, Gershwin, Rodgers, et al.—
Youmans left Harms and established Vincent Youmans, Inc. Another mistake. Distrustful of everyone, Youmans took personal control of everything
and everything began to self-destruct.

SHOW GIRL
July 2, 1929
Ziegfeld Theatre • 111 performances
Music mostly by George Gershwin (see
Gershwin: July 2, 1929); Lyrics mostly by Gus
Kahn and Ira Gershwin; Book and Direction
by Wm. Anthony McGuire (based on the
novel by J. P. McEvoy); Produced by Florenz

Ziegfeld, Jr.; With Ruby Keeler Jolson and
"(Lew) Clayton, (Eddie) Jackson & (Jimmy)
Durante."

Published Song
Mississippi Dry [lyric by J. Russel
Robinson]—added after opening

Faced with major troubles during the tryout of
GREAT DAY! [October 17, 1929], Youmans arranged a badly needed cash advance from Ziegfeld against the promise of a future musical. More
as a slap in the face to Gershwin than an improvement to the mediocre SHOW GIRL, Ziegfeld requested a post-opening interpolation from
Youmans—who was to receive his own Ziegfeldian slaps in the face during production of
SMILES [November 18, 1930].

GREAT DAY!
October 17, 1929
Cosmopolitan Theatre • 36 performances
"A Musical Play of the Southland." Lyrics by
William (Billy) Rose and Edward Eliscu; Book
by John Wells and Wm. Cary Duncan;
Directed by R. H. Burnside and Frank M.
Gillespie; Conceived and Produced by
Youmans; With Mayo Methot, Allen Prior,
Lois Deppe, and (Flournoy) Miller & (Aubrey)
Lyles.

Published Songs
Great Day!
Happy Because I'm in Love
**More Than You Know*
One Love—cut; advertised but not published
Open up Your Heart
**Without a Song*

Over a half-dozen librettists and directors came
and went—along with scores of performers (including young singer Harold Arlen)—as Youmans
prepared and wrote and conceived and produced
his GREAT DAY! But the long-in-gestation show,
known around town as "Great Delay!", retained
its problems and quickly closed. Three songs
nevertheless escaped the collapse and became all-
time standards: the rhythmic, spiritualistic *Great
Day!*; the moving anthem *Without a Song*; and
the first of four great Youmans ballads, *More Than
You Know* (which was sung by Mayo Methot, the

penultimate Mrs. Humphrey Bogart). Lyricists were Edward Eliscu, who had helped on RAINBOW [November 21, 1928], and Tin Pan Alley rhymester Billy Rose. Publisher Youmans decided that Billy sounded too undignified for serious theatre, hence "William" Rose.

SMILES
November 18, 1930
Ziegfeld Theatre • 63 performances
Lyrics mostly by Harold Adamson; Book and Direction by Wm. Anthony McGuire (based on a story by Noël Coward); Choreographed by Ned Wayburn; Produced by Florenz Ziegfeld, Jr.; With Marilyn Miller, Fred & Adele Astaire, Tom Howard, Eddie Foy, Jr., and Paul Gregory.

Published Songs
*Be Good to Me [lyric by Ring Lardner]
Blue Bowery—initial publication upon reuse with new lyric as My Lover in TAKE A CHANCE [November 26, 1932]
*Carry On, Keep Smiling
He Came Along—cut; initial publication as 1965 non-show song
*If I Were You, Love (I'd Jump Right in the Lake) [lyric by Lardner]
I'm Glad I Waited [lyric by Adamson and Clifford Grey]
More Than Ever—cut; published in U.K.
**Time on My Hands [lyric by Adamson and Mack Gordon]

Additional Song Recorded
Say, Young Man of Manhattan

With three enormous stars and a typically lavish Ziegfeld production, SMILES was sure-fire; Ziegfeld, devastated by the stock market crash, certainly hoped so. But the material was weak and Ziegfeld, Youmans, and McGuire—leading names in 1920s musical comedy—were each on their last professional legs. Sometime-lyricist Ring Lardner, a close Youmans friend on a similar self-destructive course, stepped in to help with some of his unique songwords (as in If I Were You, Love, I'd Jump Right in the Lake). Youmans's consistent failures since HIT THE DECK [April 25, 1927] combined with financial pressures and emotional problems to transform the difficult perfectionist into an impossible-to-deal-with alcoholic. Remarkably, his music was not affected by this. The forgettable SMILES contained the unforgettable Time on My Hands (which Marilyn Miller refused to sing) and two fascinating rhythmical experiments, Be Good to Me and Carry On, Keep Smiling.

THROUGH THE YEARS
January 28, 1932
Manhattan Theatre • 20 performances
Lyrics by Edward Heyman; Book by Brian Hooker (based on Smilin' Through [play] by Allan Langdon Martin); Directed by Edgar MacGregor; Choreographed by Jack Haskell and Max Scheck; Produced by Youmans; With Natalie Hall, Michael Bartlett, and Charles Winninger. Pre-Broadway title: SMILIN' THROUGH.

Published Songs
Drums in My Heart
It's Every Girl's Ambition
Kathleen Mine
Kinda Like You
**Through the Years
You're Everywhere

Youmans once more displayed his inability to assemble the elements needed to produce a successful show: THROUGH THE YEARS was a much-doctored shambles. Again Youmans managed two hits—Drums in My Heart and one of his very best songs, Through the Years. The show's failure took Youmans out of the producing business, and his difficult reputation made him virtually unemployable.

TAKE A CHANCE
November 26, 1932
Apollo Theatre • 243 performances
Music mostly by Richard A. Whiting and "Herb Brown Nacio" [Nacio Herb Brown]; Lyrics by B. G. DeSylva; Book by B. G. DeSylva and Laurence Schwab; Directed by Edgar MacGregor; Choreographed by Bobby Connolly; Produced by Laurence Schwab and B. G. DeSylva; With Ethel Merman, Jack Haley, and Jack Whiting. Pre-Broadway title: HUMPTY DUMPTY.

Published Songs
**I Want to Be with You*—cut
My Lover—cut; new lyric for *Blue Bowery*
    (unpublished) from SMILES [November
    18, 1930]
Oh, How I Long to Belong to You
Rise 'n Shine
Should I Be Sweet?
So Do I

When the pre-Broadway tryout of HUMPTY DUMPTY opened on September 12, 1932, to disastrous notices, producers Schwab and DeSylva decided to take a chance and totally overhaul it. Star comics Lou Holtz and Eddie Foy, Jr., were replaced (while singer Ethel Merman was retained), and lyricist DeSylva took an even bigger chance by hiring Youmans to supplement the score. TAKE A CHANCE was transformed into a fair-sized hit, though Youmans's contributions (except the revivalist *Rise 'n Shine*) were overshadowed by HUMPTY DUMPTY leftover *Eadie Was a Lady*. Youmans's last great ballad, the melancholy *I Want to Be with You*, was cut and remains unjustly neglected. Youmans left Broadway for Hollywood, where he wrote songs for the 1933 film *Flying down to Rio* (which introduced the Fred Astaire/Ginger Rogers team). Despite three fine contributions—*The Carioca*, *Orchids in the Moonlight*, and the title tune—the composer quickly alienated himself from future movie work. Years of heavy drinking and heavy living, meanwhile, caused Youmans to contract tuberculosis; he was forced into a long, discouraging retirement at the age of thirty-four.

VINCENT YOUMANS' BALLET REVUE
January 27, 1944
Lyric Theatre {Baltimore, Md.} •
    Closed during tryout
Music by Nicolai Rimsky-Korsakov, Maurice Ravel, and Ernesto Lecuona; Lyrics by

Maria Shelton and Gladys Shelley; Choreographed by Leonide Massine and Eugene von Groza; Directed by Eric Hatch; Produced by Youmans; With Glenn Anders, Deems Taylor, Mason Adams, and Herbert Ross.

Published Songs
None

During a brief period of remission, Youmans came back into view with this curious dance program featuring music by Mexican Ernesto Lecuona and others (but no Youmans!). The amateurishly assembled fiasco lasted three weeks, sending Youmans back to his sickbed. After another two years of illness, Vincent Youmans finally succumbed and died on April 5, 1946, in Denver, Colorado.

Vincent Youmans arrived on Broadway in the early twenties, experimenting with the same "hot" music as his lyricist's kid brother, the one-day-older, up-and-coming George Gershwin. Early success came via WILDFLOWER [February 7, 1923], a mild operetta with a touch of refreshing syncopation. Within two years, jazz-based dance rhythms were dominating Broadway, with Youmans's NO, NO, NANETTE [September 16, 1925] in the vanguard. After which the composer's myriad self-inflicted problems—physical, emotional, financial—began to overtake his career. His last projects were all hopelessly troubled and ended in failure. In the midst of this, Youmans developed an incredibly rich melodic style and wrote three of the musical theatre's all-time most beautiful songs (*More Than You Know, Time on My Hands*, and *Through the Years*). And then his career was over, after only twelve years.

RICHARD RODGERS

Born: June 28, 1902, New York, New York
Died: December 30, 1979, New York, New York

RICHARD RODGERS grew up steeped in show tunes. His parents, operetta enthusiasts, kept music in the house, and from the age of seven Rodgers's ambition was clearly set on musical theatre. In 1916 Rodgers discovered Kern—via a subway-circuit touring production of VERY GOOD EDDIE [1915] [Kern: December 23, 1915]—and began writing songs of his own. The following spring Rodgers's older brother took him to the annual Columbia Varsity Show. The fourteen-year-old lad was impressed by the lyrics, so Richard's brother Mortimer introduced him to the writer, fraternity brother Oscar Hammerstein 2nd. Richard immediately determined that he himself would go to Columbia and write varsity shows. Meanwhile, Rodgers self-published his first song in June 1917: *Auto Show Girl* [lyric by David Dyrenforth].

ONE MINUTE PLEASE
December 29, 1917
Plaza Hotel Grand Ballroom • 1 performance
Lyrics mostly by Richard C. Rodgers and Ralph G. Engelsman; Book by Ralph G. Engelsman; Directed by Milton Bender; Produced by Milton Bender for The Akron Club.

Published Songs
Auto Show Girl [lyric by David Dyrenforth]
Whispers [lyric by Engelsman and Rodgers]

Mortimer Rodgers was a member of the Akron Club, just then preparing a benefit to raise funds to send tobacco to the doughboys Over There. None of the club members wrote music, so Mortimer volunteered his brother. Richard Rodgers was to continue writing musicals for sixty-two years. *Auto Show Girl*, which had not yet created a stir, was used; so was Rodgers's

second self-published effort, *Whispers*. Milton "Doc" Bender, a Broadway dentist, served as director and producer. The unsavory Bender was to become Lorenz Hart's agent, hanger-on, and all-around bad influence. As it turns out, Rodgers—who loathed Bender even more than everyone else did—worked with him two years before Hart first came together with his Svengali.

UP STAGE AND DOWN
March 8, 1919
Waldorf-Astoria Grand Ballroom •
   1 performance
Lyrics mostly by Rodgers; Book by Myron D. Rosenthal; Directed by Dr. Harry A. Goldberg; Produced by Infants Relief Society; With Phillip Leavitt, Ralph G. Engelsman, and Myron D. Rosenthal.

Revival
As TWINKLING EYES: May 18, 1919
44th Street Theatre • 1 performance
Book revised by Larry Lea Strong; Directed by Lorenz M. Hart; With Phillip Leavitt and Ralph G. Engelsman.

Published Songs
Asiatic Angles
Butterfly Love
Love Is Not in Vain
Love Me by Parcel Post [lyric by Mortimer W. Rodgers]
There's Room for One More [lyric by Oscar Hammerstein 2nd]—initial publication upon reuse in FLY WITH ME [March 24, 1920]
Twinkling Eyes

Rodgers wrote his second complete score for another benefit. He also wrote most of the lyrics, with assists from his brother, theatrical lawyer Benjamin M. Kaye (*Prisms, Plums and Prunes* [unpublished]), and Oscar Hammerstein 2nd, whose first Broadway show was about to go into rehearsal. Uncle Arthur Hammerstein presented the drama *The Light* [May 21, 1919], which went out after only four New Haven performances. UP STAGE AND DOWN at least made it to Broadway: TWINKLING EYES, a revised version directed by Lorenz Hart (and revised by Larry Lea Strong—"Larry Least Wrong"?—which sounds suspiciously like a Hart pseudonym) was presented at the 44th Street Theatre on May 18, 1919, as a benefit for the Soldiers and Sailors Benefit Fund. Thus, the Broadway debuts of Rodgers and Hammerstein and Hart as well. Hammerstein contributed two lyrics besides the published song listed above, the others being *Can It* and *Weaknesses*.

A LONELY ROMEO
June 10, 1919
Shubert Theatre • 87 performances
Music mostly by Malvin M. Franklin and Robert Hood Bowers; Lyrics mostly by Robert B. Smith; Book by Harry B. Smith and Lew Fields; Directed and Produced by Lew Fields; With Lew Fields.

Published Song
Any Old Place with You [lyric by Lorenz Hart]—added after opening

Rodgers had long been looking for a real collaborator. Phillip Leavitt, classmate and friend of Mortimer (and actor in UP STAGE AND DOWN), introduced high school student Rodgers to yet another Columbia man who was looking for a composer. Would-be lyricist Lorenz Hart had made little professional headway since graduation. Hart's first theatrical assignment was to provide translations for the German-language DIE TÖLLE DOLLY† [October 23, 1916], which played in the Yorkville section of Manhattan. The strangely matched pair shared an admiration for the Princess Theatre shows of Kern, Bolton, and Wodehouse and decided to get together for a few songs. Leavitt took songs and songwriters to his neighbor, Broadway star-producer-director Lew Fields (see HOKEY-POKEY [Berlin: February 8, 1912]).

Fields liked *Any Old Place with You* enough to add it to his current show, A LONELY ROMEO, on August 26, 1919 (by which point it had moved to the Casino Theatre). It was Rodgers's first commercially published song. Three of Hart's DOLLY songs had already been published, including *Meyer, Your Tights Are Tight* [music by Walter Kollo].

YOU'D BE SURPRISED
March 6, 1920
Plaza Hotel Grand Ballroom • 1 performance
"An Atrocious Musical Comedy." Lyrics mostly by Lorenz Hart and Milton Bender; Book and Direction by Milton Bender; Produced by The Akron Club; With Dorothy Fields, Ralph G. Engelsman, and Phillip Leavitt.

Published Songs
A Breath of Springtime [lyric by Hart]
Don't Love Me Like Othello [lyric by Hart]—initial publication upon reuse in FLY WITH ME [March 24, 1920]
Mary, Queen of Scots [lyric by Herbert Fields]—initial publication upon reuse in POOR LITTLE RITZ GIRL [July 28, 1920]
Princess of the Willow Tree [lyric by Bender]—see POOR LITTLE RITZ GIRL
When We Are Married [lyric by Bender]

Broadway composer Rodgers, now a Columbia man, wrote yet another benefit show for the Akron Club. Lyricists included Hart, Milton Bender, and Lew Fields's younger son Herbert, who had played a small role in A LONELY ROMEO [June 10, 1919]. During the five years of struggle before Rodgers, Hart, and Fields found Broadway success, Herb filled in as occasional lyricist, choreographer, whatever. YOU'D BE SURPRISED also made use of Lew Fields's fifteen-year-old daughter Dorothy, who twenty-five years later brought Rodgers the idea for ANNIE GET YOUR GUN [Berlin: May 16, 1946].

FLY WITH ME
March 24, 1920
Hotel Astor Grand Ballroom • 4 performances
"A Futurist Musical Comedy." Lyrics mostly by Lorenz Hart; Book by Milton Kroopf

and Phillip Leavitt; Directed by Ralph Bunker; Choreographed by Herbert Fields; Produced by The Columbia University Players.

Songs Published in Vocal Score

Another Melody in F

A College on Broadway

Don't Love Me Like Othello—originally used in YOU'D BE SURPRISED [March 6, 1920]; also see POOR LITTLE RITZ GIRL [July 28, 1920]

Dreaming True—see POOR LITTLE RITZ GIRL

Gone Are the Days

Gunga Din

If You Were You—different than *If I Were You* from BETSY [December 28, 1926]

Inspiration

Peek in Pekin—see POOR LITTLE RITZ GIRL

A Penny for Your Thoughts

There's Room for One More [lyric by Oscar Hammerstein 2nd]—initial publication of song originally used in UP STAGE AND DOWN [March 8, 1919]

Working for the Government

Additional Songs Recorded

Kid, I Love You

Moonlight and You

The Third Degree of Love

Freshman Rodgers was selected to write the Columbia Varsity Show in his first year of eligibility. Among the three judges who accepted FLY WITH ME was alumnus Oscar Hammerstein, whose first Broadway musical had just opened (ALWAYS YOU [January 5, 1920], music by Herbert Stothart). Lew Fields, of A LONELY ROMEO [June 10, 1919], attended FLY WITH ME and immediately hired Rodgers and Hart to write his next musical.

POOR LITTLE RITZ GIRL

July 28, 1920

Central Theatre • 119 performances

Music also by Sigmund Romberg; Lyrics to Rodgers songs by Lorenz Hart; Book by George Campbell and Lew Fields; Directed by Ned Wayburn; Produced by Lew Fields; With Charles Purcell and Lulu McConnell.

Published Songs

Boomerang—cut; advertised but not published

Lady Raffles Behave—cut

Let Me Drink in Your Eyes—cut; advertised but not published, see YOU'LL NEVER KNOW [April 20, 1921]

Love Will Call—new lyric for *Dreaming True* from FLY WITH ME [March 24, 1920]

Love's Intense in Tents—new lyric for *Peek in Pekin* from FLY WITH ME

Mary, Queen of Scots [lyric by Herbert Fields]—originally used (unpublished) in YOU'D BE SURPRISED [March 6, 1920]

Will You Forgive Me?—cut; advertised but not published, new lyric for *Princess of the Willow Tree* from YOU'D BE SURPRISED; also see YOU'LL NEVER KNOW

You Can't Fool Your Dreams—new lyric for *Don't Love Me Like Othello* from YOU'D BE SURPRISED

POOR LITTLE RITZ GIRL tried out in Boston, where it was the opening attraction at the Wilbur Theatre. Rodgers and Hart spent the tryout period in the Adirondacks, as summer camp counselors. Back in Boston, Fields threw out half the score and brought in Sigmund Romberg. Rodgers didn't discover this until he arrived for the Broadway opening; thereafter he paid more attention—*much* more attention—to the proper use of his work. It was to be five years before Rodgers and Hart had another Broadway musical opportunity. It should be noted that POOR LITTLE RITZ GIRL (and Rodgers's other early work) was rather bland and not especially interesting. Of course, he was still only eighteen years old.

SAY MAMA!

February 12, 1921

Plaza Hotel Grand Ballroom • 1 performance

"A Musical Entertainment." Lyrics by Lorenz Hart; Directed by Herbert Fields; Produced by The Akron Club; With Ralph G. Engelsman, Dorothy Fields, and Phillip Leavitt.

Published Song

Jack and Jill—for initial publication see HALF MOON INN [March 19, 1923]

Rodgers and Hart wrote at least eight songs for this amateur show. All have disappeared except

Jack and Jill, which was salvaged and reused in 1923.

YOU'LL NEVER KNOW
April 20, 1921
Hotel Astor Grand Ballroom • 4 performances
"Columbia 15th Anniversary Varsity Show."
Lyrics by Lorenz Hart; Choreographed by Herbert Fields; Directed by Oscar Hammerstein 2nd and others; Produced by the Players' Club of Columbia University.

Songs Published in Vocal Score
Chorus Girl Blues
I'm Broke
Jumping Jack
Just a Little Lie
Let Me Drink in Your Eyes—originally used (cut, unpublished) in POOR LITTLE RITZ GIRL [July 28, 1920]
Virtue Wins the Day
Watch Yourself
When I Go on the Stage [1st]—different than song from SHE'S MY BABY [January 3, 1928]
Will You Forgive Me?—originally used (cut, unpublished) in POOR LITTLE RITZ GIRL
You'll Never Know
Your Lullaby

Rodgers wrote his second consecutive Columbia Varsity Show, after which he left Columbia to enter the Institute of Musical Art (Juilliard). Rodgers, Hart, and Fields's benefit-show career continued with a number of other offerings (with no songs published), but the boys remained ignored by Broadway. Meanwhile, Rodgers went on the road with Papa Fields to conduct the post-Broadway tour of SNAPSHOTS OF 1921 [Gershwin: June 2, 1921]. Also in the cast were Herbert Fields and soubrette Lulu McConnell of POOR LITTLE RITZ GIRL, who was Rodgers's girlfriend for many years.

WINKLE TOWN
[circa 1922]
Unproduced musical. Lyrics by Lorenz Hart; Book by Oscar Hammerstein 2nd and Herbert Fields.

Published Songs
I Want a Man—for initial publication see LIDO LADY [December 1, 1926] and AMERICA'S SWEETHEART [February 10, 1931]
**Manhattan*—for initial publication see GARRICK GAIETIES [1st] [May 17, 1925]

Additional Songs Recorded
The Hermits—for initial publication see DEAREST ENEMY [September 18, 1925]
Old Enough to Love—for initial publication see DEAREST ENEMY

The unproduced WINKLE TOWN included what was to be Rodgers's first song hit, *Manhattan*, written sometime in 1921 or 1922.

HALF MOON INN
March 19, 1923
Hotel Astor Grand Ballroom • 6 performances
"Columbia Varsity Show of 1923." Music mostly by Morris Watkins; Lyrics mostly by Perry Ivans and Corey Ford; Produced by the Players' Club of Columbia University.

Song Published in "Special Edition" Vocal Selection
Jack and Jill [lyric by Lorenz Hart]—initial publication of song originally used in SAY MAMA! [February 12, 1921]

THE MELODY MAN
May 13, 1924
Central Theatre • 56 performances
Play with songs by "Herbert Richard Lorenz"; Directed by Lawrence Marston and Alexander Leftwich; Produced by Lew Fields; With Lew Fields, Frederic Bickel (March), Eva Puck, and Sammy White. Pre-Broadway title: THE JAZZ KING.

Published Songs
I'd Like to Poison Ivy (Because She Clings to Me)
Moonlight Mama

Unable to raise enthusiasm as musical show writers, Herbert, Richard, and Lorenz combined to create this hackneyed comedy; not unwisely, they kept their names off it. Another year of non-productive collaboration followed THE MELODY

MAN. Things for the pair were bad: Hart managed a few assignments with other composers, and the discouraged Rodgers was on the verge of going into babies' underwear.

GARRICK GAIETIES ✦ First Edition
May 17, 1925
Garrick Theatre • 161 performances
"A Bubbling Satirical Musical Revue of Plays, Problems and Persons." Music mostly by Rodgers; Lyrics mostly by Lorenz Hart; Sketches by Benjamin M. Kaye, Morrie Ryskind, and others; Directed by Philip Loeb; Choreographed by Herbert Fields; Produced by The Theatre Guild; With Sterling Holloway, Edith Meiser, Romney Brent, and June Cochrane.

Published Songs
April Fool
Do You Love Me? (I Wonder)
**Manhattan—initial use of song written for WINKLE TOWN [circa 1922]
Old Fashioned Girl [lyric by Meiser]
On with the Dance
Sentimental Me (And Romantic You)
The Three Musketeers—advertised but not published; initial use of song written for WINKLE TOWN

Additional Song Published in Non-show Folio
Opening (Gilding the Guild/Soliciting Subscriptions)

Benjamin Kaye, lyricist of *Prisms, Plums and Prunes* (in UP STAGE AND DOWN [March 8, 1919]), asked Rodgers to write yet another benefit. The Theatre Guild, long in residence at the Garrick Theatre (65 West 35th Street), was building its own Guild Theatre (now the Virginia). An energetic group of younger Guild actors and understudies was planning a benefit to raise money to buy curtains for the new theatre, and Kaye—who had become lawyer for the Guild—wondered if Rodgers would help. Rodgers and Hart put together a bright and inventive score, and the two scheduled performances were so successful that the GARRICK GAITIES reopened for a commercial run. *Manhattan* was an imme-

diate and enormous song hit, taking Rodgers and Hart out of the benefit business for good. The GAITIES also included *Do You Love Me? (I Wonder)*, a nicely sweeping waltz with deft chromatic key shifts; *Sentimental Me (And Romantic You)*, a pleasant boy/girl duet; and *Gilding the Guild*, a clever opening number.

JUNE DAYS
August 6, 1925
Astor Theatre • 84 performances
Music mostly by J. Fred Coots; Lyrics mostly by Clifford Grey; Book by Cyrus Wood (based on THE CHARM SCHOOL [Kern: August 2, 1920]); Directed by J. J. Shubert; Produced by Lee and J. J. Shubert.

Published Songs
None

Rodgers and Hart contributed one song, *Anytime, Anywhere, Anyhow.*

DEAREST ENEMY
September 18, 1925
Knickerbocker Theatre • 286 performances
Lyrics by Lorenz Hart; Book by Herbert Fields; Directed by John Murray Anderson; Produced by George Ford; With Helen Ford and Charles Purcell.

Published Songs
Bye and Bye
Cheerio!
Here in My Arms—also used in LIDO LADY [December 1, 1926]
Here's a Kiss
Sweet Peter

Additional Songs Recorded
Full-Blown Roses
Gavotte
Heigh-Ho, Lackaday
The Hermits—initial use of song written for WINKLE TOWN [circa 1922]
I Beg Your Pardon
I'd Like to Hide It
Old Enough to Love—initial use of song written for WINKLE TOWN
War Is War
Where the Hudson River Flows

With a hit revue playing and a super-hit song playing everywhere, Rodgers, Hart, and Fields were finally able to get on one of their already written musicals. Musical-comedy star Helen Ford had long been interested in DEAREST ENEMY; with Rodgers and Hart now bankable, Ford's husband was able to raise the money. Revue director John Murray Anderson joined in, and the result was a freshly unpretentious hit. The ballad *Here in My Arms* joined *Manhattan* as a popular 1925 song success, while *Sweet Peter* was an amusing tale of a certain Governor of olde Nieuw Amsterdam whose philandering wife would send her caller away when she heard his peg leg coming up the stairs.

FIFTH AVENUE FOLLIES
[circa January 1926]
Fifth Avenue Nightclub
"A Revue Superb." Lyrics by Lorenz Hart; Directed by Seymour Felix; Produced by Billy Rose; With Cecil Cunningham and Bert Hanlon.

Published Songs
Maybe It's Me—see COCHRAN'S 1926 REVUE [April 29, 1926] and PEGGY-ANN [December 27, 1926]
Where's That Little Girl (*In the Little Green Hat*)—see LIDO LADY [December 1, 1926]

Rose's first nightclub venture was unsuccessful and short-lived. During his early pop-lyricist days, Rose occasionally used the slightly older (and taller) Hart as ghostwriter. Was it Hart—lyricist of *I'd Like to Poison Ivy* (*Because She Clings to Me*) (1923)—who first asked *Does the Spearmint Lose Its Flavor on the Bedpost Overnight* (1924)? The *Green Hat* song, incidentally, was suggested by Michael Arlen's scandalous best-selling novel, just then on Broadway as a Katharine Cornell vehicle.

THE GIRL FRIEND
March 17, 1926
Vanderbilt Theatre • 301 performances
Lyrics by Lorenz Hart; Book by Herbert Fields; Directed by John Harwood; Produced by Lew Fields; With Eva Puck, Sammy White, and June Cochrane.

Published Songs
*The Blue Room
The Girl Friend
Good Fellow Mine
**Sleepyhead—cut; also used in GARRICK GAIETIES [2nd] [May 10, 1926]
*Why Do I?

Additional Songs Published (No Lyric) in Piano Selection
Look for the Damsel
What Is It?

Back in 1926, Broadway gladly accepted musicals about six-day bicycle races and such. This second hit firmly established the Rodgers, Hart, and Fields team, with papa Lew Fields once again producing. THE GIRL FRIEND was written for the husband-and-wife dance team Puck and White, who had been featured in THE MELODY MAN [May 13, 1924]. Their biggest success came as "Frank and Ellie," the husband-and-wife dance team in SHOW BOAT [Kern: December 27, 1927]. *The Blue Room* was yet another major song hit, with the peppy title song also achieving popularity. *Why Do I?* is an endearing rhythm song, but the prize of the score is the unjustly neglected *Sleepyhead*—a truly superb, bluesy lullaby.

COCHRAN'S 1926 REVUE
April 29, 1926
London Pavilion {London} •
149 performances
Music mostly by others; Book by Ronald Jeans; Produced by Charles B. Cochran.

Published Song
I'm Crazy 'bout the Charleston [lyric by Donovan Parsons]—new lyric for *Maybe It's Me* from FIFTH AVENUE FOLLIES [circa January, 1926] and PEGGY-ANN [December 27, 1926]

In an era when song revisions and reuses were not exactly uncommon, *Maybe It's Me* stands out. It was initially performed and published in January 1926. When reused in London in April with a non-Hart lyric, the published sheet also included a second Hart version of the first lyric. In December, a third Hart version of *Maybe It's Me* appeared. All four were similarly unsuccessful.

GARRICK GAIETIES ✦ Second Edition

May 10, 1926
Garrick Theatre • 174 performances
Music mostly by Rodgers; Lyrics mostly by
Lorenz Hart; Sketches by Herbert Fields,
Benjamin M. Kaye, and others; Directed by
Philip Loeb; Choreographed by Herbert Fields;
Produced by The Theatre Guild; With Sterling
Holloway, Romney Brent, Edith Meiser, and
Betty Starbuck.

Published Songs

Idles of the King—for initial publication see
  LONDON PAVILION REVUE [May 20,
  1927]
Keys to Heaven
A Little Souvenir
**Mountain Greenery*
Queen Elizabeth
**Sleepyhead*—originally used (cut) in THE
  GIRL FRIEND [March 17, 1926]
What's the Use of Talking

Additional Songs Published in USO's
  At Ease

The Rose of Arizona [one-act operetta]—
  including:
Back to Nature
Davey Crockett
It May Rain
Say It with Flowers

Rodgers and Hart returned for a second successful edition of this Theatre Guild revue, with *Mountain Greenery* a song hit on the level of *Manhattan*. The rest of the score is merely adequate,
although the boys contributed an amusing one-
act operetta spoof, *The Rose of Arizona*.

LIDO LADY

December 1, 1926
Gaiety Theatre {London} • 259 performances
Lyrics by Lorenz Hart; Book by Guy Bolton,
Bert Kalmar and Harry Ruby, and Ronald
Jeans; Directed by Herbert M. Darsey;
Produced by Jack Hulbert and Paul Murray;
With Jack Hulbert, Cicely Courtneidge
(Hulbert), and Phyllis Dare.

Published Songs

Atlantic Blues—see PRESENT ARMS [April
  26, 1928]

Here in My Arms—originally used in DEAR-
  EST ENEMY [September 18, 1925]
I Want a Man—new lyric for song written for
  WINKLE TOWN [circa 1922]; also see
  AMERICA'S SWEETHEART [February 10,
  1931]
Lido Lady
Morning Is Midnight—also used in SHE'S MY
  BABY [January 3, 1928]
**A Tiny Flat Near Soho Square*—see SHE'S
  MY BABY
Try Again To-morrow
What's the Use?—new lyric for *Where's That
  Little Girl (In the Little Green Hat)* from
  FIFTH AVENUE FOLLIES [circa January
  1926]
You're on the Lido Now

Additional Songs Published (No Lyric) in
  Piano Selection

I Must Be Going
My Heart Is Sheba Bound

Rodgers and Hart went to London to write this
rather negligible show which was nevertheless a
big hit. As with Kern and Gershwin, Rodgers became immensely popular with British audiences
through the early thirties. One of the songs, *A Tiny
Flat Near Soho Square*, is quite lovely, while *Atlantic Blues* is a nice raggy rhythm number. Both
were quickly Americanized for Broadway use.

PEGGY-ANN

December 27, 1926
Vanderbilt Theatre • 333 performances
"The Utterly Different Musical Comedy." Lyrics
by Lorenz Hart; Book by Herbert Fields (based
on *Tillie's Nightmare* [musical] by Edgar
Smith); Directed by Robert Milton; Produced
by Lew Fields and Lyle D. Andrews; With
Helen Ford, Lulu McConnell, Edith Meiser,
and Betty Starbuck.

Published Songs

The Country Mouse [lyric by Desmond
  Carter]—written for London production
  [July 29, 1927]; new lyric for *A Little
  Birdie Told Me So*
Give That Little Girl a Hand—initial publica-
  tion (as professional copy) upon use in
  London production

Hello—initial publication upon use in London production

Howdy to Broadway—initial publication (as professional copy) upon use in London production

A Little Birdie Told Me So

Maybe It's Me—revised lyric for song originally used in FIFTH AVENUE FOLLIES [circa January 1926]; also see COCHRAN'S 1926 REVUE [April 29, 1926]

A Tree in the Park

Where's That Rainbow?

Additional Songs Published (No Lyric) in Piano Selection

Chuck It!

Havana

Rodgers, Hart, and Fields next undertook a somewhat futuristic musical fantasy, with the musical numbers taking place during the heroine's dreams. PEGGY-ANN was another hit for the boys, with Helen Ford (of DEAREST ENEMY [September 18, 1925]) headlining as the title character. The gentle *Tree in the Park* joined *Here in My Arms* and *The Blue Room* as top-selling Rodgers and Hart songs. Two other numbers are rather noteworthy: the early torch song *Where's That Rainbow* and the risqué *A Little Birdie Told Me So* (the birdie being the stork, which rhymes with New York).

BETSY

December 28, 1926

New Amsterdam Theatre • 39 performances
Music mostly by Rodgers (see Berlin: December 28, 1926); Lyrics mostly by Lorenz Hart; Book by Irving Caesar and David Freedman; Book revisions and Direction by Wm. Anthony McGuire; Produced by Florenz Ziegfeld, Jr.; With Belle Baker, Al Shean, and Dan Healy.

Published Songs

Come and Tell Me—cut

If I Were You—different than *If You Were You* from FLY WITH ME [March 24, 1920]; also used in LADY LUCK [April 27, 1927] and SHE'S MY BABY [January 3, 1928]

Sing—also used in LADY LUCK and LADY FINGERS [January 31, 1929]

Stonewall Moscowitz March [by Caesar, Hart, and Rodgers]

**This Funny World*

You're the Mother Type

After six quick hits in eighteen months, Rodgers and Hart met failure the night after the opening of PEGGY-ANN [December 27, 1926] with this Ziegfeldian showcase for vaudeville balladeer Belle Baker. The songwriters were rudely surprised opening night when Ziegfeld slipped in Irving Berlin's new *Blue Skies*; the song didn't help BETSY any, but it did all right by Berlin. Rodgers and Hart's contributions included one of their finest forgotten songs, the plaintive *This Funny World*. The drawing on the sheet music cover shows Ms. Baker tying strings around three slightly embarrassed gentlemen. The first two look disconcertingly like the composer and lyricist.

LADY LUCK

April 27, 1927

Carlton Theatre {London} •
324 performances
Music mostly by H. B. Hedley; Lyrics mostly by Greatrex Newman; Lyrics to Rodgers songs by Lorenz Hart; Book by Firth Shephard; With Laddie Cliff and Leslie Henson.

Published Songs

If I Were You—originally used in BETSY [December 28, 1926]; also used in SHE'S MY BABY [January 3, 1928]

Sing—originally used in BETSY; also used in LADY FINGERS [January 31, 1929]

LONDON PAVILION REVUE ◆ ONE DAM THING AFTER ANOTHER

May 20, 1927

London Pavilion {London} •
237 performances
Lyrics by Lorenz Hart; Book by Ronald Jeans; Directed by Frank Collins; Produced by Charles B. Cochran; With Jessie Matthews, Sonnie Hale, and Melville Cooper.

Published Songs

I Need Some Cooling Off—also used (unpublished) in SHE'S MY BABY [January 3, 1928]

My Heart Stood Still—also used in A CON-
NECTICUT YANKEE [November 3, 1927]
My Lucky Star—also used (unpublished) in
SHE'S MY BABY

Additional Songs Published (No Lyric) in Piano Selection

Danse Grotesque à la Nègre [instrumental]
Idles of the King—originally used in GARRICK
GAIETIES [2nd] [May 10, 1926]
Make Hey! Make Hey! While the Moon Shines
One Dam Thing after Another
Sandwich Girls
Shuffle

Rodgers and Hart returned to London with a
second hit musical. Among the songs was *My
Heart Stood Still*, inspired by the near-collision
of a Paris taxicab containing the songwriters.
The Prince of Wales—Edward, not Charles—
loved the song, so much so that he immediately
went out and requested it at a society dance. The
conductor didn't know it, so the Prince actually
hummed the song and taught it to the band. This
was front page news, naturally, and *My Heart
Stood Still* quickly became the boys' biggest
ballad hit. A second song from the show, the
gentle *My Lucky Star*, is also quite lovely but
long forgotten.

A CONNECTICUT YANKEE [1927]

November 3, 1927
Vanderbilt Theatre • 418 performances
Also see November 17, 1943. Lyrics by Lorenz
Hart; Book by Herbert Fields (based on *A
Connecticut Yankee in King Arthur's Court*
[novel] by Mark Twain); Directed by
Alexander Leftwich; Produced by Lew Fields
and Lyle D. Andrews; With William Gaxton,
Constance Carpenter, and June Cochrane.

Published Songs

I Blush—cut
I Feel at Home with You
My Heart Stood Still—originally used in
LONDON PAVILION REVUE [May 20,
1927]
On a Desert Island with Thee!
Someone Should Tell Them—cut; see AMERICA'S
SWEETHEART [February 10, 1931]
Thou Swell

Additional Songs Published (No Lyric) in Piano Selection

Here's a Toast
Nothing's Wrong

Another smashingly successful musical from
Rodgers, Hart, and Fields. A CONNECTICUT
YANKEE was Rodgers and Hart's eighth hit
show in three years. Unforeseeably, they were
to be without further Broadway success until
1936. The transatlantic song smash *My Heart
Stood Still* was joined by a second hit, the ana-
chronistically slangy *Thou Swell*. Hart, who had
displayed inventive rhyming skill all along,
began to exercise his talent for sustained comedy lyrics with the deft *I Feel at Home with You*
and *On a Desert Island with Thee!* Rodgers, meanwhile, wrote the first of his breathtaking waltzes,
Nothing's Wrong. (Only the music of this stun-
ner seems to exist; it is still hoped that the lyric
will turn up someday, somewhere.) Rodgers was
to develop a distinctive, sweeping waltz style
resulting in a dozen classics (*Lover; The Most
Beautiful Girl in the World; Out of My Dreams;
It's a Grand Night for Singing; Hello, Young Lovers*, and more).

SHE'S MY BABY

January 3, 1928
Globe Theatre • 71 performances
Lyrics by Lorenz Hart; Book by Guy Bolton,
Bert Kalmar, and Harry Ruby; Directed by
Edward Royce; Produced by Charles B.
Dillingham; With Beatrice Lillie, Clifton
Webb, Jack Whiting, and Irene Dunne.

Published Songs

A Baby's Best Friend (Is Her Mother)
How Was I to Know?—cut; see HEADS UP!
[November 11, 1929]
If I Were You—cut; originally used in BETSY
[December 28, 1926] and LADY LUCK
[April 27, 1927]
I Need Some Cooling Off—originally used in
(and only published as from) LONDON
PAVILION REVUE [May 29, 1927]
A Little House in Soho—revised lyric for *A
Tiny Flat Near Soho Square* from LIDO
LADY [December 1, 1926]

Morning Is Midnight—cut; originally used in
LIDO LADY

My Lucky Star—originally used in (and only
published as from) LONDON PAVILION
REVUE

When I Go on the Stage [2nd]—different than
song from YOU'LL NEVER KNOW [April
20, 1921]

Whoopsie!

You're What I Need

Rodgers and Hart were no more successful with
Beatrice Lillie's unique talents than Vincent Youmans had been on OH, PLEASE! [Youmans: December 17, 1926]; both composers found her difficult to please and were unable to suit her special
performing style. Rodgers and Hart eventually did
come up with a Lillie gem, *Rhythm*, for the British revue PLEASE! [November 16, 1933].

PRESENT ARMS!
April 26, 1928
Mansfield Theatre • 155 performances
Lyrics by Lorenz Hart; Book by Herbert
Fields; Directed by Alexander Leftwich;
Produced by Lew Fields; With Charles King,
Flora LeBreton, Busby Berkeley, and Joyce
Barbour.

Published Songs
*Blue Ocean Blues—new lyric for *Atlantic
Blues* from LIDO LADY [December 1, 1926]
Crazy Elbows
*Do I Hear You Saying (*I Love You*)
Down by the Sea
I'm a Fool, Little One
A Kiss for Cinderella
**You Took Advantage of Me

Additional Song Published (No Lyric) in Piano Selection
Tell It to the Marines

While Rodgers and Hart were off in London work-
ing on LIDO LADY [December 26, 1926] and LON-
DON PAVILION REVUE [May 29, 1927], Herb
Fields had scored a monumental hit with his first
non–Rodgers and Hart effort, HIT THE DECK
[Youmans: April 25, 1927]. That musical had a
Navy motif; the weaker PRESENT ARMS! did
the same for the Marines. The score contained

another comic hit, *You Took Advantage of Me* (a
distant relative, musically, of *You're the Mother
Type* from BETSY [December 28, 1926]). Also
included were two pleasant boy/girl duets with
snappy music, *Do I Hear You Saying* and *I'm a
Fool, Little One*.

CHEE-CHEE
September 25, 1928
Mansfield Theatre • 31 performances
Lyrics by Lorenz Hart; Book by Herbert Fields
(based on *The Son of the Grand Eunuch* [novel]
by Charles Petit); Directed by Alexander
Leftwich; Produced by Lew Fields; With
Helen Ford, Betty Starbuck, Philip Loeb, and
William Williams.

Published Songs
Better Be Good to Me
Dear, Oh Dear!
*I Must Love You—see SIMPLE SIMON
[February 18, 1930]
Moon of My Delight
*Singing a Love Song—see SIMPLE SIMON
The Tartar Song

Rodgers, Hart, and Fields, who had broken new
ground with PEGGY-ANN [December 27, 1926],
decided to try something new—and CHEE-CHEE
certainly was: Broadway's first Chinese castration
musical. After a stony reception it was quickly
terminated, as was Rodgers and Hart's decade-
long relationship with Herb and Lew Fields. *Singing a Love Song* and *I Must Love You* are quite
pleasant, though, and were soon reused elsewhere. Herb soon found a new partner: FIFTY
MILLION FRENCHMEN [Porter: November 27,
1929] was the first of seven-out-of-seven hits he
wrote with Cole Porter. Lew's final book musical was the aptly titled HELLO, DADDY! [Decem-
ber 26, 1928]—written by Herbert and Dorothy,
with composer Jimmy McHugh.

LADY FINGERS
January 31, 1929
Vanderbilt Theatre • 132 performances
Music mostly by Joseph Meyers; Lyrics
mostly by Edward Eliscu; Lyrics to Rodgers
songs by Lorenz Hart; Book by Eddie Buzzell
(based on *Easy Come, Easy Go* [play] by Owen

Davis); Directed by Lew Levenson; Produced by Lyle D. Andrews; With Eddie Buzzell and John Price Jones.

Published Songs

I Love You More Than Yesterday
Sing—originally used in BETSY [December 28, 1926]; also used in LADY LUCK [April 27, 1927]

SPRING IS HERE
March 11, 1929
Alvin Theatre • 104 performances
Lyrics by Lorenz Hart; Book by Owen Davis (based on *Shotgun Wedding* [play] by Owen Davis); Directed by Alexander Leftwich; Produced by Alex A. Aarons and Vinton Freedley; With Glenn Hunter, Lillian Taiz, and Charles Ruggles.

Published Songs

Baby's Awake Now
The Color of Her Eyes—cut; for initial publication see EVER GREEN [December 3, 1930]
Rich Man, Poor Man
**Why Can't I?*
**With a Song in My Heart*
You Never Say Yes
Yours Sincerely

Additional Song Recorded

Spring Is Here (In Person) [1st]—different than hit song from I MARRIED AN ANGEL [May 11, 1938]

Rodgers and Hart moved from producer Lew Fields to the Gershwins' Aarons and Freedley for two inconsequential 1929 musicals. SPRING IS HERE featured yet another one of Rodgers and Hart's biggest hits, *With a Song in My Heart*. Also in the score were two lovely, long-forgotten songs, *Baby's Awake Now* and the exquisite *Why Can't I?* The title song was *not* the superb *Spring Is Here*; that one came later, in I MARRIED AN ANGEL.

HEADS UP!
November 11, 1929
Alvin Theatre • 144 performances
Lyrics by Lorenz Hart; Book by John McGowan and Paul Gerard Smith; Produced by Alex A. Aarons and Vinton Freedley; With Jack Whiting, Barbara Newberry, Victor Moore, Betty Starbuck, and Ray Bolger. Pre-Broadway title: ME FOR YOU.

Published Songs

As Though You Were There—cut; initial publication in 1940 as non-show song
I Can Do Wonders with You—cut; also used in SIMPLE SIMON [February 18, 1930]
It Must Be Heaven
Me for You!
My Man Is on the Make
**A Ship without a Sail*
Sky City—cut
Why Do You Suppose?—new lyric for *How Was I to Know?* (cut) from SHE'S MY BABY [January 3, 1928]

Additional Songs Published (No Lyric) in British Piano Selection

Daughter Grows Older
Knees

As with Aarons and Freedley's SMARTY (see FUNNY FACE [Gershwin: November 22, 1927]), ME FOR YOU—with a book by Owen Davis of SPRING IS HERE [March 11, 1929]—had grave tryout problems. Drastic surgery was performed, but HEADS UP!—unlike FUNNY FACE—failed to respond, even with FUNNY FACE funny man Victor Moore in attendance. There was yet another stunning song, though, the unrequited love song *A Ship without a Sail*.

SIMPLE SIMON
February 18, 1930
Ziegfeld Theatre • 135 performances
Lyrics by Lorenz Hart; Book by Ed Wynn and Guy Bolton; Directed by Zeke Colvan; Produced by Florenz Ziegfeld, Jr.; With Ed Wynn, Ruth Etting, Bobbe Arnst, and Harriet Hoctor.

Published Songs

Don't Tell Your Folks
**He Dances on My Ceiling (Dancing on the Ceiling)*—cut; also used in EVER GREEN [December 3, 1930]
**He Was Too Good to Me*—cut

I Can Do Wonders with You—cut; originally used (cut) in HEADS UP! [November 11, 1929]

I Still Believe in You—cut; new lyric for *Singing a Love Song* from CHEE-CHEE [September 25, 1928]

Send for Me—new lyric for *I Must Love You* from CHEE-CHEE

Sweetenheart

***Ten Cents a Dance*

With the stock market crashed and five consecutive failures to their credit, Rodgers and Hart could not afford to turn down Ziegfeld's offer (despite their troubles with BETSY [December 28, 1926]) and undertook this Ed Wynn vehicle. Matters turned out little better. The score included another three superb songs. (The boys turned them out in a steady stream, didn't they!) *He Dances on My Ceiling*, light as air, was cut but quickly found a better life. *He Was Too Good to Me*, another stunning song of lost love, was cut and forgotten. And then there's *Ten Cents a Dance*, a heart-tugging character study with which songwriter Rodgers began his transformation into America's top musical dramatist.

EVER GREEN
December 3, 1930
Adelphi Theatre {London} •
    254 performances
Lyrics by Lorenz Hart; Book by Benn W. Levy (based on an idea by Rodgers and Hart); Directed by Frank Collins; Produced by Charles B. Cochran; With Jessie Matthews, Sonny Hale, and Joyce Barbour.

Published Songs
The Colour of Her Eyes—issued as professional copy; revised lyric for *The Color of Her Eyes* (cut; unpublished) from SPRING IS HERE [March 11, 1929]

***Dancing on the Ceiling*—new title for *He Dances on My Ceiling*, originally used (cut) in SIMPLE SIMON [February 18, 1930]

Dear! Dear!

Harlemania—issued as professional copy

If I Give in to You

In the Cool of the Evening

**No Place but Home*

Additional Songs Published (No Lyric) in Piano Selection
Lovely Woman's Ever Young
When the Old World Was New

The successful EVER GREEN—buoyed by the popularity of the formerly discarded *Dancing on the Ceiling*—was Rodgers and Hart's only theatrical oasis over a long dry spell. Of particular interest in the score are the enthrallingly romantic *No Place but Home* and, for zealous Hart enthusiasts, *The Colour of Her Eyes*, one of the first of his tart "battle-of-the-sexes" comedy duets.

AMERICA'S SWEETHEART
February 10, 1931
Broadhurst Theatre • 135 performances
Lyrics by Lorenz Hart; Book by Herbert Fields; Directed by Monty Woolley; Produced by Lawrence Schwab and Frank Mandel; With Harriette Lake (Ann Southern), Jack Whiting, and Jean Aubert.

Published Songs
How about It?

**I've Got Five Dollars*

I Want a Man—revised lyric for song used in LIDO LADY [December 1, 1926], which was a revised lyric for a song written for WINKLE TOWN [circa 1922]

A Lady Must Live

There's So Much More—revised lyric for *Someone Should Tell Them* from A CONNECTICUT YANKEE [1927] [November 3, 1927]

We'll Be the Same

Additional Songs Recorded
In Californ-i-a
Innocent Chorus Girls of Yesterday
Mr. Dolan Is Passing Through
My Sweet
Now I Believe—cut

Rodgers, Hart, and Fields met up in Hollywood and decided to return to Broadway with this satire on the movie business. The show fizzled and it was back to the Coast. The trip was worthwhile, though, if only for the carefree, Depression-rouser *I've Got Five Dollars* and the outspoken *A Lady Must Live*. Rodgers and Hart remained in Hollywood until 1935, their film out-put including the 1932 *Love Me Tonight* (where Rodgers first worked with Rouben Mamoulian) and the 1933 *Hallelulah, I'm a Bum*. Both films are notable for the close integration of music and dialogue (and wonderful songs like *Mimi, **Lover*, and **Isn't It Romantic?* from the former, and *You Are Too Beautiful* from the latter). The rest of their Hollywood stay found them work-ing on negligible projects, with a few notable songs along the way: *Tell Me I Know How to Love* (1933), *Blue Moon* (1934), and *It's Easy to Remember* (1935).

CRAZY QUILT
May 19, 1931
44th Street Theatre • 79 performances
Music mostly by Harry Warren; Lyrics mostly by Mort Dixon, Billy Rose, and others; Sketches by David Freedman; Produced and Directed by Billy Rose; With Fanny Brice (Rose), Phil Baker, and Ted Healy.

Published Songs
None

For *Second-Hand* Fanny Brice Rose (*of Washing-ton Square*), Rodgers and Hart supplied *Rest-Room Rose*. (Cole Porter tried *Hot-House Rose*, but Brice rejected it.)

PLEASE!
November 16, 1933
Savoy Theatre {London} • 108 performances
Music mostly by Vivian Ellis and Austin Croom-Johnson; Lyrics mostly by Dion Titheradge; Lyric to Rodgers song by Lorenz Hart; Book by Dion Titheradge and Robert Macgunigle; Directed by Dion Titheradge; Produced by André Charlot; With Beatrice Lillie and Lupino Lane.

Recorded Song
Rhythm—also used in THE SHOW IS ON [December 25, 1936]

Rodgers and Hart supplied this very special material for the special Lillie, a mini-medley of rhythm songs which punctured most of them.

SOMETHING GAY
April 29, 1935
Morosco Theatre • 72 performances
Play by Adelaide Heilbron; Lyric by Lorenz Hart; Directed by Thomas Mitchell; Produced by the Messrs. Shubert; With Tallulah Bankhead and Walter Pidgeon.

Published Song
You Are So Lovely and I'm So Lonely

JUMBO
November 16, 1935
Hippodrome Theatre • 233 performances
Lyrics by Lorenz Hart; Book by Ben Hecht and Charles MacArthur; Book directed by George Abbott; Staged by John Murray Anderson; Produced by Billy Rose; With Jimmy Durante, Gloria Grafton, Donald Novis, and Paul Whiteman.

Published Songs
The Circus on Parade
Diavolo
**Little Girl Blue*
**The Most Beautiful Girl in the World*
My Romance
Over and over Again—song version of *Party Waltz* [instrumental] (cut, unpublished) from 1934 movie *Hollywood Party*

Additional Song Recorded
Women

Rodgers and Hart returned to New York to work on a ballet-versus-jazz musical, a proposed movie project which Fred Astaire had turned down. In the meantime, though, Billy Rose approached the pair to write songs for his jumbo circus extrava-ganza. John Murray Anderson, director of DEAREST ENEMY [September 18, 1925], was the musical comedy veteran on hand. Ben Hecht and Charles MacArthur were writing their first musi-cal, and farce playwright/director George Abbott was hired to stage the book (*his* first musical assignment). Everything about JUMBO was gar-gantuan, including Durante's elephantine costar "Big Rosie" and the costs that ultimately over-took the show and closed it. (The four-month run was shorter than the number of perfor-mances indicate, as JUMBO played twelve performances a week.) Rodgers provided one of his most beautiful waltzes, *The Most Beautiful Girl in the World*, and the stunning unrequited love-song *Little Girl Blue*—which includes a waltz interlude as well, during which the girls on the flying trapezes flew in.

ON YOUR TOES
April 11, 1936
Imperial Theatre • 315 performances
Lyrics by Lorenz Hart; Book by Rodgers and Hart and George Abbott; Directed by Worthington Minor; Choreographed by George Balanchine; Produced by Dwight Deere Wiman; With Ray Bolger, Tamara Geva (Balanchine), Luella Gear, Monty Woolley, and Doris Carson.

Revivals
October 11, 1954
46th Street Theatre • 64 performances
Directed and Produced by George Abbott; Choreographed by George Balanchine; With Vera Zorina [Geva] and Bobby Van [Bolger], Elaine Stritch [Gear], and Ben Astar [Woolley].

March 6, 1983
Virginia Theatre • 505 performances
Directed by George Abbott; Original ballet choreography by George Balanchine; Additional ballet choreography by Peter Martins; Musical numbers choreographed by Donald Saddler; With Natalia Makarova [Geva]; Lara Teeter [Bolger]; Dina Merrill [Gear], and George S. Irving [Woolley].

Published Songs
**Glad to Be Unhappy*
The Heart Is Quicker Than the Eye
It's Got to Be Love
On Your Toes
Quiet Night
**Slaughter on Tenth Avenue* [ballet]—issued in
    separate edition
There's a Small Hotel
Too Good for the Average Man

Additional Songs Published In Vocal
    Score of 1983 Revival Version
La Princess Zenobia [ballet]
The Three Bs
Two-a-Day for Keith

The non–Fred Astaire project turned into one of the finer Rodgers and Hart shows, with Ray Bolger and ballerina Tamara Geva memorable in the leads. (Marilyn Miller was announced to costar. She turned down the part, though, and as it happened died four days before TOES opened, at the age of thirty-seven.) With ON YOUR TOES, Rodgers and Hart embarked on a remarkable string of quality musicals, abetted by a strong team of collaborators. Producer (and farm machinery heir) Dwight Deere Wiman (see THE LITTLE SHOW [Schwartz: April 30, 1929]) presented five Rodgers and Hart "spring" musicals over the next seven years. Colibrettist George Abbott wrote, directed, and produced four Rodgers and Hart hits. Wiman's set designer, Jo Mielziner, became Rodgers's designer of choice for the next twenty years. Musical comedy novice George Balanchine —who contributed two integrally plotted ballets (including the legendary *Slaughter on Tenth Avenue*)—did four hit Rodgers and Hart musicals. (Hart took Balanchine, Geva, and Zorina to agent "Doc" Bender.) Along with *Slaughter*, Rodgers and Hart sparkled with *Glad to Be Unhappy*, *There's a Small Hotel*, *The Heart Is Quicker Than the Eye*, and *It's Got to Be Love*. ON YOUR TOES enjoyed two Broadway revivals; Abbott directed both, the second at the age of ninety-two.

THE SHOW IS ON
December 25, 1936
Winter Garden Theate • 237 performances
Music mostly by Vernon Duke (see Duke: December 25, 1936; also Arlen, Gershwin, and Schwartz); Lyric to Rodgers song by Lorenz Hart; Sketches mostly by David Freedman and Moss Hart; Directed by Vincente Minnelli; Produced by Lee Shubert; With Beatrice Lillie and Bert Lahr.

Recorded Song
Rhythm—originally used in PLEASE!
    [November 16, 1933]

BABES IN ARMS
April 14, 1937
Shubert Theatre • 289 performances
Lyrics by Lorenz Hart; Book by Rodgers and Hart; Directed by Robert Sinclair; Choreo-

graphed by George Balanchine; Produced by Dwight Deere Wiman; With Mitzi Green, Ray Heatherton, Wynn Murray, Alfred Drake, and the Nicholas Brothers.

Revival
March 30, 1959
Royal Poinciana Playhouse {Palm Beach, Fla.} • Stock production
Book by George Oppenheimer; With Julie Wilson [Green] and Brian Davies [Heatherton].

Concert Version
February 11, 1999
City Center • 5 performances
Directed and Choreographed by Kathleen Marshall; Produced by City Center Encores; With David Campbell (Heatherton), Erin Dilly (Green), and Melissa Rain Anderson (Murray).

Published Songs
All at Once
All Dark People
Babes in Arms
*I Wish I Were in Love Again
*Johnny One Note
*The Lady Is a Tramp
*My Funny Valentine
Way out West
**Where or When

Additional Song Published in Vocal Score of 1959 Stock Version
Imagine

Additional Song Recorded
You Are So Fair

Coming off the very good ON YOUR TOES [April 11, 1936], Rodgers and Hart wrote their most hit-laden score. Rodgers was to have other charmed periods in his career, but the late 1930s showed Hart at the very top of his form with two brilliant ballads, *Where or When?* and *My Funny Valentine* (after writing the song, they changed the hero character's name to Val); a top-flight charm song in *I Wish I Were in Love Again*; and the twin powerhouse knockouts *Johnny One Note* and *The Lady Is a Tramp*. This score is good, even by today's standards. Rodgers and Hart also provided the libretto, the one about the group of kids getting together to put on a show. Somebody's father had a barn.

I'D RATHER BE RIGHT
November 2, 1937
Alvin Theatre • 290 performances
Lyrics by Lorenz Hart; Book by George S. Kaufman and Moss Hart; Directed by George S. Kaufman; Produced by Sam H. Harris; With George M. Cohan, Joy Hodges, and Austin Marshall.

Published Songs
*Ev'rybody Loves You—issued as professional copy only; subsequently published in non-show folio
*Have You Met Miss Jones?
I'd Rather Be Right (Don't Have to Know Much) [1st]—cut; see TWO WEEKS WITH PAY [June 24, 1940]
I'd Rather Be Right (Than Influential) [2nd]
Sweet Sixty-Five
Take and Take and Take

Additional Song Recorded
Off the Record

Author/director George S. Kaufman and producer Sam Harris decided to attempt another political satire along the lines of their OF THEE I SING [Gershwin: December 26, 1931]. The casting of George M. Cohan as Franklin D. Roosevelt made I'D RATHER BE RIGHT a highly awaited event: the "Yankee Doodle Boy" had been absent from the musical stage for a decade and was performing his first non-Cohan score. However, Cohan hated Rodgers and Hart; "Gilbert and Sullivan" he called them. What he called Roosevelt in private is unknown, but the outspoken Cohan interpolated pro–Al Smith lyrics while Rodgers and Hart weren't listening. (Cohan was high on Broadway's most-hated list. When donations were sought for his statue in Times Square, few professionals contributed.) I'D RATHER BE RIGHT was weak in book, score, and satire; the big-name package sold enough tickets for success, though. The sweetly melodic ballad *Have You Met Miss Jones?* was a moderate hit. Two other worthy songs were cut and remain neglected: the charming *I'd Rather Be Right* [1st] and the team's second tender lullaby, *Ev'rybody Loves You*, which is in a class with the equally obscure 1926 *Sleepyhead* (see THE GIRL FRIEND [March 17, 1926]).

I MARRIED AN ANGEL
May 11, 1938
Shubert Theatre • 338 performances
Lyrics by Lorenz Hart; Book by Rodgers and
Hart (based on a play by John Vaszary);
Directed by Joshua Logan; Choreographed by
George Balanchine; Produced by Dwight
Deere Wiman; With Dennis King, Vera Zorina
(Balanchine), Vivienne Segal, and Walter
Slezak.

Published Songs
At the Roxy Music Hall—issued as professional
copy only; subsequently published in non-
show folio
Did You Ever Get Stung?
How to Win Friends and Influence People
I'll Tell the Man in the Street
I Married an Angel—initial use of song written
for unproduced 1933 film version
**Spring Is Here* [2nd]—different than song
(unpublished) from SPRING IS HERE
[March 11, 1929]
A Twinkle in Your Eye

Additional Song Recorded
Angel without Wings

The angelic Vera Zorina charmed Broadway in
this happy, comic-fantasy hit. Zorina had played
the lead in the London production [February 5,
1937] of ON YOUR TOES [April 11, 1936], winning Tamara Geva's part in the 1939 film version
(and Geva's husband Balanchine, too). I MAR-
RIED AN ANGEL originated as an aborted 1933
Rodgers & Hart and Hart (Moss) project for
Jeanette MacDonald at MGM. Several years later
Rodgers and Hart (Larry) obtained the rights and
wrote the piece as a stage musical (with their own
libretto). The score included the lovely, lonely
Spring Is Here; *A Twinkle in Your Eye*, a good
comedy number harking back to *A Little Birdie
Told Me So* from PEGGY-ANN [December 27,
1926]; the wild comic novelty *At the Roxy Music Hall*; and the lovely *Angel without Wings*.
Operetta stars Dennis King and Vivienne Segal,
of Friml's THE THREE MUSKETEERS [March
13,1928], were reunited; the surprise was Segal,
now a first-rate musical comedienne. The Wiman
production team included not only Balanchine
and Jo Mielziner but also up-and-coming director Joshua Logan. (P.S.: ANGEL ended up back
at MGM with Jeanette MacDonald, who starred
in the mediocre 1942 movie version, which used
only three Rodgers and Hart songs.)

THE BOYS FROM SYRACUSE
November 23, 1938
Alvin Theatre • 235 performances
Lyrics by Lorenz Hart; Book by George
Abbott (based on *The Comedy of Errors* [play]
by William Shakespeare); Directed by George
Abbott; Choreographed by George Balanchine;
Produced by George Abbott; With Eddie
Albert, Ronald Graham, Teddy Hart, Jimmy
Savo, Muriel Angelus, Wynn Murray, and
Marcy Westcott.

Revival
April 15, 1963
Theatre Four {Off Broadway} •
502 performances
Directed by Christopher Hewett; With Stuart
Damon [Albert], Clifford David [Graham],
Rudy Tronto [Hart], Danny Carroll [Savo],
Ellen Hanley [Angelus], Karen Morrow
[Murray], and Julienne Marie [Westcott].

Concert Version
May 1, 1997
City Center • 5 performances
Directed by Susan H. Schulman; Choreo-
graphed by Kathleen Marshall; Produced by
City Center Encores; With Davis Gaines
[Albert], Malcolm Gets [Graham], Michael
McGrath [Hart], Mario Cantone [Savo],
Rebecca Luker [Angelus], Debbie (Shapiro)
Gravitte [Murray], and Sarah Uriarte Berry
[Westcott].

Published Songs
**Falling in Love with Love*
Oh, Diogenes!
The Shortest Day of the Year
Sing for Your Supper
**This Can't Be Love*
Who Are You?—written for 1940 movie version
You Have Cast Your Shadow on the Sea

Additional Songs Published in Vocal Score of 1963 Revival Version
Big Brother
Come with Me

Dear Old Syracuse
He and She
*I Had Twins
Ladies of the Evening
*What Can You Do with a Man?

Additional Songs Recorded
Big Brother Ballet
Let Antipholus In

Larry Hart's younger brother Teddy bore a striking resemblance to burlesque comic Jimmy Savo.
When Rodgers and Hart began looking at Shakespeare for source material, this potentially perfect casting made *The Comedy of Errors* (about
two sets of twins) the obvious choice. They continued their association with George Abbott,
Broadway's top farce man: the result was a
sparklingly perfect BOYS FROM SYRACUSE.
The excellent score is hard to beat: two remarkable love songs, *You Have Cast Your Shadow on
the Sea* and *The Shortest Day of the Year*; another
remarkable song of unrequited love, *Falling in
Love with Love*; yet another remarkable song, the
swinging *Sing for Your Supper*; two first-rate up-
tempo numbers, *This Can't Be Love* and *Dear Old
Syracuse*; and a pair of prickly war-of-the-sexes
duets. Abbott's less-than-satisfying experiences
with dilettante producers (like Dwight Wiman)
led him to begin producing his own shows. With
SYRACUSE he moved into the musical field, soon
to be joined by Rodgers.

TOO MANY GIRLS
October 18, 1939
Imperial Theatre • 249 performances
Lyrics by Lorenz Hart; Book by George
Marion, Jr.; Directed by George Abbott;
Choreographed by Robert Alton; Produced by
George Abbott; With Marcy Westcott,
Richard Kollmar, Desi Arnaz, Eddie Bracken,
and Mary Jane Walsh.

Published Songs
All Dressed Up, Spic and Spanish
*Give It Back to the Indians
**I Didn't Know What Time It Was
*I Like to Recognize the Tune
Love Never Went to College
She Could Shake the Maracas
You're Nearer—written for 1940 movie version

Additional Song Published in Non-show Folio
'Cause We Got Cake

Additional Songs Recorded
Heroes in the Fall
Look Out
My Prince
Pottawatomie
Sweethearts of the Team
Tempt Me Not
Too Many Girls

Abbott earned a reputation for fast-paced,
youthful entertainments like this college football
musical. Though not up to the high Rodgers and
Hart caliber, TOO MANY GIRLS was enjoyable
enough to achieve hit status. Hart's years of
drinking and dissipation had begun to catch up
with him, though, and he was growing increasingly unreliable; Rodgers occasionally had to
ghost write lyrics during Hart's absences. But
once he got started, Hart was as good as ever.
GIRLS included two knockout comedy songs,
Give It Back to the Indians and *I Like to Recognize the Tune*. There were also two strong ballads,
Love Never Went to College and the haunting *I
Didn't Know What Time It Was. You're Nearer*,
a third tender ballad, was written for the 1940
film version. Abbott took most of his youthful
cast, including Cuban émigré Desi Arnaz, to
Hollywood. Leading lady Marcy Westcott—who
introduced *I Didn't Know What Time It Was,
This Can't Be Love*, and *You Have Cast Your
Shadow on the Sea*—was replaced by nonsinging
starlet Lucille Ball.

HIGHER AND HIGHER
April 4, 1940
Shubert Theatre • 108 performances
Lyrics by Lorenz Hart; Book by Gladys
Hurlbut and Joshua Logan (based on an idea
by Irvin Pincus); Directed by Joshua Logan;
Produced by Dwight Deere Wiman; With Jack
Haley, Shirley Ross, Marta Eggerth, Leif
Erickson, and Lee Dixon.

Published Songs
Ev'ry Sunday Afternoon
From Another World

**It Never Entered My Mind*
Nothing but You

Additional Songs Published in Non-show Folio
Disgustingly Rich
It's a Lovely Day for a Murder—different than
What a Lovely Day for a Wedding from
ALLEGRO [October 10, 1947]

Additional Songs Recorded
A Barking Baby Never Bites
Blue Monday
How's Your Health?
I'm Afraid
Life! Liberty!—cut
Morning's at Seven
Pretty in the City—cut

HIGHER AND HIGHER was written as a vehicle
for Vera Zorina, who wisely opted for LOUISI-
ANA PURCHASE [Berlin: May 8, 1940] and playing against Gaxton and Moore instead of Sharkey,
HIGHER AND HIGHER's scene-stealing seal. The
show was rather negligible, with what might be
Rodgers and Hart's blandest score—except for
one of their very finest songs, the stunning *It
Never Entered My Mind*. (*From Another World*
starts well but kind of fizzles out.) The 1943 film
version—a vehicle for young pop singing sensation Frank Sinatra—retained only one of the
songs, *Disgustingly Rich*.

TWO WEEKS WITH PAY
June 24, 1940
Ridgeway Theatre {White Plains, N.Y.} •
   Summer stock tryout
Music and Lyrics mostly by others; Lyrics to
Rodgers song by Lorenz Hart; Sketches by
Charles Sherman and others; Created and
Conceived by Ted Fetter and Richard Lewine;
Directed by Felix Jacoves; Choreographed by
Gene Kelly; Produced by Dorothy and Julien
Olney; With Bill Johnson, Marie Nash, Hiram
Sherman, and Pat Harrington.

Recorded Song
*Now That I Know You—new lyric for *I'd
   Rather Be Right* (*Don't Have to Know Much*)
   [1st] (cut) from I'D RATHER BE RIGHT
   [November 2, 1937]

This summer stock revue featured leftover songs
by several composers. The compilers were minor
songwriters (Ted Fetter and Richard Lewine) with
major cousins (Cole Porter and Dick Rodgers).
Rodgers and Hart rewrote their unused title song
from I'D RATHER BE RIGHT, while people like
Arlen and Porter sent over previously used songs
like *Will You Love Me Monday Morning?* from LIFE
BEGINS AT 8:40 [Arlen: August 27, 1934] and *Just
Another Page from Your Diary* from LEAVE IT TO
ME! [Porter: November 9, 1938]. TWO WEEKS
WITH PAY closed after two weeks. The dances
were staged by Gene Kelly—from the chorus of
LEAVE IT TO ME!—who had already been cast
in the next Rodgers and Hart musical.

PAL JOEY
December 25, 1940
Ethel Barrymore Theatre • 374 performances
"A Gaily Sophisticated Musical Comedy."
Lyrics by Lorenz Hart; Book by John O'Hara
(based on stories by John O'Hara); Directed by
George Abbott; Choreographed by Robert
Alton; Produced by George Abbott; With
Vivienne Segal, Gene Kelly, June Havoc, Jack
Durant, and Jean Casto.

Revivals
January 2, 1952
Broadhurst Theatre • 542 performances
Directed by David Alexander; Choreographed
by Robert Alton; Produced by Jule Styne and
Leonard Key in association with Anthony
Brady Farrell; With Vivienne Segal, Harold
Lang [Kelly], Helen Gallagher [Havoc], Lionel
Stander [Durant], and Elaine Stritch [Casto].

May 31, 1961
City Center • 31 performances
Directed by Gus Schirmer, Jr.; Choreographed
by Ralph Beaumont; Produced by City Center
Light Opera Company; With Bob Fosse [Kelly],
Carol Bruce [Segal], and Elaine Stritch [Casto].

June 27, 1976
Circle in the Square Uptown Theatre •
   73 performances
Directed by Theodore Mann; Choreographed
by Margo Sappington; With Joan Copeland
[Segal], Christopher Chadman [Kelly], Janie
Sell [Havoc], and Dixie Carter [Casto].

Concert Version
May 4, 1995
City Center • 4 performances
Adapted by Terrence McNally; Directed by
Lonny Price; Produced by City Center En-
cores; With Patti LuPone [Segal], Peter
Gallagher [Kelly], Bebe Neuwirth [Casto], and
Vicki Lewis [Havoc].

Published Songs
**Bewitched* (*Bothered and Bewildered*)
Do It the Hard Way
Happy Hunting Horn—initial individual
    publication upon use in 1952 revival
I Could Write a Book
Plant You Now, Dig You Later
Take Him—initial individual publication upon
    use in 1952 revival
**What Is a Man?*—initial individual publica-
    tion upon use in 1952 revival
**You Mustn't Kick It Around*
Zip—initial individual publication upon use in
    1962 movie version

Additional Song Published in Non-show Folio
**Den of Iniquity*

Additional Songs Published in 1962 Vocal Score
The Flower Garden of My Heart
A Great Big Town (*Chicago*)
Pal Joey (*What Do I Care for a Dame?*)
Pal Joey Ballet [instrumental]
That Terrific Rainbow

Additional Song Recorded
I'm Talking to My Pal—cut

Rodgers, Hart, O'Hara, and producer/director/
book doctor Abbott brought a new level of realism
to the musical theatre with PAL JOEY. (Abbott was
no doubt influenced by his classic melodrama
Broadway [September 16, 1926], which had many
similar elements.) Reaction was cautious, with a
considerable segment of the audience alienated by
the heel of a hero. Gene Kelly had been acclaimed
for his performance in Saroyan's *The Time of Your
Life* [October 25, 1939]; the cynical anti-heroine
Vera was written for operetta star-turned-come-
dienne Vivienne Segal. Both roles were well cast,
well written, and impeccably performed. Rodgers

and Hart provided a properly cynical score, with
top-notch book songs—*Bewitched, I Could Write
a Book, What Is a Man?, Den of Iniquity*—and a
passel of delectable dance-oriented numbers. PAL
JOEY met with far greater success when revived
by composer-turned-producer Jule Styne in 1952.
As for Gene Kelly, he left JOEY to choreograph
Abbott and Rodgers's BEST FOOT FORWARD
[Martin: October 1, 1941] before hitting Hollywood. He returned to Broadway only once, to
direct Rodgers's FLOWER DRUM SONG [Decem-
ber 1, 1958].

BEST FOOT FORWARD
October 1, 1941
Ethel Barrymore Theatre • 326 performances
"A Modern Musical Comedy." Music and Lyrics
mostly by Hugh Martin and Ralph Blane (see
Martin: October 1, 1941); Book by John Cecil
Holm; Directed by George Abbott; Choreo-
graphed by Gene Kelly; Produced by George
Abbott; With Rosemary Lane, Nancy Walker,
Gil Stratton, Jr., and June Allyson.

Song Recorded
The Guy Who Brought Me [music by Rodgers,
    lyric by Rodgers and Martin; credited to
    Martin and Blane]

Larry Hart's deteriorating condition caused
Rodgers to look to his future. Observing George
Abbott's success as producer of THE BOYS
FROM SYRACUSE [November 23, 1938], TOO
MANY GIRLS [October 18, 1939], and PAL JOEY
[December 25, 1940], Rodgers determined that he,
too, should move into production. When Abbott
undertook BEST FOOT FORWARD—composed
by Hugh Martin, vocal arranger of SYRACUSE and
TOO MANY GIRLS—Rodgers signed on as silent
producing partner. (He also ghost wrote a song for
the show.) Rodgers similarly served as unbilled
producer on Abbott's next musical, BEAT THE
BAND [October 14, 1942], composed by Johnny
Green (conductor of BY JUPITER [June 2, 1942]).

BY JUPITER
June 2, 1942
Shubert Theatre • 427 performances
Lyrics by Lorenz Hart; Book by Rodgers and
Hart (based on *The Warrior's Husband* [play]

by Julian F. Thompson); Directed by Joshua Logan; Produced by Dwight Deere Wiman and Rodgers, in association with Richard Kollmar; With Ray Bolger, Constance Moore, Ronald Graham, and Benay Venuta. Pre-Broadway title: ALL'S FAIR.

Revival
January 19, 1967
Theatre Four {Off Broadway} •
    118 performances
Additional material by Fred Ebb; Directed by Christopher Hewett; With Bob Dishy [Bolger] and Sheila Sullivan [Moore].

Published Songs
*Careless Rhapsody
*Ev'rything I've Got
Here's a Hand
Jupiter Forbid
Nobody's Heart (*Ride Amazon Ride!*)
*Wait till You See Her

Additional Songs Recorded
Bottoms Up
The Boy I Left behind Me
Finale Act One (*No, Mother, No*)
Fool Meets Fool—cut
For Jupiter and Greece
In the Gateway of the Temple of Minerva
Life Was Monotonous—cut
Life with Father
Nothing to Do but Relax—cut
Now That I've Got My Strength

Ray Bolger returned from Hollywood (where he had made *The Wizard of Oz*, among other films) to star in this wartime hit. Bolger's performance was enough to ensure success despite uneven material. Hart's condition had deteriorated to the point that much of the score was written when he was confined to the hospital between binges; Rodgers rented the adjoining patient room and moved in. They nevertheless came up with one stunning ballad, the rhapsodic *Careless Rhapsody*; a gentle waltz/love song, *Wait till You See Her*; and a very good comedy/insult duet, *Ev'rything I've Got*. Rodgers's name officially went over the title as producer for the first time; he was to be one of Broadway's most successful producers for the next twenty years. But BY JUPITER was pretty much the end of Rodgers and Hart.

OKLAHOMA!
March 31, 1943
St. James Theatre • 2,248 performances
Book and Lyrics by Oscar Hammerstein 2nd (based on *Green Grow the Lilacs* [play] by Lynn Riggs); Directed by Rouben Mamoulian; Choreographed by Agnes de Mille; Produced by The Theatre Guild; With Alfred Drake, Joan Roberts, Celeste Holm, Howard da Silva, Betty Garde, and Lee Dixon. Pre-Broadway title: AWAY WE GO!

Revivals
May 29, 1951
Broadway Theatre • 72 performances
Original direction restaged by Jerome Whyte; Choreographed by Agnes de Mille; Produced by The Theatre Guild; With Ridge Bond [Drake] and Patricia Northrup [Roberts].

June 23, 1969
New York State Theatre • 88 performances
Directed by John Kennedy; Original Choreography Restaged by Gemze de Lappe; Produced by Music Theater of Lincoln Center (Richard Rodgers); With Bruce Yarnell [Drake], Lee Beery [Roberts], Margaret Hamilton [Garde], Spiro Malas [Da Silva], and Lee Roy Reams [Dixon].

December 13, 1979
Palace Theatre • 293 performances
Directed by William Hammerstein; Original choreography restaged by Gemze de Lappe; With Laurence Guittard [Drake], Christine Andreas [Roberts], Mary Wickes [Garde], Martin Vidnovic [Da Silva], and Christine Ebersole [Holm].

July 15, 1998
Olivier Theatre (London) • 93 performances
Directed by Trevor Nunn; Choreographed by Susan Stroman; Produced by Royal National Theatre (and Cameron Mackintosh); With Hugh Jackman (Drake), Josefina Gabrielle (Roberts), Shuler Hensley (Da Silva), and Maureen Lipman (Garde).

Published Songs
*All 'er Nothin'—initial individual publication upon use in 1955 movie version
Boys and Girls Like You and Me—cut; subsequently used in stage version of STATE FAIR [March 27, 1996]

The Farmer and the Cowman—initial individual publication upon use in movie version

*I Cain't Say No

Kansas City*—initial individual publication upon use in movie version

*Many a New Day

*Oh, What a Beautiful Mornin'

*Oklahoma!

*Out of My Dreams

*People Will Say We're in Love

Pore Jud—initial individual publication upon use in movie version

The Surrey with the Fringe on Top

Additional Songs Published in Vocal Score
It's a Scandal! It's a Outrage!
Laurey Makes up Her Mind [ballet]
Lonely Room

Additional Song Published in Non-show Folio
When I Go out Walking with My Baby—cut; subsequently used in stage version of STATE FAIR

The twenty-four-year-old Theatre Guild was foundering, without a hit since the Lunts' *There Shall Be No Night* [April 29, 1940]. They decided to turn to Rodgers and Hart—whom they had launched with THE GARRICK GAIETIES [May 17, 1925]—and asked them to adapt *Green Grow the Lilacs*, an unsuccessful folk play they had produced in 1931. The unstable Hart was not interested, so Rodgers convinced the Guild to let him collaborate with one of his pre-Hart lyricists: Oscar Hammerstein, author of the landmark SHOW BOAT [Kern: December 27, 1927] and nothing but flops since 1932. Rouben Mamoulian, director of the Guild's folk opera PORGY AND BESS [Gershwin: October 10, 1935], was signed to direct; he had done pioneering work in Hollywood with both Rodgers (*Love Me Tonight* [1932]) and Hammerstein (*High, Wide and Handsome* [1937]). Choreographer Agnes de Mille had been fired from her first two Broadway jobs, but her successful staging of Aaron Copland's *Rodeo* for the Ballets Russe [October 16, 1942] indicated her suitability for the assignment. (Rodgers himself had written a less immortal cowboy ballet for the Ballets Russe, *Ghost Town* [November 12, 1939].

His choreographer, Marc Platoff [Platt], was the lead dancer in OKLAHOMA!). With Mamoulian, Rodgers, Hammerstein, and de Mille approaching their creative peaks, the separate elements of OKLAHOMA! were superior in themselves and excellently integrated. OKLAHOMA! set new long-run records—not only on Broadway but everywhere—and the unlikely team of Rodgers and Hammerstein became tops in musical comedy.

A CONNECTICUT YANKEE [1943]
November 17, 1943
Martin Beck Theatre • 135 performances
Also see November 3, 1927. Lyrics by Lorenz Hart; Book by Herbert Fields (based on *A Connecticut Yankee in King Arthur's Court* [novel] by Mark Twain); Directed by John C. Wilson; Produced by Rodgers; With Vivienne Segal, Dick Foran, Julie Warren, Vera-Ellen, and Chester Stratton.

New Published Songs
Can't You Do a Friend a Favor?
Something—advertised but not published (title was a misprint, no such song written)
This Is My Night to Howl—advertised but not published; recorded
*To Keep My Love Alive
Ye Lunchtime Follies*—advertised but not published; recorded
You Always Love the Same Girl

The new team of Rodgers and Hammerstein was making history, and OKLAHOMA! [March 31, 1943] was the biggest hit of the century—which left Hart pretty much out in the cold. Rodgers and Herb Fields determined to give Larry a lift by revisiting their 1927 hit. The updated book, revised to allow a starring role for Vivienne Segal (of I MARRIED AN ANGEL [May 11, 1938] and PAL JOEY [December 25, 1940]), was weak and creaky, though, and the show a failure. There was a handful of new songs, including the grandly macabre *To Keep My Love Alive*, with one of Hart's best comedy lyrics. But the lyricist was beyond saving. Following a two-week binge, he appeared at the CONNECTICUT YANKEE opening in a drunken stupor, was ejected from the theatre, and disappeared. He was found the next evening passed out in the gutter—literally—by

Fritz Loewe (an as-yet-unsuccessful composer friend from the Lamb's Club). Larry Hart died of pneumonia on November 22, 1943.

CAROUSEL
April 19, 1945
Majestic Theatre • 890 performances
Book and Lyrics by Oscar Hammerstein 2nd (based on *Liliom* [play] by Ferenc Molnár, as adapted by Benjamin F. Glaser); Directed by Rouben Mamoulian; Choreographed by Agnes de Mille; Produced by The Theatre Guild (and Rodgers and Hammerstein, unbilled); With John Raitt, Jan Clayton, Jean Darling, Eric Mattson, Murvyn Vye, and Bambi Linn.

Revivals
August 10, 1965
New York State Theatre • 47 performances
Directed by Edward Greenberg; Choreographed by Agnes de Mille; Produced by Music Theater of Lincoln Center (Richard Rodgers); With John Raitt, Eileen Christy [Clayton], Susan Watson [Darling], Reid Shelton [Mattson], and Jerry Orbach [Vye].

June 16, 1985
Kennedy Center Opera House •
    40 performances
Directed by James Hammerstein; Conceived by James Hammerstein and John Mauceri; Choreographed by Peter Martins; Produced by John F. Kennedy Center (and Cameron Mackintosh); With Tom Wopat [Raitt], Kathleen Buffaloe [Clayton], and Faith Prince [Darling].

March 24, 1994
Vivian Beaumont Theatre •
    322 performances
Directed by Nicholas Hytner; Choreographed by Sir Kenneth MacMillan; Produced by Lincoln Center Theater (and Cameron Mackintosh); Transferred from Royal National Theatre {London}; With Michael Hayden [Raitt]; Sally Murphy [Clayton], Fisher Stevens [Vye], and Audra Ann McDonald [Darling].

Published Songs
**Carousel Waltz* [instrumental]—issued in
    separate edition

**If I Loved You*
June Is Bustin' out All Over
Mister Snow
A Real Nice Clambake
Soliloquy (including *My Boy Bill* and *My Little Girl*)
***What's the Use of Wond'rin'?*
When the Children Are Asleep
You'll Never Walk Alone

Additional Songs Published in Vocal Score
**Ballet* [instrumental]
Blow High, Blow Low
Geraniums in the Winder
The Highest Judge of All
Stonecutters Cut It on the Stone
You're a Queer One, Julie Jordan

As with PORGY AND BESS [Gershwin: October 10, 1935] and OKLAHOMA! [March 31, 1943], the Theatre Guild had one of their plays musicalized under the supervision of director Rouben Mamoulian: in this case, the 1921 English-language version of Molnár's *Liliom*. (During Rodgers and Hart's amateur show days, the latter was known to pick up extra money as a ghost writer; some claim that he was actually responsible for much of the Glaser adaptation.) The creators of OKLAHOMA! returned with CAROUSEL, one of the very finest American musicals. The show opened with an unconventional, fully staged instrumental prelude (a waltz, naturally). This was followed by a lengthy dramatic scene, most of which was set to music (as *You're a Queer One, Julie Jordan, Mister Snow*, and the multipart *If I Loved You*). Innovations abounded, including an extended, dramatic *Soliloquy* and the telling of a key element of the story—the troubled existence of the daughter, Louise—almost entirely through ballet. Not to mention the stunning *What's the Use of Wondrin'?*—another unrequited love song, but a far cry from the ones Rodgers wrote with Larry Hart—and the hymn *You'll Never Walk Alone*. CAROUSEL was a substantial hit, although the run was far shorter than four other Rodgers and Hammerstein musicals. Nevertheless, many agree with Rodgers's personal selection of CAROUSEL as his favorite work—a judgment spectacularly borne out in the striking 1993 London revival produced by

Cameron Mackintosh and the Royal National Theatre (and remounted in New York the following year by Lincoln Center Theatre).

ANNIE GET YOUR GUN
See Berlin: May 16, 1946.

HAPPY BIRTHDAY
October 31, 1946
Broadhurst Theatre • 564 performances
Play by Anita Loos; Lyric by Oscar Hammerstein 2nd; Directed by Joshua Logan; Produced by Rodgers and Hammerstein; With Helen Hayes.

Published Song
I Haven't Got a Worry in the World

Rodgers and Hammerstein began their producing partnership with the John van Druten's comic play *I Remember Mama*, which opened on October 19, 1944 (see I REMEMBER MAMA [May 31, 1979]). This was followed by CAROUSEL [April 19, 1945] (on which they did not receive billing), ANNIE GET YOUR GUN [Berlin: May 16, 1946], and other shows. Their first four plays and ANNIE were hits; then came two 1950 failures, after which they restricted their Broadway activities to their own work. Back in 1944, before starting CAROUSEL, Rodgers and Hammerstein wrote six songs for a movie musical remake of *State Fair* (which didn't open until the summer of 1945, after CAROUSEL). The surface parallels to OKLAHOMA! [March 31, 1943] were many, although the action took place in folksy Iowa, but *State Fair* had none of OKLAHOMA's depth. Two of the songs were especially good: the grand waltz *It's a Grand Night for Singing and Oscar's second Oscar winner, the sprightly **It Might As Well Be Spring. After Hammerstein's death in 1960, Rodgers's first project was to write five more songs—music and lyrics, all forgettable—for a 1962 remake of the *State Fair* remake (also see STATE FAIR [March 27, 1996]).

ALLEGRO
October 10, 1947
Majestic Theatre • 315 performances
Book and Lyrics by Oscar Hammerstein 2nd; Directed and Choreographed by Agnes de

Mille; Produced by The Theatre Guild (and Rodgers and Hammerstein, unbilled); With John Battles, Roberta Jonay, Annamary Dickey, and Lisa Kirk.

Concert Version
March 2, 1994
City Center • 4 performances
Directed by Susan H. Schulman; Choreographed by Lar Lubovitch; Produced by City Center Encores; With Stephen Bogardus [Battles], Karen Ziemba, Jonathan Hadary, John Cunningham, Celeste Holm, and Christine Ebersole [Kirk].

Published Songs
Come Home
**A Fellow Needs a Girl*
The Gentleman Is a Dope
**Money Isn't Everything*
My Wife—cut, for initial publication see
  SOUTH PACIFIC [April 7, 1949]
*So Far
You Are Never Away

Additional Songs Published in Vocal Score
Allegro
A Darn Nice Campus
Finale Act I (Wedding Introduction)
I Know It Can Happen Again
It May Be a Good Idea
Joseph Taylor, Jr.
One Foot, Other Foot
Poor Joe
To Have and to Hold
What a Lovely Day for a Wedding—different
  than *It's a Lovely Day for a Murder* from
  HIGHER AND HIGHER [April 4, 1940]
Wildcats
Wish Them Well
Ya-Ta-Ta

ALLEGRO was ahead of its time, which is what they say when top creators come up with something that is bafflingly unusual. This folk/morality musical approached pretentiousness, and proved that even the invulnerable Rodgers and Hammerstein could fail. ALLEGRO was inventive, certainly, and its unconventional, nonstructured storytelling pointed the way towards the Sondheim/Prince shows of the 1970s. (Teenager Sondheim spent much of his time at the

Hammerstein house and at seventeen served as production assistant on ALLEGRO.) Librettist Hammerstein was working without underlying material, which resulted in some ineffective plotting, and choreographer Agnes de Mille wasn't much help as a director. Even the songs were well below what one would expect, although there are a couple of pleasant ballads (*A Fellow Needs a Girl* and *So Far*) and a good concerted number in *Money Isn't Everything*.

SOUTH PACIFIC
April 7, 1949
Majestic Theatre • 1,925 performances
Lyrics by Oscar Hammerstein 2nd; Book by Oscar Hammerstein and Joshua Logan (based on *Tales of the South Pacific* [stories] by James Michener); Directed by Joshua Logan; Produced by Rodgers and Hammerstein in association with Leland Hayward and Joshua Logan; With Mary Martin, Ezio Pinza, William Tabbert, Myron McCormick, and Juanita Hall.

Revival
June 12, 1967
New York State Theatre • 104 performances
Directed by Joe Layton; Produced by Music Theater of Lincoln Center (Richard Rodgers); With Florence Henderson [Martin] and Giorgio Tozzi [Pinza].

Published Songs
*Bali Ha'i
*A Cockeyed Optimist
Dites-Moi
Happy Talk
Honey Bun
I'm Gonna Wash That Man Right outa My Hair
Loneliness of Evening—cut; published in
    separate edition, revised version of *Bright
    Canary Yellow* (cut, unpublished)
My Girl Back Home—cut; initial publication
    upon reuse in 1958 movie version
**Some Enchanted Evening
Suddenly Lovely—cut; for initial publication
    see THE KING AND I [March 29, 1951]
There Is Nothin' Like a Dame
**This Nearly Was Mine
Will You Marry Me?—cut; initial publication
    upon reuse in PIPE DREAM [November
    30, 1955]

*A Wonderful Guy
*You've Got to Be Carefully Taught—initial
    publication upon use in movie version
**Younger Than Springtime—new lyric for *My
    Wife* (cut, unpublished) from ALLEGRO
    [October 10, 1947]

Additional Songs Published in Vocal Score
Bloody Mary
Twin Soliloquies

Additional Song Published in Non-show Folio
Now Is the Time—cut

Rodgers, Hammerstein, and Joshua Logan won the 1950 Pulitzer (for Drama) with this adaptation of James Michener's 1948 Pulitzer winner (for Fiction). Logan had directed two Rodgers and Hart hits, as well as ANNIE GET YOUR GUN [Berlin: May 16, 1946]. (The success of SOUTH PACIFIC caused a schism between the authors, with Logan feeling unfairly coerced into accepting co-librettist billing without any share of the authors' royalties.) The score is on a level with CAROUSEL [April 19, 1945], which is to say near perfection. *Some Enchanted Evening, Younger Than Springtime, A Wonderful Guy, This Nearly Was Mine, Bali Ha'i,* and more: all are magical. Hammerstein's uncompromising statement against racial intolerance—*You've Got to Be Carefully Taught*—made many 1949 audience members uncomfortable. (The song wasn't individually published until a decade later.) Mary Martin, who turned down the lead in OKLAHOMA! [March 31, 1943], was well known to the trio for her performance in the national company [March 10, 1947] of ANNIE GET YOUR GUN. She was joined by opera star Pinza, who reluctantly agreed to the necessary eight-performance schedule—but insisted on singing no more than the equivalent of two operatic appearances a week. Therefore, the role of Emile De Becque consists of two booming solos and very little else.

THE KING AND I
March 29, 1951
St. James Theatre • 1,246 performances
Book and Lyrics by Oscar Hammerstein 2nd (based on *Anna and the King of Siam* [novel] by Margaret Landon); Directed by John van

Druten; Choreographed by Jerome Robbins;
Produced by Rodgers and Hammerstein;
With Gertrude Lawrence, Yul Brynner,
Doretta Morrow, Larry Douglas, and Dorothy
Sarnoff.

Revivals
July 6, 1964
New York State Theatre • 40 performances
Directed by Edward Greenberg; Original
choreography restaged by Yuriko; Produced
by Music Theater of Lincoln Center (Richard
Rodgers); With Risë Stevens [Lawrence],
Darren McGavin [Brynner], Lee Venora
[Morrow], and Patricia Neway [Sarnoff].

May 2, 1977
Uris Theatre • 719 performances
Directed by Yuriko; Original choreography
restaged by Yuriko; With Yul Brynner and
Constance Towers [Lawrence].

January 7, 1985
Broadway Theatre • 191 performances
Directed and Produced by Mitch Leigh;
Original choreography restaged by Rebecca
West; With Yul Brynner amd Mary Beth Peil
[Lawrence].

April 11, 1996
Neil Simon Theatre • 781 performances
Directed by Christopher Renshaw; Original
choreography restaged by Susan Kikuchi;
[New] Choreography by Lar Lubovitch; With
Donna Murphy [Lawrence] and Lou Diamond
Phillips [Brynner].

Published Songs
Getting to Know You—new lyric for *Suddenly
     Lovely* (cut, unpublished) from SOUTH
     PACIFIC [April 7, 1949]
**Hello, Young Lovers*
I Have Dreamed
I Whistle a Happy Tune
March of the Siamese Children [instrumental]
My Lord and Master
Shall We Dance?
***Something Wonderful*
We Kiss in a Shadow

Additional Songs Published in Vocal Score
A Puzzlement
The Royal Bangkok Academy
Shall I Tell You What I Think of You?

The Small House of Uncle Thomas [ballet with
     words]
The Song of the King
Western People Funny

Additional Song Recorded
Waiting—cut

Rodgers and Hammerstein had explored and
expanded the boundaries of musical theatre in
each of their collaborations. They continued to
do so with THE KING AND I, which underwent
severe tryout troubles before being patched into
a hit. The experience seemed to snuff out their
adventuresome spirit; hereafter they were to be
less ambitious. The score was certainly outstanding in spots—the anthem-like *Something Wonderful*, the heartfelt waltz *Hello, Young Lovers*,
the troubled King's soliloquy *A Puzzlement*, and
the magical *March of the Siamese Children*. While
all of the rest were better than good and more
than functional, some of these songs of Siam
sounded uncomfortably Occidental (like *I Have
Dreamed*, for example). If the score was not up
to the caliber of CAROUSEL [April 19, 1945] or
SOUTH PACIFIC [April 7, 1949], well—wouldn't
that be asking a bit much? Gertrude Lawrence
brought the material to Rodgers and Hammerstein, seeing a good role for herself. There was
also a role for Alfred Drake, of OKLAHOMA!
[March 31, 1943] and KISS ME, KATE [Porter:
December 30, 1948]. He wanted too much money,
though, so Yul Brynner—whose only credit was
opposite Mary Martin in the brief LUTE SONG
[February 6, 1946]—became the King and remained so. During the second year of the run,
Gertrude Lawrence died of cancer on September
6, 1952. Brynner repeated his role in the 1956
screen version and came back to Broadway again
and again as the King until his death in 1985. A
1996 revival—which originated in Australia, of
all places—breathed new life into the show, and
achieved deserved success.

ME AND JULIET
May 28, 1953
Majestic Theatre • 358 performances
Book and Lyrics by Oscar Hammerstein 2nd;
Directed by George Abbott; Choreographed
by Robert Alton; Produced by Rodgers and

Hammerstein; With Isabel Bigley, Joan McCracken, Bill Hayes, and Ray Walston.

Published Songs

The Big Black Giant
I'm Your Girl
It Feels Good
It's Me
Keep It Gay
*Marriage Type Love
*No Other Love—revised version of *Beneath the Southern Cross* [instrumental] from 1952 TV documentary "Victory at Sea"
That's the Way It Happens
A Very Special Day
We Deserve Each Other

Additional Songs Published in Vocal Score

*Intermission Talk (The Theatre Is Dying)
Me, Who Am I?—cut; incorporated (no lyric) in *Opening of "Me and Juliet"*
Opening of "Me and Juliet"

Additional Song Published in Non-show Folio

You Never Had It So Good—cut; initial publication upon use in stage version of STATE FAIR [March 27, 1996]

George Abbott reunited with Rodgers for this weak backstage play-within-a-weak-play, their only post–PAL JOEY [December 25, 1940] collaboration. Coming on the heels of SOUTH PACIFIC [April 7, 1949] and THE KING AND I [March 29, 1951, though, ME AND JULIET was able to achieve a slightly profitable run. The glorious tango *No Other Love*, the incessantly charming *Marriage Type Love*, and the droll *Intermission Talk* stand out from an otherwise pedestrian score. Prior to ME AND JULIET, Rodgers wrote an impressive award-winning score for the twenty-six week TV documentary "Victory at Sea."

PIPE DREAM
November 30, 1955
Shubert Theatre • 245 performances
Book and Lyrics by Oscar Hammerstein 2nd (based on *Sweet Thursday* [novel] by John Steinbeck); Directed by Harold Clurman;

Produced by Rodgers and Hammerstein; With Helen Traubel, Bill Johnson, Judy Tyler, and Mike Kellin.

Published Songs

*All at Once You Love Her
*Everybody's Got a Home but Me
*The Man I Used to Be
The Next Time It Happens
*Suzy Is a Good Thing
Sweet Thursday

Additional Songs Published in Vocal Score

All Kinds of People
Bum's Opera (You Can't Get away from a Dumb Tomato)
Dance Fugue [instrumental]
Fauna's Song [2nd] *(Beguine)*
The Happiest House on the Block
How Long?
On a Lopsided Bus
The Party That We're Gonna Have Tomorrow Night
Thinkin'
The Tide Pool
We Are a Gang of Witches
Will You Marry Me?—see SOUTH PACIFIC [April 7, 1949]

Additional Song Recorded

Fauna's Song [1st]—also in vocal score (music only) as *Change of Scene*—#15

What might have made an interesting musical did not work, suffering from strangely varying points of view. Rodgers, for his part, provided his most ambitious later score: tuneful, atmospheric, and full of interest if ultimately unsatisfying. (During the rehearsal period—when problems like this first become apparent and can be worked on—Rodgers underwent emergency surgery for cancer of the mouth.) While the show proved wildly unworkable, the enjoyably rambunctious score has some worthy high spots: a nicely gentle ballad, *All at Once You Love Her*; an infectiously likable schottische *The Man I Used to Be*; an unusual but lovely song of self-esteem, *Suzy Is a Good Thing*; and the extra-special plaintively yearning *Everybody's Got a Home but Me*. John Steinbeck was a close friend of Hammerstein; his play *Burning Bright* [October 19, 1950] was the final play produced by Rodgers & Hammerstein. The protagonist of *Sweet Thursday* was fashioned after the novelist's friend Henry Fonda. Fonda's singing audition was weak, though, so the part went to Bill Johnson, who played opposite Dolores Gray in the London production [June 7, 1947] of ANNIE GET YOUR GUN [Berlin: May 16, 1946] and replaced Alfred Drake in KISMET [Notables: December 3, 1953]. Johnson and leading lady Judy Tyler (Howdy Doody's Princess Summer-Fall-Winter-Spring) both died in separate car crashes within a year of PIPE DREAM's closing. The show's nominal star, though—opera diva Helen Traubel—was grossly miscast as the proprietress of *The Happiest House on the Block*.

FLOWER DRUM SONG
December 1, 1958
St. James Theatre • 602 performances
Lyrics by Oscar Hammerstein 2nd; Book by Oscar Hammerstein 2nd and Joseph Fields (based on the novel by C. Y. Lee); Directed by Gene Kelly; Choreographed by Carol Haney; Produced by Rodgers and Hammerstein in association with Joseph Fields; With Miyoshi Umeki, Larry Blyden, Pat Suzuki, and Juanita Hall.

Published Songs
Don't Marry Me
Grant Avenue
A Hundred Million Miracles
**I Enjoy Being a Girl*
**Love, Look Away*
My Best Love—cut
Sunday
**You Are Beautiful*—initially published as
   She Is Beautiful

Additional Songs Published in Vocal Score
Chop Suey
Fan Tan Fannie
Gliding through My Memoree
I Am Going to Like It Here
Like a God
The Other Generation

Rodgers and Hammerstein returned to an Oriental theme, this time the assimilation of Chinese immigrants in San Francisco. Unlike SOUTH PACIFIC [April 7, 1949] and THE KING AND I [March 29, 1951], though, the conflicts were used for solely comedic purposes only. The results were nonexceptional, if moderately successful. Librettist Joseph Fields was number-one son to Lew and brother to Herb, partners-in-crime with Rodgers and Hart on their Oriental castration musical CHEE-CHEE [September 25, 1928]. Gene Kelly (of PAL JOEY [December 25, 1940]) returned from Hollywood to direct, bringing his former assistant Carol Haney—who had been "discovered" in Bob Fosse's THE PAJAMA GAME [Adler: May 13, 1954]—along to choreograph. Haney's not-so-Chinese husband Larry Blyden took over the male lead from Larry Storch during the tryout. The score was exceedingly uninteresting, with one strong ballad (*Love, Look Away*), one good character number (*I Enjoy Being a Girl*), and the gentle *You Are Beautiful*. Prior to FLOWER DRUM SONG, Rodgers and Hammerstein wrote the TV musical "Cinderella" [March 31, 1957] as a vehicle for Julie Andrews. Highlights of the score include *Ten Minutes Ago*, *Impossible*, and *The Stepsisters' Lament*. The piece has twice been remade for television—in 1965 and 1997—as well as being mounted in various indifferent stage versions, the score filled out with lesser-known Rodgers and Hammerstein.

THE SOUND OF MUSIC
November 16, 1959
Lunt-Fontanne Theatre • 1,433 performances
Lyrics by Oscar Hammerstein 2nd; Book by Howard Lindsay and Russel Crouse (based on *The Trapp Family Singers* [biography] by Maria Augusta Trapp); Directed by Vincent J. Donehue; Choreographed by Joe Layton; Produced by Leland Hayward, Richard Halliday, and Rodgers and Hammerstein; With Mary Martin (Halliday), Theodore Bikel, and Patricia Neway.

Revival
March 12, 1998
Martin Beck Theatre •
   532 performances
Directed by Susan H. Schulman; Choreographed by Michael Lichtefeld; With Rebecca Luker [Martin], Michael Siberry [Bikel], and Patti Cohenour [Neway].

Published Songs

*Climb Ev'ry Mountain
*Do-Re-Mi
*Edelweiss
I Have Confidence [lyric by Rodgers]—written for 1965 movie version
The Lonely Goatherd
*Maria
*My Favorite Things
An Ordinary Couple
*Sixteen Going on Seventeen
So Long, Farewell—initial individual publication upon use in movie version
Something Good [lyric by Rodgers]—written for movie version
*The Sound of Music

Additional Songs Published in Vocal Score

Alleluia
How Can Love Survive?
No Way to Stop It
Preludium

Rodgers and Hammerstein's final show was a huge hit and ultimately one of Hollywood's all-time greatest successes, despite plenty of critical carping. Serious subjects which Rodgers and Hammerstein had sensitively handled in the past came out treacly in Lindsay and Crouse's book, and the show's various elements seemed more manufactured than inspired. The score was certainly their best since THE KING AND I [March 29, 1951], with one of Broadway's most charming charm songs, My Favorite Things; the trippingly delightful nun's-schottische Maria; the requisite strong-themed anthem in the You'll Never Walk Alone/Something Wonderful vein, Climb Ev'ry Mountain; and Do-Re-Mi, so well fashioned that whole generations of children and adults assume it's a nursery rhyme. As had happened with Rodgers on PIPE DREAM, Hammerstein underwent emergency surgery for cancer (of the stomach) during rehearsals. Hammerstein's condition proved unstoppable, and he died on August 23, 1960.

NO STRINGS

March 15, 1962
54th Street Theatre • 580 performances
Lyrics by Rodgers; Book by Samuel Taylor; Directed and Choreographed by Joe Layton;

Produced by Rodgers; With Diahann Carroll, Richard Kiley, Bernice Massi, and Polly Rowles.

Published Songs

Be My Host
Eager Beaver
La-La-La
Loads of Love
Look No Further
Love Makes the World Go
Maine
The Man Who Has Everything
*No Strings
Nobody Told Me
*The Sweetest Sounds
You Don't Tell Me

Additional Songs Published in Vocal Score

How Sad
An Orthodox Fool

Working as his own lyricist, Rodgers again tried something innovative: using on-stage musicians to counterpoint the moods and emotions of the characters. This worked extremely well, as did the show's non-realistic scenery-without-walls, but NO STRINGS was hampered by the libretto. Despite the show's then-dangerous theme of interracial romance, the interesting situation wasn't developed into much of a plot. NO STRINGS did benefit from its strong star performers, Diahann Carroll—for whom Rodgers devised the show—and Richard Kiley. And if the score wasn't up to what might be expected from Rodgers and Hammerstein or Rodgers and Hart, it was really quite nice in its own intimate way (if somewhat overloaded with introspective love songs). Best of the lot was The Sweetest Sounds, with Nobody Told Me and the title song in support.

DO I HEAR A WALTZ?

March 18, 1965
46th Street Theatre • 220 performances
Lyrics by Stephen Sondheim; Book by Arthur Laurents (based on his play The Time of the Cuckoo); Directed by John Dexter; Choreographed by Herb Ross; Produced by Rodgers;

With Elizabeth Allen, Sergio Franchi, Carol Bruce, and Madeleine Sherwood.

Published Songs
Do I Hear a Waltz?
Here We Are Again
Moon in My Window
Perhaps—cut
Someone Like You
Stay
Take the Moment
Thank You So Much
Two by Two (by Two) [1st]—cut; different than song from TWO BY TWO [November 10, 1970]

Additional Songs Published in Vocal Score
Bargaining
No Understand
Perfectly Lovely Couple
Someone Woke Up
Thinking
This Week Americans
We're Gonna Be All Right
What Do We Do? We Fly!

Additional Song Recorded
Everybody Loves Leona

Rodgers and his co-workers—Hammerstein-protégé Stephen Sondheim, accomplished librettist Arthur Laurents, and English director John Dexter—did not get along poisonously. Their resulting musical romance was misconceived, miscast, misromantic, and mistaken. Despite the project's ups and (mostly) downs, much of the Rodgers and Sondheim work—which was more or less disowned by both sides—is really quite charming. *Moon in My Window, Here We Are Again, Take the Moment*, and *Someone Woke Up* all accomplish what they set out to with charm and grace; and in the title song Rodgers came up with his final sweeping waltz. He was relatively inactive as a composer for the balance of the decade, with much of his energy spent as producer of a series of full-scale summer revivals for the Music Theater of Lincoln Center (1964–1979). His sole writing project over these years was an indifferent TV musical adaptation [November 15, 1967] of Shaw's *Androcles and the Lion*. Rodgers contributed music and lyrics for eight songs, none of them of note.

TWO BY TWO
November 10, 1970
Imperial Theatre • 343 performances
Lyrics by Martin Charnin; Book by Peter Stone (based on *The Flowering Peach* [play] by Clifford Odets); Directed and Choreographed by Joe Layton; Produced with Rodgers; With Danny Kaye, Harry Goz, Joan Copeland, and Madeline Kahn.

Published Songs
Everything That's Gonna Be Has Been—cut; issued as professional copy
Hey, Girlie—issued as professional copy
I Do Not Know a Day I Did Not Love You
An Old Man
Something Doesn't Happen
Something, Somewhere
Two by Two [2nd]—different than song (cut) from DO I HEAR A WALTZ? [March 18, 1965]

Additional Songs Published in Vocal Selection
When It Dries
You
You Have Got to Have a Rudder on the Ark

Additional Songs Published in Vocal Score
As Far As I'm Concerned
The Covenant
The Gitka's Song [instrumental]
The Golden Ram
Ninety Again
Poppa Knows Best
Put Him Away
Why Me?

In 1970, the sixty-eight-year-old Rodgers suffered a heart attack. He went on to write three more musicals, each of increasing lameness. TWO BY TWO was an unhappy, unattractive show; its sole reason for existence seemed to be to sell tickets. Star Danny Kaye—making his first Broadway appearance since LET'S FACE IT [Porter: October 29, 1941]—served as the drawing card, although he turned out to be part of the problem. (Faced with mediocre material from the authors, he started to devise his own; it didn't help, but then Kaye was just fighting for survival as he stood atop a sinking ark.) The best that can be said was that there was one rather pretty romantic ballad, *I Do Not Know a Day I Did Not Love You*, as well as a second, moderately pleasing one (*Something Doesn't Happen*).

REX
April 25, 1976
Lunt-Fontanne Theatre • 48 performances
Lyrics by Sheldon Harnick; Book by Sherman Yellen; Directed by Edwin Sherin; Choreographed by Dania Krupska; Produced by Richard Adler in association with Roger Berlind and Edward R. Downe; With Nicol Williamson, Penny Fuller, Tom Aldredge, and Glenn Close.

Published Songs
As Once I Loved You
*Away from You

Additional Songs Recorded
At the Field of Cloth of Gold
The Chase
Christmas at Hampton Court
Elizabeth
From Afar
In Time
No Song More Pleasing
So Much You Loved Me
Te Deum (God Save the King)
The Wee Golden Warrior
Where Is My Son?
Why?

REX was poorly conceived, poorly executed, and badly produced. Michael Bennett was passed over early in the game; when he was refused a percentage of the profits, he went off to develop A CHORUS LINE [Hamlisch: April 15, 1975] instead. The directorial reins were entrusted to Edwin Sherin, whose musical experience consisted of being fired from SEESAW [Coleman: March 18, 1973] in Detroit (and being replaced by Michael Bennett). On REX it was Harold Prince—who had produced songwriter-turned-producer Richard Adler's two 1950s hits—who was brought to Boston. But much too late. *Away from You* was a pleasing ballad, but that's about all you can say in favor of REX.

I REMEMBER MAMA
May 31, 1979
Majestic Theatre • 108 performances
Lyrics mostly by Martin Charnin; Book by Thomas Meehan (based on the play by John van Druten and the stories by Kathryn Forbes); Directed by Cy Feuer; Produced by Alexander H. Cohen and Hildy Parks; With Liv Ullmann, George Hearn, and George S. Irving.

Published Songs
Ev'ry Day (Comes Something Beautiful)
It Is Not the End of the World
Time
You Could Not Please Me More

Additional Songs Recorded
Easy Come, Easy Go
I Remember Mama
It's Going to Be Good to Be Gone
I Write, You Read (Fair Trade)
Lars, Lars
A Little Bit More [lyric by Raymond Jessel]
Lullaby (The Hardangerfjord)
Mama Always Makes It Better
Most Disagreeable Man
Uncle Chris [lyric by Jessel]
When?
A Writer Writes at Night

Producer Alexander H. Cohen assembled a typical Alexander H. Cohen package: star composer, star actress, and the lyricist, librettist, director, designer, etc., from Broadway's most recent smash hit (in this case, the one about the little orphan girl and her dog). But Rodgers was seventy-six, tired, and ill; Liv Ullmann was a musical novice who barely spoke (let alone sang) the language; and the musical-comedy track records of the Messrs. Charnin and Cohen were less than inspiring. John Van Druten's play *I Remember Mama* had been a wartime hit (produced in 1944 by Rodgers and Hammerstein) and a popular 1950s' television series. Cohen fired Charnin during the tryout and brought in producer Cy Feuer to direct, along with lyricist Raymond Jessel (of Cohen's BAKER STREET [Bock: February 16, 1965]). The dire I REMEMBER MAMA was Richard Rodgers's final work. He died as the decade ended, on December 30, 1979, in New

York—just after the opening of a hit revival of OKLAHOMA! [March 31, 1943].

STATE FAIR
March 27, 1996
Music Box Theatre • 111 performances
Lyrics by Oscar Hammerstein 2nd; Book by Tom Briggs and Louis Mattioli (based on the screenplay by Oscar Hammerstein 2nd and the novel by Phil Strong); Directed by James Hammerstein and Randy Skinner; Choreographed by Randy Skinner; Produced by David Merrick and The Theatre Guild; With John Davidson, Kathryn Crosby, Andrea McArdle, Donna McKechnie, Scott Wise, and Ben Wright.

Published Songs (Written for Movie Version)
All I Owe Ioway
Isn't It Kinda Fun?
**It Might As Well Be Spring
*It's a Grand Night for Singing
More Than Just a Friend [lyric by Rodgers]— written for 1962 film version
Our State Fair
That's for Me

Additional Songs in Initial Stage Use, Published in Vocal Selection
Boys and Girls Like You and Me—cut from OKLAHOMA! [March 31, 1943]
When I Go out Walking with My Baby—cut from OKLAHOMA!
You Never Had It So Good—cut from ME AND JULIET [May 28, 1953]

The Rodgers and Hammerstein Estates—on the lookout for another family musical to join OKLAHOMA! and THE SOUND OF MUSIC in their rental catalogue—decided to launch a stage version of the post-OKLAHOMA! film musical *State Fair* (see HAPPY BIRTHDAY [October 31, 1946]). After an unsuccessful tryout tour and much travail, the on-again, off-again STATE FAIR limped into Broadway's Music Box Theatre under the sponsorship of the remnants of The Theatre Guild and David Merrick. (The title page of the program listed more than twenty additional producers, "in association with" producers, "pre-Broadway producers," etc.—which is what happens when a show has severe money-raising problems.) The score was rounded out by seven lesser-known Rodgers and Hammerstein show tunes, which understandably didn't fit the slight story. David Merrick tried to make headlines by suing the Tony Awards committee or some such nonsense, but to no avail, and within weeks STATE FAIR folded up its tent.

It is impossible to go through the Richard Rodgers song listings without noting that they are veritably peppered with those song asterisks. Part of this is only logical: Rodgers wrote Broadway musicals for sixty years. (Rodgers's near-contemporary George Gershwin wrote all his complete scores in a sixteen-year span.) Rodgers activity was fueled by his inordinate success—the staggering profitability of his shows eventually enabled him to self-produce his work—and his personal desire and need to keep working. While quantity does not necessarily indicate quality, it does to an impressive extent in the Rodgers song catalogue. For twenty-five years Rodgers was among the two or three leaders of the field; no one (other than possibly Jerome Kern) was as responsible for the development of the American musical theatre. During a span of less than a decade, Rodgers wrote five innovative, high-quality musicals. ON YOUR TOES [April 11, 1936] introduced bona fide ballet to musical comedy—and used it as a plot element. THE BOYS FROM SYRACUSE [November 23, 1938] was farce musical comedy *par excellence*. PAL JOEY [December 25, 1940] first brought realistic (if disreputable) characters and subjects onto the musical stage. OKLAHOMA! [March 31, 1943] combined the various theatrical elements into a cohesive whole. And all culminated in the stunning CAROUSEL [April 19, 1945], serious, dramatic musical theatre. Consider that all five scores are highly effective almost a half century later; that during these nine years Rodgers also wrote *five additional hit musicals*, including the bounteous BABES IN ARMS [April 14, 1937]; and that he wrote many of his best songs in the years *before* and *after* this golden period (including the score of SOUTH PACIFIC [April 7, 1949]). Rodgers might not have been Broadway's most famous composer, or most popular composer, or most lovable, inspired, or even most talented composer; but his output of indisputably great songs places him near the top of them all.

COLE PORTER

Born: June 9, 1891 Peru, Indiana
Died: October 15, 1964 Santa Monica, California

COLE PORTER's father, a druggist, played a very small part in his life: his maternal grandfather, however, was industrial magnate J. O. Cole. While grandpa Cole intended young Cole to take over his business, Porter's mother cultivated his love of music; she even had an early composition, *Bobolink Waltz*, published in 1902. By his fourteenth birthday Porter was at boarding school in Massachusetts, and in 1909 he entered Yale. (He majored, apparently, in writing football songs—*Bulldog* is still sung—and varsity shows.) His first professionally published song was *Bridget*, in 1910.

All Music and Lyrics by Cole Porter unless otherwise indicated.

THE POT OF GOLD
November 26, 1912
Delta Kappa Epsilon House, Yale
{New Haven, Conn.} • 2 performances
Book by Almet F. Jenks, Jr.; Directed by Almet F. Jenks, Jr., and Porter; With Porter.

Song Published in Non-show Folio
Longing for Dear Old Broadway

THE KALEIDOSCOPE
April 30, 1913
Hotel Taft {New Haven, Conn.} •
2 performances
Produced by Yale University Dramatic Association; With Newbold Noyes and Rufus F. King.

Published Songs
Absinthe—for initial publication see MISS INFORMATION [October 5, 1915]

As I Love You—for initial publication see HANDS UP [July 22, 1915]

After graduating from Yale in 1913, Porter moved to Harvard Law School for a brief visit. His heart, though, was down in New York. An early patroness was theatrical agent Elisabeth Marbury, creator of the innovative Princess Theatre series (see NOBODY HOME [Kern: April 20, 1915]). Latching onto the entertaining young sophisticate, she went about getting him a Broadway hearing.

HANDS UP
July 22, 1915
44th Street Theatre • 52 performances
"Musico-Comico-Filmo-Melo-Drama." Music mostly by E. Ray Goetz and Sigmund Romberg; Book and Lyrics mostly by E. Ray Goetz; Directed by J. H. Benrimo; Produced by the Messrs. Shubert.

Published Song
Esmeralda—initial publication of song (previously entitled *As I Love You*) from THE KALEIDOSCOPE [April 30, 1913]

MISS INFORMATION
October 5, 1915
George M. Cohan Theatre • 47 performances
"A Little Play with a Little Music." Music mostly by Jerome Kern (see Kern: October 5, 1915); Lyrics mostly by Elsie Janis; Book by Paul Dickey and Charles W. Goddard; Directed by Robert Milton; Produced by Charles Dillingham; With Elsie Janis and Irene Bordoni.

Published Song
Two Big Eyes [lyric by John Golden]—new
lyric for *Absinthe* (unpublished) from
THE KALEIDOSCOPE [April 30,
1913]

Irene Bordoni was to star in Porter's first Broadway success, PARIS [October 8, 1928], thirteen
long years later.

SEE AMERICA FIRST
March 28, 1916
Maxine Elliott Theatre • 15 performances
"A Patriotic Comic Opera." Book, Music, and
Lyrics by T. Lawrason Riggs and Porter
[Music actually by Porter alone]; Directed by
J. H. Benrimo; Produced by The Marbury-
Comstock Company; With Dorothie Bigelow,
John H. Goldsworthy, Leonard Joy, and
Clifton Webb.

Published Songs
Buy Her a Box at the Opera
Ever and Ever Yours
I've a Shooting Box in Scotland
I've Got an Awful Lot to Learn
The Language of Flowers
Lima
Oh, Bright Fair Dream—cut
Pity Me Please—cut
Prithee, Come Crusading
See America First
Slow Sinks the Sun—cut
Something's Got to Be Done
When I Used to Lead the Ballet

Elisabeth Marbury and her Princess Theatre
partner Ray Comstock launched Porter's Broadway career with this vanity production. Made
up mostly of material written for fraternity musicals, SEE AMERICA FIRST was received as an
amateurish varsity show—though with some
surprisingly adept lyrics—and quickly closed.
The cast included dancer Clifton Webb, who was
to be a feature of Broadway's most sophisticated
revues before leaving for Hollywood. Co-author
Lawrason Riggs was Porter's college roommate.
Following SEE AMERICA FIRST, Riggs became
a priest.

VERY GOOD EDDIE [1918]
May 18, 1918
Palace Theatre {London} • 46 performances
Music mostly by Jerome Kern (see Kern:
December 23, 1915); Lyrics mostly by Schuyler
Greene and Herbert Reynolds; Book by Philip
Bartholomae and Guy Bolton (based on *Over
Night* [play] by Philip Bartholomae); Directed
by Guy Bragdon; Produced by Alfred Butt and
André Charlot; With Nelson Keys.

Published Song
Alone with You [by Porter and Melville
Gideon]

Porter escaped the World War I draft by going
to France, where he was involved with a soci-
ety-sponsored food distribution program. He
spent the war attending and throwing parties
(and not in the French Foreign Legion, as he later
implied). Songwriting continued as a hobby,
with trips across the Channel to interpolate in
London musicals. With the exception of a few
attempts at revues, Porter spent the next ten
years as a very talented dilettante.

TELLING THE TALE
[circa October 1918]
Ambassador's Theatre {London}
Book by Sydney Blow and Douglas Hoare;
Produced by Gerald Kirby and John
Wyndham; With Birdie Courtenay and Gerald
Kirby.

Published Song
Altogether Too Fond of You [by Melville
Gideon, James Heard, and Porter]—also
used (cut) in BUDDIES [October 27, 1919]

HITCHY-KOO 1919 ✦ Third Edition
October 6, 1919
Liberty Theatre • 56 performances
Book by George V. Hobart; Directed by Julian
Alfred; Produced by Raymond Hitchcock;
With Raymond Hitchcock and Joe Cook.

Published Songs
Another Sentimental Song—cut
Bring Me Back My Butterfly

I Introduced
In Hitchy's Garden
I've Got Somebody Waiting
My Cozy Little Corner in the Ritz
Old Fashioned Garden
Peter Piper/The Sea Is Calling
That Black and White Baby of Mine—cut
When I Had a Uniform On

Following the war, Porter returned to America. His already growing reputation as a clever sophisticate resulted in his being commissioned to write this revue featuring lanky comedian Raymond Hitchcock. Although parts of HITCHY-KOO's score displayed Porter's sophisticated lyricism, it was the simple, sentimental *Old Fashioned Garden* that became his first (moderate) song hit.

BUDDIES
October 27, 1919
Selwyn Theatre • 259 performances
"Comedy of Quaint Brittany." Music and Lyrics mostly by B. C. Hilliam; Book by George V. Hobart; Produced by Selwyn and Co.; With Donald Brian, Peggy Wood, and Roland Young.

Published Songs
Altogether Too Fond of You [by Melville Gideon, James Heard, and Porter]—cut before opening; originally used in TELLING THE TALE [circa October 1918]
I Never Realized [music by Gideon, lyric by Porter; issued as by Gideon]—cut before opening; also used in THE ECLIPSE [November 12, 1919]
Washington Square [music by Gideon, lyric by Porter; issued as by Gideon]—cut before opening; also see AS YOU WERE [January 2, 1920] and THE ECLIPSE

THE ECLIPSE
November 12, 1919
Garrick Theatre {London} •
117 performances
Music by Herman Darewski and Melville Gideon; Lyrics mostly by Adrian Ross; Book by Fred Thompson and E. Phillips Oppenheim; Produced by Charles B. Cochran; With Nancy Gibbs and F. Pope Stamper.

Published Songs
I Never Realized [music by Gideon, lyric by Porter; issued as lyric by Ross]—originally used (cut) in BUDDIES [October 27, 1919]
In Chelsea Somewhere [music by Gideon, lyric by "Col. E. Porter" and James Heard]—revised lyric for *Washington Square* (cut) from BUDDIES

AS YOU WERE
January 27, 1920
Central Theatre • 143 performances
"A Fantastic Revue." Music mostly by Herman Darewski; Lyrics mostly by Arthur Wimperis and E. Ray Goetz; Book by Glen MacDonough (based on *Plus Ça Change* [revue] by Rip); Produced by E. Ray Goetz; With Sam Bernard and Irene Bordoni (Goetz).

Published Song
Washington Square [music by Melville Gideon, lyric by Porter and Goetz]—revised lyric for song originally used (cut) in BUDDIES [October 27, 1919]; also see THE ECLIPSE [November 12, 1919]

A NIGHT OUT [1920]
September 18, 1920
Winter Garden Theatre {London} •
311 performances
Music mostly by Willie Redstone (see Youmans: September 7, 1925); Porter Lyrics by Clifford Grey; Book by George Grossmith and Arthur Miller (based on a farce by Georges Feydeau and Maurice Desvallieres); Directed by Tom Reynolds; Produced by George Grossmith and Edward Laurillard; With Leslie Henson and Lily St. John.

Published Porter/Grey Songs
Finale (It's a Sad Day at This Hotel)
Look Around
Our Hotel
Why Didn't We Meet Before?

MAYFAIR AND MONTMARTRE
March 9, 1922
New Oxford Theatre {London} •
 77 performances
Music mostly by others; Book by John
Hastings Turner; Directed and Produced by
Charles B. Cochran; With Alice Delysia,
Evelyn Laye, and Joyce Barbour.

Published Songs
The Blue Boy Blues
Cocktail Time
Olga (Come Back to the Volga)—refrain
 adapted from *The Volga Boat Song*

PHI-PHI
AUGUST 16, 1922
Pavilion Theatre {London} •
 132 performances
Music mostly by Christiné; Lyrics mostly by
Clifford Grey; Book by Fred Thompson and
Clifford Grey (from the French by Willemetz
and Sollar); Produced by Charles B. Cochran;
With Clifton Webb.

Published Song
The Ragtime Pipes of Pan

HITCHY-KOO OF 1922 ✦ Fifth
 Edition
October 10, 1922
Shubert Theatre {Philadelphia} •
 Closed during tryout
Book by Harold Atteridge; Directed by J. C.
Huffman; Produced by the Messrs. J. J. and
Lee Shubert; With Raymond Hitchcock.

Published Songs
The American Punch
The Bandit Band
The Harbor Deep down in My Heart
Love Letter Words
When My Caravan Comes Home

Porter wrote his third complete score for this out-
of-town failure. He also wrote the ballet *Within
the Quota*—his only highbrow attempt—which
premiered in Paris on October 25, 1923.

GREENWICH VILLAGE FOLLIES ✦
 Sixth Annual Production
September 16, 1924
Shubert Theatre • 127 performances
Book by Lew Fields, Irving Caesar, and others;
Directed by John Murray Anderson; Produced
by The Bohemians, Inc.; With The Dolly
Sisters.

Published Songs
Brittany
I'm in Love Again—added after opening; also
 used in UP WITH THE LARK [August 25,
 1927]
Make Ev'ry Day a Holiday
My Long Ago Girl
Two Little Babes in the Wood—initial
 publication upon reuse in PARIS
 [October 8, 1928]
Wait for the Moon

This series had begun life as an intimate, bohe-
mian, Off Broadway revue in 1919. The Shuberts
bought the title in 1921 and undressed it. *I'm in
Love Again* and *Two Little Babes in the Wood*
both became hits—but not until Porter's first
wave of popularity in 1928.

UP WITH THE LARK
August 25, 1927
Adelphi Theatre {London}
Music mostly by Philip Braham; Lyrics mostly
by Douglas Furber; Book by Douglas Furber
and Hartley Carrick (based on *Le Zèbre* [play]
by Armont and Nancy); Directed by George
Grossmith; Produced by Westland Produc-
tions (in association with Martin Henry); With
Allen Kearns, Leslie Sarony, and Charles King.

Published Song
I'm in Love Again—originally used in
 GREENWICH VILLAGE FOLLIES [6th]
 [September 16, 1924]

LA REVUE DES AMBASSADEURS
May 10, 1928
Les Ambassadeurs {Paris} • Nightclub revue
Music and Lyrics mostly by Porter; Directed
by Bobby Connolly; Produced by Edmond

Sayag; With Morton Downey, Evelyn Hoey, Fred Waring, and Frances Gershwin.

Published Songs
Almiro
Hans
Looking at You—cut; initial publication upon reuse in WAKE UP AND DREAM [March 27, 1929]
Military Maids
An Old Fashioned Girl
You and Me

Additional Songs Published in Vocal Selection
Alpine Rose
Baby, Let's Dance
Blue Hours
Fish
Fountain of Youth
In a Moorish Garden
The Lost Liberty Blues
Pilot Me

This nightclub show was presented for expatriate Americans in Paris. Included in the cast was the Gershwins' talented kid sister, who sang a medley of songs by her brothers.

PARIS
October 8, 1928
Music Box Theatre • 195 performances
Book by Martin Brown; Directed by W. H. Gilmore; Produced by Gilbert Miller in association with E. Ray Goetz; With Irene Bordoni (Goetz), Louise Closser Hale, and Arthur Margetson.

Published Songs
Dizzy Baby—cut; advertised but not published; initial recording upon use in London revue COLE [July 2, 1974]
Don't Look at Me That Way!—see LET'S FACE IT [October 29, 1941]
The Heaven Hop
**Let's Do It*—also used in WAKE UP AND DREAM [March 27, 1929]
**Let's Misbehave*—cut
Quelque Chose—cut

Two Little Babes in the Wood—originally used in GREENWICH VILLAGE FOLLIES [6th] [September 19, 1924]
Vivienne
Which—cut; also used in WAKE UP AND DREAM

Porter's first hit show, featuring the saucy Irene Bordoni. The risqué *Let's Do It* and the playful *Let's Misbehave* (which was cut) were quick hits, placing Porter in league with Lorenz Hart as Broadway's cleverest and most sophisticated lyricists.

WAKE UP AND DREAM
March 27, 1929
Pavilion Theatre {London} • 263 performances
December 30, 1929
Selwyn Theatre {New York} • 136 performances
Music and Lyrics mostly by Porter (see Schwartz: December 30, 1929); Book by John Hastings Turner; Directed by Frank Collins. *London*: Choreography by George Balanchine; Produced by Charles B. Cochran; With Jessie Matthews, Sonny Hale, and Tilly Losch. *New York*: Choreographed by Tilly Losch and Jack Buchanan; Produced by Arch Selwyn in association with Charles B. Cochran; With Jessie Matthews and Jack Buchanan.

Published Songs
Agua Sincopada (*Tango*) [instrumental]
The Banjo (*That Man Joe Plays*)
I Loved Him but He Didn't Love Me
I Want to Be Raided by You—advertised but not published
Gigolo
**Let's Do It*—originally used in PARIS [October 8, 1928]
Looking at You—originally used (cut/unpublished) in LA REVUE DES AMBASSADEURS [May 10, 1928]
Wake Up and Dream
**What Is This Thing Called Love?*
Which—originally used (cut) in PARIS

Additional Song Published in Non-show Folio
After All I'm Only a Schoolgirl

Additional Songs Published (No Lyric) in British Piano Selection
I Dream of a Girl in a Shawl—advertised but not published individually
I've Got a Crush on You

Additional Songs Recorded
I Want to Be Raided by You
Pills

Note: Not all songs used in both editions.

London revue master Charles Cochran had successfully imported Americans Rodgers and Hart for his 1927 LONDON PAVILION REVUE ("One Dam Thing after Another") [Rodgers: May 20, 1927]. Now he tried Porter, with similarly successful results. The score included one of Porter's finest early songs, the plaintively haunting *What Is This Thing Called Love?*, as well as the uncharacteristically gentle title song. The New York production of WAKE UP AND DREAM did not do quite as well, hampered by the stock market crash and competition from Porter's just-opened hit FIFTY MILLION FRENCHMEN [November 27, 1929].

FIFTY MILLION FRENCHMEN
November 27, 1929
Lyric Theatre • 254 performances
"A Musical Comedy Tour of Paris." Book by Herbert Fields; Directed by Monty Woolley; Produced by E. Ray Goetz; With William Gaxton, Genevieve Tobin, and Helen Broderick.

Published Songs
*Find Me a Primitive Man
The Happy Heaven of Harlem
I Worship You—cut
I'm in Love
I'm Unlucky at Gambling
Let's Step Out—added after opening
Paree, What Did You Do to Me?
Please Don't Make Me Be Good—cut
The Queen of Terre Haute—cut
You Don't Know Paree
*You Do Something to Me
*You've Got That Thing

Additional Songs Published in Non-show Folio
*The Tale of the Oyster—cut
Why Don't We Try Staying Home?—cut

Additional Songs Recorded
The Boy Friend Back Home—cut
Where Would You Get Your Coat?

Herbert Fields left his long-time collaborators Richard Rodgers and Larry Hart following the debacle of CHEE-CHEE [Rodgers: September 25, 1928], joining Porter for the first of seven consecutive hits together. Billy Gaxton, whose first important role had been as Fields's CONNECTICUT YANKEE [1927] [Rodgers: November 3, 1927], now became a box office star. Porter wrote two more hits for Gaxton and future partner Victor Moore. Directing was Porter's close friend and classmate (turned Yale drama professor) Monty Woolley, making his professional debut; he soon became an accomplished actor. Porter added to his clutch of hit songs with *You Do Something to Me* and *You've Got That Thing*, while displaying his comic proclivities with *Find Me a Primitive Man* and *The Tale of the Oyster*.

THE VANDERBILT REVUE
November 5, 1930
Vanderbilt Theatre • 13 performances
Music and Lyrics mostly by Jimmy McHugh and Dorothy Fields; Directed by Lew Fields and Theodore Hammerstein; Produced by Lew Fields and Lyle D. Andrews; With Lulu McConnell, Joe Penner, and Evelyn Hoey.

Published Song
None

Porter contributed *What's My Man Gonna Be Like?* (unpublished) to this short-lived revue produced by the father of his new librettist Herb Fields.

THE NEW YORKERS [1930]
December 8, 1930
Broadway Theatre • 168 performances
Music and Lyrics mostly by Porter; Book by Herbert Fields (based on a story by Peter Arno and E. Ray Goetz); Directed by Monty Woolley; Produced by E. Ray Goetz; With Hope Williams, Ann Pennington, Charles King, and Jimmy Durante.

Published Songs

But He Never Said He Loved Me—cut; initial publication upon reuse in NYMPH ERRANT [October 6, 1933], retitled *The Physician*

The Great Indoors

I Happen to Like New York—added after opening

I'm Getting Myself Ready for You

Just One of Those Things [1st]—cut; different than hit song from JUBILEE [October 12, 1935]

Let's Fly Away

Love for Sale

Take Me back to Manhattan

Where Have You Been?

Another hit show for Porter, though not as successful as FIFTY MILLION FRENCHMEN [November 27, 1929]. Porter continued to earn a reputation for sophistication: lyrics like *Love for Sale* outraged some (but pleased many more).

STAR DUST

[circa November 1931]
Unproduced musical. Book by Herbert Fields; [Produced by E. Ray Goetz; With Peggy Wood].

Published Songs

**I Get a Kick out of You*—see ANYTHING GOES [November 21, 1934]

I've Got You on My Mind—see GAY DIVORCE [November 29, 1932]

Mister and Missus Fitch—see GAY DIVORCE

Additional Song Recorded

I Still Love the Red, White, and Blue—see GAY DIVORCE

GAY DIVORCE

November 29, 1932
Ethel Barrymore Theatre • 248 performances
Book by Dwight Taylor; Adapted by Kenneth Webb and Samuel Hoffenstein (based on an unproduced play by J. Hartley Manners); Directed by Howard Lindsay; Produced by Dwight Deere Wiman and Tom Weatherly; With Fred Astaire, Claire Luce, and Luella Gear.

Published Songs

After You (Who?)

How's Your Romance

I've Got You on My Mind—initial use of song written for STAR DUST [circa November 1931]

Mister and Missus Fitch—initial use of song written for STAR DUST; initial publication in 1954 as non-show song

***Night and Day*

You're in Love

Additional Songs Recorded

Fate—cut

I Love You Only—written for London production [November 2, 1933]; also published (no lyric) in piano selection

I Still Love the Red, White, and Blue—written for STAR DUST

Never Say No—also published (no lyric) in piano selection

Salt Air—also published (no lyric) in piano selection

A Weekend Affair—cut

Why Marry Them?

Could Fred Astaire make it on his own following sister Adele's retirement after THE BAND WAGON [Schwartz: June 3, 1931]? He did moderately well in GAY DIVORCE, which was kept alive by the popularity of *Night and Day*. The 1934 movie version *Gay Divorcee*—which threw out Porter's entire score (except *Night and Day*)—teamed Astaire with Ginger Rogers, and that was the end of Astaire and Broadway. Hollywood also cut the original scores for the 1931 version of FIFTY MILLION FRENCHMEN [November 27, 1928] and the 1937 ROSALIE [Gershwin: January 10, 1928]—for which Porter provided new songs. Librettist Dwight Taylor—son of Laurette—found the underlying material among the papers of his stepfather, J. Hartley Manners. Taylor later collaborated with Porter on the ill-fated OUT OF THIS WORLD [December 21, 1950].

NYMPH ERRANT

October 6, 1933
Adelphi Theatre {London} •
154 performances
Book and Direction by Romney Brent (based on the novel by James Laver); Produced by

Charles B. Cochran; With Gertrude Lawrence, Elisabeth Welch, and David Burns.

Published Songs
Experiment
How Could We Be Wrong?
I Look at You—cut; initial publication as 1934 non-show song with new lyric, retitled *You're Too Far Away*
It's Bad for Me
Nymph Errant
The Physician—originally used (cut/unpublished) in THE NEW YORKERS [December 8, 1930]
Solomon
When Love Comes Your Way—cut; also used in JUBILEE [October 12, 1935]

Additional Songs Recorded
Back to Nature with You—also published (no lyric) in piano selection
Casanova
The Castle—also published (no lyric) in piano selection
The Cocotte—also published (no lyric) in piano selection
Georgia Sand—also published (no lyric) in piano selection
My Louisa—cut
Neauville-Sur-Mer—also published (no lyric) in piano selection
Plumbing
Si Vous Aimez Les Poitrines
Sweet Nudity—cut
They're Always Entertaining

A suggestive romp about a staid British nymphomaniac, which thrilled Continental society but left the staid British lukewarm despite an inviting score.

HI DIDDLE DIDDLE
October 3, 1934
Comedy Theatre {London} •
198 performances
Play by William Walker and Robert Nesbitt; Produced by André Charlot; With Douglas Byng.

Published Song
Miss Otis Regrets

Miss Otis Regrets, one of Porter's party songs from the 1920s, was individually published in America in 1934 and subsequently performed later that year in this British comedy.

ANYTHING GOES
November 21, 1934
Alvin Theatre • 420 performances
Book by Guy Bolton and P. G. Wodehouse; Revised by Howard Lindsay and Russel Crouse; Directed by Howard Lindsay; Produced by Vinton Freedley; With William Gaxton, Ethel Merman, Victor Moore, and Bettina Hall

Revivals
May 15, 1962
Orpheum Theatre {Off Broadway} •
239 performances
Book revised by Guy Bolton; Directed by Lawrence Kasha; Choreographed by Ron Field; With Eileen Rodgers [Merman], Hal Linden [Gaxton], and Mickey Deems [Moore].

October 19, 1987
Vivian Beaumont Theatre •
804 performances
[New] Book by John Weidman and Timothy Crouse; Directed by Jerry Zaks; Choreographed by Michael Smuin; produced by Lincoln Center Theater; With Patti LuPone [Merman], Howard McGillin [Gaxton], and Bill McCutcheon [Moore].

Published Songs
All through the Night
Anything Goes
Blow, Gabriel, Blow
Buddie, Beware—cut after opening
The Gypsy in Me
I Get a Kick out of You—initial publication of song written for STAR DUST [circa November 1931]
There'll Always Be a Lady Fair—initial publication upon reuse in 1936 movie version
Waltz down the Aisle—cut; see KISS ME, KATE [December 30, 1948]
You're the Top

Additional Songs Published in Vocal Score
Be Like the Bluebird
Bon Voyage
Public Enemy Number One (*Opening Act Two*)
Where Are the Men?

Additional Song Published in Non-show Folio
Kate the Great—cut

Additional Songs Recorded
There's No Cure Like Travel
What a Joy to Be Young

Porter wrote his finest score (other than KISS ME, KATE [December 30, 1948]) for this top-notch musical comedy. Vinton Freedley, heretofore associated with the Gershwins, was just recovering from his insolvency (see PARDON MY ENGLISH [Gershwin: January 20, 1933]). William Gaxton and Victor Moore had first been paired in OF THEE I SING [Gershwin: December 25, 1931] and its sequel LET 'EM EAT CAKE [Gershwin: October 21, 1933]. Now they became Broadway's top comedy team. Ethel Merman, discovered in the final Aarons and Freedley hit GIRL CRAZY [Gershwin: October 14, 1930], took Broadway by storm with her renditions of several sparkling Porter gems (including the amazing trio *I Get a Kick out of You*, *You're the Top*, and the title song). ANYTHING GOES played the Alvin—the house that Aarons, Freedley, and the Gershwins' hits built—although Freedley had to rent it, having lost it after the stock market crash. The Bolton-Wodehouse libretto about the comic aftermath of a shipwreck was hastily discarded when the *Morro Castle* sank off the New Jersey coast (with 134 dead). The authors being unavailable for revisions, it fell to director Howard Lindsay (from GAY DIVORCE [November 29, 1932]) to fashion a new book around the existing songs. Press agent Russel Crouse was brought in to help, forming yet another highly successful partnership. Twenty-five years later, a cut-down revision of ANYTHING GOES was mounted for a successful Off Broadway run. Another twenty-five years later, a full-scale revision (with libretto by John Weidman and Russel Crouse's son Timothy) launched ANYTHING GOES as a hit once again.

JUBILEE

October 12, 1935
Imperial Theatre • 169 performances
Book by Moss Hart; Book directed by Monty Woolley; Staged by Hassard Short; Produced by Sam H. Harris and Max Gordon; With Mary Boland, Melville Cooper, and June Knight.

Published Songs
**Begin the Beguine*
**Just One of Those Things* [2nd]—the hit; different than song from THE NEW YORKERS [December 8, 1930]
**The Kling-Kling Bird on the Divi-Divi Tree*
Me and Marie
A Picture of Me without You
When Love Comes Your Way—originally used (cut) in NYMPH ERRANT [October 6, 1933]
Why Shouldn't I?

Additional Songs Recorded
Entrance of Eric
Ev'rybod-ee Who's Anybod-ee
My Loulou
My Most Intimate Friend
Sunday Morning, Breakfast Time
What a Nice Municipal Park
When Me, Mowgli, Love

Porter rarely needed an excuse to travel; in this case he invited Moss Hart and Monty Woolley along on a five-month world cruise, during which they put together this moderate satire on royalty. By the time *Begin the Beguine* and *Just One of Those Things* caught on, JUBILEE was gone—lasting no longer than the cruise and costing a whole lot more. The success of the *Night and Day* number in the 1934 movie version of THE GAY DIVORCE [November 29, 1932]—the *only* Porter song retained for the film—propelled the composer to Hollywood for the first of several visits. He wrote some of his most popular songs at this time, including *I've Got You under My Skin* and *Easy to Love* for the film *Born to Dance* (1936); **In the Still of the Night* for the film *Rosalie* (1937); and *Don't Fence Me In* [lyric based on a song by Bob Fletcher], which was written for an unproduced film in 1934 and finally introduced by Roy Rogers in *Hollywood Canteen* (1944).

RED, HOT AND BLUE!
October 29, 1936
Alvin Theatre • 183 performances
Book by Howard Lindsay and Russel Crouse;
Directed by Howard Lindsay; Produced by
Vinton Freedley; With Ethel Merman, Jimmy
Durante, and Bob Hope.

Published Songs
*Down in the Depths (On the Ninetieth Floor)
Goodbye, Little Dream, Goodbye—cut; see O
    MISTRESS MINE [December 3, 1936]
*It's De-Lovely
A Little Skipper from Heaven Above
Ours
The Ozarks Are Calling Me Home
Red, Hot and Blue
Ridin' High
You're a Bad Influence on Me
You've Got Something

Additional Songs Published in "Special Edition" Vocal Selection
Perennial Debutantes
What a Great Pair We'll Be

Additional Song Published in Non-show Folio
When Your Troubles Have Started—cut

Additional Songs Recorded
Bertie and Genie—cut
Who But You?—cut

An uneven successor to ANYTHING GOES [November 20, 1934], which met with some success (thanks to the stars). William Gaxton withdrew when he learned Ethel Merman had been promised equal billing, forcing Victor Moore to leave as well. Jimmy Durante, in the role intended for Moore, presented billing problems himself; they finally settled on a diagonal criss-cross design. Bob Hope, fresh from Fanny Brice and the ZIEGFELD FOLLIES OF 1936 [Duke: January 30, 1936], didn't bother with billing: he had a line of his own below the others, undiagonal and considerably more readable. Hope followed RED, HOT AND BLUE! with Hollywood, never to return. Porter's work was far below his ANYTHING GOES output, but he did come up with a worthy successor to You're the Top in It's De-Lovely. On October 24, 1937, just three months after the death of George Gershwin, Porter was critically injured in a horseback riding accident. Opting against amputation, Porter endured constant pain for the rest of his life. After twenty years and thirty operations, he finally lost his right leg (and withdrew into lonely seclusion).

O MISTRESS MINE
December 3, 1936
St. James Theatre {London}
Play by Ben Travers; Directed and Produced by William Mollison; With Yvonne Printemps and Pierre Fresnay.

Published Song
Goodbye, Little Dream, Goodbye—originally
    cut from RED, HOT AND BLUE! [October
    29, 1936]

YOU NEVER KNOW
September 21, 1938
Winter Garden Theatre • 78 performances
Music and Lyrics also by others; Book and Direction by Rowland Leigh (based on Candle Light [play] by Siegfried Geyer); Produced by John Shubert; With Clifton Webb, Lupe Velez, and Libby Holman.

Revival
March 12, 1973
Eastside Playhouse {Off Broadway} •
    8 performances
Directed by Robert Troie

Published Songs
At Long Last Love
For No Rhyme or Reason
From Alpha to Omega
Maria
What Is That Tune?
What Shall I Do?
You Never Know

Additional Songs Published in Non-show Folio
Greek to You—from unproduced musical
    GREEK TO YOU† [circa 1937]; added to
    revival
I'm Going in for Love—cut

Additional Song Recorded
Just One Step ahead of Love—cut

Writing in his hospital bed—press releases claim a song was written as he lay crushed beneath the horse, waiting for the ambulance—Porter turned out a mediocre score for a poor musical. The Shuberts brought in other songwriters to try to strengthen the show, but the major problem was the book—and the additional songs weren't even as good as Porter's.

LEAVE IT TO ME!
November 9, 1938
Imperial Theatre • 291 performances
Book by Bella and Samuel Spewack (based on their play *Clear All Wires*); Directed by Samuel Spewack; Produced by Vinton Freedley; With William Gaxton, Victor Moore, Sophie Tucker, Tamara, and Mary Martin.

Published Songs
Far Away
From Now On
Get out of Town
I Want to Go Home
Most Gentlemen Don't Like Love
*My Heart Belongs to Daddy
Taking the Steps to Russia
To-morrow

Additional Song Published in Non-show Folio
Vite, Vite, Vite—initial publication upon reuse in 1982 movie *Evil under the Sun*

Porter bounced back with a string of six hit musicals despite uniformly lackluster scores. LEAVE IT TO ME gave Victor Moore a better role than William Gaxton for a change; the latter was getting a little past the age for brash romantic leads. The red-hot Sophie Tucker was there as well, in her only musical comedy role; but they were all overshadowed by newcomer Mary Martin, who wowed 'em with her mock-striptease to *My Heart Belongs to Daddy*.

THE SUN NEVER SETS
June 9, 1939
Drury Lane Theatre {London}
Play by Pat Wallace and Guy Bolton (based on stories by Edgar Wallace); Directed by Basil Dean and Richard Llewellyn; With Todd Duncan, Leslie Banks, Adelaide Hall, and Edna Best.

Published Song
River God

THE MAN WHO CAME TO DINNER
October 16, 1939
Music Box Theatre • 739 performances
Play by Moss Hart and George S. Kaufman; Directed by George S. Kaufman; Produced by Sam H. Harris; With Monty Woolley, Edith Atwater, and David Burns.

Song Published in Acting Edition of Script
What Am I to Do?

Hart and Kaufman's play satirized their overbearing pal Alexander Woollcott (played with relish by Porter's longtime chum Monty Woolley). Among the characters was a Cowardish personality who whisked over to the piano and dashed off a little song. Porter supplied *What Am I to Do?*—credited to "Noël Porter."

DUBARRY WAS A LADY
December 6, 1939
46th Street Theatre • 408 performances
Book by Herbert Fields and B. G. DeSylva; Directed by Edgar MacGregor; Produced by B. G. DeSylva; With Bert Lahr, Ethel Merman, Betty Grable, Ronald Graham, and Benny Baker.

Concert Version
February 15, 1996
City Center • 4 performances
Directed by Charles Repole; With Faith Prince [Merman], Robert Morse [Lahr], Scott Waara [Graham], Liz Larsen [Grable], and Mark McGrath [Baker].

Published Songs
But in the Morning, No
Come on In
Do I Love You?
Ev'ry Day a Holiday
*Friendship

Give Him the Oo-La-La
It Was Written in the Stars
Katie Went to Haiti
Well, Did You Evah?—reused with revised
    lyric in 1956 movie *High Society*
When Love Beckoned (In Fifty-Second Street)

Additional Song Published in Non-show Folio
It Ain't Etiquette

Following his 1931 breakup with songwriting
partners Lew Brown and Ray Henderson (see
GEORGE WHITES SCANDALS OF 1926 [Notables: June 14, 1926]), B. G. DeSylva began a
highly successful movie producing career. He
returned to Broadway in 1939, producing (and
coauthoring librettos for) three major hits in less
than a year: two Porter shows and LOUISIANA
PURCHASE [Berlin: May 28, 1940]. DeSylva
brought Herb Fields back from Hollywood for
DUBARRY and signed Merman (star of his preceding musical, TAKE A CHANCE [Youmans:
November 26, 1932]), and Bert Lahr (star of two
DeSylva, Brown, and Henderson hits). Also on
hand was ingenue Betty Grable, who quickly
graduated to Hollywood. Porter's cheerfully energetic score included another classic list song,
Friendship.

PANAMA HATTIE
October 30, 1940
46th Street Theatre • 501 performances
Book by Herbert Fields and B. G. DeSylva;
Directed by Edgar MacGregor; Produced by
B. G. DeSylva; With Ethel Merman, James
Dunn, and Arthur Treacher.

Published Songs
All I've Got to Get Now Is My Man
Fresh As a Daisy
I've Still Got My Health
Let's Be Buddies
Make It Another Old Fashioned, Please
My Mother Would Love You
Visit Panama
Who Would Have Dreamed?

Additional Song Published in Non-show Folio
I'm Throwing a Ball Tonight

Additional Song Recorded
They Ain't Done Right by Our Nell

Another hit for the DUBARRY WAS A LADY
[December 6, 1939] team, although this wartime
entertainment was considerably weaker (only
one number, the tongue-in-cheek cheer-up song
Let's Be Buddies, achieved popularity). Following
his threefold success, producer Buddy DeSylva
was called back to Hollywood to head Paramount
Studios.

LET'S FACE IT
October 29, 1941
Imperial Theatre • 547 performances
Music and Lyrics mostly by Porter; Book by
Herbert and Dorothy Fields (based on *The
Cradle Snatchers* [play] by Norma Mitchell and
Russell Medcraft); Directed by Edgar
MacGregor; Produced by Vinton Freedley;
With Danny Kaye, Eve Arden, Benny Baker,
Edith Meiser, and Mary Jane Walsh.

Published Songs
Ace in the Hole
Ev'rything I Love
Farming
I Hate You Darling
Jerry, My Soldier Boy
Let's Not Talk about Love—revised version of
    Don't Look at Me That Way! from PARIS
    [October 8, 1928]
A Little Rumba Numba
Rub Your Lamp
You Irritate Me So

Additional Songs Recorded
Get Yourself a Girl
A Lady Needs a Rest
Pets—cut
What Are Little Husbands Made Of?—cut

This wartime hit was bolstered by the starring
debut of Danny Kaye (fresh from LADY IN THE
DARK [Weill: January 23, 1941]). The score again
was weak, with nothing standing out other than
a couple of clever comedy songs (*Farming* and
Let's Not Talk about Love). Herb Fields partnered
with his sister Dorothy on the book; he did most
of his future work teamed with her.

SOMETHING FOR THE BOYS
January 7, 1943
Alvin Theatre • 422 performances
Book by Herbert and Dorothy Fields; Directed by Hassard Short and Herbert Fields; Produced by Michael Todd; With Ethel Merman, Bill Johnson, Allen Jenkins, Betty Garrett, and Paula Laurence.

Published Songs
By the Mississinewah
Could It Be You?
He's a Right Guy
Hey, Good Lookin'
I'm in Love with a Soldier Boy
The Leader of a Big-Time Band
See That You're Born in Texas
Something for the Boys
When My Baby Goes to Town

Additional Songs Recorded
Announcement of Inheritance (Prologue)
There's a Happy Land in the Sky
Washington, D.C.—cut
When We're Home on the Range

Porter (and Fields) continued their string of hit musical comedies. The presence of Merman and the wartime atmosphere ensured popularity, even for such inferior material as SOMETHING FOR THE BOYS—a long-run success without even one hit song. Dorothy Fields, meanwhile, came up with a new idea: Ethel Merman playing sharp-shooter Annie Oakley, as in ANNIE GET YOUR GUN [Berlin: May 16, 1946]. (SOMETHING FOR THE BOYS was originally entitled "Jenny Get Your Gun.")

MEXICAN HAYRIDE
January 28, 1944
Winter Garden Theatre • 481 performances
Book by Herbert and Dorothy Fields; Directed by Hassard Short; Produced by Michael Todd; With Bobby Clark, June Havoc, George Givot, and Wilbur Evans.

Published Songs
Abracadabra
Carlotta
Count Your Blessings
Girls

The Good-Will Movement
*I Love You
It Must Be Fun to Be You—cut
Sing to Me, Guitar
There Must Be Someone for Me

Additional Song Published in Non-show Folio
It's Just Yours—cut

Additional Songs Recorded
A Humble Hollywood Executive—cut
What a Crazy Way to Spend Sunday

MEXICAN HAYRIDE, Porter's final collaboration with Herb Fields, was also the final success in his wartime string. Comic Bobby Clark carried the ragtag show, with Porter providing the (rather corny) hit ballad I Love You.

SEVEN LIVELY ARTS
December 7, 1944
Ziegfeld Theatre • 183 performances
Ballet music by Igor Stravinsky; Sketches by Moss Hart, George S. Kaufman, Ben Hecht, and others; Directed by Hassard Short; Produced by Billy Rose; With Beatrice Lillie, Bert Lahr, and Benny Goodman.

Published Songs
The Band Started Swinging a Song
*Ev'ry Time We Say Goodbye
Frahugee-Pahnee
Hence It Don't Make Sense
Is It the Girl (Or Is It the Gown)?
Only Another Boy and Girl
When I Was a Little Cuckoo
Wow-Ooh-Wolf

Additional Songs Recorded
Big Town
Dainty, Quainty Me—cut
I Wrote a Play—cut
Pretty Little Missus Bell—cut

Billy Rose followed his greatest theatrical success—Oscar Hammerstein's adaptation of Bizet, CARMEN JONES [December 2, 1943]—by purchasing the Ziegfeld Theatre. He determined to open it with a spectacularly Rose-ian spectacle, with Lillie and Lahr and Benny Goodman, Salvador Dali scenic conceptions, and a Broadway ballet composed by no less than Igor Stravinsky. All to no avail, and no thanks to Porter's pedestrian score.

AROUND THE WORLD
May 31, 1946
Adelphi Theatre • 75 performances
Book and Direction by Orson Welles (based on *Around the World in Eighty Days* [novel] by Jules Verne); Produced by The Mercury Theatre (Orson Welles); With Arthur Margetson, Julie Warren, and Orson Welles.

Published Songs
If You Smile at Me
Look What I Found
Pipe-Dreaming
Should I Tell You I Love You
There He Goes, Mister Phileas Fogg
Wherever They Fly the Flag of Old England

Orson Welles, who had earned a Hollywood reputation for being wildly creative and totally uncontrollable, returned to Broadway—where he ran amuk with this wildly insane extravaganza. AROUND THE WORLD was Porter's biggest flop, losing a record $300,000 in a day when a big musical could be produced for less than half of that. (The lavish KISS ME, KATE [December 30, 1948] was mounted for $180,000). In trying to cover ballooning costs, Welles sold the motion picture rights to Porter's previous producer Mike Todd—who made the highly successful 1958 movie version without Welles (or, for that matter, Porter).

KISS ME, KATE
December 30, 1948
New Century Theatre • 1,077 performances
Book by Bella and Samuel Spewack (incorporating *The Taming of the Shrew* [play] by William Shakespeare); Directed by John C. Wilson; Choreographed by Hanya Holm; Produced by Arnold Saint Subber and Lemuel Ayers; With Alfred Drake, Patricia Morison, Harold Lang, and Lisa Kirk.

Published Songs
*Always True to You in My Fashion
*Another Op'nin', Another Show

*Bianca
*Brush up Your Shakespeare
*From This Moment On—added to 1953 movie version; originally used (cut) in OUT OF THIS WORLD [December 21, 1950]
I Am Ashamed That Women Are So Simple [lyric by Shakespeare]
I Hate Men
I Sing of Love
*I've Come to Wive It Wealthily in Padua
**So in Love
Tom, Dick or Harry
*Too Darn Hot
We Open in Venice
*Were Thine That Special Face
*Where Is the Life That Late I Led?
*Why Can't You Behave?
*Wunderbar—revised version of *Waltz down the Aisle* (cut) from ANYTHING GOES [November 21, 1934]

Additional Song Published in Vocal Score
Kiss Me, Kate

Additional Song Published in Non-show Folio
I'm Afraid, Sweetheart, I Love You—cut

Additional Songs Recorded
If Ever Married I'm—cut
It Was Great Fun the First Time—cut
We Shall Never Be Younger—cut
What Does Your Servant Dream About?—cut
A Woman's Career—cut

While Kern, Rodgers, and others had been working towards integrated musical theatre since the mid-1920s, Porter never tried for anything more than the best songs he could write at the time—many of them rather good—in whatever framework his librettists happened upon. Following a long creative slump, Porter and the Spewacks (of LEAVE IT TO ME [November 9, 1938]) suddenly and unexpectedly came up with one of the top musical comedies of its day. The contemporary backstage setting gave the composer an opportunity to have swinging musical fun, with *Too Darn Hot* and *Always True to You in My Fashion*; the Shakespearean farce-musical sections gave the adept lyricist a free dramatic reign to rhyme, with *I've Come to Wive It Wealthily in Padua* and *Where Is the Life That Late I Led?*; and the anachronistic combinations of style—*Bianca* and especially *Brush up Your Shakespeare*—were delightfully perfect. Porter also included one of his highly effective, carefully constructed ballads, *So in Love.* KISS ME, KATE was the best, most successful, and most personally gratifying show of Porter's career.

OUT OF THIS WORLD
December 21, 1950
New Century Theatre • 157 performances
Book by Dwight Taylor and Reginald Lawrence (based on the Amphitryon legend); Directed by Agnes de Mille; Choreographed by Hanya Holm; Produced by (Arnold) Saint Subber and Lemuel Ayers; With Charlotte Greenwood, William Eythe, Priscilla Gillette, and David Burns.

Revival
March 30, 1995
City Center • 4 performances
Directed by Mark Brokaw; Produced by City Center Encores; With Andrea Martin [Greenwood], Peter Scolari, Marin Mazzie [Gillette], La Chanze, Ken Page, Gregg Edelman [Eythe], and Ernie Sabella [Burns].

Published Songs
Cherry Pies Ought to Be You
Climb up the Mountain
From This Moment On—cut; reused in 1953 motion picture version of KISS ME, KATE [December 30, 1948]
Hark to the Song of the Night
**I Am Loved*
**Nobody's Chasing Me*
**No Lover*
**Use Your Imagination*
**Where, Oh Where?*
You Don't Remind Me—cut

Additional Song Published in Non-show Folio
Oh, It Must Be Fun—cut

Additional Songs Recorded
Entrance of Juno (*Hail, Hail, Hail*)
I Got Beauty
I Jupiter, I Rex
I Sleep Easier Now

Maiden Fair
Prologue
**They Couldn't Compare to You*
What Do You Think about Men?
Why Do You Wanta Hurt Me So?—cut

As was generally the case, a major hit was followed up with a similarly conceived, highly awaited major flop. Porter provided some of his most intricate work ever, but his skill was overshadowed by a labored book. OUT OF THIS WORLD was also roundly attacked for questionable taste, verbal and visual. The uncredited George Abbott took over from director Agnes de Mille, but the problems needed more than doctoring. Porter provided some uncharacteristically lovely songs (the delicate *I Am Loved* and the sweeping waltz *Where, Oh Where*) and some characteristically sparkling comedy songs (*They Couldn't Compare to You* and *Nobody's Chasing Me*). Not to mention *From This Moment On*, which was lost in Boston. OUT OF THIS WORLD also featured the most colorful, lavish physical production yet seen on Broadway: coproducer Lem Ayers was an inventive, gifted designer (with OKLAHOMA! [Rodgers: March 31, 1943] and KISS ME, KATE [December 30, 1948] to his credit). But OUT OF THIS WORLD proved unworkable.

CAN-CAN
May 7, 1953
Shubert Theatre • 892 performances
Book by Abe Burrows; Direction by Abe Burrows; Choreographed by Michael Kidd; Produced by Cy Feuer and Ernest Martin; With Lilo, Peter Cookson, Erik Rhodes, Hans Conried, and Gwen Verdon.

Revival
April 30, 1981
Minskoff Theatre • 5 performances
Directed by Abe Burrows; Staged and Choreographed by Roland Petit; With Zizi Jeanmaire (Petit) [Lilo], Ron Husmann [Cookson], and Pamela Sousa [Verdon].

Published Songs
Allez-Vous En
Can-Can
**C'est Magnifique*

Come along with Me
I Am in Love
If You Loved Me Truly
I Love Paris
It's All Right with Me
Live and Let Live
Montmart'
Never Give Anything Away

Additional Songs Published in Vocal Score
Every Man Is a Stupid Man
Maidens Typical of France
Never, Never Be an Artist

Additional Songs Published in Non-show Folio
To Think That This Could Happen to Me—cut; see SILK STOCKINGS [February 24, 1955]
When Love Comes to Call—cut
Who Said Gay Paree—cut

Additional Songs Recorded
The Garden of Eden Ballet [instrumental]
Her Heart Was in Her Work—cut

Feuer and Martin followed their first two shows —hit Loesser musicals—with Porter's final two works. Porter had been undergoing a rough period, with increasing deterioration of his injured legs, a 1951 nervous breakdown, and the death of his mother (to whom he was devoted) in 1952. CAN-CAN managed a fair-sized success despite a lukewarm critical reception, with dancer Gwen Verdon stealing the show in her first major role. Porter provided his final hit show tune, *I Love Paris*, and a couple of other pleasant songs as well (*C'est Magnifique, It's All Right with Me*). But CAN-CAN was intrinsically weak, as was highly evident when the show was ill-advisedly revived.

SILK STOCKINGS
February 24, 1955
Imperial Theatre • 478 performances
Book by George S. Kaufman, Leueen MacGrath [Kaufman], and Abe Burrows (based on *Ninotchka* [movie] from a story by Melchior Lengyel); Directed by Cy Feuer; Choreographed by Eugene Loring; Produced by Cy

Feuer and Ernest Martin; With Don Ameche, Hildegarde Neff, and Gretchen Wyler.

Published Songs
All of You—revised version of *To Think That This Could Happen to Me* from CAN-CAN [May 7, 1953]
As on through the Seasons We Sail
Fated to Be Mated—written for 1957 movie version
It's a Chemical Reaction, That's All
Josephine
Paris Loves Lovers
Ritz Roll and Rock—written for 1957 movie version
Satin and Silk
Siberia
Silk Stockings
Stereophonic Sound
Without Love

Additional Song Published in Non-show Folio
Give Me the Land—cut

Additional Songs Recorded
Hail Bibinski
Let's Make It a Night—cut
The Red Blues
Too Bad
Under the Dress—cut

Porter ended his Broadway career with the painfully assembled, second-rate SILK STOCKINGS. Facing severe out-of-town troubles, librettists George S. Kaufman and wife Leueen MacGrath were fired and replaced by Burrows (from GUYS AND DOLLS [Loesser: November 24, 1950] and CAN-CAN [May 7, 1953]). Producer Cy Feuer himself took over from Kaufman as director; he would also step in to finish off the final Richard Rodgers musical, I REMEMBER MAMA [Rodgers: May 31, 1979]). Porter followed SILK STOCKINGS with some miscellaneous work in Hollywood, including *True Love* for the 1956 film *High Society* and a 1958 TV musical, "Aladdin." In April 1958 he finally lost his long-time medical battle: his leg had to be amputated. Porter withdrew from public view and stopped writing. After several years of ill health and severe depression, Cole Porter died of pneumonia in Santa Monica,

California, on October 15, 1964. Broadway has seen two additional musical comedies inexpertly culled from the Porter songbook. Both were adapted from successful plays by Philip Barry, both were well known thanks to first-rate film versions starring Katharine Hepburn, both added songs *for no rhyme or reason* (to quote an old Porter song title), and neither was any good. HAPPY NEW YEAR [April 27, 1980], Burt Shevelove's adaptation of the 1928 comedy *Holiday* (play), ran for 17 performances at the Morosco. HIGH SOCIETY [April 27, 1998; 144 performances], Arthur Kopit's adaptation of the 1939 comedy *The Philadelphia Story* (play), opened eighteen years later to the day for performances at the St. James. Porter himself tried his hand at the latter play for a 1956 film version (as mentioned above), but with little success. HAPPY NEW YEAR was quickly forgotten and HIGH SOCIETY will be, too, leaving the films *Holiday* and *The Philadelphia Story* and Cole Porter unscathed.

Following a lackadaisical twelve-year apprenticeship, Cole Porter startled New York and London in 1928 with sharp, dazzling lyrics and tuneful (if sometimes less than dazzling) music. His work continued to be fresh and imaginative until 1937, when his riding accident seems to have had a permanent effect on his writing: the fun was gone. The next decade contained an impressive number of successful shows, mostly energetic wartime hits, but few of the songs were at all comparable to the earlier work. With the brilliant KISS ME, KATE [December 30, 1948], Porter instantly caught up with his contemporaries and the newcomers who had passed him by. But the creative renaissance proved to be temporary. It is disconcerting (and somewhat surprising) to play through all of Porter's work and discover that much of it is quite ordinary. But the good music is often very good, and the good lyrics are always superb, and there are enough great songs to justify Porter's place among Broadway's best songwriters.

ARTHUR SCHWARTZ

Born: November 25, 1900, Brooklyn, New York
Died: September 3, 1984, Kintnersville, Pennsylvania

ARTHUR SCHWARTZ displayed an early interest in music—despite objections from his father, a lawyer—and by the age of fourteen was playing piano accompaniment in Brooklyn movie houses. After graduating from NYU, he went on to Columbia Law School while supporting himself by teaching high school English. Schwartz continued his music hobby, though, with his first published song coming in 1923, the rhythmic *Baltimore, Md., That's the Only Doctor for Me* [lyric by Eli Dawson]. More important, while working at a summer camp (circa 1923) he met a fellow counselor who was a brilliant but as yet unsuccessful lyricist. Lorenz Hart already had a collaborator, but he wrote a few songs with Schwartz—including one that six years later, with a new lyric by Howard Dietz, would become Schwartz's first song hit. In 1926, lawyer Schwartz got his first professional chance, writing for an intimate, sophisticated revue.

THE GRAND STREET FOLLIES OF 1926 ✦ Third Edition
June 15, 1926
Neighborhood Playhouse {Off Broadway} • 55 performances
Music also by Lily Hyland and Randall Thompson; Book, Lyrics, and Direction by Agnes Morgan; Produced by The Neighborhood Playhouse; With Albert Carroll and Agnes Morgan.

Published Songs
If You Know What I Mean [lyric by Theodore Goodwin and Carroll]
Little Igloo for Two
Polar Bear Strut

THE GRAND STREET FOLLIES was what would today be considered an Off Broadway revue, providing amusing, contemporary competition to the uptown annuals. The Schwartz contributions were entertaining, though certainly unremarkable.

THE NEW YORKERS [1927]
March 10, 1927
Edyth Totten Theatre • 52 performances
Music also by Edgar Fairchild and Charles M. Schwab; Lyrics by Henry Myers; Book by Jo Swerling; Directed by Milton Bender; Produced by Milton Bender and Henry Myers.
Pre-Broadway title: 1928.

Published Song
Floating thru the Air

THE NEW YORKERS was assembled by Larry Hart's close friend, dentist Milton Bender (see ONE MINUTE PLEASE [Rodgers: December 29, 1917]). "Doc" Bender held Machiavellian power over Hart, soon giving up his dental career to become the lyricist's agent. His Broadway presence increased as Hart brought Bender friends like Tamara Geva, George Balanchine, Vernon Duke, and Vera Zorina.

GOOD BOY
September 5, 1928
Hammerstein's Theatre • 253 performances
Music mostly by Harry Ruby and Herbert Stothart; Lyrics mostly by Bert Kalmar; Book by Otto Harbach, Oscar Hammerstein 2nd, and Henry Myers; Directed by Reginald Hammerstein; Produced by Arthur Hammerstein; With Eddie Buzzell and Helen Kane.

Published Song
You're the One [lyric by Harbach]

This musical comedy featured Helen Kane introducing Kalmar and Ruby's song-hit *I Wanna Be Loved by You*, sweeping her to fame as the "Boop-Boop-a-Doop Girl."

WELL! WELL! WELL!
December 10, 1928
Shubert Theatre {New Haven, Conn.} •
 Closed during tryout
"The Musical Comedy Surprise." Music by Muriel Pollock and Schwartz; Lyrics by Max and Nathaniel Lief; Book by Montague Glass, Jules Erhart Goodman, and Harold Atteridge; Directed by Lew Morton; Produced by the Messrs. Shubert; With Jack Pearl.

Published Songs
I'll Always Remember—for initial publication see GRAND STREET FOLLIES OF 1929 [May 1, 1929]
I Love You and I Like You—for initial publication see GRAND STREET FOLLIES OF 1929
She's Such a Comfort to Me [lyric by Douglas Furber and Donovan Parsons]—for initial publication see THE HOUSE THAT JACK BUILT [November 8, 1929]

Schwartz's first full-scale Broadway opportunity shuttered after a three-week tryout. Revamped into a revue, PLEASURE BOUND [February 18, 1929] had a 136-performance run—without the use of Schwartz's material, though.

THE RED ROBE
December 25, 1928
Shubert Theatre • 167 performances
Music mostly by Jean Gilbert; Book and Lyrics mostly by Harry B. Smith (based on the novel by Stanley Weyman); Directed by Stanley Logan; Produced by the Messrs. Shubert; With Walter Woolf and José Ruben.

Published Song
Believe in Me

This dreary operetta was one of seven Broadway shows to open on Christmas Night of 1928, none

of them distinguished. Larry Hart, meanwhile, prodded Schwartz into giving up his law practice to concentrate on songwriting.

NED WAYBURN'S GAMBOLS
January 15, 1929
Knickerbocker Theatre • 31 performances
Music mostly by Walter G. Samuels; Lyrics by Morrie Ryskind; Produced and Directed by Ned Wayburn.

Published Song
*The Sun Will Shine

Ned Wayburn, formerly staff director for Lew Fields, Ziegfeld, and the Shuberts, staged an impressively large number of early revues and musicals. The totally unknown and neglected *The Sun Will Shine* was the first of Schwartz's beautiful ballads. Morrie Ryskind wrote the lyric; he went on to become an important satirist (see STRIKE UP THE BAND [1930] [Gershwin: January 14, 1930]).

THE LITTLE SHOW
April 30, 1929
Music Box Theatre • 321 performances
Music mostly by Schwartz; Lyrics mostly by Howard Dietz; Sketches by Howard Dietz, George S. Kaufman, and others; Directed by Dwight Deere Wiman and Alexander Leftwich; Produced by William A. Brady, Jr., and Dwight Deere Wiman, in association with Tom Weatherly; With Clifton Webb, Fred Allen, and Libby Holman.

Published Songs
**I Guess I'll Have to Change My Plan (*The Blue Pajama Song*)—new lyric for *I Love to Lie Awake in Bed* [lyric by Lorenz Hart]
I've Made a Habit of You
Song of the Riveter [lyric by Lew Levinson]—published in non-show edition

Additional Songs Published (No Lyric) in Piano Selection
Get up on a New Routine
The Theme Song

Following the lead of the MUSIC BOX REVUE [Berlin: September 22, 1921] and other intimate revues of the twenties, THE LITTLE SHOW added sophistication and contemporary sensibilities to the mix. The new-style revue had great success during the depression, with Schwartz and Dietz leading the field. Howard Dietz already had something of a name around town. His first song hit was *Alibi Baby* [music by Stephen Jones] from POPPY† [September 3, 1923], although Dorothy Donnelly, the show's contractual lyricist, refused to allow him credit. But publisher Max Dreyfus was impressed and sent Dietz to Jerome Kern for the unsuccessful DEAR SIR [Kern: September 23, 1924]. Schwartz was impressed, if no one else was: he recognized something in Dietz akin to Hart and tried to collaborate with Dietz (a Columbia classmate of both Hart and Hammerstein). Dietz preferred not to go from Kern to an unknown lawyer but was able to find little Broadway work (except filling in during Ira Gershwin's appendicitis on OH, KAY! [Gershwin: November 8, 1926]). Dietz didn't need Broadway work, exactly; he was director of promotion for Louis B. Mayer at MGM (and its predecessor companies) from 1924 to 1957. (A top Dietz idea: creating that famous animal icon, Leo the Lion). By 1929 he was ready to reconsider Schwartz's offer, and the successful collaboration began with THE LITTLE SHOW. *I Guess I'll Have to Change My Plan* is an especially felicitous schottische, with Dietz's risqué postprandial second refrain causing it to be subtitled *The Blue Pajama Song*. It was originally written as *I Love to Lie Awake in Bed* [lyric by Lorenz Hart] for the summer camp show DREAM BOY† [circa 1923]. The song-hit of THE LITTLE SHOW, though, was the non-Schwartz *Moanin' Low*, which Dietz wrote with Ralph Rainger.

THE GRAND STREET FOLLIES OF 1929 ✦ Sixth Edition
May 1, 1929
Booth Theatre • 93 performances
Music also by Max Ewing and others; Lyrics mostly by Agnes Morgan; Book and Direction by Agnes Morgan; Produced by The Actor-Managers, Inc., in association with Paul Moss; With Albert Carroll, Paula Trueman, and James Cagney.

Published Songs

I Love You and I Like You [lyric by Max and Nathaniel Lief]—originally used in WELL! WELL! WELL! [December 10, 1928]; also used in HERE COMES THE BRIDE [February 20, 1930]

I Need You So [lyric by David Goldberg and Howard Dietz]

What Did Della Wear (*When Georgie Came Across?*) [lyric by Morgan]

The Shuberts bought the successful GRAND STREET FOLLIES revue and brought it uptown. Schwartz's contributions included the Revolutionary War novelty *What Did Della Wear*, which according to the sheet music was introduced by Albert Carroll impersonating Fanny Brice.

THE HOUSE THAT JACK BUILT
November 8, 1929
Adelphi Theatre {London} •
270 performances
Music mostly by Ivor Novello; Lyrics mostly by Donovan Parsons; Book by Ronald Jeans and Douglas Furber; Directed and Produced by Jack Hulbert; With Cicely Courtneidge (Hulbert) and Jack Hulbert.

Published Song

She's Such a Comfort to Me [lyric by Furber and Parsons]—revised lyric for song originally used in WELL! WELL! WELL! [December 10, 1928]; also used in the New York production of WAKE UP AND DREAM [December 30, 1929]

WAKE UP AND DREAM
December 30, 1929
Selwyn Theatre • 136 performances
Music and Lyrics mostly by Cole Porter (see Porter: March 27, 1929); Book by John Hastings Turner; Directed by Frank Collins; Produced by Arch Selwyn in association with Charles B. Cochran; With Jack Buchanan and Jessie Matthews.

Published Song

She's Such a Comfort to Me [lyric by Douglas Furber, Max and Nathaniel Lief, and

Donovan Parsons]—see THE HOUSE THAT JACK BUILT [November 8, 1929]

HERE COMES THE BRIDE
February 20, 1930
Piccadilly Theatre {London} •
175 performances
"A Musical Farcical Comedy." Lyrics mostly by Desmond Carter; Book by R. P. Weston and Bert Lee (based on the play by Edgar MacGregor and Otto Harbach); Produced by Julian Wylie; With Clifford Mollison and Edmund Gwenn.

Published Songs
High and Low [lyric by Howard Dietz and Carter]—also used in THE BAND WAGON [June 3, 1931]
Hot [lyric by Carter and Lew Levinson]
I'll Always Remember [lyric by Max and Nathaniel Lief and Carter]—revised lyric for song originally used in WELL! WELL! WELL! [December 10, 1928]
I Love You and I Like You [lyric by Max and Nathaniel Lief]—see GRAND STREET FOLLIES OF 1929 [May 1, 1929]
I'm Like a Sailor (*Home from the Sea*) [lyric by Dietz and Carter]
Rose in Your Hair

Additional Song Published (No Lyric) in Piano Selection
Why Not Have a Little Party?

Schwartz went to London to write his first of three 1930s West End book musicals. It is to be assumed that the two songs credited to "Dietz and Carter" are actually by Dietz, with Carter credited due to contractual obligations; *High and Low*, the only notable song of the score, was credited solely to Dietz when it reappeared the following year—with exactly the same lyric—in THE BAND WAGON.

THE CO-OPTIMISTS OF 1930
April 4, 1930
Hippodrome {London}
"A Pierrotic Entertainment." Book and Lyrics mostly by Greatrex Newman; Directed by Leslie Henson; With Stanley Holloway, Cyril Ritchard, and Elsie Randolph.

Published Songs
Dancing Town
The Moment I Saw You [lyric by Howard Dietz and Newman]—also used in THREE'S A CROWD [October 15, 1931]
Steeplejack
Sunday Afternoon

Additional Songs Published (No Lyrics) in Piano Selections
Nothing up Our Sleeves
The Stuff to Give the Troops

The lyric to *The Moment I Saw You* was credited to Dietz alone in its American printing.

THE SECOND LITTLE SHOW
September 2, 1930
Royale Theatre • 63 performances
Music mostly by Schwartz; Lyrics mostly by Howard Dietz; Directed by Dwight Deere Wiman and Monty Woolley; Choreographed by Dave Gould; Produced by Dwight Deere Wiman and William A. Brady, Jr., in association with Tom Weatherly; With Al Trahan, J. C. Flippen, and Gloria Grafton.

Published Songs
I Like Your Face—initially issued as *Foolish Face*
Lucky Seven
What a Case I've Got on You!—see NICE GOINGS ON [September 13, 1933]
You're the Sunrise

The producers of THE LITTLE SHOW [April 30, 1929] decided to do a follow-up. Attempting to establish themselves independent of stars, they went ahead without Webb, Allen, and Holman of the first edition. THE SECOND and the non–Schwartz and Dietz THIRD LITTLE SHOW [Lane: June 1, 1931] did poorly, while Webb, Allen, and Holman went on to immediate success—in another Schwartz and Dietz revue under different management.

PRINCESS CHARMING
October 13, 1930
Imperial Theatre • 56 performances
Music by Albert Sirmay and Schwartz; Lyrics by Arthur Swanstrom; Book by Jack Donahue

(based on Arthur Wimperis and Lauri Wylie's British adaptation of the Austrian book by Ferencz Martos); Directed by Bobby Connolly; Choreographed by Albertina Rasch; Produced by Bobby Connolly and Arthur Swanstrom; With Evelyn Herbert, Robert Halliday, George Grossmith, Jeanne Aubert, and Victor Moore.

Published Songs
I'll Be There
I'll Never Leave You
I Must Be One of Those Roses
Just a Friend of Mine
Never Mind How
Trailing a Shooting Star
You

The continental operetta PRINCESS CHARMING was not especially distinguished, though it contained one song hit—the snappy, interpolated *I Love Love* [music by Robert Dolan, lyrics by Walter O'Keefe]. Hungarian-born composer Albert Sirmay went on to become a major behind-the-scenes figure at Max Dreyfus's music publishing house Chappell & Co., the successor to Harms.

THREE'S A CROWD
October 15, 1930
Selwyn Theatre • 271 performances
Music mostly by Schwartz (see Duke, Lane: October 15, 1930); Lyrics mostly by Howard Dietz; Sketches by Howard Dietz, Groucho Marx, and others; Directed by Hassard Short; Choreographed by Albertina Rasch; Produced by Max Gordon; With Clifton Webb, Fred Allen, Libby Holman, and Tamara Geva.

Published Songs
The Moment I Saw You—see THE CO-OPTIMISTS OF 1930 [April 4, 1930]
Right at the Start of It
**Something to Remember You By*—new lyric for *I Have No Words* (*To Say How Much I Love You*) from LITTLE TOMMY TUCKER [November 19, 1930]

With the authors and cast of the highly successful LITTLE SHOW [April 30, 1929] available and willing, enterprising vaudeville producer Max Gordon logically concluded that an unofficial

sequel—with stars Clifton Webb, Fred Allen, and Libby Holman—had a better chance than THE SECOND LITTLE SHOW [September 2, 1930]. He was right. Gordon became a major force in the Broadway theatre for the next fifteen years. While *Something to Remember You By* was a substantial hit, it was Holman singing the interpolated *Body and Soul* [music by Johnny Green, lyric by Edward Heyman and Robert Sour], which created a furor.

LITTLE TOMMY TUCKER
November 19, 1930
Daly's Theatre {London}
Music mostly by Vivian Ellis; Lyrics by Desmond Carter; Book by Desmond Carter, Caswell Garth, Bert Lee, and R. P. Weston; Directed by William Mollison; Produced by Herbert Clayton; With Ivy Tresmand, Rita Pepe, Jane Welsh, and Melville Cooper.

Published Songs
I Have No Words—see THREE'S A CROWD [October 15, 1930]
Out of the Blue [music by Ellis and Schwartz]

Although LITTLE TOMMY TUCKER opened after THREE'S A CROWD, *I Have Words* was published two weeks before the Dietz lyric for the same music, *Something to Remember You By*.

THE BAND WAGON
June 3, 1931
New Amsterdam Theatre • 260 performances
Lyrics by Howard Dietz; Sketches by George S. Kaufman and Howard Dietz; Directed by Hassard Short; Choreographed by Albertina Rasch; Produced by Max Gordon; With Fred & Adele Astaire, Frank Morgan, Helen Broderick, and Tilly Losch.

Published Songs
Confession
**Dancing in the Dark*
High and Low (*I've Been Looking for You*)—see HERE COMES THE BRIDE [February 20, 1930]
Hoops
I Love Louisa
Miserable with You

New Sun in the Sky
*Sweet Music
**That's Entertainment—written for 1953
   movie version *The Bandwagon*
*Triplets—added to 1953 movie version; see
   BETWEEN THE DEVIL [December 22, 1937]

Additional Number Published in Piano Selection

Beggar's Waltz [instrumental]—subsequently
   published (1932) as non-show song *Is It
   All a Dream?* [lyric by Dietz]

Additional Songs Recorded

Ballet Music [instrumental]
*It Better Be Good (*Opening*)
Nanette
Where Can He Be?
White Heat

Having learned the advantages of having
the fewest possible writers creating a revue,
Schwartz and Dietz suggested that the sketches
for their next revue come from one man only:
George S. Kaufman, who had contributed important sketches to THE LITTLE SHOW [April
30, 1929]. Like Dietz, the immensely successful Kaufman kept a full-time "real" job—as drama
editor of the *New York Times*. Director Hassard
Short, a prime force in the MUSIC BOX REVUES
[Berlin: September 22, 1921], experimented with
moving turntables, mirrors, and novel lighting effects. Songs, sketches, and dances were carefully tailored to the exceptional cast, led by the
Astaires. The resulting BAND WAGON was considered the finest musical revue of its time. The
score contains several fine songs, including one
of the all-time great show tunes: *Dancing in the
Dark*. THE BAND WAGON marked the final professional appearance of Adele Astaire; after spending most of her first thirty years on the stage,
she retired to become a lady (as wife of Lord
Cavendish). Broadway wondered if her brother—
the less charming, weak-voiced, balding straight
man of the team—could succeed on his own.

FLYING COLORS

September 15, 1932
Imperial Theatre • 188 performances
"The Howard Dietz Revue." Lyrics, Sketches,
and Direction by Howard Dietz; Choreo-
graphed by Albertina Rasch; Produced by
Max Gordon; With Clifton Webb, Charles
Butterworth, Tamara Geva, and Patsy Kelly.

Published Songs

**Alone Together
Fatal Fascination
Louisiana Hayride
A Rainy Day
*A Shine on Your Shoes
Smokin' Reefers
*Triplets—cut; for initial publication see
   BETWEEN THE DEVIL [December 22,
   1937]
Two-Faced Woman—added after opening;
   published in separate edition

Additional Song Published (No Lyric) in Piano Selection

Mein Kleine Acrobat—initial publication upon
   reuse in FOLLOW THE SUN [February 4,
   1936]

Additional Song Recorded

Mother Told Me So

In their fifth revue together, Schwartz and Dietz
had a difficult time coming through with FLY-
ING COLORS. Grave conditions were faced in
Philadelphia, including producer Max Gordon's
nervous breakdown and attempted suicide (by
jumping from the balcony lobby of the Forrest Theatre) and the last-minute firing of novice choreographer Agnes de Mille. The show
certainly couldn't compare with THE BAND
WAGON, although the score contained three
hits: *A Shine on Your Shoes, Louisiana Hayride,*
and the worthy successor to *Dancing in the Dark,*
the similarly stunning *Alone Together.*

NICE GOINGS ON

September 13, 1933
Strand Theatre {London} • 221 performances
Lyrics mostly by Frank Eyton; Book by
Douglas Furber; Directed by Leslie Henson;
Produced by Leslie Henson and Firth Shephard;
With Leslie Henson and Zelma O'Neal.

Published Songs

I Know the Kind of Girl [lyric by Furber]
Sweet One

'Twixt the Devil and the Deep Blue Sea
What a Young Girl Ought to Know—revised
    version of *What a Case I've Got on You*
    from SECOND LITTLE SHOW [September
    2, 1930]
Whatever You Do
With You Here and Me Here

SHE LOVES ME NOT
November 20, 1933
46th Street Theatre • 248 performances
Play by Howard Lindsay (based on a novel by
Edward Hope); Lyrics by Edward Heyman;
Directed by Howard Lindsay; Produced by
Dwight Deere Wiman and Tom Weatherly.

Published Songs
After All, You're All I'm After
She Loves Me Not

ZIEGFELD FOLLIES OF 1934
January 4, 1934
Winter Garden Theatre • 182 performances
Music mostly by Vernon Duke (see Duke:
January 4, 1934); Lyrics mostly by E. Y.
Harburg; Directed by Bobby Connolly and
John Murray Anderson; Produced by "Mrs.
Florenz Ziegfeld" [the Messrs. Shubert]; With
Fanny Brice, Willie & Eugene Howard, and
Jane Froman.

Song Recorded
Then I'll Be Tired of You

BRING ON THE GIRLS
October 22, 1934
National Theatre {Washington, D.C.} •
    Closed during tryout
Play by George S. Kaufman and Morrie
Ryskind; Directed by George S. Kaufman;
Produced by Sam H. Harris; With Jack Benny,
Porter Hall, Claire Carleton, and Oscar Polk.

Published Song
Down on the Old-Time Farm [lyric by Ryskind]

This Kaufman/Ryskind New Deal satire simply
didn't work and closed during the tryout. Audiences expecting another OF THEE I SING

[Gershwin: December 26, 1931] were greatly disappointed. To begin with, BRING ON THE GIRLS
wasn't even a musical.

REVENGE WITH MUSIC
November 28, 1934
New Amsterdam Theatre • 158 performances
Book and Lyrics by Howard Dietz (based on
The Three-Cornered Hat [novel] by Pedro
de Alarcon); Directed by Komisarjevsky
and Worthington Miner; Choreographed
by Michael Mordkin; Produced by Arch
Selwyn and Harold B. Franklin; With Charles
Winninger, Libby Holman, Georges Metaxa,
Ilka Chase, and Rex O'Malley.

Published Songs
If There Is Someone Lovelier than You
Maria
That Fellow Manuelo
Wand'ring Heart
When You Love Only One
**You and the Night and the Music*—revised
    version of *To-Night* [lyric by Desmond
    Carter] from 1934 movie *The Queen*.

Additional Song Recorded
In the Noonday Sun

REVENGE WITH MUSIC brought the scandalous Libby Holman (of THE LITTLE SHOW [April
30, 1929]) back to Broadway after her brief marriage to Zachary Smith Reynolds, which ended
in the young tobacco heir's suicide. Even the
abundant publicity wasn't enough to salvage
Schwartz and Dietz's first book musical. The
tempestuous *You and the Night and the Music* was
originally written as a sweeping waltz, *To-Night*.

AT HOME ABROAD
September 19, 1935
Winter Garden Theatre • 198 performances
"*A Musical Holiday.*" Lyrics by Howard Dietz;
Sketches by Howard Dietz and others;
Directed by Vincente Minnelli and Thomas
Mitchell; Choreographed by Gene Snyder
and Harry Losee; Produced by the Messrs.
Shubert; With Beatrice Lillie, Ethel Waters,
Herb Williams, Eleanor Powell, and Reginald
Gardiner.

Published Songs
Farewell, My Lovely
Got a Bran' New Suit
The Hottentot Potentate
Love is a Dancing Thing
O Leo
That's Not Cricket
Thief in the Night
What a Wonderful World

Additional Songs Published [with Non-Dietz Lyric Revisions] in USO's *At Ease*
Get Away from It All—retitled *Come along to Our Show*
The Lady with the Tap-Tap-Tap—retitled *The Soldier with the Tap-Tap-Tap*

Additional Songs Recorded
*Get Yourself a Geisha
Loadin' Time
*Paree

Schwartz and Dietz met Beatrice Lillie in this first of two hit revues they did together. The score was not up to their previous standards —the "big" songs, *Farewell, My Lovely* and *Thief in the Night*, don't quite make it—but *Get Yourself a Geisha* (with Lillie at the end of a Japanese chorus line) and *Paree* are delights. Also on this worldwide travelogue were comic foils Herb Williams and Reginald Gardiner, while Ethel Waters sang and Eleanor Powell tapped her way to Hollywood. Despite their continued Broadway success, Dietz kept his day job at MGM. Schwartz—a full-time composer stuck with a highly complementary but part-time lyricist—began to search for a new collaborator.

FOLLOW THE SUN
February 4, 1936
Adelphi Theatre {London} •
204 performances
Lyrics by Howard Dietz and Desmond Carter; Book by Ronald Jeans and John Hastings Turner; Produced by Charles B. Cochran; With Claire Luce and Nick Long, Jr.

Published Songs
Dangerous You [lyric by Carter]
How High Can a Little Bird Fly? [lyric by Dietz]—initially used in the 1934 radio serial *The Gibson Family*
Nicotina [lyric by Carter]
Sleigh Bells [lyric by Dietz]—published in separate edition

Additional Songs Published (No Lyric) in Piano Selection
Follow the Sun
Mein Kleine Acrobat—originally used (unpublished) in FLYING COLORS [September 15, 1932]
The Steamboat Whistle

THE SHOW IS ON
December 25, 1936
Winter Garden Theatre • 237 performances
Music mostly by Vernon Duke (see Duke: December 25, 1936; also Arlen, Gershwin, and Rodgers; Lyric to Schwartz song by Howard Dietz; Sketches mostly by David Freedman and Moss Hart; Directed and Designed by Vincente Minnelli; Choreographed by Robert Alton; Produced by Lee Shubert; With Beatrice Lillie, Bert Lahr, Reginald Gardiner, and Mitzi Mayfair.

Song Published [with Non-Dietz Lyric Revisions] in USO's *At Ease*
Shakespearean Opening

VIRGINIA
September 2, 1937
Center Theatre • 60 performances
"The American Musical Romance." Lyrics by Albert Stillman; Book by Laurence Stallings and Owen Davis; Book directed by Edward Clark Lilley; Staged by Leon Leonidoff; Produced by The Center Theatre; With Anne Booth, Gene Lockhart, Ronald Graham, and Nigel Bruce.

Published Songs
Good and Lucky
Good-Bye Jonah

If You Were Someone Else
My Bridal Gown [lyric by Stillman and
    Stallings]
My Heart Is Dancing
An Old Flame Never Dies [lyric by Stillman
    and Stallings]
Virginia
You and I Know [lyric by Stillman and Stallings]

The Rockefellers' initial theatrical attraction at their Music Hall twin had been Max Gordon's spectacular production of the Strauss-filled THE GREAT WALTZ[†] [September 22, 1934]. The overwhelming scale of the house made it difficult to come up with suitable future attractions—a fact which was soon to end the theatre's legitimate career. The colonial operetta VIRGINIA was overblown and represented a major financial loss.

BETWEEN THE DEVIL
December 22, 1937
Imperial Theatre • 93 performances
Book and Lyrics by Howard Dietz; Directed by Hassard Short; Choreographed by Robert Alton; Produced by the Messrs. Shubert; With Jack Buchanan, Evelyn Laye, and Adele Dixon.

Published Songs
*By Myself
Don't Go Away, Monsieur
Double Trouble—advertised but not published
I Believe in You—issued as professional copy
*I See Your Face before Me
Triplets—written for FLYING COLORS
    [September 15, 1932] (unused); initial
    publication upon reuse in 1953 movie
    version of THE BAND WAGON [June 3,
    1931]
Why Did You Do It?
You Have Everything

Additional Song Published [with Non-Dietz Lyric Revisions] in USO's *At Ease*
The Uniform

Additional Song Recorded
Imaginist Rhythm

This second Schwartz and Dietz book musical was a dated marital farce, notable only for two fine songs (*By Myself* and the evocative *I See Your Face before Me*). Neither Dietz nor Schwartz ever found Broadway success outside the revue format. Following BETWEEN THE DEVIL the team terminated their collaboration after eight full scores in as many years. Dietz continued his MGM work—he became a vice president in 1940—and entered a wartime collaboration with Vernon Duke. Schwartz worked with various top lyricists in New York and Hollywood, including Dorothy Fields, Johnny Mercer, Frank Loesser, and Ira Gershwin.

STARS IN YOUR EYES
February 9, 1939
Majestic Theatre • 127 performances
Lyrics by Dorothy Fields; Book by J. P. McEvoy; Directed by Joshua Logan; Choreographed by Carl Randall; Produced by Dwight Deere Wiman; With Ethel Merman, Jimmy Durante, Tamara Toumanova, Richard Carlson, and Mildred Natwick.

Published Songs
All the Time
I'll Pay the Check
It's All Yours
Just a Little Bit More
A Lady Needs a Change
Terribly Attractive
This Is It

Additional Song Recorded
Where Do I Go from You?

What was intended to be a politically tinged satire of the movie industry—with Jimmy Durante as a union organizer—lost its bite early on. All that remained were Merman and Durante, which was nothing to be sneezed at. This time, incidentally, Merman got first billing without a fight (see RED, HOT AND BLUE! [Porter: October 29, 1936]). Schwartz's new lyricist was Dorothy Fields, Jimmy McHugh's former collaborator on BLACKBIRDS OF 1928 [Notables: May 9, 1928]) and a recent Oscar winner for *The Way You Look Tonight* [music by Jerome Kern].

AMERICAN JUBILEE
May 12, 1940
American Jubilee Theatre {New York World's Fair}
Book and Lyrics by Oscar Hammerstein 2nd; Directed by Leon Leonidoff; Produced by Albert Johnson; Presented by the New York World's Fair Corporation; With Lucy Monroe "and a cast of 350."

Published Songs
How Can I Ever Be Alone?
My Bicycle Girl
Tennessee Fish Fry
We Like It over Here

A patriotic pageant mounted for the New York World's Fair. The only item of interest was Schwartz's catchy *Tennessee Fish Fry*, which composer Leroy Anderson appears to have caught. (He added bells and called it *Sleigh Ride* [1950], now a winter-time standard.) Following AMERICAN JUBILEE, Schwartz went to Hollywood—though not to MGM—where he produced two notable movie musicals: the 1944 Kern/Ira Gershwin *Cover Girl* and the 1946 Cole Porter–pseudo-biography *Night and Day*. Schwartz also wrote some especially tuneful movie songs, such as *Thank Your Lucky Stars*, *Love Isn't Born (It's Made)*, and *Ice Cold Katy*—all with nifty Loesser lyrics—and the lovely *A Gal in Calico* [lyric by Leo Robin].

PARK AVENUE
November 4, 1946
Shubert Theatre • 72 performances
Lyrics by Ira Gershwin; Book by Nunnally Johnson and George S. Kaufman; Directed by George S. Kaufman; Choreographed by Helen Tamiris; Produced by Max Gordon; With Leonora Corbett, Arthur Margetson, Raymond Walburn, Mary Wickes, and David Wayne.

Published Songs
For the Life of Me
**Goodbye to All That
There's No Holding Me

Additional Song Published in Non-show Folio
Don't Be a Woman If You Can

Additional Song Recorded
My Son-in-Law

A highly disappointing show from a distinguished set of authors. Left behind was the exquisite ballad *Goodbye to All That*. For the fifty-year-old Ira Gershwin, two consecutive flops—the other being THE FIREBRAND OF FLORENCE [Weill: March 22, 1945]—were enough; he went back home to Beverly Hills and stayed for good. Gershwin soon retired, but not before writing one last song classic, *The Man That Got Away* [music by Harold Arlen], for the 1954 movie remake of *A Star Is Born*.

INSIDE U.S.A.
April 30, 1948
New Century Theatre • 399 performances
Lyrics by Howard Dietz; Sketches by Arnold Auerbach, Moss Hart, and Arnold Horwitt (title suggested by the book by John Gunther); Directed by Robert H. Gordon; Choreographed by Helen Tamiris; Produced by Schwartz; With Beatrice Lillie, Jack Haley, Herb Shriner, and Valerie Bettis.

Published Songs
Blue Grass
First Prize at the Fair
Haunted Heart
My Gal Is Mine Once More
*Rhode Island Is Famous for You

Additional Songs Recorded
Atlanta
At the Mardi Gras
Come O Come (to Pittsburgh)
Inside U.S.A.
Protect Me

Schwartz reunited with Dietz and Bea Lillie for this stateside follow-up to AT HOME ABROAD [September 19, 1935], produced by the composer himself. The score was only fair, ranging from the charming *Rhode Island Is Famous for You* to the big ballad *Haunted Heart* (which is a little too haunted for my taste); but Bea Lillie at her finest was more than enough to make INSIDE U.S.A. a moderate hit. It was also to be the final success Dietz or Schwartz were to have, although the latter was still to create some of his finest work.

A TREE GROWS IN BROOKLYN
April 19, 1951
Alvin Theatre • 267 performances
Lyrics by Dorothy Fields; Book by Betty Smith and George Abbott (based on the novel by Betty Smith); Directed by George Abbott; Choreographed by Herbert Ross; Produced by George Abbott in association with Robert Fryer; With Shirley Booth, Johnnie Johnston, Marcia Van Dyke, and Nathaniel Frey.

Published Songs
Growing Pains
If You Haven't Got a Sweetheart
**I'll Buy You a Star*
I'm Like a New Broom
Look Who's Dancing
Love Is the Reason
**Make the Man Love Me*

Additional Songs Recorded
Don't Be Afraid of Anything
Halloween [instrumental]
He Had Refinement
Is That My Prince?
Mine 'til Monday
Payday
That's How It Goes
Tuscaloosa—cut; see BY THE BEAUTIFUL SEA
    [April 8, 1954]

One of Schwartz's richest scores and clearly his finest book musical, based on the popular novel. The librettists sought to balance the story's tragic elements by building up the humorous subplot; this proved a fatal mistake, as the casting of Shirley Booth made a star role out of a subordinate character. Booth's fine performance helped the show achieve a respectable, if unprofitable, run. The usually urbane Schwartz revealed a powerful, emotional side in writing for the unsophisticated, uneducated characters. Resulting treasures (adorned by Dorothy Fields's best stage work) included *Make the Man Love Me, I'll Buy You a Star*, and *Don't Be Afraid of Anything*.

BY THE BEAUTIFUL SEA
April 8, 1954
Majestic Theatre • 270 performances
Lyrics by Dorothy Fields; Book by Herbert and Dorothy Fields; Directed by Marshall Jamison; Choreographed by Helen Tamiris; Produced by Robert Fryer and Lawrence Carr; With Shirley Booth, Wilbur Evans, Cameron Prud'homme, Richard France, and Mae Barnes.

Published Songs
Alone Too Long
Hang Up!
**Happy Habit*
More Love Than Your Love
The Sea Song (*By the Beautiful Sea*)

Additional Songs Recorded
Coney Island Boat
Good Time Charlie
Hooray for George the Third
**I'd Rather Wake Up by Myself*
Old Enough to Love—new lyric for *Tuscaloosa*
    (cut, unpublished) from A TREE GROWS
    IN BROOKLYN [April 19, 1951]
Please Don't Send Me down a Baby Brother
Thirty Weeks of Heaven—cut
Throw the Anchor Away

Trying to come up with a more successful Shirley Booth vehicle than A TREE GROWS IN BROOKLYN [April 19, 1951], Dorothy and Herb Fields fashioned a second turn-of-the-century Brooklyn vehicle for their star. But without a powerful basic story and/or the strong hand of George Abbott, the result was pallid. The score was especially disappointing, with Schwartz and Fields's two big ballads—*Alone Too Long* and *More Love Than Your Love*—proving boomingly bombastic. *I'd Rather Wake Up by Myself* is a good comedy number, though, and the rhythmic *Happy Habit* is "habit forming." Schwartz next collaborated with playwright/lyricist Maxwell Anderson on a one-performance television version of the latter's play *High Tor*. Bing Crosby starred opposite the soon-to-be-famous Julie Andrews. (The show aired five days before the opening of MY FAIR LADY (Loewe: March 15, 1956]). Included was one especially beautiful ballad, **When You're in Love*.

MRS. 'ARRIS GOES TO PARIS
[circa February 1960]
Unfinished musical. Lyrics by Howard Dietz; Book by Howard Teichmann (based on the

novel by Paul Gallico); [Produced by Kermit Bloomgarden and Ray Stark].

Published Song

*Before I Kiss the World Goodbye—initial publication upon use in JENNIE [October 17, 1963]

THE GAY LIFE

November 18, 1961
Shubert Theatre • 113 performances
Lyrics by Howard Dietz; Book by Fay and Michael Kanin (based on *Anatol* [play] by Arthur Schnitzler); Directed by Gerald Freedman; Choreographed by Herbert Ross; Produced by Kermit Bloomgarden; With Walter Chiari, Barbara Cook, Jules Munshin, and Loring Smith.

Published Songs

Bloom Is Off the Rose
Come A-Wandering with Me
For the First Time
I'm Glad I'm Single
**Magic Moment
Oh, Mein Leibchen
*Something You Never Had Before—revised version of *Oh, but I Do* [lyric by Leo Robin] from 1946 movie *The Time, the Place and the Girl*
Who Can? You Can!
**Why Go Anywhere at All?

Additional Songs Recorded

Bring Your Darling Daughter
I Never Had a Chance
I Wouldn't Marry You
The Label on the Bottle
Now I'm Ready for a Frau
This Kind of a Girl
What a Charming Couple
You're Not the Type
You Will Never Be Lonely

Dietz retired his vice presidency at MGM in 1957 and reunited with Schwartz for three final Broadway projects (the first of which went unproduced). THE GAY LIFE was saddled with a lifeless book and a lifeless star (Chiari), which defeated its attributes: a fine, sweepingly Viennese score by Schwartz, a *sacher-torte*

physical production—with Tony Award–winning costumes by Lucinda Ballard (Dietz)—and a luscious performance by Barbara Cook. *Magic Moment*, *Why Go Anywhere at All?*, and *Something You Never Had Before* are all top-grade Schwartz, which is to say absolutely lovely.

JENNIE

October 17, 1963
Majestic Theatre • 82 performances
Lyrics by Howard Dietz; Book by Arnold Schulman (based on *Laurette* [biography] by Marguerite Taylor Courtney); Directed by Vincent J. Donehue; Choreographed by Matt Mattox; Produced by Cheryl Crawford and Richard Halliday; With Mary Martin, George Wallace, Robin Bailey, and Ethel Shutta.

Published Songs

*Before I Kiss the World Goodbye—initial use of song written for MRS. 'ARRIS GOES TO PARIS [circa February 1960]
Born Again
High Is Better Than Low
I Believe in Takin' a Chance
I Still Look at You That Way
On the Other Hand—cut
Waitin' for the Evening Train
When You're Far Away from New York Town
Where You Are

Additional Songs Recorded

For Better or Worse
Lonely Nights
The Night May Be Dark
Over Here
Sauce Diable [instrumental]
See Seattle

Mary Martin turned down both Fanny Brice and Dolly Gallagher Levi to portray the feisty, alcoholic "Peg o' My Heart" Laurette Taylor. The final produced work of both Schwartz and Dietz was an unhappy experience for all. Dietz had engaged in lyric-suitability battles with Ethel Merman on SADIE THOMPSON [Duke: November 16, 1944], resulting in her dropping out during rehearsals. The same problems arose here with Mary Martin, except that Mary's husband was the controlling producer of the show. JENNIE was a shambles and quickly went the way of all shambles. (A 1960 nonmusical dramatization of the biography by Taylor's daughter, starring Judy Holliday, had bombed in New Haven; hence the name change from *Laurette*.) Schwartz provided one final beautiful ballad, though, *Before I Kiss the World Goodbye*. Following their heralded return to Broadway with two embarrassing flops, Schwartz and Dietz both went into virtual retirement. Dietz, who suffered from Parkinson's disease, died July 30, 1983. Schwartz, following a stroke, died September 3, 1984, at his home in Kintnersville, Pennsylvania.

Arthur Schwartz wrote some of the finest theatre music of his time—particularly the haunting minor-key ballads of the thirties (*Dancing in the Dark*, *Alone Together*, *You and the Night and the Music*) and the later, considerably warmer ones (*Make the Man Love Me*, *I'll Buy You a Star*, *Magic Moment*). His skill also displayed itself in outstanding rhythmic work (*I Guess I'll Have to Change My Plan*, the 1953 movie song *That's Entertainment*). All of which make it difficult to explain Schwartz's record of *no* successful Broadway book musicals. Not having a full-time lyricist to develop and experiment with was certainly part of it, although Dietz's later lyrics suggest that Schwartz might have done better with, say, Dorothy Fields. However—and happily—he left behind a healthy clutch of glorious songs.

HAROLD ARLEN

Born: February 15, 1905, Buffalo, New York
Died: April 23, 1986, New York, New York

Harold Arlen was the son of a cantor, whose melodic and colorful improvisatory style was to be a tremendous influence on Arlen's work. But Arlen's interest was firmly rooted in popular music. By the age of fourteen he was playing piano in Buffalo gin mills with his band, Hyman Arluck's Snappy Trio. He spent the early 1920s as a pianist and vocalist, arriving in New York in 1925. His first three published pieces were piano solos, starting with the 1926 *Minor Gaff* (*Blues Fantasy*) (by Harold Arluck and Dick George). By 1928, he was singing in GEORGE WHITE'S SCANDALS† [9th] [July 2, 1928], under the name Harold Arlen. He moved into a small role in the pre-Broadway tryout of GREAT DAY! [Youmans: October 17, 1929], also serving as rehearsal pianist and sometime musical secretary to the troubled Youmans. Youmans, who had set up his own publishing company, published one of Arlen's three 1929 songs, the promising ballad *Rising Moon* [lyric by Jack Ellis].

While serving as dance accompanist for GREAT DAY! [Youmans: October 17, 1929], Arlen developed a catchy two-measure pickup. Songwriter Harry Warren heard it, liked it, suggested Arlen turn it into a song, and sent over lyricist Ted Koehler. *Get Happy* was the result, Arlen was immediately signed as a staff composer at Remick's, and a distinctive songwriter was born. (Arlen remained a remarkable blues singer, making definitive recordings of many of his hits.) NINE-FIFTEEN REVUE featured interpolations by some sixteen different composers, but it was Arlen's *Get Happy* which stood out—for the week of the run, anyway. Ruth Etting, who had introduced *Love Me or Leave Me* in WHOOPEE [Notables: December 4, 1928], sang Arlen's first hit. With the quick closing of NINE-FIFTEEN REVUE, Etting was rushed into the cast of SIMPLE SIMON [Rodgers: February 18, 1930]—in which she introduced her second song classic in eight days, *Ten Cents a Dance*.

NINE-FIFTEEN REVUE

February 11, 1930
George M. Cohan Theatre • 7 performances
Music and Lyrics mostly by others (see
Gershwin: February 11, 1930); Lyrics to Arlen
songs by Ted Koehler; Sketches by Eddie
Cantor, George S. Kaufman, Ring Lardner,
Wm. Anthony McGuire, and others; Directed
by Alexander Leftwich; Produced by Ruth
Selwyn; With Ruth Etting.

Published Songs
**Get Happy*
You Wanted Me, I Wanted You

EARL CARROLL VANITIES ✦

Eighth Edition
July 1, 1930
New Amsterdam Theatre • 215 performances
"America's Greatest Revue." Music also by Jay
Gorney; Lyrics to Arlen songs by Ted Koehler;
Book by Eddie Welch and Eugene Conrad;
Directed by Priestly Morrison; Produced by
Earl Carroll; With Jack Benny, Jimmy Savo,
and Herb Williams.

Published Songs
Contagious Rhythm
Hittin' the Bottle

The March of Time
One Love
Out of a Clear Blue Sky

The pop success of *Get Happy* earned Arlen and Koehler the assignment to write half the score of the next edition of the VANITIES, the weakest of the three major annual revue series. The rest of the songs were written by another young team, composer Jay Gorney and lyricist E. Y. Harburg—who soon took Koehler's place as Arlen's primary collaborator.

BROWN SUGAR
[circa December, 1930]
Cotton Club {Harlem} • Nightclub revue
"Sweet but Unrefined." Lyrics by Ted Koehler; Directed by Dan Healy; Produced by The Cotton Club; With Duke Ellington and His Orchestra.

Published Songs
*Linda
Song of the Gigolo

Having tried out Arlen and Koehler material at their Silver Slipper nightclub, proprietors Owney Madden and associates—i.e., the Mob—sent the songwriters uptown to replace Jimmy McHugh and Dorothy Fields, who had graduated to Broadway with BLACKBIRDS OF 1928 [Notables: May 9, 1928]. The Cotton Club catered to an exclusively white clientele "slumming in Harlem." They offered elaborate midnight floor shows to lubricate the main business, selling bootleg liquor. The Arlen/Koehler team did some of their best work for The Cotton Club, starting with the liquidly melodic *Linda*.

YOU SAID IT
January 19, 1931
46th Street Theatre • 168 performances
"The Musicollegiate Comedy Hit." Lyrics by Jack Yellen; Book by Jack Yellen and Sid Silvers; Directed by John Harwood; Produced by Jack Yellen and Lou Holtz; With Lou Holtz and Lyda Roberti.

Published Songs
If He Really Loves Me
It's Different with Me

Learn to Croon
*Sweet and Hot
What Do We Care?
While You Are Young
You Said It
You'll Do

Jack Yellen, a successful Tin Pan Alley lyricist (*Happy Days Are Here Again*) and former member of Arlen's father's congregation in Buffalo, pressed the brilliant new composer of *Get Happy* to collaborate on this undistinguished book musical. The score was eminently forgettable, except for the sweet and hot and sassy *Sweet and Hot*. Arlen returned to Ted Koehler and The Cotton Club.

RHYTH-MANIA
[circa December 1931]
Cotton Club {Harlem} • Nightclub revue
Lyrics by Ted Koehler; Directed by Dan Healy; Produced by The Cotton Club; With Aida Ward and Cab Calloway.

Published Songs
*Between the Devil and the Deep Blue Sea
Breakfast Dance
Get up, Get out, Get under the Sun
I Love a Parade—issued in separate edition
Kickin' the Gong Around
'Neath the Pale Cuban Moon
Without Rhythm

Arlen's second Cotton Club show featured two more song hits: the lively, liquid *Between the Devil and the Deep Blue Sea*, and the march-time *I Love a Parade*. The latter song was so effective, in fact, that the subsequent shows in the series were officially entitled COTTON CLUB PARADE.

COTTON CLUB PARADE ✦
Twentieth Edition
[circa April 1932]
Cotton Club {Harlem} • Nightclub revue
Lyrics by Ted Koehler; Directed by Dan Healy; Produced by The Cotton Club; With Cab Calloway and His Orchestra.

Published Songs
In the Silence of the Night
Minnie the Moocher's Wedding Day
You Gave Me Everything but Love

Although labeled the twentieth edition, this was actually the first COTTON CLUB PARADE. (It was the twentieth Cotton Club revue, and the third written by Arlen and Koehler).

EARL CARROLL VANITIES ✦
Tenth Edition
September 27, 1932
Broadway Theatre • 87 performances
"America's Greatest Revue." Music also by others; Lyrics to Arlen songs by Ted Koehler; Sketches by Jack McGowan; Directed by Edgar J. McGregor; Produced by Earl Carroll; With Will Fyffe, Milton Berle, and Helen Broderick.

Published Songs
****I Gotta Right to Sing the Blues*
Rockin' in Rhythm

For his second VANITIES, Arlen came up with another brilliant song, *I Gotta Right to Sing the Blues*. Influenced by the improvisatory style of the black jazz underground, Arlen's distinctive blues outclassed the synthetic-but-popular torch songs of the 1920s and met with immediate popular acceptance.

AMERICANA ✦ Third Edition
October 5, 1932
Shubert Theatre • 77 performances
Music mostly by Jay Gorney; Lyrics mostly by E. Y. Harburg; Book by J. P. McEvoy; Directed by Harold Johnsrud; Produced by J. P. McEvoy; Presented by Lee Shubert.

Published Song
Satan's Li'l Lamb [lyric by Harburg and John Mercer]

This short-lived revue, best known for Jay Gorney and Yip Harburg's *Brother, Can You Spare a Dime*, marked the first time Arlen worked with his two most important collaborators. Johnny Mercer was, like Arlen, a fine singer. He was just then struggling through the Depression as one of Paul Whiteman's Rhythm Boys (along with Arlen's younger brother Jerry).

COTTON CLUB PARADE ✦
Twenty-first Edition
October 23, 1932
Cotton Club {Harlem} • Nightclub revue
Lyrics by Ted Koehler; Directed by Dan Healy; Produced by The Cotton Club; With Aida Ward and Cab Calloway.

Published Songs
Harlem Holiday
****I've Got the World on a String*
That's What I Hate about Love
The Wail of the Reefer Man

Another PARADE with yet another great song, the light-as-air *I've Got the World on a String*.

GEORGE WHITE'S MUSIC HALL VARIETIES
November 22, 1932
Casino Theatre • 71 performances
Music mostly by others; Book by George White and William K. Wells; Produced by White; With Harry Richman, Bert Lahr, and Lily Damita.

Published Song
Two Feet in Two-Four Time [lyric by Irving Caesar]

THE GREAT MAGOO
December 2, 1932
Selwyn Theatre • 11 performances
Play by Ben Hecht and Gene Fowler; Directed by George Abbott; Produced by Billy Rose; With Paul Kelly.

Published Song
****If You Believed in Me* [lyric by E. Y. Harburg and Rose]—initial publication upon reuse in CRAZY QUILT OF 1933 [July 28, 1933], retitled *It's Only a Paper Moon*

Yip Harburg, who had written one AMERICANA [October 5, 1932] song with Arlen, sought out the composer for this incidental song in this quick flop. *It's Only a Paper Moon* soon found widespread popularity via interpolation in the 1933 movie version of TAKE A CHANCE [Youmans: November 26, 1932]. Billy Rose, producer of THE

GREAT MAGOO (and co-lyricist of GREAT DAY! [Youmans: October 17, 1929]), demanded and received a share of the authorship credit.

COTTON CLUB PARADE ✦
Twenty-second Edition
April 6, 1933
Cotton Club {Harlem} • Nightclub revue
Lyrics by Ted Koehler; Directed by Dan Healy; Produced by The Cotton Club; With Ethel Waters, George Dewey Washington, and Duke Ellington and His Orchestra.

Published Songs
Calico Days
Get Yourself a New Broom (And Sweep the Blues Away)
Happy As the Day Is Long
Muggin' Lightly
Raisin' the Rent
***Stormy Weather*

Additional Song Published in 1985 in Non-show Folio
Stormy Weather—original extended version

The most successful edition of the COTTON CLUB PARADE, highlighted by the phenomenal *Stormy Weather*. Ethel Waters's tear-filled rendition of the song convinced Irving Berlin to write her a starring role in his upcoming revue, AS THOUSANDS CHEER [Berlin: September 30, 1933].

CRAZY QUILT OF 1933
July 28, 1933
{Albany, N.Y.} • Post-Broadway tour
Music mostly by others; Produced by Billy Rose; With Anita Page.

Published Song
***It's Only a Paper Moon* [lyric by E. Y. Harburg and Rose]—initial publication of *If You Believed in Me* (unpublished) from THE GREAT MAGOO [December 2, 1932]

COTTON CLUB PARADE ✦
Twenty-fourth Edition
March 23, 1934
Cotton Club {Harlem} • Nightclub revue
Lyrics by Ted Koehler; Directed by Dan Healy; Produced by The Cotton Club; With

Adelaide Hall and Jimmie Lunceford and His Orchestra.

Published Songs
**As Long As I Live*
Breakfast Ball
Here Goes
**Ill Wind*
Primitive Prima Donna

Arlen's final Cotton Club revue starred Adelaide Hall, singing the *Stormy Weather* follow-up *Ill Wind*. Sixteen-year-old chorine Lena Horne was given a featured spot, singing and dancing the rambunctiously joyous *As Long As I Live*.

LIFE BEGINS AT 8:40
August 27, 1934
Winter Garden Theatre • 237 performances
Lyrics by Ira Gershwin and E. Y. Harburg; Sketches mostly by David Freedman; Directed and Produced by John Murray Anderson; Presented by the Messrs. Shubert; With Ray Bolger, Bert Lahr, Luella Gear, and Frances Williams.

Published Songs
Fun to Be Fooled
**Let's Take a Walk around the Block*
Shoein' the Mare
What Can You Say in a Love Song?
**You're a Builder Upper*

Additional Songs Published [with Non–Gershwin/Harburg Lyric Revisions] in USO's *At Ease*
I Couldn't Hold My Man—retitled *I Look Bad in Uniform*
Life Begins Introduction
Spring Fever

Additional Songs Recorded
C'est La Vie
The Elks and the Masons
I'm Not Myself
Quartet Erotica
Things
Will You Love Me Monday Morning?

Having parted ways with Vernon Duke during the stormy tryout of the ZIEGFELD FOLLIES OF 1934 [Duke: January 4, 1934], Yip Harburg astutely selected his *Paper Moon* composer as his new collaborator, effectively ending the Arlen/Koehler partnership. The pair had turned out eight superb songs in four years—*Get Happy, Between the Devil and the Deep Blue Sea, I've Gotta Right to Sing the Blues, I've Got the World on a String, Stormy Weather,* **Let's Fall in Love* (for the 1934 movie of the same title), *Ill Wind,* and *As Long As I Live*—but Arlen could not afford to turn down the opportunity to write a first-class musical. Harburg's college classmate and mentor Ira Gershwin joined the project as co-lyricist; brother George was busy working with DuBose Heyward on PORGY AND BESS [Gershwin: October 10, 1935]. Arlen wrote his finest work with lyricists Harburg, Gershwin, and Johnny Mercer, creating songs that were beyond the abilities of his Cotton Club collaborator. (Koehler's post-Arlen output was workmanlike but undistinguished, the most notable song being Shirley Temple's *Animal Crackers in My Soup* [1935, with Ray Henderson and Irving Caesar].) LIFE BEGINS AT 8:40 was highlighted by the performances of Ray Bolger (Arlen's roommate when he first moved to New York), Frances Williams (Arlen's girlfriend from when he first moved to New York)—and Bert Lahr. Song hits included *Fun to Be Fooled* and the charming *Let's Take a Walk around the Block.*

THE SHOW IS ON
December 25, 1936
Winter Garden Theatre • 237 performances
Music mostly by Vernon Duke (see Duke: December 25, 1936; also Gershwin, Rodgers, and Schwartz); Lyrics to Arlen song by E. Y. Harburg; Sketches by David Freedman and Moss Hart; Directed and Designed by Vincente Minnelli; Produced by Lee Shubert; With Beatrice Lillie and Bert Lahr.

Song Recorded
**Song of the Woodman*

Arlen and Harburg provided Lahr with this spoof of an art song, a worthy follow-up to *Things* from LIFE BEGINS AT 8:40 [August 27, 1934] (and a prequel to **If I Were King of the Forest* from the 1939 movie *The Wizard of Oz*).

HOORAY FOR WHAT!
December 1, 1937
Winter Garden Theatre • 200 performances
Lyrics by E. Y. Harburg; Book by Howard Lindsay and Russel Crouse; Conceived by E. Y. Harburg; Production supervised by Vincente Minnelli; Directed by Howard Lindsay; Choreographed by Robert Alton; Produced by the Messrs. Shubert; With Ed Wynn, Jack Whiting, June Clyde, and Vivian Vance.

Published Songs
Buds Won't Bud—cut
Down with Love
**God's Country*
**In the Shade of the New Apple Tree*
I've Gone Romantic on You
Life's a Dance
**Moanin' in the Mornin'*

Additional Song Published [with Non-Harburg Lyric Revisions] in USO's *At Ease*
Hooray for What!—retitled *Hooray for Us!*

Additional Song Recorded
Hero Ballet

What started out as a strong antiwar satire lost much of its bite during the tryout, as well as losing original choreographer Agnes de Mille and costars Kay Thompson and Hannah Williams (Mrs. Jack Dempsey). What remained—comedian Ed Wynn and fine songs like *In the Shade of the New Apple Tree, God's Country,* and *Moanin' in the Mornin'*—was enough to make HOORAY FOR WHAT! a moderate hit. More important, the score convinced Hollywood executive (and former lyricist) Arthur Freed that Arlen and Harburg were the ideal team to write MGM's upcoming musical fantasy *The Wizard of Oz*. Since 1934 Arlen had written scores for five undistinguished films (with two fine songs along the way, Koehler's **Let's Fall in Love* and Harburg's **Fancy Meeting You*). *The Wizard of Oz* was written like a stage musical—with leading roles for Bolger and Lahr from LIFE BEGINS AT 8:40 [August 27, 1934]—rather than a movie. The score was highly theatrical, with songs which were unusually character specific like **If I Only Had a Brain* and *If I Were King of the Forest*. Arlen and Harburg received a Best Song Oscar for *Over the Rainbow.

Oz was followed by one last undistinguished film—the Marx Bros.' *At the Circus*, for which they wrote the deft **Lydia the Tattooed Lady*. Harburg headed back East to write HOLD ON TO YOUR HATS [Lane: September 11, 1940]. Arlen stayed in Hollywood and found a new lyricist: Johnny Mercer, who had written a string of hits (including *Too Marvelous for Words*, *I'm an Old Cowhand*, *Jeepers Creepers*, and *Hooray for Hollywood*) since the pair's one-song collaboration on AMERICANA [October 5, 1932]. The new team immediately wrote a string of the finest popular songs ever, led by the incomparable ***Blues in the Night* for the 1941 movie with the same title. The film featured a second great song, ***This Time the Dream's on Me*. Within three years Arlen and Mercer added ***One for My Baby (And One for the Road)*, ***That Old Black Magic*, **Hit the Road to Dreamland*, ***Ac-cent-u-ate the Positive*, and **Out of This World*. Arlen also reunited with Yip Harburg for **Happiness Is Just a Thing Called Joe*, one of several additional songs written for the 1943 film version of CABIN IN THE SKY [Duke: October 25, 1940].

SYMPHONY IN BROWN
[circa March 1942]
Trocadero • Nightclub revue

Published Song
Life Could Be a Cakewalk with You [lyric by Ted Koehler]

BLOOMER GIRL
October 5, 1944
Shubert Theatre • 654 performances
Lyrics by E. Y. Harburg; Book by Sig. Herzig and Fred Saidy (based on an unproduced play by Dan and Lilith James); Production staged by E. Y. Harburg; Book directed by William Schorr; Choreographed by Agnes de Mille; Produced by John C. Wilson in association with Nat Goldstone; With Celeste Holm, David Brooks, Joan McCracken, and Dooley Wilson.

Published Songs
*The Eagle and Me
*Evelina

*I Got a Song—initial publication of song cut from 1943 movie version of CABIN IN THE SKY [Duke: October 25, 1940]
Right As the Rain
T'morra, T'morra
*When the Boys Come Home

Additional Song Published in 1985 Non-show Folio
Promise Me Not to Love Me—non-show song [circa 1940s] added to Goodspeed revival [September 27, 1981]

Additional Songs Recorded
Civil War Ballet
The Farmer's Daughter
It Was Good Enough for Grandma
Liza Crossing the Ice
Lullaby (Satin Gown and Silver Shoe)
Man for Sale
Never Was Born
The Rakish Young Man with the Whiskahs
Sunday in Cicero Falls
Welcome Hinges

Arlen and Harburg returned to Broadway with this Civil War–period costume musical which followed in the footsteps of OKLAHOMA! [Rodgers: March 31, 1943], employing the earlier musical's choreographer, designers, and (two) leading players. BLOOMER GIRL was entertaining, colorful, and nostalgic enough to please wartime audiences (despite Harburg's abolitionist outspokenness). The artful score included *Evelina*, a lilting and felicitous ballad of intervals; *When the Boys Come Home*, a fine waltz which was especially effective with wartime audiences, and a fine paean to freedom, *The Eagle and Me*.

ST. LOUIS WOMAN
March 30, 1946
Martin Beck Theatre • 113 performances
Also see FREE AND EASY [December 17, 1959].
Lyrics by Johnny Mercer; Book by Arna Bontemps and Countee Cullen (based on *God Sends Sunday* [novel] by Arna Bontemps); Directed by Rouben Mamoulian; Choreographed by Charles Walters; Produced by Edward Gross; With Ruby Hill, Harold Nicholas, Fayard Nicholas, Rex Ingram, June Hawkins, and Pearl Bailey.

Concert Version
April 30, 1998
City Center • 5 performances
Directed and Adapted by Jack O'Brien;
Choreographed by George Faison; Produced
by City Center Encores; With Vanessa L.
Williams [Hill], Charles S. Dutton [Ingram],
Stanley Wayne Mathis [H. Nicholas], Victor
Trent Cook [F. Nicholas], Helen Goldsby
[Hawkins], and Yvette Cason [Bailey].

Published Songs
*Any Place I Hang My Hat Is Home
Cakewalk Your Lady
*Come Rain or Come Shine
**I Had Myself a True Love
**I Wonder What Became of Me—cut
Legalize My Name
Ridin' on the Moon

Additional Song Published in Non-show Folio
A Woman's Prerogative

Additional Songs Recorded
Chinquapin Bush
I Feel My Luck Comin' Down
*Leavin' Time
Least That's My Opinion
L'il Augie Is a Natural Man
*Lullaby
*Sleep Peaceful, Mr. Used-to-Be
Sweeten' Water

Lemuel Ayers—better known as set designer of
OKLAHOMA! [March 31, 1943] and BLOOMER
GIRL [October 5, 1944] and MGM's 1944 film
Meet Me in St. Louis—undertook ST. LOUIS
WOMAN as a directing project. Arthur Freed of
MGM (which financed BLOOMER GIRL) provided both the backing and MGM star Lena
Horne. But Horne withdrew, finding the script
condescending and stereotyped; colibrettist
Countee Cullen died just before the start of re-
hearsals; and director Ayers was fired on the
road, as was choreographer Anthony Tudor and
leading lady Ruby Hill. Then the cast refused to
perform the Broadway opening unless Hill's replacement was fired and Hill rehired. While ST.
LOUIS WOMAN suffered from a lumbering book
and a lack of focus, it did possess a fine score.
Come Rain or Come Shine is a strong ballad with

an arrestingly bluesy "B" section; the free and
easy *Any Place I Hang My Hat Is Home* is a lazy
delight in a rolling, rocking rhythm; the tender
and exquisite *I Wonder What Became of Me* was
cut and remains relatively obscure, as does *I Had
Myself a True Love, Sleep Peaceful, Mr. Used-To-
Be,* and the gentle *Lullaby.* Arlen later reworked
the ST. LOUIS WOMAN material into the ill-
fated "blues opera" FREE AND EASY [Decem-
ber 17, 1959]. A painstakingly reconstructed
1998 concert version of ST. LOUIS WOMAN re-
affirmed the strength of the score (and the
weakness of the story). Arlen followed the failure of ST. LOUIS WOMAN by returning to Hollywood, where he wrote lackluster scores for
six poor film musicals. His seventh assignment,
Judy Garland's 1954 remake of *A Star Is Born*
[lyrics by Ira Gershwin], contained two important songs: the rhythmic delight *Gotta Have Me
Go with You* and the searing **The Man That Got
Away.*

HOUSE OF FLOWERS [1954]
December 30, 1954
Alvin Theatre • 165 performances
Also see January 28, 1968. Lyrics by Truman
Capote and Arlen; Book by Truman Capote
(based on his novella); Directed by Peter
Brook; Choreographed by Herbert Ross;
Produced by Saint Subber; With Pearl Bailey,
Diahann Carroll, Juanita Hall, Ray Walston,
and Geoffrey Holder.

Published Songs
*House of Flowers—revised version of *Let's
Go, Sailor* (cut, unpublished) from 1942
movie *Star Spangled Rhythm* and *I Love a
New Yorker* from 1950 movie *My Blue
Heaven*
*I Never Has Seen Snow
**A Sleepin' Bee
Smellin' of Vanilla (Bamboo Cage)
*Two Ladies in de Shade of de Banana Tree

Additional Songs Published in Vocal Selection
Can I Leave Off Wearin' My Shoes?—also
recorded as *I'm Gonna Leave Off Wearin'
My Shoes*
Don't Like Goodbyes

One Man Ain't Quite Enough
Waitin'
What Is a Friend For?

Additional Songs Recorded
Can You Explain?—cut
Has I Let You Down?
Love's No Stranger to Me—cut
Mardi Gras
Slide, Boy, Slide
Turtle Song (One Brave Man against the Sea)
Waltz [instrumental]

Producer Saint Subber of KISS ME, KATE and OUT OF THIS WORLD brought Arlen together with the young, eccentric Truman Capote. The intention was to follow the plot of Capote's award-winning novella, a boy/girl story offering atmosphere and color but little more. (Pearl Bailey's "Madame Fleur" character doubled as Royal's grandmother, a voodoo witch, in the original second act.) With an unassuming composer, an inexperienced librettist, an untried director, an out-of-place choreographer (George Balanchine), and an ineffectual producer, someone had to take charge. It was the survival of the fittest, who happened to be Ms. Bailey (who had stolen the show in ST. LOUIS WOMAN [March 30, 1946]). The production period was one continuous, many-sided battle, with Bailey winning most of the backstage bouts as her role grew larger and larger. Nevertheless, HOUSE OF FLOWERS has one of Arlen's finest scores, with *A Sleepin' Bee*, *I Never Has Seen Snow*, the title song, and the cyclonic *Two Ladies in de Shade of de Banana Tree*. Arlen managed to get through the failure of HOUSE OF FLOWERS unscathed, but it was to be his final worthwhile work.

JAMAICA
October 31, 1957
Imperial Theatre • 557 performances
Lyrics by E. Y. Harburg; Book by E. Y. Harburg and Fred Saidy; Directed by Robert Lewis; Choreographed by Jack Cole; Produced by David Merrick; With Lena Horne, Ricardo Montalban, Adelaide Hall, Josephine Premice, and Ossie Davis.

Published Songs
*Ain' It de Truth?—originally used (cut) in 1943 movie version of CABIN IN THE SKY [Duke: October 25, 1940]
Cocoanut Sweet
I Don't Think I'll End It All Today
Incompatibility
Little Biscuit
*Napoleon
Pretty to Walk With (That's How a Man Gets Got)
*Push de Button
Savannah
Take It Slow, Joe
What Good Does It Do?

Additional Song Published in 1985 Non-show Folio
There's a Sweet Wind Blowin' My Way—cut

Additional Songs Recorded
For Every Fish There's a Little Bigger Fish
Leave de Atom Alone
Monkey in the Mango Tree
Noah—cut
Pity de Sunset
Savannah's Wedding Day
(Hooray for) The Yankee Dollar

When calypso star Harry Belafonte withdrew from the JAMAICA project, the show was refashioned for Lena Horne. (Horne started her career in Arlen's final COTTON CLUB PARADE [24th] [March 23, 1934] and rode to stardom singing *Stormy Weather* in the 1943 movie with the same title.) Yip Harburg intended JAMAICA to be a pointed social satire, but the bite withered away until the show seemed little more than Lena Horne singing a string of sultry songs. Ironically, JAMAICA was Arlen's first and only hit after BLOOMER GIRL [October 5, 1944]. It will be noted that Arlen's four hit musicals—and *The Wizard of Oz* as well—were all collaborations with Harburg.

SARATOGA
December 7, 1959
Winter Garden Theatre • 80 performances
Music mostly by Arlen; Lyrics by Johnny Mercer; Book and Direction by Morton

DaCosta (based on *Saratoga Trunk* [novel] by Edna Ferber); Produced by Robert Fryer; With Howard Keel, Carol Lawrence, Carol Brice, and Edith King.

Published Songs
A Game of Poker
⁺Goose Never Be a Peacock
Love Held Lightly
The Man in My Life
Saratoga

Additional Songs Published in Vocal Selection
Dog Eat Dog
The Parks of Paris—cut
Petticoat High
You for Me—cut

Additional Songs Recorded
Countin' Our Chickens
The Cure
Gettin' a Man [music by Mercer]
Have You Heard (Gossip Song)
I'll Be Respectable
The Men Who Run the Country [music by Mercer]
One Step—Two Step
Why Fight This? [music by Mercer]
You or No One

Director Morton DaCosta was on an impressive winning streak—with the plays *No Time for Sergeants* [October 20, 1955] and *Auntie Mame* [October 31, 1956] and THE MUSIC MAN [Willson: December 19, 1957]—when he undertook the lavish SARATOGA. Writing his own libretto as well as directing, DaCosta was clearly influenced by and aspiring to the earlier Ferber-based musical, SHOW BOAT [Kern: December 27, 1927]. But SARATOGA wasn't SHOW BOAT, just an incredibly top-heavy costume operetta with only one standout song, the beautiful plaint *Goose Never Be a Peacock*. As with Arlen's three previous musicals, the tryout was a battle-strewn mess; so much so that the battle-shy composer decamped, claiming illness. (Hence three last-minute songs composed by Mercer.) SARATOGA was Arlen's shortest-running—and final—Broadway show.

FREE AND EASY
December 17, 1959
Carré Theatre {Amsterdam}
Also see ST. LOUIS WOMAN [*March 30, 1946*]. Lyrics by Johnny Mercer, Ted Koehler, and others; Book by Robert and Wilva Breen (based on the libretto for ST. LOUIS WOMAN by Arna Bontemps and Countee Cullen); Directed by Robert Breen; Produced by Stanley Chase; With Irene Williams and Harold Nicholas.

New Songs Recorded [Music Only] As Blues-Opera Suite
Champagne fo' de Lady
Dis Little While
Song of the Conjur Man
Streak o' Lightnin'

Arlen reworked the ST. LOUIS WOMAN material into the "blues opera" FREE AND EASY, an ill-conceived mishmash which unwisely incorporated some of Arlen's greatest hits (*Blues in the Night, One for My Baby, Ill Wind, That Old Black Magic*). FREE AND EASY shakily embarked on what was to be a long European tour, hopefully following the success of director Robert Breen's 1953 international PORGY AND BESS [Gershwin: October 10, 1935]. The new work opened in Amsterdam—with Arlen far away, recovering from SARATOGA [December 7, 1959]—only to close five weeks later in Paris. The back-to-back failures SARATOGA and FREE AND EASY would be Arlen's final shows. He joined with Yip Harburg to write the 1962 animated feature *Gay Purr-ee* for Judy Garland, but Arlen was soon in virtual retirement.

SOFTLY
[circa October 1966]
Unproduced musical. Lyrics by Martin Charnin; Book by Hugh Wheeler (based on a novella by Santha Rama Rau); [Produced by Saint Subber].

Songs Published in Non-show Folio
Come On, Midnight
I Could Be Good for You
Little Travelbug
Suddenly the Sunrise

Arlen tried one final musical, collaborating with Marty Charnin (who formed similar partnerships with the old and ailing Vernon Duke [ZENDA: August 5, 1963] and Richard Rodgers [TWO BY TWO: November 10, 1970]). SOFTLY—about the romance of an American man and a Japanese woman during the postwar occupation of Japan— never made it into production, although several songs have been published.

HOUSE OF FLOWERS [1968]
January 28, 1968
Theatre De Lys {Off Broadway} •
  57 performances
Also see December 30, 1954. Lyrics by Truman Capote and Arlen; Book by Truman Capote (based on his novella); Directed by Joseph Hardy; Choreographed by Talley Beatty; Produced by Saint Subber; With Josephine Premice, Yolande Bavan, Novella Nelson, and Robert Jackson.

New Songs Published in Vocal Selection
Jump de Broom [lyric by Capote]
Madame Tango's Particular Tango—written
    for revival, different than *Madame Tango's
    Tango* (cut, unpublished) from original
    version
Somethin' Cold to Drink
Wife Never Understan'

Neither Arlen, Capote, nor Saint Subber had been pleased with what happened to the original production of HOUSE OF FLOWERS. With Saint Subber flush from a string of Neil Simon comedies and Capote basking *"In Cold Blood,"* they decided to revisit their legendary failure. The new HOUSE OF FLOWERS story was much closer to Capote's novella, concentrating on the young lovers; but the flawed 1954 version was a whole lot more fun, alas. Arlen continued his unhappy retirement, with a brief period of activity in 1973 writing an unproduced, hippie-themed TV musical "Clippety Clop and Clementine" (book by Leonard Melfi). It contained one exceptional song, though. ********I Had a Love Once—* which was apparently Arlen's final song—is heart-breakingly beautiful, in a league with Arlen's very best work. After a ten-year battle with Parkinson's disease, Harold Arlen died on April 23, 1986.

If I were to have to list my favorite twenty songs, they would include a couple by Kern, a couple by Gershwin, and five or six by Harold Arlen. Many music lovers place Gershwin and Arlen at the top of the list of American songwriters. Gershwin led the way, certainly, scattering delightful surprises ("blue notes," catchy rhythms, musical whimsy) throughout his work. Arlen used these same elements, but not for effect: to Arlen they were a natural part of his musical vocabulary. Gershwin's fascinatin' rhythms were carefully built and marvelously effective. Arlen's—*Get Happy*, for example—were infectious and light as air. Gershwin's blues relied on that distinctive "blue note," as in the superb *The Man I Love*. Arlen's blues—*Stormy Weather, Blues in the Night—* relied on nothing but his limitless imagination. The music of Harold Arlen remains ageless, the songs filled with never-ending wonder.

VERNON DUKE

Born: October 10, 1903, Parafianovo (Minsk), Russia
Died: January 17, 1969, Santa Monica, California

VLADIMIR ALEXANDROVITCH DUKELSKY hailed from a White Russian family, the son of a civil engineer. A precocious musical prodigy, the preteen enrolled in the Kiev Conservatory and studied with Glière. Then came the Bolshevik Revolution in 1917 and the various upheavals that followed. The situation became especially dire as the Soviets approached Kiev in December 1919, causing Dukelsky—with his mother and younger brother—to flee to Constantinople. His ballet *Conte d'une Nuit Syrienne* was produced there in 1921. He then emigrated to America, where he worked at musical odd-jobs (accompanying gypsy violinists in restaurants, composing for magic acts). When one of his "modernist" songs was performed at a concert by recitalist Eva Gauthier, he was befriended by another by Gauthier song-provider, the up-and-coming George Gershwin. Gershwin became Duke's mentor, finding him bits and pieces of work along the way. Duke wrote the sheet music arrangement of *Somebody Loves Me*—with its marvelous inner harmonies—and (for $100) the piano solo version of *Rhapsody in Blue*. Gershwin also provided him with an Americanized name, Vernon Duke, although he retained Dukelsky for his serious works. The twenty-year old Duke went to Paris in 1924, where he fell in with other Russian expatriates and was quickly commissioned to write a ballet for Sergei Diaghilev's Ballets Russe. *Zephyr et Flore* had its Paris première June 15, 1925. While it was in preparation, Duke started interpolating songs into British musical comedies.

KATJA THE DANCER
February 21, 1925
Gaiety Theatre {London} • 505 performances
Music mostly by Jean Gilbert; Book by Frederick Lonsdale and Harry Graham (based on the Austrian musical by Leopold Jacobson and Rudolph Oesterreicher); Produced by George Edwardes; With Lilian Davies and Maida Vale.

Published Songs
Back to My Heart [lyric by Percy Greenbank]—added after opening
Try a Little Kiss [lyric by Greenbank and Arthur Wimperis]—added after opening

YVONNE
May 22, 1926
Daly's Theatre {London} • 280 performances
Music also by Jean Gilbert; Book and Lyrics by Percy Greenbank (based on the Austrian musical); Directed by Herbert Mason; Produced by George Edwardes; With Ivy Tresmand and Hal Sherman.

Published Songs
Day Dreams
It's Nicer to Be Naughty
Lucky
The Magic of the Moon
We Always Disagree

Additional Songs Published in Vocal Score
All Men Are the Same
Charming Weather (*Opening*)
Don't Forget the Waiter

Duke wrote a half-score's worth of negligible material to this import, which Noël Coward dubbed "Yvonne the Terrible."

TWO LITTLE GIRLS IN BLUE [1927]
[circa April 1927]
{Portsmouth, England} •
    Closed during tryout
Music mostly by Paul Lannin and Vincent Youmans (see Youmans: May 3, 1921); Lyrics

mostly by Ira Gershwin; Book by Fred Jackson; Produced by Norman J. Norman and David Marks; With The Barry Twins and Barrie Oliver.

Published Song
Somebody's Sunday [music and lyric by Duke]

THE BOW-WOWS
October 12, 1927
Prince of Wales's Theatre {London} •
    124 performances
"A Hare-m Scare-m Musical Show." Music and Lyrics mostly by others; Directed and Produced by Laddie Cliff; With Elsie Gregory and Georges Metaxa.

Published Song
For Goodness' Sake [lyric by James Dyrenforth]

THE YELLOW MASK
February 8, 1928
Carlton Theatre {London} • 218 performances
"A Mystery Thriller Musical." Lyrics mostly by Desmond Carter; Book by Edgar Wallace; Directed by Laddie Cliff; Produced by Julian Wylie and Laddie Cliff; With Bobby Howes, Phyllis Dare, and Leslie Henson.

Published Songs
The Bacon and the Egg
Blowing the Blues Away [lyric by Eric Little]
Deep Sea
Half a Kiss [lyric by Little]
I Love You So
I'm Wonderful
I Still Believe in You [lyric by Duke and Carter]
You Do, I Don't

Additional Songs Published (No Lyrics) in Piano Selection
Chinese Ballet
Chinese March
March
Opening Chorus Act One
Walking on Air
Yellow Mask

Duke, already attracting notice with his distinctive interpolations in Gershwin-crazy London, wrote his first complete score for this Edgar Wallace musical thriller. *Blowing the Blues Away* is in the Gershwin *Sweet and Low Down/Kickin' the Clouds Away* tradition, and the only one of Duke's early London songs worth noting.

OPEN YOUR EYES
[circa August 1929]
Empire Theatre {Edinburgh} •
    Closed during tryout
Lyrics by Collie Knox; Book by Frederick Jackson; Directed by John Harwood; With Ella Logan, Marie Burke, and Geoffrey Gwyther.

Published Songs
Happily Ever After
Jack and Jill
Open Your Eyes
Such a Funny Feeling
Too, Too Divine—see GARRICK GAIETIES [3rd]
    [June 4, 1930]
You'd Do for Me—I'd Do for You

Dukelsky's First Symphony was introduced on March 15, 1929, by the Boston Symphony and conductor Serge Koussevitzky (who was also Duke's classical music publisher). Duke permanently moved to America in June—before OPEN YOUR EYES opened (and closed)—and became a citizen in 1938.

GARRICK GAIETIES ✦
    Third Edition
June 4, 1930
Guild Theatre • 170 performances
"Music and Lyrics by Everybody" (see Blitzstein: June 4, 1930); Lyrics to Duke songs by E. Y. Harburg; Directed by Philip Loeb; Produced by The Theatre Guild; With Sterling Holloway, Edith Meiser, and Imogene Coca.

Published Songs
I Am Only Human after All [lyric by Ira Gershwin and Harburg]
Too, Too Divine—cut after opening; new lyric for song from OPEN YOUR EYES [circa August 1929]; also used with third lyric as *Shavian Shivers* (unpublished)

Ira Gershwin teamed bankrupt electrical-appliance salesman E. Y. Harburg (a friend and former

CCNY classmate) with George's difficult friend
Dukie; the three collaborated on Duke's first
American show tune, *I Am Only Human after All*.
While looking for Broadway work, Duke took a
background music job at the Paramount Studios
in Astoria. Duke and Harburg also wrote additional songs (unpublished) for the post-Broadway tour of this final GARRICK GAIETIES.

THREE'S A CROWD
October 15, 1930
Selwyn Theatre • 271 performances
Music mostly by Arthur Schwartz (see
Schwartz: October 15, 1930; also Lane); Lyrics
mostly by Howard Dietz; Sketches by Howard
Dietz and others; Directed by Hassard Short;
Choreographed by Albertina Rasch; Produced
by Max Gordon; With Clifton Webb, Fred
Allen, Libby Holman, and Tamara Geva.

Published Songs
None

Duke contributed Tamara Geva's memorable
Talkative Toes (unpublished, lyric by Howard
Dietz). Geva, at the time married to George
Balanchine, was the first of Duke's Ballets Russe
friends to achieve Broadway success.

SHOOT THE WORKS
July 21, 1931
George M. Cohan Theatre • 87 performances
Music and Lyrics mostly by others (see Berlin:
July 21, 1931); Sketches by Nunnally Johnson,
Heywood Broun, and others; Directed by Ted
Hammerstein; Produced by Heywood Broun,
with Milton Raison; With Heywood Broun,
George Murphy, and Imogene Coca.

Published Song
Mu-Cha-Cha [music by Duke and Jay Gorney,
lyric by E. Y. Harburg]

WALK A LITTLE FASTER
December 7, 1932
St. James Theatre • 119 performances
Lyrics by E. Y. Harburg; Sketches by S. J. Perel-
man; Directed by Monty Woolley; Produced by
Courtney Burr; With Beatrice Lillie, Bobby Clark
& Paul McCullough, and Evelyn Hoey.

Published Songs
**April in Paris*
Off Again, on Again
A Penny for Your Thoughts
So Nonchalant [lyric by Harburg and Charles
Tobias]
Speaking of Love
That's Life
**Where Have We Met Before?*

Duke wrote his most famous song—the beauteous
April in Paris—for his first complete Broadway
score. Trained in concert music and jazz ballet,
he quickly attracted notice with his intriguingly
advanced theatre songs. Not popularity or fame,
or money; but an ardent "highbrow" following,
which his work maintains sixty years later.

ZIEGFELD FOLLIES OF 1934
January 4, 1934
Winter Garden Theatre • 182 performances
Music mostly by Duke (also see Schwartz:
January 4, 1934); Lyrics mostly by E. Y. Harburg;
Directed by Bobby Connolly and John Murray
Anderson; Produced by "Mrs. Florenz Ziegfeld"
[the Messrs. Shubert]; With Fanny Brice, Willie
& Eugene Howard, and Jane Froman.

Published Songs
**I Like the Likes of You*
**Suddenly* [lyric by Billy Rose and Harburg]
This Is Not a Song [lyric by Harburg and E.
Hartman]
**What Is There to Say?*

Additional Song Recorded
Water under the Bridge

Following Ziegfeld's death in 1932, the Shuberts
—whose annual Winter Garden revues and PASS-
ING SHOWS had provided low-grade competition
to the showman—bought the rights to the title
from Ziegfeld's debt-ridden widow, Billie Burke.
Unbilled but acknowledged, they produced two
successful editions with Duke scores.

THUMBS UP
December 27, 1934
St. James Theatre • 156 performances
Music and Lyrics mostly by others; Directed
by John Murray Anderson and Edward Clarke

Lilley; Produced by Eddie Dowling; With
Bobby Clark & Paul McCullough, Hal LeRoy,
and J. Harold Murray.

Published Song
Autumn in New York [lyric by Duke]

Duke's one contribution to this revue was his follow-up to *April in Paris* from WALK A LITTLE
FASTER [December 7, 1932]. Both shows starred
the comedy team of Clark & McCullough—who,
needless to say, did not sing either song.

ZIEGFELD FOLLIES OF 1936
January 30, 1936
Winter Garden Theatre • 115 performances
Music mostly by Duke; Lyrics mostly by Ira
Gershwin; Sketches by David Freedman;
Directed by John Murray Anderson; Choreo-
graphed by George Balanchine and Robert
Alton; Produced by "Mrs. Florenz Ziegfeld"
[the Messrs. Shubert]; With Fanny Brice, Bob
Hope, Eve Arden, and Josephine Baker.

Concert Version
March 25, 1999
City Center • 6 performances
Directed and Adapted by Mark Waldrop;
Choreographed by Thommie Walsh and
Christopher Wheeldon; Produced by City
Center Encores; With Christine Ebersole
(Arden), Ruthie Henshall, Howard McGillin,
Stephanie Pope (Baker), Mary Testa (Brice),
and Peter Scolari (Hope).

Published Songs
The Gazooka
**I Can't Get Started*
Island in the West Indies
I Used to Be above Love—cut; published in
    1936 as a non-show song
My Red Letter Day
That Moment of Moments
Words without Music

Additional Songs Published [with Non-
Gershwin Lyric Revisions] in USO's
At Ease
Dancing to Our Score—retitled *We Somehow
    Feel That You Enjoyed Our Show*
The Economic Situation—retitled *New War
    Situation*
Fancy! Fancy!

He Hasn't a Thing Except Me—retitled *She
    Hasn't a Thing Except Me*
Time Marches On!

Additional Songs Recorded [In Preparation]
Dancing to Our Score
Does a Duck Love Water?
The Economic Situation
Fancy! Fancy!
5 A.M.
He Hasn't a Thing Except Me
Maharanee
Modernistic Moe [lyric by Gershwin and Billy
    Rose]
Sentimental Weather
Time Marches On!

Duke and Harburg—both volatile and opinionated
songwriters—broke up over disagreements on the
previous FOLLIES. Ira Gershwin was temporarily
available, as George was busy with PORGY AND
BESS [Gershwin: October 10, 1935]. Memorable
moments: Fanny Brice's creation of her "Baby
Snooks" character, and the up-and-coming Bob
Hope introducing the immortal *I Can't Get Started*.
Also introduced to America was Duke's Ballets
Russe pal, choreographer George Balanchine.

THE SHOW IS ON
December 25, 1936
Winter Garden Theatre • 237 performances
Music mostly by Duke (see Arlen, Gershwin,
Rodgers, and Schwartz: December 25, 1936);
Lyrics mostly by Ted Fetter; Sketches mostly by
David Freedman and Moss Hart; Directed by
Vincente Minnelli; Produced by Lee Shubert;
With Beatrice Lillie and Bert Lahr.

Published Song
Now

Additional Song Published [with Non-
Harburg/Fetter Lyric Revision] in
USO's *At Ease*
The Finale Marches On [lyric by E. Y. Harburg
    and Fetter]

Additional Songs Recorded
Casanova
What Has He Got?

Duke oversaw the musical department of this
third Shubert revue, with interpolations from

most of Broadway's top composers—including George Gershwin's final show tune, *By Strauss*. Following the shock of Gershwin's death on July 11, 1937, Duke went to Hollywood to help complete his friend's posthumously produced 1938 movie *The Goldwyn Follies*.

A VAGABOND HERO

December 26, 1939
National Theatre {Washington, D.C.} •
    Closed during tryout
"A Dashing Musical Romance." Music also by Samuel D. Pokrass; Book and Lyrics mostly by Charles O. Locke; (based on *Cyrano de Bergerac* [play] by Edmond Rostand); Directed by George Houston; Produced by the Messrs. Shubert; With George Houston, Ruby Mercer, Hope Emerson, and Bill Johnson. Previous title: THE WHITE PLUME.

Songs Published as Professional Copies
Bonjour, Goodbye
I Cling to You (Roxane's Song) [lyric by Locke and Ted Fetter]
Shadow of Love [lyric by Locke and Fetter]

The Shuberts' 1932 operetta CYRANO DE BERGERAC†, with music by Samuel Pokrass and lyrics by Charles O. Locke, had quickly failed on the road in its original incarnation. In 1939 they decided to remount it—they already had sets and costumes—and hired Duke to supplement the score. A week in Washington as THE WHITE PLUME, a week in Pittsburgh as A VAGABOND HERO, and that was that (although there have been several other Cyrano musicals over the years, all failures). One of Duke's ballads, *I Cling to You*, is particularly lovely, though.

KEEP OFF THE GRASS

May 23, 1940
Broadhurst Theatre • 44 performances
Music mostly by Jimmy McHugh; Lyrics by Al Dubin and Howard Dietz; Sketches by Parke Levy, Norman Panama & Melvin Frank, and others; Directed by Fred de Cordova and Edward Duryea Dowling; Choreographed by George Balanchine; Produced by the Messrs. Shubert; With Ray Bolger, Jimmy Durante, José Limon, Larry Adler, and Jane Froman.

Published Song
None

Balanchine called Duke to Boston to write a ballet for this faltering revue. Star Ray Bolger had danced Balanchine's classic *Slaughter on Tenth Avenue* in ON YOUR TOES [Rodgers: April 11, 1936]. *Raffles*, as it turned out, was not quite so legendary.

ICE CAPADES OF 1941

[circa September 1940]
"The Magnificent Ice-travaganza." Music mostly by others; Produced by Russell Markert; With Vera Hruba, Belita, and Lois Dworshak.

Published Song
Yankee Doodle Polka [lyric by John Latouche]

IT HAPPENS ON ICE

October 10, 1940
Center Theatre • 180 performances
"An Ice Extravaganza." Music also by others; Lyrics by Al Stillman; Staged and Devised by Leon Leonidoff; Produced by Sonja Henie and Arthur Wirtz; With Joe Cook.

Published Songs
Don't Blow That Horn, Gabriel [lyric by Stillman and Will Hudson]
Long Ago

CABIN IN THE SKY

October 25, 1940
Martin Beck Theatre • 156 performances
Lyrics by John Latouche; Book by Lynn Root; Dialogue staged by Albert Lewis; Directed and Choreographed by George Balanchine; Produced by Albert Lewis in association with Vinton Freedley; With Ethel Waters, Todd Duncan, Rex Ingram, Dooley Wilson, and Katherine Dunham.

Revival
January 21, 1964
Greenwich Mews Theatre {Off Broadway} •
    47 performances
Directed by Brian Shaw; With Rosetta LeNoire [Waters], Tony Middleton [Wilson], and Ketty Lester [Dunham].

Published Songs
*Cabin in the Sky
Do What You Wanna Do
*Honey in the Honeycomb
*In My Old Virginia Home (On the River Nile)—cut
Livin' It Up [lyric by Duke]—written for revival
*Love Me Tomorrow
*Love Turned the Light Out
*Not a Care in the World—added to revival; originally used in BANJO EYES [December 26, 1941]
Savannah [lyric by Latouche and Ted Fetter]
**Taking a Chance on Love

Additional Songs Recorded
Great Day
Make Way
The Man Upstairs
Not So Bad to Be Good
Wade in the Water
We'll Live All Over Again—cut

Duke wrote his best and most successful score for this fantasy musical, with friend and compatriot Balanchine not only choreographing but directing as well. Ethel Waters introduced *Taking a Chance on Love* in her greatest musical role. Also standing out from the sparkling score: *Cabin in the Sky, Love Me Tomorrow, Love Turned the Light Out*, and the cut *In My Old Virginia Home*. Duke was in the Coast Guard when MGM made their 1943 movie version, so Harold Arlen and E. Y. Harburg (of *The Wizard of Oz*) supplemented the score with three additional songs, including *Happiness Is Just a Thing Called Joe*.

BANJO EYES
December 25, 1941
Hollywood Theatre • 126 performances
Music mostly by Duke; Lyrics mostly by John Latouche; Book by Joe Quillan and Izzy Elinson (based on *Three Men on a Horse* [play] by John Cecil Holm and George Abbott); Directed by Hassard Short; Produced by Albert Lewis; With Eddie Cantor, Audrey Christie, June Clyde, and Lionel Stander.

Published Songs
Banjo Eyes
Don't Let It Happen Again—cut; issued as professional copy
I Always Think of Sally—issued as professional copy
I'll Take the City—issued as professional copy
Make with the Feet [lyric by Harold Adamson]
My Song without Words
A Nickel to My Name
*Not a Care in the World—see CABIN IN THE SKY [October 25, 1940]
We're Having a Baby (My Baby and Me) [lyric by Adamson]
Who Made the Rumba?—advertised but not published

Eddie Cantor's only Broadway appearance after WHOOPEE [Notables: December 4, 1928] was in this undistinguished wartime vehicle, with the run cut short by the star's illness. The title character, incidentally, was not Cantor but a rumba-ing racehorse (of the two-person variety). A second musical version of the play was Ray Livingston and Jay Evans's even more hapless LET IT RIDE† [October 12, 1961]. George Abbott, no fool, knew enough to stay away from both attempts at altering his classic farce.

THE LADY COMES ACROSS
January 9, 1942
44th Street Theatre • 3 performances
Lyrics by John Latouche; Book by Fred Thompson and Dawn Powell; Book directed by Romney Brent; Production supervised by Morrie Ryskind; Choreographed by George Balanchine; Produced by George Hale; With Evelyn Wyckoff, Joe E. Lewis, Ronald Graham, and Gower Champion & Jeanne Tyler (Champion).

Songs Issued in Professional Copies
I'd Like to Talk about the Weather
*Lady
Summer Is a-Comin' In—also used in THE LITTLEST REVUE [May 25, 1956]
*This Is Where I Came In
You Took Me By Surprise

Talk about getting lost on the road. This ill-fated musical started life as SHE HAD TO SAY YES†, produced and coauthored by (and starring) Dennis King with a score from Sammy Fain and Al Dubin. Duke and Latouche were called in to doctor, but King decided just to shutter instead. At which point producer George Hale bought the sets and costumes and plunged ahead. Then the trouble *really* started. British musical comedy star Jessie Matthews (see EVER GREEN [Rodgers: December 3, 1930]) came across to star, but the lady was apparently shell-shocked by the Blitz and disappeared during the Boston tryout. Understudy Evelyn Wyckoff bravely took over for the Broadway opening, but the show got bombed. Duke entered the Coast Guard.

DANCING IN THE STREETS
March 22, 1943
Shubert Theatre {Boston} •
  Closed during tryout
Lyrics by Howard Dietz; Book by John Cecil Holm and Matt Taylor; Directed by Edgar MacGregor; Produced by Vinton Freedley; With Mary Martin, Dudley Digges, and Ernest Cossart.

Published Songs
Dancing in the Streets
Got a Bran' New Daddy
Indefinable Charm
Irresistible You

Additional Song Recorded
Swattin' the Fly—cut

Lt. Duke wrote this wartime musical while safely stationed in Brooklyn. He had collaborated with Dietz before, on *Talkative Toes* from THREE'S A CROWD [October 15, 1930]. Mary Martin had first stormed Broadway in LEAVE IT TO ME [Porter: November 9, 1938], after which she hied to Hollywood. Meeting with little success as a contract player, Martin returned to the stage to star in the Ralph Rainger/Leo Robin NICE GOIN'[†] [October 21, 1939], which closed in Boston (as did DANCING IN THE STREETS, which Mary chose to do over OKLAHOMA! [Rodgers: March 31, 1943]). It wasn't till her next try that she came up roses, with ONE TOUCH OF VENUS [Weill: October 7, 1943].

NANTUCKET
[circa 1943]
Unproduced musical. Lyrics by Harold Rome; Book by Samuel Hoffenstein and Gottfried Reinhardt.

Songs Recorded
The Devil Played the Fiddle

I Knew You Well
Je T'aime—I Love You
My Heart Decided
Song of Our Love
There You Are Again
They Never Told Me
When It's Love
You after All These Years

The Coast Guard's Lt. Duke hooked up with the Army's Corporal Harold Rome (also stationed in Brooklyn) to write this long-forgotten musical comedy score—much of which, unaccountably, was recorded in 1994 by Duke-enthusiast Ben Bagley.

JACKPOT
January 13, 1944
Alvin Theatre • 69 performances
Lyrics by Howard Dietz; Book by Guy Bolton, Sidney Sheldon, and Ben Roberts; Directed by Roy Hargrave; Produced by Vinton Freedley; With Nanette Fabray, Betty Garrett, Allan Jones, and Benny Baker.

Published Songs
I've Got a One Track Mind
Sugarfoot
There Are Yanks (From the Banks of the Wabash)
What Happened?

JACKPOT was yet another undistinguished wartime musical comedy, with an undistinguished score.

TARS AND SPARS
May 5, 1944
Strand Theatre
"*A Tabloid Recruiting Revue for the United States Coast Guard.*" Music by "Lt. Vernon Duke USCGR(T)"; Book and Lyrics by Howard Dietz; Choreographed by Ted Gary and "Gower Champion Seaman 1C"; Directed and Produced by Max Liebman; With "Victor Mature CBM," "Sidney Caesar Seaman 1C," and Gower Champion.

Published Songs
Arm in Arm
Civilian

Farewell for a While
Silver Shield—published in non-show edition

Additional Songs Published in Vocal Selection
Apprentice Seaman
Palm Beach

The Army had Irving Berlin (THIS IS THE ARMY [Berlin: July 4, 1942]), Frank Loesser, and Harold Rome; the Coast Guard had Duke and assigned him to put together a recruiting show. The cast was assembled from the ranks of enlisted men, like Gower Champion from THE LADY COMES ACROSS [January 9, 1942]. Sid Caesar was found playing saxophone in the base band (give that boy some comedy routines!). TARS AND SPARS toured the country, keeping Duke, Caesar, and Champion stateside. SPARS, incidentally, were the Coast Guard's equivalent to WACS.

SADIE THOMPSON
November 16, 1944
Alvin Theatre • 60 performances
Lyrics by Howard Dietz; Book by Howard Dietz and Rouben Mamoulian (based on *Rain* [play] by W. Somerset Maugham and John Colton); Directed by Rouben Mamoulian; Produced by A. P. Waxman; With June Havoc, Lansing Hatfield, and Ralph Dumke.

Published Songs
Any Woman Who Is Willing Will Do—
advertised but not published
If You Can't Get the Love You Want
Life's a Funny Present from Someone
The Love I Long For
Poor As a Churchmouse
**Sailing at Midnight*
When You Live on an Island
You—U.S.A.—advertised but not published

Poor SADIE's fate was sealed during the first week of rehearsals, when star Ethel Merman found Dietz's lyrics lacking and quit. Her replacement: "Baby June" Havoc. (There's a connection there somewhere, isn't there?) Duke's adventurous score was quickly forgotten, including *When You Live on an Island* and the exceedingly lovely *Sailing at Midnight*.

SWEET BYE AND BYE
October 10, 1946
Shubert Theatre {New Haven, Conn.} •
Closed during tryout
Lyrics by Ogden Nash; Book by S. J. Perelman and Al Hirschfeld; Directed by Curt Conway; Produced by Nat Karson; With Dolores Gray, Erik Rhodes, and Percy Helton.

Published Songs
***Born Too Late*—cut; initial publication upon
use in THE LITTLEST REVUE [May 22, 1956]
Just Like a Man—also used in TWO'S COMPANY [December 15, 1952]
Low and Lazy
An Old Fashioned Tune
**Round About*—also used in TWO'S COMPANY
Sweet Bye and Bye

Additional Song Recorded
The Sea-gull and the Ea-gull—cut

Yet another out-of-town disaster for Duke. Beginning with Eddie Cantor's illness, which cut short the run of BANJO EYES [December 26, 1941], Duke wrote ten consecutive flops—four of which shuttered en route to Broadway. Not surprisingly, it became increasingly difficult for him to get produced, despite the high degree of quality and inventiveness in his work.

CASEY JONES
[circa 1950]
Unproduced musical. Lyrics by Sammy Cahn; Book by Arthur Carter and George Abbott; [Produced by Richard Krakeur and George Abbott].

Song Recorded
Once I Fall

Lyricist Sammy Cahn—who had split with Jule Styne after HIGH BUTTON SHOES [Styne: October 9, 1947]—chose Duke as his new collaborator. They worked together for three years, completing this unproduced musical about the legendary railroad engineer and a couple of negligible film scores. They had already embarked on their next project, a Broadway revue for Bette Davis, when Cahn received a Hollywood producing offer and withdrew. Duke turned back to his previous lyricist, Ogden Nash.

TWO'S COMPANY
December 15, 1952
Alvin Theatre • 90 performances
Music mostly by Duke; Lyrics mostly by
Ogden Nash; Sketches mostly by Charles
Sherman and Peter DeVries; Production
supervised by John Murray Anderson;
Sketches directed by Jules Dassin; Choreo-
graphed by Jerome Robbins; Produced by
James Russo and Michael Ellis; With Bette
Davis, Hiram Sherman, and Nora Kaye.

Published Songs
Good Little Girls [lyric by Sammy Cahn]—cut;
    also used in THE LITTLEST REVUE [May
    22, 1956]
It Just Occurred to Me
Just Like a Man—originally used in SWEET
    BYE AND BYE [October 10, 1946]
Out of the Clear Blue Sky
*Round About—originally used in SWEET BYE
    AND BYE

Additional Songs Recorded
Esther [lyric by Cahn]
Haunted Hot Spot
Purple Rose
Roll along Sadie
The Theatre Is a Lady
Turn Me Loose on Broadway

A turmoil-wracked Broadway failure, with
Bette Davis making her musical debut. Twenty
years later she appeared in her second and final
musical, the troubled, Broadway-bound MISS
MOFFAT† [October 7, 1974]. She sold tickets,
too, but they were suddenly forced to close when
she developed a "sudden illness."

DILLY
[circa 1954]
Unproduced musical. Lyrics by Duke, Jerome
Lawrence, and Robert E. Lee; Book by Jerome
Lawrence and Robert E. Lee (based on *Miss
Dilly Says No* [novel] by Theodore Pratt);
[Produced by Gala Ebin].

Songs Recorded
Roses in the Rain
Small World
What If You're Not?
Who's Excited?

THE LITTLEST REVUE
May 22, 1956
Phoenix Theatre {Off Broadway} •
    32 performances
Music mostly by Duke (also see Blitzstein
and Strouse: May 22, 1956); Lyrics mostly
by Ogden Nash; Sketches by Nat Hiken,
Michael Stewart, and others; Directed by Paul
Lammers; Produced by T. Edward Hambleton
and Norris Houghton by arrangement with
Ben Bagley; With Charlotte Rae, Tammy
Grimes, Joel Grey, and Larry Storch.

Published Songs
**Born Too Late—initial publication of song
    cut from SWEET BYE AND BYE [October
    10, 1946]
Good Little Girls—originally used in TWO'S
    COMPANY [December 15, 1952]
*Madly in Love
Summer Is a-Comin' In [lyric by John
    Latouche]—originally used in THE LADY
    COMES ACROSS [January 9, 1942]
You're Far from Wonderful

Additional Songs Recorded
I'm Glad I'm Not a Man
A Little Love, a Little Money
Love Is Still in Town
Second Avenue and Twelfth Street Rag

The Phoenix Theatre had ended its inaugural season with the award-winning Jerome Moross/John
Latouche GOLDEN APPLE [Notables: March 11,
1954]. Looking for another musical success, the
Phoenix and producer Ben Bagley commissioned
Duke to prepare this intimate revue. Unlike
GOLDEN APPLE, the show was unable to transfer to Broadway and closed after its limited engagement. Duke's score included the intricate and
incredibly moving *Born Too Late*.

TIME REMEMBERED
November 2, 1957
Morosco Theatre • 248 performances
Play by Jean Anouilh; English version by
Patricia Moyes; Incidental music and Lyrics
by Duke; Directed by Albert Marre (see APRIL
SONG [Leigh: July 9, 1980]); Produced by The
Playwrights' Company in association with

Milton Sperling; With Helen Hayes, Richard Burton, and Susan Strasberg.

Published Songs

Ages Ago
Time Remembered

Duke provided two songs for this successful drama, his final effort to reach Broadway.

THE PINK JUNGLE

October 14, 1959
Alcazar Theatre {San Francisco}   •
    Closed during tryout
Music and Lyrics by Duke; Book by Leslie Stevens; Choreographed by Matt Maddox; Directed by Joseph Anthony; Produced by Paul Gregory; With Ginger Rogers, Leif Erickson, and Agnes Moorehead.

Published Songs

Just Like Children—issued in 1965 as non-
    show song
Paris in New York—issued in 1965 as non-
    show song

Ginger Rogers's first Broadway musical since GIRL CRAZY [Gershwin: October 14, 1930] was not to be; it closed under a pink cloud of unpaid bills. THE PINK JUNGLE of the title, for the record, was the cosmetics game.

ZENDA

August 5, 1963
Curran Theatre {San Francisco}   •
    Closed during tryout
"A Romantic Musical." Lyrics mostly by Martin Charnin; Book by Everett Freeman (based on *The Prisoner of Zenda* [novel] by Anthony Hope); Directed by George Schaefer; Choreographed by Jack Cole; Produced by Edwin Lester (Civic Light Opera); With Alfred Drake, Anne Rogers, and Chita Rivera.

Published Songs

Let Her Not Be Beautiful (*You Are All That's*
    Beautiful)
The Night Is Filled with Wonderful Sounds

Additional Songs Recorded

Alive at Last
Alone at Night

Bounce
Enchanting Girls
I Wonder What He Meant by That
In This Life—also published in fake book
Love Is the Worst Possible Thing
The Man Loves Me
My Heart Has Come A'tumbling Down
My Royal Majesty
No Ifs! No Ands! No Buts!
No More Love
Now the World Begins Again
A Royal Confession
Words, Words, Words
Yesterday's Forgotten
Zenda

Ed Lester, the West Coast producer responsible for originating SONG OF NORWAY† [August 21, 1944], KISMET [Notables: December 3, 1953], and other costume operettas, devised this show as a vehicle for KISMET star Alfred Drake. But ZENDA turned out to be just another road disaster, with multiple problems (and multiple lyricists, with Marty Charnin's work supplemented by Lenny Adelson and Sid Kuller). ZENDA was Duke's final show. He died of lung cancer on January 17, 1969, in Santa Monica, California.

Vernon Duke began his Broadway career at the worst possible time—right after the stock market crash. Harold Arlen and Burton Lane were also 1930 newcomers; they countered by going to Hollywood, not a viable alternative for the musically highbrow Dukelsky. Duke's Broadway (and Broadway-bound) record is spotty: fourteen complete scores with only three (early) successes. It made for a discouraging career, as Duke was very much convinced that his work was better than most of his contemporaries. (And it often was.) Duke's advanced harmonies and complex forms were, and remain, fascinating. His work rarely appealed to the public at large, though. His official "hit" songs were few—*April in Paris, I Can't Get Started,* and *Taking a Chance on Love*—but over the years Duke has attracted, and continues to attract, many devotees.

BURTON LANE

Born: February 2, 1912, New York, New York
Died: January 5, 1997, New York, New York

BURTON LANE began his musical career at the age of fifteen, leaving school to work as a pianist at Remick's (where both Gershwin and Youmans started a decade earlier). Lane's expert playing attracted attention—Gershwin himself was a fan—and a Shubert offer to write a new revue. The show, which was to be the 1928 edition of the GREENWICH VILLAGE FOLLIES, was never produced. The teenager had to wait another two years before being heard on Broadway.

ARTISTS AND MODELS ✦ PARIS-RIVIERA EDITION
June 10, 1930
Majestic Theatre • 65 performances
Music mostly by others; Lane lyrics by Samuel Lerner; Book uncredited (based on *Dear Love* [British musical]); Directed by Frank Smithson; Produced by the Messrs. Shubert; With Aileen Stanley and Phil Baker.

Published Songs
My Real Ideal
Two Perfect Lovers

Book troubles on this British import were dealt with by throwing out the book (and title). The Shuberts tacked on the name of one of their perennial revues, with the label "Paris-Riviera Edition" explaining the sets and costumes. The eighteen-year-old Lane's first Broadway songs were bright and tuneful.

THREE'S A CROWD
October 15, 1930
Selwyn Theatre • 271 performances
Music mostly by Arthur Schwartz (see Schwartz: October 15, 1930; also Duke); Lyrics mostly by Howard Dietz; Sketches by Dietz, Groucho Marx, and others; Directed by Hassard Short; Produced by Max Gordon; With Clifton Webb, Fred Allen, Libby Holman, and Tamara Geva.

Published Songs
Forget All Your Books [lyric by Dietz and Samuel Lerner]
Out in the Open Air [lyric by Dietz and Ted Pola]

Impressed with Lane's work, lyricist Howard Dietz fixed up the lyrics of these songs and inserted them into this follow-up to THE LITTLE SHOW [Schwartz: April 30, 1929].

THE THIRD LITTLE SHOW
June 1, 1931
Music Box Theatre • 136 performances
Music mostly by others; Sketches by Noel Coward, S. J. Perelman, Marc Connelly, and others; Directed by Alexander Leftwich; Produced by Dwight Deere Wiman in association with Tom Weatherly; With Beatrice Lillie, Ernest Truex, and Constance Carpenter.

Published Song
Say the Word [lyric by Harold Adamson]

THE SECOND LITTLE SHOW [Schwartz: September 2, 1930]—without Webb, Holman, and Allen—had done poorly. This final edition, without Schwartz and Dietz, fared little better despite the presence of Bea Lillie.

EARL CARROLL'S VANITIES ✦
Ninth Edition
August 27, 1931
Earl Carroll Theatre • 278 performances
Music also by others; Lyrics to Lane songs by Harold Adamson; Sketches by Ralph Spence

and Eddie Welch; Directed by Edgar
MacGregor; Produced by Earl Carroll; With
Will Mahoney, Lillian Roth, and William
Demarest.

Published Songs
Goin' to Town
Have a Heart
Love Came into My Heart

The early years of the Depression were not a
good time for teenage songwriters on Broadway.
Lane and collaborator Harold Adamson went to
Hollywood, quickly coming up with the hit
Everything I Have Is Yours for the 1933 *Dancing
Lady*. Lane's Hollywood collaborators over the
years included Frank Loesser, Alan Jay Lerner,
Dorothy Fields, and Ira Gershwin, with songs
like *The Lady's in Love with You, *Too Late Now,
*You're All the World to Me, *Swing High Swing
Low, *I Love to Dance, and **How about You?

HOLD ON TO YOUR HATS
September 11, 1940
Shubert Theatre • 158 performances
Lyrics by E. Y. Harburg; Book by Guy Bolton,
Matt Brooks, and Eddie Davis; Directed by
Edgar MacGregor; Produced by Al Jolson and
George Hale; With Al Jolson, Martha Raye,
Jack Whiting, and Bert Gordon.

Published Songs
*Don't Let It Get You Down (Love Is a Lovely
Thing)*
Swing Your Calico—cut; issued as professional
copy
There's a Great Day Coming Mañana
The World Is in My Arms
Would You Be So Kindly

Additional Songs Recorded
Down on the Dude Ranch
Hold on to Your Hats
Life Was Pie for the Pioneer
Old Timer
She Came, She Saw, She Can-Canned
Then You Were Never in Love
Walking along Minding My Business
Way Out West

Al Jolson returned to Broadway after a decade,
bringing along Yip Harburg (who with Harold

Arlen had written some fine Jolson songs for the
1936 movie *The Singing Kid*). The star/producer
also brought along wife Ruby Keeler, who disappeared from the show and the marriage during the tryout. The Lane/Harburg score was
bright and tuneful—although, curiously, without any hits for Jolson. After five months the star
lost heart, closed the show, and left Broadway
for good.

LAFFING ROOM ONLY!
December 23, 1944
Winter Garden Theatre • 233 performances
Lyrics mostly by Lane; Sketches by Ole Olsen,
Chic Johnson, and others; Directed by John
Murray Anderson; Produced by the Messrs.
Shubert, Ole Olsen, and Chic Johnson; With
Ole Olsen, Chic Johnson, and Betty Garrett.

Published Songs
Feudin' and Fightin' [lyric by Lane and Al
Dubin]—initial publication upon reuse as
non-show song
Got That Good Time
Stop That Dancing

HELLZAPOPPIN'!† [September 22, 1938], the
Olsen and Johnson vaudeville revue, had run
a staggering 1,404 performances. The Shuberts
followed it with a string of offshoots, including LAFFING ROOM ONLY! *Feudin' and Fightin'*
resurfaced several years later via radio and became
a surprise hit. Heavy-drinking Hollywood lyricist
Al Dubin (*Lullaby of Broadway*) was slated to do
LAFFING ROOM ONLY! but became indisposed,
as they say, and died soon after the show opened.
Lane himself wasn't a lyricist, certainly; it now
appears that the LAFFING lyrics—including
Feudin' and Fightin'—were ghosted by Lane's late-
1930s collaborator Frank Loesser, who was just
then serving in the Army.

FINIAN'S RAINBOW
January 10, 1947
46th Street Theatre • 725 performances
"A Completely Captivating Musical." Lyrics by
E. Y. Harburg; Book by E. Y. Harburg and
Fred Saidy; Directed by Bretaigne Windust;
Choreographed by Michael Kidd; Produced by

Lee Sabinson and William R. Katzell; With Ella Logan, David Wayne, Albert Sharpe, Donald Richards, and Anita Alvarez.

Revival
May 23, 1960
46th Street Theatre • 12 performances
Directed and Choreographed by Herbert Ross; Transferred from City Center Light Opera Company; With Jeannie Carson [Logan], Howard Morris [Wayne], Biff McGuire [Richards], Carol Brice, and Anita Alvarez.

Published Songs
*The Begat
**How Are Things in Glocca Morra?
*If This Isn't Love
Look to the Rainbow
*Necessity
**Old Devil Moon
*Something Sort of Grandish
That Great Come-and-Get-It Day
**When I'm Not Near the Girl I Love
When the Idle Poor Become the Idle Rich

Additional Songs Published in Vocal Score
Dance of the Golden Crock [instrumental]
This Time of the Year

Lane's twenty-year track record hardly indicated that he was likely to write a perfect musical comedy score, yet he turned up in 1947 with the glorious FINIAN'S RAINBOW. Mixing a little social significance with some fantasy and lots of entertainment, FINIAN'S got its several messages across with wit, satire, and good-natured rambunctiousness. Lane wrote a superb, highly melodic score with bits of Irish charm. Harburg did the best work of his career, probably because he was a leprechaun by nature. The songs are gems, with the shifting harmonies of *Old Devil Moon* and the grand, sweeping-but-hesitating waltz *When I'm Not Near the Girl I Love* enchanting standouts. Harburg's deftly crafted *Necessity* and *The Begat* are perfectly complemented by Lane, the first in hot-house blues style, the second in (Broadway) gospel; so is the nursery-like, Eisenhowsish tongue twister *Something Sort of Grandish*. While the music certainly doesn't sound like that of Lane's mentor Gershwin, the songs are filled with surprising but pleasing blue notes and startling key changes (like those in *Old Devil Moon*). As it turned out, FINIAN was to be the talented Lane's only fully satisfying Broadway work. But what a score!

JOLLYANNA
[September 11, 1952]
Curran Theatre {San Francisco} •
    Closed during tryout
A revised version of FLAHOOLEY [*Notables: May 14, 1951*]. Music mostly by Sammy Fain; Lyrics by E. Y. Harburg; Book by E. Y. Harburg and Fred Saidy; Directed by Jack Donohue; Produced by Edwin Lester (San Francisco and Los Angeles Civic Light Opera); With Bobby Clark, Mitzi Gaynor, John Beal, and Biff McGuire.

Recorded Song
Santa Claus

West Coast impresario Ed Lester attempted to commercialize the outspoken FLAHOOLEY by removing the social significance (and Yma Sumac). No soap(box), though, despite the presence of Broadway's Bobby Clark and Hollywood's Mitzi Gaynor. The plan was to bring the reconstituted JOLLYANNA back to Broadway in triumph, but in less than a month it was back in the Fascinating Flop File.

ON A CLEAR DAY YOU CAN SEE FOREVER
October 17, 1965
Mark Hellinger Theatre • 280 performances
Book and Lyrics by Alan Jay Lerner; Directed by Robert Lewis; Choreographed by Herbert Ross; Produced by Alan Jay Lerner in association with Rogo Productions (Robert Goulet); With Barbara Harris, John Cullum, Titos Vandis, and William Daniels.

Published Songs
*Come Back to Me
Go to Sleep—written for 1970 movie version
*Hurry! It's Lovely up Here!
Love with All the Trimmings—written for
    movie version
*Melinda
*On a Clear Day (You Can See Forever)

On the S.S. Bernard Cohn
She Wasn't You
Wait till We're Sixty-Five
What Did I Have That I Don't Have?
When I'm Being Born Again

Additional Songs Published in Vocal Score

Solicitor's Song
When I Come Around Again—new lyric
    for When I'm Being Born Again

Additional Songs Recorded

Don't Tamper with My Sister
Tosy and Cosh

Following the 1960 retirement of Frederick Loewe, Alan Jay Lerner had been unsuccessfully searching for a collaborator. He began his ESP project—initially entitled I PICKED A DAISY—with Richard Rodgers, who found Lerner even less reliable than Larry Hart and withdrew. (Rodgers next tried Lionel Bart of OLIVER! [January 6, 1963]—who was even *more* impossible—before turning to Stephen Sondheim for DO I HEAR A WALTZ? [March 18, 1965].) Lerner turned to Lane, with whom he'd written two film scores, the 1951 *Royal Wedding* (including the Oscar-nominee *Too Late Now*) and an unproduced musicalization of Mark Twain's *Huckleberry Finn*. The pair combined for an exceedingly fine score, mostly, with the popular *On a Clear Day* and *Come Back to Me*; two delectably perfect character songs in *What Did I Have That I Don't Have?* and *Hurry! It's Lovely up Here!*; and the hauntingly melodic ballads *She Wasn't You* and *Melinda*. But all of these, plus the performances of Barbara Harris and John Cullum (who replaced Louis Jourdan during the tryout), weren't enough to carry ON A CLEAR DAY past a contrived book.

CARMELINA
April 8, 1979
St. James Theatre • 17 performances
Lyrics by Alan Jay Lerner; Book by Alan Jay Lerner and Joseph Stein; Directed by José

Ferrer; Choreographed by Peter Gennaro; Produced by Roger L. Stevens, J. W. Fisher, Joan Cullman, and Jujamcyn Productions; With Georgia Brown, Cesare Siepi, John Michael King, Virginia Martin, and Josie de Guzman.

Published Songs

It's Time for a Love Song
One More Walk around the Garden
Why Him?—issued in separate edition

Additional Songs Recorded

All That He Wants Me to Be
Carmelina
The Image of Me
I'm a Woman
I Must Have Her
Love before Breakfast
Prayer
Signora Campbell
Someone in April
Yankee Doodles Are Coming to Town

Alan Jay Lerner prevailed upon Lane to return to Broadway, but the property was poorly selected, poorly executed, and exceedingly old fashioned. Lane's work was the best of the evening, with a few especially nice songs including *One More Walk around the Garden*, *I'm a Woman*, and *Someone in April*. Lane went back into retirement for almost twenty years more, until his death on January 5, 1997.

In a career that spanned fifty years, Burton Lane chose to limit his Broadway output to only four musical comedies. Only one of these shows was successful; another remains familiar due to its indifferent Hollywood incarnation. But with *Old Devil Moon*, *When I'm Not Near the Girl I Love*, *How Are Things in Glocca Morra?*, *On a Clear Day*, and *What Did I Have That I Don't Have?* to his credit—not to mention non-show tunes like *Too Late Now*, *How about You?*, and *You're All the World to Me*—the underemployed Lane earned a high ranking among his peers.

KURT WEILL

Born: March 2, 1900, Dessau, Germany
Died: April 3, 1950, New York, New York

KURT WEILL, the son of a cantor, evinced an early interest in music. He went to Berlin in 1918, where he studied with Engelbert Humperdinck (*Hansel und Gretl*) before moving on to avant-garde composer Ferruccio Busoni. Weill soon moved from concert to contemporary work and started writing for the theatre. Caught up in Germany's inflammatory political situation, he began a collaboration in 1927 with outspoken playwright/lyricist Bertolt Brecht. The pair attracted international attention with their controversial *Die Dreigroschenoper* [August 28, 1928] (see THE THREEPENNY OPERA [April 13, 1933, and March 10, 1954]). Weill's German-language songs are not discussed in *Show Tunes*, except for material subsequently used in English-language productions. However, one would be remiss not to mention *Surabaya-Johnny and *Bilbao Song from *Happy End* [lyrics by Bertolt Brecht] [September 2, 1929]; **Alabama Song from *Aufstieg und Fall der Stadt Mahagonny* [lyric by Bertolt Brecht] [March 9, 1930]; and *Fennimores Lied, *Cäsars Tod (about the death of a dictator), and *Das Lied vom Schlaraffenland from *Der Silbersee* [lyrics by Georg Kaiser] [February 18, 1933]. Weill's political views and Jewish heritage made it impossible for him to stay in Germany, and he was forced to flee following Nazi protests at the première of *Der Silbersee*.

THE THREEPENNY OPERA [1933]
April 13, 1933
Empire Theatre • 12 performances
Also see March 10, 1954. Original book and Lyrics by Bertolt Brecht (based on *The Beggar's Opera* [play] by John Gay); English adaptation by Gifford Cochran and Jerrold Krimsky; Directed by Francesco von Mendelssohn; Produced by John Krimsky and Gifford Cochran; With Robert Chisholm, Steffi Duna, Rex Weber, and Burgess Meredith.

Published Songs
None

Note: The complete German vocal score of the 1928 version is published.

This early, indifferent translation of *Die Dreigroschenoper* was out of place on Broadway in the midst of the depression. Neither of the authors was involved with or in attendance for this quick failure. Weill's personal reviews, however, were quite positive.

MARIE GALANTE
December 22, 1934
Theatre de Paris {Paris}
Play and Lyrics by Jacques Deval (based on his novel); Directed by Andre Lefour; Produced by Leon Volterra; With Florelle, Inkijinoff, Alcover, Serge Nadoud, and Joe Alex.

Published Songs
Les Filles de Bordeaux—revised version of *In der Jugend Gold'nem Schimmer* from the 1929 German-language production *Happy End*; also revised as *The Trouble with Women* from ONE TOUCH OF VENUS [October 7, 1943]
Le Grand Lustucru
**J'Attends un Navire*
Marche de l'Armée Paneméeenne [instrumental]
Le Roi d'Aquitaine—see A KINGDOM FOR A COW [June 28, 1935]
Scène au Dancing [instrumental]

Tango—advertised but not published, initial publication as 1946 non-show song *Youkali* [lyric by Roger Fernay]

Le Train du Ciel

Weill spent his first two years of exile in France, where he continued his concert compositions, composed the ballet with songs *Die Sieben Todsünden* (The Seven Deadly Sins), and wrote music for this unsuccessful musical play with songs. *J'Attends un Navire*, though, is especially moving and quite beautiful.

A KINGDOM FOR A COW
June 28, 1935
Savoy Theatre {London}
Lyrics by Desmond Carter; Book by Reginald Arkell and Desmond Carter (based on *Der Kuhhandel* [musical], book and lyrics by Robert Vambery); Directed by Ernest Matrai and Felix Weissberger.

Published Songs
As Long As I Love
Two Hearts—new lyric for *Le Roi D'Aquitaine* from MARIE GALANTE [December 22, 1934]

Unable to get his unfinished satirical operetta *Der Kuhhandel* mounted in Paris or Zurich, Weill arranged a London production. Translated into English as A KINGDOM FOR A COW, this satire about munitions manufacturers was poorly received and closed within three weeks. Weill moved on to America for the mounting of Max Reinhardt's THE ETERNAL ROAD, a 1934 piece which wasn't ultimately produced until January 7, 1937. Weill and his wife Lotte Lenya emigrated on September 10, 1935.

JOHNNY JOHNSON
November 19, 1936
44th Street Theatre • 68 performances
"A Legend." Book and Lyrics by Paul Green; Directed by Lee Strasberg; Produced by The Group Theatre; With Russell Collins, Phoebe Brand, Paula Miller, Lee J. Cobb, Robert Lewis, Luther Adler, and Elia Kazan.

Published Songs
*Mon Ami, My Friend
Oh, Heart of Love
Oh the Rio Grande (*Cowboy Song*)

To Love You and to Lose You [lyric by Edward Heyman]—non-show lyric for *Listen to My Song* (*Johnny's Song*)

Additional Song Published in Non-show Folio
Listen to My Song (*Johnny's Song*)

Additional Songs Published in Vocal Score
Aggie's Song (*Sewing Machine*)
The Allied High Command
Asylum Chorus
The Ballad of San Juan Hill
The Battle [instrumental]
Captain Valentine's Song
Democracy's Call
A Hymn to Peace
In No Man's Land [instrumental]
Interlude after Scene III [instrumental]
In Times of War and Tumults
Introduction [instrumental]
Johnny's Dream [instrumental]
Laughing Generals [instrumental]
Music of the Stricken Redeemer [instrumental]
Over in Europe
The Psychiatry Song
The Sea Song
Song of the Goddess
Song of the Guns
Song of the Wounded Frenchmen

Additional Song Recorded
The Westpointer—cut

The socially conscious Group Theatre (Harold Clurman, Lee Strasberg, and Cheryl Crawford) commissioned this antiwar musical. North Carolina folk-playwright Paul Green wrote a muddled book, and the production suffered from unfocused direction. Although JOHNNY JOHNSON was a failure, Weill's work was well received, and he attracted notice in both Broadway and Hollywood. The score is fascinating, although saddled by inexpert lyrics.

THE ETERNAL ROAD
January 7, 1937
Manhattan Opera House • 153 performances
Play and Lyrics by Franz Werfel; Adapted by William A. Drake (from a translation by Ludwig Lewisohn); Directed by Max

Reinhardt; Produced by Meyer W. Weisgal and Crosby Gaige; With Thomas Chalmers, Sam Jaffe, Dickie (Dick) Van Patten, Katherine Carrington, and Lotte Lenya (Weill).

Songs Published in Vocal Selection
Dance of the Golden Calf
David's Psalm
The March to Zion
Promise
Song of Miriam
Song of Ruth

Philanthropist Meyer Weisgal brought Weill to America to work with fellow emigrés Max Reinhardt and Franz Werfel on this eternally-in-preparation Biblical spectacle meant to illustrate the history of Jewish persecution. In the cast were Katherine Carrington (Mrs. Arthur Schwartz at the time) and Lotte Lenya, whose career had virtually ended when she joined her husband in exile. Twenty years later, American audiences finally discovered her in THE THREE-PENNY OPERA [1954] [March 10, 1954].

KNICKERBOCKER HOLIDAY
October 19, 1938
Ethel Barrymore Theatre • 168 performances
Book and Lyrics by Maxwell Anderson (based on *Knickerbocker History of New York* [stories] by Washington Irving); Directed by Joshua Logan; Produced by The Playwrights' Company (including Maxwell Anderson); With Walter Huston, Jean Madden, Richard Kollmar, and Ray Middleton.

Concert Version
April 19, 1977
Town Hall • 16 performances
Directed by John Bowab; With Richard Kiley [Huston], Maureen Brennan [Madden], Edward Evanko [Kollmar], and Kurt Peterson [Middleton].

Published Songs
It Never Was You
**September Song*
There's Nowhere to Go but Up
Will You Remember Me?

Additional Songs Published in Vocal Selections
Ballad of the Robbers
Dirge for a Soldier
How Can You Tell an American?
May and January
The One Indispensable Man
Our Ancient Liberties
The Scars
To War!
Washington Irving's Song
We Are Cut in Twain
Young People Think about Love

Additional Songs Published in Vocal Score
The Algonquins from Harlem [instrumental]
Clickety-Clack
Entrance of the Council
Hush, Hush
No Ve Vouldn't Gonto Do It
One Touch of Alchemy (All Hail the Political Honeymoon)
Opening (Introduction to Washington Irving's Song)
Sitting in Jail

Additional Song Recorded
Bachelor Song—cut

Pulitzer Prize–winning playwright Maxwell Anderson saw the tyrannical Pieter Stuyvesant (and his councilors) as perfect counterparts to Franklin Roosevelt (and his cabinet). Anderson chose Weill on the strength of JOHNNY JOHNSON [November 19, 1936], and the two men became close friends and neighbors. The Playwrights' Company was formed by five distinguished, dissatisfied Theatre Guild dramtists—Anderson, S. N. Behrman, Sidney Howard, Elmer Rice, and Robert E. Sherwood—who banded to present their own works by committee. Weill became closely associated with The Playwrights' Company, eventually becoming a full member. KNICKERBOCKER HOLIDAY, their first production, just missed becoming a hit; Anderson's anti–New Deal tract was perhaps too bitter, or maybe just not funny enough. Highlights of the score include *September Song* (one of Weill's few popular song hits), the exuberant *There's Nowhere to Go but Up*, and two exciting propoganda songs, *How Can You Tell an American?* and *Ballad of the Robbers*.

RAILROADS ON PARADE
April 30, 1939
New York World's Fair
"Fantasia on Rail Transport." Pageant by
Edward Hungerford; Incidental music by
Weill; Directed by Charles Alan; Produced by
Eastern Railroad Presidents' Conference;
"With 250 Men & Women, 50 Horses & 20
Locomotives, all operating on their own
steam."

Published Song
Mile after Mile [lyric by Charles Alan and
    Buddy Bernier]

Weill scored this World's Fair spectacle presented by the railroad industry. The composer,
who left behind most of his money and property
when fleeing Germany, needed the work.

ULYSSES AFRICANUS
[circa August 1939]
Unfinished musical. Book and Lyrics by
Maxwell Anderson (based on *Aeneas Africanus*
[novel] by Harry Stillwell Edwards).

Published Songs
The Little Gray House—initial publication
    upon reuse in LOST IN THE STARS
    [October 30, 1949]
Lost in the Stars—published in 1942 as non-
    show song; initial use in LOST IN THE
    STARS
Lover Man—published in 1942 as non-show
    song; initial use in LOST IN THE STARS
    retitled *Trouble Man*
Stay Well—initial publication upon reuse in
    LOST IN THE STARS

Weill and Anderson\ tried to follow KNICKER-
BOCKER HOLIDAY [October 19, 1938] with this
vehicle for Paul Robeson about a wandering ex-
slave during the post–Civil War Reconstruction
era. Robeson turned down the project, though,
and that was the end of ULYSSES. Weill and
Anderson effectively incorporated a third of the
score into their next collaboration, LOST IN THE
STARS.

MADAM, WILL YOU WALK?
November 13, 1939
Ford's Theatre {Baltimore, Md.} •
    Closed during tryout
Play by Sidney Howard; Incidental music by
Weill; Directed by Margaret Webster; Pro-
duced by The Playwrights' Company; With
George M. Cohan, Peggy Conklin, and Arthur
Kennedy.

Published Songs
None

TWO ON AN ISLAND
January 22, 1940
Broadhurst Theatre • 96 performances
Play by Elmer Rice; Incidental music by Weill;
Directed by Elmer Rice; Produced by The
Playwrights' Company (including Elmer Rice);
With Betty Field (Rice), John Craven, and
Luther Adler.

Published Songs
None

LADY IN THE DARK
January 23, 1941
Alvin Theatre • 467 performances
Lyrics by Ira Gershwin; Book by Moss Hart;
Directed by Hassard Short; Choreographed by
Albertina Rasch; Produced by Sam H. Harris;
With Gertrude Lawrence, Victor Mature,
Macdonald Carey, and Danny Kaye.

Concert Version
May 4, 1994
City Center • 4 performances
Directed by Larry Carpenter; Produced by
City Center Encores; With Christine Ebersole
[Lawrence], Patrick Cassidy [Mature], Tony
Goldwyn [Carey], and Edward Hibbert
[Kaye].

Published Songs
Girl of the Moment
Jenny (The Saga of Jenny)
My Ship
One Life to Live
The Princess of Pure Delight

This Is New
*Tschaikowsky (And Other Russians)

Additional Song Published in Vocal Score
*The Best Years of His Life
Dance of the Tumblers [instrumental]
The Greatest Show on Earth
Huxley
It Looks Like Liza
Mapleton High Chorale
Oh, Fabulous One

Additional Songs Recorded
It's Never Too Late to Mendelssohn—cut;
    recorded with revisions by Sylvia Fine
    (Kaye)
No Matter under What Star You're Born—cut;
    see THE FIREBRAND OF FLORENCE
    [March 22, 1945]
You Are Unforgettable—cut
Zodiac Song—cut; see THE FIREBRAND OF
    FLORENCE

Moss Hart's personal experience with psycho-analysis provided the inspiration for this musical play. The score was made up of three extended dream sequences, with the heroine's dilemma solved in the final song (*My Ship*). Ira Gershwin, in a dazed retirement since George's death, came back with absolutely dazzling lyrics to match Weill's music. Producer Sam Harris provided Broadway's most technically complicated production to date, as Hassard Short made novel use of two turntables simultaneously. The show's very greatest asset was its LADY; Gertrude Lawrence sat on an acrobat's swing and bumped-and-ground *The Saga of Jenny*, topping all else (including young Danny Kaye's startling verbal acrobatics).

LUNCHTIME FOLLIES
June 22, 1942
Todd Shipyards {Brooklyn}
Music also by others (see Blitzstein and Rome: June 22, 1942); Lyrics by Maxwell Anderson, Howard Dietz, Dorothy Fields, Archibald MacLeish, Oscar Hammerstein 2nd, and others; Sketches by George S. Kaufman and Moss Hart, Maxwell Anderson, Zero Mostel,

and others; Production supervised by Weill; Produced by The American Theatre Wing. Alternate title: LUNCH HOUR FOLLIES.

Published Song
The Song of the Free [lyric by MacLeish]—
    initial publication as 1947 non-show song;
    first performed as part of stage show at the
    Roxy Theatre on June 4, 1942

Additional Songs Published in 1982 in Non-Show Folio
Buddy on the Nightshift [lyric by Hammerstein]
Schickelgruber [lyric by Dietz]

The LUNCHTIME FOLLIES was a series of forty-five-minute presentations mounted as morale builders at war-materiel production plants. Weill—who was in the process of applying for citizenship—took on the post of production manager for the volunteer project, which featured songs and sketches by well-known writers (performed by volunteer Broadway actors). The contents varied, based on the available cast; the initial performance featured David Burns, as Hitler, in the sketch "Gee, But It's Cold in Russia." Over a two-year period, LUNCHTIME FOLLIES played to more than 700,000 war-workers. Weill became an American citizen on August 27, 1943.

ONE TOUCH OF VENUS
Imperial Theatre
October 7, 1943 • 567 performances
Lyrics by Ogden Nash; Book by S. J. Perelman and Ogden Nash (based on "The Tinted Venus" [story] by F. Anstey); Directed by Elia Kazan; Choreography by Agnes de Mille; Produced by Cheryl Crawford; With Mary Martin, Kenny Baker, John Boles, Paula Laurence, Teddy Hart, and Sono Osato.

Concert Version
March 28, 1996
City Center • 4 performances
Directed by Leonard Foglia; Produced by City Center Encores; With Melissa Errico [Martin],

Andy Taylor [Baker], David Alan Grier [Boles], and Carol Woods [Laurence].

Published Songs

*Foolish Heart—reused in 1948 movie version as (*Don't Look Now, But*) *My Heart Is Showing* [lyric by Ann Ronell]

**Speak Low*

That's Him

The Trouble with Women—see *Les Filles de Bordeaux* from MARIE GALANTE [December 22, 1934]

West Wind—reused in movie version as *My Week* [lyric by Ronell]

Additional Songs Published in Vocal Selection

How Much I Love You

I'm a Stranger Here Myself

One Touch of Venus

Wooden Wedding

Additional Songs Recorded

Dr. Crippen

Forty Minutes for Lunch [ballet]

Love in the Mist—cut

Venus in Ozone Heights [ballet]

Very, Very, Very

Vive la Difference—cut

Way Out West in Jersey—also known as *The Jersey Plunk*

Who Am I?—cut

Weill's two wartime musical comedies proved to be his only Broadway hits. Mary Martin (see DANCING IN THE STREETS [Duke: March 22, 1943]) finally achieved stardom, in a role intended for Marlene Dietrich. Ogden Nash and S. J. Perelman's work was witty, if at times verbose. Weill provided a flavorful score featuring the exceptional *Speak Low* (*When You Speak Love*). Also of note: *Foolish Heart, That's Him,* the title song, and *I'm a Stranger Here Myself.* There were also two interesting modernist ballets (featuring Sono Osato) from the unlikely team of Weill and de Mille. Former Group Theatre producer Cheryl Crawford brought in Elia Kazan (who had appeared in her JOHNNY JOHNSON [November 19, 1936]) to direct his first of two Weill/Crawford musicals.

THE FIREBRAND OF FLORENCE

March 22, 1945

Alvin Theatre • 43 performances

Lyrics by Ira Gershwin; Book by Edwin Justus Mayer (based on his play *The Firebrand*); Book directed by John Haggott; Staged by John Murray Anderson; Produced by Max Gordon; With Earl Wrightson, Melville Cooper, Beverly Tyler, and Lotte Lenya (Weill). Pre-Broadway title: MUCH ADO ABOUT LOVE.

Published Songs

A Rhyme for Angela

Sing Me Not a Ballad

There'll Be Life, Love, and Laughter

You're Far Too Near Me

Additional Songs Recorded

Alessandro the Wise

Come to Florence

Cozy Nook Trio

Dizzily Busily

Hangman's Song (*Under the Gallows Tree*)

Just in Case

The Little Naked Boy

Love Is My Enemy

My Lords and Ladies

The Nighttime Is No Time for Thinking

No Matter under What Star You're Born—revised version of song from LADY IN THE DARK [January 23, 1941]

Souvenirs

When the Duchess Is Away

The World Is Full of Villains

*You Have to Do What You Do Do—revised version of *Zodiac Song* from LADY IN THE DARK

Weill and Gershwin fashioned FIREBRAND OF FLORENCE as a slyly playful light operetta satire. The librettist, director, and designers, though, encased it in the trappings of a costume operetta and the result was a quick failure (with a fascinating score). In their final musical comedies, Ira and George Gershwin had pioneered a musical theatre form featuring extended through-composed operetta sections. This device was further explored in both LADY IN THE DARK and FIREBRAND OF FLORENCE. The failure of the latter put an end to Ira Gershwin's experiments, and he soon retired altogether. Gershwin had a past association with the source material: as "Arthur Francis" he had written *The Voice of Love* [music by (Robert) Russell Bennett and Maurice Nitke] in the original 1924 production of Edwin Justus Mayer's play. FIREBRAND also marked Lotte Lenya's first and only Broadway appearance in a Weill musical comedy (although she also appeared in the pageant THE ETERNAL ROAD [January 7, 1937]). In FIREBRAND she was woefully miscast—as were the other leads— and scathingly reviewed.

A FLAG IS BORN

September 5, 1946
Alvin Theatre • 120 performances
Play by Ben Hecht; Incidental music by Weill; Directed by Luther Adler; Produced by The American League for a Free Palestine (Jules J. Leventhal); With Paul Muni, Marlon Brando, Quentin Reynolds, and Sidney Lumet.

Published Songs
None

Ben Hecht spearheaded this propaganda play in support of the establishment of the state of Israel.

STREET SCENE

January 9, 1947
Adelphi Theatre • 148 performances
Lyrics by Langston Hughes; Book and Additional lyrics by Elmer Rice (based on his play); Directed by Charles Friedman; Choreographed by Anna Sokolow; Produced by Dwight Deere Wiman in association with The Playwrights' Company (including Weill and Elmer Rice); With Polyna Stoska, Anne Jeffreys, and Norman Cordon.

Published Songs
A Boy Like You
Lonely House
Moon-Faced, Starry-Eyed
We'll Go Away Together
What Good Would the Moon Be?

Additional Songs Published in Vocal Score
Ain't It Awful, the Heat? [lyric by Hughes and Rice]

Blues (I Got a Marble and a Star)
Catch Me If You Can [lyric by Hughes and Rice]
Don't Forget the Lilac Bush [lyric by Hughes and Rice]
Get a Load of That [lyric by Hughes and Rice]
Ice Cream Sextet [lyric by Hughes and Rice]
I Loved Her Too [lyric by Hughes and Rice]
Let Things Be Like They Was
Lullaby [lyric by Rice]
Remember That I Care [lyric by Hughes, incorporating the poem "When Lilacs Last in the Dooryard Bloomed" by Walt Whitman]
Somehow I Never Could Believe
There'll Be Trouble [lyric by Hughes and Rice]
When a Woman Has a Baby [lyric by Hughes and Rice]
The Woman Who Lived up There
Wouldn't You Like to Be on Broadway? [lyric by Hughes and Rice]
Wrapped in a Ribbon and Tied with a Bow [lyric by Hughes and Rice]

Additional Song Recorded
Italy in Technicolor—cut

Since coming to America, Weill had been hoping to create a new musical theatre form combining opera and drama. He did not quite succeed with STREET SCENE, a quasi-opera which eventually found success in the opera house. Weill wrote a fine, rich score, and novice lyricists Elmer Rice (the playwright) and Langston Hughes (the poet) did fairly well, though their efforts are stilted in spots. Particularly effective were *Somehow I Never Could Believe, Blues, Lonely House, What Good Would the Moon Be?*, and *Lullaby*. But STREET SCENE was overlong and overly melodramatic. Weill was by now a full member (with Rice) of the Playwrights' Company, which coproduced the show.

DOWN IN THE VALLEY

July 15, 1948
University Auditorium {Bloomington, Ind.} • 1 performance
"A Folk Opera." Libretto and Lyrics by Arnold Sundgaard; Directed by Hans Busch; With

Marion Bell, James Welch, and Charles Campbell.

Published Song
The Lonesome Dove (based on the folk song)

Additional Songs Published in Vocal Score
Brack Weaver, My True Love
Down in the Valley (based on the folk song)
Hoe-Down
Hop up, My Ladies (based on the folk song)
The Little Black Train (based on the folk song)
Where Is the One Who Will Mourn Me When I'm Gone?

DOWN IN THE VALLEY was commissioned as a twenty-minute ballad opera for radio in 1945. It went unproduced until 1948, when a thirty-five minute version was prepared for production by the opera department at the University of Indiana. (The female lead was sung by Marion Bell of BRIGADOON [Loewe: March 13, 1947], who was married at the time to Alan Jay Lerner, Weill's collaborator on the upcoming LOVE LIFE [October 7, 1948].) DOWN IN THE VALLEY soon became somewhat popular with non-professional choral groups—"wherever a chorus, a few singers, and a few actors are available," per Weill.

LOVE LIFE
October 7, 1948
46th Street Theatre • 252 performances
"A Vaudeville." Book and Lyrics by Alan Jay Lerner; Directed by Elia Kazan; Produced by Cheryl Crawford; With Nanette Fabray and Ray Middleton.

Revival
June 6, 1990
Walnut Street Theatre {Philadelphia} •
    Regional production
Additional book material by Thomas Babe; Directed by Barry Harman; Choreographed by Christopher Chadman; Produced by American Music Theater Festival; With Debbie Shapiro [Fabray], Richard Muenz [Middleton], and Neal Ben-Ari.

Published Songs
Economics
Green-up Time

Here I'll Stay
Ho! Billy O! (Madrigal)—issued in choral arrangement
Is It Him or Is It Me?
Love Song
Mr. Right
Susan's Dream—cut
This Is the Life

Additional Songs Recorded
I Remember It Well—different than song from GIGI [Loewe: November 13, 1973]
I'm Your Man
Locker Room
My Kind of Night
My Name Is Samuel Cooper
What More Do I Want?—cut
Who Is Samuel Cooper?
You Understand Me So

Producer Cheryl Crawford's previous musical had been the hit BRIGADOON [Loewe: March 13, 1947]. Loewe wasn't interested in undertaking LOVE LIFE, so Crawford teamed Lerner with Weill. They attempted an examination of marriage in vaudeville style, illustrated by one family moving through different eras of American history—not unlike Thornton Wilder's 1942 play *The Skin of Our Teeth* (which was also directed by Elia Kazan). But the novel concept didn't work; Lerner went back to Loewe, Weill to Anderson. A 1990 regional theatre revival—using Weill's original orchestrations —and recent recordings only confirm my contention that LOVE LIFE is the composer's least interesting American work. Outside of the pretty ballads *Here I'll Stay* and *Love Song*, and the clever novelty song *Economics* (a cousin to *The Begat* from FINIAN'S RAINBOW [Lane: January 10, 1947]), LOVE LIFE is surprisingly restrained.

LOST IN THE STARS
October 30, 1949
Music Box Theatre • 281 performances
Book and Lyrics by Maxwell Anderson (based on *Cry the Beloved Country* [novel] by Alan Paton); Directed by Rouben Mamoulian; Produced by The Playwrights' Company (including Maxwell Anderson

and Weill); With Todd Duncan, Inez Matthews, Leslie Banks, and Julian Mayfield.

Published Songs
Big Mole
A Bird of Passage—issued in choral edition
The Little Gray House—see ULYSSES
    AFRICANUS [circa August 1939]
Lost in the Stars—see ULYSSES AFRICANUS
Stay Well—see ULYSSES AFRICANUS
Thousands of Miles
Trouble Man—see ULYSSES AFRICANUS

Additional Songs Included in Published Vocal Score
Cry the Beloved Country
Fear!
Four o'Clock
The Hills of Ixopo
Murder in Parkwold
O Tixo, Tixo, Help Me
The Search
Train to Johannesburg
The Wild Justice
Who'll Buy

Additional Songs Recorded
Gold—cut
Little Tin God—cut

Weill's final work was this musical tragedy dealing with racial prejudice in South Africa. While Anderson had great success as a dramatic playwright, he displayed a heavy hand with his two musical librettos. This heaviness worked against the chances of popular success for LOST IN THE STARS (as it had with KNICKER-BOCKER HOLIDAY [October 19, 1938]). The music is quite expert, though the lyrics are somewhat heavy-handed. It will also be noted that the strongest material (including the effective title song) had been written—music and lyrics—not for these characters in Alan Paton's South Africa (circa 1945), but for ex-slaves in the American South (circa 1870) in the unfinished ULYSSES AFRICANUS. Shortly after Weill's fiftieth birthday, while LOST IN THE STARS was still struggling at the box office, Kurt Weill had a sudden heart attack. He died April 3, 1950, in New York.

HUCKLEBERRY FINN
[circa April 1950]
Unfinished musical. Book and Lyrics by Maxwell Anderson (based on the novel by Mark Twain); [Directed by Rouben Mamoulian].

Published Songs
Apple Jack
The Catfish Song
Come in, Mornin'
River Chanty
This Time Next Year

Weill, whose deep interest in American themes had been displayed in several of his musicals (as well as the one-act folk opera DOWN IN THE VALLEY [July 15, 1948]), was collaborating with Anderson and Rouben Mamoulian on this project at the time of his death. The five completed songs were published, and an adaptation of the work was seen on German television.

THE THREEPENNY OPERA [1954]
March 10, 1954
Theatre de Lys {Off Broadway} •
    95 performances
September 20, 1955
Theatre de Lys {Off Broadway} •
    2,611 performances
Also see April 13, 1933. Original book and Lyrics by Bertolt Brecht (based on *The Beggar's Opera* by John Gay); English adaptation by Marc Blitzstein; Directed by Carmen Capalbo; Produced by Carmen Capalbo and Stanley Chase; With Scott Merrill, Jo Sullivan, Lotte Lenya (Weill), Beatrice Arthur, and Charlotte Rae.

Revivals
May 1, 1976
Vivian Beaumont Theatre • 307 performances
New translation by Ralph Manheim and John Willett; Directed by Richard Foreman; Produced by the New York Shakespeare Festival (Joseph Papp); With Raul Julia [Merrill], Blair Brown [Arthur], Ellen Greene [Lenya], and Elizabeth Wilson [Rae].

As 3 PENNY OPERA: November 5, 1989
Lunt-Fontanne Theatre • 65 performances
Translated by Michael Feingold; Directed by John Dexter; Choreographed by Peter

Gennaro; With Sting [Merrill], Maureen McGovern [Sullivan], Kim Criswell [Arthur], and Georgia Brown [Rae].

Published Song
**Mack the Knife* [lyric by Marc Blitzstein]

Additional Songs Published in Vocal Selection of Blitzstein Adaptation
Army Song
Ballad of Dependency
Ballad of the Easy Life
Barbara Song
Instead-of Song
Love Song
Pirate Jenny
Solomon Song
Tango Ballad
Useless

Additional Songs Recorded
Call from the Grave
Death Message
Finale (Reprieved)
How to Survive
Melodrama
Jealousy Duet
Morning Anthem
The Mounted Messenger
**Overture* [instrumental]
Polly's Song
Wedding Song
The World Is Mean

By mid-century Weill's 1928 *Die Dreigroschenoper* was languishing, unperformed in Europe and virtually unknown in America. (The work had been outlawed in Germany in the early thirties, and the haphazard 1933 Broadway adaptation was long forgotten.) Early in 1950, Weill's peer and sometime rival Marc Blitzstein tried his hand at an English translation of *Pirate Jenny*. Weill—long hoping to find new life for his score—was interested in working with Blitzstein on a new adaptation, but within the month Weill was dead. Blitzstein went ahead with the project, scrupulously adhering to Weill's score (although being somewhat freer with Brecht's words). A production scheduled for the spring of 1952 at City Center was suddenly canceled due to political pressures (Brecht was a Communist, Blitzstein was suspect). Blitzstein's protegé Leonard Bern-

stein was arranging an arts festival at Brandeis College (Waltham, Massachusetts); he arranged for the piece to debut there (see TROUBLE IN TAHITI [Bernstein: April 19, 1955]). Bernstein conducted the première of Blitzstein's adaptation there on June 14, 1952, with the score sung by Lotte Lenya, David Brooks, and Jo Sullivan. Two years later, THE THREEPENNY OPERA was finally staged Off Broadway for a limited ten-week engagement. Popular demand caused it to reopen, and it became a six-year phenomenon. Lenya, re-creating her original role of Jenny, began a successful American career as the prime interpreter of her husband's music. And *Mack the Knife*—Blitzstein's version of the *Moritat*—became Kurt Weill's biggest song hit, some thirty years after it was written. New York has seen two other THREEPENNY translations. Both sought to improve on Blitzstein, explaining that the 1954 adaptation of the 1928 adaptation of the 1728 musical was outdated for our modern times. Both "improved" versions made Blitzstein look very good indeed.

BRECHT ON BRECHT
January 3, 1962
Theatre de Lys {Off Broadway} •
  440 performances
Staged reading from the works of Bertolt Brecht; Arranged and Translated by George Tabori; Music mostly by others; Directed by Gene Frankel; Produced by ANTA and Cheryl Crawford; With Lotte Lenya (Weill), Dane Clark, Anne Jackson, Viveca Lindfors, and George Voskovec.

Song Recorded
None

THE RISE AND FALL OF THE CITY OF MAHAGONNY
April 28, 1970
Phyllis Anderson Theatre {Off Broadway} •
  8 performances
Original book and Lyrics by Bertolt Brecht; English adaptation by Arnold Weinstein; Conceived and Directed by Carmen Capalbo; Produced by Carmen Capalbo and Abe

Margolies; With Barbara Harris, Estelle Parsons, and Frank Poretta.

Songs Recorded
**Alabama Song*
As You Make Your Bed
Deep in Alaska
Oh, Heavenly Salvation

Carmen Capalbo, producer/director of THE THREEPENNY OPERA [1954] [March 10, 1954], attempted a misguided adaptation of Weill and Brecht's 1929 followup to the work. But on THREEPENNY, Marc Blitzstein was on hand as Weill's surrogate (and had in fact completed the adaptation before Capalbo became involved). MAHAGONNY was a large-scale mess, closing down during previews "for revision," at which point male lead Mort Shuman (of JACQUES BREL IS ALIVE AND WELL [Notables: January 22, 1968]) was replaced by Frank Poretta. A revised MAHAGONNY reopened, faced the critics, and quickly closed.

HAPPY END
May 7, 1977
Martin Beck Theatre • 75 performances
Original book and Lyrics by Bertolt Brecht (based on a play by Elisabeth Hauptmann); English adaptation by Michael Feingold; Directed by Robert Kalfin and Patricia Birch; Produced by Michael Harvey and the Chelsea Theatre Center; With Meryl Streep, Christopher Lloyd, and Tony Azito.

Songs Recorded
Bilbao Song
Childhood's Bright Endeavor
Don't Be Afraid
God Bless Rockefeller

Mandalay Song
March ahead to the Fight
Sailor Tango (*Matrosensong*)

Another unsuccessful attempt to retain the magic of the Weill-Brecht agitprop style in an American translation. This production was a Broadway transfer from the Chelsea Theatre's home at the Brooklyn Academy of Music; the first had been the artistically successful CANDIDE [1974] [Bernstein: March 10, 1974]. But CANDIDE had Hal Prince, Hugh Wheeler, Stephen Sondheim, and the composer himself in attendance. HAPPY END did not.

Kurt Weill was in America less than fifteen years, little more than half of his creative life. During that time he wrote eight complete musicals, only two of which were successful. Similarly, only two of his Broadway songs—*September Song* and *Speak Low*—became well-loved standards. In the fifty years since Weill's death, though, his long-obscure early work has gradually achieved wide recognition. This was propelled by the astounding success of the Off Broadway adaptation of THE THREEPENNY OPERA [1954] [March 10, 1954], with the Hit Parade–caliber rebirth of *Mack the Knife*. Weill's American musicals don't lend themselves easily to revival, saddled with libretto and production problems; only STREET SCENE is staged frequently, thanks to its suitability to the opera house. Nevertheless, there is fine musical theatre work throughout all of Weill's eight American scores (only four of which have been fully recorded at this date, alas). Those readers interested in serious musical theatre will be well rewarded by delving into lesser-known Weill and his early, European works (despite the language barrier).

MARC BLITZSTEIN

Born: March 2, 1905, Philadelphia, Pennsylvania
Died: January 22, 1964, Martinique, West Indies

MARC BLITZSTEIN, a pampered child from a prosperous banking family, was playing piano by ear at the age of three. At sixteen he performed as a soloist with the Philadelphia Philharmonic; at nineteen he wrote his first theatre score for Jasper Deeter's semi-professional Hedgerow Theatre outside Philadelphia. (The play, not coincidentally, was Leonid Andreyev's *King Hunger*, a Soviet propaganda tract.) At twenty-one Blitzstein left Philadelphia's newly established Curtis Institute of Music and headed for Europe, where he studied composition with both Nadia Boulanger (Aaron Copland's teacher) and Arnold Schoenberg. He returned to Philadelphia in 1927, concentrating on writing "serious" music but keeping up with musical doings on the continent: on a 1929 European trip he detoured to Wiesbaden (with Copland) to see a mounting of *Die Dreigroschenoper* (see THE THREEPENNY OPERA [1954] [Weill: March 10, 1954]).

All Music and Lyrics by Marc Blitzstein unless otherwise indicated.

GARRICK GAIETIES ✦ Third Edition
June 4, 1930
Guild Theatre • 170 performances
"Music and Lyrics by Everybody" (see Duke: June 4, 1930); Directed by Philip Loeb; Produced by The Theatre Guild; With Sterling Holloway, Edith Meiser, and Imogene Coca.

Published Song
Triple Sec [opera] [text by Ronald Jeans]

The first two editions of the GARRICK GAIETIES [Rodgers: May 17, 1925, and May 10, 1926] had included Rodgers and Hart's mock-operettas *The Joy Spreader* and *The Rose of Arizona*. This final, non–Rodgers and Hart edition included Blitzstein's 1928 "progressive opera" *Triple Sec*, which was favorably received despite its avant-garde nature.

PARADE [1935]
May 20, 1935
Guild Theatre • 40 performances
"A Social Revue." Music mostly by Jerome Moross; Lyrics mostly by others; Directed by Philip Loeb; Produced by The Theatre Guild; With Jimmy Savo and Eve Arden.

Song Recorded
Send for the Militia

Blitzstein spent the early Depression years writing, teaching, and developing his left-wing tendencies. PARADE was devised by a group of young Theatre Guild actors, as the initial GARRICK GAIETIES had been. But PARADE was extremely political, much to the embarrassment of the Guild elders, and stormily received. Blitzstein was developing a strong interest in the potential of popular music as an instrument of social message, as evidenced by the deftly satirical *Send for the Militia*. Principal composer of PARADE was the twenty-one-year-old Jerome Moross, whose one full-theatre piece was to be the superlative GOLDEN APPLE [Notables: March 11, 1954].

THE CRADLE WILL ROCK
June 16, 1937
Venice Theatre • 14 performances
December 5, 1937
Mercury Theatre • 5 performances

January 3, 1938
Windsor Theatre • 104 performances
"A Play in Music." Book by Blitzstein;
Directed by Orson Welles; Produced by Orson
Welles and John Houseman; With Howard da
Silva, Olive Stanton, Will Geer, and Blitzstein.

Revivals
December 26, 1947
Mansfield Theatre • 34 performances
Directed by Howard da Silva; Orchestra
conducted by Leonard Bernstein; Transferred
from City Center; With Alfred Drake [da Silva],
Muriel Smith [Stanton], Will Geer, Vivian
Vance, and Leonard Bernstein [Blitzstein].

November 8, 1964
Theatre Four {Off Broadway} •
    82 performances
Directed by Howard da Silva; "Musical
Consultant" Leonard Bernstein; With Jerry
Orbach [da Silva], Lauri Peters [Stanton], Nancy
Andrews, Joseph Bova, and Micki Grant.

May 9, 1983
American Place Theatre {Off Broadway} •
    29 performances
Directed by John Houseman; With Randle
Mell [da Silva], Patti LuPone [Stanton], Gerald
Gutierrez, and John Houseman.

Published Songs
*The Cradle Will Rock
Croon-Spoon
Doctor and Ella
Drugstore Scene
The Freedom of the Press
Gus and Sadie Love Song*—also included in
    Drugstore Scene
Honolulu
*Joe Worker
Leaflets! [and Art for Art's Sake]
**Nickel under the Foot
The Rich*

Additional Songs Recorded
*Let's Do Something
Moll Song
Mrs. Mister and Reverend Salvation
Oh, What a Filthy Night Court*

In 1935 Blitzstein played a sketch—including
Nickel under the Foot (a song of prostitution)—

for the visiting Bertolt Brecht. The latter suggested that he write a full-length music/theatre
piece in song, showing all members of the establishment as prostitutes. This Blitzstein did,
choosing as his hero a union organizer in Steel-
town, USA. (The year 1936 saw armed riots at
Flint, Michigan, automobile factories.) THE
CRADLE WILL ROCK was produced by the Federal Theatre Project of the Works Progress Administration (WPA), under the supervision of
Houseman and twenty-two-year-old director
Orson Welles. The government agency—which
had approved and funded the project—became
nervous after the first preview and suddenly
suspended all new WPA activities "to facilitate
budget cuts." That night the doors of the sold-
out Maxine Elliott Theatre were padlocked;
Welles had actor Will Geer perform on the side-
walk to hold the audience while Houseman
looked for an empty theatre. Eight hundred
people paraded twenty blocks uptown to the
Venice (Jolson/New Century) Theatre, where
the performance finally began two hours late.
Actors' Equity had forbidden its members to
appear; half the cast showed up anyway, de-
livering their lines from seats in the house while
Blitzstein and Welles played and narrated from
the stage. THE CRADLE WILL ROCK continued
at the Venice for two weeks, retaining the exciting performance style borne of necessity.
Welles and Houseman left the WPA to begin
their Mercury Theatre Company (with Blitzstein
as resident composer) and revived the piece for
Sunday night performances. In January, THE
CRADLE WILL ROCK finally began a commercial run.

JULIUS CAESAR
November 11, 1937
Mercury Theatre • 157 performances
Play by William Shakespeare; Incidental music
by Blitzstein; Directed by Orson Welles;
Produced by The Mercury Theatre (Orson
Welles and John Houseman); With Orson
Welles, George Coulouris, Joseph Cotten,
Hiram Sherman, and Martin Gabel.

Published Song
Orpheus (Lucius' Song) [lyric by Shakespeare]

Orson Welles continued to assault the theatre world with a modern-dress version of JULIUS CAESAR (in which he played Brutus). The Mercury Theatre Group was to have a brief but notable life, dying in Boston with a spectacularly Wellesian failure (the 1939 Shakespearean omnibus *Five Kings*). Orson went to Hollywood and made *Citizen Kane* (1941).

DANTON'S DEATH
November 2, 1938
Mercury Theatre • 21 performances
"A Drama in Individual Scenes Vignetted by Spotlight." Play by Georg Buchner; Translated by Geoffrey Dunlop; Songs by Blitzstein; Directed by Orson Welles; Produced by The Mercury Theatre (Orson Welles and John Houseman); With Orson Welles, Joseph Cotten, Martin Gabel, Arlene Francis (Gabel), and Ruth Ford.

Song Recorded
Ode to Reason

NO FOR AN ANSWER
January 5, 1941
Mecca Theatre {City Center} •
    3 performances
Book by Blitzstein; Directed by Walter E. Watts; Produced by "A Committee including Bennett Cerf, Lillian Hellman (Kober), Arthur Kober and Herman Shumlin"; With Martin Wolfson, Curt Conway, and Carol Channing.

Song Published in *People's Songs Magazine*
The Purest Kind of Guy

Additional Songs Recorded
Dimples
Francie
Fraught
Gina
In the Clear
Make the Heart Be Stone
Mike
Nick
No for an Answer

Penny Candy
Secret Singing
Song of the Bat
Take the Book

Unable to arrange a full production of NO FOR AN ANSWER, a distinguished group of theatrefolk sponsored three Sunday-night staged readings. Public reaction was even stormier than for THE CRADLE WILL ROCK [June 16, 1937], and the city threatened to close the theatre for "licensing violations." In the earlier work Blitzstein used stereotyped characters to make his point; here he tried to create a contemporary, realistic play with a musical base. The subject matter was again left wing, dealing with a strike of hotel restaurant workers. Despite the exciting nature of the work—and the overwhelmingly positive critical reaction—it was impossible to find backing for a commercial production. Among the cast was nineteen-year-old Carol Channing, fresh from Bennington. Blitzstein next went to war, serving with the 8th Air Force in London. His assignments included Director of Music for the American Broadcasting Station in Europe, supervision of the 1943 American Negro Troops Choral Concert at Royal Albert Hall, and composition of his 1944 *Airborne Symphony*.

LUNCHTIME FOLLIES
June 22, 1942
Todd Shipyards {Brooklyn}
Music and Lyrics also by others (see Rome and Weill: June 22, 1942); Sketches by George S. Kaufman and Moss Hart, Maxwell Anderson, Zero Mostel, and others; Production supervised by Kurt Weill; Produced by The American Theatre Wing. Alternate title: LUNCH HOUR FOLLIES.

Song Published
A Quiet Girl

LUNCHTIME FOLLIES was a morale-building revue mounted for workers at war-materiel production plants, produced under Kurt Weill's direction. Blitzstein contributed this little ditty about a formerly *Quiet Girl* who—now that she's involved in the war effort—wants "to make the bullet that gets Hitler."

ANOTHER PART OF THE FOREST
November 20, 1946
Fulton Theatre • 182 performances
Play by Lillian Hellman (based on characters from her play *The Little Foxes*); Incidental music by Blitzstein; Directed by Lillian Hellman; Produced by Kermit Bloomgarden; With Patricia Neal and Mildred Dunnock.

Published Songs
None

Blitzstein continued his association with Lillian Hellman, who had cosponsored NO FOR AN ANSWER [January 5, 1941]. ANOTHER PART OF THE FOREST was actually a prequel to THE LITTLE FOXES [Willson: February 15, 1939]. Blitzstein became engrossed in Hellman's rapacious Hubbard family; with the help of a grant from the American Academy of Arts and Letters, he began work on his major musical theatre piece, REGINA [October 31, 1949].

ANDROCLES AND THE LION
December 19, 1946
International Theatre • 40 performances
Play by George Bernard Shaw; Incidental music by Blitzstein; Directed by Margaret Webster; Produced by American Repertory Theatre (Eva Le Gallienne, Cheryl Crawford and Margaret Webster); With Ernest Truex, Richard Waring, and Eli Wallach.

Published Songs
None

REGINA
October 31, 1949
46th Street Theatre • 56 performances
Book by Blitzstein (based on *The Little Foxes* [play] by Lillian Hellman); Directed by Robert Lewis; Produced by Cheryl Crawford in association with Clinton Wilder; With Jane Pickens, Priscilla Gillette, Brenda Lewis, and Russell Nype.

Published Songs
*The Best Thing of All
**Blues
Chinkypin

Greedy Girl
The Rain—published in choral edition; partial version of *Make a Quiet Day*
Summer Day—non-show version of *Two Old Drybones*
*What Will It Be?

Additional Songs Published in Vocal Score
Away!
Big Rich
Deedle-Doodle
*Finale (Certainly, Lord)
Gallop
Greetings
Horace's Entrance
I Don't Know
I'm Sick of You (Horace's Last)
**Lionnet (Birdie's Aria)
*Make a Quiet Day (Rain Quartet)
*Music, Music
Regina's Aria
Sing Hubbard
Small Talk (Marshall)
*Things (Regina's Waltz)
*Transition (Bonds)
Two Old Drybones
*The Veranda [instrumental]
Want to Join the Angels

Following the war, Blitzstein began to separate his politics from his work. Sharing Kurt Weill's vision of an opera-inspired American "music drama" form, Blitzstein wrote the masterful REGINA. The advantage of being his own lyricist/librettist enabled a free combination of song, recitative, and extended multivoiced musical scenes (unlike in STREET SCENE [Weill: January 9, 1947], where the composer was somewhat restrained by inexpert collaborators). Blitzstein used his music to elaborate on the already highly pitched emotions of Lillian Hellman's little Hubbards (THE LITTLE FOXES [Willson: February 15, 1939]. And Broadway finally heard the composer's orchestrations; for economic reasons, his previous musicals had been performed with piano accompaniments. The score abounds with delights: Alexandra's touching *What Will It Be?*, Addie's sympathetic *Blues*, Regina's dangerous *Things*, Birdie's defeated *Lionnet*, the *Rain Quartet* and more. The relatively little-known REGINA ranks high among dramatic musical theatre.

KING LEAR
December 25, 1950
National Theatre • 48 performances
Play by William Shakespeare; Incidental music
by Blitzstein; Directed by John Houseman;
Produced by Robert L. Joseph and Alexander
H. Cohen; With Louis Calhern, Martin Gabel,
Nina Foch, Jo Van Fleet, and Edith Atwater.

Published Songs
None

THE THREEPENNY OPERA
See Weill: March 10, 1954.

REUBEN REUBEN
October 10, 1955
Shubert Theatre {Boston} •
   Closed during tryout
Book by Blitzstein; Directed by Robert Lewis;
Choreographed by Hanya Holm; Produced by
Cheryl Crawford; With Eddie Albert, Evelyn
Lear, Kaye Ballard, and George Gaynes.

Published Songs
Be with Me
*The Hills of Amalfi
Miracle Song
*Monday Morning Blues
*Never Get Lost

Additional Songs Recorded
Love at First Sight
Rose Song
Such a Little While

REGINA [October 31, 1949] had been built upon
Lillian Hellman's strong play *The Little Foxes.*
The highly ambitious REUBEN REUBEN was not
related to the popular novel by Peter de Vries;
it was original material by Blitzstein, and far from
ready for audiences when it opened in Boston.
REUBEN REUBEN—about a psychotic, suicidal,
tightrope-walking war veteran—suffered from
an overall lack of focus and direction, perplexing audiences, critics, and cast. What survives
of the score is original, highly imaginative, and
often incredibly lovely: *Never Get Lost*, *Monday
Morning Blues*, and *The Hills of Amalfi* are especially tender and fascinating. (Leonard Bernstein

called Blitzstein's work-failures "falling angels"
and named his daughter Nina for the REUBEN
REUBEN heroine.) Cheryl Crawford, who entered the musical theatre with the not dissimilar JOHNNY JOHNSON [Weill: November 19,
1936], produced both REGINA and REUBEN
REUBEN. The failures of these last two (along
with LOVE LIFE [Weill: October 7, 1948],
FLAHOOLEY [Notables: May 14, 1951], and
PAINT YOUR WAGON [Loewe: November 12,
1951]) forced the groundbreaking Crawford—
unable to raise sufficient backing—to drop out
of WEST SIDE STORY [Bernstein: September 26,
1957].

THE LITTLEST REVUE
May 22, 1956
Phoenix Theatre {Off Broadway} •
   32 performances
Music mostly by Vernon Duke (see Duke: May
22, 1956; also Strouse); Lyrics mostly by Ogden
Nash; Sketches by Nat Hiken, Michael
Stewart, and others; Directed by Paul
Lammers; Produced by T. Edward Hambleton
and Norris Houghton by arrangement with
Ben Bagley; With Charlotte Rae, Tammy
Grimes, Joel Grey, and Larry Storch.

Recorded Song
Modest Maid (*I Love Lechery*)—initial use of
   1944 non-show song

Modest Maid was written as special material for
Beatrice Lillie when Corporal Blitzstein was stationed in London. Lillie didn't perform it, but
Charlotte Rae of THE THREEPENNY OPERA
[1954] [Weill: March 10, 1954] used it in her
nightclub act and brought it with her into THE
LITTLEST REVUE.

A MIDSUMMER NIGHT'S DREAM
June 20, 1958
American Shakespeare Festival {Stratford, Conn.}
Play by William Shakespeare; Incidental music
by Blitzstein; Directed by Jack Landau;
Choreographed by George Balanchine;
Produced by American Shakespeare Festival
(John Houseman); With Richard Waring, June

Havoc, Barbara Barrie, John Colicos, Hiram Sherman, Morris Carnovsky, Will Geer, and Ellis Rabb.

Songs Published in *Six Elizabethan Songs*
Court Song [lyric Anonymous]
Lullaby (*You Spotted Snakes with Double Tongue*) [lyric by Shakespeare]
Sweet Is the Rose [lyric by Edmund Spenser]

THE WINTER'S TALE [1958]
July 20, 1958
American Shakespeare Festival {Stratford, Conn.}
Play by William Shakespeare; Incidental music by Blitzstein; Directed by John Houseman and Jack Landau; Choreographed by George Balanchine; Produced by American Shakespeare Festival (John Houseman); With John Colicos, Nancy Wickwire, Richard Waring, Hiram Sherman, Will Geer, Inga Swenson, Richard Easton, and Ellis Rabb.

Songs Published in *Six Elizabethan Songs*
Shepherd's Song (*When Daffodils Begin to Peer*) [lyric by Shakespeare]
Song of the Glove [lyric by Ben Jonson]
Vendor's Song (*Lawn as White as Driven Snow*) [lyric by Shakespeare]

JUNO
March 9, 1959
Winter Garden Theatre • 16 performances
Book by Joseph Stein (based on *Juno and the Paycock* [play] by Sean O'Casey); Directed by José Ferrer; Choreographed by Agnes de Mille; Produced by The Playwrights' Company, Oliver Smith, and Oliver Rea; With Shirley Booth, Melvyn Douglas, Jack MacGowran, Jean Stapleton, and Sada Thompson.

Revivals
As DAARLIN' JUNO: May 19, 1976
Long Wharf Theatre {New Haven, Conn.} • 28 performances
Additional lyrics by Richard Maltby, Jr.; Adaptation by Richard Maltby, Jr., and Geraldine Fitzgerald; Directed by Arvin Brown; With Geraldine Fitzgerald

[Booth], Milo O'Shea [Douglas], and Victor Garber.

As JUNO: October 14, 1992
Vineyard Theatre {Off Off Broadway} • 34 performances
Additional lyrics by Ellen Fitzhugh; Directed by Lonny Price; Choreographed by Joey McKneeley; With Anita Gillette [Booth] and Dick Latessa [Douglas].

Published Songs
*I Wish It So
The Liffey Waltz
My True Heart
One Kind Word

Additional Songs Recorded
Bird upon the Tree
*Daarlin' Man
Farewell, Me Butty—cut
For Love
From This Out—cut
Hymn
Ireland's Eye—cut
It's Not Irish
Johnny
Music in the House
Old Sayin's
On a Day Like This
Quarrel Song—cut
Song of the Ma
We Can Be Proud
*We're Alive
What Is the Stars? (*Life on the Sea*)
*Where
*You Poor Thing
You're the Girl—cut

Blitzstein was perhaps the perfect choice for this adaptation of O'Casey's strong comedy-drama of the Irish Revolution. However, the commercial management tried to give the show popular appeal, using miscast box-office stars Shirley Booth (who had appeared in Blitzstein's 1937 radio play "I've Got the Tune") and Melvyn Douglas. The entire project was troubled: the director was musical novice Tony Richardson, who was replaced by musical novice Vincent J. Donehue, who was replaced by musical novice José Ferrer. The dramatic and volatile score worked well, particularly effective in expressing the tragic aspects of O'Casey. But the show proved heavy and muddled, and JUNO suffered a quick death. Subsequent attempted rewrites has proven the material stubbornly problematic, despite Blitzstein's fine score.

TOYS IN THE ATTIC
February 25, 1960
Hudson Theatre • 556 performances
Play by Lillian Hellman; Incidental music by Blitzstein; Directed by Arthur Penn; Produced by Kermit Bloomgarden; With Maureen Stapleton, Jason Robards, Jr., and Irene Worth.

Published Songs
None

Blitzstein provided incidental music for this long-running Lillian Hellman play, his fourth association with the playwright. He then turned to his next projects: the opera "Sacco and Vanzetti," commissioned by the Metropolitan Opera; and IDIOTS FIRST[†], based on short stories by Bernard Malamud. Neither was completed, though. While vacationing on the island of Martinique, Blitzstein was attacked and killed. He died on January 22, 1964.

Marc Blitzstein's strong commitment and uncompromising artistic viewpoint worked against popular success. After making a prominent debut with THE CRADLE WILL ROCK [June 16, 1937], the composer had nothing but failed "falling angels." His one successful and profitable project was the labor-of-love adaptation of the work of another composer, THE THREEPENNY OPERA [1954] [Weill: March 10, 1954]. Blitzstein's own work and name are virtually forgotten. But his contributions to the serious musical theatre are of great importance and point in a direction which has not yet been fully realized.

HAROLD ROME

Born: May 27, 1908, Hartford, Connecticut
Died: October 26, 1993, New York, New York

HAROLD ROME began his musical career in college, playing in dance bands to help finance his studies. Upon graduation with an architecture degree, Rome came to New York in 1934. With high qualifications and seven years at Yale, the only architectural work he could find was a twenty-four-dollar-a-week job with the Works Progress Administration (WPA), measuring roads and mapping the course of the Hudson River. Spare-time money could be earned at the keyboard, so Rome put his musical abilities to use. In 1935 he got a musical summer job at the Green Mansions resort hotel. Assembling amateur shows for the adult campers to perform, architect Rome began writing his own songs. He spent three summers at Green Mansions, writing comic character material for weekly amateur shows.

All Music and Lyrics by Harold Rome unless otherwise indicated.

PINS AND NEEDLES
November 27, 1937
Labor Stage • 1,108 performances
Music and Lyrics mostly by Rome; Sketches by Charles Friedman and others; Directed by Charles Friedman; Choreographed by Benjamin Zemach and Gluck Sandor; Produced by the ILGWU; With the ILGWU Players.

Revival
May 19, 1967
Roundabout Theatre {Off Broadway} •
    214 performances
Directed by Gene Feist.

Published Songs
Back to Work

*Chain Store Daisy (Vassar Girl Finds Job)
Doing the Reactionary
Four Little Angels of Peace
The General Unveiled (A Satirical Ballet)
*It's Better with a Union Man (Or Bertha, the
    Sewing Machine Girl)
I've Got the Nerve to Be in Love
Mene, Mene, Tekel*—issued in separate edition
*Nobody Makes a Pass at Me
Not Cricket to Picket
One Big Union for Two
Papa Don't Love Mama Any More
Sing Me a Song with Social Significance
Stay out, Sammy!
Sunday in the Park
We Sing America*—issued in separate edition
*What Good Is Love?
When I Grow Up (G-Man Song)—issued in
    separate edition

Additional Songs Published in Vocal Score
*Cream of Mush Song
I'm Just Nuts about You
Room for One*

Additional Song Recorded
Status Quo

Note: Due to the topical nature of the piece, various songs cut or added after opening.

Louis Schaefer, entertainment director of the International Ladies Garment Workers Union (ILGWU), was looking for an extracurricular morale-building activity. Having heard Rome's work at Green Mansions, Schaefer commissioned PINS AND NEEDLES. The cast was drafted from garment workers; rehearsals were held evenings and weekends; and the ILGWU leased famed former Princess Theatre, renaming it "Labor Stage." The amateur show finally opened and quickly became a crowd-pleaser. PINS AND NEEDLES moved to the larger Windsor Theatre and went on to become Broadway's longest-running musical (for a while), outlasting the likes of IRENE [Notables: November 1, 1919], SHOW BOAT [Kern: December 27, 1927], and OF THEE I SING [Gershwin: December 26, 1931]. Rome became the first new voice to have an impact on Broadway since Arlen and Duke arrived in 1930. His breezy, lightly rhythmic musical style and pointed-but-gentle lyrics proved an attractive alternative to other depression-era attempts at Social Significance. *Sunday in the Park*, a jaunty rhythm number, enjoyed some success, but Rome really shined in comedy numbers like *Chain Store Daisy*, *Nobody Makes a Pass at Me*, and *It's Better with a Union Man*. PINS AND NEEDLES flourished, and the WPA lost an architect.

SING OUT THE NEWS
September 24, 1938
Music Box Theatre • 105 performances
Sketches by George S. Kaufman and Moss Hart (unbilled); Directed by Charles Friedman; Choreographed by Ned McGurn, Dave Gould, and Charles Walters; Produced by Max Gordon in association with George S. Kaufman and Moss Hart; With Philip Loeb, Hiram Sherman, Mary Jane Walsh, Will Geer, and Rex Ingram.

Published Songs
**F.D.R. Jones*
How Long Can Love Keep Laughing?
My Heart Is Unemployed
One of These Fine Days
Ordinary Guy
Plaza 6-9423—issued as professional copy only
Yip-Ahoy—issued as professional copy only

The unparalleled success of PINS AND NEEDLES [November 27, 1937] immediately brought its composer into top Broadway circles. Max Gordon and his usually silent partners Kaufman and Hart were excited by Rome's new voice and sponsored this full-scale revue. Without the ingratiating, nonprofessional charm of the still-running earlier show, SING OUT THE NEWS was unable to compete; but Rome came up with one of his best songs, the jubilantly joyous *F.D.R. Jones* (later to be heard sung by victorious Allied troops marching into Germany). What a song!

SING FOR YOUR SUPPER
April 24, 1939
Adelphi Theatre • 60 performances
Music mostly by others; Lyrics mostly by Robert Sour; Directed by Robert H. Gordon; Produced by WPA Federal Theatre Project; With Paula Laurence and Sonny Tufts.

Published Song
Papa's Got a Job [music by Ned Lehak, lyric by Hector Troy (Harold Rome)

Rome was asked to come up with a lyric in the *F.D.R. Jones* vein: hence the celebratory *Papa's Got a Job*. Not interested in being approached with lyric-only offers, he came up with the pseudonym Hector Troy (Rome's nickname was "Heckie").

STREETS OF PARIS
June 19, 1939
Broadhurst Theatre • 274 performances
Music mostly by Jimmy McHugh; Lyrics mostly by Al Dubin; Directed by Edward Duryea Dowling and Dennis Murray; Choreographed by Robert Alton; Produced by the Shuberts in association with (Ole) Olsen and (Chic) Johnson; With Bobby Clark, Luella Gear, Bud Abbott & Lou Costello, and Carmen Miranda.

Published Song
History Is Made at Night

The highlight of this revue was Carmen Miranda, who came out of nowhere with a bowl of fruit on her head and the McHugh/Dubin *South American Way*.

THE LITTLE DOG LAUGHED
July 13, 1940
Garden Pier {Atlantic City, N.J.} •
    Closed during tryout
"A Modern Music Comedy." Book by Joseph
Schrank; Produced and Directed by Eddie
Dowling; With Mili Monti, Philip Loeb, and
Augustin Duncan.

Published Songs
*Easy Does It
I Have a Song
I Want Romance
*Of the People Stomp—see LET FREEDOM
    SING [October 5, 1942]
You're Your Highness to Me

This extravagant, idealistic fantasy was backed
by a wealthy society matron in order to showcase her singing "discovery" Mili Monti, who
did not overwhelm 'em in Atlantic City. Rome
provided a swinging ballad, Easy Does It, and
another infectiously energetic song in the F.D.R.
Jones style, Of the People Stomp.

LUNCHTIME FOLLIES
June 22, 1942
Todd Shipyards {Brooklyn}
Music and Lyrics also by others (see Blitzstein
and Weill: June 22, 1942); Sketches by George
S. Kaufman & Moss Hart, Maxwell Anderson,
Zero Mostel, and others; Production super-
vised by Kurt Weill; Produced by the Ameri-
can Theatre Wing. Alternate title: LUNCH
HOUR FOLLIES.

Published Songs
The Ballad of Sloppy Joe
Dear Joe
The Lady's on the Job
Men behind the Man behind the Gun—issued as
    professional copy
On That Old Production Line
On Time
That's My Pop
Victory Symphony, Eight to the Bar—see LET
    FREEDOM SING [October 5, 1942]

Rome's PINS AND NEEDLES [November 27,
1937] experience made him especially well

suited to write for this series of wartime propaganda revues. By year's end, Rome himself was
in uniform.

STAR AND GARTER
June 24, 1942
Music Box Theatre • 605 performances
Music and Lyrics mostly by others; Directed
by Hassard Short; Produced by Michael Todd;
With Bobby Clark and Gypsy Rose Lee.

Published Song
Bunny, Bunny, Bunny

Rome wrote this song for Gypsy Rose Lee, for
whom he'd provided special material in his
Green Mansions days. Mike Todd's burlesque
revue was an overwhelmingly popular wartime
hit of little distinction (and little wardrobe).

LET FREEDOM SING
October 5, 1942
Longacre Theatre • 8 performances
Music and Lyrics also by others; Sketches by
Sam Locke; Directed by Joseph C. Pevney and
Robert H. Gordon; Produced by the Youth
Theatre; With Mitzi Green, Betty Garrett, and
Lee Sullivan.

Published Songs
History Eight to the Bar—revised lyric for
    Victory Symphony, Eight to the Bar,
    published only as from LUNCHTIME
    FOLLIES [June 22, 1942]
Of the People Stomp—published only as from
    THE LITTLE DOG LAUGHED [July 13, 1940]

This good-natured but amateurish revue was
poorly done and quickly gone. The only bright
spot was the unknown Betty Garrett, unani-
mously singled out by the critics and rushed into
a featured role in Merman's SOMETHING FOR
THE BOYS [Porter: January 7, 1943]. Rome, meanwhile, rushed into uniform and off to Brooklyn.

STARS AND GRIPES
July 13, 1943
War Department Theatre {Brooklyn}
"Fort Hamilton All-Soldier Show." Music and
Lyrics by PFC Harold Rome; Sketches mostly

by T4G Ace Goodrich; Directed by PFC Glenn
Jordan and PFC Martin Gabel.

Published Songs
The Army Service Forces
Hup! Tup! Thrup! Four! (*Jack the Sleepy Jeep*)
Jumping to the Jukebox—also used in SKIRTS
    [January 25, 1944]
The Little Brown Suit My Uncle Bought Me—
    also used in SKIRTS
Love Sometimes Has to Wait
My Pin-up Girl—also used in SKIRTS

A morale-building soldier show, which served
its purpose but certainly wasn't another THIS IS
THE ARMY [Berlin: July 4, 1942].

NANTUCKET
See Duke: circa 1943.

SKIRTS
January 25, 1944
Cambridge Theatre {London}
"An All-American Musical Adventure." Music
and Lyrics mostly by PFC Harold Rome and
PFC Frank Loesser; Directed by Lt. Arthur G.
Brest; Choreographed by Wendy Toye;
Produced by U.S. 8th Air Force, Special
Service Section.

Published Songs
Jumping to the Juke Box—originally used in
    STARS AND GRIPES [July 13, 1943]
The Little Brown Suit My Uncle Bought Me—
    originally used in STARS AND GRIPES
My Pin-up Girl—originally used in STARS
    AND GRIPES

The Air Force borrowed these songs from the
Army for this brief West End visit.

CALL ME MISTER
April 18, 1946
National Theatre • 734 performances
Sketches by Arnold Auerbach with Arnold
Horwitt; Directed by Robert H. Gordon;
Choreographed by John Wray; Produced by
Melvyn Douglas and Herman Levin; With
Betty Garrett, Jules Munshin, Bill Callahan,
and Lawrence Winters.

Published Songs
Along with Me
*Call Me Mister
The Drugstore Song
*The Face on the Dime
Going Home Train
His Old Man
*Little Surplus Me
Love Remains
Military Life (*The Jerk Song*)
The Red Ball Express
*South America, Take It Away
When We Meet Again

Additional Song Recorded
Yuletide, Park Avenue

Rome's joy on returning to civilian life was expressed in his infectiously jaunty *Call Me Mister* (as opposed to "Private"). Staffed and cast
mostly by ex-servicemen and USO women, CALL
ME MISTER was a happy and energetic entertainment. Betty Garrett established herself as a
first-rate comedienne, and Rome's attorney Herman Levin went into the producing business
(partnered with actor Melvyn Douglas). The
score showed Rome moving away from his socially relevant PINS AND NEEDLES [November
27, 1937] days: while he could still create hapless characters in comedy lyrics like *Poor Little
Surplus Me*, he chose broader subjects for lam-
pooning (like *South America, Take It Away*).
Rome's music had heretofore principally served
as support for the lyric; with songs like the noble
Roosevelt eulogy *Face on the Dime*, he began to
develop his gift for dramatic melody.

THAT'S THE TICKET!
September 24, 1948
Shubert Theatre {Philadelphia} •
    Closed during tryout
Book by Julius J. and Philip G. Epstein;
Directed by Jerome Robbins; Choreographed
by Paul Godkin; Produced by Joseph Kipness,
John Pransky, and Al Beckman; With Leif
Erickson, Loring Smith, and Kaye Ballard.

Published Songs
I Shouldn't Love You—see FANNY [November
    4, 1954]

The Money Song
Take off the Coat—also used in BLESS YOU
ALL [December 14, 1950]
*You Never Know What Hit You (When It's
Love)*—also used in PRETTY PENNY [June
20, 1949] and BLESS YOU ALL

Additional Song Recorded
Gin Rummy Rhapsody

This misguided effort was written by Hollywood's Epstein brothers, authors of the 1941 film
Casablanca, with Jerry Robbins attempting his
first Abbott-less effort. After a week, everybody
went home. *The Money Song*, a clever calypso
take on Yankee Dollars, managed to achieve some
radio popularity.

PRETTY PENNY
June 20, 1949
Bucks County Playhouse {New Hope, Pa.} •
Summer stock tryout
Sketches by Jerome Chodorov; Directed by
George S. Kaufman; Choreographed by
Michael Kidd; Produced by Leonard Field;
With David Burns, Lenore Lonergan, Carl
Reiner, Onna White, Peter Gennaro, and
Michael Kidd.

Published Songs
Pocketful of Dreams—initial publication upon
reuse in MICHAEL TODD'S PEEP SHOW
[June 28, 1950]
*You Never Know What Hit You (When It's
Love)*—originally used in (and only
published as from) THAT'S THE TICKET
[September 24, 1948]

Additional Songs Recorded
Cry, Baby, Cry—also used in ALIVE AND
KICKING [January 7, 1950]
French with Tears—also used in ALIVE AND
KICKING

ANGEL IN THE WINGS [December 11, 1947], a
shoestring Broadway revue with a "looking for
investors" motif starring Paul and Grace Hartman,
had been a sleeper hit. The similarly schemed
PRETTY PENNY played the stock circuit while
actually looking for investors. One night Davey
Burns, a thorough professional with an otherwise unblemished reputation, uncharacteristically castigated and physically assaulted director George Kaufman. The actor received a repri-
mand from Actors' Equity, tendered his resigna-
tion, and the show did not go on.

ALIVE AND KICKING
January 17, 1950
Winter Garden Theatre • 46 performances
Music and Lyrics mostly by others; Sketches
by Joseph Stein & Will Glickman, I. A. L.
Diamond, and others; Directed by Robert H.
Gordon; Choreographed by Jack Cole; Pro-
duced by William R. Katzell and Ray Golden;
With Jack Cole, David Burns, Jack Gilford,
Carl Reiner, Gwen Verdon, and Jack Cassidy.

Published Song
Love, It Hurts So Good

Additional Songs Recorded
Cry, Baby, Cry—originally used in PRETTY
PENNY [June 20, 1949]
French with Tears—originally used in PRETTY
PENNY

The hapless ALIVE AND KICKING had little to
recommend it except Jack Cole, Davey Burns,
and newcomers Jack Gilford, Carl Reiner, Gwen
Verdon, and Jack Cassidy.

MICHAEL TODD'S PEEP SHOW
June 28, 1950
Winter Garden Theatre • 278 performances
Music and Lyrics mostly by others (see Styne:
June 28, 1950); Sketches by Bobby Clark,
William K. Wells, and others; Scenes directed
by "Mr. R. Edwin Clark, Esq."; Directed by
Hassard Short; Choreographed by James
Starbuck; Produced by Michael Todd; With
Lina Romay, Clifford Guest, and Lilly Christine.

Published Songs
Gimme the Shimmy
Pocketful of Dreams—originally used (unpub-
lished) in PRETTY PENNY [June 20, 1949]

BLESS YOU ALL
December 14, 1950
Mark Hellinger Theatre • 84 performances
Sketches by Arnold Auerbach; Directed by

John C. Wilson; Choreographed by Helen Tamiris; Produced by Herman Levin and Oliver Smith; With Mary McCarty, Jules Munshin, Pearl Bailey, Valerie Bettis, and Donald Saddler.

Published Songs
I Can Hear It Now
*Little Things (*Meant So Much to Me*)
Love Letter to Manhattan
A Rose Is a Rose
Summer Dresses
Take off the Coat—originally used in THAT'S THE TICKET! [September 24, 1948]
You Never Know What Hit You (*When It's Love*) —originally used in THAT'S THE TICKET!

Additional Song Recorded
Don't Wanna Write about the South

The eagerly awaited follow-up to CALL ME MISTER [April 18, 1946] was a distinct disappointment and struggled through a brief run. MISTER had spirit, energy, and a point of view; BLESS YOU ALL was simply a dressed-up vehicle for making money, so it didn't. *Little Things* (*Meant So Much to Me*) is an unknown but good comedy song in a Charles Addams vein, lest anyone be looking for an unknown but good, macabre comedy song.

WISH YOU WERE HERE
June 24, 1952
Imperial Theatre • 598 performances
Book by Arthur Kober and Joshua Logan (based on *Having Wonderful Time* [play] by Arthur Kober); "Direction and Dances" by Joshua Logan; Produced by Leland Hayward and Joshua Logan; With Jack Cassidy, Patricia Marand, Sheila Bond, and Paul Valentine.

Published Songs
Could Be
Don José of Far Rockaway
Everybody Loves Everybody
Flattery
Glimpse of Love—cut
Relax
Shopping Around
Summer Afternoon
They Won't Know Me

There's Nothing Nicer Than People—added after opening
Tripping the Light Fantastic
*Where Did the Night Go?
*Wish You Were Here

Additional Songs Published in Vocal Score
Ballad of a Social Director
Camp Kare-Free (*Opening Act One*)
Certain Individuals
Mix and Mingle
Waiter's Song (*Bright College Days*)

Additional Song Recorded
Good-Bye Love—cut after opening

The enormous popularity of the sultry title song—and the novelty of a featured swimming pool—carried WISH YOU WERE HERE past poor reviews to a long, successful run. The 1937 comedy by Arthur Kober (one-time husband to Lillian Hellman) took place at an adult summer camp very much like Green Mansions, where Rome began his career. For the record, this was *not* Broadway's first swimming pool: the Majestic had one for the five-performance run of Broadway's first Mexican musical comedy, VIVA O'BRIEN† [October 9, 1941], which made very little splash indeed.

FANNY
November 4, 1954
Majestic Theatre • 888 performances
Book by S. N. Behrman and Joshua Logan (based on the trilogy by Marcel Pagnol); Directed by Joshua Logan; Choreographed by Helen Tamiris; Produced by David Merrick and Joshua Logan; With Ezio Pinza, Walter Slezak, Florence Henderson, and William Tabbert.

Published Songs
Be Kind to Your Parents
*Fanny
*I Have to Tell You—revised version of *I Shouldn't Love You* from THAT'S THE TICKET! [September 24, 1948]
I Like You
Love Is a Very Light Thing
Never Too Late for Love
Octopus

*Restless Heart
*To My Wife
*Welcome Home
Why Be Afraid to Dance?

Additional Songs Published in Vocal Score

Cold Cream Jar Song
Hakim's Cellar
Happy Birthday (Nursery Round)
Oysters, Cockles and Mussels
Panisse and Son
The Thought of You

Producer David Merrick spent a decade apprenticing in the theatre before determining to make his musical debut with an adaptation of Marcel Pagnol's trilogy. After many obstacles, he enlisted Josh Logan as director and coproducer; Logan brought along Rome, with whom he'd worked on WISH YOU WERE HERE [June 25, 1952]. (Rodgers and Hammerstein, a more obvious choice, agreed to do FANNY—but only if Merrick sold them his rights and disappeared.) FANNY was somewhat overlong and uneven, but Merrick's promotional talents enabled the show to become a long-running hit. Rome departed from his "clever" musical style to write a moving, highly melodic score. He came up with a trio of tempestuous ballads for his lovers—Restless Heart, I Have to Tell You, and the soaring title song; two gentler but similarly warm songs for Pinza, Never Too Late for Love and Welcome Home; and—perhaps best of all—the tenderly touching To My Wife.

ROMANOFF AND JULIET
October 10, 1957
Plymouth Theatre • 389 performances
Play by Peter Ustinov; Incidental music by Rome; Directed by George S. Kaufman; Produced by David Merrick; With Peter Ustinov, Jack Gilford, Henry Lascoe, and Elizabeth Allen.

Published Songs
None

Rome provided a guitar solo for George S. Kaufman's final production. The great director/playwright died on June 2, 1961.

DESTRY RIDES AGAIN
April 23, 1959
Imperial Theatre • 472 performances
Book by Leonard Gershe (based on the story by Max Brand); Directed and Choreographed by Michael Kidd; Produced by David Merrick in association with Max Brown; With Andy Griffith, Dolores Gray, Scott Brady, Jack Prince, and Libi Staiger.

Published Songs
Anyone Would Love You
*Are You Ready, Gyp Watson?
Every Once in a While
Fair Warning
Hoop de Dingle
I Know Your Kind
*I Say Hello
Once Knew a Fella
Ring on the Finger
Rose Lovejoy of Paradise Alley

Additional Songs Published in Vocal Score
Ballad of a Gun
Don't Take Me Back to Bottleneck (Opening)
I Hate Him
Ladies
Not Guilty
Only Time Will Tell
Respectability
Tomorrow Morning

Merrick and Rome followed FANNY [November 4, 1954] with a musical version of the 1939 classic western. The lavish production and Michael Kidd's exciting staging helped, but the musical DESTRY couldn't compete with the memory of James Stewart and Marlene Dietrich. Some of the songs have their adherents, but the score leaves me cold except for the moderately pleasing ballad I Say Hello and the well-turned mock dirge Are You Ready, Gyp Watson?

I CAN GET IT FOR YOU WHOLESALE
March 22, 1962
Shubert Theatre • 300 performances
Book by Jerome Weidman (based on his novel); Directed by Arthur Laurents; Choreo-

graphed by Herbert Ross; Produced by David Merrick; With Elliot Gould, Lillian Roth, Marilyn Cooper, Harold Lang, Bambi Linn, and Barbra Streisand.

Published Songs

A Gift Today (The Bar Mitzvah Song)
*Have I Told You Lately
*Miss Marmelstein
Momma, Momma
On My Way to Love
The Sound of Money
*Too Soon
*What's in It for Me?
*Who Knows?

Additional Songs Published in Vocal Score

Ballad of the Garment Trade
Eat a Little Something
The Family Way
I'm Not a Well Man
The Way Things Are
What Are They Doing to Us Now?
When Gemini Meets Capricorn

Rome set to work on his third consecutive Merrick musical with Jerome Weidman (of FIORELLO [Bock: November 23, 1959]), an adaptation of the 1944 movie National Velvet. The authors decided that Weidman's 1937 novel was a better idea, though, and Merrick concurred. Rome returned to his PINS AND NEEDLES [November 27, 1937] terrain, the New York City garment district during the depression; but the music was far richer now, reflecting his warmly melodic work on FANNY [November 4, 1954]. Especially effective were the ballads Too Soon and Who Knows?, as well as the lilting soft shoe Have I Told You Lately. The combination of an unsympathetic antihero and downbeat subject matter worked against the show, though, and WHOLESALE missed as a big ticket item. The brightest spot was an awkward young singer from Brooklyn named Streisand, who breezed into auditions and was immediately cast in a minor role. Rome went off and fashioned Miss Marmelstein (a follow-up to Nobody Makes a Pass at Me from PINS AND NEEDLES) and What Are They Doing to Us Now? to her talents, and she achieved quite a following.

THE ZULU AND THE ZAYDA

November 10, 1965
Cort Theatre • 179 performances
Play by Howard da Silva and Felix Leon; Directed by Dore Schary; Produced by Theodore Mann and Dore Schary; With Menasha Skulnik, Ossie Davis, and Louis Gossett.

Published Songs

How Cold, Cold, Cold an Empty Room
It's Good to Be Alive
Like the Breeze Blows—see GONE WITH THE WIND [August 28, 1973]
May Your Heart Stay Young (L'Chayim)
Out of This World (Oisgetzaichnet)
*Rivers of Tears
Some Things
Tkambuza (Zulu Hunting Song)
The Water Wears down the Stone
Zulu Love Song (Wait for Me)

Additional Song Published in Vocal Selection

Crocodile Wife

This left-wing soap opera with songs told of an unlikely South African friendship between a Yiddish grandfather and a young Zulu. The play didn't work; but Rome, a collector and student of African art, provided a fascinating score in the styles of the two cultures. For a good example of creative song reuse, take a look at Like the Breeze Blows. While its highly idiomatic content suggested no life outside the quickly shuttered ZAYDA, Rome effectively transformed it into the rousing wake Bonnie Gone in GONE WITH THE WIND [May 3, 1972].

LA GROSSE VALISE

December 14, 1965
54th Street Theatre • 7 performances
Music by Gerard Calvi; Lyrics by Rome; Book and Direction by Robert Dhery; Produced by Joe Kipness and Arthur Lesser; With Ronald Fraser, Victor Spinetti, and Joyce Jillson.

Published Songs

Delilah Done Me Wrong (The No Haircut Song)
For You
Slippy Sloppy Shoes
Xanadu

David Merrick and Joe Kipness had imported Robert Dhery's previous French revue, *La Plume de ma Tante*, which opened November 11, 1958, and ran a remarkable 835 performances. Merrick passed on the sequel, which was a quick failure.

GONE WITH THE WIND
August 28, 1973
Dorothy Chandler Pavilion {Los Angeles} •
    Closed during tryout
"The Epic Musical." Book by Horton Foote (based on the novel by Margaret Mitchell); Directed and Choreographed by Joe Layton; Produced by Harold Fielding; With Lesley Ann Warren, Pernell Roberts, Terence Monk, Robert Nichols, and Theresa Merritt.

Published Songs
Blueberry Eyes
Gone with the Wind
How Often
Lonely Stranger
Strange and Wonderful
We Belong to You

Additional Songs Published in Vocal
    Selection
Little Wonders
Scarlett
A Time for Love
Where Is My Soldier Boy?

Additional Songs Recorded
Because There's You—cut
Blissful Christmas
Bonnie Blue Flag—cut
*Bonnie Gone—revised version of *Like the Breeze Blows* from THE ZULU AND THE ZAYDA [November 10, 1965]
Gambling Man
Goodbye, My Honey—cut
Home Again
It Doesn't Matter Now
Johnny Is My Darling—cut
Marrying for Fun

My Soldier
Newlywed's Song
O'Hara
A Southern Lady
Tara
Today's the Day (*He Loves Me*)
Tomorrow Is Another Day
Two of a Kind
What Is Love?
Which Way Is Home?
Why Did They Die?—cut

Rome's final musical began *very* far out of town, when the composer and director/choreographer Joe Layton were invited to Tokyo to create SCARLETT [January 1, 1970]. The show—produced by the Japanese in Japanese with a Japanese cast—was highly successful. Retitled, retooled, and retranslated back into English, GONE WITH THE WIND jumped across the globe to London, where the burning of Atlanta took the West End by storm for 397 performances (starring June Ritchie and Harve Presnell). GONE WITH THE WIND eventually leapfrogged to Hollywood, but never made it back East—not even to Atlanta.

Harold Rome began his career during the musical theatre drought of the mid-1930s. He first achieved success with PINS AND NEEDLES [November 27, 1937], displaying a light but pointed touch at political satire. Rome quickly found a place in the revitalized topical revue. His specialty: sparkling comedy lyrics for everyday characters, set to bright, refreshing music. But competition from the modern book musical and the hugely successful television variety shows put an end to topical revues. After a period of adjustment, Rome responded with surprisingly rich scores for FANNY [November 4, 1954] and I CAN GET IT FOR YOU WHOLESALE [March 22, 1962]. Then came the musical theatre drought of the mid-1960s, which forced Rome (along with Schwartz, Arlen, and others) into permanent retirement.

PART II

New Composers of the 1940s and 1950s

The Depression ended as the nation geared up for war, and Broadway did its share by providing lively, energetic entertainments. Hugh Martin brought in the swinging sound of pop music, first as a vocal arranger and then as a composer. Leonard Bernstein made the first of his theatre visits with an extra-lively musical comedy (albeit with a large chunk of modern ballet). A touch of the light European style returned with Viennese emigrant Frederick Loewe. The 1940s ended with the entrance of two immensely talented Hollywood veterans—Jule Styne and Frank Loesser—whose work quickly established them as important composers of "modern musical comedy." Within a few years Loesser was grooming protégés of his own, such as pop composer Richard Adler, who enjoyed brief but notable success in the mid-1950s. Styne, meanwhile, introduced the more enduring Jerry Bock, who turned out a series of satisfying, well-written scores. Three new composer/lyricists turned up in 1957. Pop-songwriter Bob Merrill had a few early successes, after which he hit nothing but roadblocks. Pop-songwriter Meredith Willson had only one hit show, but it was a massive one. And then came the great Stephen Sondheim, who wasn't firmly established (as a composer) until 1970—and who has been at the forefront of the field ever since.

Hugh Martin   205

Leonard Bernstein   211

Frederick Loewe   221

Jule Styne   227

Frank Loesser   243

Richard Adler   251

Jerry Bock   255

Bob Merrill   263

Meredith Willson   269

Stephen Sondheim   273

HUGH MARTIN

Born: August 11, 1914, Birmingham, Alabama

HUGH MARTIN left Birmingham Southern College as a sophomore to embark on a musical career. Smitten by Gershwin and Kern, he came to Broadway as a member of Kay Thompson's backup quartet in HOORAY FOR WHAT! [Arlen: December 1, 1937]. By the end of the tryout Thompson had been replaced; Martin remained and attracted immediate notice with his contemporary, swing-oriented vocals. He created an incredible, "hot" choral arrangement for the *Sing for Your Supper* number in THE BOYS FROM SYRACUSE [Rodgers: November 23, 1938], which brought similar assignments on TOO MANY GIRLS [Rodgers: October 18, 1939] and CABIN IN THE SKY [Duke: October 25, 1940]. Martin formed a singing quartet (The Martins), which sang his arrangements in LOUISIANA PURCHASE [Berlin: May 28, 1940]. The Martins included fellow songwriter Ralph Blane (born July 26, 1914, in Broken Arrow, Oklahoma).

BEST FOOT FORWARD
October 1, 1941
Ethel Barrymore Theatre • 326 performances
"A Modern Musical Comedy." Music and Lyrics mostly by Hugh Martin and Ralph Blane (see Rodgers: October 1, 1941); Book by John Cecil Holm; Directed by George Abbott; Choreographed by Gene Kelly; Produced by George Abbott (and Richard Rodgers); With Rosemary Lane, Nancy Walker, Gil Stratton, Jr., and June Allyson.

Revival
April 2, 1963
Stage 73 • 224 performances
Directed and Choreographed by Danny

Daniels; With Paula Wayne [Lane], Liza Minnelli [Walker], Glenn (Christopher) Walken [Stratton], and Kay Cole [Allyson].

Published Songs
Buckle down, Winsocki [by Blane]—also published in 1942 with a revised non-show lyric as *Buckle Down Buck Private*
***Ev'ry Time* [by Martin]
I Know You by Heart
Just a Little Joint with a Juke Box
A Raving Beauty—added to revival; originally used in MEET ME IN ST. LOUIS [1960] [June 9, 1960]
Shady Lady Bird [by Blane]
That's How I Love the Blues [by Martin]
The Three Bs
What Do You Think I Am? [by Martin]
Wish I May—written for 1943 movie version
**You Are for Loving* [by Martin]—added to revival; originally used in MEET ME IN ST. LOUIS [1960]
You're Lucky—written for movie version

Additional Songs Recorded
Alive and Kicking—written for movie version
Don't Sell the Night Short
The Guy Who Brought Me [music by Richard Rodgers, lyric by Rodgers and Martin; credited to Martin & Blane]
Hollywood Story
Three Men on a Date

Note: All songs credited to Martin & Blane, although most were written separately. Precise authorship given where known.

George Abbott was always looking for new talent, and the fox-trotting director/producer couldn't fail to appreciate Martin's show-stopping arrangements of *Sing for Your Supper* in THE BOYS FROM SYRACUSE [Rodgers: November 23, 1938] and *I Like to Recognize the Tune* in TOO MANY GIRLS [Rodgers: October 18, 1939]. For his next "youth" musical, Abbott (and his silent producing partner Richard Rodgers) gave the song-writing assignment to novices Martin and Blane. Rodgers had decided to move into the producing field as a way of occupying himself during Larry Hart's increasing bouts of incapacitation; Rodgers also ghost-wrote a song during the tryout. BEST FOOT FORWARD was a happy success, with the score featuring the hit "football" song *Buckle down, Winsocki* [by Blane] and Martin's exquisitely poignant *Ev'ry Time*. Abbott discovery Nancy Walker stole the show, moving on to a series of Abbott-helmed vehicles; June Allyson, though, went right to Hollywood—as did Martin and Blane. Work there included three superlative songs (**The Boy Next Door*, ***Have Yourself a Merry Little Christmas*, and **The Trolley Song*) for Judy Garland in the 1944 movie *Meet Me in St. Louis* (see June 9, 1960, and November 2, 1989). Nineteen years later, Garland and director Vincente Minnelli's seventeen-year-old daughter Liza made her New York debut in the successful Off Broadway revival of BEST FOOT FORWARD.

LOOK, MA, I'M DANCIN'!
January 29, 1948
Adelphi Theatre • 188 performances
Music and Lyrics by Martin; Book by Jerome Lawrence and Robert E. Lee; Directed by George Abbott and Jerome Robbins; Conceived and Choreographed by Jerome Robbins; Produced by George Abbott; With Nancy Walker, Harold Lang, Janet Reed, Loren Welch, and Alice Pearce.

Published Songs
If You'll Be Mine
I'm Not So Bright
I'm Tired of Texas—initial publication of 1944 non-show song
The Little Boy Blues
Shauny O'Shay
Tiny Room
The Way It Might Have Been

Additional Songs Recorded
**Gotta Dance*
**I'm the First Girl in the Second Row*—new lyric for 1944 non-show song *I'm the First Man* (unpublished)
Mlle. Scandale Ballet [instrumental]
The Two of Us

George Abbott, Jerry Robbins, and Nancy Walker of ON THE TOWN [Bernstein: December 28, 1944] reunited for this comical ballet musical about a brewer's daughter bankrolling the ballet in order to get on her toes. Robbins had his first directing experience here, while Martin first worked without a collaborator. The result was moderately entertaining but not quite successful. Martin provided two harmonically remarkable ballads, *Little Boy Blues* and *Tiny Room*, as well as the lyrically spectacular *I'm the First Girl in the Second Row* "of the third scene in the fourth number in fifth position at ten o'clock on the nose." Martin wrote the latter in 1944 for a Special Services show while stationed at Camp Hood, Texas ("the first man in the second platoon of the fourth company"); this was also the origin of *I'm Tired of Texas*.

MAKE A WISH
April 18, 1951
Winter Garden Theatre • 102 performances
Music and Lyrics by Martin; Book by Preston Sturges (based on *The Good Fairy* [play] by Ferenc Molnár); Directed by John C. Wilson; Choreographed by Gower Champion; Produced by Harry Rigby and Jule Styne with Alexander H. Cohen; With Nanette Fabray, Melville Cooper, Harold Lang, Stephen Douglass, and Helen Gallagher.

Published Songs
Over and Over
Paris, France
Suits Me Fine
That Face—advertised but not published; recorded
What I Was Warned About
**When Does This Feeling Go Away?*

Additional Songs Recorded
Hello, Hello, Hello
I'll Never Make a Frenchman out of You
I Wanna Be Good 'n' Bad

Janette
Make a Wish
The Sale [instrumental] [music by Richard Prybor]
Take Me Back to Texas with You
Tonight You Are in Paree
The Tour Must Go On
The Two of Us
Who Gives a Sou?

Martin began work on a Paris-based musical with his librettists from LOOK, MA, I'M DANCIN'! [January 29, 1948], Jerome Lawrence and Robert E. Lee. When they withdrew from the project, Martin searched for another plot upon which to graft some of his already-written songs. Molnár's play—which Preston Sturges had successfully adapted into a semi-classic 1935 Margaret Sullavan film—was selected somewhat after the fact. The result was a somewhat less-than-well-made vehicle for Nanette Fabray. Composer Jule Styne was eager to enter the Broadway producing field and undertook MAKE A WISH as his first project. (Martin had done vocal arrangements for both HIGH BUTTON SHOES [Styne: October 9, 1947] and GENTLEMEN PREFER BLONDES [Styne: December 8, 1949].) Producer Alexander H. Cohen also entered the book musical field, with his first of eight (out of eight) failures. Martin's score was merely adequate, although he did manage another fine chromatic ballad (*When Does This Feeling Go Away?*) and a couple of better than average rhythmic duets for dancing duo Harold Lang and Helen Gallagher (*Suits Me Fine* and *That Face*). Martin then put on his dinner jacket and went to the Palace, playing for Judy Garland's record-breaking nineteen-week engagement (beginning October 16, 1951). Martin had a long history as arranger, coach and composer for Garland, for whom he wrote those classic *Meet Me in St. Louis* songs. The two made headlines in 1953 when they had an extremely visible battle—over the out-of-control star's interpretation of the Arlen-Gershwin *The Man That Got Away*—on a sound stage full of musicians during the making of *A Star Is Born*.

LOVE FROM JUDY
September 25, 1952
Saville Theatre {London} • 594 performances
Lyrics by Hugh Martin and Jack (Timothy) Gray; Book by Eric Maschwitz and Jean

Webster (based on *Daddy Longlegs* [novel] by Jean Webster); Directed by Charles Hickman; Choreographed by Pauline Grant; Produced by Emile Littler; With Jeannie Carson, Bill O'Connor, and Adelaide Hall.

Published Songs
Daddy Longlegs
Go and Get Your Old Banjo
Love from Judy
My True Love

Additional Songs Published in Vocal Score
Ain't Gonna Marry
Ballet [instrumental]
Dum Dum Dum
Goin' Back to School
Here We Are
I Never Dream When I Sleep
It's Better Rich
It's Great to Be an Orphan
Kind to Animals
Mardi Gras
A Touch of Voodoo
What Do I See in You?

Martin followed the failure of MAKE A WISH [April 18, 1951] with the highly successful if old-fashioned London musical LOVE FROM JUDY, collaborating with Timothy Gray (who had contributed uncredited lyrics to MAKE A WISH). Both shows, oddly enough, were about innocent waiflike foundlings who find happiness in the world outside the orphanage. JUDY's score was only moderately pleasing, lacking the typical colors of Martin's better work. But London loved it, making JUDY his most successful show. Martin returned to Hollywood, where he was an important part of the musical team at MGM through the 1940s and 1950s. A Martin/Blane stage musicalization of Colette's play *Gigi*—yet another *gamin*—was announced in 1953 but ultimately abandoned. MGM, which owned the rights, found another use for the property.

MEET ME IN ST. LOUIS [1960]
June 9, 1960
Municipal Opera {St. Louis, Mo.} •
    Summer stock tryout
Also see November 2, 1989. Music and Lyrics by Hugh Martin and Ralph Blane; Book by

Sally Benson (based on *The Kensington Stories* by Sally Benson and the 1944 movie).

Published Songs
Almost
The Boy Next Door [by Martin]—originally
    used in 1944 movie version
Diamonds in the Starlight [probably by Blane]
Have Yourself a Merry Little Christmas—
    originally used in movie version
How Do I Look?
If I Had an Igloo [by Martin]
A Raving Beauty—also used in 1963 revival of
    BEST FOOT FORWARD [October 1, 1941]
Skip to My Lou [adapted from traditional]—
    originally used in movie version
The Trolley Song—originally used in movie
    version
What's-His-Name [probably by Martin]
You Are for Loving [by Martin]—also used in
    revival of BEST FOOT FORWARD

Note: All songs credited to Martin & Blane, although most were written separately. Precise authorship given where known.

The summer of 1960 saw several stock productions of this stage adaptation of Martin and Blane's nostalgic Judy Garland film, featuring those three superb songs and not much else. (A Canadian mounting later that summer featured Robert Goulet as "The Boy Next Door," just prior to making his Broadway debut in CAMELOT [Loewe: December 3, 1960]). This adaptation of MEET ME IN ST. LOUIS never reached Broadway, but the new songs included yet another touchingly wistful beauty, *You Are for Loving*, as well as a rather novel novelty entitled *If I Had an Igloo*.

A LITTLE NIGHT MUSIC [1963]
[circa 1963]
Unproduced musical. Lyrics by Marshall Barer.

Songs Recorded
Here Come the Dreamers
On Such a Night Like This

This unproduced musical—about a group of eccentrics living by night on a Hollywood soundstage—was written for Hollywood soprano Kathryn Grayson and Liza Minnelli; Martin had just introduced the latter in his 1963 revival of BEST FOOT FORWARD [October 1, 1941]. A concert version was mounted in Los Angeles, rather belatedly, on February 12, 1998, under the title HAPPY LOT!

HIGH SPIRITS
April 7, 1964
Alvin Theatre • 375 performances
"An Improbable Musical Comedy." Book, Music, and Lyrics by Hugh Martin and Timothy Gray (based on *Blithe Spirit* [play] by Noël Coward); Choreographed by Danny Daniels; Directed by Noël Coward; Produced by Lester Osterman, Robert Fletcher, and Richard Horner; With Beatrice Lillie, Tammy Grimes, Edward Woodward, and Louise Troy.

Published Songs
The Bicycle Song—advertised but not published; recorded
Forever and a Day
If I Gave You
I Know Your Heart
Something Tells Me
Was She Prettier Than I?
You'd Better Love Me

Additional Song Published in "Professional Vocal Selection"
Faster Than Sound

Additional Songs Recorded
Go into Your Trance
Home Sweet Heaven
Something Is Coming to Tea
Talking to You
What in the World Did You Want?
Where Is the Man I Married?

Martin returned to Broadway with this final Tammy Grimes/Bea Lillie vehicle. Coward's five-character farce seemed out of place in musical comedy; the addition of an extraneous chorus seemed rather jarring. This was unfortunate, as much of the score is quite enjoyable. Up-tempo charmers include *I Know Your Heart*, *Something Tells Me*, and *You'd Better Love Me*, while *Home Sweet Heaven* is an especially well-turned list song in the Cole Porter tradition.

MEET ME IN ST. LOUIS [1989]
November 2, 1989
Gershwin Theatre • 253 performances
Also see June 9, 1960. Music and Lyrics by
Hugh Martin and Ralph Blane; Book by Hugh
Wheeler (based on *The Kensington Stories* by
Sally Benson and the 1944 movie); Directed by
Louis Burke; Choreographed by Joan
Brickhill; Produced by Brickhill-Burke
Productions, Christopher Seabrooke, and EPI
Products; With George Hearn, Milo O'Shea,
Charlotte Moore, Betty Garrett, Donna Kane,
and Courtney Peldon.

New Song Published
Ice [by Martin]—originally used in (and only
    published as from) the 1958 television
    musical "Hans Brinker"

Additional Songs Recorded
*Banjos
Be Anything but a Girl [by Martin]—originally
    used in "Hans Brinker"
The Boy Next Door (extended version) [by
    Martin]—includes refrain of *I Happen to
    Love You* [by Martin] from "Hans Brinker"
A Day in New York
*Ghosties and Ghoulies That Go Bump in the
    Night*
Irish Jig (*The Ball*)
Paging Mr. Sousa
A Touch of the Irish
Wasn't It Fun?

Note: All songs credited to Martin & Blane, although most were written separately. Precise
authorship given where known.

Husband-and-wife team Joan Brickhill and Louis
Burke, experts at staging American musicals in
their native South Africa, decided to show Broadway a thing or two and hang the expense. They
chose MEET ME IN ST. LOUIS as their vehicle and
spent an awful lot of money on an awfully amateurish show. (The famous *Trolley Song* featured a
big-as-life trolley which, after a flashy entrance,
simply turned around and around and around and
around but never went anywhere; it was that kind
of evening.) One of the new songs, *Banjos*, was
quite peppy; the rest, though, were considerably

below Martin's standards. It's hard to say exactly
when these songs were actually written, but Martin and Blane were both seventy-five when ST.
LOUIS finally hit Broadway.

I WILL COME BACK
February 25, 1998
Players Theatre {Off Broadway} •
    71 performances
Play by Timothy Gray; New songs by Hugh
Martin and Timothy Gray; Directed by
Timothy Gray; Produced by New Journeys
Ahead Ltd.; With Tommy Femia and Kristine
Zbornik.

Published Songs
None

Martin contributed four unexceptional new songs
(along with *The Boy Next Door* and *The Trolley
Song*) to this one-woman Judy Garland evening
written and directed by Martin's long-time collaborator Timothy Gray (of LOVE FROM JUDY
[September 25, 1952] and HIGH SPIRITS [April 7,
1964]). Actually it was a two-woman show. Actually it was a two-*man* show playing two women
(i.e., Judy and Barbra). You get the picture?

Hugh Martin deserves a great deal of credit for
revolutionizing the sound of the Broadway musical as a masterful vocal arranger for important
musicals by the Messrs. Berlin, Rodgers, Arlen,
Porter, and Styne. (These remain a treat and can
be heard on cast albums of numerous shows,
including Styne's HIGH BUTTON SHOES [Oc-
tober 9, 1947], GENTLEMEN PREFER BLONDES
[December 8, 1949], and HAZEL FLAGG [Febru-
ary 11, 1953]). Martin's distinctive melodic freedom and colorful harmonies made him stand out
as a possible successor to Gershwin and Arlen,
or at least Duke and Lane. His songwriting output over the years was, unfortunately, exceedingly small. It's truly unfortunate that we heard
so little from him, but how can one be but grateful for such gems as *Ev'ry Time, Little Boy Blues,
Tiny Room, You Are for Loving, Have Yourself a
Merry Little Christmas*, and *The Boy Next Door*?

LEONARD BERNSTEIN

Born: August 25, 1918, Lawrence, Massachusetts
Died: October 14, 1990, New York, New York

LEONARD BERNSTEIN's first theatre experience came when the twenty-one-year-old Harvard music major mounted the 1939 Boston première of THE CRADLE WILL ROCK [Blitzstein: June 16, 1937]. Bernstein played the onstage accompaniment; the composer attended, was impressed, and the two began a close friendship. Following graduation, Bernstein entered the Curtis Institute of Music in Philadelphia—where Blitzstein had studied—to train for a career in symphonic music. Three years assisting conductors Serge Koussevitzky and Artur Rodzinski led to Bernstein's big break on November 14, 1943: a last-minute illness and the absence of a suitable, European-born replacement resulted in Bernstein—a young American Jew—conducting a concert by the New York Philharmonic. The event attracted front page coverage, and Bernstein did his best to remain in the news for the next forty-seven years. He made his composing debut with Ballet Theatre's **Fancy Free [April 18, 1944], choreographed by (and featuring) Jerome Robbins. Robbins had been a show dancer in musicals like GREAT LADY [Loewe: December 1, 1938] and KEEP OFF THE GRASS [Duke: May 23, 1940]. Fancy Free took the ballet and music world by storm, as the two twenty-five-year-olds brought contemporary dance and jazz into the Metropolitan Opera House. Fancy Free's twenty-five-year-old scenic designer Oliver Smith determined that the piece could serve as the basis for a musical comedy and set to work with Bernstein and Robbins.

ON THE TOWN
December 28, 1944
Adelphi Theatre • 463 performances
Book and Lyrics by Betty Comden and Adolph Green (based on Fancy Free [ballet] by Bernstein and Jerome Robbins); Directed by George Abbott; Choreographed by Jerome Robbins; Produced by Oliver Smith and Paul Feigay; With Nancy Walker, Sono Osato, John Battle, Cris Alexander, Betty Comden, and Adolph Green.

Revivals
January 15, 1959
Carnegie Hall Playhouse • 70 performances
Directed by Gerald Freedman; Choreographed by Joe Layton; With Harold Lang [Battles], Pat Carroll [Walker], Evelyn Russell [Comden], Joe Bova [Green], and William Hickey [Alexander].

October 31, 1971
Imperial Theatre • 73 performances
Directed and Choreographed by Ron Field; With Phyllis Newman [Comden], Bernadette Peters [Walker], Ron Husmann [Battles], and Donna McKechnie [Osato].

November 19, 1998
Gershwin Theatre • 65 performances
Directed by George C. Wolfe; Choreographed by Keith Young; Produced by New York Shakespeare Festival (George C. Wolfe); With Lea DeLaria [Walker], Sarah Knowlton [Comden], Tai Jimenez [Osato], Robert Montano [Green], Jesse Tyler Ferguson [Alexander], and Perry Laylon Ojeda [Battles].

Published Songs
*I Can Cook Too [lyric by Bernstein; additional lyric by Comden and Green]
*Lonely Town
*Lucky to Be Me
*New York, New York
*Some Other Time
Ya Got Me

Additional Songs Published in Non-show Folio

Carried Away

I Feel Like I'm Not out of Bed Yet

**New York, New York* [complete version]

Additional Songs Published in 1997 Vocal Score

Carnegie Hall Pavane (Do-Do-Re-Do)

Come up to My Place

**The Dream Coney Island Ballet* (including the *Great Lover Displays Himself*)—also called *The Imaginary Coney Island Ballet*

Gabey's Comin'—cut; added to 1997 revival

I'm Blue

I Understand

I Wish I Was Dead

The Intermission's Great—cut; music subsequently revised for use in 1946 ballet *Facsimile*

**Lonely Town Pas de Deux* [instrumental]

**Presentation of Miss Turnstiles* [instrumental] —also called *Miss Turnstile Variations*

**The Real Coney Island Ballet* [instrumental]

Say When—cut

She's a Home Loving Girl

So Long, Baby

**Times Square Ballet* [instrumental]

Fancy Free's scenic designer Oliver Smith (who'd never produced or designed a Broadway show) determined that the piece could serve as the basis for a musical comedy, so he set to work with Bernstein and Robbins (who'd never composed or choreographed a Broadway show). He hired nightclub performers Betty Comden and Adolph Green (who'd never written book or lyrics or appeared in a Broadway show) to write the book and lyrics and play major roles. George Abbott—who at fifty-seven was more than twice as old as anyone involved—came in to direct, and ON THE TOWN was a refreshing, modernistic hit. Bernstein's score mixed five ballet sections (no *Fancy Free* music was used) with his first songs, including *New York, New York, Lonely Town, Some Other Time*, and some extremely effective comedy numbers. Robbins, Comden, and Green made sparklingly impressive debuts and began long, healthy Broadway careers. Bernstein, having conquered Broadway, returned to the world of symphonic music. As for ON THE TOWN, the material remains first class but re-

vivals remain problematic: without someone like Jerry Robbins, there are a whole bunch of holes throughout the whole show—as has been displayed in two high-profile, failed Broadway revivals.

PETER PAN [1950]

April 24, 1950

Imperial Theatre • 321 performances

Play by James M. Barrie; Incidental music by Alec Wilder; Incidental songs (Music and Lyrics) by Bernstein; Directed by John Burrell; Produced by Peter Lawrence and Roger L. Stevens; With Jean Arthur and Boris Karloff.

Published Songs

My House

Never-Land

Peter, Peter

Pirate Song—issued in choral arrangement only

Plank Round—issued in choral arrangement only

Who Am I?

Additional Song Recorded

Dream with Me—cut

Bernstein ended the forties with an assortment of serious compositions including his *Jeremiah Symphony*. He made a brief theatre visit in 1950 with these songs for the Jean Arthur production of the whimsical Barrie play. He also wrote a popular-song-inspired contemporary opera, the 1952 TROUBLE IN TAHITI (which arrived on Broadway on April 19, 1955).

WONDERFUL TOWN

February 25, 1953

Winter Garden Theatre • 559 performances

Lyrics by Betty Comden and Adolph Green; Book by Joseph Fields and Jerome Chodorov (based on their play *My Sister Eileen*, from stories by Ruth McKenney); Directed by George Abbott; Choreographed by Donald Saddler; Produced by Robert Fryer; With Rosalind Russell, Edith Adams, George Gaynes, and Henry Lascoe.

Published Songs

It's Love

A Little Bit in Love

My Darlin' Eileen ("based on an Irish Reel")
*Ohio
A Quiet Girl
*Swing!
*The Wrong Note Rag

Additional Songs Published in Non-show Folio

One Hundred Easy Ways
Pass the Football

Additional Songs Recorded

Ballet at the Village Vortex (*Let It Come Down*)
   [instrumental]
Christopher Street (*Opening*)
Conga!
Conquering the City—cut
Conversation Piece [words by Comden and
   Green]
Lonely Me—cut
The Story of My Life—cut
What a Waste

With Bernstein dedicated to his serious music career, Comden and Green had searched for a new collaborator since ON THE TOWN [December 28, 1944], trying out Morton Gould (on the Abbott/Robbins BILLION DOLLAR BABY[†] [December 21, 1945]), Saul Chaplin (on the Broadway-bound BONANZA BOUND[†] [December 26, 1947]), and Jule Styne (on the revue TWO ON THE AISLE [Styne: July 19, 1951]). The Styne collaboration seemed particularly promising, but none of the shows were successful. Late in 1952, Comden and Green were in Hollywood finishing their screenplay for *Singin' in the Rain* when George Abbott called for help. His musical version of *My Sister Eileen* was a month from rehearsals and "artistic differences" among the authors resulted in the withdrawal of songwriters Leroy Anderson and Arnold Horwitt. Comden and Green accepted the salvage job, bringing Bernstein along. ON THE TOWN had been experimental, mixing show tunes with large helpings of pure ballet. WONDERFUL TOWN was mere musical comedy—but a well-executed and highly successful example. The score was delightfully evocative of the 1930s and in places playfully creative (like *Ohio*, *Swing!* and the skillful *Wrong Note Rag*). George Abbott kept things moving at his usual fast pace, and

star Rosalind Russell made the whole package immensely enjoyable.

TROUBLE IN TAHITI ✦ Part of ALL IN ONE

April 19, 1955
Playhouse Theatre • 49 performances
Opera by Bernstein; Directed by David Brooks;
Produced by Charles Bowden and Richard Barr;
With Alice Ghostley and John Tyers.

Published Songs
None

Note: The complete vocal score is published.

The fascinating one-act opera TROUBLE IN TAHITI was first performed in June 1952 at a Brandeis College [Waltham, Mass.] arts festival put together by Bernstein; also introduced was the Marc Blitzstein adaptation of THE THREEPENNY OPERA [1954] [Weill: March 10, 1954]. (Bernstein dedicated TROUBLE IN TAHITI to Blitzstein, wrote Blitzstein's mother-in-law—pre-World War I operetta star Lina Abarbanell—into the opening number, and made him godfather of his first child.) Bernstein's opera found its way to a limited Broadway in the three-part ALL IN ONE, sharing the program with a Paul Draper dance recital and Tennessee Williams's *27 Wagons Full of Cotton*. Bernstein found his way to Milan in 1953, when he was the first American ever to conduct opera at La Scala.

THE LARK

November 17, 1955
Longacre Theatre • 229 performances
Play by Jean Anouilh; Adaptation by Lillian Hellman; Incidental music and Lyrics by Bernstein; Directed by Joseph Anthony; Produced by Kermit Bloomgarden; With Julie Harris, Boris Karloff, and Christopher Plummer.

Published Songs
Soldier's Song
Spring Song

Additional Songs Published in *Choruses from "The Lark"*

Benedictus
Court Song

Gloria
Prelude
Requiem Sanctus [1st]—different than song
    from MASS [September 8, 1971]

A QUIET PLACE [1955]
[November 23, 1955]
Shubert Theatre {New Haven, Conn.} •
    Closed during tryout
Play by Julian Claman; Title song by
Bernstein; Directed by Delbert Mann; Pro-
duced by The Playwrights' Company; With
Tyrone Power and Leora Dana.

Published Song
A Quiet Place—published only in vocal score
    of TROUBLE IN TAHITI [April 19, 1955]

A Quiet Place was an aria from TROUBLE IN
TAHITI. It was reused as title song of this quick
failure, written by a friend of Bernstein. Years
later, Bernstein wrote a continuation of TROUBLE
IN TAHITI—also entitled A QUIET PLACE [July
22, 1984].

CANDIDE [1956]
December 1, 1956
Martin Beck Theatre • 73 performances
"A Comic Operetta." Also see March 10, 1974.
Lyrics mostly by Richard Wilbur, Additional
lyrics by John Latouche, Lillian Hellman,
Leonard Bernstein, and Dorothy Parker; Book
by Lillian Hellman (based on the satire by
Voltaire); Directed by Tyrone Guthrie;
Produced by Ethel Linder Reiner in associa-
tion with Lester Osterman, Jr.; With Max
Adrian, Barbara Cook, Robert Rounseville, and
Irra Petina.

Revival
July 6, 1971
Curran Theatre {San Francisco} •
    Closed during tryout
Choreographed by Michael Smuin; Conceived
and Directed by Sheldon Patinkin; Produced
by Edwin Lester; With Douglas Campbell
[Adrian], Mary Costa [Cook], Frank Poretta
[Rounseville], and Rae Allen [Petina].

Published Songs
*The Best of All Possible Worlds [lyric by
    Latouche]—issued in choral edition and
    vocal selection
*Buenos Aires Tango (*I Am Easily Assimilated*)
    [lyric by Bernstein]
**Glitter and Be Gay—issued in separate
    edition
It Must Be Me—subsequently published in
    vocal selections with revised lyric as *It
    Must Be So*
*Make Our Garden Grow—issued in choral
    edition and vocal selection
*What's the Use?

Additional Songs Published in Vocal Score
Ballad of Eldorado [lyric by Hellman]
Bon Voyage
Dear Boy—cut
Lisbon Sequence [lyric by Bernstein]
My Love [lyric by Latouche and Wilbur]
Oh, Happy We
**Overture [instrumental]
Pilgrims Procession
Quartet Finale
Quiet
*Venice Gambling Scene (*Money, Money*) [lyric
    by Wilbur and Parker]
Wedding Chorale
You Were Dead, You Know [lyric by
    Latouche]

Note: For additional songs, see March 10,
1974.

Bernstein wrote one of Broadway's most glorious scores for this glorious failure. The production, though, was misconceived and misguided,
with Voltaire's satire played as light operetta.
John Latouche, best known for CABIN IN THE
SKY [Duke: October 25, 1941], was fresh from his
artistic triumph with THE GOLDEN APPLE
[Notables: March 11, 1954]. He suffered a heart
attack and died August 7, 1956, at the age of
thirty-eight. Dorothy Parker, librettist Lillian
Hellman, and even Bernstein contributed lyrics
before poet Richard Wilbur came in. The resulting score is treasure filled, though the show has
had a checkered existence over the last forty
years.

WEST SIDE STORY
September 26, 1957

Winter Garden Theatre • 734 performances
Lyrics by Stephen Sondheim (initially credited to Sondheim and Bernstein); Book by Arthur Laurents (suggested by *Romeo and Juliet* [play] by William Shakespeare); Conceived and Directed by Jerome Robbins; Choreographed by Jerome Robbins and Peter Gennaro; Produced by Robert E. Griffith and Harold S. Prince by arrangement with Roger L. Stevens; With Larry Kert, Carol Lawrence, Chita Rivera, and Lee Becker.

Return Engagement
April 27, 1960

Winter Garden Theatre • 249 performances
With Larry Kert, Carol Lawrence, Allyn Ann McLerie [Rivera], and Lee Becker.

Revivals
June 24, 1968

New York State Theater • 89 performances
Original direction and Choreography reproduced by Lee Becker Theodore; Produced by Music Theater of Lincoln Center (Richard Rodgers); With Kurt Peterson [Kert], Victoria Mallory [Lawrence], and Barbara Luna [Rivera].

February 14, 1980

Minskoff Theatre • 333 performances
Directed by Jerome Robbins and Gerald Freedman; Original choreography restaged by Tom Abbott and Lee Becker Theodore; With Josie De Guzman [Lawrence], Ken Marshall [Kert], and Debbie Allen [Rivera].

Published Songs
America!
*Cool
Gee, Officer Krupke—initial publication upon use in 1960 return engagement
I Feel Pretty
*Maria
One Hand, One Heart
**Something's Coming (Could Be)
*Somewhere
*Tonight

Additional Songs Published in Vocal Score
*A Boy Like That (and I Have a Love)
*The Dance at the Gym [instrumental]
**Jet Song
*Prologue [instrumental]
*The Rumble [instrumental]
*Somewhere Ballet [instrumental]
*Taunting Scene [instrumental]
*Tonight (Quintet)

Additional Song Recorded
Like Everybody Else

Arthur Laurents entered the theatre with the fine postwar drama *Home of the Brave* [December 27, 1945]. Discussions with Jerome Robbins at that time brought about the idea for an "East Side Story"—a modern-day *Romeo and Juliet* using an interfaith romance. Bernstein became involved, but the project fell through. Big-city racial gang wars became news ten years later, and the idea was reborn. Bernstein started the lyrics himself; when help was needed, Laurents brought in Sondheim—known only for his unproduced SATURDAY NIGHT [circa August 1955]—as co-lyricist. Bernstein relinquished his lyric credit during the tryout, although his name remained on early posters and the first printing of the sheet music. (It has long been rumored that Sondheim himself wrote some of the music while Bernstein was off struggling with CANDIDE [December 1, 1956]. In fact, Sondheim wrote part of *Something's Coming*, taking the verse written by Bernstein and developing it into the main section of the chorus.) Producer Cheryl Crawford, whose recent musicals had been progressive, unconventional flops (LOVE LIFE [Weill: October 7, 1948], FLAHOOLEY [Notables: May 14, 1951], and REUBEN REUBEN [Blitzstein: October 10, 1955]), was unable to come up with the financing and abandoned the production. Robert Griffith and Harold Prince, producers of three hit Abbott/Fosse musicals (see NEW GIRL IN TOWN [Merrill: May 14, 1957]), stepped in and took over. As with ON THE TOWN [December 28, 1944], WEST SIDE STORY was built on ballet; not for musical comedy purposes, though, but as a form of expression for the inarticulate characters. As might be expected, the exceptional WEST SIDE STORY was not a major hit: THE MUSIC MAN [Willson: December 19, 1957] took all the awards (except Best Choreographer) and outran it by almost two years. The show's legendary status did not develop until the release of the Oscar-winning 1961 movie version. Just after WEST SIDE opened, Bernstein became music director of the New York Philharmonic and once again left the theatre.

THE FIRST BORN
April 29, 1958
Coronet Theatre • 38 performances
Play by Christopher Fry; Songs by Leonard Bernstein; Directed by Anthony Quayle; Produced by Katharine Cornell and Roger L. Stevens; With Katharine Cornell, Anthony Quayle, and Mildred Natwick.

Published Songs
None

Katharine Cornell made one of her final stage appearances in this limited engagement.

A PRAY BY BLECHT
[circa February 16, 1969]
[Broadhurst Theatre]
Unfinished musical. Lyrics by Stephen Sondheim; Book by John Guare (based on *The Exception and the Rule* [play] by Bertolt Brecht); [Directed and Choreographed by Jerome Robbins;
Produced by Stuart Ostrow; With Zero Mostel].

Published Songs
None

A rather fascinating assemblage of talents converged for A PRAY BY BLECHT. The collaborators were unable to complete the piece to their satisfaction, though, and the already-booked theatre was released. BLECHT resurfaced in the spring of 1987 as THE ROAD TO URGA, a Lincoln Center Theater developmental workshop (with Josh Mostel in his father's role). Once again, the piece was withdrawn and appears likely to remain so.

MASS
September 8, 1971
Kennedy Center Opera House {Washington, D.C.} • 12 performances
June 28, 1972
Metropolitan Opera House • 22 performances
"A Theatre Piece for Singers, Players and Dancers." Text from the Liturgy of the Roman Mass; Additional text by Stephen Schwartz and Bernstein; Directed by Gordon Davidson; Choreographed by Alvin Ailey; Produced by Roger L. Stevens; With Alan Titus.

Published Songs
Almighty Father
Gloria Tibi
Sanctus [2nd]—different than song from THE LARK [November 17, 1955]
*A Simple Song
*The Word of the Lord

Additional Songs Published in Vocal Score
Agnus Dei
Alleluia [1st]
Confiteor Alleluia [2nd]
Credo in Unum Deum
De Profundis
Dominus Vobiscum
*Easy
Epiphany
Gloria in Excelsis
*God Said (And It Was Good)
*Half of the People [partial lyric by Paul Simon]
Hurry
I Believe in God
*I Don't Know
*I Go On
In Nomine Patris
Kyrie Eleison
Meditation No. 1 [instrumental]
Meditation No. 2 [on a sequence by Beethoven] [instrumental]
Non Credo (Possibly Yes, Probably No)
Our Father
Pax: Communion (Secret Songs)
Prefatory Prayers (Street Chorus)—see 1600 PENNSYLVANIA AVENUE [May 4, 1976]
Thank You
Things Get Broken
*World without End

Bernstein returned to the stage with this spectacular "theatre piece for singers, players and dancers" commissioned in 1966 for the opening of the John F. Kennedy Center for the Performing Arts. Bernstein's score is incredibly rich, though controversy arose over the inclusion of rock music in the religious MASS. Others protested objectionable messages, political and philosophical: the piece was sponsored by the government, but the composer was no friend of President Nixon. MASS was remounted for a three-week New York engagement, and the Kennedy Center staged a tenth-anniversary revival; but the size and scope of the piece—soloists, chorus, dance company, boys' choir, full orchestra, etc.—precluded much of an afterlife. MASS, most fortunately, remains in full glory on the original cast album.

CANDIDE [1974]
March 10, 1974
Broadway Theatre • 740 performances
Also see December 1, 1956. Lyrics mostly by Richard Wilbur; New lyrics by Stephen Sondheim; Book by Hugh Wheeler (based on the satire by Voltaire); Directed by Harold Prince; Choreographed by Patricia Birch; Produced by Chelsea Theatre Center of Brooklyn in conjunction with Harold Prince and Ruth Mitchell; With Lewis J. Stadlen, Mark Baker, Maureen Brennan, and June Gable.

Revival
April 29, 1997
Gershwin Theatre • 103 performances
Directed by Harold Prince; Choreographed by Patricia Birch; Produced by Livent (U.S.) Inc. [Garth Drabinsky]; With Jim Dale [Stadlen], Andrea Martin [Gable], Harolyn Blackwell [Brennan], and Jason Danieley [Baker].

Revised Songs Published in Choral Arrangements (and Vocal Selection)
Life Is Happiness Indeed [lyric by Sondheim]—new lyric for *Venice Gambling Scene*
This World (*Candide's Lament*) [lyric by Sondheim]—new lyric for *Quartet Finale*

Additional Songs Published in Vocal Score of 1974 Version
Alleluia [2nd]
Auto-da-fé (*What a Day*) [lyric by John Latouche and Sondheim]—revised lyric for *Ringaroundarosie* (cut) from [1956]
Barcarolle [instrumental]
The Best of All Possible Worlds—new lyric by Sondheim for song of same name
Sheep's Song [lyric by Sondheim]

Additional Songs Recorded (Various Versions)
Candide's Lament [lyric by Latouche]
The King's Barcarolle
Nothing More Than This [lyric by Bernstein]
Ringaroundarosie—cut
Universal Good [lyric by Bernstein and Lillian Hellman]
We Are Women [lyric by Bernstein]—written for 1959 London production
Westphalia Chorale [lyric by Bernstein]
Words, Words, Words (*Martin's Laughing Song*) [lyric by Bernstein]

The original CANDIDE had been unsuccessful in New York and London, and a 1971 full-scale revival had closed during its pre-Broadway tour. The remarkable score had always cried out for help, though; so when Harold Prince was asked to direct the piece, he brought along Sondheim, librettist Hugh Wheeler, and choreographer Pat Birch from A LITTLE NIGHT MUSIC [Sondheim: February 25, 1973]. They removed the costume operetta trappings which had smothered the original and moved somewhat closer to Voltaire. Acclaim in Brooklyn brought the new CANDIDE triumphantly to Broadway—where the costs were too high, the capacity too low, and the union musicians too many. Another failure, but a clear artistic success (although the musical elements of the show were reduced and somewhat undernourished). Director Prince revisited CANDIDE for the New York City Opera in 1982, amalgamating the material into a so-called "opera house version." More productions with more changes have come along since; most recently, an overblown Broadway revival—directed yet again by Prince, under the aegis of Livent—proved a quick flop. What is the best of all possible CANDIDEs? Hard to say; but the 1956 version still wins as the best of all possible CANDIDE scores.

BY BERNSTEIN
November 23, 1975
Chelsea Westside Theatre {Off Broadway} • 17 performances
New lyrics mostly by Bernstein; Conceived and Written by Betty Comden and Adolph Green; Directed by Michael Bawtree; Produced by Chelsea Theatre Center of Brooklyn; With Patricia Elliott, Kurt Peterson, and Janie Sell.

Recorded Songs
Ain't Got No Tears Left—based on theme from 1949 symphony *Age of Anxiety*
Another Love [lyric by Comden and Green]
It's Got to Be Good to Be Bad
Rio Bamba—based on *Danzon* from 1944 ballet *Fancy Free*

Lenny's friends Betty and Adolph compiled this poorly received revue, consisting of miscellaneous cut and never-performed Bernstein material.

1600 PENNSYLVANIA AVENUE
May 4, 1976
Mark Hellinger Theatre • 7 performances
Book and Lyrics by Alan Jay Lerner; Directed by Gilbert Moses; Choreographed by George Faison; Produced by Roger L. Stevens and Robert Whitehead; With Ken Howard, Patricia Routledge, Gilbert Price, and Emily Yancy.

Published Songs
Bright and Black
The President Jefferson Sunday Luncheon Party March—revised version of *Prefatory Prayers (Street Chorus)* from MASS [September 8, 1971]
Take Care of This House

Additional Songs Published in Vocal Selection
Pity the Poor
The Red White and Blues
Seena
We Must Have a Ball

Additional Songs Recorded
Duet for One (The First Lady of the Land)
Lud's Wedding

Bernstein returned to Broadway for the first time since WEST SIDE STORY [September 26, 1957] with this ill-conceived behemoth. The combination of Bernstein, Lerner, and the Bicentennial was enough to get the Coca-Cola Company to underwrite the entire production. Lerner, though, proved unable to turn the story of one hundred years upstairs and downstairs at the White House into a viable script. ON THE TOWN [December 28, 1944] and WEST SIDE had been close music/dance collaborations, with Jerome Robbins and discernible plots; WONDERFUL TOWN [February 25, 1953] had just been fast and funny. 1600 PENNSYLVANIA AVENUE was simply unworkable, with a fair amount of highly interesting music buried in the show's demise. There have been several unsuccessful attempts to rescue the material from oblivion, and parts of the score have been published or recorded. Still absent is the fascinating *Overture*, which also served as an 1812 mini-operetta as the British occupied Washington and set fire to the White House. It was that kind of evening.

THE MADWOMAN OF CENTRAL PARK WEST
June 13, 1979
22 Steps Theatre {Off Broadway} • 86 performances
Music mostly by others (also see Kander: June 13, 1979); Book by Phyllis Newman and Arthur Laurents; Directed by Arthur Laurents; Produced by Gladys Rackmil, Fritz Holt, and Barry M. Brown; With Phyllis Newman.

Song Published in Non-show Folio
My New Friends [lyric by Bernstein]

Additional Song Recorded
Up, Up, Up [lyric by Betty Comden and Adolph Green]

Bernstein contributed these songs to Phyllis (Mrs. Adolph Green) Newman's one-woman show.

A QUIET PLACE [1984]
July 22, 1984
Kennedy Center Opera House {Washington,
    D.C.} • 6 performances
Opera by Bernstein; Libretto by Stephen
Wadsworth (based on characters from
TROUBLE IN TAHITI [April 19, 1955]);
Directed by Stephen Wadsworth; Produced by
Houston Grand Opera, Kennedy Center, and
Teatro alla Scala; With Robert Galbraith,
Beverly Morgan, and Peter Kazaras.

Published Songs
None

Note: The complete vocal score is published.

A QUIET PLACE was a continuation of Bernstein's
1952 opera TROUBLE IN TAHITI. Following negative reactions to the piece in Houston, the two
operas—about succeeding generations of the
same family—were combined into a new version
for engagements at La Scala and Kennedy Center.
After a long and perhaps overly active career as
the world's most renowned music man of his time,
Bernstein suddenly announced his retirement at
the age of seventy-two. He died of a heart attack
five days later, on October 14, 1990.

Leonard Bernstein took time from his serious
music career to write just five book musicals
over forty-five busy years. Only two of these
are frequently performed: WEST SIDE STORY
[September 26, 1957] and (various versions of)
CANDIDE [December 1, 1956], but these scores
—along with ON THE TOWN [December 28,
1944]—were more than enough to earn Bernstein a reputation as one of America's leading
theatre composers.

FREDERICK LOEWE

Born: June 10, 1904, Berlin, Germany
Died: February 14, 1988, Palm Springs, California

FREDERICK LOEWE was the son of Austrian tenor Edmund Loewe, who created the role of Prince Danilo in the 1906 Berlin première of Lehar's DIE LUSTIGE WITWE† (THE MERRY WIDOW†). At the age of fifteen, Frederick wrote the European pop hit *Katrina*, which sold over a million copies. He determined upon a career in serious music, however, and studied piano and composition with Ferruccio Busoni (Kurt Weill's teacher). Arriving in America in 1924, Loewe was unable to succeed in music and went through a string of unlikely occupations, including prospecting, cowpoking, and professional boxing. In the mid-thirties he turned once again to songwriting.

PETTICOAT FEVER
March 4, 1935
Ritz Theatre • 137 performances
Play by Mark Reed; Directed by Alfred DeLiagre, Jr.; Produced by Richard Aldrich and DeLiagre, With Dennis King, Ona Munson, and Leo G. Carroll.

Published Song
Love Tiptoed through My Heart [lyric by Irene Alexander]

Former operetta star Dennis King was a Lambs' Club friend of Loewe's. He liked this song enough to interpolate it into his next play, resulting in Loewe's Broadway debut. (Loewe returned the favor, more or less, by giving King's son John Michael *On the Street Where You Live* to introduce in MY FAIR LADY [March 15, 1956].)

THE ILLUSTRATORS' SHOW
January 22, 1936
48th Street Theatre • 5 performances
Music and Lyrics mostly by others (see Loesser: January 22, 1936); Sketches by Max Liebman, Otto Soglow, and others; Directed by Allen Delano; Produced by Tom Weatherly and The Society of Illustrators.

Published Song
A Waltz Was Born in Vienna [lyric by Earle Crooker]—also used in SALUTE TO SPRING [June 12, 1937]

The short-lived ILLUSTRATORS' SHOW also marked Frank Loesser's Broadway debut. Loesser got a long-term Hollywood contract for his efforts; Loewe didn't.

SALUTE TO SPRING
[June 12, 1937]
Municipal Opera {St. Louis, Mo.} • Summer stock tryout
Book and Lyrics by Earle Crooker; Directed by Richard H. Berger; Produced by St. Louis Municipal Opera; With Guy Robertson, Berenice Claire, and Olive Olsen.

Published Songs
April Day
One Robin Doesn't Make a Spring—also used in LIFE OF THE PARTY [October 8, 1942]
Salute to Spring
Somehow—also used in LIFE OF THE PARTY
A Waltz Was Born in Vienna—originally used in THE ILLUSTRATORS' SHOW [January 22, 1936]

Loewe's first full musical score was for this out-door summer pageant.

GREAT LADY
December 1, 1938
Majestic Theatre • 20 performances
Lyrics by Earl Crooker; Book by Earl Crooker and Lowell Brentano; Directed by Bretaigne Windust; Produced by Dwight Deere Wiman and J. H. Del Bondio by arrangement with Frank Crumit; With Norma Terris, Irene Bordoni, Helen Ford, and Tullio Carminati.

Published Songs
I Have Room in My Heart
May I Suggest Romance?
There Had to Be the Waltz
Why Can't This Night Last Forever?

Dwight Deere Wiman, in the midst of his successful series of Rodgers and Hart musicals (see ON YOUR TOES [Rodgers: April 11, 1936]), produced this failed operetta. Heading the cast were leading ladies of SHOW BOAT [Kern: December 27, 1927], PARIS [Porter: October 8, 1928], and PEGGY-ANN [Rodgers: December 27, 1926]—with very little to sing about. Dancing in the chorus: twenty-year-old Jerome Robbins.

LIFE OF THE PARTY
October 8, 1942
Wilson Theatre {Detroit, Mich.} •
   Closed during tryout
Lyrics by Earle Crooker; Book by Alan Jay Lerner (based on *The Patsy* [play] by Barry Connors); Directed by Russell Filmore; Produced by Henry Duffy; With Dorothy Stone, Charles Collins, Charles Ruggles, and Margaret Dumont.

Published Songs
One Robin Doesn't Make a Spring—originally used in SALUTE TO SPRING [June 12, 1937]
Somehow—originally used in SALUTE TO SPRING

Henry Duffy successfully operated a number of stock companies on the West Coast beginning in the mid-twenties. Duffy first presented Fred

Stone's dancing daughter Dorothy (with husband Charles Collins) in PATRICIA, a non-Loewe musicalization of *The Patsy*. When Loewe and Crooker were hired to do a quick rewrite, the composer invited fellow Lambs' Club member Alan Jay Lerner—an aspiring lyricist/librettist recently out of Harvard—to patch together a new book. LIFE OF THE PARTY was quickly forgotten, but Lerner and Loewe decided to join together and write musicals.

WHAT'S UP?
November 11, 1943
National Theatre • 63 performances
"A Merry Musical." Lyrics by Alan Jay Lerner; Book by Arthur Pierson and Alan Jay Lerner; Staged and Choreographed by George Balanchine; Book directed by Robert H. Gordon; Produced by Mark Warnow; With Jimmy Savo, Johnny Morgan, Gloria Warren, and Pat Marshall.

Published Songs
Joshua
My Last Love
You Wash and I'll Dry
You've Got a Hold on Me

Lerner and Loewe's first Broadway effort was this poor wartime musical about aviators quarantined in a girls' boarding school. WHAT'S UP? marked George Balanchine's second and final directing attempt; the first had been the more successful CABIN IN THE SKY [Duke: October 25, 1940].

THE DAY BEFORE SPRING
November 22, 1945
National Theatre • 165 performances
Book and Lyrics by Alan Jay Lerner; Book Directed by Edward Padula; Staged and Produced by John C. Wilson; With Bill Johnson, Irene Manning, and Pat Marshall.

Published Songs
The Day before Spring
God's Green World
I Love You This Morning
A Jug of Wine
My Love Is a Married Man

This Is My Holiday
You Haven't Changed at All

This psychoanalytical fantasy received good reviews, but the run was disappointingly short, the show apparently too intellectual for wartime audiences. The oncoming talents of the songwriters are indicated in some of the songs, particularly *A Jug of Wine*, *God's Green World*, and the sweeping Viennese-American waltz *This Is My Holiday*.

BRIGADOON
March 13, 1947
Ziegfeld Theatre • 581 performances
Book and Lyrics by Alan Jay Lerner; Directed by Robert Lewis; Choreographed by Agnes de Mille; Produced by Cheryl Crawford; With David Brooks, Marion Bell, Pamela Britton, and James Mitchell.

Revival
October 16, 1980
Majestic Theatre • 134 performances
Directed by Vivian Matalon; Original choreography restaged by James Jamieson; With Martin Vidnovic [Brooks], Meg Bussert [Bell], and John Curry [Mitchell].

Published Songs
*Almost Like Being in Love
Brigadoon
Come to Me, Bend to Me
Down on MacConnachy Square
**From This Day On
*The Heather on the Hill
I'll Go Home with Bonnie Jean
The Love of My Life
My Mother's Wedding Day
**There but for You Go I
Waitin' for My Dearie

Additional Song Published in Vocal Selection
Jeannie's Packin' Up

Additional Songs Published in Vocal Score
The Chase
Funeral [instrumental]
Prologue (*Once in the Highlands*)
Sword Dance

Vendors' Calls
Wedding Dance [instrumental]

Lerner and Loewe's colorful fantasy of the Scottish Highlands was a surprise but welcome hit. The fine work of choreographer Agnes de Mille and the colorful physical production helped sustain the magical mood, but it was the remarkable score which supported the sentiment of the evening. The songs were literate yet emotional: popular hits like *Almost Like Being in Love* and *The Heather on the Hill*, as well as the exquisitely heartfelt *From This Day On* and *There but for You Go I*. It should be pointed out that the two hit musicals of that postwar season were both fantasies, normally an impossible musical comedy form: the escapist BRIGADOON, with its concentrated use of (but not reliance on) dance; and the longer-running (but more quickly dated) FINIAN'S RAINBOW [Lane: January 10, 1947], which used elfin charm, a similarly glorious score, and strong social satire.

PAINT YOUR WAGON
November 12, 1951
Shubert Theatre • 289 performances
Book and Lyrics by Alan Jay Lerner; Directed by Daniel Mann; Choreographed by Agnes de Mille; Produced by Cheryl Crawford; With James Barton, Olga San Juan, Tony Bavaar, and James Mitchell.

Published Songs
*Another Autumn
Cariño Mio
I'm on My Way
*I Still See Elisa
*I Talk to the Trees
Sh!—cut
*They Call the Wind Maria
Wand'rin' Star

Additional Songs Published in Vocal Score
All for Him
Hand Me down That Can o' Beans
How Can I Wait?
In Between
Lonely Men [instrumental]
Movin'
Rope Dance [instrumental]

Rumson Town
There's a Coach Comin' In
Trio (Mormons' Prayer)
What's Goin' on Here?
Whoop-ti-ay!

Loewe took a break from Lerner following the financial windfall of BRIGADOON [March 13, 1947]. The latter, meanwhile, wrote the unsuccessful LOVE LIFE [Weill: October 7, 1948] and the Oscar-winning screenplay for the highly successful 1951 movie *An American in Paris*. Lerner and Loewe reunited for PAINT YOUR WAGON, an ambitious but leaden saga of the California Gold Rush. The interwoven use of ballet that worked so well in the Highlands was less effective on the Prairies, and the subject matter was harsh and cold. In spite of the show's failure, Loewe displayed—as in all his major work—an uncanny ability to write scores indigenous to the time and locale of the characters and plots. Four of the songs are especially lovely; *I Talk to the Trees, They Call the Wind Maria, I Still See Elisa, and Another Autumn.*

MY FAIR LADY
March 15, 1956
Mark Hellinger Theatre • 2,717 performances
Book and Lyrics by Alan Jay Lerner (based on *Pygmalion* [play] by George Bernard Shaw); Directed by Moss Hart; Choreographed by Hanya Holm; Produced by Herman Levin; With Rex Harrison, Julie Andrews, Stanley Holloway, and Robert Coote.

Revivals
March 25, 1976
St. James Theatre • 377 performances
Orignal direction restaged by Jerry Adler; Original choreography restaged by Crandall Diehl; Produced by Herman Levin; With Ian Richardson [Harrison], Christine Andreas [Andrews], George Rose [Holloway], and Robert Coote.

August 18, 1981
Uris Theatre • 119 performances
Directed by Patrick Garland; Original choreography restaged by Crandall Diehl; With Rex Harrison, Nancy Ringham [Andrews], Milo O'Shea [Holloway], and Jack Gwillim [Coote].

December 9, 1993
Virginia Theatre • 165 performances
Directed by Howard Davies; Choreographed by Donald Saddler; With Richard Chamberlain [Harrison], Melissa Errico [Andrews], Julian Holloway [Holloway], and Paxton Whitehead [Coote].

Published Songs
Get Me to the Church on Time
*I Could Have Danced All Night
*I've Grown Accustomed to Her Face
Just You Wait ('enry 'iggins)
*On the Street Where You Live [2nd]—revised version of [1st]
The Rain in Spain [instrumental]
*The Rain in Spain [song version]
Say a Prayer for Me Tonight—cut; initial publication upon reuse in 1958 movie *Gigi*
Show Me
*Why Can't the English?
With a Little Bit of Luck
Without You
*Wouldn't It Be Loverly?

Additional Songs Published in Vocal Score
*Ascot Gavotte
The Embassy Waltz [instrumental]
A Hymn to Him (Why Can't a Woman Be More Like a Man?)
*I'm an Ordinary Man
Servants' Chorus
You Did It!

Additional Songs Recorded
Come to the Ball—cut
On the Street Where You Live [1st]—cut; original version

Lerner and Loewe's masterpiece broke the long-run record of OKLAHOMA! [Rodgers: March 31, 1943], back at a time when six-year runs were still unheard of. Shaw had ruled all his work off musical limits, having loathed THE CHOCOLATE SOLDIER[†] (the 1909 Oscar Straus operetta of *Arms and the Man*). But Shaw died in 1950, and *Pygmalion* went through several hands before Lerner and Loewe got the chance. Loewe wrote an intelligent and sweeping score, while Lerner wisely retained much of Shaw's sparkling language in the libretto and was able to deftly match the master's voice in the lyrics. The entire production enterprise was impeccable, the score containing no less than five ever-popular standards (although without the heart-filling emotional warmth of the music for BRIGADOON [March 13, 1947]). Lerner and Loewe seemed poised to overtake the faltering Rodgers and Hammerstein—although it turned out that the temperamental incompatibilities of the MY FAIR LADY boys were soon to scuttle the partnership.

CAMELOT
December 3, 1960
Majestic Theatre • 873 performances
Book and Lyrics by Alan Jay Lerner (based on *The Once and Future King* [book] by T. H. White); Directed by Moss Hart; Choreographed by Hanya Holm; Produced by Alan Jay Lerner, Loewe, and Moss Hart; With Richard Burton, Julie Andrews, Roddy McDowall, Robert Coote, and Robert Goulet.

Revivals
July 8, 1980
New York State Theatre • 56 performances
Directed by Frank Dunlop; Choreographed by Buddy Schwab; With Richard Burton, Christine Ebersole [Andrews], Richard Muenz [Goulet], and Paxton Whitehead [Coote].

November 15, 1981
Winter Garden Theatre • 48 performances
Directed by Frank Dunlop; Choreographed by Buddy Schwab; With Richard Harris [Burton], Meg Bussert [Andrews], Richard Muenz [Goulet], and Barrie Ingham [Coote].

June 21, 1993
Gershwin Theatre • 56 performances
Directed and Choreographed by Norbert Joerder; With Robert Goulet [Burton], Patricia Kies [Andrews], and James Valentine [Coote].

Published Songs
*Camelot
Follow Me
How to Handle a Woman
I Loved You Once in Silence
*If Ever I Would Leave You
The Lusty Month of May
The Simple Joys of Maidenhood
What Do the Simple Folk Do?

Additional Songs Published in Vocal Score
Before I Gaze at You Again
C'est Moi
The Enchanted Forest
Fie on Goodness
Guenevere
The Invisible Wall [instrumental]
I Wonder What the King Is Doing Tonight
The Jousts
Madrigal
The Persuasion
The Seven Deadly Virtues
Tent Scene [instrumental]
The Tumblers [instrumental]

Additional Songs Recorded
Then You May Take Me to the Fair—cut after opening, published in score (no lyric) as *Tent Scene and The Tumblers*

MY FAIR LADY [March 15, 1956] was followed by the Oscar-winning 1958 movie *Gigi*, after which Loewe suffered a massive heart attack. Lerner, Loewe, and Moss Hart then began work on the ill-fated CAMELOT, during the tryout of which Hart had a heart attack—causing his death within the year—and Lerner suffered a nervous breakdown. CAMELOT was poorly received but did considerably well, thanks to the strong advance sale built on MY FAIR LADY'S success and the popularity of the title song and *If Ever I Would Leave You*. Loewe's near-fatal illness and the stress caused by the collaborators' personal differences were enough to convince him to retire. In 1971 he briefly worked with Lerner on the score for the unsuccessful movie musical adaptation of Saint-Exupéry's *The Little Prince*. Lerner, for his part, went on to write another six musicals—all of which failed.

GIGI
November 13, 1973
Uris Theatre • 103 performances
Book and Lyrics by Alan Jay Lerner (based on the novel by Colette and the motion picture by Lerner and Loewe); Directed by Joseph Hardy; Choreographed by Onna White; Produced by Saint Subber and Edwin Lester (for the Los Angeles and San Francisco Light Opera

Company); With Alfred Drake, Agnes Moorehead, Maria Karnilova, and Daniel Massey.

Published Songs (Written for Movie Version)

*Gigi

*I'm Glad I'm Not Young Anymore

*I Remember It Well

*The Night They Invented Champagne

**She Is Not Thinking of Me (Waltz at Maxim's)

*Thank Heaven for Little Girls

New Songs Published in Vocal Selection

The Earth and Other Minor Things

In This Wide, Wide World

Paris Is Paris Again

Additional New Songs Published in Vocal Score

The Contract—revised version of À Toujours (cut) from motion picture version

I Never Want to Go Home Again

It's a Bore—originally used (unpublished) in motion picture version

The Telephone (Opening Act Two)

Loewe's final effort was this expanded stage version of the Oscar-winning 1958 Gigi. Inferior to the original, it quickly failed; ironically, inconsistencies in the Tony Award eligibility rules allowed GIGI to win that year's award for best score. Loewe retired to Palm Springs, where he remained until his death at eighty-three on February 14, 1988—outliving the hard-working, heavy-living Lerner, who died on June 14, 1986, at the age of sixty-eight.

Frederick Loewe's musicals were skillfully written, his music often deeply moving. All of his mature work, from BRIGADOON [March 13, 1947] on, is of consistently high quality and carefully, professionally crafted. Still, something keeps him out of the first rank of Broadway composers. By comparing him with contemporaries Frank Loesser and Jule Styne, I think I can pinpoint what's missing: the fun. Loewe was at least as strong as the others melodically, certainly; what's lacking is playfulness, joy, a sense of humor. Loewe nevertheless provided us with a trove of stunning songs—Almost Like Being in Love, The Heather on the Hill, From This Day On, There but for You Go I, I Talk to the Trees, I Still See Elisa, Another Autumn, If Ever I Would Leave You, and several from MY FAIR LADY and Gigi—and these titles, surely, speak for themselves.

JULE STYNE

Born: December 31, 1905, London, England
Died: September 20, 1994, New York, New York

JULE STYNE was born in the slums of London, son of a butter-and-egg man (and sometime wrestler). The family moved to Chicago in 1912, where Styne had a short career as a piano prodigy: a drill-press accident desensitized a finger, and the preteen switched from the concert hall to the burlesque pit. By the mid-1920s Styne was leading his own band on the South Side of Chicago and writing an occasional song as well, including the 1926 pop hit *Sunday* (words and music by Ned Miller, Chester Cohn, Jules Stein—the composer's real name—and Bennie Kruger). In 1934 Styne set up in New York as a vocal coach; four years later he was in Hollywood, working with major stars like Shirley Temple. By 1940 Styne was writing cowboy songs for B pictures. A short collaboration with lyricist Frank Loesser brought the 1941 hit *I Don't Want to Walk without You*, and Styne moved onto the Hollywood A-list.

ICE CAPADES OF 1942
[circa September 1941]
"The Magnificent Ice-travaganza." Music mostly by others; Produced by Arena Managers Association (John Harris); With Vera Hruba and Belita.

Published Song
Forever and Ever [music and lyric by Styne, Sol Meyer, and George Brown]

This ice show featured the Czech refugee skater Vera Hruba (Ralston), who looked a lot prettier than she skated (and she was pretty good on ice).

ICE CAPADES OF 1943
September 4, 1942
Madison Square Garden
"The Magnificent Ice-travaganza." Music mostly by others; Directed and Choreographed by Chester Hale; Produced by Arena Managers Association (John Harris); With Vera Hruba.

Published Song
The Guy with the Polka-Dot Tie [lyric by Sol Meyer]—see DARLING OF THE DAY [January 27, 1968]

Styne recalled a jaunty tune from his high school days—the first song he ever wrote, apparently—for this novelty number.

GLAD TO SEE YOU!
November 13, 1944
Shubert Theatre {Philadelphia} •
    Closed during tryout
Lyrics by Sammy Cahn; Book by Eddie Davis and Fred Thompson; Directed by Busby Berkeley; Produced by David Wolper; With Eddie Foy, Jr., Jane Withers, and June Knight.

Published Songs
Any Fool Can Fall in Love
Guess I'll Have to Hang My Tears out to Dry
I Don't Love You No More

In 1942 Styne began a hit-filled Hollywood collaboration with Sammy Cahn, bolstered by a close association with Frank Sinatra. Styne and Cahn made a brief visit to Broadway—or, rather, Philadelphia—with the dismal GLAD TO SEE YOU! Then it was quickly back to Hollywood, where they wrote *It's Been a Long, Long Time*.

Styne's non-show standards over the years included *I'll Walk Alone, I've Heard That Song Before, *Let It Snow, It's Magic, *Time after Time,* and **I Fall in Love Too Easily.*

HIGH BUTTON SHOES
October 9, 1947
Century Theatre • 727 performances
Lyrics by Sammy Cahn; Book by Stephen Longstreet (based on his novel *The Sisters Liked Them Handsome*); Directed by George Abbott; Choreographed by Jerome Robbins; Produced by Monte Proser and Joseph Kipness; With Phil Silvers, Nanette Fabray, Jack McCauley, Joey Faye, and Helen Gallagher.

Published Songs
Betwixt and Between—cut; for initial publication see GYPSY [May 21, 1959]
Can't You Just See Yourself?
Get Away for a Day in the Country
I Still Get Jealous
On a Sunday by the Sea
Papa, Won't You Dance with Me
There's Nothing Like a Model 'T'
You're My Girl

Additional Songs Recorded
**Bathing Beauty Ballet* [instrumental]
Bird Watcher's Song—cut
Nobody Ever Died for Dear Old Rutgers

Styne and Cahn gave Broadway another try, coming up with a rag-tag, long-running hit. The score was not very theatrical; more a collection of pop songs, two of which (*I Still Get Jealous* and *Papa, Won't You Dance with Me*) proved popular. Styne's outstanding contribution, rather surprisingly, was his spectacular comedic score for the *Bathing Beauty Ballet*. Styne and choreographer Jerome Robbins began a profitable association: Robbins was to direct six Broadway musicals, four of which had scores by Styne. George Abbott's musical comedy expertise, Phil Silvers's expert con-man, and the wonderful ballet made HIGH BUTTON SHOES fast and funny (if rather old fashioned). Styne—already forty-five years old, with dozens of lucrative Hollywood song hits to his credit—realized that the theatre was where he actually wanted to be.

GENTLEMEN PREFER BLONDES
December 8, 1949
Ziegfeld Theatre • 740 performances
Also see LORELEI [*January 27, 1974*]. Lyrics by Leo Robin; Book by Joseph Fields and Anita Loos (based on the novel by Anita Loos); Directed by John C. Wilson; Choreographed by Agnes de Mille; Produced by Herman Levin and Oliver Smith; With Carol Channing, Yvonne Adair, Jack McCauley, and George S. Irving.

Revival
April 10, 1985
Lyceum Theatre • 24 performances
Directed by Charles Repole; Choreographed by Michael Lichtefeld; Produced by National Actors Theatre; Transferred from Goodspeed Opera House; With KT Sullivan [Channing] and Karen Prunzik [Adair].

Published Songs
**Bye, Bye, Baby*
**Diamonds Are a Girl's Best Friend*
It's Delightful down in Chile
Just a Kiss Apart
**A Little Girl from Little Rock*
Sunshine
**You Say You Care*

Additional Songs Published in Vocal Selections
Coquette
Gentlemen Prefer Blondes
Homesick Blues
I Love What I'm Doing
I'm A'tingle, I'm Aglow
It's High Time
Keeping Cool with Coolidge
Mamie Is Mimi

Additional Songs Recorded
Button up with Esmond
Scherzo [instrumental]—see THE RED SHOES [December 16, 1993]

The bright and lively GENTLEMEN PREFER BLONDES was dominated by Carol Channing, who proved *Diamonds Are a Girl's Best Friend* as she portrayed *A Little Girl from Little Rock*. Styne's score also included a nice ballad, *Bye, Bye, Baby,* and the effective comedy duet *It's*

Delightful down in Chile. Styne's new lyricist was Leo Robin, who had HIT THE DECK [Youmans: April 25, 1927] and not very much else in his past; Sammy Cahn preferred to stay in Hollywood. With GENTLEMEN PREFER BLONDES a second consecutive hit, Styne remained in New York and set out to educate himself in the theatre.

MICHAEL TODD'S PEEP SHOW

June 28, 1950
Winter Garden Theatre • 278 performances
Music mostly by others (see Rome: June 28, 1950); Lyrics to Styne songs by Bob Hilliard; Sketches by Bobby Clark and others; Scenes directed by "Mr. R. Edwin Clark, Esq."; Directed by Hassard Short; Produced by Michael Todd; With Lina Romay, Clifford Guest, and Lilly Christine.

Published Songs
Francie—published in non-show edition
Stay with the Happy People—published in non-show edition

MAKE A WISH
See Martin: April 18, 1951.

TWO ON THE AISLE

July 19, 1951
Mark Hellinger Theatre • 276 performances
Sketches and Lyrics by Betty Comden and Adolph Green; Directed by Abe Burrows; Choreographed by Ted Cappy; Produced by Arthur Lesser; With Bert Lahr, Dolores Gray, Elliot Reid, and Colette Marchand.

Published Songs
Everlasting
Give a Little, Get a Little
Hold Me—Hold Me—Hold Me
How Will He Know?
So Far—So Good—cut; issued as professional copy; revised version of *Give Me a Song with a Beautiful Melody* from 1949 movie *It's a Great Feeling*
There Never Was Another Baby

Additional Songs Published in Vocal Selection
Catch Our Act at the Met—initial publication upon reuse in A PARTY WITH COMDEN AND GREEN [December 23, 1958]
If You Hadn't but You Did—initial publication upon reuse in A PARTY WITH COMDEN AND GREEN

Additional Songs Recorded
The Clown
Here She Comes Now
Show Train
Vaudeville Ain't Dead

Styne first collaborated with Comden and Green on this slapdash summer revue. The comic potential of their partnership was demonstrated by the rapid-fire *If You Hadn't but You Did*, the deliciously corny *Catch Our Act at the Met*, and the patter section of the opening number *Show Train*. Bert Lahr, Dolores Gray, and some good comedy sketches helped TWO ON THE AISLE to a respectable run.

HAZEL FLAGG

February 11, 1953
Mark Hellinger Theatre • 190 performances
Lyrics by Bob Hilliard; Book by Ben Hecht (based on "Letter to the Editor" [story] by James Street and *Nothing Sacred* [movie] by Ben Hecht); Directed by David Alexander; Choreographed by Robert Alton; Produced by Styne in association with Anthony Brady Farrell; With Helen Gallagher, Jack Whiting, Benay Venuta, and Thomas Mitchell.

Published Songs
Champagne and Wedding Cake—written for the 1954 movie version *Living It Up,*
Ev'ry Street's a Boulevard (In Old New York)—initial publication upon use in movie version
How Do You Speak to an Angel?
I Feel Like I'm Gonna Live Forever
Money Burns a Hole in My Pocket—added after opening; initial publication upon use in movie version
Salomee (With Her Seven Veils)

That's What I Like—written for movie version
Think How Many People Never Find Love—cut
You're Gonna Dance with Me, Willie

Additional Songs Recorded
Autograph Chant
Everybody Loves to Take a Bow
Hello, Hazel
I'm Glad I'm Leaving
Laura De Maupassant
A Little More Heart
Rutland Bounce [instrumental]
Who Is the Bravest?
The World Is Beautiful Today

With two quick hit shows to his credit, Styne determined to become a Broadway producer. His first show was a poorly produced mess of a failure, MAKE A WISH! [Martin: April 18, 1951]), which was followed by the highly successful revival [January 3, 1952] of PAL JOEY [Rodgers: December 25, 1940]. Styne determined to make a star out of Helen Gallagher, who had been prominent in HIGH BUTTON SHOES [October 9, 1947], MAKE A WISH!, and PAL JOEY (with a Tony Award). The vehicle built around her was weak, alas, and failed; Gallagher's career suffered, with her next big opportunity coming eighteen years later, when she won another Tony for the revival [January 19, 1971] of NO, NO, NANETTE [Youmans: September 16, 1925]. As for HAZEL FLAGG, the score is pleasant fun, with at least three worthwhile songs: the romantic ballad *How Do You Speak to an Angel?*, the frisky *I Feel Like I'm Gonna Live Forever*, and the nostalgic charmer *Ev'ry Street's a Boulevard* (*In Old New York*).

PETER PAN [1954]
October 20, 1954
Winter Garden Theatre • 149 performances
Music also by Moose Charlap; Lyrics also by Carolyn Leigh; Lyrics to Styne songs by Betty Comden and Adolph Green; Book adapted from *Peter Pan* [play] by James M. Barrie; Directed and Choreographed by Jerome Robbins; Produced by Richard Halliday and Edwin Lester; With Mary Martin, Cyril Ritchard, Margalo Gilmore, and Sondra Lee.

Revivals
September 6, 1979
Lunt-Fontanne Theatre • 550 performances
Directed and Choreographed by Rob Iscove; With Sandy Duncan [Martin] and George Rose [Ritchard].

December 13, 1990
Lunt-Fontanne Theatre • 45 performances
Directed by Fran Soeder; Choreographed by Marilyn Magness; With Cathy Rigby [Martin] and Stephen Hanan [Ritchard].

November 23, 1998
Marquis Theatre • 48 performances
Directed by Glenn Casale; Choreographed by Patti Colombo; With Cathy Rigby [Martin] and Paul Schoeffler [Ritchard].

Published Styne Songs
*Captain Hook's Waltz
Distant Melody
*Never Never Land
*Wendy

Additional Songs Written for (and Published in Vocal Selection of) 1974 "Arena Version"
Hook's Hook [music and lyric by Styne and Tom Adair]
Youth, Joy and Freedom [music and lyric by Styne and Adair]

Additional Songs Recorded
Oh My Mysterious Lady
Ugg-a-Wugg

The Mary Martin PETER PAN began as a summer presentation of Ed Lester's West Coast Civic Light Opera circuit. Martin returned in her first musical role since SOUTH PACIFIC [Rodgers: April 7, 1949], with Jerome Robbins serving as director (as well as choreographer) for the first time. The score, by theatre novices Moose Charlap and Carolyn Leigh, was weak, though, so Robbins called in Styne, Comden, and Green to revamp the show for Broadway. They did, contributing the effective theme song (*Never Never Land*), the felicitous *Wendy*, and the blimey, slimey *Captain Hook's Waltz*. (The Charlap/Leigh half of the score had its own highpoints, including *I've Gotta Crow, I Won't Grow Up, Tender Shepherd*, and *I'm Flyin'*.) The new, hybrid version proved effective, if understandably uneven, and played a successful four-month limited engagement. The show closed to allow a previously scheduled live television broadcast on March 7, 1955, which brought Mary Martin and PETER PAN and a real Broadway musical to children across the country. The show remains a favorite with family audiences, with Sandy Duncan scoring a notable success in the first Broadway revival. Styne, meanwhile, won an Oscar for the 1954 song *Three Coins in the Fountain* [lyric by Sammy Cahn].

MR. WONDERFUL
See Bock: March 22, 1956.

WAKE UP, DARLING
May 2, 1956
Ethel Barrymore Theatre • 5 performances
Play by Alec Gottlieb; Directed by Ezra Stone; Produced by Gordon W. Pollock in association with Lee Segall and Richard Cook; With Barry Nelson, Barbara Britton, Russell Nype, and Kay Medford.

Published Songs
None

The (bad) playwright in the (bad) play was writing a (bad) musical about the Civil War, so Styne and Leo Robin (of GENTLEMEN PREFER BLONDES [December 8, 1949]) provided a (good) parody of Southern songs entitled *L'il Ol' You and L'il Ol' Me.*

BELLS ARE RINGING
November 29, 1956
Shubert Theatre • 924 performances
Book and Lyrics by Betty Comden and Adolph Green; Directed by Jerome Robbins; Choreographed by Jerome Robbins and Bob Fosse; Produced by The Theatre Guild; With Judy Holliday, Sydney Chaplin, Jean Stapleton, Eddie Lawrence, and Peter Gennaro.

Published Songs
Bells Are Ringing
Better Than a Dream—written for 1960 movie version

Do It Yourself—written for movie version
Drop That Name
Hello, Hello There
I Met a Girl
Independent (On My Own)
*Just in Time
Long before I Knew You
Mu-cha-cha
**The Party's Over

Additional Songs Published in Vocal Score
*I'm Going Back
Is It a Crime?
It's a Perfect Relationship
It's a Simple Little System
The Midas Touch
Salzburg

Comden and Green's sometimes wild comic vision was perfect for this vehicle created for their former nightclub-act partner, Judy Holliday. The score was consistently good, including two pop standards (*Just in Time, The Party's Over*) and some very special special material (*I'm Going Back, It's a Simple Little System*). The whole production worked like a well-made George Abbott musical, which—with Abbott alumni Robbins, Fosse, Styne, Comden, and Green on hand—was not exactly surprising. Costarring was Sydney (son of Charles) Chaplin, not much of a singer but charming and handsome enough to star in two more Styne musicals. The composer used his vocal coach experience to fashion songs that even Chaplin could sing—like *Just in Time* (which is built pretty much on two notes) and *You Are Woman, I Am Man* (in FUNNY GIRL [March 26, 1964]).

SAY, DARLING
April 3, 1958
Anta Theatre • 332 performances
"A Play about a Musical." Lyrics by Betty Comden and Adolph Green; Book by Richard and Marian Bissell and Abe Burrows (based on the novel by Richard Bissell); Choreographed by Matt Mattox; Directed by Abe Burrows; Produced by Styne and Lester Osterman; With David Wayne, Vivian Blaine, Johnny Desmond, and Robert Morse.

Published Songs

Dance Only with Me
It's the Second Time You Meet That Matters
Let the Lower Lights Be Burning
My Little Yellow Dress—cut
Say, Darling—revised version of *Some Other Time* [lyric by Sammy Cahn] from 1944 movie *Step Lively*
Something's Always Happening on the River
Try to Love Me Just As I Am

Additional Songs Recorded

The Carnival Song
Chief of Love
The Husking Bee
It's Doom

Richard Bissell was a Dubuque-born, Harvard-educated former steamboat pilot who came to Broadway to adapt his first novel into THE PAJAMA GAME [Adler: May 13, 1954]. Bissell's book, *Say, Darling*, was a very funny "fictionalized" account of Bissell's adventures in musical comedy, complete with caricatures of Abbott, Adler, and producers Griffith and Prince. But the musical-comedy adaptation of the second novel, about the making of the musical-comedy adaptation of the first novel, wasn't as good as any of 'em. Styne, Comden, and Green's pastiche score was of little interest. The only true bright spot was young Robert Morse playing the affected-but-lovable boyish coproducer.

GYPSY

May 21, 1959
Broadway Theatre • 702 performances
Lyrics by Stephen Sondheim; Book by Arthur Laurents (based on the memoirs by Gypsy Rose Lee); Directed and Choreographed by Jerome Robbins; Produced by David Merrick and Leland Hayward; With Ethel Merman, Jack Klugman, Sandra Church, and Maria Karnilova.

Revivals
September 23, 1974
Winter Garden Theatre • 120 performances
Directed by Arthur Laurents; Choreography restaged by Robert Tucker; With Angela Lansbury [Merman], Rex Robbins [Klugman], and Zan Charisse [Church].

November 16, 1989
St. James Theatre • 476 performances
Directed by Arthur Laurents; Choreography restaged by Bonnie Walker; With Tyne Daly [Merman], Jonathan Hadary [Klugman], and Crista Moore [Church].

Published Songs

*All I Need Is the Girl
**Everything's Coming up Roses—revised version of *Betwixt and Between* (cut, unpublished) from HIGH BUTTON SHOES [October 9, 1947]
Let Me Entertain You
*Little Lamb
Mama's Talkin' Soft—cut
Mr. Goldstone
Small World
*Some People
Together Wherever We Go
*You'll Never Get Away from Me—revised version of *I'm in Pursuit of Happiness* from 1956 TV musical "Ruggles of Red Gap"

Additional Songs Published in Vocal Selection

*If Momma Was Married
*You Gotta Get a Gimmick

Additional Songs Published in Vocal Score

Baby June and Her Newsboys
Broadway
Extra! Extra!
Farm Sequence (*Caroline*)
*Rose's Turn

Additional Songs Recorded

Nice She Ain't—cut
Three Wishes for Christmas—cut

In 1957 producer David Merrick optioned Gypsy Rose Lee's memoirs and put Styne, Comden, and Green—fresh from BELLS ARE RINGING [November 29, 1956]—to work. They couldn't figure out how to do the adaptation, though, and withdrew. Merrick turned to librettist Arthur Laurents—fresh from WEST SIDE STORY [Bernstein: September 26, 1957]—who came up with the key to musicalizing Gypsy Rose Lee's autobiography: concentrating on the character of the monster-mother. Laurents brought in his WEST

SIDE STORY collaborators Robbins and Sondheim, the latter hoping to make his composing debut. But star Ethel Merman insisted on an experienced composer; she'd just done the wretched HAPPY HUNTING† [December 6, 1956] with untried songwriters Harold Karr and Matt Dubey. Cole Porter and Irving Berlin both turned GYPSY down, and the assignment finally found its way back to Styne (who had played pit piano in burlesque as a thirteen-year-old). Styne's talent and background were particularly suited to the material, and the combined Styne/Sondheim GYPSY ranks high among the theatre's very best. *Everything's Coming up Roses, Some People, Little Lamb, All I Need Is the Girl, You Gotta Get a Gimmick, Rose's Turn*—these are only a few high spots in the excellent score. The original production of GYPSY was somewhat overshadowed by the financial bonanza THE SOUND OF MUSIC [Rodgers: November 16, 1959] and the Pulitzer-winning FIORELLO! [Bock: November 23, 1959]. But GYPSY appreciation has grown over the years, with two smashingly successful revivals and a 1993 television version (starring, respectively, Angela Lansbury, Tyne Daly, and Bette Midler).

FREEDOMLAND, U.S.A.
[June 19, 1960]
Freedomland {Bronx}
"The World's Largest Outdoor Family Entertainment Center." Lyrics by George [David] Weiss; With Johnny Horton, Richard Hayes, Charlie Weaver and Earl Wrightson.

Published Song
Johnny Freedom

Additional Songs Published in Vocal Selection
The Chicago Fire
Danny the Dragon
The Jalopy Song
Little Old New York
On the Showboat
Pine Country
San Francisco Fran!
Satellite City
So Long Ma! (Headin' for New Orleans)

Freedomland—just minutes from the Bronx Zoo and Yankee Stadium—re-created "the most fa-mous actual and fictional events that represent Americana from its birth to its future" over eighty acres ("bigger than Disneyland"). Styne's songs were pre-recorded and piped in for the main attractions. Freedomland proved a mammoth failure. The site is now a gargantuan housing project, Co-op City.

DO RE MI
December 26, 1960
St. James Theatre • 400 performances
Lyrics by Betty Comden and Adolph Green; Book by Garson Kanin (based on his novella); Directed by Garson Kanin; Choreographed by Marc Breaux and Dee Dee Wood; Produced by David Merrick; With Phil Silvers, Nancy Walker, Nancy Dussault, John Reardon, and David Burns.

Published Songs
All You Need Is a Quarter
Asking for You
Cry Like the Wind
Fireworks
*Make Someone Happy
What's New at the Zoo?

Additional Songs Published in Vocal Score
Adventure
All of My Life
Ambition
He's a V.I.P.
I Know about Love
It's Legitimate
The Late, Late Show
Take a Job
Venezuela [instrumental with partial lyric]
Waiting
Who Is Mr. Big?

Additional Songs Recorded
Don't Be Ashamed of a Teardrop—cut; music only recorded
Life's Not Simple—cut

Styne reunited with Comden and Green for this comical musical comedy, which had a disappointing run despite clowns Silvers, Walker, and Dussault, good reviews, and the song hit *Make

Someone Happy. The score also included lots of fine comedy material like *Adventure*, *Ambition*, and *It's Legitimate*, as well as a delightfully hideous rock-and-roll pastiche, *What's New at the Zoo?* DO RE MI was also the show in which expressionistic designer Boris Aronson began his drive to change the way Broadway musicals looked. For this pop music business satire, he designed a spectacular show curtain consisting of stage-to-ceiling jukeboxes, wired for neon and sound.

SUBWAYS ARE FOR SLEEPING
December 27, 1961
St. James Theatre • 205 performances
Book and Lyrics by Betty Comden and Adolph Green (based on stories by Edmund G. Love); Directed and Choreographed by Michael Kidd; Produced by David Merrick; With Sydney Chaplin, Carol Lawrence, Orson Bean, and Phyllis Newman (Green).

Published Songs
Be a Santa
*Comes Once in a Lifetime
How Can You Describe a Face?
I'm Just Taking My Time
Who Knows What Might Have Been?

Additional Songs Recorded
Getting Married—cut
Girls Like Me
I Just Can't Wait
I Said It and I'm Glad
I Was a Shoo-In
Let's Talk—cut
Now I Have Someone—cut
Ride through the Night
Strange Duet—see DARLING OF THE DAY [January 27, 1968]
Subway Directions
Subways Are for Sleeping
Swing Your Projects
What Is This Feeling in the Air?

Producer David Merrick pulled the publicity coup of his distinguished career in support of SUBWAYS, which needed all the help it could get. Using gentlemen with names legitimately identical to the most powerful drama critics of the day, he composed the full-page quote ad of everyone's dreams: "No doubt about it—SUBWAYS ARE FOR SLEEPING is the best musical of the century! . . . John Chapman." In order to pull this off, Merrick had to wait for Brooks Atkinson to retire—there was only one Brooks Atkinson in the phone book. Then he had to wait for a big-budget show sure to get dismal reviews. "One of the few great musicals of the last thirty years," said Merrick's Howard Taubman, while Taubman of the *Times* called SUBWAYS "dull and vapid." Photographs accompanying the seven-out-of-seven raves indicate that in a liberal (for 1961) move, Merrick chose to include a Mr. Richard Watts from Harlem. All this in service of a sub-standard 1950s-era musical. The score was somewhat better than the rest of the show, with a nice comic production number, *Be a Santa*; the comic tour-de-force *I Was a Shoo-In*, which won a Tony Award for Adolph's wife Phyllis; and a fine Styne show tune, the jaunty *Comes Once in a Lifetime*.

ARTURO UI
November 11, 1963
Lunt-Fontanne Theatre • 8 performances
Play by Bertolt Brecht; Adapted by George Tabori; Incidental music by Jule Styne; Directed by Tony Richardson; Produced by David Merrick; With Christopher Plummer, Lionel Stander, Murvyn Vye, and Madeleine Sherwood.

Song Recorded
Opening Sequence [instrumental]

Styne supplied a barrel-house jazz accompaniment to director Tony Richardson's view of Hitler-as-Capone in prohibition Chicago. (In 1927, Capone asked if he could lead Styne's orchestra in *Rhapsody in Blue*. Styne said sure.)

FUNNY GIRL
March 26, 1964
Winter Garden Theatre • 1,348 performances
Lyrics by Bob Merrill; Book by Isobel Lennart (based on a story by Isobel Lennart and the life of Fanny Brice); Production supervised by Jerome Robbins; Directed by

Garson Kanin; Choreographed by Carol Haney; Produced by Ray Stark; With Barbra Streisand, Sydney Chaplin, Kay Medford, and Jean Stapleton.

Published Songs

*Don't Rain on My Parade
Funny Girl*—cut; published in standard edition
His Love Makes Me Beautiful—initial individual publication upon use in 1968 version
I'm the Greatest Star—initial individual publication upon use in movie version
**The Music That Makes Me Dance
**People
Who Are You Now?
You Are Woman, I Am Man
You're a Funny Girl—written for movie version

Additional Songs Published in Vocal Selection

Cornet Man
Henry Street
I Want to Be Seen with You Tonight
Individual Thing—cut; for initial publication see PRETTYBELLE [February 1, 1971]

Additional Songs Published in Vocal Score

Downtown Rag [instrumental]
Find Yourself a Man
If a Girl Isn't Pretty
Private Schwartz
Rat-Tat-Tat-Tat
Sadie, Sadie
Who Taught Her Everything

Additional Songs Recorded

Absent Minded Me—cut
The Baltimore Sun—cut
Do Puppies Go to Heaven?—cut
He's Got Larceny in His Heart—cut
I Did It on Roller Skates—cut
It's Home—cut
My Daughter Fanny, the Star—cut
Racing Form Lullaby—cut
Roller Skate Rag—cut; initial recording upon use in movie version
A Temporary Arrangement—cut

What started as Mary Martin's follow-up to THE SOUND OF MUSIC [Rodgers: November 16, 1959] traveled a particularly tortuous path before finally arriving as the hit which made Barbra Streisand a star. (Or was it Streisand who made FUNNY GIRL?) Mary Martin suggested the project to Hollywood producer (and Fanny Brice's son-in-law) Ray Stark. Stark brought the show to David Merrick, his coproducer on the 1958 play The World of Suzie Wong. Merrick assembled his GYPSY [May 21, 1959] team of Styne, Sondheim, and Robbins. Mary Martin realized she wasn't exactly particularly quite right to play Fanny Brice; she moved on instead to Laurette Taylor (see JENNIE [Schwartz: October 17, 1963]). Sondheim bowed out, and Bob Merrill (from Merrick's CARNIVAL! [Merrill: April 13, 1961]) signed on as lyricist. Barbra Streisand (from Merrick's I CAN GET IT FOR YOU WHOLESALE [Rome: March 22, 1962]) became Fanny Brice, and everything was ready. Then Robbins quit. Bob Fosse came in, Bob Fosse went out. Garson Kanin (from Merrick's DO RE MI [December 26, 1960]) came in and FUNNY GIRL breezed into rehearsal. Without David Merrick, who grew tired of it all and withdrew shortly before the beginning of rehearsals. (Besides, he had HELLO, DOLLY! [Herman: January 16, 1964] to keep him busy.) Tryout troubles unexpectedly (?) arose, and Stark replaced Kanin with—Jerome Robbins again, who managed to pull FUNNY GIRL into presentable if unexceptional shape. Styne's work was good, though the score ultimately seemed to be a string of solos for the star. (This is okay, I guess, if you happen to have Barbra Streisand.) Don't Rain on My Parade, I'm the Greatest Star, and the extra special The Music That Makes Me Dance were particularly effective, both musically and dramatically. And Streisand sang People, too.

WONDERWORLD

May 7, 1964
World's Fair Amphitheatre-in-the-Lake • 250 performances
Lyrics by Stanley Styne; Choreographed by Michael Kidd; Conceived and Directed by Leon Leonidoff; With Chita Rivera and Gretchen Wyler.

Published Song

Wonderworld

Additional Song Recorded
Welcome

This twenty-eight-show-a-week spectacle—at the old Billy Rose *Aquacade* arena—closed with debts of two-and-a-half million dollars. Styne collaborated on the score with his son Stanley.

FADE OUT—FADE IN
May 26, 1964
Mark Hellinger Theatre • 199 performances
Book and Lyrics by Betty Comden and Adolph Green; Directed by George Abbott; Choreographed by Ernest Flatt; Produced by Lester Osterman and Jule Styne; With Carol Burnett, Jack Cassidy, Lou Jacobi, and Tiger Haynes.

Published Songs
Fade Out—Fade In
I'm with You
*You Mustn't Feel Discouraged

Additional Songs Published in Vocal Selection
Call Me Savage—see HALLELUJAH, BABY! [April 26, 1967]
Go Home Train
It's Good to Be Back Home
The Usher from the Mezzanine

Additional Songs Recorded
Close Harmony
The Dangerous Age
Fear
The Fiddler and the Fighter
Lila Tremaine
L. Z. in Quest of His Youth [ballet]
My Fortune Is My Face
My Heart Is Like a Violin
Oh Those Thirties

ABC-Paramount saw fit to invest three million musical-producing dollars with producers Lester Osterman and Jule Styne, despite their track record of MR. WONDERFUL [Bock: March 22, 1956], SAY, DARLING [April 3, 1958] and FIRST IMPRESSIONS [March 19, 1959]). The money went to produce HIGH SPIRITS [Martin: April 7, 1964], FADE OUT—FADE IN, and Sammy Fain's SOMETHING MORE [November 5, 1964] (the last directed by Styne himself). After which ABC-Paramount—and Styne—reassessed their

Broadway producing careers. FADE OUT—FADE IN featured a live seal and did very well until Carol Burnett became "indisposed," as they say. The music was lively and perky (as were most Styne scores), with undistinguished but enjoyable songs like *Call Me Savage* and *Go Home Train*. The best number: Burnett playing Shirley Temple—Styne's vexation in his days as a Hollywood vocal coaching days—to Tiger Haynes's Bill Robinson in *You Mustn't Feel Discouraged*. While awaiting production of his much-delayed next project, Styne collaborated with Bob Merrill on the 1965 Cyril Ritchard/Liza Minnelli TV musical "The Dangerous Christmas of Little Red Riding Hood." The score included two rather good songs, **My Red Riding Hood* and *Ding-a-Ling, Ding-a-Ling.*

HALLELUJAH, BABY!
April 26, 1967
Martin Beck Theatre • 293 performances
Lyrics by Betty Comden and Adolph Green; Book by Arthur Laurents; Directed by Burt Shevelove; Choreographed by Kevin Carlisle; Produced by Albert W. Selden and Hal James, Jane C. Nusbaum, and Harry Rigby; With Leslie Uggams, Robert Hooks, Allen Case, and Lillian Hayman.

Published Songs
*Being Good Isn't Good Enough
*Hallelujah, Baby!
*My Own Morning
*Not Mine—see BAR MITZVAH BOY [October 31, 1978]
Now's the Time
Talking to Yourself
When the Weather's Better—cut

Additional Song Published in Vocal Selection
I Wanted to Change Him

Additional Songs Recorded
Another Day
Big Talk—cut
Feet Do Yo' Stuff
I Don't Know Where She Got It
The Slice
*Smile, Smile

Ugly, Ugly Gal—cut; see ONE NIGHT STAND
[October 20, 1980]
Watch My Dust
Witches' Brew—revised version of *Call Me
Savage* from FADE OUT—FADE IN [May
26, 1964]

Styne, composer of BELLS ARE RINGING [November 29, 1956] and GYPSY [May 21, 1959], finally received a Tony Award for this unsuccessful musical (which had long since closed). An unclear—or maybe just poorly executed—concept and a jumbled book made for confusion; racial tensions between cast and staff didn't help, and a better-than-average score wasn't enough. Styne provided a couple of moodily introspective ballads (*Being Good Isn't Good Enough, Not Mine*), some good comedy material (*Smile, Smile, I Don't Know Where She Got It*), and a strongly revivalist title song. Lost in the shuffle: the rhythmic *When the Weather's Better*. Leslie Uggams—in a role intended for Lena Horne—gave a strong performance, and Lillian Hayman was an unforgettable treasure.

DARLING OF THE DAY
January 27, 1968
George Abbott Theatre • 32 performances
Lyrics by E. Y. Harburg; Book by Nunnally
Johnson (credit removed) (based on *Buried
Alive* [novel] and *The Great Adventure* [play]
by Arnold Bennett); Directed by Noel
Willman; Choreographed by Lee Becker
Theodore; Produced by The Theatre Guild and
Joel Schenker; With Vincent Price, Patricia
Routledge, Brenda Forbes, and Teddy Green.

Published Songs
I've Got a Rainbow Working for Me
*It's Enough to Make a Lady Fall in Love—
revised version of *The Guy with the Polka-
Dot Tie* from ICE CAPADES OF 1943
[September 4, 1942]
*Let's See What Happens
*Not on Your Nellie
Under the Sunset Tree

Additional Songs Recorded
A Blushing Bride—cut
Butler in the Abbey
A Gentleman's Gentleman

He's a Genius
Money, Money, Money
Panache
Putney on the Thames—cut; revised version of
Strange Duet from SUBWAYS ARE FOR
SLEEPING [December 27, 1961]
*That Something Extra Special
That Stranger in Your Arms—cut
To Get out of This World Alive
What Makes a Marriage Merry?

It is always a bad sign when a show reaches Broadway with no book writer credited. DARLING OF THE DAY went through five librettists, four directors, and two choreographers before limping into town, a clear sign of ineffective producing. The score, though, was a delight. Styne returned to his roots—turn-of-the-century London—with panache, while Yip Harburg's lyrics are second only to his set for FINIAN'S RAINBOW [Lane: March 13, 1947]. Standing out among the score were the lovely ballad *That Something Extra Special*, the gentle waltz *Let's See What Happens*, and the endearing schottische *It's Enough to Make a Lady Fall in Love* (with Harburg's talk of "the stork of Damocles"). The lack of interest engendered by Vincent Price (playing the title role) ruined the little chance DARLING OF THE DAY might have had under its ill-fated star. Patricia Routledge was superhuman in her efforts and became the only foreign-born, unknown-to-Broadway nonstar ever to make her musical debut in a short-run flop and win the Best Actress Tony Award anyway (with thanks due her knockout production number *Not on Your Nellie*). DARLING OF THE DAY was based on Arnold Bennett's novel *Buried Alive*, which proved a fitting epitaph.

LOOK TO THE LILIES
March 29, 1970
Lunt-Fontanne Theatre • 25 performances
Lyrics by Sammy Cahn; Book by Leonard
Spigelgass (based on *Lilies of the Field* [novel]
by William Barrett); Directed by Joshua
Logan; Produced by Edgar Lansbury, Max
Brown, Richard Lewine, and Ralph Nelson;
With Shirley Booth, Al Freeman, Jr., Taina
Elg, and Carmen Alvarez.

Songs Issued as Professional Copies
I'd Sure Like to Give It a Shot
Kick the Door—cut; see ONE NIGHT STAND
[October 20, 1980]

Additional Songs Published in Vocal Selection
Follow the Lamb!
I! Yes, Me! That's Who!—see THE RED
SHOES [December 16, 1993]
Look to the Lilies
One Little Brick at a Time
Some Kind of Man
There Comes a Time

Additional Song Recorded
First Class Number One Bum

Styne reunited with his early lyricist Sammy Cahn (of HIGH BUTTON SHOES [October 9, 1947]) for this attempt at social relevance. Cahn had already returned to Broadway with a couple of flops, SKYSCRAPER† [November 13, 1965] and WALKING HAPPY† [November 26, 1966] (both with music by Jimmy Van Heusen). LOOK TO THE LILIES was even worse, with the songwriters making a rather pitiful attempt at a contemporary sound. Even the always interesting Shirley Booth, in her final musical, was uninteresting.

PRETTYBELLE
February 1, 1971
Shubert Theatre {Boston} •
    Closed during tryout
Book and Lyrics by Bob Merrill (based on the novel by Jean Arnold); Directed and Choreographed by Gower Champion; Produced by Alexander H. Cohen; With Angela Lansbury, Jon Cypher, Mark Dawson, Peter Lombard, and Charlotte Rae.

Songs Issued as Professional Copies
How Could I Know?
To a Small Degree

Additional Songs Published in Vocal Selection
I Met a Man
I'm in a Tree
Individual Thing—initial publication of song
cut from FUNNY GIRL [March 26, 1964]

Prettybelle
When I'm Drunk I'm Beautiful

Additional Songs Recorded
Back from the Great Beyond
God's Garden
I Never Did Imagine
In the Japanese Gardens
Manic Depressives
The No-Tell Motel
You Ain't Hurtin' Your Ole Lady None
You Never Looked Better

Styne followed his blandest musical—LOOK TO THE LILIES [March 29, 1970]—with his biggest disaster. PRETTYBELLE had its work cut out for it, being "a lively tale of rape and resurrection" about an alcoholic manic depressive nymphomaniac. Producer Alexander H. Cohen assembled one of his typical theatre party specials certain to attract easy financing and large advance sales, with an assemblage of star names: director of HELLO, DOLLY! [Herman: January 16, 1964], composer of GYPSY [May 21, 1959], lyricist of FUNNY GIRL, star of MAME [Herman: May 24, 1966]. All of whom were more recently coming off enormous flops, as director of THE HAPPY TIME [Kander: January 18, 1968], composer of LOOK TO THE LILIES, lyricist of BREAKFAST AT TIFFANY'S [Merrill: December 14, 1966], star of DEAR WORLD [Herman: February 6, 1969]. I am told by eyewitnesses that PRETTYBELLE was rather fascinating, in its way, and the score is not uninteresting (with melodic songs like *God's Garden, Individual Thing*, and the title number). But PRETTYBELLE's subject matter foretold its doom.

SUGAR
April 9, 1972
Majestic Theatre • 505 performances
Lyrics by Bob Merrill; Book by Peter Stone (based on *Some Like It Hot* [movie] by Billy Wilder and I. A. L. Diamond); Directed and Choreographed by Gower Champion; Produced by David Merrick; With Robert Morse, Tony Roberts, Cyril Ritchard, and Elaine Joyce.

Published Song
(Doing It For) Sugar

Additional Songs Recorded

All You Gotta Do Is Tell Me—cut
Beautiful Through and Through
The Beauty That Drives Men Mad
Hey, Why Not!
I'm Naïve—added to 1973 tour; revised lyric
    for song from the 1965 TV musical "The
    Dangerous Christmas of Red Riding Hood"
It's Always Love
Lament for Ten Men [music and lyric by
    Merrill]—added to London production,
    retitled SOME LIKE IT HOT [March 19,
    1992]; originally used in BREAKFAST AT
    TIFFANY'S [Merrill: December 14, 1966]
Magic Nights
Nice Ways—cut
November Song (*Even Dirty Old Men Need Love*)
Penniless Bums
The People in Your Life—cut; revised from
    Look at You, Look at Me [music by Styne,
    lyric by Frank Loesser] from 1941 movie
    Sis Hopkins
Some Like It Hot—added to London production
Sun on My Face—different song than *Sun on
    Your Face* (cut)
Sun on Your Face—cut; different song than
    Sun on My Face
We Could Be Close
*What Do You Give to a Man Who's Had
    Everything?*
When You Meet a Man in Chicago

Producer David Merrick took Billy Wilder's great 1960 film *The Apartment* and turned it into the hit musical PROMISES, PROMISES [Notables: December 1, 1968]. Why not try the same with Wilder's even better 1959 classic *Some Like it Hot?* Well, it's not so easy. SUGAR underwent a number of twists and turns and authors along the way, starting with the HELLO, DOLLY! [Herman: January 16, 1964] team of Jerry Herman and Michael Stewart. Styne himself knew a thing or two about the subject matter: he had been a bandleader in Prohibition Chicago (see ARTURO UI [November 11, 1963]). But SUGAR was a directionless mess. The score was bafflingly uneven, with some fairly entertaining songs (*Penniless Bums, The Beauty That Drives Men Mad, Hey, Why Not!, Doing It for Sugar*) in the first act and some rather atrocious ones in the second. This can happen

when a show undergoes extensive second act rewrites with the songwriters locked out of rehearsals by the director. (Champion, Styne, and Merrill had just come off PRETTYBELLE [February 1, 1971], which was perhaps not a good omen.) Even so, Bobby Morse's performance of *We Could Be Close* was well worth the price of admission (SUGAR opened with a record-high $15 top). The show was ill-advisedly resuscitated twenty years later for London as SOME LIKE IT HOT [March 19, 1992], with Tommy Steele directing as well as playing the Tony Curtis role.

LORELEI, OR "GENTLEMEN STILL PREFER BLONDES"

January 27, 1974
Palace Theatre • 320 performances
Also see GENTLEMEN PREFER BLONDES [*December 8, 1949*]. New lyrics by Betty Comden and Adolph Green; New book material by Kenny Solms and Gail Parent (based on GENTLEMEN PREFER BLONDES); Directed by Robert Moore; Choreographed by Ernest Flatt; Produced by Lee Guber and Shelly Gross; With Carol Channing, Dody Goodman, Tamara Long, and Peter Palmer.

Published New Songs

I Won't Let You Get Away
Lorelei [1st]—cut
Men!

Additional Songs Recorded

Looking Back
Lorelei [2nd]
Paris, Paris [lyric by Comden, Green, and
    Robin]—cut; revised version of *Sunshine*
    from GENTLEMEN PREFER BLONDES

With a lack of suitable new properties for surefire box office draw Carol Channing, an attempt was made to give Lorelei Lee a facelift. Outfitted with new material and a streamlined book, the charmingly old-fashioned original was destroyed. LORELEI preceded its Broadway run with a year-long troubled tryout tour, initially under the helm of director/choreographer Joe Layton.

HELLZAPOPPIN'!

November 22, 1976

Mechanic Theatre {Baltimore, Md.} •
 Closed during tryout

Music also by Hank Beebe and Cy Coleman (see Coleman: November 22, 1976); Lyrics by Carolyn Leigh and Bill Heyer; Book by Abe Burrows and others (based on a format by Olsen and Johnson); Directed by Jerry Adler; Choreographed by Donald Saddler; Produced by Alexander H. Cohen in association with Maggie and Jerome Minskoff; With Jerry Lewis, Lynn Redgrave, Joey Faye, and Brandon Maggart.

Styne/Leigh Songs Recorded

Hellzapoppin'
Only One to a Customer

Alexander H. Cohen's second attempt to revamp the 1,404-performance Olsen-and-Johnson original [September 22, 1938] died aborning. An earlier version, which premièred (and died) at Expo '67 in Montreal, starred TV pie-in-the-face comedian Soupy Sales.

BAR MITZVAH BOY

October 31, 1978

Her Majesty's Theatre {London} •
 77 performances

Lyrics by Don Black; Book by Jack Rosenthal (based on his teleplay); Directed by Martin Charnin; Choreographed by Peter Gennaro; Produced by Peter Witt; With Joyce Blair, Harry Towb, and Barry Angel.

Revival

May 9, 1987

American Jewish Theatre {Off Off
 Broadway} • 17 performances

American adaptation by Martin Gottfried; Directed by Robert Kalfin; With Mary Gutzi [Blair] and Michael Callan [Towb].

Songs Recorded

The Bar Mitzvah of Eliot Green
*The Harolds of This World—revised version
 of *Not Mine* from HALLELUJAH, BABY!
 [April 26, 1967]
I've Just Begun
If Only a Little Bit Sticks

Rita's Request
Simchas
*The Sun Shines out of Your Eyes
This Time Tomorrow
Thou Shalt Not
*We've Done Alright
*Where Is the Music Coming From?
Why?
*You Wouldn't Be You

Styne went back home to England to write BAR MITZVAH BOY, a quickly forgotten and unlamented failure. But this is one of Styne's better scores, with no less than five tender and lovely songs: *Where Is the Music Coming From?*, *The Harolds of This World*, *The Sun Shines out of Your Eyes*, *We've Done Alright*, and *You Wouldn't Be You*. And then there were good rhythm songs, comedy songs, etc. Not a great score, certainly, and certainly a poor show; but BAR MITZVAH BOY showed that the seventy-two year old Styne could still write a song with a beautiful melody. A poor American production was attempted Off Off Broadway in 1987 but received scant notice.

ONE NIGHT STAND

October 20, 1980

Nederlander Theatre •
 Closed during previews

Book and Lyrics by Herb Gardner; Directed by John Dexter; Choreographed by Peter Gennaro; Produced by Joseph Kipness, Lester Osterman, Joan Cullman, James M. Nederlander, and Alfred Taubman; With Jack Weston, Charles Kimbrough, and Catherine Cox.

Songs Recorded

Don't Kick My Dreams Around
For You—revised version of *Kick the Door* (cut)
 from LOOK TO THE LILIES [March 29, 1970]
Go out Big
Here Comes Never
I'm Writing a Love Song for You
Let Me Hear You Love Me
A Little Travellin' Music Please
Long Way from Home
Somebody Stole My Kazoo
Someday Soon—revised version of *Ugly, Ugly
 Gal* (cut) from HALLELUJAH, BABY!
 [April 26, 1967]

There Was a Time
*Too Old to Be So Young

Styne returned with his first new Broadway musical to open since SUGAR [April 9, 1972]. Well, not open; ONE NIGHT STAND closed after eight previews. This strange project about a composer planning his suicide was underwritten and undeveloped. Lyricist/librettist Herb Gardner was an award-winning playwright who'd never written lyrics or libretto, director John Dexter was also inexpert at musical theatre. Both of them had outsized egos, both disagreed on everything, neither could be fired. So much for ONE NIGHT STAND, although Styne wrote one good song, his last: the jazzy *Too Old to Be So Young*.

PIECES OF EIGHT

November 27, 1985
Citadel Theatre {Edmonton, Canada} •
    Regional tryout
Lyrics by Susan Birkenhead; Book by Michael Stewart and Mark Bramble (based on *Treasure Island* [novel] by Robert Louis Stevenson); Directed and Choreographed by Joe Layton; Produced by Citadel Theatre and the Edmonton Journal; With George Hearn, George Lee Andrews, Graeme Campbell, and Jonathan Ross.

Published Songs
None

An old-fashioned *Treasure Island*, without that extra-added dimension which made hits of OLIVER! [January 6, 1963] and Styne's own PETER PAN [October 20, 1954]. PIECES OF EIGHT—which, as TREASURE ISLAND, had previously been announced for Broadway by both Harry Rigby and David Merrick—disappeared after its six-week Canadian tryout.

THE RED SHOES

December 16, 1993
Gershwin Theatre • 5 performances
Lyrics by Marsha Norman and Paul Stryker (a.k.a. Bob Merrill); Book by Marsha Norman (based on the movie by Emeric Pressburger

and Michael Powell); Directed by Stanley Donen; Choreographed by Lar Lubovitch; Produced by Martin Starger in association with MCA/Universal and James M. Nederlander; With Steve Barton, Margaret Illman, Hugh Panaro, and George De La Peña.

Songs Recorded
My Reason for Being—new lyric for *I! Yes, Me! That's Who!* from LOOK TO THE LILIES [March 29, 1970]; recorded [no lyrics] as *Melody from "The Red Shoes"*
Red Shoes Ballet [instrumental]
When It Happens to You [lyric by Stryker (Merrill)]

Jule Styne apparently saw the long-in-developing RED SHOES as a new kind of challenge, with the score meant to incorporate large stretches of ballet as in ON THE TOWN [Bernstein: December 28, 1944] and WEST SIDE STORY [Bernstein: September 26, 1957]. Styne—who had done five shows with Jerry Robbins—was presumably inspired and rejuvenated by the reception accorded his *Bathing Beauty Ballet* (originally from HIGH BUTTON SHOES [October 9, 1947]) in the anthology revue JEROME ROBBINS' BROADWAY [February 26, 1989]. But THE RED SHOES was not to be HIGH BUTTON SHOES; more like Low Button Shoes (or No Button Shoes). The famously energetic Styne was eighty-eight tired years old. His final score consisted of half-remembered tunes from HAZEL FLAGG [February 11, 1953], LOOK TO THE LILIES, and elsewhere; the climactic *Red Shoes Ballet* was merely a retread of a dance specialty (*Scherzo*) from GENTLEMEN PREFER BLONDES. If Styne was tired, his final vehicle was amateurishly assembled. After discarding Styne's initial collaborators, the producer snapped up the lyricist/librettist and director of THE SECRET GARDEN [Notables: April 25, 1991]. Marsha Norman and Susan H. Schulman had given that show a refreshingly revolutionary point of view (i.e., girls are not automatically inferior to boys). The grafting of a similar sensibility on THE RED SHOES exploded into a generational battle of the sexes, with the rich old white men winning (but losing). The fortyish Schulman was fired, replaced by the seventyish Broadway novice Stanley Donen. The fortyish Norman and her libretto were not so expendable, but sixtyish producer Starger brought in seventy-three-year-old Bob Merrill to rework the lyrics. Styne's collaborator from FUNNY GIRL [March 26, 1964] knew enough to keep his name off the show—hence "Paul Stryker"—and stayed far away, faxing in his contributions from California. (When Styne went to Republic Pictures to write cowboy songs in 1941, the studio wanted him to change his name to something less ethnic and more suitable for assignments like *I Love Watermelon*, sung by Roy Rogers. A neutral, American name like Paul Stryker, they suggested. Jule Styne—who as a beginner had been "persuaded" to change his name from Jules Stein, to avoid confusion with the powerful agent of the same name—refused, but remembered Paul Stryker fifty years later.) THE RED SHOES inevitably failed, setting a new Broadway record with a loss in the eight million dollar range. It was also Jule's Last Jam: Styne died of heart failure in New York on September 20, 1994.

Arriving on Broadway in 1947, forty-two-year-old Jule Styne walked away from a successful Hollywood career and committed his future to the theatre. (Richard Rodgers, only three years older than Styne, was already on Broadway back in 1919.) Styne compensated for his late start by becoming the most prolific theatre composer of the next twenty-five years. With BELLS ARE RINGING [November 29, 1956] he established himself as a master of musical comedy. Then came the classic GYPSY [May 21, 1959], which proved him a top musical dramatist as well. The heavy demands of juggling multiple projects—and the selection of less-than-inspired material—resulted in quantity at the expense of quality, perhaps. But even the lesser scores were marked by optimism, warmth, and Styne's exciting musical professionalism. And GYPSY, by itself, is enough to ensure Styne a place in the top rank of Broadway songwriters.

FRANK LOESSER

Born: June 29, 1910, New York, New York
Died: July 28, 1969, New York, New York

FRANK LOESSER came from a musical family. His father, Henry, was a Prussian-born piano teacher, while older brother Arthur was a renowned concert pianist. Frank, though, was a musical black sheep: refusing to study the classics, he taught himself piano and immersed himself in popular music. After being expelled from college, Loesser supported himself with whatever jobs he could get (including knit-goods editor at *Women's Wear* and a stint as a process server). Always intrigued by word-play, Loesser turned to lyric writing. His first published song was *In Love with the Memory of You* (1931), with music by William Schuman (later a classical composer and the president of Juilliard). By the mid-1930s Loesser was singing and playing in nightclubs, as well as writing special material with composer Irving Actman.

All Music and Lyrics by Frank Loesser unless otherwise indicated.

THE ILLUSTRATORS' SHOW
January 22, 1936
48th Street Theatre • 5 performances
Music and Lyrics mostly by others (see Loewe: January 22, 1936); Sketches by Max Liebman, Otto Soglow, and others; Directed by Allen Delano; Produced by Tom Weatherly.

Published Song
Bang—The Bell Rang [music by Irving Actman, lyric by Loesser]

This short-lived revue had very little to distinguish it—except early contributions by both Loesser and Frederick Loewe. A Hollywood scout liked the Loesser/Actman offerings enough to sign the pair to a contract at Universal. He soon wrote his first hit, *The Moon of Manakoora* [music by Alfred Newman] for the 1937 film *The Hurricane*. Loesser quickly moved on to work with some of the top movie composers of the time, successfully collaborating with Hoagy Carmichael (*Heart and Soul*, *Two Sleepy People*), Burton Lane (*The Lady's in Love with You*), Jule Styne (*I Don't Want to Walk without You*), and Arthur Schwartz (*Thank Your Lucky Stars*, *Love Isn't Born*). Then came the war, and Loesser enlisted. Without a composer on hand, he started writing his own tunes. The first were quick wartime hits: *Praise the Lord and Pass the Ammunition* (1942) and *What Do You Do in the Infantry?* (1943).

SKIRTS
January 25, 1944
Cambridge Theatre {London}
"An All American Musical Adventure." Music and Lyrics mostly by PFC Frank Loesser and PFC Harold Rome (see Rome: January 25, 1944); Directed by Lt. Arthur G. Brest; Choreography by Wendy Toye; Produced by U.S. 8th Air Force.

Published Loesser Song
Skirts

Loesser, along with other Broadway and Hollywood professionals in the Armed Forces, had been assigned to Special Services—the morale-building entertainment branch of the Army—to write material for soldier shows. *Skirts* was borrowed by the Air Force, becoming the title song of this West End morale-building visit.

ABOUT FACE!
May 26, 1944

Camp Shanks {New York}

"An Army 'Blueprint Special.'" Music and Lyrics mostly by PFC Frank Loesser; Additional music and Lyrics by PFC Jerry Livingston and others; Sketches by PFC Arnold Auerbach and others; Directed by Robert H. Gordon; With Jules Munshin and Vincente Gomez.

Published Songs

First Class Private Mary Brown—also used in PFC MARY BROWN [circa November 1944]
One Little WAC [music by Eddie Dunstedter]
Why Do They Call a Private a Private? (*When His Life's a Public Event*) [lyric by T/Sgt. Peter Lind Hayes]

Additional Songs Published in Script

Dogface [lyric by Loesser and Peter Lind Hayes]
Gee but It's Great to Be in the Army!
PX Parade [probably by Loesser]
When He Comes Home—also used in (and individually published as from) OK, U.S.A.! [circa June 1945]

Special Services decided to issue a series of do-it-yourself soldier shows, complete with script, songs, designs, publicity material, etc. Loesser headed the songwriting branch and wrote a considerable amount of material over the next two years. *First Class Private Mary Brown* became another wartime pop hit for Loesser.

HI, YANK!
August 7, 1944

Theatre No. 5, Fort Dix {New Jersey}

"An Army 'Blueprint Special.'" Music and Lyrics mostly by PFC Frank Loesser; Additional music and Lyrics by Lt. Alex North and others; Skits by PFC Arnold Auerbach and others; Directed by Cpl. David E. Fitzgibbon; Choreographed by PFC José Limon; Produced by Capt. Hy Gardner; With David Brooks and Joshua Shelley.

Songs Published in Script

Classification Blues
Little Red Rooftops

The Most Important Job
My Gal and I (*My Gal Works at Lockheed*) [lyric by Lt. Jack Hill]
Saga of a Sad Sack [lyric by PFC Hy Zaret]
Yank, Yank, Yank

PFC MARY BROWN
[circa November 1944]

"A WAC Musical Revue." Music and Lyrics by Ruby Jane Douglass, PFC Frank Loesser, and others; Sketches by PFC Arnold Auerbach and others.

Published Songs

First Class Private Mary Brown—originally used in ABOUT FACE! [May 26, 1944]
The WAC Hymn

Additional Songs Published in Script

Come on Honey
Lonely M.P.
Lost in a Cloud of Blue
New Style Bonnet
Something New
Twenty Five Words or Less

This WAC show was inspired by Loesser's *First Class Private Mary Brown* from ABOUT FACE! [May 26, 1944]. The song had become a pop hit, resulting in this eponymous revue. Exact authorship of the non-individually published songs is unknown, but the score was credited as being "mostly by Loesser." *Lost in a Cloud of Blue* is a melodic and fairly adventurous ballad. Meanwhile, Loesser made an uncredited visit to Broadway, ghosting lyrics for his Hollywood pal Burton Lane's LAFFING ROOM ONLY! [Lane: December 23, 1944].

OK, U.S.A.!
[circa June 1945]

"An Army 'Blueprint Special.'" Music and Lyrics mostly by PFC Frank Loesser.

Published Song

When He Comes Home—originally used in ABOUT FACE! [May 26, 1944]

Additional Songs Published in Script

My Chicago
The Tall Pines

Tonight in San Francisco
A Trip 'round the U.S.A.
'Way down Texas Way
You're OK, U.S.A.!

Again, exact authorship of the songs in the script is unknown, but probably by Loesser. *My Chicago* is a schottische with a nice lilt and some surprising harmonics; *'Way down Texas Way* is a fairly entertaining cowboy song spoof. After the war, Loesser resumed his movie work, usually providing music as well as lyrics. Among the songs: *Baby, It's Cold Outside* (1948) from *Neptune's Daughter*, for which Loesser picked up an Oscar.

WHERE'S CHARLEY?

October 11, 1948
St. James Theatre • 792 performances
Book by George Abbott (based on *Charley's Aunt* [play] by Brandon Thomas); Directed by George Abbott; Choreographed by George Balanchine; Produced by Cy Feuer and Ernest Martin in association with Gwen Rickard (Bolger); With Ray Bolger, Allyn McLerie, and Doretta Morrow.

Revival
December 19, 1974
Circle in the Square Uptown Theatre •
    78 performances
Directed by Theodore Mann; Choreographed by Margo Sappington; With Raul Julia [Bolger].

Published Songs
At the Red Rose Cotillion—advertised but not
    published (except in vocal score)
*Lovelier Than Ever
*Make a Miracle
*My Darling, My Darling
*The New Ashmolean Marching Society and
    Students' Conservatory Band*
*Once in Love with Amy
Pernambuco
The Train That Brought You to Town—cut;
    advertised but not published
Where's Charley?
The Years before Us—issued in choral
    arrangement

Additional Songs Published in Vocal
    Score
*Better Get out of Here
The Gossips
*Serenade with Asides
*The Woman in His Room

Additional Songs Recorded
Saunter Away—cut
Your Own College Band—cut

When Hollywood executives Cy Feuer and Ernest Martin decided to become Broadway producers, they invited Loesser along as composer/lyricist. They also had the foresight to hire veteran George Abbott to direct and adapt the 1892 farce. Abbott frequently shepherded talented newcomers through their first important shows, including Hugh Martin, Leonard Bernstein, Jule Styne, Richard Adler, Jerry Bock, Bob Merrill, Stephen Sondheim, and John Kander. Loesser and Abbott came up with an energetic showcase for Ray Bolger. The score was intelligent and surprisingly literate—the delightful opening quartet *Better Get out of Here* is built on a gavotte, in fact—although the book was somewhat creaky. Loesser's songbag included two warmly sentimental ballads, *Lovelier Than Ever* and *My Darling, My Darling*; a clever novelty duet in *Baby, It's Cold Outside* style, *Make a Miracle*; two effective comic character studies, *Serenade with Asides* and *The Woman in His Room*; and a charm song to end all charm songs, *Once in Love with Amy*. Pretty good for a pop-tune writer from Hollywood.

GUYS AND DOLLS

November 24, 1950
46th Street Theatre • 1,200 performances
"A Musical Fable of Broadway." Book by Jo Swerling and Abe Burrows (based on stories and characters by Damon Runyon); Directed by George S. Kaufman; Choreographed by Michael Kidd; Produced by Cy Feuer and Ernest Martin; With Sam Levene, Isabel Bigley, Robert Alda, and Vivian Blaine.

Revivals
July 21, 1976
Broadway Theatre • 239 performances
Directed and Choreographed by Billy Wilson, under the Supervision of Abe Burrows; With

Norma Donaldson [Blaine], Robert Guillaume [Levene], Ernestine Jackson [Bigley], and James Randolph [Alda].

April 14, 1992
Martin Beck Theatre • 1,143 performances
Directed by Jerry Zaks; Choreographed by Christopher Chadman; With Faith Prince [Blaine], Nathan Lane [Levene], Peter Gallagher [Alda], and Josie de Guzman [Bigley].

Published Songs
Adelaide—written for 1955 movie version
*Adelaide's Lament
A Bushel and a Peck
Follow the Fold
*Fugue for Tinhorns
Guys and Dolls
Guys and Dolls Preamble (*Roxy*)
*If I Were a Bell
I'll Know
It Feels Like Forever—cut; advertised but not
    published
*I've Never Been in Love Before
*Luck Be a Lady
*Marry the Man Today
More I Cannot Wish You
*My Time of Day
The Oldest Established
Pet Me, Poppa—written for movie version
Shango—cut; advertised but not published
*Sit down You're Rockin' the Boat
Sue Me—non-show version
Sue Me Argument [duet]—show version
Take Back Your Mink
Three Cornered Tune—non-show version of
    Fugue for Tinhorns
Travelin' Light—cut; advertised but not
    published except in 1994 non-show folio
A Woman in Love—written for movie version

Loesser's sophomore effort turned out to be one of the finest modern-day musical comedies. Loesser displayed his ability to lovingly (and with dignity) capture his characters and their vernacular: his "Hot-Box Doll" Adelaide, for example, is as sympathetic and real as Nellie Forbush; her chronic dilemma, while more humorous than serious to us, is every bit as important to her. Loesser turned out a hit-filled score and quickly transformed himself into a music publishing tycoon.

(Along with the many familiar numbers, there is a cut song worth noting: the felicitously tricky *Travelin' Light*.) The happy fact that these hits were endemic to the characters not only put Loesser in the top rank of theatre composers but made GUYS AND DOLLS an instant classic. An important force on the show was director George S. Kaufman (of OF THEE I SING [Gershwin: December 26, 1931]). Radio writer Abe Burrows was brought in to replace librettist Jo Swerling and provided a fine book in Runyonese. But it was the astonishing score that made GUYS AND DOLLS a true "musical fable of Broadway." Loesser made a quick return to Hollywood for the 1952 Danny Kaye musical *Hans Christian Andersen*, for which he wrote eight songs including *Thumbelina*, the charming duet *No Two People*, and the joyous waltz *Wonderful Copenhagen*. (Stage adaptations of the film—with non-Loesser interpolations—have been attempted in London's West End, without success.)

THE MOST HAPPY FELLA
May 3, 1956
Imperial Theatre • 676 performances
Book by Loesser (based on *They Knew What They Wanted* [play] by Sidney Howard); Directed by Joseph Anthony; Choreographed by Dania Krupska; Produced by Kermit Bloomgarden and Lynn Loesser; With Robert Weede, Jo Sullivan, Art Lund, and Susan Johnson.

Revivals
October 11, 1979
Majestic Theatre • 53 performances
Directed by Jack O'Brien; Choreographed by Graciela Daniele; With Giorgio Tozzi [Weede], Sharon Daniels [Sullivan], and Richard Muenz [Lund].

February 13, 1992
Booth Theatre • 229 performances
Directed by Gerald Gutierrez; Choreographed by Liza Gennaro; Transferred from the Goodspeed Opera House; With Spiro Malas [Weede] and Sophie Hayden [Sullivan].

Published Songs
*Big D
Don't Cry

I Like Ev'rybody
Joey, Joey, Joey
The Most Happy Fella
My Heart Is So Full of You
Somebody, Somewhere
Standing on the Corner
Warm All Over

Additional Songs Published in Vocal Score

Abbondanza
Aren't You Glad?
Benvenuta
Fresno Beauties (Cold and Dead)
Goodbye, Darlin'
Happy to Make Your Acquaintance
Hoedown [instrumental]
How Beautiful the Days
I Don't Like This Dame
I Know How It Is
I Love Him
I Made a Fist
The Letter
Love and Kindness
Mama, Mama
Ooh, My Feet
Please Let Me Tell You That I Love You
Plenty Bambini
Rosabella
Seven Million Crumbs
She's Gonna Come Home with Me
Song of a Summer Night
Soon You Gonna Leave Me, Joe
Special Delivery! (One Bride)
Sposalizio
Tony's Thoughts
Young People Gotta Dance

Additional Songs Recorded

House and Garden—cut
How's about Tonight?—cut
I'll Buy Everybody a Beer—cut
Wanting to Be Wanted—cut

Loesser confounded everyone by following the raucous GUYS AND DOLLS [November 24, 1950] with this rich, operatic "musical musical." Writing his own libretto, Loesser came up with this heartwarming piece which, unlike PORGY AND BESS [Gershwin: October 10, 1935], STREET SCENE [Weill: January 9, 1947], and REGINA [Blitzstein: October 31, 1949], was a long-running money-making hit. The bountiful score is over-brimming with fine, flavorful material. Three of the songs—Standing on the Corner, Big D, and Joey, Joey, Joey—were extractable as pop hits. Loesser also came up with a new wife, divorcing coproducer Lynn and marrying Jo "Rosabella" Sullivan. The 1992 revival, which originated at the Goodspeed Opera House, handled the dilemma of outsized production costs simply by cutting the orchestra. The dramatic aspects of the show were effective with the two-piano accompaniment, prepared by Robert Page under Loesser's supervision; but if there was ever a musical that called for a lush accompaniment, it is THE MOST HAPPY FELLA. A "Frank" note on authorship: It is known that Loesser from time to time recycled material from his pre-1945 days, legally purchasing the rights from his early collaborators. Some material written in the 1930s with Irving Actman—who was musical director of GUYS AND DOLLS while Loesser was writing THE MOST HAPPY FELLA—apparently went into the Cleo/Herman scenes. For notes on other show tunes possibly ghostwritten by Loesser, see LAFFING ROOM ONLY [Lane: December 23, 1944], THE PAJAMA GAME [Adler: May 13, 1954], and THE MUSIC MAN [Willson: December 19, 1957].

GREENWILLOW

March 8, 1960
Alvin Theatre • 95 performances
Book by Lesser Samuels and Frank Loesser (based on the novel by B. J. Chute); Directed by George Roy Hill; Choreographed by Joe Layton; Produced by Robert A. Willey in association with Frank (Loesser) Productions, Inc.; With Anthony Perkins, Cecil Kellaway, Pert Kelton, and Ellen McCown.

Published Songs

Faraway Boy
Gideon Briggs, I Love You
Greenwillow Christmas
The Music of Home
Never Will I Marry
Summertime Love
Walking Away Whistling

Additional Song Published in Vocal Selection
Clang Dang the Bell

Additional Songs Recorded
Bless This Day—cut
Could've Been a Ring
A Day Borrowed from Heaven
Dorrie's Wish
Greenwillow Walk [instrumental]
He Died Good
Heart of Stone—cut
The Sermon
*What a Blessing (To Know There's a Devil)

Throughout his career Loesser demonstrated a reluctance to repeat himself, choosing to follow each project with a radical change of pace. GREENWILLOW was a pastoral, folksy, tender musical that played whimsical and dull in performance. Loesser's score had no life outside the theatre (and very little in it), but it is enchanting. Never Will I Marry is a fine, introspective song of yearning; The Music of Home and Summertime Love are strongly evocative; and there is a deliciously playful waltz for the friendly reverend, What a Blessing (To Know There's a Devil). The failure of the heartfelt GREENWILLOW was a major disappointment for Loesser.

HOW TO SUCCEED IN BUSINESS WITHOUT REALLY TRYING
October 14, 1961
46th Street Theatre • 1,417 performances
Book by Abe Burrows, Jack Weinstock, and Willie Gilbert (based on the book by Shepherd Mead); Directed by Abe Burrows; Choreographed by Hugh Lambert; Musical staging by Bob Fosse; Produced by Cy Feuer and Ernest H. Martin in association with Frank (Loesser) Productions, Inc.; With Robert Morse, Rudy Vallee, Bonnie Scott, Virginia Martin, and Charles Nelson Reilly.

Revival
March 23, 1995
Richard Rodgers Theatre • 548 performances
Directed by Des McAnuff; Choreographed by Wayne Cilento; With Matthew Broderick [Morse], Ronn Carroll [Vallee], Megan Mullally [Scott], and Jeff Blumenkrantz [Reilly].

Published Songs
*Brotherhood of Man
Grand Old Ivy
Happy to Keep His Dinner Warm
How to Succeed
*I Believe in You
Love from a Heart of Gold
Paris Original

Additional Songs Published in Vocal Selection
Cinderella, Darling
Coffee Break
*The Company Way
Rosemary
*A Secretary Is Not a Toy

Additional Songs Published in Vocal Score
Been a Long Day
*Finale Act One [trio]—including extended version of Rosemary
The Yo-Ho-Ho [instrumental]

Additional Song Recorded
Organization Man—cut

This Pulitzer Prize–winning musical cartoon remains one of the funniest evenings in Broadway history. All elements seemed to merge, though not easily: Burrows again provided a replacement libretto—as he had on GUYS AND DOLLS [November 24, 1950] and SILK STOCKINGS [Porter: February 24, 1955]—as well as directing, while Bob Fosse was rushed in to replace the show's TV-trained choreographer. Loesser provided a tongue-in-cheek score of song satires, perfectly complementing the libretto (though perhaps crimping his own melodic style). Only two of the songs proved extractable, (the hypocritical) Brotherhood of Man and (the narcissistic) I Believe in You. But the entire score is a slyly well-crafted joy, with Rosemary, The Company Way, and the playful A Secretary Is Not a Toy among the standouts.

PLEASURES AND PALACES
March 11, 1965
Fisher Theatre {Detroit, Mich.} •
    Closed during tryout
Book by Sam Spewack and Frank Loesser (based on Once There Was a Russian [play] by

Sam Spewack); Directed and Choreographed by Bob Fosse; Produced by Allen B. Whitehead in association with Frank (Loesser) Productions, Inc.; With Phyllis Newman, Jack Cassidy, Hy Hazell, and John McMartin.

Songs Issued in Professional Copies
Barabanchik
Far, Far, Far Away
In Your Eyes
Oh to Be Home Again
Pleasures and Palaces
Thunder and Lightning
Truly Loved

Sam Spewack had been highly successful with his two previous musicals, LEAVE IT TO ME [Porter: November 9, 1938] and KISS ME, KATE [Porter: December 30, 1948]. This comic costume-operetta—about Catherine the Great, Potemkin, and John Paul Jones—was a full-scale disaster which shuttered after its Detroit tryout. The 1961 play version, for that matter, had lasted only one performance on Broadway. It was Loesser's final complete score.

SEÑOR DISCRETION HIMSELF
[circa March 1968]
Unfinished musical. Book by Frank Loesser (based on a story by Budd Schulberg).

Songs Recorded
I Cannot Let You Go
You Understand Me

Loesser spent two years working on this Budd Schulberg story about a small-town, middle-aged Mexican baker. (In 1952, a Loesser/Burrows, Feuer & Martin musicalization of the 1938 film *La Femme du Boulanger*—about a small-town, middle-aged French baker—had been an-

nounced as a Bert Lahr vehicle. It was quickly withdrawn, although the source material was eventually used for THE BAKER'S WIFE [S. Schwartz: May 11, 1976]. Loesser turned instead to THE MOST HAPPY FELLA [May 3, 1956], about a small-town, middle-aged Italian-American grape rancher.) Anyway, Loesser wrote seventeen songs for SEÑOR DISCRETION; the two which have been recorded are quite good. He eventually chose to drop the project, though, as he couldn't quite figure out how to solve problems with the book. (A developmental workshop was mounted in 1985, with inconclusive results.) A heavy chain-smoker, Frank Loesser died of lung cancer on July 28, 1969, in New York.

Lyricist Frank Loesser came from Hollywood with no theatrical experience and only a few years of composing credits. In the next thirteen years he wrote five Broadway scores, three of them good and the other two quite exceptional. GUYS AND DOLLS [November 24, 1950], THE MOST HAPPY FELLA [May 3, 1956], and HOW TO SUCCEED IN BUSINESS WITHOUT REALLY TRYING [October 14, 1961] all remain among the finest of their genre. Quite significantly, these shows had first-rate work from librettists, directors, choreographers, designers, and producers: perfectionist Loesser kept a careful eye on all elements of production. His innate cleverness and ease with words, combined with a deep respect for his characters, made him one of the best comedy lyricists of his time. His music was tuneful, functional, always highly skillful, and —most importantly—usually great fun. Frank Loesser's relatively small body of work remains bright, funny, and golden.

RICHARD ADLER

Born: August 3, 1921, New York, New York

RICHARD ADLER, like Frank Loesser, was the son of a serious musician, concert pianist Clarence Adler; like Loesser, young Adler stayed away from the piano. Following wartime Navy service, Adler went into advertising. In the early 1950s he began writing pop songs with Jerry Ross (born March 9, 1926, in the Bronx), including the 1953 pop hit *Rags to Riches*. Loesser, who had set up as a music publisher following the success of GUYS AND DOLLS [Loesser: November 24, 1950], began looking for writers to supplement his own output. Adler and Ross were put under contract.

taste and lavish use of color, he had gravitated to spectacles and spent much of the 1940s doing pageants and the Ringling Brothers Circus. His career virtually at an end, Leonard Sillman gave him one last opportunity with NEW FACES OF 1952[†] [May 16, 1952]. (Sillman had similarly used the name of the fallen Charles Dillingham for his first NEW FACES[†] [March 15, 1934].) The surprising success of NEW FACES OF 1952 prompted the far inferior JOHN MURRAY ANDERSON'S ALMANAC; Anderson himself died early in the run. But Adler and Ross received their first Broadway experience.

JOHN MURRAY ANDERSON'S ALMANAC

December 10, 1953
Imperial Theatre • 229 performances
Music and Lyrics mostly by Adler and Jerry Ross; Additional music and Lyrics by others (see Coleman: December 10, 1953); Sketches by Jean Kerr, William K. Wells, and others; Directed by John Murray Anderson and Cyril Ritchard; Choreographed by Donald Saddler; Produced by Michael Grace, Stanley Gilkey, and Harry Rigby; With Hermione Gingold, Billy DeWolfe, Harry Belafonte, and Orson Bean.

Published Songs
Acorn in the Meadow
Fini
You're So Much a Part of Me

Anderson was a veteran revue director with credits including THE GREENWICH VILLAGE FOLLIES [Porter; September 16, 1924] and JUMBO [Rodgers: November 16, 1935]. Known for his

THE PAJAMA GAME

May 13, 1954
St. James Theatre • 1,063 performances
Music and Lyrics by Adler and Jerry Ross; Book by George Abbott and Richard Bissell (based on *7 ½ Cents* [novel] by Richard Bissell); Directed by George Abbott and Jerome Robbins; Choreographed by Bob Fosse; Produced by Frederick Brisson, Robert E. Griffith, and Harold S. Prince; With John Raitt, Janis Paige, Eddie Foy, Jr., and Carol Haney.

Revival
December 9, 1973
Lunt-Fontanne Theatre • 65 performances
Directed by George Abbott; Original choreography restaged by Zoya Leporska; Produced by Adler and Bert Wood in association with Nelson Peltz; With Barbara McNair [Paige], Hal Linden [Raitt], and Cab Calloway [Foy].

Published Songs
*Hernando's Hideaway
*Hey There

*I'm Not at All in Love

A New Town Is a Blue Town—issued as
  professional copy

Once-a-Year-Day—initial individual publication in connection with revival

Small Talk

*Steam Heat

There Once Was a Man

Additional Songs Published in Vocal Score

Her Is

*I'll Never Be Jealous Again

The Pajama Game (Opening)

Racing with the Clock

7 ½ Cents

Sleep-Tite

Think of the Time I Save

Additional Song Recorded

Watch Your Heart [music and lyric by Adler]
  —recorded as If You Win, You Lose;
  written for revival, revised version of
  What's Wrong with Me from KWAMINA
  [October 23, 1961]

Bobby Griffith was a long-time Abbott stage
manager, just then on WONDERFUL TOWN
[Bernstein: February 25, 1953] with young Harold
Prince (Abbott's former office boy) as his assistant. The newly formed producing team optioned
Richard Bissell's folksy best-seller and brought
it to their mentor. Unconventional musical comedy material—about a labor strike in a Midwest
garment factory—made it difficult to find established songwriters, but Frank Loesser (Abbott's
collaborator on WHERE'S CHARLEY? [Loesser:
October 11, 1948]) sent around his fledgling
protegés. Jerome Robbins, Abbott's choreographer of choice since ON THE TOWN [Bernstein:
December 28, 1944], also turned down the show—
but agreed to back up novice Bob Fosse in ex-
change for codirector billing. Fosse was recommended by his wife Joan McCracken, star of
Abbott's then-current ME AND JULIET [Rodgers:
May 28, 1953]. Thus was this Abbott-trained trio
of future musical theatre giants first brought
together. Griffith and Prince called in Frederick
Brisson, husband of Rosalind Russell (of WON-
DERFUL TOWN) for financing. The gamble on
young talents Adler, Ross, and Fosse paid off
with a staggeringly successful hit, with a little

help from Loesser and Robbins. A "Frank" note
on authorship: it has been rumored that four of
the songs were written wholly or partially by
Loesser, who ultimately reaped a fortune as publisher of the score and licensor of the stock &
amateur rights. Since I was only a year old at the
time, I can't vouch for them—but the information seems credible. The story goes that Adler
and Ross went to Frank, unable to come up with
the necessary "big ballad." Frank said something
like: "Easy. Just take any old thing"—here he
dashed off a bit of Mozart—"and play it in a
slow, leisurely 4/4." The main melodic phrase of
Hey There is, of course, the first two measures of
Mozart's Sonata in C (K 545) played in a slow,
leisurely four; Mozart didn't think of the dicta-
phone, though. Also cited are A New Town Is a
Blue Town, which does sound to me like a logical Loesserian stepping stone from My Time of
Day (GUYS AND DOLLS [November 24, 1950])
to Joey, Joey, Joey (THE MOST HAPPY FELLA
[May 3, 1956]); the mock-hillbilly duet There
Once Was a Man, the sort of novelty Loesser used
to play at parties; and Her Is.

DAMN YANKEES
May 5, 1955
46th Street Theatre • 1,019 performances
Music and Lyrics by Adler and Jerry Ross;
Book by George Abbott and Douglas Wallop
(based on The Year the Yankees Lost the
Pennant [novel] by Douglas Wallop); Directed
by George Abbott; Choreographed by Bob
Fosse; Produced by Frederick Brisson, Robert
E. Griffith, and Harold S. Prince in association
with Albert Taylor; With Gwen Verdon,
Stephen Douglass, and Ray Walston.

Revival
March 3, 1994
Marquis Theatre • 510 performances
Book revision by Jack O'Brien; Directed by
Jack O'Brien; Choreographed by Rob
Marshall; With Bebe Neuwirth [Verdon],
Victor Garber [Walston], and Jarrod Emick
[Douglass].

Published Songs
Goodbye, Old Girl

*Heart

A Man Doesn't Know
Near to You
Shoeless Joe from Hannibal, Mo.
There's Something about an Empty Chair [music
   and lyric by Adler]—written for 1958
   movie version
Two Lost Souls
Whatever Lola Wants (Lola Gets)
Who's Got the Pain

Additional Songs Published in Vocal Score
The Game
A Little Brains—A Little Talent
Six Months out of Every Year
Those Were the Good Old Days

The follow-up to THE PAJAMA GAME [May 13,
1954] was the equally successful—if less well
made—DAMN YANKEES. The same team (less
Robbins) took another popular off-beat novel
and turned it into a fast, funny 1950s musical.
Gwen Verdon, a Jack Cole dancer who stole the
show as Michael Kidd's featured dancer in CAN-
CAN [Porter: May 7, 1953], became Broadway's
new musical comedy dancing star in her first of
five Fosse shows. Adler and Ross had another
two hit songs, *Heart* and *Whatever Lola Wants*.
But on November 11, 1955, Ross died of leuke-
mia. Adler has been without success in the theatre since.

THE SIN OF PAT MULDOON
March 13, 1957
Cort Theatre • 5 performances
Play by John McLiam; Directed by Jack
Garfein; Produced by Adler and Roger L.
Stevens; With James Barton and Elaine Stritch.

Published Song
The Sin of Pat Muldoon—non-show instrumental, inspired by the play

Adler began his producing career with this quick
failure. In the fall of 1957 he wrote and produced
two 1957 television musicals, "The Gift of the
Magi" (starring Sally Ann Howes) and "Little
Women." Adler married soprano Howes—best
known as Julie Andrews's replacement in MY
FAIR LADY [Loewe: March 15, 1956]—and undertook a project for her.

KWAMINA
October 23, 1961
54th Street Theatre • 32 performances
Music and Lyrics by Adler; Book by Robert
Alan Aurthur; Directed by Robert Lewis;
Choreographed by Agnes de Mille; Produced
by Alfred de Liagre, Jr.; With Sally Ann
Howes, Terry Carter, and Brock Peters.

Published Songs
Another Time, Another Place
I'm Seeing Rainbows—cut
Nothing More to Look Forward To
Ordinary People
Something Big
What's Wrong with Me?—see THE PAJAMA
   GAME [May 13, 1954]

Additional Songs Recorded
Cocoa Bean Song
Did You Hear That?
A Man Can Have No Choice
One Wife
Seven Sheep, Four Red Shirts, and a Bottle of Gin
The Sun Is Beginning to Crow (You Are Home)
Welcome Home
What Happened to Me Tonight?
You're As English As

With all good intentions, the authors created a
contemporary "The King and I Goes to Africa."
Hammerstein and Rodgers had carefully handled
their racial intolerance theme in Siam and Bali
H'ai; the KWAMINA book was a poor retread,
with bits of Eliza Doolittle thrown in. Adler,
though, came up with a worthy, dramatic score
with especially good choral numbers. He went
back to pop work, wrote the catchy *Let Hertz
Put You in the Driver's Seat* jingle, and produced
special events for the Kennedy and Johnson ad-
ministrations (including the infamous JFK birthday party featuring Marilyn Monroe).

A MOTHER'S KISSES
September 23, 1968
Shubert Theatre {New Haven, Conn.} •
   Closed during tryout
Music and Lyrics by Adler; Book by Bruce Jay
Friedman (based on his novel); Directed by
Gene Saks; Choreographed by Onna White;

Produced by Lester Osterman, Richard Homer, and Lawrence Kasha; With Beatrice Arthur (Saks), Bill Callaway, and Carl Ballantine.

Songs Recorded
Don't Live inside of Yourself
There Goes My Life
When You Gonna Learn?—recorded as *Put Your Money on Me*

In the late 1960s, Jewish mothers were good for a laugh. Hoping to mine theatre party business, two Jewish mother shows were mounted: the Herbert Martin/Michael Leonard HOW TO BE A JEWISH MOTHER† [December 28, 1967], which died after three weeks on Broadway, and A MOTHER'S KISSES, which played three deadly weeks on the road. The former was a two-character musical starring the formidable team of Molly Picon and Godfrey Cambridge; the latter was an attempt at making a star out of the acid-tongued Bea Arthur, who created both Yente the Matchmaker in FIDDLER [Bock: September 22, 1964] and Vera Charles in MAME [Herman: May 24, 1966]. Adler next returned to Broadway in 1973 as producer of the unsuccessful interracial revival of THE PAJAMA GAME [May 13, 1954].

REX
See Rodgers: April 25, 1976.

MUSIC IS
December 20, 1976
St. James Theatre • 8 performances
Music by Adler; Lyrics by Will Holt; Book

and Direction by George Abbott (based on *Twelfth Night* [play] by William Shakespeare); Choreographed by Patricia Birch; Produced by Adler, Roger Berlind, and Edward R. Downe, Jr.; With Joel Higgins, Catherine Cox, and Christopher Hewett.

Song Recorded
Should I Speak of Loving You

Adler rejoined George Abbott twenty-two years after their initial collaboration. Abbott had done well enough with the Bard's THE BOYS FROM SYRACUSE [Rodgers: November 23, 1938]. But *The Comedy of Errors* lent itself to the farcical treatment that *Twelfth Night* didn't; and, after all, Rodgers and Hart and Balanchine weren't along to help. Adler wrote a couple of catchy tunes—*Sing High* was especially good—but to little avail. MUSIC IS was dreary, old-fashioned, and of far less interest than the off-Broadway rock adaptation of the same play, YOUR OWN THING† [January 13, 1968]. PLAY ON!† [March 20, 1997]—yet another *Twelfth Night*, Harlemized to the music of Duke Ellington—turned up twenty years later, with similar results.

Richard Adler arrived on Broadway with sturdy scores for two consecutive musical hits. Then collaborator Jerry Ross died, and Adler's career never recovered. KWAMINA [October 23, 1961] showed his potential as a composer of serious theatre work, but nothing of worth has come along since.

JERRY BOCK

Born: November 23, 1928, New Haven, Connecticut

JERRY BOCK grew up in Flushing, New York, where his father was a salesman. He began playing the piano at nine and was soon writing songs (including his high school musical BIG DREAMS, a fundraiser for a Navy hospital ship). In 1945 he went to the University of Wisconsin as a music major.

ultimately unsatisfying. Following graduation in 1949, Bock teamed with lyricist Larry Holofcener. They began writing songs and material for television, including Sid Caesar's *Your Show of Shows*. They also wrote amateur revues at Tamiment, a Pennsylvania summer resort similar to Green Mansions (where Harold Rome began his career).

BIG AS LIFE
[circa May 1948]
"University of Wisconsin Golden Jubilee Production." Music by Jerrold Bock; Lyrics by Jack Royce; Book by Dave Pollard; Produced by The Haresfoot Club.

Published Songs
Everybody Loses
Forest in the Sky—advertised but not
    published
Great Wisconsin
Starway Lullaby
Today—advertised but not published
Why Sing a Love Song?

A struggle between the radio industry and ASCAP over licensing fees caused formation of the competing Broadcast Music Inc. (BMI). For a brief period ASCAP songs were kept from the airwaves, and BMI went searching for substitute material. A scouring of college campuses resulted in the publishing of varsity shows by Bock and Sondheim (PHINNEY'S RAINBOW [circa May 1948]), among others. None of this material proved popular, but the college experiment paid off well: while Sondheim quickly moved to ASCAP, Bock remained with BMI and eventually provided them with a strong group of song hits. As for BIG AS LIFE, *Why Sing a Love Song?* is interesting, if

CATCH A STAR
September 6, 1955
Plymouth Theatre • 23 performances
Music mostly by Sammy Fain and Philip Charig; Lyrics to Bock songs by Larry Holofcener; Sketches by Danny and Neil Simon; Conceived and Supervised by Ray Golden; Produced by Sy Kleinman; With Pat Carroll, David Burns, and Marc Breaux.

Published Songs
None

The Simon brothers were television comedy writers who had worked at Tamiment. They gave Broadway a try, bringing along a few Bock/Holofcener songs. CATCH A STAR quickly closed, and the Simon boys went back to television. The younger brother would return to Broadway, though.

MR. WONDERFUL
March 22, 1956
Broadway Theatre • 383 performances
Music and Lyrics mostly by Bock, Larry Holofcener, and George Weiss; Book by Joseph Stein and Will Glickman; "Production Conceived by Jule Styne"; Directed by Jack Donohue; Produced by Jule Styne and George

Gilbert in association with Lester Osterman, Jr.; With Sammy Davis, Jr., Jack Carter, Pat Marshall, and Chita Rivera.

Published Songs
Ethel, Baby
Jacques D'Iraque
Mr. Wonderful
There
*Too Close for Comfort
Without You I'm Nothing

Additional Songs Recorded
Charlie Welch
I'm Available
I've Been Too Busy
Miami
1617 Broadway
Talk to Him

Producer Jule Styne determined to become a major Broadway producer like Richard Rodgers, with less than remarkable results (see HAZEL FLAGG [Styne: February 11, 1953). Too busy to write the score for this Sammy Davis, Jr., vehicle, Styne gambled on newcomers Bock and Holofcener (later adding pop composer George Weiss to help). The resulting MR. WONDERFUL was not much of a show—the Davis character rose to stardom and did his nightclub act, with impressions of Jimmy Cagney, etc.—but the star's presence and two hit songs (the title number and *Too Close for Comfort*) kept it alive despite dismal reviews.

THE ZIEGFELD FOLLIES OF 1956
April 16, 1956
Shubert Theatre {Boston} •
    Closed during tryout
Music mostly by others (see Coleman: April 16, 1956); Lyrics to Bock songs by Larry Holofcener; Sketches by Arnold B. Horwitt, Ronny Graham, and others; Directed by Christopher Hewett; Choreographed by Jack Cole; Produced by Richard Kollmar and James W. Gardiner by arrangement with Billie Burke Ziegfeld; With Tallulah Bankhead, David Burns, Mae Barnes, Joan Diener, Carol Haney, Lee Becker, and Larry Kert.

Published Songs
None

The last successful ZIEGFELD FOLLIES[†] was the Shuberts' wartime edition [April 1, 1943] starring Milton Berle. This one, headlined by Tallulah Bankhead, died after a four-week tryout. Meanwhile, actor Jack Cassidy introduced Bock to Sheldon Harnick at the opening night party of Harry Warren's phenomenal flop SHANGRI-LA[†] [June 13, 1956]. (Cassidy was the juvenile lead, Harnick provided additional lyrics.) Green Mansions veteran Harnick had interpolated clever songs—music and lyrics—into several revues, including the deft *Boston Beguine* in NEW FACES OF 1952[†] [May 16, 1952]. Publisher Tommy Valando signed up Bock and Harnick and went about getting the new team their first assignment.

THE BODY BEAUTIFUL
January 23, 1958
Broadway Theatre • 60 performances
Lyrics by Sheldon Harnick; Book by Joseph Stein and Will Glickman; Directed by George Schaefer; Choreographed by Herbert Ross; Produced by Richard Kollmar and Albert W. Selden; With Jack Warden, Mindy Carson, Steve Forrest, and Barbara McNair.

Published Songs
All of These and More
Hidden in My Heart—cut
Just My Luck
Leave Well Enough Alone
Uh-Huh, Oh Yeah

Additional Song Published in Non-show Folio
Summer Is

Bock and Harnick's debut came with this quick failure about the prizefight game. But the score was promising enough to attract the notice of producers Bobby Griffith and Hal Prince, who were looking to produce their fifth consecutive hit. The BODY BEAUTIFUL score included a catchy rhythm number, *Just My Luck*, and a throwaway song called *Gloria* (unpublished) with notably delectable comedy lyrics.

FIORELLO!

November 23, 1959
Broadhurst Theatre • 795 performances
Lyrics by Sheldon Harnick; Book by Jerome
Weidman and George Abbott; Directed by
George Abbott; Choreographed by Peter
Gennaro; Produced by Robert E. Griffith and
Harold S. Prince; With Tom Bosley, Patricia
Wilson, Howard da Silva, Eileen Rodgers, and
Pat Stanley.

Concert Version
February 9, 1994
City Center • 4 performances
Directed by Walter Bobbie; Choreographed by
Christopher Chadman; Produced by City
Center Encores; With Jerry Zaks [Bosley],
Faith Prince [Wilson], Philip Bosco [da Silva],
Donna McKechnie [Rodgers], Liz Callaway
[Stanley].

Published Songs
Gentleman Jimmy
*I Love a Cop—advertised but not published
    (except in vocal selection)
Little Tin Box
*Politics and Poker
'Til Tomorrow
*(I'll Marry) The Very Next Man
*When Did I Fall in Love?
Where Do I Go from Here?—cut

Additional Songs Recorded
The Bum Won
Home Again
Marie's Law
The Name's La Guardia
On the Side of the Angels
Unfair

Arthur Penn, director of the hit drama *Two for the Seesaw* [January 16, 1958], came to Griffith and Prince with the idea for this Fiorello LaGuardia biomusical. The producers, who had successfully gambled on novices Adler, Ross, Merrill, and Sondheim, gave Bock and Harnick the job. The book assignment went to novice librettist Jerome Weidman, author of the 1937 New York City/Depression novel *I Can Get it for You Wholesale*. As the La Guardia biography moved further into the musical comedy vein, Penn left and Griffith/Prince mentor George

Abbott took over as director and colibrettist. The resulting FIORELLO! was a moderate success— the competing SOUND OF MUSIC [Rodgers: November 16, 1959] doubled FIORELLO's run— but it went into the record books as the third Pulitzer Prize–winning Broadway musical. The score handily displays Bock and Harnick's strong feel for character work, expressing the thoughts and emotions of the more-or-less contemporary common man in a variety of forms: a delicious charm song (*I Love a Cop*); a contrapuntal character duet (*Marie's Law*); a strong rhythmic number (*Gentleman Jimmy*); two stunning novelty septets (*Politics and Poker* and *Little Tin Box*); and a very pretty romantic ballad (*When Did I Fall in Love?*).

TENDERLOIN

October 17, 1960
46th Street Theatre • 216 performances
Lyrics by Sheldon Harnick; Book by George
Abbott and Jerome Weidman (based on the
novel by Samuel Hopkins Adams); Directed by
George Abbott; Choreographed by Joe Layton;
Produced by Robert E. Griffith and Harold S.
Prince; With Maurice Evans, Ron Husmann,
Eileen Rodgers, and Margery Gray.

Published Songs
Artificial Flowers
Good Clean Fun
I Wonder What It's Like—cut
Lovely Laurie—cut
**My Gentle Young Johnny
My Miss Mary
Tommy, Tommy

Additional Song Published in Non-show Folio
*The Picture of Happiness

Additional Songs Recorded
The Army of the Just
Bless This Land
Dear Friend [1st]—different from song in SHE
    LOVES ME [April 23, 1963]
Dr. Brock
How the Money Changes Hands
*Little Old New York
Reform

The Trial
What's in It for You?

Once again, the creators of a landmark musical attempted to follow up with a close copy; once again, the attempt failed. TENDERLOIN took place in a little older New York than FIORELLO! [November 23, 1959] and switched from inside politics to inside vice. The creators did a fine job with the colorful bad guys (and dolls) in numbers like *Little Old New York* and the sparkling *Picture of Happiness*; but the good guys in the story—a reforming reverend and his Army of the Just—were bland and sappy. The songs for the good men (and women) are also slightly stilted, but the fun stuff far outweighs the rest. And Bock included a truly stunning waltz, *My Gentle Young Johnny.*

NEVER TOO LATE
November 27, 1962
Playhouse Theatre • 1,007 performances
Play by Sumner Arthur Long; Incidental music mostly by John Kander (see Kander: November 27, 1962); Directed by George Abbott; Produced by Elliot Martin and Daniel Hollywood; With Paul Ford, Maureen O'Sullivan, and Orson Bean.

Published Song
Never Too Late [lyric by Sheldon Harnick]

MAN IN THE MOON
April 11, 1963
Biltmore Theatre • 7 performances
A Marionette Show. Lyrics by Sheldon Harnick; Book by Arthur Burns (based on a story by Bil Baird); Directed by Gerald Freedman; Produced by Arthur Cantor and Joseph Harris; With Bil and Cora Baird's Marionettes.

Published Song
Worlds Apart

Additional Songs Recorded
Ain't You Never Been Afraid?
Itch to Be Rich
Look Where I Am
You Treacherous Man

This marionette show made a brief stop on Broadway en route to an overseas State Department tour.

SHE LOVES ME
April 23, 1963
Eugene O'Neill Theatre • 302 performances
"The Happiest Musical." Lyrics by Sheldon Harnick; Book by Joe Masteroff (based on *The Shop around the Corner* [play] by Miklos Laszlo); Directed by Harold Prince; Choreographed by Carol Haney; Produced by Harold Prince in association with Lawrence J. Kasha and Philip C. McKenna; With Barbara Cook, Daniel Massey, Barbara Baxley, Ludwig Donath, and Jack Cassidy.

Concert Version
March 29, 1977
Town Hall • 24 performances
Directed by John Bowab; With Madeline Kahn [Cook], Barry Bostwick [Massey], Rita Moreno [Baxley], George Rose [Donath], and Laurence Guittard [Cassidy].

Revival
September 28, 1993
Brooks Atkinson Theatre • 294 performances
Directed by Scott Ellis; Choreographed by Rob Marshall; Transferred from the Roundabout Theatre; With Boyd Gaines [Massey], Diane Fratantoni [Cook], Sally Mayes [Baxley], Louis Zorich [Donath], and Howard McGillin [Cassidy].

Published Songs
Days Gone By
*Dear Friend [2nd]—different from song in TENDERLOIN [October 17, 1960]
Grand Knowing You
*Ice Cream—issued in 1994 in separate edition as *Vanilla Ice Cream*
Ilona—advertised but not published (except in vocal selection)
*She Loves Me
*Tonight at Eight
*Will He Like Me?

Additional Song Published in 1994 Vocal Selection
*A Trip to the Library

Additional Songs Recorded

Good Morning, Good Day—music published [no lyric] in piano selection from London production [April 29, 1964; 189 performances]

Good Bye, Georg

*Heads I Win—added to London production

I Don't Know His Name

I Resolve

Letters—extended choral version of *Three Letters*; added to London production

No More Candy

Perspective

A Romantic Atmosphere

Sounds While Selling—music published [no lyric] in London piano selection

Tango Tragique

Tell Me I Look Nice—cut

Thank You, Madam

Three Letters

Try Me

Twelve Days to Christmas—music published [no lyric] in London piano selection

Where's My Shoe?

Director Harold Prince, whose Broadway debut had been as replacement on A FAMILY AFFAIR [Kander: January 27, 1962], now prepared his first musical from inception. Bock and Harnick wrote their finest score for this romantic/comic valentine, which was given a cream-puff production and perfectly played. Barbara Cook had her best role as the heroine, and Jack Cassidy (who had introduced Bock and Harnick) received a Tony Award for his supporting role. Yet SHE LOVES ME failed, despite exceedingly mild competition. The show was effectively revived by the Roundabout Theatre in 1993, but the commercial transfer (with Diane Fratantoni replacing Judy Kuhn in the female lead) also had a disappointing run. Both Broadway productions were remounted in London, and they failed, too. Four out of four is not an especially good record, but somehow it doesn't seem to matter (except to the backers). For Bock and Harnick provided SHE LOVES ME with an overstuffed candy box of a score: *Dear Friend, Ice Cream, She Loves Me, Will He Like Me?, Heads I Win* (for London), *A Trip to the Library*, and on and on.

TO BROADWAY WITH LOVE

April 22, 1964

Texas Pavilion Music Hall
    {New York World's Fair}

Title theme and Original material by Bock; Lyrics to Bock songs by Sheldon Harnick; Conceived and Directed by Morton DaCosta; Choreographed by Donald Saddler; Produced by George Schaeffer and Angus G. Wynne, Jr.; With Carmen Alvarez, Patti Karr, Rod Perry, and Sheila Smith.

Songs Recorded

Beautiful Lady

Mata Hari Mine

Popsicles in Paris

Remember Radio

To Broadway with Love

Bock and Harnick contributed several new songs to this anthology revue—using mostly old material—which was unsuccessfully mounted at the 1964 World's Fair.

FIDDLER ON THE ROOF

September 22, 1964

Imperial Theatre • 3,242 performances

Lyrics by Sheldon Harnick; Book by Joseph Stein (based on stories by Sholom Aleichem); Directed and Choreographed by Jerome Robbins; Produced by Harold Prince; With Zero Mostel, Maria Karnilova, and Beatrice Arthur.

Revivals

December 28, 1976

Winter Garden Theatre • 167 performances

Original direction reproduced by Ruth Mitchell; Original choreography reproduced by Tommy Abbott; With Zero Mostel, Thelma Lee [Karnilova], and Ruth Jaroslow [Arthur].

July 9, 1981

New York State Theatre • 53 performances

Directed and Choreographed by Jerome Robbins; With Herschel Bernardi [Mostel] and Maria Karnilova.

November 18, 1990

Gershwin Theatre • 241 performances

Original direction reproduced by Ruth Mitchell; Original choreography reproduced by Sammy Dallas Bayes; With Topol [Mostel], Marcia Lewis [Karnilova], and Ruth Jaroslow [Arthur].

Published Songs

Anatevka—initial individual publication upon use in 1971 movie version

Do You Love Me?—initial individual publication upon use in movie version

*Far from the Home I Love—initial individual publication upon use in movie version

Fiddler on the Roof (*Theme*)—non-show lyric

*If I Were a Rich Man

Matchmaker, Matchmaker

Miracle of Miracles—initial individual publication upon use in movie version

Now I Have Everything

*Sabbath Prayer—initial individual publication upon use in movie version

*Sunrise, Sunset

To Life—initial individual publication upon use in movie version

*Tradition—initial individual publication upon use in movie version

Additional Songs Published in Vocal Score

Chava Sequence (*Little Chavaleh*)

The Dream

The Rumor

Tevye's Monologue (*They Gave Each Other a Pledge*)

Tevye's Rebuttal

Wedding Dance [instrumental]

Additional Song Published in Non-show Folio

*When Messiah Comes—cut

Additional Songs Recorded

*Dear Sweet Sewing Machine—cut

How Much Richer Could One Man Be?—cut

Bock and Harnick joined with Joseph Stein—librettist of Bock's first two musicals—for this landmark musical based on stories by Sholom Aleichem. Producer Fred Coe had trouble raising the financing—a musical about a milkman in a pogrom?—so Harold Prince came into the project after the opening of SHE LOVES ME [April 23, 1963]. Prince enlisted Jerome Robbins (who had just dropped out of FUNNY GIRL

[Styne: March 26, 1964]), raised the money, and bought out Coe's interest. FIDDLER'S universal theme—as interpreted by Robbins—brought the piece worldwide acclaim, and Bock and Harnick provided excellent work in songs like *Tradition*, *Sabbath Prayer*, *If I Were a Rich Man*, and the *Chava Sequence*. There are also a couple of especially good cut songs—*When Messiah Comes* and *Dear Sweet Sewing Machine*—an indication that the things didn't work out exactly as expected. But FIDDLER, for good reason, remains one of America's favorite musicals.

BAKER STREET

February 16, 1965

Broadway Theatre • 313 performances

Music and Lyrics mostly by Marian Grudeff and Raymond Jessel; Lyrics to Bock songs by Sheldon Harnick; Book by Jerome Coopersmith (based on stories by Sir Arthur Conan Doyle); Directed by Harold Prince; Choreographed by Lee Becker Theodore; Produced by Alexander H. Cohen; With Fritz Weaver, Inga Swenson, and Martin Gabel.

Published Songs

Buffalo Belle—cut

Cold, Clear World

I'm in London Again

I Shall Miss You (*Holmes*)

Bock and Harnick answered director Hal Prince's calls for help on this bloated extravaganza by interpolating four songs, with Harnick seizing the opportunity to come up with a nifty pun about "the stately Holmes of England." The interpolations were publicly credited to the songwriters of record; the sheet music, curiously, carries no composer/lyricist credits whatsoever.

GENERATION

October 6, 1965

Morosco Theatre • 300 performances

Play by William Goodhart; Incidental music by Bock; Directed by Gene Saks; Produced by Frederick Brisson; With Henry Fonda and Holly Turner.

Published Songs
None

Bock wrote a title song to a lyric by the play-wright.

THE APPLE TREE
October 18, 1966
Shubert Theatre • 463 performances
Lyrics by Sheldon Harnick; Book by Bock and Harnick; Additional material by Jerome Coopersmith (based on stories by Mark Twain, Frank R. Stockton, and Jules Feiffer); Directed by Mike Nichols; Choreographed by Lee Becker Theodore; "Additional Musical Staging by Herbert Ross"; Produced by Stuart Ostrow; With Barbara Harris, Larry Blyden, and Alan Alda.

Published Songs
The Apple Tree (Forbidden Fruit)
Beautiful, Beautiful World
I'm Lost—cut
I've Got What You Want
What Makes Me Love Him?

Additional Songs Published in Vocal
    Selection
Oh, to Be a Movie Star
Wealth
You Are Not Real

Additional Songs Published in Vocal Score
Ai, Ai!
Eve
Feelings
Fish
Forbidden Love (In Gaul)
Friends
Gorgeous
Here in Eden
I Know
I'll Tell You a Truth
Lullaby (Go to Sleep Whatever You Are)
Make Way
Prisoner, Choose!
Razor Teeth
Tiger, Tiger
Which Door?
Who Is She?

An interesting idea—an evening of three one-act musicals—proved difficult to pull off. Jerome Robbins and Jerome Coopersmith left the project early on; musical novice Mike Nichols came in, bringing along "Passionella," which he'd staged in a previous version (THE WORLD OF JULES FEIFFER [Sondheim: July 2, 1962]). THE APPLE TREE proved uneven, hindered by the imposition of the Man/Woman/Devil concept over three unequal parts. The song-filled score has its high spots, though, showing Bock and Harnick at their best in *What Makes Me Love Him?*, *Go to Sleep Whatever You Are*, and *Oh, to Be a Movie Star*. Bock and Harnick next wrote a musical about the final years of Lord Horatio Nelson, TRAFALGAR[†] (with a book by John Arden). The show was scheduled for a London opening on October 21, 1967, but was ultimately never produced.

HER FIRST ROMAN
October 20, 1968
Lunt-Fontanne Theatre • 17 performances
Music and Lyrics mostly by Ervin Drake; Additional music by Bock; Lyrics to Bock songs by Sheldon Harnick; Book by Ervin Drake (based on *Caesar and Cleopatra* [play] by George Bernard Shaw); Directed by Derek Goldby; Choreographed by Dania Krupska; Produced by Joseph Cates and Henry Fownes (in association with Warner Brothers–7 Arts); With Richard Kiley, Leslie Uggams, and Claudia McNeil.

Published Bock Songs
None

Joseph Cates was successful, at least, in securing the closely guarded rights to Shaw's *Caesar and Cleopatra*. Then he assigned the score to pop composer Ervin Drake (who had written Cates's unsuccessful WHAT MAKES SAMMY RUN? [February 27, 1964]), hiring Drake as librettist as well. The director and choreographer (and their several replacements) were replaced en route, with Bock and Harnick finally rushing to Boston for last-minute cosmetic surgery. They contributed three songs (*Caesar Is Wrong*, *Old Gentleman*, and *Ptolemy* [all unpublished]), but to no avail.

THE ROTHSCHILDS
October 19, 1970
Lunt-Fontanne Theatre • 507 performances
Lyrics by Sheldon Harnick; Book by Sherman Yellen (based on the biography by Frederic Morton); Directed and Choreographed by Michael Kidd; Produced by Lester Osterman and Hillard Elkins; With Hal Linden, Leila Martin, Paul Hecht, Keene Curtis, and Jill Clayburgh.

Revival
April 27, 1990
Circle in the Square Downtown
    {Off Broadway} • 379 performances
Directed by Lonny Price; With Mike Burstyn [Linden].

Published Songs
I'm in Love! I'm in Love!
*In My Own Lifetime
One Room
Valse de Rothschild (Never Again)

Additional Songs Published in Vocal Selection
Everything
Rothschild and Sons
Sons

Additional Song Published in Non-show Folio
Just a Map—cut; new lyric for *Mayer's Lullaby* (cut/unpublished)

Additional Songs Recorded
Allons
Bonds
Give England Strength
Have You Ever Seen a Prettier Little Congress?
He Tossed a Coin
Pleasure and Privilege
Stability
*They Say
This Amazing London Town

A theatre-party special, calculated to please audiences who were still thronging to the six-year-old FIDDLER ON THE ROOF [September 22, 1964]. But Mayer Rothschild and his five sons hadn't the charm of Tevye and his gals. The weak book lacked warmth and interest, Bock and Harnick were a century out of their element, and there was no Robbins or Prince in sight. There was no clear point of view, either; just desperate producers and numerable directors and choreographers. And a couple of effective songs, *In My Own Lifetime*, a deftly comic choral number (*They Say*), and a lovely antiwar lullaby called *Just a Map* (which was cut). Disagreements during the troubled tryout of THE ROTHSCHILDS caused Bock to terminate his collaboration with Sheldon Harnick. Their final song, apparently, was *Should I, Should I, Should I*, written for Mayor Lindsay to sing in the mini-musical THE MAYOR'S REBUTTAL[†] at the Inner Circle dinner on March 3, 1973, at the New York Hilton. (Lindsay supporters Bock and Harnick also wrote material for the mayor's appearance at the 1966 Inner Circle dinner.) Bock withdrew into near retirement, happily collecting his never-ending FIDDLER royalties. He wrote an unproduced mystery-musical (with his own lyrics) and more recently 1040[†], another unproduced musical based on the tax code (with his own lyrics, after an aborted collaboration with William Finn). Harnick has been more active but decidedly unsuccessful, working with composers like Richard Rodgers (see REX [Rodgers: April 25, 1976]), Michel Legrand, and Joseph Raposo.

The final two Bock and Harnick shows were criticized for not being as good as FIDDLER ON THE ROOF [September 22, 1964]. Of course they were not as good as FIDDLER ON THE ROOF; how many shows are? Bock and Harnick were together for only twelve years and have been parted for more than a quarter of a century. Their names, though—and, perhaps, their talent—remain intrinsically linked. Bock leaves us with more than enough wonderful songs to make us rue his self-imposed exile from Broadway of almost three decades.

BOB MERRILL

Born: May 17, 1920, Atlantic City, New Jersey
Died: February 17, 1998, Beverly Hills, California

BOB MERRILL grew up in Philadelphia, where his father was a candy manufacturer. By his late teens he was working as a nightclub singer. Following military service, Merrill went to Hollywood in 1943 as an NBC radio writer, then served as dialogue director at Columbia Pictures. An interest in songwriting led to a highly profitable pop song career, highlighted by the 1950 *If I Knew You Were Comin' I'd've Baked a Cake* (written with Al Hoffman and Clem Watts) and the unforgettable *How Much Is That Doggie in the Window?* in 1953. His success with novelty songs was such that he had difficulty getting a serious hearing.

All Music and Lyrics by Bob Merrill unless otherwise indicated.

NEW GIRL IN TOWN
May 14, 1957
46th Street Theatre • 431 performances
Book by George Abbott (based on *Anna Christie* [play] by Eugene O'Neill); Directed by George Abbott; Choreographed by Bob Fosse; Produced by Frederick Brisson, Robert E. Griffith, and Harold S. Prince; With Gwen Verdon, Thelma Ritter, George Wallace, and Cameron Prud'homme.

Published Songs
At the Check Apron Ball
Did You Close Your Eyes?
Elegance—cut; for initial publication see
    HELLO, DOLLY! [January 16, 1964]
Flings
Here We Are Again—cut
If That Was Love
It's Good to Be Alive
Look at 'Er

Theme from "New Girl in Town" [instrumental]—non-lyric version of *Anna Lilla*
Sunshine Girl
You're My Friend, Ain'tcha?

Additional Songs Recorded
Anna Lilla
Chess and Checkers
On the Farm
Roll Yer Socks Up
There Ain't No Flies on Me
When I Valse

George Abbott, Bobby Griffith, and Hal Prince were looking for a project to follow their twin hits THE PAJAMA GAME [Adler: May 13, 1954] and DAMN YANKEES [Adler: May 5, 1955]. (Jerry Ross, the shows' co-composer, had died—and Richard Adler apparently had nothing to offer.) When MGM dropped *A Saint She Ain't*, the proposed Doris Day musical remake of *Anna Christie*, George Abbott heard the score, called for Griffith and Prince, and brought Bob Merrill to Broadway. Extreme tryout disagreements resulted in an ugly rift between the Abbott/Prince camp and Fosse/Verdon, resulting in a permanent separation. NEW GIRL was nevertheless moderately successful, thanks to costars Gwen Verdon and Thelma Ritter (who shared the Tony Award for Best Actress in a Musical). The score was of little interest—the ballads were particularly bald—except for the delectable turn-of-the-century novelty *The Sunshine Girl* and a cheery trio for over-the-hill floozies, *Flings*. Griffith, Prince, and Abbott went off looking for new songwriters (see FIORELLO! [Bock: November 23, 1959]); Fosse and Verdon went looking for new producers (see REDHEAD [Notables: February 5, 1959]); and Merrill got a call from David Merrick.

TAKE ME ALONG

October 22, 1959
Shubert Theatre • 448 performances
Book by Joseph Stein and Robert Russell
(based on *Ah, Wilderness* [play] by Eugene
O'Neill); Directed by Peter Glenville; Choreo-
graphed by Onna White; Produced by David
Merrick; With Jackie Gleason, Eileen Herlie,
Walter Pidgeon, and Robert Morse.

Revival
April 14, 1985
Martin Beck Theatre • 1 performance
Directed by Thomas Gruenewald; Choreo-
graphed by Dan Siretta; Transferred from
Goodspeed Opera House; with Robert Nichols
[Pidgeon], Kurt Knudson [Gleason], and Beth
Fowler [Herlie].

Published Songs

But Yours
I Get Embarrassed
I Would Die
Little Green Snake
Nine o'Clock
*Promise Me a Rose
Sid, Ol' Kid
Staying Young
*Take Me Along

Additional Songs Recorded

Oh, Please
The Parade
That's How It Starts
*Volunteer Firemen Picnic (Ladies with a Liberal
    Point of View)*
We're Home
Wint's Song

Merrill tried a second O'Neill adaptation, this
time using the playwright's more suitable turn-
of-the-century comedy. But the show's focus
was thrown out of kilter when TV comedian
Jackie Gleason was hired to play the wastrel uncle.
Walter Pidgeon, in the part created by George M.
Cohan, certainly couldn't compete, so Gleason
and his role ballooned. TAKE ME ALONG might
have succeeded anyway; it had fine performances
from Gleason, Eileen Herlie, and Robert Morse; a
nostalgic physical production; and a charming
score (including the snappy title song and the
tender *Promise Me a Rose*). But off-stage problems

developed between star and producer, eventually
causing Gleason to ankle. Merrill's NEW GIRL IN
TOWN [May 14, 1957] had been successful although not very good; TAKE ME ALONG was
considerably better but barely managed to break
even. A summer stock revival without stars, fixes,
or imagination came to Broadway on April 14,
1985, closing on April 14, 1985.

CARNIVAL!

April 13, 1961
Imperial Theatre • 719 performances
Book by Michael Stewart (based on material
by Helen Deutsch); Directed and Choreo-
graphed by Gower Champion; Produced by
David Merrick; With Anna Maria Alberghetti,
Jerry Orbach, Kaye Ballard, James Mitchell,
and Pierre Olaf.

Published Songs

*Beautiful Candy
Grand Imperial Cirque de Paris
Her Face
It Was Always You
Mira (Can You Imagine That?)
She's My Love
**Theme from Carnival! (Love Makes the World
    Go Round)*
*Three Puppet Songs: Golden, Delicious Fish, The
    Rich, Yum-Ticky-Tum-Tum*
*Yes, My Heart

Additional Song Published in *Puppet Songs from "Carnival!"*

Fairyland

Additional Songs Recorded

Direct from Vienna—also published (no lyric)
    in piano selection
Everybody Likes You
Humming
I Hate Him
I've Got to Find a Reason
Magic, Magic
Sword, Rose and Cape
A Very Nice Man

David Merrick had been particularly successful
with Gallic shows, from FANNY [Rome: November 4, 1954] to the revue LA PLUME DE MA
TANTE[†] [September 29, 1960]. Securing the

rights to the 1953 movie *Lili*,—about a small-time French traveling circus—Merrick wisely put the project in the hands of Gower Champion and librettist Michael Stewart (direct from the sleeper hit BYE BYE BIRDIE [Strouse: April 14, 1960]). Merrill, who did well enough on his first Merrick assignment, came up with his best score. CARNIVAL! was magical: staging, songs, puppets, and all. Merrill even managed to match the movie's hit theme song (*Hi-Lili, Hi-Lo*) with *Love Makes the World Go Round*. The entire score, in fact, is friendly, charming, and sweet.

HELLO, DOLLY!

January 16, 1964
St. James Theatre • 2,844 performances
Music and Lyrics mostly by Jerry Herman (also see Strouse: January 16, 1964); Book by Michael Stewart; (based on *The Matchmaker* [play] by Thornton Wilder); Directed and Choreographed by Gower Champion; Produced by David Merrick; With Carol Channing, David Burns, Eileen Brennan, and Charles Nelson Reilly.

Songs Published in Vocal Selection
Elegance [by Merrill and Herman]
Motherhood March [by Merrill and Herman]

Awaiting the start of rehearsals for his third consecutive Merrick musical, FUNNY GIRL [Styne: March 26, 1964], Merrill was called to Detroit when DOLLY! underwent tryout transfusions. For details, see [Herman: January 16, 1964].

FUNNY GIRL

See Styne: March 26, 1964.

BREAKFAST AT TIFFANY'S

December 14, 1966
Majestic Theatre • Closed during previews
Book "Adapted" by Edward Albee (based on the novella by Truman Capote); Directed by Joseph Anthony; Choreographed by Michael Kidd; Produced by David Merrick; With Mary Tyler Moore, Richard Chamberlain, Art Lund, and Sally Kellerman. Pre-Broadway title: HOLLY GOLIGHTLY.

Songs Issued as Professional Copies
*Breakfast at Tiffany's
Ciao, Compare
*Holly Golightly
I've Got a Penny—cut
Travellin'—cut
You've Never Kissed Her

Additional Songs Recorded
Freddy Chant
Grade "A" Treatment
*Home for Wayward Girls
I'm Not the Girl Who Used to Be
Lament for Ten Men—reused in SOME LIKE IT HOT, the London production [March 2, 1992] of SUGAR [Styne: April 9, 1972]
Same Mistakes
Stay with Me
When Daddy Comes Home
Who Needs Her?

Merrill, in his fourth Merrick assignment, came up with one of Broadway's all-time fiascos. A popular novel, a smash movie, and two major TV stars added up to a record advance sale; but Merrick chose to close what he considered a hopelessly poor show. A satisfactory point of view for the treatment of the prostitute heroine was never found, even with a drastic tryout revision by Edward Albee (who replaced Abe Burrows, who replaced Nunnally Johnson). Merrill's work, though, had charm in places, particularly in the two title songs and the cheery *Home for Wayward Girls*.

HENRY, SWEET HENRY

October 23, 1967
Palace Theatre • 80 performances
Book by Nunnally Johnson (based on *The World of Henry Orient* [novel] by Nora Johnson); Directed by George Roy Hill; Choreographed by Michael Bennett; Produced by Edward Specter Productions and Norman Twain; With Don Ameche, Carol Bruce, Robin Wilson, Louise Lasser, Neva Small, and Alice Playten.

Published Songs
Dearest Darling—cut; issued as professional copy
Do You Ever Go to Boston?

Henry, Sweet Henry
*Here I Am
I Wonder How It Is to Dance with a Boy
Love of My Life—cut; issued as professional
    copy
My Kind of Person—cut; issued as professional
    copy
Somebody Someplace—cut; issued as profes-
    sional copy
Weary Near to Dyin'
You Might Get to Like Me—cut; issued as
    professional copy; revised version of *We
    Only Remember* (cut, unpublished) from
    HELLO, DOLLY! [January 16, 1964]

Additional Songs Recorded
Academic Fugue
I'm Blue Too
*In Some Little World
Nobody Steps on Kafritz
People Watchers
Pillar to Post
Poor Little Person—revised version of *My Kind
    of Person* (cut)
To Be Artistic
Woman in Love

Merrill tried yet another adaptation of a popular movie, again meeting with failure. The teenage girls of HENRY, SWEET HENRY were (mostly)
amusing and sympathetic; the adults, though,
were obnoxious and uninteresting. Merrill's tender material for the girls (including *Here I Am*
and *In Some Little World*) was overpowered by
the grown-up songs, and the show—in a season
where it should have been a hit—defeated itself.
Broadway found a new choreographer, though:
Michael Bennett, a Michael Kidd dancer in SUB-
WAYS ARE FOR SLEEPING [Styne: December
27, 1961] and HERE'S LOVE [Willson: October 3,
1963]. This was Bennett's second attempt, following the equally unsuccessful A JOYFUL NOISE
[December 15, 1966].

PRETTYBELLE
See Styne: February 1, 1971.

SUGAR
See Styne: April 9, 1972.

THE PRINCE OF GRAND STREET
March 7, 1978
Forrest Theatre {Philadelphia} •
    Closed during tryout
Book by Bob Merrill; Directed by Gene Saks;
Choreographed by Lee Becker Theodore;
Produced by Robert Whitehead, Roger L.
Stevens, and The Shubert Organization; With
Robert Preston, Sam Levene, Neva Small,
Werner Klemperer, and Bernice Massi.

Song Recorded
Sew a Button—cut; initial recording upon
    reuse in HANNAH . . . 1939 [May 31,
    1990]

The combination of BREAKFAST AT TIFFANY'S
[December 14, 1966], PRETTYBELLE [February
1, 1971], and THE PRINCE OF GRAND STREET
—three disastrous big-star vehicles with great
potential and heavy advance theatre-party book-
ings—virtually ended Merrill's Broadway career. (Theatre owners hate to give back ticket
money.) THE PRINCE OF GRAND STREET was
patterned after Jacob Adler, patriarch of the
Yiddish Theatre. Robert Preston was one of Broadway's finest and most charming actors, equally
at home in drama and musical—but *Jacob Adler?*
(In the second act, the aging Yiddish Prince portrayed Huckleberry Finn. Seems that Adler was
a great chum of Mark Twain.) Preston also closed
out of town when Stuart Ostrow cast him as
Pancho Villa in WE TAKE THE TOWN [Febru-
ary 19, 1962]. The writers get blamed for these
things, and the actors suffer through the painful performances (no matter how few). But what
about the producers who choose the material?

HANNAH . . . 1939
May 31, 1990
Vineyard Theatre {Off Off Broadway} •
    46 performances
Book by Bob Merrill; Directed by Douglas
Aibel; Choreographed by Tina Paul; Produced
by The Vineyard Theatre; With Julie Wilson,
Leigh Beery, Neva Small, and Tony Carlin.

Songs Recorded
Ah, Our Germans
Gentle Afternoon

Hannah Will Take Care of You
Kissed on the Eyes
Learn about Life
Martina
No Give, No Take
Opening
The Pearl We Called Prague
Pretty Thing
Radio Dance
Sew a Button—cut; originally used in THE
    PRINCE OF GRAND STREET [March 7,
    1978]
So Good to See You
Someday
Wear a Little Grin
We Dance
Who Is Hannah?

HANNAH . . . 1939—cheery title, isn't it?—was the story of a Jewish fashion designer whose Prague factory is commandeered to manufacture Nazi uniforms. Hannah becomes fond (in a motherly way) of the young lieutenant who oversees the operation, never dreaming what the Nazis—*Ah, Our Germans,* she sings—are really up to. This from the guy who wrote *How Much Is That Doggie in the Window?* Grisly, man, real grisly. The Vineyard Theatre had previously presented

a Merrill anthology musical, WE'RE HOME [October 19, 1984], which attracted scant attention during its twenty-four-performance run.

THE RED SHOES
See Styne: December 16, 1993.

Merrill did his RED SHOES patching via fax from his home in Beverly Hills. After several years of ill health and prolonged depression—and facing increased incapacitation—Merrill committed suicide on February 17, 1998.

Bob Merrill wrote seven full scores for the theatre, as well as three sets of lyrics to Jule Styne's music. His best work—CARNIVAL! [April 13, 1961], plus sections of TAKE ME ALONG [October 22, 1959] and HENRY, SWEET HENRY [October 23, 1967]—displayed a wistful innocence. His more "sophisticated" efforts were coarse, less appealing, and at times tasteless. Since joining composer Jule Styne to write *People* and FUNNY GIRL [March 26, 1964]—for whatever reason—Bob Merrill did little of interest (except collect FUNNY GIRL royalties).

MEREDITH WILLSON

Born: May 8, 1902, Mason City, Iowa
Died: June 15, 1984, Santa Monica, California

MEREDITH WILLSON, as a small-town child, did not take up the trumpet and lisp (like Winthrop Paroo in THE MUSIC MAN [December 19, 1957]). Rather, he sang barber shop and became proficient on flute and piccolo. His mother gave piano lessons, though. Willson spent the early 1920s in John Philip Sousa's band, then moved over to the New York Philharmonic. After the stock market crash, Willson went to the West Coast and began a profitable career in radio as performer and conductor.

All Music and Lyrics by Meredith Willson unless otherwise indicated.

THE LITTLE FOXES
February 15, 1939
National Theatre • 410 performances
Play by Lillian Hellman; Incidental music by Willson; Produced and Directed by Herman Shumlin; With Tallulah Bankhead.

Published Song
Never Feel Too Weary to Pray—initial publication upon use in movie version

Willson's career somehow led him to this first of two seemingly unlikely assignments. In 1940 he composed and arranged the score for Charles Chaplin's film *The Great Dictator*. His first song hit was the 1941 pop song *You and I*. *May the Good Lord Bless and Keep You*, theme song for Tallulah Bankhead's 1950 radio show, was an inspirational hit during the Korean War. In 1948 Willson wrote a slight, nostalgic semiautobiography. Frank Loesser, who had just successfully made the Hollywood-to-Broadway trip with WHERE'S CHARLEY? [Loesser: October 11, 1948], suggested that Willson write a musical comedy based on his early days in small-town America.

THE MUSIC MAN
December 19, 1957
Majestic Theatre • 1,375 performances
Book by Willson with Franklin Lacey (based on *And There I Stood with My Piccolo* [memoir] by Willson); Directed by Morton DaCosta; Choreographed by Onna White; Produced by Kermit Bloomgarden with Herbert Greene, in association with Frank (Loesser) Productions; With Robert Preston, Barbara Cook, David Burns, Iggie Wolfington, and Pert Kelton.

Revival
June 5, 1980
City Center • 21 performances
Directed and Choreographed by Michael Kidd; With Dick Van Dyke [Preston], Meg Bussert [Cook], Iggie Wolfington [Burns], and Christian Slater.

Published Songs
Being in Love—written for 1962 movie version
*Goodnight, My Someone
It's You
Lida Rose
*Seventy-Six Trombones
Till There Was You—revised lyric for 1950 non-show song *Till I Met You*
Ya Got Trouble—initial individual publication in 1966

Additional Songs Published in Vocal Selection
Gary, Indiana
*My White Knight
The Wells Fargo Wagon

Additional Songs Published in Vocal Score
Iowa Stubborn
*Marian the Librarian
Piano Lesson (If You Don't Mind My Saying So)
Pick-a-Little, Talk-a-Little
*Rock Island (Train Talk)
The Sadder-but-Wiser Girl
Shipoopi
Sincere
Will I Ever Tell You?

Additional Song Recorded
You Don't Have to Kiss Me Goodnight—cut

After eight years and many different versions, Willson's nostalgic musical finally made it to Broadway. With no theatre experience, the composer used inventiveness and humor to come up with a delightful score. THE MUSIC MAN became the biggest hit of the late 1950s, far outdistancing the likes of WEST SIDE STORY [Bernstein: September 26, 1957] and GYPSY [Styne: May 21, 1959]. The heretofore non-singing Robert Preston was an inspired casting choice; besides, no established stage star wanted to do it. Barbara Cook graduated from CANDIDE [Bernstein: December 1, 1956] to become a favorite musical comedy heroine. Frank Loesser, instigator of the project, reaped multiple benefits as associate producer, publisher of the score, and licenser of rights.

Another "Frank" note on authorship: Willson's mentor Loesser appears to have ghosted the glorious *My White Knight*. (It can be musically traced to two MOST HAPPY FELLA [May 3, 1956] themes, Marie's cut aria *Eyes Like a Stranger*, and underscoring developed from *Somebody, Somewhere*.) When THE MUSIC MAN went to Hollywood, Willson discarded *My White Knight* and replaced it with a pallid ballad of his own, *Being in Love*.

THE UNSINKABLE MOLLY BROWN
November 3, 1960
Winter Garden Theatre • 532 performances
Book by Richard Morris; Directed by Dore Schary; Choreographed by Peter Gennaro; Produced by The Theatre Guild and Dore Schary; With Tammy Grimes, Harve Presnell, Cameron Prud'homme, and Edith Meiser.

Published Songs
Are You Sure?
Bea-u-ti-ful People of Denver
Belly up to the Bar Boys
Bon Jour (The Language Song)
Chick-a-Pen
Dolce Far Niente
He's My Friend—written for 1964 movie
    version
*I Ain't Down Yet
I Ain't Down Yet ("March")
If I Knew
I'll Never Say No
I've A'ready Started In
Keep-a-Hoppin'

Additional Song Published in Vocal Selection
Leadville Johnny Brown (Soliloquy)

Additional Songs Published in Vocal Score
Colorado, My Home
Denver Police
Happy Birthday, Mrs. J. J. Brown
My Brass Bed
Up Where the People Are [instrumental]

Willson's second musical was another homespun hit, with much less appeal than THE MUSIC MAN [December 19, 1957]. What had been spontaneous inventiveness in 1957 was too calculated here; but Willson's energetic tunefulness, Tammy Grimes's star-making performance, and a large advance sale carried the show to moderate success.

HERE'S LOVE
October 3, 1963
Shubert Theatre • 334 performances
Book by Willson (based on "Miracle on 34th Street" [story] by Valentine Davies); Directed by Stuart Ostrow; Choreographed by Michael Kidd; Produced by Stuart Ostrow; With Janis Paige, Craig Stevens, Laurence Naismith, and Fred Gwynne.

Published Songs
Arm in Arm
The Big Clown Balloons
Dear Mister Santa Claus—cut

Expect Things to Happen
Here's Love
Love, Come Take Me Again—cut
My State, My Kansas, My Home
My Wish
Pine Cones and Holly Berries—
    countermelody to Willson's 1951 non-
    show song *It's Beginning to Look Like
    Christmas*
That Man Over There
You Don't Know

Additional Songs Recorded
The Bugle
Look Little Girl
She Hadda Go Back

A sure-fire family hit based on a Christmas movie classic, HERE'S LOVE had no chance: if you can't do something better, don't do it. Director Norman Jewison departed during the tryout; Ostrow, a former Frank Music administrator with good theatre sense but little experience, took. Outside of choreographer Michael Kidd's inventive Thanksgiving Day Parade opening, HERE'S LOVE had nothing going for it other than a decent-sized advance sale.

| 49 |
September 2, 1969
Dorothy Chandler Pavilion {Los Angeles} •
    Closed during tryout
"A Romantic Speculation." Book by Willson and Richard Morris (based on an idea by Ed Ainsworth); Directed by Richard Morris; Choreographed by Danny Daniels; Produced by Edwin Lester (Los Angeles Civic Light Opera); With John Cullum, Chita Rivera, Jean Fenn, and Steve Arlen.

Published Songs
None

Willson's final attempt for the theatre was this charmless Christopher Columbus operetta which suffered a severe critical trouncing and quickly sank. Willson went back into retirement and died June 15, 1984, in Santa Monica.

Meredith Willson was not really a theatre composer; rather, he was an inventive novelty writer with one great show in him. THE MUSIC MAN [December 19, 1957] will always remain a one-of-a-kind classic. The composer's three other scores, however, are of little interest.

STEPHEN SONDHEIM

Born: March 22, 1930, New York, New York

STEPHEN SONDHEIM moved at the age of eleven from Manhattan to Doylestown, Pennsylvania—Doylestown, country home of Oscar Hammerstein 2nd. A friendship with young James Hammerstein led to a close teacher/student relationship with James's father, the man who helped create "dramatic" musical theatre in his work with Jerome Kern and who over the next few years would write OKLAHOMA! [Rodgers: March 31, 1943] and CAROUSEL [Rodgers: April 19, 1945]. The teen-aged Sondheim was soon struggling through formative musicals written under Hammerstein's tutelage. He also watched as Hammerstein struggled through his own problematic musical, the free-form ALLEGRO [Rodgers: October 10, 1947]; as a Williams College sophomore, Sondheim served as production assistant.

All Music and Lyrics by Stephen Sondheim unless otherwise indicated.

PHINNEY'S RAINBOW
[circa May 1948]
Adams Memorial Theatre
{Williamstown, Mass.} • 4 performances
Williams College Show. Book by Sondheim and Josiah T. S. Horton; Directed by David C. Bryant; Produced by Cap and Bells, Inc.

Published Songs
How Do I Know?
Phinney's Rainbow
Still Got My Heart

Sondheim's first published theatre work came from this college show, courtesy of the BMI talent search (see BIG AS LIFE [Bock: circa May 1948]). The college president was named James Phinney Baxter, and the title was borrowed from a recent Broadway hit. The songs, though, were far removed from *How Are Things in Glocca Morra*. Sondheim was fourteen years away from his first Broadway musical (as composer), so it's interesting to see how advanced these early songs are. *Phinney's Rainbow* has a strong, complex rhythm (which gets *too* complex along the way); the lyric, as it happens, is a take-off on Hammerstein's hymn *You'll Never Walk Alone*. *Still Got My Heart* is particularly interesting for its effective harmonic wanderings, combined with a couple of syncopational tricks.

ALL THAT GLITTERS
March 19, 1949
Adams Memorial Theatre
{Williamstown, Mass.} • 4 performances
Williams College Show. Book by Sondheim (based on *Beggar on Horseback* [play] by George S. Kaufman and Marc Connelly}; Directed by David C. Bryant; Produced by Cap and Bells, Inc.; With Ronald Moir, Betty Dissell, Jeanette Forsey, and Donald Rackerby.

Songs Published in Vocal Selection
I Love You, Etcetera
I Must Be Dreaming
I Need Love
Let's Not Fall in Love
When I See You

Teacher Hammerstein instructed student Sondheim to take a play he liked and turn it into a musical; ALL THAT GLITTERS, from Kaufman and Connelly's *Beggar on Horseback*, was the result. *When I See You* stands out; the complexities are striking—nineteen-year-old Sondheim tried things no one else in those days (except Blitzstein or Duke) was doing. One wonders, though, how a 1949 college soprano coped with the key shifts into and throughout the fascinating bridge. *Let's Not Fall in Love* is the best of the others, a light rhythm number. In these first eight published, teenage songs, Sondheim was somewhat less adept with words and melody; rhythmically, he was often *too* intricate.

I KNOW MY LOVE

November 2, 1949

Shubert Theatre • 247 performances

Play by S. N. Behrman (based on *Aupres de Ma Blonde* [play] by Marcel Achard); Directed by Alfred Lunt; Produced by The Theatre Guild and John C. Wilson; With Alfred Lunt, Lynn Fontanne, and Geoffrey Kerr.

Published Songs

None

While still at Williams, Sondheim had his first Broadway hearing with a Christmas carol written for this Lunt/Fontanne vehicle. (The Sondheim name was not exactly unknown along Broadway; his father, a dress manufacturer, had taken full-page ads in late-1920s theatre programs with testimonials—signed by Flo Ziegfeld, no less—for Sondheim wedding gowns.) Upon graduation, Sondheim studied with avant-garde composer Milton Babbitt on a fellowship. His first professional writing job came in the fall of 1953, when he went to Hollywood to assist George Oppenheimer—a friend of Hammerstein —with a season of scripts for the TV series *Topper*. He also wrote the song *Rag Me That Mendelssohn March* for the summer stock tryout of the Claudette Colbert comedy *A Mighty Man Is He*, by Oppenheimer and Arthur Kober, which played the Falmouth/Cape/Ogunquit summer stock circuit in August 1955. (The 1960 Broadway production of the play used a different song, by pop songwriter Sherman Edwards, who would write one musical: 1776 [Notables: March 16, 1969].)

SATURDAY NIGHT

[circa August 1955]

Unproduced musical. Book by Julius J. Epstein (based on *Front Porch in Brooklyn* [play] by Julius J. Epstein and Philip G. Epstein); [Produced by Lemuel Ayers].

Songs Published in Non-show Folios

Isn't It?

So Many People—initial use in MARRY ME A LITTLE [March 12, 1981]

What More Do I Need?—initial use in MARRY ME A LITTLE

Additional Songs Recorded

All for You

Class—initial use in 1982 London production of MARRY ME A LITTLE

Exhibit A

In the Movies

I Remember That

It's That Kind of a Neighborhood (including *Fair Brooklyn*)

Love's a Bond

A Moment with You

One Wonderful Day

Saturday Night

Returning from his *Topper* assignment in Hollywood, Sondheim was commissioned to write his first Broadway musical by Lemuel Ayers. Ayers was producer/set designer of KISS ME KATE [Porter: December 30, 1948] and OUT OF THIS WORLD [Porter: December 21, 1950], as well as designer of shows like OKLAHOMA! [Rodgers: March 31, 1943] and THE PAJAMA GAME [Adler: May 13, 1954]). The money was only partially raised when Ayers died on August 14, 1955, at the age of forty; nobody bothered to pick up SATURDAY NIGHT, and that was that. After the successful opening of GYPSY [Styne: May 21, 1959], composer-turned-producer Jule Styne announced it for December 1959, with Bob Fosse at the helm. Sondheim himself pulled the plug, feeling that SATURDAY NIGHT would be a step backward. After restricting the rights to his firstborn for many years, Sondheim finally allowed the Bridewell Theater Company in London to do a reading in 1995, which was followed by the British equivalent to an Off Off Broadway production [December 17, 1997]. The results were as one might have expected: an interesting if unremarkable score surrounded by an uninteresting book. A second production was mounted May 19, 1999, by the non-Equity Pegasus Players in Chicago, with Sondheim contributing two new songs, *Delighted I'm Sure* and *Montana Chem* (presently unpublished). While there are some songs of note—*So Many People*, the title song—none of SATURDAY NIGHT could be considered major Sondheim. If produced in 1955 it would presumably have paled besides THE PAJAMA GAME, FANNY [Rome: November 4, 1954], or even PLAIN AND FANCY [Notables: January 27, 1955].

GIRLS OF SUMMER
November 19, 1956
Longacre Theatre • 56 performances
Play by N. Richard Nash; Incidental music by Sondheim; Directed by Jack Garfein; Produced by Cheryl Crawford; With Shelley Winters, Pat Hingle, and George Peppard.

Published Song
Girls of Summer

On the basis of the unproduced SATURDAY NIGHT, Sondheim was selected as co-lyricist of the upcoming WEST SIDE STORY [Bernstein: September 26, 1957]. Cheryl Crawford, who was WEST SIDE's producer at the time, gave Sondheim his first real Broadway hearing with the incidental music assignment on GIRLS OF SUMMER. The title song is Sondheim at his jazziest until MERRILY WE ROLL ALONG [November 16, 1981].

WEST SIDE STORY
See Bernstein: September 26, 1957.

TAKE FIVE
October 10, 1957
Downstairs at the Upstairs Room •
    Nightclub revue
Music and Lyrics mostly by Ronny Graham, Bart Howard, and others; Sketches by Don Adams, Dee Caruso, Bill Levine, and Steven Vinaver; Directed by Max Adrian and John Heawood; Produced by Julius Monk; With Ronny Graham, Ellen Hanley, and Gerry Matthews.

Sond Recorded
Pour le Sport—written for unfinished 1956 musical THE LAST RESORTS[†], initial use in MARRY ME A LITTLE [March 12, 1981]

Back in 1955 young Sondheim's young producer friend Harold Prince—picture them as two kids on a tenement rooftop, á la MERRILY WE ROLL ALONG [November 16, 1981]—had optioned Cleveland Amory's novel *The Last Resorts*. Sond heim was to write music and lyrics, with a book by Jean Kerr (whose *Please Don't Eat the Daisies* was a current best-seller). Little was written before THE LAST RESORTS was dropped; *Pour le Sport* was salvaged and placed in this edition of Julius Monk's nightclub series. Other TAKE FIVE contributors worthy of note were composer Jonathan Tunick (working with lyricist Steven Vinaver) and lyricist Carolyn Leigh (working with composer Philip Springer). Prince ultimately produced Sondheim's first musicals as both lyricist and composer, although he originated neither. Prince and partner Bobby Griffith took over WEST SIDE STORY [Bernstein: September 26, 1957] when it was dropped by Cheryl Crawford. A FUNNY THING HAPPENED ON THE WAY TO THE FORUM [May 8, 1962] was a post-GYPSY [Styne: May 21, 1959] project of David Merrick. Jerry Robbins, originally slated to direct, decided to withdraw from the show. He then decided he wanted to direct it after all—but only if Prince were the producer. The authors duly refused to extend Merrick's option on the property and gave it to Prince—after which Robbins decided he didn't want to direct it again. Thus FORUM became an Abbott/Prince show, with Robbins stepping in at the last moment for some critical doctoring.

GYPSY
See Styne: May 21, 1959.

INVITATION TO A MARCH
October 29, 1960
Music Box Theatre • 113 performances
Play by Arthur Laurents; Incidental music by Sondheim; Directed by Arthur Laurents; Produced by The Theatre Guild; With Celeste

Holm, Madeleine Sherwood, Eileen Heckart, Jane Fonda, and James MacArthur.

Song Recorded
Incidental Music [selection]

Arthur Laurents had been responsible for bringing Sondheim in on WEST SIDE STORY [Bernstein: September 26, 1957] and GYPSY [Styne: May 21, 1959]—which, oddly enough, was Laurents's final Broadway hit as a writer. The two close friends were to create one more musical together, the ill-fated ANYONE CAN WHISTLE [April 4, 1964].

A FUNNY THING HAPPENED ON THE WAY TO THE FORUM
May 8, 1962
Alvin Theatre • 964 performances
Book by Burt Shevelove and Larry Gelbart (based on plays by Plautus); Directed by George Abbott; Choreographed by Jack Cole; Produced by Harold Prince; With Zero Mostel, Jack Gilford, David Burns, and John Carradine.

Revivals
March 30, 1972
Lunt-Fontanne Theatre • 156 performances
Directed by Burt Shevelove; Choreographed by Ralph Beaumont; With Phil Silvers [Mostel], Larry Blyden [Gilford], and Carl Ballantine [Carradine].

April 18, 1996
St. James Theatre • 715 performances
Directed by Jerry Zaks; Choreographed by Rob Marshall; With Nathan Lane [Mostel], Mark Linn-Baker [Gilford], Lewis J. Stadlen [Burns], and Ernie Sabella [Carradine].

Published Songs
*Comedy Tonight
*Everybody Ought to Have a Maid
I Do Like You—cut
Love, I Hear
Love Is in the Air—cut
*Lovely
That'll Show Him
Your Eyes Are Blue—cut

Additional Songs Published in Vocal Selection
*Impossible
Pretty Little Picture

Additional Songs Published in Vocal Score
*Bring Me My Bride
*Free
Funeral Sequence
The House of Marcus Lycus [2nd]—underscoring version
I'm Calm
That Dirty Old Man

Additional Songs Recorded
Echo Song—cut
The House of Marcus Lycus [1st]—cut; song version
There's Something about a War

Composer Sondheim—already highly successful as a lyricist—was finally heard on Broadway with this extremely funny vaudeville-based farce musical. Sondheim's lyrics were on a level with the lovingly slapdash book by Burt Shevelove (a longtime friend) and Larry Gelbart (with whom Sondheim had collaborated on an unproduced screenplay in the mid-1950s). The music was suitably witty but slightly tame, except for the brashly delectable *Everybody Ought to Have a Maid*. *Comedy Tonight*, *Impossible*, *Free*, and *Bring Me My Bride* all display great verbal dexterity, but the only truly melodic song in the score is the purposely vapid *Lovely*. It wasn't until COMPANY [April 26, 1970]—a depressingly long eight years later—that Sondheim's music began to receive true recognition. (FORUM predated GYPSY [Styne: May 21, 1959]; the authors completed their first draft late in 1958.) FORUM was producer Harold Prince's first musical on his own; partner Bobby Griffith died while the show was in preparation on June 7, 1961. It also turned out to be George Abbott's final musical success—with an assist from Jerome Robbins.

THE WORLD OF JULES FEIFFER
July 2, 1962
Hunterdon Hills Playhouse {Clinton, N.J.} • Summer stock tryout
Sketches by Jules Feiffer; Music and Lyrics by Sondheim; Directed by Mike Nichols; Pro-

duced by Lewis Allen and Harry Rigby; With Ronny Graham, Dorothy Loudon, and Paul Sand.

Song Published in Non-show Folio
Truly Content

Mike Nichols first tried his hand at legit directing with this summer stock revue based on Jules Feiffer's work. Sondheim composed incidental music for "George's Moon" and "Passionella," with one song—*Truly Content*—for the latter. It is quite a delight, comparing favorably to the similarly first-rate *Oh, to Be a Movie Star* from Nichols's second try at "Passionella" in THE APPLE TREE [Bock: October 18, 1966]. Dorothy Loudon, who spent the next fifteen years giving life to a string of musical fatalities—until Nichols put her in ANNIE [Strouse: April 21, 1977])—surely must have made an interesting chimney sweep.

HOT SPOT
April 19, 1963
Majestic Theatre • 43 performances
Music by Mary Rodgers; Lyrics mostly by Martin Charnin; Book by Jack Weinstock and Willie Gilbert; Directed by Morton Da Costa; Choreographed by Onna White; Produced by Robert Fryer and Lawrence Carr, in association with John Herman; With Judy Holliday, Joseph Campanella, Joe Bova, Mary Louise Wilson, and George Furth.

Song Recorded
Don't Laugh [music and lyrics by Rodgers, Charnin, and Sondheim]—advertised but not published; initial recording upon reuse in THE MADWOMAN OF CENTRAL PARK WEST [Bernstein/Kander: June 13, 1979]

Sondheim stepped in to help out his close friend Mary Rodgers (the pair had served as summer stock apprentices at the Westport Country Playhouse) and Martin Charnin (who played "Big Deal" in WEST SIDE STORY [Bernstein: September 26, 1957]). Sondheim had collaborated with Rodgers a decade earlier on an unproduced TV musical; here she wrote the music and he provided the lyric, which was then supplemented

by Charnin. A FUNNY THING [May 8, 1962] was "saved" at the very last minute, they say, when ghost-director Jerome Robbins requisitioned a new opening number. *Comedy Tonight* told the audience precisely what to expect and the show magically turned into a hit. The last-minute balm for the tepid HOT SPOT was *Don't Laugh*, and it told the audience precisely what to expect.

ANYONE CAN WHISTLE
April 4, 1964
Majestic Theatre • 9 performances
"*A Wild New Musical.*" Book by Arthur Laurents; Directed by Arthur Laurents; Choreographed by Herbert Ross; Produced by Kermit Bloomgarden and Diana Krasny; With Angela Lansbury, Lee Remick, and Harry Guardino.

Concert Version
April 8, 1995
Carnegie Hall • 1 performance
Directed by Herbert Ross; Benefit for Gay Men's Health Crisis; With Bernadette Peters [Remick], Madeline Kahn [Lansbury], Scott Bakula [Guardino], and Angela Lansbury.

Published Songs
Anyone Can Whistle
Come Play Wiz Me
Everybody Says Don't
I've Got You to Lean On
A Parade in Town
See What It Gets You
There Won't Be Trumpets—cut
With So Little to Be Sure Of

Additional Songs Published in Vocal Score
A-1 March
Cora's Chase (Lock 'Em Up)
I'm Like the Bluebird
Me and My Town
Miracle Song
Opposites
Run for Your Lives
Simple (A Is One)
Watchcries

Additional Song Recorded
There's Always a Woman—cut

This "wild, new musical" was too wild and new (and muddled) to compete with the likes of HELLO, DOLLY! [Herman: January 16, 1964] and FUNNY GIRL [Styne: March 26, 1964] and was gone in a week. Sondheim's score was impressively well developed, and rather startling sounding at the time. The melodic *With So Little to Be Sure Of* and the title song are effective, if pessimistic, ballads; *A Parade in Town* and the rhythmically playful *Me and My Town* make good character material for the show's offbeat villainess. But it is the fascinating extended musical scenes, with their intricate choral work, that immediately marked Sondheim as the most distinctive theatre composer of his time. The first-act sanity sequence (*Simple, Watchcries, Opposites*) and the third-act chase (*Lock 'Em Up*) are unlike anything that came before. Unfortunately for Sondheim, the mammoth failure of the complex ANYONE CAN WHISTLE was enough to scare away producers bearing composing jobs for the rest of the decade. Angela Lansbury—who was to come back with a legendary Sondheim performance—became an important musical comedy star overnight. But via Jerry Herman.

DO I HEAR A WALTZ?
See Rodgers: March 18, 1965.

THE MAD SHOW
January 9, 1966
New Theatre {Off Broadway} •
    871 performances
Music by Mary Rodgers; Lyrics mostly by Marshall Barer; Book by Larry Siegel and Stan Hart (based on *Mad* magazine); Directed by Steven Vinaver; Produced by Ivor David Balding; With Linda Lavin, Paul Sand, Dick Libertini, and Jo Anne Worley.

Song Published in Non-show Folio
The Boy From [music by Rodgers, lyric by "Esteban Ria Nido"]

Sondheim again lent a hand to his friend Mary Rodgers, contributing this nonsense lyric in the *Girl from Ipanema* vein. The only Sondheim music to be heard between ANYONE CAN WHISTLE [April 4, 1964] and COMPANY [April 26, 1970] was for the TV mini-musical "Evening Primrose" [November 16, 1966], which starred Anthony Perkins. Sondheim provided four songs, including *Take Me to the World* (which harkens back to *With So Little to Be Sure Of*) and the evocative *I Remember*.

ILLYA DARLING
April 11, 1967
Mark Hellinger Theatre • 320 performances
Music by Manos Hadjidakis; Lyrics mostly by Joe Darion; Book by Jules Dassin (based on his screenplay *Never on Sunday*); Directed by Jules Dassin; Choreographed by Onna White; Produced by Kermit Bloomgarden in association with United Artists; With Melina Mercouri [Dassin] and Orson Bean.

Published Songs
None

Sondheim was called in by producer Kermit Bloomgarden (of ANYONE CAN WHISTLE [April 4, 1964]) to help on this ill-assembled Melina Mercouri vehicle; composer of record Manos Hadjidakis—who had written the international song hit *Never on Sunday*—was out of place on Broadway (to say the least). Sondheim did some rewrites on the lyric of an unused opening number as well as contributing lyrics for one song, *Piraeus*, which was dropped just before the Broadway opening. (This is not to be confused with *Piraeus, My Love*, which was not by Sondheim.)

A PRAY BY BLECHT
See Bernstein: circa February 16, 1969.

COMPANY
April 26, 1970
Alvin Theatre • 706 performances
Book by George Furth; Directed by Harold Prince; Choreographed by Michael Bennett; Produced by Harold Prince in association with Ruth Mitchell; With Dean Jones, Elaine Stritch, Barbara Barrie, John Cunningham, Charles Kimbrough, Beth Howland, Pamela Myers, Susan Browning, and Donna McKechnie.

Concert Version
April 11, 1993
Vivian Beaumont Theatre • 2 performances
Benefit for Broadway Cares/Equity Fights
AIDS; With the Original Cast and Patti
LuPone.

Revival
October 5, 1995
Roundabout Theatre • 68 performances
Directed by Scott Ellis; Choreographed by Rob
Marshall; Produced by Roundabout Theatre
(Todd Haimes); With Boyd Gaines [Jones],
Debra Monk [Stritch], Kate Burton [Barrie],
Robert Westenberg [Kimbrough], Veanne Cox
[Howland], and La Chanze [Myers].

Published Songs
*Another Hundred People
*Being Alive
*Company
The Ladies Who Lunch
The Little Things You Do Together
Side by Side by Side
*Someone Is Waiting
*Sorry-Grateful
*You Could Drive a Person Crazy

Additional Songs Published in Vocal Selection
Barcelona
What Would We Do without You?

Additional Songs Published in Vocal Score
*Getting Married Today
Have I Got a Girl for You
Poor Baby
Tick-Tock [instrumental]

Additional Songs Published in Non-show Folios
Happily Ever After—cut
*Marry Me a Little—cut

Additional Song Recorded
Multitudes of Amys—cut

Sondheim returned to Broadway with the most
important new musical since FIDDLER ON THE
ROOF [Bock: September 22, 1964]. Producer/di-
rector Harold Prince had broken new ground
with CABARET [Kander: November 20, 1966],

despite a score which lagged several paces behind staging and production. In Sondheim,
Prince found the perfect collaborator (or was it
the other way around?). The pair had been
friends for years; when WEST SIDE STORY
[Bernstein: September 26, 1957] lost its producer
and was about to be shelved, it was Prince whom
Sondheim called for help. COMPANY was something new for Broadway, a musical for Our
Times. (It should be noted, though, that while
Sondheim's work has been hailed and lauded by
sophisticates, the mass audience has at every step
preferred lesser competition like APPLAUSE
[Strouse: March 30,1970], PIPPIN [S. Schwartz:
October 23, 1972], ANNIE [Strouse: April 21,
1977], LA CAGE AUX FOLLES [Herman: August
21, 1983], and even BEAUTY AND THE BEAST
[Menken: April 18, 1994].) While Sondheim's
COMPANY score was filled with contemporary
rhythms, it was anything but "pop." Words
and music revealed character in a highly personal, self-analytical way. *Being Alive, Sorry-
Grateful, Another Hundred People, Company*, and
Getting Married Today told more about the characters—and the times—than any monologue or
book scene could hope to do. There had been
exceptional character studies before—Billy Bigelow's *Soliloquy*, the King of Siam's *A Puzzlement*,
Tevye's *If I Were a Rich Man*—but these were
exceptions. The age of Sondheim, if you will, has
been distinguished by scoresful of analytical,
personalized musical portraits (and has spawned
scores of bad songs from Sondheim imitators). At
any rate, Sondheim and Prince—abetted by a
highly complementary company of coworkers
headed by designer Boris Aronson and orchestrator Jonathan Tunick—undertook six major
musicals over the next eleven years: two hits,
three failures (financially, that is), and one dis-
cordant disaster which ended it all. But the work
towers over anything else done during this period and has influenced most of what has come
along since.

FOLLIES
April 4, 1971
Winter Garden Theatre • 522 performances
Book by James Goldman; Directed by Harold
Prince and Michael Bennett; Choreographed

by Michael Bennett; Produced by Harold
Prince in association with Ruth Mitchell; With
Alexis Smith, Dorothy Collins, Gene Nelson,
John McMartin, and Yvonne de Carlo.

Concert Version
September 6, 1985
Avery Fisher Hall • 2 performances
Directed by Herbert Ross; With Lee Remick
[Smith], Barbara Cook [Collins], George Hearn
[McMartin], Mandy Patinkin [Nelson], Carol
Burnett [de Carlo], and Elaine Stritch.

Revival
April 24, 1998
Paper Mill Playhouse {Millburn, N.J.} •
    Regional production
Directed by Robert Johanson; Choreographed
by Jerry Mitchell; With Dee Hoty [Smith],
Donna McKechnie [Collins], Tony Roberts
[Nelson], Laurence Guittard [McMartin], and
Ann Miller [de Carlo].

Published Songs
*Broadway Baby
Follies (Beautiful Girls)
**Losing My Mind
*Too Many Mornings

Additional Songs Published in Vocal Selections
Ah, but Underneath—written for 1987 London
    production
Ah, Paris!
Could I Leave You?
*Country House—written for London production
The God-Why-Don't-You-Love-Me Blues
    (Buddy's Blues)
**I'm Still Here
In Buddy's Eyes
Loveland [2nd]—written for London produc-
    tion
Make the Most of Your Music—written for
    London production
One More Kiss
*Waiting for the Girls Upstairs
*Who's That Woman?

Additional Songs Published in Vocal Score
Don't Look at Me
Fox-Trot [instrumental]—non-lyric version of
    Can That Boy Fox-Trot! (cut)

Live, Laugh, Love
Loveland [1st]
Love Will See Us Through
Lucy and Jessie
Prologue [instrumental]—non-song version of
    All Things Bright and Beautiful (cut)
Rain on the Roof
The Road You Didn't Take
Vincent and Vanessa Dance [instrumental]—
    dance version of Bolero D'Amour (cut);
    developed by Richard De Benedictis
You're Gonna Love Tomorrow

Additional Songs Published in Non-show Folios
*All Things Bright and Beautiful—cut; song
    version of Prologue; initial use in MARRY
    ME A LITTLE [March 12, 1981]
Can That Boy Fox-Trot!—cut
Little White House—cut; initial use in MARRY
    ME A LITTLE
Uptown, Downtown—cut; initial use in
    MARRY ME A LITTLE
Who Could Be Blue?—cut; initial use in
    MARRY ME A LITTLE

Additional Songs Recorded
*Bring on the Girls—cut
It Wasn't Meant to Happen—cut; initial use in
    MARRY ME A LITTLE
Pleasant Little Kingdom—cut
That Old Piano Roll—cut

One of Sondheim's richest scores was overwhelmed by a bloated concept, aiming for surre-
alism but winding up overly pretentious. The
"layered ghosts" approach, intended to illustrate
the characters' many psychoneuroses—Sally flirting with Young Ben fighting with Phyllis commiserating Young Buddy mooning over Young
Sally, while a couple of Heidis sang soprano—
came across as rather silly, capsizing the otherwise
adventurous work. (Sondheim and Goldman had
been working on the project for five years; as THE
GIRLS UPSTAIRS—for GYPSY [May 21, 1959]
producers Merrick and Heyward—it had no
ghosts, no flashbacks, and only one set of suffering characters.) The score, staging, and production values made FOLLIES a staggering experience by the third viewing; but that wasn't good
enough for the bored hordes who stormed out of

the Winter Garden. For the listener, the rewards were—and are—numerous: *Losing My Mind, I'm Still Here, Too Many Mornings, Broadway Baby, Who's That Woman?, One More Kiss, Waiting for the Girls Upstairs*, and on. An all-star concert version in 1985—and the success of the resulting live recording—led producer Cameron Mackintosh to mount a revised FOLLIES in London in 1987. Things didn't work out much better than in 1971, though. Only one of Sondheim's new songs was of FOLLIES quality, a remarkable duet/battle called *Country House*. A 1998 regional revival caused quite a stir and considerable talk of transfer, but cooler heads (and FOLLIES' tradition of losing money) prevailed.

TWIGS

November 14, 1971
Broadhurst Theatre • 312 performances
Play by George Furth; Directed by Michael Bennett; Produced by Frederick Brisson in association with Plum Productions, Inc. (Michael Bennett); With Sada Thompson.

Published Songs
None

George Furth, a comic character actor from HOT SPOT [April 19, 1963], wrote a series of eleven short playlets about marriage. Seven of them were combined into "A Husband, a Wife, and a Friend," a vehicle intended for Kim Stanley (with Ron Leibman and John McMartin). This unproduced script served as the genesis for the musical of the same name, although only one-and-a-half of the playlets were ultimately used. After the successful opening of COMPANY [April 26, 1970], Furth went back to the remaining material and fashioned it into the wildly funny TWIGS, with a wildly funny performance by Sada Thompson (under the direction of COMPANY's Michael Bennett). Sondheim contributed the song *Hollywood and Vine*, with a lyric by George Furth.

A LITTLE NIGHT MUSIC [1973]

February 25, 1973
Shubert Theatre • 601 performances
Book by Hugh Wheeler (based on *Smiles of a Summer Night* [film] by Ingmar Bergman);

Directed by Harold Prince; Choreographed by Patricia Birch; Produced by Harold Prince in association with Ruth Mitchell; With Glynis Johns, Len Cariou, Hermione Gingold, and Victoria Mallory.

Published Songs
A Little Night Music (The Sun Won't Set) [instrumental version]
*The Miller's Son
Remember?
*Send in the Clowns
*You Must Meet My Wife

Additional Songs Published in Vocal Selection
**Every Day a Little Death
The Glamorous Life (Pack up the Luggage) [1st]
Liaisons

Additional Songs Published in Vocal Score
In Praise of Women
*It Would Have Been Wonderful
*Later
Night Waltz II (The Sun Sits Low)
*Now
Perpetual Anticipation
*Soon
The Sun Won't Set [song version]
**A Weekend in the Country

Additional Songs Published in Non-show Folios
Bang!—cut; initial use in MARRY ME A LITTLE [March 12, 1981]
The Glamorous Life (The Letter Song) [2nd]—written for 1978 movie version
Silly People—cut
Two Fairy Tales—cut

Additional Songs Recorded
Love Takes Time—written for movie version; new lyric for *The Sun Won't Set*
My Husband the Pig—recorded upon use in PUTTING IT TOGETHER [March 2, 1993]

A waltzing operetta hit, with a book only half as tangled as FOLLIES [April 4, 1971] and one of Sondheim's most enjoyable scores. Everything is well done, everything is inventive, and in song after song music and lyric are delectably matched.

The three opening character soliloquies, *Now, Soon,* and *Later,* combine into a spectacular trio (which propels itself into something even grander than its individual parts). *A Weekend in the Country* is another marvel, interweaving six characters and seven "scenes" into a grand first act finale—and covering what would otherwise have been pages and pages and pages of librettical explication. There are three remarkable duets for strangely paired characters: a man rhapsodizing to his ex-mistress about his child bride (*You Must Meet My Wife*); the man and his ex-mistress's current lover jealously jousting (*It Would Have Been Wonderful*); and the mistress's ex-lover's child bride commiserating with the mistress's current lover's long-suffering wife (*Every Day a Little Death*). (Before his breakthrough with COMPANY [April 26, 1970], Sondheim created word puzzles for *New York Magazine.*) And finally there is *The Glamorous Life,* which interweaves letters from three generations of women with the comments of the Greek Chorus (Swedish Chorus?). For the film version Sondheim wrote a second version of this song, as a solo for the teenaged daughter, which is probably even better; but the first—with its "Pack up the Luggage" refrain—is a constant for anyone who's ever hit the road with a bus & truck. Sondheim also came up with *Send in the Clowns,* his only popular hit (as composer) to date.

THE ENCLAVE
November 15, 1973
Theatre Four {Off Broadway} •
    22 performances
Play by Arthur Laurents; Incidental music by Sondheim; Directed by Arthur Laurents; Produced by Edgar Lansbury, Joseph Beruh, and Clinton Wilder; With Peg Murray, Laurence Hugo, and Barton Heyman.

Song Recorded
Incidental Music [selection]

Sondheim provided pre-recorded music for Arthur Laurent's gay-themed play, the final collaboration of the two longtime friends. Sondheim also wrote his first full-length movie score for Alain Resnais's 1974 French-language mystery *Stavisky.* The lush, moody work sounds like a tapestry of (future) Sondheim themes and should not be overlooked by fans of the composer.

CANDIDE [1974]
See Bernstein: March 10, 1974.

THE FROGS
May 20, 1974
Yale University Swimming Pool
    {New Haven, Conn.} • 8 performances
Book by Burt Shevelove (based on the play by Aristophanes); Directed by Burt Shevelove; Choreographed by Carmen de Lavallade; Produced by Yale Repertory Theatre; With Larry Blyden, Alvin Epstein, Carmen de Lavallade, Anthony Holland, Christopher Durang, Meryl Streep, and Sigourney Weaver.

Songs Published in Non-show Folio
Fear No More [lyric by William Shakespeare]
Invocation to the Gods and Instructions to the Audience

This musical experiment performed in the swimming pool at Yale created quite a splash. The built-in obstacles, though, made it more curious than theatrical. (It was kind of boring, actually.) And there were severe echo problems.

PACIFIC OVERTURES
January 11, 1976
Winter Garden Theatre • 193 performances
Book by John Weidman; Additional material by Hugh Wheeler; Directed by Harold Prince; Choreographed by Patricia Birch; Produced by Harold Prince in association with Ruth Mitchell; With Mako, Soon-Teck Oh, Sab Shimono, Yuki Shimoda, and Isao Sato

Revival
October 25, 1984
Promenade Theatre {Off Broadway} •
    109 performances
Directed by Fran Soeder; Choreographed by Janet Watson; Transferred from York Theater Company; With Ernest Abuba and Kevin Gray [Sato].

Song Published in Non-show Folio
*Pretty Lady

Additional Songs Published in Vocal Score

The Advantages of Floating in the Middle of the Sea
****A Bowler Hat*
Chrysanthemum Tea [2nd]—replacement for [1st] version (cut/unpublished)
**Four Black Dragons*
Lion Dance [instrumental]
Next!
Please Hello
Poems
**Someone in a Tree*
There Is No Other Way
Welcome to Kanagawa

Sondheim and Prince attempted something different, and they certainly succeeded. Once again, the work was inaccessible due to an uninvolving book (although that was by no means the only problem). But the score was uniformly interesting (although it took repeated hearings to enjoy), containing some of Sondheim's finest writing. *Pretty Lady* is Sondheim at his most beautifully melodic, and I gladly hold it up to those who criticize his work as being cold and unemotional. *Someone in a Tree* and *Four Black Dragons* are wonderful, multipart story/songs, deftly covering a great deal of information and similarly building to glorious musical/choral conclusions. And *A Bowler Hat* is truly exceptional writing: a lucid statement of the show's overall theme, with the character himself ironically illustrating his point. But PACIFIC OVERTURE's book and artsy production scheme overwhelmed the score; the high point of the evening was designer Boris Aronson's battleship.

SIDE BY SIDE BY SONDHEIM
May 4, 1976
Mermaid Theatre {London}
July 7, 1976
Wyndham's Theatre {London}
April 18, 1977
Music Box Theatre {New York} •
    384 performances
Directed by Ned Sherrin; With Millicent Martin, Julia McKenzie, David Kernan, and Ned Sherrin; London: Produced by H. M. Tennent, Ltd., and Cameron Mackintosh; New York: Produced by Harold Prince in association with Ruth Mitchell and the Incomes Company, Ltd.

Published Song
I Never Do Anything Twice (Madam's Song)— published in separate edition, originally used in 1976 movie *The Seven Percent Solution*

Additional Song Recorded
The Two of You—added to tour; initial use of song written in 1952 for the TV puppet show *Kukla, Fran, and Ollie*

Note: Songs written for previously produced musicals are listed with their original scores.

David Kernan, who played the Carl-Magnus in the 1975 London production of A LITTLE NIGHT MUSIC [February 25, 1973], came up with the idea of a three-singers-on-barstools revue of Sondheim songs. The London SIDE BY SIDE played a nine-week engagement beginning May 4, 1976, at the Mermaid Theatre (more or less equivalent to Off Broadway); it then transferred to Wyndham's Theatre in the West End for a fifteen-month run. After a six-week stand at the Royal Alexandra in Toronto, the show returned to London's Garrick on October 4, 1977, for an additional seven months. In the midst of this, Hal Prince imported the original cast to Broadway's Music Box, where it did quite well (though not as well as in London). New York replacements included Nancy Dussault, Larry Kert, Georgia Brown, Hermione Gingold, and puppets Kukla and Ollie (with Burr Tillstrom), who joined the show in Chicago before moving to Broadway for the end of the run; hence the addition of the charming *The Two of You*. SIDE BY SIDE marked the first time that the public at large became aware of the phrase "Sondheim musical," despite his impressive track record on the Bernstein musical, the Merman musical, and several Prince musicals.

SWEENEY TODD ✦ THE DEMON BARBER OF FLEET STREET
March 1, 1979
Uris Theatre • 558 performances
Book by Hugh Wheeler (based on a play by Christopher Bond); Directed by Harold Prince;

Choreographed by Larry Fuller; Produced by Richard Barr, Charles Woodward, Robert Fryer, Mary Lea Johnson, and Martin Richards; With Len Cariou, Angela Lansbury, Victor Garber, Ken Jennings, and Edmund Lyndeck.

Revival
September 14, 1989
Circle in the Square Uptown •
    189 performances
Directed by Susan H. Schulman; Choreographed by Michael Lichtefeld; Transferred from York Theater Company; With Bob Gunton [Cariou], Beth Fowler [Lansbury], and Jim Walton [Garber].

Published Songs
*Johanna
*Not While I'm Around
**Pretty Women

Additional Songs Published in Vocal Selection
The Ballad of Sweeney Todd
By the Sea
Green Finch and Linnet Bird
Wait

Additional Songs Published in Vocal Score
Ah, Miss
The Barber and His Wife
City on Fire!
The Contest
**Epiphany
*Final Scene
*God, That's Good!
Kiss Me
*Johanna (*Turpin Version*)—cut
Ladies in Their Sensitivities
The Letter (Quintet)
*A Little Priest
*My Friends
No Place Like London
Parlor Songs
Pirelli's Miracle Elixir
Poor Thing
The Worst Pies in London

Sondheim and Prince once again chose unconventional subject matter for the fifth of their six collaborations. This time the gamble paid off,

with Sondheim producing what is arguably his finest work to date. The other Sondheim/Prince shows were saddled by their books; SWEENEY TODD, though, was told mostly in music. And what music! Sondheim wrote an extensive and varied score, ranging from moments of tender beauty to madness. The exquisitely lovely *Pretty Women*, sung as our hero prepares to slice the villain's throat; the gentle lullaby *Not While I'm Around*, sung by a half-wit who couldn't be more wrong in his every word; *A Little Priest*, set to a crunchily cannibalistic waltz; *God, That's Good!*, peppered with ghoulish puns about shepherd's pie made with actual shepherd; and two wonderfully different songs called *Johanna*, one quite beautiful and the other quite mad. And the *Epiphany*—in which our hero crosses into insanity before our eyes—is unquestionably one of the most extraordinary segments in musical theatre. Len Cariou (of A LITTLE NIGHT MUSIC [February 25, 1973]) and Angela Lansbury (who had followed ANYONE CAN WHISTLE [April 4, 1964] with Tony Award–winning performances in two Jerry Herman musicals) created breathtakingly larger-than-life characters, but it was Sondheim's exquisite score that made SWEENEY TODD the best musical of the decade.

MARRY ME A LITTLE
March 12, 1981
Actors Playhouse • 96 performances
Conceived and Developed by Craig Lucas and Norman René; Directed by Norman René; Produced by Diane de Mailly in association with William B. Young; With Craig Lucas and Suzanne Henry.

Song Recorded
Pour le Sport—see TAKE FIVE [October 10, 1957]

Note: Songs written for previously produced musicals are listed with their original scores.

A singer in SWEENEY TODD [March 1, 1979] came up with the idea of taking previously cut/unused Sondheim material and working it into an intimate boy/girl courtship revue. The results were moderate, although they did manage to introduce some worthy material (and the singer in question—Craig Lucas—turned out to be a pretty good playwright). Sondheim, meanwhile, wrote a background score for Warren Beatty's 1981 movie *Reds*, which included an evocative theme subsequently set with a lyric as *Goodbye for Now*.

MERRILY WE ROLL ALONG
November 16, 1981
Alvin Theatre • 16 performances
Book by George Furth (based on the play by George S. Kaufman and Moss Hart); Directed by Harold Prince; Choreographed by Larry Fuller; Produced by Lord Grade, Martin Starger, Robert Fryer, and Harold Prince; With Jim Walton, Ann Morrison, Lonny Price, and Jason Alexander.

Revivals
June 16, 1985
La Jolla Playhouse {San Diego} • Regional production
Directed by James Lapine; With John Rubinstein [Walton], Heather MacRae [Morrison], and Chip Zien [Price].

May 26, 1994
St. Peter's Church {Off Off Broadway} • 54 performances
Directed by Susan H. Schulman; Choreographed by Michael Lichtefeld; Produced by York Theater Company; With Malcolm Gets [Walton], Amy Ryder [Morrison], and Adam Heller [Price].

Published Songs
*Good Thing Going
*Not a Day Goes By

Additional Songs Published in Vocal Selection
The Hills of Tomorrow
Honey—cut
Like It Was
Merrily We Roll Along
*Old Friends
Our Time

Additional Songs Published in Vocal Score
Bobby and Jackie and Jack
Franklin Shepard, Inc.
*It's a Hit
Meet the Blob

Now You Know
Opening Doors
Rich and Happy
Who Wants to Live in New York?—alternate lyric for *Good Thing Going*

Additional Songs Recorded
Growing Up—written for 1985 production
Opening Act II—alternate verse for *Good Thing Going*
That Frank—written for 1985 production; revised version of *Rich and Happy*

The Sondheim/Prince collaboration ran aground on the curious MERRILY WE ROLL ALONG. Kaufman and Hart's 1934 play had been top-heavy and melodramatic; its main distinctions were an astounding (for the depression) nine full sets and the then-revolutionary device of moving backwards in time. ("Merrily We Roll Backwards" cynics named it; there was also considerable gossip about characters who appeared to be modeled on former Kaufman collaborators Dorothy Parker and George Gershwin.) By 1981 the reverse-time novelty was no longer novel, and the musical MERRILY proved unworkable despite an interesting premise. The songs came off best, as in all Sondheim shows: the anthem-like *Our Time*, the moving *Not a Day Goes By*, the delectable *Old Friends*, the brash *Now You Know*, the well-crafted quartet *It's a Hit*. The use of *Merrily We Roll Along* to move back through time worked better than the other conceptual choices of the evening. And mention must be made of the composer's choral work and the dazzling jazz orchestrations by Jonathan Tunick. But the unhappy MERRILY served to sever the Sondheim/Prince collaboration after six remarkable shows in eleven years.

SUNDAY IN THE PARK WITH GEORGE
May 2, 1984
Booth Theatre • 604 performances
Book and Direction by James Lapine; Produced by The Shubert Organization and Emanuel Azenberg in association with Playwrights Horizons (André Bishop); With Mandy Patinkin, Bernadette Peters, Dana Ivey, and Charles Kimbrough.

Concert Version
May 15, 1994
St. James Theatre • 1 performance
Benefit for Friends in Deed; With the Original
Cast

Songs Published in Vocal Selection
Beautiful
Children and Art
**Finishing the Hat*
Move On
Putting It Together—solo version as revised for
    Barbra Streisand's *The Broadway Album*;
    issued in non-show edition.
Sunday

Additional Songs Published in Vocal
    Score
Chromolume #7 [instrumental]
Color and Light
The Day Off
Everybody Loves Louis
Gossip
It's Hot up Here
Lesson #8
No Life
Putting It Together—show version
Sunday in the Park with George
We Do Not Belong Together

Working without Harold Prince for the first time
since 1970, Sondheim joined with James Lapine
(author/director of Playwrights Horizons' Off
Broadway hit *Table Settings* [January 14, 1980])
for SUNDAY IN THE PARK WITH GEORGE.
The score, here, was the thing; and Broadway
musicalizing did not work in the piece's favor.
What seemed like a magical chamber musical—
to me, at least—in the 1983 developmental production at Playwrights Horizons appeared relatively charmless with full trappings at the bigger
Booth. (Even so, it was clearly superior to its
competition. While SUNDAY won the Pulitzer,
the show and Sondheim's score were passed over
for the Tony Awards by a *vastly* inferior Jerry
Herman musical.) Taking his cue from the pal-
ette of painter Seurat, Sondheim attempted musical pointillism and produced a first act of color
and light: *Sunday*, lyric and music, illustrated
the painting illustrating the painter. The people
of 1884 on the island in the Seine were real and

relevant and interesting. Not so the Impres-
sionist's model's grandson in Chicago, with his
laser-beam art and his doddering musical-
comedy grandmother. Whatever the authors'
intentions, their 1884 was far more relevant to
modern times than their 1984. As for musical
laserism, there seems to be no such thing; and
practical lasers beamed over the head of the audience bought spectacle at the expense of imag-
ery. Meanwhile, Sondheim was at the top of his
form (make that anyone's form) in *Finishing the
Hat*. This was his second perfect hat song, following the *Bowler*; one can only hope for more.
(Does anyone still wear a hat? . . .)

INTO THE WOODS
November 5, 1987
Martin Beck Theatre • 764 performances
Book by James Lapine; Directed by James
Lapine; Choreographed by Lar Lubovitch;
Produced by Heidi Landesman, Rocco
Landesman, Rick Steiner, M. Anthony Fisher,
Frederic H. Mayerson, and Jujamcyn Theatres;
With Bernadette Peters, Joanna Gleason, Chip
Zien, Tom Aldredge, and Robert Westenberg.

Concert Version
November 9, 1997
Broadway Theatre • 2 performances
Benefit for Friends in Deed and God's Love
We Deliver; With the Original Cast.

Published Songs
Children Will Listen
No One Is Alone
Stay with Me

Additional Songs Published in Vocal
    Selection
Agony
*Any Moment (Anything Can Happen in the
    Woods)*
Into the Woods (Prologue Act One)
It Takes Two (You're Different in the Woods)
No More

Additional Songs Published in Vocal Score
Cinderella at the Grave
Ever After
First Midnight
Giants in the Sky

Greens
Hello, Little Girl
I Guess This Is Goodbye
I Know Things Now
Lament (Children Won't Listen)
*Last Midnight
Maybe They're Magic (Magic Beans)
Moments in the Woods
On the Steps of the Palace
So Happy (Prologue Act Two)
A Very Nice Prince
Your Fault

Additional Song Recorded
Our Little World—added to 1990 London
    production

SUNDAY IN THE PARK [May 2, 1984] was worthwhile, in my opinion, despite its conceptual flaws. I enjoyed INTO THE WOODS more, but found it more disappointing despite its attributes. Once again, Sondheim and Lapine's socially significant second act strived to show us the evils of Our Modern Times; once again, the darker side of the show was—well, dark. While SUNDAY attempted to grapple with the weighty theme of Life versus Art, INTO THE WOODS took a potentially intriguing idea and spun it out in hit-or-miss fashion. No Sondheim score is without interest, certainly; there are always layers of textures, treasures, and tricks to enjoy. But WOODS, for me, didn't quite pay off. The twelve-minute prologue (*Into the Woods*) was a perfect example: Sondheim took us on a musical journey of bits and pieces, building to a glorious choral cacophony as in *A Weekend in the Country* from A LITTLE NIGHT MUSIC [February 25, 1973]. But while *Weekend* went on to a rousingly exciting finish, *Woods* merely ended with a restatement of the refrain. Similar letdowns muted the fleetingly lovely *Any Moment* and *It Takes Two*; Sondheim seemed to cut all of his loveliest *Moments in the Woods* short without satisfactory resolution. Presumably he was doing this on purpose, in a Rapunzelish attempt at weaving a continuous musical thread without stopping for individual highspots. (If so, how does one explain *Agony*, a reworking of NIGHT MUSIC's *It Would Have Been Wonderful*?) The only exhilarating moments came in the *Your Fault/Last Midnight* segment, which was similar

to—though not nearly as effective as—the exceptional *Epiphany* of SWEENEY TOOD [March 1, 1979]. Much of the score, in fact, recalled similar but better moments in NIGHT MUSIC and SWEENEY. The foregoing notwithstanding, this is how Sondheim saw fit to write the material; and to paraphrase George Abbott, if it's good enough for Sondheim, it's good enough for us.

ASSASSINS
January 27, 1991
Playwrights Horizons {Off Off Broadway} •
    72 performances
Book by John Weidman; Directed by Jerry Zaks; Choreographed by D. J. Giagni; Produced by Playwrights Horizons (André Bishop); With Victor Garber, Terrence Mann, Jonathan Hadary, Eddie Korbich, Annie Golden, and Debra Monk.

Published Song
Something Just Broke—written for 1993
    London production

Additional Songs Published in Vocal Selection
The Ballad of Booth
The Ballad of Czolgosz
The Ballad of Guiteau
*Everybody's Got the Right
*Unworthy of Your Love

Additional Songs Published in Vocal Score
*Another National Anthem
*Gun Song
How I Saved Roosevelt

What a wonderful system where a true artist (i.e., Sondheim) can work on whatever he is compelled to work on (ASSASSINS) and can hear it mounted under optimum conditions (like at Playwrights Horizons) without the overpowering commercial and financial pressures of our legitimate theatre. (As a commercial exercise, Sondheim wrote five songs for Warren Beatty's 1990 movie *Dick Tracy*—and won an Oscar in the process, for *Sooner or Later*.) Did ASSASSINS work? No. Was it conceptually flawed? Perhaps. Was it worth Sondheim's time and energy? Absolutely. ASSASSINS was an interesting idea which didn't quite make it off the page and onto the stage. Sondheim and John Weidman format-ted the show as a series of revue sketches, which was probably the best way to do it; but it seems that they were writing sketches for two differ-ent revue/musicals. If ASSASSINS had a brief life, so did the original productions of ANYONE CAN WHISTLE [April 4, 1964] and MERRILY WE ROLL ALONG [November 16, 1981]—two scores surely appreciated by anyone interested in musical theatre (except, perhaps, the inves-tors). Mark ASSASSINS an unsuccessful experi-ment, perhaps; but who among us would want Sondheim to stop experimenting?

PUTTING IT TOGETHER
March 2, 1993
Manhattan Theatre Club Stage One
   {Off Broadway} • 96 performances
Directed by Julia McKenzie; Choreographed by Bob Avian; Produced by Manhattan Theatre Club by special arrangement with Cameron Mackintosh; With Julie Andrews, Stephen Collins, Christopher Durang, Michael Rupert, and Rachel York.

Published Songs
Back in Business—written for and published
   as from the 1990 movie *Dick Tracy*
Live Alone and Like It—written for and
   published as from *Dick Tracy*
Sooner or Later—written for and published as
   from *Dick Tracy*

Note: Songs written for previously produced musicals are listed with their original scores.

With Sondheim the long-acknowledged master of the Broadway musical, a new revue of his songs—with Julie Andrews making her first theatrical appearance since CAMELOT [Loewe: December 3, 1960], no less!—was a much antici-pated, sold-out-in-advance event. But PUTTING IT TOGETHER simply wasn't very appealing, despite (or because) of its surefire appeal, and expired after its limited Off Broadway engage-ment. A flat-footed follow-up to SIDE BY SIDE BY SONDHEIM [May 4, 1976]—directed by that show's Julia McKenzie, starring Diana Rigg—PUTTING IT TOGETHER premièred under the aegis of Cameron Mackintosh in Oxford in 1992.

A third version, incorporating some different songs and with plot revisions, opened at the Mark Taper Forum in Los Angeles on October 4, 1998, for a nine-week limited run. Carol Burnett led the cast, under the direction of Eric D. Schaeffer, with choreography by Bob Avian. This last PUT-TING IT TOGETHER is scheduled to finally reach Broadway in the fall of 1999.

PASSION
May 9, 1994
Plymouth Theatre • 280 performances
Book by James Lapine (based on the film *Passione D'Amore*); Directed by James Lapine; Produced by The Shubert Organization, Capital Cities/ABC, Roger Berlind, and Scott Rudin in association with Lincoln Center Theater (André Bishop); With Donna Murphy, Jere Shea, Gregg Edelman, Tom Aldredge, and Marin Mazzie.

Songs Published in Vocal Selection
*Happiness
*I Read
I Wish I Could Forget You
Love Like Ours
*Loving You
No One Has Ever Loved Me
*They Hear Drums

Additional Songs Published in Vocal Score
Fifth Letter
Finale (Scene 15)
First Letter
*Flashback
Forty Days
Fosca's Entrance
Fourth Letter
Nightmare
Scene 3
Scene 6/Three Weeks
Scene 7
Scene 9
Scene 10
Scene 11
Scene 12
Scene 13
Scene 14
Second Letter
Sunrise Letter Transition (Scenes 4–5)
Third Letter

Three Days
Transition (*Scenes 7–8*)
Transition (*Scenes 10–11*)
Transition from Train Scene (*Scenes 11–12*)
Transition to Scene 14

Additional Song Recorded

*No One Has Ever Loved Me (climactic
version)—cut from Broadway production,
added to London production

Note: Due to the nature of the material, no attempt has been made to label the score contents
with individual song titles.

For years Sondheim seemed to be heading toward
a new form of musical theatre, with the score composed not of individual songs but a collection
of recurring, puzzle-like themes which—in the
end—would form a glorious interwoven tapestry.
Musical themes sung by the same character from
a different context (as their views and feelings
change); a different character from the same context (i.e., reading a letter, telling or retelling a
story); or a different character in a different context altogether. In PASSION he was able to do just
that, thanks to his innate talent, his advanced
craftsmanship, and a property which called for
such a treatment. (Sondheim also had in James
Lapine a collaborator with a strong and complementary visual sense). PASSION was musical theatre unlike anything which had come before, and
paid a heavy price: the show was much maligned,
misunderstood, and disliked by the majority. The
painter has the opportunity to stand back from
the nearly completed canvas and make changes;
Sondheim and Lapine needed that opportunity for
PASSION and took it but were forced to do so
while their work was on all-too-public display.
Due to the inherent difficulties in weaving miracu-
lous tapestries, it wasn't quite ready for the on-
slaught it faced during previews; nor was it in
perfect form at the time of the official opening.
PASSION—in the theatre—suffered a dismal fate;
but the score is quite passionately wondrous and
will hopefully have the afterlife it deserves.

GETTING AWAY WITH MURDER
March 17, 1996
Broadhurst Theatre • 17 performances
Play by Sondheim and George Furth; Directed
by Jack O'Brien; Produced by Roger Berlind;
With John Rubinstein, Terrence Mann, and
Christine Ebersole.

Published Songs
None

Inveterate puzzler Sondheim and his COMPANY
[April 26, 1970]/MERRILY [November 16, 1981]
librettist George Furth saw fit to collaborate on
this tricky murder mystery which, alas, had one
trick too few. (In 1973 Sondheim—with Tony
Perkins—had written his only screenplay, the
murder mystery movie *The Last of Sheila*.) GET-
TING AWAY WITH MURDER got more press
coverage for its clever artwork—a gargoyle with
a smoking gun—than for the show itself, and
quickly expired.

Stephen Sondheim has written fifteen book musicals (including three for which he provided lyrics only). Virtually all of his work is exceptional,
although half of the shows—and a few of the
scores—leave something to be desired. (Of the
musicals he composed, only FORUM [May 8,
1962], COMPANY [April 26, 1970], and A LITTLE
NIGHT MUSIC [February 25, 1973] returned their
investments and can be considered "hits"—but
that is of little matter.) Sondheim has never
settled for the merely adequate; virtually every
song is interesting and intriguing. In the 1991
edition of "*Show Tunes*," I found it somewhat
disconcerting that the scores since SWEENEY
TODD [March 1, 1979] had been problematic. I
sensed that he was trying to move towards a new
style of musical theatre and hoped it would all
make sense in his next score. As it turns out, it
did; PASSION [May 9, 1994] wove a magical
musical tapestry. It also was one of Sondheim's
bigger failures (*see what it gets you?*—to quote
an old Sondheim song-title). Sondheim meanwhile continues to write and explore, slowly
but steadily. A new musical, presently entitled
WISE GUYS, will presumably be finished, tested,
and mounted on Broadway by the composer's
seventieth birthday in 2000. Hit (hopefully) or
miss, we can be sure that it will be intriguing,
expertly crafted, and up to Mr. Sondheim's overwhelmingly high standard.

PART III

New Composers of the 1960s and Beyond

The 1960s began with a burst of new voices—voices which, as it happened, would seem pretty passé by the dawning of the age of Aquarius in 1968. Charles Strouse, Harvey Schmidt, and Cy Coleman all made their debuts in 1960; in the 1961–62 season they were joined by Jerry Herman, John Kander, and Stephen Sondheim (who had already written lyrics for two epochal musicals of the late 1950s and is thus discussed in part 2). One more composer of this generation came along, the one-hit wonder Mitch Leigh, but in 1966 opportunities for writers of Broadway musicals dried up. (Sondheim will turn seventy in the year 2000—and he is marginally younger than Bock, Strouse, Schmidt, Coleman, Leigh, and Kander, all of whom were born within a three-year period.) While all of these gentlemen made numerous Broadway appearances, the musical theatre slowdown of the 1970s and 1980s resulted in limited exposure for composers arriving more recently. Larry Grossman came along in 1970—a particularly dire time—and has seen only four musicals reach Broadway in thirty years. Stephen Schwartz appeared in 1971, the first successful theatre composer of the rock era; despite some enormous early hits, he, too, has also only made it to Broadway four times. Marvin Hamlisch debuted in 1975, another one-hit wonder (so far) with yet another four musicals. (This compares with a dozen or more Broadway scores from Strouse, Kander, Coleman, and Sondheim.) Alan Menken debuted in 1979 and had a long-running Off Broadway hit in 1982; only one of his projects has made it to Broadway (in 1994), via Hollywood. The unorthodox William Finn appeared Off Broadway, with much acclaim, in 1981; he didn't make it to Broadway until 1992 (his only appearance to date). Maury Yeston made an acclaimed Broadway debut in 1982; he didn't reappear with a full score—and not for want of trying—until 1997. Things have been somewhat easier for Stephen Flaherty, the youngest composer examined in *Show Tunes* and the only one (other than Billy Finn) who was born this side of 1950. Flaherty has written three Broadway musicals in eight years; the success of the most recent is likely to move him to a prime position among his peers.

Charles Strouse   293

Harvey Schmidt   305

Cy Coleman   313

Jerry Herman   323

John Kander   331

Mitch Leigh   343

Larry Grossman   349

Stephen Schwartz   355

Marvin Hamlisch   359

Alan Menken   363

William Finn   369

Maury Yeston   375

Stephen Flaherty   381

CHARLES STROUSE

Born: June 7, 1928, New York, New York

CHARLES STROUSE began his musical career training for the concert hall. After graduating from the Eastman School of Music in Rochester (New York), he studied with Nadia Boulanger in Paris and Aaron Copland before changing over to popular music. His first theatre composing came in 1953, writing summer amateur shows at Green Mansions (Harold Rome's training ground); his collaborator was Lee Adams, a magazine editor. For three years Strouse supported himself as a rehearsal pianist and accompanist, returning to Green Mansions for summers of high-pressure songwriting.

SHOESTRING REVUE
February 28, 1955
President Theatre {Off Broadway} •
    100 performances
Music and Lyrics mostly by others; Lyrics to Strouse songs by Michael Stewart; Sketches by Michael Stewart, Sheldon Harnick, and others; Directed by Christopher Hewett; Produced by Ben Bagley in association with Mr. and Mrs. Judson S. Todd; With Dorothy Greener, Beatrice Arthur, Dody Goodman, and Chita Rivera.

Songs Recorded
The History of the World
Man's Inhumanity to Man
Three Loves

Twenty-two-year-old Ben Bagley came to New York and compiled three memorable (if not overly successful) Off Broadway revues in two seasons; featured were early songs and sketches by novices Charles Strouse, Mike Stewart, Lee Adams, Sheldon Harnick, Harvey Schmidt, and

Tom Jones. Strouse was musical director for the first SHOESTRING REVUE and placed interpolations in all three Bagley revues.

THE LITTLEST REVUE
May 22, 1956
Phoenix Theatre {Off Broadway} •
    32 performances
Music mostly by Vernon Duke (see Duke: May 22, 1956; also Blitzstein); Lyrics mostly by Ogden Nash; Sketches by Nat Hiken, Michael Stewart, and others; Directed by Paul Lammers; Produced by T. Edward Hambleton and Norris Houghton, by arrangement with Ben Bagley; With Tammy Grimes, Charlotte Rae, Joel Grey, and Larry Storch.

Songs Recorded
I Lost the Rhythm [lyric by Strouse]
*Spring Doth Let Her Colours Fly [lyric by Lee Adams]

Strouse and lyricist Lee Adams made their first New York appearance with *Spring Doth Let Her Colours Fly*, a very funny cartoon in words and (Wagnerian) music for comedienne Charlotte Rae.

SIXTH FINGER IN A FIVE FINGER GLOVE
October 8, 1956
Longacre Theatre • 2 performances
Play by Scott Michel; Incidental music by Strouse; Directed by John Holden; Produced by Gertrude Caplin and Thelma Fingar; With Jimmie Komack and Salome Jens.

Published Songs
None

Strouse made his Broadway debut with this little horror, instantly proclaimed one of the worst plays of the decade. The critics had virtually nothing favorable to say except that Strouse's music—which included an impressionistic ballet and "a daybed that folds up to music"—deserved a better fate.

SHOESTRING '57
November 5, 1956
Barbizon Plaza Theatre {Off Broadway} •
110 performances
Music mostly by others (see Schmidt: November 5, 1956); Lyrics by Sheldon Harnick, Michael Stewart, Tom Jones, Carolyn Leigh, and others; Lyrics to Strouse songs by Lee Adams; Directed by Paul Lammers; Choreographed by Danny Daniels; Produced by Ben Bagley in association with E. H. Morris; With Dody Goodman, Dorothy Greener, and Paul Mazursky.

Song Recorded
The Arts

Music publisher Edwin H. (Buddy) Morris found a new method for arranging interpolations: coproducing the show himself. While nothing of interest came from SHOESTRING '57, Morris signed three of the most important composers of the 1960 crop: Strouse (with Lee Adams), Cy Coleman (with Carolyn Leigh), and Jerry Herman.

BYE BYE BIRDIE
April 14, 1960
Martin Beck Theatre • 607 performances
Lyrics by Lee Adams; Book by Michael Stewart; Directed and Choreographed by Gower Champion; Produced by Edward Padula in association with L. Slade Brown; With Chita Rivera, Dick Van Dyke, Susan Watson, Dick Gautier, and Kay Medford.

Revival
[May 9, 1991]
Terrace Theatre {Long Beach, Calif.} •
Touring company
Directed by Gene Saks; Choreographed by Edmund Kresley; With Tommy Tune [Van

Dyke], Ann Reinking [Rivera], Susan Egan [Watson], and Marilyn Cooper [Medford].

Published Songs
*Baby, Talk to Me
Bye Bye Birdie*—written for 1963 movie version
*How Lovely to Be a Woman
*Kids!
*A Lot of Livin' to Do
*One Boy
*One Last Kiss
*Put on a Happy Face
Rosie

Additional Songs Published in 1995 Vocal Selection
Let's Settle Down—written for 1995 TV version
Take a Giant Step—written for 1991 touring revival
When a Mother Doesn't Matter Anymore—written for 1995 TV version

Additional Songs Published in Vocal Score
*An English Teacher
A Healthy, Normal American Boy
Honestly Sincere
*Hymn for a Sunday Evening (Ed Sullivan)
One Hundred Ways Ballet [instrumental]
Shriner's Ballet [instrumental]
Spanish Rose
*The Telephone Hour
We Love You Conrad
What Did I Ever See in Him?*

Additional Song Recorded
Older and Wiser—cut

To the surprise of everyone (including the authors), this cartoon musical was an enormously popular hit. After going through a number of different librettists (including nightclub comic Mike Nichols), Michael Stewart—a TV writer for Sid Caesar and Strouse's lyricist for SHOE-STRING REVUE [February 28, 1955]—came up with a book that worked. Gower (and Marge) Champion had been approached to star; instead, he directed his first book musical and became a major musical comedy force for twenty years. Strouse, who had done some arrangements for

the two-week flop GIRLS AGAINST THE BOYS†
[November 2, 1959], brought along that show's
featured comic Dick Van Dyke. He was joined by
SHOESTRING REVUE alumna Chita Rivera, just
back from the London production of WEST SIDE
STORY [Bernstein: September 26, 1957]. Strouse
wrote a score of simple pop tunes and rock lam-
poons—and found himself with sturdy crowd
pleasers like *Put on a Happy Face, A Lot of Livin'
to Do,* and *Rosie.* There was also fine musical
comedy material like *Kids!* and *Hymn for a Sunday Evening,* the mellow *Baby, Talk to Me,* and
the artful concerted number *The Telephone Hour.*

ALL AMERICAN
March 19, 1962
Winter Garden Theatre • 80 performances
Lyrics by Lee Adams; Book by Mel Brooks
(based on *Professor Fodorski* [novel] by Robert
Lewis Taylor); Choreographed by Danny
Daniels; Directed by Joshua Logan; Produced
by Edward Padula in association with L. Slade
Brown; With Ray Bolger, Eileen Herlie, Fritz
Weaver, Ron Husmann, and Anita Gillette.

Published Songs
The Fight Song
If I Were You
I'm Fascinating
It's Fun to Think
I've Just Seen Her (*As Nobody Else Has Seen
    Her*)
Nightlife
*Once upon a Time
Our Children
We Speak the Same Language
What a Country!

Additional Song Published in Vocal
    Selection
The Immigration and Naturalization Rag
    (*Melt Us*)

Additional Songs Recorded
Have a Dream
I Couldn't Have Done It Alone
Physical Fitness
The Real Me
Search Your Heart
Which Way?

Success quickly split the BYE BYE BIRDIE [April
14, 1960] team, as David Merrick snapped up
Gower Champion and Mike Stewart for his CAR-
NIVAL! [Merrill: April 13, 1961]. Strouse, Adams,
and their BIRDIE producers turned to veteran
Joshua Logan, directing his first of five musicals
since FANNY [Rome: November 4, 1954]—all
failures, of increasingly dire proportions. Librettist Stewart was replaced by another Sid Caesar
comedy writer whom Strouse knew from his days
writing dance music for "Your Show of Shows."
Mel Brooks's one previous musical comedy had
been SHINBONE ALLEY† [April 13, 1957], the
stage version of "archie and mehitabel." The
charm of Ray Bolger and Eileen Herlie wasn't
enough to carry this charmless college football
musical, which did include the gentle hit *Once
upon a Time* and the feathery soft-shoe *I'm
Fascinating.*

HELLO, DOLLY!
January 16, 1964
St. James Theatre • 2,844 performances
Music and Lyrics mostly by Jerry Herman (see
Herman: January 16, 1964; also Merrill); Book
by Michael Stewart (based on *The Matchmaker*
[play] by Thornton Wilder); Directed and
Choreographed by Gower Champion;
Produced by David Merrick; With Carol
Channing, David Burns, Eileen Brennan, and
Charles Nelson Reilly.

Published Songs
None

When Gower Champion (of BYE BYE BIRDIE
[April 14, 1960]) found his new musical ailing on
the road, he called in Strouse and Adams for first
aid. (For details, see Herman: January 16, 1964.)

GOLDEN BOY
October 20, 1964
Majestic Theatre • 569 performances
Lyrics by Lee Adams; Book by Clifford Odets
and William Gibson (based on the play by
Clifford Odets); Choreographed by Donald
McKayle; Directed by Arthur Penn; Produced
by Hillard Elkins; With Sammy Davis, Jr.,
Billy Daniels, and Paula Wayne.

Published Songs
Can't You See It?
Gimme Some
Golden Boy
**I Want to Be with You*
**Lorna's Here*
*Night Song
Stick Around
Theme from Golden Boy [instrumental]—issued
    as professional copy; piano solo version of
    Night Song
This Is the Life
**While the City Sleeps*

Additional Songs Published in Vocal Selection
Colorful
Don't Forget 127th Street
Everything's Great
No More

Additional Song Published in Non-show Folio
What Am I Gonna Do without You?—written
    for 1989 stock revival

Additional Songs Recorded
What Became of Me?—written for 1968
    London production, also published in fake
    book; see DANCE A LITTLE CLOSER
    [May 11, 1983]
Workout

Sammy Davis's second Broadway vehicle had as many problems as the first (MR. WONDERFUL [Bock: March 22, 1956]), though with better basic material and a far stronger score. But Clifford Odets's 1937 play was already clichéd; the young newcomer who makes it big, the harried white manager, etc., were familiar enough from both MR. WONDERFUL and the boxing musical THE BODY BEAUTIFUL [Bock: January 23, 1958]. Strouse, though, had his first Broadway opportunity to write emotional, romantic music; what seemed like a complex departure from BYE BYE BIRDIE [April 14, 1960] was actually a return to his abstract training. *Night Song, Lorna's Here, I Want to Be with You*, and the title song were all highly moving and fascinating in structure, while the seductive *While the City Sleeps* seemed to perfectly express the

intended tone of the entire production. With GOLDEN BOY's failure Strouse went back to writing contemporary, pop musicals, sacrificing much in inventiveness and musical texture.

"IT'S A BIRD, IT'S A PLANE, IT'S SUPERMAN"
March 29, 1966
Alvin Theatre • 129 performances
Lyrics by Lee Adams; Book by David Newman and Robert Benton (based on *Superman* [comic strip]); Directed by Harold Prince; Choreographed by Ernest Flatt; Produced by Harold Prince in association with Ruth Mitchell; With Jack Cassidy, Patricia Marand, Bob Holiday, Michael O'Sullivan, and Linda Lavin.

Published Songs
It's Superman
Love Theme from "Superman" [instrumental]—
    non-lyric version of *What I've Always*
    Wanted
Superman March [instrumental]
Superman Theme
What I've Always Wanted
**You've Got Possibilities*

Additional Songs Published in Vocal Selection
Doing Good
I'm Not Finished Yet
It's Super Nice
Ooh, Do You Love You!
Pow! Bam! Zonk!
Revenge
So Long, Big Guy
The Strongest Man in the World
We Don't Matter at All
We Need Him
The Woman for the Man (*Who Has Everything*)
**You've Got What I Need, Baby*

Additional Songs Recorded
Did You See That?—cut
Dot, Dot, Dot—cut
A Woman Alone—cut; see DANCE A LITTLE
    CLOSER [May 11, 1983]

Strouse turned to comic-strip music for this comic-strip musical, with a particularly fine set of pun-filled comedy lyrics by the underrated Lee Adams. The music was generally peppy if lightweight, with a couple of especially felicitous tunes in *You've Got Possibilities* and *You've Got What I Need, Baby*. Librettists David Newman and Robert Benton held on to their Superman treatment and successfully duplicated it a decade later in Hollywood—without Strouse, Adams, Prince. For director/producer Prince it was the end of his musical comedy days: he determined to move away from the old-fashioned world of Abbott to the progressive world of Robbins. First stop: CABARET [Kander: November 20, 1966].

APPLAUSE
March 30, 1970
Palace Theatre • 896 performances
Lyrics by Lee Adams; Book by Betty Comden and Adolph Green (based on "All about Eve" [story] by Mary Orr); Directed and Choreographed by Ron Field; Produced by Joseph Kipness, Lawrence Kasha, James M. Nederlander, and George Steinbrenner III; With Lauren Bacall, Len Cariou, Penny Fuller, and Bonnie Franklin.

Revival
October 22, 1996
Tampa Bay Performing Arts Center
{Tampa, Fla.} • Closed during tryout
Directed by Gene Saks; Choreographed by Ann Reinking; With Stephanie Zimbalist [Bacall] and John Dossett [Cariou].

Published Songs
Applause
Backstage Babble
The Best Night of My Life
But Alive
*Good Friends
Hurry Back
It Was Always You—cut
Love Comes First—cut
One of a Kind
She's No Longer a Gypsy
Something Greater
Think How It's Gonna Be (When We're Together Again)
Welcome to the Theatre

Additional Songs Published in Vocal Selection
Fasten Your Seat Belts
One Hallowe'en
Who's That Girl?

Additional Song Published in Vocal Score
Inner Thoughts

Strouse and Adams had their only hit since BYE BYE BIRDIE [April 14, 1960] with this vehicle for Lauren Bacall. The star ably carried her first musical, with assists from Len Cariou and the energetic Bonnie Franklin; and Ron Field, fresh from two Harold Prince shows, did a fine job in his first directing attempt. But Strouse's score was not very good at all; his poorest to date, in fact. *Welcome to the Theatre* has emotional pull, and *Good Friends* is folksy but joyful. Comden and Green provided book without lyrics for the first time in their career, coming in during the tryout to replace Sidney Michaels. All told, APPLAUSE was a very weak and very empty hit, as was demonstrated by a 1996 pre-Broadway tour which folded after three dreary weeks.

SIX
April 12, 1971
Cricket Theatre {Off Broadway} •
8 performances
Book and Lyrics by Strouse; Directed by Peter Coe; Produced by Slade Brown; With Lee Beery, Gilbert Price, Hal Watters, and Alvin Ing.

Published Songs
None

Finally reestablished on Broadway with the hit APPLAUSE [March 30, 1970], Strouse expressed his abstract background with the experimental SIX. Produced on a small scale, the piece baffled audiences and was quickly withdrawn.

I AND ALBERT
November 6, 1972
Piccadilly Theatre {London} •
120 performances
Lyrics by Lee Adams; Book by Jay Presson Allen; Directed by John Schlesinger; Produced

by Lewis M. Allen and Si Litvinoff; With Polly James and Sven-Bertil Taube.

Published Songs

I and Albert
Just You and Me—see RAGS [August 21, 1986]
This Gentle Land
Victoria
**Victoria and Albert Waltz* [instrumental]

Additional Songs Recorded

All Bless the Genius of Man
Draw the Blinds
Enough!
Go It, Old Girl!
Hans
His Royal Highness
It Has All Begun
**I've 'Eard the Bloody 'Indoos 'As It Worse*
Leave It Alone
No One to Call Me Victoria
When You Speak with a Lady
The Widow at Windsor

Strouse and Adams seemed an unlikely pair to write a Victorian British musical about Queen and Consort. London audiences were not amused. This was actually an American project under the title H.R.H., but David Merrick dropped it (as he had IT'S SUPERMAN [March 29, 1966]). The score is not without its charms, though, like the crisp *Victoria and Albert Waltz* and the rhythmic *I've 'Eard the Bloody 'Indoos 'As It Worse.*

ANNIE

April 21, 1977
Alvin Theatre • 2,377 performances
Lyrics by Martin Charnin; Book by Thomas Meehan (based on *Little Orphan Annie* [comic strip]); Choreographed by Peter Gennaro; Directed by Martin Charnin; Produced by Mike Nichols, Irwin Meyer, Stephen Friedman, and Lewis Allen; With Reid Shelton, Dorothy London, Andrea McArdle, and Robert Fitch.

Revival

March 26, 1997
Martin Beck Theatre • 240 performances
Directed by Martin Charnin; Choreographed by Peter Gennaro; With Nell Carter [Loudon] and Conrad John Schuck [Shelton].

Published Songs

Annie
Easy Street
I Don't Need Anything but You
It's the Hard-Knock Life
Let's Go to the Movies—written for 1982 movie version
Little Girls—new lyric for *Just Wait* (cut)
Maybe
A New Deal for Christmas
N.Y.C.
Sandy (Dumb Dog)—written for movie version
Sign—written for movie version
Tomorrow
**We Got Annie!*—cut; initial publication upon reuse in movie version
**You're Never Fully Dressed without a Smile*

Additional Songs Published in Vocal Selection

I Think I'm Gonna Like It Here
Something Was Missing—revised version of *You Rat, You* from 1968 movie *The Night They Raided Minsky's*
We'd Like to Thank You, Herbert Hoover
You Won't Be an Orphan for Long

Additional Songs Recorded

Apples—cut
I've Never Been So Happy—cut
Just Wait—cut; see *Little Girls*
Parents—cut
That's the Way It Goes—cut

An unlikely, impossible-to-get-produced cartoon musical finally got mounted and became the runaway smash hit of the decade, second only to A CHORUS LINE [Hamlisch: July 25, 1975]. A 1976 summer stock tryout at the Goodspeed Opera House finally got ANNIE on her feet, but just barely. Then Mike Nichols came in to produce, assuring financing and offering helpful suggestions. Like expanding the part of Miss Hannigan into a starring role for Dorothy Loudon, his original "Passionella" in THE WORLD OF JULES FEIFFER [Sondheim: July 2, 1962]). The resulting blockbuster was a great crowd-pleaser, although it never pleased this viewer much. The score is cheerily perky but rarely distinguished, with musical quality several notches above the lyrics. *Tomorrow*, of course, was a monstrous song hit.

A couple of the other songs are pleasing—*It's the Hard-Knock Life* and *You're Never Fully Dressed without a Smile*, for example—and *We Got Annie!* is quite delightful. (Unfortunately, they cut out the melody, cut out the rhythm, and retained the countermelody for an insipid title song.) ANNIE returned with a twentieth-anniversary revival, which was soundly trounced as being synthetic, contrived, and of questionable taste—pretty much my sentiments back in 1977.

A BROADWAY MUSICAL
December 21, 1978
Lunt-Fontanne Theatre • 1 performance
Lyrics by Lee Adams; Book by William F. Brown; Directed and Choreographed by Gower Champion; Produced by Norman Kean and Garth H. Drabinsky; With Warren Berlinger, Larry Marshall, Patti Karr, and Tiger Haynes.

Songs Published in Non-show Folios
A Broadway Musical
The 1934 Hot Chocolate Jazz Babies Revue
Smashing New York Times

Additional Song Recorded
Lawyers

A poorly produced Broadway musical about a poorly produced Broadway musical, A BROADWAY MUSICAL played its out-of-town tryout *uptown*—in Harlem. Librettist Brown (of THE WIZ [Notables: January 5, 1975]) and Strouse and Adams (of GOLDEN BOY [October 20, 1964]) good-naturedly addressed their experiences as white writers on black musicals. Things took on the very racial overtones they were trying to avoid, though, when black director/choreographer George Faison (hot from THE WIZ) was replaced by the white Gower Champion (cold since 1966). A BROADWAY MUSICAL closed opening night, the first of six Strouse efforts to shutter in less than a week. So far.

FLOWERS FOR ALGERNON
June 14, 1979
Queen's Theatre {London} • 28 performances
[and]

CHARLIE AND ALGERNON
September 14, 1980
Helen Hayes Theatre {New York} •
    17 performances
Book and Lyrics by David Rogers (based on "Flowers for Algernon" [story] by Daniel Keyes). *London*: Directed by Peter Coe; Produced by Michael White in association with Isobel Robins Konecky; With Michael Crawford and Cheryl Rogers. *New York*: Directed by Louis W. Scheeder; Produced by Kennedy Center, Isobel Robins Konecky, Fisher Theatre Foundation, and Folger Theatre Group; With P. J. Benjamin and Sandy Faison.

Published Songs
Charlie
I Got a Friend
Midnight Riding
No Surprises
Whatever Time There Is

Additional Songs Recorded
Charlie and Algernon
Dream Safe with Me
Hey Look at Me!
His Name Is Charlie Gordon
I Can't Tell You
I Really Loved You
The Maze
Now
Our Boy Charlie
Reading
Some Bright Morning

Strouse and his collaborator David Rogers undertook a musical about mental retardation and a tap-dancing mouse. The material was sensitively handled in the 1968 film adaptation, *Charly*, but the well-meaning CHARLIE AND ALGERNON proved painful.

BOJANGLES
[circa April 1980]
Unproduced musical. Lyrics by Sammy Cahn (based on the life of Bill Robinson).

Songs Published in Non-show Folio
Da-Da, Da-Da, Da-Da!
A Dancin' Man
Follow the Way of the Lord

Hollywood songwriter Sammy Cahn returned to Broadway with WORDS AND MUSIC† [April 16, 1974], a surprisingly successful anthology revue. Other than that, though, the formerly prolific wordsmith had been pretty much unoccupied since the mid-1960s. Cahn joined with Strouse for one last attempt, a biomusical about Bill Robinson. BOJANGLES was initially announced for the spring of 1980, resurfaced again with different producers and a new book by Samm-Art Williams for 1984–85, and disappeared. Following Cahn's death on January 15, 1993, BOJANGLES was given a nonprofessional workshop production—with yet another book—on July 9, 1993, in Richmond, Virginia. And that, presumably, is the last of that.

BRING BACK BIRDIE
March 5, 1981
Martin Beck Theatre • 4 performances
Lyrics by Lee Adams; Book by Michael Stewart (based on characters from BYE BYE BIRDIE [April 14, 1960]); Directed and Choreographed by Joe Layton; Produced by Lee Guber, Shelly Gross, Slade Brown, and Jim Milford; With Donald O'Connor, Chita Rivera, Maria Karnilova, and Maurice Hines.

Songs Published in Non-show Folios
Baby, You Can Count on Me
Middle Age Blues
Young

Additional Songs Recorded
Back in Show Biz Again
Bring Back Birdie
Half of a Couple
I Like What I Do
I Love 'Em All
Inner Peace
A Man Worth Fightin' For
Movin' Out
There's a Brand New Beat in Heaven
Twenty Happy Years
Well, I'm Not
When Will Grown-Ups Grow Up?
You Can Never Go Back

BYE BYE BIRDIE's phenomenal success as a school and community theatre staple prompted the authors to write a sequel, specifically for the school and community theatre market. BRING BACK BIRDIE was not intended or suitable for Broadway, but that didn't prevent summer tent producers Lee Guber and Shelly Gross from forging ahead with this sad and pathetically amateurish piece. They'd have been much better off just bringing back BIRDIE.

UPSTAIRS AT O'NEAL'S
October 28, 1982
O'Neal's Restaurant {Off Broadway} •
    308 performances • Cabaret revue
Music and Lyrics mostly by others; Conceived and Directed by Martin Charnin; Produced by Martin Charnin and Michael & Patrick O'Neal; With Douglas Bernstein, Randall Edwards, Bebe Neuwirth, and Michon Peacock.

Song Recorded
Boy Do We Need It Now [music and lyric by Strouse]

Strouse contributed this song to a cabaret revue devised by ANNIE [April 21, 1977]–collaborator Charnin.

THE NIGHTINGALE
December 18, 1982
Lyric Theatre {Hammersmith, England}
Book and Lyrics by Strouse; Directed by Peter James; Choreographed by Gillian Gregory; Produced by the Lyric Theatre; With Sarah Brightman, Susannah Fellows, and Gordon Sandison.

Songs Published in Vocal Score
Charming
Death Duet
The Emperor Is a Man
I Was Lost
The Mechanical Bird
Never Speak Directly to an Emperor
The Nightingale
Perfect Harmony
Please Don't Make Me Hear That Song Again
Rivers Cannot Flow Upwards
A Singer Must Be Free
Take Us to the Forest
We Are China
Who Are These People?
Why Am I So Happy?

Despite his string of post-ANNIE [April 21, 1977] failures, Strouse continued to get productions of almost everything he turned out. THE NIGHT-INGALE was an all-Strouse children's opera, initially mounted April 25, 1982, by The First All Children's Theatre (a New York-based amateur group). *Please Don't Make Me Hear That Song Again* was not about ANNIE's *Tomorrow*, though it might as well have been.

DANCE A LITTLE CLOSER
May 11, 1983
Minskoff Theatre • 1 performance
Book and Lyrics by Alan Jay Lerner (based on *Idiot's Delight* [play] by Robert E. Sherwood); Choreography by Billy Wilson; Directed by Alan Jay Lerner; Produced by Frederick Brisson, Jerome Minskoff, James Nederlander, and Kennedy Center; With Len Cariou, Liz Robertson (Lerner), and George Rose.

Published Songs
*Another Life
Dance a Little Closer*—new lyric for *What Became of Me?* written for 1968 London production of GOLDEN BOY [October 20, 1964]
**I Never Want to See You Again*
**There's Always One You Can't Forget*

Additional Songs Published in Non-show Folios
No Man Is Worth It
There's Never Been Anything Like Us

Additional Songs Recorded
Anyone Who Loves
Auf Wiedersehen—revised version of *A Woman Alone* (cut) from "IT'S SUPER-MAN" [March 29, 1966]
Happy Happy New Year
He Always Comes Home to Me
Homesick
I Don't Know
I Got a New Girl
It Never Would've Worked
Mad
On Top of the World
What Are You Going to Do about It?
**Why Can't the World Go and Leave Us Alone?*
A Woman Who Thinks I'm Wonderful

A contemporary update of Robert Sherwood's pre–World War II cautionary tale "Idiot's Delight" must have seemed like a good idea to Alan Jay Lerner. It wasn't, though, and DANCE A LITTLE CLOSER was quickly forgotten. Strangely enough, this was Strouse's most pleasing and inventive score since GOLDEN BOY [October 20, 1964]. *I Never Want to See You Again* and *There's Always One You Can't Forget* are heart-felt, emotional songs somewhat in the same vein as Lerner's stunning (but far superior) *There but for You Go I* and *From This Day On* from BRIGA-DOON [Loewe: March 13, 1947]. *Anyone Who Loves* is effective, the title song is pleasant, and there's a stunning waltz in *Why Can't the World Go and Leave Us Alone?* Not a great score, certainly, and saddled with some wildly uneven lyrics by Lerner; but the DANCE A LITTLE CLOSER songs deserve more attention than they received.

MAYOR
May 13, 1985
Village Gate Upstairs {Off Broadway} • 268 performances
Music and Lyrics by Strouse; Book by Warren Leight (based on the autobiography by Edward I. Koch); Choreographed by Barbara Siman (Strouse); Directed by Jeffrey B. Moss; Produced by Martin Richards, Jerry Kravat, Mary Lea Johnson with the New York Music Company; With Lenny Wolpe.

Published Songs
Good Times
I'll Never Leave You (We Are One)
Mayor
My City

Additional Songs Published in Vocal Selection
Ballad
Hootspa
How'm I Doin'?
I Want to Be the Mayor
The Last "I Love New York" Song
March of the Yuppies
What You See Is What You Get
You Can Be a New Yorker, Too!
You're Not the Mayor

Strouse wrote his own lyrics for this harmless, charmless cabaret revue based on the autobiography of the then-mayor of New York.

RAGS
August 21, 1986
Mark Hellinger Theatre • 4 performances
"The New American Musical." Lyrics by Stephen Schwartz; Book by Joseph Stein; Choreographed by Ron Field; Directed by Gene Saks; Produced by Lee Guber, Martin Heinfling, and Marvin A. Krauss; With Teresa Stratas, Larry Kert, Dick Latessa, Terrence Mann, Lonny Price, and Judy Kuhn.

Songs Published in Vocal Selection
*Blame It on the Summer Night
*Brand New World—revised version of Just You and Me from I AND ALBERT [November 6, 1972]
Children of the Wind—show version
Children of the Wind—standard version
Dancing with the Fools
For My Mary
Penny a Tune (East Side Melodies)
Rags
Three Sunny Rooms
Wanting
Yankee Boy

Additional Songs Recorded
Bread and Freedom (Sisters We Stand)
The Cherry Street Cafe
Easy for You
*Greenhorns
Hard to Be a Prince
I Remember
Kaddish
Nothing Will Hurt Us Again
The Sound of Love (Gramophone Sequence)
Uptown
What's Wrong with That?

A new musical from the composer of ANNIE [April 21, 1977]!, the lyricist of PIPPIN [S. Schwartz: October 23, 1972]!, and the librettist of FIDDLER ON THE ROOF [Bock: September 22, 1964]! Couldn't miss, right? Of course these same gents were also guilty of the more recent BRING BACK BIRDIE [March 5, 1981], WORKING [S. Schwartz: May 14, 1978], and SO LONG, 174TH STREET [May 9, 1976]. More to the point, the three collaborators seemed to be working in three separate vacuums. RAGS was misguided, misconceived, and misproduced. As it happens, Strouse again provided several fine songs amidst a rather uneven score. What was apparently the musical concept—taking Old World melodies and throwing them into the melting pot of New World ragtime—worked extremely well on *Brand New World, Greenhorns,* and the exquisitely bluesy *Blame It on the Summer Night.* The rest of the music ranged from ordinary to n.s.g. [not-so-good] but oh those lyrics! "Oy," as the characters in RAGS would say, and did.

ANNIE 2 (MISS HANNIGAN'S REVENGE)
January 4, 1990
Kennedy Center Opera House {Washington, D.C.} • Closed during tryout
Also see ANNIE WARBUCKS [August 9, 1993].
Lyrics by Martin Charnin; Book by Thomas Meehan (based on *Little Orphan Annie* [comic strip] and the musical ANNIE [April 21, 1977]); Directed by Martin Charnin; Choreographed by Danny Daniels; Produced by Lewis Allen, Roger Berlind, Martin Heinfling, and Fifth Avenue Productions/Margo Lion Ltd.; With Dorothy Loudon, Harve Presnell, Ronny Graham, Lauren Mitchell, Marian Seldes, and Danielle Findley.

Published Songs
*When You Smile (I Smile)
A Younger Man

Additional Song Recorded
You You You (Could Be Annie 2)—see ANNIE WARBUCKS

The smell of money once again lured successful show folk down the primrose path. I readily admit that I didn't much like ANNIE 1, but it was at least humorous in a simplistic way. ANNIE 2 was remarkable in that it was one of the most mirthless musicals in memory. (I saw it twice, and counted one good joke.) One good song, too, the cheery *When You Smile (I Smile).* To those who say we should be less critical at "family shows" and heed audience reaction, I offer this eyewitness report: a sweet little ribboned-and-bowed miss sitting two rows in front of me threw up in the first act, 'round about the time the lyricist rhymed *squash* with *galoshes*. The daughter of an investor, perhaps?

NICK & NORA
December 8, 1991
Marquis Theatre • 9 performances
Lyrics by Richard Maltby, Jr.; Book by Arthur Laurents (based on characters created by Dashiell Hammett and the *Thin Man* movies); Directed by Arthur Laurents; Choreographed by Tina Paul; Produced by Terry Allen Kramer, Charlene and James M. Nederlander, Daryl Roth, and Elizabeth Ireland McCann; With Barry Bostwick, Joanna Gleason, Christine Baranski, Chris Sarandon, Faith Prince, and Debra Monk.

Songs Published in Vocal Selection
As Long As You're Happy
Boom Chicka Boom
Class
Everybody Wants to Do a Musical
Is There Anything Better Than Dancing?
Look Who's Alone Now
Married Life (Let's Go Home)
May the Best Man Win
Men
Swell

Additional Songs Recorded
Busy Night at Lorraine's
Max's Story
People Get Hurt

The very notion of a murder mystery musical spoof is fraught with peril. How do you maintain the tension when your characters stop to sing? NICK & NORA had an even bigger problem: somebody else had just succeeded with a murder mystery musical spoof of their own. Not only that, but the competing musical—Larry Gelbart's CITY OF ANGELS [Coleman: December 11, 1989], an award-winning hit in its second year—was similarly set in Hollywood, with detective-heroes solving movieland murders. And NICK & NORA had to compete with the audiences' fond memories of William Powell and Myrna Loy (and Asta) as well. Add to that a

couple of long postponements, a change of producers, and an unhappy and troubled preview period, and it's no wonder that NICK & NORA was as miserable as RAGS [August 21, 1986]. Strouse nevertheless managed to come up with some enjoyably melodic songs—*Is There Anything Better Than Dancing?*, *As Long As You're Happy*, *Married Life*, and a couple of effective concerted numbers—but to no avail. It almost seems that as Strouse's writing got better, his shows got worse.

ANNIE WARBUCKS
August 9, 1993
Variety Arts Theatre {Off Broadway} •
   200 performances
Also see ANNIE 2 [*January 4, 1990*]. Lyrics by Martin Charnin; Book by Thomas Meehan; (based on *Little Orphan Annie* [comic strip] and the musical ANNIE [April 21, 1977]); Directed by Martin Charnin; Choreographed by Peter Gennaro; Produced by Ben Sprecher, William Miller, and Dennis Grimaldi; With Kathryn Zaremba, Harve Presnell, Alene Robertson, and Donna McKechnie.

Published Songs
When You Smile (I Smile)—published as from
   ANNIE 2
A Younger Man—published as from ANNIE 2

Additional Songs Published in Vocal Selection
All Dolled Up
Annie Ain't Just Annie Anymore
But You Go On
Changes
I Always Knew
It Would Have Been Wonderful
Leave It to the Girls
Love
The Other Woman
Somebody's Gotta Do Somethin'

Additional Songs Recorded
Above the Law—new lyric for *You You You
   (Could Be Annie 2)* (unpublished) from
   ANNIE 2
I Got Me
That's the Kind of Woman

Having failed miserably with the can't-miss ANNIE 2, the ANNIE boys grit their teeth and tried again. (Strouse and Charnin and Meehan had little else to do, having each suffered nothing but flops since ANNIE 1.) The basic plot complication of ANNIE 2—Warbucks needing to find a wife in order to keep his little orphan—was carried over to ANNIE WARBUCKS, allowing the retention of a good chunk of not good material. The Miss Hannigan character (and Dorothy Loudon), though—the sparkplug of ANNIE and ANNIE 2—was retired. When the final set of producers could not find the money to do ANNIE WARBUCKS on Broadway—surprise, surprise—they cut it down to Off Broadway size, in effect saving themselves millions of dollars in additional losses. The results were foreseeably dire, putting an end—presumably—to Annie's theatrical escapades.

Charles Strouse's record shows fifteen full-scale musicals, twelve of which have been failures.

Only two of his scores have been particularly exciting, BYE BYE BIRDIE [April 14, 1960] and GOLDEN BOY [October 20, 1964]. And then there was ANNIE [April 21, 1977], as big a hit as anyone ever needs in order to be set for life. ANNIE'S *Tomorrow* has brought eight quick flops so far, seven of them—A BROADWAY MUSICAL [December 21, 1978], BRING BACK BIRDIE [March 5, 1981], DANCE A LITTLE CLOSER [May 11, 1983], RAGS [August 21, 1986], ANNIE 2 [January 4, 1990], NICK & NORA [December 8, 1991], and ANNIE WARBUCKS [August 9, 1993]—lighting the lights of Broadway for a total of only nineteen performances combined. How's that for a record?? Nevertheless, Strouse's recent scores demonstrate that he is still capable of writing a highly catchy show tune. He deserves credit for not throwing in the proverbial sponge, at least, though one might fault his project selection. And no matter what the record shows, the man can certainly write a good song. Once in a while, at least.

HARVEY SCHMIDT

Born: September 12, 1929, Dallas, Texas

HARVEY SCHMIDT, the son of a Methodist minister, was studying art at the University of Texas when he met fellow Texan Tom Jones (born February 17, 1928). A mutual interest in theatre led the pair to a songwriting collaboration on college shows. The fledgling team moved to New York in the early fifties, with Schmidt supporting himself as a commercial artist.

SHOESTRING '57

November 5, 1956
Barbizon Plaza Theatre {Off Broadway} •
    110 performances
Music mostly by others (see Strouse: November 5, 1956); Lyrics by Sheldon Harnick, Michael Stewart, Lee Adams, Carolyn Leigh, and others; Directed by Paul Lammers; Choreographed by Danny Daniels; Produced by Ben Bagley in association with E. H. Morris; With Dody Goodman, Dorothy Greener, and Paul Mazursky.

Song Recorded
At Twenty-Two [lyric by Tom Jones]

This revue was a sequel to Ben Bagley's first SHOESTRING REVUE [Strouse: February 28, 1955]. Bagley was to leave Off Broadway for a record producing career, specializing in long lost theatre music revisited—with Schmidt himself providing distinctive jacket cover paintings for the series.

DEMI-DOZEN

October 11, 1958
Upstairs at the Downstairs • Nightclub show
Music also by others (see Coleman: October 11, 1958); Lyrics to Schmidt songs by Tom Jones; Directed by John Heawood; Produced by Julius Monk; With Gerry Matthews and Jane Connell.

Songs Recorded
Grand Opening
The Holy Man and the Yankee
Mr. Off Broadway
One and All [lyric by Schmidt]
Race of the Lexington Avenue Express
A Seasonal Sonatina
Statehood Hula

Jones and Schmidt received their first real New York break—though little notice—in Julius Monk's DEMI-DOZEN. Monk assembled an intermittent series of revues at his various nightclubs, Downstairs at the Upstairs (on upper Sixth Avenue), Upstairs at the Downstairs (on West 56th Street), and Plaza-9 (in the hotel).

THE FANTASTICKS

May 3, 1960
Sullivan Street Theatre {Off Broadway} •
    Still playing April 1, 1999
Book and Lyrics by Tom Jones (based on *Les Romanesques* [play] by Edmond Rostand); Directed by Word Baker; Produced by Lore Noto; With Jerry Orbach, Kenneth Nelson, Rita Gardner, and Thomas Bruce (Tom Jones).

Published Songs
**Soon It's Gonna Rain*
They Were You
**Try to Remember*

Additional Songs Published in Vocal Selection
I Can See It
Much More

Never Say No
Plant a Radish

Additional Songs Published in Vocal Score

Happy Ending
It Depends on What You Pay
Metaphor
*Overture [instrumental]
Rape Ballet [instrumental]
'Round and Round
This Plum Is Too Ripe

Additional Song Published in Revised Playscript

Abductions (*And So Forth*)—song version of *Rape Ballet* written for 1990 road tour

Additional Songs Recorded

Come on Along—cut; initial recording upon reuse in THE SHOW GOES ON [December 17, 1997]
I Have Acted Like a Fool—cut

Fellow University of Texas student Word Baker renewed acquaintance with Schmidt and Jones when he served as associate director/producer of DEMI-DOZEN [October 11, 1958]. With the opportunity to mount an original one-act musical at a Barnard College (New York) summer program, Baker asked Schmidt and Jones if they had anything suitable. They provided their work-in-progress, THE FANTASTICKS, for the week of August 3, 1959. Novice producer Lore Noto optioned the show and brought an expanded version to Greenwich Village's Sullivan Street Theatre. This was back in 1960, when Jerry Orbach was twenty-four years old. The popularity of *Try to Remember* sustained the show for a dozen years or so, and *Soon It's Gonna Rain* accounted for another decade. The show's simplicity and theatrical inventiveness (and relatively low operating cost) keep THE FANTASTICKS running and running and running.

I IO IN THE SHADE

October 24, 1963
Broadhurst Theatre • 330 performances
Lyrics by Tom Jones; Book by N. Richard Nash (based on his play *The Rainmaker*);

Directed by Joseph Anthony; Choreographed by Agnes de Mille; Produced by David Merrick; With Inga Swenson, Robert Horton, Stephen Douglass, and Lesley Ann Warren.

Published Songs

Everything Beautiful Happens at Night
Is It Really Me?
Love, Don't Turn Away
A Man and a Woman
110 in the Shade—added to 1967 London production
Simple Little Things
Too Many People Alone—cut

Additional Songs Published in Vocal Selection

*Gonna Be Another Hot Day
Little Red Hat
Raunchy

Additional Songs Published in Vocal Score

Cinderella
The Hungry Men
Lizzie's Comin' Home
Melisande
*Old Maid
Poker Polka
*The Rain Song
Wonderful Music
You're Not Fooling Me

Additional Songs Recorded

Desseau Dance Hall—cut; initial recording upon reuse in THE SHOW GOES ON [December 17, 1997]
*Evening Star—cut
Flibbertigibbet—cut
I Can Dance—cut; initial recording upon reuse in THE SHOW GOES ON
Inside My Head—cut
Just Fine—cut
*Sweetriver—cut

Producer David Merrick brought Schmidt and Jones to Broadway, joining them with N. Richard Nash and his 1954 hit drama *The Rainmaker*. The trio came up with a surprisingly effective and well-crafted piece; not strong enough to withstand the season's two Merrick-generated smashes, HELLO, DOLLY! [Herman: January 16,

1964] and FUNNY GIRL [Styne: March 26, 1964], though. The 110 score is nevertheless quite impressive, with songs like *Gonna Be Another Hot Day*, *The Rain Song*, and the searing soliloquy *Old Maid*. A whole bushelful of songs were cut along the way, including the lovely *Sweetriver* and the evocative *Evening Star*.

I DO! I DO!
December 5, 1966
46th Street Theatre • 561 performances
Book and Lyrics by Tom Jones (based on *The Fourposter* [play] by Jan de Hartog); Directed and Choreographed by Gower Champion; Produced by David Merrick; With Mary Martin and Robert Preston.

Revival
March 28, 1996
Lambs Theatre • 68 performances
Directed by Will Mackenzie; Choreographed by Janet Watson [Jones]; With Karen Ziemba [Martin] and David Garrison [Preston].

Published Songs
The Honeymoon Is Over
I Do! I Do! [2nd]
Love Isn't Everything
*My Cup Runneth Over
**Thousands of Flowers*—cut
Together Forever
What Is a Woman?

Additional Songs Published in Vocal Selection
I Love My Wife
Roll up the Ribbons
Someone Needs Me
This House
Where Are the Snows?

Additional Songs Published in Vocal Score
All the Dearly Beloved
The Father of the Bride
Flaming Agnes
Goodnight
Nobody's Perfect
Something Has Happened

A Well Known Fact
When the Kids Get Married

Additional Songs Recorded
Guess We May As Well Stay Married Now— cut
I Do! I Do! (I Do Adore You) [1st]—cut; initial recording upon reuse in THE SHOW GOES ON [December 17, 1997]
I Do! I Do! (Who Loves to Touch You?) [3rd]— written for proposed film version; initial recording upon reuse in THE SHOW GOES ON
Man and Wife—cut
Throw it Away—cut

Although inventiveness and sparseness were Schmidt and Jones's stock in trade, I DO! I DO! was a curious paradox: an intimate, two-character, sentimental valentine capable of sustaining full-scale staging with boffo star-performances from a pair of big name inveterate scene-stealers. The results were functional, which was more than enough for a profitable run (cut short by the 1968 Actors' Equity strike). The score contains a fair amount of charming material, but little stands out besides the countryish waltz *My Cup Runneth Over*. *Thousands of Flowers*—which was cut in Boston due to ineffective staging—is a treasure, though.

CELEBRATION
January 22, 1969
Ambassador Theatre • 110 performances
Book, Lyrics, and Direction by Tom Jones; Choreographed by Vernon Lusby; Produced by Cheryl Crawford and Richard Chandler; With Keith Charles, Susan Watson, Ted Thurston, and Michael Glenn-Smith.

Published Songs
Celebration
*I'm Glad to See You've Got What You Want
Love Song
My Garden
*Under the Tree

Additional Songs Published in Vocal Selection
It's You Who Makes Me Young
Somebody

Additional Songs Published in Vocal
 Score
Beautician Ballet [instrumental]
Bored
Fifty Million Years Ago
Not My Problem
Orphan in the Storm
Saturnalia [instrumental]
Survive
Where Did It Go?
Winter and Summer

After two successful (but relatively conventional) Merrick musicals, Schmidt and Jones returned to the experimental field of THE FANTASTICKS [May 3, 1960]. Both shows shared a similar theatrical simplicity, but while THE FANTASTICKS was slightly metaphoric, CELEBRATION was heavily symbolic, anti-establishment, anti-war, and anti-Broadway. After the show's quick failure, Schmidt and Jones retreated to their Off Off Broadway studio to work on future experiments away from commercial theatre pressures.

COLETTE [1970]
May 6, 1970
Ellen Stewart Theatre {Off Broadway} •
 101 performances
Play by Elinor Jones (based on *Earthly Paradise* [autobiographical stories] by Colette); Incidental music by Harvey Schmidt; Lyrics by Tom Jones; Directed by Gerald Freedman; Produced by Cheryl Crawford in association with Mary W. John; With Zoe Caldwell, Mildred Dunnock, Keene Curtis, Barry Bostwick, and Harvey Schmidt.

Published Song
Earthly Paradise

Additional Songs Recorded
The Bouilloux Girls
Femme Du Monde

Tom Jones's wife (at the time) wrote this acclaimed stage biography of the French writer, featuring a bravura performance by Zoe Caldwell (and Schmidt providing an on-stage piano accompaniment). The boys caught Colette fever, though, which was to haunt them and their work for two decades.

PHILEMON
January 3, 1975
Portfolio Theatre {Off Off Broadway} •
 60 performances
Book and Lyrics by Tom Jones; Directed by Lester Collins (Tom Jones); Produced by Portfolio Productions (Tom Jones and Harvey Schmidt); With Dick Latessa, Michael Glenn-Smith, Leila Martin, and Kathrin King Segal.

Songs Published in Non-show Folio
The Greatest of These
I Love His Face

Additional Songs Recorded
Antioch Prison
Come with Me
Don't Kiki Me
He's Coming
How Free I Feel
*I'd Do Almost Anything to Get out of Here and
 Go Home*
I Love Order
My Secret Dream
Name: Cockian
The Nightmare
Oh, How Easy to Be Scornful!
Sometimes
The Streets of Antioch Stink
Within This Empty Space

Another experiment in the CELEBRATION [January 22, 1969] mode, this one about third-century Christian martyrs and clowns. Limited commercial possibilities.

THE BONE ROOM
February 28, 1975
Portfolio Theatre {Off Off Broadway} •
 12 performances
Book and Lyrics by Tom Jones; Directed by John Schak; Produced by Portfolio Productions (Tom Jones and Harvey Schmidt); With John Cunningham, Susan Watson, and Ray Stewart.

Songs Published in Non-show Folio
Postcards
A Wonderful Way to Die

Additional Song Recorded
Wishes Won't Wash Dishes

This was a developmental "work in progress" of another macabre work, which was ultimately left unfinished.

COLETTE [1982]
February 9, 1982
Fifth Avenue Theatre {Seattle, Wash.} •
    Closed during tryout
Book and Lyrics by Tom Jones; Directed by Dennis Rosa; Choreographed by Carl Jablonski; Produced by Harry Rigby and The John F. Kennedy Center in association with the Denver Center and James M. Nederlander; With Diana Rigg, Robert Helpmann, John Reardon, Martin Vidnovic, and Marta Eggerth.

Song Published in Non-show Folio
**The Room Is Filled with You*

Additional Songs Recorded
See COLETTE COLLAGE [1991] [April 24, 1991].

Schmidt and Jones returned to the world of the commercial theatre with a full-scale, extravagant musical that quickly collapsed on the road. This COLETTE was inspired by but not actually based on the Elinor Jones play [May 6, 1970]. It was subsequently recycled into two further versions, both entitled COLETTE COLLAGE.

COLETTE COLLAGE [1983]
March 31, 1983
Church of the Heavenly Rest
    {Off Off Broadway} • 17 performances
Also see April 24, 1991. Book and Lyrics by Tom Jones (based on COLETTE [1982]); Directed by Fran Soeder; Choreographed by Janet Watson (Jones); Produced by York Theatre Company (Janet Hayes Walker); With Jana Robbins, Timothy Jerome, Steven F. Hall, Joanne Beretta, and George Hall.

Published Songs
See COLETTE COLLAGE [1991] [April 24, 1991].

Schmidt and Jones quickly responded to the failure of the top-heavy COLETTE [1982 ed.] [February 9, 1982] by radically cutting it down to vest-pocket size. This did not solve the problem, though, leaving the boys to spend another decade puzzling out how to fix COLETTE.

GROVER'S CORNERS
July 29, 1987
Marriott's Lincolnshire (Illinois) Theatre •
    Regional production
Book and Lyrics by Tom Jones (based on *Our Town* [play] by Thornton Wilder); Directed by Dominic Missimi; Produced by Kary M. Walker in association with the National Alliance of Musical Theatre Producers; With Deanna Wells, Michael Bartsch, Tom Jones, and Harvey Schmidt.

Published Songs
None

Sometimes things just don't seem to work out. Jones and Schmidt's adaptation of Thornton Wilder's 1938 classic began as a developmental workshop at Westbeth on December 15, 1984, with a Broadway transfer slated for May 1, 1985. Producers Tyler Gatchell and Peter Neufeld were unable to attract sufficient backing, though, and GROVER'S CORNERS entered unproduced musical limbo. A plan was formulated to mount the show at various regional theatres around the country, although it ultimately played only one engagement. (The semi-professional cast was bolstered by Tom Jones, as the Stage Manager, with Harvey Schmidt at the piano. The workshop cast had featured Liz Callaway and Scott Waara, with John Cunningham as the Stage Manager). GROVER languished once more, until a full-scale national tour was announced to begin in November 1989, starring Mary Martin —of I DO! I DO! [December 5, 1966]—as the Stage Manager. Well, why not? But Mary withdrew when she was diagnosed with cancer—she died November 4, 1990—and the production was canceled. At this writing we might still someday get to see GROVER'S CORNERS, the score for which contains at least two songs too good to languish, *Our Town* and the rhapsodic *Time Goes By*.

COLETTE COLLAGE [1991]
April 24, 1991
Saint Peter's Church {Off Off Broadway} •
  26 performances
Two Musicals about Colette ["Willy" *and*
"Maurice"]. Also see March 31, 1983. Book and
Lyrics by Tom Jones (based on COLETTE
[1982] [February 9, 1982]); Directed by Tom
Jones and Harvey Schmidt; Choreographed by
Janet Watson (Jones) and Scott Harris;
Produced by Musical Theatre Works; With
Betsy Joslyn, Kenneth Kantor, James J.
Mellon, Joanne Beretta, and Ralston Hill.

Song Published in Non-show Folio
**The Room Is Filled with You*

Songs Recorded
Autumn Afternoon
Be My Lady
Claudine
*Come to Life
Decorate the Face
The Dog and Cat Duet
Do It for Willy
The Father of Claudine
Growing Older
*I Miss You
*Joy
Love Is Not a Sentiment Worthy of Respect
The Music Hall
Ooh-La-La
Riviera Nights
A Simple Country Wedding
Something for the Summer
Two Claudines
La Vagabonde
Victory
Why Can't I Walk through That Door?
You Could Hurt Me

Schmidt and Jones followed their GROVER'S
CORNERS [July 29, 1987] disappointment by returning to their long-in-development COLETTE
project. The show—covering seventy years in the
heroine's life—remained aimlessly puzzling and
unwieldy on stage. The score itself, though, has
much to recommend it, as displayed in a 1994
studio recording. There are no fewer than four
beautiful songs written in the best Harvey
Schmidt style: *Joy, Come to Life*, the haunting

I Miss You, and the extra-special *The Room Is
Filled with You.*

THE SHOW GOES ON
December 17, 1997
Saint Peter's Church {Off Off Broadway} •
  88 performances
Lyrics by Tom Jones; Directed by Drew Scott
Harris; Choreographed by Janet Watson
(Jones); Produced by York Theatre Company
(James Morgan); With Tom Jones, Harvey
Schmidt, JoAnn Cunningham, Emma Lampert,
and J. Mark McVey.

Songs Recorded
Everyone Looks Lonely—written for 1962
  television special "New York Scrapbook"
I Know Loneliness Quite Well—written for
  "New York Scrapbook"
The Story of My Life—written for "New York
  Scrapbook"

Note: All other songs are listed with the shows
for which they were written.

Despite the fact that Jones and Schmidt had been
absent from Broadway for almost thirty years,
the late 1990s saw a revival of interest in their
work (helped by a flurry of recordings of their
lesser-known work). This led to an "and then we
wrote" anthology revue which was intelligent,
unpretentious, and enjoyable—pretty much like
the overall work of Jones and Schmidt.

MIRETTE
July 1, 1998
Goodspeed Opera House {East Haddam, Conn.} •
  96 performances
Lyrics by Tom Jones; Book by Elizabeth Diggs
(based on *Mirette on the High Wire* [children's
book] by Emily Arnold McCully); Directed by
André Ernotte; Choreographed by Janet
Watson (Jones); Produced by Goodspeed
Musicals (Michael P. Price); With Cassandra
Kubinski and James J. Mellon.

Song Recorded
The Show Goes On—initial recording upon use
  in THE SHOW GOES ON [December 17,
  1997]

After all those years of work on various versions of COLETTE, Schmidt and Jones rather surprisingly turned to yet another turn-of-the-century Parisian musical (with a not dissimilar music hall background). As with COLETTE, the finished piece was rather perplexing; in this case, too simplistic for an "adult" musical but too morose for kids. Goodspeed first mounted MIRETTE in a developmental production [August 1, 1996] at their intimate Norma Terris Theatre. They then expanded it for the mainstage, but with similar results. Two songs stood out, *Sometimes You Just Need Someone* and *Keep Your Feet upon the Ground.*

Harvey Schmidt and collaborator Tom Jones displayed creativity and inventiveness in their work during the sixties. Despite two Broadway hits, the pair were uncomfortable working on the large scale necessary for the commercial theatre. After many years of self-imposed exile, they found themselves stymied in their attempts to return. Broadway is always in great need of creativity and inventiveness, certainly, and Schmidt and Jones might very well have more to contribute. Meanwhile, THE FANTASTICKS [May 3, 1960] keeps running.

CY COLEMAN

Born: June 14, 1929, Bronx, New York

Cy COLEMAN, a child prodigy at the keyboard, was giving recitals at the age of five. The budding concert pianist took a turn to pop as a teenager, when he played at servicemen's clubs during World War II. He formed a jazz trio and was soon playing successfully in nightclubs. Coleman also started writing songs with lyricist Joseph McCarthy, Jr. (whose father wrote IRENE [Notables: November 1, 1919]).

JOHN MURRAY ANDERSON'S ALMANAC

December 10, 1953
Imperial Theatre • 229 performances
Music mostly by Richard Adler and Jerry Ross (see Adler and Ross: December 10, 1953); Sketches by Jean Kerr, William K. Wells, and others; Directed by John Murray Anderson and Cyril Ritchard; Choreographed by Donald Saddler; Produced by Michael Grace, Stanley Gilkey, and Harry Rigby; With Hermione Gingold, Billy DeWolfe, Harry Belafonte, and Orson Bean.

Published Song

Tin Pan Alley [lyric by Joseph McCarthy, Jr.]

Coleman came to Broadway with an interpolation into this mediocre revue. JOHN MURRAY ANDERSON'S ALMANAC quickly earned Richard Adler and Jerry Ross a full-scale assignment (see THE PAJAMA GAME [Adler: May 13, 1954]). Coleman, though, had to wait seven years for a full Broadway hearing. He spent his time, meanwhile, doing night club and TV work (including a composing stint for the Kate Smith Hour).

THE ZIEGFELD FOLLIES OF 1956

April 16, 1956
Shubert Theatre {Boston} • Closed during tryout
Music and Lyrics mostly by others (see Bock: April 16, 1956); Sketches by Arnold B. Horwitt, Ronny Graham, and others; Directed by Christopher Hewett; Choreographed by Jack Cole; Produced by Richard Kollmar and James W. Gardiner by arrangement with Billie Burke Ziegfeld; With Tallulah Bankhead, David Burns, Mae Barnes, Joan Diener, Carol Haney, Lee Becker, and Larry Kert.

Published Songs

None

COMPULSION

October 24, 1957
Ambassador Theatre • 140 performances
Play by Meyer Levin; Incidental music by Coleman; Directed by Alex Segal; Produced by Michael Myerberg; With Roddy McDowall and Dean Stockwell.

Published Song

Compulsion [instrumental]

Coleman provided incidental music and served as musical director for this drama based on the Leopold and Loeb case. At about the same time, Coleman found a new lyricist: Carolyn Leigh, best known for her work on the Mary Martin PETER PAN [1954] [Styne: October 20, 1954]. Their collaboration quickly turned out pop hits, like *Witchcraft, Firefly*, and the chromatically swingy *The Best Is Yet to Come*.

DEMI-DOZEN
October 11, 1958
Upstairs at the Downstairs {Off Broadway} •
    Nightclub revue
Music mostly by Harvey Schmidt; Directed by
John Heawood; Produced by Julius Monk;
With Jane Connell and Gerry Matthews.

Published Song
You Fascinate Me So [lyric by Carolyn Leigh]

MEDIUM RARE
June 29, 1960
Happy Medium Theatre {Chicago} •
    1,210 performances
"An Intimate Musical Revue." Music mostly
by others; Directed by Bill Penn; Produced by
Robert Weiner; With Anne Meara, Jerry
Stiller, and Bobo Lewis.

Published Song
The Tempo of the Times [lyric by Carolyn Leigh]

WILDCAT
December 16, 1960
Alvin Theatre • 172 performances
Lyrics by Carolyn Leigh; Book by N. Richard
Nash; Directed and Choreographed by Michael
Kidd; Produced by Michael Kidd and N.
Richard Nash; With Lucille Ball, Keith Andes,
Edith King, Paula Stewart, Clifford David, and
Swen Swenson.

Published Songs
Angelina—cut
Give a Little Whistle
**Hey, Look Me Over!*
One Day We Dance
Tall Hope
What Takes My Fancy
You're Far Away from Home—cut
**You've Come Home*

Additional Songs Published in Vocal
    Score
Corduroy Road
Dancing on My Tippy-Tippy Toes
El Sombrero
Oil!
You're a Liar!

Additional Songs Recorded
Bouncing Back for More—cut; subsequently
    used in HELLZAPOPPIN'! [November 22,
    1976]
That's What I Want for Jamie
Wildcat—cut; music published as part of
    Overture in vocal score

Reeling from the end of her twenty-year marriage
to Desi Arnaz, Lucille Ball left Hollywood looking for new fields to conquer. Lucy commissioned
WILDCAT—she was the actual producer and sole
backer—and put the project in the hands of di-
rector/choreographer Michael Kidd (who, as it
turned out, had already had his final hit). Coleman
and Leigh's pop-song success earned them the
assignment. They came up with a fairly bland
score, showing promise in songs like the march-
tempo *Hey, Look Me Over!* and the rather pretty
You've Come Home. WILDCAT was blessed with
an understandably enormous advance sale, but the
star/producer eventually grew tired of doing eight
shows a week, "became ill," and closed the show.

LITTLE ME
November 17, 1962
Lunt-Fontanne Theatre • 257 performances
Lyrics by Carolyn Leigh; Book by Neil Simon
(based on the novel by Patrick Dennis);
Directed by Cy Feuer and Bob Fosse; Choreo-
graphed by Bob Fosse; Produced by Cy Feuer
and Ernest Martin; With Sid Caesar, Virginia
Martin, Nancy Andrews, and Swen Swenson.

Revivals
January 21, 1982
Eugene O'Neill Theatre • 36 performances
Directed by Robert Drivas; Choreographed by
Peter Gennaro; With James Coco [1/2 Caesar],
Victor Garber [1/2 Caesar], Mary Gordon
Murray [Martin], Jessica James [Andrews],
and Don Correia [Swenson].

November 12, 1998
Roundabout Theatre • 101 performances
Directed and Choreographed by Rob Marshall;
with Martin Short [Caesar] and Faith Prince
[Martin and Andrews].

Published Songs
Deep down Inside
Dimples

Don't Ask a Lady—written for revival
Le Grand Boom-Boom
Here's to Us
I've Got Your Number
I Wanna Be Yours—written for revival
Little Me
On the Other Side of the Tracks
Poor Little Hollywood Star
Real Live Girl
To Be a Performer!—revised lyric for 1958
   non-show song

Additional Songs Recorded
Goodbye (The Prince's Farewell)
I Love You
Rich Kids' Rag [instrumental]
Smart People Stay Single—cut
The Truth

Feuer and Martin followed HOW TO SUCCEED IN BUSINESS WITHOUT REALLY TRYING [Loesser: October 14, 1961] with this second fast-paced, brash musical. They brought along Bob Fosse, making him codirector as well choreographer, and Virginia (Hedy LaRue) Martin to play the title role. Librettist Neil Simon—who at this point had only one play on his resumé, the negligible 1961 hit *Come Blow Your Horn*—suggested making a star role out of LITTLE ME's seven lovers and putting his ex-boss Sid Caesar into the part. (In addition to his *Your Show of Shows* chores, Simon had written a 1955 TV musicalization of *Heidi* for Caesar's producer Max Liebman—with lyrics by Carolyn Leigh.) LITTLE ME had a fine score, with Coleman combining his two strongest musical traits—rhythmic jazz and humor—into a gem of a score set to sparkling Leigh lyrics. *I've Got Your Number, To Be a Performer!, Poor Little Hollywood Star, On the Other Side of the Tracks*, and the *Rich Kids' Rag*—all blend music and comedy to delightful results. Yet despite its wildly funny humor, LITTLE ME was a disappointing failure—possibly because it had no heart. When the authors tried to "fix" LITTLE ME twenty years later, the alterations proved ill-fitting. Yet another revival sixteen years later also proved stubbornly problematic. After writing LITTLE ME, Coleman went to Hollywood, were he scored the 1964 movie *Father Goose*, which included a second fine march in *Hey, Look Me Over!* style, *Pass Me By* [lyric by Carolyn Leigh].

SWEET CHARITY
January 29, 1966
Palace Theatre • 608 performances
Lyrics by Dorothy Fields; Book by Neil Simon (based on *Nights of Cabiria* [movie] by Federico Fellini, Tullio Pinelli, and Ennio Flaiano); Conceived, Directed, and Choreographed by Bob Fosse; Produced by Fryer, Carr, and Harris; With Gwen Verdon, John McMartin, Helen Gallagher, and Thelma Oliver.

Revival
April 27, 1986
Minskoff Theatre • 368 performances
Directed and Choreographed by Bob Fosse; With Debbie Allen [Verdon], Michael Rupert [McMartin], and Bebe Neuwirth [Gallagher].

Published Songs
Baby, Dream Your Dream
Big Spender
Gimme a Rain Check—cut
If My Friends Could See Me Now
I Love to Cry at Weddings
I'm a Brass Band
I'm the Bravest Individual (I Have Ever Met) [1st]
It's a Nice Face—written for 1969 movie version
Keep It in the Family—cut; for initial publication see KEEP IT IN THE FAMILY [September 27, 1967]
My Personal Property—written for movie version
Poor Everybody Else—cut; also used in SEESAW [March 18, 1973]
The Rhythm of Life
Sweet Charity [1st] (*Charity's Theme*) [instrumental]
Sweet Charity [2nd]—new lyric for *You Wanna Bet* (cut)
Sweet Charity [3rd]—written for movie version; new music for lyric of *Sweet Charity* [2nd]
There's Gotta Be Something Better Than This
Too Many Tomorrows
Where Am I Going?
You Should See Yourself
You Wanna Bet—cut; used with new lyric as *Sweet Charity* [2nd]

Additional Songs Published in Vocal Score
Charity's Soliloquy
Rich Man's Frug [1st] [instrumental]

Additional Songs Recorded
Big Fat Heart—cut
I Can't Let You Go—cut
I'm the Bravest Individual (I Have Ever Met) [2nd]—new music for [1st] lyric; written for revival
Pink Taffeta Sample Size 10—cut
Pompeii Club (Rich Man's Frug) [2nd] [instrumental]—written for movie version
Rebirth (Finale) [instrumental]—written for movie version

Since REDHEAD [Notables: February 5, 1959], Bob Fosse's only success had been as replacement choreographer on HOW TO SUCCEED IN BUSINESS WITHOUT REALLY TRYING [Loesser: October 14, 1961]. With SWEET CHARITY, Fosse left the confines of the Abbott-influenced well-made book musical and began to imprint his style on the material more fully than even Robbins did. CHARITY boasted the return to the stage of Gwen Verdon, who had followed REDHEAD by marrying Fosse and having a daughter. Fosse brought Coleman together with REDHEAD lyricist Dorothy Fields. (Carolyn Leigh's personality had alienated her collaborators on LITTLE ME [November 17, 1962]. When a song was cut during the tryout, Leigh actually dragged a Philadelphia patrolman into the theatre during the performance and demanded that he arrest producer/director Cy Feuer.) Fosse also tried writing the book himself (under the pseudonym Bert Lewis, as in Robert Louis Fosse), eventually calling Neil Simon to take over. The score was bright and perky throughout, entertaining if not overly distinguished. But there was a handful of good songs—*If My Friends Could See Me Now, Where Am I Going?*, and *Baby, Dream Your Dream*—and in the *Big Spender* number all theatrical elements blended perfectly. If CHARITY was uneven in places, Verdon and Fosse more than made up for its lapses.

KEEP IT IN THE FAMILY
September 27, 1967
Plymouth Theatre • 5 performances
Play by Bill Naughton; Directed by Allan Davis; Produced by David Merrick; With Maureen O'Sullivan, Patrick Magee, and Karen Black.

Published Song
Keep It in the Family [lyric by Dorothy Fields]—initial publication of song cut from SWEET CHARITY [January 29, 1966]

ELEANOR
[circa 1969]
Unproduced musical. Lyrics by Dorothy Fields; Book by Jerome Coopersmith (based on the life of Eleanor Roosevelt).

Published Song
It's Not Where You Start—initial publication upon use in SEESAW [March 18, 1973]

Additional Song Recorded
After Forty It's Patch, Patch, Patch

SEESAW
March 18, 1973
Uris Theatre • 296 performances
Lyrics by Dorothy Fields; Book and Direction by Michael Bennett (based on *Two for the Seesaw* [play] by William Gibson); Choreographed by Michael Bennett and Grover Dale (with Tommy Tune); Produced by Joseph Kipness, Lawrence Kasha, James Nederlander, and George Steinbrenner III; With Michele Lee, Ken Howard, Tommy Tune, and Giancarlo Esposito.

Published Songs
He's Good for Me
If There Were More People Like You—cut; issued as professional copy
I'm Way Ahead
In Tune
It's Not Where You Start—see ELEANOR [circa 1969]
My City
Nobody Does It Like Me
Poor Everybody Else—originally used (cut) in SWEET CHARITY [January 29, 1966]
Ride out the Storm
Seesaw
Spanglish
Welcome to Holiday Inn

We've Got It
You're a Lovable Lunatic

Additional Songs Recorded
*Chapter 54, Number 1909 (The Late Great State
    of New York)*
Pick up the Pieces—cut

William Gibson's intimate two-character play
was blown up into a massive, trouble-ridden
production. Star Lainie Kazan and director
Edwin Sherin were fired in Detroit, with Michael
Bennett stepping in to reconceive the show.
(Bennett also took credit for the book after Mike
Stewart departed.) But SEESAW was ultimately
unsalvageable. The Coleman/Fields score was a
strange mixture of traditional, contemporary,
and (horrid) rock; only a couple of songs stood
out, *It's Not Where You Start*—written for
ELEANOR—and the soliloquy *I'm Way Ahead*.
SEESAW was the final show of Dorothy Fields's
fifty years in show business. She died March 28,
1974.

STRAWS IN THE WIND
February 21, 1975
American Place Theatre {Off Broadway} •
    33 performances
Music mostly by others; Lyrics to Coleman
songs by Betty Comden and Adolph Green;
Directed by Phyllis Newman; Produced by
American Place Theatre; With Tovah
Feldshuh, Brandon Maggart, and Josh Mostel.

Songs Recorded
The Lost Word
Simplified Language

HELLZAPOPPIN'!
November 22, 1976
Mechanic Theatre {Baltimore} •
    Closed during tryout
Music mostly by Hank Beebe and Jule Styne
(see Styne: November 22, 1976); Lyrics by
Carolyn Leigh and Bill Heyer; Book by Abe
Burrows and others (based on a format by
Olsen and Johnson); Directed by Jerry Adler;
Choreographed by Donald Saddler; Produced
by Alexander H. Cohen in association with

Maggie and Jerome Minskoff; With Jerry
Lewis, Lynn Redgrave, Joey Faye, and
Brandon Maggart.

Song Recorded
Bouncin' Back for More—see WILDCAT
    [December 16, 1960]

Coleman's former collaborator Carolyn Leigh
wrote four songs for HELLZAPOPPIN'! with Jule
Styne. She also placed WILDCAT-cut *Bouncin'
Back for More* in the score.

I LOVE MY WIFE
April 17, 1977
Ethel Barrymore Theatre • 857 performances
Book and Lyrics by Michael Stewart (based on
a play by Luis Rego); Directed by Gene Saks;
Choreographed by Onna White; Produced by
Terry Allen Kramer and Harry Rigby by
arrangement with Joseph Kipness; With
Lenny Baker, James Naughton, Joanna
Gleason, and Ilene Graff.

Published Songs
*Hey There, Good Times
I Love My Wife
Love Revolution
Someone Wonderful I Missed

Additional Songs Published in Vocal
    Selection
By Threes
Ev'rybody Today Is Turning On
Lovers on Christmas Eve
Married Couple Seeks Married Couple
Monica
A Mover's Life
Scream
Sexually Free
We're Still Friends

Following the death of Dorothy Fields, Coleman
teamed up with Comden and Green for ON THE
TWENTIETH CENTURY [February 19, 1978].
While that show was in preparation, Mike
Stewart (who had worked with Coleman on SEE-
SAW [March 18, 1973]) found this French com-
edy and proposed an intimate musical. Stewart
undertook the lyric assignment himself, and I
LOVE MY WIFE proved a surprise hit—boast-

ing the charm of Lenny Baker, an on-stage combo wearing Santa Claus suits (in the jaunty *Hey There, Good Times*), and little else.

ON THE TWENTIETH CENTURY
February 19, 1978
St. James Theatre • 449 performances
Book and Lyrics by Betty Comden and Adolph Green (based on *Twentieth Century* [play] by Ben Hecht and Charles MacArthur); Directed by Harold Prince; Choreographed by Larry Fuller; Produced by Robert Fryer, Mary Lea Johnson, James Cresson, and Martin Richards; With John Cullum, Madeline Kahn, Imogene Coca, and Kevin Kline.

Published Songs
Never
On the Twentieth Century
Our Private World

Additional Songs Published in Vocal Selection
Five Zeros
I Rise Again
I've Got It All
The Legacy
Life Is Like a Train
Mine
Repent
She's a Nut
Sign, Lily, Sign (Sextet)
Together
Veronique

Additional Songs Recorded
Babette
Lily, Oscar

Despite Tony Award–winning performances by John Cullum and Kevin Kline and a lavish art deco production by Robin Wagner, ON THE TWEN-TIETH CENTURY was top-heavy and ran out of steam. The score was somewhat enjoyable, more for performance and arrangement than music; Coleman deserted his normal rhythmic style for a land between comic operetta and mock, an experiment which didn't quite work. But Wagner's train, in life-size and miniature, did.

HOME AGAIN, HOME AGAIN
March 12, 1979
American Shakespeare Theatre
{Stratford, Conn.} • Closed during tryout
Lyrics by Barbara Fried; Book by Russell Baker; Directed by Gene Saks; Choreographed by Onna White; Produced by Irwin Meyer and Stephen R. Friedman; With Lisa Kirk, Dick Shawn, Anita Morris, and Mike Kellin.

Published Songs
None

With a book by *New York Times* columnist Russell Baker and staging by the I LOVE MY WIFE [April 17, 1977] team, HOME AGAIN, HOME AGAIN had a promising premise. But the producers—money men from ANNIE [April 21, 1977] team—ran into severe problems, and HOME AGAIN was stranded on the road. Not only did Meyer and Freidman produce three flops in ten months, they also landed in the hoosegow for a coal mining tax shelter fraud. (Their biggest victim was one E. Presley, deceased pop singer, who dropped $510,000.)

BARNUM
April 30, 1980
St. James Theatre • 854 performances
Lyrics by Michael Stewart; Book by Mark Bramble; Directed and Choreographed by Joe Layton; Produced by Coleman, Judy Gordon, and Maurice and Lois F. Rosenfield; With Jim Dale, Glenn Close, and Marianne Tatum.

Published Songs
The Colors of My Life
Come Follow the Band
Join the Circus
One Brick at a Time
There Is a Sucker Born Every Minute

Additional Songs Published in Vocal Selection
Bigger Isn't Better
Black and White
I Like Your Style
Love Makes Such Fools of Us All
Museum Song
Out There

The Prince of Humbug
Thank God I'm Old

The concept of BARNUM—a circus atmosphere overtaking the theatre, spilling through the audience—combined with Jim Dale's bravura performance to make for a moderate hit. The music, though not especially memorable, was highly energetic; the lyrics, once again, came from Mike Stewart, of I LOVE MY WIFE [April 17, 1977]. After less than inspiring management on SEESAW [March 18, 1973] and HOME AGAIN, HOME AGAIN [March 12, 1979], Coleman tried his hand at coproducing, with more satisfactory results.

DIAMONDS
November 29, 1984
Circle in the Square Downtown
    {Off Broadway} • 122 performances
Music mostly by Larry Grossman (also see Kander and Menken: November 29, 1984); Lyrics mostly by Ellen Fitzhugh; Additional lyrics by Howard Ashman, Betty Comden, Fred Ebb, Adolph Green, David Zippel, and others; Sketches by Ralph G. Allen, Roy Blount, Jr., John Lahr, John Weidman, and others; Directed by Harold Prince; Choreographed by Theodore Pappas; Produced by Stephen G. Martin, Harold DeFelice, Louis W. Scheeder, Kenneth John Productions, Inc., in association with Frank Basile; With Loni Ackerman, Susan Bigelow, Jackee Harry, Dick Latessa, and Chip Zien.

Published Songs
None

Coleman, Betty Comden, and Adolph Green contributed two songs—*Cleaning Crew* and *Vendors*—to this Hal Prince curiosity.

13 DAYS TO BROADWAY ✦
    FORMERLY 10 DAYS TO BROADWAY
[circa 1985]
Unproduced musical. Lyrics by Barbara Fried; Book by Russell Baker; [Directed and Choreographed by Joe Layton; Produced by Coleman and Robin Wagner].

Song Published in Non-show Folio
You There in the Back Row

Coleman joined his HOME AGAIN [March 12, 1979] collaborators to write this musical about writing a flop musical (namely HOME AGAIN). Work on 13 DAYS, etc., began in 1983, there was workshop in 1985, and it was again announced for a late 1987 opening. (Given the twenty-year gestation of THE LIFE [April 26, 1997], nothing, I guess, is impossible.) Coleman, incidentally, performed *You There in the Back Row* "from his upcoming musical" on the 1985 Tony Awards telecast.

WELCOME TO THE CLUB
April 13, 1989
Music Box Theatre • 12 performances
Lyrics by Coleman and A. E. Hotchner; Book by A. E. Hotchner; Directed by Peter Mark Schifter; Choreographed by Patricia Birch; Produced by Coleman, A. E. Hotchner, William H. Kessler, Jr., and Michael M. Weatherly; With Avery Schreiber, Marilyn Sokol, Marcia Mitzman, and Sally Mayes.

Published Song
At My Side

Additional Songs Published in Non-show Folio
Piece of Cake
Rio
Southern Comfort

Additional Song Recorded
In the Name of Love

Coleman was to round out the decade with his best musical, but not before things got pretty gruesome indeed. WELCOME TO THE CLUB—a hateful hate-filled entertainment about divorce—tried out under the title LET 'EM ROT. Enough said? EXACTLY LIKE YOU, another courtroom opus sharing WELCOME TO THE CLUB's authors and a good chunk of the score, was mounted by the Off Broadway York Theatre Company on April 14, 1999, following a 1998 developmental production at the Goodspeed Opera House's Norma Terris Theatre. EXACTLY LIKE YOU was much less offensive than WELCOME TO THE CLUB, if only marginally better. But Coleman supplied three attractive tunes, *At My Side*, *In the Name of Love*, and *Ain't He Cute*.

CITY OF ANGELS

December 11, 1989
Virginia Theatre • 878 performances
Lyrics by David Zippel; Book by Larry Gelbart; Directed by Michael Blakemore; Choreographed by Walter Painter; Produced by Nick Vanoff, Roger Berlind, Jujamcyn Theatres, Suntory International Corp., and The Shubert Organization; With James Naughton, Gregg Edelman, Randy Graff, Dee Hoty, Kay McClelland, and Rene Auberjonois.

Published Songs
Funny
Lost and Found
*With Every Breath I Take
You Can Always Count on Me

Additional Songs Published in Vocal Selection
Alaura's Theme—song version with cut lyric
*Ev'rybody's Gotta Be Somewhere
L. A. Blues—song version with cut lyric
Stay with Me
The Tennis Song (*The Ball Is in Your Court*)
*Theme from "City of Angels"
What You Don't Know about Women
You're Nothing without Me

Additional Songs Published in Vocal Score
Alaura's Theme [instrumental]
All You Have to Do Is Wait
The Buddy System
*Double Talk
It Needs Work
L. A. Blues [instrumental]
You Gotta Look out for Yourself

Cy Coleman and neophyte lyricist David Zippel ended the 1980s with what might be deemed Broadway's Best Score of the Decade. (This is not as complimentary as it might sound, I'm afraid, as a glance at Appendix 1, the "Chronological Listing of Productions," will show. My choice for Best of the Decade: the Off Broadway MARCH OF THE FALSETTOS [Finn: April 1, 1981].) Cole-

man harkened back to his jazz background to create some incredibly liquid melodies, like *Double Talk*, *Theme from "City of Angels,"* *What You Don't Know about Women*, and *Ev'rybody's Gotta Be Somewhere*. He was matched—and then some—by Zippel, Broadway's most impressive new songwriter since Maury Yeston debuted with NINE [Yeston: May 9, 1982]. But the score eventually suffered from a certain lack of restraint, with perhaps too many inventive novelty numbers exploiting the plot's double exposure. Assorted combinations of real and "reel" characters, in and out of disguise, sang with (and against) themselves; but of true emotion there was virtually none. The best element of CITY OF ANGELS, though, was the jokebook: the score couldn't quite keep up with that Gelbartian plot packed with purposely contrived contrivances.

THE WILL ROGERS FOLLIES

May 1, 1991
Palace Theatre • 983 performances
Lyrics by Betty Comden and Adolph Green; Book by Peter Stone; Directed and Choreographed by Tommy Tune; Produced by Pierre Cossette, Martin Richards, Sam Crothers, James M. Nederlander, Stewart F. Lane, and Max Weitzenhoffer in association with Japan Satellite Broadcasting, Inc.; With Keith Carradine, Dee Hoty, Dick Latessa, and Cady Hoffman

Published Songs
Look Around
*Never Met a Man I Didn't Like

Additional Songs Published in Vocal Selection
The Big Time
Favorite Son
Give a Man Enough Rope
It's a Boy!
Marry Me Now
My Big Mistake
My Unknown Someone
No Man Left for Me
Will-a-Mania

Additional Songs Recorded
I Got You/First Act Finale
Let's Go Flying

Presents for Mrs. Rogers
So Long Pa
We're Heading for a Wedding
Wild West Show/Dog Act [instrumental]
Without You

THE WILL ROGERS FOLLIES was one of those shows that you either loved or hated. I belong in the latter category, having found the proceedings highly offensive. The sort of thing where they lecture you with dollops of social significance while treating women (and chorus girls) like cattle in skin-tight pantsuits, with tails. The score was tuneful, if overwhelmed by the ugliness of the evening, and contained some pleasantly jingly tunes like *Give a Man Enough Rope* and *Never Met a Man I Didn't Like*. Coleman joined once more with the venerable Comden and Green, who within two days of the opening turned one hundred fifty-one years old. Director/choreographer/magician Tommy Tune once more pulled a tip-tapping rabbit out of his top hat, although the show was ultimately unable to recoup its investment. THE WILL ROGERS FOLLIES, in sum, seemed to be a rough copy of BARNUM [April 30, 1980] without the entertainment value or good-natured charm of Coleman's earlier showbiz-life-in-revue. Yes, the score and the show won Tony Awards; but, then, so did REDHEAD [Notables: February 5, 1959] and WOMAN OF THE YEAR [Kander: March 29, 1981].

THE LIFE
April 26, 1997
Ethel Barrymore Theatre • 465 performances
"An American Musical Masterpiece." Lyrics by Ira Gasman; Book by David Newman, Ira Gasman, and Coleman (based on an original idea by Ira Gasman); Directed by Michael Blakemore; Choreographed by Joey McNeely; With Pamela Isaacs, Kevin Ramsey, Lillias White, Chuck Cooper, and Sam Harris.

Published Songs
Easy Money
He's No Good
My Body
My Friend

Additional Songs Published in Vocal Selection
Don't Take Much
The Hooker's Ball
I'm Leaving You
*A Lovely Day to Be out of Jail
Mr. Greed
My Way Or the Highway
The Oldest Profession
People Magazine
A Piece of the Action
Someday Is for Suckers
Use What You Got
We Gotta Go
We Had a Dream
Why Don't They Leave Us Alone?
You Can't Get to Heaven

Additional Songs Recorded
Check It Out!
Go Home
Step Right Up
Was That a Smile?—cut; recorded as piano solo (no lyric)

During the multi-city success of his topical 1973 Off Broadway revue WHAT'S A NICE COUNTRY LIKE YOU DOING IN A STATE LIKE THIS?†, lyricist Ira Gasman turned his thoughts to the pimps and hookers of Forty-second Street. THE LIFE, too, was topical—twenty years before it was produced, that is. By the time the show made it to Broadway, though, life and art and music and Forty-second Street had changed. The results were strangely out of place; the piece itself obscene at times and at other times obscenely corny. (If THE LIFE, WILL ROGERS FOLLIES [May 1, 1991], and WELCOME TO THE CLUB [April 13, 1989] are any indication, Coleman has an incredibly demeaning attitude toward women.) The strangest thing about THE LIFE, though, was the music: some of the best material Coleman has ever written. Anchored, alas, to fatally low-grade lyrics. *A Lovely Day to Be out of Jail*, for example, is possibly the sweetest music Coleman ever wrote, but the lyric—about Riker's Island and Legal Aid—makes it an unlikely candidate for popular performance. *The Oldest Profession*, *The Hooker's Ball*, *Easy Money*, *People Magazine*—were well-written, effective theatre music in seamy surroundings. It must be added that

Coleman and Gasman also attempted some laughably primitive stretches of recitative. Pimp-opretta, you might call it.

Cy Coleman's early Neil Simon/Bob Fosse collaborations—LITTLE ME [November 17, 1962] and SWEET CHARITY [January 30, 1966]—had bright, exciting scores. Slightly lacking in heart, perhaps, but well suited to the material. CHARITY was followed by a long inactive period, with only one produced show in eleven years. His nine musicals since 1966 have ranged from tunefully adequate to bafflingly poor, with one exceptional exception. A capable musician with good ideas, Coleman has always been kept—by indifferent luck and unfavorable circumstance—in the shadows of contemporaries Strouse, Herman, and Kander. Suddenly and unexpectedly, he came through at the age of sixty with his most impressive work, CITY OF ANGELS [December 11, 1989]—one of the best scores written by any of his generation (not including Sondheim and Bock, of course) and arguably the first exciting work from any of them since the dawning of the Age of Aquarius [i.e., the late 1960s]. But considering Coleman's innate talent, a depressingly large chunk of his work has been merely functional. *The Best Is Yet to Come* predicted one of Coleman's 1959 pop tunes. While he has written several rhythmic songs of the same high caliber over the last forty years, he has still not managed to top his highly promising early hit.

JERRY HERMAN

Born: July 10, 1933, New York, New York

JERRY HERMAN grew up in Jersey City, son of a summer-camp owner. A self-taught musician, Herman started training as an interior decorator at the Parsons School of Design before switching to drama at the University of Miami.

All Music and Lyrics by Jerry Herman unless otherwise indicated.

I FEEL WONDERFUL
October 18, 1954
Theatre de Lys {Off Broadway} •
    48 performances
Sketches by Barry Alan Grael; Directed by Herman; Produced by Sidney S. Oshrin; With Phyllis Newman and Richard Tone.

Published Songs
None

Herman graduated from Miami and returned to New York, bringing back this collegiate college revue (backed by fans back in Miami). For what it's worth, I FEEL WONDERFUL followed the initial limited engagement of Marc Blitzstein's adaptation of THE THREEPENNY OPERA [Weill: March 10, 1954] into the Theatre de Lys. THREEPENNY soon returned, and ran and ran and ran until—well, until Herman reached Broadway with MILK AND HONEY [October 10, 1961].

NIGHTCAP
May 18, 1958
Showplace {Off Broadway} •
    Nightclub revue
Directed by Herman; Choreographed by Phyllis Newman; Produced by Jim Paul Eilers; With Kenneth Nelson, Charles Nelson Reilly, Fia Karin, and Estelle Parsons.

Published Songs
Show Tune in 2/4—initial publication upon reuse in PARADE [1960] [January 20, 1960]; see MAME [May 24, 1966]
Your Good Morning—initial publication upon reuse in PARADE

Additional Songs Recorded
Confession to a Park Avenue Mother—initial recording upon reuse in PARADE
Jolly Theatrical Season—initial recording upon reuse in PARADE

While working as a pianist at the nightclub Showplace, Herman talked the owner into putting on this intimate, late-night revue. Two of the songs were worth attention, *Show Tune in 2/4*—a lively, catchy show tune in 2/4—and the cleverly amusing *Jolly Theatrical Season*.

PARADE [1960]
January 20, 1960
Players Theatre {Off Broadway} •
    95 performances
Book and Direction by Herman; Choreographed by Richard Tone; Produced by Lawrence N. Kasha; With Dody Goodman, Charles Nelson Reilly, Fia Karin, and Richard Tone.

Published Songs
Next Time I Love
Show Tune in 2/4—originally used in NIGHTCAP [May 18, 1958]; see MAME [May 24, 1966]
The Wonderful World of the Two-a-Day

Your Good Morning—originally used in
NIGHTCAP
Your Hand in Mine

Additional Songs Recorded
Another Candle
The Antique Man
Confession to a Park Avenue Mother—origi-
nally used in NIGHTCAP
Jolly Theatrical Season—originally used in
NIGHTCAP
Just Plain Folks
Maria in Spats
Overture—see MACK AND MABEL [October 6,
1974]
Save the Village

Herman first attracted attention with the Off
Broadway revue PARADE. Although the score
was small scale and somewhat primitive, Herman
already displayed bright, friendly music and
cheerful, humorous lyrics. Charles Nelson Reilly
—who repeated his songs from NIGHTCAP [May
18, 1958]—left the cast to go to Broadway with
BYE BYE BIRDIE [Strouse: April 14, 1960]. After
creating the mock-villainous Bud Frump in HOW
TO SUCCEED [Loesser: October 14, 1961], he returned to Herman as the unlikely romantic juvenile in HELLO, DOLLY! [January 16, 1964].

FROM A TO Z
April 20, 1960
Brooks Atkinson Theatre • 21 performances
Music mostly by others; Lyrics mostly by Fred
Ebb and others; Sketches by Woody Allen and
others; Directed by Christopher Hewett; Pro-
duced by Carroll and Harris Masterson; With
Hermione Gingold, Bob Dishy, and Elliot Reid.

Published Songs
None

Herman contributed the opening number, *Best
Gold*, to this short-lived revue which also introduced Fred Ebb and Woody Allen to Broadway.

MILK AND HONEY
October 10, 1961
Martin Beck Theatre • 543 performances
Book by Don Appell; Directed by Albert
Marre; Choreographed by Donald Saddler;
Produced by Gerard Ostreicher; With Robert
Weede, Mimi Benzell, Molly Picon, and
Tommy Rall.

Revival
April 30, 1994
American Jewish Theatre • 59 performances
Directed by Richard Sabellico; With Ron
Holgate [Weede], Jeanne Lehman [Benzell],
and Chevi Colton [Picon].

Published Songs
As Simple As That
Chin up, Ladies
I Will Follow You
Independence Day Hora
Let's Not Waste a Moment
Milk and Honey
*Shalom
That Was Yesterday
There's No Reason in the World

Additional Songs Published in Vocal Score
*Hymn to Hymie
Like a Young Man
Sheep Song
The Wedding

An Israel-based musical seemed a safe bet for
theatre parties—particularly with Yiddish-the-
atre favorite Molly Picon on hand. The novice
producer believed in the novice composer and
the novice librettist and gave them the assignment. Herman did well enough, providing the
highly melodic, minor-key *Shalom*, a couple of
adequate ballads (*I Will Follow You, Let's Not
Waste a Moment*), and some effective old lady
material for comedienne Picon (*Hymn to Hymie*).
But the show as a whole was turgid. MILK AND
HONEY set a new Broadway record, becoming
the first Broadway musical to run over five hundred performances and still lose money.

MADAME APHRODITE
December 29, 1961
Orpheum Theatre {Off Broadway} •
13 performances
Book by Tad Mosel; Directed by Robert
Turoff; Produced by Howard Barker, Cynthia
Baer, and Robert Chambers; With Nancy
Andrews, Cherry Davis, and Jack Drummond.

Published Songs
Beautiful—see LA CAGE AUX FOLLES
    [August 21, 1983]
The Girls Who Sit and Wait
Only, Only Love
Take a Good Look Around

HELLO, DOLLY!
January 16, 1964
St. James Theatre • 2,844 performances
Music and Lyrics mostly by Herman; Book by
Michael Stewart (based on *The Matchmaker*
[play] by Thornton Wilder); Directed and
Choreographed by Gower Champion;
Produced by David Merrick; With Carol
Channing, David Burns, Eileen Brennan, and
Charles Nelson Reilly.

Restaging
November 12, 1967
St. James Theatre •
    [Continuation of original run]
Original direction restaged by Lucia Victor;
Original choreography restaged by Jack Craig;
Produced by David Merrick; With Pearl Bailey
[Channing], Cab Calloway [Burns], Emily
Yancy [Brennan], and Jack Crowder [Reilly].

Revivals
March 5, 1978
Lunt-Fontanne Theatre • 147 performances
Original direction restaged by Lucia Victor;
Original choreography restaged by Jack Craig;
Production supervised by Herman; With Carol
Channing, Eddie Bracken [Burns], Florence
Lacey [Brennan], and Lee Roy Reams [Reilly].

November 6, 1975
Minskoff Theatre • 42 performances
Original direction restaged by Lucia Victor;
Original choreography restaged by Jack Craig;
With Pearl Bailey [Merman], Billy Daniels
[Burns], and Mary Louise [Brennan].

October 19, 1995
Lunt-Fontanne Theatre • 118 performances
Original direction and choreography restaged
by Lee Roy Reams; With Carol Channing, Jay
Garner [Burns], and Florence Lacey [Brennan].

Published Songs
*Before the Parade Passes By—(see commen-
    tary, below)

Dancing
*Hello, Dolly!
It Only Takes a Moment
It Takes a Woman—initial individual publica-
    tion upon use in 1965 London production
Leave Everything to Me—added to 1969 movie
    version
Love Is Only Love—added to movie version
Love, Look in My Window—added after
    opening (1970)
*Put on Your Sunday Clothes
Ribbons down My Back
*So Long, Dearie
World, Take Me Back—added after opening
    (1970)

Additional Songs Published in Vocal Selection
*Elegance [music by Bob Merrill, lyric by
    Merrill and Herman]
I Put My Hand In
Motherhood March [by Merrill and Herman]

Additional Song Published in Vocal Score
Waiter's Gallop [instrumental]

Additional Songs Recorded
Come and Be My Butterfly—cut after opening
Penny in My Pocket—cut

HELLO, DOLLY! galloped on to Broadway as the
biggest hit of the young decade and remained so
despite competition from the illustrious FIDDLER
ON THE ROOF [Bock: September 22, 1964] and
MAN OF LA MANCHA [Leigh: November 22,
1965]. Gower Champion's magical staging; Carol
Channing's charisma, in a part which no musical
comedy leading lady originally wanted to play
(but everybody eventually did); David Merrick's
showmanship, especially with his canny rejuve-
nation of a fading hit into a sellout simply by
adding Pearl Bailey; and Jerry Herman's title song
all played a part in making DOLLY a record-breaking hit despite a score of mixed parentage. Herman
paid a six-figure settlement (without admission of
infringement) on a plagiarism claim against the
title song brought by Mack David (brother of Hal
David, lyricist of Merrick's PROMISES, PROM-
ISES [Notables: December 1, 1968]). *Hello, Dolly!*
is certainly more than similar to David's 1948 pop
hit *Sunflower*, but surely an unconscious borrowing on Herman's part. During the troubled try-

out, Merrick called in Bob Merrill (from the Champion/Stewart hit CARNIVAL [Merrill: April 13, 1961]) to doctor the score. Champion, meanwhile, brought in Charles Strouse and Lee Adams (from the Champion/Stewart hit BYE BYE BIRDIE [Strouse: April 14, 1960]). Two Merrill offerings (with revisions by Herman) were used, *Motherhood March* and the artful *Elegance* (left over from NEW GIRL IN TOWN [Merrill: May 14, 1957]). A third Merrill song, the ballad *We Only Remember*, was unused but recycled for HENRY, SWEET HENRY [Merrill: October 23, 1967]. (When Merrill died in 1998, Merrick ran a paid obituary in the *Times* specifically thanking Merrill for "his contribution to HELLO, DOLLY!") Strouse and Adams came up with a big number to end the first act, *Before the Parade Passes By*. This version was not used, though; instead, Herman wrote his own song with the same title. While Herman received sole public credit for all of these songs, the actual authorship —per Mr. Herman—is as given in the song listings above. (ASCAP, which licenses songs by their members for public performance, lists *Before the Parade Passes By* as by Adams, Herman, and Strouse in the official ASCAP "Index of Performed Compositions." *Elegance* and *Motherhood March* are credited to Merrill alone.) At any rate, DOLLY! was immensely entertaining and, after thirty-five years, is still "glowin' and crowin' and goin' strong."

BEN FRANKLIN IN PARIS
October 27, 1964
Lunt-Fontanne Theatre • 215 performances
Music mostly by Mark Sandrich, Jr.; Book and Lyrics (mostly) by Sidney Michaels; Directed and Choreographed by Michael Kidd; Produced by George W. George and Harvey Granat; With Robert Preston, Ulla Sallert, Susan Watson, and Franklin Kiser.

Published Song
*To Be Alone with You

Additional Song Published in Vocal Selection
Too Charming

BEN FRANKLIN IN Boston was having the miseries. Surgeons were called in but the troubles were terminal. This time Herman was the song doctor, with his two ghosted contributions credited to Sandrich and Michaels. Herman has since taken public credit for authorship, as well he should: *To Be Alone with You* is a very pretty ballad, on a level with his best work.

MAME
May 24, 1966
Winter Garden Theatre • 1,508 performances
Book by Jerome Lawrence and Robert E. Lee (based on *Auntie Mame* [novel] by Patrick Dennis); Directed by Gene Saks; Choreographed by Onna White; Produced by Fryer, Carr, and Harris; With Angela Lansbury, Beatrice Arthur (Saks), Jane Connell, Charles Braswell, and Frankie Michaels.

Revival
July 24, 1983
Gershwin Theatre • 41 performances
Directed by John Bowab; Original choreography re-created by Diana Baffa-Brill; Produced by the Mitch Leigh Company; With Angela Lansbury, Anne Francine [Arthur], and Jane Connell.

Published Songs
**If He Walked into My Life*
**It's Today*—revised version of *Show Tune in 2/4* from NIGHTCAP [May 18, 1958]
Loving You—added to 1974 movie version
**Mame*
My Best Girl
**Open a New Window*
**That's How Young I Feel*
**We Need a Little Christmas*

Additional Songs Published in Vocal Selection
**Bosom Buddies*
Gooch's Song
The Man in the Moon
St. Bridget

Additional Song Published in Vocal Score
The Fox Hunt (Fall Off, Auntie Mame)

Additional Song Recorded
Camouflage—cut

Herman followed DOLLY with the entertaining, stylish MAME. Needing no last-minute "help" this time, Herman provided a fine, first-class score. The big ballad, *If He Walked into My Life*, was quite good; his comedy numbers, *Gooch's Song* and *Bosom Buddies*, were expert; and he provided an infectiously charming charm song in *We Need a Little Christmas. Mame* joined *Hello, Dolly!* in the popular title-song sweepstakes, and the show had a long and successful run (though not so spectacular as her step-sister from Yonkers). MAME, incidentally, was produced in tandem with yet another lady, SWEET CHARITY [Coleman: January 29, 1966].

DEAR WORLD
February 6, 1969
Mark Hellinger Theatre • 132 performances
Book by Jerome Lawrence and Robert E. Lee (based on *The Madwoman of Chaillot* [play] by Jean Giraudoux); Directed and Choreographed by Joe Layton; Produced by Alexander H. Cohen; With Angela Lansbury, Milo O'Shea, Jane Connell, and Carmen Matthews.

Published Songs
And I Was Beautiful
Dear World
Garbage [instrumental]
I Don't Want to Know
I've Never Said I Love You
Kiss Her Now
One Person

Additional Songs Published in Vocal Selection
Dickie
Each Tomorrow Morning
Memories
Pearls
The Spring of Next Year
Thoughts
Voices

Additional Song Recorded
Garbage [song version]

Alexander H. Cohen assembled the authors and stars of MAME [May 24, 1966] for this lavishly packaged, sure-fire hit—which proved to be a massive, misguided failure. Herman's music was actually rather tuneful, but the lyrics were far below his usual level. (The title song lyric is absolutely frightful, atoned for in part by a de-

lightful contrapuntal *Tea Party* trio.) Aside from the score and the book, DEAR WORLD suffered from lack of (or surplus of?) direction, the director being Joe Layton who replaced Peter Glenville who replaced Lucia Victor.

MACK & MABEL
October 6, 1974
Majestic Theatre • 65 performances
Book by Michael Stewart (based on an idea by Leonard Spigelgass); Directed and Choreographed by Gower Champion; Produced by David Merrick; With Robert Preston, Bernadette Peters, Lisa Kirk, and James Mitchell.

Published Songs
Hundreds of Girls
I Promise You a Happy Ending
I Won't Send Roses
Tap Your Troubles Away
Time Heals Everything
Today I'm Gonna Think about Me—cut; issued in separate edition
When Mabel Comes in the Room
Wherever He Ain't

Additional Songs Published in Vocal Selection
Big Time
I Wanna Make the World Laugh—new lyric for unspecified song originally used in PARADE [1960] [January 20, 1960]
Look What Happened to Mabel
Movies Were Movies

Additional Song Recorded
Hit 'Em on the Head—cut; initial recording upon use in 1995 London production
My Heart Leaps Up

Another poorly conceived, ill-manufactured musical comedy. Herman displayed his ability to write perfect material for his female lead in *Look What Happened to Mabel* and *Time Heals Everything*, but the rest of the score was pretty barren. (The MABEL score has adherents, who go weak in the knees over *I Won't Send Roses*, but I'm not among them.) Robert Preston gave his usual superb performance, and Bernadette Peters was highly sympathetic in an unsympathetic role. Producer David Merrick put the show in the hands of Gower Champion, who had long since lost his touch. His career following I DO! I DO! [Schmidt: December 5, 1966] was marked by six of the bigger financial disasters of the era, including THE HAPPY TIME [Kander: January 18, 1968], PRETTYBELLE [Styne: February 1, 1971], and the incomprehensible ROCKABYE HAMLET† [February 17, 1976]. For twenty years people kept threatening to bring MACK & MABEL back to the *Big Time*. (I recall a short-lived stock tour with Lucie Arnaz as Bernadette and Tommy Tune *Tapping his Troubles Away* in the Lisa Kirk role.) MABEL finally got another shot, a full-scale London production [November 7, 1995] with uncredited book revisions by Stewart's sister Francine Pascal. The good things worked well, but the impossible things remained impossible. *Time Heals Everything* except misconceived musical comedies.

THE GRAND TOUR
January 11, 1979
Palace Theatre • 61 performances
Book by Michael Stewart and Mark Bramble (based on *Jacobowsky and the Colonel* [play] by Franz Werfel); Directed by Gerald Freedman; Choreographed by Donald Saddler; Produced by James Nederlander, Diana Shumlin, and Jack Schlissel; With Joel Grey, Ron Holgate, and Florence Lacey.

Published Songs
*I'll Be Here Tomorrow
Marianne
You I Like

Additional Songs Published in Vocal Selection
For Poland
I Belong Here
I Think I Think
Mazel Tov
More and More/Less and Less
Mrs. S. L. Jacobowsky
One Extraordinary Thing
We're Almost There

A charmless show, not helped by a miscast star, two pedestrian featured players, and a drab production. Herman provided a fine, dramatic open-

ing number—*I'll Be Here Tomorrow*—which set the story off to a fine start. Then things hit bottom, more or less idling through the rest of the evening. As with DEAR WORLD [February 6, 1969], the lyrics in places were quite frightful.

A DAY IN HOLLYWOOD/A NIGHT IN THE UKRAINE
May 1, 1980
John Golden Theatre • 588 performances
Music mostly by Frank Lazarus; Book and Lyrics mostly by Dick Vosburgh; Additional music and lyrics by Herman; Directed and Choreographed by Tommy Tune; Produced by Alexander H. Cohen and Hildy Parks; With Priscilla Lopez, David Garrison, and Frank Lazarus.

Published Song
The Best in the World

Additional Songs Published in Vocal Selection
Just Go to the Movies
Nelson

The DAY IN HOLLYWOOD section of this two-part revue needed some beefing up, so Alexander Cohen (of DEAR WORLD [February 6, 1969]) called for Jerry. Herman, at the nadir of his career, contributed three numbers including the amusing Nelson Eddy spoof *Nelson*.

LA CAGE AUX FOLLES
August 21, 1983
Palace Theatre • 1,761 performances
Also see THE QUEEN OF BASIN STREET [Yeston: circa March 1982]. Book by Harvey Fierstein (based on the play by Jean Poiret); Directed by Arthur Laurents; Choreographed by Scott Salmon; Produced by Allan Carr, Kenneth-Mark Productions, Marvin A. Krauss, Stewart F. Lane, James M. Nederlander, Martin Richards, Fritz Holt, and Barry Brown; With George Hearn and Gene Barry.

Published Songs
The Best of Times
La Cage aux Folles
*I Am What I Am
Look Over There

Song on the Sand (La Da Da Da)
With You on My Arm

Additional Songs Published in Vocal Selection

A Little More Mascara—revised version of
Beautiful from MADAME APHRODITE
[December 29, 1961]
Masculinity
We Are What We Are—alternate lyric for *I
Am What I Am*

Additional Song Recorded

Cocktail Counterpoint—revised version of
Have a Nice Day (cut/unpublished,
subsequently used in JERRY'S GIRLS
[December 18, 1985])

Herman had been without a hit since MAME [May
24, 1966]. It was assumed that his "popular touch"
was outdated, too old-fashioned. Then came LA
CAGE AUX FOLLES, Broadway's biggest hit since
ANNIE [Strouse: April 21, 1977]. Curiously
enough, considering the diversity in subject matter, the award-winning LA CAGE and ANNIE
were pretty much equally matched in quality of
score, book, and direction. Many theatregoers
loved both, while neither was to my personal
taste. Oh, well, a hit is a hit is a hit. Right?

JERRY'S GIRLS

December 18, 1985
St. James Theatre • 139 performances
"A Musical Entertainment." Concept by
Herman and Larry Alford; Directed by Larry
Alford; Choreographed by Wayne Cilento;
Produced by Zev Bufman and Kenneth-John
Productions, in association with Agnese/
Raibourn; With Dorothy Loudon, Chita
Rivera, and Leslie Uggams.

Song Published in Vocal Selection
Take It All Off

Note: Songs written for previously produced
musicals are listed with their original scores.

Herman has not returned to Broadway since LA
CAGE AUX FOLLES [August 21, 1983] except
for revivals of his two mid-1960s hits and this
unsuccessful anthology revue. JERRY'S GIRLS
began as an Off Off Broadway revue [August 17,
1981], with the composer himself supported by
four non-star girls. This led to a full-scale road
tour [February 28, 1984] headed by Carol
Channing, Leslie Uggams, and Andrea McArdle.
That didn't work, either, so they mounted yet
another version for Broadway. JERRY'S GIRLS
staggered into the St. James—DOLLY's [January
16, 1964] old stomping grounds—and limped
along for four underattended months. Herman's
only completed project since LA CAGE was the
1996 Angela Lansbury TV musical "Mrs. Santa
Claus," for which he wrote a pleasant set of songs
in typical Herman style. He returned to Broadway—playing the piano himself—with another
anthology revue that limped through twenty-eight
weary performances at the Booth, AN EVENING
WITH JERRY HERMAN [July 28, 1998].

Jerry Herman wrote one of the most successful
musicals of the sixties, as well as one of the biggest hits of the eighties. A third show, MAME
[May 24, 1966], was also a major box office hit.
Herman's record compares more than favorably
with many of his peers, yet his work is continually attacked for its common touch. There's a
reason for this, perhaps. However, it must be
remembered that he has proven himself highly
capable with the score for MAME and a half-
dozen fine songs scattered through his other
shows. Perhaps he has been better off not writing constantly through the years. (Look at Charles
Strouse's post-ANNIE [April 21, 1977] record, for
comparison.) In any event, Mr. Herman has a fine
enough record to retire on.

JOHN KANDER

Born: March 18, 1927, Kansas City, Missouri

JOHN KANDER attended Oberlin College, where he wrote songs with childhood friend James Goldman. Coming to New York to get a master's degree from Columbia, Kander began working as an accompanist. His first Broadway assignments came as dance music arranger for two David Merrick hits, GYPSY [Styne: May 21, 1959] and Marguerite Monnot's IRMA LA DOUCE† [September 29, 1960]—both of which had especially good dance arrangements.

A FAMILY AFFAIR
January 27, 1962
Billy Rose Theatre • 65 performances
"By James Goldman, John Kander, and William Goldman"; Directed by Harold Prince; Produced by Andrew Siff; With Shelley Berman, Eileen Heckart, Morris Carnovsky, Larry Kert, and Rita Gardner.

Published Songs
Beautiful
A Family Affair
*Harmony
Mamie in the Afternoon—cut; see THE ACT
   [October 2, 1977]
There's a Room in My House

Additional Songs Recorded
Anything for You
Every Girl Wants to Get Married
Football Game (Marching Songs)
I'm Worse Than Anybody
Kalua Bay
*My Son, the Lawyer
Now Morris
Revenge
Right Girls
Summer Is Over

What I Say Goes
Wonderful Party

The authors of A FAMILY AFFAIR had never done a Broadway show, the producer had never done a Broadway show, the director—Word Baker of THE FANTASTICKS [Schmidt: May 3, 1960]—had never done a Broadway show, even the choreographer had never done a Broadway show. The same could be said, more or less, for BYE BYE BIRDIE [Strouse: April 14, 1960]; but A FAMILY AFFAIR was no BIRDIE. After the dismal Philadelphia opening a call went to Harold Prince, who had produced James Goldman's 1961 play *They Might Be Giants*, which closed during its pre–West End tryout (and a few other smash hits), but had never directed anything. Prince helped improve the show somewhat, which was the best he could do under the circumstances, but he would produce Kander's next two musicals (as well as James Goldman's FOLLIES [Sondheim: April 4, 1971]). William Goldman went to Hollywood to become a top screenwriter, visiting Broadway to write the fascinating 1969 chronicle *The Season*. As for the problematic FAMILY AFFAIR, two concerted comedy numbers—*Harmony* and *My Son, the Lawyer*—displayed a composer with a definite affinity for the theatre. (While the three authors received joint billing, the music was written by Kander, the lyrics by Kander and James Goldman, and the book by the Goldman brothers.)

NEVER TOO LATE
November 27, 1962
Playhouse Theatre • 1,007 performances
Play by Sumner Arthur Long; Incidental music by Kander; Song by Jerry Bock and

Sheldon Harnick (see Bock: November 27, 1962); Directed by George Abbott; Produced by Elliot Martin and Daniel Hollywood; With Paul Ford, Maureen O'Sullivan, and Orson Bean.

Published Songs
None

Kander provided incidental music for this surprise hit, George Abbott's final smash. The one song used, though, was provided by Bock and Harnick.

FLORA, THE RED MENACE
May 11, 1965
Alvin Theatre • 87 performances
Lyrics by Fred Ebb; Book by George Abbott and Robert Russell (based on *Love Is Just around the Corner* [novel] by Lester Atwell); Directed by George Abbott; Choreographed by Lee Theodore; Produced by Harold Prince; With Liza Minnelli, Bob Dishy, Mary Louise Wilson, Cathryn Damon, and James Cresson.

Revival
December 6, 1987
Vineyard Theatre {Off Off Broadway} •
    46 performances
[New] Book by David Thompson; Directed by Scott Ellis; Choreographed by Susan Stroman; With Veanne Cox [Minnelli] and Peter Frechette [Dishy].

Published Songs
All I Need (*Is One Good Break*)
*Dear Love
Express Yourself
I Believe You—cut
Knock Knock
Not Every Day of the Week
*A Quiet Thing
*Sing Happy

Additional Songs Recorded
The Flame
Hello, Waves
The Joke—written for revival
Keepin' It Hot—written for revival
The Kid Herself—cut
Palomino Pal

Sign Here
Street Songs
Unafraid
Where Did Everybody Go?—written for revival
You Are You

Publisher Tommy Valando—who had launched composer Jerry Bock and published the four Bock-Prince musicals—matched Kander with lyricist Fred Ebb, who had been writing undistinguished revue material (see FROM A TO Z [Herman: April 20, 1960]). The new team immediately came up with a 1962 pop hit, *My Coloring Book*. Prince, who had been impressed with Kander on A FAMILY AFFAIR [January 27, 1962], gave the pair their first Broadway assignment. FLORA, THE RED MENACE was the last of the Abbott-Prince shows; the formula which worked so well in the 1950s was becoming outmoded, and Prince determined to move on and direct his future shows himself. If FLORA was unworkable, it featured a staggeringly bright new star in Liza Minnelli and a highly spirited score with three fine songs, *A Quiet Thing*, *Dear Love*, and *Sing Happy*.

CABARET
November 20, 1966
Broadhurst Theatre • 1,165 performances
Lyrics by Fred Ebb; Book by Joe Masteroff (based on *I Am a Camera* [play] by John van Druten, from stories by Christopher Isherwood); Directed by Harold Prince; Choreographed by Ronald Field; Produced by Harold Prince in association with Ruth Mitchell; With Jill Haworth, Jack Gilford, Lotte Lenya, Bert Convy, and Joel Grey.

Revivals
October 29, 1987
Imperial Theatre • 262 performances
Directed by Harold Prince; Choreographed by Ronald Field; With Joel Grey, Alyson Reed [Haworth], Gregg Edelman [Convy], Regina Resnick [Lenya], and Werner Klemperer [Gilford].

March 19, 1998
Kit Kat Klub (Henry Miller's Theatre) •
    Still playing April 1, 1999

Directed by Sam Mendes and Rob Marshall; Choreographed by Rob Marshall; Produced by Roundabout Theatre; With Natasha Richardson [Haworth], Alan Cumming [Grey], Ron Rifkin [Gilford], Mary Louise Wilson [Lenya], and John Benjamin Hickey [Convy].

Published Songs
*Cabaret
I Don't Care Much—cut; added to 1987 revival
Married
Maybe This Time—added to 1972 movie version and 1998 revival; initial use of 1963 non-show song
Meeskite
Mein Herr—written for movie version and added to 1998 revival
Money, Money (Makes the World Go Round)—written for movie version and added to 1998 revival
Tomorrow Belongs to Me
Why Should I Wake Up?
*Wilkommen (Welcome)

Additional Songs Published in Vocal Selections
Don't Tell Mama
If You Could See Her
It Couldn't Please Me More (The Pineapple Song)
Perfectly Marvelous
*So What
**What Would You Do?

Additional Songs Published in Vocal Score
Sitting Pretty (Money Song)
*Telephone Song
Two Ladies

Additional Songs Recorded
Don't Go—written for 1987 revival
Good Time Charlie—cut
It'll All Blow Over—cut
Roommates—cut

Kander and Ebb's first hit and most important show came with this first of the new-style Harold Prince musicals. Prince had already directed four unsuccessful, traditional musicals; he now forged ahead into a more conceptualized musical theatre. CABARET's score was good but

strangely uneven (as was the show itself): the Kit Kat Club solos (Wilkommen and Cabaret) and the M.C.'s comic specialties were quite good, mixed in with rather bland songs accompanying the weak story sections. (One of the story section songs was top rate, though, the searing What Would You Do?) The considerably altered 1972 movie version, under the directorial hand of Bob Fosse, solved some of CABARET's dramaturgical problems. These were thus all the more apparent when the original was resuscitated in a lackluster twentieth-anniversary revival. Kander and Ebb added an indifferent new song, Don't Go, and reinstated the cut I Don't Care Much. Sam Mendes and Rob Marshall's 1998 revival—based on Mendes's 1993 London production—took a new and darker look at the material with exhilarating results, coming up with presumably the best of all possible CABARETs.

THE HAPPY TIME
January 18, 1968
Broadway Theatre • 286 performances
Lyrics by Fred Ebb; Book by N. Richard Nash (based on the novel by Robert L. Fontaine); Directed and Choreographed by Gower Champion; Produced by David Merrick; With Robert Goulet, David Wayne, Mike Rupert, and George S. Irving.

Published Songs
(Walking) Among My Yesterdays
*A Certain Girl—written for the unproduced 1965 musical THE EMPEROR OF SAN FRANCISCO† (also called GOLDEN GATE)
The Happy Time
I Don't Remember You
*The Life of the Party
Seeing Things
Tomorrow Morning
Without Me

Additional Songs Published in Vocal Selection
Please Stay
St. Pierre

Additional Songs Recorded
Catch My Garter
He's Back
If You Leave Me Now—cut

The success of CABARET [November 20, 1966] brought commercial Broadway calling, in the guise of David Merrick and Gower Champion. Kander and Ebb wrote a slight but charming score for what turned out to be an overblown, ponderous production. For lack of a better idea, Champion turned THE HAPPY TIME into a multimedia photography show and all was lost. Broadway had its first million-dollar bomb, with Champion nevertheless receiving two Tony Awards. Kander and Ebb provided two endearing songs, though, *A Certain Girl* and *The Life of the Party.*

ZORBÁ
November 17, 1968
Imperial Theatre • 305 performances
Lyrics by Fred Ebb; Book by Joseph Stein (based on *Zorbá the Greek* [novel] by Nikos Kazantzakis); Directed by Harold Prince; Choreographed by Ronald Field; Produced by Harold Prince in association with Ruth Mitchell; With Herschel Bernardi, Maria Karnilova, John Cunningham, and Lorraine Serabian.

Revival
October 16, 1983
Broadway Theatre • 362 performances
Directed by Michael Cacoyannis; Choreographed by Graciela Daniele; With Anthony Quinn [Bernardi], Lila Kedrova [Karnilova], Debbie Shapiro [Serrabian], and Robert Westenberg [Cunningham].

Published Songs
The First Time
Happy Birthday to Me
No Boom Boom
Only Love
Why Can't I Speak?
Woman—written for revival
Zorbá Theme (Life Is) [instrumental]

Additional Songs Published in Vocal Selection
I Am Free
The Top of the Hill—see KISS OF THE SPIDER WOMAN [1993] [May 3, 1993]

Additional Songs Recorded
The Butterfly (Not Too Fast)
The Crow

Goodbye, Canavaro
Grandpapa (Zorbá's Dance)
Life Is [song version]
Y'assou

Once again, the purveyors of one hit—Kander, Ebb, Prince, and Fields's CABARET [November 20, 1966]—followed up with a similarly assembled advance-sale blockbuster which quickly busted. There were also strong overtones of Prince's long-running FIDDLER ON THE ROOF [Book: September 22, 1964], represented by librettist Joseph Stein, Herschel Bernardi (a long-time Tevye), and Maria Karnilova. ZORBÁ was a gray and muddy entertainment, overwhelmed by layers of theatrically pretentious concept. Kander and Ebb broke through with some nice writing in spots—*No Boom Boom, Life Is, Why Can't I Speak?*—but everything was so utterly *depressing.*

70, GIRLS, 70
April 15, 1971
Broadhurst Theatre • 35 performances
Lyrics by Fred Ebb; Book by Fred Ebb and Norman L. Martin (based on *Breath of Spring* [play] by Peter Coke); Directed by Paul Aaron; Choreographed by Onna White; Produced by Arthur Whitelaw; With Mildred Natwick, Lillian Roth, Lillian Hayman, and Hans Conried.

Published Songs
The Elephant Song
Yes

Additional Songs Published in Vocal Selection
Believe
Boom Ditty Boom
Broadway, My Street
Coffee (in a Cardboard Cup)
Do We?
Go Visit Your Grandmother
Home
Old Folks
70, Girls, 70

Additional Songs Recorded
The Caper
Hit It, Lorraine

See the Light
You and I, Love

Kander and Ebb bounced back from the ponderous ZORBÁ [Nobember 17, 1968] with an intimate, charming-but-hopelessly-flawed show. 70, GIRLS, 70 had an amateurish, loosely-put-together feel to it which belied its production history. Librettist Joe Masteroff and choreographer-turned-director Ron Field—both from CABARET [November 20, 1966]—left early on. Ebb brought in his pre-Kander collaborator Norman Martin to work on the book, while the show went through at least three directors. Two star comedians departed along the way, Eddie Foy, Jr., and David Burns (who suffered a fatal heart attack onstage during the tryout. Talk about dying in Philadelphia . . .). Kander and Ebb, meanwhile, wrote their friendliest score, with the corny-but-sweet *Broadway, My Street*, the endearing soft-shoe *Go Visit Your Grandmother*, and the upbeat, life-affirming *Yes*. 70, GIRLS, 70 was Kander's quickest failure—though not his biggest flop, as THE HAPPY TIME, THE ACT, WOMAN OF THE YEAR, THE RINK, both versions of KISS OF THE SPIDER WOMAN, and STEEL PIER all suffered infinitely larger losses.

CHICAGO
June 1, 1975
46th Street Theatre • 923 performances
"A Musical Vaudeville." Lyrics by Fred Ebb; Book by Fred Ebb and Bob Fosse (based on the play by Maurine Dallas Watkins); Directed and Choreographed by Bob Fosse; Produced by Robert Fryer and James Cresson; With Gwen Verdon, Chita Rivera, Jerry Orbach, and Barney Martin.

Revival
November 14, 1996
Shubert Theatre • still playing April 1, 1999
Directed by Walter Bobbie; Choreographed by Ann Reinking "in the style of Bob Fosse"; Transferred from City Center Encores [May 2, 1996]; With Ann Reinking [Verdon], Bebe Neuwirth [Rivera], and James Naughton [Orbach].

Published Songs
*And All That Jazz
I Can't Do It Alone*

Me and My Baby
**Mr. Cellophane*
My Own Best Friend
Razzle Dazzle
Roxie

Additional Songs Published in Vocal Selection
All I Care About
Class
Funny Honey
A Little Bit of Good
Nowadays
When You're Good to Mama

Additional Songs Recorded
**Cell Block Tango*
Hot Honey Rag [instrumental]—initial recording in connection with revival
I Know a Girl—initial recording in connection with revival
It—cut
Loopin' de Loop—cut
Ten Percent—cut
We Both Reached for the Gun
When Velma Takes the Stand

In his previous projects—PIPPIN [S. Schwartz: October 23, 1972] and the 1972 film version of CABARET [November 20, 1966]—Bob Fosse had taken already-written material and altered it, effectively so, to fit his needs. CHICAGO, though, was conceived and controlled by Fosse; the songs were written to order to fill the director/choreographer's "musical vaudeville" needs instead of the other way around. Kander and Ebb, thus constrained, came up with a score full of highly stageable "numbers" rather than dramatic theatre songs. *Razzle Dazzle, And All That Jazz, My Own Best Friend,* and *Me and My Baby*, though not without their charms, could be inserted into just about any carelessly integrated musical. Only one of the CHICAGO songs managed to break through this wall, working as an effective performance vehicle with emotional force, the heart-rending *Mr. Cellophane*. I also pause to praise the delightfully contrived contrapuntal choral ensemble *Cell Block Tango*, a sister to *Big Spender* from Fosse's SWEET CHARITY [Coleman: January 29, 1966]. But Fosse, Gwen Verdon (in her first musical since CHARITY), and

Chita Rivera (in her first since BAJOUR[†] [November 23, 1964]) provided enough entertainment to give Kander and Ebb their second-biggest hit. CHICAGO looked even better in the scaled-down 1996 revival, which seems likely to surpass CABARET in longevity and profitability (though not in overall importance).

THE ACT
October 29, 1977
Majestic Theatre • 233 performances
Lyrics by Fred Ebb; Book by George Furth;
Directed by Martin Scorsese; Choreographed
by Ron Lewis; Produced by The Shubert
Organization, and Cy Feuer and Ernest Martin;
With Liza Minnelli and Barry Nelson. Pre-
Broadway titles: IN PERSON and SHINE
IT ON.

Published Songs
City Lights
It's the Strangest Thing
My Own Space
Shine It On

Additional Song Published in Vocal Selection of AND THE WORLD GOES 'ROUND [March 18, 1991]
Arthur in the Afternoon—revised lyric for
  Mamie in the Afternoon (by Kander, James
  Goldman, and William Goldman) from A
  FAMILY AFFAIR [January 27, 1962]

Additional Songs Recorded
Bobo's
Hot Enough for You?
*Little Do They Know (Gypsies' Song)
The Money Tree
The Only Game in Town—cut
*Please, Sir—cut
There When I Need Him
Turning (Shaker Hymn)
Walking Papers

CHICAGO [June 1, 1975] had Bob Fosse to help triumph over its weaknesses; THE ACT had weaker material, no Fosse, and one Liza in place of Gwen and Chita. Minnelli's popularity at the time made her a sure-fire ticket seller during the pre-Broadway tryout, but her vehicle underwent severe rewrites, changes, firings, etc. The

whole thing wound up as little more than a parade of nondistinguished songs with unusually drab music—surprising from Kander—and worse lyrics. *Little Do They Know* is an amusing novelty number for the dancers, but the rest of the songs can best be described as "noisy." (Did someone say "disco"?) However, there might be extenuating circumstances: *Please, Sir*—a cut number which has been recorded—searingly and expertly defines the leading character. If this is any indication of what was lost along the way, then maybe there was a lot more to THE ACT than the dismal entertainment that limped into town.

THE MADWOMAN OF CENTRAL PARK WEST
June 13, 1979
22 Steps Theatre {Off Broadway} •
  86 performances
Music mostly by others (also see Bernstein:
June 13, 1979); Lyric to Kander song by Fred
Ebb; Book by Phyllis Newman and Arthur
Laurents; Directed by Arthur Laurents;
Produced by Gladys Rackmil, Fritz Holt, and
Barry M. Brown; With Phyllis Newman.

Song Recorded
Cheerleader

WOMAN OF THE YEAR
March 29, 1981
Palace Theatre • 770 performances
Lyrics by Fred Ebb; Book by Peter Stone
(based on the screenplay by Ring Lardner,
Jr., and Michael Kanin); Directed by Robert
Moore; Choreographed by Tony Charmoli;
Produced by Lawrence Kasha, David S.
Landay, James M. Nederlander, Warner
Communications, Carole J. Shorenstein,
and Stewart F. Lane; With Lauren Bacall,
Harry Guardino, Roderick Cook, and Rex
Everhart.

Published Songs
One of the Girls
See You in the Funny Papers
Sometimes a Day Goes By
We're Gonna Work It Out

Additional Songs Published in Vocal Selection
*The Grass Is Always Greener
*I Wrote the Book
Woman of the Year

Additional Songs Recorded
Happy in the Morning
*It Isn't Working
I Told You So
The Poker Game
Shut up, Gerald
So What Else Is New?
Table Talk
When You're Right, You're Right
Who Would Have Dreamed—cut

The well-written and literate Oscar-winning screenplay for the deft 1941 Tracy/Hepburn movie was turned into a one-sided comic strip, leaving nothing much to amuse audiences except Marilyn Cooper (playing a character highly reminiscent of Agnes Gooch from MAME [Herman: May 24, 1966]). The abysmal competition—ONE NIGHT STAND [Styne: October 20, 1980], BRING BACK BIRDIE [Strouse: March 5, 1981]—allowed the authors to win Tony Awards, and Lauren Bacall's star power was strong enough to keep the show running almost two years (at a massive financial loss). Kander and Ebb provided a one-note score, with many similar-sounding songs and some especially vapid ballads (for performers who couldn't sing). The songwriters' humor shone through, at least, in a grandly wacky concerted number (It Isn't Working) and the insult-duet slugfest The Grass Is Always Greener. But WOMAN OF THE YEAR was pretty desperate.

THE RINK
February 9, 1984
Martin Beck Theatre • 204 performances
Lyrics by Fred Ebb; Book by Terrence McNally; Directed by A. J. Antoon; Choreographed by Graciela Daniele; Produced by Jules Fisher, Roger Berlind, Joan Cullman, Milbro Productions, and Kenneth-John Productions in association with Jonathan Farkas; With Chita Rivera, Liza Minnelli, Jason Alexander, Ronn Carroll, and Scott Ellis.

Songs Published in Vocal Selection
All the Children in a Row
Blue Crystal
Chief Cook and Bottle Washer
*Colored Lights—see KISS OF THE SPIDER WOMAN [1993] [May 3, 1993]
Marry Me
The Rink
Under the Roller-Coaster
Wallflower
We Can Make It

Additional Songs Recorded
After All These Years
Angel's Rink and Social Center
The Apple Doesn't Fall
Don't "Ah, Ma" Me
Mrs. A.
Not Enough Magic
What Happened to the Old Days?
Wine and Peaches—cut

Not even the combined presence of Liza Minnelli and Chita Rivera could breathe any life into THE RINK, yet another heartless musical built around nothing. Minnelli went way back with Kander and Ebb, starting with FLORA, THE RED MENACE [May 11, 1965]. She became a superstar in the 1972 film of CABARET [November 20, 1966] and the TV special "Liza with a Z," which featured special material by her favorite songwriters. When Minnelli stepped in for two months to cover the ailing Gwen Verdon in CHICAGO [June 1, 1975], she pushed the show to sellout status. But then came THE ACT [October 29, 1977], which so tarnished Minnelli's star that her name didn't even provide an advance sale for THE RINK. Which was a somewhat vulgar and vile show anyway, with only one interesting song (Colored Lights) to recommend it.

DIAMONDS
November 29, 1984
Circle in the Square Downtown {Off Broadway} • 122 performances
Music mostly by Larry Grossman (also see Coleman and Menken: November 29, 1984); Lyrics mostly by Ellen Fitzhugh; Additional lyrics by Howard Ashman, Betty Comden, Fred Ebb, Adolph Green, David Zippel, and

others; Sketches by Ralph G. Allen, Roy Blount, Jr., John Lahr, John Weidman, and others; Directed by Harold Prince; Choreographed by Theodore Pappas; Produced by Stephen G. Martin, Harold DeFelice, Louis W. Scheeder, Kenneth John Productions, Inc., in association with Frank Basile; With Loni Ackerman, Susan Bigelow, Jackee Harry, Dick Latessa, and Chip Zien.

Published Songs
None

Kander and Ebb contributed two songs—*Diamonds Are Forever* and *Winter in New York*—to Hal Prince's indifferent baseball revue.

HAY FEVER
December 12, 1985
Music Box Theatre • 124 performances
Play by Noël Coward; Directed by Brian Murray; Produced by Roger Peters in association with MBS Co.; With Rosemary Harris and Roy Dotrice.

Published Songs
None

Kander and Ebb contributed one song, *No, My Heart*, to this short-lived revival of Coward's comedy.

KISS OF THE SPIDER WOMAN [1990]
May 1, 1990
Performing Arts Center {Purchase, N.Y.} •
    "Developmental Workshop"
Also see May 3, 1993. Lyrics by Fred Ebb; Book by Terrence McNally (based on the novel by Manuel Puig); Directed by Harold Prince; Choreographed by Susan Stroman; Produced by New Musicals (Marty Bell); With John Rubinstein, Kevin Gray, Lauren Mitchell, and Harry Goz.

Published Songs
See KISS OF THE SPIDER WOMAN [1993]
    [May 3, 1993].

It has become the norm for new musicals to be mounted in workshops before braving the wilds of Broadway. The theory: see whether or not the material works before spending five or six million dollars. The only trouble with this system is that shows that clearly don't, won't, and shouldn't work—like THE RINK [February 9, 1984], RAGS [Strouse: August 21, 1986], and LEGS DIAMOND[†] [December 26, 1988]—blithely continue on towards sure disaster. How bad does a workshop need to be in order to convince the creators to throw in the towel? What price ego? The New Musicals organization was founded to give still-developing works like KISS OF THE SPIDER WOMAN full-scale mountings; the inevitable failure of their maiden effort was pretty much apparent. Unlike other developmental workshop, New Musicals peddled tickets to the theatre public. Thus, the all-powerful *New York Times* reviewed the show—despite protestations from the SPIDER WOMAN men that they weren't "ready"—and the deservably awful reviews killed SPIDER WOMAN (temporarily, as it happens) and the New Musicals organization as well. Two of their three other scheduled projects eventually made it to Broadway, the interesting-but-flawed THE SECRET GARDEN [Notables: April 25, 1991] and the not as interesting-and-flawed MY FAVORITE YEAR [Flaherty: December 10, 1992].

AND THE WORLD GOES 'ROUND ✦
THE SONGS OF KANDER & EBB
March 18, 1991
Westside Theatre {Off Broadway} •
    408 performances
Lyrics by Fred Ebb; Conceived by Scott Ellis, Susan Stroman, and David Thompson; Directed by Scott Ellis; Choreographed by Susan Stroman; Produced by R. Tyler Gatchell, Jr., Peter Neufeld, Patrick J. Patek, and Gene R. Korf in association with the McCarter Theatre; With Bob Cuccioli, Karen Mason, Brenda Pressley, Jim Walton, and Karen Ziemba.

Songs (in Initial Theatrical Use) Published in Vocal Selection
But the World Goes 'Round—originally used in 1977 movie *New York, New York*
How Lucky Can You Get—originally used in 1975 movie *Funny Lady*
Isn't This Better?—initial publication of song originally used in *Funny Lady*

Kiss of the Spider Woman—initial publication of song originally used in KISS OF THE SPIDER WOMAN [1990] [May 1, 1990]

Maybe This Time—see CABARET [November 20, 1966]

Money, Money (Makes the World Go Round)—see CABARET

My Coloring Book—written as 1962 non-show song

Pain

Ring Them Bells—previously used in 1972 TV special "Liza with a Z"

Sara Lee—initial publication of non-show song

There Goes the Ball Game—originally used in 1977 movie *New York, New York*

Note: Songs written for previously produced musicals are listed with their original scores.

AND THE WORLD GOES 'ROUND proved to be a friendly, upbeat, and likable anthology revue. This was the first Kander and Ebb show, as it happens, that I found enjoyable since the ill-fated but endearing 70, GIRLS, 70 [April 15, 1971]. A good deal of the material seemed to work better here than in the show for which it was written. Altogether, a pleasant surprise.

KISS OF THE SPIDER WOMAN
[1993]
May 3, 1993
Broadhurst Theatre • 906 performances
Also see May 1, 1990. Lyrics by Fred Ebb; Book by Terrence McNally (based on the novel by Manuel Puig); Directed by Harold Prince; Choreographed by Vincent Paterson and Rob Marshall; Produced by Livent (U.S) [Garth Drabinsky]; With Chita Rivera, Brent Carver, and Anthony Crivello.

Published Songs
Anything for Him
The Day after That—revised version of verse of *Colored Lights* from THE RINK [February 9, 1984]
*Dear One
Dressing Them Up
I Do Miracles
The Kiss of the Spider Woman

The Morphine Tango
Only in the Movies
Over the Wall II
She's a Woman
Where You Are

Additional Songs Recorded
Bluebloods
Gabriel's Letter/My First Woman
Gimme Love
Good Times
Her Name Is Aurora
I Draw the Line
Mama, It's Me
Marta
Over the Wall I—revised version of *The Top of the Hill* from ZORBÁ [November 17, 1968]
Prologue
A Visit
You Could Never Shame Me

Canadian producer Garth Drabinsky took up the defeated SPIDER WOMAN, allowing Kander, Ebb, librettist Terrence McNally, and director Hal Prince the opportunity to rethink the show and providing the funds with which to mount it. (Livent's Creative Affairs department was headed by Marty Bell, Producing Director of the brief-lived New Musicals.) The revised version of SPIDER WOMAN premiered in Toronto in June 1992 and stopped in London in October before heading to Broadway. The show was hailed as a great creative achievement by many, although soundly detested by others. SPIDER WOMAN won awards left and right, simultaneously losing money left and right. (Once you start losing a chunk of money every week, the overall size of your loss will correspond to the number of weeks you continue to run. The publicly traded Livent saw fit to run SPIDER WOMEN 114 weeks, amassing a deficit in the neighborhood of six million dollars. And Wall Street was shocked when Livent went bankrupt in 1998). Broadway acclaim vindicated the quick failure of the New Musicals developmental production of the show, artistically anyway. Those who consider the show a classic will argue that it doesn't matter how much money it lost. For myself, I had a strongly negative reaction to the book and lyrics at Purchase and a similar response on Broadway. I even went back a third time, hoping to be won over. The music is not without interest, certainly—especially the moving ballad *Dear One*—but I found Kander's work for the most part diminished by his collaborators' extremely distasteful contributions.

STEEL PIER
April 24, 1997
Richard Rodgers Theatre • 76 performances
Lyrics by Fred Ebb; Book by David Thompson; Conceived by Scott Ellis, Susan Stroman, and David Thompson; Directed by Scott Ellis; Choreographed by Susan Stroman; Producer by Roger Berlind; With Gregory Harrison, Karen Ziemba, Daniel McDonald, and Debra Monk.

Songs Published in Vocal Selection
Dance with Me
Everybody's Girl
First You Dream—revised version of *Why Can't I Speak* from ZORBÁ [November 17, 1968]
The Last Girl
Lovebird
Rita's Theme (*Opening*) [instrumental]
Second Chance
Somebody Older
Steel Pier
Wet
Willing to Ride (*Here I Go Again*)

Additional Songs Recorded
Everybody Dance
Leave the World Behind
A Powerful Thing
Running in Place
The Shag [instrumental]
Two Little Words
Two Step [instrumental]

Scott Ellis, Susan Stroman, and David Thompson first joined together in 1987 to revise and rethink an Off Off Broadway revival of Kander and Ebb's FLORA, THE RED MENACE [May 11, 1965]. The experience was positive enough for the songwriters to allow them to conceive a full-scale Off Broadway revue of their work, AND THE WORLD GOES 'ROUND [March 18, 1991]. This experience was positive enough for the

songwriters to allow them to conceive a full-scale new musical, STEEL PIER. (And choreographer Stroman's prominence was strong enough to attract financing, thanks to CRAZY FOR YOU [February 19, 1992].) Kander and Ebb provided STEEL PIER with their best work in many years, including a good character song (*Willing to Ride*); some fine ensemble dance numbers (like *Everybody Dance*); a perky and functional charm duet (*Second Chance*); and one of Kander and Ebb's best ballads, *First You Dream*. But the concept—a mid-depression dance marathon soap opera, with a ghost hero no less—left the creators with very little leeway, and the promising STEEL PIER simply couldn't find firm footing. OVER AND OVER—a long-in-gestation musicalization of Thornton Wilder's Pulitzer Prize–winning *The Skin of Our Teeth*, with libretto by Joe Stein (of ZORBÁ [November 17, 1968])—received a regional production [February 4, 1999] at the Signature Theatre in Arlington, Virginia. The reception did not bode well for an afterlife, although KISS OF THE SPIDER WOMAN [1993] [May 3, 1993] surmounted even steeper obstacles.

John Kander's first six musicals (through 70, GIRLS, 70 [April 15, 1971]) were interesting and worthwhile, although only CABARET [November 20, 1966] was a hit. The latter part of his career (to date) consisted of three drab star vehicles (which displayed little of the composer's creativity) followed by the controversial KISS OF THE SPIDER WOMAN [May 3, 1993] and the worthy failure STEEL PIER [April 24, 1997]. I have left out the show that came in the middle of all this, and purposely so: the much-heralded, glossy-but-heartless CHICAGO [June 1, 1975], was a great disappointment in its time, which was precisely eleven days after the première of A CHORUS LINE [Hamlisch: May 21, 1975]. Twenty years later, though, in the midst of the glossy-but-heartless 1990s, CHICAGO returned and became one of Broadway's biggest blockbusters. Rewarding for Kander and Ebb, emotionally and (especially) financially, but somewhat bittersweet when your heartfelt STEEL PIER is slammed, slighted, and shuttered. (CABARET returned two years later in an even better revival, although its site-specific production made it less adaptable for reproduction than CHICAGO.) That's twelve musicals, all told, in thirty-five years. Only two were money-making hits, with two more having lengthy if unsuccessful runs. But that's not to say the other shows should be dismissed; FLORA, THE RED MENACE [May 11, 1965], HAPPY TIME [January 18, 1968], and 70, GIRLS, 70 had enjoyable scores, while SPIDER WOMAN was startlingly artistic. Kander has written some very good music over the years—always professional, often interesting, and occa-sionally superb. Fred Ebb's writing style is witty, biting, and sarcastic; it suits him well, but how well does it suit Kander? Many of the projects the team has selected—like THE ACT [October 29, 1977], WOMAN OF THE YEAR [March 29, 1981], and THE RINK [February 9, 1984]—seemed suitable for Ebb, but I can't help thinking that there is another side to Kander, a strongly melodic, highly emotional side which he has rarely had the opportunity to develop and explore.

MITCH LEIGH

Born: January 31, 1928, Brooklyn, New York

MITCH LEIGH prepared for his musical career at Yale, studying composition with Paul Hindemith. Upon receiving his master's, he entered the world of advertising and became an expert at lucrative television jingles. (His most popular work—other than *The Impossible Dream*—remains *Nobody Doesn't Like Sara Lee*.) By the early 1960s, the highly successful ad man was ready to put his musical training to a more "legitimate" use.

TOO TRUE TO BE GOOD
March 12, 1963
54th Street Theatre • 94 performances
Play by George Bernard Shaw; Incidental music by Leigh; Directed by Albert Marre; Produced by Paul Vroom, Buff Cobb, and Burry Frederick; With Lillian Gish, Robert Preston, David Wayne, Cedric Hardwicke, Eileen Heckart, Cyril Ritchard, Glynis Johns, and Ray Middleton.

Published Songs
None

Leigh began a career-long association with director Albert Marre on this all-star revival. Marre's only successful musical was KISMET [Notables: December 3, 1953]; more recently, he'd helmed the soggy MILK AND HONEY [Herman: October 10, 1961]. Leigh and Marre began discussing a musical adaptation of Dale Wasserman's 1960 teleplay "I, Don Quixote." The ambitious Leigh began work—with, unaccountably, poet W. H. Auden as lyricist.

NEVER LIVE OVER A PRETZEL FACTORY
March 28, 1964
Eugene O'Neill Theatre • 9 performances
Play by Jerry Devine; Incidental music by Leigh; Directed by Albert Marre; Produced by Paul Vroom, Buff Cobb, and Albert Marre; With Dennis O'Keefe and Martin Sheen.

Published Songs
None

Leigh's first Broadway song to be heard—for a week—was *In This Town* [lyric by Jack Wohl]

MAN OF LA MANCHA
November 22, 1965
Anta Washington Square Theatre • 2,328 performances
Lyrics by Joe Darion; Book by Dale Wasserman (based on *Don Quixote* [novel] by Miguel de Cervantes); Directed by Albert Marre; Choreographed by Jack Cole; Produced by Albert W. Selden and Hal James; With Richard Kiley, Joan Diener (Marre), Irving Jacobson, Ray Middleton, and Robert Rounseville.

Revivals
June 22, 1972
Vivian Beaumont Theatre • 140 performances
Directed by Albert Marre; With Richard Kiley, Joan Diener, Eugene Varrato [Jacobson]; Jack Dabdoub [Middleton], and Robert Rounseville.

September 15, 1977
Palace Theatre • 120 performances

Directed by Albert Marre; Produced by Eugene V. Wolsk (and Leigh); With Richard Kiley and Emily Yancy [Diener].

April 24, 1992
Marquis Theatre • 108 performances
Directed by Albert Marre; Produced by The Mitch Leigh Company; With Raul Julia [Kiley] and Sheena Easton [Diener].

Published Songs

Aldonza
*Dulcinea
***The Impossible Dream* (*The Quest*)
I Really Like Him
Knight of the Woeful Countenance (*The Dubbing*)
Little Bird, Little Bird
A Little Gossip
Man of La Mancha (*I, Don Quixote*)
**To Each His Dulcinea* (*To Every Man His Dream*)

Additional Songs Published in Vocal Score

Barber's Song
The Combat
Golden Helmet
I'm Only Thinking of Him
It's All the Same
Knight of the Mirrors
The Psalm
**What Do You Want of Me?*—recorded as *What Does He Want of Me?*

A summer season at the Goodspeed Opera House in East Haddam, Connecticut, brought forth this monumental worldwide hit (for details see CHU-CHEM [1966] [November 15, 1966]). Lyricist Joe Darion, W. H. Auden's replacement, had one Broadway musical—the negligible SHINBONE ALLEY[†] [April 13, 1957]—to his credit; composer Leigh and librettist Wasserman had none. While the separate elements were not perfect in themselves, everything joined together effectively. Leigh's highly theatrical, strongly rhythmic score played an important part in overriding the sometimes saccharine book, with *The Impossible Dream* affecting the public conscience as Lerner and Loewe's *Camelot* had. There were other fine songs as well, like the contemplative *What Do You Want of Me?*, and two gentle waltzes, *Dulcinea* and *To Each His Dulcinea*. LA

MANCHA enjoyed a long run and has been frequently revived—with composer Leigh usually doubling as producer.

CHU-CHEM [1966]
November 15, 1966
New Locust Street Theatre {Philadelphia} • Closed during tryout
"A Zen Buddhist–Hebrew Musical Comedy, in English." Also see April 7, 1989. Lyrics by Jim Haines and Jack Wohl; Book by Ted Allan; Directed by Albert Marre; Choreographed by Jack Cole; Produced by Cheryl Crawford and Leigh; With Menasha Skulnick and Molly Picon.

Published Songs
None

The summer of 1965 saw an ambitious project at the newly restored Goodspeed Opera House in East Haddam, Connecticut: producer Albert Selden and director Albert Marre planned a season of three new musicals, all with music by the unknown Mitch Leigh. Their intention was to move each show to Broadway, in turn, for four-week runs. The first opened June 24 at Goodspeed and took several months to get to New York, but MAN OF LA MANCHA [November 22, 1965] ultimately lasted longer than four weeks. The second was an adaptation of Sean O'Casey's 1940 comedy *Purple Dust*, a play Marre had been trying to mount in America since 1952. The third, CHU-CHEM, was canceled in place of a return engagement of the Broadway-bound LA MANCHA. CHU-CHEM was finally mounted the following year, with veteran Cheryl Crawford joining Leigh in the production. The baffling show quickly expired in Philadelphia, only to finally brave (?) Broadway two decades later.

CRY FOR US ALL
April 8, 1970
Broadhurst Theatre • 9 performances
Lyrics by William Alfred and Phyllis Robinson; Book by William Alfred and Albert Marre (based on *Hogan's Goat* [play] by William Alfred); Directed by Albert Marre; Produced by Leigh in association with

L. Gerald Goldsmith; With Robert Weede, Joan Diener (Marre), Steve Arlen, Helen Gallagher, and Tommy Rall. Alternate tryout title: WHO TO LOVE.

Published Songs
Cry for Us All
That Slavery Is Love
*The Verandah Waltz

Additional Songs Recorded
*Aggie, Oh Aggie
*The Cruelty Man
The End of My Race
How Are Ya, Since?
The Leg of the Duck
The Mayor's Chair
Search Your Heart
Swing Your Bag
This Cornucopian Land
The Wages of Sin
Who to Love If Not a Stranger

Leigh returned to Broadway with a work even more ambitious than MAN OF LA MANCHA [November 22, 1965]. CRY FOR US ALL was musical drama verging on the operatic; but a muddy book weighed down the already heavy subject matter, and matters weren't helped by some especially stilted lyrics. Yet much of the score was finely written, Leigh working with constantly shifting rhythms for highly emotional effects. There was a strong if overly dramatic aria, *Who to Love If Not a Stranger*; an infectiously tuneful street urchin trio, *The Cruelty Man*; and—as in LA MANCHA—two lovely waltzes, *Aggie, Oh Aggie* and *The Verandah Waltz*. (If Mr. Leigh has written a good song since, though, I haven't heard it.)

HALLOWEEN
September 20, 1972
Bucks County Playhouse {New Hope, Pa.} • Closed during tryout
Book and Lyrics by Sidney Michaels; Directed by Albert Marre; Produced by Albert W. Selden and Jerome Minskoff; With David Wayne, Margot Moser, and Dick Shawn.

Published Songs
None

Again working with a collaborator undistinguished in the musical theatre—Sidney Michaels's biggest credit was getting fired from APPLAUSE [Strouse: March 30, 1970]—Leigh turned out this strange, experimental opus filled with midgets, which was long gone before Halloween. Yes, I said midgets.

HOME SWEET HOMER
January 4, 1976
Palace Theatre • 1 performance
Lyrics by Charles Burr and Forman Brown; Book by Roland Kibbee and Albert Marre (based on *The Odyssey* by Homer); Directed by Albert Marre; Produced by The John F. Kennedy Center; With Yul Brynner, Joan Diener (Marre), Russ Thacker, Diana Davila, and Martin Vidnovic. Pre-Broadway title: ODYSSEY.

Published Songs
None

Despite impressive grosses on its year-long pre-Broadway odyssey, all was not well with the wandering ODYSSEY. So much so that lyricist/librettist Erich ("Love Story") Segal quit, taking his material with him (as he had on his previous musical comedy, I'M SOLOMON† [April 23, 1968]). ODYSSEY was rewritten, more or less, renamed HOME SWEET HOMER (why??) and sailed into port at the Palace. One laughably inane performance, and everyone set sail for home.

SARAVÁ
February 23, 1979
Mark Hellinger Theatre • 177 performances
Book and Lyrics by N. Richard Nash (based on *Dona Flor and Her Two Husbands* [novel] by Jorge Amado); Directed and Choreographed by Rick Atwell; Produced by Eugene V. Wolsk (and Leigh); With Tovah Feldshuh, P. J. Benjamin, and Michael Ingraham.

Published Song
Saravá

Additional Song Recorded
You Do

Leigh, who never met a lyricist he could work with, chose yet another novice to collaborate with. Playwright N. Richard Nash had provided the rather good book for 110 IN THE SHADE [Schmidt: October 24, 1963], as well as the less happy HAPPY TIME [Kander: January 18, 1968] and WILDCAT [Coleman: December 16, 1960]; but a lyricist he wasn't. SARAVÁ was without distinction, and even a skillfully contrived advertising campaign—designed by TV commercial expert Mitch Leigh—didn't help.

APRIL SONG
July 9, 1980
John Drew Theatre {East Hampton, N.Y.} •
    Summer stock tryout
Lyrics by Sammy Cahn; Book by Albert Marre (based on *Leocadia* [play] by Jean Anouilh); Directed by Albert Marre; Produced by Albert Marre and Leigh; With Glynis Johns.

Published Songs
None

Something impelled Marre to take the Anouilh play—which he had successfully directed in an earlier nonmusical translation (TIME REMEMBERED [Duke: November 2, 1957])—and turn it into a play with songs. Another Mitch Leigh show with no future, this time with lyrics by Sammy Cahn.

MIKE
April 6, 1988
Walnut Street Theatre {Philadelphia} •
    Regional tryout
Also see AIN'T BROADWAY GRAND [*April 18, 1993*]. Lyrics by Lee Adams; Book by Thomas Meehan (based on the biography *A Valuable Property* by Michael Todd, Jr., and Susan McCarthy Todd); Directed by Martin Charnin; Produced by Walnut Street Theatre Company and Cyma Rubin; With Michael Lembeck, Loni Ackerman, Leslie Easterbrook, and Robert Morse.

Published Songs
See AIN'T BROADWAY GRAND

Mike Todd's AS THE GIRLS GO[†] [November 13, 1948] was a star vehicle for Bobby Clark, with a bland score by Jimmy McHugh and Harold Adamson. A dismal failure during its tryout, producer Todd threw out most of the book (about the first lady President, with Bobby as "the First Man") and made it into a glorified revue. AS THE GIRLS GO came into New York as the first show with a $7.20 top—SOUTH PACIFIC [Rodgers: April 7, 1949] charged only $6—unaccountably received a bunch of raves, and ran for 414 performances (losing money nevertheless). MIKE not only told the story of the making of AS THE GIRLS GO; it also imitated it, up to the part where the show is triumphantly transformed. Mike Todd (1909–58) wasn't around to fix it, of course, so they brought in Martin Charnin. MIKE died in Philadelphia, only to rise again as AIN'T BROADWAY GRAND.

CHU CHEM [1989]
March 17, 1989
Ritz Theatre • 44 performances
"The 1st Chinese-Jewish Musical." Also see November 15, 1966. Lyrics by Jim Haines and Jack Wohl; Book by Ted Allan; Directed by Albert Marre; Produced by The Mitch Leigh Company and William D. Rollnick; With Mark Zeller, Emily Zacharias, Thom Sesma, and Irving Burton.

Songs Recorded
Boom!
I'll Talk to Her
I Once Believed
It Must Be Good for Me
It's Possible
Love Is
Orient Yourself
Our Kind of War
The River
Shame on You
We Dwell in Our Hearts
Welcome
What Happened, What?
You'll Have to Change

Broadway finally got to see CHU CHEM (hyphen removed) after twenty-two years, and it was still pretty awful. This from the guy who wrote MAN OF LA MANCHA [November 22, 1965]?

AIN'T BROADWAY GRAND
April 18, 1993
Lunt-Fontanne Theatre • 25 performances
"A Brand-New 1948 Musical Comedy." Also see
MIKE *[April 6, 1988]*. Lyrics by Lee Adams; Book
by Thomas Meehan and Lee Adams; Directed
by Scott Harris; Choreographed by Randy
Skinner; Produced by Arthur Rubin (and
Leigh); With Mike Burstyn, Debbie Shapiro
Gravitte, Maureen McNamara, and Gerry Vichi.

Songs Published in Vocal Selection
Ain't Broadway Grand
Class
Girls Ahoy!
He's My Guy
It's Time to Go
The Man I Married
Maybe, Maybe Not
On the Street
Tall Dames and Low Comedy
They'll Never Take Me Alive
Waiting in the Wings
You're My Star

This "Brand-New 1948 Musical Comedy" wasn't
exactly brand-new, and it wasn't as good as your
typical 1948 musical (like KISS ME, KATE [Porter: December 30, 1948]). As with CHU CHEM
[1989] [March 17, 1989], Leigh resuscitated a
dead show, put up most of the financing himself, and took a Broadway bath. Ain't Broadway
grand??

Mitch Leigh entered the musical theatre with the
instant classic MAN OF LA MANCHA [November 22, 1965]. He also wrote the admirable (if
flawed) CRY FOR US ALL [April 8, 1970]. Otherwise, things have been pretty bleak. Leigh has
pretty much controlled the artistic content of his
shows, not only as strong-willed author but usually as not-so-silent coproducer as well. If his
nine consecutive flops have been the result of
poor decisions (or plain bad luck), the decisions
(or luck) have been made by Leigh himself. But
he did write *The Impossible Dream*, an inspirational hit which has had widespread influence
outside the cloistered world of the theatre. And
that's not chicken liver, as they'd say in CHU
CHEM (with schmaltz). Although one may well
wonder, as Walter Kerr once asked, just how
does one right an unrightable wrong?

LARRY GROSSMAN

Born: September 3, 1938, Chicago, Illinois

LARRY GROSSMAN determined to be a songwriter at an early age. He attended Northwestern University, known in theatrical circles for their annual Waa-Mu shows. Grossman wrote several Waa-Mu shows as an undergraduate. (For the last forty years he has served on an informal basis as a Waa-Mu adviser and occasional contributor.) Grossman came to New York in 1962—and quickly placed a song in a nightclub revue.

NO SHOESTRINGS

October 11, 1962
Upstairs at the Downstairs • Nightclub revue
Music and Lyrics mostly by others; Sketches by Woody Allen and others; Directed by Ben Bagley; Produced by Upstairs at the Downstairs; With Danny Carroll, Jane Connell, and Bill McCutcheon.

Published Songs
None

In 1962, Julius Monk left the Upstairs at the Downstairs nightclub for Plaza 9 (at the Plaza Hotel). Ben Bagley (see SHOESTRING REVUE [Strouse: February 28, 1955]) took over, with NO SHOESTRINGS. (The title was a play on the then-current NO STRINGS [Rodgers: March 15, 1962]; the revue featured a sketch with Bill McCutcheon as a gloating Rodgers, dismissively glad to be free of his former lyricists). Grossman contributed one of his Waa-Mu songs (music and lyric), the topical *I Was a Pawn for Werner von Braun*. He found work as a coach and accompanist, began composing for television, and in 1965 was signed by Tommy Valando, publisher of Bock & Harnick and Kander & Ebb. Grossman started writing pop songs, and in 1968 Valando partnered him with lyricist Hal Hackady.

PLAY IT AGAIN, SAM

February 12, 1969
Broadhurst Theatre • 453 performances
Play by Woody Allen; Directed by Joseph Hardy; Produced by David Merrick in association with Jack Rollins and Charles Joffe; With Woody Allen, Anthony Roberts, and Diane Keaton.

Published Song
Play It Again, Sam [lyric by Hal Hackady]—cut

Grossman and Hackady wrote this title song for Woody Allen's Bogartian comedy. It was recorded by Tony Bennett; for a brief while during the tryout, part of the recording was "played" on an onstage phonograph. Grossman and Hackady were already at work on their first Broadway musical.

MINNIE'S BOYS

March 26, 1970
Imperial Theatre • 80 performances
"A Rollicking New Marx Brothers Musical."
Lyrics by Hal Hackady; Book by Arthur Marx and Robert Fisher (based upon the lives of the Marx Brothers); Production consultant: Groucho Marx; Directed by Stanley Prager; Choreographed by Marc Breaux; Produced by Arthur Whitelaw, Max Brown, and Byron Goldman; With Shelley Winters, Arny Freeman, Mort Marshall, Julie Kurnitz, Lewis J. Stadlen, and Daniel Fortus.

Published Songs
*Be Happy
Empty—cut
He Gives Me Love—recorded as *They Give Me Love*
*Mama, a Rainbow

Minnie's Boys
Rich Is
Theme from "Minnie's Boys" (*Ninety-Third Street*) [instrumental]
Where Was I When They Passed out Luck?

Additional Songs Published in Vocal Selection
You Don't Have to Do It for Me
You Remind Me of You

Additional Songs Recorded
The Act
Five Growing Boys
The Four Nightingales
Underneath It All

If they could make Gypsy Rose Lee's mom a star, why not Groucho's? (Perhaps Laurents and Styne and Sondheim could have, but not this group—which included Minnie's grandson Arthur Marx.) Whenever MINNIE'S BOYS got funny—which was not infrequently—their mom, in the shape of Shelley Winters, would come in and Gummo up the works. Larry Grossman's melodies were bright and perky, with a couple of nice rhythm numbers—the title number and *Rich Is*—and two especially tender ballads, *Mama, a Rainbow* and the melancholically minor-key *Be Happy*. But severe flaws in the book, direction, production, and star casting were enough to scuttle poor old MINNIE. To add insult to insult, the man in the *Times* characterized the score as "gross and hack."

GOODTIME CHARLEY
March 3, 1975
Palace Theatre • 104 performances
Lyrics by Hal Hackady; Book by Sidney Michaels; Directed by Peter Hunt; Choreographed by Onna White; Produced by Max Brown and Byron Goldman in association with Robert Victor and Stone Widney; With Joel Grey, Ann Reinking, Susan Browning, Richard B. Schull, and Jay Garner.

Published Songs
Goodtime Charley
I Leave the World
To Make the Boy a Man
Tomorrow's Good Old Days—cut

Additional Songs Recorded
Bits and Pieces
Born Lover
Confessional (*I Did It and I'm Sorry*)
History
I Am Going to Love (*The Man You're Going to Be*)
Merci, Bon Dieu
One Little Year
Voices and Visions
Why Can't We All Be Nice?
You Still Have a Long Way to Go

A song-and-dancer about that live-wire Joan of Arc? Why not? As with MINNIE'S BOYS, a big star was cast in the lead—playing not Groucho or Joan but a less memorable, subsidiary character. (Yes, yes, I know it worked with Gypsy Rose Lee; but, then, she was no saint.) Compounding GOODTIME CHARLEY'S problems was that the whole thing was pretty poor. There was a tender little duet about plague and venereal disease and lost digits (toes), *Merci, Bon Dieu*, but that was the high spot. The producers no doubt figured they had another PIPPIN [S. Schwartz: October 23, 1972], this one with a bona fide ticket-selling star. Seems not.

SNOOPY!!!
December 9, 1975
Little Fox Theatre {San Francisco; Off Broadway} • Closed during tryout
Lyrics by Hal Hackady; Book by Warren Lockhart, Arthur Whitelaw, and Michael R. Grace (based on *Peanuts* [comic strip] by Charles M. Schulz); Directed by Arthur Whitelaw; Choreographed by Marc Breaux; Produced by Arthur Whitelaw, Michael R. Grace, Susan Bloom, and Warren Lockhart in association with Charles M. Schulz Creative Associates; With Don Potter, Jimmy Dodge, and Pamela Myers.

Revival
December 20, 1982
Lambs Theatre {Off Broadway} • 152 performances
Directed by Arthur Whitelaw; Choreographed by Marc Breaux; With David Garrison, Kay Cole, and Vicki Lewis.

Songs Published in Vocal Selection
Clouds
Daisy Hill
Don't Be Anything Less
Friend
I Know Now
Just One Person
Poor Sweet Baby
Where Did That Little Dog Go?
Woodstock's Theme [instrumental]
The World According to Snoopy

Additional Songs Recorded
The Big Bow-Wow
Dime a Dozen—written for subsequent production
Edgar Allan Poe
The Great Writer
Hurry up Face—written for subsequent production
Mother's Day—written for subsequent production
Snoopy's Song—written for subsequent production
The Vigil
When Do the Good Things Start?—written for subsequent production

Producer Arthur Whitelaw—who'd lost his shirt on MINNIE'S BOYS [March 26, 1970]—devised this sequel to his early goldmine YOU'RE A GOOD MAN, CHARLIE BROWN [Notables: March 7, 1967]. He eschewed that show's creative team, though, replacing them with Grossman and Hackady and himself (as director and coauthor). Despite it's exclamation points, SNOOPY!!! closed after seven months and never made it to town. The rights were then tied up for years by legal wranglings; a revised production appeared Off Broadway seven years later. But SNOOPY!!! certainly didn't recapture the magic of the long-running YOU'RE A GOOD MAN, CHARLIE BROWN. Grossman and Hackady wrote another four complete musicals during their collaboration, none of which was produced. Then Grossman got a call from Hal Prince.

A DOLL'S LIFE
September 23, 1982
Mark Hellinger Theatre • 5 performances
Book and Lyrics by Betty Comden and Adolph Green (suggested by characters from *A Doll's*

House [play] by Henrik Ibsen); Directed by Harold Prince; Choreographed by Larry Fuller; Produced by James M. Nederlander, Sidney L. Shlenker, Warner Theatre Productions, Joseph Harris, Mary Lea Johnson, Martin Richards, and Robert Fryer in association with Harold Prince; With George Hearn, Betsy Joslyn, Peter Gallagher, and Edmund Lyndeck.

Revival
December 13, 1994
Saint Peter's Church {Off Broadway} • 34 performances
Revisions by Grossman, Betty Comden, and Adolph Green; Directed by Robert Brink; Produced by York Theatre Company; With Jill Geddes [Joslyn].

Songs Published in Vocal Selection
A Doll's Life
Learn to Be Lonely
No More Mornings
Power
Rare Wines
*Stay with Me, Nora
You Interest Me

Additional Songs Recorded
The Arrival
At Last
Can You Hear Me Now?
The Departure
The Grand Café
Jailer, Jailer
Letter from Klemnacht
Letter to the Children
Loki and Baldur
New Year's Eve
Rats and Mice and Fish
She Thinks That's the Answer
There She Is
A Woman Alone

What happened when Nora slammed that door and walked out on Torvald? Nora. Remember Nora? The one from *A Doll's House*? You remember *A Doll's House*? Only vaguely, if at all? As Marian the Librarian's mother might have said, "Excuse me for living but I never read it." Or as William Saroyan did say, "No foundation, all the way down the line." Saroyan, in *The Time of Your Life*? . . . The preceding illustrates only one of the problems of A DOLL'S LIFE. There would be a built-in audience for a musical about what happened after Rhett slammed that door and walked out on Scarlett, perhaps, or maybe even Blanche & Stella & Stanley, but you certainly can't compare Ibsen to Margaret Mitchell. The whole thing—from the post-EVITA [September 25, 1979] Hal Prince, with book and lyrics by the facile and witty Betty Comden and Adolph Green, of all people—was extremely murky, about women's rights and emancipated mistresses and starving composers at the opera house and fish. Buried beneath it all was a surprisingly intelligent and richly textured score by Grossman, worlds away from his previous earlier work and well worthwhile. But hopelessly hidden by the excesses on stage.

THE END OF THE WORLD
May 6, 1984
Music Box Theatre • 33 performances
Play by Arthur Kopit; Incidental music by Grossman; Directed by Harold Prince; Produced by John F. Kennedy Center and Michael Frazier; With John Shea, Linda Hunt, and Barnard Hughes.

Published Songs
None

Grossman, in the midst of two Harold Prince musicals, provided incidental music for this Arthur Kopit drama. One song was included, *What Can One Man Do?* [lyric by Ellen Fitzhugh].

DIAMONDS
November 29, 1984
Circle in the Square Downtown
{Off Broadway} • 122 performances
Music mostly by Grossman; Additional music by Cy Coleman, John Kander, Alan Menken and others (see Coleman, Kander, and Menken: November 29, 1984); Lyrics mostly by Ellen Fitzhugh; Additional lyrics by Howard Ashman, Betty Comden, Fred Ebb, Adolph Green, David Zippel, and others; Sketches by Ralph G. Allen, Roy Blount, Jr., John Lahr, John Weidman, and others; Directed by

Harold Prince; Choreographed by Theodore Pappas; Produced by Stephen G. Martin, Harold DeFelice, Louis W. Scheeder, Kenneth John Productions, Inc., in association with Frank Basile; With Loni Ackerman, Susan Bigelow, Jackee Harry, Dick Latessa, and Chip Zien.

Published Songs
None

Hal Prince's baseball revue was a strange and unsatisfying entertainment with contributions from no fewer than thirty-two writers, none of them distinguished. (The contributions, not the writers). Grossman and Fitzhugh contributed four songs; Prince's occasional collaborators Kander & Ebb and Comden, Green, & Coleman two songs each, with one contribution from Alan Menken and David Zippel, one from Craig Carnelia, one from Gerard Alessandrini. All eminently forgettable and forgotten except for *Hundreds of Hats* by Jonathan Sheffer and Howard Ashman (which has been recorded), and something called *Escorte-Moi* (which turned out to be Harry von Tilzer's *Take Me out to the Ballgame* in French).

GRIND
April 16, 1985
Mark Hellinger Theatre • 79 performances
Lyrics by Ellen Fitzhugh; Book by Fay Kanin; Directed by Harold Prince; Choreographed by Lester Wilson; Produced by Kenneth D. Greenblatt, John J. Pomerantz, Mary Lea Johnson, Martin Richards, James M. Nederlander, Harold Prince, and Michael Frazier; With Ben Vereen, Leilani Jones, Timothy Nolen, and Stubby Kaye.

Songs Published in Vocal Selection
All Things to One Man
The Grind
Katie, My Love
My Daddy Always Taught Me to Share
Never Put It in Writing
New Man
A Sweet Thing Like Me
These Eyes of Mine
This Must Be the Place
Who Is He?

Additional Songs Recorded
Down
I Get Myself Out
I Talk, You Talk
The Line
Timing
Why, Mama, Why?

Here was yet another wildly misguided musical attempt, mixing racial prejudice, the depression, the Irish Republican Army, and burlesque. Pretty much baffling on the whole; yet a good part of the score—taken out of the theatre—is quite interesting. (In the theatre it seemed as unfathomable as the rest of the proceedings). As was the case with the vaudeville-based MINNIE'S BOYS [March 26, 1970], Grossman's burlesque-flavored music was for the most part bright and cheerful (as in *This Must Be the Place*, *A Sweet Thing Like Me*, and *Why, Mama, Why?*). There was also an artful sequence combining three separate solos into one effective solo, not unlike the *Now/Soon/Later* sequence in Prince's A LITTLE NIGHT MUSIC [Sondheim: February 25, 1973]. Other parts of the score, though, were problematic, especially Ben Vereen's "star" material and some unfortunate "Irish" songs. The dismal back-to-back failures of two inordinately expensive musicals—both with Hal Prince, no less—effectively ended Grossman's Broadway usefulness. At least he made it to the Tony Awards: he scored several Tony and Oscar telecasts, winning six Emmys along the way. He also found success writing for *Sesame Street* and other television shows; lucrative, perhaps, but it ain't Broadway.

PAPER MOON
September 17, 1993
Paper Mill Playhouse {Millburn, N.J.} •
    Regional tryout
Lyrics by Ellen Fitzhugh and Carol Hall; Book by Martin Casella (based on *Addie Pray* [novel]

by Joe David Brown and the film *Paper Moon*); Directed by Matt Casella; Choreographed by Alan Johnson; Produced by Paper Mill Playhouse (Angelo del Rossi and Robert Johanson) by arrangement with Roger Berlind; With Gregory Harrison, Christine Ebersole, Linda Hart, John Dossett, and Natalie DeLucia.

Song Recorded
I Do What I Can

Grossman's fifth Broadway musical was given the equivalent of a pre-Broadway tryout at the regional Paper Mill Playhouse. Results were uneven, causing producer Roger Berlind to close it on the eve of its December 5 Broadway opening (with the marquee already up at the Marquis). Grossman, lyricist Ellen Fitzhugh, and Carol Hall (of BEST LITTLE WHOREHOUSE IN TEXAS [Notables: April 17, 1978])—who contributed last-minute lyrics for four songs— came up with a strangely stagnant evening. Once again, Grossman provided some clearly superior music to the project; but there were also some oddly bland spots. A revised PAPER MOON (with the Hall material removed) was given a second shot in a 1996 production mounted by the Goodspeed Opera House and the Walnut Street Theatre; but the overall effect remained emotionless and cold.

Larry Grossman's career is rather puzzling. Here is a composer of obvious talent who has met with failure after failure after failure. He has five Broadway shows to his credit, along with one Off Broadway score; most can be described as highly interesting and often impressive. He has also written no fewer than six unproduced musicals, which presumably will remain so. It is impossible to say whether Grossman's problem has been poor subject selection, the inability of his collaborators, or just excessively bad luck. But the man can surely write. He will, presumably, be heard from again; hopefully under happier circumstances.

STEPHEN SCHWARTZ

Born: March 6, 1948, Roslyn Heights, New York

STEPHEN SCHWARTZ became enamored of musical theatre at the age of nine, when he attended SHINBONE ALLEY† [April 13, 1957], a flop musical composed by his next-door neighbor George Kleinsinger. During high school he attended weekend classes at Juilliard and then headed for Carnegie Tech (now Carnegie-Mellon University), where he wrote a college musical called PIPPIN, PIPPIN (see PIPPIN [October 23, 1972]). He returned to New York, began working as a record producer, and got himself an agent—Leonard Bernstein's sister Shirley.

All Music and Lyrics by Stephen Schwartz unless noted.

BUTTERFLIES ARE FREE
October 21, 1969
Booth Theatre • 1,128 performances
Play by Leonard Gershe; Directed by Milton Katselas; Produced by Arthur Whitelaw, Max J. Brown, and Byron Goldman; With Keir Dullea, Eileen Heckart, and Blythe Danner.

Published Song
Butterflies Are Free

Shirley Bernstein got Schwartz his first Broadway hearing with this folk-like song for singer-and-guitar. (She also set him up with brother Leonard, who was struggling through his long-in-gestation MASS [Bernstein: September 8, 1971].) BUTTERFLIES was a surprise hit, the title song low key but pleasant.

GODSPELL
May 17, 1971
Cherry Lane Theatre {Off Broadway} •
  2,124 performances

June 22, 1976
Broadhurst Theatre • 527 performances
Book and Direction by John-Michael Tebelak (based on *The Gospel According to St. Matthew*); Produced by Edgar Lansbury, Stuart Duncan, and Joseph Beruh; With Stephen Nathan and David Haskell.

Published Songs
All for the Best
All Good Gifts
Beautiful City—written for the 1973 movie
  version
By My Side [music and lyrics by Jay Hamburger and Peggy Gordon]
*Day by Day
Finale (Long Live God)
Learn Your Lessons Well
Light of the World
O Bless the Lord
On the Willows
Prepare Ye the Way of the Lord
Save the People
Turn Back, O Man
We Beseech Thee

Additional Songs Published in Vocal
  Score
Alas for You
Prologue
Tower of Babble

Schwartz's success began with this pop-biblical revue, the FANTASTICKS [Schmidt: May 3, 1960] of the seventies (although GODSPELL's run was far shorter; only six years). The score was easy and tuneful, with the pop hit *Day by Day* bringing Schwartz to the attention of Broadway.

MASS
See Bernstein: September 8, 1971.

PIPPIN
October 23, 1972
Imperial Theatre • 1,944 performances
Book by Roger O. Hirson; Directed and
Choreographed by Bob Fosse; Produced
by Stuart Ostrow; With Eric Berry, Jill
Clayburgh, Leland Palmer, Irene Ryan, Ben
Vereen, and John Rubinstein.

Published Songs
*Corner of the Sky
*Goodtime Ladies Rag [instrumental]
I Guess I'll Miss the Man
Just between the Two of Us—cut
Morning Glow

Additional Songs Published in Vocal Selection
Extraordinary
Kind of Woman
Love Song
*Magic to Do
No Time at All
Pippin
*Simple Joys
Spread a Little Sunshine
With You

Additional Songs Published in Vocal Score
Glory
On the Right Track
Prayer for a Duck
There He Was
War Is a Science
Welcome Home, Son

Additional Song Recorded
Marking Time—cut

With the success of GODSPELL [May 17, 1971], a college project of Schwartz's found its way to Broadway. Inability to raise money resulted in a drastically cut budget; hence, the imaginative, minimal production (and a skeletal replacement for the intended set). What PIPPIN did have was Bob Fosse at his inventive best, more than making up for the less-than-staggering score and more-than-lackluster book. There were some nice tunes, though, including *Corner of the Sky, Goodtime Ladies Rag, Magic to Do*, and *Simple Joys*. Leading Player Ben Vereen and designers Tony Walton and Patricia Zipprodt made valuable contributions, and a revolutionary (for the theatre) TV advertising campaign kept PIPPIN running for almost five years.

THE MAGIC SHOW
May 28, 1974
Cort Theatre • 1,920 performances
Book by Bob Randall (based on magic by Doug Henning); Directed and Choreographed by Grover Dale; Produced by Edgar Lansbury, Joseph Beruh, and Ivan Reitman; With Doug Henning, Dale Soules, Anita Morris (Dale), and David Ogden Stiers.

Published Song
Lion Tamer

Additional Songs Published in Vocal Selection
Before Your Very Eyes
Charmin's Lament
Solid Silver Platform Shoes
Style
Sweet, Sweet, Sweet
Two's Company
Up to His Old Tricks
West End Avenue

The great magic feat here was pulling a long-run hit out of a very empty hat. THE MAGIC SHOW ran 1,920 performances; A LITTLE NIGHT MUSIC [Sondheim: February 25, 1973], in comparison, barely broke 600. During the 1976–77 season, Schwartz had an unheard-of three musicals on Broadway. (Unheard of until Andrew Lloyd Webber, that is.) Schwartz has not been back on Broadway since 1978, though, except for four dismal performances in 1986.

THE BAKER'S WIFE
May 11, 1976
Dorothy Chandler Pavilion {Los Angeles} • Closed during tryout
Book by Joseph Stein (based on *La Femme de Boulanger* [movie] by Marcel Pagnol and Jean

Giono); Directed by John Berry; Choreographed by Robert Tucker; Produced by David Merrick; With Topol (eventually replaced by Paul Sorvino), Patti LuPone, Kurt Peterson, Keene Curtis, David Rounds, and Portia Nelson.

Songs Published in Vocal Selection
If I Have to Live Alone
Meadowlark
Where Is the Warmth?

Additional Songs Recorded
Any-Day-Now Day
Bread
Buzz-a-Buzz—added to 1989 British
    production
Chanson
Endless Delights
Feminine Companionship—added to British
    production
Gifts of Love
If It Wasn't for You—added to British
    production
Look for the Woman
The Luckiest Man in the World
Merci, Madame
Plain and Simple—added to British production
Proud Lady
Romance
Serenade

Stephen Schwartz's track record led to this assignment on the "big" musical of the season. David Merrick brought together Topol, the Israeli-born star of the London and Hollywood FIDDLER ON THE ROOF [Bock: September 21, 1964], and Joe Stein, that musical's librettist, for a big-budget, sure-fire hit. . . . Director Joseph Hardy left midway through the six-month tryout; Topol lasted till the next-to-last stop. Merrick, who didn't like anything about THE BAKER'S WIFE, canceled the Broadway booking and pulled the plug. (Merrick so disliked the big ballad *Meadowlark*—"Dickie Bird," he called it—that he once climbed into the orchestra pit after the matinee and pulled the parts off the music stand, effectively forcing the song to be cut.) An "improved" London production [October 27, 1989], directed by Trevor Nunn, also proved to be half-baked.

WORKING
May 14, 1978
46th Street Theatre • 25 performances
Music and Lyrics mostly by others; Book and Direction by Schwartz (based on the book by Studs Terkel); Choreographed by Onna White; Produced by Stephen R. Friedman and Irwin Meyer (in association with Joseph Harris); With Lenora Nemetz, Rex Everhart, Bobo Lewis, Patti LuPone, Lynne Thigpen, David Patrick Kelly, and Arny Freeman.

Songs Published in Vocal Selection
All the Livelong Day [lyric incorporating the
    poem "I Hear America Singing" by Walt
    Whitman]
Fathers and Sons
It's an Art
Neat to Be a Newsboy

If Broadway can be said to take retribution for undeserved hits, then Broadway took retribution on composer Schwartz with THE BAKER'S WIFE [May 11, 1976]. Then they did it again—publicly so, with treacherous in-town previews—with the highly unworkable WORKING, which Schwartz conceived, directed, and coauthored. The non-Schwartz sections of the score—contributed by a handful of writers—contained a couple of good songs, *Just a Housewife* (by Craig Carnelia) and **If I Could've Been* (by Micki Grant).

PERSONALS
November 8, 1985
Minetta Lane Theatre • 265 performances
Music mostly by others (see Menken: November 8, 1985); Lyrics and Sketches by David Crane, Seth Friedman, and Marta Kauffman; Directed by Paul Lazarus; Choreographed by D. J. Giagni; Produced by John-Edward Hill, Arthur Mackenzie, and Jon D. Silverman; With Jason Alexander, Laura Dean, Jeff Keller, Dee Hoty, Nancy Opel, and Trey Wilson.

Songs Recorded
Moving in with Linda [lyric by David Crane,
    Seth Friedman, and Marta Kauffman]
Nothing to Do with Love [lyric by Crane,
    Friedman, and Kauffman]

Some Things Don't End [lyric by Crane, Friedman, and Kauffman]

RAGS
See Strouse: August 21, 1986.

CHILDREN OF EDEN
January 8, 1991
Prince Edward Theatre {London} •
103 performances
Book by John Caird (based on the Old Testament); Directed by John Caird; Choreographed by Matthew Bourne; Produced by William MacDonald and Patricia MacNaughton; With Ken Page, Martin Smith, Shezwae Powell, and Frances Ruffelle.

Published Song
Children of Eden

Additional Songs Published in Vocal Selection
Ain't It Good?
The Hardest Part of Love
In the Beginning
In Whatever Time We Have
Lost in the Wilderness
The Spark of Creation
Stranger to the Rain
A World without You

Additional Songs Recorded
Childhood's End
Civilized Society
Close to Home
The Death of Abel
Degenerations
The Dove Song
The End of a Perfect Day
The Expulsion
Father's Day
The Flood
The Gathering Storm
Generations
Grateful Children
The Hour of Darkness

In Pursuit of Excellence
Let There Be
The Mark of Cain
The Naming
Noah's Lullaby
A Piece of Eight
Perfect
Precious Children
The Return of the Animals
A Ring of Stones
Sailor of the Skies
Shipshape
The Tree of Knowledge
The Wasteland
What Is He Waiting For?
Words of Doom

The story of Adam and Eve and the Serpent and Noah, from the guy who wrote GODSPELL [May 17, 1971] (and John Caird, the co-director of LES MISÉRABLES[†] [March 12, 1987]). CHILDREN OF EDEN was Schwartz's fourth consecutive mammoth disaster. The score, though, is surprisingly enjoyable, second only to PIPPIN [October 23, 1972] among the composer's work. CHILDREN OF EDEN eventually made its way to America when a 1997 revision opened at the regional Papermill Playhouse in Millburn, New Jersey. The cast album of the latter production might well result in a stock and amateur afterlife for this tuneful score. Schwartz remained pretty much inactive until the mid-1990s, when he journeyed to Disneyland to write lyrics to Alan Menken's music for the animated features *Pocohantas* (1995) and *The Hunchback of Notre Dame* (1996). Schwartz then went back to the Bible, with music and lyrics for Dreamworks' first animated musical, *Prince of Egypt* (1998).

The highpoint of Stephen Schwartz's career was unquestionably PIPPIN [October 23, 1972]. The low point has been—well—everything since. With three long-running goldmines to his credit and a reemergence on the scene following a long hibernation, though, Schwartz will presumably be back one of these days to try anew.

MARVIN HAMLISCH

Born: June 2, 1944, New York, New York

MARVIN HAMLISCH studied at Juilliard and went on to receive his bachelor's degree from Queens College. In his early twenties, he wrote his first pop hit, *Sunshine, Lollipops and Rainbows* [1965, lyric by Howard Liebling]. But Hamlisch was just another one of your Broadway piano players, serving as rehearsal accompanist for FUNNY GIRL [Styne: March 26, 1964] and doing dance arrangements on minor musicals like HENRY, SWEET HENRY [Merrill: October 23, 1967] and GOLDEN RAINBOW† [February 4, 1968]. Then Hollywood producer Sol Siegel heard him playing piano at a party, hired him to score the 1968 Burt Lancaster film *The Swimmer*, and Hamlisch was on his way (although he returned to Broadway to do dance arrangements for MINNIE'S BOYS [Grossman: March 26, 1970]). He became an instant celebrity on Oscar night, 1974, when he picked up an unprecedented three Oscars for his work on the 1973 films *The Sting* and *The Way We Were*. The choreographer of HENRY, SWEET HENRY was just then working on an idea for a novel new-form dance musical, so he called on his now famous former arranger.

A CHORUS LINE
May 21, 1975
Public Theatre {Off Broadway} •
    101 performances
July 25, 1975
Shubert Theatre • 6,137 performances
Lyrics by Edward Kleban; Book by James Kirkwood and Nicholas Dante; Conceived and Directed by Michael Bennett; Choreographed by Michael Bennett and Bob Avian; Produced by New York Shakespeare Festival (Joseph Papp); With Donna McKechnie, Priscilla Lopez, Carole (Kelly) Bishop, Sammy Williams, and Pamela Blair.

Published Songs
*Dance: Ten, Looks: Three
I Can Do That
The Music and the Mirror
One
What I Did for Love

Additional Songs Published in Vocal Selection
*At the Ballet
*Hello Twelve, Hello Thirteen, Hello Love
I Hope I Get It
*Nothing
Sing!

Additional Songs Published in Vocal Score
And . . .
Who Am I Anyway?

Michael Bennett, who had codirected FOLLIES [Sondheim: April 4, 1971] and served as replacement director/librettist on SEESAW [Coleman: March 18, 1973], decided to create a musical of his own. Rather than placing it in the hands of writers, he assembled a group of dancers and developed the idea himself in workshop. Only then did he bring in the writers, including Marvin Hamlisch, to fill in the words and music. Bennett's idea was brilliantly realized, and A CHORUS LINE went on to become Broadway's long-run champ (until overtaken by CATS† [October 7, 1982]). The score is quite good in parts, especially character numbers like *At the Ballet, Nothing*, and *Dance: Ten, Looks: Three*. (The big song hit of the show, *What I Did for Love*, is sturdy but more pop than theatrical; you could put it in almost any contemporary show.) Much of the score, though, sounds like dance routines converted—after the fact—into music and words. Given the overall scope of A CHORUS LINE and the strong vision of Bennett, this worked perfectly fine. But even in the initial flush of CHORUS LINE excitement, one wondered whether Hamlisch's immense success in his Broadway debut was merely a one-shot, right-place-in-the-right-time fluke. Twenty-three years and four musicals later, Hamlisch has yet to write a single satisfying stage song—let alone score—since CHORUS LINE.

THEY'RE PLAYING OUR SONG
February 11, 1979
Imperial Theatre • 1,082 performances
Lyrics by Carole Bayer Sager; Book by Neil Simon; Directed by Robert Moore; Choreographed by Patricia Birch; Produced by Emanuel Azenberg; With Robert Klein and Lucie Arnaz.

Published Song
They're Playing My Song

Additional Songs Published in Vocal Selection
Fallin'
Fill in the Words
I Still Believe in Love
If You Really Knew Me
Just for Tonight
When You're in My Arms

Additional Songs Recorded
Right
Workin' It Out

Broadway's top comedy writer Neil Simon found another odd couple in composer Hamlisch and his then girlfriend, lyricist Carole Bayer Sager. This translated into an exceedingly sketchy, gimmick of a musical which—thanks to competition like KING OF HEARTS† [October 22, 1978] and BALLROOM† [December 14, 1978]—proved enormously successful. But no thanks to the songwriters, except as models for the characters. So they got married and divorced. (The songwriters, not the characters.)

JEAN SEBERG
December 1, 1983
Olivier Theatre {London} • 60 performances
"*A Musical Tragedy.*" Lyrics by Christopher Adler; Book by Julian Barry (based on an original idea by Christopher Adler); Directed

by Peter Hall; Choreographed by Irving Davies; Produced by the National Theatre (Peter Hall); With Elisabeth Counsell, Kelly Hunter, Joss Ackland, and John Savident.

Song Published in Non-show Folio
Dreamers

Christopher Adler—son of composer/lyricist Richard Adler, stepson of Sally Ann Howes—came up with the idea of a musical exploring the life and death of movie actress Jean Seberg. "Not a bio," explained director Peter Hall, "a metaphor of something larger. It's about civil rights, the black power movement," etc. The British public was angry that the subsidized National Theatre was mounting a pre-Broadway tryout of a for-profit venture. Then they saw the show, and they were just angry. The plan was to keep JEAN SEBERG in repertory for eighteen months, but it was gone in eight weeks (replaced by a remounted revival of GUYS AND DOLLS [Loesser: November 24, 1950]).

SMILE
November 24, 1986
Lunt-Fontanne Theatre • 48 performances
Book and Lyrics by Howard Ashman (based on the screenplay by Jerry Belson); Directed by Howard Ashman; Choreographed by Mary Kyte; Produced by Lawrence Gordon, Richard M. Kagan, and Sidney L. Shlenker; With Marsha Waterbury, Jeff McCarthy, Anne Marie Bobby, Jodi Benson, Dick Patterson, and Veanne Cox.

Songs Published in Non-show Folio
Disneyland
In Our Hands
Smile

Additional Songs Recorded
Maria's Song
Nightlife in Santa Rosa [lyric by Carolyn Leigh]—cut
Six O'Clock News [lyric by Leigh]—cut

A bunch of kids stripped naked (emotionally), auditioning their acts with a Broadway choreographer on the loose. Sound familiar? With A CHORUS LINE [May 21, 1975] still happily chugging away on Shubert Alley, Hamlisch returned to Broadway with his fourth musical. With his fourth completely different group of collaborators, stagers, and producers; nobody had chosen to work with him more than once (or vice versa), which is a pretty bad omen. On SMILE alone, Hamlisch worked with a whole phalanx of theatre pros—lyricist Carolyn Leigh, librettists Tom Meehan and Jack Heifner (one at a time), and director Graciela Daniele—before starting from scratch again with Howard Ashman. Which is a pretty bad omen. Ashman was best known for the Off Broadway spoof LITTLE SHOP OF HORRORS [Menken: July 27, 1982]. SMILE was pretty much a mess, with Hamlisch's efforts having little to offer besides a pleasantly jingly title tune. (When Ashman died in 1991, he was lionized as a great Broadway songwriter; odd, as SMILE—which was scuttled by indifferent book, lyrics, and direction—was Ashman's sole Broadway credit.)

THE GOODBYE GIRL
March 4, 1993
Marquis Theatre • 188 performances
Lyrics by David Zippel; Book by Neil Simon (based on the screenplay by Neil Simon); Directed by Michael Kidd; Choreographed by Graciela Daniele; Produced by Office Two-One Inc., Gladys Nederlander, Stewart F. Lane, James M. Nederlander, Richard Kagan, and Emanuel Azenberg; With Bernadette Peters, Martin Short, Carol Woods, and Tammy Minoff.

Songs Published in Vocal Selection
A Beat Behind
Don't Follow in My Footsteps
Good News, Bad News
How Can I Win?
I Can Play This Part
My Rules
No More
No More ("Pop Version")
Paula (An Improvised Love Song)
What a Guy

Additional Songs Recorded
Am I Who I Think I Am? [lyric by Don Black]—new lyric for *I Can Play This Part*, written for 1997 London production

Body Talk [lyric by Black]—written for London production
Do You Want to Be in My Movie? [lyric by Black]—written for London production
Elliot Garfield Grant
The Future Isn't What It Used to Be [lyric by Black]—written for London production
Get a Life [lyric by Black]—written for London production
If You Break Their Hearts [lyric by Black]—written for London production
I'll Take the Sky [lyric by Black]—written for London production
Richard Interred
Too Good to Be Bad
Who Would've Thought?

Hamlisch teamed with lyricist David Zippel (of CITY OF ANGELS [Coleman: December 11, 1989]) and reunited with Neil Simon for a sure-fire musical comedy hit. Things don't work out sometimes, though, and THE GOODBYE GIRL was a resounding failure. The collaborators did not get along during the Chicago tryout so loudly that word quickly reached Shubert Alley; and if it was impossible to fire the lyricist, they did fire Simon's long-time director of choice Gene Saks. Choreographer Michael Kidd, who hadn't had a hit in thirty-seven years (see LI'L ABNER [Notables: November 15, 1956]) and was never much of a director anyway, was brought in from California and out of retirement to referee rewrites. All of this with two charismatic stars wasting away on stage, the always dependable Bernadette Peters and the surprisingly adept Martin Short. The score was marginally better than Hamlisch's previous efforts, although it had a disconcerting tendency to sound like the Neal Hefti background music from Simon's *Odd Couple* television series. Zippel's lyrics were clearly stronger than the work of the other collaborators; when the time came for a 1997 London mounting, Hamlisch tossed most of them out. With replacement lyrics by Don Black, the new GOODBYE GIRL did even worse than the first and bid a quick adieu.

A CHORUS LINE [May 21, 1975] is unquestionably a great Broadway musical, although much of the effective score was perhaps more atmospheric than artistic. That one show alone unquestionably gives Hamlisch a place in Broadway history. It's just as well, as his other four scores have been singularly devoid of distinction or any interest whatsoever. He will presumably be back, though: his next announced project is a musicalization of the 1957 motion picture *The Sweet Smell of Success*, for which he seems stylistically well suited. With stronger source material than he has previously worked from and first-rate dramatist John Guare as librettist, Hamlisch will have the opportunity to demonstrate that CHORUS LINE was no mere fluke.

ALAN MENKEN

Born: July 22, 1949, New Rochelle, New York

ALAN MENKEN was a highly musical child, making up songs from his early years. His family was highly supportive—his father was a musical dentist—and after he graduated from NYU, his parents suggested that he enroll in Lehman Engel's BMI Workshop. He did and was soon working with lyricist/librettist Howard Ashman.

GOD BLESS YOU, MR. ROSEWATER
October 14, 1979
Entermedia Theatre {"Mid" Broadway} •
    49 performances
Book and Lyrics by Howard Ashman (based on the novel by Kurt Vonnegut); Additional lyrics by Dennis Green; Directed by Howard Ashman; Choreographed by Mary Kyte; Produced by Edith Vonnegut in association with Warner Theatre Productions and Mark Gasarch; With Frederick Coffin, Janie Sell, and Jonathan Hadary.

Published Songs
None

Menken and his BMI partner Howard Ashman's first musical was an adaptation of a minor Kurt Vonnegut novel. A well-received mounting at the Off Off Broadway WPA Theatre—of which Ashman was artistic director and co-founder—resulted in a transfer to the 500-seat, "Mid Broadway" Entermedia (original home of GREASE [Notables: February 14, 1972] and THE BEST LITTLE WHOREHOUSE IN TEXAS [Notables: April 17, 1978]). ROSEWATER proved extremely uneven, though. The strongest element in the show was the music, but Menken seemed constrained by the needs of his lyricist: interesting strains of melody seemed to disappear in a tor-

rent of words, leaving the whole thing extremely unmemorable. (I can recall entire songs from other bad musicals I've worked on, like TRICKS[†] [January 8, 1973], SOON[†] [January 12, 1971], and SPOTLIGHT[†] [January 14, 1978]. I only remember about twelve measures of ROSEWATER— the *Cheese Nips* song—despite having heard the score dozens of times.)

REAL LIFE FUNNIES
February 11, 1981
Manhattan Theatre Club/Upstage
    {Off Broadway} • 23 performances
Lyrics and Adaptation by Howard Ashman (based on the comic strip by Stan Mack); Directed by Howard Ashman; Produced by Manhattan Theatre Club; With Pamela Blair, Merwin Goldsmith, Janie Sell, Dale Soules, and Chip Zien.

Song Recorded
Ah, Men

Menken and Ashman followed ROSEWATER [October 14, 1979] with the short-lived REAL LIFE, based on Stan Mack's idiosyncratic comic strip.

BABE
[circa 1981]
Unfinished musical. Book and Lyrics by Howard Ashman.

Songs Recorded
Growin' Boy
Hero

This musical biography of Babe Ruth was abandoned midway by the authors. Menken simultaneously wrote BATTLE OF THE GIANTS, a gay musical spoof with lyrics by Steve Brown which never got past a Tom O'Horgan-directed workshop.

LITTLE SHOP OF HORRORS
May 6, 1982
WPA Theatre • 24 performances
July 27, 1982
Orpheum Theatre {Off Broadway} •
   2,209 performances
Book and Lyrics by Howard Ashman (based on the film by Roger Corman); Directed by Howard Ashman; Choreographed by Mary Kyte; Produced by WPA Theatre (Kyle Rennick), David Geffen, Cameron Mackintosh, and The Shubert Organization; With Ellen Greene and Lee Wilkof.

Songs Published in Vocal Selections
Dentist!
Don't Feed the Plants (Finale)
Git It!
Grow for Me
Little Shop of Horrors
Mean Green Mother from Outer Space—written for 1986 film version
The Meek Shall Inherit
Skid Row (Downtown)
Somewhere That's Green
Suddenly Seymour
Ya Never Know

Additional Songs Recorded
Closed for Renovation
Crystal, Ronnette & Chiffon—written for film version (unused)
Dardos
A Little Dental Music—cut
Mushnik & Son
Now/It's Just the Gas
Sominex
Suppertime
We'll Have Tomorrow—cut

Menken and Howard Ashman's second transfer from WPA proved a big time Off Broadway smash, about a man-eating plant. LITTLE SHOP OF HORRORS was an offbeat spoof with an impressive group of high-powered Broadway pro-

ducers, and it enjoyed a long New York run, numerous companies, and a motion picture adaptation. The pastiche score was adequate for its purposes, although it certainly didn't have the charm or appeal (or song hits) of Broadway's first rock & roll spoof, BYE BYE BIRDIE [Strouse: April 14, 1960]. LITTLE SHOP did quite well nevertheless, and the 1986 film version earned Menken his first (of many) Oscar nominations, for the movie's new song *Mean Green Mother from Outer Space*.

KICKS: THE SHOWGIRL MUSICAL
[circa February 1984]
Unproduced musical. Book, Lyrics, and Direction by Tom Eyen.

Songs Recorded
I Want to Be a Rockette
You Are the Only One

Menken next collaborated with lyricist/librettist/director Tom Eyen on KICKS: THE SHOWGIRL MUSICAL, which got as far as a couple of workshops in the winter of 1984. DREAMGIRLS [Notables: December 20, 1981] started similarly; Michael Bennett saw it in workshop, agreed to produce it, and eventually took over from Eyen as director. KICKS, though, never got past its workshops. In the meanwhile, Menken provided music for the television series *Sesame Street* and *Love of Life*.

DIAMONDS
November 29, 1984
Circle in the Square Downtown
   {Off Broadway} • 122 performances
Music mostly by Larry Grossman (see Grossman: November 29, 1984); Additional music by Cy Coleman, John Kander, and others (see Coleman and Kander: November 29, 1984); Lyrics mostly by Ellen Fitzhugh; Additional lyrics by Howard Ashman, Betty Comden, Fred Ebb, Adolph Green, David Zippel, and others; Sketches by Ralph G. Allen, Roy Blount, Jr., John Lahr, John Weidman, and others; Directed by Harold Prince; Choreographed by Theodore Pappas; Produced by Stephen G. Martin, Harold

DeFelice, Louis W. Scheeder, Kenneth John Productions, Inc., in association with Frank Basile; With Loni Ackerman, Susan Bigelow, Jackee Harry, Dick Latessa, and Chip Zien.

Published Songs
None

Menken contributed one song—*In the Cards* [lyric by David Zippel]—to Hal Prince's indifferent baseball revue.

PERSONALS
November 8, 1985
Minetta Lane Theatre • 265 performances
Music mostly by others (see S. Schwartz: November 8, 1985); Lyrics and Sketches by David Crane, Seth Friedman, and Marta Kauffman; Directed by Paul Lazarus; Choreographed by D. J. Giagni; Produced by John-Edward Hill, Arthur Mackenzie, and Jon D. Silverman; With Jason Alexander, Laura Dean, Jeff Keller, Dee Hoty, Nancy Opel, and Trey Wilson.

Songs Recorded
I Could Always Go to You [lyric by David Crane, Seth Friedman, and Marta Kauffman]
I'd Rather Dance Alone [lyric by Crane, Friedman, and Kauffman]

THE APPRENTICESHIP OF DUDDY KRAVITZ
September 30, 1987
Zellerbach Theatre {Philadelphia} • Regional tryout
Lyrics by David Spencer; Book by Austin Pendleton and Mordecai Richler (based on the novel by Mordecai Richler); Directed by Austin Pendleton; Choreographed by D. J. Giagni; Produced by American Theater Music Festival; With Lonny Price and Anne Marie Bobby.

Published Songs
None

Mordecai Richler's novel—which had been made into a popular 1974 movie, starring Richard Dreyfus—proved difficult to adapt to the stage. An earlier version, with a score by Jerry Leiber and Mike Stoller, had failed after a 1984 tryout at the Citadel Theatre in Edmunton, Canada. Menken's version apparently had some rather interesting music, but the story's monster of a central character remained unworkable. After a decade of struggle, Menken and Ashman took a slight detour from Broadway to the moribund feature animation department at Disney Studios. Their celebrated 1989 film *The Little Mermaid* quickly changed the face of feature animation (and the fortunes of Disney). This was followed by the 1991 *Beauty and the Beast* and the 1992 *Aladdin*. The three films garnered Menken six Oscars, three for best original scores and another three for the songs *Under the Sea, Beauty and the Beast*, and *A Whole New World*. While writing *Aladdin*, though, Ashman died (with only one Broadway show to his credit, the mirthless SMILE [Hamlisch: November 24, 1986]). Tim Rice, of EVITA[†] [September 25, 1979], stepped in to finish the *Aladdin* lyrics. Menken tried a non-animated movie musical, the 1992 *Newsies* [lyrics by Jack Feldman], which was a quick failure. He also wrote a score for the 1992 TV miniseries *Lincoln*.

WEIRD ROMANCE
May 12, 1992
WPA Theatre {Off Off Broadway} • 50 performances
Two One-Act Musicals. Lyrics by David Spencer; Book by Alan Brennert (based on the stories "The Girl Who Was Plugged In" by James Tiptree, Jr., and "Her Pilgrim Soul" by Alan Brennert); Directed by Barry Harman; Choreographed by John Carrafa; Produced by WPA Theatre (Kyle Rennick); With Jonathan Hadary and Ellen Greene.

Songs Published in Vocal Selection
Eyes That Never Lie
Feeling No Pain
I Can Show You a Thing or Two
A Man
My Orderly World
Need to Know
Pop! Flash!
Someone Else Is Waiting

Stop and See Me
Weird Romance
Worth It

Additional Songs Recorded
Amazing Penetration
Another Woman
Great Unknown
No One Can Do It
Pressing Onward
That's Where We Came in
You Remember

Menken returned to his WPA roots, presumably looking to escape the family-oriented "Disney" tag with which his name had been linked. WEIRD ROMANCE was certainly not for children; the strange science fiction musical wasn't much for adults either and quickly disappeared. Disney, meanwhile, decided to enter the Broadway arena—with a stage version of one of Menken's film hits.

BEAUTY AND THE BEAST
April 18, 1994
Palace Theatre • Still playing April 1, 1999
Music by Alan Menken; Lyrics by Howard Ashman and Tim Rice; Book by Linda Woolverton (based on the 1991 movie); Choreographed by Matt West; Directed by Robert Jess Roth; Produced by Walt Disney Productions; With Susan Egan, Terrence Mann, Tom Bosley, Burke Moses, Gary Beach, and Beth Fowler.

Published Song
Beauty and the Beast [lyric by Ashman]—written for movie version

Additional Songs Published in Vocal Selection
*Be Our Guest [lyric by Ashman]—written for movie version
Belle [lyric by Ashman]—written for movie version
*Gaston [lyric by Ashman]—written for movie version
Home [lyric by Rice]
How Long Must This Go On? [lyric by Rice]
Human Again [lyric by Ashman]—written for movie version

If I Can't Love Her [lyric by Rice]
Maison des Lunes [lyric by Rice]
Me [lyric by Rice]
The Mob Song [lyric by Ashman]—written for movie version
No Matter What [lyric by Rice]
Something There [lyric by Ashman]—written for movie version
Transformation [lyric by Rice]

Additional Song Recorded
The Battle [lyric by Ashman]—written for movie version

Fourteen years after GOD BLESS YOU, MR. ROSEWATER [October 14, 1979], Menken finally made it to Broadway. Not with a Broadway show, exactly, but with a stage adaptation of the 1991 film *Beauty and the Beast*. While there were a half-dozen new songs written with Tim Rice, the basic score (and the most effective songs) were all written in the late 1980s for the film. The show itself was assembled in theme-park manner, aimed at unsophisticated mass audiences (who eagerly thronged to it) rather than actual theatregoers (who were jadedly dismissive or—in some cases—just plain bored). BEAUTY AND THE BEAST was not taken seriously by critics or Broadwayites, just by ticket-buyers with plenty of spare cash for official BEAUTY AND THE BEAST souvenirs. So Menken finally had his Broadway hit—and a big one—although earning little respect for it. (Disney learned from their experience: for their next Broadway foray, they successfully combined commerce with high art in the stage adaptation of the non-Menken 1994 animated blockbuster *The Lion King* [Notables: November 24, 1997].)

A CHRISTMAS CAROL
December 1, 1994
Paramount Theatre {Arena Show} •
71 performances
Lyrics by Lynn Ahrens; Book by Mike Ockrent and Lynn Ahrens (based on the novel by Charles Dickens); Directed by Mike Ockrent; Choreographed by Susan Stroman; Produced by Madison Square Garden, Dodger Productions, and Tim Hawkins; With Walter Charles, Ken Jennings, Jeff Keller, Robert Westenberg, and Emily Skinner.

Songs Published in Vocal Selection
*Abundance and Charity
Christmas Together
God Bless Us, Everyone
The Lights of Long Ago
Link by Link
Mr. Fezziwig's Annual Christmas Ball
A Place Called Home
The Years Are Passing By
Yesterday, Tomorrow and Today

Additional Songs Recorded
Dancing on Your Grave
Jolly, Rich and Fat
Money Montage
Nothing to Do with Me

Madison Square Garden decided to get in on New York City's holiday spirit with their own annual extravaganza (and wrestle some business from Radio City Music Hall's Christmas Spectacular). Who better to sign up as composer than Disney's own music man? Money was no object—some thirteen million was poured into A CHRISTMAS CAROL, custom designed to fit into the awkward, low-ceilinged 5,100-seat Paramount Theatre. A CHRISTMAS CAROL was functional, workable, and bland; the score professional, fully adequate, and bland. One song, *Abundance and Charity*, was totally out of place and out of time and out of tune with the rest of the piece; it was also the most interesting thing in the score, a bit of inspired lunacy like Menken's movie songs *Under the Sea* and *Be My Guest*. But the atmospheric score has none of the high-spirited buoyancy of other Dickensian musicals like Lionel Bart's OLIVER![†] [January 6, 1963] or even Cyril Ornadel and Leslie Bricusse's somewhat spotty PICKWICK[†] [October 4, 1965]. Nevertheless, Madison Square Garden seems to have gotten what they wanted: a seasonal, popular-priced, ninety-minute, three-a-day spectacle for the mass market family audience. Since its opening, A CHRISTMAS CAROL has been remounted every year (at this writing), usually with a yesteryear star—Tony Randall, Roddy McDowall, Hal Linden, Roger Daltrey—as curmudgeonly old Ebenezer. For Menken it was back to feature animation—though with diminishing returns. His 1995 effort *Pocahontas*, with lyrics by Stephen Schwartz, was less pleasing than its predecessors (though Menken picked up his customary two Oscars). There were no awards, though, for the 1996 *Hunchback of Notre Dame* (with Schwartz) or the 1997 *Hercules* (with David Zippel).

KING DAVID
May 18, 1997
New Amsterdam Theatre • 5 performances
Lyrics by Tim Rice; Directed by Mike Ockrent; Produced by Walt Disney Theatrical Productions; With Marcus Lovett, Roger Bart, Stephen Bogardus, Judy Kuhn, Alice Ripley, and Martin Vidnovic.

Songs Recorded
Absalom, My Absalom
The Caravan Moves On
The Death of Saul
The Enemy Within
Entry into Jerusalem [incorporating Psalm 24]
Goliath of Gath
How Are the Mighty Fallen
Hunted Partridge on the Hill
Israel and Saul
The Long, Long Day
Never Again
Psalm 8
Samuel Anoints David
Saul Has Slain His Thousands
Sheer Perfection
This New Jerusalem
Warm Spring Night
When in Love
You Have It All

Menken returned to Disney, this time with—of all things—a biblical oratorio. Lyricist Tim Rice, of course, made his reputation and millions on Joseph and Jesus (not to mention Santa Evita). DAVID's score was adventurous, certainly, and contained one real rouser in the gospel vein, *Saul Has Slain His Thousands*; but the piece—which was mounted as a concert as the opening attraction at Disney's renovated New Amsterdam Theatre—proved to have little appeal and questionable prospects. But think of all those potential biblical action figures they could peddle. Disney being Disney, one should never count anything out.

Alan Menken was trained and reared in the theatre and clearly has a highly theatrical musicality. Yet his stage work over the course of twenty years has had little effect. One tends to blame Disney for stealing him away; without Disney, though, Menken would very possibly still be unknown and unheard and millions of dollars poorer. He has, in fact, done a sizable amount of stage work, including several musicals that remain unproduced. At this juncture, with animated film musicals on a seeming decline while stage musicals surge (at least temporarily), one hopes that Menken will turn back to Broadway —and finally write a *real* musical.

WILLIAM FINN

Born: February 28, 1952, Boston, Massachusetts

WILLIAM FINN grew up in Natick, Massachusetts. He went to school at Williams College—Stephen Sondheim's alma mater—as an English major. While there he wrote three musicals, RAPE, SCRAMBLED EGGS, and SIZZLE. Upon graduation, he won the Hutchinson Fellowship (like Sondheim) and endeavored to become a composer. He supported himself in the meanwhile as a writer for in-flight magazines, a temp worker, and a play reader for the New York Shakespeare Festival. He also wrote music and served as musical director for a showcase production of a play by Paul Leavin, BENNY LEONARD AND THE BROOKLYN BRIDGE [March 31, 1977], at the Open Space in Soho; among the cast were singers Alison Fraser and Mary Testa. Then André Bishop of Playwrights Horizons heard Finn's early work, recognized his wild (though undeveloped) talent, and offered him a home base.

All Music and Lyrics by William Finn unless indicated.

IN TROUSERS

February 21, 1979
Playwrights Horizons {Off Off Broadway} •
  24 performances
Directed by Finn; Produced by Playwrights Horizons (André Bishop); With Chip Zien, Alison Fraser, Mary Testa, and Joanna Green.

Songs Recorded
Another Sleepless Night
A Breakfast over Sugar
High School Ladies at Five o'Clock
How Marvin Eats His Breakfast
How the Body Falls Apart
I Am Wearing a Hat (Marvin Takes a Wife)

I'm Breaking Down—added to 1981 revival;
  also used in MARCH OF THE FALSETTOS
  [April 1, 1981]
In Trousers (The Dream)
*Love Me for What I Am
Marvin Takes a Victory Shower
Marvin's Giddy Seizures
My Chance to Survive the Night
My High School Sweetheart
The Nausea before the Game
The Rape of Miss Goldberg
Set Those Sails
*Whizzer Going Down
Your Lips and Me

The idiosyncratic Finn's first produced musical was about an idiosyncratic fellow named Marvin, who in the course of the rather unwieldy action grows up, passes through high school, marries, and leaves his wife for a fellow called Whizzer. Though IN TROUSERS was somewhat scattered, much of the score was unquestionably remarkable (if clearly startling). Like *Love Me for What I Am*, a beautiful, soaring ballad; *I'm Breaking Down*, a psychoneurotic tour de force; and the rambunctious *Whizzer Going Down*, which is quite unlike anything heard elsewhere. Playwrights Horizons initially mounted the piece as a developmental workshop [December 8, 1978, 8 performances], with Finn himself playing Marvin. A revised version (with a different cast and creative staff) was mounted Off Off Broadway on Februry 22, 1981, by Second Stage for fifteen performances. Following the success of the show's sequel, MARCH OF THE FALSETTOS, a further revision of IN TROUSERS was produced by Roger Berlind and Gregory Harrison at the Promenade Theatre

[March 26, 1985]. Still hampered by structural problems and dramatic immaturity, the fascinating IN TROUSERS closed (for good?) after sixteen performances.

MARCH OF THE FALSETTOS
April 1, 1981
Playwrights Horizons {Off Off Broadway} •
   170 performances
November 9, 1981
Westside Arts Center {Off Broadway} •
   128 performances
Also see FALSETTOS [*April 29, 1992*]. Directed by James Lapine; Produced by Mary Lea Johnson, Francine Lefrak, Martin Richards, Warner Theatre Productions, Inc., and Playwrights Horizons (André Bishop); With Michael Rupert, Alison Fraser, Chip Zien, Stephen Bogardus, and James Kushner.

Songs Initially Published in FALSETTOS
   Vocal Selection
Father to Son
Four Jews in a Room Bitching
*The Games I Play
*I'm Breaking Down—added to Los Angeles
   production; originally used in 1981 revival
   of IN TROUSERS [February 21, 1979]
*I Never Wanted to Love You
Making a Home
March of the Falsettos
A Marriage Proposal

Additional Songs Recorded
*The Chess Game
Everyone Tells Jason to See a Psychiatrist
Jason's Therapy
*Love Is Blind
Marvin at the Psychiatrist (A 3-Part Mini-
   Opera)
Marvin Hits Trina
*My Father's a Homo
Please Come to My House
This Had Better Come to a Stop
*The Thrill of First Love
A Tight-Knit Family
*Trina's Song

This sequel to IN TROUSERS [February 21, 1979] was a highly original, highly exciting piece which —surprisingly—was immediately recognized and found an enthusiastic following. Finn adhered to no structure: music and lyrics just went where they needed to go, forming a tapestry of strong, emotional musical themes. The author displayed a keen ability at drawing his characters in songs like *Four Jews in a Room Bitching*, *Trina's Song*, *The Games I Play*, and the unlikely soft-shoe *My Father's a Homo*. Particularly stunning were the intricately written musical conversations for combinations of his five characters: *This Had Better Come to a Stop*, *Love Is Blind*, *The Chess Game*, and *I Never Wanted to Love You*. A very special theatre work, and arguably the best score of the 1980s.

AMERICA KICKS UP ITS HEELS
March 2, 1983
Playwrights Horizons {Off Off Broadway} •
   28 performances
Also see ROMANCE IN HARD TIMES [*December 28, 1989*]. Book by Charles Rubin; Directed by Mary Kyte and Ben Levit; Choreographed by Mary Kyte; Produced by Playwrights Horizons (André Bishop); With Patti LuPone, Lenora Nemetz, Dick Latessa, I. M. Hobson, Alix Korey, and Peggy Hewett.

Song Recorded
All Fall Down

Finn found it exceedingly difficult to follow up his two contemporary Marvin Musicals. He next attempted AMERICA KICKS UP ITS HEELS, a free-form depression-era musical set in a soup kitchen in Hell's Kitchen. But the undisciplined work proved baffling, closing without an official opening. In 1984, Finn received a Guggenheim Fellowship.

TANGO APASIONADO
November 6, 1987
Westbeth Theater Center {Off Off Broadway} •
   47 performances
Also see DANGEROUS GAMES [*October 19, 1989*]. Music by Astor Piazzolla; Lyrics by Finn; Adaptation by Jim Lewis and Graciela Daniele (based on the works of Jorge Luis Borges); Conceived, Choreographed, and

Directed by Graciela Daniele; Produced by INTAR Hispanic American Arts Center; With Leonardo Cimino, Tina Paul, John Mineo, Gregory Mitchell, and Camille Saviola.

Published Songs
None

With his formerly promising career as the "new Sondheim" at a long standstill, Finn contributed lyrics to TANGO APASIONADO. This dance project of Graciela Daniele—based on the works of the great Argentine writer Jorge Luis Borges—was set to music by internationally acclaimed tango master Astor Piazzolla.

THE WINTER'S TALE [1989]
February 21, 1989
Public/Anspacher Theatre {Off Broadway} • 24 performances
Play by William Shakespeare; Incidental music by Finn and Michael Starobin; Directed by James Lapine; Produced by New York Shakespeare Festival (Joseph Papp); With Mandy Patinkin, Christopher Reeve, and Alfre Woodard.

Published Songs
None

DANGEROUS GAMES
October 19, 1989
Nederlander Theatre • 4 performances
Also see TANGO APASIONADO [*November 6, 1987*]. Music by Astor Piazzolla; Lyrics by Finn; Book by Jim Lewis and Graciela Daniele; Conceived, Choreographed, and Directed by Graciela Daniele; Co-choreographed by Tina Paul; Produced by Jules Fisher, James M. Nederlander, and Arthur Rubin in association with Mary Kantor; With Tina Paul, John Mineo, and Gregory Mitchell.

Published Songs
None

TANGO APASIONADO was remounted for Broadway, with most of the same cast but with the character names changed (and the "based on Borges" credit removed). "Not recommended for

children," it said, in big print on the ads; not recommended for anyone, said the critics.

ROMANCE IN HARD TIMES
December 28, 1989
Public/Anspacher Theatre
{Off Off Broadway} • 6 performances
Book by Finn (based on AMERICA KICKS UP ITS HEELS [March 2, 1983]); Directed by David Warren; Choreographed by Marcia Milgrom Dodge; Produced by New York Shakespeare Festival (Joseph Papp); With Lillias White, Cleavant Derricks, Lawrence Clayton, Alix Korey, and Peggy Hewett.

Song Recorded
All Fall Down

Joe Papp established a Musical Lab of three-week workshops, with the second entry being Finn's revised version of AMERICA KICKS UP ITS HEELS. Revised, rewritten, and rethought as well, with the main characters (and their songs) now being of a different color. ROMANCE IN HARD TIMES was even more unwieldy than its predecessor had been, and its workshop even more problematic (with two of the major players replaced en route). The performances by Lillias White and Cleavant Derricks were quite remarkable, but Finn's Depression piece remained an undisciplined enigma of enormous (if enormously unrealized) talent.

FALSETTOLAND
June 28, 1990
Playwrights Horizons {Off Off Broadway} • 75 performances
September 16, 1990
Lucille Lortel Theatre {Off Broadway} • 165 performances
Also see FALSETTOS [*April 29, 1992*]. Conceived by Finn and James Lapine (based on characters from MARCH OF THE FALSETTOS [April 1, 1981]); Directed by James Lapine; Produced by Maurice Rosenfield & Lois F. Rosenfield, Inc., with Steven Suskin, in association with Playwrights Horizons (André Bishop); With Michael Rupert, Stephen Bogardus, Faith Prince, Lonny Price, Danny Gerard, Heather MacRae, and Janet Metz.

Songs Published in Vocal Selection
*The Baseball Game
A Day in Falsettoland
*Everyone Hates His Parents
*Holding to the Ground (Trina's Song)
Something Bad Is Happening
*Unlikely Lovers
*What More Can I Say?
*What Would I Do?
*You Gotta Die Sometime

Additional Songs Recorded
*Another Miracle of Judaism
Canceling the Bar Mitzvah
Days Like This
Do You Know How Great My Life Is?
Falsettoland
I Don't Get It
Jason's Bar Mitzvah
Miracle of Judaism
More Racquetball
Planning a Bar Mitzvah (Round Tables, Square Tables)
Racquetball
Trina Works It Out
Year of the Child

Nine frustrating years after first bursting into prominence with MARCH OF THE FALSETTOS [April 1, 1981], Finn returned to his characters from IN TROUSERS [February 21, 1979] for his third and final Marvin musical. FALSETTOLAND followed them from 1981—when Marvin's world discovered that Something Bad Is Happening— through to the moment when Whizzer dies (and Marvin, finally, grows up). The somber theme, as seen through Finn's off-center brilliance, was simultaneously tragic and invigorating; the manic/comic numbers were as effective (and somewhat more polished) than in the earlier works. Finn's score was also uncharacteristically beautiful in spots, such as the moving What Would I Do? and the glorious quartet Unlikely Lovers; and bitterly fatalistic in others, such as the wife's desperate Holding to the Ground and the victim's macabre You Gotta Die Sometime. Most impressive, perhaps, was Finn's ability to express plot through song—the show was entirely through-composed, like MARCH OF THE FALSETTOS—in such sections as the hilarious Baseball Game ("We're watching Jewish boys

who cannot play baseball play baseball"); More Racquetball, in which the tragedy of the piece starkly springs from nowhere (as in real life); and in the heart-wrenching Another Miracle of Judaism, in which Marvin's thirteen-year-old grapples with the reality of death. FALSETTOLAND was a major accomplishment, fulfilling Finn's early promise and finally bringing him to Broadway.

FALSETTOS
April 29, 1992
John Golden Theatre • 487 performances
Book by Finn and James Lapine (combining MARCH OF THE FALSETTOS [November 9, 1981] and FALSETTOLAND [June 28, 1990]); Directed by James Lapine; Produced by Fran and Barry Weissler; With Michael Rupert, Stephen Bogardus, Chip Zien, Barbara Walsh, Heather MacRae, Carolee Carmello, and Jonathan Kaplan.

Published Songs
See MARCH OF THE FALSETTOS and FALSETTOLAND.

The possibility of combining the two FALSETTO musicals had been considered when FALSETTOLAND transferred from Playwrights Horizons, but for various reasons it was at that time impractical. The two pieces were successfully combined the following year when Graciela Daniele (of DANGEROUS GAMES [October 19, 1989]) directed the first post–New York FALSETTOLAND, at Hartford Stage Company in October 1991. This led, in turn, to a Broadway production of FALSETTO/FALSETTOLAND, with James Lapine recreating his original stagings (with his original leading men). FALSETTOS, happily, proved a success, and Finn—finally on Broadway—picked up two well-deserved Tony Awards for his efforts.

A NEW BRAIN
June 18, 1998
Mitzi Newhouse Theatre {Off Broadway} • 116 performances
Book by Finn and James Lapine; Directed and Choreographed by Graciela Daniele; Produced by Lincoln Center Theater (André Bishop); With Kristin Chenoweth, Penny Fuller, Malcolm

Gets, Liz Larsen, Christopher Innvar, John Jellison, Keith Byron Kirk, Michael Mandell, Mary Testa, and Chip Zien.

Songs Published in Vocal Selection
And They're Off
Change
Don't Give In
Eating Myself up Alive
Gordo's Law of Genetics
Heart and Music
I'd Rather Be Sailing
I Feel So Much Spring
The Music Still Plays On
Poor, Unsuccessful and Fat
A Really Lousy Day in the Universe

Additional Songs Recorded
Brain Dead
Calamari
Family History
Frogs Have So Much Spring
The Homeless Lady's Revenge
I Have So Many Songs
In the Middle of the Room
An Invitation to Sleep In My Arms
Just Go
Mother's Gonna Make Things Fine
911 Emergency
Sitting Becalmed in the Lee of Cuttyhunk
Throw It Out
Time
Time and Music
Trouble In His Brain
Whenever I Dream
Yes
You Boys Are Gonna Get Me in Trouble

Following the successful opening of FALSETTOS [April 29, 1992], Finn was diagnosed with an inoperable brain tumor. This proved to be a misdiagnosis, but he understandably went through a nightmare until it was all cleared up. Finn then returned to work on no fewer than three projects, all of which remain unproduced to date: a lyrics-only collaboration with Jerry Bock on the tax-code–inspired 1040 (from which Finn ultimately withdrew, with Bock taking over the lyric-writing assignment and eventually withdrawing from the project as well); THE ROYAL FAMILY, a musical comedy version of George S. Kaufman

and Edna Ferber's play; and MUSCLE, a collaboration with James Lapine. (This last had begun as a Lapine/Sondheim companion piece to PASSION [Sondheim: May 9, 1994], which at the time was intended as a one-act.) Finn finally returned with his first produced piece in eight years, since FALSETTOLAND [June 28, 1990]: A NEW BRAIN, about a composer misdiagnosed with an inoperable brain tumor. Finn's quirky style and richly entertaining humor were still in evidence—and richly welcome—and there were a handful of remarkable songs: *The Music Still Plays On, An Invitation to Sleep in My Arms, I Feel So Much Spring, Gordo's Law of Genetics* (*The Bad Traits Will Always Predominate*), and the exquisite *Sailing*. But the overall piece was weakened by the connective plot material, and the high emotional pitch of Finn's more important work was missing. While semi-autobiographical, A NEW BRAIN somehow seemed far less personal than the non-autobiographical FALSETTOs musicals. I, for one, am always glad to hear anything Finn cares to write.

LOVE'S FIRE ✦ FRESH NUMBERS BY SEVEN AMERICAN PLAYWRIGHTS
June 22, 1998
Public/Newman {Off Off Broadway} •
    16 performances
One-act plays by Finn, Eric Bogosian, John Guare, Tony Kushner, Marsha Norman, Ntozake Shange, and Wendy Wasserstein (inspired by sonnets by William Shakespeare); Music also by Adam Guettel and Chico Freeman; Directed by Mark Lamos; Produced by The Acting Company (Margot Harley) in association with Ira Pittleman and Jonathan C. Herzog.

Published Songs
None

The Acting Company celebrated their twenty-fifth anniversary with an evening of Shakespeare-inspired one-acts, contributed by all-star writers. Following a cross-country tour (beginning January 3, 1998) and a brief visit to the Royal Shakespeare Company's London base at the Barbican Center, LOVE'S FIRE came to the

New York Shakespeare Festival for two weeks. Among the offerings were Wendy Wasserstein's *Waiting for Philip Glass* (from Sonnet 94); John Guare's *The General of Hot Desire: An Essay*, with music by Adam Guettel (from Sonnet 154); and Finn's *Painting* (from Sonnet 102).

William Finn burst forth on the scene with MARCH OF THE FALSETTOS [April 1, 1981] and was immediately hailed as the new Sondheim, the first great composer of the post-1950 generation. This is a rather heavy burden to place on anyone, and Finn responded by remaining relatively silent until FALSETTOLAND [June 28, 1990], nine years later. These two scores are exceptional and received due acclaim, but Finn has always veered toward non-mainstream material; more noncommercial than Sondheim, even. He has reached Broadway only once—not with a show intended for Broadway but with FALSETTOS [April 29, 1992], the combined version of the two aforementioned shows. (THE ROYAL FAMILY† is presently scheduled for the 1999–2000 season.) Three Off Broadway musicals, three Off Off Broadway workshops, and several incidental contributions is not a whole lot to show for twenty years, quantity-wise; but Finn seems not to care much about quantity. Or Broadway, for that matter. Finn does what he wants, the way he wants it. While his creative choices sometimes seem wrongheaded or just plain indecipherable— what, exactly, was ROMANCE IN HARD TIMES [December 29, 1989]?—it is his very unruliness that has resulted in some of the most remarkable musical theatre material of the last twenty years.

MAURY YESTON

Born: October 23, 1945, Jersey City, New Jersey

MAURY YESTON developed an early interest in musical theatre. He graduated from Yale in 1967 with twin ambitions: to teach music and write Broadway hits. After getting his master's at Cambridge, he returned to Yale for his doctorate in 1971 and simultaneously entered Lehman Engel's BMI Workshop. Through the 1970s Yeston taught at Yale and worked on a rather unlikely project, a musical theatre adaptation of Fellini's *8 ½*.

All Music and Lyrics by Maury Yeston unless otherwise noted.

CLOUD NINE
May 18, 1981
Theatre de Lys {Off Broadway} •
    971 performances
Play by Caryl Churchill; Incidental music and Title song by Maury Yeston; Directed by Tommy Tune; Produced by Michel Stuart and Harvey J. Klaris in association with Michel Kleinman Productions; With Zeljko Ivanek, Concetta Tomei, E. Catherine Kerr, Veronica Castang, and Nicholas Surovy.

Published Songs
None

In 1980, Tommy Tune became attached to Yeston's Fellini project, which was to be produced as NINE [May 9, 1982]. In the meanwhile, the director, composer, and producers of the forthcoming NINE did CLOUD NINE, a fascinating puzzle of a piece which enjoyed a successful run.

THE QUEEN OF BASIN STREET
[circa March, 1982]
Also see LA CAGE AUX FOLLES [Herman: August 21, 1983]. Unproduced musical. Book by Jay Presson Allen (based on *La Cage aux Folles* [play] by Jean Poiret); [Directed by Mike Nichols and Tommy Tune; Choreographed by Tommy Tune; Produced by Allan Carr].

Published Songs
None

Hollywood producer Allan Carr saw Jean Poiret's farce in Paris in 1976 and quickly optioned the musical stage rights. The 1977 French film version was an enormous international hit, attracting mainstream audiences across Europe and the United States (where it was released in 1979). Carr enlisted Jay Presson Allen to reset the piece in New Orleans and brought in Mike Nichols (a producing partner of Allen's husband on ANNIE [Strouse: April 21, 1977] and other projects) and Tommy Tune (fresh from WHOREHOUSE [Notables: April 17, 1978]). Jerry Herman and Marvin Hamlisch were early candidates for the score, but Tune had his new discovery write four songs on spec. Yeston got the job, the show was announced, work progressed, and a sure-fire hit seemed to be in the making. Then Nichols suddenly quit—apparently over a profit participation dispute—Tune followed him, and Allen was fired. So much for Maury Yeston and THE QUEEN OF BASIN STREET. Carr enlisted a new staff for his LA CAGE, and Yeston went back to Yale and Fellini. (Nichols filed his ideas away for the future; in 1996 he filmed THE BIRDCAGE, a remake of the material set in Miami Beach—with music by Sondheim.)

NINE
May 9, 1982
46th Street Theatre • 739 performances
Book by Arthur Kopit (based on Mario Fratti's adaptation of *8 ½* [movie] by Federico Fellini, Tullio Pinelli, and Ennio Flaiano);

Directed by Tommy Tune; Choreographed by Thommie Walsh; Produced by Michel Stuart, Harvey J. Klaris, Roger S. Berlind, James M. Nederlander, Francine Lefrak, and Kenneth D. Greenblatt; With Raul Julia, Liliane Montevecchi, Karen Akers, Anita Morris, Taina Elg, and Shelly Burch.

Published Songs
Be Italian
*Be on Your Own
Only with You
*Simple
*Unusual Way

Additional Songs Published in Vocal Selections
Amor
*The Bells of St. Sebastian
A Call from the Vatican
Folies Bergères
Getting Tall
Guido's Song
I Can't Make This Movie
*My Husband Makes Movies
Nine
*Waltz from Nine

Additional Songs Recorded
The Germans at the Spa
Grand Canal Sequence
A Man Like You
Not Since Chaplin
Overture Delle Donne
Ti Voglio Bene

After almost a decade in development, Yeston's unheralded NINE arrived as the sleeper hit of the 1981–82 season. A novel concept—the white-garbed hero surrounded by a cast of women in black and four little boys with tambourines—allowed for a striking if ultimately one-gimmick show. But Yeston—arriving out of nowhere, as it were—made an immediate impact with Broadway's first intelligent score since SWEENEY TODD [Sondheim: March 1, 1979]. Yeston's score was at once vibrant, emotional, and lyrical (though suffering from a few embarrassing patches of lyrics). Unusual Way, Simple, Be on Your Own, My Husband Makes Movies, The Bells of St. Sebastian, Waltz from Nine—this was an uncommonly rich musical score. The success of NINE

allowed Yeston to leave Yale and devote his full energy to the Broadway musical—except that it would be fifteen years before another real Yeston musical reached town. Yeston's next project was Goya—A Life in Song. It was decided to start with a concept record album with Placido Domingo, though, and the 1989 disc was the last of Goya.

1-2-3-4-5
December 20, 1988
City Center Stage One {Off Broadway} •
    51 performances
Book by Larry Gelbart (suggested by the first five books of the Bible); Directed by Gerald Gutierrez; Produced by Manhattan Theatre Club; With Pamela Blair, Jonathan Hadary, Lauren Mitchell, and Mary Testa.

Published Song
*New Words—issued in 1991 as from HISTORY LOVES COMPANY (see commentary, below)

Six long years after NINE [May 9, 1982], Yeston turned up with librettist Larry Gelbart on 1-2-3-4-5, a satiric look at Genesis as seen by "the neighbors of the main stars." Things did not proceed smoothly, however: the long-announced Manhattan Theatre Club production was at the last minute hastily labeled a work-in-progress and not offered to the critics. Yeston—without Gelbart—later tried a second version of the show under the title HISTORY LOVES COMPANY and a third version (called IN THE BEGINNING—as well. One song found its way into print, the tender but complex, lullaby-like New Words.

GRAND HOTEL ✦ THE MUSICAL
November 12, 1989
Martin Beck Theatre • 1,018 performances
Music and Lyrics by Robert Wright and George Forrest; Additional music and lyrics by Yeston; Book by Luther Davis (based on the novel by Vicki Baum and AT THE GRAND† [July 7, 1958] by Robert Wright, George Forrest, and Luther Davis); Directed and Choreographed by Tommy Tune; Produced by Martin Richards, Mary Lea Johnson, Sam Crothers, Sander Jacobs,

Kenneth D. Greenblatt, Paramount Pictures, and Jujamcyn Theaters; With David (James) Carroll, Liliane Montevecchi, Jane Krakowski, Michael Jeter, Timothy Jerome, and Karen Akers.

Note: Certain songs by Wright and Forrest were revised by Yeston during the pre-Broadway tryout. These have been published in their original versions, as indicated, though recorded in the show versions.

Published Song
The Grand Parade (*Theme from "Grand Hotel"*) [by Yeston]

Additional Songs Published in Vocal
     Selections
As It Should Be [by Wright and Forrest]—preliminary version
At the Grand Hotel [by Yeston]
Bonjour, Amour [by Yeston]
The Grand Charleston (*H-A-P-P-Y*) [by Wright and Forrest]
The Grand Fox-Trot (*Trottin' the Fox/*Who Couldn't Dance with You*) [by Wright and Forrest "with Wally Harper"]
*The Grand Tango (*Table with a View*) [by Wright and Forrest]—preliminary version; originally used in AT THE GRAND
*I Waltz Alone [by Wright and Forrest]—preliminary version; originally used in AT THE GRAND
I Want to Go to Hollywood [by Yeston]
*Love Can't Happen [by Yeston]
Maybe My Baby Loves Me [by Wright and Forrest]
Roses at the Station [by Yeston]
*Villa on a Hill [by Wright and Forrest]
We'll Take a Glass Together [by Wright and Forrest]—preliminary version; originally used in AT THE GRAND
*What You Need [by Wright and Forrest]—originally used in AT THE GRAND

Additional Songs Recorded
After Autumn [by Wright and Forrest]—cut
Bolero [instrumental]
The Crooked Path [by Wright and Forrest]
Fire and Ice [by Wright and Forrest]
Flaemchen (*The Flame Girl*) [by Wright and Forrest]—cut

The Grand Waltz [by Wright and Forrest]
How Can I Tell Her? [by Wright and Forrest]—new lyric for *Alone* (unpublished) from AT THE GRAND
Some Have, Some Have Not [by Wright and Forrest]
Twenty-Two Years [by Yeston]

AT THE GRAND[†], a lugubrious operetta from the KISMET [Notables: December 3, 1953] boys, opened in Los Angeles on July 7, 1958. Paul Muni starred in the Lionel Barrymore role, with the director's wife Joan Diener Marre as Greta Garbo. Two months later THE GRAND closed its doors—but not forever. The piece unaccountably resurfaced in Boston, twenty-one years later, as GRAND HOTEL. When the tryout proved turbulent, director Tommy Tune called in Yeston (from NINE [May 9, 1982])—over vehement protests from Wright and Forrest—to revise and supplement the score. The book was similarly overhauled, without credit, by Peter Stone. After all of which the show remained lugubrious, despite some dynamically stylish staging (with vestiges of FOLLIES [Sondheim: April 4, 1971] and CABARET [Kander: November 20, 1966] abounding). The producers proclaimed GRAND HOTEL "The Mega-Hit of the '90s!," although it was long gone by the summer of '92.

PHANTOM
January 25, 1991
Theatre Under the Stars {Houston} •
     Regional tryout
"The American Musical Sensation." Book by Arthur Kopit (based on *Phantom of the Opera* [novel] by Gaston Leroux); Directed by Charles Abbott; Produced by Theatre Under the Stars (Frank Young and John Holly); With Richard White, Glory Crampton, Jack Dabdoub, and Patti Alinson.

Songs Published in Vocal Selection
*Home
Mélodie de Paris
My True Love
This Place Is Mine
You Are Music
You Are My Own

Additional Songs Recorded
As You Would Love Paree
Dressing for the Night
The Music Lessons/Phantom Fugue
My Mother Bore Me
Paree Is a Lark
Paris Is a Tomb
Sing
Where in the World
Who Could Ever Have Dreamed up You
Without Your Music

Negotiating stage rights to a popular novel or play is often difficult and sometimes impossible, while public domain material requires no permissions whatsoever. The problem with public domain, though, is that it's so damn public; you always run the risk that somebody else will get the same idea and beat you to it. Geoffrey Holder approached Yeston and Peter Stone in the fall of 1983 with his idea for PHANTOM and the rights to the novel. The *American* rights to the novel, that is—turns out it was already in the public domain in England. On October 9, 1986, the Andrew Lloyd Webber/Harold Prince/Cameron Mackintosh version of PHANTOM OF THE OPERA† opened in London; so much for Maury Yeston and librettist Arthur Kopit (who had replaced Stone). PHANTOM languished, although Kopit was able to cash in with a 1990 NBC mini-series version. At which point a Houston regional theatre offered to mount the American PHANTOM. (There was yet another version floating around the country just then, also from England, by Ken Hill.) The Yeston PHANTOM did rather well in Houston, leading to a string of regional productions—although Broadway remains out of the question while Lloyd Webber's masked man remains in town. The most surprising thing about this twisted PHANTOM tale is that Yeston's score is actually far more tuneful than you-know-who's. Songs like *Home* and *Mélodie de Paris* stand out individually, but much of the music weaves an enchanting spell (though suffering from a few embarrassing patches of lyrics).

TITANIC
April 23, 1997
Lunt-Fontanne Theatre • 804 performances

Book by Peter Stone; Directed by Richard Jones; Choreographed by Lynne Taylor-Corbett; Produced by Dodger Endemol Theatricals, Richard S. Pechter, and The John F. Kennedy Center for the Performing Arts; With Michael Cerveris, David Garrison, John Cunningham, Victoria Clark, Judith Blazer, and Brian d'Arcy James.

Published Songs
*Autumn
Godspeed Titanic (Sail On)

Additional Songs Published in Vocal Selection
Barrett's Song
Doing the Latest Rag
How Did They Build Titanic?
I Have Danced
I Must Get on That Ship
In Every Age
Lady's Maid
The Night Was Alive
**No Moon (Sailing)*
The Proposal
Still
There She Is
To Be a Captain
We'll Meet Tomorrow

Additional Songs Recorded
The Blame
Canons
Dressed in Your Pyjamas in the Grand Salon
The First Class Roster
Getting in the Lifeboat
Hymn
The Largest Moving Object
Loading Inventory
Mr. Andrews' Vision
The Staircase
Wake up, Wake Up!
What a Remarkable Age This Is!

A musical about the sinking of the Titanic is bound to be either a hit or a flop of Titanic dimensions. The worthy-but-flawed TITANIC managed to skirt an enormous critical iceberg, took advantage of fair trade winds (which scuttled the competition), and worked itself into a sea-worthy audience pleaser—although within two years the producers gave up the ship, in a sea of red ink. The high-water mark of the piece was, not surprisingly, Yeston's bounteous score (despite being a bit bloated at times, and suffering from a few embarrassing patches of lyrics). A Herculean and admirable effort nonetheless, with *Autumn, No Moon, Lady's Maid, We'll Meet Tomorrow*, and the momentous opening scene standing out.

Two musicals in fifteen years is not anybody's idea of a satisfying Broadway career, but Yeston —with little more than NINE [May 9, 1982] and TITANIC [April 23, 1997] to show for his efforts—must clearly be considered an important Broadway composer (although he is a couple of notches below some of his lyric-writing contemporaries). After a series of unfortunate derailments, the success of TITANIC seems finally to have put his career on track. It is to be hoped and expected that he take advantage of the situation and forge ahead. Success or failure are never guaranteed in this business; but whatever Yeston might come up with, NINE and TITANIC (as well as PHANTOM and his GRAND HOTEL contributions) indicate that the man is incapable of writing a score that is less than intelligent and interesting.

STEPHEN FLAHERTY

Born: September 18, 1960, Pittsburgh, Pennsylvania

STEPHEN FLAHERTY decided on a career in the musical theatre early on, when he saw a local production of GODSPELL [S. Schwartz: May 17, 1971]. While attending the Cincinnati College Conservatory of Music, he was invited by Lehman Engel to join the BMI Workshop. Flaherty moved to New York in 1982, just after Engel's death, and began working the following year with Lynn Ahrens, a writer/producer of children's television shows. The pair's early BMI work drew an avid supporter in Ira Weitzman, the musical theatre program director at Playwrights Horizons. After writing a one-act children's musical version of "The Emperor's New Clothes" for Theatreworks, U.S.A., Flaherty and Ahrens undertook a project for Playwrights Horizons.

LUCKY STIFF
April 26, 1988
Playwrights Horizons {Off Off Broadway} •
    15 performances
Book and Lyrics by Lynn Ahrens (based on
The Man Who Broke the Bank at Monte Carlo
[novel] by Michael Butterworth); Directed by
Thommie Walsh; Produced by Playwrights
Horizons (André Bishop); With Stephen Stout,
Julie White, Mary Testa, and Paul Kandel.

Songs Published in Vocal Selection
Dogs versus You
Fancy Meeting You Here
Good to Be Alive
Lucky
Nice
The Phone Call
Rita's Confession
Something Funny's Going On
Times Like This

Additional Songs Recorded
Him, Them, It, Her
Mr. Witherspoon's Friday Night
Monte Carlo!
Uncle's Last Request
Welcome Back, Mr. Witherspoon (The Nightmare)

The macabre LUCKY STIFF attracted little attention during its brief limited run. A 1994 studio cast album demonstrated that Flaherty and Ahrens's first score was a tuneful, black comedy delight. Most impressive were the refreshingly outlandish plot numbers, like *Rita's Confession*, the opening number *Something Funny's Going On*, and *Welcome Back, Mr. Witherspoon*. The gentler songs—*Fancy Meeting You Here, Times Like This* (a tender ballad about a girl's best friend)—were also pleasing, if less expert. But the long-forgotten LUCKY STIFF marked an auspicious beginning. Flaherty and Ahrens clearly showed promise right from the beginning, although it would be a decade before their breakthrough show broke through. Another early project, ANTLER†—with a libretto by George C. Wolfe —went unfinished.

ONCE ON THIS ISLAND
April 6, 1990
Playwrights Horizons {Off Off Broadway} •
    60 performances
October 18, 1990
Booth Theatre • 469 performances
Book and Lyrics by Lynn Ahrens (based on
My Love, My Love [novel] by Rosa Guy);
Directed and Choreographed by Graciela
Daniele; Produced by The Shubert Organization, Capital Cities/ABC Inc., Suntory International Corp., and James Walsh in association

with Playwrights Horizons (André Bishop);
With La Chanze, Sheila Gibbs, Jerry Dixon,
Ellis E. Williams, and Kecia Lewis-Evans.

Songs Published in Vocal Selection

*Forever Yours
The Human Heart
*Mama Will Provide
Rain
*Some Girls
Ti Moune
*Waiting for Life
We Dance

Additional Songs Recorded

And the Gods Heard Her Prayer
*Come down from the Tree—cut
One Small Girl
A Part of Us
Pray
The Sad Tale of the Beauxhommes
Some Say
When Daniel Marries—cut
Why We Tell the Story

Ahrens and Flaherty came to Broadway with
ONCE ON THIS ISLAND, which was also developed at Playwrights Horizons. ISLAND was a
pastoral story with a Caribbean beat, far more
lyrical than the brash LUCKY STIFF [April 26,
1988]. I personally found the piece's artsy, story
theatre–like production off-putting from the very
first number—so much so that that I failed to
appreciate the worthy score that followed. (And
I'm not the only one; the show limped along for a
season but never did find much of an audience.)
Flaherty provided two melodic love songs, *Some
Girls* and the duet *Forever Yours*, as well as two
energetic character numbers, *Waiting for Life* and
the show-stopping *Mama Will Provide*. More
important, the composer/lyricist team demonstrated a growing skill at expressing narrative in
music, with *Rain*—which ably illustrates the action—and *The Sad Tale of the Beauxhommes*, an
impressive expository history in song. There was
also a very special cut song, the lovely and exceedingly moving *Come down from the Tree*.

MY FAVORITE YEAR

December 10, 1992
Vivian Beaumont Theatre • 37 performances
Lyrics by Lynn Ahrens; Book by Joseph

Dougherty (based on the screenplay by
Norman Steinberg and Dennis Palumbo);
Directed by Ron Lagomarsino; Choreographed
by Thommie Walsh; Produced by Lincoln
Center Theater (André Bishop); With Evan
Pappas, Tim Curry, Lainie Kazan, Josh Mostel,
and Andrea Martin.

Songs Published in Vocal Selection

Funny
If the World Were Like the Movies
Larger Than Life
Manhattan
My Favorite Year
Professional Showbizness Comedy
Rookie in the Ring
Shut up and Dance
Twenty Million People
Welcome to Brooklyn

Additional Songs Recorded

Exits
The Duck Joke
Gospel According to King
The King Kaiser Comedy Cavalcade
The Lights Come Up
Maxford House
The Musketeer Sketch
Naked in Bethesda Fountain

Even before the Playwrights Horizons production of ONCE ON THIS ISLAND, Flaherty and
Ahrens had written their first full-blown musical comedy. MY FAVORITE YEAR was scheduled for a January 8, 1991, première as part of
the New Musicals season, on a subscription series
with KISS OF THE SPIDER WOMAN [1990]:
[Kander: May 1, 1990]. SPIDER WOMAN was the
kiss of death for New Musicals, though, strand-
ing both MY FAVORITE YEAR and THE SE-
CRET GARDEN [Notables: April 25, 1991]. In
the meanwhile, though, Playwrights Horizons
André Bishop had become Artistic Director of
Lincoln Center Theater. He quickly snapped up
Flaherty and Ahrens' orphan and gave it a full-
scale, first-class mounting. The show wasn't
quite workable, though. MY FAVORITE YEAR
told of a week back in 1954 when an over-the-
top ex-movie star (like Errol Flynn) guested on
a top-rated live television comedy hour (like Sid
Caesar's), as seen through the eyes of a resident
comedy writer (like Mel Brooks, who produced

the 1982 film on which the musical was based). Of course, the stage version of MY FAVORITE YEAR did not have Errol Flynn, Sid Caesar, or Mel Brooks in attendance, and the controlled insanity of *Your Show of Shows* was not so easily manufactured. (Only Broadway newcomer Andrea Martin was able to pull it off, as an Imogene Coca–like comedy writer.) The score was fashioned to sound like it came from a 1950s musical comedy, but it was more HAZEL FLAGG [Styne: February 11, 1953] than THE PAJAMA GAME [Adler: May 13, 1954] and especially weak in its attempts at musicalized Sid Caesar. Nice bits of melody came through in places—*If the World Were Like the Movies, Larger Than Life, Rookie in the Ring*—but most of the score missed. Following the failure of MY FAVORITE YEAR, Ahrens received an offer she couldn't refuse and temporarily parted with Flaherty for Madison Square Garden's A CHRISTMAS CAROL [Menken: December 1, 1994].

PROPOSALS
November 6, 1997
Broadhurst Theatre • 76 performances
Play by Neil Simon; Incidental music by Flaherty; Directed by Joe Mantello; Produced by Emanuel Azenberg; With L. Scott Caldwell, Dick Latessa, Kelly Bishop, and Suzanne Cryer.

Songs Published
None

While waiting for the Broadway première of RAGTIME [January 18, 1998]—which had already established itself as a major hit during its pre-Broadway stands in Toronto and Los Angeles—Flaherty and Ahrens wrote the score for the 1997 animated movie musical *Anastasia*. Flaherty also contributed atmospheric incidental music for Neil Simon's short-lived PROPOSALS.

RAGTIME
January 18, 1998
Ford Center • Still playing April 4, 1999
Lyrics by Lynn Ahrens; Book by Terrence McNally (based on the novel by E. L. Doctorow); Directed by Frank Galati; Choreographed by

Graciela Daniele; Produced by Livent (U.S.) Inc. (Garth Drabinsky); With Brian Stokes Mitchell, Peter Friedman, Marin Mazzie, Audra McDonald, Mark Jacoby, and Judy Kaye.

Published Song
Ragtime

Additional Songs Published in Vocal Selection
Back to Before
Buffalo Nickel Photoplay, Inc.
Gliding
Goodbye, My Love
Make Them Hear You
New Music
Our Children
Sarah Brown Eyes
'Till We Reach That Day
Wheels of a Dream
Your Daddy's Son

Additional Songs Recorded
Atlantic City
Coalhouse Demands
Coalhouse's Soliloquy
The Crime of the Century
Gettin' Ready Rag
Harry Houdini, Master Escapist
He Wanted to Say
Henry Ford
His Name Was Coalhouse Walker
I Have a Feeling—cut; recorded in instrumental version
Journey On
Justice
Look What You've Done
The Night That Goldman Spoke in Union Square
Nothing Like the City
President
The Show Biz—cut
A Shtetl Iz Amereke
Success
What a Game!
What Kind of Woman

Flaherty and Ahrens finally arrived in the big time with RAGTIME, the most heralded new musical in two months. Unfortunately for producer Garth Drabinsky, the sound of RAGTIME was somewhat drowned out by the roar of THE LION KING [Notables: November 13, 1997], putting a crimp in Livent's plans of dominating Broadway and the road and the world with the hit of the century. RAGTIME was good enough to stand on its own, certainly, despite some flaws and weaknesses; the production was expertly assembled and bursting with talent, though the overall effect was one of high-gloss craft at the expense of art and heart. THE LION KING was not all perfect, of course, and clearly inferior to RAGTIME in score, book, and star performances. But the Disney show rooted audiences to their seats, while the Livent show was merely very good. It is unfair, perhaps, to judge RAGTIME by comparing it with its neighbor; if it had come along a year or even six months earlier, it no doubt would have been universally lauded and applauded. But it's hard to build an empire when the hottest ticket in town is at the box office across the street.

It is too early to assess Stephen Flaherty's Broadway career; he has only just finally arrived. His first musical, LUCKY STIFF [April 26, 1988], displayed his knack for comedy and narrative composing; the second, ONCE ON THIS ISLAND [April 6, 1990], hinted at a strong and sometimes glorious melodic gift; and MY FAVORITE YEAR [December 10, 1992] gave him a chance to learn from his mistakes. The lessons all paid off admirably with RAGTIME [January 18, 1998], which despite its disappointing reception has a fine score which will surely prove enduring and endearing over the years. As the new century begins, Flaherty is perhaps in the best position of all his peers: he appears to have the ability and capability to write whatever he pleases, and whatever he writes—for now—is sure to be produced. The same can be said for Stephen Sondheim, of course; but Sondheim, who is in some ways Broadway's "youngest" composer, is approaching seventy. The other composers still active—John Kander, Cy Coleman, Charles Strouse, Harvey Schmidt— are all *older* than Sondheim. Flaherty is the youngest composer discussed in *Show Tunes*; he and Billy Finn (who is eight years older) are the only two born since 1950. So Broadway eagerly waits and looks forward to Mr. Flaherty's future efforts.

PART IV

Notable Scores by Other Composers

Since the 1920s, a core group of composers—from Kern and Berlin, to Gershwin, Porter and Rodgers, to Styne, Sondheim, Strouse, and Kander—has been responsible for the vast majority of America's great musicals. The following section contains notable shows by other composers which merit discussion. Some were enormous hits and are included for that reason only; others were written by popular or interesting composers who never found Broadway success; and a handful are included simply due to the high quality of the work.

IRENE   387

SHUFFLE ALONG   387

GEORGE WHITE'S SCANDALS OF 1926   388

GOOD NEWS!   388

BLACKBIRDS OF 1928   389

WHOOPEE   389

FINE AND DANDY   390

WALK WITH MUSIC   390

EARLY TO BED   391

BEGGAR'S HOLIDAY   391

FLAHOOLEY   392

TOP BANANA   392

KISMET   393

THE GOLDEN APPLE   394

PLAIN AND FANCY   394

LI'L ABNER   395

GOLDILOCKS   396

REDHEAD   396

ONCE UPON A MATTRESS   397

YOU'RE A GOOD MAN, CHARLIE BROWN   397

JACQUES BREL IS ALIVE AND WELL AND LIVING IN PARIS   398

HAIR   399

PROMISES, PROMISES   400

1776   400

PROMENADE   401

PURLIE   402

GREASE   402

THE WIZ   403

SHENANDOAH   403

THE ROBBER BRIDEGROOM   404

THE BEST LITTLE WHOREHOUSE IN TEXAS   404

DREAMGIRLS   405

BABY   405

BIG RIVER   406

THE SECRET GARDEN   406

JELLY'S LAST JAM   407

VICTOR/VICTORIA   408

FLOYD COLLINS   408

BRING IN 'DA NOISE, BRING
    IN 'DA FUNK   409

BIG   409

RENT   410

JEKYLL & HYDE   411

SIDE SHOW   412

THE LION KING   413

SATURN RETURNS: A CONCERT   413

PARADE   414

IRENE
November 1, 1919
Vanderbilt Theatre • 675 performances
Music by Harry Tierney; Lyrics by Joseph
McCarthy; Book by James Montgomery;
Directed by Edward Royce; Produced by
Vanderbilt Producing Corp.; With Edith
Day.

Revival
March 13, 1973
Minskoff Theatre • 594 performances
Additional songs by Charles Gaynor and
others; (New) book by Hugh Wheeler and
Joseph Stein; Directed by Gower Champion;
Choreographed by Peter Gennaro; With
Debbie Reynolds [Day], Patsy Kelly, Monte
Markham, and George S. Irving.

Published Songs
Alice Blue Gown
Castle of Dreams
The Family Tree [additional lyric by Charles
    Gaynor]—initial publication upon use in
    revival
Hobbies
Irene
Irene Valse [instrumental]—non-song version
The Last Part of Ev'ry Party
The "Paul Jones"
Skyrocket
Talk of the Town
To Be Worthy (Worthy of You)
We're Getting Away with It
You've Got Me out on a Limb—written for 1940
    movie version

Additional Songs Published in Vocal
    Score
To Love You—countermelody to *To Be Worthy*
*Too Much Bowden (Opening Chorus Act 2,
    Scene 2)*

Harry Tierney (1895–1965) was one of many Tin
Pan Alley composers who made occasional Broad-
way visits. His first and most successful effort,
IRENE, set the mold for the "American Cinderella" musicals. (The Shuberts, ever on the lookout for a catchy title, actually came up with
SALLY, IRENE & MARY† [September 4, 1922];
SALLY being Kern's [December 21, 1920] and
MARY† [October 18, 1920] being Louis Hirsch's
Love Nest musical.) IRENE waltzed to a record-
length run in her *Alice Blue Gown*, unsurpassed
until the Depression-era PINS AND NEEDLES
[Rome: November 27, 1937] set a new mark of
1,108. Tierney and McCarthy wrote two other
moderately successful shows, both for Ziegfeld:
Eddie Cantor's KID BOOTS† [December 31, 1923]
and RIO RITA† [February 2, 1927].

SHUFFLE ALONG
May 23, 1921
63rd Street Music Hall • 484 performances
"A Musical Melange." Music by Eubie Blake;
Lyrics by Noble Sissle; Book by Flournoy
Miller and Aubrey Lyles; Conceived by
Flournoy Miller and Aubrey Lyles; Directed
by Flournoy Miller; Produced by Nikko
Producing Co.; With Eubie Blake, Noble Sissle,
Flournoy Miller, Aubrey Lyles, and Florence
Mills.

Published Songs
Aintcha Comin' Back, Mary Ann, to Maryland
Baltimore Buzz
Bandana Days
Daddy Won't You Please Come Home
Everything Reminds Me of You
Gypsy Blues
Good Night, Angeline [by Jim Europe, Sissle,
    and Blake]—originally issued as 1919 non-
    show song

If You've Never Been Vamped by a Brown Skin
  (*You've Never Been Vamped at All*)
I'm Craving for That Kind of Love (*Kiss Me*)
I'm Just Simply Full of Jazz
I'm Just Wild about Harry—new melody for
  lyric revised from 1916 non-show song *My
  Loving Baby*
In Honeysuckle Time (*When Emaline Said She'd
  Be Mine*)
Kentucky Sue
Love Will Find a Way
Liza Quit Vamping Me—advertised but not
  published
Low Down Blues
Old Black Joe and Uncle Tom
Oriental Blues
Pickaninny Shoes
Shuffle Along
Sing Me to Sleep Dear Mammy (*With a Hush-a-
  Bye Pickaninny Tune*)
Vision Girl—originally used in MIDNIGHT
  ROUNDERS[†] [July 12, 1920]

Note: Various songs cut or added after opening.

This shoestring revue set a standard for rag-tag
black musicals. A surprise hit, SHUFFLE
ALONG outran most Broadway musicals of the
time and toured for many years. Two revised
versions [December 26, 1932] and [May 8,
1952]—both headed by Sissle and Blake—
lasted only twenty-one performances combined. Eubie Blake (1883–1983) had no success
with his other Broadway work, including the
anthology revue EUBIE![†] [September 20, 1978]
which attempted to cash in on the overflow
business from the Fats Waller anthology AIN'T
MISBEHAVIN'[†] [May 8, 1978].

GEORGE WHITE'S SCANDALS OF 1926 ✦ Eighth Edition
June 14, 1926
Apollo Theatre • 432 performances
Music by Ray Henderson; Lyrics by B. G.
DeSylva and Lew Brown; Sketches by George
White and W. K. Wells; Directed and Pro-
duced by George White; With Ann
Pennington, Willie and Eugene Howard, and
Harry Richman.

Published Songs
**The Birth of the Blues*
*Black Bottom
The Girl Is You and the Boy Is Me
Here I Am—added after opening; published in
  separate edition
*It All Depends on You—added after opening;
  published in separate edition
Lucky Day
Sevilla
Tweet Tweet

Ray Henderson (1896–1970) established himself
on Tin Pan Alley with song hits like *That Old Gang
of Mine* and *Bye Bye Blackbird*. When George
Gershwin left the SCANDALS after the Sixth Edition [June 30, 1924] to concentrate on book musicals, White joined Henderson with pop lyricist
Lew Brown (1893–1958) and Gershwin's SCAN-
DALS collaborator Buddy DeSylva (1895–1950).
Thus was born the most successful songwriting
team of the late 1920s. The 1926 edition of the
SCANDALS alone had four hits, all of them quite
good: *Black Bottom*—which launched a dance
craze—*Lucky Day*, *It All Depends on You* (*I Can
Be Happy, I Can Be Blue*), and the extra-special
Birth of the Blues. Gershwin's five editions had
brought forth only two worthwhile songs, *I'll
Build a Stairway to Paradise* and *Somebody Loves
Me*—both with DeSylva lyrics.

GOOD NEWS!
September 6, 1927
Chanin's 46th Street Theatre •
  551 performances
"The Collegiate Musical." Music by Ray
Henderson; Lyrics by B. G. DeSylva and Lew
Brown; Book by Laurence Schwab and B. G.
DeSylva; Directed by Edgar MacGregor;
Choreographed by Bobby Connolly; Produced
by Laurence Schwab and Frank Mandel; With
Mary Lawlor, John Price Jones, Zelma O'Neal,
and George Olsen and His Orchestra.

Revival
December 23, 1974
St. James Theatre • 16 performances
Adaptation by Garry Marshall; Directed by
Michael Kidd; With Alice Faye, Gene Nelson,
and Stubby Kaye.

Published Songs
*The Best Things in Life Are Free
A Girl of the Pi Beta Phi
Good News
Happy Days
He's a Ladies' Man
Just Imagine
Lucky in Love
*The Varsity Drag

Additional Songs Published in Vocal Score
Baby! What?
Flaming Youth
In the Meantime
On the Campus
Tait Song
Today's the Day

DeSylva, Brown, and Henderson entered the book musical field with five consecutive hits. Following the Bert Lahr vehicle FLYING HIGH† [March 3, 1930], the team went to Hollywood—where the ambitious DeSylva ended up running Paramount Studios (see DUBARRY WAS A LADY [Porter: December 6, 1939]). Henderson and Brown continued writing (together and individually) but never equaled the success of D., B., & H. GOOD NEWS! was a mindless football musical in the LEAVE IT TO JANE [Kern: August 28, 1917] tradition; The Best Things in Life Are Free and The Varsity Drag were hits in the DeSylva, Brown, and Henderson tradition.

BLACKBIRDS OF 1928
May 9, 1928
Liberty Theatre • 519 performances
Music by Jimmy McHugh; Lyrics by Dorothy Fields; Directed and Produced by Lew Leslie; With Bill Robinson, Adelaide Hall, and Aida Ward.

Published Songs
Baby!
Bandanna Babies
Diga-Diga-Doo
Dixie
Doin' the New Low Down
Here Comes My Blackbird
**I Can't Give You Anything but Love

I Must Have That Man!
Magnolia's Wedding Day
Porgy
Shuffle Your Feet and Roll Along

Pop songwriter Jimmy McHugh (1894–1969) began contributing material to Harlem's Cotton Club in 1921. In 1927 he found a new lyricist: Dorothy Fields, daughter of Lew and sister of Herb. Cotton Club work got them the assignment for the successful BLACKBIRDS OF 1928. The score brought McHugh and Fields immediate acclaim, with I Can't Give You Anything but Love and Diga-Diga-Doo leading the way. Following LEW LESLIE'S INTERNATIONAL REVUE† [February 25, 1930], which was a quick failure but included *On the Sunny Side of the Street, Fields and McHugh moved to Hollywood. The team did quite well—with songs like *I'm in the Mood for Love—until Jerome Kern needed a lyric for a new song added to the 1935 movie version of ROBERTA [November 18, 1933]. Fields got the assignment and the pair came up with Lovely to Look At. (As Fields and McHugh were signed as a team, McHugh shared lyricist credit.) Kern immediately took Fields as his partner for films like the 1936 Swing Time. McHugh continued writing for Broadway and Hollywood for another twenty-five years, but never as memorably or successfully as he had with Fields.

WHOOPEE
December 4, 1928
New Amsterdam Theatre • 255 performances
Music mostly by Walter Donaldson; Lyrics mostly by Gus Kahn; Book and Direction by Wm. Anthony McGuire (based on The Nervous Wreck [play] by Owen Davis); Produced by Florenz Ziegfeld, Jr.; With Eddie Cantor, Ruth Etting, and George Olsen and His Orchestra.

Revival
February 14, 1979
ANTA Theatre • 204 performances
Directed by Frank Corsaro; Choreographed by Dan Siretta; Transferred from Goodspeed Opera House; With Charles Repole [Cantor].

Published Songs
Come West, Little Girl, Come West
A Girl Friend of a Boy Friend of Mine—written
    for 1930 movie version
Gypsy Joe
The Gypsy Song (*Where Sunset Meets the Sea*)
Here's to the Girl of My Heart!
I'm Bringing a Red, Red Rose
*Love Me or Leave Me
*Makin' Whoopee!
My Baby Just Cares for Me—written for movie
    version
The Song of the Setting Sun
Until You Get Somebody Else

Walter Donaldson (1893–1947) was another top
Tin Pan Alley composer, with hits like *How Ya
Gonna Keep 'Em Down on the Farm?*, **My Blue
Heaven*, and Al Jolson's *My Mammy*. Although
he occasionally contributed interpolations to
Broadway shows, his only full stage score was
this Flo Ziegfeld/Eddie Cantor hit. Donaldson's
popular touch was evident in *Makin' Whoopee!*
and *Love Me or Leave Me*.

FINE AND DANDY
September 23, 1930
Erlanger Theatre • 255 performances
Music by Kay Swift; Lyrics by Paul James;
Book by Donald Ogden Stewart; "Many
Nonsensical Moments Created by Joe Cook";
Directed by Morris Green; Produced by
Morris Green and Lewis Gensler; With Joe
Cook, Nell O'Day, Dave Chasen, and Eleanor
Powell.

Published Songs
**Can This Be Love?
*Fine and Dandy
The Jig Hop
Let's Go Eat Worms in the Garden
Nobody Breaks My Heart
Rich or Poor
Starting at the Bottom

A handful of female lyricists have been success-
ful in the theatre, starting with Anne Caldwell (of
SHE'S A GOOD FELLOW [Kern: May 5, 1919]),
Dorothy Donnelly (of Romberg's THE STUDENT
PRINCE[†] [December 2, 1924]), and Dorothy Fields.
But for some unaccountable reason, almost no
women composers have had success on Broadway.
Kay Swift (1907–93) made a promising start with
notable interpolations in THE LITTLE SHOW
[Schwartz: April 30, 1929] and NINE-FIFTEEN
REVUE [Arlen: February 11, 1930]. (Earlier, she
had served as rehearsal pianist for A CONNECTI-
CUT YANKEE [Rodgers: November 3, 1927].)
Her first and only book musical was FINE AND
DANDY, with one of the best scores of the sea-
son. She then left her lyricist-husband Paul James
(Warburg) and put her career on hold to become
involved (personally and artistically) with George
Gershwin. Her only return to Broadway was with
songs for Cornelia Otis Skinner's one-woman
PARIS '90[†] [March 4, 1952]. But back in 1929–30,
Swift composed three extra-special songs: **Can't
We Be Friends?* (from THE LITTLE SHOW), *Can
This Be Love?*, and the dandy *Fine and Dandy*.
Other early women composers included Alma
Sanders (who wrote a string of unimportant pre-
Depression musicals with lyricist-husband Monte
Carlo) and Ann Ronell, another Gershwin protégé
best known for her lyric to the 1933 *Who's Afraid
of the Big Bad Wolf?* In more recent times, Mary
Rodgers and Carol Hall were both successful with
transfers from Off Broadway's old Yiddish Art
(Phoenix/Entermedia) Theatre, ONCE UPON A
MATTRESS [Notables: May 11, 1959] and THE
BEST LITTLE WHOREHOUSE IN TEXAS [No-
tables: April 17, 1978]. The nineties began with
another impressive debut, Lucy Simon with THE
SECRET GARDEN [Notables: April 25, 1991].

WALK WITH MUSIC
June 4, 1940
Ethel Barrymore Theatre • 55 performances
Music mostly by Hoagy Carmichael; Lyrics
mostly by Johnny Mercer; Book by Guy
Bolton, Parke Levy, and Alan Prescott (based
on *Three Blind Mice* [play] by Stephen Powys
[aka Virginia De Lanty, Mrs. Guy Bolton]);
Directed by Clarke Lilley; Produced by Ruth
Selwyn in association with the Messrs.
Shubert; With Kitty Carlisle, Mitzi Green, Jack
Whiting and Stepin' Fetchit. Pre-Broadway
title: THREE AFTER THREE.

Published Songs
Darn Clever, These Chinee—advertised but not
    published

Everything Happens to Me—advertised but not published

How Nice for Me—issued in professional copy only

I Walk with Music

Ooh! What You Said

The Rumba Jumps!

Way Back in 1939 A.D.

What'll They Think of Next

Additional Songs Published [with Non-Mercer Lyric Revisions] in USO's *At Ease*

Break It Up, Cinderella—retitled *Break It Now, Buck Private*

Wait till You See Me in the Morning

Hoagy Carmichael (1899–1981) was one of America's finest (and most unique) melodists. His credits include such fascinating stunners as **Stardust*, **Lazy River*, **Georgia on My Mind*, and **How Little We Know*. A prewar Hollywood collaboration with Frank Loesser turned out hits like *Two Sleepy People* and *Heart and Soul* (which is second only to *Chopsticks* in popularity with piano duelists). His periodic work with Johnny Mercer resulted in *Lazy Bones* and the 1951 Oscar winner *In the Cool, Cool, Cool of the Evening*. WALK WITH MUSIC, Carmichael's only complete score, was a quick failure; his one Broadway song hit was *Little Old Lady* [lyric by Stanley Adams], interpolated into THE SHOW IS ON [Duke: December 25, 1936].

EARLY TO BED
June 17, 1943
Broadhurst Theatre • 380 performances
Music by Thomas (Fats) Waller; Book and Lyrics by George Marion, Jr.; Directed and Choreographed by Robert Alton; Produced by Richard Kollmar and Alfred Bloomingdale; With Richard Kollmar, Muriel Angelus, and Mary Small.

Published Songs
The Ladies Who Sing with a Band
Slightly Less Than Wonderful
There's a Man in My Life
This Is So Nice
When the Nylons Bloom Again—issued as professional copy only

Additional Song Recorded
Hi-De-Ho-Hi

Fats Waller (1904–43) was a jazz pianist/singer with a distinctive style and overloaded personality. One of his very few Broadway visits brought *Ain't Misbehavin'*, from the revue HOT CHOCOLATES [June 20, 1929]. Waller's other complete Broadway score was for the book musical EARLY TO BED, a mediocre wartime hit which opened shortly before the composer's death. An anthology revue of his work, AIN'T MISBEHAVIN' [May 8, 1978], was an award-winning, long-running hit.

BEGGAR'S HOLIDAY
December 26, 1946
Broadway Theatre • 108 performances
Music by Duke Ellington; Book and Lyrics by John Latouche (based on *The Beggar's Opera* by John Gay); Directed by Nicholas Ray; Choreographed by Valerie Bettis; Produced by Perry Watkins and John R. Sheppard, Jr.; With Alfred Drake, Bernice Parks, Marie Bryant, and Zero Mostel.

Published Songs
On the Wrong Side of the Railroad Tracks
Take Love Easy
Tomorrow Mountain
When I Walk with You

Additional Songs Published in Vocal Selection
Brown Penny [instrumental]
I've Got Me—lyric revised for song of same title in BALLET BALLADS [May 9, 1948] (with different music by Jerome Moross)
Maybe I Should Change My Ways
Tooth and Claw
Wanna Be Bad
Where Is My Hero?

Additional Songs Recorded
In Between
Lullaby for Junior
Ore from a Goldmine
The Scrimmage of Life

This ambitious musical was the first book show by bandleader/composer Duke Ellington (1899–

1974). Based on *The Beggar's Opera*—at a time when the Weill/Brecht adaptation was virtually unknown in this country (see THE THREE-PENNY OPERA [1954] [Weill: March 10, 1954])—BEGGAR'S HOLIDAY ran into tryout trouble when star Libby Holman quit. Audiences looking for a happy, black revusical from the Duke were confronted by Zero Mostel's perplexing Poppa Peachum. Ellington came back once more with the *Blue Angel* musical POUSSE-CAFÉ† [March 18, 1966], which lasted three performances. The black composer anthology fad of the late 1970s brought forth a successful Ellington revue, SOPHISTICATED LADIES† [March 1, 1981]. His songbook was also recycled into Shakespeare's *Twelfth Night* as PLAY ON!† [March 20, 1997], with less happy results.

FLAHOOLEY

May 14, 1951
Broadhurst Theatre • 40 performances
Also see JOLLYANNA [*Lane: September 11, 1952*]. Music mostly by Sammy Fain; Lyrics mostly by E. Y. Harburg; Book by E. Y. Harburg and Fred Saidy; Directed by E. Y. Harburg and Fred Saidy; Choreographed by Helen Tamiris; Produced by Cheryl Crawford in association with E. Y. Harburg and Fred Saidy; With Ernest Truex, Yma Sumac, Barbara Cook, Edith Atwater, and Irwin Corey.

Published Songs

Come Back, Little Genie—advertised but not published; recorded
Flahooley
Here's to Your Illusions
He's Only Wonderful
How Lucky Can You Get?—written for revised 1952 version, JOLLYANNA
*The Springtime Cometh
Who Says There Ain't No Santa Claus?—issued as professional copy
The World Is Your Balloon

Additional Songs Recorded

B. G. Bigelow, Inc.
Birds [music and lyric by Moises Vivanco]
Come Back, Little Genie
Happy Hunting

Jump, Little Chillun!
Najla's Lament [music and lyric by Vivanco]
Najla's Song of Joy [music and lyric by Vivanco]
Scheherazade
Sing the Merry
The Spirit of Capsulanti
*You, Too, Can Be a Puppet

Successful Hollywood composer Sammy Fain (1902–89) made eight Broadway visits during his career, all failures. The unconventional FLAHOOLEY stands out for its above-average score and outspoken intentions. In FINIAN'S RAINBOW [Lane: January 10, 1947], Yip Harburg slyly cloaked his social commentary with humor; but he found less to laugh at during the witch-hunt days of FLAHOOLEY. (He could, though, provide the lyrically dazzling *You, Too, Can Be a Puppet* and the sprightly *Springtime Cometh*.) Cheryl Crawford once again gambled on an intelligent, uncommercial musical and paid the price.

TOP BANANA

November 1, 1951
Winter Garden Theatre • 350 performances
Music and Lyrics by Johnny Mercer; Book by H. S. Kraft; Directed by Jack Donohue; Choreographed by Ron Fletcher; Produced by Paula Stone and Mike Sloane; With Phil Silvers, Rose Marie, Joey Faye, and Bob Scheerer.

Published Songs

Be My Guest
My Home Is in My Shoes
O.K. for T.V.
Only If You're in Love
Sans Souci
That's for Sure
Top Banana

Additional Songs Recorded

A Dog Is a Man's Best Friend
The Elevator Song (Going Up)
I Fought Every Step of the Way
The Man of the Year This Week
Meet Miss Blendo
Slogan Song
A Word a Day
You're So Beautiful That . . .

Exceptional pop lyricist Johnny Mercer (1909–76) wrote his own music on occasion, including such songs as *I'm an Old Cowhand* and *Something's Gotta Give*. With TOP BANANA he tried an entire score on his own, with mixed results. The rag-tag burlesque show featured Phil Silvers, a handful of clowns, and a dog named Ted "Sport" Morgan (who sang an inspired duet with Silvers)—all rather more enjoyable than distinguished. TOP BANANA was produced by Paula Stone (see RIPPLES [Kern: February 11, 1930]) and her husband, Mike Sloane.

KISMET
December 3, 1953
Ziegfeld Theatre • 583 performances
"A Musical Arabian Night." Music by Alexander Borodin; Musical adaptation and Lyrics by Robert Wright and George Forrest; Book by Charles Lederer and Luther Davis (based on the play by Edward Knoblock); Choreographed by Jack Cole; Directed by Albert Marre; Produced by Charles Lederer; With Alfred Drake, Doretta Morrow, Richard Kiley, Joan Diener, and Henry Calvin.

Revival
June 22, 1965
New York State Theatre • 39 performances
Directed by Edward Greenberg; Choreographed by Jack Cole; Produced by Music Theater of Lincoln Center (Richard Rodgers); With Alfred Drake, Lee Venora [Morrow], Anne Jeffreys [Diener], and Henry Calvin.

Revision
As TIMBUKTU: April 1, 1978
Mark Hellinger Theatre • 243 performances
New songs by Robert Wright and George Forrest "from African folk music"; New book by Luther Davis; Produced by Luther Davis; With Eartha Kitt [Diener], Melba Moore [Morrow], Gilbert Price [Kiley], and Ira Hawkins [Drake].

Published Songs
*And This Is My Beloved
*Baubles, Bangles, and Beads
Bored—written for 1955 movie version
He's in Love
Night of My Nights

Sands of Time
*Stranger in Paradise

Additional Song Published in Vocal Selection
Not Since Nineveh

Additional Songs Published in Vocal Score
Fate
Gesticulate
The Olive Tree
Rahadlakum
Rhymes Have I
Was I Wazir?
Zubbediya [instrumental]

Additional Songs Published in Vocal Selection for TIMBUKTU
Golden Land, Golden Life [music and lyric by Wright and Forrest]—written for TIMBUKTU
In the Beginning, Woman [music and lyric by Wright and Forrest]—written for TIMBUKTU
My Magic Lamp—cut from KISMET; revised for TIMBUKTU

Additional Song Recorded
Power [music and lyric by Wright and Forrest]—written for TIMBUKTU

Robert Wright and George Forrest made a career of "borrowing" tunes from dead composers and transferring them into pop operettas. The first, Eddie Grieg's SONG OF NORWAY[†] [August 21, 1944], moved from Los Angeles to Broadway for an 860-performance wartime run. This was followed by quick flops set to Vic Herbert, Frank Lehar, and Brazilian Heitor Villa-Lobos (who was alive, but certainly highbrow). Then came KISMET with tunes by Al Borodin, the only man to win a Tony Award sixty-seven years after he'd kicked off, this thanks to his famous ditty *Stranger in Paradise*, better known—to him, anyway—as a section of the *Polovtsian Dances* from the opera *Prince Igor*. Wright and Forrest then decided it was time to write their own music—or maybe they just ran out of dead composers?—and penned three "original" flops, only one of which even made it to Broadway (the Alfred Drake–starrer KEAN[†] [November 2, 1961]). The boys next turned to the works of Serge Rachmaninoff (d. 1943) for one last floperetta, ANYA[†] [November 29, 1965]. And that was that for a quarter of a century—

when AT THE GRAND† [July 7, 1958], one of their
out-of-town mishaps, was dusted off, overhauled,
and considerably Tuned up under the title GRAND
HOTEL [Yeston: November 12, 1989].

THE GOLDEN APPLE
March 11, 1954
Phoenix Theatre {Off Broadway} •
    46 performances
April 20, 1954
Alvin Theatre • 127 performances
Music by Jerome Moross; Book and Lyrics by
John Latouche (based on *The Odyssey* by
Homer); Directed by Norman Lloyd; Choreo-
graphed by Hanya Holm; Produced by The
Phoenix Theatre (T. Edward Hambleton and
Norris Houghton); With Priscilla Gillette,
Stephen Douglass, Kaye Ballard, Jack Whiting,
and Jonathan Lucas.

Revival
February 12, 1962
York Playhouse {Off Broadway} •
    112 performances
Directed by Robert Turoff; With Jan McArt
[Gillette], Stan Page [Douglass], and Swen
Swenson [Whiting].

Published Songs
Goona-Goona
*It's the Going Home Together
**Lazy Afternoon
Store-Bought Suit
Windflowers—initially issued as *When We
    Were Young*

Additional Songs Recorded
Calypso
Circe, Circe
Come along, Boys (Raise a Ruckus Tonight)
Departure for Rhododendron (1st Act Finale)
Doomed, Doomed, Doomed
Hector's Song (People Like You and Like Me)
Helen Is Always Willing
The Heroes Come Home
It Was a Glad Adventure
Judgement of Paris
Mother Hare's Prophecy
My Love Is on the Way
My Picture in the Papers

Overture [instrumental]
Scylla and Charybdis
Sewing Bee
The Tirade (Finale)
*Ulysses' Soliloquy (Despair Cuts through Me
    Like a Knife)*

Jerome Moross (1913–83) and John Latouche
(1917–56) had first collaborated on BALLET BAL-
LADS† [May 9, 1948], three one-act "dance plays"
which played a seven-week Broadway run.
Moross made his Broadway debut with the radical PARADE [1935] [Blitzstein: May 20, 1935], but
most of his career was spent scoring motion pictures (including his superb work on the 1958
Western *The Big Country*). John Latouche's only
hit show was CABIN IN THE SKY [Duke: October
25, 1940], although his work was typically clever
and literate. His untimely death was the first of the
many obstacles which beset CANDIDE [1956]
[Bernstein: December 1, 1956]. THE GOLDEN
APPLE benefited from imaginative theatricality in
all departments, but it was the more-than-glorious
score that carried this brilliant musical theatre experiment from Off Broadway to the Alvin.

PLAIN AND FANCY
January 27, 1955
Mark Hellinger Theatre • 461 performances
Music by Albert Hague; Lyrics by Arnold B.
Horwitt; Book by Joseph Stein and Will
Glickman; Directed by Morton Da Costa;
Choreographed by Helen Tamiris; Produced
by Richard Kollmar and James W. Gardiner in
association with Yvette Schumer; With
Richard Derr, Barbara Cook, David Daniels,
Shirt Conway, and Nancy Andrews.

Published Songs
City Mouse, Country Mouse
*Follow Your Heart
*It Wonders Me
Plain We Live
Plenty of Pennsylvania
This Is All Very New to Me
*Young and Foolish

Additional Songs Published in Vocal
    Score
How Do You Raise a Barn?

It's a Helluva Way to Run a Love Affair
I'll Show Him
Take Your Time and Take Your Pick
Why Not Katie?
You Can't Miss It

By the mid-1950s, musical comedy had been Abbottized into slick, well-made, slightly satirical laugh machines like WONDERFUL TOWN [Bernstein: February 25, 1953] and THE PAJAMA GAME [Adler: May 13, 1954]. Along came PLAIN AND FANCY, an old-fashioned, low-pressure alternative set among the Pennsylvania Dutch. While the material was no more than adequate, it was pleasant and certainly suitable for the family trade. The show was buoyed by the work of first-time composer Albert Hague, providing some of the loveliest melodies of the season (*It Wonders Me, Young and Foolish, Follow Your Heart*). The moderate success of PLAIN AND FANCY encouraged the mounting of a second slice of folksy Americana, one that had been kicking around since 1951: Meredith Willson's THE MUSIC MAN [December 19, 1957], with Morton Da Costa and Barbara Cook from PLAIN AND FANCY. PLAIN AND FANCY's basic plot —unmarried big-city couple go to small-town U.S.A., observe quaint customs, suffer romantic discord, and patch things up by the final curtain—was also retread, more or less, into the upcoming BYE BYE BIRDIE [Strouse: April 14, 1960].

LI'L ABNER

November 15, 1956
St. James Theatre • 693 performances
Music by Gene de Paul; Lyrics by Johnny Mercer; Book by Norman Panama and Melvin Frank (based on the comic strip by Al Capp); Directed and Choreographed by Michael Kidd; Produced by Norman Panama, Melvin Frank, and Michael Kidd; With Edith Adams, Peter Palmer, Stubby Kaye, and Charlotte Rae.

Concert Version
March 26, 1998
City Center • 5 performances
Directed by Christopher Ashley; Choreographed by Kathleen Marshall; Produced by City Center Encores; With Burke Moses

[Palmer], Alice Ripley [Adams], Lea DeLaria [Kaye], Dick Latessa, and Dana Ivey [Rae].

Published Songs
*If I Had My Druthers
It's a Nuisance Having You Around—cut
*Jubilation T. Cornpone
Love in a Home
*Namely You
Otherwise (I Wish It Could Be)—written for 1959 movie version
Unnecessary Town

Additional Songs Published in Vocal Score
*The Country's in the Very Best of Hands
Dogpatch Dance [instrumental]
*It's a Typical Day
The Matrimonial Stomp
Oh, Happy Day
*Past My Prime
Progress Is the Root of All Evil
Put 'Em Back
Rag Off'n the Bush
*Sadie Hawkins Ballet [instrumental]
There's Room Enough for Us
What's Good for General Bullmoose

Choreographer Michael Kidd came to Broadway with the magical FINIAN'S RAINBOW [Lane: January 10, 1947]. He quickly attained genius status (and three quick Tony Awards) with his work on GUYS AND DOLLS [Loesser: November 24, 1950] and CAN-CAN [Porter: May 7, 1953]. Kidd was in league with Jerome Robbins, setting a new dance style for Broadway. (They were no strangers, either: Kidd and Robbins had played two of the three sailors in the premiere of Robbins's ballet *Fancy Free* (see ON THE TOWN [Bernstein: December 28, 1944]). Kidd went to MGM for their 1953 version of THE BAND WAGON [Schwartz: June 3, 1931], followed by the 1954 movie musical classic *Seven Brides for Seven Brothers*. Kidd then joined *Seven Brides* songwriters Gene de Paul and Johnny Mercer for the exuberant L'IL ABNER. Al Capp's cartoon characters had been looking for a stage role for several years, but Broadway writers like Lerner and Loewe and Lane had given up on them. Kidd and company did just fine, with Mercer providing one of Broadway's best sets of comedy lyrics ever. The choreographer won his fourth Tony and was to receive another for his next musical (DESTRY RIDES AGAIN [Rome: April 23, 1959]). The talented Kidd had nothing but flops thereafter, though.

GOLDILOCKS
October 11, 1958
Lunt-Fontanne Theatre • 161 performances
Music by Leroy Anderson; Lyrics by Joan Ford, Walter and Jean Kerr; Book by Walter and Jean Kerr; Directed by Walter Kerr; Choreographed by Agnes de Mille; Produced by The Producers Theatre and Robert Whitehead; With Don Ameche, Elaine Stritch, Russell Nype, Pat Stanley, Nathaniel Frey, and Margaret Hamilton.

Published Songs
Guess Who—cut
Heart of Stone (*Pyramid Song*)
*I Never Know When (*To Say When*)
Lady in Waiting
Lazy Moon
*The Pussy Foot
Save a Kiss
Shall I Take My Heart and Go?

Additional Songs Recorded
Bad Companions
Give the Little Lady (*A Great Big Hand*)
I Can't Be in Love
If I Can't Take It with Me—cut
No One Will Ever Love You (*Like You Do*)
There Never Was a Woman (*Who Couldn't Be Had*)
Two Years in the Making
*Who's Been Sitting in My Chair?

Pop composer Leroy Anderson (1908–75) was best known for orchestral compositions like *The Syncopated Clock* and *Sleigh Ride*. The songs from GOLDILOCKS—his only musical—might not be great, but they sure are a lot of fun. *I Never Know When* is a stunning torch song; *Who's Been Sitting in My Chair?* a fine comic lament; and *The Pussy Foot* is infectiously delectable. There were also some pretty good comedy songs, with especially smart lyrics from the Kerrs and Joan Ford. The show itself had problems, but GOLDILOCKS was certainly tuneful.

REDHEAD
February 5, 1959
46th Street Theatre • 452 performances
Music by Albert Hague; Lyrics by Dorothy Fields; Book by Herbert and Dorothy Fields, Sidney Sheldon, and David Shaw; Directed and Choreographed by Bob Fosse; Produced by Robert Fryer and Lawrence Carr; With Gwen Verdon, Richard Kiley, and Leonard Stone.

Published Songs
I Feel Merely Marvelous
I'm Back in Circulation
It Doesn't Take a Minute—cut
Just for Once
Look Who's in Love
My Girl Is Just Enough Woman for Me
The Right Finger of My Left Hand
Two Faces in the Dark

Additional Songs Published in Vocal Score
Behave Yourself
Chase [instrumental]
Dream Dance [instrumental]
'Erbie Fitch's Dilemma
I'll Try
Pickpocket Tango [instrumental]
The Simpson Sisters
Uncle Sam Rag
We Loves Ya, Jimey

Albert Hague (of PLAIN AND FANCY [Notables: January 27, 1955]) teamed up with veteran lyricist Dorothy Fields for this Gwen Verdon/Bob Fosse vehicle. While Hague's earlier score had a few pretty tunes, this one was extremely mediocre. REDHEAD nevertheless won the Best Musical Tony Award—with Hague, the librettists, choreographer Fosse, and stars Verdon and Kiley all winning as well (against negligible competition from GOLDILOCKS [Notables: October 11, 1958], FLOWER DRUM SONG [Rodgers: December 1, 1958], and DESTRY RIDES AGAIN [Rome: April 23, 1959]). This was Fosse's third Tony in five years, Verdon's fourth in six. Fosse's next project was THE CONQUERING HERO† [January 16, 1961], from which he was fired, out of town; the show finally stumbled in with no director or choreographer credited. Fosse's next show as full director/choreographer, PLEA-SURES AND PALACES [Loesser: March 11, 1965], didn't even make it to Broadway. Seven years after the seven-Tony REDHEAD, Fosse and Verdon (with REDHEAD's producers and lyricist) finally returned with SWEET CHARITY [Coleman: January 30, 1966]. As for Hague, his Broadway future was hopelessly hapless: CAFE CROWN† [April 17, 1964], THE FIG LEAVES ARE FALLING† [January 2, 1969], and Bette Davis's out-of-town flop MISS MOFFAT† [October 7, 1974].

ONCE UPON A MATTRESS
May 11, 1959
Phoenix Theatre {Off Broadway} •
    216 performances

November 25, 1959
Alvin Theatre • 244 performances
Music by Mary Rodgers; Lyrics by Marshall Barer; Book by Jay Thompson, Marshall Barer, and Dean Fuller; Directed by George Abbott; Choreographed by Joe Layton; Produced by T. Edward Hambleton, Norris Houghton, and William and Jean Eckart; With Carol Burnett, Joe Bova, Jack Gilford, and Jane White.

Revival
December 19, 1996
Broadhurst Theatre • 187 performances
Directed by Gerald Gutierrez; Choreographed by Liza Gennaro; With Sarah Jessica Parker [Burnett].

Published Songs
*In a Little While
*Normandy
Shy
Yesterday I Loved You

Additional Songs Published in Vocal Score
Happily Ever After
Man to Man Talk
Many Moons Ago
The Minstrel, the Jester and I
An Opening for a Princess
Quiet
Sensitivity
Song of Love (I'm in Love with a Girl Named Fred)

Spanish Panic [instrumental]
The Swamps of Home
Very Soft Shoes

Additional Song Recorded
Goodnight, Sweet Princess—written for revival

Yet another group of musical comedy novices were shepherded in by Old Man Abbott. The best work came from composer Mary Rodgers, whose father had pioneered modern musical comedy with Mr. A. (beginning with ON YOUR TOES [Rodgers: April 11, 1936]). Rodgers provided some especially lilting melodies, including *In a Little While* and *Normandy*. Her next musical, the Judy Holliday vehicle HOT SPOT [Sondheim: April 19, 1963], was one of those big-budget, big-advance-sale bonanzas which go wrong and turn into highly public busts. Rodgers returned once more with the long-running Off Broadway hit THE MAD SHOW [Sondheim: January 9, 1966], after which she threw down her composer's pencil. MATTRESS is best remembered as the launching pad for comedienne Carol Burnett. The absence of a suitable clown proved fatal to the professionally mounted but ineffective 1996 revival.

YOU'RE A GOOD MAN, CHARLIE BROWN
March 7, 1967
Theatre 80 St. Marks {Off Broadway} •
    1,597 performances

"*A New Entertainment.*" Music and Lyrics by Clark Gesner; Book by John Gordon (Clark Gesner) (based on the comic strip by Charles M. Schulz); Directed by Joseph Hardy; Choreographed by Patricia Birch; Produced by Arthur Whitelaw and Gene Persson; With Bill Hinnant, Reva Rose, Karen Johnson, Bob Balaban, Skip Hinnant, and Gary Burghoff.

Revivals
June 1, 1971
John Golden Theatre • 31 performances
Directed by Joseph Hardy; Choreographed by Patricia Birch; With Dean Stolber (Burghoff) and Liz O'Neal (Rose).

February 4, 1999
Ambassador Theatre • 150 performances
Additional music and Lyrics by Andrew

Lippa; Directed by Michael Mayer; Choreographed by Jerry Mitchell; With Roger Bart (Bill Hinnant), Ilana Levine (Rose), Stanley Wayne Mathis (Skip Hinnant), Anthony Rapp (Burghoff), B. D. Wong (Balaban), and Kristin Chenoweth.

Published Songs
Book Report
*Happiness
You're a Good Man, Charlie Brown

Additional Songs Published in Vocal Selection
Baseball Game (T.E.A.M.)
The Doctor Is In
The Kite
Little Known Facts
My Blanket and Me
Schroeder (music by Beethoven)
Snoopy
*Suppertime

Additional Songs Recorded
Beethoven Day (music and lyric by Andrew Lippa)—added to 1999 revival
Glee Club Rehearsal
*My New Philosophy (music and lyric by Lippa)—added to 1999 revival
Peanuts Potpourri
Queen Lucy
The Red Baron
When Do the Good Things Start? (music and lyric by Lippa)—added to 1999 revival

Charles M. Schulz's gentle-but-knowing comic strip came to Off Broadway with this good-natured and friendly revue (which began life as a children's record album). YOU'RE A GOOD MAN, CHARLIE BROWN amassed an impressive four-year run, with multiple, profitable companies; a healthy afterlife as a stock & amateur staple; and even a not-very-successful sequel, SNOOPY [Grossman: December 9, 1975]. (It didn't hurt that CHARLIE BROWN opened during one of the most dismal stretches Broadway had ever known, with sixteen consecutive flop musicals in a row—including BREAKFAST AT TIFFANY'S [Merrill: December 14, 1966], SHERRY† [March 28, 1967], MATA HARI† [December 9, 1967], GOLDEN RAINBOW† [February 4, 1968], and I'M SOLO-

MON† [April 23, 1968].) Shortly after finishing its original run, the producers of CHARLIE BROWN decided to storm an undernourished Broadway—which proved a poor idea. The good-natured-but-brittle entertainment was given new life with a full-scale mounting in 1999, but good ol' Charlie Brown seemed a bit out of place in the age of Bart Simpson.

JACQUES BREL IS ALIVE AND WELL AND LIVING IN PARIS
January 22, 1968
Village Gate {Off Broadway} •
    1,847 performances
Music mostly by Jacques Brel; Lyrics by Mort Shuman and Eric Blau, from the French Lyrics by Jacques Brel; Production conception and Additional material by Eric Blau and Mort Shuman; Directed by Moni Yakim; Produced by 3W Productions (including Eric Blau); With Elly Stone, Mort Shuman, Shawn Elliott, and Alice Whitfield.

Note: All music and French lyrics by Brel; all English lyrics by Shuman and Blau unless indicated.

Published Songs
Fanette
If We Only Have Love (Quand On N'a Que l'Amour)
Marathon (Les Flamandes) [English lyric by Blau]

Additional Songs Published in Vocal Selections
Alone (Seul) [English lyric by Blau]
*Amsterdam
Bachelor's Dance (La Bouree du Célibataire) [English lyric by Blau]
*Brussels (Bruxelles) [music by Brel and Gerard Jouannest, English lyric by Blau]
*The Bulls (Les Toros) [music by Brel, Jouannest and Jean Corti]
*Carousel (La Valse à Mille Temps) [English lyric by Blau]—initially used in Blau's Off Broadway revue O OYSTERS!!!† [January 26, 1961]
*The Desperate Ones (Les Déséspéres) [music by Jouannest]

Funeral Tango (La Tango Funebre) [music by
    Jouannest]
*I Loved (J'aimais) [music by Jouannest and
    François Rauber]
Jackie (La Chanson de Jacky) [music by Jouannest]
Madeleine [music by Brel, Jouannest, and
    Corti, English lyric by Blau]
*Marieke [music by Brel and Jouannest,
    English lyric by Blau]
Mathilde [music by Jouannest]
*My Death (La Mort)
Next (Au Suivant)
*The Old Folks (Les Vieux) [music by Brel,
    Jouannest, and Corti]
*Sons Of (Fils De) [music by Jouannest]
Timid Frieda (Les Timides)
You're Not Alone (Jef)

JACQUES BREL IS ALIVE AND WELL AND
LIVING IN PARIS—a string of songs about the
human condition—perfectly captured the mood
of its time. (While it would be unfair to classify
it as a Vietnam protest piece, the message clearly
came across.) BREL was phenomenally successful in Greenwich Village; this despite the fact
that the majority of the audience had never heard
of the Belgian-born Brel (1929–78). Someone listening to the score today for the first time might
wonder what all the fuss was about; all I can say
is that it was magically spellbinding at the time
(and remains so, mostly, for me at least). The two
dozen songs touched on just about every emotion. A good part of the credit must be ascribed
to the masterful English lyrics by Mort Shuman
and Eric Blau; one wonders how literal the translations were, though, especially in the "gutsy"
spellbinders Shuman himself performed (*Amsterdam, Funeral Tango, Next*). Accompanying the
often trenchant lyrics were melodies of exquisite loveliness (*Old Folks, You're Not Alone, My
Death, Marieke, Fanette*) as well as others of out-
right jubilation (*Carousel, Brussels, Sons Of*).

HAIR
April 29, 1968
Biltmore Theatre • 1,742 performances
"The American Tribal Love-Rock Musical."
Music by Galt MacDermot; Book and Lyrics
by James Rado and Gerome Ragni; Directed by
Tom O'Horgan; Choreographed by Julie

Arenal; Produced by Michael Butler; With
James Rado, Gerome Ragni, Lynn Kellogg,
Melba Moore, and Diane Keaton.

Revival
October 5, 1977
Biltmore Theatre • 43 performances
Directed by Tom O'Horgan; Choreographed
by Julie Arenal; Produced by Michael Butler
in association with K. H. Nezhad; With Ellen
Foley, Cleavant Derricks, Loretta Devine, Peter
Gallagher, Kristen Vigard, and Charlaine
Woodard.

Published Songs
*Aquarius
*Easy to Be Hard
Frank Mills
Good Morning Starshine
Hair
*Let the Sunshine In—initially issued as *The
    Flesh Failures*
*Where Do I Go?

Additional Songs Published in Vocal
    Selections
Abie Baby/Fourscore
Ain't Got No
Air
Black Boys
Donna
Electric Blues/Old Fashioned Melody
Hashish
I Got Life
I'm Black
Initials
Manchester England
Somebody to Love—written for 1979 movie
    version
Three-Five-Zero-Zero
Walking in Space
What a Piece of Work Is Man [lyric by William
    Shakespeare]
White Boys

Additional Songs Recorded
The Bed
Be-In
Colored Spade
Don't Put It Down
My Conviction
Sodomy

Note: Various cut and/or unused songs have been recorded.

HAIR had a pre-Broadway tour of sorts, playing three months at the New York Shakespeare Festival [October 29, 1967] before briefly moving to the Cheetah discothèque. A new production team was then assembled, led by director Tom O'Horgan (replacing Gerald Freedman). Invading the sacred precincts of Broadway, HAIR shocked, insulted, enraged, etc. But the show quickly won over most of the audience, with its strong overall viewpoint (credit O'Horgan) and a very good, tuneful score: *Where Do I Go?, Easy to Be Hard, Aquarius, Let the Sunshine In*, etc. Broadway audiences were comfortable enough with the songs, and non-Broadway audiences first discovered theatre courtesy of the "American Tribal Love-Rock Musical." Canadian-born composer Galt MacDermot's next project was John Guare's successful pop adaptation of TWO GENTLEMEN OF VERONA† [December 1, 1971]. His subsequent Broadway adventures were unwieldy failures (DUDE† [October 9, 1972], VIA GALACTICA† [November 28, 1972], and the more intimate THE HUMAN COMEDY† [April 5, 1984]); but the man can sure write a tune.

PROMISES, PROMISES
December 1, 1968
Shubert Theatre • 1,281 performances
Music by Burt Bacharach; Lyrics by Hal David; Book by Neil Simon (based on *The Apartment* [movie] by Billy Wilder and I. A. L. Diamond); Directed by Robert Moore; Choreographed by Michael Bennett; Produced by David Merrick; With Jerry Orbach, Jill O'Hara, Edward Winter, A. Larry Haines, Marian Mercer, and Donna McKechnie.

Concert Version
February 20, 1997
City Center • 5 performances
Directed and Choreographed by Rob Marshall; Produced by City Center Encores; With Martin Short [Orbach], Kerry O'Malley [O'Hara], Terrence Mann [Winter], Dick Latessa [Haines], and Christine Baranski [Mercer].

Published Songs
Christmas Day

*I'll Never Fall in Love Again
Knowing When to Leave
*Promises, Promises
Wanting Things
Whoever You Are I Love You

Additional Songs Published in Vocal Score
A Fact Can Be a Beautiful Thing
Grapes of Roth [instrumental]
Half As Big As Life
It's Our Little Secret
She Likes Basketball
Turkey Lurkey Time
Upstairs
Where Can You Take a Girl?
You'll Think of Someone
A Young Pretty Girl Like You

Additional Songs Recorded
Tick Tock Goes the Clock—cut
What Am I Doing Here?—cut

The mid-1960s saw composer Burt Bacharach rise to celebrity status, with a personable personality and a string of pop hits (*What the World Needs Now, Alfie*, etc.). David Merrick brought Bacharach and his lyricist Hal David to Broadway, putting them together with Neil Simon and a classic Billy Wilder screenplay. Simon wrote his best libretto to Bacharach and David's lively score (bordering on the over-bouncy). Also making significant contributions were choreographer Michael Bennett (who had performed salvage work on Merrick's unsalvagable HOW NOW, DOW JONES† [December 7, 1967]) and designer Robin Wagner (who made his Broadway musical debut with HAIR [Notables: April 29, 1968]). Bennett and Wagner began experimenting with choreographed set changes, with immediately gratifying results. The assignment of adapting Bacharach's pop recording sound to live theatre went to Jonathan Tunick, who immediately moved on (with Bennett) to COMPANY [Sondheim: April 26, 1970] and began his reign as the musical theatre's finest modern-day orchestrator.

1776
March 16, 1969
46th Street Theatre • 1,217 performances
Music and Lyrics by Sherman Edwards; Book by Peter Stone; Directed by Peter Hunt;

Choreographed by Onna White; Produced by Stuart Ostrow; With William Daniels, Howard Da Silva, Ken Howard, Virginia Vestoff, Paul Hecht, and Ronald Holgate.

Revival
August 14, 1997
Criterion Theatre • 333 performances
Directed by Scott Ellis; Choreographed by Kathleen Marshall; Produced by Roundabout Theatre Company; With Brent Spiner [Adams], Pat Hingle [Da Silva], Tom Aldredge, and Gregg Edelman.

Published Songs
*He Plays the Violin
Is Anybody There?
*Momma Look Sharp
Yours, Yours, Yours!

Additional Songs Published in Vocal Selection
But, Mr. Adams
*Cool, Cool, Considerate Men
The Egg
The Lees of Old Virginia
Molasses to Rum
Piddle, Twiddle and Resolve
Sit Down, John
Till Then

Theatrical novice Sherman Edwards (1919–81) decided to musicalize the suspenseful(?) tale of John Adams, Ben Franklin, and Tom Jefferson writing the Declaration of Independence. Edwards received encouragement and tutelage from Frank Loesser, as had Meredith Willson with THE MUSIC MAN [Willson: December 19, 1957]. Producer Stuart Ostrow, a former Frank (Loesser) Music executive, took up the unlikely project and persuaded the author to allow him to bring in a real bookwriter. The result was not particularly well made, but 1776 proved highly effective and a sleeper hit. A 1997 revival at the Roundabout Theatre proved the show still worked quite well, though not well enough to survive a transfer to Broadway's largest barn of a theatre, the Gershwin.

PROMENADE
June 4, 1969
Promenade Theatre {Off Broadway} •
  259 performances

Music by Al Carmines; Book and Lyrics by Maria Irene Fornes; Directed by Lawrence Kornfeld; Produced by Edgar Lansbury and Joseph Beruh; With Madeline Kahn, George S. Irving, Gilbert Price, Shannon Bolin, and Alice Playten.

Published Song
Promenade Theme [instrumental]

Additional Songs Published in Vocal Selection
Capricious and Fickle
The Cigarette Song
A Flower
I Saw a Man
The Moment Has Passed
Unrequited Love

Additional Songs Recorded
All Is Well in the City
Chicken Is He
Clothes Make the Man (Who Could Marry a Gigolo?)
Crown Me
Four (Naked Ladies)
Isn't That Clear?
Listen, I Feel
Little Fool
The Passing of Time
A Poor Man
Two Little Angels

PROMENADE was avant-garde, experimental, unconventional, and pretty strange—which is perhaps how 1928 Berliners described *Die Dreigroschenoper* (see THE THREEPENNY OPERA [1933] [Weill: April 13, 1933]). Not that it belongs in the same class as the Weill/Brecht masterwork; PROMENADE quickly dated, and the book and lyrics by Maria Irene Fornes were closer in style to Gert (Stein) than Bert (Brecht). But Al Carmines's music was vibrant, alive, unconventional, and pretty strange. Carmines, pastor of the Judson Memorial Church in Greenwich Village, has written dozens of Off and Off Off Broadway musicals since 1964, usually with gay themes. PROMENADE has been his only "commercial" success; his only Broadway stab was W.C.†, a Bill Fields stage bio starring Mickey Rooney and Bernadette Peters, which closed during its 1971 summer stock tryout. PROMENADE, incidentally, seems to be the only musical in history that actually had a theatre named after it.

PURLIE
March 15, 1970
Broadway Theatre • 689 performances
Music by Gary Geld; Lyrics by Peter Udell;
Book by Ossie Davis, Philip Rose, and Peter
Udell (based on *Purlie Victorious* [play] by
Ossie Davis); Directed by Philip Rose; Choreographed by Louis Johnson; Produced by
Philip Rose; With Cleavon Little, Melba
Moore, John Heffernan, Sherman Hemsley,
and Novella Nelson.

Published Songs
*He Can Do It
*I Got Love
Purlie
*Walk Him up the Stairs

Additional Songs Published in Vocal Selection
Big Fish, Little Fish
*Down Home
First Thing Monday Mornin'
New Fangled Preacher Man
The World Is Comin' to a Start

Additional Songs Recorded
The Barrels of War
God's Alive
Great White Father (Of the Year)
The Harder They Fall
Skinnin' a Cat
The Unborn Love

PURLIE had a lot going for it, including a trio of good songs (*I Got Love, Walk Him up the Stairs*, and *Down Home*) from pop songwriters Gary Geld and Peter Udell. There were also Tony-caliber performances by Cleavon Little and Melba Moore. But the unheralded PURLIE faced a series of struggles. PURLIE was the first full-scale Broadway musical aiming to attract a substantial black audience, which—believe it or not—made some older white theatregoers uncomfortable. (These were the days before TV's *All in the Family* came along and began battering away at bigotry.) Perhaps PURLIE's biggest problem was that it was an indepen-

dently produced show with no financial backing from the Broadway establishment. Forced into three expensive theatre moves to make way for presumably "surefire hits" (like PRETTY-BELLE [Styne: February 1, 1971]) and FOLLIES [Sondheim: April 4, 1971]), PURLIE was finally defeated and closed at a loss.

GREASE
February 14, 1972
Eden Theatre {"Mid" Broadway} •
128 performances
June 7, 1972
Broadhurst Theatre • 3,388 performances
Book, Music, and Lyrics by Jim Jacobs and
Warren Casey; Directed by Tom Moore; Choreographed by Patricia Birch; Produced by Kenneth
Waissman and Maxine Fox; With Barry
Bostwick, Carole Demas, and Adrienne Barbeau.

Revival
May 11, 1994
Eugene O'Neill Theatre • 1,501 performances
"The Tommy Tune Production." Directed and
Choreographed by Jeff Calhoun; With Ricky
Paull Goldin [Bostwick]; Susan Wood [Demas],
and Rosie O'Donnell [Barbeau].

Published Songs
Freddy, My Love
Summer Nights
There Are Worse Things I Could Do
Those Magic Changes

Additional Songs Published in Vocal Selection
All Choked Up
Alone at a Drive-in Movie
Beauty School Dropout
Born to Hand Jive
Greased Lightnin'
It's Raining on Prom Night
Look at Me, I'm Sandra Dee
Mooning
Rock 'n Roll Party Queen
Rydell Alma Mater
We Go Together

Additional Songs Published in Vocal Score
Rydell's Fight Song
Shakin' at the High School Hop

Like BYE BYE BIRDIE [Strouse: April 14, 1960], but without its quality or charm, GREASE satirized late-1950s rock & roll. Like HAIR [Notables: April 29, 1968], but without *its* quality or charm, GREASE moved from downtown and attracted many, many theatregoers for many, many years. Most of them left GREASE satisfied; a significant number returned to see it again and again. Some of them have become the theatregoers of today, so who are we to complain if GREASE had a score-ful of ultimately monotonous parodies, as opposed to BIRDIE's clever pastiches which were memorable in their own right? GREASE's 1994 revival had a similarly successful run, helped by a policy of rotating guest stars.

THE WIZ
January 5, 1975
Majestic Theatre • 1,672 performances
Music and Lyrics mostly by Charlie Smalls; Book by William F. Brown (based on *The Wonderful Wizard of Oz* [novel] by L. Frank Baum); Directed by Geoffrey Holder; Choreographed by George Faison; Produced by Ken Harper; With Stephanie Mills, Tiger Haynes, Hinton Battle, and DeeDee Bridgewater.

Revival
May 24, 1984
Lunt-Fontanne Theatre • 13 performances
Directed by Geoffrey Holder; Choreographed by George Faison; With Stephanie Mills.

Published Songs
Be a Lion
Don't Cry Girl
Ease on down the Road
Everybody Rejoice [music by Luther Vandross]
He's the Wizard
Home
If You Believe
A Rested Body Is a Rested Mind

Additional Songs Published in Vocal Selections
Don't Nobody Bring Me No Bad News
The Feeling We Once Had
I'm a Mean Ole Lion
I Was Born on the Day before Yesterday

Slide Some Oil to Me
So You Want to See the Wizard
Soon As I Get Home
Tornado [music by Timothy Graphenreed and Harold Wheeler]
What Would I Do If I Could Feel
Who, Who Do You Think You Are?
Y'all Got It
You Can't Win—initial publication upon use in 1978 movie version

Another negligible but highly successful musical. *Ease on Down the Road* became the first blockbuster Broadway song hit of the 1970s and helped carry THE WIZ past a dismal initial reception. The 1978 film and 1984 revival were both failures, though.

SHENANDOAH
January 7, 1975
Alvin Theatre • 1,050 performances
Music by Gary Geld; Lyrics by Peter Udell; Book by James Lee Barrett, Philip Rose, and Peter Udell (based on the screenplay by James Lee Barrett); Directed by Philip Rose; Choreographed by Robert Tucker; Produced by Philip Rose, and Gloria and Louis K. Sher; With John Cullum, Donna Theodore, Joel Higgins, and Penelope Milford.

Revival
August 8, 1989
Virginia Theatre • 31 performances
Directed by Philip Rose; Choreographed by Robert Tucker; With John Cullum.

Published Songs
*Freedom
Pass the Cross
We Make a Beautiful Pair

Additional Songs Published in Vocal Score
It's a Boy
I've Heard It All Before
Meditation (This Land Don't Belong to Virginia)
Next to Lovin' (I Like Fightin' Best)
The Only Home I Know
Over the Hill
Papa's Gonna Make It Alright
The Pickers Are Comin'

Raise the Flag
Violets and Silverbells
Why Am I Me?

Gary Geld, Peter Udell, and Philip Rose returned with a second musical which—unlike their somewhat superior PURLIE [Notables: March 15, 1970]—managed to run two and a half years and make a little money. (Very little money.) John Cullum carried the show with his strong performance in a heavy singing/acting role (written for Robert Ryan, who died before rehearsals). The property had potential as a serious musical in the CAROUSEL [Rodgers: April 19, 1945] vein; but no Hammerstein, Mamoulian, or Rodgers was on hand. The final Geld, Udell, and Rose musical was the Thomas Wolfe–based ANGEL† [May 10, 1978], which played five performances before giving up the ghost.

THE ROBBER BRIDEGROOM
October 9, 1976
Biltmore Theatre • 145 performances
Music by Robert Waldman; Book and Lyrics by Alfred Uhry (based on the novella by Eudora Welty); Directed by Gerald Freedman; Choreographed by Donald Saddler; Produced by John Houseman, Margot Harley, and Michael B. Kapon; With Barry Bostwick, Rhonda Coullet, and Barbara Lang.

Published Songs
Deeper in the Woods
Nothin' Up
Sleepy Man

Additional Songs Published in Vocal
    Selection
Goodbye Salome
Love Stolen
Once upon the Natchez Trace
The Pricklepear Bloom
Poor Tied up Darlin'
Riches
Rosamund's Dream
Steal with Style
Two Heads
Where Oh Where

Additional Songs Recorded
Company's Comin'
Gallop to Your Treasure Thy Wife

Grab Your Mate and Skedaddle All
Poor Little Baby Darlin
That's the Way the People Blend
You Got a Suckling Pig

Robert Waldman and Alfred Uhry's THE ROBBER BRIDEGROOM was inventive and highly unconventional. It was also highly noncommercial and died after an underattended four-month run. The authors had even less luck with their first musical—the one-performance HERE'S WHERE I BELONG† [March 3, 1968], based on John Steinbeck's *East of Eden*—while their third, SWING† [February 25, 1980], closed during its Washington tryout. Uhry was infinitely more successful when he tried his hand at playwriting, with the 1987 *Driving Miss Daisy* and its 1996 sequel *The Last Night at Ballyhoo*. He returned to the Broadway musical as librettist—though not as lyricist—for PARADE [Notables: December 17, 1998]. THE ROBBER BRIDEGROOM was initially presented for a limited engagement at the Harkness Theatre [October 7, 1975] by John Houseman's Acting Company (made up of Juilliard graduates). Playing the bridegroom and his stolen bride: beginners Kevin Kline and Patti LuPone.

THE BEST LITTLE WHOREHOUSE
    IN TEXAS
April 17, 1978
Entermedia Theatre {"Mid" Broadway} •
    85 performances
June 19, 1978
46th Street Theatre • 1,584 performances
Music and Lyrics by Carol Hall; Book by Larry L. King and Peter Masterson (based on an article by Larry L. King); Directed by Peter Masterson and Tommy Tune; Choreographed by Tommy Tune; Produced by Universal Pictures; With Carlin Glynn, Henderson Forsythe, Pamela Blair, Delores Hall, and Jay Garner.

Songs Published in Vocal Selection
The Aggie Song
Bus from Amarillo
Doatsy Mae
Girl, You're a Woman
Good Old Girl
Hard Candy Christmas

A Li'l Ole Billy Pissant Country Place
No Lies
The Sidestep
Texas Has a Whorehouse in It
Twenty Fans
Twenty-Four Hours of Lovin'
Watch Dog Theme

Additional Song Recorded
Have a Memory on Me—cut

A potentially good musical settled for being just a crowd-pleasing li'l ole hit. Theatrical novices Carol Hall and Larry L. King did well enough, although the effectiveness of their material was diminished by pre-opening "improvements." Theatrical novice Hall's score had some very nice highpoints, actually, like *Bus from Amarillo*, *Doatsy Mae*, and *Hard Candy Christmas*. The production team reassembled sixteen years later for THE BEST LITTLE WHOREHOUSE GOES PUBLIC[†] [May 10, 1994], which was tasteless (which is not a sin) and unfunny (which is) for fifteen embarrassingly painful performances.

DREAMGIRLS
December 20, 1981
Imperial Theatre • 1,522 performances
Music by Henry Krieger; Book and Lyrics by Tom Eyen; Directed by Michael Bennett; Choreographed by Michael Bennett and Michael Peters; Produced by Michael Bennett, Bob Avian, Geffen Records, and the Shubert Organization; With Jennifer Holliday, Loretta Devine, Sheryl Lee Ralph, Cleavant Derricks, Obba Babatunde, and Ben Harney.

Revival
June 28, 1987
Ambassador Theatre • 177 performances
Directed by Michael Bennett; Choreographed by Michael Bennett and Michael Peters; Production supervised by Bob Avian; With Lillias White [Halliday]; Alisa Gyse [Ralph], and Arnetia Walker [Devine].

Songs Published in Vocal Selection
Ain't No Party
*And I Am Telling You I'm Not Going
Cadillac Car
Dreamgirls

Fake Your Way to the Top
Family
Hard to Say Goodbye, My Love
I Am Changing
Move (You're Steppin' on My Heart)
*One Night Only
*Steppin' to the Bad Side
When I First Saw You

Additional Songs Recorded
Firing of Jimmy
I Meant You No Harm
I Miss You Old Friend
Press Conference
The Rap

Michael Bennett, Hal Prince, and Bob Fosse perfected the concept musical, built on plenty of concept and (at times) little else. Artistic vision freed them from relying on book, music, lyrics: instead of assembling a production around written material, they seemed to start with movement and add on songs, plot, etc. During large chunks of DREAMGIRLS, Bennett seemed to be working closer with his set and lighting designers than with the authors. This was not ineffective, as it turned out: the show was entertaining while the material itself seemed functional. The score is somewhat more than adequate, with fine numbers like *And I Am Telling You I'm Not Going*, *Steppin' to the Bad Side*, and *One Night Only*. But the authors displayed a rather puzzling tendency to switch from high-gear Motown to decidedly non-Motown quasi-recitative, with less-than-satisfactory results.

BABY
December 4, 1983
Ethel Barrymore Theatre • 241 performances
Music by David Shire; Lyrics by Richard Maltby, Jr.; Book by Sybille Pearson (based on a story by Susan Yankowitz); Directed by Richard Maltby, Jr.; Choreographed by Wayne Cilento; Produced by James B. Freydberg and Ivan Bloch, Kenneth-John Productions, and Suzanne J. Schwartz; With Liz Callaway, James Congdon, Catherine Cox, Beth Fowler, Todd Graff, and Martin Vidnovic.

Published Songs
I Want It All

Additional Songs Published in Vocal Selections
And What If We Had Loved Like That?
At Night She Comes Home to Me
Baby, Baby, Baby
Easier to Love
Fatherhood Blues
I Chose Right—song version of unpublished theme from 1981 movie *Only When I Laugh*
Patterns—cut
The Story Goes On
Two People in Love
With You

Additional Songs Recorded
The Birth
The Ladies Singing Their Song
Opening
The Plaza Song
Romance
We Start Today
What Could Be Better Than That?

The very special BABY came bouncing along in the midst of one of Broadway's most distressingly barren stretches. Audiences never discovered it in sufficient numbers, though, resulting in a disappointing failure. BABY was warm, pink, and tender, with a more melodic score than Broadway had heard in a long while: *Baby, Baby, Baby, And What If We Had Loved Like That*, the especially moving *The Story Goes On*, and more. BABY was weakened, though, by the lack of Broadway experience among authors and production staff. David Shire and Richard Maltby had been around since the Off Broadway SAP OF LIFE[†] [October 2, 1961]. Their cabaret revue STARTING HERE, STARTING NOW[†] [March 7, 1977] was far more successful, but two Broadway attempts—HOW DO YOU DO, I LOVE YOU[†] [1967] and LOVE MATCH[†] [November 3, 1968]—closed during their tryouts. Maltby had reached Broadway a few years' earlier, as director of the Off Broadway transfer AIN'T MISBEHAVIN'[†] [May 8, 1978]. He also found work as a co-lyricist on Cameron Mackintosh musicals, beginning with Andrew Lloyd Webber's SONG AND DANCE[†] [September 18, 1985]. Maltby and Shire's next theatre piece was

a pleasant but mild Off Broadway revue, CLOSER THAN EVER[†] [November 6, 1989]. They finally returned to Broadway, unhappily so, with BIG [Notables: April 28, 1996].

BIG RIVER
April 25, 1985
Eugene O'Neill Theatre • 1,408 performances
Music and Lyrics by Roger Miller; Book by William Hauptman (based on *Huckleberry Finn* [novel] by Mark Twain); Directed by Des McAnuff; Produced by Rocco Landesman, Heidi Landesman, Rick Steiner, M. Anthony Fisher, and Dodger Productions; With Daniel H. Jenkins, Ron Richardson, Bob Gunton, and René Auberjonois.

Published Songs
Muddy Water
River in the Rain
Waitin' for the Light to Shine
Worlds Apart

Additional Songs Published in Vocal Selection
Arkansas/How Blest We Are
The Boys
The Crossing
Do Ya Wanna Go to Heaven?
Free at Last
Guv'ment
Hand for the Hog
I, Huckleberry, Me
Leavin's Not the Only Way to Go
The Royal Nonesuch
When the Sun Goes down in the South
You Oughta Be Here with Me

BIG RIVER was the best musical of the worst (?) season for Broadway musicals in seventy years. The score by country songwriter Roger Miller was dramatically ineffective and the book was weak, but Mark Twain and the lack of competition—with an assist from director Des McAnuff and designer Heidi Landesman—managed to give BIG RIVER some life.

THE SECRET GARDEN
April 25, 1991
St. James Theatre • 706 performances
Music by Lucy Simon; Book and Lyrics by Marsha Norman (based on the novel by

Frances Hodgson Burnett); Directed by Susan H. Schulman; Choreographed by Michael Lichtefeld; Produced by Heidi Landesman, Rick Steiner, Frederic H. Mayerson, Elizabeth Williams, Jujamcyn Theatres [Rocco Landesman]/TV ASAHI and Dodger Productions; With Daisy Eagen, Mandy Patinkin, Rebecca Luker, Alison Fraser, and Robert Westenberg.

Published Songs
Come to My Garden
Hold On
How Could I Ever Know

Additional Songs Published in Vocal Selections
A Bit of Earth
Clusters of Crocus
The Girl I Mean to Be
If I Had a Fine White Horse
*Lily's Eyes
Race You to the Top of the Morning
Round-Shouldered Man
Where in the World
Wick
*Winter's on the Wing

Additional Songs Published in Vocal Score
Come Spirit, Come Charm
Final Storm
A Girl in the Valley
The House upon the Hill
*I Heard Someone Crying
It's a Maze
Letter Song
Quartet
Show Me the Key
Storm I
Storm II
There's a Girl

From rather unlikely visitors to the musical theatre—pop songwriter Lucy Simon and Pulitzer Prize–winning dramatist Marsha Norman—came an admirable and intriguing musical drama. Imperfect, perhaps; unconventional, certainly; but a breath of fresh wind in a Broadway garden grown stale. The moody score was overstuffed and a bit murky, at times tending toward operetta; but overall it was rather effective, with some lovely work in *Lily's Eyes*, *I Heard Someone Crying*, and *Winter's on the Wing*.

JELLY'S LAST JAM
April 26, 1992
Virginia Theatre • 569 performances
Music by Jelly Roll Morton; Musical adaptation and Additional music by Luther Henderson; Lyrics by Susan Birkenhead; Book and Direction by George C. Wolfe; Choreographed by Hope Clarke; Tap choreography by Gregory Hines and Ted L. Levy; Produced by Margo Lion and Paula Koslow in association with Polygram Diversified Entertainment, 126 Second Avenue Corp./Hal Luftig, Rodger Hess, Jujamcyn Theatres/TV Asahi, and Herb Alpert; With Gregory Hines, Savion Glover, Stanley Wayne Mathis, Tonya Pinkins, and Keith David.

Songs Published in Vocal Selection
Creole Boy [music by Henderson]
Doctor Jazz [music by Joseph "King" Oliver and Walter Melrose, lyric adapted by Birkenhead]—new version of 1927 non-show song
Good Ole New York
In My Day
Jelly's Jam—new lyric for *King Porter Stomp*
The Last Chance Blues
Michigan Water [music traditional]
Play the Music for Me
Somethin' More
That's How You Jazz [music by Henderson]
Too Late, Daddy [music by Henderson]
The Whole World's Waitin' to Sing Your Song [music by Bob Cloud and Ben Garrison]—new lyric for *My Little Dixie Home* [original lyric by Harrison Godwin Smith]

Additional Songs Recorded
The Banishment
The Chicago Strut
The Creole Way [music by Henderson]
Get Away Boy [music by Henderson]
Jelly's Isolation Dance [instrumental]
The Last Rites [music by Henderson and Morton]
Lonely Boy Blues [music traditional]

Lovin' Is a Lowdown Blues
Street Scene [music by Henderson]
That's the Way We Do Things in New Yawk
We Are the Rhythms That Color Your Song

Note: Much of the score was compiled from existing music, in most cases newly arranged and with new lyrics.

Gregory Hines and director/librettist George C. Wolfe invaded Broadway with the dynamic, original JELLY'S LAST JAM. The piece was unusual, and perhaps a bit startling, but that was presumably the intention. The score seemed more atmospheric than theatrical, but that was also presumably the intention. JELLY marked Wolfe's Broadway debut; he soon established an important presence, with his remarkable direction of *Angels in America* [May 4, 1993] and as producer of the New York Shakespeare Festival.

VICTOR/VICTORIA

October 25, 1995
Marquis Theatre • 738 performances
Music by Henry Mancini; Additional music by Frank Wildhorn; Lyrics by Leslie Bricusse; Book by Blake Edwards (based on his screenplay); Directed by Blake Edwards; Choreographed by Rob Marshall; Produced by Blake Edwards, Tony Adams, John Scher, Endemol Theatre Productions, Inc., and Polygram Broadway Ventures, Inc.; With Julie Andrews, Tony Roberts, Michael Nouri, Rachel York, and Gregory Jbara.

Additional Songs Published in Vocal Selection

Almost a Love Song
Chicago, Illinois—written for movie version
Crazy World—written for movie version
If I Were a Man
Le Jazz Hot—written for movie version
King's Dilemma
Living in the Shadows [music by Frank Wildhorn]
Paris by Night
Paris Makes Me Horny
Louis Says [music by Frank Wildhorn]
Trust Me [music by Frank Wildhorn]
Victor/Victoria
You & Me—written for movie version

Additional Songs Recorded

Cat and Mouse
The Tango

There was a time when the presence of a big enough star—like Katharine Hepburn in COCO† [December 18, 1969] or Danny Kaye in TWO BY TWO [Rodgers: November 10, 1970]—could sell enough tickets to ensure a profit (assuming they stayed with the show long enough). But with the excessive costs of mounting a musical nowadays, it can take years and years and years to work your way into the black. Julie Andrews was game enough to give VICTOR/VICTORIA her all, despite the back-breaking work and some demeaningly bad material. (Her husband—who conceived it, wrote it, misdirected it, and produced it—had his ego on the line, after all. Whereas a star like Glenn Close is more likely to take her check, serve her time, and get out as soon as possible, even as her vehicle's chances trail off into the sunset.) But how much can you ask of a sixty-year-old woman playing a girl playing a man playing a girl, etc.? Blake Edwards took his rather good 1982 movie and—apparently out of a lack of any film work—determined to turn the thing into a Broadway hit. After a decade of obstacles—including the death of composer Henry Mancini, who won an Oscar for his original score—VICTOR/VICTORIA made it to Broadway. You could blame the show's troubles on the lack of Broadway experience among the creators, except that the worst work came from the one veteran on hand, lyricist Leslie Bricusse. VICTOR/VICTORIA nevertheless did sellout business. For a while, that is, after which even Julie Andrews couldn't fill the house. She finally withdrew, was replaced by Raquel Welch, and seven weeks later the whole thing sunk in a vat of red ink.

FLOYD COLLINS

March 3, 1996
Playwrights Horizons {Off Off Broadway} • 24 performances
Music and Lyrics by Adam Guettel; Book and Additional lyrics by Tina Landau; Directed by Tina Landau; Produced by Playwrights Horizons (Tim Sanford); With Christopher Innvar and Jason Danieley.

Songs Recorded

The Ballad of Floyd Collins
*The Call
The Carnival [instrumental]
Daybreak [lyric by Guettel and Landau]
The Dream
Git Comfortable
*Heart an' Hand
How Glory Goes
I Landed on Him [lyric by Guettel and Landau]
*Is That Remarkable?
It Moves [lyric by Guettel and Landau]
Lucky
The Riddle Song [lyric by Guettel and Landau]
Through the Mountain
Time to Go [lyric by Guettel and Landau]
'Tween a Rock an' a Hard Place

A budding young musical theatre composer is sure to attract some attention when he's the son of the composer of a well-remembered musical comedy hit, especially if his grandfather wrote a dozen or so of Broadway's greatest musicals. Distinguished lineage alone won't get you listed in *Show Tunes*, however; so let's just ignore family connections. (Oddly enough, the musical theatre's only other three-generation family [that I can think of] is the Hammersteins. Four generations, actually: Oscar/Willie/Oscar 2nd/ William & James.) Adam Guettel—who was born just before grandpa went into rehearsals for DO I HEAR A WALTZ?—provided a fascinating, folk-like score for the unconventional chamber musical FLOYD COLLINS. The downbeat subject matter—a 1925 mining disaster in Kentucky— made the piece an unlikely candidate for transfer. But Guettel seems a likely candidate for musical theatre prominence. His emotional music soars to great heights, and anyone who can write a great concerted number like *Is That Remarkable?* clearly belongs on Broadway.

BRING IN 'DA NOISE, BRING IN 'DA FUNK

April 25, 1996
Ambassador Theatre • 1,130 performances
Music by Daryl Waters, Zane Mark, and Ann Duquesnay; Book and Lyrics by Reg E. Gaines (based on an idea by Savion Glover and George C. Wolfe); Conceived and Directed by George C. Wolfe; Choreographed by Savion Glover; Produced by Joseph Papp Public Theatre/New York Shakespeare Festival (George C. Wolfe); With Savion Glover, Anne Duquesnay, and Jeffrey Wright.

Songs Recorded

Bring in 'da Noise, Bring in 'da Funk
Chicago Bound
The Chicago Riot Rag
The Door to Isle Gorée
Gospel/Hip Hop Rant
Hot Fun
I Got the Beat/Dark Tower
Kid Go!
Lost Beat Swing
The Lynching Blues
Now That's Tap
Quittin' Time
Shifting Sounds
Slave Ships
Som'thin' from Nuthin'
Them Conkheads
The Uncle Huck-a-Buck Song

BRING IN 'DA NOISE, BRING IN 'DA FUNK might seem out of place in a book called *Show Tunes*, as the score is about as far away from show tunes as you can get. One thing's for sure, though: Savion Glover and George Wolfe created a masterful piece of musical theatre. Few people left whistling the songs, certainly; but few people left unmoved. Classify it as you will, BRING IN 'DA NOISE brought excitement back to Broadway.

BIG

April 28, 1996
Shubert Theatre • 193 performances
Music by David Shire; Lyrics by Richard Maltby, Jr.; Book by John Weidman (based on the screenplay by Gary Ross and Anne Spielberg); Directed by Mike Ockrent; Choreographed by Susan Stroman; Produced by James R. Freydberg, Kenneth Feld, Lawrence Mark, and Kenneth D. Greenblatt in association with FAO Schwartz; With Daniel Jenkins, Crista Moore, Jon Cypher, and Barbara Walsh.

Songs Published in Vocal Selection
Coffee, Black!
Cross the Line
*Dancing All the Time
Fun
I Want to Go Home
I Want to Know
One Special Man
Stars, Stars, Stars
*Stop, Time

Additional Songs Recorded
Can't Wait
Carnival
Do You Want to Play Games?
Here We Go Again
It's Time
Josh's Welcome
The Nightmare
The Real Thing
Talk to Her
This Isn't Me
The Time of Your Life
Turning into Something—cut
When You're Big
Zoltar Speaks

BIG was big, all right, dropping more than ten million dollars down the Broadway rabbit-hole. The songwriters and producer of the well-intentioned BABY [Notables: December 4, 1983] came up with an intrinsically unworkable idea: To create a stage musicalization of *Big*, the fantasy film hit about a teenager is being magically transformed into an adult's body (with all those hormones). With a clear view of the BIG central problem and no idea how to solve it, they nevertheless went ahead and optioned the film. Unable to solve it in the writing, they nevertheless undertook several developmental workshops. Unable to solve it in the workshops, they nevertheless went into full-scale production. Unable to solve it in their pre-Broadway tryout, they nevertheless spent more and more and more money trying to fix the unfixable instead of just admitting defeat and closing in Detroit. And then they were shocked when they met with bad reviews and bad business and—horrors!—they weren't even nominated as the best musical of the year. Blame for this shouldn't go to the writers alone, certainly, as they were just trying to do what they were hired to do. Shire and Maltby's score was the best element in the show, which is not much of a recommendation. But the music was generally pleasant, with a couple of rather good songs (*Dancing All the Time* and *Stop, Time*). But BIG was a big waste of time, money, and the efforts of talented people. A cut-down and rewritten version for the family trade was mounted as a national tour with better results, but not better enough.

RENT
April 29, 1996
Nederlander Theatre •
    Still playing April 1, 1999
Book, Music, and Lyrics by Jonathan Larson; Directed by Michael Greif; Produced by Jeffrey Seller, Kevin McCollum, Allan S. Gordon, and New York Theatre Workshop; With Wilson Jermaine Heredia, Jesse L. Martin, Idina Menzel, Adam Pascal, Anthony Rapp, Daphne Rubin-Vega, and Fredi Walker.

Published Song
*Seasons of Love

Additional Songs Published in Vocal Selection
Another Day
Halloween
I'll Cover You
*One Song Glory
Out Tonight
Rent
Santa Fe
Take Me or Leave Me
*Without You
Your Eyes

Additional Songs Recorded
Christmas Bells
Contact
Finale
Goodbye Love
Happy New Year
I Should Tell You
La Vie Boheme
Life Support
Light My Candle
On the Street

Over the Moon
Tango: Maureen
Today 4 U
Tune Up #1
Tune Up #2
Tune Up #3
Voice Mail #1
Voice Mail #2
Voice Mail #3
Voice Mail #4
Voice Mail #5
We're Okay
What You Own
Will I?
You Okay Honey?
You'll See

Through the 1980s and 1990s, Broadway had become accustomed to seeing only one or two new musicals a season. The final Tony-eligible week of 1995–96 saw three all-new musicals: One was traditional (and pretty bad), while two were astoundingly unconventional shows which achieved instant "hit" status. RENT turned into the biggest hit of the year and presumably the biggest hit of the decade. (But how do you compare the RENT receipts—or anyone else's—to those of the ongoing PHANTOM OF THE OPERA[†] [January 26, 1988], which opened in England back in 1986?) Jonathan Larson gave RENT a far-reaching and bounteous score, and of course the poor fellow died before seeing his show open. RENT had a strong impact on the theatre and even on society, as HAIR [Notables: April 28, 1968] had done back in the 1960s. Like HAIR it became a high-profile media event with far-reaching effect, although HAIR was infinitely more friendly and entertaining. At any rate, after the quick and sudden emergence of BRING IN 'DA NOISE [Notables: April 25, 1996] and RENT, Broadway was no longer accused of being the old-fashioned province of the middle-aged middle-class.

JEKYLL & HYDE
April 28, 1997
Plymouth Theatre • Still playing April 1, 1999
Music by Frank Wildhorn; Book and Lyrics by Leslie Bricusse (based on *The Strange Case of Dr. Jekyll and Mr. Hyde* [novella] by Robert Louis Stevenson); Conceived for the stage by Steve Cuden and Frank Wildhorn; Directed by Robin Phillips; Produced by PACE Theatrical Group and Fox Theatricals, in association with Jerry Frankel, Magicworks Entertainments, and The Landmark Entertainment Group; With Robert Cuccioli, Linda Eder, Christiane Noll, George Merritt, Robert Evan, and Barrie Ingham.

Published Songs
It's a Dangerous Game
A New Life
Someone Like You
This Is the Moment

Additional Songs Published in Vocal Selections
Alive!
Confrontation
Façade
Good and Evil
Hospital Board—cut
In His Eyes
It's Over Now—cut
Letting Go
Lost in the Darkness
Love Has Come of Age—cut
Murder, Murder!
No One Knows Who I Am
No One Must Ever Know—cut
Once upon a Dream
Possessed—cut
Retribution—cut
Seduction—cut
Sympathy, Tenderness
Take Me As I Am
Till You Came into My Life—cut
Transformation—cut; revised to *First Transformation*
We Still Have Time—cut

Additional Songs Recorded
Bitch, Bitch, Bitch—cut
Board of Governors—cut
Bring on the Men—cut
Emma's Reasons
The Engagement Party—cut
First Transformation—revised version of *Transformation*
The Girls of the Night—cut

How Can I Continue On?—cut
I Must Go On
I Need to Know—cut
Lisa Carew—cut
Lucy Meets Hyde—cut
Lucy Meets Jekyll—cut
Mass—cut
Now There Is No Choice
Obsession
Pursue the Truth
Reflections in His Eyes—cut
Streak of Madness—cut
The Wedding Reception—cut
The World Has Gone Insane—cut
Your Work—*and Nothing More*

Frank Wildhorn was a pop songwriter with no theatrical experience. Leslie Bricusse was a composer/lyricist with vast experience and a handful of early-1960s hit show tunes (with a pop sound) like *What Kind of Fool Am I?* and *Who Can I Turn To?* They joined to write an adaptation of JEKYLL & HYDE, which premièred in 1990 at the Alley Theatre in Houston in 1990, was rewritten and revised for a new production in 1995 at Theatre Under the Stars in Houston, and was then once again rewritten and revised for Broadway. (In the interim, Bricusse wrote the lyrics for VICTOR/VICTORIA [Notables: October 25, 1995]—with Wildhorn stepping in after Henry Mancini's death to compose three songs.) JEKYLL & HYDE was roundly roasted for its substandard material by critics and Broadwayites alike, but it proved to be one of those so-called "audience shows," which enjoy a respectable run but eventually close several million dollars in the red. The writing is, perhaps, baldly bad at times; but, then, the final director of the enterprise, Robin Phillips, wisely dressed things up with excessive, effective theatricality. Wildhorn quickly returned with THE SCARLET PIMPERNEL[†] [November 9, 1997], similar in style and quality (or lack of). With the opening of THE CIVIL WAR[†] [April 22, 1999], Wildhorn had three Broadway musicals running (briefly) simultaneously, which he trumpeted loudly in the press. When the final accounting is done, though, the three combined may well represent a loss in excess of 15 million dollars, which Wildhorn presumably will not trumpet loudly in the press.

SIDE SHOW
October 16, 1997
Richard Rodgers Theatre • 91 performances
Music by Henry Krieger; Book and Lyrics by Bill Russell; Directed and Choreographed by Robert Longbottom; Produced by Emanuel Azenberg, Joseph Nederlander, Herschel Waxman, Janice McKenna, and Scott Nederlander; With Alice Ripley, Emily Skinner, Jeff McCarthy, Hugh Panaro, Norm Lewis, and Ken Jennings.

Songs Published in Vocal Selection
Come Look at the Freaks
The Devil You Know
Feelings You've Got to Hide
Happy Birthday to You and to You
I Will Never Leave You
Leave Me Alone
Like Everyone Else
One Plus One Equals Three
Private Conversation
Say Goodbye to the Freak Show
Tunnel of Love
We Share Everything
When I'm By Your Side
Who Will Love Me As I Am?
You Should Be Loved

Additional Songs Recorded
Beautiful Day for a Wedding
Buddy Kissed Me
Buddy's Confession
I'm Daisy, I'm Violet
Marry Me, Terry
More Than We Bargained For
New Year's Day
Rare Songbirds on Display Stuck with You/
    Ready to Play—cut

Composer Henry Krieger followed the distinctive DREAMGIRLS [Notables: December 20, 1981] with the formulaic THE TAP DANCE KID[†] [December 21, 1983], which was of little interest. Fourteen years later he reappeared with the fascinating but intrinsically flawed SIDE SHOW. The show—about an abused pair of Siamese twins struggling in a Depression-era freak circus—aimed to be a searing indictment of the human condition. I guess. Unfortunately, the writing veered from that of serious social drama (like *The Elephant Man*) to the sort of thing you'd see in a bad 1930s Hollywood backstage musical. The lyrics were especially simplistic, given to clumsy rhyming (far more apparent on the cast album than in the theatre) and the same type of banal recitative which hampered much of DREAMGIRLS. The moment they mixed in a couple of out-of-context "camp" musical numbers—director and lyricist came from the 1991 Off Broadway beauty contest musical PAGEANT[†]—they lost the benefit of the doubt, and this viewer as well.

THE LION KING
November 13, 1997
New Amsterdam Theatre •
    Still playing April 1, 1999
Music by Elton John; Lyrics by Tim Rice; Additional music and Lyrics by Lebo M, Mark Mancina, Jay Rifkin, Julie Taymor, and Hans Zimmer; Book by Roger Allers and Irene Mecchia (based on the screenplay by Irene Mecchi, Jonathan Roberts, and Linda Woolverton); Directed by Julie Taymor; Choreographed by Garth Fagan; Produced by Walt Disney Theatrical Productions; With John Vickery, Samuel E. Wright, Geoff Hoyle, Tsidii Le Loka, Tom Alan Robbins, and Max Casella.

Published Songs
Can You Feel the Love Tonight—originally used in movie version
Circle of Life—originally used in movie version

Additional Songs Published in Vocal Selection
Be Prepared—originally used in movie version
Hakuna Matata—originally used in movie version
I Just Can't Wait to Be King—originally used in movie version

Additional Songs Recorded
Chow Down
Endless Night [music by Lebo M, Hans Zimmer, and Jay Rifkin; Lyric by Julie Taymor]
Grasslands Chant [by Lebo M]
King of Pride Rock [music by Hans Zimmer, Lyric by Lebo M]
The Lioness Hunt [by Lebo M]

The Morning Report
The Madness of King Scar
One by One [by Lebo M]
Rafiki Mourns [by Tsidii Le Loka]
Shadowland [music by Hans Zimmer and Lebo M, Lyric by Mark Mancina and Lebo M]
Simba Confronts Scar [instrumental] [music by Mark Mancina and Robert Elhai]
The Stampede [instrumental] [music by Zimmer]
They Live in You [by Mark Mancina, Jay Rifkin, and Lebo M]

The folks at Disney observed the amounts of money that a Broadway musical like BEAUTY AND THE BEAST [Menken: April 18, 1994] could generate, and determined to go full scale into the Broadway business. As with BEAUTY, they took one of their top-grossing animated musicals and adapted it for the stage. Unlike BEAUTY, they did so with a great deal of imagination. THE LION KING was a rather spectacular spectacle, and well worth the adulation heaped upon it. If the score was the weakest link, that was to be expected (with new songs written for the stage version by no fewer than nine writers). The show included a snippet of the 1961 pop song *The Lion Sleeps Tonight* [by George David Weiss, Hugo Peretti, and Luigi Creatore] as some kind of a gag; this was inadvisable, as this was the best music in the show. Few people went to THE LION KING for the music, though. And few were disappointed, thanks to Julie Taymor's remarkable stage wizardry.

SATURN RETURNS: A CONCERT
April 11, 1998
Public/Luesther Lab {Off Off Broadway} •
    20 performances
Music and Lyrics by Adam Guettel; Additional lyrics by Ellen Fitzhugh; Directed by Tina Landau; Produced by New York Shakespeare Festival; With Vivian Cherry, Lawrence Clayton, Annie Golden, José Llana, Theresa McCarthy, and Bob Stillman.

Songs Recorded (under the Title *Myths and Hymns*)
At the Sounding [lyric from *The Temple Trio* (1886 hymnal)]
Awaiting You

Children of the Heavenly King [lyric from *The Temple Trio*]

**Come to Jesus*

The Great Highway

Hero & Leander

How Can I Lose You?

**Icarus*

Migratory V

Pegasus [lyric by Ellen Fitzhugh]

Saturn Returns: The Flight

Saturn Returns: The Return

Sisyphus [lyric by Ellen Fitzhugh]

There's a Land [lyric from *The Temple Trio*]

There's a Shout [lyric from *The Temple Trio*]

Having no completed project with which to follow up FLOYD COLLINS [March 3, 1996]—which despite a brief run had attained cult following, thanks to an unexpected but highly welcome cast album—Adam Guettel and his collaborator Tina Landau fashioned nineteen interrelated non-theatre songs into SATURN RETURNS: A CONCERT. The mythological parts of SATURN dated back to 1987, when Guettel began writing about the search for self—and making your own mark despite the shadow of your father, as he explains in the masterful *Icarus*. He began a second song cycle in 1993, inspired by texts from nineteenth-century religious hymns. These were combined into a surprisingly effective recital and—despite a spare, singers-on-barstools production—rapturously received. And no wonder. In song after song, Guettel immediately established a high emotional pitch—and then kept building on it, taking his audience on an emotional roller coaster (as in *Saturn Returns: The Flight*). Along the way, he effortlessly threw in a few first-rate musical comedy numbers. Guettel can no longer be called a promising young writer; despite his limited output, he is clearly a major talent in search of inspiration and the right project. Hopefully, the acclaim accorded FLOYD and SATURN will spur him onward to Broadway—and soon.

PARADE [1998]
December 17, 1998
Mitzi Newhouse Theatre • 84 performances
Music and Lyrics by Jason Robert Brown;
Book by Alfred Uhry; Directed by Harold

Prince; Choreographed by Patricia Birch; Produced by Lincoln Center Theater (André Bishop and Bernard Gersten) in association with Livent (U.S.) Inc. With Brent Carver and Carolee Carmello.

Songs Recorded

All the Wasted Time

Big News

Come Up to My Office

Do It Alone

The Dream of Atlanta

The Factory Girls

Feel the Rain Fall

Frankie's Testimony

Interrogation: I Am Trying to Remember

It's Hard to Speak My Heart

How Can I Call This Home?

Leo at Work/What Am I Waiting For?

Letter to the Governor

My Child Will Forgive Me

The Old Red Hills of Home

People of Atlanta

The Picture Show

Pretty Music

Real Big News

A Rumblin' and a Rollin'

Sh'ma

Summation and Cakewalk

That's What He Said

There Is a Fountain/It Don't Make Sense

This Is Not Over Yet

Twenty Miles from Marietta

Where Will You Stand When the Flood Comes?

You Don't Know This Man

Director Harold Prince joined with *Driving Miss Daisy* author Alfred Uhry (see THE ROBBER BRIDEGROOM [Notables: October 9, 1976]) to create this uncompromising, fact-based piece about an anti-Semitic lynching in 1915 Atlanta. Prince plucked twenty-eight-year-old composer/lyricist Jason Robert Brown from near anonymity to write the score. (His song cycle SONGS FOR A NEW WORLD [October 11, 1995] had been produced for twelve performances Off Off Broadway by the WPA—directed by Prince's daughter Daisy.) Brown's leap to Broadway might have been too much too soon; parts of PARADE were expertly crafted—the up-tempo numbers, especially—while other sections were admirable-but-difficult. (Although I'd wager that John Kander or Charles Strouse or Cy Coleman or even Andrew Lloyd Webber would have had their hands full fulfilling Hal Prince's bleak vision.) A combination of mixed reviews, the downbeat theme, and the lack of financial support from bankrupt backer Livent sidetracked the worthy PARADE after a mere ten weeks. Nevertheless, I feel sure that this is one of those shows destined to have a longer and happier life on the CD player than in the theatre.

APPENDIX I

Chronological Listing of Productions

All productions discussed in this book are listed on the pages that follow in chronological order.

Dates represent the official New York or London opening. Shows which did not open in New York or London are listed by the date of the out-of-town opening or first public performance. Where exact date is unknown, year and month (if known) are given as "circa [month] [year]."

Where more than one composer contributed to the same production, each is named. Songs written by those composers will be found in the respective chapters.

The page number in the final column represents the primary discussion(s) of each production; for further mention of the show, see the Show Index.

1904

| January 18, 1904 | An English Daisy | Kern | 3 |
| September 19, 1904 | Mr. Wix of Wickham | Kern | 3 |

1905

circa April 1905	The Silver Slipper	Kern	3
August 28, 1905	The Catch of the Season	Kern	3
October 14, 1905	The Babes and the Baron	Kern	4
November 4, 1905	The Earl and the Girl	Kern	4

1906

March 19, 1906	The Beauty of Bath	Kern	4
circa March 1906	The Spring Chicken	Kern	4
August 6, 1906	The Little Cherub	Kern	5
September 20, 1906	My Lady's Maid	Kern	5
October 22, 1906	The Rich Mr. Hoggenheimer	Kern	5

1907

March 25, 1907	The White Chrysanthemum	Kern	5
April 8, 1907	The Orchid	Kern	5
May 20, 1907	Fascinating Flora	Kern	6
August 26, 1907	The Dairymaids	Kern	6
October 7, 1907	The Gay White Way	Kern	6
November 18, 1907	The Morals of Marcus	Kern	6
December 1, 1907	Peter Pan [1907]	Kern	6

1908

January 27, 1908	A Waltz Dream	Kern	6
September 2, 1908	The Girls of Gottenberg	Kern	7
September 7, 1908	Fluffy Ruffles	Kern	7
November 2, 1908	The Boys and Betty	Berlin	37

1909

January 25, 1909	Kittie Grey	Kern	7
July 29, 1909	The Gay Hussars	Kern	7
September 6, 1909	The Dollar Princess	Kern	7
September 27, 1909	The Girl and the Wizard	Kern	8
		Berlin	37
October 26, 1909	The Golden Widow	Kern	8

1910

January 6, 1910	The Jolly Bachelors	Berlin	37
January 10, 1910	King of Cadonia	Kern	8
circa April 1910	Are You a Mason?	Berlin	37
June 20, 1910	Ziegfeld Follies of 1910	Berlin	38
July 18, 1910	Up and Down Broadway	Berlin	38
August 17, 1910	The Echo	Kern	8

	1910 (*continued*)		
August 29, 1910	Our Miss Gibbs	Kern	8
circa August 1910	The Girl and the Drummer	Kern	8
		Berlin	38
September 21, 1910	He Came from Milwaukee	Berlin	38
November 7, 1910	Getting a Polish	Berlin	38
circa December 1910	Two Men and a Girl	Berlin	38
	1911		
February 4, 1911	The Henpecks	Kern	9
March 6, 1911	Jumping Jupiter	Berlin	39
March 20, 1911	La Belle Paree	Kern	9
April 3, 1911	Little Miss Fix-It	Kern	9
April 27, 1911	Gaby	Berlin	39
May 28, 1911	Friars' Frolic of 1911	Berlin	39
June 26, 1911	Ziegfeld Follies of 1911	Kern	9
		Berlin	39
August 28, 1911	The Siren	Kern	9
September 11, 1911	The Fascinating Widow	Berlin	39
September 18, 1911	The Kiss Waltz	Kern	10
September 25, 1911	The Little Millionaire	Berlin	40
October 5, 1911	The Never Homes	Berlin	40
circa October 1911	A Real Girl	Berlin	40
circa November 1911	Winter Garden Vaudeville	Berlin	40
	1912		
January 15, 1912	She Knows Better Now	Berlin	40
February 8, 1912	Hokey-Pokey [. . .]	Berlin	40
February 12, 1912	The Opera Ball	Kern	10
March 5, 1912	The Whirl of Society	Berlin	41
April 11, 1912	A Winsome Widow	Kern	10
circa April 1912	Cohan and Harris Minstrels	Berlin	41
July 22, 1912	The Passing Show of 1912	Berlin	41
August 5, 1912	The Girl from Montmartre	Kern	10
August 5, 1912	Hanky Panky	Berlin	41
August 31, 1912	A Polish Wedding	Kern	10
September 9, 1912	The "Mind-the-Paint" Girl	Kern	10
September 12, 1912	My Best Girl	Berlin	41
October 7, 1912	The Woman Haters	Kern	11
October 21, 1912	Ziegfeld Follies of 1912	Berlin	41
November 13, 1912	The Red Petticoat	Kern	11
November 26, 1912	The Pot of Gold	Porter	117
November 30, 1912	The Sun Dodgers	Berlin	41
December 23, 1912	Hullo, Ragtime!	Berlin	42
	1913		
February 3, 1913	The Sunshine Girl	Kern	11
April 28, 1913	The Amazons	Kern	11
April 30, 1913	The Kaleidoscope	Porter	117

(*continued*)

DAY		COMPOSER	PAGE
	1913 *(continued)*		
June 5, 1913	All Aboard!	Berlin	42
August 25, 1913	The Doll Girl	Kern	11
September 3, 1913	Lieber Augustin	Kern	12
September 22, 1913	The Marriage Market	Kern	12
circa September 1913	Die Ballkönigin	Kern	12
circa September 1913	The Trained Nurses	Berlin	42
October 30, 1913	Oh, I Say!	Kern	12
	1914		
January 12, 1914	The Queen of the Movies	Berlin	42
February 2, 1914	The Laughing Husband	Kern	13
February 2, 1914	When Claudia Smiles	Kern	13
February 23, 1914	Along Came Ruth	Berlin	42
August 24, 1914	The Girl from Utah	Kern	13
circa October 1914	The Society Buds	Berlin	42
December 8, 1914	Watch Your Step	Berlin	42
	1915		
January 25, 1915	Ninety in the Shade	Kern	13
February 8, 1915	A Girl of Today	Kern	14
March 8, 1915	Fads and Fancies	Kern	14
March 22, 1915	Rosy Rapture	Kern	14
April 20, 1915	Nobody Home	Kern	14
April 28, 1915	Tonight's the Night!	Kern	15
circa April 1915	Winter Garden Vaudeville	Berlin	43
May 3, 1915	A Modern Eve	Kern	15
July 22, 1915	Hands Up	Porter	117
August 27, 1915	Cousin Lucy	Kern	15
October 5, 1915	Miss Information	Kern	15
		Porter	117
December 23, 1915	Very Good Eddie [1915]	Kern	16
December 25, 1915	Stop! Look! Listen!	Berlin	43
	1916		
March 28, 1916	See America First	Porter	118
May 28, 1916	Friars' Frolic of 1916	Berlin	43
May 29, 1916	Step This Way	Berlin	44
June 12, 1916	Ziegfeld Follies of 1916	Kern	16
		Berlin	44
June 22, 1916	Passing Show of 1916	Gershwin	57
September 19, 1916	Theodore and Co.	Kern	17
September 25, 1916	Miss Springtime	Kern	17
October 24, 1916	Go to It	Kern	17
November 6, 1916	The Century Girl	Berlin	44
	1917		
January 11, 1917	Have a Heart	Kern	17
January 15, 1917	Love o' Mike	Kern	18

DAY		COMPOSER	PAGE

DAY		COMPOSER	PAGE
February 20, 1917	Oh, Boy!	Kern	18
circa April 1917	Dance and Grow Thin	Berlin	44
June 12, 1917	Ziegfeld Follies of 1917	Kern	19
August 28, 1917	Leave It to Jane	Kern	19
September 10, 1917	Rambler Rose	Berlin	44
September 24, 1917	The Riviera Girl	Kern	19
October 16, 1917	Jack O'Lantern	Berlin	44
November 5, 1917	Miss 1917	Kern	20
December 25, 1917	Going Up	Berlin	45
December 29, 1917	One Minute Please	Rodgers	85
December 31, 1917	The Cohan Revue of 1918	Berlin	45

1918

February 1, 1918	Oh Lady! Lady!!	Kern	20
March 11, 1918	Toot-Toot!	Kern	20
May 18, 1918	Very Good Eddie [1918]	Porter	118
May 22, 1918	Rock-a-bye Baby	Kern	21
June 6, 1918	Hitchy-Koo of 1918	Gershwin	57
June 18, 1918	Ziegfeld Follies of 1918	Berlin	45
August 19, 1918	Yip-Yip-Yaphank	Berlin	45
August 22, 1918	Everything	Berlin	46
August 29, 1918	Head over Heels	Kern	21
October 24, 1918	Ladies First	Gershwin	57
circa October 1918	Telling the Tale	Porter	118
November 4, 1918	The Canary	Kern	21
		Berlin	46
November 27, 1918	Oh, My Dear!	Kern	21
December 9, 1918	Half Past Eight	Gershwin	58

1919

February 6, 1919	Good Morning Judge	Gershwin	58
February 17, 1919	The Royal Vagabond	Berlin	46
March 8, 1919	Up Stage and Down	Rodgers	85
May 5, 1919	She's a Good Fellow	Kern	22
May 12, 1919	The Lady in Red	Kern	22
		Gershwin	58
May 26, 1919	La La Lucille	Gershwin	58
June 10, 1919	A Lonely Romeo	Rodgers	86
June 23, 1919	Ziegfeld Follies of 1919	Berlin	46
October 2, 1919	Ziegfeld Midnight Frolic	Berlin	46
October 6, 1919	Hitchy-Koo 1919	Porter	118
October 24, 1919	Demi Tasse [Capitol Revue]	Gershwin	59
October 27, 1919	Buddies	Porter	119
November 1, 1919	Irene	Notables	387
November 12, 1919	The Eclipse	Porter	119
December 8, 1919	Zip, Goes a Million	Kern	22
December 27, 1919	Morris Gest's Midnight Whirl	Gershwin	59
circa December 1919	Sinbad	Gershwin	59

(*continued*)

	1920		
January 13, 1920	The Passion Flower	Berlin	47
January 27, 1920	As You Were	Porter	119
February 2, 1920	The Night Boat	Kern	23
February 2, 1920	Dere Mable	Gershwin	59
March 6, 1920	You'd Be Surprised	Rodgers	86
March 8, 1920	Ziegfeld Girls of 1920	Berlin	47
March 24, 1920	Fly with Me	Rodgers	86
April 5, 1920	The Ed Wynn Carnival	Gershwin	59
June 7, 1920	George White's Scandals [2nd]	Gershwin	60
June 22, 1920	Ziegfeld Follies of 1920	Berlin	47
July 28, 1920	Poor Little Ritz Girl	Rodgers	87
August 2, 1920	The Charm School	Kern	23
August 31, 1920	The Sweetheart Shop	Gershwin	60
September 18, 1920	A Night Out [1920]	Porter	119
September 27, 1920	Piccadilly to Broadway	Gershwin	60
		Youmans	77
September 29, 1920	Broadway Brevities of 1920	Berlin	47
		Gershwin	60
October 19, 1920	Hitchy-Koo 1920	Kern	23
December 21, 1920	Sally	Kern	23

	1921		
February 12, 1921	Say Mama!	Rodgers	87
March 21, 1921	A Dangerous Maid	Gershwin	60
April 20, 1921	You'll Never Know	Rodgers	88
May 3, 1921	Two Little Girls in Blue [1921]	Youmans	77
May 23, 1921	Shuffle Along	Notables	387
June 2, 1921	Snapshots of 1921	Gershwin	61
June 21, 1921	Ziegfeld Follies of 1921	Kern	24
July 11, 1921	George White's Scandals [3rd]	Gershwin	61
September 19, 1921	The Cabaret Girl	Kern	24
September 22, 1921	Music Box Revue [1st]	Berlin	47
November 1, 1921	Good Morning Dearie	Kern	25
November 7, 1921	The Perfect Fool	Gershwin	61

	1922		
Februry 20, 1922	For Goodness Sake	Gershwin	61
February 20, 1922	The French Doll	Gershwin	62
March 9, 1922	Mayfair and Montmartre	Porter	120
July 6, 1922	Spice of 1922	Gershwin	62
August 16, 1922	Phi-Phi	Porter	120
August 28, 1922	George White's Scandals [4th]	Gershwin	62
October 10, 1922	Hitchy-Koo of 1922	Porter	120
October 23, 1922	Music Box Revue [2nd]	Berlin	47
November 28, 1922	The Bunch and Judy	Kern	25
December 4, 1922	Our Nell	Gershwin	62
December 25, 1922	Rose Briar	Kern	25
circa 1922	Winkle Town	Rodgers	88

1923

January 24, 1923	The Dancing Girl	Gershwin	63
February 7, 1923	Wildflower	Youmans	78
March 19, 1923	Half Moon Inn	Rodgers	88
April 3, 1923	The Rainbow	Gershwin	63
June 18, 1923	George White's Scandals [5th]	Gershwin	63
August 28, 1923	Little Miss Bluebeard	Gershwin	63
September 5, 1923	The Beauty Prize	Kern	26
September 22, 1923	Music Box Revue [3rd]	Berlin	48
September 25, 1923	Nifties of 1923	Gershwin	64
October 4, 1923	Hammerstein's Nine O'Clock Revue	Youmans	78
November 6, 1923	The Stepping Stones	Kern	26
December 25, 1923	Mary Jane McKane	Youmans	79

1924

January 21, 1924	Sweet Little Devil	Gershwin	64
January 21, 1924	Lollipop	Youmans	79
April 8, 1924	Sitting Pretty	Kern	26
May 13, 1924	The Melody Man	Rodgers	88
May 21, 1924	The Punch Bowl	Berlin	48
June 30, 1924	George White's Scandals [6th]	Gershwin	64
September 11, 1924	Primrose	Gershwin	64
September 16, 1924	Greenwich Village Follies	Porter	120
September 23, 1924	Dear Sir	Kern	27
September 23, 1924	Charlot's Revue	Youmans	79
November 6, 1924	Peter Pan [1924]	Kern	27
December 1, 1924	Music Box Revue [4th]	Berlin	48
December 1, 1924	Lady, Be Good!	Gershwin	65

1925

April 13, 1925	Tell Me More!	Gershwin	65
May 17, 1925	Garrick Gaieties [1st]	Rodgers	89
August 6, 1925	June Days	Rodgers	89
September 7, 1925	A Night Out [1925]	Youmans	79
September 16, 1925	No, No, Nanette	Youmans	80
September 18, 1925	Dearest Enemy	Rodgers	89
September 22, 1925	Sunny	Kern	27
October 26, 1925	The City Chap	Kern	28
December 8, 1925	The Cocoanuts	Berlin	49
December 28, 1925	Tip-Toes	Gershwin	66
December 30, 1925	Song of the Flame	Gershwin	67

1926

circa January 1926	Fifth Avenue Follies	Rodgers	90
February 21, 1926	Katja the Dancer	Duke	159
March 17, 1926	The Girl Friend	Rodgers	90

(continued)

1926 (continued)

DAY		COMPOSER	PAGE
April 29, 1926	Cochran's 1926 Revue	Rodgers	90
May 10, 1926	Garrick Gaieties [2nd]	Rodgers	91
May 22, 1926	Yvonne	Duke	159
June 14, 1926	George White's Scandals of 1926	Notables	388
June 15, 1926	The Grand Street Follies of 1926	Schwartz	135
July 26, 1926	Americana [1st]	Gershwin	67
October 12, 1926	Criss-Cross	Kern	28
November 8, 1926	Oh, Kay!	Gershwin	67
December 1, 1926	Lido Lady	Rodgers	91
December 17, 1926	Oh, Please!	Youmans	80
December 27, 1926	Peggy-Ann	Rodgers	91
December 28, 1926	Betsy	Rodgers	92
		Berlin	49

1927

March 10, 1927	The New Yorkers [1927]	Schwartz	135
March 22, 1927	Lucky	Kern	28
April 25, 1927	Hit the Deck	Youmans	81
April 27, 1927	Lady Luck	Rodgers	92
circa April 1927	Two Little Girls in Blue [1927]	Duke	159
May 20, 1927	London Pavilion Revue	Rodgers	92
August 16, 1927	Ziegfeld Follies of 1927	Berlin	49
August 25, 1927	Up with the Lark	Porter	120
August 29, 1927	Strike up the Band [1927]	Gershwin	68
September 6, 1927	Good News!	Notables	388
October 12, 1927	The Bow-Wows	Duke	160
November 3, 1927	A Connecticut Yankee [1927]	Rodgers	93
November 22, 1927	Funny Face	Gershwin	68
December 27, 1927	Show Boat	Kern	29

1928

January 3, 1928	She's My Baby	Rodgers	93
January 10, 1928	Rosalie	Gershwin	69
February 8, 1928	The Yellow Mask	Duke	160
February 23, 1928	Lady Mary	Kern	30
April 26, 1928	Present Arms!	Rodgers	94
April 27, 1928	Blue Eyes	Kern	30
May 9, 1928	Blackbirds of 1928	Notables	389
May 10, 1928	La Revue des Ambassadeurs	Porter	120
September 5, 1928	Good Boy	Schwartz	135
September 25, 1928	Chee-Chee	Rodgers	94
October 8, 1928	Paris	Porter	121
November 8, 1928	Treasure Girl	Gershwin	69
November 21, 1928	Rainbow	Youmans	81
December 4, 1928	Whoopee	Notables	389
December 10, 1928	Well! Well! Well!	Schwartz	136
December 25, 1928	The Red Robe	Schwartz	136

1929

DAY		COMPOSER	PAGE
January 15, 1929	New Wayburn's Gambols	Schwartz	136
circa January 1929	East Is West	Gershwin	70
January 31, 1929	Lady Fingers	Rodgers	94
March 11, 1929	Spring Is Here	Rodgers	95
March 27, 1929	Wake up and Dream	Porter	121
April 30, 1929	The Little Show	Schwartz	136
May 1, 1929	The Grand Street Follies of 1929	Schwartz	137
July 2, 1929	Show Girl	Gershwin	70
		Youmans	82
circa August 1929	Open Your Eyes	Duke	160
September 3, 1929	Sweet Adeline	Kern	31
October 17, 1929	Great Day!	Youmans	82
November 8, 1929	The House That Jack Built	Schwartz	137
November 11, 1929	Heads Up!	Rodgers	95
November 27, 1929	Fifty Million Frenchmen	Porter	122
December 30, 1929	Wake up and Dream	Schwartz	137

1930

DAY		COMPOSER	PAGE
January 14, 1930	Strike up the Band [1930]	Gershwin	70
February 11, 1930	Ripples	Kern	31
February 11, 1930	Nine-Fifteen Revue	Arlen	149
		Gershwin	71
February 18, 1930	Simple Simon	Rodgers	95
February 20, 1930	Here Comes the Bride	Schwartz	138
April 4, 1930	The Co-Optimists of 1930	Schwartz	138
June 4, 1930	Garrick Gaieties [3rd]	Duke	160
		Blitzstein	185
June 10, 1930	Artists and Models	Lane	169
July 1, 1930	Earl Carroll Vanities [8th]	Arlen	149
September 2, 1930	The Second Little Show	Schwartz	138
September 23, 1930	Fine and Dandy	Notables	390
October 13, 1930	Princess Charming	Schwartz	138
October 14, 1930	Girl Crazy	Gershwin	71
October 15, 1930	Three's a Crowd	Schwartz	139
		Duke	161
		Lane	169
November 5, 1930	The Vanderbilt Revue	Porter	122
November 18, 1930	Smiles	Youmans	83
November 19, 1930	Little Tommy Tucker	Schwartz	139
December 3, 1930	Ever Green	Rodgers	96
December 8, 1930	The New Yorkers [1930]	Porter	122
circa December 1930	Brown Sugar	Arlen	150

1931

DAY		COMPOSER	PAGE
January 19, 1931	You Said It	Arlen	150
February 10, 1931	America's Sweetheart	Rodgers	96
May 19, 1931	Crazy Quilt	Rodgers	97
June 1, 1931	The Third Little Show	Lane	169

(continued)

1931 *(continued)*

June 3, 1931	The Band Wagon	Schwartz	139
July 21, 1931	Shoot the Works	Duke	161
		Berlin	50
August 27, 1931	Earl Carroll's Vanities [9th]	Lane	169
October 15, 1931	The Cat and the Fiddle	Kern	32
circa November 1931	Star Dust	Porter	123
December 26, 1931	Of Thee I Sing	Gershwin	72
circa December 1931	Rhyth-Mania	Arlen	150

1932

January 28, 1932	Through the Years	Youmans	83
February 17, 1932	Face the Music	Berlin	50
circa April 1932	Cotton Club Parade [20th]	Arlen	150
September 15, 1932	Flying Colors	Schwartz	140
September 27, 1932	Earl Carroll Vanities [10th]	Arlen	151
October 5, 1932	Americana [3rd]	Arlen	151
October 23, 1932	Cotton Club Parade [21st]	Arlen	151
November 8, 1932	Music in the Air	Kern	32
November 22, 1932	George White's Music Hall Varieties	Arlen	151
November 26, 1932	Take a Chance	Youmans	83
November 29, 1932	Gay Divorce	Porter	123
December 2, 1932	The Great Magoo	Arlen	151
December 7, 1932	Walk a Little Faster	Duke	161

1933

January 20, 1933	Pardon My English	Gershwin	72
April 6, 1933	Cotton Club Parade [22nd]	Arlen	152
April 13, 1933	The Threepenny Opera [1933]	Weill	173
July 28, 1933	Crazy Quilt of 1933	Arlen	152
September 13, 1933	Nice Goings On	Schwartz	140
September 30, 1933	As Thousands Cheer	Berlin	50
October 6, 1933	Nymph Errant	Porter	123
October 21, 1933	Let 'Em Eat Cake	Gershwin	73
November 16, 1933	Please!	Rodgers	97
November 18, 1933	Roberta	Kern	33
November 20, 1933	She Loves Me Not	Schwartz	141

1934

January 4, 1934	Ziegfeld Follies of 1934	Duke	161
		Schwartz	141
March 23, 1934	Cotton Club Parade [24th]	Arlen	152
April 19, 1934	Three Sisters	Kern	33
August 27, 1934	Life Begins at 8:40	Arlen	152
October 3, 1934	Hi Diddle Diddle	Porter	124
October 22, 1934	Bring on the Girls	Schwartz	141
November 21, 1934	Anything Goes	Porter	124
November 28, 1934	Revenge with Music	Schwartz	141
December 22, 1934	Marie Galante	Weill	173
December 27, 1934	Thumbs Up	Duke	161

1935

March 4, 1935	Petticoat Fever	Loewe	221
April 29, 1935	Something Gay	Rodgers	97
May 20, 1935	Parade [1935]	Blitzstein	185
June 28, 1935	A Kingdom for a Cow	Weill	174
September 19, 1935	At Home Abroad	Schwartz	141
October 10, 1935	Porgy and Bess	Gershwin	74
October 12, 1935	Jubilee	Porter	125
November 16, 1935	Jumbo	Rodgers	97

1936

January 22, 1936	The Illustrators' Show	Loewe	221
		Loesser	243
January 30, 1936	Ziegfeld Follies of 1936	Duke	162
February 4, 1936	Follow the Sun	Schwartz	142
April 11, 1936	On Your Toes	Rodgers	98
October 29, 1936	Red, Hot and Blue!	Porter	126
November 19, 1936	Johnny Johnson	Weill	174
December 3, 1936	O Mistress Mine	Porter	126
December 25, 1936	The Show Is On	Duke	162
		Arlen	153
		Gershwin	75
		Rodgers	98
		Schwartz	142

1937

January 7, 1937	The Eternal Road	Weill	174
April 14, 1937	Babes in Arms	Rodgers	98
June 12, 1937	Salute to Spring	Loewe	221
June 16, 1937	The Cradle Will Rock	Blitzstein	185
September 2, 1937	Virginia	Schwartz	142
November 2, 1937	I'd Rather Be Right	Rodgers	99
November 11, 1937	Julius Caesar	Blitzstein	186
November 27, 1937	Pins and Needles	Rome	193
December 1, 1937	Hooray for What!	Arlen	153
December 22, 1937	Between the Devil	Schwartz	143

1938

May 11, 1938	I Married an Angel	Rodgers	100
June 3, 1938	Gentlemen Unafraid	Kern	34
September 21, 1938	You Never Know	Porter	126
September 24, 1938	Sing Out the News	Rome	194
October 19, 1938	Knickerbocker Holiday	Weill	175
November 2, 1938	Danton's Death	Blitzstein	187
November 9, 1938	Leave It to Me!	Porter	127
November 23, 1938	The Boys from Syracuse	Rodgers	100
December 1, 1938	Great Lady	Loewe	222

(continued)

DAY		COMPOSER	PAGE
	1939		
January 3, 1939	Mamba's Daughters	Kern	34
February 9, 1939	Stars in Your Eyes	Schwartz	143
February 15, 1939	The Little Foxes	Willson	269
April 24, 1939	Sing for Your Supper	Rome	194
April 30, 1939	Railroads on Parade	Weill	176
May 17, 1939	Very Warm for May	Kern	34
June 9, 1939	The Sun Never Sets	Porter	127
June 19, 1939	Streets of Paris	Rome	194
circa August 1939	Ulysses Africanus	Weill	176
October 16, 1939	The Man Who Came to Dinner	Porter	127
October 18, 1939	Too Many Girls	Rodgers	101
November 13, 1939	Madam, Will You Walk?	Weill	176
December 6, 1939	DuBarry Was a Lady	Porter	127
December 26, 1939	A Vagabond Hero	Duke	163
	1940		
January 22, 1940	Two on an Island	Weill	176
April 4, 1940	Higher and Higher	Rodgers	101
May 12, 1940	American Jubilee	Schwartz	144
May 23, 1940	Keep Off the Grass	Duke	163
May 28, 1940	Louisiana Purchase	Berlin	51
June 4, 1940	Walk with Music	Notables	390
June 24, 1940	Two Weeks with Pay	Rodgers	102
July 13, 1940	The Little Dog Laughed	Rome	195
September 11, 1940	Hold on to Your Hats	Lane	170
circa September 1940	Ice Capades of 1941	Duke	163
October 10, 1940	It Happens on Ice	Duke	163
October 25, 1940	Cabin in the Sky	Duke	163
October 30, 1940	Panama Hattie	Porter	128
December 25, 1940	Pal Joey	Rodgers	102
	1941		
January 5, 1941	No for an Answer	Blitzstein	187
January 23, 1941	Lady in the Dark	Weill	176
September 30, 1941	Ice Capades of 1942	Styne	227
October 1, 1941	Best Foot Forward	Martin	205
		Rodgers	103
October 29, 1941	Let's Face It	Porter	128
December 25, 1941	Banjo Eyes	Duke	164
	1942		
January 9, 1942	The Lady Comes Across	Duke	164
circa March 1942	Symphony in Brown	Arlen	154
June 2, 1942	By Jupiter	Rodgers	103
June 22, 1942	Lunchtime Follies	Weill	177
		Rome	195
		Blitzstein	187
June 24, 1942	Star and Garter	Rome	195

DAY		COMPOSER	PAGE
	1942 (continued)		
July 4, 1942	This Is the Army	Berlin	52
September 4, 1942	Ice Capades of 1943	Styne	227
October 5, 1942	Let Freedom Sing	Rome	195
October 8, 1942	Life of the Party	Loewe	222
	1943		
January 7, 1943	Something for the Boys	Porter	129
March 22, 1943	Dancing in the Streets	Duke	165
March 31, 1943	Oklahoma!	Rodgers	104
June 17, 1943	Early to Bed	Notables	391
July 13, 1943	Stars and Gripes	Rome	195
October 7, 1943	One Touch of Venus	Weill	177
November 11, 1943	What's Up?	Loewe	222
November 17, 1943	A Connecticut Yankee [1943]	Rodgers	105
circa 1943	Nantucket	Duke	165
	1944		
January 13, 1944	Jackpot	Duke	165
January 25, 1944	Skirts	Rome	196
		Loesser	243
January 27, 1944	Vincent Youmans' Ballet Revue	Youmans	84
January 28, 1944	Mexican Hayride	Porter	129
May 5, 1944	Tars and Spars	Duke	165
May 26, 1944	About Face!	Loesser	244
August 7, 1944	Hi, Yank!	Loesser	244
October 5, 1944	Bloomer Girl	Arlen	154
November 13, 1944	Glad to See You!	Styne	257
November 16, 1944	Sadie Thompson	Duke	166
circa November 1944	PFC Mary Brown	Loesser	244
December 7, 1944	Seven Lively Arts	Porter	129
December 23, 1944	Laffing Room Only!	Lane	170
December 28, 1944	On the Town	Bernstein	211
	1945		
March 22, 1945	The Firebrand of Florence	Weill	178
April 19, 1945	Carousel	Rodgers	106
circa June 1945	OK, U.S.A.!	Loesser	244
November 22, 1945	The Day before Spring	Loewe	222
	1946		
March 30, 1946	St. Louis Woman	Arlen	154
April 18, 1946	Call Me Mister	Rome	196
May 16, 1946	Annie Get Your Gun	Berlin	53
May 31, 1946	Around the World	Porter	130
September 5, 1946	A Flag Is Born	Weill	179
October 10, 1946	Sweet Bye and Bye	Duke	166
October 31, 1946	Happy Birthday	Rodgers	107

(continued)

DAY		COMPOSER	PAGE

1946 (*continued*)

November 4, 1946	Park Avenue	Schwartz	144
November 20, 1946	Another Part of the Forest	Blitzstein	188
December 19, 1946	Androcles and the Lion	Blitzstein	188
December 26, 1946	Beggar's Holiday	Notables	391

1947

January 9, 1947	Street Scene	Weill	179
January 10, 1947	Finian's Rainbow	Lane	170
March 13, 1947	Brigadoon	Loewe	223
October 9, 1947	High Button Shoes	Styne	228
October 10, 1947	Allegro	Rodgers	107

1948

January 29, 1948	Look, Ma, I'm Dancin'!	Martin	206
April 30, 1948	Inside U.S.A.	Schwartz	144
circa May 1948	Big as Life	Boc	255
circa May 1948	Phinney's Rainbow	Sondheim	273
July 15, 1948	Down in the Valley	Weill	179
September 24, 1948	That's the Ticket!	Rome	196
October 7, 1948	Love Life	Weill	180
October 11, 1948	Where's Charley?	Loesser	245
December 30, 1948	Kiss Me, Kate	Porter	130
circa 1948	Stars on My Shoulders	Berlin	53

1949

March 19, 1949	All That Glitters	Sondheim	273
April 7, 1949	South Pacific	Rodgers	108
June 20, 1949	Pretty Penny	Rome	197
July 15, 1949	Miss Liberty	Berlin	54
October 30, 1949	Lost in the Stars	Weill	180
October 31, 1949	Regina	Blitzstein	188
November 2, 1949	I Know My Love	Sondheim	274
December 8, 1949	Gentlemen Prefer Blondes	Styne	228

1950

January 17, 1950	Alive and Kicking	Rome	197
April 24, 1950	Peter Pan [1950]	Bernstein	212
circa April 1950	Huckleberry Finn	Weill	181
June 28, 1950	Michael Todd's Peep Show	Rome	197
		Styne	229
October 12, 1950	Call Me Madam	Berlin	54
November 24, 1950	Guys and Dolls	Loesser	245
December 14, 1950	Bless You All	Rome	197
December 21, 1950	Out of This World	Porter	131
December 25, 1950	King Lear	Blitzstein	189
December 31, 1950	Casey Jones	Duke	166

1951

Day		Composer	Page
March 9, 1951	Let Me Hear the Melody	Gershwin	75
March 29, 1951	The King and I	Rodgers	108
April 18, 1951	Make a Wish	Martin	206
April 19, 1951	A Tree Grows in Brooklyn	Schwartz	145
May 14, 1951	Flahooley	Notables	392
July 19, 1951	Two on the Aisle	Styne	229
November 1, 1951	Top Banana	Notables	392
November 12, 1951	Paint Your Wagon	Loewe	223

1952

Day		Composer	Page
May 7, 1952	Can-Can	Porter	131
June 24, 1952	Wish You Were Here	Rome	198
September 11, 1952	Jollyanna	Lane	171
September 25, 1952	Love from Judy	Martin	207
December 15, 1952	Two's Company	Duke	167

1953

Day		Composer	Page
February 11, 1953	Hazel Flagg	Styne	229
February 25, 1953	Wonderful Town	Bernstein	212
May 28, 1953	Me and Juliet	Rodgers	109
December 3, 1953	Kismet	Notables	393
December 10, 1953	John Murray Anderson's Almanac	Adler	251
		Coleman	313

1954

Day		Composer	Page
March 10, 1954	The Threepenny Opera [1954]	Weill	181
March 11, 1954	The Golden Apple	Notables	394
April 8, 1954	By the Beautiful Sea	Schwartz	145
May 13, 1954	The Pajama Game	Adler	251
October 18, 1954	I Feel Wonderful	Herman	323
October 24, 1954	Peter Pan [1954]	Styne	230
November 4, 1954	Fanny	Rome	198
December 30, 1954	House of Flowers [1954]	Arlen	155
circa 1954	Dilly	Duke	167

1955

Day		Composer	Page
January 27, 1955	Plain and Fancy	Notables	394
February 24, 1955	Silk Stockings	Porter	132
February 28, 1955	Shoestring Revue	Strouse	293
April 19, 1955	Trouble in Tahiti [All in One]	Bernstein	213
May 5, 1955	Damn Yankees	Adler	252
circa August 1955	Saturday Night	Sondheim	274
September 6, 1955	Catch a Star	Bock	255
October 10, 1955	Reuben Reuben	Blitzstein	189
November 17, 1955	The Lark	Bernstein	213
November 23, 1955	A Quiet Place [1955]	Bernstein	213
November 30, 1955	Pipe Dream	Rodgers	110

(continued)

DAY		COMPOSER	PAGE
	1956		
March 15, 1956	My Fair Lady	Loewe	224
March 22, 1956	Mr. Wonderful	Bock	255
April 16, 1956	Ziegfeld Follies of 1956	Bock	256
		Coleman	313
May 2, 1956	Wake up, Darling	Styne	231
May 3, 1956	The Most Happy Fella	Loesser	246
May 22, 1956	The Littlest Revue	Duke	167
		Blitzstein	189
		Strouse	293
October 8, 1956	Sixth Finger in a Five Finger Glove	Strouse	293
November 5, 1956	Shoestring '57	Strouse	294
		Schmidt	305
November 15, 1956	Li'l Abner	Notables	395
November 19, 1956	Girls of Summer	Sondheim	275
November 29, 1956	Bells Are Ringing	Styne	231
December 1, 1956	Candide [1956]	Bernstein	214
circa December 1956	The Mizner Story	Berlin	55
	1957		
March 13, 1957	The Sin of Pat Muldoon	Adler	253
May 14, 1957	New Girl in Town	Merrill	263
September 26, 1957	West Side Story	Bernstein	215
October 10, 1957	Romanoff and Juliet	Rome	199
October 10, 1957	Take Five	Sondheim	275
October 24, 1957	Compulsion	Coleman	313
October 31, 1957	Jamaica	Arlen	156
November 2, 1957	Time Remembered	Duke	167
December 19, 1957	The Music Man	Willson	269
	1958		
January 23, 1958	The Body Beautiful	Bock	256
April 3, 1958	Say, Darling	Styne	231
April 29, 1958	The First Born	Bernstein	216
May 18, 1958	Nightcap	Herman	323
June 20, 1958	A Midsummer Night's Dream	Blitzstein	189
July 20, 1958	The Winter's Tale [1958]	Blitzstein	190
October 11, 1958	Demi-Dozen	Schmidt	305
		Coleman	314
November 11, 1958	Goldilocks	Notables	396
December 1, 1958	Flower Drum Song	Rodgers	111
	1959		
February 5, 1959	Redhead	Notables	396
March 9, 1959	Juno	Blitzstein	190
April 23, 1959	Destry Rides Again	Rome	199
May 11, 1959	Once upon a Mattress	Notables	397
May 21, 1959	Gypsy	Styne	232
October 14, 1959	The Pink Jungle	Duke	168

1959 (*continued*)

October 22, 1959	Take Me Along	Merrill	264
November 16, 1959	The Sound of Music	Rodgers	111
November 23, 1959	Fiorello!	Bock	257
December 7, 1959	Saratoga	Arlen	156
December 17, 1959	Free and Easy	Arlen	157

1960

January 20, 1960	Parade [1960]	Herman	323
circa February 1960	Mrs. 'Arris Goes to Paris	Schwartz	145
March 8, 1960	Greenwillow	Loesser	247
April 14, 1960	Bye Bye Birdie	Strouse	294
April 20, 1960	From A to Z	Herman	324
May 3, 1960	The Fantasticks	Schmidt	305
June 6, 1960	Meet Me in St. Louis [1960]	Martin	207
June 19, 1960	Freedomland, U.S.A.	Styne	233
June 29, 1960	Medium Rare	Coleman	314
October 17, 1960	Tenderloin	Bock	257
October 29, 1960	Invitation to a March	Sondheim	275
November 3, 1960	The Unsinkable Molly Brown	Willson	270
December 3, 1960	Camelot	Loewe	225
December 16, 1960	Wildcat	Coleman	314
December 25, 1960	Toys in the Attic	Blitzstein	191
December 28, 1960	Do Re Mi	Styne	233

1961

April 13, 1961	Carnival!	Merrill	264
October 10, 1961	Milk and Honey	Herman	324
October 14, 1961	How to Succeed [. . .] without Really Trying	Loesser	248
October 23, 1961	Kwamina	Adler	253
November 18, 1961	The Gay Life	Schwartz	146
December 27, 1961	Subways Are for Sleeping	Styne	234
December 29, 1961	Madame Aphrodite	Herman	324

1962

January 3, 1962	Brecht on Brecht	Weill	182
January 27, 1962	A Family Affair	Kander	331
March 15, 1962	No Strings	Rodgers	112
March 19, 1962	All American	Strouse	295
March 22, 1962	I Can Get It for You Wholesale	Rome	199
May 8, 1962	A Funny Thing Happened [. . .] Forum	Sondheim	276
July 2, 1962	The World of Jules Feiffer	Sondheim	276
October 11, 1962	No Shoestrings	Grossman	349
October 20, 1962	Mr. President	Berlin	55
November 17, 1962	Little Me	Coleman	314
November 27, 1962	Never Too Late	Bock	258
		Kander	331

(*continued*)

1963

DAY		COMPOSER	PAGE
March 12, 1963	Too True to Be Good	Leigh	343
April 19, 1963	Hot Spot	Sondheim	277
August 5, 1963	Zenda	Duke	168
October 3, 1963	Here's Love	Willson	270
October 17, 1963	Jennie	Schwartz	146
October 24, 1963	110 in the Shade	Schmidt	306
November 11, 1963	Arturo Ui	Styne	234
November 11, 1963	Man in the Moon	Bock	258
November 23, 1963	She Loves Me	Bock	258
circa 1963	A Little Night Music [1963]	Martin	208

1964

DAY		COMPOSER	PAGE
January 16, 1964	Hello, Dolly!	Herman	325
		Merrill	265
		Strouse	295
March 26, 1964	Funny Girl	Styne	234
March 28, 1964	Never Live over a Pretzel Factory	Leigh	343
April 4, 1964	Anyone Can Whistle	Sondheim	277
April 7, 1964	High Spirits	Martin	208
April 22, 1964	To Broadway with Love	Bock	259
May 7, 1964	Wonderworld	Styne	235
May 26, 1964	Fade Out—Fade In	Styne	236
September 22, 1964	Fiddler on the Roof	Bock	259
October 20, 1964	Golden Boy	Strouse	295
October 27, 1964	Ben Franklin in Paris	Herman	326

1965

DAY		COMPOSER	PAGE
February 16, 1965	Baker Street	Bock	260
March 11, 1965	Pleasures and Palaces	Loesser	248
March 18, 1965	Do I Hear a Waltz?	Rodgers	112
May 11, 1965	Flora, the Red Menace	Kander	332
October 3, 1965	Generation	Bock	260
October 10, 1965	The Zulu and the Zayda	Rome	200
October 17, 1965	On a Clear Day You Can See Forever	Lane	171
November 22, 1965	Man of La Mancha	Leigh	343
December 14, 1965	La Grosse Valise	Rome	200

1966

DAY		COMPOSER	PAGE
January 9, 1966	The Mad Show	Sondheim	278
January 29, 1966	Sweet Charity	Coleman	315
March 29, 1966	"It's a Bird, It's a Plane, It's Superman"	Strouse	296
May 24, 1966	Mame	Herman	326
October 18, 1966	The Apple Tree	Bock	261
circa October 1966	Softly	Arlen	157
November 15, 1966	Chu-Chem [1966]	Leigh	344
November 20, 1966	Cabaret	Kander	332
December 5, 1966	I Do! I Do!	Schmidt	307
December 14, 1966	Breakfast at Tiffany's	Merrill	265

1967

Day		Composer	Page
March 7, 1967	You're a Good Man, Charlie Brown	Notables	397
April 11, 1967	Illya Darling	Sondheim	278
April 26, 1967	Hallelujah, Baby!	Styne	236
September 27, 1967	Keep It in the Family	Coleman	316
October 23, 1967	Henry, Sweet Henry	Merrill	265

1968

Day		Composer	Page
January 18, 1968	The Happy Time	Kander	333
January 22, 1968	Jacques Brel Is Alive and Well [. . .] Paris	Notables	398
January 27, 1968	Darling of the Day	Styne	237
January 28, 1968	House of Flowers [1968]	Arlen	158
circa March 1968	Senor Discretion Himself	Loesser	249
April 29, 1968	Hair	Notables	399
September 23, 1968	A Mother's Kisses	Adler	253
October 20, 1968	Her First Roman	Bock	261
November 17, 1968	Zorbá	Kander	334
December 1, 1968	Promises! Promises!	Notables	400

1969

Day		Composer	Page
January 22, 1969	Celebration	Schmidt	307
February 6, 1969	Dear World	Herman	327
February 12, 1969	Play It Again, Sam	Grossman	349
circa February 16, 1969	A Pray by Blecht	Bernstein	216
March 16, 1969	1776	Notables	400
June 4, 1969	Promenade	Notables	401
September 2, 1969	1491	Willson	271
October 21, 1969	Butterflies Are Free	S. Schwartz	355
circa 1969	Eleanor	Coleman	316

1970

Day		Composer	Page
March 15, 1970	Purlie	Notables	402
March 26, 1970	Minnie's Boys	Grossman	349
March 29, 1970	Look to the Lilies	Styne	237
March 30, 1970	Applause	Strouse	297
April 8, 1970	Cry for Us All	Leigh	344
April 26, 1970	Company	Sondheim	278
April 28, 1970	The Rise and Fall of the City of Mahagonny	Weill	182
May 6, 1970	Colette [1970]	Schmidt	308
October 19, 1970	The Rothschilds	Bock	262
November 10, 1970	Two by Two	Rodgers	113

1971

Day		Composer	Page
February 1, 1971	Prettybelle	Styne	238
April 4, 1971	Follies	Sondheim	279
April 12, 1971	Six	Strouse	297
April 15, 1971	70, Girls, 70	Kander	334
May 17, 1971	Godspell	S. Schwartz	355

(continued)

	1971 (*continued*)	

DAY		COMPOSER	PAGE
September 8, 1971	Mass	Bernstein	216
November 14, 1971	Twigs	Sondheim	281

	1972	

February 14, 1972	Grease	Notables	402
April 9, 1972	Sugar	Styne	230
September 20, 1972	Halloween	Leigh	345
October 23, 1972	Pippin	S. Schwartz	356
November 6, 1972	I and Albert	Strouse	297

	1973	

February 25, 1973	A Little Night Music [1973]	Sondheim	281
March 18, 1973	Seesaw	Coleman	316
August 28, 1973	Gone with the Wind	Rome	201
November 13, 1973	Gigi	Loewe	225
November 15, 1973	The Enclave	Sondheim	282

	1974	

January 27, 1974	Lorelei	Styne	239
March 10, 1974	Candide [1974]	Bernstein	217
May 20, 1974	The Frogs	Sondheim	282
May 28, 1974	The Magic Show	S. Schwartz	356
October 6, 1974	Mack & Mabel	Herman	327

	1975	

January 3, 1975	Philemon	Schmidt	308
January 5, 1975	The Wiz	Notables	403
January 7, 1975	Shenandoah	Notables	403
February 21, 1975	Straws in the Wind	Coleman	317
February 28, 1975	The Bone Room	Schmidt	308
March 3, 1975	Goodtime Charley	Grossman	350
May 21, 1975	A Chorus Line	Hamlisch	359
June 1, 1975	Chicago	Kander	335
November 23, 1975	By Bernstein	Bernstein	218
December 9, 1975	Snoopy!!!	Grossman	350

	1976	

January 4, 1976	Home Sweet Homer	Leigh	345
January 11, 1976	Pacific Overtures	Sondheim	282
April 25, 1976	Rex	Rodgers	114
May 4, 1976	1600 Pennsylvania Avenue	Bernstein	218
May 4, 1976	Side by Side by Sondheim	Sondheim	283
May 11, 1976	The Baker's Wife	S. Schwartz	356
October 9, 1976	The Robber Bridegroom	Notables	404
November 22, 1976	Hellzapoppin'!	Styne	240
		Coleman	317
December 20, 1976	Music Is	Adler	254

1977

April 17, 1977	I Love My Wife	Coleman	317
April 21, 1977	Annie	Strouse	298
May 7, 1977	Happy End	Weill	183
October 29, 1977	The Act	Kander	336

1978

February 19, 1978	On the Twentieth Century	Coleman	318
March 7, 1978	The Prince of Grand Street	Merrill	266
April 17, 1978	The Best Little Whorehouse in Texas	Notables	404
May 14, 1978	Working	S. Schwartz	357
October 31, 1978	Bar Mitzvah Boy	Styne	240
December 21, 1978	A Broadway Musical	Strouse	299

1979

January 11, 1979	The Grand Tour	Herman	328
February 11, 1979	They're Playing Our Song	Hamlisch	360
February 21, 1979	In Trousers	Finn	369
February 23, 1979	Saravá	Leigh	345
March 1, 1979	Sweeney Todd	Sondheim	283
March 12, 1979	Home Again, Home Again	Coleman	318
April 8, 1979	Carmelina	Lane	172
May 31, 1979	I Remember Mama	Rodgers	114
June 13, 1979	The Madwoman of Central Park West	Bernstein	218
		Kander	336
June 14, 1979	Flowers for Algernon	Strouse	299
October 14, 1979	God Bless You, Mr. Rosewater	Menken	363

1980

circa April 1980	Bojangles	Strouse	299
April 30, 1980	Barnum	Coleman	318
May 1, 1980	A Day in Hollywood/A Night in the Ukraine	Herman	328
July 9, 1980	April Song	Leigh	346
September 14, 1980	Charlie and Algernon	Strouse	299
October 20, 1980	One Night Stand	Styne	240

1981

February 11, 1981	Real Life Funnies	Menken	363
March 5, 1981	Bring Back Birdie	Strouse	300
March 12, 1981	Marry Me a Little	Sondheim	284
March 29, 1981	Woman of the Year	Kander	336
April 1, 1981	March of the Falsettos	Finn	370
May 18, 1981	Cloud Nine	Yeston	375
November 16, 1981	Merrily We Roll Along	Sondheim	285
December 20, 1981	Dreamgirls	Notables	405
circa 1981	Babe	Menken	363

(continued)

DAY		COMPOSER	PAGE

1982

February 9, 1982	Colette [1982]	Schmidt	309
circa March 1982	The Queen of Basin Street	Yeston	375
May 6, 1982	Little Shop of Horrors	Menken	364
May 9, 1982	Nine	Yeston	375
September 23, 1982	A Doll's Life	Grossman	351
October 28, 1982	Upstairs at O'Neal's	Strouse	300
December 18, 1982	The Nightingale	Strouse	300

1983

March 2, 1983	America Kicks up Its Heels	Finn	370
March 31, 1983	Colette Collage [1983]	Schmidt	309
May 11, 1983	Dance a Little Closer	Strouse	301
August 21, 1983	La Cage aux Folles	Herman	328
December 1, 1983	Jean Seberg	Hamlisch	360
December 4, 1983	Baby	Notables	405

1984

February 9, 1984	The Rink	Kander	337
circa February 1984	Kicks: The Showgirl Musical	Menken	364
May 2, 1984	Sunday in the Park with George	Sondheim	285
May 6, 1984	The End of the World	Grossman	352
July 22, 1984	A Quiet Place [1984]	Bernstein	219
November 29, 1984	Diamonds	Grossman	352
		Coleman	319
		Kander	337
		Menken	364

1985

April 16, 1985	Grind	Grossman	352
April 25, 1985	Big River	Notables	406
May 13, 1985	Mayor	Strouse	301
November 8, 1985	Personals	S. Schwartz	357
		Menken	365
November 27, 1985	Pieces of Eight	Styne	241
December 12, 1985	Hay Fever	Kander	338
December 18, 1985	Jerry's Girls	Herman	329
circa 1985	13 Days to Broadway	Coleman	319

1986

| August 21, 1986 | Rags | Strouse | 302 |
| November 24, 1986 | Smile | Hamlisch | 360 |

1987

July 29, 1987	Grover's Corners	Schmidt	309
November 5, 1987	Into the Woods	Sondheim	286
November 6, 1987	Tango Apasionado	Finn	370
November 30, 1987	The Apprenticeship of Duddy Kravitz	Menken	365

1988

April 6, 1988	Mike	Leigh	346
April 26, 1988	Lucky Stiff	Flaherty	381
December 20, 1988	1-2-3-4-5	Yeston	376

1989

February 21, 1989	The Winter's Tale [1989]	Finn	371
March 17, 1989	Chu Chem [1989]	Leigh	346
April 13, 1989	Welcome to the Club	Coleman	319
October 19, 1989	Dangerous Games	Finn	371
November 2, 1989	Meet Me in St. Louis [1989]	Martin	209
November 12, 1989	Grand Hotel	Yeston	376
December 11, 1989	City of Angels	Coleman	320
December 28, 1989	Romance in Hard Times	Finn	371

1990

January 4, 1990	Annie 2	Strouse	302
April 6, 1990	Once on This Island	Flaherty	381
May 1, 1990	Kiss of the Spider Woman [1990]	Kander	338
May 31, 1990	Hannah . . . 1939	Merrill	266
June 28, 1990	Falsettoland	Finn	371

1991

January 8, 1991	Children of Eden	S. Schwartz	358
January 25, 1991	Phantom	Yeston	377
January 27, 1991	Assassins	Sondheim	287
March 18, 1991	And the World Goes 'Round	Kander	338
April 24, 1991	Collete Collage [1991]	Schmidt	310
April 25, 1991	The Secret Garden	Notables	406
May 1, 1991	The Will Rogers Follies	Coleman	320
December 8, 1991	Nick & Nora	Strouse	303

1992

April 26, 1992	Jelly's Last Jam	Notables	407
April 29, 1992	Falsettos	Finn	372
May 12, 1992	Weird Romance	Menken	365
December 10, 1992	My Favorite Year	Flaherty	382

1993

March 2, 1993	Putting It Together	Sondheim	288
March 4, 1993	The Goodbye Girl	Hamlisch	361
April 18, 1993	Ain't Broadway Grand	Leigh	347
May 3, 1993	Kiss of the Spider Woman [1993]	Kander	339
August 9, 1993	Annie Warbucks	Strouse	303
September 17, 1993	Paper Moon	Grossman	353
December 16, 1993	The Red Shoes	Styne	241

(continued)

1994

Day		Composer	Page
April 18, 1994	Beauty and the Beast	Menken	366
May 9, 1994	Passion	Sondheim	288
December 1, 1994	A Christmas Carol	Menken	366

1995

October 25, 1995	Victor/Victoria	Notables	408

1996

March 3, 1996	Floyd Collins	Notables	408
March 17, 1996	Getting Away with Murder	Sondheim	289
March 27, 1996	State Fair	Rodgers	115
April 25, 1996	Bring in 'da Noise, Bring in 'da Funk	Notables	409
April 28, 1996	Big	Notables	409
April 29, 1996	Rent	Notables	410

1997

April 23, 1997	Titanic	Yeston	378
April 24, 1997	Steel Pier	Kander	340
April 26, 1997	The Life	Coleman	321
April 28, 1997	Jekyll & Hyde	Notables	411
May 18, 1997	King David	Menken	367
October 16, 1997	Side Show	Notables	412
November 6, 1997	Proposals	Flaherty	383
November 13, 1997	The Lion King	Notables	413
December 17, 1997	The Show Goes On	Schmidt	310

1998

January 18, 1998	Ragtime	Flaherty	383
February 25, 1998	I Will Come Back	Martin	209
April 11, 1998	Saturn Returns	Notables	413
June 18, 1998	A New Brain	Finn	372
June 22, 1998	Love's Fire	Finn	373
July 1, 1998	Mirette	Schmidt	310
December 17, 1998	Parade [1998]	Notables	414

APPENDIX 2

Collaborator Reference Listing

The reader will have noted certain collaborators regularly mentioned throughout this book. A core group of lyricists, librettists, directors, choreographers, and producers shared responsibility for most of Broadway's better shows and more important innovations.

Many of the lyricists, especially, made essential contributions to the field. Most have been praised far too little (or not at all); that's not to say they are unappreciated.

Forty-two of these collaborators have been included in this appendix. Productions they collaborated on are listed, giving a partial view of their careers. Only shows discussed in this book are listed, and the collaborators are included even in cases where they did not receive official credit.

The usual function(s) they performed are mentioned. The collaborator did not necessarily serve in all capacities on each production.

This reference guide can serve as just that—a guide. Though work of the collaborators has been discussed only as it affected the composers, most of them are worthy of separate study. The collaborators represented in this appendix are as follows:

George Abbott 442
Lee Adams 442
George Balanchine 443
Michael Bennett 443
Guy Bolton 443
Gower Champion 444
Betty Comden & Adolph Green 444
Cheryl Crawford 445
Agnes de Mille 445
B. G. DeSylva 446
Howard Dietz 446
Charles B. Dillingham 447
Fred Ebb 447
Dorothy Fields 448
Herbert Fields 448
Bob Fosse 449
Vinton Freedley 449
Robert Fryer 450
Ira Gershwin 450
Oscar Hammerstein 2nd 451
Otto Harbach 452

E. Y. (Yip) Harburg 452
Sheldon Harnick 452
Sam H. Harris 453
Lorenz Hart 453
Moss Hart 454
Tom Jones 454
George S. Kaufman 455
Michael Kidd 455
Joe Layton 456
Alan Jay Lerner 456
Joshua Logan 457
Rouben Mamoulian 457
David Merrick 457
Harold Prince 458
Jerome Robbins 459
Joseph Stein 459
Michael Stewart 459
Tommy Tune 460
P. G. Wodehouse 460
Florenz Ziegfeld, Jr. 460

DATE	COMPOSER(S)	PRODUCTION

GEORGE ABBOTT, librettist, director, producer
Born: June 25, 1887, Forrestville, New York
Died: January 31, 1995, Miami Beach, Florida

DATE	COMPOSER(S)	PRODUCTION
December 2, 1932	Arlen	The Great Magoo
November 16, 1935	Rodgers	Jumbo
April 11, 1936	Rodgers	On Your Toes
November 23, 1938	Rodgers	The Boys from Syracuse
October 18, 1939	Rodgers	Too Many Girls
December 25, 1940	Rodgers	Pal Joey
October 1, 1941	Martin, Rodgers	Best Foot Forward
December 28, 1944	Bernstein	On the Town
October 9, 1947	Styne	High Button Shoes
January 29, 1948	Martin	Look, Ma, I'm Dancin'!
October 11, 1948	Loesser	Where's Charley?
October 12, 1950	Berlin	Call Me Madam
December 21, 1950	Porter	Out of This World
April 19, 1951	Schwartz	A Tree Grows in Brooklyn
February 25, 1953	Bernstein	Wonderful Town
May 28, 1953	Rodgers	Me and Juliet
May 13, 1954	Adler	The Pajama Game
May 5, 1955	Adler	Damn Yankees
May 14, 1957	Merrill	New Girl in Town
May 11, 1959	Notables	Once upon a Mattress
November 23, 1959	Bock	Fiorello!
October 17, 1960	Bock	Tenderloin
May 8, 1962	Sondheim	A Funny Thing Happened [. . .] Forum
November 27, 1962	Bock, Kander	Never Too Late
May 26, 1964	Styne	Fade Out—Fade In
May 11, 1965	Kander	Flora, the Red Menace
December 20, 1976	Adler	Music Is

LEE ADAMS, lyricist
Born: August 14, 1924, Springfield, Ohio

DATE	COMPOSER(S)	PRODUCTION
May 22, 1956	Strouse	The Littlest Revue
November 5, 1956	Strouse	Shoestring '57
April 14, 1960	Strouse	Bye Bye Birdie
March 19, 1962	Strouse	All American
January 16, 1964	Strouse	Hello, Dolly!
October 20, 1964	Strouse	Golden Boy
March 29, 1966	Strouse	"It's a Bird, It's a Plane, It's Superman"
March 30, 1970	Strouse	Applause
November 6, 1972	Strouse	I and Albert
December 21, 1978	Strouse	A Broadway Musical
March 5, 1981	Strouse	Bring Back Birdie
April 6, 1988	Leigh	Mike
April 18, 1993	Leigh	Ain't Broadway Grand

DATE	COMPOSER(S)	PRODUCTION

GEORGE BALANCHINE, choreographer
Born: January 9, 1904, St. Petersburg, Russia
Died: April 30, 1983, New York, New York

DATE	COMPOSER(S)	PRODUCTION
March 27, 1929	Porter	Wake up and Dream
January 30, 1936	Duke	Ziegfeld Follies of 1936
April 11, 1936	Rodgers	On Your Toes
April 14, 1937	Rodgers	Babes in Arms
May 11, 1938	Rodgers	I Married an Angel
November 23, 1938	Rodgers	The Boys from Syracuse
May 23, 1940	Duke	Keep Off the Grass
May 28, 1940	Berlin	Louisiana Purchase
October 25, 1940	Duke	Cabin in the Sky
January 9, 1942	Duke	The Lady Comes Across
November 11, 1943	Loewe	What's Up?
October 11, 1948	Loesser	Where's Charley?
June 20, 1958	Blitzstein	A Midsummer Night's Dream
July 20, 1958	Blitzstein	The Winter's Tale [1958]

MICHAEL BENNETT, director, choreographer, producer
Born: April 8, 1943, Buffalo, New York
Died: July 2, 1987, Tucson, Arizona

DATE	COMPOSER(S)	PRODUCTION
October 23, 1967	Merrill	Henry, Sweet Henry
December 1, 1968	Notables	Promises! Promises!
April 26, 1970	Sondheim	Company
April 4, 1971	Sondheim	Follies
November 14, 1971	Sondheim	Twigs
March 18, 1973	Coleman	Seesaw
May 21, 1975	Hamlisch	A Chorus Line
December 20, 1981	Notables	Dreamgirls

GUY BOLTON, librettist
Born: November 23, 1884, Broxbourne, England
Died: September 5, 1979, London, England

DATE	COMPOSER(S)	PRODUCTION
January 25, 1915	Kern	Ninety in the Shade
April 20, 1915	Kern	Nobody Home
December 23, 1915	Kern	Very Good Eddie [1915]
September 25, 1916	Kern	Miss Springtime
January 11, 1917	Kern	Have a Heart
February 20, 1917	Kern	Oh, Boy!
August 28, 1917	Kern	Leave It to Jane
September 24, 1917	Kern	The Riviera Girl
November 5, 1917	Kern	Miss 1917
February 1, 1918	Kern	Oh Lady! Lady!!
May 18, 1918	Porter	Very Good Eddie [1918]
November 27, 1918	Kern	Oh, My Dear!
December 21, 1920	Kern	Sally
April 8, 1924	Kern	Sitting Pretty
September 11, 1924	Gershwin	Primrose

(continued)

DATE	COMPOSER(S)	PRODUCTION

DATE	COMPOSER(S)	PRODUCTION
December 1, 1924	Gershwin	Lady, Be Good!
December 28, 1925	Gershwin	Tip-Toes
November 8, 1926	Gershwin	Oh, Kay!
January 3, 1928	Rodgers	She's My Baby
January 10, 1928	Gershwin	Rosalie
April 27, 1928	Kern	Blue Eyes
February 18, 1930	Rodgers	Simple Simon
October 14, 1930	Gershwin	Girl Crazy
November 21, 1934	Porter	Anything Goes
June 9, 1939	Porter	The Sun Never Sets
June 4, 1940	Notables	Walk with Music
January 13, 1944	Duke	Jackpot

GOWER CHAMPION, director, choreographer
Born: June 22, 1920, Geneva, Illinois
Died: August 25, 1980, New York, New York

DATE	COMPOSER(S)	PRODUCTION
January 9, 1942	Duke	The Lady Comes Across
May 5, 1944	Duke	Tars and Spars
April 18, 1951	Martin	Make a Wish
April 14, 1960	Strouse	Bye Bye Birdie
April 13, 1961	Merrill	Carnival!
January 16, 1964	Herman, Merrill, Strouse	Hello, Dolly!
December 5, 1966	Schmidt	I Do! I Do!
January 18, 1968	Kander	The Happy Time
February 1, 1971	Styne	Prettybelle
April 9, 1972	Styne	Sugar
October 6, 1974	Herman	Mack & Mabel
October 29, 1977	Kander	The Act
December 21, 1978	Strouse	A Broadway Musical

BETTY COMDEN, lyricist, librettist
Born: May 3, 1915, New York, New York

ADOLPH GREEN, lyricist, librettist
Born: December 2, 1915, New York, New York

DATE	COMPOSER(S)	PRODUCTION
December 28, 1944	Bernstein	On the Town
July 19, 1951	Styne	Two on the Aisle
February 25, 1953	Bernstein	Wonderful Town
October 24, 1954	Styne	Peter Pan [1954]
November 29, 1956	Styne	Bells Are Ringing
April 3, 1958	Styne	Say, Darling
December 28, 1960	Styne	Do Re Mi
December 27, 1961	Styne	Subways Are for Sleeping
May 26, 1964	Styne	Fade Out—Fade In
April 26, 1967	Styne	Hallelujah, Baby!
March 30, 1970	Strouse	Applause
January 27, 1974	Styne	Lorelei
February 21, 1975	Coleman	Straws in the Wind
November 23, 1975	Bernstein	By Bernstein

DATE	COMPOSER(S)	PRODUCTION

DATE	COMPOSER(S)	PRODUCTION
February 19, 1978	Coleman	On the Twentieth Century
June 13, 1979	Bernstein	The Madwoman of Central Park West
September 23, 1982	Grossman	A Doll's Life
November 29, 1984	Coleman	Diamonds
May 1, 1991	Coleman	The Will Rogers Follies

CHERYL CRAWFORD, producer
Born: September 24, 1902, Akron, Ohio
Died: October 7, 1986, New York, New York

November 19, 1936	Weill	Johnny Johnson
October 7, 1943	Weill	One Touch of Venus
December 19, 1946	Blitzstein	Androcles and the Lion
March 13, 1947	Loewe	Brigadoon
October 7, 1948	Weill	Love Life
October 31, 1949	Blitzstein	Regina
May 14, 1951	Notables	Flahooley
November 12, 1951	Loewe	Paint Your Wagon
October 10, 1955	Blitzstein	Reuben Reuben
November 19, 1956	Sondheim	The Girls of Summer
January 3, 1962	Weill	Brecht on Brecht
October 17, 1963	Schwartz	Jennie
November 15, 1966	Leigh	Chu-Chem [1966]
January 22, 1969	Schmidt	Celebration
May 6, 1970	Schmidt	Colette [1970]

AGNES DE MILLE, choreographer
Born: September 18, 1905, New York, New York
Died: October 6, 1993, New York, New York

September 15, 1932	Schwartz	Flying Colors
October 6, 1933	Porter	Nymph Errant
December 1, 1937	Arlen	Hooray for What!
March 31, 1943	Rodgers	Oklahoma!
October 7, 1943	Weill	One Touch of Venus
October 5, 1944	Arlen	Bloomer Girl
April 19, 1945	Rodgers	Carousel
March 13, 1947	Loewe	Brigadoon
October 10, 1947	Rodgers	Allegro
December 8, 1949	Styne	Gentlemen Prefer Blondes
December 21, 1950	Porter	Out of This World
November 12, 1951	Loewe	Paint Your Wagon
November 11, 1958	Notables	Goldilocks
March 9, 1959	Blitzstein	Juno
October 23, 1961	Adler	Kwamina
October 24, 1963	Schmidt	110 in the Shade

(*continued*)

DATE	COMPOSER(S)	PRODUCTION

B. G. DESYLVA, lyricist, producer
Born: January 27, 1895, New York, New York
Died: July 11, 1950, Los Angeles, California

DATE	COMPOSER(S)	PRODUCTION
May 26, 1919	Gershwin	La La Lucille
December 8, 1919	Kern	Zip, Goes a Million
December 27, 1919	Gershwin	Morris Gest's Midnight Whirl
circa December 1919	Gershwin	Sinbad
December 21, 1920	Kern	Sally
June 21, 1921	Kern	Ziegfeld Follies of 1921
November 7, 1921	Gershwin	The Perfect Fool
February 20, 1922	Gershwin	The French Doll
July 6, 1922	Gershwin	Spice of 1922
August 28, 1922	Gershwin	George White's Scandals [4th]
June 18, 1923	Gershwin	George White's Scandals [5th]
August 28, 1923	Gershwin	Little Miss Bluebeard
January 21, 1924	Gershwin	Sweet Little Devil
June 30, 1924	Gershwin	George White's Scandals [6th]
September 11, 1924	Gershwin	Primrose
November 6, 1924	Kern	Peter Pan [1924]
April 13, 1925	Gershwin	Tell Me More
June 14, 1926	Notables	George White's Scandals of 1926
September 6, 1927	Notables	Good News!
November 26, 1932	Youmans	Take a Chance
December 6, 1939	Porter	DuBarry Was a Lady
May 28, 1940	Berlin	Louisiana Purchase
October 30, 1940	Porter	Panama Hattie

HOWARD DIETZ, lyricist
Born: September 8, 1896, New York, New York
Died: July 30, 1983, New York, New York

DATE	COMPOSER(S)	PRODUCTION
September 23, 1924	Kern	Dear Sir
November 8, 1926	Gershwin	Oh, Kay!
April 30, 1929	Schwartz	The Little Show
May 1, 1929	Schwartz	The Grand Street Follies of 1929
February 20, 1930	Schwartz	Here Comes the Bride
April 4, 1930	Schwartz	The Co-Optimists of 1930
September 2, 1930	Schwartz	The Second Little Show
October 15, 1930	Schwartz, Duke, Lane	Three's a Crowd
June 3, 1931	Schwartz	The Band Wagon
September 15, 1932	Schwartz	Flying Colors
November 28, 1934	Schwartz	Revenge with Music
September 19, 1935	Schwartz	At Home Abroad
February 4, 1936	Schwartz	Follow the Sun
December 25, 1936	Schwartz	The Show Is On
December 22, 1937	Schwartz	Between the Devil
May 23, 1940	Duke	Keep Off the Grass
June 22, 1942	Weill	Lunchtime Follies
March 22, 1943	Duke	Dancing in the Streets
January 13, 1944	Duke	Jackpot

DATE	COMPOSER(S)	PRODUCTION
	Howard Dietz (*continued*)	
May 5, 1944	Duke	Tars and Spars
November 16, 1944	Duke	Sadie Thompson
April 30, 1948	Schwartz	Inside U.S.A.
circa February, 1960	Schwartz	Mrs. 'Arris Goes to Paris
November 18, 1961	Schwartz	The Gay Life
October 17, 1963	Schwartz	Jennie

CHARLES B. DILLINGHAM, producer
Born: May 30, 1868, Hartford, Connecticut
Died: August 30, 1934, New York, New York

August 17, 1910	Kern	The Echo
December 8, 1914	Berlin	Watch Your Step
October 5, 1915	Kern, Porter	Miss Information
December 25, 1915	Berlin	Stop! Look! Listen!
November 6, 1916	Berlin	The Century Girl
circa April 1917	Berlin	Dance and Grow Thin
October 16, 1917	Berlin	Jack O'Lantern
November 5, 1917	Kern	Miss 1917
August 22, 1918	Berlin	Everything
November 4, 1918	Kern, Berlin	The Canary
May 5, 1919	Kern	She's a Good Fellow
February 2, 1920	Kern	The Night Boat
November 1, 1921	Kern	Good Morning Dearie
November 28, 1922	Kern	The Bunch and Judy
November 6, 1923	Kern	The Stepping Stones
November 6, 1924	Kern	Peter Pan [1924]
September 22, 1925	Kern	Sunny
October 26, 1925	Kern	The City Chap
October 12, 1926	Kern	Criss-Cross
December 17, 1926	Youmans	Oh, Please!
March 22, 1927	Kern	Lucky
January 3, 1928	Rodgers	She's My Baby
February 11, 1930	Kern	Ripples

FRED EBB, lyricist
Born: April 8, 1932, New York, New York

April 20, 1960	Herman	From A to Z
May 11, 1965	Kander	Flora, the Red Menace
November 20, 1966	Kander	Cabaret
January 18, 1968	Kander	The Happy Time
November 17, 1968	Kander	Zorbá
April 15, 1971	Kander	70, Girls, 70
June 1, 1975	Kander	Chicago
October 29, 1977	Kander	The Act
June 13, 1979	Kander	The Madwoman of Central Park West
March 29, 1981	Kander	Woman of the Year
February 9, 1984	Kander	The Rink

(*continued*)

DATE	COMPOSER(S)	PRODUCTION

Fred Ebb (*continued*)

DATE	COMPOSER(S)	PRODUCTION
November 29, 1984	Kander	Diamonds
December 12, 1985	Kander	Hay Fever
May 1, 1990	Kander	Kiss of the Spider Woman [1990]
March 18, 1991	Kander	And the World Goes 'Round
May 3, 1993	Kander	Kiss of the Spider Woman [1993]
April 24, 1997	Kander	Steel Pier

DOROTHY FIELDS, lyricist, librettist
Born: July 15, 1905, Allenhurst, New Jersey
Died: March 28, 1974, New York, New York

DATE	COMPOSER(S)	PRODUCTION
March 6, 1920	Rodgers	You'd Be Surprised
May 9, 1928	Notables	Blackbirds of 1928
November 5, 1930	Porter	The Vanderbilt Revue
February 9, 1939	Schwartz	Stars in Your Eyes
October 29, 1941	Porter	Let's Face It
January 7, 1943	Porter	Something for the Boys
January 28, 1944	Porter	Mexican Hayride
May 16, 1946	Berlin	Annie Get Your Gun
April 19, 1951	Schwartz	A Tree Grows in Brooklyn
April 8, 1954	Schwartz	By the Beautiful Sea
January 29, 1966	Coleman	Sweet Charity
September 27, 1967	Coleman	Keep It in the Family
circa 1969	Coleman	Eleanor
March 18, 1973	Coleman	Seesaw

HERBERT FIELDS, librettist
Born: July 26, 1897, New York, New York
Died: March 24, 1958, New York, New York

DATE	COMPOSER(S)	PRODUCTION
March 6, 1920	Rodgers	You'd Be Surprised
March 24, 1920	Rodgers	Fly with Me
July 28, 1920	Rodgers	Poor Little Ritz Girl
April 20, 1921	Rodgers	You'll Never Know
circa 1922	Rodgers	Winkle Town
May 13, 1924	Rodgers	The Melody Man
May 17, 1925	Rodgers	Garrick Gaieties [1st]
September 18, 1925	Rodgers	Dearest Enemy
March 17, 1926	Rodgers	The Girl Friend
May 10, 1926	Rodgers	Garrick Gaieties [2nd]
December 27, 1926	Rodgers	Peggy-Ann
April 25, 1927	Youmans	Hit the Deck
November 3, 1927	Rodgers	A Connecticut Yankee [1927]
April 26, 1928	Rodgers	Present Arms!
September 25, 1928	Rodgers	Chee-Chee
November 27, 1929	Porter	Fifty Million Frenchmen
December 8, 1930	Porter	The New Yorkers [1930]
February 10, 1931	Rodgers	America's Sweetheart

DATE	COMPOSER(S)	PRODUCTION

Herbert Fields (*continued*)

January 20, 1933	Gershwin	Pardon My English
December 6, 1939	Porter	DuBarry Was a Lady
October 30, 1940	Porter	Panama Hattie
October 29, 1941	Porter	Let's Face It
January 7, 1943	Porter	Something for the Boys
November 17, 1943	Rodgers	A Connecticut Yankee [1943]
January 28, 1944	Porter	Mexican Hayride
May 16, 1946	Berlin	Annie Get Your Gun
April 8, 1954	Schwartz	By the Beautiful Sea
February 5, 1959	Notables	Redhead

BOB FOSSE, director, choreographer
Born: June 23, 1927, Chicago, Illinois
Died: September 23, 1987, Washington, DC

May 13, 1954	Adler	The Pajama Game
May 5, 1955	Adler	Damn Yankees
November 29, 1956	Styne	Bells Are Ringing
May 14, 1957	Merrill	New Girl in Town
February 5, 1959	Notables	Redhead
October 14, 1961	Loesser	How to Succeed [. . .] without Really Trying
November 17, 1962	Coleman	Little Me
March 11, 1965	Loesser	Pleasures and Palaces
January 29, 1966	Coleman	Sweet Charity
October 23, 1972	S. Schwartz	Pippin
June 1, 1975	Kander	Chicago
April 16, 1985	Grossman	Grind

VINTON FREEDLEY, producer
Born: November 5, 1891, Philadelphia, Pennsylvania
Died: June 5, 1969, New York, New York

December 1, 1924	Gershwin	Lady, Be Good!
December 28, 1925	Gershwin	Tip-Toes
November 8, 1926	Gershwin	Oh, Kay!
November 22, 1927	Gershwin	Funny Face
November 8, 1928	Gershwin	Treasure Girl
March 11, 1929	Rodgers	Spring Is Here
November 11, 1929	Rodgers	Heads Up!
October 14, 1930	Gershwin	Girl Crazy
January 20, 1933	Gershwin	Pardon My English
November 21, 1934	Porter	Anything Goes
October 29, 1936	Porter	Red, Hot and Blue!
November 9, 1938	Porter	Leave It to Me!
October 25, 1940	Duke	Cabin in the Sky
October 29, 1941	Porter	Let's Face It
March 22, 1943	Duke	Dancing in the Streets
January 13, 1944	Duke	Jackpot

(*continued*)

DATE	COMPOSER(S)	PRODUCTION

ROBERT FRYER, producer
Born: November 18, 1920, Washington, D.C.

DATE	COMPOSER(S)	PRODUCTION
April 19, 1951	Schwartz	A Tree Grows in Brooklyn
April 8, 1954	Schwartz	By the Beautiful Sea
February 5, 1959	Notables	Redhead
December 7, 1959	Arlen	Saratoga
April 19, 1963	Sondheim	Hot Spot
January 29, 1966	Coleman	Sweet Charity
May 24, 1966	Herman	Mame
June 1, 1975	Kander	Chicago
February 19, 1978	Coleman	On the Twentieth Century
March 1, 1979	Sondheim	Sweeney Todd
November 16, 1981	Sondheim	Merrily We Roll Along
September 23, 1982	Grossman	A Doll's Life

IRA GERSHWIN, lyricist
Born: December 6, 1896, New York, New York
Died: August 17, 1983, Beverly Hills, California

DATE	COMPOSER(S)	PRODUCTION
October 24, 1918	Gershwin	Ladies First
August 31, 1920	Gershwin	The Sweetheart Shop
September 27, 1920	Youmans	Piccadilly to Broadway
March 21, 1921	Gershwin	A Dangerous Maid
May 3, 1921	Youmans	Two Little Girls in Blue [1921]
August 28, 1922	Gershwin	George White's Scandals [4th]
August 28, 1923	Gershwin	Little Miss Bluebeard
September 11, 1924	Gershwin	Primrose
December 1, 1924	Gershwin	Lady, Be Good!
April 13, 1925	Gershwin	Tell Me More
September 7, 1925	Youmans	A Night Out [1925]
December 28, 1925	Gershwin	Tip-Toes
July 26, 1926	Gershwin	Americana
November 8, 1926	Gershwin	Oh, Kay!
circa April 1927	Duke	Two Little Girls in Blue [1927]
August 29, 1927	Gershwin	Strike up the Band [1927]
November 22, 1927	Gershwin	Funny Face
January 10, 1928	Gershwin	Rosalie
November 8, 1928	Gershwin	Treasure Girl
circa January 1929	Gershwin	East Is West
July 2, 1929	Gershwin, Youmans	Show Girl
January 14, 1930	Gershwin	Strike up the Band [1930]
February 11, 1930	Gershwin	Nine-Fifteen Revue
June 4, 1930	Duke	Garrick Gaieties [3rd]
October 14, 1930	Gershwin	Girl Crazy
December 26, 1931	Gershwin	Of Thee I Sing
January 20, 1933	Gershwin	Pardon My English
October 21, 1933	Gershwin	Let 'Em Eat Cake
August 27, 1934	Arlen	Life Begins at 8:40
October 10, 1935	Gershwin	Porgy and Bess
January 30, 1936	Duke	Ziegfeld Follies of 1936
December 25, 1936	Gershwin	The Show Is On
January 23, 1941	Weill	Lady in the Dark

DATE	COMPOSER(S)	PRODUCTION
	Ira Gershwin (*continued*)	
March 22, 1945	Weill	The Firebrand of Florence
November 4, 1946	Schwartz	Park Avenue
March 9, 1951	Gershwin	Let Me Hear the Melody

OSCAR HAMMERSTEIN 2ND, lyricist, librettist, producer
Born: July 12, 1895, New York, New York
Died: August 23, 1960, Doyleston, Pennsylvania

March 8, 1919	Rodgers	Up Stage and Down
March 24, 1920	Rodgers	Fly with Me
circa 1922	Rodgers	Winkle Town
February 7, 1923	Youmans	Wildflower
October 4, 1923	Youmans	Hammerstein's Nine O'Clock Revue
December 25, 1923	Youmans	Mary Jane McKane
September 22, 1925	Kern	Sunny
December 30, 1925	Gershwin	Song of the Flame
December 27, 1927	Kern	Show Boat
September 5, 1928	Schwartz	Good Boy
November 21, 1928	Youmans	Rainbow
September 3, 1929	Kern	Sweet Adeline
November 8, 1932	Kern	Music in the Air
April 19, 1934	Kern	Three Sisters
June 3, 1938	Kern	Gentlemen Unafraid
May 17, 1939	Kern	Very Warm for May
May 12, 1940	Schwartz	American Jubilee
June 22, 1942	Weill	Lunchtime Follies
March 31, 1943	Rodgers	Oklahoma!
April 19, 1945	Rodgers	Carousel
May 16, 1946	Berlin	Annie Get Your Gun
October 31, 1946	Rodgers	Happy Birthday
October 10, 1947	Rodgers	Allegro
April 7, 1949	Rodgers	South Pacific
March 29, 1951	Rodgers	The King and I
May 28, 1953	Rodgers	Me and Juliet
November 30, 1955	Rodgers	Pipe Dream
December 1, 1958	Rodgers	Flower Drum Song
November 16, 1959	Rodgers	The Sound of Music
March 27, 1996	Rodgers	State Fair

OTTO HARBACH, lyricist, librettist
Born: August 18, 1873, Salt Lake City, Utah
Died: January 24, 1963, New York, New York

September 11, 1911	Berlin	The Fascinating Widow
December 25, 1917	Berlin	Going Up
February 7, 1923	Youmans	Wildflower
September 16, 1925	Youmans	No, No, Nanette
September 22, 1925	Kern	Sunny
December 30, 1925	Gershwin	Song of the Flame

(*continued*)

DATE	COMPOSER(S)	PRODUCTION

Otto Harbach (*continued*)

DATE	COMPOSER(S)	PRODUCTION
October 12, 1926	Kern	Criss-Cross
December 17, 1926	Youmans	Oh, Please!
March 22, 1927	Kern	Lucky
September 5, 1928	Schwartz	Good Boy
February 20, 1930	Schwartz	Here Comes the Bride
October 15, 1930	Kern	The Cat and the Fiddle
November 18, 1933	Kern	Roberta
June 3, 1938	Kern	Gentlemen Unafraid

E. Y. (YIP) HARBURG, lyricist, librettist
Born: April 8, 1898, New York, New York
Died: March 5, 1981, Los Angeles, California

June 4, 1930	Duke	Garrick Gaieties [3rd]
July 1, 1930	Arlen	Earl Carroll Vanities [8th]
October 5, 1932	Arlen	Americana
December 2, 1932	Arlen	The Great Magoo
December 7, 1932	Duke	Walk a Little Faster
July 28, 1933	Arlen	Crazy Quilt of 1933
January 4, 1934	Duke, Schwartz	Ziegfeld Follies of 1934
August 27, 1934	Arlen	Life Begins at 8:40
December 25, 1936	Arlen	The Show Is On
December 1, 1937	Arlen	Hooray for What!
September 11, 1940	Lane	Hold on to Your Hats
October 25, 1940	Duke	Cabin in the Sky
October 5, 1944	Arlen	Bloomer Girl
January 10, 1947	Lane	Finian's Rainbow
May 14, 1951	Notables	Flahooley
September 11, 1952	Lane	Jollyanna
October 31, 1957	Arlen	Jamaica
January 27, 1968	Styne	Darling of the Day

SHELDON HARNICK, lyricist
Born: December 27, 1924, Chicago, Illinois

February 28, 1955	Strouse	Shoestring Revue
November 5, 1956	Strouse	Shoestring '57
January 23, 1958	Bock	The Body Beautiful
November 23, 1959	Bock	Fiorello!
October 17, 1960	Bock	Tenderloin
November 27, 1962	Bock	Never Too Late
November 11, 1963	Bock	Man in the Moon
November 23, 1963	Bock	She Loves Me
September 22, 1964	Bock	Fiddler on the Roof
February 16, 1965	Bock	Baker Street
October 3, 1965	Bock	Generation
October 18, 1966	Bock	The Apple Tree
October 20, 1968	Bock	Her First Roman
October 19, 1970	Bock	The Rothschilds
April 25, 1976	Rodgers	Rex

DATE	COMPOSER(S)	PRODUCTION

SAM H. HARRIS, producer
Born: February 3, 1872, New York, New York
Died: July 3, 1941, New York, New York

DATE	COMPOSER(S)	PRODUCTION
September 25, 1911	Berlin	The Little Millionaire
circa April 1912	Berlin	Cohan and Harris Minstrels
August 31, 1912	Kern	A Polish Wedding
May 28, 1916	Berlin	Friars' Frolic of 1916
December 25, 1917	Berlin	Going Up
December 31, 1917	Berlin	The Cohan Revue of 1918
February 17, 1919	Berlin	The Royal Vagabond
September 22, 1921	Berlin	Music Box Revue [1st]
October 23, 1922	Berlin	Music Box Revue [2nd]
September 22, 1923	Berlin	Music Box Revue [3rd]
December 1, 1924	Berlin	Music Box Revue [4th]
December 8, 1925	Berlin	The Cocoanuts
December 26, 1931	Gershwin	Of Thee I Sing
February 17, 1932	Berlin	Face the Music
September 30, 1933	Berlin	As Thousands Cheer
October 21, 1933	Gershwin	Let 'Em Eat Cake
October 12, 1935	Porter	Jubilee
November 2, 1937	Rodgers	I'd Rather Be Right
January 23, 1941	Weill	Lady in the Dark

LORENZ HART, lyricist
Born: May 2, 1895, New York, New York
Died: November 22, 1943, New York, New York

DATE	COMPOSER(S)	PRODUCTION
March 8, 1919	Rodgers	Up Stage and Down
June 10, 1919	Rodgers	A Lonely Romeo
March 6, 1920	Rodgers	You'd Be Surprised
March 24, 1920	Rodgers	Fly with Me
July 28, 1920	Rodgers	Poor Little Ritz Girl
February 12, 1921	Rodgers	Say Mama!
April 20, 1921	Rodgers	You'll Never Know
circa 1922	Rodgers	Winkle Town
March 19, 1923	Rodgers	Half Moon Inn
May 13, 1924	Rodgers	The Melody Man
May 17, 1925	Rodgers	Garrick Gaieties [1st]
August 6, 1925	Rodgers	June Days
September 18, 1925	Rodgers	Dearest Enemy
circa January 1926	Rodgers	Fifth Avenue Follies
March 17, 1926	Rodgers	The Girl Friend
April 29, 1926	Rodgers	Cochran's 1926 Revue
May 10, 1926	Rodgers	Garrick Gaieties [2nd]
December 1, 1926	Rodgers	Lido Lady
December 27, 1926	Rodgers	Peggy-Ann
December 28, 1926	Rodgers, Berlin	Betsy
April 27, 1927	Rodgers	Lady Luck
May 20, 1927	Rodgers	London Pavilion Revue
November 3, 1927	Rodgers	A Connecticut Yankee [1927]
January 3, 1928	Rodgers	She's My Baby

(continued)

DATE	COMPOSER(S)	PRODUCTION

Lorenz Hart (*continued*)

DATE	COMPOSER(S)	PRODUCTION
April 26, 1928	Rodgers	Present Arms!
September 25, 1928	Rodgers	Chee-Chee
January 31, 1929	Rodgers	Lady Fingers
March 11, 1929	Rodgers	Spring Is Here
November 11, 1929	Rodgers	Heads Up!
February 18, 1930	Rodgers	Simple Simon
December 3, 1930	Rodgers	Ever Green
February 10, 1931	Rodgers	America's Sweetheart
May 19, 1931	Rodgers	Crazy Quilt
November 16, 1933	Rodgers	Please!
April 29, 1935	Rodgers	Something Gay
November 16, 1935	Rodgers	Jumbo
April 11, 1936	Rodgers	On Your Toes
December 25, 1936	Rodgers	The Show Is On
April 14, 1937	Rodgers	Babes in Arms
November 2, 1937	Rodgers	I'd Rather Be Right
May 11, 1938	Rodgers	I Married an Angel
November 23, 1938	Rodgers	The Boys from Syracuse
October 18, 1939	Rodgers	Too Many Girls
April 4, 1940	Rodgers	Higher and Higher
June 24, 1940	Rodgers	Two Weeks with Pay
December 25, 1940	Rodgers	Pal Joey
October 1, 1941	Rodgers	Best Foot Forward
June 2, 1942	Rodgers	By Jupiter
November 17, 1943	Rodgers	A Connecticut Yankee [1943]

MOSS HART, librettist, director
Born: October 24, 1904, New York, New York
Died: December 20, 1961, Palm Springs, California

DATE	COMPOSER(S)	PRODUCTION
February 17, 1932	Berlin	Face the Music
September 30, 1933	Berlin	As Thousands Cheer
October 12, 1935	Porter	Jubilee
December 25, 1936	Duke	The Show Is On
November 2, 1937	Rodgers	I'd Rather Be Right
September 24, 1938	Rome	Sing out the News
October 16, 1939	Porter	The Man Who Came to Dinner
January 23, 1941	Weill	Lady in the Dark
June 22, 1942	Weill, Rome	Lunchtime Follies
December 7, 1944	Porter	Seven Lively Arts
April 30, 1948	Schwartz	Inside U.S.A.
July 15, 1949	Berlin	Miss Liberty
March 15, 1956	Loewe	My Fair Lady
December 3, 1960	Loewe	Camelot

TOM JONES, lyricist, librettist
Born: February 17, 1928, Littlefield, Texas

DATE	COMPOSER(S)	PRODUCTION
November 5, 1956	Schmidt	Shoestring '57
October 11, 1958	Schmidt	Demi-Dozen

DATE	COMPOSER(S)	PRODUCTION

Tom Jones (*continued*)

DATE	COMPOSER(S)	PRODUCTION
May 3, 1960	Schmidt	The Fantasticks
October 24, 1963	Schmidt	110 in the Shade
December 5, 1966	Schmidt	I Do! I Do!
January 22, 1969	Schmidt	Celebration
May 6, 1970	Schmidt	Colette [1970]
January 3, 1975	Schmidt	Philemon
February 28, 1975	Schmidt	The Bone Room
February 9, 1982	Schmidt	Colette [1982]
March 31, 1983	Schmidt	Colette Collage [1983]
July 29, 1987	Schmidt	Grover's Corners
April 24, 1991	Schmidt	Collete Collage [1991]
December 17, 1997	Schmidt	The Show Goes On
July 1, 1998	Schmidt	Mirette

GEORGE S. KAUFMAN, librettist, director
Born: November 14, 1889, Pittsburgh, Pennsylvania
Died: June 2, 1961, New York, New York

DATE	COMPOSER(S)	PRODUCTION
September 22, 1923	Berlin	Music Box Revue [3rd]
December 8, 1925	Berlin	The Cocoanuts
August 29, 1927	Gershwin	Strike up the Band [1927]
April 30, 1929	Schwartz	The Little Show
January 14, 1930	Gershwin	Strike up the Band [1930]
February 11, 1930	Arlen	Nine-Fifteen Revue
June 3, 1931	Schwartz	The Band Wagon
December 26, 1931	Gershwin	Of Thee I Sing
February 17, 1932	Berlin	Face the Music
October 21, 1933	Gershwin	Let 'Em Eat Cake
October 22, 1934	Schwartz	Bring on the Girls
December 25, 1936	Duke	The Show Is On
November 2, 1937	Rodgers	I'd Rather Be Right
September 24, 1938	Rome	Sing out the News
October 16, 1939	Porter	The Man Who Came to Dinner
June 22, 1942	Weill	Lunchtime Follies
December 7, 1944	Porter	Seven Lively Arts
November 4, 1946	Schwartz	Park Avenue
June 20, 1949	Rome	Pretty Penny
November 24, 1950	Loesser	Guys and Dolls
February 24, 1955	Porter	Silk Stockings
circa December 1956	Berlin	The Mizner Story
October 10, 1957	Rome	Romanoff and Juliet

MICHAEL KIDD, director, choreographer
Born: August 12, 1919, Brooklyn, New York

DATE	COMPOSER(S)	PRODUCTION
January 10, 1947	Lane	Finian's Rainbow
June 20, 1949	Rome	Pretty Penny
November 24, 1950	Loesser	Guys and Dolls
May 7, 1952	Porter	Can-Can
November 15, 1956	Notables	Li'l Abner

(*continued*)

DATE	COMPOSER(S)	PRODUCTION

Michael Kidd (*continued*)

DATE	COMPOSER(S)	PRODUCTION
April 23, 1959	Rome	Destry Rides Again
December 16, 1960	Coleman	Wildcat
December 27, 1961	Styne	Subways Are for Sleeping
October 3, 1963	Willson	Here's Love
May 7, 1964	Styne	Wonderworld
October 27, 1964	Herman	Ben Franklin in Paris
December 14, 1966	Merrill	Breakfast at Tiffany's
October 19, 1970	Bock	The Rothschilds
March 4, 1993	Hamlisch	The Goodbye Girl

JOE LAYTON, director, choreographer
Born: May 3, 1931, Brooklyn, New York
Died: May 5, 1995, Key West, Florida

May 11, 1959	Notables	Once upon a Mattress
November 16, 1959	Rodgers	The Sound of Music
March 8, 1960	Loesser	Greenwillow
October 17, 1960	Bock	Tenderloin
March 15, 1962	Rodgers	No Strings
February 6, 1969	Herman	Dear World
November 10, 1970	Rodgers	Two by Two
August 28, 1973	Rome	Gone with the Wind
January 27, 1974	Styne	Lorelei
April 30, 1980	Coleman	Barnum
March 5, 1981	Strouse	Bring Back Birdie
November 27, 1985	Styne	Pieces of Eight

ALAN JAY LERNER, lyricist, librettist
Born: August 31, 1918, New York, New York
Died: June 14, 1986, New York, New York

October 8, 1942	Loewe	Life of the Party
November 11, 1943	Loewe	What's Up?
November 22, 1945	Loewe	The Day before Spring
March 13, 1947	Loewe	Brigadoon
October 7, 1948	Weill	Love Life
November 12, 1951	Loewe	Paint Your Wagon
March 15, 1956	Loewe	My Fair Lady
December 3, 1960	Loewe	Camelot
October 17, 1965	Lane	On a Clear Day You Can See Forever
November 13, 1973	Loewe	Gigi
May 4, 1976	Bernstein	1600 Pennsylvania Avenue
April 8, 1979	Lane	Carmelina
May 11, 1983	Strouse	Dance a Little Closer

DATE	COMPOSER(S)	PRODUCTION

JOSHUA LOGAN, director
Born: October 5, 1908, Texarkana, Texas
Died: July 12, 1988, New York, New York

DATE	COMPOSER(S)	PRODUCTION
May 11, 1938	Rodgers	I Married an Angel
October 19, 1938	Weill	Knickerbocker Holiday
February 9, 1939	Schwartz	Stars in Your Eyes
April 4, 1940	Rodgers	Higher and Higher
June 2, 1942	Rodgers	By Jupiter
July 4, 1942	Berlin	This Is the Army
May 16, 1946	Berlin	Annie Get Your Gun
October 31, 1946	Rodgers	Happy Birthday
April 7, 1949	Rodgers	South Pacific
June 24, 1952	Rome	Wish You Were Here
November 4, 1954	Rome	Fanny
March 19, 1962	Strouse	All American
October 20, 1962	Berlin	Mr. President
May 24, 1966	Herman	Mame
March 29, 1970	Styne	Look to the Lilies

ROUBEN MAMOULIAN, director
Born: October 8, 1889, Tiflis, Russia
Died: December 4, 1987, Woodland Hills, California

DATE	COMPOSER(S)	PRODUCTION
October 10, 1935	Gershwin	Porgy and Bess
March 31, 1943	Rodgers	Oklahoma!
November 16, 1944	Duke	Sadie Thompson
April 19, 1945	Rodgers	Carousel
March 30, 1946	Arlen	St. Louis Woman
October 30, 1949	Weill	Lost in the Stars
circa April, 1950	Weill	Huckleberry Finn

DAVID MERRICK, producer
Born: November 27, 1911, St. Louis, Missouri

DATE	COMPOSER(S)	PRODUCTION
November 4, 1954	Rome	Fanny
October 10, 1957	Rome	Romanoff and Juliet
October 31, 1957	Arlen	Jamaica
April 23, 1959	Rome	Destry Rides Again
May 21, 1959	Styne	Gypsy
October 22, 1959	Merrill	Take Me Along
December 28, 1960	Styne	Do Re Mi
April 13, 1961	Merrill	Carnival
December 27, 1961	Styne	Subways Are for Sleeping
March 22, 1962	Rome	I Can Get It for You Wholesale
October 24, 1963	Schmidt	110 in the Shade
November 11, 1963	Styne	Arturo Ui
January 16, 1964	Herman, Merrill, Strouse	Hello, Dolly!
March 26, 1964	Styne	Funny Girl
December 5, 1966	Schmidt	I Do! I Do!
December 14, 1966	Merrill	Breakfast at Tiffany's
September 27, 1967	Coleman	Keep It in the Family

(continued)

DATE	COMPOSER(S)	PRODUCTION

David Merrick (continued)

DATE	COMPOSER(S)	PRODUCTION
January 18, 1968	Kander	The Happy Time
December 1, 1968	Notables	Promises! Promises!
April 9, 1972	Styne	Sugar
October 6, 1974	Herman	Mack & Mabel
May 11, 1976	S. Schwartz	The Baker's Wife
March 27, 1996	Rodgers	State Fair

HAROLD PRINCE, producer, director
Born: January 30, 1928, New York, New York

May 13, 1954	Adler	The Pajama Game
May 5, 1955	Adler	Damn Yankees
May 14, 1957	Merrill	New Girl in Town
September 26, 1957	Bernstein	West Side Story
November 23, 1959	Bock	Fiorello!
October 17, 1960	Bock	Tenderloin
January 27, 1962	Kander	A Family Affair
May 8, 1962	Sondheim	A Funny Thing Happened [. . .] Forum
November 27, 1962	Bock, Kander	Never Too Late
November 23, 1963	Bock	She Loves Me
September 22, 1964	Bock	Fiddler on the Roof
February 16, 1965	Bock	Baker Street
May 11, 1965	Kander	Flora, the Red Menace
March 29, 1966	Strouse	"It's a Bird, It's a Plane, It's Superman"
November 20, 1966	Kander	Cabaret
January 18, 1968	Kander	The Happy Time
November 17, 1968	Kander	Zorbá
April 26, 1970	Sondheim	Company
April 4, 1971	Sondheim	Follies
February 25, 1973	Sondheim	A Little Night Music [1973]
March 10, 1974	Bernstein	Candide [1974]
January 11, 1976	Sondheim	Pacific Overtures
April 25, 1976	Rodgers	Rex
May 4, 1976	Sondheim	Side by Side by Sondheim
February 19, 1978	Coleman	On the Twentieth Century
March 1, 1979	Sondheim	Sweeney Todd
November 16, 1981	Sondheim	Merrily We Roll Along
November 29, 1984	Grossmith, Coleman, Kander, Menken	Diamonds
May 1, 1990	Kander	Kiss of the Spider Woman [1990]
May 3, 1993	Kander	Kiss of the Spider Woman [1993]
December 17, 1998	Notables	Parade [1998]

DATE	COMPOSER(S)	PRODUCTION

JEROME ROBBINS, director, choreographer
Born: October 1, 1918, New York, New York
Died: July 29, 1998, New York, New York

DATE	COMPOSER(S)	PRODUCTION
December 28, 1944	Bernstein	On the Town
October 9, 1947	Styne	High Button Shoes
January 29, 1948	Martin	Look, Ma, I'm Dancin'!
September 24, 1948	Rome	That's the Ticket
July 15, 1949	Berlin	Miss Liberty
October 12, 1950	Berlin	Call Me Madam
March 29, 1951	Rodgers	The King and I
December 15, 1952	Duke	Two's Company
May 13, 1954	Adler	The Pajama Game
October 24, 1954	Styne	Peter Pan [1954]
November 29, 1956	Styne	Bells Are Ringing
September 26, 1957	Bernstein	West Side Story
May 21, 1959	Styne	Gypsy
March 26, 1964	Styne	Funny Girl
September 22, 1964	Bock	Fiddler on the Roof
circa February 16, 1969	Bernstein	A Pray by Blecht

JOSEPH STEIN, librettist
Born: May 30, 1912, New York, New York

DATE	COMPOSER(S)	PRODUCTION
January 27, 1955	Notables	Plain and Fancy
March 22, 1956	Bock	Mr. Wonderful
January 23, 1958	Bock	The Body Beautiful
March 9, 1959	Blitzstein	Juno
October 22, 1959	Merrill	Take Me Along
September 22, 1964	Bock	Fiddler on the Roof
November 17, 1968	Kander	Zorbá
May 11, 1976	S. Schwartz	The Baker's Wife
April 8, 1979	Lane	Carmelina
August 21, 1986	Strouse	Rags

MICHAEL STEWART, librettist
Born: August 1, 1929, New York, New York
Died: September 20, 1987, New York, New York

DATE	COMPOSER(S)	PRODUCTION
February 28, 1955	Strouse	Shoestring Revue
May 22, 1956	Strouse	The Littlest Revue
November 5, 1956	Strouse	Shoestring '57
April 14, 1960	Strouse	Bye Bye Birdie
April 13, 1961	Merrill	Carnival!
January 16, 1964	Herman	Hello, Dolly!
March 18, 1973	Coleman	Seesaw
October 6, 1974	Herman	Mack & Mabel
April 17, 1977	Coleman	I Love My Wife
January 11, 1979	Herman	The Grand Tour
April 30, 1980	Coleman	Barnum
March 5, 1981	Strouse	Bring Back Birdie
November 27, 1985	Styne	Pieces of Eight

(continued)

DATE	COMPOSER(S)	PRODUCTION

TOMMY TUNE, director, choreographer
Born: February 28, 1939, Wichita Falls, Texas

DATE	COMPOSER(S)	PRODUCTION
March 18, 1973	Coleman	Seesaw
April 17, 1978	Notables	The Best Little Whorehouse in Texas
May 1, 1980	Herman	A Day in Hollywood/ A Night in the Ukraine
May 18, 1981	Yeston	Cloud Nine
circa March 1982	Yeston	The Queen of Basin Street
May 9, 1982	Yeston	Nine
November 12, 1989	Yeston	Grand Hotel
May 1, 1991	Coleman	The Will Rogers Follies

P. G. WODEHOUSE, lyricist, librettist
Born: October 15, 1881, Guildford, England
Died: February 14, 1975, Southampton, New York

DATE	COMPOSER(S)	PRODUCTION
March 19, 1906	Kern	The Beauty of Bath
September 25, 1916	Kern	Miss Springtime
January 11, 1917	Kern	Have a Heart
February 20, 1917	Kern	Oh, Boy!
August 28, 1917	Kern	Leave It to Jane
September 24, 1917	Kern	The Riviera Girl
November 5, 1917	Kern	Miss 1917
February 1, 1918	Kern	Oh Lady! Lady!!
November 27, 1918	Kern	Oh, My Dear!
December 21, 1920	Kern	Sally
September 19, 1921	Kern	The Cabaret Girl
September 5, 1923	Kern	The Beauty Prize
April 8, 1924	Kern	Sitting Pretty
November 8, 1926	Gershwin	Oh, Kay!
December 27, 1927	Kern	Show Boat
January 10, 1928	Gershwin	Rosalie
November 21, 1934	Porter	Anything Goes

FLORENZ ZIEGFELD, JR., producer
Born: March 15, 1867, Chicago, Illinois
Died: July 22, 1932, Los Angeles, California

DATE	COMPOSER(S)	PRODUCTION
June 20, 1910	Berlin	Ziegfeld Follies of 1910
June 26, 1911	Kern, Berlin	Ziegfeld Follies of 1911
April 11, 1912	Kern	A Winsome Widow
October 21, 1912	Berlin	Ziegfeld Follies of 1912
June 12, 1916	Kern, Berlin	Ziegfeld Follies of 1916
November 6, 1916	Berlin	The Century Girl
circa April 1917	Berlin	Dance and Grow Thin
June 12, 1917	Kern	Ziegfeld Follies of 1917
November 5, 1917	Kern	Miss 1917
June 18, 1918	Berlin	Ziegfeld Follies of 1918
June 23, 1919	Berlin	Ziegfeld Follies of 1919
October 2, 1919	Berlin	Ziegfeld Midnight Frolic
March 8, 1920	Berlin	Ziegfeld Girls of 1920

DATE	COMPOSER(S)	PRODUCTION
	Florenz Ziegfeld (*continued*)	
June 22, 1920	Berlin	Ziegfeld Follies of 1920
June 21, 1921	Kern	Ziegfeld Follies of 1921
December 25, 1922	Kern	Rose Briar
September 22, 1925	Kern	Sunny
December 28, 1926	Rodgers, Berlin	Betsy
March 22, 1927	Kern	Lucky
August 16, 1927	Berlin	Ziegfeld Follies of 1927
December 27, 1927	Kern	Show Boat
January 10, 1928	Gershwin	Rosalie
December 4, 1928	Notables	Whoopee
circa January 1929	Gershwin	East Is West
July 2, 1929	Gershwin, Youmans	Show Girl
February 18, 1930	Rodgers	Simple Simon
November 18, 1930	Youmans	Smiles

APPENDIX 3

Bibliography and a Word about Finding Music

Bibliography

This section lists the more helpful sources used in the preparation of this book. The most important material has been the songs, over 7,000 of them: for obvious reasons, printed music, scores, and collections are not listed individually below. Neither are invaluable newspaper reviews and articles, theatre programs, souvenir programs, liner notes, etc.

Abbott, George. *Mister Abbott*. New York: Random House, 1963.

ASCAP. *Index of Performed Compositions* (Four editions). New York: American Society of Composers, Authors, and Publishers, 1952–78.

Astaire, Fred. *Steps in Time*. New York: Harper & Brothers, 1959.

Banfield, Stephen. *Sondheim's Broadway Musicals*. Ann Arbor: University of Michigan Press, 1993.

Bergreen, Laurence. *As Thousands Cheer: The Life of Irving Berlin*. New York: Viking, 1990.

Bernstein, Leonard. *Findings*. New York: Simon and Schuster, 1982.

Bloom, Ken. *American Song: The Complete Musical Theatre Companion, 1877–1995*. Second edition. New York: Schirmer Books, 1996.

Blum, Daniel, ed. *Theatre World*, vols. 1–4. New York: Daniel C. Blum/Theatre World, 1945–48; vols. 5–13. New York: Greenberg Publisher, 1949–57; vols. 14–20. Philadelphia: Chilton Books, 1958–64.

Bordman, Gerald. *American Musical Theatre*. New York: Oxford University Press, 1978.

———. *Days to Be Happy, Years to Be Sad*. New York: Oxford University Press, 1982.

———. *Jerome Kern*. New York: Oxford University Press, 1980.

Burrows, Abe. *Honest Abe*. Boston: Little, Brown & Co., 1980.

Cantor, Eddie. *My Life Is in Your Hands*. New York: Blue Ribbon Books, 1932.

Chapman, John, ed. *The Best Play Series, Vols. 1947–1948* through *1951–1952*. New York: Dodd, Mead & Co., 1948–52.

[Chappell Group]. *Comprehensive Catalogue of Vocal Solos*. New York: Chappell Group, [1953].

Connors, Martin, and Jim Craddock, eds. *Videohound's Golden Movie Retriever 1998*. Detroit: Visible Ink Press, 1998.

Crawford, Cheryl. *One Naked Individual*. Indianapolis: Bobbs-Merrill Co., 1977.

de Mille, Agnes. *Dance to the Piper*. Boston: Little, Brown and Co., 1952.

Dietz, Howard. *Dancing in the Dark*. New York: Quadrangle, 1974.

Drew, David. *Kurt Weill: A Handbook*. Berkeley: University of California Press, 1987.

Duke, Vernon. *Passport to Paris*. Boston: Little, Brown & Co., 1955.

Ewen, David. *New Complete Book of the American Musical Theatre*. Holt, Rinehart and Winston, 1970.

———. *Popular American Composers*. New York: H. W. Wilson Co., 1962. First Supplement, 1972.

Feinstein, Michael. *Nice Work If You Can Get It: My Life in Rhythm and Rhyme*. New York: Hyperion, 1995.

Fordin, Hugh. *Getting to Know Him*. New York: Random House, 1977.

Freedland, Michael. *Irving Berlin*. New York: Stein & Day, 1974.

Gershwin, Ira. *Lyrics on Several Occasions*. New York: Alfred A. Knopf, 1959.

Goldberg, Isaac, supplemented by Edith Garson. *George Gershwin: A Study in American Music*. New York: Frederick Ungar Publishing Co., 1958.

Gordon, Eric A. *Mark the Music: The Life and Work of Marc Blitzstein*. New York: St. Martin's Press, 1989.

Gordon, Max, and Lewis Funke. *Max Gordon Presents*. New York: Bernard Geis, 1963.

Green, Stanley. *Encyclopedia of the Musical Theatre*. New York: Dodd, Mead & Co., 1976.

———. *Ring Bells! Sing Songs!* New York: Arlington House, 1971.

———. *The World of Musical Comedy*. Revised and enlarged 4th edition. San Diego: A. S. Barnes and Co., 1980.

Green, Stanley, ed. *Rodgers and Hammerstein Fact Book*. New York: Lynn Farnol Group, 1980.

Guernsey, Jr., Otis L., ed. *The Best Plays Series*, Vols. *1964–1965* through *1984–1985*. New York: Dodd, Mead & Co., 1965–85.

Guernsey, Jr., Otis L., ed. *The Best Plays Series*. Vols. *1996–97*. New York: Limelight Editions, 1997.

Guernsey, Jr., Otis L., and Jeffrey Sweet, eds. *The Best Plays Series*. Vols. *1985–1986* through *1986–1987*. New York: Dodd, Mead & Co., 1987–88.

Guernsey, Jr., Otis L., and Jeffrey Sweet, eds. *The Best Plays Series*, Vols. *1987–88* through *1991–92*. New York: Applause, 1989–92.

Guernsey, Jr., Otis L., and Jeffrey Sweet, eds. *The Best Plays Series*, Vols. *1992–93* through *1995–96*. New York: Limelight Editions, 1993–96.

Halliwell, Leslie. *Halliwell's Film Guide*. 7th ed. New York: Harper & Row, 1989.

Hart, Dorothy. *Thou Swell, Thou Witty*. New York: Harper & Row, 1976.

Hart, Dorothy, and Robert Kimball, eds. *The Complete Lyrics of Lorenz Hart*. New York: Alfred A. Knopf, 1986.

Hellman, Lillian. *Pentimento: A Book of Portraits*. Boston: Little, Brown and Co., 1973.

Hewes, Henry, ed. *The Best Plays Series*. Vols. *1961–62* through *1963–64*. New York: Dodd, Mead & Co., 1962–64.

Higham, Charles. *Ziegfeld*. Chicago: Henry Regnery, 1972.

Hughes, Elinor. *Passing through to Broadway*. Boston: Waverly House, 1948.

Hummel, David. *The Collector's Guide to the Musical Theatre*. Metuchen, N.J.: Scarecrow Press, 1984.

Jablonski, Edward. *Harold Arlen: Rhythm, Rainbows, and Blues*. Boston: Northeastern University Press, 1996.

Jablonski, Edward, and Lawrence D. Stewart. *The Gershwin Years*. Garden City, N.Y.: Doubleday and Co., Inc., 1973.

Jay, Dave. *The Irving Berlin Songography*. New Rochelle: Arlington House, 1969.

Kimball, Robert, ed. *Cole*. New York: Holt, Rinehart and Winston, 1971.

———. *The Complete Lyrics of Cole Porter*. New York: Alfred A. Knopf, 1983.

———. *The Complete Lyrics of Ira Gershwin*. New York: Alfred A. Knopf, 1993.

Kimball, Robert, and Alfred Simon. *The Gershwins*. New York: Atheneum, 1973.

Kronenberger, Louis, ed. *The Best Plays Series*. Vols. *1952–53* through *1960–61*. New York: Dodd, Mead & and Co., 1953–61.

Lamb, Andrew. *Jerome Kern in Edwardian London*. East Preston, West Sussex, England: Andrew Lamb, 1981.

Leonard, William Torbert. *Broadway Bound*. Metuchen, N.J.: Scarecrow Press, 1983.

Lerner, Alan Jay. *The Street Where I Live*. New York: W. W. Norton & Co., 1978.

Lewine, Richard, and Alfred Simon. *Encyclopedia of Theatre Music*. New York: Random House, 1961.

———. *Songs of the American Theatre*. New York: Dodd, Mead & Co., 1973.

Loesser, Susan. *A Most Remarkable Fella: Frank Loesser and the Guys and Dolls in His Life*. New York: Donald I. Fine, 1993.

Logan, Joshua. *Josh*. New York: Delacorte Press, 1976.

Lynch, Richard Chigley. *Broadway on Record*. New York: Greenwood Press, 1987.

McNamara, Daniel, ed. *The ASCAP Biographical Dictionary of Composers, Authors and Publishers*. New York: Thomas Y. Crowell Co., 1948.

McNeil, Alex. *Total Television*. 4th edition. New York: Penguin, 1996.

Mandelbaum, Ken. *Not Since "Carrie."* New York: St. Martin's, 1991.

Mantle, Burns, ed. *The Best Plays Series*. Vols. *1919–20* through *1923–24*. Boston: Small, Maynard & Co., 1920–1924; Vols. *1924–25* through *1946–47*. New York: Dodd, Mead & Co., 1925–47.

Mantle, Burns, and Garrison P. Sherwood, eds. *The Best Plays of 1899–1909*. New York: Dodd, Mead & Co., 1944.

Mantle, Burns, and Garrison P. Sherwood. *The Best Plays of 1909–1919*. New York: Dodd, Mead, & Co., 1933.

Marx, Samuel, and Jan Clayton. *Rodgers & Hart: Bewitched, Bothered, and Bedeviled*. New York: G. P. Putnam's Sons, 1976.

Meredith, Scott. *George S. Kaufman and His Friends*. Garden City: Doubleday & Co., 1974.

Meyerson, Harold, and Ernie Harburg. *Who Put the Rainbow in the Wizard of Oz?* Ann Arbor: University of Michigan Press, 1993.

Nathan, George Jean. *The Theatre Book of the Year.* Vols. *1941–42* through *1950–51.* New York: Alfred A. Knopf, 1943–51.

New York Theatre Critics Reviews. Vols. 1–30. New York: Critics' Theatre Reviews, Inc., 1940–70.

The New York Times Directory of the Film. New York: Arno Press, 1971.

The New York Times Directory of the Theatre. New York: Arno Press, 1973.

Nolan, Frederick. *Lorenz Hart: A Poet on Broadway.* New York: Oxford University Press, 1994.

———. *The Sound of Their Music.* New York: Walker & Co., 1978.

Parker, John, ed. *Who's Who in the Theatre.* 1st through 16th editions. London: Sir Isaac Pitman & Sons, 1912–77.

Prince, Hal. *Contradictions: Notes on Twenty-Six Years in the Theatre.* New York: Dodd, Mead & Co., 1974.

Raymond, Jack. *Show Music on Record: The First 100 Years.* Washington, D.C.: Smithsonian Institution Press, 1992.

Rigdon, Walter, ed. *Biographical Encyclopedia and Who's Who of the American Theatre.* New York: Heineman, 1966.

Rodgers, Richard. *Musical Stages.* New York: Random House, 1975.

Sanders, Ronald. *The Days Grow Short: The Life and Music of Kurt Weill.* New York: Holt, Rinehart & Winston, 1980.

Schwartz, Charles. *Cole Porter.* New York: Dial Press, 1977.

———. *Gershwin: His Life and Music.* New York: Bobbs-Merrill, 1973.

Stagg, Jerry. *The Brothers Shubert.* New York: Random House, 1968.

Stone, Fred. *Rolling Stone.* New York: Whittlesey House, 1945.

Stott, William, with Fred Fehl and Jane Stott. *On Broadway.* Austin: University of Texas Press, 1978.

Stubblebine, Donald J. *Broadway Sheet Music: A Comprehensive Listing, 1918–93.* Jefferson, N.C.: McFarland & Co., Inc., 1996.

———. *Cinema Sheet Music.* Jefferson, N.C.: McFarland & Co., Inc., 1991.

Suskin, Steven. *Berlin, Kern, Rodgers, Hart, and Hammerstein: A Complete Song Catalogue.* Jefferson, N.C.: McFarland & Co., 1990.

———. *More Opening Nights on Broadway.* New York: Schirmer Books, 1997.

———. *Opening Night on Broadway.* New York: Schirmer Books, 1990.

Symonette, Lys. and Kim H. Kowalke, eds. and trans. *Speak Low (When You Speak Love).* Berkeley: University of California Press, 1996.

Taylor, Theodore. *Jule: The Story of Composer Jule Styne.* New York: Random House, 1979.

Teichmann, Howard. *George S. Kaufman: An Intimate Portrait.* New York: Atheneum, 1972.

Toohey, John L. *A History of the Pulitzer Prize Plays.* New York: Citadel Press, 1967.

[U.S. Army Service Forces]. *About Face!* New York: Special Services Division, [circa 1944].

———. *Hi, Yank!* New York: Special Services Division, [circa 1944].

———. *OK, U.S.A.!* New York: Special Services Division, [circa 1945].

———. *PFC Mary Brown.* New York: Special Services Division, [circa 1944].

Wharton, John. *Life among the Playwrights.* New York: Quadrangle, 1974.

Willis, John, ed. *Theatre World.* Vols. 21–46. New York: Crown Publishers, 1965–91. Vols. 47–51. New York: Applause Theatre Book Publishers, 1992–97.

Wintergreen, John P. *Diary of an Ex-President.* New York: Minton, Balch and Co., 1932.

[Writers and Material Committee for Soldier Shows]. *At Ease.* Vols. 3 and 4. USO-Camp Shows, Inc., 1943.

Zadan, Craig. *Sondheim & Co.* 2d ed. New York: Harper & Row, 1989.

A Word about Finding Music

Recently issued songs and still-popular standards can best be found in local music stores. Many vocal scores and selections are still in print. Since *Show Tunes* was first published in 1986, publishers have begun reissuing long-out-of-print songs in new editions of vocal selections and composer anthologies; in some cases these include previously unpublished work. Chain stores that sell only contemporary hits won't be of much help; but any place that carries instruction books, classical music, and such will have or gladly order these items. (Much of this material is now becoming available for purchase over the Internet.)

The majority of the recorded songs mentioned in this book are included on original cast albums, with a goodly amount showing up in the last decade on revival and studio cast albums. Other, more obscure songs have shown up on personality albums and collections of cut songs. Jack Raymond's *Show Music on Record* and Richard Lynch's *Broadway on Record* are helpful guides to finding what you are looking for.

Some long-established music stores still have out-of-print music in stock. An increasing number of antique and used book dealers now carry out-of-print songs; if they don't handle music, they will generally know of other dealers who do. There are dozens of mail-order dealers specializing in music; they advertise in newspapers and journals for antique dealers and collectors. Flea markets and antique shows can also be good places to find music.

The best place to find specific out-of-print songs is in one of several public or university libraries with specialized collections. Your local librarian—or a quick check of the Internet—can guide you to the likeliest collection in your area. Individual policies vary, but many of these facilities allow photocopying of out-of-print material for noncommercial use. The most helpful and complete collection—incorporating the actual copyright deposit copies of the songs—can be found in the ever-helpful Music Division at the Library of Congress in Washington.

SONG TITLE INDEX

A Is One, 277
A-1 March, 277
À Toujours, 226
Abbondanza, 247
Abductions (And So Forth), 306
Abe Lincoln Had Just One Country, 34
Abie Baby/Fourscore, 399
Above the Law, 303
Abracadabra, 129
Absalom, My Absalom, 367
Absent Minded Me, 235
Absinthe, 117, 118
Abundance and Charity, 367
Academic Fugue, 266
Ac-cent-u-ate the Positive, 154
Ace in the Hole, 128
Acorn in the Meadow, 251
Across the Sea, 62
Act, The, 350
Adelaide, 246
Adelaide's Lament, 246
Advantages of Floating in the Middle of the Sea, The, 283
Adventure, 233, 234
After All, I'm Only a Schoolgirl, 121
After All These Years, 337
After All, You're All I'm After, 141
After Autumn, 377
After Forty It's Patch, Patch, Patch, 316
After You (Who?), 123
Age of Anxiety, 218
Ages Ago, 168
Aggie Oh Aggie, 345
Aggie Song, The [Hall], 404
Aggie's Song (Sewing Machine) [Weill], 174
Agnus Dei, 216
Agony, 286, 287
Agua Sincopada (Tango), 121
Ah, but Underneath, 280
Ah, Men, 363
Ah, Miss, 284
Ah, Our Germans, 266, 267

Ah, Paris!, 280
Ai, Ai!, 261
Aida McCluskie, 7
Ain't Broadway Grand, 347
Ain't Gonna Marry, 207
Ain't Got No, 399
Ain't Got No Tears Left, 218
Ain't He Cute, 320
Ain't It a Grand and Glorious Feeling?, 18
Ain't It Awful, the Heat?, 179
Ain't It de Truth?, 156
Ain't It Funny What a Difference Just a Few Drinks Make?, 17
Ain't It Good?, 358
Ain't Misbehavin', 391
Ain't No Party, 405
Ain't You Never Been Afraid?, 258
Aintcha Comin' Back, Mary Ann, to Maryland, 387
Air, 399
Airborne Symphony, 187
Alabama Song, 173, 183
Alas for You, 355
Alaura's Theme, 320
Aldonza, 344
Alessandro the Wise, 178
Alexander's Bag-Pipe Band, 40
Alexander's Ragtime Band, 39, 40
Algonquins from Harlem, The, 175
Alibi Baby, 137
Alice Blue Gown, 387
Alice in Wonderland [Berlin—1st], 44
Alice in Wonderland [Berlin—2nd], 48
Alice in Wonderland [Kern], 13
Alive!, 411
Alive and Kicking, 205
Alive at Last, 168
All Alone, 48
All at Once, 99
All at Once You Love Her, 110
All Bless the Genius of Man, 298
All by Myself, 62

All Choked Up, 402
All Dark People, 99
All Dolled Up, 303
All Dressed Up, Spic and Spanish, 101
All Er Nothin', 104
All Fall Down, 370, 371
All for Him, 223
All for the Best, 355
All for You, 274
All Full of Talk, 17
All Good Gifts, 355
All Hail the Political Honeymoon, 175
All I Care About, 335
All I Need (Is One Good Break), 332
All I Need Is the Girl, 232, 233
All I Owe Ioway, 115
All I Want Is You, 5
All I've Got to Get Now Is My Man, 128
All in Fun, 35
All Is Well in the City, 401
All Kinds of People, 110
All Lanes Must Reach a Turning, 27, 30
All Men Are the Same, 159
All of My Life, 233
All of These and More, 256
All of You, 132
All Over Town, 63
All That He Wants Me to Be, 172
All That I Want Is Somebody to Love Me, 17
All the Children in a Row, 337
All the Dearly Beloved, 307
All the Livelong Day, 357
All the Things You Are, 35, 76
All the Time, 143
All the Wasted Time, 414
All the World Is Dancing Mad, 27
All the World Is Swaying, 21
All Things Bright and Beautiful, 280
All Things to One Man, 352
All through the Night, 124
All You Gotta Do Is Tell Me, 239
All You Have to Do Is Wait, 320
All You Need Is a Girl, 26
All You Need Is a Quarter, 233
Allegro, 107
Alleluia [Bernstein—1st], 216
Alleluia [Bernstein—2nd], 217
Alleluia [Rodgers], 112
Allez-Vous En, 131
Allied High Command, The, 174
Allons, 262
Almighty Father, 216
Almiro, 121
Almost, 208
Almost a Love Song, 408

Almost Like Being in Love, 223, 226
Alone (Seul), 398
Alone at Last [Duke], 168
Alone at Last [Kern—1st], 13
Alone at Last [Kern—2nd], 16, 31
Alone at Night, 168
Alone at the Drive-In Movie, 402
Alone Together, 140, 147
Alone Too Long, 145
Alone with You, 118
Along Came Ruth, 42
Along with Me, 196
Alpine Rose, 121
Altogether Too Fond of You, 118, 119
Always, 48
Always True to You in My Fashion, 130
Am I Who I Think I Am?, 361
Amazing Penetration, 366
Ambition, 233, 234
America!, 215
American Eagles, 52
American in Paris, An, 70, 74
American Punch, The, 120
Amor, 376
Amsterdam, 398, 399
Anatevka, 260
Ancient Tunes, 27
And . . . , 359
And All That Jazz, 335
And Father Wanted Me to Learn a Trade, 43
And I Am All Alone, 17
And I Am Telling You I'm Not Going, 405
And I Was Beautiful, 327
And Love Was Born, 32
And the Gods Heard Her Prayer, 382
And They're Off, 373
And This Is My Beloved, 393
And What If We Had Loved Like That?, 406
Angel without Wings, 100
Angel's Rink and Social Center, 337
Angelina, 314
Angelo, 39
Angling by the Babbling Brook, 3
Animal Crackers in My Soup, 153
Anna Lilla, 263
Annie, 298, 301
Annie Ain't Just Annie Anymore, 303
Announcement of Inheritance (Prologue),
    129
Another Autumn, 223, 224, 226
Another Candle, 324
Another Day [Larson], 410
Another Day [Styne], 236
Another Hundred People, 279
Another Life, 301

Another Little Girl, 14
Another Love, 218
Another Melody in F, 87
Another Miracle of Judaism, 372
Another National Anthem, 287
Another Op'nin', Another Show, 130
Another Sentimental Song, 118
Another Sleepless Night, 369
Another Time, Another Place, 253
Another Day [Larson], 410
Another Woman, 366
Answer Me, 39
Anthem for Presentation, 54
Antioch Prison, 308
Antique Man, The, 324
Any Day Now Day, 357
Any Fool Can Fall in Love, 227
Any Little Tune, 63
Any Moment (Anything Can Happen in the Woods), 286, 287
Any Old Night (Is a Wonderful Night), 14, 15
Any Old Place with You, 86
Any Place I Hang My Hat Is Home, 155
Any Woman Who Is Willing Will Do, 166
Anyone Can Whistle, 277
Anyone Who Loves, 301
Anyone Would Love You, 199
Anything Can Happen in the Woods, 286, 287
Anything for Him, 339
Anything for You [Gershwin], 61
Anything for You [Kander], 331
Anything Goes, 124
Anything May Happen Any Day, 32
Anything You Can Do, 53
Anytime, Anywhere, Anyhow, 89
Applause, 297
Apple Doesn't Fall, The, 337
Apple Jack, 181
Apple Tree, The, 261
Apples, 298
Apprentice Seaman, 165
April Day, 221
April Fool, 89
April in Paris, 161, 162, 168
Aquarius, 399, 400
Are You Ready, Gyp Watson?, 199
Are You Sure?, 270
Aren't You Glad?, 247
Argentina, 62
Arkansas, 406
Arm in Arm [Duke], 165
Arm in Arm [Willson], 270
Armful of Trouble, 33
Armful of You, 81
Army of the Just, The, 257

Army Service Forces, The, 196
Army Song, 182
Army's Made a Man out of Me, The, 52
Arrival, The, 351
Art for Art's Sake, 185
Arthur in the Afternoon, 336
Artificial Flowers, 257
Arts, The, 294
As Far As I'm Concerned, 113
As I Love You, 117
As It Should Be, 377
As Long As I Live [Arlen], 152, 153
As Long As I Love [Weill], 174
As Long As You're Happy, 303
As on through the Seasons We Sail, 132
As Once I Loved You, 114
As Simple As That, 324
As Though You Were There, 95
As You Make Your Bed, 183
As You Would Love Paree, 378
Ascot Gavotte, 224
Asiatic Angles, 85
Ask Me Again, 67
Asking for You, 233
Asylum Chorus, 174
At Half Past Seven, 64
At Last, 351
At Long Last Love, 126
At My Side, 319, 320
At Night She Comes Home to Me, 406
At Stony Brook, 33
At That San Francisco Fair, 14
At the Ball, 24
At the Ballet, 359
At the Casino, 3
At the Check Apron Ball, 263
At the Court around the Corner, 47
At the Field of Cloth of Gold, 114
At the Grand Hotel, 377
At the Mardi Gras, 144
At the Picture Show, 41
At the Red Rose Cotillion, 245
At the Roxy Music Hall, 100
At the Sounding, 413
At Twenty-Two, 305
Atlanta, 144
Atlantic Blues, 91, 94
Atlantic City, 383
Auf Wiedersehen, 301
Auto da fé (What a Day), 217
Auto Show Girl, 85
Autograph Chant, 230
Autumn, 378, 379
Autumn Afternoon, 310
Autumn in New York, 162

Awaiting You, 413
Away!, 188
Away from You, 114

B. G. Bigelow, Inc., 392
Babbitt and the Bromide, The, 68
Babbling Babette, 26
Babes in Arms, 99
Babes in the Wood, 16, 19
Babette, 318
Baby [Gershwin—1st], 66
Baby [Gershwin—2nd], 66
Baby [McHugh], 389
Baby, Baby, Baby, 406
Baby Blues, 60
Baby, Dream Your Dream, 315, 316
Baby, It's Cold Outside, 245
Baby June and Her Newsboys, 232
Baby, Let's Dance, 121
Baby, Talk to Me, 294
Baby Vampire, The, 18
Baby, What!, 389
Baby, You Can Count on Me, 300
Baby's Awake Now, 95
Baby's Best Friend, A (Is Her Mother), 93
Bachelor Song, 175
Bachelor's Dance, 398
Back from the Great Beyond, 238
Back Home, 59
Back in Business, 288
Back in Show Business Again, 300
Back to Before, 383
Back to My Heart, 159
Back to Nature [Rodgers], 91
Back to Nature with You [Porter], 124
Back to the Heather, 30
Back to Work, 193
Backstage Babble, 297
Bacon and the Egg, The, 160
Bad Companions, 396
Bagpipe Serenade, 5
Bali Ha'i, 108
Ballad [Strouse], 301
Ballad of a Gun, 199
Ballad of a Social Director, 198
Ballad of Booth, The, 287
Ballad of Czolgosz, The, 287
Ballad of Dependency, 182
Ballad of Eldorado, 214
Ballad of Floyd Collins, The, 409
Ballad of Guiteau, The, 287
Ballad of San Juan Hill, The, 174
Ballad of Sloppy Joe, The, 195
Ballad of Sweeney Todd, The, 284
Ballad of the Easy Life, 182

Ballad of the Garment Trade, 200
Ballad of the Robbers, 175
Ballet [Carousel], 106
Ballet [Love from Judy], 207
Ballet [Lucky], 29
Ballet at the Village Vortex, 213
Ballet Music [Band Wagon], 140
Ballooning, 6
Baltimore Buzz, 387
Baltimore Sun, The, 235
Baltimore, Md., That's the Only Doctor for Me,
135
Bambalina, 78
Bamboo Cage, 155
Band Started Swinging a Song, The, 129
Bandana Days, 387
Bandanna Babies, 389
Bandit Band, The, 120
Bang!, 281
Bang the Bell Rang, 243
Banishment, The, 407
Banjo (That Man Joe Plays), The, 121
Banjo Eyes, 164
Banjos, 209
Bar Mitzvah of Eliot Green, The, 240
Bar Mitzvah Song, 200
Barabanchik, 249
Barbara Song, 182
Barbary Coast, 71
Barber and His Wife, The, 284
Barber's Song, 344
Barcarolle, 217
Barcelona, 279
Bargaining, 113
Barking Baby Never Bites, A, 102
Barrels of War, The, 402
Barrett's Song, 378
Baseball Game, The [Finn], 372
Baseball Game (T.E.A.M) [Gesner], 398
Bathing Beauty Ballet, 288, 241
Battle, The [Menken], 366
Battle, The [Weill], 174
Baubles, Bangles, and Beads, 393
Be a Lion, 403
Be a Little Sunbeam, 18
Be a Santa, 234
Be Anything but a Girl, 209
Be Good to Me, 83
Be Happy, 349, 350
Be Italian, 376
Be Kind to Your Parents, 198
Be Like the Bluebird, 125
Be My Guest [Mercer], 392
Be My Host [Rodgers], 112
Be My Lady, 310

Be on Your Own, 376
Be Our Guest [Menken], 366
Be Prepared, 413
Be with Me, 189
Be-In, 399
Beat Behind, A, 361
Beau Brummel, 65
Beautician Ballet, 308
Beautiful [Herman], 325, 329
Beautiful [Kander], 331
Beautiful [Sondheim], 286
Beautiful, Beautiful World, 261
Beautiful Candy, 264
Beautiful City, 355
Beautiful Day in Brooklyn, A, 53
Beautiful Day for a Wedding, 412
Beautiful Faces, 47
Beautiful Girls, 280
Beautiful Gypsy, 69
Beautiful Lady, 259
Beautiful People of Denver, 270
Beautiful through and Through, 239
Beauty and the Beast, 365, 366
Beauty School Dropout, 402
Beauty That Drives Men Mad, The, 239
Because, Because, 72
Because There's You, 201
Because You Love the Singer, 26
Bed, The, 399
Been a Long Day, 248
Beethoven Day, 398
Before I Gaze at You Again, 225
Before I Kiss the World Goodbye, 146, 147
Before I Met You, 20
Before the Parade Passes By, 325, 326
Before Your Very Eyes, 356
Begat, The, 171
Beggar's Waltz, 140
Begging for Love, 50
Begin the Beguine, 125
Behave Yourself, 396
Behind the Fan, 47
Being Alive, 279
Being Good Isn't Good Enough, 236
Being in Love, 269, 270
Believe, 334
Believe in Me, 136
Belle, 366
Bells, 47
Bells Are Ringing, 231
Bells of St. Sebastian, The, 376
Belly up to the Bar, Boys, 270
Beneath the Eastern Moon, 63
Beneath the Southern Cross, 110
Benedictus, 213

Benvenuta, 247
Berkeley Square and Kew, 65
Bertha, the Sewing Machine Girl, 193
Bertie and Gertie, 126
Bess, You Is My Woman, 74
Best Gold, 324
Best in the World, The, 328
Best is Yet to Come, The, 313, 322
Best Night of My Life, The, 297
Best of All Possible Worlds, The, 214, 217
Best of Everything, The, 58, 61
Best of Friends Must Part, 37
Best of Times, The, 328
Best Sort of Mother, Best Sort of Child, 14
Best Thing for You, The, 54
Best Thing of All, The, 188
Best Things in Life Are Free, The, 389
Best Years of His Life, The, 177
Better Be Good to Me, 94
Better Get out of Here, 245
Better Than a Dream, 231
Between the Devil and the Deep Blue Sea [Arlen], 150, 153
Betwixt and Between, 228, 232
Bevo, 45, 46
Bewitched (Bothered and Bewildered), 103
Bianca, 130, 131
Bicycle Song, The, 208
Bidin' My Time, 71
Big Black Giant, The, 110
Big Bow-Wow, The, 351
Big Brother, 100
Big Brother Ballet, 101
Big Clown Balloons, The, 270
Big D, 246, 247
Big Fat Heart, 316
Big Fish, Little Fish, 402
Big Mole, 181
Big News, 414
Big Rich, 188
Big Show, The, 21
Big Spender, 315, 316, 335
Big Spring Drive, The, 21
Big Talk, 236
Big Time [Herman], 327, 328
Big Time, The [Coleman], 320
Big Town, 129
Bigger Isn't Better, 318
Bilbao Song, 173, 183
Bill, 20, 22, 29
Bill's a Liar, 5
Bird of Paradise (My Honolulu Girl), 43
Bird of Passage, A, 181
Bird upon the Tree, 190
Bird Watcher's Song, 228

Birdie's Aria, 188
Birds, 392
Birth, The, 406
Birth of the Blues, The, 388
Bit of Earth, A, 407
Bitch, Bitch, Bitch, 411
Bits and Pieces, 350
Black and White, 318
Black Bottom, 388
Black Boys, 399
Blame, The, 378
Blame It on the Summer Night, 302
Bless This Day, 248
Bless This Land, 257
Blissful Christmas, 201
Bloody Mary, 108
Bloom Is off the Rose, 146
Blow Gabriel Blow, 124
Blow High, Blow Low, 106
Blow Your Horn, 43
Blowing the Blues Away, 160
Blue, Blue [Kern], 5
Blue, Blue, Blue [Gershwin], 73, 74
Blue Bowery, 83, 84
Blue Boy Blues, The, 120
Blue Bulgarian Band, The, 8
Blue Crystal, 337
Blue Danube Blues, 25
Blue Devils of France, The, 45
Blue Eyes, 30
Blue Grass, 144
Blue Hours, 121
Blue Monday [Rodgers], 102
Blue Monday Blues [Gershwin], 62, 74
Blue Moon, 97
Blue Ocean Blues, 94
Blue Pajama Song, The, 137
Blue Room, The, 90, 92
Blue Skies, 49, 92
Blueberry Eyes, 201
Bluebloods, 339
Blues [Blitzstein], 188
Blues (I Got a Marble and a Star) [Weill], 179
Blues Fantasy, 149
Blues in the Night, 154, 157, 158
Blues Theme, 70
Blushing Bride, A, 237
Board of Governors, 411
Boat Sails on Wednesday, A, 7
Bob White, 23
Bobby and Jackie and Jack, 285
Bobo's, 336
Bobolink Waltz, 117
Body and Soul, 139
Body Talk, 361

Bohemia, 10
Bolero, 377
Bon Jour (The Language Song), 270
Bon Voyage [Bernstein], 214
Bon Voyage [Porter], 125
Bonds [Blitzstein], 188
Bonds [Bock], 262
Bongo on the Congo, 26
Bonjour, Amour, 377
Bonjour, Goodbye, 163
Bonnie Blue Flag, 201
Bonnie Gone, 201
Book Report, 398
Boom!, 345
Boom Chicka Boom, 303
Boom Ditty Boom, 335
Boomerang, 87
Bored [Borodin], 393
Bored [Schmidt], 307
Born Again, 146
Born Loser, 350
Born to Hand Jive, 402
Born Too Late, 166, 167
Bosom Buddies, 326, 327
Boston Beguine, 256
Bottoms Up, 104
Bought and Paid For, 13, 28
Bouilloux Girls, The, 308
Bounce, 168
Bouncing Back for More, 314
Bow Belles, 31
Bowler Hat, A, 283, 286
Boy, Do We Need It Now, 300
Boy Friend Back Home, The, 122
Boy From, The, 278
Boy I Left Behind Me, The, 104
Boy Like That, A, 215
Boy Like You, A, 179
Boy Next Door, The [Martin], 206, 208, 209
Boy Next Door, The [Youmans], 80
Boy Wanted, 61, 64
Boy! What Love Has Done to Me!, 71, 72
Boys, The, 406
Boys and Girls Like You and Me, 104, 115
Brack Weaver, My True Love, 180
Brain Dead, 373
Brand New World, 302
Bread, 357
Bread and Butter, 28
Bread and Freedom (Sisters We Stand), 302
Break It Now, Buck Private, 391
Break It Up, Cinderella, 391
Breakfast at Tiffany's, 265
Breakfast Ball, 152
Breakfast Dance, 150

Breakfast over Sugar, A, 369
Breath of Springtime, A, 86
Breeze Kissed Your Hair, The, 32
Bride and Groom, 68
Bride Was Dressed in White, The, 81
Bridget, 117
Brigadoon, 223
Bright and Black, 218
Bright Canary Yellow, 108
Bright College Days, 198
Bright Lights, 18
Bring 'Em Back, 23
Bring Back Birdie, 300
Bring Back My Lena to Me, 38
Bring in 'da Noise, Bring in 'da Funk, 409
Bring Me Back My Butterfly, 118
Bring Me My Bride, 276
Bring on the Girls, 280
Bring on the Men, 411
Bring on the Pepper, 48
Bring Your Darling Daughter, 146
Brittany, 120
Broadway, 232
Broadway Baby, 280, 281
Broadway Musical, A, 299
Broadway, My Street, 334, 335
Broncho Busters, 71
Brother, Can You Spare a Dime?, 151
Brotherhood of Man, 248
Brown Penny, 391
Brush up Your Shakespeare, 130, 131
Brussels (Bruxelles), 398, 399
Buckle Down, Buck Private, 205
Buckle Down, Winsocki, 205, 206
Buddie Beware, 124
Buddy Kissed Me, 412
Buddy on the Nightshift, 177
Buddy System, The, 320
Buddy's Blues, 280
Buddy's Confession, 412
Buds Won't Bud, 153
Buenos Aires Tango (I Am Easily Assimilated), 214
Buffalo Belle, 260
Buffo Dance, 16
Buffalo Nickel Photoplay, Inc., 383
Buggy Riding, 23
Bugle, The, 271
Bull Frog Patrol, The, 22
Bulldog, 117
Bulls (Les Toros), The, 398
Bum Won, The, 257
Bum's Opera (You Can't Get away from a Dumb Tomato), 110
Bungalow in Quogue, 20
Bunny, Bunny, Bunny, 195

Bus from Amarillo, 404, 405
Bushel and a Peck, A, 246
Business for a Good Girl Is Bad, 54
Business of Our Own, A, 22
Busy Night at Lorraine's, 303
But Alive, 297
But He Never Said He Loved Me, 123
But in the Morning, No, 127
But Mr. Adams, 401
But Not for Me, 71, 72
But the World Goes 'Round, 338
But You Go On, 303
But Yours, 264
Butler in the Abbey, 237
Butterflies Are Free, 355
Butterfly (Not Too Fast), The, 334
Butterfly Love, 85
Button up with Esmond, 228
Buy Her a Box at the Opera, 118
Buzz-A-Buzz, 357
Buzzard Song, 74
By and By [Gershwin], 62
By My Side, 355
By Myself, 143
By Strauss, 75, 163
By the Beautiful Sea, 145
By the Blue Lagoon, 8
By the Country Stile, 12
By the Mississinewah, 129
By the Sea, 284
By Threes, 317
Bye and Bye [Rodgers], 89
Bye, Bye, Baby, 228
Bye Bye Birdie, 294
Bye Bye Blackbird, 388
Bygone Days, 10

C'est la Vie, 152
C'est Magnifique, 131, 132
C'est Moi, 225
C'mon Folks, We'se Rarin' to Go, 30
Cab-Horse Trot, The, 65
Cabaret, 333
Cabin in the Sky, 164
Cadillac Car, 405
Caesar Is Wrong, 261
Cäsars Tod, 173
Cakewalk Your Lady, 155
Calamari, 373
Calico Days, 152
Call, The, 409
Call from the Grave, 182
Call from the Vatican, A, 376
Call Me Flo, 10
Call Me Madam, 55

Call Me Mister, 196
Call Me Savage, 236, 237
Call of the Sea, 80
Call of the South, The, 49
Calypso, 394
Camelot, 225
Camouflage, 326
Camp Kare-free, 198
Can I Leave Off Wearin' My Shoes?, 155
Can That Boy Fox Trot!, 280
Can This Be Love?, 390
Can We Do Anything?, 65
Can You Explain?, 156
Can You Feel the Love Tonight, 413
Can You Hear Me Now?, 351
Can You Imagine That?, 264
Can You Use Any Money Today?, 54
Can't Help Lovin' Dat Man, 29
Can't Wait, 410
Can't We Be Friends?, 390
Can't You Do a Friend a Favor?, 105
Can't You Just See Yourself?, 228
Can't You See I Mean You?, 14, 16, 17
Can't You See It?, 296
Can't You Tell?, 49
Can-Can, 131
Canceling the Bar Mitzvah, 372
Candide's Lament, 217
Cane Dance, 26
Canons, 378
Cantabile (Song without Words), 34, 35
Caper, The, 334
Capricious and Fickle, 401
Captain Andy's Entrance and Ballyhoo, 29
Captain Hook's Waltz, 230
Captain Valentine's Song, 174
Caravan Moves On, The, 367
Careless Rhapsody, 104
Cariño Mio, 223
Carioca, The, 84
Carlotta, 129
Carmelina, 172
Carnegie Hall Pavanne (Do-Do-Re-Do), 212
Carnival [Shire], 410
Carnival, The [Guettel], 409
Carnival Song, The [Styne], 232
Carnival Time, 65
Caroline, 232
Carousel (La Valse à Mille Temps), 398, 399
Carousel Waltz, 106
Carried Away, 212
Carry On, Keep Smiling, 83
Casanova [Duke], 162
Casanova [Porter], 124
Casino Music Hall, The, 17

Castle, The, 124
Castle of Dreams, 387
Cat and Mouse, 408
Catamarang, 8, 24
Catch Me If You Can, 179
Catch My Garter, 333
Catch our Act at the Met, 229
Catfish Song, The, 181
'Cause We Got Cake, 101
Celebration, 307
Cell Block Tango, 335
Certain Girl, A, 333, 334
Certain Individuals, 198
Certainly, Lord, 188
Chain Story Daisy (Vassar Girl Finds Job), 193, 194
Champagne and Wedding Cake, 229
Champagne fo' de Lady, 157
Change, 373
Change of Scene [Pipe Dream], 110
Changes, 303
Chanson, 357
Chaplin Walk, The, 14
Chapter 54, Number 1909 (The Late Great State of New York), 317
Charity's Soliloquy, 316
Charity's Theme, 315
Charlie [Kern], 31
Charlie [Strouse], 299
Charlie and Algernon, 299
Charlie Welch, 256
Charmin's Lament, 356
Charming, 300
Charming Weather, 159
Chase [Hague], 396
Chase, The [Kern], 28
Chase, The [Loewe], 223
Chase, The [Rodgers], 114
Chase, The [Youmans], 78
Chava Sequence, 260
Check It Out!, 321
Cheek to Cheek, 51
Cheer Up Girls, 6
Cheerio!, 89
Cheerleader, 336
Cheese Nips, 363
Cherry Pies Ought to Be You, 131
Cherry Street Cafe, The, 302
Chess and Checkers, 263
Chess Game, The, 370
Chicago, 103
Chicago Bound, 409
Chicago Fire, The, 233
Chicago, Illinois, 408
Chicago Riot Rag, The, 409
Chicago Strut, The, 407

Chick! Chick! Chick!, 23
Chick-a-Pen, 270
Chicken Is He, 401
Chicken Walk, The, 44
Chief Cook and Bottle Washer, 337
Chief of Love, 232
Childhood's Bright Endeavor, 183
Childhood's End, 358
Children and Art, 286
Children of Eden, 358
Children of the Heavenly King, 414
Children of the Wind, 302
Children Will Listen, 286
Chin Up, Ladies, 324
Chinese Ballet, 160
Chinese Firecrackers, 47
Chinese March, 160
Chinkypin, 188
Chinquapin Bush, 155
Chop Suey, 111
Chopin Ad Lib, 24
Chopsticks, 391
Chorus Girl Blues, 88
Chow Down, 413
Christmas at Hampton Court, 114
Christmas Bells, 410
Christmas Day, 400
Christmas Together, 367
Christopher Street, 213
Chromolume #7, 286
Chrysanthemum Tea, 283
Chuck It!, 92
Church 'round the Corner, The, 24
Ciao, Compare, 265
Cigarette Song, The, 401
Cinderelatives, 62
Cinderella, 306
Cinderella at the Grave, 286
Cinderella Darling, 248
Cinderella Girl, 28
Circe, Circe, 394
Circle of Life, 413
Circus Is Coming to Town, The, 46
Circus on Parade, The, 97
Circus Queen, 34
City Lights, 336
City Mouse, Country Mouse, 394
City on Fire!, 284
Civil War Ballet, 154
Civilian, 165
Civilized Society, 358
Clang Dang the Bell, 248
Clap Yo' Hands, 67
Clara, Clara, 74
Class [Kander], 335

Class [Leigh], 347
Class [Sondheim], 274
Class [Strouse], 303
Classification Blues, 244
Claudine, 310
Cleaning Crew, 319
Cleopatterer, 19
Clickety-Clack, 175
Climb Ev'ry Mountain, 112
Climb up the Mountain, 131
Climb up the Social Ladder, 73
Climbing up the Scale, 48
Close Harmony, 236
Close to Home, 358
Closed for Renovation, 364
Closing [This Is the Army], 52
Clothes Make the Man (Who Could Marry a
    Gigolo?), 401
Clouds, 351
Clown, The, 229
Clusters of Crocus, 407
Coaching, 27
Coalhouse Demands, 383
Coalhouse's Soliloquy, 383
Cockeyed Optimist, A, 108
Cocktail Counterpoint, 329
Cocktail Time, 120
Cocoa Bean Song, 253
Cocoanut Sweet, 156
Cocotte, The, 124
Coffee, Black!, 410
Coffee Break, 248
Coffee in a Cardboard Cup, 334
Cold and Dead, 247
Cold, Clear World, 260
Cold Cream Jar Song, 199
College on Broadway, A, 87
Colonel Buffalo Bill, 53
Color and Light, 286
Color of Her Eyes, The, 95, 96
Colorado, My Home, 270
Colored Lights, 337, 339
Colored Spade, 399
Colorful, 296
Colors of My Life, The, 318
Colour of Her Eyes, The, 96
Combat, The, 344
Come A-Wandering with Me, 146
Come Along Boys (Raise a Ruckus), 394
Come Along, Pretty Girl, 8, 9
Come Along Sextette, 47
Come Along to Our Show, 142
Come Along to Toy Town, 45, 46
Come Along with Me, 132
Come and Be My Butterfly, 325

Come and Tell Me, 92
Come Around on Our Veranda, 6
Come Back, Little Genie, 392
Come Back to Me, 171, 172
Come Follow the Band, 318
Come Home, 107
Come In, Mornin', 181
Come Let's Dance through the Night, 78
Come Look at the Freaks, 412
Come-Look-at-the-War Choral Society, 68
Come O Come (To Pittsburgh), 144
Come on Along, 306
Come on and Pet Me, 79
Come on Honey, 244
Come on In, 127
Come on, Midnight, 157
Come on Over Here, 11
Come Play Wiz Me, 277
Come Rain or Come Shine, 155
Come Spirit, Come Charm, 407
Come Tiny Goldfish to Me, 8
Come to Florence, 178
Come to Jesus, 414
Come to Life [Schmidt], 310
Come to Me, Bend to Me, 223
Come to My Garden, 407
Come to the Ball, 224
Come to the Land of the Argentine, 42
Come to the Moon, 59, 63
Come up to My Office, 414
Come up to My Place, 212
Come West, Little Girl, Come West, 390
Come with Me [Rodgers], 100
Come with Me [Schmidt], 308
Comedy Tonight, 276, 277
Comes Once in a Lifetime, 234
Comes the Revolution, 73, 74
Company, 279
Company Way, The, 248
Company's Comin', 404
Compulsion, 313
Concerto in F, 66, 74
Coney Island Boat, 145
Confession, 139
Confession to a Park Avenue Mother, 323, 324
Confessional (I Did It and I'm Sorry), 350
Confiteor Alleluia, 216
Confrontation, 411
Conga!, 213
Conquering the City, 213
Contact, 410
Contagious Rhythm, 149
Contest, The, 284
Contract, The, 226
Conversation Piece, 213

Coo-coo Coo-coo (Marie), 8
Cool, 215
Cool, Cool Considerate Men, 401
Coquette, 228
Cora's Chase (Lock 'Em Up), 277
Corduroy Road, 314
Corn Muffins, 72
Corner of the Sky, 356
Cornet Man, 235
Cossack Love Song, 67
Cottage in Kent, A, 26
Cotton Blossom, 29
Could Be, 198
Could I Leave You?, 280
Could It Be You?, 129
Could You Use Me?, 71, 72
Could've Been a Ring, 248
Count Your Blessings, 129
Countin' Our Chickens, 157
Country Cousin, 77
Country House, 280, 281
Country Mouse, The, 91
Country Side (This Is the Life for a Man), 64
Country's in the Very Best of Hands, The, 395
'Course I Will, 78
Court Song [Bernstein], 213
Court Song [Blitzstein], 190
Covenant, The, 113
Cozy Nook Trio, 178
Cradle Will Rock, The, 186
Crap Game, 74
Crazy Elbows, 94
Crazy World, 408
Cream of Mush Song, 193
Credo in Unum Deum, 216
Creole Boy, 407
Creole Love Song, The, 30
Creole Way, The, 407
Crickets Are Calling, The, 19
Crime of the Century, The, 383
Crinoline Days, 48
Crocodile Wife, 200
Crooked Path, The, 377
Croon-Spoon, 186
Cross the Line, 410
Crossing, The, 406
Crow, The, 334
Crown Me, 401
Cruelty Man, The, 345
Cry, Baby, Cry, 197
Cry for Us All, 345
Cry Like the Wind, 233
Cry the Beloved Country, 181
Crystal, Ronnette & Chiffon, 364
Cuddle Up, 40

Cupid, the Winner, 23
Cure, The, 157
Curtsey, The, 31

D'ye Love Me?, 27
Daarlin' Man, 190
Da-Da, Da-Da, Da-Da!, 299
Daddy Longlegs, 207
Daddy, Won't You Please Come Home?, 387
Dahomey, 30
Dainty, Quainty Me, 129
Daisy, 18
Daisy Hill, 351
Dance a Little Closer, 301
Dance Alone with You, 68, 69
Dance and Grow Thin, 44
Dance at the Gym, The, 215
Dance Away the Night, 29
Dance Fugue, 110
Dance of the Golden Calf, 175
Dance of the Golden Crock, 171
Dance of the Grizzly Bear, The, 38
Dance of the Tumblers, 177
Dance Only with Me, 232
Dance: Ten, Looks: Three, 359
(Dance to the Music of) The Ocarina, 54
Dance Trio, 16
Dance with Me [Kander], 340
Dance with Me (Tonight at the Mardi Gras)
   [Berlin], 51
Dancin' Man, A [Berlin], 299
Dancing, 325
Dancing All the Time, 410
Dancing Honeymoon, 48
Dancing in the Dark, 139, 147
Dancing in the Streets [Duke], 165
Dancing in the Streets [Gershwin], 73
Dancing on My Tippy-Tippy Toes, 314
Dancing on the Ceiling, 95, 96
Dancing on Your Grave, 367
Dancing Shoes, 61
Dancing Time, 24
Dancing to Our Score, 162
Dancing Town, 138
Dancing with the Fools, 302
Dandies on Parade, 30
Dangerous Age, The, 236
Dangerous You, 142
Danny the Dragon, 233
Danse Grotesque à la Nègre, 93
Dardanella, 25
Dardos, 364
Dark Tower, 409
Darn Clever, These Chinee, 390
Darn Nice Campus, A, 107

Das Lied vom Schlaraffenland, 173
Daughter Grows Older, 95
Davey Crockett, 91
David's Psalm, 175
Day after That, The, 339
Day before Spring, The, 222
Day Borrowed from Heaven, A, 248
Day by Day, 355
Day Dreams, 159
Day in Falsettoland, A, 372
Day in New York, A, 209
Day Off, The, 286
Daybreak, 409
Days Gone By [Bock], 258
Days Gone By [Kern], 27
Days Like This, 372
De Goblin's Glide, 9
De Profundis, 216
Dear Boy, 214
Dear! Dear!, 96
Dear Friend [1st], 257
Dear Friend [2nd], 258, 259
Dear Joe, 195
Dear Little Girl, 67
Dear Little Peter Pan, 26
Dear Love, 332
Dear Mister Santa Claus, 270
Dear Oh Dear!, 94
Dear Old Prison Days, 20
Dear Old Syracuse, 101
Dear One, 339, 340
Dear Sweet Sewing Machine, 260
Dear World, 327
Dearest Darling, 265
Death Duet, 300
Death Message, 182
Death of Abel, The, 358
Death of Saul, 367
Debts, 51
Decorate the Face, 310
Deedle-Doodle, 188
Deep down Inside, 314
Deep in Alaska, 183
Deep in My Heart, 79
Deep Sea, 160
Deeper in the Woods, 404
Degenerations, 358
Delighted, I'm Sure, 275
Delilah Done Me Wrong (The No Haircut Song),
   200
Democracy's Call, 174
Den of Iniquity, 103
Dentist!, 364
Denver Police, 270
Departure, The, 351

Departure for Rhododendron, 394
Despair Cuts through Me Like a Knife, 394
Desperate Ones (Les Désésperés), The, 398
Desseau Dance Hall, 306
Devil Played the Fiddle, The, 165
Devil You Know, The, 412
Diamond Horseshoe, 48
Diamonds Are a Girl's Best Friend, 228
Diamonds Are Forever, 338
Diamonds in the Starlight, 208
Diavolo, 97
Dickie, 327
Did You Close Your Eyes?, 263
Did You Ever Get Stung?, 100
Did You Hear That?, 253
Did You See That?, 296
Didn't You Believe?, 25
Die Süsse Pariserin (Fraulein de Loraine), 12, 26, 30
Diga-Diga-Doo, 389
Dime a Dozen, 351
Dimple on My Knee, The, 72
Dimples [Blitzstein], 187
Dimples [Coleman], 314
Ding-a-Ling, Ding-a-Ling, 236
Ding Dong [Berlin], 45, 46
Ding Dong [Gershwin], 71
Ding Dong, It's Kissing Time, 23
Dining Out, 7
Direct from Vienna, 264
Dirge for a Soldier, 175
Dis Little While, 157
Disgustingly Rich, 102
Disneyland, 360
Distant Melody, 230
Dites-Moi, 108
Dixie, 389
Dixie Rose, 59
Dizzily, Busily, 178
Dizzy Baby, 121
Do I Do Wrong?, 31, 33
Do I Hear a Waltz?, 113
Do I Hear You Saying (I Love You), 94
Do I Love You?, 127
Do It Again, 62
Do It Alone, 414
Do It For Willy, 310
Do It Now, 20
Do It the Hard Way, 103
Do It Yourself, 231
Do Look at Him, 20
Do Puppies Go to Heaven?, 235
Do We?, 334
Do What You Do!, 70
Do What You Wanna Do, 164

Do Ya Wanna Go to Heaven?, 406
Do You Ever Go to Boston?, 265
Do You Know How Great My Life Is?, 372
Do You Love Me? [Bock], 260
Do You Love Me? (I Wonder) [Rodgers], 89
Do You Want to Be in My Movie?, 361
Do You Want to Play Games?, 410
Do-Do-Do, 67, 68
Do-Do-Re-Do, 212
Do-Re-Mi, 112
Doatsy Mae, 404, 405
Doctor and Ella, 186
Dr. Brock, 257
Dr. Crippen, 178
Doctor Is In, The, 398
Doctor Jazz, 407
Does a Duck Love Water?, 162
Does the Spearmint Lose Its Flavor on the Bedpost Overnight?, 90
Dog and Cat Duet, The, 310
Dog Eat Dog, 157
Dog Gone That Chilly Man, 39
Dog Is a Man's Best Friend, A, 392
Dogs versus You, 381
Dogface, 244
Dogpatch Dance, 395
Doin' the New Low Down, 389
Doin' What Comes Natur'lly, 53
Doing Good, 296
(Doing It For) Sugar, 238, 239
Doing the Latest Rag, 378
Doing the Reactionary, 193
Dolce Far Niente, 270
Doll's Life, A, 351
Dolly, 77, 78
Dominus Vobiscum, 216
Don Jose of Far Rockaway, 198
Don't "Ah, Ma" Me, 337
Don't Ask, 68
Don't Ask a Lady, 315
Don't Ask Me Not to Sing, 32, 33
Don't Be a Woman If You Can, 144
Don't Be Afraid, 183
Don't Be Afraid of Anything, 145
Don't Be Afraid of Romance, 55
Don't Be Anything Less, 351
Don't Be Ashamed of a Teardrop, 233
Don't Blow That Horn, Gabriel, 163
Don't Cry, 246
Don't Cry, Girl, 403
Don't Ever Leave Me, 31
Don't Feed the Plants (Finale), 364
Don't Fence Me In, 125
Don't Follow in My Footsteps, 361
Don't Forget 127th Street, 296

Don't Forget the Lilac Bush, 179
Don't Forget the Waiter, 159
Don't Give In, 373
Don't Go, 333
Don't Go Away, Monsieur, 143
Don't Kick My Dreams Around, 240
Don't Kiki Me, 308
Don't Laugh, 277
Don't Let It Get You Down, 170
Don't Let It Happen Again, 164
Don't Like Goodbyes, 155
Don't Live inside of Yourself, 254
Don't Look at Me [Sondheim], 280
Don't Look at Me That Way [Porter], 121, 128
Don't Look Now but My Heart Is Showing, 178
Don't Love Me Like Othello, 86, 87
Don't Marry Me, 111
Don't Nobody Bring Me No Bad News, 403
Don't Put It Down, 399
Don't Rain on My Parade, 235
Don't Sell the Night Short, 205
Don't Send Me Back (To Petrograd), 49
Don't Take Me Back to Bottleneck, 199
Don't Take Much, 321
Don't Take Your Beau to the Seashore, 39
Don't Tamper with My Sister, 172
Don't Tell Mama, 333
Don't Tell Your Folks, 95
Don't Tempt Me, 18
Don't Turn My Picture to the Wall, 10
Don't Wait Too Long, 49
Don't Wanna Write about the South, 198
Don't You Want a Paper, Dearie?, 5
Don't You Want to Take Me?, 23
Donna, 399
Doomed, Doomed, Doomed, 394
Door to Isle Gorée, The, 409
Dorrie's Wish, 248
Dot, Dot, Dot, 296
Double Talk (Stine's Opening), 320
Double Trouble, 143
Dove Song, The, 358
Down, 353
Down by the Sea, 94
Down Home, 402
Down in My Heart, 40
Down in the Depths (On the Ninetieth Floor), 126
Down in the Valley, 180
Down on MacConnachy Square, 223
Down on the Dude Ranch, 170
Down on the Old-Time Farm, 141
Down to the Folies Bergère, 39
Down Where the Jack O'Lanterns Grow, 45
Down with Love, 153
Downcast Eye, The, 3

Downtown Rag, 235
Draw the Blinds, 298
Dream, The [Bock], 260
Dream, The [Finn], 369
Dream, The [Guettel], 409
Dream a Dream, 27
Dream Coney Island Ballet, The, 212
Dream of a Ladies Cloak Room Attendant, 29
Dream of Atlanta, The, 414
Dream on Little Soldier Boy, 45
Dream Safe with Me, 299
Dream with Me, 212
Dreamers, 360
Dreamgirls, 405
Dreaming True, 87
Dresden Northwest Mounted, 73
Dressed in Your Pyjamas in the Grand Salon, 378
Dressing for the Night, 378
Dressing Them Up, 339
Drift with Me, 18
Drifting along with the Tide, 61
Drop That Name, 231
Drugstore Scene [Blitzstein], 186
Drugstore Song, The [Rome], 196
Drums in My Heart, 83
Dubbing, The, 344
Duck Joke, The, 382
Duet for One (The First Lady of the Land), 218
Dulcinea, 344
Dum Dum Dum, 207
Dumb Dog, 298

Each Pearl a Thought, 13
Each Tomorrow Morning, 327
Eadie Was a Lady, 84
Eager Beaver, 112
Eagle and Me, The, 154
Earth and Other Minor Things, The, 226
Earthly Paradise, 308
Ease on down the Road, 403
Easier to Love, 406
Easter Parade, 51
Eastern Moon, 6
Easy, 216
Easy Come, Easy Go, 114
Easy Does It, 195
Easy for You, 302
Easy Money, 321
Easy Pickin's, 25
Easy Street, 298
Easy to Be Hard, 399, 400
Easy to Love, 125
Eat a Little Something, 200
Eating Myself up Alive, 373
Echo Song, 276

Economic Situation, The, 162
Economics, 180
Edelweiss, 112
Edinboro Jig, The, 9
Edinboro Wriggle, The, 9
Edgar Allan Poe, 351
Edna May's Irish Song, 4
Egg, The, 401
Eight Little Girls, 8
El Sombrero, 314
Electric Blues/Old Fashioned Melody, 399
Elegance, 263, 265, 325, 326
Elephant Song, The, 334
Elevator Song (Goin' Up), 392
Elizabeth, 114
Elks and the Masons, The, 152
Elliot Garfield Grant, 361
Embassy Waltz, The, 224
Embraceable You, 71
Emma's Reasons, 411
Emperor Is a Man, The, 300
Empty, 349
Empty Pockets Filled with Love, 55
Enchanted Forest, The, 225
Enchanted Train, The, 26
Enchanting Girls, 168
End of a Perfect Day, The, 358
End of a String, 65
End of My Race, The, 345
Endless Delights, 357
Endless Night, 413
Enemy Within, The, 367
England Every Time for Me, 43
Engagement Party, The, 411
English Teacher, An, 294
Enough!, 298
Entrance of Eric, 125
Entrance of Juno (Hail, Hail, Hail), 131
Entrance of the Council, 175
Entry into Jerusalem, 367
Ephraham Played upon the Piano, 39
Epiphany [Bernstein], 216
Epiphany [Sondheim], 284, 287
Erbie Fitch's Dilemma, 396
Escorte-Moi, 352
Esmeralda, 117
Esther, 167
Ethel, Baby, 256
Eulalie, 7
Ev'ry Day (Comes Something Beautiful), 114
Ev'ry Day a Holiday, 127
Ev'ry Street's a Boulevard (In Old New York), 229, 230
Ev'ry Sunday Afternoon, 101
Ev'ry Time, 205, 209

Ev'ry Time We Say Goodbye, 129
Ev'rybod-ee Who's Anybod-ee, 125
Ev'rybody Knows I Love Somebody, 69
Ev'rybody Loves You, 99
Ev'rybody Today Is Turning On, 317
Ev'rybody's Gotta Be Somewhere, 320
Ev'rything I Love, 128
Ev'rything I've Got, 104
Eve, 261
Evelina, 154
Even Dirty Old Men Need Love, 239
Evening Star [Gershwin], 65, 66
Evening Star [Schmidt], 306, 307
Ever After, 286
Ever and Ever Yours, 118
Ever Since I Put on a Uniform, 45
Everlasting, 229
Every Day, 19
Every Day a Little Death, 281, 282
Every Day in Every Way, 25
Every Girl I Meet, 8
Every Girl in All America, 21
Every Girl Wants to Get Married, 331
Every Man Is a Stupid Man, 132
Every Once in a While, 199
Everybody Calls Me Little Red Riding Hood, 26
Everybody Dance, 340
Everybody Likes You, 264
Everybody Loses, 255
Everybody Loves Everybody, 198
Everybody Loves Leona, 113
Everybody Loves Louis, 286
Everybody Loves to Take a Bow, 230
Everybody Ought to Have a Maid, 276
Everybody Rejoice, 403
Everybody Says Don't, 277
Everybody Step, 47
Everybody Wants to Do a Musical, 303
Everybody's Girl, 340
Everybody's Got a Home but Me, 110
Everybody's Got the Right, 287
Everyone Hates His Parents, 372
Everyone in the World Is Doing the Charleston, 49
Everyone Looks Lonely, 310
Everyone Tells Jason to See a Psychiatrist, 370
Everything [Bock], 262
Everything Beautiful Happens at Night, 306
Everything Happens to Me, 391
Everything I Have Is Yours, 170
Everything in America Is Ragtime, 43
Everything Reminds Me of You, 387
Everything That's Gonna Be Has Been, 113
Everything's Coming up Roses, 232, 233
Everything's Great, 296
Exhibit A, 274

Exits, 382
Expect Things to Happen, 271
Experiment, 124
Express Yourself, 332
Expulsion, The, 358
Extra, Extra [Berlin], 54
Extra, Extra [Styne], 232
Extraordinary, 356
Eyes Like a Stranger, 270
Eyes of Youth See the Truth, The, 45
Eyes That Never Lie, 365

F.D.R. Jones, 194
Façade, 411
Face on the Dime, The, 196
Fact Can Be a Beautiful Thing, A, 400
Factory Girls, The, 414
Fade Out—Fade In, 236
Faded Rose, 81
Fair Brooklyn, 274
Fair Lady, A, 31
Fair Trade, 114
Fair Warning, 199
Fairyland, 264
Fake Your Way to the Top, 405
Fallin', 360
Falling in Love with Love, 100, 101
Falling out of Love Can Be Fun, 54
Falsettoland, 372
Family, 405
Family Affair, A, 331
Family History, 373
Family Tree, The, 387
Family Way, The, 200
Fan Me with a Movement Slow, 10
Fan Tan Fannie, 111
Fancy! Fancy!, 162
Fancy Meeting You [Arlen], 153
Fancy Meeting You Here [Flaherty], 381
Fanette, 398, 399
Fanny, 198
Far Away [Porter], 127
Far Far Far Away [Loesser], 249
Far from the Home I Love, 260
Faraway Boy, 247
Farewell, Dear Toys, 4
Farewell for a While, 166
Farewell, Me Butty, 190
Farewell, My Lovely, 142
Farm Sequence (Caroline), 232
Farmer and the Cowman, The, 105
Farmer's Daughter, The, 154
Farming, 128
Fascinating Rhythm, 65, 76
Fasten Your Seat Belts, 297

Faster Than Sound, 208
Fatal Fascination, 140
Fate [Borodin], 393
Fate [Porter], 123
Fated to Be Mated, 132
Father of Claudine, The, 310
Father of the Bride, The, 307
Father to Son, 370
Fatherhood Blues, 406
Fatherland, Mother of the Band, 73
Fathers and Sons, 357
Father's Day, 358
Fauna's Song [1st], 110
Fauna's Song (Beguine) [2nd], 110
Favorite Son, 320
Fear [Styne], 236
Fear [Weill], 181
Fear No More, 282
Feel the Rain Fall, 414
Feeling I'm Falling, 70
Feeling No Pain, 365
Feeling Sentimental, 70
Feeling We Once Had, The, 403
Feelings, 261
Feelings You've Got to Hide, 412
Feet Do Yo' Stuff, 236
Fellow Needs a Girl, A, 107, 108
Feminine Companionship, 357
Femme Du Monde, 308
Fennimores Lied, 173
Feudin' and Fightin', 170
Fiddler and the Fighter, The, 236
Fiddler on the Roof (Theme), 260
Fidgety Feet, 67
Fie on Goodness, 225
Fifth Army's Where My Heart Is, The, 52
Fifth Letter, 288
Fifty Million Years Ago, 308
Fight Over Me, 80
Fight Song, The, 295
Fill in the Words, 360
Final Scene [Sweeney Todd], 284
Final Storm, 407
Finale [A Night Out], 119
Finale [Godspell], 355
Finale (Scene 15) [Passion], 288
Finale [Regina], 188
Finale [Rent], 410
Finale [The Threepenny Opera], 182
Finale Act One [Allegro], 107
Finale Act One [Blue Eyes], 31
Finale Act One [By Jupiter], 104
Finale Act One [Have a Heart], 18
Finale Act One [How to Succeed . . .], 248
Finale Act One [Oh Lady! Lady!!], 20

Finale Act 1 (Wedding) [*Show Boat*], 30
Finale Act Two [*Cabaret Girl*], 24
Finale Marches On, The, 162
Finaletto Act One [*Cabaret Girl*], 24
Find Me a Primitive Man, 122
Find Yourself a Man, 235
Fine and Dandy, 390
Fini, 251
Finishing the Hat, 286
Fire and Ice, 377
Firefly, 313
Fireworks, 233
Firing of Jimmy, 405
First Class Number One Bum, 238
First Class Private Mary Brown, 244
First Class Roster, The, 378
First Day of May, The, 18
First Lady, The, 55
First Lady and First Gent, 73
First Letter, 288
First Midnight, 286
First Prize at the Fair, 144
First Rose of Summer, 22, 24
First There Was Fletcher, 71
First Thing Monday Mornin', 402
First Time, The, 334
First Transformation, 411
First You Dream, 340
Fish [Bock], 261
Fish [Porter], 121
5 A.M., 162
Five Growing Boys, 350
Five O'Clock Tea, 49
Five Zeros, 318
Flaemchen (The Flame Girl), 377
Flahooley, 392
Flame, The, 332
Flaming Agnes, 307
Flaming Youth, 389
Flannel Petticoat Girl, 78, 79
Flappers Are We, 80
Flashback, 288
Flattery, 198
Flesh Failures, The, 399
Fletcher's American Cheese Chorale Society, 68
Fletcher's American Chocolate Chorale Society, 71
Flibbertigibbet, 306
Flings, 263
Floating thru the Air, 135
Flood, The, 358
Florida by the Sea, 49
Flower, A, 401
Flower Garden of My Heart, 103
Flubby Dub, 19
Flying down to Rio, 84

Foggy Day, A, 75
Folies Bergères, 376
Follies (Beautiful Girls), 280
Follow Me, 225
Follow Me Around [Berlin], 41
Follow Me Round [Kern], 9
Follow the Crowd, 42
Follow the Drum, 69
Follow the Fold, 246
Follow the Lamb!, 238
Follow the Sun, 142
Follow the Way of the Lord, 299
Follow Your Heart, 394, 395
Fool Meets Fool, 104
Foolish Face, 138
Foolish Heart, 178
Fools Fall in Love, 51, 52
Football Game (Marching Songs), 331
Football Song (Opening Act Two), 19
For Better or Worse, 146
For Every Fish There's a Little Bigger Fish, 156
For Goodness' Sake, 160
For Jupiter and Greece, 104
For Love, 190
For My Mary, 302
For No Rhyme or Reason, 126
For Poland, 328
For the First Time [Schwartz], 146
For the Life of Me, 144
For the Man I Love, 26
For the Very First Time, 54
For You [Rome], 200
For You [Styne], 240
Forbidden Fruit, 261
Forbidden Love (In Gaul), 261
Forest in the Sky, 255
Forever and a Day, 208
Forever and Ever, 227
Forever Yours, 382
Forget All Your Books, 169
Forget Me Not, 22
Forty Days, 288
Forty Minutes for Lunch, 178
Fosca's Entrance, 288
Fountain of Youth, 121
Four (Naked Ladies), 401
Four Black Dragons, 283
Four Jews in a Room Bitching, 370
Four Little Angels of Peace, 193
Four Little Sirens, 65
Four Nightingales, The, 350
Four O'Clock, 181
Fourscore, 399
Fourth Letter, 288
Fox Has Left His Lair, The, 28

Fox Hunt (Fall off, Auntie Mame), The, 326
Fox-Trot [Sondheim], 280
Frahngee-Pahnee, 129
Francie [Blitzstein], 187
Francie [Styne], 229
Frank Mills, 399
Frankie's Testimony, 414
Franklin Shepard, Inc., 285
Frantzi, 8
Fraught, 187
Freddy Chant, 265
Freddy My Love, 402
Free [Berlin], 54
Free [Sondheim], 276
Free at Last, 406
Freedom, 403
Freedom of the Press, The, 186
Freida, 7
French with Tears, 197
Fresh As a Daisy, 128
Fresno Beauties, 247
Freud, Jung and Adler, 73
Friars' Parade, 44
Friend [Grossman], 351
Friends [Bock], 261
Friendship, 127, 128
Frogs Have So Much Spring, 373
Frolic of a Breeze, The, 3, 4
From Afar, 114
From Alpha to Omega, 126
From Another World, 101, 102
From Now On [Gershwin], 58
From Now On [Porter], 127
From Saturday to Monday, 3
From This Day On, 223, 226, 301
From This Moment On, 130, 131
From This Out, 190
Fugue for Tinhorns, 246
Full-Blown Roses, 89
Fun, 410
Fun to Be Fooled, 152, 153
Funeral [Loewe], 223
Funeral Sequence [Sondheim], 276
Funeral Tango (La Tango Funebre) [Brel], 399
Funnies, The, 51
Funny [Coleman], 320
Funny [Flaherty], 382
Funny Face, 69
Funny Girl, 235
Funny Honey, 335
Funny Little Something, 21
Funny Old House, 34
Furnishing a House for Two, 42
Future Isn't What It Used to Be, The, 361

G-Man Song, 193
Gabey's Comin', 212
Gabriel's Letter, 339
Gal in Calico, A, 144
Gallivantin' Aroun', 30
Gallop, 188
Gallop to Your Treasure Thy Wife, 404
Gambling Man, 201
Game, The, 253
Game of Poker, A, 157
Games I Play, The, 370
Garbage, 327
Garçon, S'il Vous Plait, 72
Garden of Eden Ballet, The, 132
Gary, Indiana, 269
Gaston, 366
Gathering Storm, The, 358
Gavotte, 89
Gay Lothario, The, 7
Gazooka, The, 162
Gee, but It's Great to Be in the Army!, 244
Gee, Officer Krupke, 215
General Unveiled, The, 193
General's Gone to a Party, The, 73
Generations, 358
Gentle Afternoon, 266
Gentleman Is a Dope, The, 107
Gentleman Jimmy, 257
Gentleman's Gentleman, A, 237
Gentlemen Prefer Blondes [Berlin], 49
Gentlemen Prefer Blondes [Styne], 228
Georgia on My Mind, 391
Georgia Sand, 124
Geraniums in the Winder, 106
Germans at the Spa, The, 376
Gesticulate, 393
Get a Life, 361
Get a Load of That, 179
Get Away Boy, 407
Get Away for a Day in the Country, 228
Get Away from It All, 142
Get Happy, 149, 150, 153, 158
Get Me to the Church on Time, 224
Get out of Town, 127
Get up, Get out, Get under the Sun, 150
Get up on a New Routine, 136
Get Yourself a Geisha, 142
Get Yourself a Girl, 128
Get Yourself a New Broom (And Sweep the Blues Away), 152
Gettin' a Man, 157
Gettin' Ready Rag, 383
Getting in the Lifeboat, 378
Getting Married [Styne], 234
Getting Married Today [Sondheim], 279

Getting Tall, 376
Getting to Know You, 109
Ghosties and Ghoulies That Go Bump in the Night, 209
Giants in the Sky, 286
Gideon Briggs, I Love You, 247
Gift Today, A (Bar Mitzvah Song), 200
Gifts of Love, 357
Gigi, 226
Gigolo, 121
Gilding the Guild, 89
Gimme a Rain Check, 316
Gimme Love, 339
Gimme Some, 296
Gimme the Shimmy, 197
Gin Rummy Rhapsody, 197
Gina, 187
Ginger Town, 22
Girl Friend, The, 90
Girl Friend of a Boy Friend of Mine, 390
Girl from Ipanema, 278
Girl I Mean to Be, The, 407
Girl in the Valley, A, 407
Girl Is You and the Boy Is Me, The, 388
Girl of the Moment, 176
Girl of the Pi Beta Phi, A, 389
Girl on the Magazine, The, 43
Girl That I Marry, The, 53
Girl, You're a Woman, 404
Girlie, 21
Girls, 129
Girls Ahoy!, 347
Girls in the Sea, 23
Girls Like Me, 234
Girls of My Dreams, The, 47
Girls of Summer, 275
Girls of the Night, The, 411
Girls Who Sit and Wait, The, 325
Git Comfortable, 409
Git It!, 364
Gitka's Song, The, 113
Give a Little, Get a Little, 229
Give a Little Thought to Me, 22
Give a Little Whistle, 314
Give a Man Enough Rope, 320, 321
Give England Strength, 262
Give Him the Oo-La-La, 128
Give It Back to the Indians, 101
Give Me a Song with a Beautiful Melody, 229
Give Me My Mammy, 63
Give Me the Land, 132
Give Me Your Tired, Your Poor, 54
Give That Little Girl a Hand, 91
Give the Little Lady (A Great Big Hand), 396
Glad to Be Home, 55

Glad to Be Unhappy, 98
Glamorous Life, The [1st], 281, 282
Glamorous Life, The [2nd], 281, 282
Glee Club Rehearsal, 398
Gliding, 383
Gliding through My Memoree, 111
Glimpse of Love, 198
Glitter and Be Gay, 214
Gloria [Bernstein], 214
Gloria [Bock], 256
Gloria in Excelsis, 216
Gloria Tibi, 216
Glory, 356
Go and Get Your Old Banjo, 207
Go Home, 321
Go Home Train, 236
Go into Your Trance, 208
Go It, Old Girl!, 298
Go Little Boat, 20, 22
Go out Big, 240
Go to Sleep [Lane], 171
Go to Sleep Whatever You Are [Bock], 261
Go Visit Your Grandmother, 334, 335
God Bless Rockefeller, 183
God Bless Us, Everyone, 367
God Said (And It Was Good), 216
God That's Good, 284
God's Alive, 402
God's Country, 153
God's Garden, 238
God's Green World, 222
God-Why-Don't-You-Love-Me Blues (Buddy's Blues), The, 280
Godspeed Titanic (Sail On), 378
Goin' Back to School, 207
Goin' to Town, 170
Goin' Up (The Elevator Song), 392
Going Home Train, 196
Going Rowing, 79
Gold, 181
Golden Boy, 296
Golden Delicious Fish, 264
Golden Helmet, 344
Golden Land, Golden Life, 393
Golden Ram, The, 113
Goldfarb, That's 'Im, 71
Goliath of Gath, 367
Gone Are the Days, 87
Gone, Gone, Gone, 74
Gone with the Wind, 201
Gonna Be Another Hot Day, 306, 307
Gooch's Song, 326, 327
Good and Evil, 411
Good and Lucky, 142
Good Bye, Georg, 259

Good Clean Fun, 257
Good Fellow Mine, 90
Good Friends, 297
Good Little Girls, 167
Good Morning Dearie, 25
Good Morning, Good Day, 259
Good Morning Starshine, 399
Good News, 389
Good News, Bad News, 361
Good Night, Angeline, 387
Good Old Atwater, 19
Good Old Girl, 404
Good Ole New York, 407
Good Thing Going, 285
Good Time Charlie [Schwartz], 145
Good Time Charlie [Kander], 333
Good Times [Kander], 339
Good Times [Strouse], 301
Good to Be Alive, 381
Good Will Movement, The, 129
Good-Bye, Becky Cohen, 38
Good-Night Boat, 23
Good-Night, My Dear, 63
Goodbye (The Prince's Farewell), 315
Goodbye Love, 410
Goodbye, My Love, 383
Goodbye to All That, 144
Goodbye, Canavaro, 334
Goodbye, Darlin', 247
Goodbye for Now, 285
Goodbye, Jonah, 142
Goodbye, Little Dream, Goodbye, 126
Goodbye, Love, 198
Goodbye, My Honey, 201
Goodbye, Old Girl, 252
Goodbye, Salome, 404
Goodnight, 307
Goodnight, My Someone, 269
Goodnight, Sweet Prince, 397
Goodtime Charley [Grossman], 350
Goodtime Ladies Rag, 356
Goona-Goona, 394
Goose Never Be a Peacock, 157
Gordo's Law of Genetics (The Bad Traits Will
    Always Predominate), 373
Gorgeous, 261
Gossip [Sondheim], 286
Gossips, The [Loesser], 245
Gospel, 409
Gospel According to King, 382
Got a Bran' New Daddy, 165
Got a Bran' New Suit, 142
Got a Rainbow, 70
Got That Good Time, 170
Gotta Have Me Go with You, 155

Gotta Dance, 206
Grab Your Mate and Skedaddle All, 404
Grade "A" Treatment, 265
Grand Cafe, The, 351
Grand Canal Sequence, 376
Grand Charleston, The (H-A-P-P-Y), 377
Grand Fox-Trot, The, 377
Grand Imperial Cirque de Paris, 264
Grand Knowing You, 258
Grand Old Ivy, 248
Grand Opening [Demi-Dozen], 305
Grand Parade (Theme from Grand Hotel), 377
Grand Tango, The, 377
Grand Waltz, The, 377
Grandpapa (Zorba's Dance), 334
Grant Avenue, 111
Grapes of Roth, 400
Grass Is Always Greener, The, 337
Grasslands Chant, 413
Grateful Children, 358
Greased Lightnin', 402
Great Big Town (Chicago), A, 103
Great Day [Duke], 164
Great Day! [Youmans], 82
Great Highway, The, 414
Great Indoors, The, 123
Great Unknown, 366
Great White Father (Of the Year), 402
Great Wisconsin, 255
Great Writer, The, 351
Greatest of These, The, 308
Greatest Show on Earth, The, 177
Greedy Girl, 188
Greek to You, 126
Green Finch and Linnet Bird, 284
Green-Up Time, 180
Greenhorns, 302
Greens, 287
Greenwich Village, 20
Greenwillow Christmas, 247
Greenwillow Walk, 288
Greetings, 188
Grind, The, 352
Grow for Me, 364
Growin' Boy, 363
Growing Older, 310
Growing Pains, 145
Growing Up, 285
Guenevere, 225
Guess I'll Have to Hang My Tears out to Dry, 227
Guess We May As Well Stay Married Now, 307
Guess Who, 396
Guido's Song, 376
Gun Song, 287
Gunga Din, 87

Gus and Sadie Love Song, 185
Guv'ment, 406
Guy Who Brought Me, The, 103, 205
Guy with the Polka-Dot Tie, The, 227, 237
Guys and Dolls, 246
Guys and Dolls Preamble, 246
Gypsy Blues, 387
Gypsy Caravan, 27
Gypsy in Me, The, 124
Gypsy Joe, 390
Gypsy's Song, 336

Hail, Bibinski, 132
Hail, Hail, Hail, 131
Hair, 399
Hakim's Cellar, 199
Hakuna Matata, 413
Half a Kiss, 160
Half As Big As Life, 400
Half of a Couple, 300
"Half of It Dearie" Blues, The, 65
Half of the People, 216
Hallelujah!, 81
Hallelujah, Baby!, 236
Halloween [Larson], 410
Halloween [Schwartz], 145
Hand for the Hog, 406
Hand in Hand, 34
Hand Me down That Can o' Beans, 223
Hang on to Me, 65
Hang Up!, 145
Hangin' Around with You, 70
Hanging Throttlebottom in the Morning, 73
Hangman's Song (Under the Gallow Tree), 178
Hannah Will Take Care of You, 267
Hans [Porter], 121
Hans [Strouse], 298
Happiest House on the Block, The, 110, 111
Happily Ever After [Duke], 160
Happily Ever After [Rodgers], 397
Happily Ever After [Sondheim], 279
Happiness [Gesner], 398
Happiness [Sondheim], 288
Happiness Is Just a Thing Called Joe, 154
H-A-P-P-Y, 377
Happy As the Day Is Long, 152
Happy Because I'm in Love, 82
Happy Birthday (Nursery Round), 199
Happy Birthday, Mrs. J.J. Brown, 270
Happy Birthday to Me, 334
Happy Birthday to You and to You, 412
Happy Days, 389
Happy Days Are Here Agin, 150
Happy Ending, 306
Happy Habit, 145

Happy Happy New Year [Strouse], 301
Happy Heaven of Harlem, 122
Happy Hunting, 392
Happy Hunting Horn, 103
Happy in the Morning, 337
Happy New Year [Larson], 410
Happy Talk, 108
Happy Time, The, 333
Happy to Keep His Dinner Warm, 248
Happy to Make Your Acquaintance, 247
Happy Wedding Day, 22
Harbor Deep down in My Heart, The, 120
Harbor of My Heart, 81
Hard Candy Christmas, 404, 405
Hard to Be a Prince, 302
Hard to Say Goodbye, My Love, 405
Harder They Fall, The, 402
Hardest Part of Love, The, 358
Harem Life (Outside of That Every Little Thing's All Right), 46
Hark to the Song of the Night, 131
Harlem Boogie-Woogie, 35
Harlem Holiday, 150
Harlem on My Mind, 51
Harlem River Chanty, 66
Harlem Serenade, 70
Harlemania, 96
Harmony, 331
Harolds of This World, The, 240
Harry Houdini, Master Escapist, 383
Has Anyone Seen My Joe?, 62
Has I Let You Down?, 156
Hashish, 399
Haunted Heart, 144
Haunted Hot Spot, 167
Havana, 92
Have a Dream, 295
Have a Heart [Kern—1st], 17
Have a Heart [Kern—2nd], 18
Have a Heart [Lane], 170
Have a Memory on Me, 405
Have a Nice Day, 329
Have I Got a Girl for You, 279
Have I Told You Lately, 200
Have You Ever Seen a Prettier Little Congress?, 262
"Have You Forgotten Me?" Blues, 25
Have You Heard (Gossip Song), 157
Have You Met Miss Jones?, 99
Have Yourself a Merry Little Christmas, 206, 208, 209
Hay Ride, The, 6
Hay, Straw, 81
He Always Comes Home to Me, 301
He and She, 101

He Came Along, 83
He Can Do It, 402
He Dances on My Ceiling (Dancing on the Ceiling), 95, 96
He Died Good, 248
He Gives Me Love, 349
He Had Refinement, 145
He Hasn't a Thing Except Me, 162
He Is the Type, 28
He Knows Milk, 71
He Loves and She Loves, 69
He Must Be Nice to Mother, 10
He Plays the Violin, 401
He Sympathized with Me, 38
He Tossed a Coin, 262
He Wanted to Say, 383
He Was Too Good to Me, 95, 96
He's a Genius, 237
He's a Ladies' Man, 389
He's a Right Guy, 129
He's a V.I.P., 233
He's Back, 333
He's Coming, 308
He's Good for Me, 316
He's Got Larceny in His Heart, 235
He's in Love, 393
He's My Friend, 270
He's My Guy, 347
He's No Good, 321
He's Not Himself, 73
He's Only Wonderful, 392
He's Oversexed, 73
He's the Wizard, 403
Head Over Heels, 21
Heads I Win, 259
Healthy Normal American Boy, A, 294
Heart, 252, 253
Heart an' Hand, 409
Heart and Music, 373
Heart and Soul, 243, 391
Heart for Sale, A, 23
Heart Is Quicker Than the Eye, The, 98
Heart of Stone [Loesser], 248
Heart of Stone (Pyramid Song) [Anderson], 396
Heat Wave, 51
Heather on the Hill, The, 223, 226
Heaven Hop, The, 121
Heaven in My Arms (Music in My Heart), 35
Heaven on Earth, 67
Hector's Song (People Like You and Like Me), 394
Heigh-Ho, Lackaday, 89
Helen Is Always Willing, 394
Hello, 92
Hello, Dolly!, 325
Hello, Good Morning, 72

Hello, Hazel, 230
Hello, Hello, Hello, 206
Hello, Hello There, 231
Hello, Little Girl, 287
Hello Twelve, Hello Thirteen, Hello Love, 359
Hello, Waves, 332
Hello, Young Lovers, 93, 109
Hellzapoppin', 240
Hence It Don't Make Sense, 129
Henry, 31
Henry Ford, 383
Henry Street, 235
Henry, Sweet Henry, 266
Her Face, 264
Her Heart Was in Her Work, 132
Her Is, 252
Her Name is Aurora, 339
Here Am I [Kern], 31
Here Come the Dreamers, 208
Here Comes My Blackbird, 389
Here Comes Never, 240
Here Goes, 152
Here I Am [Henderson], 388
Here I Am [Merrill], 266
Here I'll Stay, 180
Here in Eden, 261
Here in My Arms, 89, 90, 91, 92
Here It Comes, 34
Here She Comes Now, 229
Here We Are [Martin], 207
Here We Are Again [Merrill], 263
Here We Are Again [Rodgers], 113
Here We Are Together Again [Kern], 28
Here We Go Again, 410
Here's a Hand, 104
Here's a Kiss, 89
Here's a Toast, 93
Here's Love, 271
Here's to the Girl of My Heart, 390
Here's to Us, 315
Here's to Your Illusions, 392
Herman, Let's Dance That Beautiful Waltz, 38
Hermits, The, 88, 89
Hernando's Hideaway, 251
Hero, 363
Hero & Leander, 414
Hero Ballet, 153
Heroes Come Home, The, 394
Heroes in the Fall, 101
Hey, Fellah!, 30
Hey, Girlie, 113
Hey, Good Lookin', 129
Hey! Hey! Let 'Er Go!, 64
Hey, Look at Me!, 299
Hey, Look Me Over!, 314

Hey There, 251, 252
Hey There, Good Times, 317, 318
Hey, Why Not!, 239
Hh! Cha Cha!, 32
Hi-De-Ho-Hi, 391
Hi-Ho!, 75
Hi-Lili, Hi-Lo, 265
Hidden in My Heart, 256
High and Low (I've Been Looking for You), 138
High Hat, 69
High Is Better Than Low, 146
High School Ladies at Five O'Clock, 369
High Up in Harlem, 35
Highest Judge of All, The, 106
Hills of Amalfi, The, 189
Hills of Ixopo, The, 181
Hills of Tomorrow, The, 285
Him, Them, It, Her, 381
Hip Hop Rant, 409
Hippopotamus, 8
Hiram's Band, 42
His Love Makes Me Beautiful, 235
His Majesty's Dragoons, 31
His Name Is Charlie Gordon, 299
His Name Was Coalhouse Walker, 383
His Old Man, 196
His Royal Highness, 298
History, 350
History Eight to the Bar, 195
History Is Made at Night, 194
History of the World, The, 293
Hit It Lorraine, 334
Hit the Road to Dreamland, 154
Hit with the Ladies, A, 49
Hittin' the Bottle, 149
Ho! Billy O!, 180
Hobbies, 387
Hoe-Down [Weill], 180
Hoedown [Loesser], 247
Hold On, 407
Hold Me—Hold Me—Hold Me, 229
Hold on to Your Hats, 170
Hold Your Head up High, 33
Holding to the Ground, 372
Holly Golightly, 265
Hollywood and Vine, 281
Hollywood Story, 205
Holy Man and the Yankee, The, 305
Home [Kander], 334
Home [Menken], 366
Home [Smalls], 403
Home [Yeston], 377, 378
Home Again [Bock], 257
Home Again [Rome], 201
Home Blues, 70

Home for Wayward Girls, 265
Home Sweet Heaven, 208
Home Sweet Home, 22
Homeless Lady's Revenge, The, 373
Homesick [Strouse], 301
Homesick Blues [Styne], 228
Homeward Bound, 42, 68
Homework, 54
Hon'rable Profession of the Fourth Estate, The, 54
Honestly Sincere, 294
Honey, 285
Honey Bun [Rodgers], 108
Honey Bun [Youmans], 79
Honey in the Honeycomb, 164
Honeymoon Inn, 18
Honeymoon Is Over, The, 307
Honeymoon Isle, 26
Honeymoon Land, 21, 23
Honeymoon Lane, 11
Honolulu, 186
Hook's Hook, 230
Hooker's Ball, The, 321
Hoop De Dingle, 199
Hoop-La-La, Papa!, 10
Hoops, 139
Hooray for George the Third, 145
Hooray for Hollywood, 154
Hooray for Us, 153
Hooray for What!, 153
Hootspa, 301
Hop Up, My Ladies, 180
Hoping That Someday You'd Care, 68
Horace's Entrance, 188
Horace's Last, 188
Hospital Board, 411
Hostess with the Mostes' on the Ball, The, 54
Hot, 138
Hot Dog!, 25
Hot Enough for You?, 336
Hot Fun, 409
Hot Honey Rag, 335
Hot House Rose, 97
Hot Spot, 33
Hottentot Potentate, The, 142
Hour of Darkness, The, 358
House and Garden, 247
House of Flowers, 155
House of Marcus Lycus [1st], 276
House of Marcus Lycus [2nd], 276
House upon the Hill, The, 407
How about a Boy Like Me?, 71
How about a Cheer for the Navy, 52
How about a Man, 68, 71
How about It?, 96
How about You?, 170, 172

How Are Things in Glocca Morra?, 171, 172, 273
How Are the Mighty Fallen, 367
How Are Ya, Since?, 345
How Beautiful the Days, 247
How Blest We Are, 406
How Can I Call This Home?, 414
How Can I Continue On?, 412
How Can I Ever Be Alone?, 144
How Can I Lose You?, 414
How Can I Tell Her?, 377
How Can I Wait?, 223
How Can I Win?, 361
How Can Love Survive?, 112
How Can You Describe a Face?, 234
How Can You Tell an American?, 175
How Cold Cold Cold an Empty Room, 200
How Could I Ever Know [Simon], 407
How Could I Know? [Styne], 238
How Could We Be Wrong?, 124
How Did They Build Titanic?, 378
How Do I Know?, 273
How Do I Look?, 208
How Do You Do, Katinka?, 25
How Do You Raise a Barn?, 394
How Do You Speak to an Angel?, 229, 230
How Free I Feel, 308
How Glory Goes, 409
How High Can a Little Bird Fly?, 142
How I Saved Roosevelt, 287
How Little We Know, 391
How Long, 110
How Long Can Love Keep Laughing?, 194
How Long Has This Been Going On?, 69
How Lovely to Be a Woman, 294
How Lucky Can You Get? [Fain], 392
How Lucky Can You Get? [Kander], 338
How Marvin Eats His Breakfast, 369
How Much I Love You, 178
How Much Is That Doggie in the Window?, 263, 267
How Much Richer Could One Man Be?, 260
How Nice for Me, 301
How Often, 201
How Sad, 112
How the Body Falls Apart, 369
How the Money Changes Hands, 257
How to Handle a Woman, 225
How to Succeed, 248
How to Survive, 182
How to Win Friends and Influence People, 100
How Was I to Know?, 93, 95
How Will He Know?, 229
How Ya Gonna Keep 'Em down on the Farm, 390
How'd You Like to Spoon with Me?, 4, 5
How'm I Doin'?, 301

How's About Tonight?, 247
How's Chances, 51
How's Your Health?, 102
How's Your Romance, 123
Howdy! How D'You Do?, 8
Howdy to Broadway, 92
Human Heart, The, 382
Humble Hollywood Executive, A, 129
Humming, 264
Hundred Million Miracles, A, 111
Hundreds of Girls, 327
Hundreds of Hats, 352
Hungry Men, The, 306
Hunt Ball, The, 28
Hunted Partridge on the Hill, 367
Hup! Tup! Thrup! Four! (Jack, the Sleepy Jeep), 196
Hurry, 216
Hurry Back, 297
Hurry! It's Lovely up Here!, 171, 172
Hurry up Face, 351
Hush, Hush, 175
Husking Bee, The, 232
Huxley, 177
Hymn [Blitzstein], 190
Hymn [Yeston], 378
Hymn for a Sunday Evening (Ed Sullivan), 294, 295
Hymn to Him (Why Can't a Woman Be More Like a Man), A, 224
Hymn to Hymie, 324
Hymn to Peace, A, 174

I Ain't down Yet, 270
I Ain't Got No Shame, 74
I Always Knew, 303
I Always Think of Sally, 164
I Am Ashamed That Women Are So Simple, 130
I Am Changing, 405
I Am Easily Assimilated, 214
I Am Free, 334
I Am Going to Like It Here, 111
I Am Going to Love (The Man You're Going to Be), 350
I Am in Love, 131
I Am Loved, 131
I Am Only Human after All, 160, 161
I Am So Eager, 32
I Am Wearing a Hat, 369
I Am What I Am, 328, 329
I and Albert, 298
I Beg Your Pardon, 89
I Beg Your Pardon, Dear Old Broadway, 39
I Believe in God, 216
I Believe in Takin' a Chance, 146

I Believe in You [Loesser], 248
I Believe in You [Schwartz], 143
I Believe You [Kander], 332
I Believed All They Said, 21
I Belong Here, 328
I Blush, 93
I Cain't Say No, 105
I Can Always Find a Little Sunshine in the YMCA, 45
I Can Always Find Another Partner, 78
I Can Dance, 306
I Can Cook Too, 211
I Can Do That, 359
I Can Do Wonders with You, 95, 96
I Can Hear It Now, 198
I Can Play This Part, 361
I Can See It, 305
I Can Show You a Thing or Two, 365
I Can't Be in Love, 396
I Can't Do It Alone, 335
I Can't Forget Your Eyes, 13, 28
I Can't Get Started, 162, 168
I Can't Give You Anything but Love, 389
I Can't Let You Go [Coleman], 316
I Can't Make This Movie, 376
I Can't Say You're the Only One, 7
I Can't Tell You, 299
I Cannot Let You Go [Loesser], 249
I Chose Right, 406
I Cling to You (Roxane's Song), 163
I Could Always Go to You, 365
I Could Be Good for You, 157
I Could Have Danced All Night, 224
I Could Write a Book, 103
I Couldn't Have Done It Alone, 295
I Couldn't Hold My Man, 152
I Did It on Roller Skates, 235
I Didn't Know What Time It Was, 101
I Do, I Do (I Do Adore You) [1st], 307
I Do! I Do! [2nd], 307
I Do, I Do (Who Loves to Touch You?) [3rd], 307
I Do Like You, 276
I Do Miracles, 339
I Do Not Know a Day I Did Not Love You, 113, 114
I Do What I Can, 353
I, Don Quixote, 344
I Don't Care Much, 333
I Don't Get It, 372
I Don't Know [Bernstein], 216
I Don't Know [Blitzstein], 188
I Don't Know [Strouse], 301
I Don't Know His Name, 259
I Don't Know Where She Got It, 236
I Don't Like This Dame, 247

I Don't Love You No More, 227
I Don't Need Anything but You, 298
I Don't Remember You, 333
I Don't Think I'll End It All Today, 156
I Don't Think I'll Fall in Love Today, 70
I Don't Wanna Be Married, I Just Wanna Be Friends, 50
I Don't Want a Girlie, 80
I Don't Want to Know, 327
I Don't Want to Walk without You, 227, 243
I Don't Want You to Be a Sister to Me, 8
I Draw the Line, 339
I Dream of a Girl in a Shawl, 122
I Enjoy Being a Girl, 111
I Fall in Love Too Easily, 228
I Feel at Home with You, 93
I Feel Like I'm Gonna Live Forever, 229, 230
I Feel Like I'm Not out of Bed Yet, 212
I Feel Merely Marvelous, 396
I Feel My Luck Comin' Back, 155
I Feel Pretty, 215
I Feel So Much Spring, 373
I Fought Every Step of the Way, 392
I Found a Four Leaf Clover, 62
I Get a Kick out of You, 123, 124, 125
I Get Along with the Aussies, 52
I Get Embarrassed, 264
I Get Myself Out, 353
I Go On, 216
I Got a Friend, 299
I Got a New Girl, 301
I Got a Song, 154
I Got Beauty, 131
I Got Life, 399
I Got Lost in His Arms, 53
I Got Love, 402
I Got Me, 303
I Got Plenty o' Nuttin', 74
I Got Rhythm, 71, 72
I Got the Beat, 409
I Got the Sun in the Morning, 53
I Got You, 320
I Gotta Right to Sing the Blues, 151
I Guess I'll Have to Change My Plan (The Blue Pajama Song), 136, 137, 147
I Guess I'll Miss the Man, 356
I Guess This Is Goodbye, 287
I Had a Love Once, 158
I Had Myself a True Love, 155
I Had Twins, 101
I Happen to Like New York, 123
I Happen to Love You, 209
I Hate Him [Merrill], 264
I Hate Him [Rome], 199
I Hate Men, 130

I Hate You, 43
I Hate You Darling, 128
I Have a Feeling, 383
I Have a Love, 215
I Have a Song, 195
I Have Acted Like a Fool, 306
I Have Confidence, 112
I Have Danced, 378
I Have Dreamed, 109
I Have Just One Heart for Just One Boy, 46
I Have No Words (To Say How Much I Love You),
     139
I Have Room in My Heart, 222
I Have So Many Songs, 373
I Have the Room Above, 29
I Have to Tell You, 198, 199
I Haven't Got a Worry in the World, 107
I Heard Someone Crying, 407
I Hope I Get It, 359
I, Huckleberry, Me, 406
I Introduced, 119
I Jupiter, I Rex, 131
I Just Can't Wait, 234
I Just Can't Wait to Be King, 413
I Just Couldn't Do without You, 5
I Knew You Well, 165
I Know, 261
I Know a Foul Ball, 73
I Know a Girl, 335
I Know about Love, 233
I Know and She Knows [Kern], 13
I Know How It Is, 247
I Know It Can Happen Again, 107
I Know Loneliness Quite Well, 310
I Know That Now, 351
I Know That You Know [Youmans], 81
I Know the Kind of Girl, 140
I Know Things Now, 287
I Know You by Heart, 205
I Know Your Heart, 208
I Know Your Kind, 199
I Landed on Him, 409
I Leave the World, 350
I Left My Heart at the Stage Door Canteen, 52
I Like Ev'rybody, 247
I Like the Likes of You, 161
I Like to Recognize the Tune, 101, 206
I Like What I Do, 300
I Like You, 198
I Like You As You Are, 81
I Like Your Face, 138
I Like Your Style, 318
I Look at You, 124
I Look Bad in Uniform, 158
I Look for Love, 81

I Lost the Rhythm, 293
I Love 'Em All [Kern], 33
I Love 'Em All [Strouse], 300
I Love a Cop, 257
I Love a New Yorker, 155
I Love a Parade, 150
I Love a Piano, 43
I Love Him, 247
I Love His Face, 308
I Love Lechery, 189
I Love Louisa, 139
I Love Love, 139
I Love My Wife [Coleman], 317
I Love My Wife [Schmidt], 307
I Love Order, 308
I Love Paris, 132
I Love the Lassies (I Love 'Em All), 23
I Love to Cry at Weddings, 315
I Love to Dance [Berlin], 43
I Love to Dance [Lane], 170
I Love to Have the Boys around Me, 43
I Love to Lie Awake in Bed, 136, 137
I Love Watermelon, 242
I Love What I'm Doing, 228
I Love You [Coleman], 315
I Love You [Gershwin], 61
I Love You [Porter], 129
I Love You and I Like You, 136, 137, 138
I Love You Etcetera, 273
I Love You I Love You I Love You, 78
I Love You More Than Yesterday, 95
I Love You Only, 123
I Love You So, 160
I Love You This Morning, 222
I Loved (J'aimais), 399
I Loved Her Too, 179
I Loved Him but He Didn't Love Me, 121
I Loved You Once in Silence, 225
I Loves You, Porgy, 74
I Made a Fist, 247
I Make Hay While the Moon Shines, 65
I Married an Angel, 100
I Mean to Say, 70
I Meant You No Harm, 405
I Met a Girl, 231
I Met a Man, 238
I Might Fall Back on You, 29
I Might Grow Fond of You, 28
I Miss You [Schmidt], 310
I Miss You Old Friend, 405
I Must Be Dreaming, 273
I Must Be Going, 91
I Must Be Home by Twelve O'Clock, 70
I Must Be One of the Roses, 139
I Must Get on That Ship, 378

I Must Go On, 412
I Must Have Her, 172
I Must Have That Man!, 389
I Must Love You, 94, 96
I Need a Garden, 64
I Need Love, 273
I Need Some Cooling Off, 92, 93
I Need to Know, 412
I Need You So, 137
I Never Did Imagine, 238
I Never Do Anything Twice (Madam's Song), 283
I Never Dream When I Sleep, 207
I Never Had a Chance, 146
I Never Has Seen Snow, 155, 156
I Never Know When (To Say When), 396
I Never Realized, 119
I Never Thought, 21
I Never Want to Go Home Again, 226
I Never Want to See You Again, 301
I Never Wanted to Love You, 370
I Once Believed, 345
I Promise You a Happy Ending, 327
I Put My Hand In, 325
I Read, 288
I Really Like Him, 344
I Really Loved You, 299
I Remember [Sondheim], 278
I Remember [Strouse], 302
I Remember It Well [Loewe], 226
I Remember It Well [Weill], 180
I Remember Mama, 114
I Remember That, 274
I Resolve, 259
I Rise Again, 318
I Said It and I'm Glad, 234
I Saw a Man, 401
I Saw the Roses and Remembered You, 26
I Say Hello, 199
I Say It's Spinach, 50
I See Your Face before Me, 143
I Shall Miss You (Holmes), 260
I Should Tell You, 410
I Shouldn't Love You, 196, 198
I Sing of Love, 130
I Sleep Easier Now, 131
I Still Believe in Love [Hamlisch], 360
I Still Believe in You [Duke], 160
I Still Believe in You [Rodgers], 96
I Still Get Jealous, 228
I Still Look at You That Way, 146
I Still Love the Red, White and Blue, 123
I Still See Elisa, 223, 224, 226
I Still Suits Me, 29
I Talk to the Trees, 223, 224, 226
I Talk, You Talk, 353

I Think, I Think, 328
I Think I'm Gonna Like It Here, 298
I Told You So, 337
I Understand, 212
I Used to Be above Love, 162
I Walk with Music, 391
I Waltz Alone, 377
I Wanna Be Good 'n' Bad, 206
I Wanna Be Loved by You, 136
I Wanna Be Yours, 315
I Wanna Make the World Laugh, 327
I Want a Man [Rodgers], 88, 91, 96
I Want a Man [Youmans], 81
I Want a Yes Man, 79
I Want It All, 406
I Want My Little Gob, 22
I Want Romance, 195
I Want to Be a Ballet Dancer, 49
I Want to Be a Rockette, 364
I Want to Be a War Bride, 71
I Want to Be Happy, 80
I Want to Be in Dixie, 41, 42
I Want to Be Raided by You, 121, 122
I Want to Be Seen with You Tonight, 235
I Want to Be the Mayor, 301
I Want to Be There, 27
I Want to Be with You [Strouse], 296
I Want to Be with You [Youmans], 84
I Want to Go Home [Porter], 127
I Want to Go Home [Shire], 410
I Want to Go to Hollywood, 377
I Want to Know, 410
I Want to Sing in Opera, 9
I Wanted to Change Him, 236
I Was a Pawn for Werner von Braun, 349
I Was a Shoo-In, 234
I Was Alone, 28
I Was Born on the Day before Yesterday, 403
I Was Lonely, 21
I Was Lost, 300
I Was So Young (You Were So Beautiful), 58
I Was the Most Beautiful Blossom, 72
I Watch the Love Parade, 32
I Whistle a Happy Tune, 109
I Will Follow You, 324
I Will Never Leave You, 412
I Will Knit a Suit o' Dreams, 21
I Wish I Could Forgive You, 288
I Wish I Was Dead, 212
I Wish I Were in Love Again, 99
I Wish It So, 190
I Won't Dance, 33, 34
I Won't Grow Up, 230
I Won't Let You Get Away, 239
I Won't Say I Will (But I Won't Say I Won't), 63

I Won't Send Roses, 327
I Wonder, 11
I Wonder How It Is to Dance with a Boy, 266
I Wonder What Became of Me, 155
I Wonder What He Meant by That, 168
I Wonder What It's Like, 257
I Wonder What the King Is Doing Tonight, 225
I Wonder Why [Berlin], 55
I Wonder Why [Kern], 18
I Worship You, 122
I Would Die, 264
I Would Like to Play a Lover's Part, 30
I Wouldn't Give That for the Man Who Couldn't Dance, 46
I Wouldn't Marry You, 146
I Write, You Read (Fair Trade), 114
I Wrote a Play, 129
I Wrote the Book, 337
I! Yes Me! That's Who!, 238, 241
I'd Do Almost Anything to Get Out of Here and Go Home, 308
I'd Like a Lighthouse, 23
I'd Like My Picture Took, 54
I'd Like to Have a Million in the Bank, 16
I'd Like to Hide It, 89
I'd Like to Meet Your Father, 6
I'd Like to Poison Ivy (Because She Clings to Me), 88, 90
I'd Like to Talk about the Weather, 164
I'd Love to Be Shot out of a Cannon with You, 51
I'd Love to Dance through Life with You, 15
I'd Much Rather Stay at Home, 7
I'd Rather Be Right (Don't Have to Know Much) [1st], 99, 102
I'd Rather Be Right (Than Influential) [2nd], 99
I'd Rather Be Sailing, 373
I'd Rather Charleston, 65
I'd Rather Dance Alone, 365
I'd Rather See a Minstrel Show, 46
I'd Rather Wake up by Myself, 145
I'd Sure Like to Give It a Shot, 238
I'll Always Remember, 136, 138
I'll Cover You, 410
I'll Be Hard to Handle, 33
I'll Be Here Tomorrow, 328
I'll Be Respectable, 157
I'll Be There, 139
I'll Be Waiting 'neath Your Window, 10
I'll Build a Stairway to Paradise, 61, 62, 64, 388
I'll Buy Everybody a Beer, 247
I'll Buy You a Star, 145, 147
I'll Go Home with Bonnie Jean, 223
I'll Know, 246
I'll Marry the Very Next Man, 257
I'll Never Be Jealous Again, 252

I'll Never Fall in Love Again, 400
I'll Never Leave You [Schwartz], 139
I'll Never Leave You (We Are One) [Strouse], 301
I'll Never Make a Frenchman out of You, 206
I'll Never Say No, 270
I'll Pay the Check, 143
I'll See You in C-U-B-A, 47
I'll Share It All with You, 53
I'll Show Him, 395
I'll Take the City, 164
I'll Take the Sky, 361
I'll Take You Back to Italy, 45
I'll Talk to Her, 345
I'll Tell the Man in the Street, 100
I'll Tell You a Truth, 261
I'll Try, 396
I'll Walk Alone, 228
I'm a Bad, Bad Man, 53
I'm a Brass Band, 315
I'm a Crazy Daffydil, 9
I'm a Dancing Teacher Now, 42
I'm a Dumb-Bell, 47
I'm a Fool, Little One, 94
I'm a Mean Ole Lion, 403
I'm a Prize, 26
I'm a Stranger Here Myself, 178
I'm a Woman, 172
I'm A'Tingle, I'm A'Glow, 228
I'm Afraid, 102
I'm Afraid, Sweetheart, I Love You, 130
I'm Alone, 32
I'm an Indian Too, 53
I'm an Old Cowhand, 154, 393
I'm an Ordinary Man, 224
I'm Available, 256
I'm Back in Circulation, 396
I'm Black, 399
I'm Blue, 212
I'm Blue, Too, 266
I'm Breaking Down, 369, 370
I'm Bringing a Red, Red Rose, 390
I'm Broke, 88
I'm Calm, 276
I'm Craving for That Kind of Love (Kiss Me), 388
I'm Crazy 'bout the Charleston, 90
I'm Daisy, I'm Violet, 412
I'm Fascinating, 295
I'm Flyin', 230
I'm Getting Myself Ready for You, 123
I'm Getting Tired So I Can Sleep, 52
I'm Glad I Waited, 83
I'm Glad I'm Leaving, 230
I'm Glad I'm Not a Man, 167
I'm Glad I'm Not Young Anymore, 226
I'm Glad I'm Single, 146

I'm Glad to See You've Got What You Want, 307
I'm Going Away, 12
I'm Going Back, 231
I'm Going Back to Dixie, 40
I'm Going in for Love, 126
I'm Going on a Long Vacation, 37
I'm Going to Find a Girl, 19
I'm Gonna Get Him, 55
I'm Gonna Leave off Wearin' My Shoes, 155
I'm Gonna Pin a Medal on the Girl I Left Behind, 45
I'm Goin' to See My Mother, 62
I'm Gonna Wash That Man Right Outa My Hair, 108
I'm Here, Little Girls, I'm Here, 18
I'm in a Tree, 238
I'm in London Again, 260
I'm in Love, 122
I'm in Love Again, 120
I'm in Love, I'm in Love, 262
I'm in Love with a Girl Named Fred, 397
I'm in Love with a Soldier Boy, 129
I'm in Pursuit of Happiness, 232
I'm in the Mood for Love, 389
I'm Just Nuts about You, 193
I'm Just Simply Full of Jazz, 388
I'm Just Taking My Time, 234
I'm Just Wild about Harry, 388
I'm Leaving You, 321
I'm Like a New Broom, 145
I'm Like a Sailor, 138
I'm Like the Bluebird, 277
I'm Looking for a Daddy Long Legs, 48
I'm Looking for an Irish Husband, 12
I'm Lost, 261
I'm Naïve, 239
I'm Not a Well Man, 200
I'm Not at All in Love, 252
I'm Not Finished Yet, 296
I'm Not Myself, 152
I'm Not So Bright, 206
I'm Not the Girl Who Used to Be, 265
I'm Old Fashioned, 35
I'm on My Way, 223
I'm Only Thinking of Him, 344
I'm Seeing Rainbows, 253
I'm Sick of You (Horace's Last), 188
I'm So Busy, 18
I'm Still Here, 280, 281
I'm Talking to My Pal, 103
I'm the Bravest Individual (I Have Ever Met), 315, 316
I'm the First Girl in the Second Row, 206
I'm the First Man, 206
I'm the Greatest Star, 235

I'm the Guy That Guards the Harem (And My Heart's in My Work), 46
I'm the Human Brush (That Paints the Crimson on Paree), 9
I'm the Old Man in the Moon, 19
I'm Throwing a Ball Tonight, 128
I'm Tired of Texas, 206
I'm Unlucky at Gambling, 122
I'm Waiting for a Wonderful Girl, 81
I'm Way Ahead, 316, 317
I'm Well Known, 6
I'm Wise, 27
I'm with You, 236
I'm Wonderful, 160
I'm Worse Than Anybody, 331
I'm Writing a Love Song for You, 240
I'm Your Girl [Rodgers], 110
I'm Your Man, 180
I've 'Eard the Bloody 'Indoos 'As It Worse, 298
I've a Little Favor, 5
I've a Million Reasons Why I Love You, 6
I've a Shooting Box in Scotland, 118
I've A'ready Started In, 270
I've Been Too Busy, 256
I've Been Waiting for You All the Time, 22
I've Brushed My Teeth, 73
I've Come to Wive It Wealthily in Padua, 130
I've Confessed to the Breeze, 80
I've Gone Romantic on You, 153
I've Got a Crush on You [Gershwin], 70, 71
I've Got a Crush on You [Porter], 122
I've Got a Go Back to Texas, 43
I've Got a One Track Mind, 165
I've Got a Penny, 265
I've Got a Rainbow Working for Me, 237
I've Got a Sweet Tooth Bothering Me, 44
I've Got an Awful Lot to Learn, 118
I've Got Five Dollars, 96
I've Got It All, 318
I've Got Me, 391
I've Got Money in the Bank, 12
I've Got Somebody Waiting, 119
I've Got the Nerve to Be in Love, 193
I've Got the World on a String, 150, 153
I've Got to Be Around, 55
I've Got to Be There, 73
I've Got to Crow, 230
I've Got to Dance, 16
I've Got to Find a Reason, 264
I've Got What You Want, 261
I've Got You on My Mind, 123
I've Got You to Lean On, 277
I've Got You under My Skin, 125
I've Got Your Number, 315
I've Gotta Right to Sing the Blues, 153

I've Grown Accustomed to Her Face, 224
I've Heard It All Before, 403
I've Heard That Song Before, 228
I've Just Been Waiting for You, 15
I've Just Begun, 240
I've Just Seen Her (As Nobody Else Has Seen Her), 295
I've Looked for Trouble, 28
I've Made a Habit of You, 136
I've Never Been in Love Before, 246
I've Never Been So Happy, 298
I've Never Said I Love You, 327
I've Still Got My Health, 128
I've Taken Such a Fancy to You, 10
I've Told Ev'ry Little Star, 32
Icarus, 414
Ice, 209
Ice Cold Katy, 144
Ice Cream [Bock], 258, 259
Ice Cream Sextet [Weill], 179
Idle Dreams, 60
Idles of the King, 91, 93
If (There's Anything You Want), 21
If a Girl Isn't Pretty, 235
If Ever I Would Leave You, 225
If Ever Married 'Im, 130
If He Really Loves Me, 150
If He Walked into My Life, 326, 327
If I Became the President, 71
If I Can't Love Her, 366
If I Can't Take It with Me, 396
If I Could've Been, 357
If I Find the Girl, 16
If I Gave You, 208
If I Give in to You, 96
If I Had a Fine White Horse, 407
If I Had an Igloo, 208
If I Had My Druthers, 395
If I Have to Live Alone, 357
If I Knew, 270
If I Knew You Were Comin' I'd've Baked a Cake, 263
If I Loved You, 106
If I Only Had a Brain, 153
If I Told You, 78, 82
If I Were a Bell, 246
If I Were a Man, 408
If I Were a Rich Man, 260, 279
If I Were King of the Forest, 153
If I Were You [Rodgers], 87, 92, 93
If I Were You [Strouse], 295
If I Were You Love, 83
If It Wasn't for You, 357
If Momma Was Married, 232
If My Friends Could See Me Now, 315, 316

If Only a Little Bit Sticks, 240
If That Was Love, 263
If the Girl Wants You (Never Mind the Color of Her Eyes), 7
If the Managers Only Thought the Same As Mother, 37
If the World Were Like the Movies, 382, 383
If There Is Someone Lovelier Than You, 141
If There Were More People Like You, 316
If This Isn't Love, 171
If We Could Lead a Merry Mormon Life, 27
If We Only Have Love (Quand On N'a Que l'Amour), 398
If We Were on Our Honeymoon (Railway Duet), 11
If You Believe, 403
If You Believed in Me, 151, 152
If You Break Their Hearts, 361
If You Can't Get the Love You Want, 166
If You Could See Her, 333
If You Don't Mind My Saying So, 270
If You Don't Want Me (Why Do You Hang Around), 42
If You Hadn't but You Did, 229
If You Haven't Got an Ear for Music, 55
If You Haven't Got a Sweetheart, 145
If You Know What I Mean, 135
If You Leave Me Now, 333
If You Loved Me Truly, 132
If You Only Care Enough, 21
If You Really Knew Me, 360
If You Smile at Me, 130
If You Think It's Love You're Right, 27
If You Were Someone Else, 143
If You Were You, 87, 92
If You Will Be My Morganatic Wife, 27
If You Win, You Lose, 251
If You Would Only Love Me, 11
If You'll Be Mine, 206
If You're a Friend of Mine, 30
If You've Never Been Vamped by a Brown Skin, 388
Ill Wind, 152, 153, 157
Illegitimate Daughter, The, 72
Ilona, 258
Image of Me, The, 172
Imaginary Coney Island Ballet, The, 212
Imagine, 99
Imaginist Rhythm, 143
Immigration and Naturalization Rag (Melt Us), The, 295
Impossible [Rodgers], 111
Impossible [Sondheim], 276
Impossible Dream, The (The Quest), 344, 347
In a Cozy Kitchenette Apartment, 47

In a Little While, 397
In a Moorish Garden, 121
In Araby with You, 28
In Arcady, 15
In Between [Ellington], 391
In Between [Loewe], 223
In Buddy's Eyes, 280
In Californ-i-a, 96
In Chelsea Somewhere, 119
In Der Jugend Gold'nem Schimmer, 173
In Every Age, 378
In Egern on the Tegern Sea, 32
In Florida Among the Palms, 44
In Gaul, 261
In His Eyes, 411
In Hitchy's Garden, 119
In Honeysuckle Time, When Emaline Said She'd
    Be Mine, 388
In Love, 31
In Love with Love, 26, 30
In Love with the Memory of You, 243
In My Day, 407
In My Old Virginia Home (On the River Nile), 164
In My Own Lifetime, 262
In No Man's Land, 174
In Nomine Patris, 216
In Other Words, Seventeen, 35
In Our Hands, 360
In Our Hide-Away, 55
In Praise of Women, 281
In Pursuit of Excellence, 358
In Sardinia, 66
In Society, 24
In Some Little World, 266
In the Beginning, 358
In the Beginning, Woman, 393
In the Cards, 365
In the Clear, 187
In the Cool Cool Cool of the Evening [Carmichael],
    391
In the Cool of the Evening [Rodgers], 96
In the Gateway of the Temple of Minerva, 104
In the Heart of the Dark, 35
In the Japanese Gardens, 238
In the Mandarin's Orchid Garden, 70
In the Meantime, 389
In the Middle of the Room, 373
In the Movies, 274
In the Name of Love, 319, 320
In the Noonday Sun, 141
In the Rain, 63
In the Rattle of the Battle, 71
In the Shade of a Sheltering Tree, 49
In the Shade of the New Apple Tree, 153
In the Silence of the Night, 150

In the Still of the Night, 125
In the Swim, 69
In the Valley of Montbijou, 9
In This Life, 168
In This Town, 343
In This Wide, Wide World, 226
In Three-Quarter Time, 73
In Time, 114
In Times of War and Tumults, 174
In Trousers (The Dream), 369
In Tune, 316
In Whatever Time We Have, 358
In Your Eyes, 249
Incidental Music [The Enclave], 282
Incidental Music [Invitation to a March], 276
Incompatibility, 156
Indefinable Charm, 165
Independence Day Hora, 324
Independent (On My Own), 231
Individual Thing, 235, 238
Initials, 399
Inner Peace, 300
Inner Thoughts, 297
Innocent Chorus Girls of Yesterday, 96
Innocent Ingenue Baby, 62, 63
Innocent Lonesome Blue Baby, 63
Inside My Head, 306
Inside U.S.A., 144
Inspiration, 87
Instead-Of Song, 182
Interlude after Scene III [Johnny Johnson], 174
Intermission Talk (The Theater is Dying), 110
Intermission's Great, The, 212
Interrogation: I Am Trying to Remember, 414
Into the Woods, 286, 287
Introduction [Johnny Johnson], 174
Introduction to Finale Act One [Let 'Em Eat Cake],
    73
Invisible Wall, The, 225
Invitation to Sleep in My Arms, 373
Invocation to the Gods, 282
Iowa Stubborn, 270
Ireland's Eye, 190
Irene, 387
Irish Jig (The Ball), 209
Irresistible You, 165
Is Anybody There?, 401
Is He the Only Man in the World?, 55
Is It a Crime?, 231
Is It All a Dream?, 140
Is It Him or Is It Me?, 180
Is It Really Me?, 306
Is It the Girl (Or Is It the Gown)?, 129
Is She the Only Girl in the World?, 55
Is That My Prince?, 145

Is That Remarkable?, 409
Is There Anything Better Than Dancing?, 303
Is This Not a Lovely Spot?, 27
Island in the West Indies, 162
Israel and Saul, 367
Isn't It a Pity?, 73, 76
Isn't It Great to Be Married?, 16, 17
Isn't It Kinda Fun?, 115
Isn't It Romantic?, 97
Isn't It Terrible What They Did to Mary Queen of Scots?, 65
Isn't It Wonderful, 64
Isn't That Clear?, 401
Isn't There a Crowd Everywhere?, 17
Isn't This Better?, 338
It [Berlin], 50
It [Kander], 335
It Ain't Etiquette, 128
It Ain't Necessarily So, 74
It All Belongs to Me, 50
It All Depends on You, 388
It Better Be Good, 140
It Can't Be Did, 39
It Can't Be Done, 18
It Couldn't Please Me More, 333
It Depends on What You Pay, 306
It Doesn't Matter Now, 201
It Doesn't Take a Minute, 396
It Don't Make Sense, 414
It Feels Good, 110
It Feels Like Forever, 246
It Gets Lonely in the White House, 53, 55
It Has All Begun, 298
It Is Not the End of the World, 114
It Is the Fourteenth of July, 65
It Isn't What You Did (It's What You Didn't Do), 73
It Isn't Working, 337
It Isn't Your Fault, 14, 18
It Just Occurred to Me, 167
It Looks Like Liza, 177
It May Be a Good Idea, 107
It May Rain, 91
It Might As Well Be Spring, 107, 115
It Moves, 409
It Must Be Fun to Be You, 129
It Must Be Good for Me, 345
It Must Be Heaven, 95
It Must Be Love, 79
It Must Be Me, 214
It Needs Work, 320
It Never Entered My Mind, 102
It Never Was You, 175
It Never Would've Worked, 301
It Only Takes a Moment, 325

It Takes a Long Pull to Get There, 74
It Takes a Woman, 325
It Takes an Irishman to Make Love, 44
It Takes Two (You're Different in the Woods), 286, 287
It Was a Glad Adventure, 394
It Was Always You [Merrill], 264
It Was Always You [Strouse], 297
It Was Good Enough for Grandma, 154
It Was Great Fun the First Time, 130
It Was Written in the Stars, 128
It Wasn't Meant to Happen, 280
It Wasn't My Fault, 18
It Won't Mean a Thing, 28
It Wonders Me, 394, 395
It Would Have Been Wonderful [Sondheim], 281, 287
It Would Have Been Wonderful [Strouse], 303
It'll All Blow Over, 333
It'll Come to You, 51
It's a Bore, 226
It's a Boy! [Coleman], 320
It's a Boy! [Geld], 403
It's a Chemical Reaction, That's All, 132
It's a Dangerous Game, 411
It's a Grand Night for Singing, 93, 107, 115
It's a Great Big Land, 19
It's a Great Little World, 66
It's a Hard, Hard World, 20
It's a Helluva Way to Run a Love Affair, 395
It's a Hit, 285
It's a Long, Long Day, 26
It's a Lovely Day for a Murder, 101, 107
It's a Lovely Day for a Walk, 53
It's a Lovely Day Today, 54
It's a Lovely Day Tomorrow, 51
It's a Maze, 407
It's a Nice Face, 315
It's a Nuisance Having You Around, 395
It's a Perfect Relationship, 231
It's a Sad Day at This Hotel, 119
It's a Scandal! It's an Outrage!, 105
It's a Simple Little System, 231
It's a Sure Sign, 18
It's a Typical Day, 395
It's All Right with Me, 132
It's All the Same, 344
It's All Yours, 143
It's Always Love, 239
It's an Art, 357
It's Bad for Me, 124
It's Been a Long, Long Time, 227
It's Beginning to Look a Lot Like Christmas, 271
It's Better Rich, 207

It's Better with a Union Man (Or Bertha, the Sewing Machine Girl), 193, 194
It's De-Lovely, 126
It's Delightful down in Chile, 228–29
It's Different with Me, 150
It's Doom, 232
It's Easy to Remember, 97
It's Enough to Make a Lady Fall in Love, 237
It's Every Girl's Ambition, 83
It's Fun to Think, 295
It's Getting Hotter in the North, 30
It's Going to Be Good to Be Gone, 114
It's Good to Be Alive [Merrill], 263
It's Good to Be Alive [Rome], 200
It's Good to Be Back Home, 236
It's Got to Be Good to Be Bad, 218
It's Got to Be Love, 98
It's Great to Be an Orphan, 207
It's Greek to Me, 21
It's Hard to Speak My Heart, 414
It's High Time, 228
It's Home, 235
It's Hot up Here, 286
It's Just the Gas, 364
It's Just Yours, 129
It's Legitimate, 233, 234
It's Love, 212
It's Magic, 228
It's Me, 110
It's Never Too Late to Mendelssohn, 177
It's Nicer to Be Naughty, 159
It's Not Irish, 190
It's Not Where You Start, 316, 317
It's Only a Paper Moon, 151, 152
It's Our Little Secret, 400
It's Over Now, 411
It's Possible, 345
It's Raining on Prom Night, 402
It's Super Nice, 296
It's Superman, 296
It's That Kind of Neighborhood, 274
It's the Going Home Together, 394
It's the Hard-Knock Life, 298, 299
It's the Little Bit of Irish, 46
It's the Second Time You Meet, 232
It's the Strangest Thing, 336
It's Time, 410
It's Time for a Love Song, 172
It's Time to Go, 347
It's Today, 326
It's up to the Band, 50
It's You, 269
It's You Who Makes Me Young, 307
Italy in Technicolor, 179
Itch to Be Rich, 258

J'Attends un Navire, 173, 174
Jack and Jill [Duke], 160
Jack and Jill [Rodgers], 87, 88
Jack, the Sleepy Jeep, 196
Jackie (La Chanson de Jacky), 399
Jacques d'Iraque, 256
Jailer, Jailer, 351
Jalopy Song, The, 233
Janette, 207
Jap-German Sextet, 52
Jason's Bar Mitzvah, 372
Jason's Therapy, 370
Je T'aime—I Love You, 165
Jealousy Duet, 182
Jeannie's Packin' Up, 223
Jeepers Creepers, 154
Jelly's Isolation, 407
Jelly's Jam, 407
Jenny (The Saga of Jenny), 176
Jeremiah Symphony, 212
Jerk Song, The, 196
Jerry, My Soldier Boy, 128
Jersey Plunk, The, 178
Jet Song, 215
Jig Hop, The, 390
Jijibo, The, 64
Jilted, Jilted!, 72
Jimmy, 50
Joan of Arc, 24
Joe Worker, 186
Joey, Joey, Joey, 247, 252
Johanna, 284
Johanna (Turpin Version), 284
Johnny, 190
Johnny Freedom, 233
Johnny Is My Darling, 201
Johnny One Note, 99
Johnny's Dream, 174
Johnny's Song, 174
Join the Circus, 318
Join the Navy!, 81
Joke, The, 332
Jolly, Rich and Fat, 367
Jolly Theatrical Season, 323, 324
Josh's Welcome, 410
Joseph Taylor, Jr, 107
Josephine, 132
Joshua, 222
Journey On, 383
Journey's End, 24, 28
Jousts, The, 225
Joy [Schmidt], 310
Joy Bells, 26
Juanita, 65
Jubilation T. Cornpone, 395

Jubilo, 22
Judgement of Paris, 394
Jug of Wine, A, 222
Jump de Broom, 158
Jump, Little Chillun!, 392
Jumping Jack, 88
Jumping to the Jukebox, 196
June Is Bustin' out All Over, 106
Jungle Jingle, 50
Jupiter Forbid, 104
Just a Friend of Mine, 139
Just a Housewife, 357
Just a Kiss Apart, 228
Just a Little Bit More, 143
Just a Little Joint with a Juke Box, 205
Just a Little Lie, 88
Just a Little Line, 22
Just a Map, 262
Just Another Page from Your Diary, 102
Just Because You're You, 19
Just between the Two of Us, 356
Just Fine, 306
Just for Once, 396
Just for Tonight, 360
Just Go, 373
Just Go to the Movies, 328
Just Good Friends, 7
Just Imagine, 389
Just in Case, 178
Just in Time, 231
Just Like a Man, 166, 167
Just Like Children, 168
Just My Luck, 256
Just One of Those Things [1st], 123
Just One of Those Things [2nd], 125
Just One Person, 351
Just One Step ahead of Love, 126
Just One Way to Say I Love You, 54
Just Plain Folks, 324
Just to Know You Are Mine, 61
Just Wait [Kern], 27
Just Wait [Strouse], 298
Just You and Me, 298, 302
Just You Wait ('enry 'iggins), 224
Just You Watch My Step, 19
Justice, 383

Ka-Lu-A, 24, 25
Kaddish, 302
Kalua Bay, 331
Kansas City, 105
Kate the Great, 125
Kathleen Mine, 83
Katie, My Love, 352
Katie Went to Haiti, 128

Katrina, 221
Katy Was a Business Girl, 6
Katy-did, 13
Keep a Taxi Waiting Dear, 39
Keep A-Hoppin', 270
Keep It Gay, 110
Keep It in the Family, 315, 316
Keep Smiling, 34
Keep Your Feet upon the Ground, 311
Keepin' It Hot, 332
Keepin' Myself for You, 81
Keeping Cool with Coolidge, 228
Kentucky Sue, 388
Kettle Song, The, 21
Keys to Heaven, 91
Kick in the Pants, The, 52
Kick the Door, 238, 240
Kickin' the Clouds Away, 66, 160
Kickin' the Gong Around, 150
Kid Go!, 409
Kid Herself, The, 332
Kid, I Love You, 87
Kids!, 294, 295
Kind of Woman, 356
Kind to Animals, 207
Kinda Like You, 83
King Kaiser Comedy Cavalcade, The, 382
King of Pride Rock, 413
King Porter Stomp, 407
Kingdom Comin', 22
King's Barcarolle, The, 217
King's Dilemma, 408
Kiss a Four Leaf Clover, 28
Kiss for Cinderella [Gershwin], 72
Kiss for Cinderella, A [Rodgers], 94
Kiss Her Now, 327
Kiss Me [Blake], 388
Kiss Me [Sondheim], 284
Kiss Me, Kate, 130
Kiss of the Spider Woman, 339
Kissed on the Eyes, 267
Kissing, 79
Kitchen Police (Poor Little Me), 45
Kite, The, 398
Kling-Kling Bird on the Divi-Divi Tree, The, 125
Knees, 95
Knight of the Mirrors, 344
Knight of the Woeful Countenance (The Dubbing), 344
Knock Knock, 332
Knowing When to Leave, 400
Kongo Kate, 64
K-ra-zy for You, 70
Kyrie Eleison, 216

La Vagabonde, 310
La Vie Boheme, 410
L'Chayim, 200
L'il Augie Is a Natural Man, 155
L'il Ole Bitty Pissant Country Place, 405
L. A. Blues, 320
L. Z. in Quest of His Youth, 236
La Cage aux Folles, 328
La Princess Zenobia, 98
La-La-La, 112
Label on the Bottle, The, 146
Ladies [Rome], 199
Ladies in Their Sensitivities, 284
Ladies of the Chorus, 45, 52
Ladies of the Evening, 101
Ladies Singing Their Song, The, 406
Ladies Who Lunch, The, 279
Ladies Who Sing with a Band, The, 391
Ladies with a Liberal Point of View, 264
Lady [Duke], 164
Lady in Waiting, 396
Lady Is a Tramp, The, 99
Lady Must Live, A, 96
Lady Needs a Change, A, 143
Lady Needs a Rest, A, 128
Lady of the Evening, 48
Lady Raffles Behave, 87
Lady with the Tap-Tap-Tap, The, 142
Lady's in Love with You, The, 170, 243
Lady's Maid, 378, 379
Lady's on the Job, The, 195
Lament (Children Won't Listen) [Sondheim], 287
Lament for Ten Men, 239, 265
Land of Let's Pretend, The, 13
Land of the Gay Caballero, 71
Land Where the Good Songs Go, The, 20
Language of Flowers, The, 118
Language of Love, The [Kern], 22
Larger Than Life, 382
Largest Moving Object, The, 378
Lars, Lars, 114
Last Chance Blues, The, 407
Last Girl, The, 340
Last "I Love New York" Song, The, 301
Last Midnight, 287
Last Part of Ev'ry Party, The, 387
Last Rites, The, 407
Last Time I Saw Paris, The, 35
Late, Late Show, The, 233
Later, 281, 282, 353
Latins Know How, 51
Laugh It Up, 55
Laughing Generals, 174
Laura De Maupassant, 230
Laurey Makes up Her Mind, 105

Law Must Be Obeyed, The, 43
Lawyer Frazier Scene, 74
Lawyers, 299
Lazy Afternoon, 394
Lazy Bones, 391
Lazy Moon, 396
Lazy River, 391
Le Grand Boom-Boom, 315
Le Grand Lustucru, 173
Le Jazz Hot, 408
Le Roi d'Aquitaine, 173, 174
Le Train du Ciel, 174
Lead Me to Love, 43
Lead Me to That Beautiful Band, 41
Leader of a Big-Time Band, The, 129
Leadville Johnny Brown (Soliloquy), 270
Leaflets!, 186
League of Nations, The [Gershwin], 73
Learn about Life, 267
Learn to Be Lonely, 351
Learn to Croon, 150
Learn to Do the Strut, 48
Learn to Sing a Love Song, 50
Learn Your Lessons Well, 355
Least That's My Opinion, 155
Leave de Atom Alone, 156
Leave Everything to Me, 325
Leave It Alone, 298
Leave It to Jane, 19
Leave It to the Girls, 303
Leave Me Alone, 412
Leave the World Behind, 340
Leave Well Enough Alone, 256
Leavin' fo' de Promise' Lan', 74
Leavin' Time, 155
Leavin's Not the Only Way to Go, 406
Leaving Town While We May, 65
Lees of Old Virginia, The, 401
Left All Alone Again Blues, 23
Leg of Nations, The [Berlin], 47
Leg of the Duck, The, 345
Legacy, The, 318
Legalize My Name, 155
Legend of the Pearls, 47
Lena, Lena, 8
Leo at Work, 414
Les Filles de Bordeaux, 173, 178
Lesson #8, 286
Let Antipholus In, 101
Let 'Em Eat Cake, 73
Let Her Not Be Beautiful (You Are All That's Beautiful), 168
Let Hertz Put You in the Driver's Seat, 253
Let It Snow, 228
Let Me Drink in Your Eyes, 87, 88

Let Me Entertain You, 232
Let Me Give All My Love to Thee, 81
Let Me Hear You Love Me, 240
Let Me Sing and I'm Happy, 50
Let the Lower Lights Be Burning, 232
Let the Sunshine In, 399, 400
Let There Be, 358
Let Things Be Like They Was, 179
Let Us Build a Little Nest, 10
Let's Be Buddies, 128
Let's Be Lonesome Together, 63
Let's Begin, 33
Let's Build a Little Nest, 21
Let's Call the Whole Thing Off, 75
Let's Do It, 121
Let's Do Something, 186
Let's Face the Music and Dance, 51
Let's Fall in Love, 153
Let's Fly Away, 123
Let's Go, 21
Let's Go 'round the Town, 43
Let's Go Back to the Waltz, 55
Let's Go Eat Worms in the Garden, 390
Let's Go Flying, 320
Let's Go Sailor, 155
Let's Go to the Movies, 298
Let's Go West Again, 53
Let's Have Another Cup of Coffee, 50
Let's Kiss and Make Up, 69
Let's Make It a Night, 132
Let's Misbehave, 121
Let's Not Fall in Love, 273, 274
Let's Not Talk about Love, 128
Let's Not Waste a Moment, 324
Let's Say Good-Night, 28
Let's See What Happens, 237
Let's Settle Down, 294
Let's Step Out, 122
Let's Take a Walk around the Block, 152, 153
Let's Take an Old-Fashioned Walk, 54
Let's Talk, 234
Letter, The [Loesser], 247
Letter, The [Sondheim], 288
Letter from Klemnacht, 351
Letter Song [Kern], 288
Letter Song [Simon], 407
Letter to the Children, 351
Letter to the Governor, 414
Letters [Bock], 259
Letter 1 [Sondheim], 288
Letter 3 [Sondheim], 288
Letter 4 [Sondheim], 288
Letter 5 [Sondheim], 288
Letting Go, 411
L'Histoire de Madame de la Tour, 35

L'il Augie Is a Natural Man, 155
Li'l Ol' You and Li'l Ol' Me, 231
Liaisons, 281
Lichtenburg, 54
Lida Rose, 269
Lido Lady, 91
Life Begins Introduction, 152
Life Could Be a Cakewalk with You, 154
Life Is, 334
Life Is Happiness Indeed, 217
Life Is Like a Train, 318
Life! Liberty!, 102
Life of a Rose, The, 63
Life of the Party, The, 333, 334
Life on the Sea, 190
Life Support, 410
Life upon the Wicked Stage, 29
Life Was Monotonous, 104
Life Was Pie for the Pioneer, 170
Life with Father, 104
Life's a Dance [Arlen], 153
Life's a Dance [Kern], 18
Life's a Funny Present from Someone, 166
Life's Not Simple, 233
Liffey Waltz, The, 190
Light My Candle, 410
Light of the World, 355
Lights Come Up, The, 382
Lights of Long Ago, The, 367
Like a Bird on the Wing, 79
Like a God, 111
Like a Young Man, 324
Like Everybody Else [Burnstein], 215
Like Everyone Else [Krieger], 412
Like He Loves Me, 81
Like It Was, 285
Like the Breeze Blows, 200, 201
Lila Tremaine, 236
Lily, Oscar, 318
Lily's Eyes, 407
Lima, 118
Limehouse Nights, 59
Linda, 150
Line, The, 353
Linger in the Lobby, 65
Link by Link, 367
Lion Dance, 283
Lion Sleeps Tonight, The, 413
Lioness Hunt, The, 413
Lion Tamer, 356
Lionnet, 188
Lisa Carew, 412
Lisbon Sequence, 214
Listen, I Feel, 401
Listen to My Song (Johnny's Song), 174

Listening, 49
Little Angel Cake, 26
Little Back-Yard Band, The, 22
Little Billie, 19
Little Bird, Little Bird, 344
Little Birdie Told Me So, A, 91, 92, 100
Little Biscuit, 156
Little Bit in Love, A, 212
Little Bit More, A, 114
Little Bit of Everything, A, 41
Little Bit of Good, A, 335
Little Bit of Silk, A, 12
Little Black Train, The, 180
Little Boy Blues, The, 206, 209
Little Brains, a Little Talent, A, 253
Little Brown Suit My Uncle Bought Me, The, 196
Little Bungalow, A, 49
Little Butterfly, 48
Little Chavaleh, 260
Little Church around the Corner, The, 6
Little Dental Music, A, 364
Little Do They Know, 336
Little Eva, 6
Little Fish in a Big Pond, 54
Little Fool, 401
Little Girl Blue, 97, 98
Little Girl from Little Rock, A, 228
Little Girls, 298
Little Golden Maid, 11
Little Gossip, A, 344
Little Gray House, The, 176, 181
Little Green Snake, 264
Little House in Soho, A, 93
Little Igloo for Two, 135
Little Jazz Bird, 65
Little Known Facts, 398
Little Lamb, 232, 233
Little Love, A (But Not for Me), 15, 16
Little Love, a Little Money, A, 167
Little Me, 315
Little More Heart, A, 230
Little More Mascara, A, 329
Little Naked Boy, The, 178
Little Night Music, A, (The Sun Won't Set), 281
Little Old Lady, 391
Little Old New York [Bock], 257, 258
Little Old New York [Styne], 233
Little Priest, A, 284
Little Red Hat, 306
Little Red Lacquer Cage, The, 48
Little Red Rooftops, 244
Little Rumba Numba, A, 128
Little Shop of Horrors, 364
Little Skipper from Heaven Above, A, 126
Little Souvenir, A, 91

Little Surplus Me, 196
Little Thing Like a Kiss, A, 11, 20
Little Things (Meant So Much to Me), 198
Little Things You Do Together, The, 279
Little Tin Box, 257
Little Tin God, 181
Little Travelbug, 157
Little Travellin' Music Please, A, 240
Little Tune, Go Away, 21
Little White House, 280
Little Wonders, 201
Live Alone and Like It, 288
Live and Let Live, 132
Live, Laugh, Love, 280
Livin' It Up, 164
Living in the Shadows, 408
Liza (All the Clouds'll Roll Away), 70
Liza Crossing the Ice, 154
Liza Quit Vamping Me, 388
Lizzie's Comin' Home, 306
Lo-La-Lo, 63
Loadin' Time, 142
Loading Inventory, 378
Loads of Love, 112
Lock 'Em Up, 278
Lock Me in Your Harem, and Throw Away the
  Key, 43
Locker Room, 180
Loki and Baldur, 351
London, Dear Old London, 24
Loneliness of Evening, 108
Lonely Boy, 74
Lonely Boy Blues, 407
Lonely Feet, 31, 34
Lonely Goatherd, The, 112
Lonely Heart, 51
Lonely House, 179
Lonely M. P., 244
Lonely Me, 213
Lonely Men, 223
Lonely Nights, 146
Lonely Room, 105
Lonely Stranger, 201
Lonely Town, 211, 212
Lonely Town Ballet, 212
Lonesome Cowboy, The, 72
Lonesome Dove, The, 180
Lonesome Walls, 34
Long Ago [Duke], 163
Long Ago (And Far Away) [Kern], 35
Long before I Knew You, 231
Long Live God, 355
Long Live Nancy, 31
Long, Long Day, The, 367
Long Way from Home, 240

Longing for Dear Old Broadway, 117
Loo-Loo [Youmans], 81
Look Around [Coleman], 320
Look Around [Porter], 119
Look Around [Strouse], 320
Look at 'Er, 263
Look at Me, I'm Sandra Dee, 402
Look at You, Look at Me, 239
Look for the Damsel, 90
Look for the Silver Lining, 22, 23, 24, 25
Look for the Woman, 357
Look in Her Eyes, 12, 18
Look in His Eyes, 12, 18
Look in the Book, 18
Look Little Girl, 271
Look Me Over Dearie, 9
Look No Further, 112
Look Out, 101
Look out for the Bolsheviki Man, 46
Look Over There, 328
Look to the Lilies, 238
Look to the Rainbow, 171
Look What Happened to Mabel, 327
Look What I Found, 130
Look What You've Done, 383
Look Where I Am, 258
Look Who's Alone Now, 303
Look Who's Dancing, 145
Look Who's in Love, 396
Looking All Over for You, 24
Looking at You, 121
Looking Back, 239
Looking for a Boy, 66
Loopin' de Loop, 335
Lord Done Fixed up My Soul, The, 51
Lorelei, The [Gershwin], 73
Lorelei [Kern], 23, 24
Lorelei [Styne—1st], 239
Lorelei [Styne—2nd], 239
Lorna's Here, 296
Losing My Mind, 280, 281
Lost and Found, 320
Lost Beat Swing, 409
Lost in a Cloud of Blue, 244
Lost in the Darkness, 411
Lost in the Stars, 176, 181
Lost in the Wilderness, 358
Lost Liberty Blues, The, 121
Lost Word, The, 317
Lot of Livin' to Do, A, 294, 295
Louis Says, 408
Louisiana Hayride, 140
Louisiana Purchase, 51
Love, 303
Love and Kindness, 247

Love and the Moon, 25
Love at First Sight, 189
Love before Breakfast, 172
Love Blossoms, 14
Love Can't Happen, 377
Love Came in to My Heart, 170
Love Come Take Me Again, 271
Love Comes First, 297
Love Don't Turn Away, 306
Love for Sale, 123
Love from a Heart of Gold, 248
Love from Judy, 207
Love Has Come of Age, 411
Love Held Lightly, 157
Love, I Hear, 276
Love I Long For, The, 166
Love I Never Knew, 66
Love in a Home, 395
Love in the Mist, 178
Love Is, 345
Love Is a Dancing Thing, 142
Love Is a Very Light Thing, 198
Love Is Blind, 370
Love Is Here to Stay, 75
Love Is in the Air, 66
Love Is Like a Rubber Band (Hoop Song), 10
Love Is Like a Violin, 13
Love Is My Enemy, 178
Love Is Not a Sentiment Worthy of Respect, 310
Love Is Not in Vain, 85
Love Is Only Love, 325
Love Is Still in Town, 167
Love Is Sweeping the Country, 72
Love Is the Reason, 145
Love Is the Worst Possible Thing, 168
Love Isn't Born (It's Made), 144, 243
Love Isn't Everything, 307
Love, It Hurts So Good, 197
Love Leads to Marriage, 55
Love Letter to Manhattan, 198
Love Letter Words, 120
Love Like Ours, 288
Love, Look Away, 111
Love, Look in My Window, 325
Love Makes Such Fools of Us All, 318
Love Makes the World Go, 112
Love Makes the World Go Round, 264, 265
Love Me by Parcel Post, 85
Love Me for What I Am, 369
Love Me or Leave Me, 149, 390
Love Me Tomorrow, 164
Love Nest, 387
Love Never Went to College, 101
Love of a Wife, The, 58
Love of My Life, The, 223

Love Remains, 196
Love Revolution, 317
Love Sometimes Has to Wait, 196
Love Song [S. Schwartz], 356
Love Song [Schmidt], 307
Love Song [Weill—1st], 180
Love Song [Weill—2nd], 182
Love Stolen, 404
Love Takes Time, 281
Love Theme from "Superman", 296
Love Tiptoed through My Heart, 221
Love Turned the Light Out, 164
Love Will Call, 87
Love Will Find a Way, 388
Love Will See Us Through, 280
Love with All the Trimmings, 171
Love's a Bond, 274
Love's Charming Art, 10
Love's Intense in Tents, 87
Love's No Stranger to Me, 156
Lovebird, 340
Loveland [1st], 280
Loveland [2nd], 280
Lovelier Than Ever, 245
Lovely, 276
Lovely Day to Be out of Jail, A, 321
Lovely Laurie, 257
Lovely to Look At, 33, 389
Lovely Woman's Ever Young, 96
Lover, 93, 97
Lover Man, 176
Lovers on Christmas Eve, 317
Lovin' Is a Lowdown Blues, 408
Loving You [Herman], 326
Loving You [Sondheim], 288
Low and Lazy, 166
Low Down Blues, 388
Lu Lu [Gershwin], 60
Lucius' Song, 186
Luck Be a Lady, 246
Luckiest Man in the World, The [Gershwin], 73
Luckiest Man in the World, The [S. Schwartz], 357
Lucky [Duke], 159
Lucky [Flaherty], 381
Lucky [Guettel], 409
Lucky Bird, 81
Lucky Boy, 49
Lucky Day, 388
Lucky in Love, 389
Lucky Seven, 138
Lucky to Be Me, 211
Lucy and Jessie, 280
Lucy Meets Hyde, 412
Lucy Meets Jekyll, 412
Lud's Wedding, 218

Lullaby [Arlen], 154, 155
Lullaby [Blitzstein], 190
Lullaby (Go to Sleep Whatever You Are) [Bock], 261
Lullaby [Gershwin], 62
Lullaby [Kern], 21
Lullaby (The Hardangerfjord) [Rodgers], 114
Lullaby [Weill], 179
Lullaby for Junior, 391
Lullaby of Broadway, 170
Lunchtime Follies, Ye, 105
Lusty Month of May, The, 225
Lynching Blues, The, 409
Lydia, the Tattooed Lady, 154

Mack the Knife, 182, 183
Mad, 301
Madame Tango's Particular Tango, 158
Madame Tango's Tango, 158
Madeleine, 399
Mademoiselle in New Rochelle, 71
Madly in Love, 167
Madrigal [Kern], 33
Madrigal [Loewe], 225
Madness of King Scar, The, 413
Magic, Magic, 264
Magic Melody, The, 15
Magic Moment, 146, 147
Magic Nights, 239
Magic of the Moon, The, 159
Magic to Do, 356
Magnolia's Wedding Day, 389
Maharanee, 162
Mah-Jongg, 64
Maid of Mesh, 48
Maiden Fair, 131
Maidens Typical of France, 132
Maine, 112
Maison des Lunes, 366
Make a Miracle, 245
Make a Quiet Day, 188
Make a Wish, 207
Make Believe, 29
Make Every Day a Holiday, 120
Make Hey! Make Hey! (While the Moon Shines), 93
Make It Another Old-Fashioned, Please, 128
Make Our Garden Grow, 214
Make Someone Happy, 233
Make the Heart Be Stone, 187
Make the Man Love Me, 145, 147
Make the Most of Your Music, 280
Make Them Hear You, 383
Make Way [Bock], 261
Make Way [Duke], 164

Make with the Feet, 164
Makin' Whoopee!, 390
Making a Home, 370
Making of a Girl, The, 57
Mama, a Rainbow, 349, 350
Mama Always Makes It Better, 114
Mama, It's Me, 339
Mama, Mama [Loesser], 247
Mama Will Provide, 382
Mama's Talkin' Soft, 232
Mame, 326, 327
Mamie in the Afternoon, 331
Mamie Is Mimi, 228
Man, A, 365
Man and a Woman, A, 306
Man and Wife, 307
Man around the House, A, 22
Man Bites Dog, 51
Man Can Have No Choice, A, 253
Man Doesn't Know, A, 253
Man for Sale, 154
Man I Love, The, 65, 68, 69
Man I Married, The, 347
Man I Used to Be, The, 110
Man in My Life, The, 157
Man in the Moon, The, 326
Man Like You, A, 376
Man Loves Me, The, 168
Man of High Degree, A, 71
Man of La Mancha (I, Don Quixote), 344
Man of the Year This Week, The, 392
Man That Got Away, The, 144, 155, 158, 207
Man to Man Talk, 397
Man Upstairs, The, 164
Man Who Has Everything, The, 112
Man Worth Fightin' For, A, 300
Man's Inhumanity to Man, 293
Manchester, England, 399
Mandalay Song, 183
Mandy, 45, 46
Manhattan [Flaherty], 382
Manhattan [Rodgers], 81, 88, 89, 90, 91
Manhattan Madness, 50
Manic Depressives, 238
Manicure Girl, The, 9
Many a New Day, 105
Many Moons Ago, 397
Mapleton High Chorale, 177
Marathon, 398
March [Yellow Mask], 160
March Ahead to the Fight, 183
March of the Falsettos, 370
March of the Siamese Children, 109
March of the Yuppies, 301
March of Time, The, 150

March to Zion, The, 175
Marche de l'Armee Panameene, 173
Mardi Gras [Arlen], 156
Mardi Gras [Martin], 207
Maria [Bernstein], 215
Maria [Porter], 126
Maria [Rodgers], 112
Maria [Schwartz], 141
Maria in Spats, 324
Maria's Song, 360
Marian the Librarian, 270
Marianne, 328
Marie from Sunny Italy, 37
Marie's Law, 257
Marie-Louise, 10
Marieke, 399
Mark of Cain, The, 358
Marking Time, 356
Marriage Proposal, A, 370
Marriage Type Love, 110
Married, 333
Married Couple Seeks Married Couple, 317
Married Life (Let's Go Home), 303
Marry Me, 337
Marry Me a Little, 279
Marry Me Now, 320
Marry Me, Terry, 412
Marry the Man Today, 246
Marrying for Fun, 201
Marrying for Love, 54
Martina, 267
Marvin at the Psychiatrist, 370
Marvin Hits Trina, 370
Marvin Takes a Victory Shower, 369
Marvin Takes a Wife, 369
Marvin's Giddy Seizures, 369
Mary McGee, 6
Mary, Queen of Scots, 86, 87
Masculinity, 329
Mass, 412
Mata Hari Mine, 259
Matchmaker, Matchmaker, 260
Mathilde, 399
Matrimonial Stomp, The, 395
Max's Story, 303
Maxford House, 382
May and January, 175
May I Suggest Romance?, 222
May the Best Man Win, 303
May the Good Lord Bless and Keep You, 269
May Your Heart Stay Young (L'Chayim), 200
Maybe [Gershwin], 67, 68
Maybe [Strouse], 298
Maybe I Should Change My Ways, 391
Maybe It's Me, 90, 92

Maybe, Maybe Not, 347
Maybe My Baby Loves Me, 377
Maybe They're Magic (Magic Beans), 287
Maybe This Time, 333, 339
Mayer's Lullaby, 262
Mayor, 301
Mayor's Chair, The, 345
Maze, The, 299
Mazel Tov, 328
Me, 366
Me an' My Bundle, 54
Me and Marie, 125
Me and My Baby, 335
Me and My Town, 277, 278
Me for You!, 95
Me, Who Am I?, 110
Meadow Serenade, 68
Meadowlark, 357
Mean Green Mother from Outer Space, 364
Meat and Potatoes, 55
Mechanical Bird, The, 300
Meditation [Geld], 403
Meditation No. 1 [Bernstein], 216
Meditation No. 2 [Bernstein], 216
Meek Shall Inherit, The, 364
Meeskite, 333
Meet Her with a Taximeter, 7
Meet Me at Twilight, 5
Meet Me down on Main Street, 26
Meet Miss Blendo, 392
Meet the Blob, 285
Mein Herr, 333
Mein Kleine Acrobat, 140, 142
Melinda, 171, 172
Melisande, 306
Melodie de Paris, 377, 378
Melodies of May, 33
Melodrama, 182
Melody from "The Red Shoes," 241
Melt Us, 295
Memories [Herman], 327
Men [Strouse], 303
Men! [Styne], 239
Men behind the Man behind the Gun, 195
Men Who Run the Country, The, 157
Mene, Mene, Tekel, 193
Merci, Bon Dieu, 350
Merci, Madame, 357
Merrily We Roll Along, 285
Merry Andrew, 69
Metaphor, 306
Metropolitan Ladies, 47
Metropolitan Nights, 43
Metropolitan Opening, 51
Meyer, Your Tights Are Tight, 86

Miami, 256
Michigan Water, 407
Midas Touch, The, 231
Middle Age Blues, 300
Midnight Bells, 67
Midnight Riding, 299
Migratory V, 414
Mike, 187
Mile after Mile, 176
Military Dancing Drill, 68, 71
Military Life (The Jerk Song), 196
Military Maids, 121
Milk and Honey, 324
Miller's Son, The, 281
Million Dollar Ball, The, 41
Mimi, 97
Mind the Paint, 11
Mine [Coleman], 318
Mine [Gershwin], 73
Mine 'Til Monday, 145
Minnie the Moocher's Wedding Day, 150
Minnie's Boys, 350
Minor Gaff (Blues Fantasy), 149
Minstrel Days, 49
Minstrel Parade, The, 43
Minstrel, the Jester and I, The, 397
Mira (Can You Imagine That?), 264
Miracle of Judaism, 372
Miracle of Miracles, 260
Miracle Song [Blitzstein], 189
Miracle Song [Sondheim], 277
Miserable with You, 139
Misery's Comin' Aroun', 30
Miss Liberty, 54
Miss Marmelstein, 200
Miss Otis Regrets, 124
Miss Turnstile Variations, 212
Mississippi Dry, 82
Mrs. A., 337
Mrs. Cockatoo, 7
Mrs. Mister and Reverend Salvation, 186
Mrs. Monotony, 54
Mrs. S. L. Jacobowsky, 328
Mrs. Sally Adams, 54
Mister and Missus Fitch, 123
Mr. and Mrs. Rorer, 26
Mr. Andrew's Vision, 378
Mr. Cellophane, 335
Mr. Dolan Is Passing Through, 96
Mr. Chamberlain, 4
Mr. Fezziwig's Annual Christmas Ball, 367
Mr. Goldstone, 232
Mr. Gravvins—Mr. Gripps, 24
Mr. Greed, 321
Mr. Monotony, 54

Mr. Off Broadway, 305
Mr. Right, 180
Mister Snow, 106
Mr. Witherspoon's Friday Night, 381
Mr. Wonderful, 256
Misunderstood, 32
Mitzi's Lullaby, 21
Mix and Mingle, 198
Mlle. Scandale Ballet, 206
Moanin' in the Mornin', 153
Moanin' Low, 137
Mob Song, The, 366
Modernistic Moe, 162
Modest Maid (I Love Lechery), 189
Molasses to Rum, 401
Moll Song, 186
Molly O'Hallerhan, 4
Moment Has Passed, The, 401
Moment I Saw You, The, 138, 139
Moment with You, A, 274
Moments in the Woods, 287
Moments of the Dance, 21
Momma Look Sharp, 401
Momma, Momma [Rome], 200
Mon Ami, My Friend, 174
Monday Morning Blues, 189
Money Burns a Hole in My Pocket, 229
Money Isn't Everything, 107, 108
Money Montage, 367
Money Song, The [Kander], 333
Money Song, The [Rome], 197
Money Tree, The, 336
Money, Money (Makes the World Go Round), 333, 339
Money, Money (Venice Gambling Scene), 214
Money, Money, Money [Styne], 237
Monica, 237
Monkey Doodle-Doo, The [1st], 42
Monkey Doodle-Doo, The [2nd], 49
Monkey in the Mango Tree, 156
Mont Martre [Berlin], 48
Montana Chem, 275
Monte Carlo!, 381
Montmart' [Porter], 132
Moon in My Window, 113
Moon Love, 26
Moon of Love, 23
Moon of Manakoora, The, 243
Moon of My Delight, 94
Moon Over Napoli, 51
Moon Song, 20
Moon-Faced, Starry-Eyed, 179
Mooning, 402
Moonlight and You, 87
Moonlight in Versailles, 63

Moonlight Mama, 88
Moonshine Lullaby, 53
Mophams, The, 65
More and More/Less and Less, 328
More I Cannot Wish You, 246
More Love Than Your Love, 145
More Racquetball, 372
More Than Ever, 83
More Than Just a Friend, 115
More Than We Bargained For, 412
More Than You Know, 82, 84
Moritat, 182
Mormon's Prayer, 224
Morning Anthem, 182
Morning Glory, 25
Morning Glow, 356
Morning Is Midnight, 91, 94
Morning Report, The, 413
Mornings at Seven, 102
Morphine Tango, The, 339
Most Beautiful Girl in the World, The, 93, 97, 98
Most Disagreeable Man, 114
Most Expensive Statue in the World, The, 54
Most Gentlemen Don't Like Love, 127
Most Happy Fella, The, 247
Most Important Job, The, 244
Mother and Father, 8
Mother Hare's Prophecy, 394
Mother Told Me So, 140
Mother's Day, 351
Mother's Gonna Make Things Fine, 373
Motherhood March, 265, 325, 326
Mothers of the Nation, 73
Mountain Greenery, 91
Mounted Messenger, The, 182
Move (You're Steppin' on My Heart), 405
Move On, 286
Move Over, 43
Mover's Life, A, 317
Movies Were Movies, 327
Movin' Out, 300
Movin', 223
Mu-Cha-Cha [Duke], 161
Mu-Cha-Cha [Styne], 231
Much More, 305
Muddy Water, 406
Muggin' Lightly, 152
Multitudes of Amys, 279
Murder in Parkwold, 181
Murder, Murder!, 411
Murderous Monty and Light-Fingered Jane, 66
Museum Song, 318
Music and the Mirror, The, 359
Music Hall, The, 310
Music in the House, 190

Music Lesson, The, 378
Music, Music, 188
Music of Home, The, 247, 248
Music of the Stricken Redeemer, 174
Music Still Plays On, The, 373
Music That Makes Me Dance, The, 235
Musketeer Sketch, The, 382
My Baby Just Cares for Me, 390
My Best Girl, 326
My Best Love, 111
My Bicycle Girl, 144
My Big Mistake, 320
My Blanket and Me, 398
My Blue Heaven, 390
My Body, 321
My Boy, 21
My Boy and I, 79, 80
My Boy Bill, 106
My Brass Bed, 270
My Bridal Gown, 143
My British Buddy, 52
My Castle in the Air, 17
My Celia, 3
My Chance to Survive the Night, 369
My Chicago, 244
My Child Will Forgive Me, 414
My City [Coleman], 316
My City [Strouse], 301
My Coloring Book, 332, 339
My Conviction, 399
My Cousin in Milwaukee, 73
My Cozy Little Corner in the Ritz, 119
My Cup Runneth Over, 307
My Daddy Always Taught Me to Share, 352
My Darlin' Eileen, 213
My Darling, My Darling, 245
My Daughter Fanny, the Star, 235
My Death (La Mort), 399
My Defenses Are Down, 53
My Fair Lady, 66
My Father's a Homo, 370
My Favorite Things, 112
My Favorite Year, 382
My First Woman, 339
My Fortune Is My Face, 236
My Friend [Coleman], 321
My Friends [Sondheim], 284
My Funny Valentine, 99
My Gal and I (My Gal Works at Lockheed), 244
My Gal Is Mine Once More, 144
My Garden, 307
My Gentle Young Johnny, 257, 258
My Girl Back Home, 108
My Girl Is Just Enough Woman for Me, 396

My Heart Belongs to Daddy, 127
My Heart Decided, 165
My Heart Has Come A'Tumbling Down, 168
My Heart I Cannot Give to You, 9
My Heart Is Dancing, 143
My Heart Is Like a Violin, 236
My Heart Is Sheba Bound, 91
My Heart Is So Full of You, 247
My Heart Is Unemployed, 194
My Heart Leaps Up, 327
My Heart Stood Still, 93
My High School Sweetheart, 369
My Home Is in My Shoes, 392
My Honolulu Girl, 43
My House, 212
My Hungarian Irish Girl, 5
My Husband Makes Movies, 376
My Husband the Pig, 281
My Kind of Night, 180
My Kind of Person, 266
My Lady, 60
My Lady of the Nile, 17
My Lady's Dress, 25
My Last Love, 22
My Little Book of Poetry, 47
My Little Dixie Home, 407
My Little Girl, 106
My Little Yellow Dress, 232
My Log-Cabin Home, 61
My Long Ago Girl, 120
My Lord and Master, 109
My Lords and Ladies, 178
My Louisa, 124
My Loulou, 125
My Love, 214
My Love Is a Married Man, 222
My Love Is on the Way, 394
My Lover, 83, 84
My Loving Baby, 388
My Lucky Star, 93, 94
My Magic Lamp, 393
My Mammy, 390
My Man Is on the Make, 95
My Man's Gone Now, 74, 75
My Miss Mary, 257
My Most Intimate Friend, 125
My Mother Bore Me, 378
My Mother Told Me Not to Trust a Soldier, 82
My Mother Would Love You, 128
My Mother's Wedding Day, 223
My Name is Samuel Cooper, 180
My New Friends, 218
My New York, 50
My New Philosophy, 398

My Old Love Is My New Love, 60
My One and Only, 69
My Orderly World, 365
My Otaheitee Lady, 11
My Own Best Friend, 335
My Own Morning, 236
My Own Space, 336
My Peaches and Cream, 11
My Personal Property, 315
My Picture in the Papers, 394
My Pin-Up Girl, 196
My Prince, 101
My Real Ideal, 169
My Reason for Being, 241
My Red Letter Day, 162
My Red Riding Hood, 236
My Rhinestone Girl, 50
My Romance, 97
My Royal Majesty, 168
My Rules, 361
My Secret Dream, 308
My Sergeant and I Are Buddies, 52
My Ship, 176, 177
My Soldier, 201
My Son, the Lawyer, 331
My Son-in-Law, 144
My Song without Words [Duke], 164
My Southern Belle, 4
My State, My Kansas, My Home, 271
My Sweet, 96
My Tambourine Girl, 46
My Time of Day, 246, 252
My True Heart, 190
My True Love [Martin], 207
My True Love [Yeston], 377
My Unknown Someone, 320
My Way Or the Highway, 321
My Week, 178
My White Knight, 269, 270
My Wife, 107, 108
My Wife Bridget, 38
My Wish, 271

N.Y.C, 298
Najla's Lament, 392
Najla's Song of Joy, 392
Naked in Bethesda Fountain, 382
Name: Cockian, 308
Name's LaGuardia, The, 257
Namely You, 395
Naming, The, 358
Nanette, 140
Napoleon [Arlen], 156
Napoleon [Kern], 18
Nashville Nightingale, 64

Naughty Baby, 64
Nausea before the Game, The, 369
Near to You, 253
Neat to Be a Newsboy, 357
'Neath the Pale Cuban Moon, 150
Neauville-Sur-Mer, 124
Necessity, 171
Need to Know, 365
Nelson, 328
Nerves, 24
Nesting Time in Flatbush, 18
Never, 318
Never Again [Bock], 262
Never Again [Menken], 367
Never Feel Too Weary to Pray, 269
Never Get Lost, 189
Never Give Anything Away, 132
Never Marry a Girl with Cold Feet, 6
Never Met a Man I Didn't Like, 320, 321
Never Mind How, 139
Never, Never Be an Artist, 132
Never Never Land [Styne], 230
Never on Sunday, 278
Never Put It in Writing, 352
Never Say No [Porter], 123
Never Say No [Schmidt], 306
Never Speak Directly to an Emperor, 300
Never Too Late, 258
Never Too Late for Love, 198, 199
Never Was Born, 154
Never Was There a Girl So Fair, 72
Never Will I Marry, 247, 248
Never-Land [Bernstein], 212
New Ashmolean Marching Society and Students'
    Conservatory Band, The, 245
New Deal for Christmas, A, 298
New Fangled Preacher Man, 402
New Life, A, 411
New Love Is Old, A, 32
New Man, 352
New Music, 383
New Style Bonnet, 244
New Sun in the Sky, 140
New Town Is a Blue Town, A, 252
New War Situation, 162
New Worlds, 376
New Year's Day, 412
New Year's Eve, 351
New York, New York, 211, 212
Newlywed's Song, 201
Next (Au Suivant) [Brel], 399
Next [Sondheim], 283
Next Time I Love, 323
Next Time It Happens, The, 110
Next to Lovin' (I Like Fightin' Best), 403

Niagara Falls, 25
Nice, 381
Nice Baby, 66
Nice She Ain't, 232
Nice Ways, 239
Nice Work If You Can Get It, 75
Nick, 187
Nickel to My Name, A, 164
Nickel under the Foot, 186
Nicodemus, 81
Nicotina, 142
Night and Day, 123, 125
Night Is Filled with Wonderful Sounds, The, 168
Night May Be Dark, The, 146
Night of My Nights, 393
Night Song, 296
Night That Goldman Spoke in Union Square, The, 383
Night They Invented Champagne, The, 226
Night Time, The, 24
Night Time in Araby, 64
Night Waltz (The Sun Sits Low), 281
Night Was Alive, The, 378
Night Was Made for Love, The, 32
Nightie-Night, 66
Nightingale, The (Turk's Song) [Kern], 18
Nightingale, The [Strouse], 300
Nightlife, 295
Nightlife in Santa Rosa, 360
Nightmare [Sondheim], 288
Nightmare, The [Flaherty], 381
Nightmare, The [Schmidt], 308
Nightmare, The [Shire], 410
Nighttime Is No Time for Thinking, The, 178
Nine, 376
Nine O'Clock, 264
911 Emergency, 373
1934 Hot Chocolate Jazz Babies Revue, The, 299
Ninety Again, 113
Ninety-Third Street, 350
No Boom Boom, 334
No Comprenez, No Capish, No Versteh!, 73
No for an Answer, 187
No Give, No Take, 267
No Ifs! No Ands! No Buts!, 168
No Lies, 405
No Life, 286
No Lover, 131
No Man Is Worth It, 301
No Man Left for Me, 320
No Matter under What Star You're Born, 177, 178
No Matter What, 366
No Moon, 378, 379
No More [Sondheim], 286
No More [Hamlisch], 361

No More [Strouse], 296
No More Candy, 259
No More Love, 168
No More Mornings, 351
No, Mother, No, 104
No, No, Nanette!, 80
No One Can Do It, 366
No One Else but That Girl of Mine, 61, 63
No One Else but You, 31
No One Has Ever Loved Me, 288, 289
No One Is Alone, 286
No One Knows (How Much I'm in Love), 28
No One Knows Who I Am, 411
No One Must Ever Know, 411
No One to Call Me Victoria, 298
No One Will Ever Love You (Like You Do), 396
No Other Love, 110
No Place but Home, 96
No Place Like London, 284
No Song More Pleasing, 114
No Strings, 112
No Surprises, 299
No Time at All, 356
No Understand, 113
No Ve Vouldn't Gonto Do It, 175
No Way to Stop It, 112
No-Tell Motel, The, 238
Noah, 156
Noah's Lullaby, 358
Nobody Breaks My Heart, 390
Nobody but You, 58
Nobody Does It Like Me, 316
Nobody Doesn't Like Sara Lee, 343
Nobody Else but Me, 29, 35
Nobody Ever Died for Dear Old Rutgers, 228
Nobody Makes a Pass at Me, 193, 194, 200
Nobody Steps on Kaffritz, 266
Nobody Told Me, 112
Nobody's Chasing Me, 131
Nobody's Heart (Ride Amazon Ride!), 104
Nobody's Perfect, 307
Nodding Roses, 16
Non Credo, 216
Non-Stop Dancing, 26
Normandy, 397
Not a Care in the World, 164
Not a Day Goes By, 285
Not Cricket to Picket, 193
Not Enough Magic, 337
Not Every Day of the Week, 332
Not for All the Rice in China, 51
Not Guilty, 199
Not Here! Not Here!, 8
Not Mine, 236, 240
Not My Problem, 308

Not on Your Nellie, 237
Not Since Chaplin, 376
Not Since Nineveh, 393
Not So Bad to Be Good, 164
Not While I'm Around, 284
Not Yet, 20
Not You, 21
Nothin' Up, 404
Nothing, 359
Nothing at All, 7
Nothing but You, 102
Nothing Could Be Sweeter, 81
Nothing Like the City, 383
Nothing More Than This, 217
Nothing More to Look Forward To, 253
Nothing More to Say, 53
Nothing to Do but Relax, 104
Nothing to Do with Me, 367
Nothing up Our Sleeves, 138
Nothing Will Hurt Us Again, 302
Nothing's Wrong, 93
November Song (Even Dirty Old Men Need Love), 239
Now [Duke], 162
Now [Menken], 364
Now [Sondheim], 281, 282, 353
Now [Strouse], 299
Now I Believe, 96
Now I Have Everything, 260
Now I Have Someone, 234
Now I'm Ready for a Frau, 146
Now Is the Time, 108
Now It Can Be Told, 51
Now, Morris, 331
Now That I Have Springtime, 34
Now That I Know You, 102
Now That I've Got My Strength, 104
Now That We're Mr. and Mrs., 77
Now That's Tap, 409
Now the World Begins Again, 168
Now There Is No Choice, 412
Now You Know, 285
Now's the Time, 236
Nowadays, 335
Nursery Clock, 26
Nursery Fanfare, 21
Nurses Are We, 10
Nymph Errant, 124

O Bless the Lord, 355
O Leo, 142
O Tixo, Tixo, Help Me, 181
O'Hara, 201
O.K. for T.V., 392
Obsession, 412

Ocarina, The, 54
Octopus, 198
Ode to Reason, 187
Of the People Stomp, 195
Of Thee I Sing, 72
Off Again, on Again, 161
Off the Record, 99
Office Hours, 43
Official Resume (First There Was Fletcher), 71
Oh Bess, Oh Where's My Bess?, 74
Oh, Bright Fair Dream, 118
Oh, but I Do, 146
Oh, de Lawd Shake de Heavens, 74
Oh, Diogenes!, 100
Oh, Doctor Jesus, 74
Oh, Fabulous One, 177
Oh, Gee! Oh Joy!, 69
Oh, Happy Day, 395
Oh, Happy We, 214
Oh, Heart of Love, 174
Oh, Heavenly Salvation, 183
Oh, How Easy to Be Scornful!, 308
Oh, How I Hate to Get up in the Morning, 45, 46, 52
Oh, How I Long to Belong to You, 84
Oh, How That German Could Love, 37
Oh, I Can't Sit Down, 74
Oh, It Must Be Fun, 131
Oh, Kay!, 67
Oh, Lady Be Good, 65
Oh Lady! Lady!!, 20
Oh, Lawd, I'm on My Way, 74
Oh, Me! Oh My!, 77, 78
Oh, Mein Leibchen, 146
Oh, Mr. Chamberlain, 4
Oh, My Mysterious Lady, 230
Oh! Nina, 63
Oh, Please, 264
Oh, Promise Me You'll Write to Him Today, 21, 22
Oh, So Nice, 70
Oh, That Beautiful Rag, 37, 38
Oh, the Rio Grande, 174
Oh, This Is Such a Lovely War, 68
Oh, Those Thirties, 236
Oh, to Be a Movie Star, 261, 277
Oh, to Be Home Again, 249
Oh, What a Beautiful Mornin', 105
Oh, What a Filthy Night Court, 186
Oh, What She Hangs Out, 62
Oh, You Beautiful Person, 22
Oh, You Beautiful Spring, 11
Ohio, 213
Oil!, 314
Oisgetzaichnet, 200

Oklahoma!, 105
Ol' Man River, 29
Old Bill Baker (The Undertaker), 16
Old Black Joe and Uncle Tom, 388
Old Boy Neutral, 16
Old Devil Moon, 171, 172
Old Enough to Love [Rodgers], 88, 89
Old Enough to Love [Schwartz], 145
Old Fashioned Garden, 119
Old Fashioned Girl, An [Porter], 121
Old Fashioned Girl [Rodgers], 89
Old Fashioned Melody, 399
Old Fashioned Tune, An, 166
Old Fashioned Wedding, An, 53, 55
Old Fashioned Wife, An, 18
Old Flame Never Dies, An, 143
Old Folks [Kander], 334
Old Folks, The (Les Vieux) [Brel], 399
Old Friends, 285
Old Gentleman, 261
Old Maid, 306, 307
Old Man, An, 113
Old Red Hills of Home, The, 414
Old Sayin's, 190
Old Timer, 170
Old Town, The, 23
Older and Wiser, 294
Oldest Established, The, 246
Oldest Profession, The, 321
Olga (Come Back to the Volga), 120
Olive Tree, The, 393
On a Clear Day (You Can See Forever), 171, 172
On a Day Like This, 190
On a Desert Island with Thee! [Rodgers], 93
On a Desert Island with You [Kern], 26
On a Lopsided Bus, 110
On a Roof in Manhattan, 50
On a Sunday by the Sea, 228
On and on and On, 73
On My Mind the Whole Night Long, 60
On My Own, 231
On My Way to Love, 200
On Such a Night Like This, 208
On That Matter No One Budges, 72
On That Old Production Line, 195
(On the Beach At) How've You Been, 63
On the Brim of Her Old-Fashioned Bonnet, 60
On the Campus, 389
On the Farm, 263
On the Other Hand, 146
On the Other Side of the Tracks, 315
On the Right Track, 356
On the S.S. Bernard Cohm, 172
On the Sands of Wa-Ki-Ki, 16
On the Shore at Le Lei Wi, 16

On the Showboat, 233
On the Side of the Angels, 257
On the Steps of the Palace, 287
On the Street [Larson], 410
On the Street [Leigh], 347
On the Street Where You Live [Loewe], 224
On the Sunny Side of the Street, 389
On the Twentieth Century, 318
On the Willows, 355
On the Wrong Side of the Railroad Tracks, 391
On Time, 195
On Top of the World, 301
On with the Dance [Kern], 24
On with the Dance [Rodgers], 89
On Your Toes, 98
Once a Year Day, 252
Once Every Four Years, 55
Once I Fall, 166
Once in a Blue Moon, 26
Once in Love with Amy, 245
Once Knew a Fella, 199
Once upon a Dream, 411
Once upon a Time [Strouse], 295
Once upon a Time Today [Berlin], 54
Once upon the Natchez Trace, 404
One, 359
One and All, 305
One Big Union for Two, 193
One Boy, 294
One Brave Man Against the Sea, 156
One Brick at a Time, 318
One by One, 413
One Dam Thing after Another, 93
One Day We Dance, 314
One Extraordinary Thing, 328
One Foot, Other Foot, 107
One for My Baby (And One for the Road), 154, 157
One Girl [Berlin], 48
One Girl, The [Youmans], 82
One Hallowe'en, 297
One Hand, One Heart, 215
One Hundred Easy Ways, 213
110 in the Shade, 306
One Hundred Ways Ballet, 294
One Indispensable Man, The, 175
One Kind Word, 190
One Last Kiss, 294
One Life to Live, 176
One Little Brick at a Time, 238
One Little WAC, 244
One Little Year, 350
One Love [Arlen], 150
One Love [Youmans], 82

One Man Ain't Quite Enough, 156
One Moment Alone, 32
One More Dance, 32
One More Kiss, 280, 281
One More Walk around the Garden, 172
One Night Only, 405
One o'Clock in the Morning, 40
One of a Kind, 297
One of the Girls, 336
One of These Fine Days, 194
One Person, 327
One Plus One Equals Three, 412
One Robin Doesn't Make a Spring, 221, 222
One Room, 262
One Small Girl, 382
One Song Glory, 410
One Special Man, 410
One Step—Two Step, 157
One Touch of Alchemy (All Hail the Political Honeymoon), 175
One Touch of Venus, 178
One, Two, Three, 21
One Wife, 253
One Wonderful Day, 274
Only a Moment Ago, 80
Only Another Boy and Girl, 129
Only Dance I Know, The, 55
Only for Americans, 54
Only Game in Town, The, 336
Only Home I Know, The, 403
Only If You're in Love, 392
Only in the Movies, 339
Only Love, 334
Only One to a Customer, 240
Only Only Love, 325
Only Time Will Tell, 199
Only with You, 376
Oo, How I Love to Be Loved by You, 60
Ooh, Do You Love You!, 296
Ooh-La-La, 310
Ooh, Maybe It's You, 50
Ooh, My Feet, 247
Ooh! What You Said, 391
Ooo, Ooo, Lena!, 10
Open a New Window, 326
Open up Your Heart, 82
Open Your Eyes, 160
Opening [Baby], 406
Opening [Garrick Gaieties], 89
Opening [Hannah . . . 1939], 267
Opening [Knickerbocker Holiday], 175
Opening [This Is the Army], 52
Opening Act One [Oh, Boy!], 19
Opening Act One [Tip-Toes], 66
Opening Act One (Coaching) [Sitting Pretty], 27

Opening Act One (Street Vendors) [Cat and the Fiddle], 32
Opening Act Two [Have a Heart], 18
Opening Act II [Merrily We Roll Along], 285
Opening Act Two [Pardon My English], 73
Opening Act Two (Ancient Tunes) [Sitting Pretty], 27
Opening Act Two (In Society) [Sally], 24
Opening Act Two (Russian Dance) [Doll Girl], 12
Opening Chorus [Louisiana Purchase], 52
Opening Chorus (Office Hours) [Watch Your Step], 43
Opening Chorus (Some Dough for the Army Relief) [This Is the Army], 52
Opening Chorus Act One [The Yellow Mask], 160
Opening Chorus Act One [For Goodness Sake], 62
Opening Chorus Act One [Stop Flirting], 62
Opening Chorus Act One [Tell Me More!], 66
Opening Chorus Act One (Wedding Day) [Oh Lady! Lady!!], 20
Opening Doors, 285
Opening for a Princess, An, 397
Opening Letter [Louisiana Purchase], 52
Opening of "Me and Juliet," 110
Opening of "Mr. President," 55
Opening of Second Act (Jane Cow Number) [This Is the Army], 52
Opening Sequence [Arturo Ui], 234
Opera Burlesque (On the Sextette from Lucia de Lammermoor), 41
Opposites, 277, 278
Orange Grove in California, An, 48
Orchids in the Moonlight, 84
Ordinary Couple, An, 112
Ordinary Guy, 194
Ordinary People, 253
Organization Man, 248
Ore from a Goldmine, 391
Orient Yourself, 345
Orienta, 78
Oriental Blues, 388
Oriental Dreams, 24
Orphan Girl, 79
Orphan in the Storm, 308
Orpheus (Lucius' Song), 186
Orthodox Fool, An, 112
Other Generation, The, 111
Other Woman, The, 303
Otherwise (I Wish It Could Be), 395
Our Ancient Liberties, 175
Our Boy Charlie, 299
Our Children [Flaherty], 383
Our Children [Strouse], 295
Our Day of Independence, 54
Our Father, 216

Our Hotel, 119
Our Kind of War, 345
Our Little Nest, 20
Our Little World, 287
Our Lovely Rose, 26
Our Private World, 318
Our State Fair, 115
Our Time, 285
Our Town, 309
Out Tonight, 410
Our Wedding Day, 51
Ours, 126
Out in the Open Air, 169
Out of a Clear Blue Sky [Arlen], 150
Out of a Clear Blue Sky [Duke], 167
Out of My Dreams, 93, 105
Out of the Blue [Kern], 31
Out of the Blue [Schwartz], 139
Out of the Clear Blue Sky [Duke], 167
Out of This World [Arlen], 154
Out of This World (Oisgetzaichnet) [Rome], 200
Out There, 318
Out There in an Orchard, 30
Outside of That I Love You, 51
Over and Over, 206
Over and Over Again, 97
Over Here, 146
Over in Europe, 174
Over the Hill, 403
Over the Moon, 411
Over the Rainbow, 153
Over the Wall I, 339
Over the Wall II, 339
Overflow, 74
Overture [Parade], 324
Overture [Candide], 214
Overture [Fantasticks], 306
Overture [Golden Apple], 394
Overture [1600 Pennsylvania Avenue], 218
Overture [The Threepenny Opera], 182
Overture [Wildcat], 314
Overture Delle Donne [Nine], 376
Oysters, Cockles and Muscles, 199
Ozarks Are Calling Me Home, The, 126

Pack of Cards, A, 30
Pack up the Luggage, 281
Pack up Your Sins and Go to the Devil, 48
Package of Seeds, A, 14, 18
Paging Mr. Sousa, 209
Pain, 339
Pair of Ordinary Coons, A, 43
Pajama Game, The (Opening), 252
Pal Joey (What Do I Care for a Dame?), 103
Pal Joey Ballet, 103

Pal Like You, A, 18
Palace Dance, 26
Pale Venetian Moon, The, 25
Palm Beach, 165
Palomino Pal, 332
Panache, 237
Panisse and Son, 199
Pantry Scene, 30
Papa Don't Love Mama Anymore, 193
Papa, Won't You Dance with Me?, 228
Papa's Gonna Make It Alright, 403
Papa's Got a Job, 194
Paper Moon, 153
Parade, The, 264
Parade in Town, A, 277, 278
Paree, 142
Paree Is a Lark, 378
Paree, What Did You Do to Me?, 122
Parents, 298
Paris by Night, 408
Paris, France, 206
Paris in New York, 168
Paris Is a Paradise for Coons, 9
Paris Is a Tomb, 378
Paris Is Paris Again, 226
Paris Loves Lovers, 132
Paris Makes Me Horny, 408
Paris Original, 248
Paris, Paris, 239
Paris Wakes up and Smiles, 54
Parks of Paris, The, 157
Parlor Songs, 284
Part of Us, A, 382
Party That We're Gonna Have Tomorrow Night,
   The, 110
Party Waltz, 97
Party's Over, The, 231
Pass the Cross, 403
Pass the Football, 213
Passing of Time, The, 401
Passion Flower, The, 47
Past My Prime, 395
Patriotic Rally, 68
Patterns, 406
Paul Jones, The, 387
Paula, 361
Pax: Communion (Secret Songs), 216
Payday, 145
Peach Girl, 25
Peach of a Wife, A, 19
Peach on the Beach, 80
Peaches, 20
Pearl of Ceylon, 29
Pearl We Call Prague, The, 267
Pearls, 327

Peanuts Potpourri, 398
Peek in Pekin, 87
Pegasus, 414
Penniless Bums, 239
Penny a Tune (East Side Melodies), 302
Penny Candy, 187
Penny for Your Thoughts [Duke], 161
Penny for Your Thoughts, A [Rodgers], 87
Penny in My Pocket, 325
People, 235, 267
People Get Hurt, 303
People in Your Life, The, 239
People Like You and Like Me, 394
People Magazine, 321
People of Atlanta, 414
People Watchers, 266
People Will Say We're in Love, 105
Pepita, 64
Perennial Debutantes, 126
Perfect, 358
Perfect Harmony, 300
Perfectly Lovely Couple, 113
Perfectly Marvelous, 333
Pergola Patrol, The, 25, 27
Perhaps, 113
Pernambuco, 245
Perpetual Anticipation, 281
Perspective, 259
Persuasion, The, 225
Pet Me, Poppa, 246
Peter, Peter, 212
Peter Piper/The Sea Is Calling, 119
Pets, 128
Petticoat High, 157
Phantom Fugue, 378
Phinney's Rainbow, 273
Phone Call, The, 381
Physical Fitness, 295
Physician, The, 123, 124
Piano Lesson (If You Don't Mind My Saying So),
  270
Pick Up the Pieces, 317
Pick-a-Little, Talk-a-Little, 270
Pickaninny Shoes, 388
Pickers Are Comin', The, 403
Pickpocket Tango, 396
Picture I Want to See, The, 20
Picture of Happiness, The, 257, 258
Picture of Me without You, A, 125
Picture Show, The, 414
Piddle, Twiddle and Resolve, 401
Pie, 26
Piece of Cake, 319
Piece of Eight, A, 358
Pigtails and Freckles, 55

Pilgrims Procession, 214
Pillar to Post, 266
Pills, 122
Pilot Me, 121
Pine Cones and Holly Berries, 271
Pine Country, 233
Pineapple Song, The, 333
Pink Taffeta Sample Size 10, 316
Pipe-Dreaming, 130
Pippin, 356
Piraeus, 278
Pirate Jenny, 182
Pirate Song, 212
Pirelli's Miracle Elixir, 284
Pity de Sunset, 156
Pity Me Please, 118
Pity the Poor, 218
Place Called Home, A, 367
Plain and Simple, 357
Plain Rustic Ride, A, 5
Plain We Live, 394
Plank Round, 212
Planning a Bar Mitzvah (Round Tables, Square
  Tables), 372
Plant a Radish, 306
Plant You Now, Dig You Later, 103
Play It Again, Sam, 349
Play the Music for Me, 407
Plaza 6-9423, 194
Plaza Song, The, 406
Pleasant Little Kingdom, 280
Please Come to My House, 370
Please Don't Make Me Be Good, 122
Please Don't Make Me Hear That Song Again, 300,
  301
Please Don't Send Me down a Baby Brother, 145
Please, Hello, 283
Please Let Me Tell You That I Love You, 247
Please, Sir, 336
Please Stay, 333
Pleasure and Privilege, 262
Pleasures and Palaces, 249
Plenty Bambini, 247
Plenty of Pennsylvania, 394
Plumbing, 124
Pocketful of Dreams, 197
Poems, 283
Poker Game, The, 337
Poker Love (Card Duet), 5
Poker Polka, 306
Polar Bear Strut, 135
Policeman's Ball, The, 54
Politics and Poker, 257
Polka (Mr. and Mrs. Castle's Specialty), 43
Polly Believed in Preparedness, 18

Polly Pretty Polly (Polly with a Past), 45
Polly's Song, 182
Polovstian Dances, 393
Pompeii Club, 316
Poor As a Churchmouse, 166
Poor Baby, 279
Poor Everybody Else, 315, 316
Poor Joe [Berlin], 55
Poor Joe [Rodgers], 107
Poor Little Baby Darlin', 404
Poor Little Hollywood Star, 315
Poor Little Me, 45
Poor Little Person, 266
Poor Little Rich Girl's Dog, 44
Poor Man, A, 401
Poor Pierrot, 32
Poor Prune, 19
Poor Sweet Baby, 351
Poor Thing, 284
Poor Tied up Darlin', 404
Poor, Unsuccessful and Fat, 373
Pop! Flash!, 365
Poppa Knows Best, 113
Poppyland, 59
Popsicles in Paris, 259
Porcelain Maid, 48
Pore Jud, 105
Porgy, 389
Possessed, 411
Postcards, 308
Pottawatomie, 101
Pour le Sport, 275, 284
Pow! Bam! Zonk!, 296
Power [Grossman], 351
Power [Wright and Forrest], 393
Powerful Thing, A, 340
Praise the Day, 31
Praise the Lord and Pass the Ammunition, 243
Pray, 382
Prayer [Kern], 33
Prayer [Lane], 172
Prayer for a Duck, 356
Precious Children, 358
Prefatory Prayers (Street Chorus), 216, 218
Prelude [Bernstein], 214
Prelude [Kern], 26
Preludium, 112
Prepare Ye the Way of the Lord, 355
Presentation of Miss Turnstiles, 212
Presents for Mrs. Rogers, 321
President, 383
President Jefferson Sunday Luncheon March, The, 218
Press Conference, 405

Pressing Onward, 366
Pretty Girl Is Like a Melody, A, 46
Pretty in the City, 102
Pretty Lady, 282, 283
Pretty Little Missus Bell, 129
Pretty Little Picture, 276
Pretty Music, 414
Pretty Thing, 267
Pretty to Walk With (That's How a Man Gets Got), 156
Pretty Women, 284
Prettybelle, 238
Pricklepear Bloom, The, 404
Primitive Prima Donna, 152
Prince of Humbug, The, 319
Princess of Pure Delight, The, 176
Princess of the Willow Tree, 86, 87
Princess Zenobia Ballet, 98
Prisms, Plums and Prunes, 86, 89
Prisoner, Choose!, 261
Prithee, Come Crusading, 118
Private Conversation, 412
Private Schwartz, 235
Professional Showbizness Comedy, 382
Progress Is the Root of All Evil, 395
Prologue [Follies], 280
Prologue [Godspell], 355
Prologue [Out of This World], 131
Prologue [West Side Story], 215
Prologue (Once in the Highlands) [Brigadoon], 223
Promenade Theme, 401
Promise [Weill], 175
Promise Me a Rose, 264
Promise Me Not to Love Me, 154
Promises, Promises, 400
Proposal, The, 378
Prosperity Is Just around the Corner, 72
Protect Me, 144
Proud Lady, 357
Psalm, The, 344
Psalm 8, 367
Psychiatry Song, The, 174
Ptolemy, 261
Public Enemy Number One, 125
Pulitzer Prize, The, 54
Purest Kind of Guy, The, 187
Purlie, 402
Purple Rose, 167
Pursue the Truth, 412
Push de Button, 156
Pussy Foot, The, 396
Put 'Em Back, 395
Put Him Away, 113
Put on a Happy Face, 294, 295

Put on Your Sunday Clothes, 325
Put Your Money on Me, 254
Putney on the Thames, 237
Puttin' on the Ritz, 50
Putting It Together, 286
Puzzlement, A, 109, 279
PX Parade, 244

Quarrel Song, 190
Quartet [The Secret Garden], 407
Quartet Erotica, 152
Quartet Finale [Candide], 214, 217
Queen Elizabeth, 91
Queen Isabella, 60
Queen Lucy, 398
Queen of Terre Haute, The, 122
Queenie's Ballyhoo (C'mon Folks We'se Rarin' to
    Go), 30
Quelque Chose, 121
Quest, The (The Impossible Dream), 344
Quiet [Bernstein], 214
Quiet [Rodgers], 397
Quiet Girl, A [Bernstein], 213
Quiet Girl, A [Blitzstein], 187
Quiet Night, 98
Quiet Place, A, 214
Quiet Thing, A, 332
Quittin' Time, 409

Race Horse and the Flea, The, 54
Race of the Lexington Avenue Express, 305
Race You to the Top of the Morning, 407
Racing Form Lullaby, 235
Racing with the Clock, 252
Racquetball, 372
Radio Dance, 267
Rafiki Mourns, 413
Raffles, 163
Rag Me That Mendelssohn March, 274
Rag off'n the Bush, 395
Raggedy Ann, 26
Rags, 302
Rags to Riches, 251
Ragtime, 383
Ragtime Jockey Man, The, 41
Ragtime Mocking Bird, The, 40
Ragtime Opera Medley, 43
Ragtime Pipes of Pan, The, 120
Ragtime Razor Brigade, 45
Ragtime Restaurant, The, 11
Ragtime Soldier Man, The, 42
Rahadlakum, 393
Railway Duet, 11
Rain [Flaherty], 382

Rain, The [Blitzstein], 188
Rain in Spain, The, 224
Rain on the Roof, 280
Rain Quartet, 188
Rain Song, The [Schmidt], 306, 307
Rainbow of Girls, 50
Raining, 4
Rainy Day, A, 140
Raise a Ruckus Tonight, 394
Raise the Flag, 404
Raisin' the Rent, 152
Rakish Young Man with the Whiskahs, The, 154
Rap, The, 405
Rape Ballet, 306
Rape of Miss Goldberg, The, 369
Rare Songbirds on Display, 412
Rare Wines, 351
Rat-Tat-Tat-Tat, 235
Rats and Mice and Fish, 351
Raunchy, 306
Raving Beauty, A, 205, 208
Razor Teeth, 261
Razzle Dazzle, 335
Reading, 299
Ready to Play, 412
Real American Folk Song (Is a Rag), 58
Real Big News, 414
Real Coney Island Ballet, The, 212
Real Live Girl, 315
Real Me, The, 295
Real Nice Clambake, A, 106
Real Thing, The, 410
Really Lousy Day in the Universe, A, 373
Rebirth, 316
Recipe, A, 5, 6
Red Ball Express, The, 196
Red Baron, The, 398
Red Blues, The, 132
Red Headed Woman, A, 74
Red, Hot and Blue, 126
Red Shoes Ballet, 241
Red, White and Blue [Kern], 8
Red White and Blues, The [Bernstein], 218
Reflections in His Eyes, 412
Reform, 257
Refugee Song (We'll Take Care of You All), 14
Regina's Aria, 188
Regina's Waltz (Things), 188
Relax, 198
Remember, 281
Remember Radio, 259
Remember That I Care, 179
Reminiscences, 18
Rent, 410

Repent, 318
Reprieved, 182
Requiem Sanctus, 214
Respectability, 199
Rest-Room Rose, 97
Rested Body Is a Rested Mind, A, 403
Restless Heart, 199
Retribution, 411
Return of the Animals, The, 358
Revenge [Kander], 331
Revenge [Strouse], 296
Revolt in Cuba, 51
Rhapsody in Blue, 63, 64, 66, 74, 76, 81, 159, 234
Rhode Island Is Famous for You, 144
Rhyme for Angela, A, 178
Rhymes Have, I, 393
Rhythm, 97, 98
Rhythm of Life, The, 315
Ribbons and Bows, 50
Ribbons down My Back, 325
Rice and Shoes, 78
Rich, The [Blitzstein], 186
Rich, The [Merrill], 264
Rich and Happy, 285
Rich Is, 350
Rich Kids' Rag, 315
Rich Man, Poor Man, 95
Rich Man's Frug, 316
Rich or Poor, 390
Richard Interred, 361
Riches, 404
Riddle Song, The, 409
Ride Amazon Ride!, 104
Ride out the Storm, 316
Ride through the Night, 234
Ridin' High, 126
Ridin' on the Moon, 155
Right, 360
Right As the Rain, 154
Right at the Start of It, 139
Right Finger of My Left Hand, The, 396
Right Girls, 331
Right Now, 6
Ring of Stones, A, 358
Ring on the Finger, 199
Ring Them Bells, 339
Ringaroundarosie, 217
Rink, The, 337
Rio, 319
Rio Bamba, 218
Rip Van Winkle and His Little Men, 23
Rise 'n Shine, 84
Rising Moon, 149
Rita's Confession, 381

Rita's Request, 240
Rita's Theme, 340
Ritz Rock and Roll, 132
River, The, 345
River Chanty, 181
River God, 127
River in the Rain, 406
Rivers Cannot Flow Upwards, 300
Rivers of Tears, 200
Riviera Nights, 310
Road That Lies Before, The, 18
Road You Didn't Take, The, 280
Robbing Your Father, 80
Rock Island (Train Talk), 270
Rock 'n Roll Party Queen, 402
Rockabye Baby, 49
Rockin' in Rhythm, 151
Roll Along Sadie, 167
Roll On, Rolling Road, 34
Roll up the Ribbons, 307
Roll Yer Socks Up, 263
Rolled into One, 18
Roller Skate Rag, 235
Romance [S. Schwartz], 357
Romance [Shire], 406
Romantic Atmosphere, A, 259
Romeo and Juliet, 31
Rookie in the Ring, 382, 383
Room for One, 193
Room Is Filled with You, The, 309, 310
Roommates, 333
Rope Dance, 223
Rosabella, 247
Rosalie [Gershwin], 69
Rosalie [Kern], 5, 13
Rosamund's Dream, 404
Rose in Your Hair, 138
Rose Is a Rose, A, 198
Rose Lovejoy of Paradise Alley, 199
Rose Marie, 25
Rose of Madrid, 64
Rose Song, 189
Rose's Turn, 232, 233
Rosemary, 248
Roses at the Station, 377
Roses in the Rain, 167
Roses of France, 65
Rosie, 294, 295
Rothschild and Sons, 262
Round About, 166, 167
Round and Round, 306
Round-Shouldered Man, 407
Roxie, 335
Royal Bangkok Academy, The, 109

Royal Confession, A, 168
Royal Nonesuch, The, 406
Rub Your Lamp, 128
Rumba Jumps!, The, 391
Rumble, The, 215
Rumblin' and a Rollin', A, 414
Rumor, The, 260
Rumson Town, 224
Run for Your Lives, 277
Running in Place, 340
Russian Dance [Gershwin], 61
Russian Dance [Kern], 12
Rutland Bounce, 230
Rydell Alma Mater, 402
Rydell's Fight Song, 402

'S Wonderful, 69
Sabbath Prayer, 260
Sad Tale of the Beauxhommes, 382
Sadder-But-Wiser Girl, The, 270
Sadie Hawkins Ballet, 395
Sadie, Sadie, 235
Saga of a Sad Sack, 244
Saga of Jenny, The, 177
Sailing at Midnight, 166
Sailor of the Skies, 358
Sailor Song, 43
Sailor Tango (Matrosensong), 183
St. Bridget, 326
St. Pierre, 333
Sale, The, 207
Sally, 24
Salomee (With Her Seven Veils), 229
Salt Air, 123
Salute to Spring, 221
Salzburg, 231
Sam and Delilah, 71, 72
Same Mistakes, 265
Same Sort of Girl, The, 13, 14
Samuel Annoints David, 367
San Francisco Fran!, 233
Sanctus [2nd], 216
Sands of Time, 393
Sandwich Girls, 93
Sandy (Dumb Dog), 298
Sans Souci, 392
Santa Claus [Lane], 171
Santa Claus [Youmans], 80
Santa Fe, 410
Sara Lee, 339
Sarah Brown Eyes, 383
Saratoga, 157
Sarava, 345
Satan's L'il Lamb, 151

Satellite City, 233
Satin and Silk, 132
Saturday Night [Kern], 17
Saturday Night [Sondheim], 274
Saturn Returns: The Flight, 414
Saturn Returns: The Return, 414
Saturnalia, 308
Sauce Diable, 146
Saul Has Slain His Thousands, 367
Saunter Away, 245
Savannah [Arlen], 156
Savannah [Duke], 164
Savannah's Wedding Day, 156
Save a Kiss, 396
Save the People, 355
Save the Village, 324
Say a Prayer for Me Tonight, 224
Say, Darling, 232
Say Goodbye to the Freak Show, 412
Say It with Flowers, 91
Say It with Music, 47
Say So!, 69
Say the Word, 169
Say When, 212
Say, Young Man of Manhattan, 83
Scandal Walk, 60
Scarlett, 201
Scars, The, 171
Scene 3 [Passion], 288
Scene 4 [Passion], 288
Scene 5 [Passion], 288
Scene 6/Three Weeks [Passion], 288
Scene 7 [Passion], 288
Scene 8 [Passion], 288
Scene 9 [Passion], 288
Scene 10 [Passion], 288
Scene 11 [Passion], 288
Scene 12 [Passion], 288
Scene 13 [Passion], 288
Scene 14 [Passion], 288
Scène au Dancing, 173
Scheherazade, 392
Scherzo, 228, 241
Schickelgruber, 177
Schnitza Komisski, The, 24
Schoolhouse Blues, The, 47
Scream, 317
Scrimmage of Life, The, 391
Schroeder, 398
Scylla and Charybdis, 394
Sea Is Calling, The, 119
Sea Song, The (By the Beautiful Sea) [Schwartz], 145
Sea Song, The [Weill], 174

Sea-gull and the Ea-gull, The, 166
Search, The, 181
Search Your Heart [Leigh], 345
Search Your Heart [Strouse], 295
Seasonal Sonatina, A, 305
Second Avenue and Twelfth Street Rag, 167
Second Chance, 340
Secret Service, The, 55
Secret Singing, 187
Secretary Is Not a Toy, A, 248
Seduction, 411
See America First, 118
See Seattle, 146
See That You're Born in Texas, 129
See the Light, 335
See What It Gets You, 277
See You in the Funny Papers, 336
Seeing Things, 333
Seena, 218
Seesaw, 316
Senatorial Roll Call, The, 72
Send a Lot of Jazz Bands Over There, 45
Send for Me, 96
Send for the Militia, 185
Send in the Clowns, 281, 282
Sensitivity, 397
Sentimental Me (And Romantic You), 89
Sentimental Weather, 162
September Song, 175, 183
Serenade, 357
Serenade with Asides, 245
Sergeant Philip of the Dancers, 10
Sermon, The, 248
Servant's Chorus, 224
Set Those Sails, 369
Setting up Exercises, 69
Settle Down in a One-Horse Town, 43
7/2 Cents, 252
Seven Deadly Virtues, The, 225
Seven Million Crumbs, 247
Seven Sheep, Four Red Shirts, and a Bottle of Gin, 253
Seventeen and Twenty-One, 68
70, Girls, 70, 334
Seventy-Six Trombones, 269
Sevilla, 388
Sew a Button, 266, 267
Sewing Bee, 394
Sex Marches On, 51
Sexually Free, 317
Sh!, 223
Shadow of Love, 163
Shadow of the Moon, 26
Shadowland, 413
Shady Lady Bird, 205

Shakespearean Opening, 142
Shakin' at the High School, 402
Shaking the Blues Away, 50
Shall I Take My Heart and Go?, 396
Shall I Tell You What I Think of You?, 109
Shall We Dance?, 109
Shalom, 324
Shame on You, 345
Shango, 246
Shauny O'Shay, 206
Shavian Shivers, 160
She Came, She Saw, She Can-Canned, 170
She Could Shake the Maracas, 101
She Didn't Say "Yes", 32
She Hadda Go Back, 271
She Hangs out in Our Alley, 62
She Hasn't a Thing Except Me, 162
She Is Beautiful, 111
She Is Not Thinking of Me, 226
She Likes Basketball, 400
She Loves Me Not, 141
She Loves Me, 258, 259
She Thinks That's the Answer, 351
She Was a Dear Little Girl, 37
She Wasn't You, 172
She's a Home Loving Girl, 212
She's a Nut, 318
She's a Woman, 339
She's Gonna Come Home with Me, 247
She's Just a Baby, 261
She's My Love, 264
She's No Longer a Gypsy, 297
She's Such a Comfort to Me, 136, 137
Sheep Song [Herman], 324
Sheep's Song [Bernstein], 217
Sheer Perfection, 367
Shepherd's Song [Blitzstein], 190
Shifting Sounds, 409
Shimmy with Me, 24
Shine It On, 336
Shine on Your Shoes, A, 140
Shine Out All You Little Stars, 7
Ship without a Sail, A, 95
Shipoopi, 270
Shipshape, 358
Shirts by the Millions, 73
Sh'ma, 414
Shoein' the Mare, 152
Shoeless Joe from Hannibal, Mo., 253
Shop, 18
Shopping Around, 198
Shortest Day of the Year, The, 100, 101
Should I Be Sweet?, 84
Should I, Should I, Should I, 262
Should I Speak of Loving You?, 254

Should I Tell You I Love You?, 130
Show Biz, The, 383
Show Goes On, The, 310
Show Me, 224
Show Me the Key, 407
Show Me the Town, 67, 69
Show Train, 229
Show Tune in 2/4, 323, 326
Show Us How to Do the Fox Trot, 43
Shriner's Ballet, 294
Shtetl Iz Amereke, A, 383
Shuffle, 93
Shuffle Along, 388
Shuffle Your Feet and Roll Along, 389
Shufflin' Sam, 26
Shut Up and Dance, 382
Shut Up, Gerald, 337
Shy, 397
Si Vous Aimez les Poitrines, 124
Siberia, 132
Sid, Ol' Kid, 264
Side by Side by Side, 279
Sidestep, The, 405
Sign, 298
Sign Here, 332
Sign, Lily, Sign (Sextet), 318
Signal, The, 67
Signora Campbell, 172
Silk Stockings, 132
Silly People, 281
Silver Shield, 166
Simba Confronts Scar, 413
Simchas, 240
Simple (A Is One) [Sondheim], 277, 278
Simple [Yeston], 376
Simple Country Wedding, A, 310
Simple Joys, 356
Simple Joys of Maidenhood, The, 225
Simple Life, The, 61
Simple Little Things, 306
Simple Little Tune, 18
Simple Melody, 43
Simple Song, A [Bernstein], 216
Simplified Language, 317
Simpson Sisters, The, 396
Sin of Pat Muldoon, The, 253
Since the Days of Grandmama, 11
Sincere, 270
Sing [Hamlisch], 359
Sing [Rodgers], 92, 95
Sing [Yeston], 378
Sing for Your Supper, 100, 101, 206
Sing Happy, 332
Sing High, 254
Sing Hubbard, 188

Sing Me a Song with Social Significance, 193
Sing Me Not a Ballad, 178
Sing Me to Sleep, Dear Mammy (With a Hush-a-
    Bye Pickaninny Tune), 388
Sing the Merry, 392
Sing to Me, Guitar, 129
Sing Trovatore, 9
Sing-Song Girl, 25
Singer Must Be Free, A, 300
Singing a Love Song, 94, 96
Sir Galahad, 19
Sirens, The, 61, 65
Siren's Song, The, 19
Sisyphus, 414
Sit Down, John, 401
Sit Down, You're Rockin' the Boat, 246
Sitting Becalmed in the Lee of Cuttyhunk, 373
Sitting in Jail, 175
Sitting Pretty [Kander], 333
Sitting Pretty [Kern], 26
Six Months out of Every Year, 253
Six O'Clock News, 360
Sixteen Going on Seventeen, 112
1617 Broadway, 256
Skating Song, 43
Skid Row (Downtown), 364
Skinnin' a Cat, 402
Skip to My Lou, 208
Skirts, 243
Sky City, 95
Skyrocket, 387
Slaughter on Tenth Avenue, 98
Slave Ships, 409
Sleep Peaceful, Mr. Used-to-Be, 155
Sleep-Tite, 252
Sleepin' Bee, A, 155, 156
Sleepy Man, 404
Sleepyhead, 90, 91, 99
Sleigh Bells, 142
Sleigh Ride, 396
Slice, The, 236
Slide, Boy, Slide, 156
Slide Some Oil to Me, 403
Slightly Less Than Wonderful, 391
Slippy Sloppy Shoes, 200
Slogan Song, 392
Slow Sinks the Sun, 118
Small House of Uncle Thomas, The, 109
Small Talk [Adler], 252
Small Talk [Blitzstein], 188
Small World [Duke], 167
Small World [Styne], 232
Smart People Stay Single, 315
Smashing New York Times, 299
Smellin' of Vanilla (Bamboo Cage), 155

Smile [Hamlisch], 360
Smile and Show Your Dimple, 51
Smile, Smile [Styne], 236, 237
Smoke Gets in Your Eyes, 33
Smokin' Reefers, 140
Snoopy, 398
Snoopy's Song, 351
Snow, 54
Snow Flakes, 60
So Am I, 65
So Are You! (The Rose is Red—Violets are Blue),
    70
So Do I, 84
So Far, 107, 108
So Far—So Good, 229
So Good to See You, 267
So Happy, 287
So in Love, 130
So Long, Baby, 212
So Long, Big Guy, 296
So Long, Dearie, 325
So Long, Farewell, 112
So Long Ma! (Headin' for New Orleans), 233
So Long, Pa, 321
So Many People, 274, 275
So Much You Loved Me, 114
So Nonchalant, 161
So What? [Gershwin], 73
So What [Kander], 333
So What Else Is New?, 337
So You Want to See the Wizard?, 403
So's Your Old Man, 28
Society, 15
Sodomy, 399
Soft Lights and Sweet Music, 50
Soldier with the Tap-Tap-Tap, The, 142
Soldier's Song, 213
Soldiers' March, 71
Solicitor's Song, 172
Solid Silver Platform Shoes, 356
Soliloquy [Rodgers], 106, 279
Solomon [Porter], 124
Solomon Song [Weill], 182
Sombrero Land, 40
Some Bright Morning, 299
Some Enchanted Evening, 108
Some Far-Away Someone, 64
Some Fine Day, 23
Some Girl Is on Your Mind, xi, 31
Some Girls, 382
Some Girls Can Bake a Pie, 72
Some Have, Some Have Not, 377
Some Kind of a Man, 238
Some Like It Hot, 239

Some Little Girl, 20
Some One [Kern], 17, 31
Some Other Time [Bernstein], 211, 212
Some Other Time [Styne], 232
Some Party, 22
Some People, 232, 233
Some Rain Must Fall, 61
Some Say, 382
Some Sort of Somebody (All of the Time), 16
Some Things, 200
Some Things Don't End, 358
Some Wonderful Sort of Someone, 58
Somebody [Schmidt], 307
Somebody Loves Me, 64, 159, 388
Somebody Older, 340
Somebody, Someplace, 266
Somebody, Somewhere, 247, 270
Somebody Stole My Heart Away, 70
Somebody Stole My Kazoo, 240
Somebody to Love, 399
Somebody Wants to Go to Sleep, 34
Somebody's Coming to My House, 42
Somebody's Gotta Do Somethin', 303
Somebody's Sunday, 160
Someday, 267
Someday Is for Suckers, 321
Someday Soon, 240
Somehow, 221, 222
Somehow I Never Could Believe, 179
Somehow It Seldom Comes True, 58
Someone [Gershwin], 62
Someone [Kern], 38
Someone Believes in You, 64
Someone Else Is Waiting, 365
Someone in a Tree, 283
Someone in April, 172
Someone Is Waiting, 279
Someone Like You [Rodgers], 113
Someone Like You [Wildhorn], 411
Someone Needs Me, 307
Someone Should Tell Them, 93, 96
Someone to Watch Over Me, 67, 68, 76
Someone Woke Up, 113
Someone Wonderful I Missed, 317
Somethin' Cold to Drink, 158
Somethin' More, 407
Something, 105
Something about Love, 65
Something Bad Is Happening, 372
Something Big, 253
Something Doesn't Happen, 113, 114
Something for the Boys, 129
Something for the Summer, 310
Something Funny's Going On, 381

Something Good, 112
Something Greater, 297
Something Had to Happen, 33
Something Has Happened, 307
Something Is Coming to Tea, 208
Something Just Broke, 287
Something New, 244
Something Somewhere, 113
Something Sort of Grandish, 171
Something Tells Me, 208
Something There, 366
Something to Dance About, 55
Something to Remember You By, 139
Something Was Missing, 298
Something Wonderful, 109
Something You Never Had Before, 146
Something's Always Happening on the River, 232
Something's Coming (Could Be), 215
Something's Got to Be Done, 118
Something's Gotta Give, 393
Sometimes, 308
Sometimes a Day Goes By, 336
Sometimes I'm Happy, 79, 80, 81
Sometimes You Just Need Someone, 311
Somewhere, 215
Somewhere Ballet, 215
Somewhere That's Green, 364
Sominex, 364
Som'thin' from Nuthin', 409
Sonata in C (K 545), 252
Song for Belly Dancer (The Only Dance I Know), 55
Song Is You, The, 32
Song of a Summer Night, 247
Song of Love, 397
Song of Miriam, 175
Song of Ruth, 175
Song of Our Love, 165
Song of the Bat, 187
Song of the Conjur Man, 157
Song of the Flame, 67
Song of the Free, The, 177
Song of the Gigolo, 150
Song of the Glove, 190
Song of the Goddess, 174
Song of the Guns, 174
Song of the King, The, 109
Song of the Ma, 190
Song of the Rivetter, 136
Song of the Setting Sun, The, 390
Song of the West, 81
Song of the Woodman, 153
Song of the Wounded Frenchman, 174
Song on the Sand (La Da Da Da), 329

Song without Words [Kern], 35
Songs of Long Ago, The, 60
Sons [Bock], 262
Sons Of (Fils De) [Brel], 399
Soon [Gershwin], 71
Soon [Sondheim], 281, 282, 353
Soon As I Get Home, 403
Soon It's Gonna Rain, 305, 306
Soon You Gonna Leave Me, Joe, 247
Sooner or Later, 287, 288
Sorry—Grateful, 279
Sound of Love, The (Gramophone Sequence), 302
Sound of Money, The, 200
Sound of Music, The, 112
Sounds While Selling, 259
South America, Take It Away, 196
South American Way, 194
South Sea Isles, 61
Southern Lady, A, 201
Souvenirs, 178
Spanglish, 316
Spanish [Berlin], 45
Spanish [Youmans], 79
Spanish Love [Berlin], 39
Spanish Love [Gershwin], 60
Spanish Panic, 397
Spanish Rose, 294
Spark of Creation, The, 358
Speak Low, 178, 183
Speaking of Love, 161
Special Delivery! (One Bride), 247
Spirit of Capsulanti, The, 392
Sports of Gay Chicago, The, 30
Sposalizio, 247
Spread a Little Sunshine, 356
Spring, 21
Spring Doth Let Her Colours Fly, 293
Spring Fever, 152
Spring Is Here [1st], 76, 95
Spring Is Here [2nd], 100
Spring of Next Year, The, 327
Spring Song, 213
Springtime Cometh, The, 392
Ssh . . . You'll Waken Mister Doyle, 13
Stability, 262
Staircase, The, 378
Stampede, The, 413
Standing on the Corner, 247
Star of Hitchy Koo, The, 23
Stardust, 391
Stars, Stars, Stars, 410
Starting at the Bottom, 390
Starway Lullaby, 255
Statehood Hula, 305

Status Quo, 193
Stay, 113
Stay Out, Sammy!, 193
Stay Well, 176, 181
Stay with Me [Coleman], 320
Stay with Me [Merrill], 265
Stay with Me [Sondheim], 286
Stay with Me, Nora, 351
Stay with the Happy People, 229
Staying Young, 264
Steal with Style, 404
Steam Heat, 252
Steamboat Whistle, The, 142
Steel Pier, 340
Steeplejack, 138
Step Right Up, 321
Step This Way, 44
Steppin' to the Bad Side, 405
Stepping Stones, 26
Stepsisters' Lament, The, 111
Stereophonic Sound, 132
Sterling Silver Moon, 45
Stick Around, 296
Still, 378
Still Got My Heart, 273
Stonecutters Cut It on the Stone, 106
Stonewall Moscowitz March, 92
Stop and See Me, 366
Stop! Look! Listen!, 43
Stop That Dancing, 170
Stop That Rag (Keep on Playing, Honey), 37
Stop, Time, 410
Store-Bought Suit, 394
Storm I, 407
Storm II, 407
Storm Prayers, 74
Stormy Weather, 76, 152, 153, 156, 158
Story Goes On, The, 406
Story of My Life, The [Bernstein], 213
Story of My Life, The [Schmidt], 310
Stranded Again, 318
Strange and Wonderful, 201
Strange Duet, 234, 237
Stranger in Paradise, 393
Stranger to the Rain, 358
Streak o' Lightnin', 157
Streak of Madness, 412
Street Cries [Gershwin], 74
Street Scene, 408
Street Songs [Kander], 332
Streets of Antioch Stink, The, 308
Strike up the Band, 68, 71
Strongest Man in the World, The, 296
Strut Lady with Me, 63
Stuck with You, 412

Stuff to Give the Troops, The, 138
Style, 356
Subway Directions, 234
Subway Express, The, 6
Subways Are for Sleeping, 234
Success, 383
Such a Funny Feeling, 160
Such a Little While, 189
Suddenly, 161
Suddenly Lovely, 108
Suddenly the Sunrise, 157
Sue Me, 246
Sue Me Argument, 246
Sugar, 238
Sugarfoot, 165
Suits Me Fine, 206
Summation and Cakewalk, 414
Summer Afternoon, 198
Summer Day, 188
Summer Dresses, 198
Summer Is, 256
Summer Is A-Comin' In, 164, 167
Summer Is Over, 331
Summer Nights, 402
Summertime, 74, 76
Summertime Love, 247, 248
Sun about to Rise, The, 31
Sun Is Beginning to Crow, The, 253
Sun on My Face, 239
Sun on Your Face, 239
Sun Shines Brighter, The, 19
Sun Shines out of Your Eyes, The, 240
Sun Sits Low, The, 281
Sun Starts to Shine Again, The, 20
Sun Will Shine, The, 136
Sun Won't Set, The, 281
Sunday [Rodgers], 111
Sunday [Sondheim], 286
Sunday [Styne], 227
Sunday Afternoon, 138
Sunday in Cicero Falls, 154
Sunday in London Town, 63
Sunday in the Park [Rome], 193, 194
Sunday in the Park with George [Sondheim], 286
Sunday Morning, Breakfast Time, 125
Sunflower, 325
Sunny, 28
Sunrise Letter Transition (Scenes 4–5), 288
Sunrise, Sunset, 260
Sunshine [Kern], 28
Sunshine [Styne], 228, 239
Sunshine Girl, 263
Sunshine, Lollipops and Rainbows, 359
Superman March, 296
Superman Theme, 296

Supper Time [Berlin], 51
Suppertime [Gesner], 398
Suppertime [Menken], 364
Surabaya-Johnny, 173
Surrey with the Fringe on Top, The, 105
Survive, 308
Susan, 3
Susan's Dream, 180
Susie (Camel Song), 28
Suzette and Her Pet, 8
Suzy Is a Good Thing, 110
Swamps of Home, The, 397
Swanee, 59
Swanee Rose, 59
Swattin' the Fly, 165
Sweet and Hot, 150
Sweet and Low-Down, 66, 160
Sweet Bye and Bye, 166
Sweet Charity (Charity's Theme) [1st], 315
Sweet Charity [2nd], 315
Sweet Charity [3rd], 315
Sweet Is the Rose, 190
Sweet Italian Love, 38
Sweet Marie, Make-a Rag-a-time Dance wid Me, 37
Sweet Music, 140
Sweet Nudity, 124
Sweet One, 140
Sweet Parisian, The, 12
Sweet Peter, 89, 90
Sweet River, 306
Sweet Sixty-Five, 99
Sweet, Sweet, Sweet, 356
Sweet Thing Like Me, A, 352, 353
Sweet Thursday, 110
Sweeten' Water, 155
Sweetenheart, 96
Sweetest Girl, Silly Boy, I Love You, 7
Sweetest Sounds, The, 112
Sweetest Thing in Life, The, 27
Sweetheart I'm So Glad That I Met You, 63, 66
Sweethearts of the Team, 101
Sweetie, 23
Sweetriver, 306, 307
Swell, 303
Swing!, 213
Swing High Swing Low, 170
Swing Your Bag, 345
Swing Your Calico, 170
Swing Your Projects, 234
Swiss Miss (The Cab-Horse Trot), 65
Sword Dance, 223
Sword, Rose and Cape, 264
Sympathetic Someone, 28
Sympathy, Tenderness, 411
Syncopated Clock, The, 396

Syncopated Cocktail, A, 46
Syncopated Vamp, The, 47
Syncopated Walk, The, 43

T'morra, T'morra, 154
Ta-ta, Little Girl, 10
Table Talk, 337
Table with a View, 377
Tait Song, 389
Take 'Im Away (He's Breakin' My Heart), 49
Take a Chance (Little Girl), 21
Take a Giant Step, 294
Take a Good Look Around, 325
Take a Job, 233
Take a Little One-Step, 79
Take a Little Wife, 48
Take a Step with Me, 13
Take and Take and Take, 99
Take Back Your Mink, 246
Take Care, 7
Take Care of This House, 218
Take Him, 103
Take It All Off, 329
Take It in Your Stride, 53
Take It Slow, Joe, 156
Take Love Easy, 391
Take Me Along, 264
Take Me As I Am, 411
Take Me Back, 42
Take Me Back to Manhattan, 123
Take Me Back to Texas with You, 207
Take Me on the Merry-Go-Round, 4
Take Me or Leave Me, 410
Take Me out to the Ballgame, 351
Take Me to the World, 278
Take Me with You, Soldier Boy, 52
Take Off a Little Bit, 43
Take Off the Coat, 197, 198
Take the Book, 187
Take the Moment, 113
Take Us to the Forest, 300
Take Your Time and Take Your Pick, 395
Taking a Chance on Love, 164, 168
Taking the Steps to Russia, 127
Tale of the Oyster, The, 122
Talk of the Town, 387
Talk to Her, 410
Talk to Him, 256
Talkative Toes, 161
Talking to You, 208
Talking to Yourself, 236
Tall Dames and Low Comedy, 347
Tall Hope, 314
Tall Pines, The, 244
Tango [Marie Galante], 174

Tango, The [Mancini], 408

Tango Ballad [*The Threepenny Opera*], 182

Tango: Maureen [Larson], 411

Tango Melody, 49

Tango Tragique, 259

Tap Your Troubles Away, 327, 328

Tara, 201

Tartar [Gershwin], 67

Tartar Song, The [Rodgers], 94

Taunting Scene, 215

Te Deum (God Save the King), 114

Tea for Two, 80

Tea Party, 327

Teach Me How to Love, 43

Teacher, Teacher, 22

Tee-Oodle-Um-Bum-Bo, 58

Teepee, 21

Telephone, The [Loewe], 226

Telephone Girlie [Youmans], 80

Telephone Girls [Kern], 22

Telephone Song [Kander], 333

Telephone Hour, The, 294, 295

Tell Her in the Springtime, 49

Tell It to the Marines, 94

Tell Me a Bedtime Story, 48

Tell Me All Your Troubles, Cutie, 20

Tell Me I Know How to Love, 97

Tell Me I Look Nice, 259

Tell Me Little Gypsy, 47

Tell Me More, 66

Tell Me with a Melody, 47

Tell the Doc, 69

Temple Trio, The, 413

Tempo of the Times, The, 314

Temporary Arrangement, A, 235

Tempt Me Not, 101

Ten Cents a Dance, 96, 149

Ten Minutes Ago, 111

Ten Percent, 335

Tender Shepherd, 230

Tennessee Fish Fry, 144

Tennis Song, The (The Ball Is in Your Court), 320

Tent Scene, 225

Terribly Attractive, 143

Tevye's Monologue (They Gave Each Other a Pledge), 260

Tevye's Rebuttal, 260

Texas Has a Whorehouse in It, 405

Thank God I'm Old, 319

Thank Heaven for Little Girls, 226

Thank You, 216

"Thank You, Kind Sir!" Said She, 39

Thank You, Madam, 259

Thank You So Much, 113

Thank Your Lucky Stars, 144, 243

That American Boy of Mine, 63

That Black and White Baby of Mine, 119

That Certain Feeling, 66

That Come Hither Look, 17

That Dirty Old Man, 276

That Face, 206

That Fellow Manuelo, 141

That Forgotten Melody, 79

That Frank, 285

That Great Come and Get It Day, 171

That Hula Hula, 43

That Little Something, 28, 29

That Lost Barber Shop Chord, 67

That Lucky Fellow, 35

That Man Over There, 271

That Moment of Moments, 162

That Mysterious Rag, 40

That New-Fangled Mother of Mine, 64

That Old Black Magic, 154, 157

That Old Gang of Mine, 388

That Old Piano Roll, 280

That Opera Rag, 38

That Peculiar Tune, 15

That Revolutionary Rag, 46

That Russian Winter, 52

That Slavery Is Love, 345

That Society Bear, 41

That Something Extra Special, 237

That Stranger in Your Arms, 237

That Terrific Rainbow, 103

That Was Yesterday, 324

That'll Show Him, 276

That's All Right for McGilligan, 9

That's Entertainment, 140, 147

That's for Me, 115

That's for Sure, 392

That's Him, 178

That's How I Love the Blues, 205

That's How It Goes, 145

That's How It Starts, 264

That's How You Jazz, 407

That's How Young I Feel, 326

That's Life, 161

That's My Idea of Paradise, 42

That's My Pop, 195

That's Not Cricket, 142

That's the Kind of Woman, 303

That's the Way It Goes, 298

That's the Way It Happens, 110

That's the Way the People Blend, 404

That's the Way We Do Things in New Yawk, 408

That's What He Did, 73

That's What He Said, 414

That's What I Hate about Love, 151
That's What I Like, 230
That's What I Want for Jamie, 314
That's What the Well-Dressed Man in Harlem Will Wear, 52
That's Where We Came In, 366
Theatre Is a Lady, The, 167
Theatre Is Dying, The, 110
Them Conkheads, 409
Theme from "Carnival!" (Love Makes the World Go Round), 264
Theme from "City of Angels," 320
Theme from "Golden Boy," 296
Theme from "Grand Hotel," 377
Theme from "Minnie's Boys," 350
Theme from "New Girl in Town," 263
Theme Song, The [*Little Show*], 136
Then I'll Be Tired of You, 141
Then You May Take Me to the Fair, 225
Then You Were Never in Love, 170
There, 256
There Ain't No Flies on Me, 263
There Are No Wings on a Foxhole, 52
There Are Worse Things I Could Do, 402
There Are Yanks (From the Banks of the Wabash), 165
There but for You Go I, 223, 226, 301
There Comes a Time, 238
There Goes My Life, 254
There Goes the Ball Game, 339
There Had to Be the Waltz, 222
There He Goes, Mister Phileas Fogg, 130
There He Was, 356
There Is a Fountain, 414
There Is a Happy Land (Tale of Woe), 9
There Is a Sucker Born Every Minute, 318
There Is No Other Way, 283
There Is Nothin' Like a Dame, 108
There Is Nothing Too Good for You, 63
There Isn't One Girl, 27
There It Is Again (When Your Favorite Girl's Not There), 19
There Must Be Someone for Me, 129
There Never Was a Woman (Who Couldn't Be Had), 396
There Never Was Another Baby, 229
There Once Was a Man, 252
There She Is, 351, 378
There Was a Time, 241
There When I Need Him, 336
There Won't Be Trumpets, 277
There You Are Again, 165
There'll Always Be a Lady Fair, 124
There'll Be Life, Love and Laughter, 178
There'll Be Trouble, 179
There's a Boat Dat's Leavin' Soon for New York, 74
There's a Brand New Beat in Heaven, 300
There's a Coach Comin' In, 224
There's a Girl, 407
There's a Girl in Havana, 40
There's a Great Day Coming Mañana, 170
There's a Happy Land in the Sky, 129
There's a Hill beyond a Hill, 32
There's a Land, 414
There's a Man in My Life, 391
There's a Resting Place for Every Girl (Sun Chair Song), 10
There's a Room in My House, 331
There's a Shout, 414
There's a Sweet Wind Blowin' My Way, 156
There's a Small Hotel, 98
There's Always a Woman, 277
There's Always One You Can't Forget, 301
There's Gotta Be Something Better Than This, 315
There's More to the Kiss Than the Sound, 58
There's More to the Kiss Than the X-X-X, 58, 59
There's Never Been Anything Like Us, 301
There's No Better Use for Time Than Kissing, 21
There's No Business Like Show Business, 53
There's No Cure Like Travel, 125
There's No Holding Me, 144
There's No Reason in the World, 324
There's Nothing Like a Model "T", 228
There's Nothing Nicer Than People, 198
There's Nowhere to Go but Up, 175
There's Room Enough for Us, 395
There's Room for One More, 85, 87
There's So Much More, 96
There's Something about a War, 276
There's Something about an Empty Chair, 253
There's Something Nice about the South, 44
There's Something Rather Odd about Augustus, 7
These Charming People, 66
These Eyes of Mine, 352
They Ain't Done Right by Our Nell, 128
They All Laughed, 75
They All Look Alike, 18
They Always Follow Me Around, 43
They Call It Dancing, 47
They Call the Wind Maria, 223, 224
They Can't Take That Away from Me, 75
They Couldn't Compare to You, 131
They Didn't Believe Me, 13, 15, 16, 19
They Gave Each Other a Pledge, 260
They Give Me Love, 349
They Hear Drums, 288
They Like Ike, 55

They Live in You, 413
They Love Me, 55
They Never Told Me, 165
They Pass by Singin', 74
They Say, 262
They Say It's Wonderful, 53
They Were You, 305
They Won't Know Me, 198
They'll Never Take Me Alive, 347
They're Always Entertaining, 124
They're Playing Our Song, 360
Thief in the Night, 142
Things [Arlen], 152, 153
Things (Regina's Waltz) [Blitzstein], 188
Things Get Broken, 216
Think How It's Gonna Be (When We're Together Again), 297
Think How Many People Never Find Love, 230
Think of the Time I Save, 252
Thinkin' [Pipe Dream], 110
Thinking [Do I Hear a Waltz?], 113
Third Degree of Love, The, 87
Third Letter, 288
Thirteen Collar, 16
Thirty Weeks of Heaven, 145
This Amazing London Town, 262
This Can't Be Love, 100, 101
This Cornucopian Land, 345
This Could Go on for Years, 71
This Funny World, 92
This Gentle Land, 298
This Had Better Come to a Stop, 370
This House, 307
This Is a Great Country, 55
This Is Not Over Yet, 414
This Is All Very New to Me, 394
This Is It, 143
This Is My Holiday, 223
This Is My Night to Howl, 105
This Is New, 177
This Is Not a Song, 161
This Is So Nice, 391
This Is the Army, Mr. Jones, 52
This Is the Life [Strouse], 296
This Is the Life [Weill], 180
This Is the Life for a Man [Gershwin], 64
This Is the Moment, 411
This Isn't Me, 410
This Is Where I Came In, 164
This Kind of a Girl, 146
This Land Don't Belong to Virginia, 403
This Must Be the Place, 352, 353
This Nearly Was Mine, 108
This New Jerusalem, 367
This Place Is Mine, 377

This Plum Is Too Ripe, 306
This Time, 52
This Time Next Year, 181
This Time of the Year, 171
This Time the Dream's on Me, 154
This Time Tomorrow, 240
This Week Americans, 113
This World (Candide's Lament), 217
Those "Come Hither" Eyes, 15, 17
Those Days Are Gone Forever, 25
Those Magic Changes, 402
Those Were the Good Old Days, 253
Thou Shalt Not, 240
Thou Swell, 93
Thought of You, The, 199
Thoughts, 327
Thousands of Flowers, 307
Thousands of Miles, 181
Three Bs, The [Martin], 205
Three Bs, The [Rodgers], 98
Three Cheers for the Red, White, and Blue, 48
Three Cheers for the Union!, 71
Three Coins in the Fountain, 231
Three Cornered Tune, 246
Three Days, 289
Three-Five-Zero-Zero, 399
365 Days, 17
Three Letters, 259
Three Loves, 293
Three Men on a Date, 205
Three Musketeers, The, 89
Three Puppet Songs, 264
Three Sunny Rooms, 302
Three Times a Day, 66
Three Wishes for Christmas, 232
Thrill of First Love, The, 370
Throttle Throttlebottom, 73
Through a Keyhole, 51
Through the Mountain, 409
Through the Years, 83, 84
Throw 'Er in High!, 63
Throw it Away, 307
Throw It Out, 373
Throw the Anchor Away, 145
Thumbelina, 246
Thunder and Lighting, 249
Ti Moune, 382
Ti Voglio Bene, 376
Tick-Tock, 279
Tick Tock Goes the Clock, 400
Tickling the Ivories, 50
Tide Pool, The, 110
Tie a String around Your Finger, 79
Tiger, Tiger, 261
Tight-Knit Family, A, 370

'Til Good Luck Comes My Way, 30
'Til Tomorrow, 257
Till I Meet Someone Like You, 65
Till I Met You, 269
Till the Clouds Roll By, 19
Till Then, 401
Till There Was You, 269
Till We Reach That Day, 383
Till You Came into My Life, 411
Time [Finn], 373
Time [Rodgers], 114
Time after Time, 228
Time and Music, 373
Time for Love, A, 201
Time Goes By, 309
Time Heals Everything, 327, 328
Time Marches On!, 162
Time of Your Life, The, 410
Time on My Hands, 83, 84
Time Remembered, 168
Time to Go, 409
Times Like This, 381
Times Square Ballet, 212
Timid Frieda (Les Timides), 399
Timing, 353
Tin Pan Alley, 313
Ting-a-Ling the Bells'll Ring, 49
Tiny Flat Near Soho Square, A, 91, 93
Tiny Room, 206, 209
Tirade, The, 394
Tkambuza (Zulu Hunting Song), 200
To a Small Degree, 238
To Be a Captain, 378
To Be a Performer!, 315
To Be Alone with You, 326
To Be Artistic, 266
To Be Worthy (Worthy of You), 387
To Broadway with Love, 259
To Each His Dulcinea (To Every Man His Dream),
  344
To Get out of This World Alive, 237
To Have and to Hold, 107
To Keep My Love Alive, 105
To Life, 260
To Love You, 387
To Love You and to Lose You, 174
To Make the Boy a Man, 350
To My Wife, 199
To Think That This Could Happen to Me, 132
To War!, 175
To-Night [Schwartz], 141
Today, 255
Today 4 U, 411
Today I'm Gonna Think about Me, 327
Today's the Day (He Loves Me) [Rome], 201

Today's the Day [Henderson], 389
Toddle, 25
Toddlin' Along, 71
Together, 318
Together at Last, 73
Together Forever, 307
Together, Wherever We Go, 232
Tokio Blues, 49
Tom, Dick or Harry, 130
Tomale, 64
Tommy, Tommy, 257
Tomorrow [Porter], 127
Tomorrow [Strouse], 298
Tomorrow Belongs to Me, 333
Tomorrow Is Another Day, 201
Tomorrow Morning [Kander], 333
Tomorrow Morning [Rome], 199
Tomorrow Mountain, 391
Tomorrow's Good Old Days, 350
Tonight [Bernstein], 215
Tonight [Gershwin], 73
Tonight at Eight, 258
Tonight at the Mardi Gras, 51
Tonight in San Francisco, 245
Tonight Quintet, 215
Tonight You Are in Paree, 207
Tonight's the Night, 70
Tony's Thoughts, 247
Too Bad, 132
Too Charming, 326
Too Close for Comfort, 256
Too Darn Hot, 130
Too Good for the Average Man, 98
Too Good to Be Bad, 361
Too Late, Daddy, 407
Too Late Now, 170, 172
Too Many Girls, 101
Too Many Mornings, 280, 281
Too Many People Alone, 306
Too Many Rings around Rosie, 80
Too Many Sweethearts, 48, 49
Too Many Tomorrows, 315
Too Marvelous for Words, 154
Too Much Bowden, 387
Too Old to Be So Young, 240
Too Soon, 200
Too, Too Divine, 160
Toodle-Oo, 79
Tooth and Claw, 391
Top Banana, 392
Top Hat, White Tie and Tails, 51
Top of the Hill, The, 334, 339
Tornado, 403
Tosy and Cosh, 172
Touch of the Irish, A, 209

Touch of Voodoo, A, 207
Touch of Your Hand, The, 33
Tour Must Go On, The, 207
Tower of Babble, 355
Tra-La-La, 62
Tradition, 260
Trailing a Shooting Star, 139
Train Du Ciel, 174
Train Talk, 270
Train That Brought You to Town, The, 245
Train to Johannesburg, 181
Transformation [Menken], 366
Transformation [Wildhorn], 411
Transition (Bonds), 188
Transition (Scenes 7–8) [Passion], 289
Transition (Scenes 10–11) [Passion], 289
Transition from Train Scene (Scenes 11–12)
    [Passion], 289
Transition to Scene 14 [Passion], 289
Traveling Light, xii, 246
Travellin', 265
Treat Me Rough!, 71
Tree in the Park, A, 92
Tree of Knowledge, The, 358
Trial, The, 258
Triangle, The, 14, 16
Trina Works It Out, 372
Trina's Song, 370
Trio (Mormon's Prayer), 224
Trip around the U.S.A., A, 245
Trip to the Library, A, 258, 259
Triple Sec, 185
Triplets, 140, 143
Tripping the Light Fantastic, 198
Trocadero Opening Chorus (New Year Song), 30
Trolley Song, The, 206, 208, 209
Trottin' the Fox, 377
Trouble about the Drama, 31
Trouble in His Brain, 373
Trouble in Tahiti, 213
Trouble Man, 181
Trouble with Women, The, 173, 178
True Love, 132
Truly Content, 277
Truly Loved, 249
Trumpeter, Blow Your Golden Horn!, 72
Trust Me, 408
Truth, The, 315
Try a Little Kiss, 159
Try Again To-morrow, 91
Try Me, 259
Try to Forget, 32
Try to Love Me Just As I Am, 232
Try to Remember, 305, 306
Tschaikowsky (And Other Russians), 177

Tulip Time in Sing-Sing, 26
Tulips (Two Lips), 4
Tum on and Tiss Me, 60
Tumblers, The, 225
Tune in to Station J.O.Y., 64
Tune Up #1, 411
Tune Up #2, 411
Tune Up #3, 411
Tunnel of Love, 412
Turkey Lurkey Time, 400
Turkey Trot, 9
Turn Back, O Man, 355
Turn Me Loose on Broadway, 167
Turning (Shaker Hymn) [Kander], 336
Turning into Something, 410
Turtle Song (One Brave Man Against the Sea), 156
Tuscaloosa, 145
'Twas Not So Long Ago, 31
Tweedledee for President, 73
'Tween a Rock an' a Hard Place, 409
Tweet Tweet, 388
Twelve Days to Christmas, 259
Twenty Fans, 405
Twenty Happy Years, 300
Twenty Miles from Marietta, 414
Twenty Million People, 382
Twenty-Five Words or Less, 244
Twenty-Four Hours of Lovin', 405
Twenty-Two Years, 377
Twin Soliloquies, 108
Twinkle in Your Eye, A, 100
Twinkling Eyes, 85
'Twixt the Devil and the Deep Blue Sea
    [Schwartz], 141
Two Big Eyes, 118
Two by Two [1st], 113
Two by Two [2nd], 113
Two Cheers instead of Three, 50
Two Claudines, 310
Two Faces in the Dark, 396
Two Fairy Tales, 281
Two Feet in Two Four Time, 151
Two Heads, 404
Two Heads Are Better Than One, 15, 21
Two Hearts, 174
Two Ladies, 333
Two Ladies in de Shade of de Banana Tree, 155,
    156
Two Little Angels, 401
Two Little Babes in the Wood, 120, 121
Two Little Bluebirds, 28
Two Little Words, 340
Two Lost Souls, 253
Two of a Kind, 201
Two of Us, The, 206, 207

Two of You, The, 283
Two Old Drybones, 188
Two People in Love, 406
Two Perfect Lovers, 169
Two Sleepy People, 243, 391
Two Step, 340
Two Waltzes in C, 73
Two Years in the Making, 396
Two's Company, 356
Two-A-Day for Keith, 98
Two-Faced Woman, 140
Typical Self-Made American, A, 68, 71

Ugg-a-Wugg, 230
Ugly, Ugly Gal, 237, 240
Uh-Huh, Oh Yeah, 256
Ulysses' Soliloquy, 394
Unafraid, 332
Unborn Love, The, 402
Uncle Chris, 114
Uncle Huck-a-Buck Song, The, 409
Uncle Sam Rag, 396
Under a One-Man Top, 64
Uncle's Last Request, 381
Under the Dress, 132
Under the Gallows Tree, 178
Under the Linden Tree, 5
Under the Roller-Coaster, 337
Under the Sunset Tree, 237
Under the Sea, 365
Under the Tree, 307
Underneath It All, 350
Unfair, 257
Uniform, The, 143
Union League, The, 73
Union Square, 73
Universal Good, 217
Unlikely Lovers, 372
Unlucky in Love, 49
Unnecessary Town, 395
Unofficial Spokesman, The, 68, 71
Unrequited Love, 401
Until I Fell in Love with You, 43
Until You Get Somebody Else, 390
Unusual Way, 376
Unworthy of Your Love, 287
Up and at 'Em, 73
Up to His Old Tricks, 356
Up, Up, Up, 218
Up Where the People Are, 270
Upstairs, 400
Uptown, 302
Uptown, Downtown, 280
Use What You Got, 321
Use Your Imagination, 131

Useless, 182
Usher from the Mezzanine, The, 236

Valse de Rothschild (Never Again), 262
Vanilla Ice Cream, 258
Varsity Drag, The, 389
Vaudeville Ain't Dead, 229
Ve Don't Like It, 52
Ven I Valse, 263
Vendors, 319
Vendor's Song [Blitzstein], 190
Vendors' Calls [Loewe], 223
Venezuela, 233
Venice Gambling Scene (Money, Money), 214
Venus in Ozone Heights, 178
Veranda, The, 188
Verandah Waltz, The, 345
Veronique, 318
Very Next Man, The, 257
Very Nice Man, A, 264
Very Nice Prince, A, 287
Very Soft Shoes, 397
Very Special Day, A, 110
Very, Very, Very, 178
Vicar Song, 24
Victor/Victoria, 408
Victoria, 298
Victoria and Albert Waltz, 298
Victory, 310
Victory Symphony, Eight to the Bar, 195
Vienna, 7
Vigil, The, 351
Villa on a Hill, 377
Villain Dance, 30
Vincent and Vanessa Dance, 280
Violets and Silverbells, 404
Virginia (Don't Go Too Far) [Gershwin], 64
Virginia [Schwartz], 143
Virginia [Youmans], 82
Virtue Wins the Day, 88
Vision Girl, 388
Visit, A, 339
Visit Panama, 128
Vite, Vite, Vite, 127
Vive la Difference, 178
Vivienne, 121
Vodka, 67
Voice Mail #1, 411
Voice Mail #2, 411
Voice Mail #3, 411
Voice Mail #4, 411
Voice Mail #5, 411
Voice of Love, The, 179
Voices, 327
Voices and Visions, 350

Volga Boat Song, The, 120
Volunteer Firemen Picnic (Ladies with a Liberal
    Point of View), 264

Wac Hymn, The, 244
Wade in the Water, 164
Wages of Sin, The, 345
Wail of the Reefer Man, The, 151
Wait, 284
Wait a Bit, Susie, 65, 69
Wait for Me, 200
Wait for the Moon, 120
Wait till Tomorrow, 19
Wait till We're Sixty-Five, 172
Wait till You See Her, 104
Wait till You See Me in the Morning, 391
Waiter's Gallop, 325
Waiter's Song (Bright College Days), 198
Waitin' [Arlen], 156
Waitin' for My Dearie, 223
Waitin' for the Evening Train, 146
Waitin' for the Light to Shine, 406
Waiting [Styne], 233
Waiting around the Comer, 20
Waiting for Life, 382
Waiting for the Girls Upstairs, 280, 281
Waiting for the Sun to Come Out, 60
Waiting for You [Kern], 3
Waiting for You [Youmans], 80
Waiting in the Wings, 347
Wake up and Dream, 121
Wake up, Wake Up!, 378
Walk Him up the Stairs, 402
Walking along Minding My Business, 170
(Walking) Among My Yesterdays, 333
Walking away Whistling, 247
Walking Home with Angeline, 62
Walking Home with Josie, 28
Walking in Space, 399
Walking on Air, 160
Walking Papers, 336
Wallflower, 337
Waltz [House of Flowers], 156
Waltz at Maxim's, 226
Waltz down the Aisle, 124
Waltz from "Nine," 376
Waltz of Long Ago, A, 48
Waltz Was Born in Vienna, A, 221
Wand'rin' Star, 223
Wand'ring Heart, 141
Wanna Be Bad, 391
Want to Join the Angels, 188
Wanting, 302
Wanting Things, 400

Wanting to Be Wanted, 247
War Is a Science, 356
War Is War, 89
War That Ended War, The, 68
Warm All Over, 247
Warm Spring Night, 367
Was I Wazir?, 393
Was She Prettier Than I?, 208
Was That a Smile?, 321
Washington, D.C., 129
Washington Irving's Song, 175
Washington Square, 119
Washington Square Dance, 55
Washington Twist, The, 55
Wasn't It Fun?, 209
Wasteland, The, 358
Watch Dog Theme, 405
Watch My Dust, 237
Watch Your Head, 73
Watch Your Heart, 252
Watch Your Step, 43
Watch Yourself, 88
Watchcries, 277, 278
Water under the Bridge, 161
Water Wears down the Stone, The, 200
Way Back in 1939 A.D., 391
Way down Texas Way, 245
Way down Town, 25
Way It Might Have Been, The, 206
Way out West [Lane], 170
Way out West [Rodgers], 99
Way out West in Jersey [Weill], 178
Way Things Are, The, 200
Way You Look Tonight, The, 143
We Always Disagree, 159
We Are a Gang of Witches, 110
We Are China, 300
We Are Cut in Twain, 175
We Are One (I'll Never Leave You), 301
We Are the Rhythms That Color Your Song, 408
We Are What We Are, 329
We Are Women, 217
We Belong to You, 201
We Belong Together, 33
We Beseech Thee, 355
We Both Reached for the Gun, 335
We Can Be Proud, 190
We Can Make It, 337
We Could Be Close, 239
We Dance [Flaherty], 382
We Dance [Merrill], 267
We Deserve Each Other, 110
We Do Not Belong Together, 286
We Don't Matter at All, 296

We Dwell in Our Hearts, 345
We Go Together, 402
We Got Annie!, 298, 299
We Gotta Go, 321
We Had a Dream, 321
We Kiss in a Shadow, 109
We Like It Over Here, 144
We Love You Conrad, 294
We Loves Ya, Jimey, 396
We Make a Beautiful Pair, 403
We Must Have a Ball, 218
We Need a Little Christmas, 326, 327
We Need Him, 296
We Only Remember, 266, 326
We Open in Venice, 130
We Shall Never Be Younger, 130
We Share Everything, 412
We Should Care (Let the Lazy Sun Refuse to Care) [1st], 49
We Should Care (Let the Sun Start to Cry) [2nd], 49
We Sing America, 193
We Somehow Feel That You Enjoyed Our Show, 162
We Speak the Same Language, 295
We Start Today, 406
We Still Have Time, 411
We Still Like Ike, 55
We Were So Young, 31
We Will Take the Road Together, 26
We'd Like to Thank You, Herbert Hoover, 298
We'll Be the Same, 96
We'll Go Away Together, 179
We'll Have Tomorrow, 364
We'll Live All Over Again, 164
We'll Meet Tomorrow, 378, 379
We'll See, 18
We'll Take a Glass Together, 377
We'll Take Care of You All (Refugee Song), 13, 14
We're Alive, 190
We're All of Us Excited, 80
We're Almost There, 328
We're Crooks, 20
We're Getting Away with It, 387
We're Going to Be Pals, 18
We're Gonna Be All Right, 113
We're Gonna Work It Out, 336
We're Gymnastic, 28
We're Having a Baby (My Baby and Me), 164
We're Heading for a Wedding, 321
We're Here Because, 65
We're Home, 264
We're Okay, 411
We're on Our Way, 16

We're on Our Way to France, 45
We're Pals, 59
We're Still Friends, 317
We've Done Alright, 240
We've Got It, 317
Wealth, 261
Wear a Little Grin, 267
Weary Near to Dyin', 266
Wedding, The [Milk and Honey], 324
Wedding [Show Boat], 30
Wedding Bells Are Calling Me, 15, 16
Wedding Chorale [Candide], 214
Wedding Dance [Brigadoon], 223
Wedding Dance [Fiddler on the Roof], 260
Wedding Knell [Sunny], 28
Wedding of Words and Music, 45
Wedding Reception, The, 412
Wedding Scene [Sunny], 28
Wedding Song [The Threepenny Opera], 182
Wee Golden Warrior, The, 114
Weekend Affair, A, 123
Weekend in the Country, A, 281, 282, 287
Weeping Willow Tree, 27, 31
Weird Romance, 366
Welcome [Leigh], 345
Welcome [Styne], 236
Welcome Back, Mr. Witherspoon, 381
Welcome Hinges, 154
Welcome Home [Adler], 253
Welcome Home [Rome], 199
Welcome Home, Son, 356
Welcome to Brooklyn, 382
Welcome to Holiday Inn, 316
Welcome to Kanagawa, 283
Welcome to the Theatre, 297
Well, Did You Evah?, 128
Well, I'm Not, 300
Well Known Fact, A, 307
Wells Fargo Wagon, The, 269
Wendy, 230
Were Thine That Special Face?, 130
West End Avenue, 356
West Wind [Weill], 178
West Wind [Youmans], 82
Western People Funny, 109
Westphalia Chorale, 217
Westpointer, The, 174
Wet, 340
What a Blessing, 248
What a Case I've Got on You!, 138
What a Charming Couple, 146
What a Country!, 295
What a Crazy Way to Spend Sunday, 129
What a Game!, 383

What a Great Pair We'll Be, 126
What a Guy, 361
What a Joy to Be Young, 125
What a Lovely Day for a Wedding, 102, 107
What a Nice Municipal Park, 125
What a Piece of Work Is Man, 399
What a Remarkable Age This Is!, 378
What a Waste, 213
What a Wonderful World, 142
What a Young Girl Ought to Know, 141
What Am I Doing Here?, 400
What Am I Gonna Do?, 69
What Am I Gonna Do without You?, 296
What Am I to Do?, 127
What Am I Waiting For?, 414
What Are Little Husbands Made of, 128
What Are They Doing to Us Now?, 200
What Are We Going to Do with All the Jeeps?, 52
What Are We Here For?, 70
What Are You Going to Do about It?, 301
What Became of Me?, 296, 301
What Can One Man Do?, 352
What Can You Do with a General?, 53
What Can You Do With a Man?, 101
What Can You Say in a Love Song?, 152
What Causes That?, 70
What Chance Have I with Love?, 51
What Could Be Better Than That?, 406
What Did Della Wear? (When Georgie Came Across), 137
What Did I Ever See in Him?, 294
What Did I Have That I Don't Have?, 172
What Do You Do in the Infantry?, 243
What Do I Care for a Dame?, 103
What Do I Have to Do to Get My Picture in the Paper?, 54
What Do I See in You?, 207
What Do the Simple Folk Do?, 225
What Do We Care?, 150
What Do We Do? We Fly!, 113
What Do You Give to a Man Who's Had Everything?, 239
What Do You Think about Men?, 131
What Do You Think I Am?, 205
What Do You Want of Me?, 344
What Does He Look Like?, 52
What Does He Want of Me?, 344
What Does Your Servant Dream About?, 130
What Good Are Words?, 34
What Good Does It Do?, 156
What Good Is Love, 193
What Good Would the Moon Be?, 179
What Happened?, 165
What Happened to Me Tonight?, 253
What Happened to the Old Days?, 337

What Happened, What?, 345
What Has He Got?, 162
What I Did for Love, 359
What I Say Goes, 331
What I Was Warned About, 206
What I'm Longing to Say, 19
What I've Always Wanted, 296
What If You're Not?, 167
What in the World Did You Want?, 208
What Is a Friend For?, 156
What Is a Man?, 103
What Is a Woman?, 307
What Is He Waiting For?, 358
What Is It?, 90
What Is Love? [Berlin], 43
What Is Love? [Rome], 201
What Is That Tune?, 126
What Is the Stars? (Life on the Sea), 190
What Is There to Say?, 161
What Is This Feeling in the Air?, 234
What Is This Thing Called Love?, 121
What Kind of Fool Am I?, 412
What Kind of Woman, 383
What Makes a Marriage Merry?, 237
What Makes Me Love Him? [Bock], 261
What Makes Me Love You? [Berlin], 50
What More Can I Say?, 372
What More Do I Need?, 274
What More Do I Want?, 180
What Shall I Do?, 126
What Sort of Wedding Is This?, 73
What Takes My Fancy, 314
What the World Needs Now, 400
What Will It Be?, 188
What Would I Do?, 372
What Would I Do If I Could Feel?, 403
What Would We Do without You?, 279
What Would You Do?, 333
What You Don't Know about Women, 320
What You Need, 377
What You Own, 411
What You See Is What You Get, 301
What You Want wid Bess?, 74
What'll I Do?, 48
What'll They Think of Next?, 391
What's Goin' on Here?, 224
What's Good for General Bullmouse, 395
What's-His-Name, 208
What's in It for Me? [Rome], 200
What's in It for You? [Bock], 258
What's My Man Gonna Be Like?, 122
What's New at the Zoo?, 233, 234
What's the Use? [Bernstein], 214
What's the Use? [Rodgers], 91
What's the Use of Talking, 91

What's the Use of Wond'rin'?, 106
What's There about Me?, 49
What's Wrong with Me?, 252, 253
What's Wrong with That?, 302
Whatever Lola Wants (Lola Gets), 253
Whatever Time There Is, 299
Whatever You Do, 141
Wheatless Day, 20
Wheels of a Dream, 383
When, 114
When a Mother Doesn't Matter Any More, 294
When a New Star, 34
When a Woman Has a Baby, 179
When Daddy Comes Home, 265
When Daniel Marries, 382
When Did I Fall in Love?, 257
When Do the Good Things Start?, 351, 398
When Do We Dance?, 66
When Does This Feeling Go Away?, 206, 207
When Gemini Meets Capricorn, 200
When He Comes Home, 244
When I Come around Again, 172
When I Discover My Man, 23
When I Discovered You, 43
When I Fell in Love with You, 28
When I First Saw You, 405
When I Get Back to the U.S.A., 43
When I Go on the Stage [1st], 88
When I Go on the Stage [2nd], 94
When I Go out Walking with My Baby, 105, 115
When I Grow up (G-Man Song), 193
When I Had a Uniform On, 119
When I Lost You, 39, 40
When I See You, 273, 274
When I Used to Lead the Ballet, 118
When I Valse, 263
When I Walk with You, 391
When I Was a Little Cuckoo, 129
When I'm Being Born Again, 172
When I'm By Your Side, 412
When I'm Drunk I'm Beautiful, 238
When I'm Not Near the Girl I Love, 171, 172
When I'm out with You, 43
When In Love, 367
When It Dries, 113
When It Happens to You, 241
When It's Cactus Time in Arizona, 72
When It's Love, 165
When It's Night Time in Dixie Land, 43
When Love Beckoned (In Fifty-second Street), 128
When Love Come to Call, 132
When Love Comes Your Way, 124, 125
When Mabel Comes in the Room, 327
When Me, Mowgli, Love, 125
When Messiah Comes, 260

When My Baby Goes to Town, 129
When My Caravan Comes Home, 120
When My Dreams Come True, 49
When Nations Get Together, 73
When Our Ship Comes Sailing In, 68
When the Bo-Tree Blossoms Again, 29
When the Boys Come Home, 154
When the Children Are Asleep, 106
When the Curtain Falls, 45
When the Duchess Is Away, 178
When the Idle Poor Become the Idle Rich, 171
When the Kids Get Married, 307
When the Lights Are Low, 17
When the Nylons Bloom Again, 391
When the Old World Was New, 96
When the Ships Come Home, 20
When the Spring Is in the Air, 33
When the Sun Goes down in the South, 406
When the Weather's Better, 236
When Three Is Company (Cupid Song), 12, 19
When Toby Is out of Town, 65
When Velma Takes the Stand, 335
When We Are Married, 86
When We Get Our Divorce, 28
When We Meet Again, 196
When We Tell Them about It All, 30
When We Were Young, 394
When We're Home on the Range, 129
When We're Running a Little Hotel of Our Own, 49
When Will Grown-Ups Grow Up?, 300
When You Gonna Learn?, 254
When You Live on an Island, 166
When You Love Only One, 141
When You Meet a Man in Chicago, 239
When You Smile (I Smile), 302, 303
When You Speak with a Lady, 298
When You Take the Road with Me, 26
When You Wake up Dancing, 21
When You Want 'Em You Can't Get 'Em (When You've Got 'Em, You Don't Want 'Em), 57
When You're Big, 410
When You're Far Away from New York Town, 146
When You're Good to Mama, 335
When You're in Love [Schwartz], 145
When You're in Love You'll Know, 17
When You're in My Arms, 360
When You're in Town, 40
When You're Right, You're Right, 337
When You're Sad, 80
When Your Favorite Girl's Not There, 19
When Your Troubles Have Started, 126
Whenever I Dream, 373
Where?, 190
Where Am I Going?, 315, 316

Where Are the Men?, 125
Where Are the Snows?, 307
Where Can He Be?, 140
Where Can You Take a Girl?, 400
Where Did Everybody Go?, 332
Where Did It Go?, 308
Where Did That Little Dog Go?, 351
Where Did the Night Go?, 198
Where Do I Go?, 399, 400
Where Do I Go from Here? [Bock], 257
Where Do I Go from Here? [Schwartz], 143
Where East Meets West, 61
Where Has My Hubby Gone? Blues, 80
Where Have We Met Before?, 161
Where Have You Been?, 123
Where in the World [Simon], 407
Where in the World [Yeston], 378
Where Is My Hero?, 391
Where Is My Little Old New York?, 49
Where Is My Soldier Boy?, 201
Where Is My Son?, 114
Where Is She?, 63
Where Is the Life That Late I Led?, 130
Where Is the Man I Married?, 208
Where Is the Man of My Dreams?, 62
Where Is the Music Coming From?, 240
Where Is the One Who Will Mourn Me When I'm
  Gone?, 180
Where Is the Song of Songs for Me?, 55
Where Is the Warmth?, 357
Where Oh Where [Porter], 131
Where Oh Where [Waldman], 404
Where or When, 99
Where Sunset Meets the Sea, 390
Where the Delicatessan Flows (In Sardinia), 66
Where the Hudson River Flows, 89
Where Was I When They Passed out Luck?, 350
Where Will You Stand When the Flood Comes?,
  414
Where Would You Get Your Coat?, 122
Where You Are [Kander], 339
Where You Are [Schwartz], 146
Where You Go, I Go, 73
Where's Charley?, 245
Where's My Shoe?, 259
Where's That Little Girl (In the Little Green Hat?),
  90, 91
Where's That Rainbow?, 92
Where's the Boy? Here's the Girl, 70
Where's the Girl for Me?, 14, 22
Where's the Mate for Me?, 30
Wherever He Ain't, 327
Wherever They Fly the Flag of Old England, 130
Which?, 121
Which Door?, 261

Which Way Is Home?, 201
Which Way?, 295
While the City Sleeps, 296
While You Are Young, 150
Whip-Poor-Will, 22, 23, 24
Whispers, 85
Whistle When You're Lonely, 8
Whistling Dan, 14, 19
White Boys, 399
White Christmas, 52
White Heat, 140
Whizzer Going Down, 369
Who? [Berlin], 49
Who? [Kern], 28
Who Am I? [Bernstein], 212
Who Am I? [Weill], 178
Who Am I? (That You Should Care for Me)
  [Youmans], 82
Who Am I, Anyway?, 359
Who Are These People?, 300
Who Are You?, 100
Who Are You Now?, 235
Who But You?, 126
Who Can I Turn To? (When Nobody Needs Me),
  412
Who Can? You Can!, 146
Who Cares? [Gershwin], 72
Who Cares? [Kern], 18
Who Could Be Blue?, 280
Who Could Ever Have Dreamed up You, 378
Who Could Marry a Gigolo?, 401
Who Couldn't Dance with You?, 377
Who Do You Love, I Hope?, 53
Who Gives a Sou?, 207
Who Is Hannah?, 267
Who Is He?, 352
Who Is Mr. Big?, 233
Who Is Samuel Cooper?, 180
Who Is She?, 261
Who Is the Bravest?, 230
Who Is the Lucky Girl to Be?, 72
Who Knows?, 200
Who Knows What Might Have Been?, 234
Who Made the Rumba?, 164
Who Needs Her?, 265
Who Said Gay Paree?, 132
Who Says There Ain't No Santa Claus?, 392
Who Taught Her Everything?, 235
Who to Love If Not a Stranger?, 345
Who Wants to Live in New York?, 285
Who, Who Do You Think You Are?, 403
Who Will Love Me As I Am?, 412
Who Would Have Dreamed? [Kander], 337
Who Would Have Dreamed? [Porter], 128
Who Would've Thought?, 361

Who'll Buy?, 181
Who's Afraid of the Big Bad Wolf?, 390
Who's Been Sitting in My Chair?, 396
Who's Excited?, 167
Who's Got the Pain?, 253
Who's That Girl?, 297
Who's That Woman?, 280, 281
Who's the Greatest?, 73
Who's Who with You?, 77, 78
Whoever You Are I Love You, 400
Whole New World, A, 365
Whole World's Waitin' to Sing Your Song, The, 407
Whoop-De-Oodle-Doo!, 25
Whoop-ti-ay!, 224
Whoopsie!, 94
Whose Baby Are You?, 23
Why? [Kern], 19
Why? [Rodgers], 114
Why? [Styne], 240
Why Am I Me?, 404
Why Am I So Happy?, 300
Why Be Afraid to Dance?, 199
Why Can't a Woman Be More Like a Man?, 224
Why Can't I?, 95
Why Can't I Speak?, 334, 340
Why Can't I Walk through That Door?, 310
Why Can't the English?, 224
Why Can't the World Go and Leave Us Alone?, 301
Why Can't This Night Last Forever?, 222
Why Can't We All Be Nice?, 350
Why Can't You Behave?, 130
Why Did They Die?, 201
Why Did You Do It?, 143
Why Didn't We Meet Before?, 119
Why Do I?, 90
Why Do I Love You? [Gershwin], 66
Why Do I Love You? [Kern], 29, 32
Why Do They Call a Private a Private? (When His Life's a Public Event), 244
Why Do You Suppose?, 95
Why Do You Want to Know Why?, 49
Why Do You Wanta Hurt Me So?, 131
Why Don't They Dance the Polka Anymore?, 13
Why Don't They Give Us a Chance?, 43
Why Don't They Leave Us Alone, 321
Why Don't We Try Staying Home?, 122
Why Fight This?, 157
Why Go Anywhere at All?, 146
Why Him?, 172
Why, Mama, Why?, 353
Why Marry Them?, 123
Why Me?, 113
Why Not Have a Little Party?, 138

Why Not Katie?, 395
Why, Oh Why?, 81
Why Should I Wake Up?, 333
Why Shouldn't I?, 125
Why Sing a Love Song?, 255
Why Speak of Money?, 73
Why Was I Born?, 31
Why We Tell the Story, 382
Wick, 407
Widow at Windsor, The, 298
Wife Never Understan', 158
Wifie of Your Own, A, 13
Wild about You, 52
Wild Justice, The, 181
Wild Rose, 24
Wild West Show/Dog Act, 321
Wildcat [Coleman], 314
Wildcats [Rodgers], 107
Wildflower, 78
Wilkommen (Welcome), 333
Will He Like Me?, 258, 259
Will I?, 411
Will I Ever Tell You?, 270
Will It All End in Smoke?, 12
Will She Come from the East? (East-North-West-or South), 48
Will You Forgive Me?, 87, 88
Will You Love Me Monday Morning?, 102, 152
Will You Marry Me?, 108, 110
Will You Remember Me? [Gershwin], 65
Will You Remember Me? [Weill], 175
Will-a-Mania, 320
Willing to Ride (Here I Go Again), 340
Windflowers, 394
Wine and Peaches, 337
Wine! Wine! (Champagne Song), 3
Wint's Song, 264
Winter and Summer, 308
Winter in New York, 338
Winter's on the Wing, 407
Wintergreen for President, 72, 73
Wish I May, 205
Wish Them Well, 107
Wish You Were Here, 198
Wishes Won't Wash Dishes, 309
Wishing, 38
Wishing Well Scene, 27
Witchcraft, 313
Witches' Brew, 237
With a Family Reputation, 49
With a Little Bit of Luck, 224
With a Song in My Heart, 95
With Every Breath I Take, 320
With Music, 53
With My Head in the Clouds, 52

With So Little to Be Sure of, 277, 278
With You [S. Schwartz], 356
With You [Shire], 406
With You Here and Me Here, 141
With You on My Arm, 329
Within the Quota, 120
Within This Empty Space, 308
Without a Song, 82
Without Love, 132
Without Me, 333
Without Rhythm, 150
Without the Girl—Inside!, 6
Without You [Coleman], 321
Without You [Larson], 410
Without You [Loewe], 224
Without You I'm Nothing, 256
Without Your Music, 378
Woman [Kander], 334
Woman Alone, A [Grossman], 351
Woman Alone, A [Strouse], 296, 301
Woman for the Man Who Has Everything, The, 296
Woman in His Room, The, 245
Woman in Love, A [Loesser], 246
Woman in Love [Merrill], 266
Woman Is a Sometime Thing, A, 74
Woman of the Year, 337
Woman Who Lived up There, The, 179
Woman Who Thinks I'm Wonderful, A, 301
Woman's Career, A, 130
Woman's Prerogative, A, 155
Woman's Touch, A, 68
Women [Rodgers], 97
Won't You Have a Little Feather?, 6
Won't You Kiss Me Once before I Go?, 4
Won't You Let Me Carry Your Parcel?, 7
Wonderful Copenhagen, 246
Wonderful Dad, 26
Wonderful Guy, A, 108
Wonderful Music, 306
Wonderful Party, 331
Wonderful Way to Die, A, 308
Wonderful World of the Two-a-Day, 323
Wonderworld, 235
Wooden Wedding, 178
Woodman, Woodman, Spare That Tree!, 39
Woodstock's Theme, 351
Word a Day, A, 392
Word of the Lord, The, 216
Words Are Not Needed, 19
Words without Music, 162
Words, Words, Words [Duke], 168
Words, Words, Words (Martin's Laughing Song) [Bernstein], 217
Words of Doom, 358

Workin' It Out, 360
Working for the Government, 87
Workout, 296
World According to Snoopy, The, 351
World Has Gone Insane, The, 412
World Is Beautiful Today, The, 230
World Is Comin' to a Start, The, 402
World Is Full of Villains, The, 178
World Is in My Arms, The, 170
World Is Mean, The, 182
World Is Mine, The, 69, 71
World Is Your Balloon, The, 392
World Take Me Back, 325
World without End, 216
World without You, A, 358
Worlds Apart [Bock], 258
Worlds Apart [Miller], 406
Worries, 27
Worst Pies in London, The, 284
Worth It, 366
Worthy of You, 387
Would You Be So Kindly, 170
Wouldn't It Be Loverly?, 224
Wouldn't You Like to Be on Broadway?, 179
Wow-Ooh-Wolf, 129
Wrapped in a Ribbon and Tied with a Bow, 179
Writer Writes at Night, A, 114
Wrong Note Rag, The, 213
Wunderbar, 130

Xanadu, 200

Y'all Got It, 403
Y'assou, 334
Ya Got Me, 211
Ya Got Trouble, 269
Ya Never Know, 364
Ya-Ta-Ta, 107
Yank, Yank, Yank, 244
Yankee Boy, 302
Yankee Dollar, (Hooray for The), 156
Yankee Doodle Blues, 62
Yankee Doodle on the Line, 21
Yankee Doodle Polka, 163
Yankee Doodle Rhythm, 68, 69
Yankee Doodles Are Coming to Town, 172
Year after Year, 64
Year from Today, A, 27
Year of the Child, 372
Years Are Passing By, The, 367
Years before Us, The, 245
Yellow Mask, 160
Yes [Finn], 373
Yes [Kander], 334, 335
Yes, Ma'am! (You're from the Show Boat), 30

Yes, My Heart, 264
Yesterday I Loved You, 397
Yesterday, Tomorrow and Today, 367
Yesterday's Forgotten, 168
Yesterdays, 33
Yip Ahoy, 194
Yip Yip Yaphanker's Introduction, 52
Yo-Ho-Ho, The, 248
You [Rodgers], 113
You [Schwartz], 139
You—U.S.A., 166
You after All These Years, 165
You Ain't Hurtin' Your Ole Lady None, 238
You Alone Would Do (I'd Want Only You), 27
You Always Love the Same Girl, 105
You and I (In Old Versailles) [Gershwin], 63
You and I [Willson], 269
You and I Know, 143
You and I, Love, 335
You & Me [Mancini], 408
You and Me [Porter], 121
You and the Night and the Music, 141, 147
You Are All That's Beautiful, 168
You Are Beautiful, 111
You Are Doing Very Well, 34
You Are for Loving, 205, 208, 209
You Are Home, 253
You Are Love, 29
You Are Music, 377
You Are My Own, 377
You Are Never Away, 107
You Are Not Real, 261
You Are So Fair, 99
You Are So Lovely and I'm So Lonely, 97
You Are the Only One, 364
You Are Too Beautiful, 97
You Are Unforgettable, 177
You Are Woman, I Am Man, 231, 235
You Are You [Gershwin], 67
You Are You [Kander], 332
You Boys Are Gonna Get Me in Trouble, 373
You Can Always Count on Me, 320
You Can Be a New Yorker, Too!, 301
You Can Dance with Any Girl at All, 80
You Can Have Him, 54
You Can Never Go Back, 300
You Can't Brush Me Off, 52
You Can't Fool Your Dreams, 87
You Can't Get a Man with a Gun, 53
You Can't Get Away from a Dumb Tomato, 110
You Can't Keep a Good Girl Down (Joan of Arc), 24
You Can't Make Love by Wireless, 26, 31
You Can't Miss It, 395
You Can't Win, 403
You Cannot Make Your Shimmy Shake on Tea, 46

You Could Drive a Person Crazy, 279
You Could Hurt Me, 310
You Could Never Shame Me, 339
You Did It!, 224
You Do, 345
You Do, I Don't, 160
You Do Something to Me, 122
You Don't Have to Do It for Me, 350
You Don't Have to Kiss Me Goodnight, 270
You Don't Know, 271
You Don't Know Paree, 122
You Don't Know This Man, 414
You Don't Remind Me, 131
You Don't Tell Me, 112
You Fascinate Me So, 314
You for Me, 157
You Found Me and I Found You, 20
You Gave Me Ev'rything but Love, 150
You Got a Suckling Pig, 404
You Gotta Die Sometime, 372
You Gotta Get a Gimmick, 232, 233
You Gotta Look out for Yourself, 320
You Have Cast Your Shadow on the Sea, 100, 101
You Have Everything, 143
You Have Got to Have a Rudder on the Ark, 13
You Have It All, 367
You Have to Do What You Do Do, 178
You Haven't Changed at All, 223
You I Like, 328
You Interest Me, 351
You Irritate Me So, 128
You Know and I Know, 14, 15
You Might Get to Like Me, 266
You Must Come Over, 24
You Must Meet My Wife, 281, 282
You Mustn't Feel Discouraged, 236
You Mustn't Kick It Around, 103
You Need a Hobby, 55
You Never Can Blame a Girl for Dreaming, 78
You Never Can Tell, 13
You Never Had It So Good, 110, 115
You Never Knew about Me, 19
You Never Know [Porter], 126
You Never Know What Hit You (When It's Love), 197, 198
You Never Looked Better, 238
You Never Say Yes, 95
You Okay Honey?, 411
You or No One, 157
You Oughta Be Here with Me, 406
You Poor Thing, 190
You Rat You, 298
You Remember, 366
You Remind Me of You, 350
You Said It, 150

You Said Something, 18
You Say You Care, 228
You Should Be Loved, 412
You Should See Yourself, 315
You Started Something, 78, 80
You Tell 'Em, 22
You There in the Back Row, 319
You, Too, Can Be a Puppet, 392
You Took Advantage of Me, 94
You Took Me by Surprise, 164
You Treacherous Man, 258
You Understand Me [Loesser], 249
You Understand Me So, 180
You Wanna Bet?, 315
You Want the Best Seats, We Have 'Em, 25
You Wanted Me, I Wanted You, 149
You Wash and I'll Dry, 222
You Were Dead, You Know, 214
You Will—Won't You?, 28
You Will Never Be Lonely, 146
You Won't Be an Orphan for Long, 298
You Wouldn't Be You, 240
You You You (Could Be Annie 2), 302, 303
You'd Be Surprised, 46
You'd Better Love Me, 208
You'd Do for Me—I'd Do for You, 160
You'll Do, 150
You'll Find Me Playing Mah-Jongg, 26
You'll Have to Change, 345
You'll Never Get Away from Me, 232
You'll Never Know [Rodgers], 88
You'll Never Walk Alone, 106, 273
You'll See, 411
You'll Think of Someone, 400
You're a Bad Influence on Me, 126
You're a Builder Upper, 152
You're a Funny Girl, 235
You're a Good Man, Charlie Brown, 398
You're a Liar!, 314
You're a Lovable Lunatic, 317
You're a Queer One, Julie Jordan, 106
You're a Sentimental Guy, 55
You're a Sucker for a Dame, 55
You're All the World to Me, 170, 172
You're As English As, 253
You're Devastating, 33
You're Everywhere, 83
You're Far Away from Home, 314
You're Far from Wonderful, 167
You're Far Too Near Me, 178
You're Gonna Dance with Me, Willie, 230
You're Gonna Love Tomorrow, 280
You're Here and I'm Here, 12, 13
You're in Love, 123
You're Just in Love (I Wonder Why?), 55

You're Lonely and I'm Lonely, 52
You're Lucky, 205
You're My Friend, Aintcha?, 263
You're My Girl [Styne], 228
You're My Star, 347
You're Nearer, 101
You're Never Fully Dressed without a Smile, 298, 299
You're Not Alone (Jef) [Brel], 399
You're Not Fooling Me, 306
You're Not the Mayor, 301
You're Not the Type, 146
You're Nothing without Me, 320
You're OK, U.S.A.!, 245
You're on the Lido Now, 91
You're So Beautiful, 46
You're So Beautiful That . . . , 392
You're So Much a Part of Me, 251
You're the Girl, 190
You're the Mother Type, 92, 94
You're the One, 136
You're the Only Girl He Loves, 10, 20
You're the Sunrise, 138
You're the Top, 124, 125
You're Too Far Away, 124
You're What I Need, 94
You're Your Highness to Me, 195
You've Built a Fire down in My Heart, 39, 40
You've Come Home, 314
You've Got a Hold on Me, 222
You've Got Me out on a Limb, 387
You've Got Possibilities, 296, 297
You've Got Something, 126
You've Got That Thing, 122
You've Got to Be Carefully Taught, 108
You've Got to Be Way Out to Be Way In, 55
You've Got What Gets Me, 71
You've Got What I Need, Baby, 296, 297
You've Never Kissed Her, 265
You-oo Just You, 57
Youkali, 174
Young, 300
Young and Foolish, 394, 395
Young People Gotta Dance, 247
Young People Think about Love, 175
Young Pretty Girl Like You, A, 400
Younger Man, A, 302, 303
Younger Than Springtime, 108
Your Daddy's Son, 383
Your Dream (Is the Same As My Dream), 34
Your Eyes, 410
Your Eyes Are Blue, 276
Your Fault, 287
Your Good Morning, 323, 324
Your Hand in Mine, 324

Your Lips and Me, 369
Your Lullaby, 88
Your Own College Band, 245
Your Work—and Nothing More, 412
Yours Sincerely, 95
Yours, Yours, Yours!, 401
Youth, Joy and Freedom, 230
Yuletide, Park Avenue, 196
Yum-Ticky-Tum-Tum, 264

Zenda, 168
Zip, 103
Zodiac Song, 177, 178
Zoltar Speaks, 410
Zorba Theme (Life Is), 334
Zorba's Dance, 334
Zubbediya, 393
Zulu Love Song (Wait for Me), 200

SHOW INDEX

This index includes all musicals and plays, as well as basic property material, motion pictures, etc. The principal listings for productions written by the major composers (or included as notable scores) are denoted by boldfaced page numbers.

About Face!, **244**
Act, The, 335, **336**, 337, 341
Addie Pray, 353
Aeneas Africanus, 176
Ah, Wilderness, 264
Ain't Broadway Grand, 346, **347**
Ain't Misbehavin', 388, 391, 406
Aladdin [film], 365
Aladdin [TV musical], 132
Alive and Kicking, **197**
All Aboard!, **42**
All about Eve, 297
All American, **295**
All in One, 213
All in the Family, 402
All That Glitters, **273–74**
Allegro, **107–108**
All's Fair, 104
Along Came Ruth, **42**
Always You, 87
Amazons, The, 11
America Kicks Up Its Heels, **370**, 371
American in Paris, 224
American Jubilee, **144**
Americana [1st], **67**, 151
Americana [3rd], **151**
America's Sweetheart, **96–97**
Amphitryon, 131
Anastasia, 383
Anatol, 146
And the World Goes 'Round, **338–39**, 340
And There I Stood with My Piccolo, 269
Androcles and the Lion, **188**
Angel, 404
Angel in the Wings, **197**
Angels in America, 408
Animal Crackers, 71
Anna and the King of Siam, 108

Anna Christie, 263
Annie, 35, 277, 279, **298–99**, 302, 303, 304, 318, 329, 375
Annie Get Your Gun, **53**, **55–56**, 86, 108, 111, 129
Annie 2 (Miss Hannigan's Revenge), **302–303**, 304
Annie Warbucks, 302, **303–304**
Another Part of the Forest, **188**
Antler, 381
Anya, 393
Anyone Can Whistle, 276, **277**, 284, 288
Anything Goes, **124–25**, 126
Apartment, The, 239, 400
Applause, 279, **297**, 345
Apple Tree, The, **261**, 277
Apprenticeship of Duddy Kravitz, The, **365**
April Song, **346**
Aquacade, 236
archie & mehitable, 295
Are You a Mason?, **37**
Arms and the Man, 224
Around the World, **130**
Around the World in Eighty Days, 130
Artists and Models, **169**
Arturo Ui, **234**, 239
As the Girls Go, 346
As Thousands Cheer, **50–51**, 152
As You Were, **119**
Assassins, **287–88**
At Ease, 91, 142, 143, 152, 153, 162
At Home Abroad, **141–42**, 144
At the Circus, 154
At the Grand, 376, 377, 394
Aufstieg und Fall der Stadt Mahagonny, 173
Auntie Mame, 157, 326
Aupres de Ma Blonde, 274
Aviator, The, 45
Away We Go!, 104

Babe, 363–64
Babes and the Baron, The, **4**
Babes in Arms, 98–99, 115
Babes in the Wood, 4
Baby, **405–406**, 410
Baby Mine, 21
Bajour, 336
Baker Street, 114, **260**
Baker's Wife, The, 249, **356–57**
Ballet Ballads, 391, 394
Ballroom, 360
Band Wagon, The, 32, 123, **139–40**
Banjo Eyes, **164**, 166
Bar Mitzvah Boy, **240**
Barnum, 318–19
Battle of the Giants, 364
Beat the Band, 103
Beauty and the Beast, 279, **366**, 413
Beauty and the Beast [film], 365, 366
Beauty of Bath, The, **4**, 17
Beauty Prize, The, **26**
Beggar on Horseback, 273
Beggar's Holiday, **391–92**
Beggar's Opera, The, 173, 181, 391, 392
Begum, The, 12
Bells Are Ringing, **231**, 232, 237, 242
Ben Franklin in Paris, **326**
Benny Leonard and the Brooklyn Bridge, 369
Best Foot Forward, 19, **103**, **205–206**, 208
Best Little Whorehouse Goes Public, The, 405
Best Little Whorehouse in Texas, The, 353, 363, 375, 390, **404–405**
Betsy, **49**, **92**
Between the Devil, **143**
Big, **409–10**
Big As Life, **255**, 273
Big Country, 394
Big River, 406
Billion Dollar Baby, 213
Birdcage, The, 375
Blackbirds of 1928, 143, 150, **389**
Bless You All, **197–98**
Blithe Spirit, 208
Bloomer Girl, **154**, 155–56
Blue Angel, 392
Blue Eyes, **30–31**
Blue Monday, 62
Blues in the Night, 154
Body Beautiful, The, **256**, 296
Bojangles, **299–300**
Bonanza Bound, 213
Bone Room, The, **308–309**
Born to Dance, 125
Bow-Wows, The, **160**
Boys and Betty, The, **37**

Boys from Syracuse, The, **100–101**, 103, 115, 205–206, 254
Breakfast at Tiffany's, 238, **265**, 266, 398
Breath of Spring, 334
Brecht on Brecht, **182**
Brewster's Millions, 22
Brigadoon, 53, 180, **223**, 224, 225, 226, 301
Bring Back Birdie, **300**, 302, 304, 337
Bring in 'da Noise, Bring in 'da Funk, **409**, 411
Bring on the Girls, **141**
Broadway, 103
Broadway Brevities of 1920, **47**, 60
Broadway Musical, A, **299**, 304
Brown Sugar, **150**
Buddies, **119**
Bunch and Judy, The, **25**
Buried Alive, 237
Burning Bright, 110–11
Butterflies Are Free, 355
By Bernstein, **218**
By Jupiter, **103–104**
By the Beautiful Sea, **145**
Bye Bye Birdie, 265, **294–95**, 296–97, 300, 304, 324, 326, 331, 364, 403

Cabaret, 279, **332–33**, 334, 335, 337, 340, 377
Cabaret Girl, The, **24–25**, 26
Cabin in the Sky, 154, **163–64**, 205, 214, 222, 394
Caesar and Cleopatra, 261
Cafe Crown, 397
Call Me Madam, **54–55**
Call Me Mister, 196, 198
Camelot, 208, **225**, 288
Canary, The, **21**, 46
Can-Can, **131–32**
Candide [1956], **214**, 215, 219, 394
Candide [1974], **217–18**, 270
Candle Light, 126
Capitol Revue, 57, 59
Carmelina, **172**
Carmen Jones, 129
Carnival!, 235, **264–65**, 267, 295, 326
Carousel, 53, **106–107**, 108, 109, 115, 273, 404
Casablanca, 197
Casey Jones, 166
Cat and the Fiddle, The, **32**, 33
Catch a Star, **255**
Catch of the Season, The, **3–4**
Cats, 359
Celebration, 307–308
Century Girl, The, 20, **44**
Charley's Aunt, 245
Charlie and Algernon, **299**
Charlot's Revue [1924], 68, **79**, 81
Charly, 299

Charm School, The, **23**, 89
Chee-Chee, **94**, 111, 122
Chicago, 335–36, 337, 340–41
Children of Eden, **358**
Chocolate Soldier, The, 224
Chorus Line, A, 114, 340, **359–60**, 361–62
Christmas Carol, A, 366–67, 383
Chu-Chem [1966], **344**
Chu Chem [1989], 346, 347
Cinderella, 111
Citizen Kane, 187
City Chap, The, **28**
City of Angels, 303, **320**, 322, 361
Civil War, The, 412
Clear All Wires, 127
Clippety Clop and Clementine, 158
Closer Than Ever, 406
Cloud Nine, **375**
Cochran's 1926 Revue, **90**
Coco, 408
Cocoanuts, The, **49**
Cohan and Harris Minstrels, **41**
Cohan Revue of 1918, The, **45**
Cole, 121
Colette [1970], 308, 311
Colette [1982], 309, 310, 311
Colette Collage [1983], **309**
Colette Collage [1991], 310
College Widow, The, 19
Come Blow Your Horn, 315
Comedy of Errors, 100, 101, 254
Company, 276, **278–79**, 281–82, 289, 400
Compulsion, 313
Connecticut Yankee, A [1927], **93**, 122, 390
Connecticut Yankee, A [1943], **105–106**
Connecticut Yankee in King Arthur's Court, A, 93, 105
Conquering Hero, The, 396
Conte d'une Nuit Syrienne, 159
Contented Woman, A, 57
Co-Optimists of 1930, The, **138**
Coquin de Printemps, 4
Cotton Club, 150–51
Cotton Club Parade [20th], **150–51**
Cotton Club Parade [21st], 151
Cotton Club Parade [22nd], 51, **152**
Cotton Club Parade [24th], 152, 156
Cousin Lucy, **15**
Cover Girl, 144
Cradle Snatchers, The, 128
Cradle Will Rock, The, **185–86**, 187, 191, 211
Crazy for You, 71–72, 340
Crazy Quilt [1931], **97**
Crazy Quilt of 1933, 152
Criss-Cross, **28**

Cry for Us All, 344–45, 347
Cry the Beloved Country, 180
Cyrano de Bergerac, 163

Daarlin' Juno, 190
Daddy Longlegs, 207
Dairymaids, The, **6**
Damn Yankees, **252–53**, 263
Damsel in Distress, 75
Dance a Little Closer, 301, 304
Dance and Grow Thin, **44**
Dancing Girl, The, **63**
Dancing in the Streets, **165**, 178
Dancing Lady, 170
Dangerous Christmas of Red Riding Hood, The, 239
Dangerous Games, **371**, 372
Dangerous Maid, A, **60–61**, 65
Danton's Death, **187**
Darling of the Day, 237
Day before Spring, The, **222–23**
Day in Hollywood/A Night in the Ukraine, 328
Dear Love, 169
Dear Sir, **27**
Dear World, 238, **327**, 328
Dearest Enemy, **89–90**, 92, 97
Demi-Dozen, 305, 306, **314**
Demi Tasse, **59**
Der Kuhhandel, 174
Der Silbersee, 173
Dere Mable, **59**
Destry Rides Again, **199**, 396
Diamonds, 319, **337–38**, 352, **364–65**
Dick Tracy, 287
Did You Ever, 43
Die Ballkönigin, **12**, 30
Die Dreigroschenoper, 173, 182. *See also* Threepenny Opera, The
Die Frauenfresser, 11
Die Lustige Witwe, 7, 221
Die Polnische Wirtschaft, 10
Die Sieben Todsünden (The Seven Deadly Sins), 174
Die Tölle Dolly, 86
Dilly, 167
Dislocated Honeymoon, A, 60–61
Do I Hear a Waltz?, **112–13**, 172, 409
Do Re Mi, **233–34**, 235
Doll Girl, The, **11–12**
Dollar Princess, The, **7–8**
Doll's House, A, 351
Doll's Life, A, **351–52**
Don Quixote, 343
Dona Flor and Her Two Husbands, 345
Down in the Valley, **179–80**, 181

Dream Boy, 137
Dreamgirls, 364, **405**, 412, 413
Driving Miss Daisy, 404, 414
DuBarry Was a Lady, **127–28**, 389
Dude, 400

Earl and the Girl, The, 4, **4**
Earl Carroll Vanities [8th], **149–50**
Earl Carroll Vanities [9th], **169–70**
Earl Carroll Vanities [10th], 151
Early to Bed, 391
Earthly Paradise, 308
East Is West, **70**
East of Eden, 404
East Side Story, 215
Easter Parade, 54
Easy Come, Easy Go, 94
Echo, The, **8**
Eclipse, The, **119**
Ed Wynn Carnival, The, **59–60**
8 1/2, 375
Eleanor, **316**, 317
Elephant Man, The, 412
Emperor of San Francisco, 333
Enclave, The, **282**
End of the World, The, **352**
English Daisy, An, **3**
Eternal Road, The, **174–75**, 179
Eubie!, 388
Evening Primrose, 278
Evening with Jerry Herman, An, 329
Ever Green, 96, 165
Everything, **46**
Evil under the Sun, 127
Evita, 352, 365
Exactly Like You, 319–20
Exception and the Rule, The, 216
Excuse Me, 20

Face the Music, **50**
Fade Out—Fade In, **236**
Fads and Fancies, **14**
Falsettoland, **371–72**, 373, 374
Falsettos, **372**, 374
Family Affair, A, 259, **331**
Fancy Free, 211, 212, 218, **395**
Fanny, **198–99**, 200–201, 275, 295
Fantasticks, The, **305–306**, 308, 311, 355
Fascinating Flora, **6**
Fascinating Widow, The, **39–40**
Father Goose, 315
Fiddler on the Roof, **259–60**, 262, 279, 302, 325, 334, 357
Fifth Avenue Follies, **90**
Fifty Million Frenchmen, 94, **122**, 123

Fig Leaves Are Falling, The, 397
Fine and Dandy, **390**
Finian's Rainbow, **170–71**, 180, 223, 392
Fiorello!, 200, 233, **257**, 258, 263
Firebrand, The, 178
Firebrand of Florence, The, 76, 144, **178–79**
Firefly, The, 31, 78
First Born, The, **216**
First Impressions, 236
Five Kings, 187
Flag Is Born, A, **179**
Flahooley, 171, 189, 215, **392**
Flame Within, The, 29
Flora, The Red Menace, **332**, 337, 340, 341
Flower Drum Song, **111**, 396
Flowering Peach, The, 113
Flowers for Algernon, **299**
Floyd Collins, **408–409**, 414
Fluffy Ruffles, **7**
Fly with Me, **86–87**
Flying Colors, **140**
Flying down to Rio, 84
Flying High, **389**
Folies Bergère Revue, 39
Follies, **279–81**, 331, 359, 377, 402
Follow the Crowd, 43
Follow the Sun, **142**
For Goodness Sake, **61–62**, 63, 65, 66
For Love of Mike, 18
Fortune Hunter, The, 28
Fourposter, The, 307
1491, **271**
Free and Easy, 155, **157**
Freedomland, U.S.A., **233**
French Doll, The, 62
Friars' Frolic of 1911, **39**
Friars' Frolic of 1916, **43–44**
Frogs, The, **282**
From A to Z, **324**
Front Porch in Brooklyn, 274
Funny Face, **68–69**, 95
Funny Girl, 231, **234–35**, 238, 241, 260, 265, 267, 307, 359
Funny Lady, 338
Funny Thing Happened on the Way to the Forum, A, 275, **276**, 277, 289

Gaby, **39**
Garrick Gaieties [1st], **89**, 105
Garrick Gaieties [2nd], **91**
Garrick Gaieties [3rd], **160–61**, 185
Gay Divorce, 123, 125
Gay Divorcee, 123
Gay Hussars, The, **7**
Gay Life, The, **146**

Gay Purr-ee, 157
Gay White Way, The, **6**
General of Hot Desire, The, 374
Generation, 260–61
Gentlemen Prefer Blondes, 207, 209, **228–29**, 231, 239, 241
Gentlemen Unafraid, **34**
George White's Music Hall Varieties, **151**
George White's Scandals [1st], 60
George White's Scandals [2nd], **60**
George White's Scandals [3rd], **61**
George White's Scandals [4th], **62**
George White's Scandals [5th], **63**
George White's Scandals [6th], **64**
George White's Scandals [8th], 60, 128, **388**
George White's Scandals [9th], 149
Getting a Polish, **38**
Getting Away with Murder, **289**
Ghost Town, 105
Gibson Family, The, 142
Gift of the Magi, The, 253
Gigi [film], 224, 225, 226
Gigi [Loewe], 225–26
Gigi [Martin], 207
Girl and the Drummer, The, **8–9**, 38
Girl and the Wizard, The, **8**, 37
Girl behind the Counter, The, 44
Girl Crazy, **71–72**, 125, 168
Girl Friend, The, **90**, 99
Girl from Kay's, The, 5
Girl from Montmartre, The, **10**
Girl from Utah, The, **13**
Girl of Today, A, **14**
Girl Who Was Plugged In, The, 365
Girls against the Boys, 295
Girls of Gottenberg, The, **7**
Girls of Summer, **275**
Girls Upstairs, The, 280
Girls Will Be Girls, 18
Glad to See You!, **227–28**
Go to It, **17**
God Bless You, Mr. Rosewater, **363**, 366
God Sends Sunday, 154
Godspell, **355**, 356, 358, 381
Going Up, **45**
Golden Apple, The, 167, 185, 214, **394**
Golden Boy, **295–96**, 299, 304
Golden Gate, **333**
Golden Rainbow, 359, **398**
Golden Widow, The, **8**
Goldilocks, **396**
Goldwyn Follies, The, 75, 162
Gone with the Wind, 200, **201**
Good Boy, **135–36**
Good Fairy, The, 206

Good Morning Dearie, **25**
Good Morning Judge, **58**
Good News!, 19, **388–89**
Goodbye Girl, The, **361**
Goodtime Charley, **350**
Gospel According to St. Matthew, 355
Gowns by Roberta, **33**
Goya—A Life in Song, 376
Grand Hotel: The Musical, **376–77**, 379
Grand Street Follies of 1926, **135**
Grand Street Follies of 1929, **137**
Grand Tour, The, **328**
Grease, 363, **402–403**
Great Adventure, The, 237
Great Day!, **82–83**, 149
Great Dictator, The, 269
Great Lady, 211, **222**
Great Magoo, The, **151–52**
Great Waltz, The, 143
Greek to You, 126
Green Grow the Lilacs, 104, 105
Greenwich Village Follies [6th], **120**
Greenwich Village Follies of 1928, 169
Greenwillow, **247–48**
Grind, **352–53**
Grover's Corners, 309, 310
Guys and Dolls, 132, **245–46**, 247, 248, 249, 251–52, 360
Gypsy, **232–33**, 237, 238, 242, 270, 274, 331

Hair, **399–400**, 403, 411
Half Moon Inn, **88**
Half Past Eight, **58**
Hallelujah, Baby!, **236–37**
Hallelulah, I'm a Bum, 97
Halloween, **345**
Hammerstein's Nine O'Clock Revue, **78**
Hands Up, **117**
Hanky Panky, **41**
Hannah . . . 1939, **266–67**
Hans Brinker, 209
Hans Christian Andersen, 246
Hansel und Gretl, 173
Happy Birthday, 53, **107**, 115
Happy End [1929], **173**
Happy End [1977], **183**
Happy Hunting, 233
Happy Lot!, 208
Happy New Year, 133
Happy Time, The, 238, **333–34**, 335, 341, 328, 346
Have a Heart, **17–18**
Having Wonderful Time, 198
Hay Fever, **338**
Hayfoot, Strawfoot, 34
Hayseed, 62

Hazel Flagg, 209, **229–30**, 241, 256, 383
He Came from Milwaukee, 38
Head Over Heels, **21**
Heads Up!, **95**
Heidi, 315
Helen of Troy, N.Y., 48
Hello, Daddy!, 94
Hello, Dolly!, 86, 235, 238–39, **265**, 278, **295**, 306, 324, **325–26**, 329
Hellzapoppin'! [1938], 170, 240
Hellzapoppin'! [1976], **240**, 317
Henpecks, The, **9**
Henry, Sweet Henry, **265–66**, 267, 326, 359
Her First Roman, **261**
Her Pilgrim Soul, 365
Hercules, 367
Here Comes the Bride, **138**
Here's Love, 266, **270–71**
Here's Where I Belong, 404
Hi Diddle Diddle, **124**
Hi, Yank!, **244**
High Button Shoes, 166, 207, 209, **228**, 230, 238, 241
High Society, 133
High Society [film], 128, 132
High Spirits, **208**, 209, 236
High Tor, 145
High, Wide and Handsome, 105
Higher and Higher, **101–102**
History Loves Company, 376
Hit the Deck, **81**, 83, 94, 229
Hitchy-Koo of 1918, **57**
Hitchy-Koo of 1919, **118–19**
Hitchy-Koo of 1920, **23**
Hitchy-Koo of 1922, **120**
Hogan's Goat, 344
Hokey-Pokey and Bunty, Bulls, and Strings, **40–41**
Hold on to Your Hats, 154, **170**
Holiday, 133
Holiday Inn, 52
Holly Golightly, 265
Hollywood Canteen, 125
Hollywood Party, 97
Home Again, Home Again, 318, 319
Home of the Brave, 215
Home Sweet Homer, **345**
Hooray for What!, **153–54**, 205
Hot Chocolates, 391
Hot Spot, **277**
House of Flowers [1954], **155–56**
House of Flowers [1968], **158**
House That Jack Built, The, **137**
How Do You Do, I Love You, 406
How Now, Dow Jones, 400
How to Be a Jewish Mother, 254

How to Succeed in Business without Really Trying, **248**, 249, 315, 316, 324
Huckleberry Finn [Lane], 172
Huckleberry Finn [novel], 406
Huckleberry Finn [Weill], **181**
Hullo, Ragtime!, **42**
Human Comedy, The, 400
Humpty Dumpty, 83–84
Hunchback of Notre Dame, 358, 367
Hurricane, The, 243
Husband, a Wife, and a Friend, A, 281

I Am a Camera, 332
I and Albert, **297–98**
I Can Get It for You Wholesale, **199–200**, 201, 235
I Do! I Do!, **307**
I, Don Quixote, 343
I Feel Wonderful, **323**
I Know My Love, 274
I Love My Wife, **317–18**, 319
I Married an Angel, 53, 95, **100**, 105
I Picked a Daisy, 172
I Remember Mama, 107, **114–15**, 132
I Will Come Back, 209
Ice Capades of 1941, **163**
Ice Capades of 1942, **227**
Ice Capades of 1943, **227**
I'd Rather Be Right, 99, 102
Idiot's Delight, 301
Idiot's First, 191
If Men Played Cards Like Women Do, 48
Illustrators' Show, The, **221**, 243
Illya Darling, **278**
I'm Solomon, 345, 398
In Person, 336
In the Beginning, 376
In Trousers, **369–70**, 372
Inside U.S.A., **144**
Into the Woods, **286–87**
Invitation to a March, **275–76**
Irene, 194, **387**
Irma la Douce, 331
It Happens on Ice, **163**
"It's a Bird, It's a Plane, It's Superman," **296–97**, 298
It's a Great Feeling, 229
I've Got the Tune, 190

Jack O'Lantern, **44–45**
Jackpot, **165**
Jacobowsky and the Colonel, 328
Jacques Brel Is Alive and Well [. . .], **398–99**
Jamaica, **156**
Jazz King, The, 88
Jean Seberg, 360

Jekyll & Hyde, 411–12
Jelly's Last Jam, 407–408
Jennie, 146–47
Jerome Robbins' Broadway, 54, 241
Jerry's Girls, 329
John Murray Anderson's Almanac, 251, 313
Johnny Johnson, 174, 175, 178, 189
Jolly Bachelors, The, 37
Jollyanna, 171
Joy Spreader, The, 185
Joyful Noise, A, 266
Jubilee, 125, 125
Julius Caesar, 186–87
Jumbo, 97–98
Jumping Jupiter, 39
June Days, 89
Juno, 190–91
Juno and the Paycock, 190

Kaleidoscope, The, 117
Katja the Dancer, 159
Kean, 393
Keep It in the Family, 316
Keep off the Grass, 163, 211
Kensington Stories, 208, 209
Kicks: The Showgirl Musical, 364
Kid Boots, 387
King and I, The, 108–109, 110–12
King David, 367
King Hunger, 185
King Lear, 189
King of Cadonia, The, 8
King of Hearts, 360
Kingdom for a Cow, A, 174
Kismet, 111, 168, 343, 377, 393–94
Kiss Me, Kate, 109, 125, 130–31, 133, 156, 249, 274, 347
Kiss of the Spider Woman [1990], 335, 338, 341, 382
Kiss of the Spider Woman [1993], 335, 339–40
Kiss Waltz, The, 10
Kittie Grey, 7
Knickerbocker History of New York, 175
Knickerbocker Holiday, 175, 176, 181
Kwamina, 253, 254

La Belle Paree, 9
La Cage aux Folles, 279, 328–29, 375
La Dame de Chez Maxim, 10
La Femme du Boulanger, 249, 356
La Grosse Valise, 200–201
La, La Lucille, 58–59, 66, 77, 78
La Plume de Ma Tante, 201, 264
La Revue des Ambassadeurs, 120–21
Ladies First, 57–58

Lady, Be Good!, 65, 66, 79
Lady Comes Across, The, 164–65, 166
Lady Fingers, 94–95
Lady in Red, The, 22, 58
Lady in the Dark, 76, 128, 176–77, 178
Lady Luck, 92
Lady Mary, 30
Lady of the Pavements, 55
Laffing Room Only!, 170, 244, 247
Lark, The, 213–14
Last Night at Ballyhoo, 404
Last of Sheila, The, 289
Last Resorts, The, 275
Laughing Husband, The, 13
Laurette, 146
Le Zèbre, 120
Leave It to Jane, 19, 22, 389
Leave It to Me, 102, 127, 130, 165, 249
Left Over, The, 79
Legendary Mizners, 55
Legs Diamond, 338
Leocadia, 346
Les Fêtards, 7
Les Misérables, 358
Les Romanesques, 305
Let 'Em Eat Cake, 73–74, 125
Let 'Em Rot, 319
Let Freedom Sing, 195
Let It Ride, 164
Let Me Hear the Melody, 75
Let's Face It, 113, 128
Let's Fall in Love, 153
Letter to the Editor, 229
Lew Leslie's International Revue, 389
Lido Lady, 91, 94
Lieber Augustin, 12
Life, The, 319, 321–22
Life Begins at 8:40, 102, 152–53
Life of the Party, 222
Light, The, 78, 86
Li'l Abner, 361, 395–96
Lilies of the Field, 237
Liliom, 106
Limelight, 48
Lincoln, 365
Lion King, The, 383–84, 413
Lion King, The [film], 366
Little Cherub, The, 5
Little Dog Laughed, The, 195
Little Foxes, The, 188, 269
Little Johnny Jones, 40
Little Me, 314–15, 322
Little Mermaid, The, 365
Little Millionaire, The, 40
Little Miss Bluebeard, 63

Little Miss Fix-It, 9
Little Miss Springtime, 17
Little Night Music, A [1963] [Martin], 208–209
Little Night Music, A [1973] [Sondheim], 217, 281–82, 283, 284, 287, 289, 353, 356
Little Orphan Annie, 298, 302, 303
Little Prince, The, 225
Little Shop of Horrors, 361, 364
Little Show, The, 27, 98, 136–37, 138–41, 169, 390
Little Tommy Tucker, 139
Little Women, 253
Littlest Revue, The, 167, 189, 293
Living It Up, 229
Liza with a Z, 337, 339
Lollipop, 79
London Pavilion Revue, 92–93, 94, 122
Lonely Romeo, A, 41, 86, 87
Look, Ma, I'm Dancin'!, 206
Look to the Lilies, 237–38, 241
Look Who's Here [1st] [Kern], 11
Look Who's Here [2nd] [Gershwin], 57
Lorelei, 239
Lost in the Stars, 180–81
Louisiana Purchase, 51–52, 102, 128, 205
Love from Judy, 207, 209
Love Is Just around the Corner, 332
Love Life, 180, 189, 215, 224
Love Match, 406
Love Me Tonight, 97, 105
Love o' Mike, 18
Love of Life, 364
Love Story, 345
Love's Fire, 373–74
Lucky, 28–29
Lucky Stiff, 381, 382, 384
Lunch Hour Follies, 177, 187, 195
Lunchtime Follies, 177, 187, 195
Lute Song, 109

Mack & Mabel, 327–28
Mad Show, The, 278
Madam, Will You Walk?, 176
Madame Aphrodite, 324–25
Madwoman of Central Park West, 218, 336
Madwoman of Chaillot, The, 327
Magic Show, The, 356
Magistrate, The, 58
Make a Wish, 206–207, 230
Mamba's Daughters, 34
Mame, 238, 254, 326–27, 329, 337
Man in the Moon, 258
Man of La Mancha, 325, 343–44, 345, 346, 347
Man Who Broke the Bank at Monte Carlo, The, 381
Man Who Came to Dinner, The, 127

March of the Falsettos, 320, 369, 370, 371, 372, 373, 374
Marie Galante, 173–74
Marriage Market, The, 12, 13
Marry Me a Little, 284–85
Mary, 387
Mary Jane McKane, 79
Mass, 216–17, 355
Mata Hari, 398
Matchmaker, The, 265, 295, 325
Mayfair and Montmartre, 120
Mayor, 301–302
Mayor's Rebuttal, The, 262
Me and Juliet, 109–10, 252
Me for You, 95
Medium Rare, 314
Meet Me in St. Louis [1960], 207–208
Meet Me in St. Louis [1989], 209
Meet Me in St. Louis [film], 155, 206, 208
Melody Man, The, 88–89, 90
Merrily We Roll Along, 275, 285, 288–89
Merry Widow, The, 7, 10, 221
Mexican Hayride, 129
Michael Todd's Peep Show, 197, 229
Midsummer Night's Dream, A, 189–90
Mighty Man Is He, A, 274
Mike, 346, 347
Milk and Honey, 324, 343
Milk White Flag, A, 17
"Mind-the-Paint" Girl, The, 10–11
Ming Toy, 70
Minnie's Boys, 349–50, 351, 359
Miracle on 34th Street, 270
Mirette, 310–11
Mirette on the High Wire, 310
Miss Caprice, 12
Miss Dilly Says No, 167
Miss Information, 15–16, 117–18
Miss Liberty, 54
Miss Moffat, 167, 397
Miss 1917, 20, 57
Miss Springtime, 17
Mrs. 'Arris Goes to Paris, 145
Mrs. Jim, 38
Mrs. Santa Claus, 329
Mr. Popple (of Ippleton), 14
Mr. President, 54, 55
Mr. Wix of Wickham, 3
Mr. Wonderful, 236, 255–56, 296
Mizner Story, The, 55
Modern Eve, A, 15
Morals of Marcus, The, 6
More Cheers, 51
Morris Gest's Midnight Whirl, 59
Most Happy Fella, The, 246–47, 249, 252, 270

Mother's Kisses, A, **253–54**
Much Ado about Love, 178
Muscle, **373**
Music Box Revue [1st], **47**, 136, 140
Music Box Revue [2nd], **47–48**
Music Box Revue [3rd], **48**
Music Box Revue [4th], **48–49**
Music in the Air, **32–33**, 82
Music Is, **254**
Music Man, The, 157, 216, 247, 269, **269–70**, 271, 401
My Best Girl, **41**
My Blue Heaven, 155
My Fair Lady [1st] [Gershwin], 66
My Fair Lady [2nd] [Loewe], 145, 221, **224–25**, 226, 253
My Favorite Year, 338, **382–83**, 384
My Lady Friends, 80
My Lady's Maid, **5**
My Love, My Love, 381
My One and Only, **68–69**
My Sister Eileen, 212, 213

Nanette, 230
Nantucket, **165**
National Velvet, 220
Naughty Marietta, 31
Ned Wayburn's Gambols, **136**
Neptune's Daughter, 245
Nervous Wreck, The, 389
Never Homes, The, **40**
Never Live over a Pretzel Factory, **343**
Never on Sunday, 278
Never Too Late, **258**, 331–32
New Brain, A, **372–73**
New Faces [1934], 251
New Faces of 1952!, 251, 256
New Girl, A, 22
New Girl in Town, 215, **263**, 264, 326
New York, New York, 338, 339
New Yorkers, The [1927] [Schwartz], **135**
New Yorkers, The [1930] [Porter], **122–23**
Newsies, 365
Next, 11
Nice Goin', 165
Nice Goings On, **140–41**
Nick & Nora, 303, 304
Nifties of 1923, **64**
Night and Day, 144
Night Boat, The, **23**
Night Out, A, **79–80**, 119
Night They Raided Minsky's, The, 298
Nightcap, **323**, 324
Nightingale, The, **300–301**
Nights of Cabiria, 315

Nine, 320, **375–76**, 379
Nine-Fifteen Revue, 71, 149, **149**, 390
1928, 135
Ninety in the Shade, **13–14**
Ninotchka, 132
No for an Answer, 185, **187**
No, No, Nanette, 79, **80**, 81, 84
No Shoestrings, **349**
No Strings, **112**, 349
No Time for Sergeants, 157
Nobody Home, 6, **14–15**, 17, 117
Nothing Sacred, 229
Nymph Errant, **123–24**

O Mistress Mine, **126**
O Oysters!!!, 398
Odd Couple, 361
Odyssey, 345, 394
Of Thee I Sing, 50, **72**, 73, 75, 99, 141, 194, 246
Oh, Boy!, **18–19**, 25
Oh, I Say!, **12–13**
Oh, Joy!, 18
Oh, Kay!, 66, **67–68**, 69, 70, 81, 137
Oh Lady! Lady!!, 20
Oh, My Dear!, **21–22**
Oh, Please!, **80–81**, 94
OK, U.S.A.!, **244–45**
Oklahoma!, 33, 66, 75, **104–105**, 106–109, 115, 131, 154–55, 165, 224, 273–74
Oliver!, 172, 241, 367
On a Clear Day You Can See Forever, **171–72**
On the Town, 206, **211–12**, 213, 215, 218–19, 241, 252
On the Twentieth Century, 318
On Your Toes, **98**, 99, 115, 163, 222
Once and Future King, The, 225
Once in a Lifetime, 50
Once on This Island, **381–82**
Once There Was a Russian, 248
Once upon a Mattress, 390, **397**
1-2-3-4-5, **376**
One Dam Thing after Another, 92–93
110 in the Shade, **306–307**, 346
One Minute Please, **85**, 135
One Night in the Tropics, 34
One Night Stand, **240–41**, 337
One Touch of Venus, 165, **177–78**
Only When I Laugh, 406
Open Your Eyes, **160**
Opera Ball, The, **10**
Orchid, The, **5–6**
Oui, Madame, 77
Our Miss Gibbs, **8**
Our Nell, **62–63**
Our Town, 309

Out of This World, 123, **131**, 156, 274
Over and Over, 340
Over Night, 16, 118

Pacific Overtures, **282–83**
Pageant, 413
Paint Your Wagon, 189, **223–24**
Painting, 374
Pajama Game, The, 111, 232, 244, **251–52**, 253–54, 263, 274, 313, 383
Pal Joey, **102–103**, 105, 230
Panama Hattie, **128**
Paper Moon, 353
Parade [1998] 404, [Notables], 151, 404, **414–15**
Parade [1935] [Blitzstein], **185**
Parade [1960] [Herman], **323–24**
Pardon My English, **72–73**, 74, 125
Paris, 52, **121**, 222
Paris '90, 390
Park Avenue, **144**
Party with Comden and Green, A, 229
Passing Show of 1912, **41**, 161
Passing Show of 1916, **57**, 161
Passion, **288–89**
Passion Flower, The, **47**
Passione D'Amore, 288
Patricia, 222
Patsy, The, 222
Peanuts, 350, 397
Peg o' My Heart, 146
Peggy-Ann, **91–92**, 94, 100, 222
Perfect Fool, The, **61**
Perfect Lady, A, 64
Personals, 357–58, **365**
Peter Pan [1907] [Kern], **6**
Peter Pan [1924] [Kern], **27**, 69
Peter Pan [1950] [Bernstein], **212**
Peter Pan [1954] [Styne], **230–31**, 241, 313
Petticoat Fever, **221**
PFC Mary Brown, **244**
Phantom [Yeston], **377–78**, 379
Phantom of the Opera [Lloyd Webber], 378, 411
Phantom of the Opera [novel], 377
Philadelphia Story, 133
Philemon, **308**
Phinney's Rainbow, 255, **273**
Phi-Phi, **120**
Piccadilly to Broadway, 60, 61, **77**
Pickwick, 367
Pieces of Eight, **241**
Pink Dominos, The, 15
Pink Jungle, The, 168, **168**
Pins and Needles, **193–94**, 195–96, 200–201, 387
Pipe Dream, **110–11**, 112
Pippin, 279, 302, 335, 350, 355, **356**, 358

Plain and Fancy, 275, **392–94**
Play It Again, Sam, **349**
Play On!, 254, 392
Please!, **97**
Please Don't Eat the Daisies, 275
Pleasure Bound, 136
Pleasures and Palaces, **248–49**, 397
Plus Ça Change, 119
Pocohantas, 358, 367
Polish Wedding, A, **10**
Poor Little Ritz Girl, **87**, 88
Poppy, 137
Porgy, 74
Porgy and Bess, 62, **74–75**, 76, 105, 106, 157, 162, 247
Pot of Gold, The, **117**
Pousse-Cafe, 392
Pray by Blecht, A, **216**
Present Arms!, **94**
Pretty Penny, 197
Prettybelle, **238**, 239, 328, 402
Primrose, **64–65**
Prince Igor, 393
Prince of Egypt, 358
Prince of Grand Street, The, 266, **266**
Princess Charming, **138–39**
Prisoner of Zenda, The, 168
Professor Fodorski, 295
Promenade, **401–402**
Promises, Promises, 239, 325, **400**
Proposals, **383**
Punch Bowl, The, **48**
Purlie, **402**, 404
Purlie Victorious, 402
Purple Dust, 344
Putting It Together, **288**
Pygmalion, 224

Queen, The, 141
Queen of Basin Street, The, 328, **375**
Queen of the Movies, the, **42**
Quiet Place, A [1955], **214**
Quiet Place, A [1984], 214, 219

Rags, 302, 303, 304
Ragtime, **383–84**
Railroads on Parade, 176
Rain, 166
Rainbow [1923] [Gershwin], **63**
Rainbow [1928] [Youmans], **81–82**, 83
Rainmaker, The, 306
Rambler Rose, **44**
Rape, 369
Real Girl, A, **40**
Real Life Funnies, **363**

Red, Hot and Blue!, 126, 143
Red Mill, The, 8, 26, 32
Red Petticoat, The, 11
Red Robe, The, 136
Red Shoes, The, 241–42, 267
Redhead, 263, 316, 321, 396–97
Regina, 188, 247
Rent, 410–11
Reuben Reuben, 189, 189, 215
Revenge with Music, 141
Rex, 114
Rhyth-Mania, 150
Rich Mr. Hoggenheimer, The, 5
Rink, The, 335, 337, 338, 341
Rio Rita, 387
Ripples, 31–32
Riquette et Sa Mère, 11
Rise and Fall of the City of Mahagonny, The, 182–83
Riviera Girl, The, 19–20
Road to Urga, The, 216
Robber Bridegroom, The, 404
Roberta, 33, 35, 389
Rock-a-Bye Baby, 21, 25
Rockabye Hamlet, 328
Rodeo, 105
Romance in Hard Times, 371, 374
Romanoff and Juliet, 199
Romeo and Juliet, 215
Rosalie, 69, 123
Rosalie [film], 125
Rose Briar, 25
Rose Marie [Friml], 28, 31, 67
Rose of Arizona, The, 91, 185
Rosy Rapture, 14
Rothschilds, The, 262
Royal Family, 373, 374
Royal Vagabond, The, 46
Royal Wedding, 172
Ruggles of Red Gap, 232

Sacco and Vanzetti, 191
Sadie Thompson, 146, 166
Saint She Ain't, A, 263
St. Louis Woman, 154–55, 156–57
Sally, 23–24, 25, 27, 387
Sally, Irene & Mary, 387
Salute to Spring, 221–22
Sap of Life, 406
Saratoga, 156–57
Saratoga Trunk, 157
Saravá, 345–46
Saturday Night, 215, 274–75
Saturn Returns: A Concert, 413–14
Say, Darling, 231–32, 236

Say Mama!, 87–88
Scarlet Pimpernel. The, 412
Scarlett, 201
Scrambled Eggs, 369
Season, The, 331
Second Little Show, The, 138, 139
Secret Garden, The, 241, 338, 382, 390, 406–407
See America First, 118
Seesaw, 114, 316–17, 359
Señor Discretion Himself, 249
Sentimental Guy, 55
Sesame Street, 353, 364
7 1/2 Cents, 251
Seven Brides for Seven Brothers, 395
Seven Deadly Sins, The (Die Sieben Todsünden), 174
Seven Lively Arts, 129–30
Seven Percent Solution, The, 283
1776, 400–401
70, Girls, 70, 334–35, 341
Shadows, 21
Shall We Dance, 75
Shangri-La, 256
She Had to Say Yes, 164
She Knows Better Now, 40
She Loves Me, 258–59, 260
She Loves Me Not, 141
Shenandoah, 403–404
Sherry, 398
She's a Good Fellow, 22, 390
She's My Baby, 81, 93–94
Shinbone Alley, 295, 344, 355
Shine It On, 336
Shoestring '57, 294, 305
Shoestring Revue, 293, 294–95
Shoot the Works, 50, 161
Shop around the Corner, The, 258
Shore Leave, 81
Shotgun Wedding, 95
Show Boat, 25, 27, 29–30, 31, 33, 35, 69, 82, 90, 105, 157, 194, 222
Show Girl, 70, 82
Show Goes On, The, 310
Show Is On, The, 75, 98, 142, 153, 162, 391
Shuffle Along, 387–88
Side by Side by Sondheim, 283
Side Show, 412–13
Silk Stockings, 132, 248
Silver Slipper, The, 3
Simple Simon, 95–96, 149
Sin of Pat Muldoon, The, 253
Sinbad, 59
Sing for Your Supper, 194
Sing Out the News, 194
Singin' in the Rain, 213

Singing Kid, The, 170
Siren, The, **9–10**
Sis Hopkins, 239
Sisters Liked Them Handsome, The, 228
Sitting Pretty, **26–27**
Six, **297**
1600 Pennsylvania Avenue, **218**
Sixth Finger in a Five Finger Glove, **293–94**
Sizzle, 369
Skin of Our Teeth, The, 180, 340
Skirts, **196**, **243**
Skyscraper, 238
Smarty, 68, 69, 95
Smile [Hamlisch], **360–61**
Smiles [Youmans], **83**
Smiles of a Summer Night, 281
Smilin' Through, 83
Smiling Faces, 32
Snapshots of 1921, 60, **61**, 88
Snoopy!!!, **350–51**
So Long, 174th Street, 302
Society Buds, The, **42**
Softly, **157–58**
Some Like It Hot [1992], 239
Some Like It Hot [film], 238, 239
Something for the Boys, **129**, 195
Something Gay, **97**
Something More, 236
Son of the Grand Eunuch, The, 94
Song and Dance, 406
Song of Norway, 168, 393
Song of the Flame, **67**
Songs for a New World, 414
Soon, 363
Sophisticated Ladies, 392
Sound of Music, The, **111–12**, 115, 233, 235, 257
South Pacific, 108, 109–11, 115, 230, 346
Spice of 1922, **62**
Spotlight, 363
Spring Chicken, The, **4–5**
Spring Is Here, 95, **95**
Star and Garter, **195**
Star Dust, **123**
Star Is Born, A, 144, 155, 207
Star Spangled Rhythm, 155
Stars and Gripes, **195–96**
Stars in Your Eyes, **143**
Stars on My Shoulders, **53–54**
Starting Here, Starting Now, 406
State Fair, **115**
Stavisky, 282
Steel Pier, 335, **340**
Step Lively, 232
Step This Way, **44**

Stepping Stones, The, **26**
Sting, The, 359
Stop Flirting!, 61–62, 65
Stop! Look! Listen!, **43**
Stop Press, 51
Stormy Weather, 156
Strange Case of Dr. Jekyll and Mr. Hyde, The, 411
Straws in the Wind, 317
Street Scene, **179**, 183, 188, 247
Streets of Paris, 194
Strike Up the Band [1927], **68**, 69
Strike Up the Band [1930], **70–71**, 72, 74–75, 136
Student Prince, The, 390
Subways Are for Sleeping, **234**, 266
Sugar, **238–39**
Sun Dodgers, The, **41–42**
Sun Never Sets, The, **127**
Sunday in the Park with George, **285–86**, 287
Sunny, **27–28**
Sunshine Girl, The, **11**
Superman, 296
Sweeney Todd, **283–84**, 287, 289, 376
Sweet Adeline, 31
Sweet Bye and Bye, **166**
Sweet Charity, **315–16**, 322, 327, 335, 397
Sweet Little Devil, **64**
Sweet Smell of Success, 362
Sweet Thursday, 110
Sweetheart Shop, The, **60**
Swimmer, The, 359
Swing, 404
Swing Time, 389
Symphony in Brown, **154**

Table Settings, 286
Take a Chance, **83–84**, 128, 151
Take Five, 275, **275**
Take Me Along, **264**, 267
Tales of the South Pacific, 108
Talk of New York, The, 68
Taming of the Shrew, The, 130
Tango Apasionado, **370–71**
Tap Dance Kid, The, 412
Tars and Spars, **165–66**
Tell Me More!, **65–66**
Telling the Tale, **118**
10 Days to Broadway, 319
Tenderloin, **257–58**
That's the Ticket, **196–97**
Theodore and Co., **17**
There Shall Be No Night, 105
They Knew What They Wanted, 246
They Might Be Giants, 331
They're Playing Our Song, **360**

Thin Man, The, 303
Third Little Show, The, 138, **169**
13 Days to Broadway, **319**
This Is the Army, 45, **52**, 196
Three after Three, 390
Three Cheers, 32
Three-Cornered Hat, The, 141
Three Blind Mice, 390
Three Men on a Horse, 164
Three Musketeers, The, 100
Three Sisters, 33–34
Threepenny Opera, The [1933], **173**
Threepenny Opera, The [1954], 175, **181–82**, 183,
    185, 189, 191, 213, 323, 392, 401
Three's a Crowd, 32, 139, 161, 165, **169**
Through the Years, 83
Thumbs Up, **161–162**
Tillie's Nightmare, 91
Timbuktu, 393
Time of the Cuckoo, The, 112
Time of Your Life, The, 103, 351
Time Remembered, **167–68**, 346
Time, The Place and the Girl, The, 146
Tinted Venus, The, 177
Tip-Toes, **66**
Titanic, **378–79**
To Broadway with Love, **259**
Tonight's the Night!, **15**
Too Many Girls, 19, **101**, 103, 205–206
Too True to Be Good, **343**
Toot-Toot!, **20–21**
Top Banana, **392–93**
Topper, 274
Toys in the Attic, **191**
Trafalgar, 261
Trained Nurses, The, **42**
Trapp Family Singers, The, 111
Treasure Girl, **69–70**
Treasure Island, 241
Tree Grows in Brooklyn, A, **145**
Tricks, 363
Trip to Chinatown, A, 10
Triple Sec, 185
Trouble in Tahiti, 212, **213**, 214, 218–19
Twelfth Night, 254, 392
Twentieth Century, 317, 318
27 Wagons Full of Cotton, 213
Twigs, **281**
Twinkling Eyes, 85–86
Two by Two, **113–14**, 408
Two for the Seesaw, 257, 316
Two Gentlemen of Verona, 400
Two Little Girls in Blue, 58, 61, 66, **77–78**, **159–60**
Two Men and a Girl, 38

Two on an Island, 176
Two on the Aisle, 213, **229**
Two Weeks with Pay, **102**
Two's Company, 167

Ulysses Africanus, 176
Unsinkable Molly Brown, The, **270**
Up and Down Broadway, **38**
Up Stage and Down, **85–86**, 89
Up with the Lark, **120**
Upstairs at O'Neal's, **300**
USO's *At Ease. See* At Ease

Vagabond Hero, A, **163**
Valuable Property, A, 346
Vanderbilt Revue, The, **122**
Very Good Eddie, 15, 16, 85, **118**
Very Warm for May, **34–35**, 53
Via Galactica, 400
Victor/Victoria, 408, 412
Victory at Sea, 110
Vincent Youmans' Ballet Revue, **84**
Virginia, **142–43**
Viva O'Brien, 198

W.C., 401
Waiting for Philip Glass, 374
Wake Up and Dream, **121–22**, **137–38**
Wake Up, Darling, **231**
Walk a Little Faster, **161**, 162
Walk with Music, **390–91**
Walking Happy, 238
Waltz Dream, A, **6–7**
Warrior's Husband, The, 103
Watch Your Step, **42–43**
Way We Were, The, 359
We Take the Town, 266
Wedding Night, The, 12–13
Weird Romance, **365–66**
Welcome to the Club, **319–20**, 321
Well! Well! Well!, **136**
We're Home, 267
West Side Story, 189, **215–16**, 218–19, 232–33,
    241, 270, 275–77, 279, 295
What Happened to Jones, 9, 38
What Makes Sammy Run?, 261
What's a Nice Country Like You Doing in a State
    Like This?, 321
What's Up?, **222**
When Claudia Smiles, 13
Where's Charley?, 245, 252, 269
Whirl of Society, The, **41**
White Christmas, 52, 54
White Chrysanthemum, The, **5**

White Plume, The, 163
Who to Love, 345
Whoopee, 149, 164, **389–90**
Wildcat, **314**, 317, 346
Wildflower, 28, 31, 67, **78**, 80, 84
Will Rogers Follies, The, **320–33**
Winkle Town, **88**
Winsome Widow, A, **10**
Winter Garden Vaudeville [1911], **40**
Winter Garden Vaudeville [1915], **43**
Winter's Tale, The [1958] [Blitzstein], **190**
Winter's Tale, The [1989] [Finn], **371**
Wise Guy, 55
Wise Guys, 55, 289
Wish You Were Here, **198**, 199
Within the Quota, 120
Wiz, The, 299, **403**
Wizard of Oz, The, 104, 153, 156, 164
Woman Haters, The, **11**
Woman of the Year, 321, 335, **336–37**, 341
Wonderful Town, **212–13**, 252
Wonderful Wizard of Oz, The, 403
Wonderworld, **235–36**
Words and Music, 300
Working, 302, **357**
World of Henry Orient, The, 265
World of Jules Feiffer, The, 261, **276–77**, 298
World of Suzie Wong, The, 235

Year the Yankees Lost the Pennant, The, 252
Yellow Mask, The, **160**
Yip-Yip-Yaphank, **45–46**, 52
You Never Know [Porter], **126–27**
You Said It, 150

You'd Be Surprised, **86**
You'll Never Know [Rodgers], **88**
Your Own Thing, 254
Your Show of Shows, 255, 315, 383
You're a Good Man, Charlie Brown, 351,
  397–98
Yvonne, **159**

Zenda, **168**
Zephyr et Flore, 159
Ziegfeld Follies, 24, 60
Ziegfeld Follies of 1907, 38
Ziegfeld Follies of 1910, 38
Ziegfeld Follies of 1911, **9**, 39
Ziegfeld Follies of 1912, **41**
Ziegfeld Follies of 1916, **16–17**, **44**
Ziegfeld Follies of 1917, **19**
Ziegfeld Follies of 1918, **45**
Ziegfeld Follies of 1919, **46**
Ziegfeld Follies of 1920, **47**
Ziegfeld Follies of 1921, 24
Ziegfeld Follies of 1927, 38, **49–50**
Ziegfeld Follies of 1931, 50
Ziegfeld Follies of 1934, **141**, 152, **161**
Ziegfeld Follies of 1936, 126, **162**
Ziegfeld Follies of 1943, 256
Ziegfeld Follies of 1956, **256**, 313
Ziegfeld Girls of 1920, 47
Ziegfeld Midnight Frolic, **46–47**
Zip, Goes a Million, **22–23**, 25, 27
Zorbá, **334**, 335
Zorbá the Greek, 334
Zulu and the Zayda, The, **200**

PEOPLE INDEX

This index contains many, but not all, of the persons mentioned in this book. Those who worked importantly or primarily in musical theater are included. Demands of space, time, and interest have limited the inclusion of some who are only tangentially associated with the songs, shows, and careers of the major composers. For ease of usage, page numbers of the primary discussion of each of the major composers and collaborators are denoted by boldfaced page numbers.

Aarons, Alexander A., 25, 59, 61–62, 65–69, 71–73, 77–79, 95
Aarons, Alfred E., 58, 59, 65, 66, 77, 78, 79
Abbott, Bud, 194
Abbott, Charles, 377
Abbott, George, 54, 97–98, 100–103, 109–10, 131, 145, 151, 164, 166, 197, 205–206, 211–13, 215, 228, 231, 236, 245, 251–52, 254, 257, 258, 263, 275–76, 287, 332, 397, **442**
Abbott, Tom, 215
Ackerman, Loni, 319, 338, 346, 352, 365
Ackland, Joss, 360
Acting Company, 373
Actman, Irving, 247
Adair, Yvonne, 228
Adams, Edith (Edie), 212, 395
Adams, Lee, 293–300, 305, 326, 346, 347, **442**
Adams, Maude, 6, 27
Adams, Tony, 408
Adamson, Harold, 83, 169–70, 346
Ade, George, 19
Adler, Bruce, 71
Adler, Christopher, 360
Adler, Jacob, 266
Adler, Jerry, 224, 317
Adler, Larry, 163
Adler, Luther, 174, 176, 179
Adler, Richard, 114, 203, 245, **251–54**, 263, 313, 360
Adrian, Max, 214, 275
Agnese/Raibourn, 329
Ahrens, Lynn, 366, 381–83
Aibel, Douglas, 266
Ailey, Alvin, 216
Akers, Karen, 376, 377
Albee, Edward, 265

Alberghetti, Anna Maria, 264
Albert, Eddie, 54, 100, 189
Alda, Alan, 261
Alda, Robert, 245
Aldredge, Tom, 114, 286, 288, 401
Aldrich, Richard, 221
Aleichem, Sholom, 259–60
Alexander, Jason, 285, 357, 365
Alford, Larry, 329
Alfred, William, 344
Alinson, Patti, 377
Allan, Ted, 344, 346
Allen, Debbie, 215
Allen, Elizabeth, 113, 199
Allen, Fred, 136, 138–39, 161, 169
Allen, Jay Presson, 297, 375
Allen, Lewis, 277, 298, 302
Allen, Ralph G., 338, 364
Allen, Woody, 324, 349
Allers, Roger, 413
Allyson, June, 103, 205–206
Alpert, Herb, 407
Alton, Robert, 101–102, 109, 142–43, 153, 162, 194, 229, 391
Alvarez, Anita, 171
Amado, Jorge, 345
Ameche, Don, 132, 265, 396
American Music Theater Festival, 180
American Shakespeare Festival, 189–90
Amory, Cleveland, 275
Anders, Glenn, 84
Anderson, Arthur, 5
Anderson, John Murray, 48, 89–90, 97, 120, 141, 152, 161–62, 167, 178, 251, 313
Anderson, Leroy, 213, 396
Anderson, Maxwell, 175–77, 180–81, 187, 195

Anderson, Melissa Rain, 99
Andreas, Christine, 104, 224
Andrews, Julie, 111, 224, 225, 288, 408
Andrews, Lyle D., 91, 93, 95, 122
Andrews, Nancy, 186, 314, 324, 394
Anouilh, Jean, 167, 213, 346
Anthony, Joseph, 168, 213, 246, 265, 306
Antoon, A. J., 337
Appell, Don, 324
Arbuckle, Fatty, 48
Arden, Eve, 35, 128, 162, 185
Arena Managers Association, 227
Arenal, Julie, 399
Arlen, Harold, 1, 82, 98, 102, 144, **149–58**, 168, 207, 209
Arlen, Steve, 271, 345
Arnaz, Desi, 101, 314
Arnaz, Lucie, 328, 360
Arno, Peter, 122
Aronson, Boris, 234, 279
Arthur, Beatrice, 181, 254, 259, 293, 326
Arthur, Jean, 212
Ashley, Christopher, 50, 395
Ashman, Howard, 337, 360–61, 363–66
Askins, Harry, 20
Astaire, Adele, 25, 61, 62, 65, 68, 83, 123, 139–40
Astaire, Fred, 25, 61, 62, 65, 68, 72, 75, 83, 84, 97, 98, 123, 139
Atteridge, Harold, 136
Atwater, Edith, 127, 189, 392
Atwell, Rick, 345
Auberjonois, Ren, 320, 406
Aubert, Jean, 96, 139
Auden, W. H., 343, 344
Auerbach, Arnold, 144, 196, 197, 244
Avian, Bob, 288, 359, 405
Ayers, Lemuel, 130–31, 155, 274
Azenberg, Emanuel, 285, 360, 361, 383, 412
Azito, Tony, 183

Babbitt, Milton, 274
Babe, Thomas, 180
Bacall, Lauren, 297, 336–37
Bacharach, Burt, 400
Baffa-Brill, Diana, 326
Bagley, Ben, 165, 167, 189, 293, 294, 305, 349
Bailey, Pearl, 154–56, 198, 325
Baird, Bil, 258
Baker, Belle, 49, 92
Baker, Benny, 127, 128, 165
Baker, Josephine, 162
Baker, Lenny, 317–18
Baker, Mark, 217
Baker, Russell, 318, 319
Baker, Word, 305–306, 331

Bakula, Scott, 277
Balaban, Bob, 397
Balanchine, George, 51, 52, 98–100, 121, 135, 156, 161–64, 189–90, 222, 245, **443**
Ball, Lucille, 101, 314
Ballantine, Carl, 276
Ballard, Kaye, 189, 264, 394
Ballard, Lucinda, 146
Bankhead, Tallulah, 97, 256, 269, 313
Baranski, Christine, 303, 400
Barbeau, Adrienne, 402
Barer, Marshall, 208, 278, 397
Barr, Richard, 213, 284
Barratt, Augustus, 7, 8, 41
Barrett, James Lee, 403
Barrie, Barbara, 190, 278
Barrie, J. M., 6, 14, 27, 212, 230
Barry, Gene, 328
Barry, Julian, 360
Barrymore, Lionel, 377
Bart, Lionel, 172, 367
Bart, Roger, 367, 398
Barton, James, 223, 253
Barton, Steve, 241
Basile, Frank, 338, 365
Battle, Hinton, 403
Baum, L. Frank, 403
Baum, Vicki, 376
Baxley, Barbara, 258
Bayes, Nora, 9, 37, 45, 57, 61
Bayes, Sammy Dallas, 260
Beach, Gary, 366
Bean, Orson, 234, 251, 258, 278, 313, 332
Beatty, Warren, 287
Beaumont, Ralph, 276
Becker (Theodore), Lee, 215, 237, 260–61, 266, 313, 332
Beebe, Hank, 317
Beery, Leigh, 266
Behrman, S. N., 55, 75, 175, 198
Belafonte, Harry, 156, 251, 313
Belita, 227
Bell, Charles W., 60–61
Bell, Marion, 180, 223
Bell, Marty, 338, 339
Belson, Jerry, 360
Ben-Ari, Neal, 180
Benchley, Robert, 48
Bender, Milton "Doc," 85–86, 98, 135
Benjamin, P. J., 299, 345
Bennett, Arnold, 237
Bennett, Michael, 114, 266, 278–81, 316–17, 359, 364, 400, 405, **443**
Bennett, Robert Russell, 179
Bennett, Tony, 349

Benny, Jack, 141, 149
Benson, Jodi, 71, 360
Benson, Sally, 208–209
Benton, Robert, 296
Benzell, Mimi, 324
Beretta, Joanne, 310
Bergman, Ingmar, 281
Berkeley, Busby, 94, 227
Berle, Milton, 151, 256
Berlin, Irving, 1, 20, **37–56**, 92, 102, 152, 166, 209, 233
Berlind, Roger, 114, 254, 288–89, 302, 320, 337, 340, 353, 369–70, 376
Berman, Shelley, 331
Bernard, Sam, 5, 8, 37, 38, 44, 47, 64, 119
Bernardi, Herschel, 259, 334
Bernstein, Leonard, 182, 186, 203, **211–19**, 245, 355
Bernstein, Shirley, 355
Berry, Eric, 356
Berry, John, 357
Berry, Sarah Uriarte, 100
Beruh, Joseph, 282, 355, 356, 401
Bettis, Valerie, 144, 198, 391
Bigelow, Susan, 338, 365
Bigley, Isabel, 110, 245
Bikel, Theodore, 111
Birch, Patricia, 183, 217, 254, 281–82, 319, 360, 397, 402, 414
Birkenhead, Susan, 241, 407
Bishop, André, 285, 287, 288, 369–72, 381, 382, 414
Bishop, Carole (Kelly), 359, 383
Bissell, Richard, 231–32, 251–52
Black, Don, 240, 361
Black, Karen, 316
Blackwell, Harolyn, 217
Blaine, Vivian, 231, 245
Blair, Pamela, 359, 363, 376, 404
Blake, Eubie, 387–88
Blakemore, Michael, 320, 321
Blane, Ralph, 103, 205–209
Blau, Eric, 398–99
Blazer, Judith, 51, 378
Bledsoe, Jules, 29
Blitzstein, Marc, 1, 181–83, **185–91**, 211, 213, 274, 323
Bloch, Ivan, 405
Bloom, Susan, 350
Bloomgarden, Kermit, 146, 188, 191, 213, 246, 269, 277–78
Bloomingdale, Alfred, 391
Blount, Roy, Jr., 338, 364
Blumenkrantz, Jeff, 248
Blumenthal, A. C., 33
Blyden, Larry, 111, 261, 276, 282

BMI Workshop, 363, 375, 381
Bobbie, Walter, 257, 335
Bobby, Anne Marie, 360, 365
Bock, Jerry, 203, 245, **255–62**, 331, 332, 373
Bogardus, Stephen, 31, 107, 367, 370–72
Bogosian, Eric, 373
Boland, Mary, 50, 125
Bolger, Ray, 95, 98, 104, 152–53, 163, 245, 295
Bolton, Guy, 13, 14, 16–23, 26, 27, 64–67, 71, 91, 93, 95, 118, 124–25, 127, 165, 170, 390, **443–44**
Booth, Shirley, 145, 190, 237–38
Boothe, Anne, 142
Bordoni (Goetz), Irene, 15, 51, 57, 62, 117–18, 121, 222
Borges, Jorge Luis, 370–71
Borodin, Alexander, 393–94
Bosco, Philip, 68, 257
Bosley, Tom, 257, 366
Bostwick, Barry, 258, 303, 308, 402, 404
Boucicault, Dion G., 11
Boulanger, Nadia, 185, 293
Bourne, Matthew, 358
Bova, Joe, 186, 211, 277, 397
Bovill, C. H., 7
Bowden, Charles, 213
Bracken, Eddie, 101, 325
Brady, William A., Jr., 9, 38, 136, 138
Bramble, Mark, 241, 318, 328
Brand, Max, 199
Brando, Marlon, 179
Breaux, Marc, 349, 350
Brecht, Bertolt, 173, 181–83, 216, 234
Brel, Jacques, 398–99
Brennan, Eileen, 265, 295, 325
Brennan, Maureen, 175, 217
Brennert, Alan, 365
Brent, Romney, 89, 91, 123, 164
Brian, Donald, 7, 9, 10, 12, 13, 35, 119
Brice, Carol, 157, 171
Brice, Fanny, 38, 39, 46–48, 97, 126, 137, 141, 146, 161–62, 234
Brickhill, Joan, 209
Bricusse, Leslie, 367, 408, 411–12
Briggs, Tom, 115
Brightman, Sarah, 300
Brink, Robert, 351
Brisson, Frederick, 251–52, 260, 263, 281, 301
Britton, Pamela, 223
Broderick, Helen, 50, 60, 77, 122, 139, 151
Broderick, Matthew, 248
Brokaw, Mark, 131
Brook, Peter, 155
Brooklyn Academy of Music, 72, 73
Brooks, David, 154, 182, 213, 223, 244
Brooks, Mel, 295, 382

Broun, Heywood, 50, 161
Brown, Anne, 74
Brown, Barry M., 218, 328, 336
Brown, Forman, 345
Brown, George, 227
Brown, Georgia, 172, 182, 283
Brown, Jason Robert, 414–15
Brown,.Joe David, 353
Brown, L. Slade, 294, 295, 297, 300
Brown, Lew, 128, 388–89
Brown, Max, 16, 199, 237, 349, 350, 355
Brown, Steve, 364
Brown, William F., 299, 403
Browning, Susan, 278
Bruce, Carol, 29, 51, 113, 201, 265
Bruce, Nigel, 142
Bryan, Alfred, 77
Brynner, Yul, 109, 345
Bubbles, John W., 74
Buchanan, Jack, 68, 73, 121, 137, 143
Buffaloe, Kathleen, 106
Bufman, Zev, 329
Burch, Shelly, 376
Burghoff, Gary, 397
Burke, Louis, 209
Burke (Ziegfeld), Billie, 11, 24, 25, 161, 256
Burnett, Carol, 236, 280, 288, 397
Burnett, Frances Hodgson, 407
Burns, David, 124, 127, 131, 177, 197, 233, 255–
    56, 265, 269, 276, 295, 313, 325, 335
Burnside, R. H., 4–6, 26, 28, 42–44, 46, 68, 82
Burr, Charles, 345
Burrows, Abe, 131–32, 229, 231, 240, 245–46, 248–
    49, 265, 317
Burstyn, Mike, 262, 347
Burton, Kate, 279
Burton, Richard, 168, 225
Busoni, Ferruccio, 173, 221
Bussert, Meg, 223, 225, 269
Butterworth, Charles, 30, 140
Butterworth, Michael, 381

Caesar, Irving, 31, 49, 57–62, 64, 78–80, 92, 120,
    153
Caesar, Sid, 165, 255, 294, 295, 314–15
Cagney, James, 137
Cahill, Marie, 10, 13, 37
Cahn, Sammy, 166, 227–29, 231, 237–38, 299–300,
    346
Caird, John, 358
Caldwell, Anne, 13, 17, 22–26, 28, 44, 58, 60, 80,
    390
Caldwell, L. Scott, 383
Caldwell, Zoe, 308
Calhoun, Jeff, 53, 68, 402

Callan, Michael, 240
Callaway, Liz, 257, 309, 405
Calloway, Cab, 74, 75, 150–51, 251, 325
Cambridge, Godfrey, 254
Campbell, David, 99
Cantone, Mario, 100
Cantor, Arthur, 258
Cantor, Eddie, 45–47, 49, 50, 60, 149, 164, 166,
    387, 389
Capalbo, Carmen, 181–83, 281
Capital Cities/ABC Inc., 288, 381
Capote, Truman, 155–56, 158, 265
Capp, Al, 395
Cariou, Len, 284, 297, 310
Carle, Richard, 4, 10, 11, 13, 39
Carlin, Tony, 266
Carlisle, Kitty, 390
Carmello, Carolee, 372, 414
Carmichael, Hoagy, 243, 390–91
Carmines, Al, 401–402
Carnelia, Craig, 357
Carnegie Hall, 51
Carnovsky, Morris, 75, 190, 331
Carpenter, Constance, 93, 169
Carpenter, Larry, 176
Carr, Allan, 328, 375
Carr, Lawrence, 145, 277, 396
Carradine, John, 276
Carradine, Keith, 320
Carrafa, John, 365
Carrington, Katharine, 32, 175
Carroll, Albert, 137
Carroll, Danny, 349
Carroll, David James, 67, 377
Carroll, Diahann, 112, 155
Carroll, Earl, 149, 151, 170
Carroll, Leo G., 221
Carroll, Ronn, 248
Carson, Jeannie, 171, 207
Carson, Yvette, 155
Carter (Stone), Aileen, 26
Carter, Arthur, 166
Carter, Desmond, 64, 65, 138–39, 142, 160, 174
Carter, Dixie, 102
Carter, Frank, 24, 45
Carter, Jack, 256
Carter, Nell, 298
Carus, Emma, 37
Carver, Brent, 339, 414
Caryll, Ivan, 4, 5, 7, 8, 21, 44, 46, 58
Casale, Glenn, 230
Casella, Martin, 353
Casella, Matt, 353
Casella, Max, 413
Casey, Warren, 402–403

Cassidy, Jack, 197–98, 236, 249, 256, 258–59, 296
Cassidy, Patrick, 176
Castang, Veronica, 375
Castle, Irene, 20, 42
Castle, Vernon, 42
Cates, Joseph, 261
Catlett, Walter, 23, 27, 29, 47, 65, 69
Cawthorn, Joseph, 11, 13, 21, 44, 46
Center Theatre, 142
Cerf, Bennett, 187
Cervantes, Miguel de, 343
Cerveris, Michael, 378
Chadman, Christopher, 102, 180, 246, 257
Chamberlain, Richard, 224, 265
Chamberlin, Kevin, 51
Champion, Gower, 164, 206, 238–39, 264–65, 294, 295, 299, 307, 325–28, 333–34, 387, **444**
Champion, Marge, 294
Channing, Carol, 187, 228, 239, 265, 295, 325, 329
Chaplin, Charles, 48, 231, 269
Chaplin, Saul, 213
Chaplin, Sydney, 231, 234–35
Charig, Philip, 30, 255
Charisse, Zan, 232
Charlap, Moose, 230
Charles, Walter, 54, 366
Charlot, Andr, 79, 97, 118, 124
Charnin, Martin, 113–14, 157–58, 168, 240, 277, 298, 300, 302–304, 346
Chenoweth, Kristin, 372, 398
Cherry, Vivian, 413
Chiari, Walter, 146
Chodorov, Jerome, 197, 212
Christin, 120
Churchill, Caryl, 375
Cilento, Wayne, 248, 329, 405
Cimino, Leonardo, 371
City Center Encores, 31, 54, 68, 99, 103, 107, 131, 155, 162, 176, 177, 257, 335, 395, 400
City Center Light Opera Company, 102
Clark, Bobby, 47, 48, 70, 129, 161–62, 171, 194–95, 197, 229, 346
Clark, Victoria, 378
Clarke, Hope, 407
Clayburgh, Jill, 262, 356
Clayton, Jan, 29, 106
Clayton, Lawrence, 371, 413
Cleale, Lewis, 54
Close, Glenn, 114, 318, 408
Cloud, Bob, 407
Clurman, Harold, 75, 110, 174
Cobb, Lee J., 174
Coca, Imogene, 50, 160–61, 185, 318
Cochran, Charles B., 90, 92, 96, 119–22, 124, 137, 142

Cochrane, June, 89–90, 93
Coco, James, 314
Coe, Fred, 260
Coe, Peter, 297, 299
Coffin, Frederick, 363
Cohan, George M., 10, 39, 40, 41, 43–46, 68, 99, 176, 264
Cohen, Alexander H., 114, 189, 206–207, 238, 240, 260, 317, 327, 328
Cohenour, Patti, 31, 111
Cole, Jack, 156, 168, 197, 256, 276, 313, 343, 344, 393
Cole, Kay, 350
Coleman, Cy, 240, 291, 294, **313–22**, 352, 364, 384, 415
Coleman, Warren, 74
Coles, Charles "Honi," 68
Colette, 207, 225, 308–10
Collier, William, 39, 40, 44, 47, 60, 64
Collins, Charles, 222
Collins, Dorothy, 280
Collins, Lester, 308
Collins, Stephen, 288
Colombo, Patti, 230
Colton, Chevi, 324
Colvan, Zeke, 29, 34, 49, 95
Comden, Betty, 211–13, 218, 229–34, 236, 239, 297, 317–20, 337, 351–52, 364, **444–45**
Comstock, F. Ray, 6, 14, 15, 19, 20, 22, 26, 118
Conklin, Peggy, 176
Connell, Jane, 305, 314, 326, 327, 349
Connelly, Marc, 48, 169, 273
Connolly, Bobby, 83, 120, 139, 141, 388
Conried, Hans, 131, 334
Convy, Bert, 332
Cook, Barbara, 29, 146, 214, 258–59, 269–70, 280, 392, 394
Cook, Joe, 58, 118, 163
Cook, Victor Trent, 155
Cookson, Peter, 131
Cooper, Chuck, 321
Cooper, Marilyn, 200, 294, 337
Cooper, Melville, 92, 125, 139, 178, 206
Coopersmith, Jerome, 260–61, 316
Coote, Robert, 224–25, 225
Copeland, Joan, 102
Copland, Aaron, 105, 185, 293
Corman, Roger, 364
Cornell, Katherine, 90, 216
Correia, Don, 314
Cossette, Pierre, 320
Costello, Lou, 194
Cotten, Joseph, 186, 187
Coullet, Rhonda, 404
Counsell, Elisabeth, 360

Courtneidge, Cicely, 91, 137
Coward, Nol, 27, 83, 159, 169, 208, 338
Cox, Catherine, 240, 254, 405
Cox, Veanne, 279, 332, 360
Craig, Jack, 325
Crampton, Glory, 377
Crane, David, 357–58, 365
Craven, Frank, 23, 45
Craven, John, 176
Crawford, Cheryl, 74, 75, 146, 174, 177–78, 180, 182, 188, 189, 215, 223, 275, 307, 308, 344, 392, **445**
Crawford, Clifton, 41
Crawford, Michael, 299
Cresson, James, 318, 332, 335
Crichton, Madge, 5
Criswell, Kim, 182
Crivello, Anthony, 339
Crosby, Kathryn, 115
Crothers, Sam, 320, 376
Crouse, Russel, 54, 55, 111–12, 124–26, 153
Crowder, Jack, 325
Cryer, Suzanne, 383
Cuccioli, Robert, 338, 411
Cuden, Steve, 411
Cullum, John, 171–72, 271, 318, 403, 404
Cumming, Alan, 333
Cunningham, JoAnn, 310
Cunningham, John, 107, 278, 308, 309, 334, 378
Curry, John, 223
Curry, Tim, 382
Curtis, Keene, 262, 308, 357
Cypher, Jon, 409

Da Silva, Howard, 401
Dabdoub, Jack, 343, 377
DaCosta, Morton, 156–57, 259, 269
Dale, Grover, 316, 356
Dale, Jim, 217, 318–19
Dali, Salvador, 129
Daltrey, Roger, 367
Daly, Tyne, 54, 232–33
Daly, William, 60, 61, 62–63, 77
Damon, Cathryn, 332
Dana, Leora, 214
Daniele, Graciela, 53, 246, 334, 337, 361, 370–72, 381, 383
Danieley, Jason, 68, 217, 408
Daniels, Billy, 171, 295, 325
Daniels, Danny, 53, 205, 208, 271, 294, 302, 305, 395
Daniels, Sharon, 246
Daniels, William, 401
Danner, Blythe, 355
Dante, Nicholas, 359
Darion, Joe, 278, 343–44

Darnley, Herbert, 3
Dassin, Jules, 167, 278
David, Hal, 325, 400
David, Keith, 407
David, Mack, 325
Davidson, Gordon, 216
Davidson, John, 115
Davies, Howard, 224
Davies, Irving, 360
Davies, Valentine, 270
Davis, Allan, 316
Davis, Bessie McCoy, 20
Davis, Bette, 166, 167, 397
Davis, Luther, 376, 393
Davis, Ossie, 156, 200, 402
Davis, Owen, 94–95, 142, 389
Davis, Sammy, Jr., 256, 295, 296
Dawn, Hazel, 44
Day, Doris, 263
Day, Edith, 45, 78, 387
De Carlo, Yvonne, 280
De La Peña, George, 241
De Lappe, Gemze, 104
De Mille, Agnes, 104–108, 131, 140, 153–54, 177–78, 190, 223, 228, 253, 306, 396, **445**
De Paul, Gene, 395
DeFelice, Harold, 338, 364–65
Del Rossi, Angelo, 353
DeLaria, Lea, 211, 395
DeLiagre, Alfred, Jr., 221
DeLucia, Natalie, 353
Demas, Carole, 402
Dennis, Patrick, 314, 326
Derricks, Cleavant, 371, 399, 405
Deslys, Gaby, 14, 43
Desmond, Johnny, 231
DeSylva, B. G., 22, 24, 27, 51, 58, 59, 61–65, 80, 83–84, 127–28, 388–89, **446**
Deval, Jacques, 173
Devine, Jerry, 343
Devine, Loretta, 399, 405
DeWolfe, Billy, 313
Dexter, John, 112–13, 181, 240–41
Diaghilev, Serge, 159
Dickens, Charles, 366
Dickson, Dorothy, 18, 21, 22, 26
Diehl, Crandall, 224
Diener (Marre), Joan, 256, 313, 343, 345, 377, 393
Dietrich, Marlene, 178, 199
Dietz, Howard, 27, 67, 68, 135–36, 139, 141–47, 161, 163, 165–66, 169, 177, **446–47**
Diggs, Elizabeth, 310
Dillingham, Charles B., 8, 15, 20–23, 25–31, 32, 33, 42–44, 46, 57, 64, 69, 80, 81, 93, 117, **447**
Dillon, Denny, 68

Dilly, Erin, 99
Dishy, Bob, 104, 324, 332
Disney Theatrical Productions, 366, 367, 413
Dixon, Jerry, 382
Dixon, Lee, 101, 104
Doctorow, E. L., 383
Dodge, Jimmy, 350
Dodge, Marcia Milgrom, 371
Dodger Endemol Theatricals, 378
Dodger Productions, 366, 406, 407
Domingo, Placido, 376
Donahue, Jack, 27, 69, 138
Donaldson, Norma, 246
Donaldson, Walter, 389–90
Donehue, Vincent J., 111, 146, 190
Donen, Stanley, 241
Donnelly, Dorothy, 137, 390
Doro, Marie, 6
Dossett, John, 297, 353
Dotrice, Roy, 338
Dougherty, Joseph, 382
Douglas, Melvyn, 75, 190, 196
Douglass, Stephen, 29, 206, 252, 306, 394
Dowling, Eddie, 46, 162, 163, 194, 195
Doyle, Sir Arthur Conan, 260
Drabinsky, Garth H., 217, 299, 339, 383
Drake, Alfred, 99, 104, 109, 111, 130, 168, 186,
  226, 391, 393
Drake, Ervin, 261
Drama Department, 51
Dresser, Louise, 8, 17, 21
Dressler, Marie, 63
Dreyfus, Max, 3, 20, 27, 30, 57, 77, 78, 82, 137,
  139
Dreyfus, Richard, 365
Drivas, Robert, 314
Drummond, Jack, 324
Dubin, Al, 163, 194
Duffy, Henry, 222
Duke, Vernon, 1, 75, 98, 135, 141–43, 152–53,
  158, 159–68, 189, 274, 293
Dukelsky, Vladimir. See Duke, Vernon
Dullea, Keir, 355
Dumont, Margaret, 49, 222
Duncan, Augustin, 195
Duncan, Sandy, 230, 231
Duncan, Todd, 74, 127, 181
Duncan, William Cary, 46, 78, 79, 82
Dunham, Katharine, 163
Dunlop, Frank, 225
Dunne, Irene, 28, 93
Dunnock, Mildred, 188, 308
Duquesnay, Ann, 409
Durang, Christopher, 282, 288
Durante, Jimmy, 70, 82, 97, 122, 125, 143, 163

Dussault, Nancy, 233, 283
Dutton, Charles S., 155

Eagen, Daisy, 407
Easton, Sheena, 344
Eaton, Mary, 29, 47
Ebb, Fred, 104, 319, 324, 332–41, 352, 364, 447–
  48
Ebersole, Christine, 104, 107, 162, 176, 289, 353
Ebin, Gala, 167
Edelman, Gregg, 131, 288, 320, 332, 401
Eder, Linda, 411
Edwards, Blake, 408
Edwards, Cliff, 65
Edwards, Sherman, 274, 400–401
Egan, Susan, 294, 366
Eggerth, Marta, 101, 309
Eilers, Jim Paul, 323
Elg, Taina, 51
Elkins, Hillard, 262, 295
Ellington, Duke, 150, 152, 254, 391–92
Elliott, Maxine, 15
Elliott, Patricia, 218
Elliott, William, 19, 20, 22
Ellis, Melville, 6
Ellis, Scott, 258, 279, 332, 337, 338, 340, 401
Eltinge, Julian, 3, 15, 39
Embersole, Christine, 225
Emick, Jarrod, 252
Endemol Theatre Productions, 408
Engel, Lehman, 363, 375, 381
Engelsman, Ralph G., 85, 86, 87
Englander, Ludwig, 5, 6
Epstein, Alvin, 282
Erickson, Leif, 101, 168
Erlanger, A. L., 17, 20, 39, 44, 61, 77, 78
Ernotte, Andr, 310
Errico, Melissa, 54, 177, 224
Errol, Leon, 23, 57, 61
Etting, Ruth, 49, 95, 149, 389
Evan, Robert, 411
Evans, Maurice, 257
Evans, Wilbur, 129, 145
Everard, George, 3
Eyen, Tom, 364, 405

Fabray, Nanette, 55, 165, 180, 206–207, 228
Fagan, Garth, 413
Fain, Sammy, 164, 171, 236, 255, 392
Faison, George, 155, 218, 299, 403
Faison, Sandy, 299
Fall, Leo, 9, 11
FAO Schwartz, 409
Farrell, Anthony Brady, 229
Faye, Alice, 388

Fears, Peggy, 32, 33
Feiffer, Jules, 261, 276–77
Feingold, Michael, 181, 183
Feist, Gene, 193
Feld, Kenneth, 409
Feldshuh, Tovah, 317, 345
Fellini, Federico, 315, 375
Femia, Tommy, 209
Fenwick, Irene, 42
Ferber, Edna, 29, 373
Ferguson, Jesse Tyler, 211
Ferrer, Jos, 55, 172, 190
Fetchit, Stepin', 390
Fetter, Ted, 102, 162–63
Feuer, Cy, 114, 131–32, 245, 249, 314–16, 336
Feydeau, Georges, 10, 119
Field (Rice), Betty, 176
Field, Ron, 29, 124, 211, 297, 302, 332, 334–35
Fielding, Harold, 201
Fields, Dorothy, 33–35, 53, 86–87, 94, 122, 128–
    29, 143, 145, 147, 150, 170, 177, 315–17, 389,
    390, 396, **448**
Fields, Herbert, 41, 53, 72, 81, 86–89, 91–92, 94,
    96, 105, 111, 122–23, 127–29, 145, **448–49**
Fields, Joseph, 111, 212, 228
Fields, Lew, 3, 9, 20, 37, 40–42, 44, 61, 81, 86–88,
    90–95, 111, 120, 122, 136
Fields, W. C., 45–47, 62, 401
Fierstein, Harvey, 328
Fifth Avenue Productions, 302
Findley, Danielle, 302
Finn, William, 262, 291, 320, **369–74**, 384
Fisher, Fred, 25
Fisher, Jules, 337, 371
Fisher, M. Anthony, 286
Fisher, Robert, 349
Fitch, Robert, 298
Fitzhugh, Ellen, 319, 337, 352, 353, 364, 413
Flaherty, Stephen, 291, **381–84**
Flatt, Ernest, 236, 239, 296
Foglia, Leonard, 177
Foley, Ellen, 399
Fonda, Henry, 111, 260
Fonda, Jane, 276
Foote, Horton, 201
Ford, Corey, 88
Ford, Helen, 60, 61, 89–92, 94, 222
Ford, Joan, 396
Ford, Paul, 258, 332
Fornes, Maria Irene, 401
Forrest, George, 376–77, 393–94
Forsythe, Henderson, 404
Fosse, Bob, 102, 111, 215, 231, 235, 248–49, 251–
    53, 263, 314–16, 322, 333, 335, 336, 356, 396–
    97, **449**

Fowler, Beth, 284, 366
Fox, Harry, 22, 43
Fox, Maxine, 402
Fox Theatricals, 411
Foy, Eddie, 4, 5, 38
Foy, Eddie, Jr., 83, 84, 227, 251, 335
Fraganza, Trixie, 41
Franchi, Sergio, 113
Francis, Arlene, 187
Francis, Arthur. *See* Gershwin, Ira
Francis, W. T., 3, 7
Frank, Melvin, 395
Frankel, Jerry, 411
Franklin, Bonnie, 297
Fraser, Alison, 369, 370, 407
Fratantoni, Diane, 258, 259
Fratti, Mario, 375
Frazee, H. H., 39, 57, 80
Frazier, Michael, 352
Frechette, Peter, 332
Freedley, Vinton, 59, 61, 65–69, 71–73, 95, 124–
    28, 163, 165, **449**
Freedman, Gerald, 211, 215, 258, 308, 328, 400,
    404
Freeman, Al, Jr., 237
Freeman, Chico, 373
Frey, Nathaniel, 145, 396
Freydberg, James B., 405, 409
Fried, Barbara, 318, 319
Friedman, Bruce Jay, 253
Friedman, Charles, 179, 193–94
Friedman, Peter, 383
Friedman, Seth, 357–58, 365
Friedman, Stephen, 298, 318, 357
Friml, Rudolf, 24, 67, 78
Frohman, Charles, 3–14, 44, 63
Froman, Jane, 141, 161, 163
Fry, Christopher, 216
Fryer, Robert, 145, 157, 212, 277, 284–85, 318,
    335, 351, **450**
Fuller, Larry, 284–85, 318, 351
Fuller, Penny, 114, 297, 372
Furth, George, 277–78, 281, 285, 289, 336

Gabel, Martin, 186–87, 189, 195, 260
Gabrielle, Josefina, 104
Gaines, Boyd, 258, 279
Gaines, Davis, 100
Gaines, Reg E., 409
Galati, Frank, 383
Gallagher, Helen, 80, 102, 206–207, 228–30, 315,
    345
Gallagher, Peter, 103, 246, 351, 399
Gallico, Paul, 146
Garber, Victor, 190, 252, 284, 287, 314

Gardiner, Reginald, 141–42
Gardner, Herb, 240–41
Gardner, Rita, 305, 331
Garland, Judy, 155, 157, 206, 207, 208, 209
Garland, Patrick, 224
Garner, Jay, 325, 350
Garrett, Betty, 129, 165, 195–96, 209
Garrison, Ben, 407
Garrison, David, 68, 307, 328, 350, 378
Gasarch, Mark, 363
Gasman, Ira, 321–22
Gatchell, R. Tyler, Jr., 309, 338
Gautier, Dick, 294
Gaxton, William, 47, 48, 51–52, 72, 73, 93, 122, 124–27
Gay, John, 173, 181
Gaynes, George, 189, 212
Gaynor, Mitzi, 171
Gear, Luella, 18, 98, 123, 152, 194
Geddes, Jill, 351
Geer, Will, 186, 190, 194
Geffen, David, 364
Gelbart, Larry, 276, 303, 320, 376
Geld, Gary, 402–404
Gennaro, Liza, 246, 397
Gennaro, Peter, 55, 172, 181–82, 197, 215, 231, 240, 257, 270, 298, 303, 314, 387
Gerard, Danny, 371
Gershe, Leonard, 199, 355
Gershwin, Frances, 121
Gershwin, George, 1, 20, 25, 46, **57–76**, 77, 79, 81, 82, 98, 105, 106, 115, 121, 126, 159, 161–63, 169, 171, 178, 207, 285, 390
Gershwin, Ira, 35, 58–80, 82, 98, 121, 137, 143–44, 152–53, 155, 158, 160, 162, 170, 176–78, **450–51**
Gersten, Bernard, 414
Gesner, Clark, 397–98
Gest, Morris, 19, 22, 26, 59
Gets, Malcolm, 100, 285, 372–73
Geva, Tamara, 98, 100, 135, 139–40, 161, 169
Ghostley, Alice, 213
Giagni, D. J., 287, 357, 365
Gibbs, Sheila, 382
Gibson, William, 295, 316–17
Gilbert, Jean, 10, 15, 42, 136, 159
Gilbert, Willie, 248, 277
Gilford, Jack, 72, 73, 80, 197, 276, 332, 397
Gillette, Anita, 55, 190, 295
Gillette, Priscilla, 131, 188, 394
Gingold, Hermione, 251, 281, 283, 313, 324
Giono, Jean, 356–57
Giraudoux, Jean, 327
Gish, Lillian, 343
Glass, Montague, 136
Gleason, Jackie, 264

Gleason, Joanna, 286, 303, 317
Glenville, Peter, 264, 327
Glover, Savion, 407, 409
Glynn, Carlin, 404
Goetz, E. Ray, 9, 39–44, 40, 60–63, 77, 117, 119, 121–23
Goldby, Derek, 261
Golden, Annie, 287, 413
Golden, John, 17, 46
Goldin, Ricky Paull, 402
Goldman, Byron, 16, 349, 350, 355
Goldman, James, 279–80, 331, 336
Goldman, William, 331, 336
Goldsby, Helen, 155
Goldsmith, Merwin, 363
Goldwyn, Tony, 176
Goodman, Benny, 129
Goodman, Dody, 293, 294, 305, 323
Goodman, Jules Erhart, 136
Goodman, Philip, 27, 81
Goodspeed Musicals, 310–11
Goodspeed Opera House, 16, 67, 246, 319, 344, 353, 389
Gordon, Allan S., 410
Gordon, John, 397
Gordon, Judy, 318
Gordon, Lawrence, 360
Gordon, Max, 32, 33, 35, 55, 125, 139–40, 143, 144, 161, 169, 178
Gordon, Robert H., 144, 194–97, 222, 244
Gorney, Jay, 149–51
Gossett, Louis, 200
Gottfried, Martin, 240
Gould, Elliot, 200
Gould, Morton, 213
Goulet, Robert, 171, 208, 225, 333
Goz, Harry, 338
Grable, Betty, 127–28
Grace, Michael R., 350
Grade, Lord Lew, 285
Graff, Randy, 320
Graff, Todd, 405
Graham, Ronald, 34, 100, 104, 127, 142, 152, 164, 256, 275, 277, 302, 313
Grant, Micki, 357
Grant, Pauline, 207
Gravitte, Debbie Shapiro, 51, 100, 347
Gray, Dolores, 111, 166, 199, 229
Gray, Kevin, 338
Gray, Margery, 257
Gray, Timothy, 207–209
Green, Adolph, 211–13, 218, 229–34, 236, 239, 297, 317–20, 337, 351–52, 364, **444–45**
Green, Dennis, 363
Green, Jack, 63

Green, Johnny, 103, 139
Green, Mitzi, 99, 195, 390
Green, Morris, 390
Green, Paul, 174
Greenbank, Percy, 4, 5, 15, 159
Greenblatt, Kenneth D., 352, 376, 377, 409
Greene, Ellen, 364, 365
Greene, Herbert, 269
Greene, Schuyler, 14–16, 18, 58, 77, 80, 118
Greenstreet, Sydney, 33
Greenwood, Charlotte, 33, 41, 47, 131
Gregory, Gillian, 300
Greif, Michael, 410
Gresham, Herbert, 7, 17, 42, 58, 60
Grey, Clifford, 17, 23, 24, 63, 79, 81, 83, 89, 118, 120
Grey, Joel, 167, 189, 293, 328, 332, 350
Grier, David Alan, 178
Griffith, Andy, 199
Griffith, Robert E., 215, 251–52, 257, 263, 275
Grimaldi, Dennis, 303
Grimes, Tammy, 167, 189, 208, 270, 293
Groener, Harry, 71
Groody, Louise, 20, 23, 25, 80, 81
Gross, Shelly, 239, 300
Grossman, Larry, 291, 319, 337, **349–53**, 364
Grossmith, George, 4, 7, 15, 17, 24–26, 64, 79, 119, 120, 139
Grossmith, Lawrence, 5
Group Theatre, 174
Grudeff, Marian, 260
Guardino, Harry, 277, 336
Guare, John, 216, 373–74
Guber, Lee, 239, 300, 302
Guettel, Adam, 373–74, 408–409, 413–14
Guillaume, Robert, 246
Guittard, Laurence, 104, 258, 280
Gunton, Bob, 284, 406
Guthrie, Tyrone, 214
Gutierrez, Gerald, 186, 246, 376, 397
Gutzi, Mary, 240
Guy, Rosa, 381
Guzman, Josie de, 246
Gwillim, Jack, 224
Gwynne, Fred, 270

Hackady, Hal, 349–51
Hadary, Jonathan, 107, 232, 287, 363, 365, 376
Hadjidakis, Manos, 278
Hague, Albert, 394–97
Haimes, Todd, 279
Haines, H. E., 4, 12
Haines, Jim, 344, 346
Hale, Chester, 227
Hale, Sonny, 92, 96, 121

Haley, Jack, 83, 101, 144
Hall, Adelaide, 127, 152, 156, 207, 389
Hall, Bettina, 32, 124
Hall, Carol, 353, 390, 404–405
Hall, Delores, 404
Hall, Juanita, 108, 111, 155
Hall, Natalie, 32, 83
Hall, Peter, 360
Halliday, Richard, 111, 146, 229
Hambleton, T. Edward, 167, 189, 293, 397
Hamilton, Margaret, 29, 104, 396
Hamlisch, Marvin, 291, **359–62**, 375
Hammerstein, Arthur, 3, 31, 33, 67, 78, 79, 86, 135
Hammerstein, James, 106, 273
Hammerstein, Oscar, 2nd, 27, 29–35, 53, 56, 67, 78, 79, 81–82, 85, 87, 106–109, 111–15, 129, 135, 137, 144, 177, 199, 215, 253, 273, **451**
Hammerstein, Reginald, 32
Hammerstein, Theodore, 122
Hammerstein, William, 104
Hammett, Dashiell, 303
Hanan, Stephen, 230
Haney, Carol, 235, 251, 256, 258, 313
Harbach, Otto, 27, 28, 32–34, 39, 45, 67, 78, 80, 135, 138, **451–52**
Harburg, E. Y. (Yip), 141, 150–54, 156–57, 160–62, 164, 170–71, 237, 392, **452**
Hardwicke, Cedric, 343
Hardy, Joseph, 158, 225, 349, 397
Harley, Margot, 373
Harman, Barry, 180, 365
Harney, Ben, 405
Harnick, Sheldon, 114, 256–62, 293–94, 305, 332, **452**
Harris, Barbara, 171–72, 183, 261
Harris, Drew Scott, 310
Harris, Henry B., 39, 41
Harris, John, 227
Harris, Joseph, 351, 357
Harris, Julie, 213
Harris, Richard, 225
Harris, Rosemary, 338
Harris, Sam H., 10, 40, 41, 43–50, 72, 73, 99, 125, 127, 141, 176–77, 321, **453**
Harris, Scott, 310, 347
Harrison, Gregory, 340, 353, 369–70
Harrison, Rex, 224
Harry, Jackee, 338, 365
Hart, Linda, 353
Hart, Lorenz (Larry), 33, 41, 49, 50, 81, 85–103, 105–106, 108, 112, 121–22, 135–37, 172, 206, **453–54**
Hart, Moss, 50–51, 54, 75, 98–100, 125, 127, 129, 142, 144, 153, 162, 176–77, 185, 187, 194, 195, 224–25, 285, **454**

Hart, Teddy, 100–101, 177
Hartman, Grace, 197
Hartman, Paul, 72, 197
Hartog, Jan de, 307
Harvey, Michael, 183
Harwood, John, 30, 65–67, 90, 150, 160
Haskell, David, 355
Hauptman, William, 406
Havoc, June, 102, 129, 166, 189–90
Hawkins, Tim, 366
Haworth, Jill, 332
Hayden, Michael, 106
Hayden, Sophie, 246
Hayes, Helen, 39, 107, 168
Hayman, Lillian, 236, 334
Haynes, Tiger, 236, 299, 403
Hayward, Leland, 54, 55, 108, 111, 198, 232
Hearn, George, 114, 209, 241, 280, 328, 351
Heatherton, Ray, 99
Hecht, Ben, 97, 129, 151, 179, 229, 318
Hecht, Paul, 262, 401
Heckart, Eileen, 276, 331, 343, 355
Heifner, Jack, 361
Heinfling, Martin, 302
Heller, Adam, 285
Hellman, Lillian, 187–89, 191, 198, 213, 214, 269
Helpmann, Robert, 309
Henderson, Florence, 108, 198
Henderson, Luther, 407–408
Henderson, Ray, 128, 153, 388–89
Henning, Doug, 356
Henshall, Ruthie, 162
Hensley, Shuler, 104
Henson, Leslie, 138
Hepburn, Katharine, 337, 408
Herbert, Joseph W., 6, 8, 11, 12, 59
Herbert, Victor, 12, 20, 24, 42, 44, 77
Heredia, Wilson Jermaine, 410
Herlie, Eileen, 264, 295
Herman, Jerry, 239, 265, 278, 284, 286, 291, 294, 295, **323–29**, 375
Herzog, Jonathan C., 373
Hess, Rodger, 407
Hewett, Christopher, 100, 104, 254, 256, 293, 313, 324
Hewett, Peggy, 370, 371
Heyer, Bill, 317
Heyman, Barton, 282
Heyman, Edward, 139, 141
Heyward, Dorothy, 34, 74
Heyward, DuBose, 34, 74–75, 153
Hibbert, Edward, 176
Hickey, John Benjamin, 333
Hickman, Charles, 207
Hicks, Seymour, 3, 4, 12

Higgins, Joel, 254, 403
Hill, George Roy, 247
Hill, Ken, 378
Hill, Ralston, 310
Hines, Gregory, 407–408
Hines, Maurice, 300
Hingle, Pat, 401
Hinnant, Bill, 397
Hinnant, Skip, 397
Hirsch, Louis, 8, 16, 21, 38, 41, 42, 44, 45, 387
Hirschfeld, Al, 166
Hirson, Roger, 356
Hitchcock, Raymond, 23, 57, 118–19, 120
Hobson, I. M., 370
Hoey, Evelyn, 122
Hoffman, Al, 263
Hoffman, Cady, 320
Holden, Hal, 72
Holden, John, 293
Holder, Geoffrey, 155, 378, 403
Holgate, Ron, 53, 324, 328, 401
Holland, Anthony, 282
Holliday, Jennifer, 405
Holliday, Judy, 147, 231, 277, 397
Holloway, Julian, 224
Holloway, Stanley, 33, 138, 224
Holloway, Sterling, 89, 91, 160, 185
Holly, John, 377
Holm, Celeste, 104, 107, 154, 275–76
Holm, Hanya, 130, 131, 189, 224–25, 394
Holman, Libby, 81, 126, 136, 138–39, 141, 161, 169
Holofcener, Larry, 255–56
Holt, Fritz, 218, 328, 336
Holt, Will, 254
Holtz, Lou, 60, 66, 84, 150
Homer, 345, 394
Homer, Richard, 254
Hooks, Robert, 236
Hope, Bob, 33, 126, 162
Hopper, DeWolf, 12, 46, 61
Hopper, Edna Wallace, 5, 39
Horne, Lena, 152, 155–56
Horner, Richard, 208
Horwitt, Arnold B., 144, 196, 213, 256, 313, 394
Hoschna, Karl, 39
Hotchner, A. E., 319
Hoty, Dee, 280, 320, 357, 365
Houghton, Norris, 167, 189, 293, 397
Houseman, John, 186, 187, 189, 190, 404
Howard, Eugene, 41, 141, 161, 388
Howard, Ken, 218, 316, 401
Howard, Sidney, 175–76
Howard, Willie, 23, 41, 71, 161, 388
Howes, Sally Ann, 253, 360

Howland, Beth, 278
Hoyle, Geoff, 413
Hoyt, Charles, 10, 17, 57
Hruba, Vera, 163, 227
Hubbell, Raymond, 9, 10, 19, 37, 39, 41, 57
Huffman, J. C., 10, 12, 41, 57, 59, 63, 120
Hughes, Barnard, 352
Hughes, Langston, 179
Hugo, Laurence, 282
Hulbert, Jack, 91, 137
Hunt, Linda, 352
Hunt, Peter, 350, 400
Hunter, Glenn, 95
Hunter, Kelly, 360
Husmann, Ron, 131, 211, 257, 295
Huston, Walter, 175
Hymer, John B., 70
Hytner, Nicholas, 106

Ibsen, Henrik, 351
Illman, Margaret, 241
Ingham, Barrie, 225, 411
Ingram, Rex, 154, 163, 194
Innvar, Christopher, 373, 408
INTAR Hispanic American Arts Center, 371
Irving, George S., 51, 98, 114, 228, 333, 387, 401
Irving, Washington, 175
Irwin, May, 38, 40
Irwin, Wallace, 7
Isaacs, Pamela, 321
Iscove, Rob, 230
Isherwood, Christopher, 332
Ivanek, Zeljko, 375
Ivans, Perry, 88
Ives, David, 68
Ivey, Dana, 285, 395

Jablonski, Carl, 309
Jackman, Hugh, 104
Jackson, Anne, 182
Jackson, Arthur, 58, 60, 61, 65
Jackson, Ernestine, 246
Jacobi, Lou, 236
Jacobi, Victor, 12, 44
Jacobs, Jim, 402–403
Jacobson, Irving, 343
Jacoby, Mark, 29, 383
Jaffe, Sam, 175
James, Brian d'Arcy, 378
James, Hal, 236, 343
James, Jessica, 314
James, Paul, 390
James, Peter, 300
Jamieson, James, 223
Janis, Elsie, 15, 44, 117

Japan Satellite Broadcasting, Inc., 320
Jaroslow, Ruth, 260
Jbara, Gregory, 408
Jeanmarie, Zizi, 131
Jeans, Ronald, 142
Jellison, John, 373
Jenkins, Daniel H., 406, 409
Jenks, Almet F., Jr., 117
Jennings, Ken, 284, 366, 412
Jessel, Raymond, 114, 260
Jeter, Michael, 377
Jewison, Norman, 271
Jimenez, Tai, 211
Joerder, Norbert, 225
Joffe, Charles, 349
Johanson, Robert, 280, 353
John, Elton, 413
John F. Kennedy Center. *See* Kennedy (John F.)
    Center
John, Kenneth, 338
Johns, Glynis, 281, 343, 346
Johnson, Alan, 353
Johnson, Bill, 102, 110–11, 129, 163, 222
Johnson, Chic, 194, 240
Johnson, Karen, 397
Johnson, Louis, 402
Johnson, Mary Lea, 284, 301, 318, 351, 352, 370,
    376
Johnson, Nora, 265
Johnson, Nunnally, 50, 144, 161, 237, 265
Johnson, Susan, 246
Johnston, Alva, 55
Johnstone, Justine, 43
Jolson, Al, 9, 41, 59, 170
Jones, Casey, 166
Jones, Dean, 278
Jones, Elinor, 308, 309
Jones, Richard, 378
Jones, Tom, 293, 294, 305–11, **454–55**
Jordan, Glenn, 196
Joseph Papp Public Theatre, 409
Joslyn, Betsy, 310, 351
Jourdan, Louis, 172
Jujamcyn Theatres, 286, 320, 377, 407
Julia, Raul, 181, 245, 344, 376

Kagan, Richard M., 360, 361
Kahn, Gus, 70, 82, 389
Kahn, Madeline, 113, 258, 277, 318, 401
Kalfin, Robert, 183, 240
Kalman, Emmerich, 7, 17, 19
Kalmar, Bert, 28, 48, 91, 93, 135–36
Kandel, Paul, 381
Kander, John, 245, 258, 291, **331–41**, 352, 364,
    384, 415

Kane, Donna, 209
Kane, Helen, 135–36
Kanin, Fay, 352
Kanin, Garson, 233, 235
Kanin, Michael, 146, 336
Kantor, Kenneth, 310
Kantor, Mary, 371
Kaplan, Jonathan, 372
Karin, Fia, 323
Karloff, Boris, 212, 213
Karnilova, Maria, 226, 232, 259, 300, 334
Karr, Patti, 259, 299
Kasha, Lawrence, 29, 124, 254, 258, 297, 316, 323, 336
Katselas, Milton, 355
Kauffman, Marta, 357–58, 365
Kaufman, George S., 40, 48–50, 55, 68, 70–73, 99, 127, 129, 132, 136, 139–41, 144, 149, 177, 187, 194–95, 197, 199, 245–46, 273, 285, 373, **455**
Kaye, Benjamin M., 86, 89, 91
Kaye, Danny, 113, 128, 176–77, 246, 408
Kaye, Judy, 383
Kaye, Nora, 167
Kaye, Stubby, 352, 388, 395
Kazan, Elia, 174, 177–78, 180
Kazan, Lainie, 317, 382
Kazantzakis, Nikos, 334
Kean, Norman, 299
Kearns, Allen, 66, 68, 71, 120
Keaton, Diane, 349, 399
Keel, Howard, 157
Keeler (Jolson), Ruby, 29, 70, 80, 82
Kellaway, Cecil, 347
Keller, Jeff, 366
Kellerman, Sally, 265
Kellin, Mike, 75, 110, 318
Kelly, Gene, 102–103, 111, 205
Kelly, Patsy, 80, 140, 387
Kelton, Pert, 247, 269
Kennedy, Arthur, 176
Kennedy (John F.) Center, 106, 217, 219, 299, 301, 309, 345, 352, 378
Kenneth John Productions, Inc., 329, 338, 365
Kent, William, 20, 68, 71
Kerker, Gustave, 6
Kern, Jerome, 1, **3–35**, 53, 56, 57, 105, 115, 117–18, 130, 137, 143–44, 158, 273, 387, 389
Kerr, E. Catherine, 375
Kerr, Jean, 251, 275, 313, 396
Kerr, Walter, 396
Kert, Larry, 72, 73, 215, 256, 283, 302, 313, 331
Kibbee, Roland, 345
Kidd, Michael, 131, 196–97, 199, 234–35, 245, 253, 262, 265–66, 269, 270–71, 314, 326, 361, 388, 395–96, **455–56**

Kies, Patricia, 225
Kikuchi, Susan, 109
Kiley, Richard, 112, 175, 261, 343, 344, 393, 396
Kimbrough, Charles, 240, 278, 285
King, Charles, 58, 81, 94, 120, 122
King, Dennis, 29, 32, 100, 164, 221
King, Edith, 157, 314
King, Larry L., 404–405
King, Rufus F., 117
Kipness, Joseph, 200–201, 228, 240, 297, 316, 317
Kirk, Keith Byron, 373
Kirk, Lisa, 130, 318, 327
Kirkwood, James, 359
Kitt, Eartha, 393
Klaris, Harvey J., 375, 376
Klaw, Marc, 17, 20, 59
Kleban, Edward, 359
Klein, Robert, 360
Klemperer, Werner, 266, 332
Kline, Kevin, 318, 404
Klugman, Jack, 232
Knowlton, Sarah, 211
Koch, Edward I., 301
Koehler, Ted, 149–50, 152–53, 157
Kollmar, Richard, 101, 104, 156, 175, 256, 313, 391, 394
Kopit, Arthur, 352, 375, 377–78
Korbich, Eddie, 287
Korey, Alix, 370, 371
Korf, Gene R., 338
Kornfeld, Lawrence, 401
Koslow, Paula, 407
Koussevitzky, Serge, 160, 211
Krakeur, Richard, 166
Krakowski, Jane, 377
Kramer, Terry Allen, 303, 317
Krasna, Norman, 53
Krauss, Marvin A., 302, 328
Kresley, Edmund, 294
Krieger, Henry, 405, 412–13
Krupska, Dania, 67, 114, 246, 261
Kubinski, Cassandra, 310
Kuhn, Judy, 51, 68, 259, 302, 367
Kushner, James, 370
Kushner, Tony, 373
Kyte, Mary, 360, 363, 364, 370

La Chanze, 131, 279, 382
Lacey, Florence, 325, 328
Lagomarsino, Ron, 382
Lahr, Bert, 75, 98, 127–29, 142, 151–53, 229, 249, 389
Lahr, John, 338, 364
Lake, Harriette, 96
Lammers, Paul, 293, 294, 305

Lamos, Mark, 373
Lampert, Emma, 310
Lancaster, Burt, 359
Landau, Tina, 408–409, 413–14
Landay, David S., 336
Landesman, Heidi, 286, 406, 407
Landesman, Rocco, 286, 406, 407
Landmark Entertainment Group, 411
Lane, Burton, 1, 68, 168, **169–72**, 243–44
Lane, Nathan, 246, 276
Lane, Rosemary, 103, 205
Lane, Stewart F., 320, 328, 336, 361
Lang, Harold, 130, 200, 206–207, 211
Lannin, Paul, 61, 77, 159
Lansbury, Angela, 232, 233, 238, 277–78, 284,
    326, 327, 329
Lansbury, Edgar, 237, 282, 355, 356, 401
Lapine, James, 285–89, 370–73
Lardner, Ring, 16, 83, 149
Lardner, Ring, Jr., 336
Larsen, Liz, 127, 373
Larson, Jonathan, 410–11
Lasky, Jesse L., 39, 42
Lasser, Louise, 265
Latessa, Dick, 190, 302, 308, 319, 320, 338, 352,
    365, 370, 383, 395, 400
Latouche, John, 163–64, 167, 214, 391, 394
Laurence, Paula, 129, 177, 194
Laurents, Arthur, 112–13, 215, 218, 232, 236, 275–
    77, 282, 303, 328, 336
Lavallade, Carmen de, 282
Lavin, Linda, 278, 296
Lawford, Ernest, 6
Lawrence, Carol, 157, 215, 234
Lawrence, Gertrude, 67–69, 81, 109, 124, 176–77
Lawrence, Jerome, 167, 206, 207, 326, 327
Laye, Evelyn, 30, 120, 143
Layton, Joe, 108, 111–13, 201, 211, 241, 247, 257,
    300, 318, 319, 327, 397, **456**
Lazarus, Frank, 328
Lazarus, Paul, 357, 365
Le Loka, Tsidii, 413
Lear, Evelyn, 189
Leavitt, Phillip, 85–87
Lebo M, 413
Lecuona, Ernesto, 84
Lederer, Charles, 393
Lederer, George W., 39
Lee, Gypsy Rose, 195, 232, 350
Lee, Michele, 316
Lee, Robert E., 167, 206–207, 326, 327
Lee, Sammy, 45
Lefrak, Francine, 370, 376
Leftwich, Alexander, 70, 71, 81, 88, 93–95, 136,
    149, 169

Lehar, Franz, 7
Lehman, Jeanne, 324
Leiber, Jerry, 365
Leigh, Carolyn, 230, 240, 275, 294, 305, 313–17,
    361
Leigh, Mitch, 109, 291, **343–47**
Leight, Warren, 301
LeMaire, George, 47, 60
LeMaire, Rufus, 47, 60, 62
Lennart, Isobel, 234
Lenya, Lotte, 174, 175, 178–79, 181–82, 332
Leonidoff, Leon, 142
Leopold and Loeb case, 313
Lerner, Alan Jay, 170–72, 180, 218, 222–25, 301,
    456
Leroux, Gaston, 377
Leroy, Hal, 162
Lesser, Arthur, 200, 229
Lester, Edwin, 168, 171, 214, 225, 230, 271
Levant, Oscar, 31
Levene, Sam, 245, 266
Levey (Cohan), Ethel, 39, 42
Levin, Herman, 196, 198, 224, 228
Levin, Meyer, 313
Levine, Ilana, 398
Levit, Ben, 370
Levy, Ted L., 407
Lewine, Richard, 102, 237
Lewis, Albert, 163–64
Lewis, Brenda, 188
Lewis, Jerry, 240, 317
Lewis, Jim, 370, 371
Lewis, Joe E., 164
Lewis, Marcia, 260
Lewis, Norm, 412
Lewis, Robert, 156, 171, 174, 188–89, 223, 253
Lewis, Ron, 336
Lewis, Ted, 46
Lewis, Vicki, 103, 350
Lewis-Evans, Kecia, 382
Lichtefeld, Michael, 111, 228, 284, 285, 407
Liebman, Max, 165, 221, 243, 315
Lief, Max, 136–37
Lief, Nathaniel, 136–37
Lilley, Clarke, 390
Lilley, Edward Clark, 142, 161
Lillie, Beatrice, 68, 75, 80–81, 93–94, 97, 98, 129,
    141–42, 144, 153, 161–62, 169, 189, 208
Limon, Jos, 163
Lincoln Center Theater, 124, 288, 372, 382, 414
Linden, Hal, 124, 251, 262, 367
Lindfors, Viveca, 182
Lindsay, Howard, 54, 55, 111–12, 123–26, 141,
    153
Linn, Bambi, 23, 106, 200

Linn-Baker, Mark, 276
Lion, Margo, 302, 407
Lipman, Maureen, 104
Lippa, Andrew, 397–98, 399
Little, Cleavon, 402
Littler, Emile, 207
Livent (U.S.), 29, 217, 339, 383–84, 414–15
Llana, Jos, 413
Lloyd, Christopher, 183
Lloyd Weber, Andrew, 356, 378, 406, 415
Lockhart, Gene, 142
Lockhart, Warren, 350
Loeb, Philip, 89, 91, 94, 160, 185, 194, 195
Loesser, Arthur, 243
Loesser, Frank, 132, 143–44, 166, 170, 196, 203, 221, 227, **243–49**, 269–70, 391, 401
Loesser, Lynn, 246–47
Loewe, Frederick, 172, 180, 203, **221–26**, 243
Logan, Ella, 160, 171
Logan, Joshua, 53, 55, 100–101, 104, 107–108, 143, 175, 198–99, 237, 295, **457**
Long, Avon, 34, 35, 74
Long, Huey, 52
Long, Nick, Jr., 142
Long, Sumner Arthur, 331
Longbottom, Robert, 412
Longstreet, Stephen, 228
Loos, Anita, 228
Lopez, Priscilla, 328, 359
Losch, Tilly, 121, 139
Loudon, Dorothy, 31, 277, 298, 302, 304, 329
Lovett, Marcus, 367
Loy, Myrna, 303
Lubovitch, Lar, 107, 109, 241, 286
Lucas, Craig, 284
Luce, Claire, 142
Ludwig, Ken, 71
Luftig, Hal, 407
Lukas, Paul, 54
Luker, Rebecca, 29, 100, 111, 407
Lumet, Sidney, 179
Lund, Art, 246, 265
LuPone, Patti, 103, 124, 186, 279, 357, 370, 404
Lusby, Vernon, 307
Lyles, Aubrey, 387
Lyndeck, Edmund, 284, 351

MacArthur, Charles, 97, 318
MacArthur, James, 276
MacDermot, Galt, 399–400
MacDonald, Audra Ann, 106
MacDonald, Jeanette, 100
MacDonald, William, 358
MacGregor, Edgar, 51, 60, 61, 64, 68, 83, 127–28, 138, 165, 170, 388

Mack, Stan, 363
Mackay (Berlin), Ellin, 48
Mackenzie, Will, 307
Mackintosh, Cameron, 104, 106–107, 281, 283, 288, 364, 378, 406
MacMillan, Sir Kenneth, 106
MacNaughton, Patricia, 358
MacRae, Heather, 285, 371, 372
Madison Square Garden, 366
Magee, Patrick, 316
Maggart, Brandon, 240, 317
Magicworks Entertainments, 411
Magness, Marilyn, 230
Mako, 282
Malas, Spiro, 246
Mallory, Victoria, 215, 281
Maltby, Richard, Jr, 190, 303, 405–406, 409
Mamoulian, Rouben, 74–75, 97, 104–106, 154, 166, 180–81, **457**
Mancina, Mark, 413
Mancini, Henry, 408, 412
Mandel, Frank, 64, 80, 96, 388
Mandell, Michael, 373
Manhattan Theatre Club, 288, 363, 376
Mann, Daniel, 223
Mann, Terrence, 287, 289, 302, 366, 400
Mann, Theodore, 102, 200, 245
Manners, J. Hartley, 8, 37, 123
Mantello, Joe, 383
Marbury, Elisabeth, 15, 18, 117–18
Marie, Rose, 392
Marion, George, 7, 11, 21, 37, 39, 42, 49, 60, 77
Marion, George, Jr., 101, 391
Mark, Lawrence, 409
Mark, Zane, 409
Markham, Monte, 387
Marre, Albert, 167, 324, 343–46, 393
Marshall, Garry, 388
Marshall, Kathleen, 51, 54, 99, 100, 395, 401
Marshall, Ken, 215
Marshall, Larry, 299
Marshall, Pat, 222
Marshall, Rob, 252, 258, 276, 279, 314, 333, 339, 400, 408
Martin, Andrea, 131, 217, 382, 383
Martin, Barney, 335
Martin, Elliot, 258, 332
Martin, Ernest H., 131–32, 245, 249, 314–15, 336
Martin, Hugh, 103, **205–209**, 245
Martin, Jesse L., 410
Martin, Leila, 262, 308
Martin, Mary, 108, 109, 111, 127, 146, 165, 177–78, 230, 231, 235, 307, 309
Martin, Millicent, 283
Martin, Norman, 334–35

Martin, Stephen G., 338, 364
Martin, Virginia, 172, 248, 314–15
Martins, Peter, 98, 106
Marx, Arthur, 349–50
Marx, Groucho, 139, 169, 349
Marx, Minnie, 349–50
Marx Brothers, 49, 71, 154
Maschwitz, Eric, 207
Mason, Karen, 338
Massey, Daniel, 226, 258
Massi, Bernice, 112, 266
Massine, Leonide, 84
Masteroff, Joe, 258, 332, 335
Masterson, Peter, 404
Matalon, Vivian, 223
Mathis, Stanley Wayne, 155, 398, 407
Matthews, Inez, 181
Matthews, Jessie, 92, 96, 121, 137, 165
Mattioli, Louis, 115
Mature, Victor, 165, 176
Mauceri, John, 106
Maugham, W. Somerset, 166
May, Edna, 3
Mayer, Edwin Justice, 178–79
Mayer, Michael, 398
Mayerson, Frederic H., 286, 407
Mayes, Sally, 258
Mayhew, Stella, 9, 37, 41, 81
Mazzie, Marin, 131, 288, 383
MBS Co., 338
MCA/Universal, 241
McAnuff, Des, 248, 406
McArdle, Andrea, 115, 298, 329
McCann, Elizabeth Ireland, 303
McCarter Theatre, 338
McCarthy, Jeff, 360, 412
McCarthy, Joseph, 387
McCarthy, Joseph, Jr., 313
McCarthy, Theresa, 413
McCarty, Mary, 54, 198
McClintic, Guthrie, 34
McCollum, Kevin, 410
McConnell, Lulu, 87, 91, 122
McCoy (Davis), Bessie, 8, 9, 20, 39, 59
McCracken, Joan, 110, 154, 252
McCullough, Paul, 47, 48, 70, 161–62
McCully, Emily Arnold, 310
McCutcheon, Bill, 124, 349
McDonald, Audra Ann, 106, 383
McDonald, Daniel, 340
McDowall, Roddy, 225, 313, 367
McGavin, Darren, 109
McGillin, Howard, 51, 124, 162, 258
McGovern, Maureen, 72, 73, 182
McGrath, Mark, 127

McGrath, Michael, 51, 100
McGuire, William Anthony, 31, 49, 69, 70, 82, 83, 92, 149, 171, 389
McHugh, Jimmy, 33, 94, 122, 143, 150, 163, 194, 346, 389
McKayle, Donald, 295
McKechnie, Donna, 115, 211, 257, 278, 280, 303, 359, 400
McKee, Lonette, 29
McKenna, Janice, 412
McKenney, Ruth, 212
McKenzie, Julia, 288
McLerie, Allyn (Ann), 54, 215, 245
McMartin, John, 29, 249, 280–81, 315
McNair, Barbara, 251, 256
McNally, Terrence, 103, 337–39, 383
McNamara, Maureen, 347
McNeely, Joey, 321
McVey, J. Mark, 310
Mead, Shepherd, 248
Meara, Anne, 314
Mecchia, Irene, 413
Medford, Kay, 231, 235, 294
Meehan, Thomas, 67, 114, 298, 302–304, 346, 347, 361
Meiser, Edith, 89, 91, 128, 160, 185, 270
Mell, Randle, 186
Mellon, James J., 310
Melrose, Walter, 407
Mendes, Sam, 333
Menken, Alan, 291, 352, 358, **363–68**
Menzel, Idina, 410
Mercer, Johnny, 35, 143, 151, 153–54, 156–57, 390, 391, 392–93, 395
Mercer, Marian, 400
Mercouri, Melina, 278
Mercury Theatre, 130, 186, 187
Meredith, Burgess, 75, 173
Merman, Ethel, 35, 53–55, 71, 72, 83, 84, 124–29, 143, 146, 195, 232–33, 325
Merrick, David, 16, 67, 115, 156, 198–201, 232–35, 238–39, 241, 263, 265, 295, 298, 306, 307, 316, 325–28, 331, 333–34, 349, 357, 400, **457–58**
Merrill, Bob, 203, 234, 236, 238–39, 241–42, 245, **263–67**, 325–26
Merritt, George, 411
Metaxa, Georges, 32, 141, 160
Methot, Mayo, 82
Metz, Janet, 371
Meyer, Irwin, 298, 318, 357
Meyer, Sol, 227
Michaels, Sidney, 297, 326, 345, 350
Michel Kleinman Productions, 375
Michel, Scott, 293
Michener, James, 108

Middleton, Ray, 53, 175, 180, 343
Mielziner, Jo, 98, 100
Milford, Penelope, 403
Millar, Gertie, 7
Miller, Alice Duer, 23, 33
Miller, Ann, 280
Miller, Flournoy, 387
Miller, Marilyn, 23–24, 27, 45, 46, 50, 51, 68, 69, 83, 98
Miller, Roger, 406
Miller, William, 303
Mills, Florence, 387
Mills, Stephanie, 403
Mineo, John, 371
Minnelli, Liza, 205–206, 208, 236, 332, 336, 337
Minnelli, Vincente, 34, 75, 98, 141–42, 153, 168, 206
Minoff, Tammy, 361
Minskoff, Jerome, 240, 301, 317, 345
Miranda, Carmen, 194
Missimi, Dominic, 309
Mitch Leigh Company, 344
Mitchell, Brian (Stokes), 67, 383
Mitchell, Gregory, 371
Mitchell, James, 223, 264, 327
Mitchell, Jerry, 280, 398
Mitchell, Julian, 9, 10, 38, 39, 41, 59
Mitchell, Lauren, 302, 338, 376
Mitchell, Margaret, 201, 240, 352
Mitchell, Ruth, 217, 259, 278, 280–83, 296, 332, 334
Mitchell, Thomas, 97, 229
Moln r, Ferenc, 106, 206–207
Monckton, Lionel, 4, 5, 7, 8, 58
Monk, Debra, 279, 287, 303, 340
Monk, Julius, 275, 305, 314, 349
Monnot, Marguerite, 331
Montalban, Ricardo, 156
Montano, Robert, 211
Montevecchi, Liliane, 376, 377
Montgomery, David, 25, 26
Monti, Mili, 195
Moore, Charlotte, 209
Moore, Constance, 104
Moore, Crista, 232, 409
Moore, Grace, 48
Moore, Mary Tyler, 265
Moore, Melba, 393, 399, 402
Moore, Robert, 336, 360, 400
Moore, Tom, 402
Moore, Victor, 51–52, 67, 68, 72, 73, 95, 122, 124–27, 139
Moorehead, Agnes, 168, 226
Moran, Lois, 72, 73
Moreno, Rita, 258

Morgan, Frank, 21, 69, 139
Morgan, Helen, 29, 30, 31
Morgan, James, 310
Morison, Patricia, 130
Moross, Jerome, 167, 185, 394
Morris, Anita, 318, 356, 376
Morris, E. H., 294, 305
Morris, Richard, 270–71
Morrison, Ann, 285
Morrow, Doretta, 109, 245, 393
Morse, Robert, 127, 231–32, 238–39, 264, 346
Morton, Jelly Roll, 407–408
Morton, Lew, 136
Mosel, Tad, 324
Moses, Burke, 366, 395
Moses, Gilbert, 218
Moss, Jeffrey B., 301
Mostel, Josh, 317, 382
Mostel, Zero, 177, 187, 195, 216, 259, 276, 391, 392
Mozart, Wolfgang Amadeus, 252
Muenz, Richard, 180, 225, 246
Mullally, Megan, 248
Muni, Paul, 179, 377
Munshin, Jules, 146, 196, 198, 244
Murphy, Donna, 109, 288
Murphy, George, 50, 161
Murphy, Sally, 106
Murray, Brian, 338
Murray, Mary Gordon, 314
Murray, Peg, 282
Murray, Wynn, 99–100
Music Theater of Lincoln Center, 29, 53, 104, 106, 108, 109, 393
Musical Theatre Works, 310
Myers, Pamela, 278, 350

Naismith, Laurence, 270
Nash, N. Richard, 275, 306, 314, 333, 345–46
Nash, Ogden, 166, 167, 177–78, 189, 293
Nathan, Stephen, 355
National Actors Theatre, 228
National Theatre, 360
Natwick, Mildred, 143, 216, 334
Naughton, Bill, 316
Naughton, James, 317, 320, 335
Neal, Patricia, 188
Nederlander, Charlene, 303
Nederlander, Gladys, 361
Nederlander, James M., 240, 241, 297, 301, 303, 309, 316, 320, 328, 336, 351, 352, 361, 371, 376
Nederlander, Joseph, 412
Nederlander, Scott, 412
Neff, Hildegarde, 132
Nelson, Barry, 231, 336

Nelson, Gene, 280, 388
Nelson, Portia, 357
Nemetz, Lenora, 357, 370
Neufeld, Peter, 309, 338
Neuwirth, Bebe, 103, 252, 335, 315
New Journeys Ahead Ltd., 209
New Musicals, 338, 339
New York Shakespeare Festival, 181, 211, 359, 371, 409, 413
New York Theatre Workshop, 410
Neway, Patricia, 109
Newman, David, 296, 321
Newman, Greatrex, 138
Newman, Phyllis, 211, 218, 234, 249, 317, 323, 336
Newsome, Paula, 51
Nichols, Mike, 261, 276, 294, 298, 375
Noll, Christiane, 411
Norden, A. M., 3
Norman, Marsha, 241, 373, 406–407
Norworth, Jack, 9, 14, 37
Noto, Lore, 305
Nouri, Michael, 408
Novello, Ivor, 17, 137
Noyes, Newbold, 117
Nunn, Trevor, 104, 357
Nype, Russell, 54, 188, 231, 396

O'Brien, Jack, 155, 246, 252, 289
O'Casey, Sean, 190–91, 344
Ockrent, Mike, 71, 366, 367, 409
O'Connor, Bill, 207
O'Connor, Donald, 29, 300
Odets, Clifford, 113, 295, 296
O'Donnell, Rosie, 402
Office Two-One Inc., 361
O'Hara, Jill, 400
O'Hara, John, 102–103
O'Horgan, Tom, 364, 399–400
Ojeda, Perry Laylon, 211
Oliver, Edna May, 18, 29, 68
Oliver, Joseph "King," 407
Olsen, George, 388, 389
Olsen, Ole, 194, 240
O'Malley, Kerry, 400
126 Second Avenue Corp., 407
O'Neal, Liz, 397
O'Neill, Eugene, 263–64
Oppenheimer, George, 99, 274
Orbach, Jerry, 53, 106, 186, 264, 305, 306, 335, 400
Ornadel, Cyril, 367
Orr, Mary, 297
Osato, Sono, 177–78, 211

O'Shea, Milo, 190, 209, 224, 327
Osterman, Lester, 208, 214, 231, 236, 240, 254, 256, 262
Ostreicher, Gerard, 324
Ostrow, Stuart, 216, 261, 266, 270–71, 356, 401
O'Sullivan, Maureen, 316, 332

PACE Theatrical Group, 411
Padula, Edward, 222, 294, 295
Page, Ken, 131, 358
Pagnol, Marcel, 199, 356
Paige, Janis, 251, 270
Painter, Walter, 320
Paley, Lou, 60, 63
Palmer, Peter, 239, 395
Palumbo, Dennis, 382
Panama, Norman, 395
Panaro, Hugh, 241, 412
Paper Mill Playhouse, 353
Papp, Joseph, 181, 359, 371
Pappas, Evan, 382
Pappas, Theodore, 319, 338, 352, 364
Paramount Pictures, 377
Parker, Dorothy, 214, 285
Parker, Sarah Jessica, 397
Parks, Hildy, 114, 328
Parsons, Estelle, 183, 323
Pascal, Adam, 410
Pascal, Francine, 328
Patek, Patrick J., 338
Paterson, Vincent, 339
Patinkin, Mandy, 280, 285, 371, 407
Paton, Alan, 180
Patterson, Dick, 71, 360
Paul, Tina, 266, 303, 371
Pearl, Jack, 63, 72, 136
Pearson, Sybille, 405
Pechter, Richard S., 378
Pegasus Players, 275
Peil, Mary Beth, 51, 109
Peldon, Courtney, 209
Pendleton, Austin, 365
Penn, Arthur, 191, 257, 295
Penn, Bill, 314
Penner, Joe, 122
Pennington, Ann, 10, 60, 61, 122, 388
Perelman, S. J., 161, 166, 169, 177–78
Perkins, Anthony, 247, 278, 289
Perkins, Edward B., 58
Persson, Gene, 397
Peters, Bernadette, 53, 211, 277, 285–86, 327, 361, 401
Peters, Brock, 253
Peters, Roger, 338

Peterson, Kurt, 175, 215, 357
Petina, Irra, 214
Petit, Roland, 131
Phillips, Lou Diamond, 109
Phillips, Robin, 411, 412
Phoenix Theatre, 394
Piazzolla, Astor, 370, 371
Pickens, Jane, 32, 188
Picon, Molly, 254, 324, 344
Pidgeon, Walter, 97, 264
Pinero, Sir Arthur Wing, 10, 11, 58
Pinkins, Tonya, 407
Pinza, Ezio, 108, 198
Pittleman, Ira, 373
Playten, Alice, 265, 401
Playwrights' Company, 167, 175, 176, 179, 180,
    190, 214
Playwrights Horizons, 285, 287, 369–70, 371, 381–
    82, 408
Plummer, Christopher, 213, 234
Poiret, Jean, 328, 375
Pollock, Muriel, 136
Polygram Broadway Ventures, Inc., 408
Polygram Diversified Entertainment, 407
Pope, Stephanie, 162
Poretta, Frank, 183, 214
Porter, Cole, 1, 16, 94, 97, 102, 109, **117–33**, 137,
    144, 209, 233
Portfolio Productions, 308
Potter, Don, 350
Powell, Eleanor, 141–42, 390
Powell, Michael, 241
Powell, Shezwae, 358
Powell, William, 303
Power, Tyrone, 214
Prager, Stanley, 349
Pratt, Theodore, 167
Presley, Elvis, 318
Presnell, Harve, 201, 270, 302, 303
Pressburger, Emeric, 241
Pressley, Brenda, 338
Preston, Robert, 266, 269–70, 307, 326, 327, 343
Price, Gilbert, 218, 297, 393, 401
Price, Leontyne, 74, 75
Price, Lonny, 103, 190, 262, 285, 302, 365, 371
Price, Michael P., 310
Price, Vincent, 237
Prince, Daisy, 414
Prince, Faith, 106, 127, 246, 257, 303, 314, 371, 372
Prince, Harold, 29, 114, 215, 217, 251–52, 256–60,
    263, 275–76, 278–86, 296–97, 318, 319, 331,
    332, 334, 338, 339, 351–53, 364, 365, 378, 414–
    15, **458**
Prud'homme, Cameron, 145, 263, 270

Prunzik, Karen, 228
Puck, Eva, 88, 90
Puig, Manuel, 338, 339
Purcell, Charles, 80, 87, 89

Quayle, Anthony, 216
Quinn, Anthony, 75, 334

Racheff, James, 67
Rackmil, Gladys, 218, 336
Rado, James, 399
Rae, Charlotte, 167, 181, 189, 238, 293, 395
Raft, George, 28
Ragni, Gerome, 399
Rainger, Ralph, 137
Raitt, John, 106, 251
Rall, Tommy, 324, 345
Ralph, Sheryl Lee, 405
Ramsey, Kevin, 321
Randall, Bob, 356
Randall, Tony, 31, 367
Rando, John, 68
Randolph, Elsie, 138
Randolph, James, 246
Rapp, Anthony, 398, 410
Rasch, Albertina, 139–40, 161, 176
Rau, Santha Rama, 157
Ravel, Maurice, 84
Raye, Martha, 170
Reams, Lee Roy, 325
Reardon, John, 234, 309
Redgrave, Lynn, 68, 240, 317
Reed, Alyson, 332
Reeve, Christopher, 371
Reilly, Charles Nelson, 248, 265, 295, 323–24, 325
Reiner, Carl, 197
Reinhardt, Max, 174–75
Reinking, Ann, 294, 297, 335, 350
Remick, Jerome H., 57
Remick, Lee, 277, 280
Rennick, Kyle, 364, 365
Renshaw, Christopher, 109
Repole, Charles, 54, 127, 228
Resnick, Regina, 332
Reynolds, Debbie, 387
Reynolds, Herbert (M. E. Rourke), 5–8, 12, 16, 18,
    21, 26, 118
Rice, Edward E., 3
Rice, Elmer, 175, 176, 179
Rice, Tim, 366, 367, 413
Richards, Donald, 171
Richards, Martin, 284, 301, 318, 320, 328, 351,
    352, 370, 376
Richardson, Ian, 224

Richardson, Natasha, 333
Richardson, Ron, 406
Richardson, Tony, 190, 234
Richler, Mordecai, 365
Richman, Harry, 151, 388
Rifkin, Jay, 413
Rigby, Cathy, 230
Rigby, Harry, 206, 236, 241, 251, 277, 309, 313, 317
Rigg, Diana, 288, 309
Riggs, Lynn, 104
Riggs, T. Lawrason, 118
Rikfin, Ron, 333
Rimsky-Korsakov, Nikolai, 84
Ring, Blanche, 13
Ringham, Nancy, 224
Ripley, Alice, 367, 395, 412
Risqué, W. H., 3
Ritchard, Cyril, 138, 230, 236, 238, 251, 343
Ritter, Thelma, 263
Rivera, Chita, 168, 215, 235, 256, 271, 293–95, 300, 329, 335–37, 339
Robards, Jason, Jr., 191
Robbins, Jerome, 54, 109, 167, 197, 206, 211–13, 215–16, 218, 222, 228, 230–32, 234–35, 241, 251–52, 259–61, 275, 277, 395, **459**
Robbins, Rex, 232
Robbins, Tom Alan, 413
Roberti, Lyda, 33, 72, 150
Roberts, Anthony, 349
Roberts, Joan, 104
Roberts, Jonathan, 413
Roberts, Pernell, 201
Roberts, Tony, 238, 280, 408
Robertson, Alene, 303
Robertson, Liz, 301
Robeson, Paul, 29, 176
Robin, Leo, 81, 228–29, 231, 239
Robinson, Bill, 299–300, 389
Robinson, Phyllis, 344
Rodgers, Eileen, 124, 257
Rodgers, Mary, 277–78, 390, 397
Rodgers, Mortimer, 85–86
Rodgers, Richard, 1, 33, 35, 41, 49, 53, 56, 61, 77, 81, 85–115, 122, 130, 132, 158, 172, 185, 199, 205–206, 209, 215, 242, 253, 262, 349, 397
Rodzinski, Artur, 211
Rogers, Cheryl, 299
Rogers, David, 299
Rogers, Ginger, 71, 72, 75, 84, 123
Rogers, Roy, 242
Rogers, Will, 32, 168, 320–21
Rollins, Jack, 349
Romberg, Sigmund, 57, 59, 63, 69, 87, 117

Rome, Harold, 1, 165–66, **193–201**, 243, 255, 293
Ronell, Ann, 390
Rooney, Mickey, 401
Roosevelt, Eleanor, 316
Root, Lynn, 163
Rosa, Dennis, 309
Rose, Billy, 32, 82–83, 90, 97, 129, 151–52, 161
Rose, George, 224, 230, 258, 301
Rose, Philip, 402–404
Rose, Reva, 397
Rosenfield, Lois F., 318, 371
Rosenfield, Maurice, 318, 371
Ross, Adrian, 4, 5, 119
Ross, Gary, 409
Ross, Herbert, 84, 112, 145–46, 155, 171, 200, 261, 277, 280
Ross, Jerry, 251–53, 263, 313
Ross, Shirley, 101
Rostand, Edmond, 163, 305
Roth, Daryl, 303
Roth, Lillian, 170, 200, 334
Roth, Murray, 57
Roth, Robert Jess, 366
Rothschild, Mayer, 262
Roundabout Theatre, 258, 279, 333, 401
Rounds, David, 357
Rounseville, Robert, 214, 343
Rourke, M. E. See Reynolds, Herbert (M. E. Rourke)
Routledge, Patricia, 218, 237
Rowland, Adele, 10, 14, 58
Royal National Theatre, 104, 106
Royce, Edward, 4, 12, 13, 17–25, 46, 47, 93, 387
Ruben, Jos, 32, 136
Rubens, Paul, 5, 6, 11, 13–15, 58
Rubin, Arthur, 347, 371
Rubin, Charles, 370
Rubin, Cyma, 67, 80, 346
Rubin-Vega, Daphne, 410
Rubinstein, John, 285, 289, 338, 356
Ruby, Harry, 28–29, 48, 91, 93, 135–36
Rudin, Scott, 288
Ruffelle, Frances, 358
Runyon, Damon, 245–46
Rupert, Michael, 288, 315, 333, 370–72
Russell, Bill, 412
Russell, Lillian, 40
Russell, Robert, 264, 332
Russell, Rosalind, 212
Ruth, Babe, 80, 363–64
Ryan, Irene, 356
Ryan, Robert, 55, 404
Ryder, Amy, 285
Ryskind, Morrie, 51, 70, 72, 73, 89, 136, 141, 164

Sabella, Ernie, 131, 276

Sabellico, Richard, 324

Saddler, Donald, 67, 80, 98, 198, 212, 224, 240, 251, 259, 313, 317, 324, 328, 404

Sager, Carole Bayer, 360

Saidy, Fred, 154, 156, 171, 392

Saint-Subber, Arnold, 130–31, 155–58, 225

Saks, Gene, 253, 260, 266, 294, 297, 302, 317, 318, 326, 361

Salmon, Scott, 328

San Juan, Olga, 223

Sand, Paul, 277–78

Sanders, Alma, 390

Sanderson, Julia, 4, 6, 7, 9, 10, 11, 13, 21, 23, 46

Sandrich, Mark, 326

Sanford, Tim, 408

Sappington, Margo, 102

Sarandon, Chris, 303

Saroyan, William, 351

Savage, Henry W., 7, 17, 20, 21, 42, 79

Savident, John, 360

Saviola, Camille, 371

Savo, Jimmy, 68, 100–101, 149, 185, 222

Schaeffer, Eric D., 31, 288

Schak, John, 308

Schary, Dore, 200, 270

Scheeder, Louis W., 299, 319, 338, 352, 365

Scher, John, 408

Schifter, Peter Mark, 319

Schlesinger, John, 297

Schlissel, Jack, 328

Schmidt, Harvey, 291, 293, **305–311**, 314, 384

Schoeffler, Paul, 230

Schoenberg, Arnold, 185

Schramm, David, 68

Schuck, Conrad John, 298

Schulberg, Budd, 249

Schulman, Susan H., 100, 107, 111, 284, 285, 407

Schulz, Charles M., 350, 397–98

Schuman, William, 243

Schwab, Buddy, 225

Schwab, Laurence, 64, 83–84, 388

Schwartz, Arthur, 1, 98, **135–47**, 161, 169, 243

Schwartz, Stephen, 216, 291, 302, **355–58**, 367

Scolari, Peter, 131, 162

Scorsese, Martin, 336

Scott, Cyril, 3

Seabrooke, Christopher, 209

Sears, Zelda, 79

Seberg, Jean, 360

Seeley, Blossom, 43

Segal, Alex, 313

Segal, Erich, 345

Segal, Vivienne, 20, 57, 61, 100, 102–103, 105

Selden, Albert W., 236, 256, 343, 344, 345

Seldes, Marian, 302

Sell, Janie, 102, 218, 363

Seller, Jeffrey, 410

Selwyn, Edgar, 21, 27, 61, 68, 70, 71

Selwyn, Ruth, 71, 149, 390

Seurat, Georges, 286

Shakespeare, William, 100–101, 130, 186–87, 189, 190, 215, 254, 282, 371, 373, 392, 399

Shange, Ntozake, 373

Shapiro, Debbie, 100, 180

Sharpe, Albert, 171

Shaw, George Bernard, 188, 224, 261, 343

Shaw, Oscar, 19, 25, 27, 48, 67, 77

Shawn, Dick, 318, 345

Shea, Jere, 288

Shea, John, 352

Shean, Al, 32, 49, 92

Sheen, Martin, 343

Sheldon, Sidney, 165, 396

Shelton, Reid, 106, 298

Sherin, Edwin, 114, 317

Sherman, Hiram, 35, 102, 167, 186, 190, 194

Sherrin, Ned, 283

Sherwood, Robert E., 54, 175, 301

Shevelove, Burt, 80, 236, 276, 282

Shipman, Samuel, 70

Shire, David, 405–406, 409–10

Shlenker, Sidney L., 351, 360

Shorenstein, Carole J., 336

Short, Hassard, 27, 29, 33, 35, 47, 48, 50, 80, 125, 129, 139, 143, 161, 164, 169, 176–77, 195, 197, 229

Short, Martin, 314, 361, 400

Shubert, Messrs., 4–6, 8–12, 18, 31, 37, 38, 40, 41, 43, 49, 50, 57–59, 63, 75, 89, 97–98, 117, 120, 126, 127, 136, 141–43, 151–53, 161–63, 169–70, 390

Shubert Organization, 266, 285, 288, 320, 336, 364, 381, 405

Shuman, Mort, 183, 398–99

Shumlin, Herman, 187, 269

Shutta, Ethel, 146

Siberry, Michael, 111

Siegel, sol, 359

Siepi, Cesare, 172

Silvers, Phil, 228, 233, 276, 392, 393

Siman, Barbara, 301

Simon, Lucy, 390, 406–407

Simon, Neil, 158, 255, 314–16, 322, 360, 361, 383, 400

Sinatra, Frank, 102, 227

Siretta, Dan, 67

Sirmay, Albert, 30, 31, 138–39

Sissle, Noble, 387–88
Skelton, Richard (Red), 34
Skinner, Cornelia Otis, 390
Skinner, Emily, 366, 412
Skinner, Randy, 347
Skulnik, Menasha, 200, 344
Slater, Christian, 269
Slezak, Walter, 32, 100, 198
Sloane, A. Baldwin, 9, 40, 41, 42, 57
Sloane, Mike, 392, 393
Small, Neva, 265–66, 266
Smalls, Charlie, 403
Smith, Alexis, 280
Smith, Betty, 145
Smith, Edgar, 3, 9, 10, 12, 38, 40, 41, 44
Smith, Harrison Goodwin, 407
Smith, Harry B., 5, 9–13, 15, 18, 21, 22, 38, 39, 41–
    44, 46, 57, 136
Smith, Kate, 313
Smith, Loring, 146
Smith, Martin, 358
Smith, Oliver, 190, 198, 211–12, 228
Smith, Queenie, 26, 66
Smith, Sheila, 259
Smith, Winchell, 22, 28
Smithson, Frank, 5, 15, 22, 58, 169
Snyder, Ted, 37–43
Soeder, Fran, 230, 309
Sohlke, Gus, 40
Sondheim, Stephen, 55, 112–13, 172, 203, 215–17,
    232, 235, 245, **273–89**, 375, 384
Sorvino, Paul, 357
Soules, Dale, 363
Sousa, John Philip, 46, 81, 269
Sousa, Pamela, 131
Southern, Ann, 96
Spencer, David, 365
Spewack, Bella, 127, 130
Spewack, Sam, 127, 130, 248–49
Spielberg, Anne, 409
Spigelgass, Leonard, 237, 327
Spiner, Brent, 401
Sprecher, Ben, 303
Stadlen, Lewis J., 217, 276, 349
Stallings, Laurence, 81, 142
Stanley, Pat, 257, 396
Stapleton, Jean, 190, 231, 235
Stapleton, Maureen, 190
Starbuck, Betty, 91, 94–95
Starger, Martin, 241, 285
Stark, Ray, 146, 235
Starobin, Michael, 371
Steele, Tommy, 239
Stein, Joseph, 172, 190, 197, 255, 256, 259–60,
    264, 302, 334, 340, 356–57, 387, 394, **459**

Steinbeck, John, 110
Steinberg, Norman, 382
Steinbrenner, George, III, 297, 316
Steiner, Rick, 286, 406, 407
Stevens, Craig, 270
Stevens, Fisher, 106
Stevens, Ris, 109
Stevens, Roger L., 172, 212, 215–16, 218, 253, 266
Stevenson, Robert Louis, 241, 411
Stewart, James, 199
Stewart, Michael, 139, 167, 189, 241, 264–65, 293–
    95, 300, 305, 317–19, 325, 327, 328, **459**
Stewart, Ray, 308
Stiller, Jerry, 314
Stillman, Albert, 142, 163
Stillman, Bob, 413
Sting, 182
Stockwell, Dean, 313
Stolber, Dean, 397
Stoller, Mike, 365
Stone, Dorothy, 26, 28, 31, 32, 222
Stone, Elly, 398
Stone, Ezra, 52, 231
Stone, Fred, 25, 26, 28, 31–32, 44, 222
Stone, Paula, 31, 32, 392, 393
Stone, Peter, 53, 68, 113, 238, 320, 336, 377, 378,
    400
Stothart, Herbert, 67, 78, 79, 87, 135
Stout, Stephen, 381
Strasberg, Lee, 174
Stratas, Teresa, 302
Straus, Oscar, 6, 224
Stravinsky, Igor, 129, 130
Streep, Meryl, 183, 282
Streisand, Barbra, 200, 235
Stritch, Elaine, 29, 98, 102, 253, 278, 280, 396
Stroman, Susan, 29, 71, 104, 332, 338, 340, 366,
    409
Stromberg, John, 40
Strouse, Charles, 291, **293–304**, 326, 329, 384
Stryker, Paul, 241, 242. See also Merrill, Bob
Stuart, Leslie, 3
Stuart, Michel, 375, 376
Sturges, Preston, 206–207
Styne, Jule, 102–103, 166, 203, 206–207, 209, 213,
    227–42, 245, 255–56, 267, 317
Styne, Stanley, 235–36
Sullivan, Jo, 181–82, 246–47
Sullivan, KT, 228
Sumac, Yma, 392
Suntory International Corp., 381
Surovy, Nicholas, 375
Suskin, Steven, 371
Suzuki, Pat, 111
Swenson, Inga, 190, 260, 306

Swenson, Swen, 314, 394
Swerling, Jo, 135, 245–46
Swift, Kay, 68, 390

Tabbert, William, 108, 198
Talbot, Howard, 5, 7, 58
Tamara, 33, 127
Tamiris, Helen, 29, 53, 144–45, 199, 392, 394
Tanguay, Eva, 41
Tarkington, Booth, 25, 38
Taylor, Andy, 178
Taylor, Charles H., 4
Taylor, Dwight, 123, 131
Taylor, Laurette, 123, 146–47, 235
Taylor, Samuel, 112
Taylor-Corbett, Lynne, 378
Taymor, Julie, 413
Teal, Ben, 3, 5, 7
Tebelak, John-Michael, 355
Teek, Angela, 67
Temple, Shirley, 153
Templeton, Fay, 33, 40
Terkel, Studs, 357
Terris, Norma, 29, 222
Terriss, Ellaline, 4
Testa, Mary, 162, 369, 373, 376, 381
Theatre Guild, 74, 89, 91, 104, 106, 107, 115, 160, 185, 231, 237, 270, 274, 275
Theatre Under the Stars, 377
Theatreworks, U.S.A., 381
Theodore, Donna., 403
Theodore, Lee Becker. *See* Becker (Theodore), Lee
Thomas, Brandon, 245
Thompson, David, 332, 338, 340
Thompson, Fred, 15, 58, 65, 66, 68, 69, 119, 120, 164, 227, 281
Thompson, Kay, 153, 205
Thompson, Sada, 190, 281
Tierney, Harry, 387
Tinney, Frank, 42, 44, 48
Tiptree, James. Jr., 365
Todd, Michael, 129, 130, 195, 197, 229, 346
Todd, Michael, Jr., 346
Todd, Susan McCarthy, 346
Tomei, Concetta, 375
Tone, Richard, 323
Topol, 260, 357
Tours, Frank A., 6, 9
Towers, Constance, 109
Tozzi, Giorgio, 246
Traubel, Helen, 110–11
Treacher, Arthur, 128
Troie, Robert, 126
Troy, Hector. *See* Rome, Harold
Truex, Ernest, 16, 169, 188, 392

Tucker, Robert, 232, 357, 403
Tucker, Sophie, 127
Tufts, Sonny, 194
Tune, Tommy, 68, 294, 316, 320–21, 328, 375–77, 404, **460**
Tunick, Jonathan, 275, 279, 285, 400
Turner, John Hastings, 142
Turoff, Robert, 324
TV Asahi, 407
Twain, Mark, 105, 172, 181, 261, 406
Twain, Norman, 275
Twiggy, 68

Udell, Peter, 402–404
Uggams, Leslie, 236, 261, 329
Uhry, Alfred, 404, 414
Ullman, Liv, 114
United Artists, 278
Universal Pictures, 404
Upstairs at the Downstairs, 349
Ustinov, Peter, 199

Valando, Tommy, 256, 332, 349
Valentine, James, 225
Vallee, Rudy, 248
Valli (Dreyfus), Valli, 7, 10
Van Druten, John, 107–109, 114, 332
Van Dyke, Dick, 269, 294, 295
Vance, Vivian, 153, 186
Vanoff, Nick, 320
Varrato, Eugene, 343
Velez, Lupe, 126
Venora, Lee, 109
Venuta, Benay, 53, 229
Verdon, Gwen, 131–32, 197, 252–53, 263, 315, 335, 337, 396–97
Vereen, Ben, 352–53, 356
Vestoff, Virginia, 401
Vichi, Gerry, 347
Vickery, John, 413
Victor, Lucia, 325, 327
Vidnovic, Martin, 104, 223, 309, 345, 367, 405
Vigard, Kristen, 399
Villa, Pancho, 266
Vineyard Theatre, 266
Voltaire, 214, 217
Vonnegut, Edith, 363
Vonnegut, Kurt, 363
Vosburgh, Dick, 328
Voskovec, George, 182

Waara, Scott, 127, 309
Wagner, John H., 3
Wagner, Robin, 40, 318, 319
Waissman, Kenneth, 402

Waldman, Robert, 404
Waldrop, Mark, 162
Walker, Bonnie, 232
Walker, Fredi, 410
Walker, Kary M., 309
Walker, Nancy, 103, 205–206, 208, 211, 233
Wallace, Edgar, 63, 127, 160
Wallach, Eli, 188
Waller, Thomas "Fats," 388, 391
Walsh, Barbara, 372, 409
Walsh, James, 381
Walsh, Mary Jane, 101, 128, 194
Walsh, Thommie, 68, 162, 376, 381, 382
Walston, Ray, 110, 155, 252
Walt Disney Productions, 366, 367, 413
Walton, Jim, 284–85, 285, 338
Walton, Tony, 356
Ward, Aida, 150–51, 389
Warden, Jack, 256
Warner Communications, 336
Warner Theatre Productions, 351, 363, 370
Warren, David, 371
Warren, Harry, 97, 149, 256
Warren, Lesley Anne, 201, 306
Wasserman, Dale, 343–44
Wasserstein, Wendy, 373–74
Waterbury, Marsha, 360
Waters, Daryl, 409
Waters, Ethel, 34, 50, 51, 141–42, 152, 163, 164
Watkins, Maurine Dallas, 335
Watkins, Morris, 88
Watson (Jones), Janet, 307, 309, 310
Watson, Susan, 29, 80, 106, 294, 307, 308, 326
Watts, Clem, 263
Waxman, Herschel, 412
Wayburn, Ned, 8, 9, 17, 19, 20, 23, 37, 40, 41, 44–47, 59, 77, 83, 87, 136
Wayne, David, 29, 144, 171, 231, 333, 343, 345
Weaver, Fritz, 260, 295
Weaver, Sigourney, 282
Webb, Clifton, 18, 50, 60, 77, 93, 118, 120, 126, 136, 138–40, 161, 169
Weber, Joe, 3, 40–41
Webster, Jean, 207
Webster, Margaret, 176, 188
Weede, Robert, 246, 324, 345
Weidman, Charles, 50
Weidman, Jerome, 199–200, 257
Weidman, John, 5, 55, 124–25, 282, 287–88, 319, 338, 352, 364, 409
Weill, Kurt, 1, **173–83**, 187–88, 195, 221
Weinstock, Jack, 248, 277
Weiss, George (David), 233, 255–56
Weissler, Barry, 372
Weissler, Fran, 372

Weitzenhoffer, Max, 320
Weitzman, Ira, 51
Welch, Elisabeth, 124
Welch, Raquel, 408
Welles, Orson, 130, 185–87
Wells, William K., 63–65, 151, 197, 251, 313, 388
Welty, Eudora, 404
Werfel, Franz, 174–75, 328
West, Matt, 366, 413
West, Rebecca, 109
Westcott, Marcy, 100, 101
Westenberg, Robert, 279, 286, 334, 366, 407
Weston, Jack, 67, 240
Wheaton, Anna, 18, 60, 77
Wheeldon, Christopher, 162
Wheeler, Hugh, 157, 209, 217, 281–83, 387
White, George, 8, 60–64, 151, 388
White, Julie, 381
White, Lillias, 321, 371
White, Michael, 299
White, Onna, 197, 225, 253, 264, 269, 277–78, 317, 318, 326, 334, 350, 357, 401
White, Richard, 377
White, Sammy, 88, 90
White, T. H., 225
Whitehead, Allen B., 249
Whitehead, Paxton, 224, 225
Whitehead, Robert, 218, 266, 396
Whitelaw, Arthur, 334, 349–51, 355, 397
Whiteman, Paul, 29, 62, 97, 151
Whiting, Jack, 35, 83, 93, 95, 96, 153, 170, 229, 390, 394
Whiting, Richard, 60, 83
Whitman, Walt, 179, 357
Wickes, Mary, 104
Wilbur, Richard, 214
Wilder, Alec, 212
Wilder, Billy, 238–39, 400
Wilder, Clinton, 188, 282
Wilder, Thornton, 180, 265, 295, 309, 325, 340
Wildhorn, Frank, 408, 411–12
Wilkof, Lee, 364
Williams, Bert, 38, 39, 46, 47, 60
Williams, Elizabeth, 407
Williams, Ellis E., 382
Williams, Hannah, 153
Williams, Hattie, 5, 7, 10, 11
Williams, Herb, 141–42, 149
Williams, Samm-Art, 300
Williams, Sammy, 359
Williams, Vanessa L., 155
Williamson, Nicol, 114
Willman, Noel, 237
Willson, Meredith, 203, **269–71**, 401
Wilson, Billy, 245, 301

Wilson, Dooley, 154, 163
Wilson, John C., 105, 130, 154, 198, 206, 222, 228, 274
Wilson, Julie, 99, 266
Wilson, Lester, 352
Wilson, Mary Louise, 277, 332, 333
Wiman, Dwight Deere, 98–101, 104, 123, 136, 138, 141, 143, 169, 179, 222
Windust, Bretaigne, 222
Winninger, Charles, 13, 29, 32, 45, 47, 80, 83, 141
Winters, Shelley, 275, 349–50
Withers, Jane, 227
Wodehouse, P. G., 4, 16–21, 24, 26–29, 67, 69, 124, **460**
Wohl, Jack, 344, 346
Wolfe, George C., 211, 381, 407–409
Wolfe, Thomas, 404
Wolfington, Iggie, 269
Wolpe, Lenny, 301
Wolper, David, 227
Wolsk, Eugene V., 344, 345
Wong, B. D., 51, 398
Wood, Peggy, 18, 119, 123
Wood, Susan, 402
Woodard, Charlaine, 399
Woods, A. H., 11, 15, 39
Woods, Carol, 178, 361
Woodward, Charles, 284
Woodward, Edward, 208
Woolley, Monty, 96, 98, 122, 125, 127, 138, 161
Woolverton, Linda, 366, 413
Wopat, Tom, 53, 106
Worley, Jo Anne, 278
Worth, Irene, 191
WPA Theatre, 364, 365, 414
Wright, Ben, 115
Wright, Jeffrey, 409

Wright, Robert, 376–77, 393–94
Wright, Samuel E., 413
Wright, Valerie, 53
Wyler, Gretchen, 132, 235
Wynn, Ed, 59, 61, 95–96, 153

Yakim, Moni, 398
Yale University Dramatic Association, 117
Yancy, Emily, 218, 325, 344
Yellen, Jack, 150
Yellen, Sherman, 114, 262
Yeston, Maury, 291, 320, **375–79**
York, Rachel, 288, 408
York Theater Company, 284, 285, 309, 310, 319, 351
Youmans, Vincent, 1, 60, **77–84**, 94, 159, 169
Young, Frank, 377
Young, Keith, 211
Young, Roland, 119
Yuriko, 109

Zaks, Jerry, 124, 246, 257, 276, 287
Zaremba, Kathryn, 303
Zbornik, Kristine, 209
Ziegfeld, Florenz, Jr., 9, 10, 17, 19, 20, 23–25, 29–30, 33, 38, 39, 41, 44–47, 49–50, 57, 60, 69, 70, 82, 83, 92, 95–96, 136, 161, 274, 389, **460–61**
Ziemba, Karen, 107, 307, 338, 340
Zien, Chip, 285–86, 319, 338, 352, 363, 365, 369, 370, 372, 373
Zimbalist, Stephanie, 297
Zimmer, Hans, 413
Zippel, David, 319, 320, 337, 352, 361, 364, 365, 367
Zipprodt, Patricia, 356
Zorich, Louis, 258
Zorina, Vera, 51, 52, 98, 100, 135